Intermediate Microeconomics
Theory and Applications

Heinz Kohler

Amherst College

Scott, Foresman and Company
Glenview, Illinois

Dallas, Texas

Oakland, New Jersey

Palo Alto, California

Tucker, Georgia

London, England

To Dorothy Ives

Library of Congress Cataloging in Publication Data

Kohler, Heinz.
    Intermediate microeconomics.

    Includes bibliographies and indexes.
    1. Microeconomics.   I. Title.
HB172.K68   338.5   81-14453
ISBN 0-673-15277-4   AACR2

Credits

p. 9   The Granger Collection, New York
p. 20   UPI
p. 28   UPI
p. 46   Courtesy News and Publications Service, Stanford University
p. 56   The Bettmann Archive
p. 57   BBC Hulton Picture Library
p. 58   Courtesy Codrington Library, All Souls College, Oxford
p. 67   Figure copyright the Society of Economic Analysts
p. 84   Courtesy Professor Sir John Hicks
p. 94   Figure reprinted with permission of Macmillan Publishing Co., Inc. Copyright © 1977 by Macmillan Publishing Co.
p. 107 Table copyright 1974 by the President and Fellows of Harvard College
p. 134 The Granger Collection, New York
p. 138 Courtesy Harvey Leibenstein
p. 141 Table © Western Economic Association, 1967 & 1968
p. 148 Table reprinted by permission of Allen R. Ferguson, President of the Public Interest Economics Center. Copyright © 1958 the American Economic Association.
p. 164 Courtesy Ellen Viner Seiler
p. 179 *Tass* from Sovfoto
p. 190 Historical Pictures Service, Chicago

p. 225 Figures copyright © 1978 by the President and Fellows of Harvard College.
p. 232 Table copyright © 1976 National Bureau of Economic Research, Inc.
p. 239 Columbiana Collection, Columbia University
p. 241 Courtesy University of Chicago
p. 252 Courtesy Department of Economics, University of Chicago
p. 264 Wide World
p. 271 Courtesy University of Chicago
p. 287 Courtesy University of Chicago
p. 312 Courtesy Harvard University
p. 329 Historical Pictures Service, Chicago
p. 353 Courtesy Harvard University
p. 380 Courtesy New York University
p. 392 Ramsey & Muspratt, Cambridge
p. 421 The Granger Collection, New York
p. 455 The Granger Collection, New York
p. 483 Courtesy Bibliotheque Cantonale et Universitaire, Lausanne
p. 485 Courtesy Wassily Leontief
p. 515 Courtesy University of Chicago
p. 528 Courtesy University Library, Cambridge, England
p. 533 Courtesy Ronald H. Coase
p. 560 Courtesy Massachusetts Institute of Technology
p. 574 Courtesy News and Publications Service, Stanford University
p. 576 Center for Study of Public Choice

Preface

Economics is an important subject. Those who master the theoretical knowledge of the discipline are able to wield a powerful set of tools capable of affecting, for better or for worse, the material welfare of vast millions of people. This book, which is aimed at students who have had only an introductory economics course or students in MBA programs, develops all of the theoretical tools traditionally found in microeconomics texts (and more).

Economics is also an exciting subject—as evidenced throughout this book by a continuous link between theory and applications. As the detailed Table of Contents shows, many of these applications have been integrated into the basic structure of chapters. Such is the case with rationing and mandated purchases (Chapter 3), import quotas (Chapter 7), the economics of natural resources (Chapter 9), the baseball players' market (Chapter 13), and highway congestion (Chapter 18), to name just a few of the nearly three dozen topics. Some 48 other applications, however, have been set off as self-contained Analytical Examples; in addition, an about equal number of Close-Ups provide somewhat less rigorous examples of how microeconomics reaches into every nook and cranny of our lives. Finally, each chapter contains one or more biographical sketches of the scholars most responsible for the material discussed. (The text Applications, Analytical Examples, Close-ups, and Biographies are all listed in the Table of Contents.)

To the Instructor

This book is divided into five parts. Part 1, "Introduction," reviews crucial lessons of the elementary economics course and lays the groundwork for the remainder of the book. Chapters 1 and 2 can easily be assigned without further class discussion of the key concepts of scarcity, choice, optimizing, and the like. Part 2, "Basic Features of the Market Economy," presents the traditional theory of the household (Chapters 3 and 4) and of the firm (Chapters 5 and 6) as well as the traditional theory of supply and demand (Chapters 7 and 8). Part 3, "The Complexity of the Market Economy," introduces intertemporal decision making and uncertainty (Chapters 9 and 10) and imperfect competition (Chapters 11-13). Part 4, "The Performance of the Market Economy," develops the key concepts of efficiency (Chapter 14), equity (Chapter 15), and general equilibrium (Chapter 16). Part 5, "Government Intervention in the Market Economy," provides in-depth discussions of antitrust policy and regulation (Chapter 17), externalities (Chapter 18), and public goods (Chapter 19).

The chapters of this book are self-contained units. It is not necessary to cover them all or even to assign them in the order in which they appear. To the extent that one chapter builds upon material in other chapters, cross references with page numbers have been provided. Instructors, therefore, can design their own courses using any desired combinations of chapters. Instructors teaching under a quarter system, for example, could assign Chapters 1 and 2 but could focus class discussion on Chapters 3-8 and 11-13, excluding appendices. If time permits, *any* remaining chapters, in any order, can be added to this nine-chapter core.

Two types of supporting materials are available: an *Instructor's Manual* and a *Student Workbook* (described below). The *Instructor's Manual* contains responses or answers for the even-numbered end-of-chapter Questions and Problems in this text. It also contains, for each chapter of the text, 35 multiple-choice and 15 true-false questions (with answers). These questions do not duplicate those in the *Student Workbook*. Instructors who wish to elaborate upon any of the materials discussed in the text will find the end-of-chapter Selected Readings particularly helpful.

To the Student

Students will find a number of aids to the study of the material presented in this book. Some of these aids have been built into the text: the figures made self-contained by carefully worded captions, the chapter Summaries, the end-of-chapter listings of Key Terms (boldfaced in the text), the end-of-chapter Questions and Problems, and the Selected Readings. In addition, a Glossary of all key terms and Answers to odd-numbered Questions and Problems appear at the end of the book. A separate *Student Workbook* is also available. For each chapter of this book, the *Student Workbook* contains 25 multiple-choice questions, 10 true-false questions, and numerous problems—as well as answers to all of these.

Acknowledgements

I would like to express my sincere gratitude to many who have helped me in the creation of this text. Many reviewers took the time to examine at least a part of the project and gave me good advice:

Jack Adams, University of Arkansas
G. O. Bierwag, University of Oregon
Robert Borengasser, St. Mary's College, Indiana
William Brown, California State University, Northridge
Louis Cain, Loyola University, Chicago
Richard Clarke, University of Wisconsin, Madison
Alvin Cohen, Lehigh University
Eleanor Craig, University of Delaware
Jacque Cremer, University of Pennsylvania
Richard Ericson, Harvard University
James Ferguson, University of Rochester
Tim Gronberg, Texas A & M University
James Hess, University of Southern California

Elisabeth Hoffman, Purdue University
Dennis Johnson, University of South Dakota
Richard Kihlstrom, University of Pennsylvania
Rodney Mabry, Northeast Louisiana University
Jeff Madura, University of North Carolina, Charlotte
J. Peter Mattila, Iowa State University
Sharon Oster, Yale University
Sam Peltzman, University of Chicago
Owen Phillips, Texas A & M University
Larry Pulley, Brandeis University
Robert Puth, University of New Hampshire
Helen Tauchen, University of North Carolina, Chapel Hill
Tom Ulen, University of Illinois, Urbana
Fred Westfield, Vanderbilt University
Robert Wolf, Boston University

I am equally grateful to George Lobell, Mary LaMont, and Randi Brill, the acquiring editor, staff editor, and designer, respectively, of the book. They have guided this project through the long process of production and have created, as most will agree, a beautiful book. Permission to use selected materials from earlier books is gratefully acknowledged from the Dryden Press of Hinsdale, Illinois *(Economics: The Science of Scarcity,* 1970); from D. C. Heath and Co. of Lexington, Massachusetts *(Economics and Urban Problems,* 1973; *Scarcity and Freedom: An Introduction to Economics,* 1977); and from the Robert E. Krieger Publishing Company, once of Huntington, New York, and now of Melbourne, Florida *(Welfare and Planning: An Analysis of Capitalism versus Socialism,* 2nd ed., 1979). Finally, Dorothy Ives, my marvellous secretary, over the years has typed more pages of mine than I dare count and, once again, did a perfect job. It is with special gratitude that I dedicate this book to her.

Heinz Kohler
Amherst College

Contents

PART 2   THE BASIC FEATURES OF THE MARKET ECONOMY

PART 3   THE COMPLEXITY OF THE MARKET ECONOMY

CHAPTER 11   Monopoly and Cartels   *318*

CHAPTER 12   Oligopoly and Monopolistic Competition   *350*

APPENDIX 12A   Game Theory   *377*

CHAPTER 13   Imperfect Markets for Resource Services   *386*

PART 4 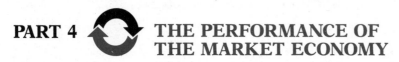 THE PERFORMANCE OF THE MARKET ECONOMY

CHAPTER 14   Efficiency   *417*

PART 5  GOVERNMENT INTERVENTION IN THE MARKET ECONOMY

PART 1

Introduction

CHAPTER 1

Scarcity, Choice, and Optimizing

A universal problem exists. Small bands of African Bushmen face it; so do Amazon Indians and Greenland Eskimos. Peasants in China, Egypt, and Peru suffer from it; so do urban dwellers in Moscow, Paris, and New York. All of them, every day, wrestle with the basic economic problem of *scarcity*. This problem, which is central to every elementary economics text, is also central to this intermediate one. This chapter will review the nature of the problem and its implications.

An Immense Desire for Goods

A thought experiment can quickly remind us of what scarcity involves. Suppose a smiling genie popped out of a bottle and offered to be at our service. Suppose he were prepared to bring us, just for the asking, any object we desired and the devoted attention of any person we named. Imagine the abundance of goods that could then be ours! If we were hungry, we could call for food, and it would be there in the wink of an eye. We could conjure up new clothes or that fancy camera we were never quite able to afford. Presents for family and friends? A flashy sports car for ourselves? Of course. A house on our favorite island in the middle of the sea? A plane to take us there? They could be ours. Lessons to

fly that plane? Lessons to gain all kinds of other skills? The best in medical care, concerts at night, visits to beautiful places? All of these we could enjoy. . . .

We need not belabor the point. More than 4 billion people live on this earth, and they do not have genies ready to serve them. But they do spend their individual lives in the pursuit of happiness. To most of them, most of the time, happiness is an elusive goal indeed. Most of them, probably, could not even name the exact ingredients that would produce it. But surely, the kinds of material things listed above would be mentioned by many. We can guess that most people, if given the chance offered by our genie, would not reject it. Most likely, they would be all too ready to prepare an impressive list of things to have and of things or people to use. And all these people would hope that somewhere hidden in their list would be at least some of the ingredients required for their happiness.

Indeed, Economists typically assume that most people on earth harbor desires for a truly staggering variety and quantity of goods. Although no one has ever measured the aggregate size of this desire, one can guess that its extent is immense. All one has to do is imagine people in their various capacities as family members, producers, government officials, and so on, and one can easily picture the lengthy lists of wishes such people would prepare if they did meet the incredible kind of genie noted above, who was ready to offer all goods at a zero price.

Two things, in particular, should be noted. First, in this book the term **goods** refers to all the varied means by which people satisfy their material wants. These means may be tangible *commodities* (like food and clothes) that users come to own completely. But goods may also be intangible *services*, either of people (such as teachers and doctors) or of commodities (such as airliners and hotels) that users enjoy temporarily without coming to own the persons or commodities involved.

Second, the term **desire for goods**, does not mean *demand* for goods, a concept that refers to desire backed up by purchasing power, which enables people in our society to acquire goods that are for sale at positive prices. Instead, *desire* refers to wishful thinking, to the quantities people would take if no purchasing power were needed because all goods were available at zero prices. It is desire for goods in this sense that economists claim is immense in most places on earth.

Resources— The Ingredients to Make Goods

Introductory economics courses teach something else that must be recalled: in the real world, goods are not made by genies with the help of magic; on the contrary, they are made by people with the help of productive ingredients called **resources**. Customarily, resources are classified into three major groups: human, natural, and capital. They are put to work in the **process of production**, a set of activities deliberately designed to make goods available to people where and when they are wanted.

Human resources are people able and willing to participate in the productive process, supplying their mental or physical labor. **Natural resources** are gifts of nature in their natural state; that is, productive ingredients not made by peo-

ple and as yet untouched by them. Think of sunlight and ocean tides, of virgin land and the plants and animals upon it, of schools of fish in the ocean, or of minerals and fuels underground. **Capital resources**, finally, are all the productive ingredients made by people. They include all types of structures used by producers of goods— structures such as factory buildings, schools, or airport control towers. They include equipment of producers, such as computers, milling machines, or fleets of trucks. And they include producer inventories of raw materials, semifinished goods, or even finished goods that have not yet reached their ultimate users.

Note: First, many items considered by people in general to be natural resources are viewed as capital resources by economists. Consider animals that have been domesticated and specially bred; soil that has been cleared, irrigated, and fertilized; or oil that has been pumped from the ground and shipped far from its original place of deposit. None of these is in its natural state; all of them are in a sense made by people. So they are capital resources, as defined above.

Second, one is almost tempted to carry this reasoning a step further. Economists know that a healthy, educated, and trained labor force (like soil that has been cleared, irrigated, and fertilized) is more productive than it would be without these qualities. Thus one might wish to classify people who are in good physical condition, educated, and trained as produced capital, too! Nevertheless, economists do not classify people as capital resources. In later chapters, however, we will recognize that different people clearly possess different amounts of an invisible kind of **human capital**, consisting of the health care, general education, and training embodied in them.

Finally, *capital resources*, as the term is used in this book, do not include **financial capital**, such as money, stocks, deeds, or bonds. For an individual in modern society, such items are important indeed, but they are not directly productive. They are only claims against real resources. People could easily increase such paper claims a millionfold. Yet, if no corresponding increase occurred in the form of blast furnaces, locomotives, oil deposits, and so on, people would not be richer at all. They could not produce more on that account. Just as a baker uses butter, eggs, flour, and milk (and not green dollar bills) to bake a cake, so the people in every society must mix *real* capital resources with natural and human ones to produce each and every good they do acquire.

Technology— The Knowledge to Make Goods

Elementary economics textbooks also teach us that the quantities of goods people are able to produce depend not only on the quantities of resources they have and put to use, but also on their **technology**, the set of known methods of production available to them. This knowledge of possible methods of production, like the recipe book available to the baker, sets limits on the quantity of goods that can be produced *per unit* of resources. Such limits are, of course, far from eternally fixed. Consider how, during the past century, people have discovered fertilizers, hormones, and high-yield crops and have used these discoveries, along with wonders of agricultural machinery, to raise incredibly the yield per acre of land. Before we run out of conventional fuel, people may well discover how to use solar power on a large scale. Should that happen, the quantities of goods produced per unit of this particular natural resource would increase dramatically. This would happen, furthermore, not because of any change in the quantity or quality of this resource (the sun radiates as much energy to us now as it will then). It would happen because of a new entry in our productive recipe book that would enable us to switch to a technique of production previously unavailable. Such an advance in technical knowledge should not be confused with a switch, in response to changing circumstances, from one known technique of production to another. While the former is akin to discovering a new recipe, the latter is about selecting a different one from among those previously known.

Limited Resources and Technology Yield Limited Goods

Just as a cake is limited in size by the quantities of ingredients and the possible recipes available to the baker, so the "pie" of goods produced by any society is limited by the resources and technology available to it. Obviously, no society has unlimited stocks of resources or of technical knowledge. At any one moment, there are only so many people able and willing to work in the productive process, and limited quantities of human capital are embodied in them. There are only so many acres of virgin timberland and so many known barrels of oil in the ground. There are only so many assembly plants and miles of highway in existence. There are only so many recipes of production from which to choose. Given the best techniques of production available, even the use of all resource stocks at the maximum possible rate (of 24 hours each day) would produce a limited set of newly produced goods in a year. In fact, of course, some resources cannot be used at such a maximum rate. This is most obvious in the case of people.

Yet, as a matter of logic, the inevitably limited size of a society's annual "pie" of goods need not be of concern. Conceivably, this set of goods might be more than sufficient to satisfy all the material desires of all the people. In fact, however, this isn't so, and therein lies the essence of the problem of scarcity.

Scarcity— The Basic Economic Problem

All nations on earth face the economic problem of **scarcity**. Everywhere, the limited set of goods that can be produced in a year is insufficient to satisfy, simultaneously, the desire for goods by all the people. When an attempt is made to give to all people all the goods they desire at zero prices, there are not enough goods to go around.

Note: The notion of scarcity employed by economists is not identical to the concept of shortages that exist at *positive* prices. Nor must it be confused with situations in which quantities supplied seem small compared to other times or places. Economists measure the desire for goods at *zero* prices and do not link scarcity to the production of small quantities of goods. On the contrary, in many nations, many goods are produced in huge quantities indeed. The essence of scarcity lies in the *relationship* between people's desire for goods (at zero prices) and their ability to produce goods. As long as that desire exceeds that ability, no matter how large that ability is, scarcity persists, as Figure 1.1 illustrates.

Because economists are forever telling people that ours is a world of scarcity wherein people can never have all they want, economics is often called "the dismal science." Yet, actually, economists are far from content with being prophets of gloom. While they recognize that scarcity is a built-in fact of life for modern Americans, Chi-

nese, and Russians as well as for isolated Bushmen, Indians, and Eskimos, the main concern of economists is to explore the exact implications of scarcity. This exploration can help people minimize the impact of scarcity.

Scarcity Requires Choice

The most obvious implication of scarcity is the need to choose—which is the second major lesson of an elementary text. Children have to learn painfully that, when confronted with the offer of ice cream or cake, "I take both" is not a permissible answer. Adult decision makers in every society, every day, face similar painful choices. Because the present technical knowledge of people falls short of that possessed by genies, there are not enough resources to do everything; hence, people cannot have all the goods they want. But they can choose within the limited realm of the possible. They can decide what will be done with the resources available—and what must be left undone. And there are literally millions of such choices to be made. Consider some of the major types of choices.

First, decision makers in each society must decide on the *rate of resource use*; for example, they must decide how many hours the available number of people or machines should work on the average day. Decision makers must then decide on the *rates of consumption and investment*; that is, they must channel the chosen flow of resource services (such as 800 million labor hours per day) toward making goods available to households in the present or toward the creation of bigger and better stocks of resources and improved methods of production. Decision makers must also determine the *detailed composition of production*; in other words, they must decide on the precise types and quantities of (individual and collective) consumption or investment goods. Some economists refer to the decisions just discussed as the big question of What. People in each society must decide, they say, *what* they will have: leisure or goods, consumption or investment goods, apples or new

FIGURE 1.1 The Scarcity Problem

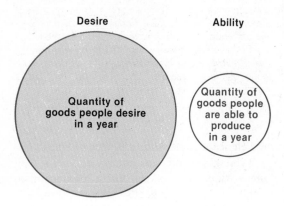

Desire   Ability

Quantity of
goods people desire
in a year

Quantity of
goods people
are able to
produce
in a year

In any nation today, the people's wish to satisfy all their desires for goods is frustrated by the unavailability of sufficient resources and technical knowledge to produce a sufficiently large quantity of goods. While resources and technology allow the production of the "pie" shown by the right-hand circle, people would like to consume the one shown by the left-hand circle. Note: This graph refers to a given year. Over time, the right-hand circle can grow, as more resources and better technology are put to work. Yet the left-hand circle can grow as well, as the number of people or desires multiply, allowing scarcity to persist.

factories . . . But people must also consider the question of How; that is, they must decide on how each of these decisions is to be carried out. Such a decision requires that people determine a *scheme of specialization*, or precisely which household provides, and which firm uses, which portion of the total flow of resource services toward what end. Finally, as some economists like to put it, there is the big question of For Whom. People in each society must choose one of many possible ways of *apportioning goods* among themselves.

Choice Brings Benefit and Cost

In a world of scarcity, the kinds of choices outlined above cannot be escaped. And every choice is a mixture of pleasure and pain, of opportunity gained and opportunity lost. This is so because every use of resources for one purpose means forgoing the opportunity to use them for another purpose that is also desired. Every act of choice gives people something they want and thus brings an advantage, or **benefit**, but with each benefit comes the disappointment of not getting something else that is also wanted; hence, a disadvantage, or **cost**. Because every desire we satisfy ''costs us'' the opportunity of satisfying a different desire, the opportunity lost is also referred to as **opportunity cost**.

Implicitly, we have noted all this in the previous section. Every hour of labor performed means an hour of leisure forgone. Every labor hour devoted to making a consumption good is an hour taken from making an investment good. Every hour of labor spent raising apples is an hour lost raising corn. Every labor hour spent raising apples in Oregon is an hour lost raising apples in Maine. Every apple given to John Doe is an apple lost to Peggy Brown. In each case, there is an opportunity gained and another one lost.

Figure 1.2, the production-possibilities frontier, is a favorite graph of elementary economics texts because it illustrates the concepts of scarcity

FIGURE 1.2
The Production-Possibilities Frontier

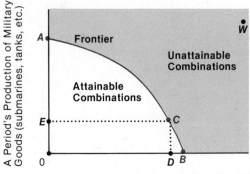

A Period's Production of Civilian Goods
(apples, sweaters, etc.)

This production-possibilities frontier shows all the alternative combinations of two groups of goods that people in a society are capable of producing in a given period by using their flow of resources fully and in the best possible way, given their present state of technology. Thus it divides the set of all conceivable combinations of goods into two: attainable ones (unshaded) and unattainable ones (shaded). In a world of scarcity, there is always some impenetrable frontier that restricts people's freedom to get all they want (such as combination W). People must choose within the (unshaded) world of the possible, along or underneath the frontier to the world of the impossible. When they do, they get a benefit, but they also incur an opportunity cost.

and choice as well as the concepts of benefit and cost. Imagine people in a society allocating their annual flow of resources to the production of nothing but military goods, such as submarines and tanks. By using their flow of resources fully and in the best possible way, given their present state of technical knowledge, the people of that society would be able to produce some maximum quantity of such goods, perhaps that shown by the distance *0A* in Figure 1.2. These same people could, of course, devote all their resources to making goods for civilian uses, such as apples or sweaters. By using all their resources for civilian instead of military purposes, they would, under similar assumptions, produce some other maximum quantity of goods, exemplified by *0B*. These people could also produce any one of the many combinations of military and civilian goods lying on line *AB*. This line is their **production-possibilities frontier**, which shows all the alternative combinations of the two groups of goods that the people in a society are capable of producing in a given period by using their flow of resources fully and in the best possible way, given their present state of technology. The existence of scarcity is illustrated by the fact that all combinations of goods lying above and to the right of line *AB* are unattainable, even though they may well be wanted by people. Combinations lying to the left and below the line are attainable, but they would require less than the total flow of resources or less efficient production methods than the people have available. The production-possibilities frontier inescapably restricts people's freedom to get all they want. They may want combination *W*, but they cannot penetrate the frontier into the (shaded) world of the impossible. In spite of scarcity, however, it is not impossible for people to choose from within the (unshaded) realm of the possible.

It is now very easy to see how each benefit comes together with an opportunity cost. If the people in this society were to produce quantity *0A* of military goods, they would have to forgo quantity *0B* of civilian goods. Thus the opportunity cost of *0A* military goods would equal *0B* of civilian goods. Alternatively, if these people were to produce *0B* of civilian goods, they would have to forgo production of *0A* of military goods. The opportunity cost of *0B* of civilian goods would equal *0A* of military goods. And if they were to produce (at point *C*) some of both types of goods, the production of *0D* of civilian goods would cost *AE* of military goods, while producing *0E* of the military goods would cost *BD* of the civilian goods. The benefit of producing a certain quantity of one good always costs people the quantity of another good that might have been made with the resources that were used to make the first.

The citizens of many a society have incurred heavy opportunity costs in order to carry forward certain national goals, whether freely chosen by all of them or imposed upon them by a few. Hitler urged Germany to forgo butter in favor of guns, and he presided over a massive national effort to cut the production of civilian goods in favor of military goods. Stalin, interested in rapid economic growth of the Soviet Union, drastically cut the production of consumption goods and greatly increased that of investment goods. The increased quantities of buildings and machines produced then, he argued, would allow a much greater production of consumption goods later. The people of the United States, in the 1960s, carried on a similar massive redirection of resources. In the midst of much controversy, such tasks as the abolition of poverty and the cleaning up of the environment were slighted in order to carry forward national commitments to land an American on the moon and to fight a war in Vietnam.

We as individuals, similarly, incur opportunity costs every day, wherever we turn. Just as the nation as a whole has limited resources to spend, each individual has a limited money income. When we spend our money on ice cream, we might have to forgo the opportunity of seeing a movie. Then the movie forgone is the opportunity cost of eating ice cream. When a family spends its money on furniture, it might have to forgo a vacation trip. The vacation trip forgone is the opportunity cost of having the furniture.

Similar costs are incurred by all of us as we allocate the limited *time* available to us. If we watch the evening newscast (or read this book), we might not be able to watch the sunset. Not enjoying the sunset is the opportunity cost of seeing the news (or reading this book). Whatever we do, because there are so many things we like to do and time is limited, we must *pay* for our benefits by incurring opportunity costs. Everything we do has its price! And that is why economics applies to every nook and cranny of human experience, and why price theory, or microeconomics, has been called the heart of economic science.

CLOSE-UP 1.1

When Space Won over Sewers

On July 20, 1969 at 10:56 P M Eastern Daylight Time, Neil A. Armstrong, commander of Apollo 11, put the first human footprint on the moon. Since then, eleven others—all Americans—have also walked on the moon. Their success followed the kind of difficult choice depicted in Figure 1.2 by the production-possibilities frontier. By forgoing $24 billion worth of other goods, Americans bought a number of benefits with the Apollo Project: a demonstration of space flight capability, rapid advances in computer technology, and important new knowledge of the solar system. Yet Americans have never been able to agree on whether the benefits were worth the cost. A 1969 poll by CBS News showed that people throughout the nation were just about evenly split on that question. A similar poll taken ten years later had identical results.

This ambivalence was reflected in Congress. In 1970, a tough fight emerged among those, like Senator Fulbright, who wanted resources used for the construction of sewer and water facilities and others who urged the construction of a *space shuttle*. This reusable, piloted vehicle would be able to carry large payloads into space, taking off like a rocket. It would orbit like a spacecraft and return to earth, landing like a plane. The program's cost was estimated at $14 to $30 billion; the perceived benefits included the shuttle's use for orbiting, servicing, repairing. and retrieving satellites, as well as ferrying people and materials between the earth and permanent space stations. These space stations might produce vast amounts of solar electric power and become the homes, eventually, of billions of people. Although Senator Mondale described the space shuttle program as one of the most indefensible items in the budget in light of domestic needs, space won over sewers.

Sources: *The New York Times*, July 21, 1969, p. 1, and July 20, 1979, p. 12; National Aeronautics and Space Administration, *Space Settlements: A Design Study* (Washington, D.C.: U. S. Government Printing Office, 1977).

The Nature of Microeconomics

The preceding sections make it easy to see why the following is such a popular definition of **economics**: *the study of how people allocate scarce resources (that usually have many alternative uses) to produce goods and of how they apportion these scarce goods among themselves.* Other, briefer definitions simply refer to economics as the study of scarcity or of choice, the need for the latter being, of course, implied by the existence of the former.

Practitioners of economics have, in turn, divided the field into **macroeconomics** and **microeconomics**. Macroeconomics, not to be dealt with in this book, studies the "big picture," the aggregate flows of resources and goods and the overall level of prices. Microeconomics, the exclusive subject matter of this book, studies the behavior of decision makers in households, firms, and governments who, individually or in groups, make the kinds of choices that determine not only the detailed composition of the aggregate flows of resources and goods, but also the relative prices among individual resources and goods. When studying how these choices are made, furthermore, microeconomists have discovered that people by and large follow a certain principle of rational behavior. Adam Smith (see Biography 1.1) stated it in a common-sense fashion; modern economists use more formal language.

The Principle of Rational Behavior

When circumstances dictate a choice among a number of possible alternatives, people who are free to make choices usually can be counted on to select the one that promotes their welfare (as they conceive it at the time) in the most effective way.

This informal version of the principle does not claim, however, that people will act selfishly. To the extent that people desire goods, for example, they might be selfishly motivated, seeking only to use goods for themselves. But they might also be altruists, seeking the satisfaction of making gifts of goods to family, friends, or the world at large. The above principle simply tells us that people in general act sensibly, intelligently, and judiciously on behalf of their goals in life, whatever these may be.

One wonders whether a statement that is so extremely vague can be put to any practical use. As Adam Smith discovered two centuries ago, the above principle, properly endowed with content, can become a surprisingly powerful tool for explaining and predicting the economic behavior of people.

BIOGRAPHY 1.1
Adam Smith

Adam Smith (1723–1790) was born in Kirkaldy, Scotland. He studied at Glasgow, then at Oxford, only to return to Glasgow as a teacher of moral philosophy (economics had not yet been invented as a separate discipline). Smith wrote only two books; both brought him instant fame. His first book, *The Theory of Moral Sentiments*, was published in 1759; his second, *An Inquiry into the Nature and Causes of the Wealth of Nations*, in 1776. The latter book has been called the fountainhead of economic science; it earned Smith the title "father of economics."

The single most important source of the wealth of nations, Smith argues in his later book, is the division of labor. "This division of labor, from which so many advantages are derived," he says, "is not originally the effect of any human wisdom, which foresees and intends that general opulence to which it gives occasion. It is the necessary, though very slow and gradual, consequence of a certain propensity in human nature which has in view no such extensive utility; the propensity to truck, barter, and exchange one thing for another."[1] Throughout his book, Smith emphasizes the importance of economic liberty; that is, of free competition among individuals pursuing their self-interest as they choose to define it. The free, spontaneous interaction of people in the marketplace—all persons having only their own narrow, but not necessarily selfish, ends in mind—would bring about, argues Smith, the general benefit of humanity that nobody intended. In contrast, governmental attempts to guide or regulate the market would end up doing more harm than good.

Indeed, the beaver-deer example cited in this chapter can be used to illustrate his point. As long as nature yielded one beaver or two deer for the same amount of effort (and all people were free to hunt what they liked), a beaver's price in the market ultimately would have to be twice that of a deer, reflecting the relative opportunity costs in the process of production. Any well-intentioned government that tried to help consumers of beavers by decreeing, let us say, a halving of their price (as measured in deer) would simply cause the supply of beavers to dry up. That would leave the very people government wanted to help without beavers altogether!

Thus Smith proved to be a brilliant microeconomist when he noted that the structure of relative prices, in a society wherein resources were mobile, was far from arbitrary and could not be altered at will (away from the structure of opportunity costs) without undesirable consequences. While it did not matter whether the absolute price of a beaver was £1 or £100, under the assumptions underlying Smith's example, any price of a deer that was not half that of a beaver in the marketplace would cause nothing but trouble.

[1]Smith, *The Nature and Causes of the Wealth of Nations*, p. 11.

The Case of Beavers and Deer

Consider, for instance, the famous example Smith used to explain the relative price of beavers and deer:[1]

> In that early and rude state of society which precedes both the accumulation of stock and the appropriation of land, the proportion between the quantities of labor necessary for acquiring different objects seems to be the only circumstance which can afford any rule for exchanging them for one another. If, among a nation of hunters, for example, it usually costs twice the labor to kill a beaver which it does to kill a deer, one beaver should naturally exchange for or be worth two deer. It is natural that what is usually the produce of two days' or two hours' labor, should be worth double of what is usually the produce of one day's or one hour's labor.

Let us examine how Smith reached his conclusion. He pictured a primitive nation of hunters all of whom, apparently, had equal access to the resources provided by nature and all of whom, apparently, relied exclusively on their own labor and not on fancy capital (''stock'' as he called it) to catch their prey. He assumed that a hunter would usually need two days to kill a beaver but only one day to kill a deer. Under these circumstances, anyone going into the forest and interacting only with nature could in fact exchange one beaver for two deer: By using two days for hunting deer, one would gain two deer (the benefit) but sacrifice one beaver (the opportunity cost). Conversely, by using two days for hunting beaver, one would catch one beaver (the benefit) but lose two deer (the opportunity cost).

Therefore, argued Smith, one beaver would also have to exchange for two deer when people met in their villages and interacted *with each other*. Smith imagined what would happen if one beaver were to be traded in the market for *one* deer: Hunters of beaver, instead of hunting for two days to get a beaver, could then hunt for one

day to get a deer and trade it for a beaver in the market. Thus they could have an extra day of leisure without any sacrifice of goods available to them. Or they could hunt for two days to get two deer, trading in one (or both) at the marketplace. Thus they could perform the same amount of work, while receiving more goods (two beavers instead of one or one beaver and one deer instead of one beaver only).

Surely, concluded Smith, with an eye on the above principle of rational behavior, many people would interpret more leisure (without an added sacrifice of goods) or more goods (without an added sacrifice of leisure) as an increase in their welfare. Therefore, many people would begin to act accordingly: the hunting of beaver would drop or even cease altogether, while the hunting of deer would increase. If the forest continued to yield a deer for every day's hunt in spite of all the extra hunters (and that Smith assumed), the supply of deer in the market would rise and rise, but the supply of beaver would all but vanish. People seeking to buy beavers with deer would have a hard time finding sellers; but any remaining hunters of beaver would find it easy to raise their price and demand more than one deer. Only when the price of beaver in the market had risen to two deer (and become equal to the ''price'' in the forest), concluded Smith, would the shortage of beaver in the marketplace disappear—along with the surplus of deer.

Thus Smith tried to explain the structure of relative prices by the relative *labor* costs of production. Under his assumptions (natural resources being abundant, capital resources being of negligible importance, human resources being freely mobile between various activities, and people acting rationally in the above sense), he was right.

Just as Adam Smith was ready to predict the behavior of people in a world of primitive hunters (if the relative prices of their goods in the market ever diverged from relative costs of production in the forest), so modern microeconomists are trained to predict the behavior of groups of people in our world. Although no one can predict the behavior of any one individual (who may act

[1] Adam Smith, *An Inquiry into the Nature and Causes of the Wealth of Nations* (Homewood, Ill.: Richard D. Irwin, 1963), Book 1, Chap. 6, p. 38.

erratically because of mental defect, passion, thoughtlessness, or plain perversity), systematic self-interested behavior is dominant in groups of people. As a result, a trained microeconomist can predict the behavior, in response to certain stimuli, of groups of people. Indeed, such an observer-turned-actor, by providing the necessary stimuli, could manipulate people into behaving in a prearranged fashion! And therein lies the promise, and the danger, of applying microeconomics to the world around us.

As was noted above, modern economists have, of course, gone far beyond the vague notion of rational behavior employed by Adam Smith. As they see it, people who want to minimize the impact of scarcity on their lives by never wasting their resources, by using them ever so frugally, by *economizing* them, must employ a special way of thinking in making decisions.

Marginalist Thinking

How do we decide on the allocation of our scarce time among the many competing activities we might engage in? How do we decide on the allocation of our scarce money income among the many goods we want? Are we successfully economizing our own "resources"?

Even a moment's reflection reveals one interesting fact: seldom do we make all-or-nothing decisions. We rarely spend *all* our time studying economics and *none* of it doing other things. We rarely spend all our income buying food and none of it buying other goods. Usually, we engage in a variety of activities in a day, just as we buy many different goods with our income. Groups of people, like the citizens of a nation, do the same thing. They never use all their scarce resources for one purpose only. Hitler did not make the Germans choose *all* guns and *no* butter (combination *A* in Figure 1.3). Rather, he moved Germany along its production-possibilities frontier from a combination like *C* (lots of civilian goods, few military goods, but some of *both*) to one nearer to but not at *A* (lots of military goods, few civilian goods, but some of both). The

decisions made did not involve choosing *all* this or *all* that. It was, rather, a matter of *a little more of this* and *a little less of that*, as Figure 1.3 illustrates.

It is easy to see why all-or-nothing decisions are rare and why people often prefer to use scarce resources for a combination of many things. Imagine how you would feel about the allocation of your daily money income if you spent all of it on food only. No matter how much you wished otherwise, you couldn't buy the same amount of food *and* more of other things as well, but by giving up a little of the food you were buying in a day, you could get a little more of other things—like clothing, housing, or medical care. And you would then feel better off.

At that moment you would have utilized, unconsciously no doubt, the very key to the economical use of resources. You would have engaged in **marginalist thinking**, or thinking about the objective possibility and the subjective welfare implication of small changes in varia-

FIGURE 1.3 Making a New Choice

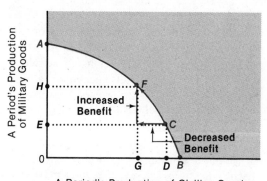

A Period's Production of Civilian Goods

The reallocation of resources in a fully employed economy can be illustrated by a movement along its production-possibilities frontier, as from *C* to *F*. As a result of this movement, one benefit is decreased—in this case, the production of civilian goods from *OD* to *OG*. At the same time, another benefit is increased—in this case, the production of military goods from *OE* to *OH*.

bles. In this case you would have determined a. that a dollar's worth of other goods could, in fact, be gained by forgoing a dollar's worth of food and b. that the potential gain to your welfare from having a little more of other goods would by far outweigh the potential loss to your welfare from doing so. (This loss would be occasioned by the necessity of having to eat less food.) By reallocating your spending accordingly, you would have squeezed from your scarce income a greater total welfare than before. And, without knowing it, you would have employed a principle of smart decision making that, consistently applied, would allow you to achieve not only greater welfare, but the greatest possible welfare.

Optimizing

When there is scarcity, any act of choice brings with it not only a benefit, but also a cost. Therefore, if we replace one choice by another choice, we will *change* both the benefit and the cost that were associated with our original choice. Economists have a special name for such changes in the overall benefit and cost of an activity. They call an increase (or decrease) in an activity's overall benefit, which is attributable to a unit increase (or decrease) in the level of that activity, its **marginal benefit (MB)**. And they call an increase (or decrease) in an activity's overall cost, which is attributable to a unit increase (or decrease) in the level of that activity, its **marginal cost (MC)** (or its marginal opportunity cost). Thus Hitler's decision to expand the production of military goods was occasioned by the judgment that the marginal benefit involved (distance *EH* in Figure 1.3) was worth more than the marginal cost (distance *DG*, the decreased benefit from the enjoyment of civilian goods, the production of which had to be decreased). Similarly, in the earlier example, your hypothetical decision to consume a larger quantity of other goods resulted from your judgment that the subjective value of the marginal benefit of doing so (the increase in your satisfaction caused by consuming more nonfood items than before)

exceeded that of the marginal cost (the decrease in your satisfaction caused by having to consume less food in order to consume more nonfood items). The decision involved nothing more difficult than applying the **optimization principle**:

> *People desiring to maximize the welfare they obtain from scarce resources must change the level of any activity as long as they do not value equally its marginal benefit, MB, and its marginal cost, MC. Whenever they value the marginal benefit more than the marginal cost, an expansion of the activity will raise their total welfare. Whenever they value the marginal benefit less than the marginal cost, a contraction of the activity will raise their total welfare. Whenever they consider the marginal benefit and marginal cost of equal value, the best possible (or optimum) level of the activity has been reached.*

If one follows this principle, any initial divergence between the values placed on marginal benefit and marginal cost tends to disappear as one changes the level of the activity in question. This surprising result occurs because the values placed on the marginal benefit tend to be smaller, and those placed on the marginal cost tend to be larger, at higher levels of an activity; at lower levels of the activity, the opposite occurs.

Declining Marginal Benefit

> *All other relevant factors being equal, the greater the overall level of any activity during a given period, the smaller will its marginal benefit usually be.*

This **principle of declining marginal benefit** is depicted in Figure 1.4 on page 14. If you were consuming no food at all during a day, you would, of course, get a zero *total* benefit from food consumption (Point *O*, upper graph). But you might place a fairly high value on *changing* your level of food consumption from zero to one

CLOSE-UP 1.2

Fish vs. Fuel at the Georges Bank

Georges Bank, lying from 50–200 miles off Massachusetts, is one of the world's most productive fishing grounds. Some 200 species of fish and shellfish spawn and feed there, including cod, haddock, flounder, lobster, and scallops. In 1978, the U. S. catch was valued at $82 million; that of foreigners at $85 million. Similar catches worth $3.34 billion were likely over the next 20 years.

Yet in 1979 some argued that Americans, if necessary, should forgo this food (incur a marginal cost) in order to get oil and gas from Georges Bank. Over the next 20 years, the drilling leases sold in 1979 were expected to yield 123 million barrels of oil and 870 billion cubic feet of gas, worth $7 billion (a larger marginal benefit).

Quite possibly, the marginal cost of $3.34 billion worth of fish did not need to be incurred at all: oil and gas leases were granted in the "safe" part of the bank, from which currents could carry any oil spill out to sea. Marine life was so diverse that only a few species were spawning at any one time (so few would have their fragile eggs and larvae harmed by any one spill). Even the harm of a spill like those at Santa Barbara and the Bay of Campeche was not expected to be permanent.

Source: *The New York Times*, October 12, 1979, p. A30.

unit. The hypothetical increase in satisfaction associated with such a one-unit change in food consumption might be designated as quantity *a*, and this *marginal* benefit is illustrated by block *a* in the lower graph. The height of block *a* would also, of course, show the total benefit associated with a daily food consumption of one unit (point *Q*, upper graph).

But, almost certainly, you would feel quite different under different circumstances. Imagine, instead, that you were consuming four units of food per day and receiving a total benefit of *R*. You would surely place a much lower value on changing your level of food consumption by one unit, from four to five units. This lower hypothetical increase in satisfaction, associated with a unit change in food consumption, might be designated as quantity *e*, and this marginal benefit is illustrated by block *e* in the lower graph. The height of block *e*, of course, also shows by how much the total benefit associated with a daily food consumption of five units (point *P*) would exceed the total benefit associated with a daily food consumption of four units (point *R*).

All this is only common sense. Can you imagine yourself placing the *same* value on getting another unit of food (or attaching the *same* importance to giving up a single unit of food) regardless of your current level of con-

sumption? Of course not. Indeed, one can easily imagine the marginal benefit of food consumption being zero at a sufficiently high level of consumption (to the right of block *e* on the lower graph). At such a point of **satiation**, the total benefit derivable from consumption could not be increased any further. The total benefit would be maximized at some point to the right of *P* in the upper graph. At that point you would feel that nothing could be gained from consuming a unit more and that nothing would be lost by consuming a unit less.

Just as one can increase daily food intake, so can one decrease it. In that case, the operation of the principle of declining marginal benefit reverses: *Because marginal benefit is lower at higher levels of an activity, marginal benefit is higher at lower levels of an activity.* You can see this reversal of the principle by noting how the size of the blocks in Figure 1.4 increases as one goes from the right-hand to the left-hand side of the graphs. This fact also corresponds to our daily experience. For example, it might make little difference to you whether you got four or five units of food per day. Your evaluation of the marginal benefit might be low (quantity *e*). Yet it might make a big difference to you to get one unit of food instead of two. Under these different circumstances, your view of the marginal benefit

FIGURE 1.4 Declining Marginal Benefit

(a)

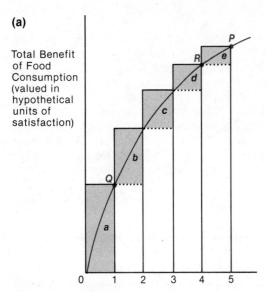

Total Benefit
of Food
Consumption
(valued in
hypothetical
units of
satisfaction)

(b)

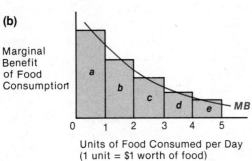

Marginal
Benefit
of Food
Consumption

Units of Food Consumed per Day
(1 unit = $1 worth of food)

This graph illustrates the principle of declining marginal benefit. All other relevant factors being equal, the higher the level of daily food consumption, the lower its marginal benefit (*MB*). The heights of blocks *a* through *e* pretend to measure the marginal benefit. Note how, in panel (b), the smooth curve drawn through the top of each block declines toward the right, while the total benefit of food consumption in panel (a)—being nothing else but the sum of the marginal benefits—rises by less and less as the amount of food consumed increases by equal units. Note: The principle is not a rigid law. Increased units of any activity may well be associated with at first rising and then constant marginal benefits (not shown here), but the principle asserts that marginal benefits always decline *eventually*.

CLOSE-UP 1.3

The Food-Safety War

When the U.S. Congress passed the Food and Drug Act of 1906, it probably made a wise decision. The marginal benefit of this act, which helped clean up unsanitary practices in the food industry and eliminated poisonous adulterants and preservatives, almost certainly exceeded its marginal cost. Marginal benefit did *not* exceed marginal cost in 1968 when Congress added the Delaney clause: this clause prohibits the use of any additives shown to cause cancer in people or animals, whether added deliberately or inadvertently during growing, processing, and packaging—and it does so regardless of the cost.

The Delaney clause was an invitation to experimenters to find conditions that render almost any substance harmful. Tests showed that all

might be high (quantity *b*). The marginal benefit of food consumption differs with your circumstances! Place this phenomenon in the context of scarcity, and you make an important discovery: *declining* marginal benefit is closely related to *rising* marginal cost.

Rising Marginal Cost

As we noted earlier, we can, in fact, always have more of one good if we are ready to give up some of another. Now we are ready to see fully the implication of making such changes. As we have more and more of one thing, the result is *declining* marginal benefits. But these benefits come to us only because we have less and less of another thing, the *rising* marginal benefits of which we have to forgo. Those forgone and rising marginal benefits of whatever we are giving up are, of course, the *rising marginal costs* of whatever we are getting more of. Given your limited money income, if you buy successively more units of clothing (Adam Smith's beaver coats), you must

kinds of manufactured and natural substances—ranging from saccharin, sodium nitrite, and food coloring agents to estrogen, vitamin D, and even eggs and ice water—could cause cancer if fed to test animals in a short enough time and in large enough quantities. As a result, the Food and Drug Administration initiated the "food-safety war." It announced its intention to ban saccharin, nitrites, and various food colorings, such as carbon black and red dye #2, from foods, drugs, and cosmetics. (Powerful new instruments allow the detection of such substances in traces of one part per billion.) While a saccharin ban affects such items as diet drinks, lipsticks, and prescription drugs, nitrites are mainly used for retarding spoilage in bacon, ham, sausages, and canned luncheon meats.

Yet critics have pointed out that the Delaney clause violates the optimization principle. Even if the FDA achieved positive marginal benefits, it would cause vastly greater marginal costs. Such costs include sickness and death as a result of tooth decay, obesity, and blood sugar problems (avoidable by saccharin) or epidemics of food poisoning (nitrites inhibit the growth of botulism toxins that used to kill many thousands each year). Regulators who would find it "unconscionable" and "despicable" to tolerate "a little bit of cancer," as they put it, are, therefore, avoiding some cancer deaths at the cost of more deaths from other causes. (In addition, the FDA would also have to ban beer, fruits, and vegetables, for all of these contain nitrites; human saliva contains a greater proportion of nitrites than canned meats!)

Source: Tom Alexander, "Time for a Cease-Fire in the Food-Safety Wars," *Fortune*, February 26, 1979, pp. 94–99.

CLOSE-UP 1.4

Benzene at the Workplace

Benzene, found in gas and oil, is one of 2000 suspected *carcinogens* (cancer-producing substances). In concentrations of over 20 parts per million (ppm), it causes leukemia. Workers have been affected by benzene in the oil industry and in plants that produce adhesives, paints, pesticides, and rubber. Acting under the authority of a 1970 law, the Occupational Safety and Health Administration (OSHA) set a 10 ppm allowable limit of benzene in the air but announced its intention to lower the limit further to 1 ppm. It was estimated that this tightened regulation would prevent one extra cancer death every three years (the marginal benefit). It would cost the industry an extra $500 million in the first year, and $150 million per year thereafter (the marginal cost).

To spend hundreds of millions of dollars in order to prevent a single death, argued the industry, was absurd. With that money, spent elsewhere, one could save *more* lives. (A mobile cardiac unit saves lives at $1,765 each, a motorcycle crash helmet campaign at $3,000 each, and a cervical cancer detection program at $3,520 each.) Indeed, a lower court set the OSHA regulation aside on grounds such as these.

Then, in 1979, the U.S. Supreme Court agreed to hear the case of *AFL-CIO Industrial Union Department* vs. *American Petroleum Institute*. Everyone thought this would decide once and for all whether government agencies had to justify the benefits of their regulations by reasonable costs, but such was not to be. The court was unable to muster a majority on any of the legal questions before it.

Sources: *The New York Times*, April 29, 1979 and October 14, 1979, p. E20; Antonin Scalia, "A Note on the Benzene Case," *Regulation*, July/August 1980, pp. 25–28.

forgo successively more units of food (his deer). As you do so, the marginal benefit to you of clothing will decline, but, simultaneously, the marginal cost to you of clothing will rise. This is so because the marginal cost to you of clothing is identical to the forgone marginal benefit to you of food, which will rise as you have less food. Consider Figure 1.5.

FIGURE 1.5   Rising Marginal Cost

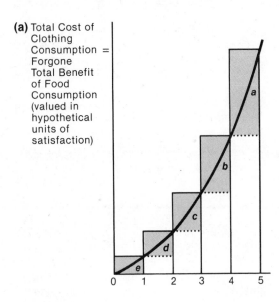

(a) Total Cost of Clothing Consumption = Forgone Total Benefit of Food Consumption (valued in hypothetical units of satisfaction)

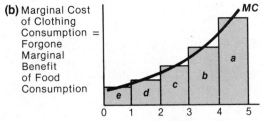

(b) Marginal Cost of Clothing Consumption = Forgone Marginal Benefit of Food Consumption

Units of Clothing Consumed per Day (1 unit = $1 worth of clothing)

The declining marginal benefit of increased food consumption implies a rising marginal benefit of decreased food consumption (Figure 1.4); this decreased food consumption constitutes the rising marginal cost of increased clothing consumption if food has to be sacrificed for clothing. Note: It is assumed here that the marginal benefit of consuming any one good is independent of the quantities consumed of any other good.

Figure 1.5 is based on Figure 1.4 and, to keep things simple, on the assumption that the marginal benefit of food is independent of the quantity of clothing, while the marginal benefit of clothing is unaffected by the quantity of food. Now imagine yourself spending $5 a day on food and clothing. If we defined a unit of each good as *a dollar's worth*, you could buy five units of food and nothing else, getting a total benefit shown by point *P* in Figure 1.4. You could, of course, get a first unit of clothing by giving up the fifth unit of food. If you did, you would gain satisfaction from clothing (a quantity we might call *f*), but your satisfaction derived from food would drop from point *P* to point *R* in Figure 1.4; that is, by quantity *e*. This would be the marginal cost of consuming one unit of clothing per day (note quantity *e* in the lower graph, Figure 1.5). Similarly, giving up the fourth unit of food (to get a second one of clothing) would involve not only a further (and smaller) gain (quantity *g*), but also a further (and larger) loss of satisfaction equal to *d* (Figure 1.4). This loss would be the marginal cost of consuming two units of clothing (note quantity *d* in the lower graph, Figure 1.5). At this point, the *total* cost of clothing consumption would be *e* + *d* (upper graph, Figure 1.5). You can proceed similarly to derive the remainder of Figure 1.5.

The Maximum Net Benefit

It is but a short step now to determine how you could gain the greatest satisfaction from your limited budget; it is just a matter of applying the optimization principle illustrated in Figure 1.6. In the upper two portions of the graph, the smooth curves representing the total and marginal cost of clothing consumption in Figure 1.5 have been redrawn. Added are total and marginal benefit curves for clothing consumption, which are analogous to those for food in Figure 1.4.

Now it can be shown that you would have to consume 2.5 units of clothing per day if you cared to maximize your **net benefit**; that is, the difference between the total benefit and total cost

FIGURE 1.6 Optimization

(a)
Total Benefit
and Total Cost
of Clothing
Consumption
(valued in
hypothetical
units of
satisfaction)

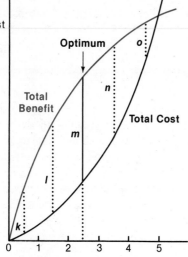

(b)
Marginal
Benefit and
Marginal Cost
of Clothing
Consumption

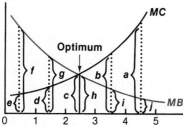

(c)
Net Benefit
of Clothing
Consumption

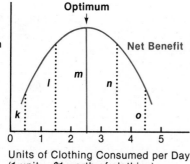

Units of Clothing Consumed per Day
(1 unit = $1 worth of clothing)

of your activities. If you consumed less, you would find the marginal benefit of clothing consumption, *MB*, exceeding the corresponding marginal cost, *MC*. Note how distance *f* exceeds *e* and how *g* exceeds *d*. In each case, by consuming more clothing at the expense of food, you would raise your total benefit (by *f* or *g*, respectively), but you would raise your total cost by less (by *e* or *d*, respectively). Because the additional satisfaction from more clothing would exceed the loss of satisfaction from less food, the difference between your total benefit and total cost, or your *net benefit*, would rise (from *k* toward *m*). Note how the net benefit is plotted separately in the lowest portion of the graph.

Similarly, you would be foolish to consume more than 2.5 units of clothing per day. If you did, you would find the marginal benefit of clothing consumption falling short of its marginal cost. Note how distance *i* falls short of *b* and how *j* falls short of *a*. In this case, by consuming less clothing but more food, you would lower your total benefit (by *j* or *i*), but you would lower your total cost more (by *a* or *b*). Since the loss of satisfaction from less clothing would be exceeded by the additional satisfaction from more food, your net benefit would again rise (from *o* toward *m*).

We can now go full circle and return to the issue raised earlier in this chapter. We make so few all-or-nothing decisions precisely because, without knowing it, we are following the optimization principle in much of our daily lives. It is rarely desirable to expand an activity in order to

This graph illustrates the principle of optimization: Anyone desiring to maximize the net benefit of an activity must expand or contract that activity up to the point at which its marginal benefit just equals its marginal cost. This optimum is reached at 2.5 units of clothing consumption in this example. Note: We abstract from the possibility that low levels of an activity may be associated with at first rising or constant marginal benefits and with at first falling or constant marginal costs in order to focus on the essentials.

maximize the total benefit from it. Note how, in the top graph of Figure 1.6, the total benefit of clothing consumption would indeed continue to rise beyond the optimum if you purchased a fourth or fifth unit. But it is the *greater* rise in total cost (the greater loss in some other benefit) that would make such action inadvisable.

Whoever follows the principle of optimization can thus reach the best possible (or *optimum*) position—not where the *total* benefit is maximized, but where the total benefit of an activity exceeds the total cost by the greatest amount, yielding the maximum *net* benefit (distance *m*). This principle is widely applicable beyond the seemingly trivial example utilized here.

A Universal Principle

The optimization principle is the universal principle of rational behavior for all who want to maximize welfare under conditions of scarcity. The people of all societies, be they members of households, managers of firms, or government officials, must apply it when deciding how to allocate their scarce resources in the best way. You must apply it if you care to allocate most effectively your scarce money income between food and clothing or your scarce time between tennis and study. Managers must apply it if they care to allocate their scarce resources most effectively between the production of cars and trucks or potatoes and wheat. Government officials must apply it if they care to allocate their scarce resources most effectively between health care and education or subways and cleaning up the environment. All these activities have marginal costs, all of which eventually rise as the activity level is increased. All these activities have declining marginal benefits also. And that is why all decision makers must be careful not to do too much of any one thing at the expense of other things that are also wanted. No matter how good or sacred any activity may seem, in a world of scarcity there is some logical stopping point beyond which an activity should be expanded no further. This is not the point of satiation, but the

point at which, in people's judgment, the marginal cost and marginal benefit have come together. Those who heed this rule will be most effective in achieving their objectives, whatever they may be. But there are complications.

Complications

Making the best of all possible choices looks simple enough in Figure 1.6. The position of the optimum is obvious no matter which one of the three graphs is considered because the example is a simple one. All the necessary data have been plotted and the necessary curves have been drawn for us, placing us in the Godlike position of an omniscient observer. A single decision maker is involved. Unfortunately, the real world is much more inconveniently arranged.

Insufficient Data or Processing Capacity

On some occasions, crucial information needed for optimizing decisions simply is not available to decision makers; on other occasions, decision makers are unable to utilize all the data that are available to them. Naturally, people who do not know the marginal benefits and marginal costs associated with their activities (perhaps because they stretch out into an uncertain future) will be unable to determine the optimum level of these activities; people who have more information than they are capable of processing will find themselves in a similar predicament. This is equally true of decision makers in households, firms, and government. Herbert Simon (see Biography 1.2) has been particularly concerned with this issue. Consider his assessment of decision making in government:[2]

> Many of the central issues of our time are questions of how we use limited information and limited computational capacity to deal with enormous problems whose shape we barely grasp. For

[2]Herbert A. Simon, "Rationality as Process and as Product of Thought," *The American Economic Review*, May 1978, p. 13.

CLOSE-UP 1.5

Russian Roulette with Skylab

The benefits and costs of choices can never be known in advance with certainty. Consider the case of Skylab, for which Americans decided to forgo $2.6 billion worth of other goods. At 77 tons, it was in 1973 the largest object ever put into orbit. Three crews of astronauts visited the lab. They gained important new knowledge about the sun, about the earth's resources, and about the ability of human beings to function in space (the longest stay was 84 days).

Potentially, though, there was an additional cost due to the space station's uncontrolled return to earth: a 1 in 152 chance that someone would be killed somewhere (or a 1 in 600 billion chance that a specific individual would be hit). There were hopes that the space shuttle would be operational by 1983 so that it could boost Skylab into a higher orbit (or at least take off the larger pieces). The space shuttle program, however, fell behind schedule—and Skylab's orbit deteriorated much faster than anticipated. (Increased sunspot activity raised the temperature and expanded the gases in the upper atmosphere, putting more air molecules in Skylab's path.) A 1979 reentry became unavoidable. Skylab would break up at an altitude of 60 miles and two thirds of it would burn up, but 500 pieces (including a 4000-pound film storage vault and a 5000-pound airlock shroud) would hit the earth. Where? Since Skylab's orbits covered the whole earth from 50° north to 50° south, and since Skylab might skip along the top of the atmosphere like a stone being skimmed along water, the 100-mile wide, 4000-mile long path of debris was unpredictable. (Predictions about paths across the continental United States and into the Amazon jungle, from the Azores to South Africa, or from Montreal to Maine and the Atlantic proved wrong.) Eventually, on July 11, 1979, during Skylab's 34,981st orbit, thousands of sparkling, glowing chunks thundered across the Indian Ocean and Australia's night sky— crackling, roaring, and trailing orange, red, and blue flames. As in the case of thousands of other space objects (and hordes of meteorites that strike the earth every year), there was no injury or damage. Last-minute unsuccessful attempts to save Skylab, or at least control its demise, cost more than the guidance rockets that could have brought it down safely but which were deleted from a 1970 appropriations bill.

Source: *The New York Times*, July 7, 1979, pp. 1 and 18; July 9, 1979, pp. A1 and B10; July 12, 1979, pp. A1 and A18.

many purposes, a modern government can be regarded as a parallel computing device. While one part of its capability for rational problem solving is directed to fire protection, another is directed to paving highways, and another to collecting refuse. For other important purposes, a government, like a human being, is a serial processing system, capable of attending to only one thing at a time. When important new policies must be formulated, public and official attention must be focused on one or a few matters. Other concerns, no matter how pressing, must wait their turn on the agenda. When the agenda becomes crowded, public life begins to appear more and more as a succession of crises. . . . There is the constant danger that attention directed to a single facet . . . will spawn solutions that disregard vital consequences for the other facets. When oil is scarce, we return to coal, but forget that we must then deal with vastly increased quantities of sulfur oxides in our urban air. Or we outlaw nuclear power stations because of radiation hazards, but fail to make alternative provision to meet our energy needs.

Multiple Decision Makers

Equally serious is the problem of multiple decision makers. As long as there is more than one decision maker in society, potential conflicts arise about the proper allocation of resources and goods. More often than not, choices that have benefits and costs for one person bring additional benefits and costs to other persons. Even if individual decision makers are not hampered by

BIOGRAPHY 1.2

Herbert A. Simon

Herbert A. Simon (1916–) was born in Milwaukee. He studied at the University of Chicago and soon became fascinated by the positive theory of human rationality. Economics to him was not just the study of the allocation of scarce resources but, above all, the study of the *rational* allocation of scarce resources. His pioneering research into the decision-making process within economic organizations is reflected in many writings, notably *Models of Man: Social and Rational* (1957). *The Sciences of the Artificial* (1969), and *Administrative Behavior*, 3rd ed. (1976). In 1978, while serving as professor of computer science and psychology at Pittsburgh's Carnegie-Mellon University, Simon was awarded the Nobel Memorial Prize in Economic Science. Simon emphasizes the fact that people who make choices may lack crucial information or be incapable of processing it. Therefore, he urges economists not to be preoccupied with *substantive* rationality at the expense of *procedural* rationality. Substantive rationality focuses on the *result* of choice and considers choice rational when the chosen level of any activity exactly yields the largest possible net benefit. Procedural rationality is concerned instead with the *process* of choice and considers choice rational when real-world people (who are neither omniscient nor omnipotent) choose tolerably effective procedures to approximate the largest possible net benefit from any activity. People are more likely to *satisfice* (approximate an optimum), Simon says, than to *maximize* (reach an optimum exactly).

> The need to approximate [is] not just a minor feature of our world to be dealt with by manufacturing larger computers or breeding smarter people. Complexity is deep in the nature of things, and discovering tolerable approximation procedures and heuristics that permit huge spaces to be searched very selectively lies at the heart of intelligence, whether human or artificial. A theory of rationality that does not give an account of problem solving in the face of complexity is sadly incomplete. It is worse than incomplete; it can be seriously misleading by providing "solutions" to economic questions that are without operational significance.[1]

[1]Simon, "Rationality as Process," p. 12.

insufficient capacities to acquire and process information relevant to maximizing their own net benefits, they may be quite unwilling (and rationally so) to take into account the external effects of their choices on others. And even in the absence of such external effects, it is, of course, always possible to increase the welfare of one person at the expense of another. Thus a difficult problem arises: How can one determine whether the separate optimizing decisions of many individuals add up to a *social* optimum as well? This is a question we must leave for later chapters.

Conclusion

What then of the optimization principle? As the biographical profile of Herbert Simon indicates (see Biography 1.2), economists are not foolish enough to assume that decision makers in households, firms, or government are omniscient and omnipotent. They know that people always have limited, and oftentimes have insufficient, capacities to acquire and process relevant information. They know that rational people so limited will be unable to settle for nothing but the best (the exact optimum) but will have to be content with approximating the optimum. Thus economists expect that people will often be unable to equate benefits and costs precisely at the margin. Yet they also expect that people, like Adam Smith's primitive hunters, will change their behavior whenever the possibility of a more satisfactory state of affairs (of reaping a larger net benefit under different circumstances) has become too obvious to be ignored. And if people who are eager to promote their own welfare at least follow the optimization principle to the best of their ability (and that seems in fact to be the case), economists who are aware of this fact have in their hands a powerful tool of prediction.

The optimization principle is helpful even in less than ideal circumstances. It helps decision makers avoid the grossest of errors in allocating their scarce resources—not a mean accomplishment in a world of scarcity—and it helps economists predict at least the direction of any changes that decision makers are likely to make. We will meet examples of this throughout the following chapters.

SUMMARY

1.   Most people on earth harbor desires for a truly staggering variety and quantity of goods. One can appreciate the extent of this desire by imagining the quantities of goods people would take if all goods were available at zero prices.

2.   Goods are produced with resources—human, natural, and capital.

3.   Technology sets limits on the quantity of goods producible per unit of resources.

4.   Limited resources and limited technology combine to yield limited quantities of goods in any given period.

5.   In all nations today, the quantity of goods that can be produced in a given period with available resources and technology falls short of the quantity required to fulfill, simultaneously, the desire for goods by all the people. This condition constitutes the economic problem of scarcity.

6.   The most obvious implication of scarcity is the need to choose. People in each society must decide on one of many possible rates at which to use their resources. They must direct their flow of resources toward consuming or investing. They must choose the detailed composition of their production and a scheme of specialization among themselves. They must choose one of many ways of apportioning their output.

7.   Choice brings a mixture of pleasure and pain because every use of resources for one purpose means forgoing the opportunity to use them for another desired purpose. Where there is scarcity, opportunity cost thus accompanies any benefit derived from a particular use of resources. This fact can be illustrated by the production-possibilities frontier.

8.   *Price theory*, or *microeconomics*, has been called the heart of economic science. It studies the behavior of decision makers in households, firms, and governments who make the kinds of choices that determine not only the detailed composition of the aggregate flows of resources and goods, but also the relative prices of individual resources and goods. Beginning with Adam Smith, economists have built this branch of economics into a powerful tool for explaining and predicting the economic behavior of people.

9.   Modern economists stress that successful economizing requires a special (marginalist) way of thinking about the objective possibility and subjective welfare implication of small changes in variables. People can always allocate another unit of their fully used resources toward one activity if they take a unit away from another activity. They can always have a marginal benefit if they are ready to pay a marginal cost.

10.   The optimization principle tells people who wish to maximize their welfare under what circumstances it is wise or foolish to expand one activity at the expense of another. The optimization principle tells people whenever a subjective evaluation of one activity shows

   a. $MB > MC$, one should expand the activity.

   b. $MB < MC$, one should contract the activity.

   c. $MB = MC$, the activity level is optimum.

11.   As a consequence of the principle of declining marginal benefit, any initial divergence between marginal benefit and marginal cost tends to disappear as one changes the level of an activity.

12.   Declining marginal benefits associated with increased levels of an activity imply rising marginal benefits associated with decreased levels of that activity. If such decreased levels are the opportunity cost of increasing some other activity, the rising marginal benefits forgone from the sacrificed activity become the rising marginal costs of the increasing activity.

13. The net benefit of any activity can be maximized by following the optimization principle.

14. The optimization principle is a universal principle of rational behavior that sets, for all activities, a logical stopping point beyond which that activity should be expanded no further.

15. Optimizing can, however, be an elusive goal, especially when crucial information needed by individual decision makers is absent or when they are unable to utilize data that are available. The presence of multiple decision makers adds further complications to the quest for optimal choices concerning the allocation of resources and goods.

KEY TERMS

benefit
capital resources
cost
desire for goods
economics
financial capital
goods
human capital
human resources
macroeconomics
marginal benefit *(MB)*
marginal cost *(MC)*
marginalist thinking
microeconomics
natural resources
net benefit
opportunity cost
optimization principle
principle of declining
marginal benefit

process of production
production-possibilities frontier
resources
satiation
scarcity
technology

QUESTIONS AND PROBLEMS

1. **a.** Which of the following are *natural resources* as defined above: 100 cubic feet of coal, a highway, a cow, an acre of land, sand at a beach not yet discovered by humans, sunshine, a school of tuna in the ocean, a college building, a can of peas? (*Hint*: Of the nine required answers, three will be *always*, three others *never* and the remaining three *maybe*.) What reasons can you give for your answers?

b. Which of the following are *capital resources*: an automobile-assembly plant, a toy truck, Ford Motor Company stock, a natural waterfall, unsold refrigerators held by an appliance dealer, an inventory of groceries held by a food store, a horse, a truck driver, a wristwatch? (*Hint*: Of the nine required answers, three will be *always*; three others *never*; and the remaining three *maybe*.) What reasons can you give for your answers?

2. Draw a production-possibilities frontier like the one in Figure 1.2. Label the vertical axis "investment goods" and the horizontal one "consumption goods." Choose some point on the curve near the middle to depict a country's present position. What do you think would eventually happen *to the entire curve* if the country's citizens

a. increased the production of investment goods (and your chosen point moved up and left along the frontier)?

b. reduced the production of investment goods (and your chosen point moved down and right along the frontier)?

c. decided to give up the "rat race" and be content with a minimum of both types of goods?

3. Consider the concept of *opportunity cost.*

a. Suppose you had to choose one of *three* items. If you chose *a*, what would be the opportunity cost: *b, c,* or both?

b. What do you think is the opportunity cost of each of the following: giving more foreign aid, stepping up the arms race, avoiding air and water pollution?

c. When people say "time is money," what can they possibly mean?

4. Consider the beaver-deer example of Adam Smith.

a. What is the shape of a production-possibilities frontier for beavers and deer implied by his example?

b. What would be the outcome of his story if the government fixed the beaver/deer price at 1:1 and also prevented people from switching occupations?

c. Do you think one could apply his price theory to determine the value of a *human* life relative to deer or any other good? Would your answer differ for people in the United States as opposed to people in India?

5. Have another look at Figure 1.1, which illustrates the scarcity problem. Residents of poor countries are almost unanimous in preferring policies that increase the right-hand circle to policies that decrease the left-hand circle; the reverse is found only among some residents of rich countries. Explain, using the principle of declining marginal benefit.

6. Explain the following statements (with the help of Figure 1.6 on optimization):

a. "It may be wise for a household to stop the consumption of any good long before satiation is reached, and it would be stupid to increase consumption beyond satiation."

b. "It may be wise for a nation to stop putting more resources into education long before the extra benefits from such action have fallen to zero."

c. "It is stupid to maximize the total bene-fit of an activity and equally stupid to minimize its total cost."

7. Mr. A: I have been looking at Figure 1.6 on optimization. It's fascinating! Just imagine how one can apply it to other things besides mundane commodities: one could put on the horizontal axis the height of trees or of buildings, the weight of people or of airplanes, the size of people's wealth or of their business organizations, the degree of pollution or the degree of race or sex discrimination in society. Or even people's sinfulness and the length of their lives! In all these cases and a million more, the graph applies. Most things are good when there is little of them and bad when there is much.

Mrs. B: Really, *you* are a little much. Your application of the optimization principle is an outrage. I am with Wordsworth: "High Heaven rejects the lore of nicely calculated less or more."

Discuss.

8. Evaluate each illustration of the following statement: "People, clearly, do *not* optimize:

a. Note how speeders end up in the hospital, bank robbers go to jail, and cheating students are thrown out of school."

b. Note how so many people do things I would never do because I know it is bad for me (and them)."

c. Note how so many people act selfishly, impulsively, or out of habit."

SELECTED READINGS

Boulding, Kenneth E. *Collected Papers* (Boulder, Colo: Associated University Press, 1971–75), *vol. 1,* "Is Economics Necessary?"; *vol. 2,* "Some Contributions of Economics to the General Theory of Value" (Chap. 1), "The Uses of Price Theory" (Chap. 19), "The Economics of the Coming Spaceship Earth" (Chap. 26); *vol. 3,* "The Economist and the Engineer" (Chap. 14), "Is Scarcity Dead?" (Chap. 20), "The Misallocation of Intellectual Resources in Economics" (Chap. 35), "After Samuelson, Who Needs Adam Smith?" (Chap. 36); *vol. 4,* "The Menace of Methuselah: Possible Consequences of Increased Life Expectancy" (Chap. 20).

Gramm, Warren S. "The Selective Interpretation of Adam Smith," *Journal of Economic Issues*, March 1980, pp. 119–41.

An argument that economists are not reading Adam Smith correctly.

Simon, Herbert A. *Administrative Behavior*, 3rd ed. (New York: Macmillan, 1976).

A study of the decision-making process within economic organizations.

Simon, Herbert A. "Rational Decision Making in Business Organizations," *The American Economic Review*, September 1979, pp. 493–513.

The 1978 Nobel Prize lecture.

Smith, Adam. *An Inquiry into the Nature and Causes of the Wealth of Nations*, (Homewood, Ill.: Richard D. Irwin, 1963, originally 1776).

The first systematic treatment of economic science.

CHAPTER 2

The Economic System and Economic Theory

As the preceding chapter has indicated, the citizens of all nations have one thing in common: everywhere and every day, people have to wrestle with scarcity and make painful choices about allocating resources and apportioning goods. Yet the people of different societies have chosen vastly different arrangements for making these choices. This chapter will discuss two major types of **economic systems**, or social arrangements by which people cooperate with each other in the allocation of resources and the apportionment of goods. This chapter will also show the role economic theory plays in helping us understand different economic systems. One thing that all modern economic systems have in common is that they are extremely complex because most people are participants in a vast scheme of specialization.

A Universal Feature: Large-Scale Specialization

Consider these facts about the United States in the 1980s: Its economy includes some 80 million households (mostly families, but also individuals living alone), some 15 million firms (single proprietorships, partnerships, and corporations), and over 80,000 separate governments (local, state, and federal). All of these make economic choices about the production and apportionment of millions of goods and the utilization of as many resources. (Consider the many types and qualities of resources contained in each of the three broad classes of resources—human, natural, and capital—discussed in Chapter 1.)

Conceivably, of course, each and every good could be produced by the very same people who consume it. Each household, for instance, could be a totally self-sufficient unit of production and consumption, very much like Robinson Crusoe. It could use whatever resources it had, produce its own food, clothing, shelter, and so on, and be totally independent of the rest of humanity. In fact, however, this is the exception rather than the rule. In the United States, people consume little, if anything, of what they themselves produce. They are part of a grand division of labor. They exchange most or all of their own production with others who similarly specialize. These others, furthermore, are apt to be not a few identifiable persons, but literally hundreds of thousands of unknown people: farmers in Kansas, factory workers in Michigan, tin miners in Bolivia, sheep ranchers in Australia, oil workers in the North Sea, typists in California. . . . All of these, in one way or another, help provide each of us with the goods we do consume.

Why this elaborate setup? Because we all get more goods when the process of production is organized on the basis of specialization and exchange rather than on the basis of self-sufficiency of every person or region. Imagine how few and primitive our goods would be if we insisted on making all of them ourselves or if, like Crusoe, we had to do so. A look at some of the small self-contained communities in this world, such as those of the African Bushmen, the Amazon Indians, or the Greenland Eskimos, illustrates this point.

Adam Smith articulated the advantages of the division of labor 200 years ago when he pointed out that a pinmaker could not produce twenty pins in a day if he himself had to do everything that was required—drawing out the wire, straightening it, cutting it, pointing it, grinding it for receiving the head, making the head, and so on. Yet Smith observed that ten people, only poorly equipped with machinery but with the proper division of labor among them, were able to make 48,000 pins in one day.

This particular example, of course, refers to specialization within a firm, but Smith was well aware of the benefits from specialization on a larger scale. He knew how the wealth of nations could be increased by the kind of regional cooperation involved in international trade among countries. Yet, as this very example serves to show, use of the division of labor is not a feature peculiar to the U.S. economy; it is a worldwide phenomenon. And the benefits, measured in greater production of goods, are enormous. Unfortunately, where there is a benefit, there is oftentimes a cost. And so it is here. Americans, Russians, and all other people who enjoy the obvious material benefits derived from a division of labor have to pay a price. They must divert valuable resources to deal with the complex problem of *coordination* to which the division of labor gives rise.

A Universal Problem: Assuring Coordination

As people interact in their economic activities, not only within each firm and each nation, but even with people throughout the world, every-thing that one person does comes to intermingle with the actions of all others in an endless web. Any one action requires, directly and indirectly, appropriate complementary actions by thousands of other people. Think of a simple good—for example, a cake—and how it typically comes to you. Imagine the countless people and the countless types of natural and capital resources that are necessary to produce the ingredients of a cake. And trace in your mind the countless stages through which each of these ingredients must travel before they turn into a cake. Consider how many more resources are involved in bringing it to you! Then think of the many other goods you consume, every day. How easy it would be for something to go wrong somewhere in the complicated sets of events that create these goods and transport them through space and time.

In 1845, Frédéric Bastiat, a famous French economist, was having just such thoughts:[1]

> On coming to Paris for a visit, I said to myself: Here are a million human beings who would all die in a few days if supplies of all sorts did not flow into this great metropolis. It staggers the imagination to try to comprehend the vast multiplicity of objects that must pass through its gates tomorrow, if its inhabitants are to be preserved from the horrors of famine, insurrection, and pillage. And yet all are sleeping peacefully at this moment without being disturbed for a single instant by the idea of so frightful a prospect. . . .
>
> How does each succeeding day manage to bring to this gigantic market just what is necessary—neither too much nor too little? What, then, is the resourceful and secret power that governs the amazing regularity of such complicated movements, a regularity in which everyone has such implicit faith, although his prosperity and his very life depend upon it?

One could write a similar story today. Think of New York. As in Bastiat's Paris, millions of

---

[1]Translated by the author from ''Il n'y a pas de principes absolus'' in *Sophismes Économiques*, in *Oeuvres Complètes de Frédéric Bastiat*, vol. 4 (Paris: Guillaume, 1907), pp. 94–97. *See* Bastiat, *Economic Sophisms* (Princeton, N.J.: D. Van Nostrand Co., 1964) for an English edition.

people are living there. In a matter of days, they would all starve without a continual influx of goods. And what variety and quantity of goods these are! Thousands of tons of bread and fruit, trainloads of meat and coal, furniture and shirts, hairspray and bobby pins! These goods come not only from the surrounding countryside, but from the farthest corners of the globe. For days and months, by air, sea, and land, they are traveling, with New York as their destination. The same is true, on a smaller scale, for every city, town, and village in this country. But who is in charge of planning and guiding all this activity on which our existence depends? Who makes sure that the activities of every person mesh perfectly with those of all other persons?

For New York and the U.S. economy, the answer to these questions is "nobody at all." For Moscow and the Soviet economy, the answer would be quite different. These two economic systems differ drastically in the way they try to achieve **economic order**, a state of affairs in which the specialized activities of all the people engaged in the division of labor are well coordinated.

Whenever people decide to engage in a division of labor, their separate activities can be coordinated in one of two ways: by **deliberate coordination** or by **spontaneous coordination**. The former approach is easier to understand; it tends to be the first solution that people consider when thinking about the coordination problem.

Deliberate Coordination

Characteristics of Deliberate Coordination

The separate economic activities of people engaged in a division of labor can be coordinated deliberately by a manager or a central planner. This deliberate coordination is also known as **managerial coordination** or the system of the **Visible Hand**. Under such circumstances, human reason is in charge (a matter most pleasing to human vanity). Ideally, the manager creates a social blueprint of everybody's activities to be

performed during a future period. This blueprint is supposed to account for the concrete actions of all individuals at every moment and to assure that the separate activities of all people mesh perfectly. If a manager decides to make locomotives, this manager would assign just the right number of other people, raw materials, and machines to produce just the right amounts of iron ore needed to make just the right amount of steel to make the locomotives. And, similarly, everything else that happens is to fit perfectly into the design: the manager would order production of just the right amount of fuel to make just the right amount of electricity to run the machines that make the ball bearings for still other machines that make locomotive wheels. Once the plan is made, specific orders are issued to all individuals, and they are expected to do nothing but obey. The entire economy is thus run like one giant factory, by the visible hand of a manager.

Unfortunately, not everything that is logically conceivable is practically possible. The kind of task outlined above is an extremely difficult one. It can be carried out perfectly only by someone who is both omniscient and omnipotent, as a simple thought experiment can illustrate:

Imagine that *you* were a country's economic dictator, and nothing could happen without your direction. Many millions of people were waiting for your commands. How would you decide what to produce and how and when and where and for whom? On what basis would you conclude that John Doe should mine iron ore to be made into steel to be made into locomotives? Why not use the steel to make orchard-spraying machines? Or plows to prepare a field for growing corn? Or should you grow red cabbages? If so, how many would you grow, where exactly should they go, and when? Your chance of making a complete mess of things would be excellent indeed. As would any central planner who is merely human, you would quickly run into the problem of being unable to gather, digest, and communicate all the knowledge that must be used to do a perfect job. Managerial coordination, therefore, has a number of inevitable costs.

The Costs of Deliberate Order

Any one person who attempted the task of managerial coordination on a large scale would be incapable of making the different actions of different people mesh. Chaos rather than order would reign. In order to achieve even the semblance of order, such a person would need the help of an elaborate bureaucracy, staffed with tens of thousands of people and equipped with fancy communications and computing devices.

All these resources, however, could be producing other goods instead. The loss of these potential goods is the first cost of managerial coordination.

Loss of output due to inefficiency is the second cost of managerial coordination. Even a large planning bureaucracy is unlikely to achieve the best possible allocation of resources. Friedrich A. von Hayek (see Biography 2.1) has been particularly eloquent in pointing out the reason for this inefficiency: large numbers of people who wish to arrange a division of labor always

BIOGRAPHY 2.1
Friedrich A. von Hayek

Friedrich August von Hayek (1899-   ) was born and educated in Vienna. He began his career as director of the Austrian Institute for Economic Research and lecturer in economics at the University of Vienna. Starting in 1931 he served as professor first at the London School of Economics, then at the University of Chicago, and finally at the University of Freiburg in Germany. In 1974, while serving as visiting professor at the University of Salzburg in Austria, von Hayek was awarded the Nobel Memorial Prize in Economic Science (jointly with Sweden's Gunnar Myrdal). Von Hayek's greatest insight, perhaps, is that markets, above all else, are mechanisms for utilizing knowledge. He considered the question of what institutional arrangement could best enable large numbers of people—each possessing only bits of knowledge—to cooperate with each other so as to achieve the best use of resources. He rejected the notion that one could put at the disposal of some center all the knowledge that ought to be used but that was initially dispersed among many. The relevant knowledge is made up of elements of such number, diversity, and variety, he argued, that its explicit, conscious combination in a single mind is impossible. Yet the spontaneous interaction of people in free markets can bring about that which could be achieved by deliberate action only by someone possessing the combined knowledge of all. Consider his own words:[1]

It is worth contemplating for a moment a very simple and commonplace instance of the action of the price system to see what precisely it accomplishes. Assume that somewhere in the world a new opportunity for the use of some raw material, say tin, has arisen, or that one of the sources of supply of tin has been eliminated. It does not matter for our purpose—and it is very significant that it does not matter—which of these two causes has made tin more scarce. All that the users of tin need to know is that some of the tin they used to consume is now more profitably employed elsewhere. . . . There is no need for the great majority of them even to know where the more urgent need has arisen. . . . If only some of them know directly of the new demand, and switch resources over to it, and if the people who are aware of the new gap thus created in turn fill it from still other sources, the effect will rapidly spread throughout the whole economic system and influence not only all the uses of tin, but also those of its substitutes and the substitutes of these substitutes, the supply of all the things made of tin, and their substitutes. . . .

The most significant fact about this system is the economy of knowledge with which it operates. . . . In abbreviated form, by a kind of symbol, only the most essential information

encounter the **knowledge problem**, the difficulty of making use jointly of all the knowledge relevant to the most effective division of labor because such knowledge is not available to a single mind in its totality but is found, in billions of dispersed fragments, in the minds of countless separate individuals. This knowledge, furthermore, is not only *scientific* knowledge, of general applicability—for example, the technical knowledge about which chemicals must be combined in what proportions to make plastics. Such scientific knowledge could conceivably be gathered in one central place. The knowledge about which Hayek is concerned is primarily *unorganized* knowledge of particular applicability, the fleeting knowledge of the particular circumstances of place and time. Consider knowledge of *production possibilities* and *preferences* that refers only to particular places and people and moments. Each individual inevitably possesses unique bits of such information.

This information may be about a **marginal**

---

is passed on, and passed on only to those concerned. . . . The marvel is that in a case like that of a scarcity of one raw material, without an order being issued, without more than perhaps a handful of people knowing the cause, tens of thousands of people whose identity could not be ascertained by months of investigation, are made to use the material or its products more sparingly. . . .

I have deliberately used the word "marvel" to shock the reader out of the complacency with which we often take the working of this mechanism for granted. I am convinced that if it were the result of deliberate human design, and if the people guided by the price changes understood that their decisions have significance far beyond their immediate aim, this mechanism would have been acclaimed as one of the greatest triumphs of the human mind. . . . But those who clamor for "conscious direction"—and who cannot believe that anything which has evolved without design (and even without our understanding it) should solve problems which we should not be able to solve consciously—should remember this: The problem is precisely how to extend the span of our utilization of resources beyond the span of the control of any one mind; and, therefore, how to dispense with the need of conscious control and how to provide inducements which will make the individuals do the desirable things without anyone having to tell them what to do.

Von Hayek is more than an economist. He is also an eminent political and legal theorist. He is convinced that markets do the best job of solving the problem of resource allocation, but only if they are free from any distortions introduced by ill-advised government. In a best-selling book, *The Road to Serfdom* (1944), von Hayek warns that the enthusiasm of governments for intervening in the market leads us down a path that ends in central planning and totalitarianism. Government intervention will thus cause the end of the free society, humanity's highest social achievement.

Von Hayek's most recent books from the University of Chicago Press are magnificent statements of all of these themes: *The Constitution of Liberty* (1960); and *Law, Legislation, and Liberty*, vol. I, *Rules and Order* (1973), vol. II, *The Mirage of Social Justice* (1976), and vol. III, *The Political Order of a Free Society* (1979).

[1]Friedrich A. von Hayek, "The Use of Knowledge in Society," *The American Economic Review*, September 1945, pp. 519–30.

rate of transformation, (MRT), the rate at which a producer is technically able to exchange, in the process of production, a little bit of one variable (say, labor or butter) for a little bit of another variable (say, apples produced with the help of that labor or produced in place of that butter). Or the information may be about a **marginal rate of substitution, (MRS)**, the rate at which a consumer is willing to exchange, as a matter of indifference, a little bit of one variable (say, the consumption of leisure or butter) for a little bit of another variable (say, the consumption of apples received for the sacrifice of leisure or butter). Let us refer to these bits of information as *MRT*s (production possibilities) and *MRS*s (preferences), respectively. Then we can follow Hayek's argument:

Consider, Hayek suggests, the enormous volume of this information. In the area of production possibilities, imagine the set of billions of *MRT*s. One *MRT* might be that of a farmer who could turn an extra day's worth of labor into 10 extra tons of wheat (given, of course, that farm's current levels and types of output, its current employment of particular people, land, and capital, and currently available technical knowledge). Another *MRT* might be the rate of a different farmer whose quite different circumstances allowed only a yield of 2 extra tons of wheat for an extra day of labor applied. Clearly, any one person who possessed knowledge of both of these *MRT*s would realize that it would be more effective to allocate extra labor to the first farm rather than the second one, if extra wheat was to be produced. Yet there might be another farmer still whose *MRT* was even more favorable. And all these *MRT*s would be conditional upon current circumstances. Every change in the volume of inputs and outputs, in technical knowledge, in the quality of people or machines, the weather, the geographic location, and a million other circumstances would change these objective possibilities.

The same is true for people's preferences. Imagine the nearly infinite set of *MRS*s: One *MRS* might be that of a man willing to exchange, indifferently, an extra hour of work for the equivalent of an extra bushel of apples. Another person might be delighted to give up income equivalent to two bushels of apples for an extra hour of leisure. Once more, a person knowing both could arrange for a mutually advantageous deal. And once more such a person would realize that there were billions of *MRS*s to consult, if the best allocation of resources was to be achieved, and that each of these *MRS*s would be conditional upon current circumstances. Hayek tells us that if the mind (or the computer) of a national central planner contained all this knowledge about the ever-changing circumstances of all individuals, that planner might search systematically for ways to improve the allocation of resources and thereby raise the welfare of people. But such is not the case. No central planner (or group of planners) can ever possess this unorganized type of knowledge. It must always remain dispersed. The central planner (or group of planners) will always be ignorant of most of what is known to all others taken together.

Even if, by some miracle, such planners could gather together all the knowledge that should be used but that was, in the first instance, held by others, it would then be impossible to integrate the information received and issue appropriate commands to the various individuals. Such an attempt would immediately founder on the problem of information overload. An infinite amount of information—all of which is relevant to the best use of resources and all of which is continually changing—simply could not be digested. Any single individual (or group of individuals), even with fancy computers, has a limited attention span and a limited capacity for comprehension or for weighing alternatives. When told absolutely everything, even if it were possible, people could simply not handle all the information received. Thus an economic commander could not help but ignore much that is relevant for issuing the best possible set of commands and for verifying their execution. The loss of output due to inefficiency would be the second cost of managerial coordination, to be added to the first cost of output lost to establishing a bureaucracy.

A third cost of managerial coordination might be the loss of output that occurs as a result of incentive problems. As we will note in Chapter 15, such problems might accompany attempts by central planners to create "distributive justice" by divorcing people's income from their contribution to production. (If people were told, for example, that they will get the same income as everyone else no matter what they did, they might just decide to work less than otherwise and produce less output.)

Given the likelihood of these heavy costs of managerial coordination, it is not surprising that the centrally planned economies of the Soviet Union and Eastern Europe have flirted with the alternative method of coordinating the interdependent activities of people through the market. And it is not surprising that in our own economy the principle of the deliberate order has survived only *within* firms. In fact, the inability of managers of large firms to escape the above costs is one of the reasons why these firms cease to grow or why they introduce market relations even internally. (General Motors, whose management must coordinate the activities of more than half a million employees, is an example of a firm introducing internal market relations among its independent divisions.)

Spontaneous Coordination

Characteristics of Spontaneous Coordination

Many economists, since the days of Adam Smith, have argued that the separate economic activities of people engaged in a division of labor can be coordinated spontaneously by price signals generated in markets. This is called the system of **market coordination** or of the **Invisible Hand**. No central planner is put in charge of anything (a situation that dooms people, critics argue, to "irrationality" and "enslavement by blind forces"). In such a system, people do not cooperate with each other because someone issues commands reinforced, no doubt, by appropriate threats for noncompliance. Gone is the motto of

the deliberate order: "You will do what I tell you, or I will do something bad to you." Instead, all individuals make their own plans on the basis of whatever limited knowledge they happen to possess. Then they meet in markets and make conditional offers to one another: "I will do something nice for you, if you do something nice for me," they say.

Coordination of these independently decided but interdependent actions of different people is achieved and maintained by the **price system**, the set of interdependent prices in all the markets for goods and resources. These prices change as long as the independent actions of households and firms are not perfectly coordinated, making households and firms, in turn, change their behavior until coordination is achieved. Prices tell people indirectly what their inability to know everybody and everything intimately keeps them from knowing directly. Being keenly aware of how their welfare is affected by the prices they can get for what they sell and by the prices they must pay for what they want, all people are habitual price watchers. When people look for 16 million tons of apples, while only 8 million are being offered, anxious would-be buyers of apples will compete against each other and drive the price up. In response to these higher prices, two changes will occur: 1. some price-watching households will change their minds and decide to seek fewer apples at the higher price (using, perhaps, oranges instead); 2. some price-watching owners of firms will change their minds, too, and decide to offer more apples at the higher price (producing more apples at the expense of something else, reducing apple inventories, increasing imports, and so on). Before you know it, a balance will be achieved between the production and consumption of apples. Similar adjustments will occur in all other realms of activity.

Adam Smith had this to say way back in 1776:[2]

[2] Adam Smith, *An Inquiry Into the Nature and Causes of the Wealth of Nations* (Homewood, Ill.: Irwin, 1963/1776), vol. 1, p. 12; vol 2, pp. 21–23.

It is not from the benevolence of the butcher, the brewer, or the baker that we expect our dinner, but from their regard of their own interest. We address ourselves not to their humanity, but to their self-love, and never talk to them of our own necessities but of their advantages. . . . Every individual is continually exerting himself to find out the most advantageous employment of whatever capital he can command . . . he intends only his own gain, and he is in this . . . led by an invisible hand to promote an end which was no part of his intention. By pursuing his own interest, he frequently promotes that of the society more effectually than when he really intends to promote it.

And Bastiat answered his own question about the secret power that governs economic activity in the market economy:[3]

That power . . . is the principle of free exchange. We put our faith in that inner light which Providence has placed in the hearts of all men, and to which has been entrusted the preservation and the unlimited improvement of our species, a light we term *self-interest*, which is so illuminating, so constant, and so penetrating, when it is left free of every hindrance. Where would you be, inhabitants of Paris, if some cabinet minister decided to substitute for that power contrivances of his own invention, however superior we might suppose them to be: if he proposed to subject this prodigious mechanism to his supreme direction, to take control of all of it into his own hands, to determine by whom, where, how, and under what conditions everything should be produced, transported, exchanged, and consumed? Although there may be much suffering within your walls, although misery, despair, and perhaps starvation, cause more tears to flow than your warmhearted charity can wipe away, it is probable, I dare say it is certain, that the arbitrary intervention of the government would infinitely multiply this suffering and spread among all of you the ills that now affect only a small number of your fellow citizens.

And thus it is in the United States. Basically, the economic choices made by a multitude of different households, firms, and governments are coordinated spontaneously, unconsciously and without the intervention of any human commander-in-chief. Economic order is generated, as if by an Invisible Hand, because self-interested decision makers take their cues from the movement of market prices and adjust their activities as needed. However, spontaneous order, like the deliberate one, is not achieved without costs.

The Costs of Spontaneous Order

Just as managerial coordination sacrifices output by tying up valuable resources in a bureaucracy to make possible the central planning and management of the economy, so market coordination sacrifices output by tying up valuable resources to make possible decentralized planning and management. Economists talk of **transactions costs**, or the **costs of exchange**, when output is sacrificed because resources are used to set up a system of voluntary exchanges and keep it functioning. Consider what is involved.

To begin with, a government bureaucracy is needed to assign **property rights**; that is, rights to the exclusive, but perhaps socially circumscribed, use of scarce things. And these rights have to be transferable from one person to another. Clearly, unless such rights to all scarce resources and goods were assigned to particular people, nobody would ever succeed in selling anything (or have any reason to buy anything).

In addition, a government agency can facilitate widespread exchange by providing a convenient medium of exchange—money. And people must also set up a system of police and courts to protect property rights. At its best, such protection assures that holders of property rights are never prevented from exercising these rights as they see fit and are never coerced (by brute force, fraud, deceit, and the like) into uses of their rights that they dislike.

Finally, the parties who have items to exchange have to expend further resources to find each other, to inform themselves about the characteristics of items to be traded, to negotiate contracts, and to arrange for payment.

[3]Bastiat, *Sophismes Économiques*.

But note: These transactions costs (which can be avoided in a pure system of managerial coordination) should not be confused with **transfer costs** (which are present in any economic system). Transfer costs might be measured as output sacrificed because resources are used to transport goods from one point in space or time to another.

Interestingly, the existence of transactions costs explains why business firms in the United States remain islands of managerial coordination within the larger sea that is the market economy. Conceivably, the owners of firms could utilize the principle of market coordination when arranging the division of labor *within* their firms, making it work in the same fashion as it works so quietly, persistently, and successfully in arranging the division of labor *among* firms. In principle, a new contract could be negotiated with each worker for every single task to be performed. Thus, a worker could be guided by differential wages to run the turret lathe now, overhaul the truck engine later, and deliver packages the next morning, just as the firm itself is guided by differential prices to produce different items, or different quantities of a given item, at different times. Yet oftentimes the transactions costs for carrying the principle of the Invisible Hand into the firm are too high. Owners of firms find it more advantageous to substitute a single contract for an infinite series of them. Within specified limits, workers pledge obedience to a boss; for that obedience they receive a wage. Within the confines of the firm, the boss becomes a central planner.

All of this discussion leaves one important issue unsettled. We have seen that the spontaneous economic order generates transactions costs that are analogous to (but not necessarily of equal size as) the costs of a central planning bureaucracy in the deliberate order. But we have not considered whether market coordination, like managerial coordination, is likely to produce additional costs of forgone output through economic inefficiency or through the pursuit of distributive justice that affects incentives adversely. These questions are addressed in the remaining chapters of this book, which are devoted exclusively to a thorough study of the market economy.

Theorizing: Making Maps of Reality

Some professors tell the story of a mythical student who demanded ''just the facts, all the facts.'' Anyone who wants to understand a modern market economy (such as that of the United States) and who wants to judge the degree of its success in allocating scarce resources in the best possible way does well not to ask for *all* the facts. It is too easy to drown in an infinite morass of incoherent detail. Contrary to the often heard cliché, facts do *not* speak for themselves.

Paradoxically, true understanding is always gained through the orderly *loss* of information. To gain such understanding of our economy, we must simplify, even ruthlessly so. We must first take something like a satellite picture of the market economy, a picture that brings into sharp relief the broad outlines of reality but fails to convey important details. Once we have come to understand the *essence* of the market economy in Part Two, we can move our vantage point and consider additional features of the bewildering complexity around us in the remaining chapters.

The process of abstracting from reality, of focusing on only its most important features, is called *theorizing*. Theorizing is akin to producing a geographic map. Because all of us have used maps, all of us are already familiar with the benefits of theorizing. Notice how geographers never provide us with a detailed picture of the world. Nowadays they draw their maps from satellite and aircraft photographs, and, before we know it, they show us the whole United States on a piece of paper twelve inches square. What could be more unrealistic? Yet realism would force the map makers to include every town, every brook, every house and tree, even every blade of grass in the landscape. This would be manifestly absurd. If we insisted on realism in maps, none of us would have the slightest idea even of the broad outlines of our physical environment. Literally, we would be lost. It is just when we create the unrealistic, when we forget about the many towns and brooks and houses, when we refuse to consider trees and blades of grass, that we create the useful. Up to a point, the more unrealistic it is, the more useful our map becomes! As we delete most of the detail and concentrate on the essentials, we extract ourselves from the chaos of fact and see things to which we were blind before. Economic theorizing does the same sort of thing. It produces a set of propositions intended to serve as an explanation of the major phenomena observed in the economy. Like a map, such **theory** is a simplified representation of reality.

Note: Just as one can draw many types of maps, even of the same geographic area, so one can create many theories for a given economic environment. One can abstract from reality in many different ways and to different degrees, and there is no single correct way of doing so.

Consider, for instance, the three maps of Logan International Airport in Figure 2.1. Each one of them depicts the airport area of Boston, Massachusetts, but each map focuses on different aspects of this reality. Which map is the most useful one depends very much on the purpose of the user. A pilot cleared by approach control "along Victor 431 to Rever" will wish to use map (a) because none of the other maps depicts this airway (V-431) and this intersection in the sky (Rever). Such a pilot would have no use whatsoever for a street map of Boston (not shown) or map (c) of Logan's taxiways.

Yet a pilot "cleared for ILS runway 4 Right approach" would find maps (a) and (c) quite useless, and map (b) of extreme importance. Map (b) depicts other aspects of the same reality: the 110.3 megahertz frequency of the instrument landing system, the 035° inbound magnetic course, the 375 megahertz frequency of the outer marker, the exact spot (MM) above which a yellow middle marker light will flash in the cockpit, and much more.

Finally, picture the same pilot on the ground, about to vacate runway 4 Right, perhaps at the runway 33 Right intersection. The ground controller might say: "Eastern 701, cleared to the ramp, via November, the Outer, and Whiskey." Could the pilot find the route to the Eastern

Airlines Terminal (EA) with the help of maps (a) or (b)? Of course not. Nothing but map (c) would do.

One day, perhaps, you will land at Boston's Logan International Airport. If you do, you are likely to be aware of none of the features of reality that are depicted on these three maps. Most likely, you will not even know whether you are landing on runway 4 Right, 33 Left, 27, or whatever. The world of your awareness will be a totally different one: filled with ships in the harbor, perhaps; with glances of a skyline, the Prudential Building; with fleeting views of gas trucks, fire engines, and baggage carts; with taxis crawling through Callahan tunnel, past Quincy Market. . . .

Yet the world depicted on our three maps will also be there: a world of electronic beacons and hypothetical lines in the sky, of men and women behind radar screens that stand in rows inside a concrete box in Nashua, of disembodied voices that come out of black boxes on the ground and in the sky. Whether you will know it or not, the maps that depict this unseen world will have served you well.

In the same way, anyone who wishes to navigate the infinitely more complex world of our economic system will be served best by a varied set of strange-looking maps, or theories, that highlight only limited aspects of reality. The remainder of this chapter introduces the first of these maps.

Mapping the Market Economy

The market economy discussed in the rest of this book will be assumed to operate under **capitalism**, an economic system in which most resources are privately owned. The major exchange relations that exist in such an economy can be depicted by the circular flows in Figure 2.2. Consider part (a). The left-hand box represents a likely multitude of households in whose adult members the property rights to most resources reside. (Even in capitalism, some resources must be owned by government so that it can perform

Figure 2.1 Maps of Logan International Airport

(a)

(b)

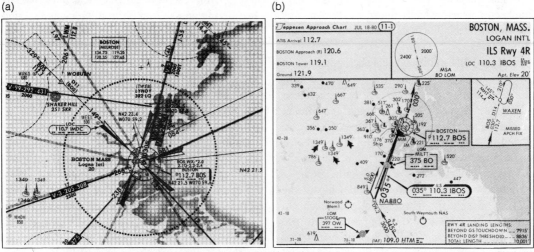

(c)

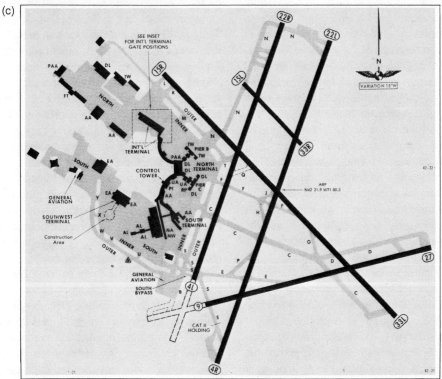

Different maps of Boston's airport area illustrate different degrees of abstraction from reality. Which map is most useful depends on the purpose of the user. In an analogous fashion, different economic theories can highlight different features of an economic system. *Copyright 1978(a), 1977(b), and 1981(c) Jeppesen Sanderson, Inc.*

whatever functions people assign to it.) The right-hand box in part (a) represents a large number of firms, which, under capitalism, any adventuresome individuals are free to form (and to liquidate).

Households and firms meet each other in two types of markets. Consider first the lower half of part (a). Its outer half-circle pictures households selling, and firms buying, services of the human, natural, and capital resource stocks that are owned by households. On a given day, perhaps, a particular household may sell 8 labor hours, 24 oil-deposit hours, and 24 turret-lathe hours— without, of course, giving up ownership of the person, oil deposit, or turret lathe as such. In return for the privilege of being allowed to use these resources temporarily, the firms involved pay out money in the form of wages and rental payments. This is a cost to them but income to the households involved. This income stream is augmented (or decreased) by positive (or negative) profits of the households that are also owners of firms. The shaded half-circle in the lower half represents this monetary counterflow to the flow of resource services.

Now consider the upper half of part (a). Its outer half-circle pictures firms selling, and households buying, consumption goods and human capital goods. As indicated, the consumption goods may be nondurable apples or airplane rides or durable cars; the human capital goods could be educational services. Once more, the shaded half-circle represents the monetary counterflow to this flow of goods.

Part (a) is fine as far as it goes. Like map (a) in Figure 2.1, it tells the truth but not all of it. If we focused our attention more closely on the household box, we might discover the relationships pictured in part (b). In a capitalist market economy, frequent exchanges occur that involve only households. Households can sell outright the stocks of natural and capital resources they own (instead of just renting them out to firms temporarily), but when they do other households come to own them. Similarly, as part (b) illustrates, households often trade corporate stock

among themselves; they lend to and borrow money from each other (which can be viewed as the buying and selling of promissory notes); and they even trade such strange things as copper futures (to be discussed in Chapter 10). Thus the circular flow in part (b), like map (b) above, adds more detail to our bird's-eye view of the market economy.

Part (c) adds detail about the behavior of firms. Additional frequent exchanges occur that involve only firms. In particular, firms sell goods to other firms. Sometimes, these goods are used up right away by their recipients in the making of other goods (as perhaps the fertilizer or insurance service in our example). Such goods, which are produced by domestic producers during a period and then used up by the same or other domestic producers during the same period in the making of other goods, are called **intermediate goods**. Their purchase gives rise to raw material costs on the part of their buyers. At other times, firms sell **final goods**, goods produced by domestic producers during a period but *not* used up by the same or other domestic producers during the same period in the making of other goods. When final goods go to households, they are called *consumption* or *human capital goods*, as noted above, but when they go to firms, they are called *investment goods*. The blast furnaces in our example are a case in point. Their purchase gives rise to investment expenditures (financed, perhaps, with a portion of revenues corresponding to depreciation allowances or with the portion of profits not paid out to the owners of firms).

Note: Figure 2.2 is so general that it could serve as a map of any capitalist market economy, however simple or complex. Because we want to study the *essence* of such a market economy before studying its complexities, we must make a number of simplifying assumptions. In order to examine the essence of the market economy, the chapters in Part Two will make assumptions about the role of government, the motivations of households and of firms, and the nature of markets that differentiate the theory in Part Two from the theory in Parts Three to Five.

FIGURE 2.2 Circular Flows

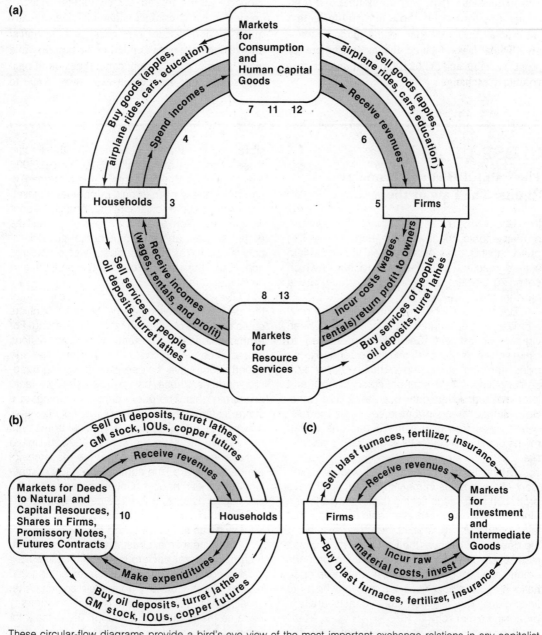

These circular-flow diagrams provide a bird's-eye view of the most important exchange relations in any capitalist market economy. They can be viewed as maps of this economy. (The numbers indicate the chapters that will focus on the particular aspect of the economy shown. Additional chapters will focus on other aspects, such as contingent-claims markets and the role of government.)

Assumption 1:   A Minimal Government

Throughout Part Two, we will assume that government performs only those minimal tasks that are crucial for a well-functioning market economy. These tasks include the establishment of property rights and the facilitation of unrestricted voluntary exchange.

Establishing Property Rights. Throughout Part Two, we will expect that government assigns property rights for all scarce things. Scarcity creates a basic conflict situation. During any given period, once resources and technical knowledge have been applied in the best possible way, people as a group cannot get additional goods. But any one person can always hope to

---

CLOSE-UP 2.1

The Painful Birth of Property Rights: The Law of the Sea

In the absence of a government that assigns property rights, the law of the jungle is likely to prevail; that is, the strong are likely to appropriate scarce resources. The world's oceans, which cover 70 percent of the earth's surface, are a case in point.

Because there has never been a world government, property rights in the ocean have been virtually nonexistent. Coastal nations used to claim sovereignty over a zone that extended three miles from the coast (the distance that a 17th century land-based cannon could shoot) and later claimed sovereignty over a 12-mile zone. Beyond that, "freedom of the sea" was the rule. Anyone was free to use the oceans as cheap routes of transport or for fishing, whaling, and the like.

During the twentieth century, however, significant improvements in maritime technology have produced long-range fishing fleets that can even pinpoint schools of fish electronically. It did not take long for conflicts of interest to arise among the developed nations (the fishing fleets of which meet each other on the richest fishing grounds around the world) and between the developed nations and the poor nations (many of which are finding that the fish near their coasts are approaching extinction).

This conflict has been exacerbated by the discovery of oil and gas on the continental shelves and in the deep sea, and by the discovery of consolidated minerals, available in potato-sized nodules that lie scattered on the Pacific Ocean floor but at depths of 12,000 to 20,000 feet. Nodules of phosphate, ferro-manganese, and manganese (with cobalt, copper, and nickel) have attracted particular interest. Additional conflicts have arisen about the uses of oceans as dumping sites, about the accidental pollution of coastal zones as a consequence of oil drilling, and about the uses of over 100 merchant and naval straits for transit.

Given the military and economic strength of the developed nations, some of these conflicts could easily be resolved in favor of the strong. For example, because certain developed nations (notably the United States, West Germany, and Japan) alone have the capability of mining deep-sea nodules, these nations possess *de facto* property rights. The poor countries, hoping for a share in the ocean's Eldoradolike riches, have, however, pressed for an international agreement on property rights in the sea. In 1970, a United Nations resolution declared that the resources of the deep sea are "the common heritage of mankind," not just happy hunting grounds for the developed nations. But a 158-nation UN Conference on the Law of the Sea that has been meeting for years was still deadlocked by 1981.

In the meantime, coastal nations, in a sudden rush of unilateral declarations, have claimed exclusive rights to economic zones extending 200 nautical miles outward from their coasts. After initial challenges, this new limit of sovereignty became the norm by the late 1970s, at least for fishing and oil-drilling operations. However, even in these zones conflicts persist on such matters as shipping lanes, overflights, and marine scientific research.

CLOSE-UP 2.2

The Painful Birth of Property Rights: The Moon's Riches

In 1979, after seven years' labor, an international treaty on the exploitation of the moon's resources was approved by the 47-member United Nations Committee on Outer Space. The agreement seeks to insure that smaller powers lacking the ability to explore space will have a stake in the mineral wealth of the moon and other celestial bodies by proclaiming these resources to be the "common heritage of mankind." Any commercial exploitation, however, is considered to be decades away.

Agreement on the new treaty was stalled for years because the Soviet Union was unwilling to accept the concept that the moon's resources should be a common heritage. The third world countries pressed for a commitment from the space powers similar to the one they sought on the mining of seabed minerals.

The controversial article designating the moon and its resources as "a common heritage" stipulates that neither the surface nor subsurface shall become the property of any country, although countries retain the right to conduct lunar explorations. Once commercial exploitation "is about to become feasible," the treaty commits countries to establishing an international regime to see that the benefits of lunar exploitation are shared equitably.

Source: *The New York Times*, July 4, 1979

---

get more goods at the expense of other persons. In the absence of government, there would surely emerge a wild scramble to appropriate scarce, goods-yielding resources. Undoubtedly, the strong and the cunning would then end up with most resources and goods at the expense of the weak and not-so-clever. Life for many would be "nasty, brutish, and short." To avoid this situation, government is needed to bully the bullies, to banish the law of the jungle.

By assigning property rights, government establishes a boundary line for the social behavior of every person and makes clear who has disposition over any particular resource or good at any one moment. In fact, by establishing property rights, government distributes **economic power**, the capacity to make and enforce decisions on the allocation of resources and the apportioning of goods.

If you were given the exclusive right to yourself (no slavery was allowed) and also to 10 acres of land, a truck, and a house, these things would delineate your area of responsibility. These would be the things with which you could make choices, the things you could use to pursue your own welfare as you cared to define it. All other scarce things would be none of your business. They would be assigned to others and would establish *their* economic power.

Note: Because we are studying capitalism, we will further assume that government assigns property rights as rarely as possible to itself and as often as possible to private individuals.

Facilitating Unrestricted Voluntary Exchange. Throughout Part Two, we will expect that government guarantees to all individuals an equal opportunity to the freest possible use of the property rights it has assigned.

First, we expect that government, with the rarest of exceptions, gives people the right to transfer their property rights to others. (In some instances, this right might be denied. For example, the government might forbid people to sell themselves into slavery or to practice the world's oldest profession.)

Second, we expect that government establishes a uniform system of weights, measures, and norms and provides money as a universally accepted medium of exchange. Money is something we tend to take for granted, but consider how impossible it would be to carry out the many trillion dollars' worth of transactions we annually handle in the United States if we had to rely on barter. If you could do nothing but paint houses and wanted bread, red cabbage, and a haircut, you would have a hard time finding a baker, a farmer, and a barber who required just a loaf of bread's worth of painting, a cabbage head's worth, or a haircut's worth. Even indirect barter would be next to impossible. You might take a pig in return for painting a farmer's house, but how could you convert such an indivisible good into bread, cabbage, and a haircut? How could you store it if you did not care to spend your income just yet? Clearly, without the existence of a convenient medium of exchange, the myriad of voluntary economic transactions occurring daily in any modern economy would be unthinkable.

Finally, we expect that government sets up a system of law, police, and courts to assure that people are never coerced into uses of property rights they do not wish to make, unless all others are equally coerced (as in the payment of taxes). We imagine, similarly, that people are never prevented from uses of property rights they do wish to make, unless all others are equally prevented (as in the production of heroin). In short, we imagine that anything one person is allowed to do all others are allowed to do; anything forbidden to one person is equally forbidden to all others.

Throughout Part Two, we will assume that government performs only the tasks just described and performs them well. Later, in the chapters that follow Part Two, we will consider a more complex world in which the government is engaged in many additional activities and frequently neglects the crucial tasks outlined here.

Assumption 2: Utility-Maximizing Households

The chapters in Part Two will assume that households follow the optimization principle in order to *maximize the utility* they derive from their economic choices. We will consider each household to be a single decision-making unit and not concern ourselves with the internal process by which the members of multiperson households

CLOSE-UP 2.3

The Painful Birth of Property Rights: The Electromagnetic Spectrum

Like the air, the world's radio spectrum used to be taken for granted. But it is a very scarce resource now. If everyone who wished to just broadcast freely, there would be serious overcrowding and bad reception around the globe. As a result, property rights in radio frequencies (for voice communication, navigation, and data transmission) are sought by the military, by space agencies, by multinational manufacturing corporations and international banks, by airlines and ocean shippers, by radio and television broadcasters, by amateurs, and by many others.

In 1979, a 140-nation General World Administrative Radio Conference convened in Geneva to assign property rights in radio frequencies for the remainder of this century. A conflict emerged because nations wanted more frequencies than are available but also because nations had ideological differences. While Western, developed nations favored the free global flow of information, the poor and Soviet-bloc nations favored a "new world information order" that would enable them to control strictly all information flows within their borders. They linked agreement on the allocation of scarce frequencies to agreements restricting the flow of information. They argued that the beaming of radio and television broadcasts by one country to another should occur only with the latter's consent and that the transmission of news via satellite should occur only with the consent of the country in which the news originates.

Source: *The New York Times*, September 23, 1979, p. E8; September 25, 1979, p. A1.

come to resolve possible conflicts of interest among themselves. Given the government framework just discussed, we will imagine households as free to follow their self-interest. If they wished, they could use their resources all alone, hermitlike, without ever relating to others at all. Or they could enter into all sorts of voluntary (and, therefore, mutually beneficial) agreements of cooperation with others, exchanging—at any terms acceptable to all parties concerned—the property rights to resources or goods or any other scarce things. In short, we will expect that no one judges the choices of households or has to approve them, that people are not subject to the will of other people, and that they are not someone else's unwilling tools. In particular, we will imagine that government makes no attempt to define the meaning of "social welfare." The term will have no meaning apart from *whatever* result actually emerges from the multitude of independent choices of all the people in society, all of whom are free to define their own happiness in their own way (and to take whatever actions seem appropriate to achieve it).

The utility-maximization assumption is often misunderstood. We are not imagining that all people are totally selfish and driven only by self-love. The utility-maximization assumption is perfectly consistent with people being selfish, selfless, or a mixture of both. Totally selfish people, who have no use for other people unless they can get something out of them, might maximize their utility by working their resources to the utmost and then spending their incomes on an army of gadgets that give pleasure to them alone: cars and snowmobiles; vacuum cleaners and refrigerators; power saws and electric toothbrushes. Yet other people, equally selfish, might prefer a minimum of work and money income and then maximize their utility by sleeping late, swinging in hammocks, lolling at the beach, and spending hours each day in lonesome meditation. Perfect altruists, on the other hand, might spend lives of hard work, only to give away most of their incomes to the church, to the college of their choice, or to the victims of the latest drought, hurricane, or war. They, too, would be maximizing their utility. Their happiness would not be derived from the pleasurable use of gadgets or free time, but from the pleasure of contemplating the help they had given to the sick, the crippled, the orphaned, or the college students who, thanks to their scholarships, need not toil in factory and field. These same altruists could, of course, like our selfish friends, forgo work and income and monetary charity, maximize their leisure time, and give their *personal* attention to those they cared to help. In each of these very different cases, people are maximizing their utility. When citing this goal as the basic motivation of households, we only assume that people will attempt to make as much progress toward their goals in life as they possibly can, whatever these goals might be. Presumably, this is as important to the egotist as to the altruist.

Assumption 3:   Profit-Maximizing Firms

Throughout Part Two, we will assume that firms follow the optimization principle in order to *maximize the profit* they derive from their economic choices. And we will likewise treat each firm as a single decision-making unit and not concern ourselves with the internal process by which multiple owners of firms resolve possible conflicts of interest among themselves.

We will expect, in short, that people setting up and running firms consider a high money income very important for achieving their particular goals in life. We will attribute to them the hope that the revenues they derive from the sale of goods will exceed, as much as possible, the costs they must incur during the production of these goods. In a world of uncertainty, running a firm clearly amounts to taking a chance: hoped-for-profits may fail to materialize. Losses may take their place if lower-than-expected revenues or higher-than-expected costs appear, at which point owners of firms may note belatedly that it would have been better not to have gone into business at all. It does not seem unreasonable, therefore, to assume that those people who nevertheless go into business—and by that very fact indicate a desire to increase their money incomes beyond what they would otherwise be—will conduct that business in such a fashion as to get the greatest possible profit. For this reason, we will assume that owners of firms keep a sharp eye on business affairs, are personally involved in their businesses, and are always ready to exploit whatever opportunity presents itself to increase profit to the maximum possible level.

Once more, a word of warning is in order. We are not assuming that all owners of firms must be selfish and exploitative, nor are we approving of such orientation. Nor are we assuming that those who make profits (rather than losses) will use their higher money incomes to promote selfish purposes. There is nothing to prevent the monetarily successful owners of a firm from using their profits to help the poor or to do any one of a million "unselfish" things. Nor is there anything, of course, to force profit makers into doing any of these "socially responsible" things. Just like wage income, profit can be large or small (and unlike wage income, it can even be negative); just like wage income, it represents power to pursue *whatever* goals the recipients wish to pursue.

Assumption 4:   Perfect Markets

Throughout Part Two, we will assume that the conditions postulated in Assumptions 1, 2, and 3 give rise to a multitude of markets. These markets, however, must not be envisioned as the open-air markets of old—with fish, flower, and vegetable stalls, under multicolored tents, located on the town square, and open only three days a week. As we will use the term, a **market** refers to an invisible framework within which owners of property rights can make contact with one another for the purpose of trading something scarce and within which they jointly determine the price of what they are trading. Thus there are as many markets as there are scarce things—markets for apples, shoes, and airplane rides; markets for the use of workers, oil deposits, and turret lathes; markets for shares of stock and deeds to land. According to our definition, two

shares of General Motors stock, traded in New York and Chicago, respectively, are being traded in the same market. But apples and shoes, traded in the same store, are being traded in two different markets.

The chapters in Part Two will assume, furthermore, that every market is a **perfect market**. To qualify as perfect, a market must possess the following four characteristics:

a. There is a large number of independent buyers and also of sellers.
b. All units of the traded item are viewed as identical.
c. All buyers and sellers possess full knowledge relevant to trading.
d. Nothing impedes entry into or exit from the market.

There is a large number of independent buyers and also of sellers. Throughout Part Two, we will assume that a large number of buyers and also of sellers can be found in each market and that each of these traders acts independently of all others.

This raises a difficult question about the meaning of largeness. Where do we draw the line? Is 1,000 a large number, while 999 is small? Fortunately, the issue is resolved quite easily: we can consider the number of buyers or sellers large if the ordinary transactions of any one buyer or seller do not appreciably affect the price at which transactions are made. This implies that even the largest buyer purchases only a trifling fraction of the total traded. Think of households buying oranges, for example. This also implies that even the largest seller sells only an insignificant percentage of the total traded. Consider farmers selling wheat, for example.

It is by no means difficult to find real-world markets in which the number of buyers is large in this sense and in which the number of sellers is large at the same time. Consider the organized stock or commodity exchanges or the foreign exchange markets. Any single buyer or seller of General Motors stock, of winter wheat, or of

German marks is in the exact position we are now attributing to all buyers and sellers in all markets.

Part Three, however, will demonstrate that there are other markets in which the number of buyers, or of sellers, or of both is small (possibly because large numbers of them act in collusion). The cigarette companies, the meatpackers, or the single employer in town are each an example of a small number of buyers; the auto companies, the teamsters union, or the OPEC cartel, are examples of a small number of sellers.

All units of the traded item are viewed as identical. Throughout Part Two, we will assume that, in the minds of buyers, all units of the item that is traded in any one market are identical. It is easy to find real-world markets that have this characteristic. Consider the market for beef or salt or Irish potatoes; for a given grade of coal, gasoline, or steel; of German marks or General Motors stock. So far as buyers are concerned, each unit is a perfect duplicate of any other unit. As a result, buyers never care from which particular seller they acquire the units they buy. They do not care whether they get farmer Brown's potatoes or farmer Green's, whether they buy the stock certificate of a given firm from a broker in Chicago or a lady next door.

Under such conditions, advertising by any one seller, aimed at taking customers away from other sellers in the same market, makes no sense. Imagine farmer Brown renting billboards, buying radio and television time, sending messages through the mail, taking out ads in magazines and newspapers, and employing an army of traveling sales representatives, telling us "Farmer Brown's Irish potatoes are the best," or (shading the truth somewhat) "Farmer Brown's Irish potatoes cure cancer," or even "Farmer Green's Irish potatoes cause cancer." With the possible exception of Green, people would just laugh at him, knowing full well that anybody's Irish potatoes were just as good as anybody else's. Brown would be pretty stupid wasting all that money.

Part Three will show that other markets exist as well—markets in which advertising is rampant and in which buyers care very much about the exact source of their supply. This is so when buyers see differences in different units of an item, regardless of whether this is objectively true. Think of aspirin brand A vs. B, of autos, cigarettes, or soap, of toothpaste, and of labor. Think of products that buyers admit to be identical but that are linked to attributes that do matter: a store closer to home, free convenient parking, more and friendlier clerks, music while you shop, carpeted floors, more trading stamps, easier credit terms, prompter delivery, better warranties, faster repair and maintenance. . . .

All buyers and sellers possess full knowledge relevant to trading. Throughout Part Two, we will assume that all buyers and sellers are effectively linked with all potential trading partners and are fully aware of the characteristics of traded items and of prices offered and demanded. People are in close contact with each other, and their communication is continuous. The ticker tape of the New York Stock Exchange, duplicated within seconds in brokerage houses all over the world, is a good example of this situation.

Once again, Part Three will demonstrate that the real world is more complex. It contains many markets in which traders have a hard time finding each other and are imperfectly informed about quality and prices. As a result, people have to incur costs to acquire the knowledge we now assume to be at their disposal.

Consider how traders have to find each other through costly classified advertising or intermediaries. Consider how some market participants often know more about quality than their trading partners: employers may know of risks attached to jobs, while employees do not; manufacturers may know that their appliances will break in four months, while purchasers do not; doctors may know of their limited experience or incompetence, while their patients do not; job applicants may know of their lack of talent or motivation, while their prospective employers do not. Such lack of knowledge about quality imposes costs on buyers in addition to those associated with finding out who the sellers are (buyers who do not care to learn from bitter experience have to protect themselves against low quality by buying service contracts, warranties, or advice). Finally, consider how prices are often quoted deceptively and how they vary widely among sellers of identical items—a fact that buyers can discover only through an expensive search.

Nothing impedes entry into and exit from the market. Throughout Part Two, we will assume that anyone, at any time, is free to become a buyer or seller in any market, is free to enter the market on the same terms as existing traders. Similarly, we will assume that there are no impediments that prevent anyone from ceasing to be a buyer or seller in a market and thus from leaving it.

There are many real-world markets in which this condition exists. If one possesses the requisite resources, one can become a buyer or seller of potatoes or piano lessons at any time, and the same holds for many other markets as well.

Part Three will look at exceptions that are just as frequent. Consider how technical conditions often dictate the existence of a single seller only, as in the case of telephone service. Consider how sellers form cartels and then conspire to keep other sellers out of the market, as in the case of labor unions. Consider how governments grant exclusive franchises to limited numbers of sellers, as in the case of taxicabs, or how they place deliberate barriers in the way of some sellers, such as foreigners.

Good Theory vs. Bad Theory

The chapters in Part Two will develop a theory of the market economy based on the assumptions presented in the preceding sections of this chapter.

While it is true that theory is indispensable for those who seek to understand a complex world, it is also true that not every theory is automatically a good one. Just as early map makers produced bad maps that falsified even the broad outlines of reality (and contributed to

confusion rather than understanding), so theorists are quite capable of producing simplified representations of the economic world that mislead rather than enlighten. This is, of course, no argument against drawing maps or constructing theory; it is an argument for making the best possible ones. And this brings us to an important question: How can we tell whether a theory is good or bad?

There are two schools of thought on the best way to test a theory. Some judge a theory by testing the validity of its *assumptions*; others by testing the validity of a theory's *predictions*.

Testing a Theory by Its Assumptions

One way to evaluate a theory is to inquire into the truth of the assumptions on which a theory is based. If the assumptions are patently false or distort reality greatly, one can rate the theory as bad and refuse to use it as a guide to reality.

Our above list, for instance, includes the assumption that owners of firms maximize profits. Some economists have argued that this is simply not so. When asked about their motivation, owners of firms, these critics say, reveal a great variety of goals besides maximum profit: a large share of their market, maximum *sales*, prestige (gained, perhaps, by improving environmental quality or giving to charity), personal power, a good life, growth of their firms, technical leadership, *average* profit (to discourage competitors, labor unions, and government regulators), stability (or the avoidance of unpleasant surprises)—the list goes on. Indeed, critics continue, firms that are corporations are run by managers and not owners; and managers couldn't care less about profit. They care a great deal about high salaries, large staffs, luxury offices, business trips to Las Vegas, and the like. These things raise costs and *reduce* profit.

In the same fashion, those focusing on assumptions to validate theory might investigate all the other assumptions listed above. They might note many exceptions (to which we have called attention ourselves), and they might, therefore, reject out of hand and right now *whatever* theory might be built upon these assumptions in Part Two. But one can test the validity of a theory in an altogether different way.

Testing a Theory by Its Predictions

Most people would describe the three maps found in Figure 2.1 as weird representations of reality, totally at odds with their mental image of Boston. Any Bostonian one might interview in the street might agree with this negative assessment. *Yet those maps work*! Every month, they help hundreds of pilots make accurate predictions, which enable them to slide down invisible glide slopes to runways shrouded in fog.

In the same way, one can argue, whether assumptions are weird or unrealistic is quite irrelevant. What matters is whether a theory allows us to make accurate predictions about past or future phenomena of which observations have not yet been made.

Milton Friedman (see Biography 2.2) has been the undisputed leader of those who would validate a theory solely on the basis of its ability to generate successful predictions. Consider, for example, his view of the profit maximization assumption. Friedman knows that many of the nonprofit goals noted above are in fact not as important as alleged. Yet proving the validity of the profit-maximizing assumption does not matter to him at all. Friedman would retain any theory based on the profit-maximizing assumption, even if the behavior of firms were apparently determined by the nonprofit goals listed above or even if owners made decisions at random—*as long as accurate predictions were derivable from this theory*. And why should such accurate predictions be generated? Because, among all the owners of firms, some may in fact (and quite unintentionally) make the kinds of decisions that maximize profits. Their firms may well prosper and grow in the long run. And all other firms may grow less, shrink, and disappear. If this were so, Friedman argues, one would be justified in assuming a nonexistent world in which owners of firms *consciously* maximized profits. A theory based on this false assumption would nevertheless produce accurate predictions about the survival of profit-maximizing firms in the real world.

Thus Friedman considers the widely held view that realistic assumptions are the criteria for a valid theory as fundamentally wrong and the cause of much mischief. Truly significant theories, he argues, necessarily have assumptions that are wildly inaccurate as descriptive representations of reality. The more significant the theory, the more unrealistic its assumptions must be. A theory is important, he says, if it explains much by little, if it abstracts crucial elements from the mass of complex and detailed circumstances surrounding the phenomena to be explained, and permits valid predictions on the basis of them alone.

This is also the position adopted in this book. The chapters of Part Two, therefore, will explore the implications of the four assumptions stated in this chapter and will test the resultant theory with respect to its ability to explain the world in which we live.

Positive Theory vs. Normative Statements

The stress on prediction as a test for the value of a theory has an added advantage. It calls attention to a crucial distinction. We will restrict ourselves here to **positive theory**, theory that makes purely descriptive statements and predictions. Positive theory is the essence of science. It explains what is and what causes what; it predicts what will be the consequences of any change in circumstances. Such positive theory must not be confused with **normative statements**, or prescriptive statements akin to preaching. Such value judgments tell us what ought to be, what is good and what is bad.

Every theorist has, of course, personal preferences. Oftentimes, these norms act as a filter for the analytic perceptions of the theorist. All of us, being human, tend to filter out aspects of reality that challenge our norms and to overemphasize those that support them. Oftentimes we

BIOGRAPHY 2.2

Milton Friedman

Milton Friedman (1912-   ) was born in Brooklyn, New York, the son of immigrant parents. After studying at Rutgers and the University of Chicago, he worked for many years at the National Bureau of Economic Research and then received his doctoral degree at Columbia University in 1946. In 1967, he was honored with the presidency of the American Economic Association; and in 1976, while serving as professor of economics at the University of Chicago, Friedman was awarded the Nobel Memorial Prize in Economic Science. He is now retired and a resident scholar at the Hoover Institution in Stanford, California.

Friedman's work covers a wide range of topics, but one underlying theme is the conviction that the market economy is the best economic system and works best when government performs only the minimal functions necessary to support it.

His most important work in macroeconomics concerns the role of money in the economy. *A Monetary History of the United States, 1867–1960* (written with Anna J. Schwartz, 1963) challenges the notions that the market economy without government intervention is inherently unstable and that monetary policy was powerless during the Great Depression. Instead, Friedman sees the Great Depression as a monument to the harm that

can be done by a few men who wield vast power over monetary policy.

In other areas, too, as Friedman sees it, the government is apt to do more harm than good when it intervenes in the operation of markets. As if led by an Invisible Hand, he says, government officials who seek to serve the public interest invariably end up serving a private interest instead. Much of this is discussed in his celebrated columns in *Newsweek* magazine, many of which are reprinted as *An Economist's Protest* (1972), and in his *Free to Choose: A Personal Statement* (1980), a book based on a series of PBS television shows of the same name.

Perhaps the most widely known of Friedman's books is *Capitalism and Freedom* (1962). He argues in this book that the kind of economic system that provides economic freedom—namely, competitive capitalism—also promotes political freedom. "Historical evidence speaks with one voice on the relation between political freedom and a free market," he says (p. 9). "I know of no example in time or place of a society that has been marked by a large measure of political freedom and that has not also used something comparable to a free market to organize the bulk of economic activity."

Finally, Friedman is the unchallenged leader

are blind to what we dislike, overperceptive to what we like. We may end up presenting as theory (as a map of reality) what is in fact our own wishful thinking.

The only known remedy for this deplorable habit of confusing our wishful thinking with reality is the criticism of others. However blind they are to the impact of their norms on their thought (as we are to that of our norms on our thought), we all seem to have an acute perception of the impact of the norms of others on their thought. We must always do our best not to shape positive conclusions to fit strongly held norma-

tive preconceptions and not to reject positive conclusions when their normative implications are unpalatable to us. Normative statements that masquerade as positive theory are the worst possible kind of "theory."

SUMMARY

1. People in different societies have chosen vastly different sets of arrangements for cooperating with each other in the allocation of resources and the apportionment of goods. Each arrangement is an *economic system*.

of the "instrumentalists," who validate theories that prove to be good instruments for making predictions. Consider his own words:[1]

> The relevant question to ask about the "assumptions" of a theory is not whether they are descriptively "realistic," for they never are, but whether they are sufficiently good approximations for the purpose in hand. And this question can be answered only by seeing whether the theory works, which means whether it yields sufficiently accurate predictions. . . . A theory or its "assumptions" cannot possibly be thoroughly "realistic." . . . A completely "realistic" theory of the wheat market would have to include not only the conditions directly underlying the supply and demand for wheat but also the kind of coins or credit instruments used to make exchanges; the personal characteristics of wheat-traders such as the color of each trader's hair and eyes, his antecedents and education, the number of members of his family, their characteristics, antecedents, and education, etc.; the kind of soil on which the wheat was grown, its physical and chemical characteristics, the weather prevailing during the growing season; the personal characteristics of the farmers growing the wheat and of the consumers who will ultimately use it; and so on indefinitely. Any attempt to move very far in achieving this kind of "realism" is certain to render a theory utterly useless. . . . A meaningful scientific hypothesis or theory typically asserts that certain forces are, and other forces are not, important in understanding a particular class of phenomena. It is frequently convenient to present such a hypothesis by stating that the phenomena it is desired to predict behave in the world of observation *as if* they occurred in a hypothetical and highly simplified world containing only the forces that the hypothesis asserts to be important. . . . Such a theory cannot be tested by comparing its "assumptions" directly with "reality." . . . Yet the belief that a theory can be tested by the realism of its assumptions independently of the accuracy of its predictions is widespread and the source of much of the perennial criticism of economic theory as unrealistic. Such criticism is largely irrelevant.

[1]Milton Friedman, *Essays in Positive Economics* (Chicago: University of Chicago Press, 1953), pp. 15, 32, 40, and 41.

2. All modern economic systems have in common a reliance on a large-scale division of labor. This specialization brings the benefit of greater production along with a cost: the problem of having to coordinate the specialized activities of people, of having to assure economic order.

3. The separate activities of people engaged in a division of labor can be coordinated deliberately by a human manager. *Managerial coordination*, while making possible increased output through a division of labor, inevitably sacrifices output by tying up resources in a planning bureaucracy. As a result of being unable to solve the knowledge problem, it is bound to sacrifice additional output through economic inefficiency. The likely pursuit of distributive justice (which creates incentive problems) may impose further output loss.

4. The separate activities of people engaged in a division of labor can also be coordinated spontaneously by price signals generated in markets. *Market coordination*, while making possible increased output through a division of labor, inevitably sacrifices output by tying up resources to set up a system of voluntary exchanges and keep it functioning. The remainder of this book is devoted exclusively to a more thorough study of the market economy.

5. Anyone who wants to understand the modern market economy, and wants to judge the degree of its success, will find it impossible to gather and digest all the relevant facts. Yet the desired understanding can be gained by a process called *theorizing*. This process is very much akin to the making of a geographic map because a map, like a theory, becomes a useful guide to reality precisely because it is unrealistic.

6. The major exchange relations that exist in any capitalist market economy can be mapped in circular-flow diagrams. These diagrams can also serve as previews to the remainder of this book. In order to study first the essential features of the capitalist market economy, we make the following simplifying assumptions:

    a. Government confines itself to the crucial tasks of establishing property rights in all scarce things and facilitating unrestricted voluntary exchange.

    b. Households follow the optimization principle with the goal of maximizing their utility.

    c. Firms follow the optimization principle with the goal of maximizing their profit.

    d. All markets are perfect. In each market: there exists a large number of independent buyers and also of sellers; all units of the traded item are viewed as identical; all buyers and sellers possess full knowledge relevant to trading; nothing impedes entry into or exit from the market.

7. A comprehensive theory that serves to explain the major phenomena observed in the market economy can be built from simple assumptions, such as those in point 6. Two schools of thought disagree on the issue of what makes a theory good or bad. Some would test the goodness of a theory by the validity of its *assumptions* (an approach rejected here); others would focus on the validity of its *predictions*. In either case, one must be careful to distinguish between *positive theory* (description and prediction) and *normative statements* (prescription or preaching).

KEY TERMS

capitalism
costs of exchange
deliberate coordination
economic order
economic power
economic systems
final goods
intermediate goods
Invisible Hand
knowledge problem
managerial coordination
marginal rate of substitution (*MRS*)
marginal rate of transformation (*MRT*)
market
market coordination
normative statements
perfect market
positive theory
price system
property rights
spontaneous coordination
theory
transactions costs
transfer costs
Visible Hand

QUESTIONS AND PROBLEMS

1. There are instances in which the assignment of property rights is clearly impossible. Consider the case of anadromous species of fish (fish that swim upstream to mate, like salmon), much debated during the Law of the Sea conference. Such fish spawn in the fresh water streams of "countries of origin," then migrate beyond the 200 mile economic zone to the high seas where everyone might catch them. How could one possibly protect such property?

2. Consider the circular-flow diagrams in Figure 2.2. Make this map of the market economy more "realistic" by introducing government. (*Hints*: Government might take away in taxes some of the revenues flowing to firms or some of the incomes flowing to households, and it might create new money. It might use these funds to buy some of the resource services supplied by households, such as the services of judges, teachers, and police officers. It might buy some of the goods supplied by firms, such as courthouses, school buildings, and police cruisers. It might buy stocks of resources outright.)

3. "It is one thing for government, in order to certify competence, to require the licensing of people in certain occupations (doctors, lawyers, barbers, and taxi drivers). It is quite another to restrict, at the same time, the number of persons who may engage in these occupations. The former promotes perfect markets; the latter destroys them." Evaluate this position.

4. *Communist*: Altruism is inconsistent with the market economy. I reject the market economy on the grounds that it is based on narrow *selfishness*, on an unadulterated lust for selfish gain by individuals—all of whom are only interested in themselves and lack identification with the rest of humanity. Because many people have a desire to identify with a body larger than their immediate families, a desire to put work for others before selfishness, the Communist promise of a society of *unselfishness*, wherein all belong to one large loving family, is exerting great moral appeal to millions of people.

Anti-Communist: Your claim of superior morality is insincere. The unselfish subordination in the Communist state of individual desires to those of others only disguises the extreme selfishness of the Communist élite, which wants to further its own goals by manipulating and exploiting the rest of the people.

Evaluate. (*Hints*: Note the text discussion of utility and profit maximization. Note that Jesus advised us to love others *as* ourselves, not *instead* of ourselves. Then apply the optimization principle to the choice between self-love and love of others. Consider what it has to say about the likelihood of all-or-nothing choices being optimal.)

5. "I don't get it. Under Stalin's system of central planning, when production was 'for use and not for profit,' inventories of consumption goods piled up that nobody wanted. So they introduced production for *profit* and the problem went away!"

Do *you* get it? Explain.

6. At one point, Castro argued that everyone should have an equal income. Because he felt it is morally wrong to let some people (like professional cane cutters) do all the heavy or dirty work for other people, he decided all people should take turns doing such work. Later, he decided that it was perfectly fine for only certain people to do such work, provided they got extra rewards (more money or longer vacations). Why do you think he changed his mind?

7. *Mr. A*: Now I have heard everything: People in the market economy are not supposed to coordinate their activities in a rational way, but they should simply submit to the blind forces of the market and all would work out for the good! That's just like announcing, as the fundamental principle of the whole system, that, *"in order to make a perfect and beautiful machine, it is not requisite to know how to make it."* This proposition will be found, on careful examination, to summarize the essential idea of the Invisible Hand. In short, Absolute Ignorance is fully qualified to take the place of Absolute Wisdom.

Ms. B: Poor A, as usual, you don't see what it's all about. Why *not* submit to something that works well, even if you don't understand it rationally? As A. N. Whitehead used to say, "Civilization advances by extending the number of important operations we can perform *without* thinking about them." Knowing full well the limitations of human reason, I vote for the Invisible Hand.

Evaluate these two opposing positions.

8. "The size of firms in a market economy can be understood with the help of the optimization principle." Explain. (*Hint*: Consider the avoidance of market coordination costs as the *benefit* of organizing a division of labor through a manager rather than through the market. Think of managerial coordination costs as the *cost* of organizing a division of labor within a firm).

SELECTED READINGS

Boland, Lawrence A. "A Critique of Friedman's Critics." *Journal of Economic Literature*, June 1979, pp. 503–22.

> A superb discussion of the methodological issues raised in the last section of this chapter; but note also the continued debate in the December 1980 issue. pp. 1553–57.

Coase, Ronald H. "The Nature of the Firm." *Economica*, November 1937, pp. 386–405. Reprinted in American Economic Association, *Readings in Price Theory*. Chicago: Irwin, 1952.

> Contains the answer to Question 8 in the "Questions and Problems" section above.

Hayek, Friedrich A. *Individualism and Economic Order*. Chicago: University of Chicago Press, 1948; *The Counter-Revolution of Science*. Glencoe: Free Press, 1952; *Studies in Philosophy, Politics, and Economics*. Chicago: University of Chicago Press, 1967.

> Earlier works on the themes discussed in Biography 2.1.

Koopmans, Tjalling. *Three Essays on the State of Economic Science*. New York: McGraw-Hill, 1957.

> A methodological discussion at odds with Friedman's view.

Machlup, Fritz, ed. *Essays on Hayek*. New York: New York University Press, 1976.

> Wide-ranging discussion of Hayek's life and work by eight authors.

Manne, Henry G. *The Economics of Legal Relationships: Readings in the Theory of Property Rights*. St. Paul: West Publishing Co., 1975.

> An excellent set of 37 readings on property rights.

Nozick, Robert. *Anarchy, State, and Utopia*. New York: Basic Books, 1974.

> A discussion of the role of government in the economy.

Robbins, Lionel. *An Essay on the Nature and Significance of Economic Science*. London: Macmillan, 1935.

> A classic work on methodology.

Samuelson, Paul. "Problems of Methodology: Discussion." *The American Economic Review*, May 1963, pp. 231–36.

> A methodological discussion at odds with Friedman's view.

Seligman, Ben B. *Main Currents in Modern Economics*. Vol. 2, pp. 342–61; Vol. 3, pp. 673–83. Chicago: Quadrangle, 1962.

> Critical reviews, respectively, of the work of Hayek and Friedman.

PART 2

The Basic Features of the Market Economy

CHAPTER 3

The Preferences of the Consumer

In the United States of 1980, some 80 million households spent privately more than $1,600 billion, or 65 percent of the gross national income. As a result, they received a vast collection of consumption and human capital goods, ranging from apples, butter, and winter coats to housing and refrigerators, to airplane rides, medical care, and vocational training. This chapter will construct a theory that highlights the major factors that explain how consumers divide their expenditures. We will treat each household as a single, utility-maximizing consumer and envision each consumer confronted with a multitude of markets in which goods are offered at given prices. Naturally, the preferences of consumers play a major role in their consumption decisions. Their tastes do not, however, play the only role; for that which is desired is always constrained by that which is possible.

The Consumption-Possibilities Frontier

Imagine a consumer who makes choices about the consumption of two goods only, apples and butter. In light of the existence of millions of goods, this request may seem unbearably restrictive, but it is made for good reasons: It makes possible the graphical exposition of our theory (graphs become awkward in three dimensions and fail us completely in more than three). More importantly, this approach yields results that can be applied to any number of goods. Consider Figure 3.1. Every point on the graph represents a different combination of two goods, quantities of which are measured along the two axes of the graph. Point A, for example, represents 120 pounds of apples and 0 pounds of butter per week; Point B, 0 pounds of apples and 30 pounds of butter per week; and Point C, 60 pounds of apples and 60 pounds of butter per week. The graph as a whole, therefore, can be looked upon as the **field of choice**, the set of all the alternative combinations of these two goods over which the consumer might conceivably exercise choice.

Note: The graph is said to be *dense* because every single point in it represents a logically possible combination of our two goods, even though some of these combinations may contain fractions, such as 200.13 pounds of apples and 10.69 pounds of butter per week. Some writers argue that our theory becomes invalid for goods that cannot be subdivided into small units in this way. Surely, this is not so: A household can consume fractions *per week* even of so-called indivisible goods. One can consume 0.1428571 automobiles or 0.2 haircuts per week because one

FIGURE 3.1 The Field of Choice

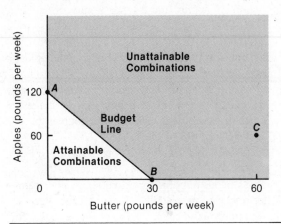

This graph shows all the alternative combinations of two goods over which a consumer might conceivably exercise choice. Given a limited budget ($120/week) and positive prices of goods ($1/pound for apples, $4/pound for butter), many conceivable bundles of goods become unattainable. The budget line is a consumption-possibilities frontier. It divides the field of choice in two: combinations of goods that can be bought (unshaded) and those that cannot be bought (shaded). The budget line, of course, satisfies a simple equation, $B = q_a \cdot p_a + q_b \cdot p_b$, where B is the size of the budget, while the q's and p's refer to the quantities and prices of apples and butter, respectively. Note: The units on the two axes are not identical. Compare the position of the 60 on each axis. The purpose of the difference in scale between axes is not to confuse but to keep the graph compact. It is important to be alert to how any graph is constructed.

can rent goods for limited periods or own them jointly with others (and hence use a car for one day a week only). One can vary the frequency of purchase (and hence buy a haircut once every five weeks). One can also vary the lifetime of so-called indivisible goods by buying different sizes or qualities.

Not every combination in Figure 3.1, however—logically conceivable though it may be—is accessible to our consumer because scarce goods do not sell at zero prices, and the consumer has only a limited budget to spend. This budget equals the consumer's income, possibly augmented by borrowing or reduced by saving. Now assume an apple price of $1 per pound, a butter price of $4 per pound, and a budget of $120 per week. Given these facts, our consumer could spend in a week $120 on apples and receive 120 pounds of them, as represented by point *A*. The consumer could instead spend $120 on butter and receive 30 pounds of it, as indicated by point *B*. Finally, by fully spending the $120 budget, the consumer could instead buy any other combination of apples and butter lying on the straight line *AB*. This line is the **budget line** or **consumption-possibilities frontier**, which shows all the alternative combinations of the two goods that the consumer is able to buy in the given period at current market prices by fully using the

given budget. Thus the budget line divides the set of all conceivable combinations of goods in two: attainable ones (unshaded) and unattainable ones (shaded). The consumer is constrained by prices and budget to choose within the unshaded world of the possible, along or underneath the consumption possibilities frontier.

Note that the *slope* of budget line *AB* reflects the ratio of prices of the two goods: The absolute value of this slope (ignoring its negative sign)[1] equals distance *OA* divided by distance *OB*, measured, of course, not in inches but in the units given on our axes. This comes to 120 pounds per week over 30 pounds per week and equals 4/1, or the price of butter, P_b, divided by the price of apples, P_a.

$$|\textbf{Budget line slope}| = \frac{P_b}{P_a}$$

In our case, because a pound of butter costs four times as much as a pound of apples, 4 pounds of apples exchange in the market for 1 pound of butter.

---

[1]It is common practice among mathematicians to depict *absolute value* by placing vertical lines before and after a number, as in |4|. This indicates that the number can represent either +4 or −4 but that the sign is irrelevant for the moment.

Similarly, the *position* of budget line *AB* reflects the size of the consumer's budget: Because we assumed a budget of $120 per week, point *A* is found by dividing $120 by the apple price of $1 (equals 120 pounds per week). Point *B* is found by dividing $120 by the butter price of $4 (equals 30 pounds per week).

$$OA = \frac{\text{Budget}}{P_a} \text{ and } OB = \frac{\text{Budget}}{P_b}$$

Naturally, any change in prices or budget also changes the slope or position of the budget line. These changing opportunities are shown in Figure 3.2. The graph comes in three panels (a), (b), and (c), and in each of these, the budget line of Figure 3.1 has been reproduced as the dashed line *AB*. In panel (*a*), we assume a fall in the butter price from $4 per pound to $2 per pound—apple price ($1 per pound) and budget ($120 per week) remaining the same. As a result, the budget line tilts outward, enlarging the unshaded subset of attainable combinations. Note the arrows and the shrinking of the shaded subset of unattainable bundles of goods. While $120 per week still buys only 120 pounds of apples per week (at $1 each), it now buys 60 rather than 30 pounds of butter per week (at $2 each). The new budget line, therefore, is *AC*. Its slope is *OA/OC*, equal in absolute value to 120/60 or 2/1, the new ratio of butter price to apple price.

Panel (*b*) depicts the opposite case of a *rise* in price, but this time the price is of apples rather than butter. Here the price rises from $1 per pound to $2 per pound—butter price ($4 per pound) and budget ($120 per week) remaining the same. As a result, the budget line tilts *inward*, reducing the unshaded subset of attainable combinations. Note the arrows and the enlargement of the shaded subset of unattainable bundles of goods. While $120 per week still buys only 30 pounds of butter per week (at $4 each), it now buys 60 rather than 120 pounds of apples per week (at $2 each). The slope of the new budget line, *BD*, is *OD/OB*, equal in absolute value to 60/30 or 2/1, the new ratio of butter price to apple price.

Panel (c) shows the effect of a higher budget only. All prices are assumed unchanged ($1 per pound of apples and $4 per pound of butter). Line *EF* represents a budget that doubles from $120 to $240 per week. As a result, there occurs a parallel outward *shift* of the budget line, enlarging the unshaded subset of attainable combinations of goods. At unchanged prices, $240 rather than $120 per week can buy exactly twice as much of either good. Distance *OA* doubles to *OE*, and distance *OB* to *OF*.

Naturally, Figure 3.2 does not show all the conceivable combinations of events that can change consumption opportunities. A higher butter price, a lower apple price, a lower budget, or simultaneous changes in prices and budget, for example, have not been illustrated. Yet the message is clear: the combinations of goods that are accessible to the consumer are always constrained by prices and budget. The graphs on page 55 depict this basic fact.

Once we know how a consumer's choices are constrained by prices and budget, can we similarly depict the one bundle of goods, among all the attainable ones, that a utility-maximizing consumer will finally select because it is of the greatest subjective value? The answer is yes, and it leads us directly into a fascinating chapter in the history of economic theorizing.

The Concept of Utility: A Historic Note

As we noted in Chapter 1, most activities have benefits as well as costs. The satisfaction a person derives from the activity of consumption has traditionally been termed **utility**. This term has been closely associated with the philosophy of Jeremy Bentham (see Biography 3.1). Yet neither philosopher Bentham nor the economists who embraced or rejected his ideas during his lifetime (and for several decades thereafter) understood the relationship between the value of goods and the utility derived by their consumers. Many economists, in fact, used to think of value as something intrinsic to a good. Karl Marx, for

FIGURE 3.2 Changing Opportunities

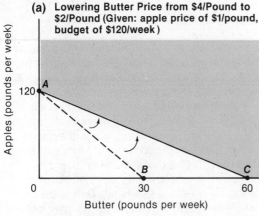

(a) Lowering Butter Price from $4/Pound to $2/Pound (Given: apple price of $1/pound, budget of $120/week)

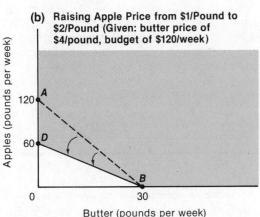

(b) Raising Apple Price from $1/Pound to $2/Pound (Given: butter price of $4/pound, budget of $120/week)

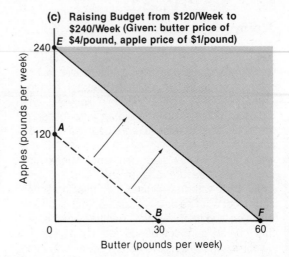

(c) Raising Budget from $120/Week to $240/Week (Given: butter price of $4/pound, apple price of $1/pound)

The consumption-possibilities frontier between the set of consumption goods that can be bought by a consumer (unshaded) and the set that cannot be bought (shaded) is far from fixed. Lower prices, as in panel (a), or a higher budget, as in panel (c), expand consumption possibilities; higher prices, as in panel (b), or a lower budget (not shown) contract them. Obviously, combinations of these events can also occur (not shown).

example, thought of value as congealed labor time that was "embodied" in a good. Presumably, if it took 4 units of labor to produce a pound of butter but only 1 unit to produce a pound of apples, a pound of butter was worth four times as much as a pound of apples. The beaver/deer example of Adam Smith, noted in Chapter 1, led to a similar conclusion. Yet economists were never too happy with this type of explanation. Marx's critics argued that the mere expenditure of labor, even of the minimum necessary amount, was surely not sufficient to establish the value of a good. What if one produced shredded bees' wings which nobody wanted? And Adam Smith found it necessary to distinguish between "value in exchange" and "value in use" when

he noted the famous paradox of diamonds and water: While diamonds have a high value in the marketplace (a high value in exchange), they are unnecessary to life (have a low value in use). On the other hand, water is fetching a low market price, while life is impossible without it. Despite its low market value, water has a high utility.

The first major breakthrough in this ageless controversy came a century after Adam Smith in the move from total utility to marginal utility. To the British economist William Stanley Jevons (see Biography 3.2), value was never intrinsic to an object but resulted from a relationship between a valuing person and an object. Even the value so determined was not a fixed number, but varied with the quantity of the object the evaluat-

BIOGRAPHY 3.1:

Jeremy Bentham

Jeremy Bentham (1748–1832) was born in London, England. He was trained as a lawyer, but he retired early to devote his life to research and the ardent advocacy of his utilitarian philosophy. This philosophy was expounded in *An Introduction to the Principles of Morals and Legislation*, published in 1789, and in many other works. "Nature has placed man," said Bentham,[1] "under the empire of *pleasure* and of *pain*. . . . He who pretends to withdraw himself from this subjection knows not what he says. His only object is to seek pleasure and to shun pain." Bentham suggested that human conduct be guided by a "felicific calculus," which approves of any action only if the pleasure it brings outweighs the pain it causes. He thought that the pleasure and pain of each action could be measured in units called *utils*, just like weight can be measured in pounds. He even believed it possible to add up these util numbers interpersonally so that 10 utils for John and 5 for Jane make a total of 15 for the pair. He identified the social total of utility produced by all actions as the common good, and he advocated that this total utility be maximized to achieve "the greatest happiness of the greatest number."

As the review of the optimization principle in Chapter 1 indicated, modern economists follow in the footsteps of Bentham when they analyze human behavior based on comparisons of *benefits* and *costs* (Bentham's "pleasure" and "pain"). Yet, unlike Jevons and Edgeworth, modern economists do not share Bentham's faith in the cardinal measurability of utility. Nor do they believe that a social utility maximum can be found by making interpersonal comparisons of utility. Nevertheless, the Benthamite search for some kind of social optimum continues (but will be more fully addressed in Parts Four and Five).

[1]Jeremy Bentham, *The Theory of Legislation* (New York: Harcourt, Brace and Co., 1931), p. 2.

---

ing person possessed. The great advance made by Jevons was, in fact, the discovery of the **principle of diminishing marginal utility:**

> *Given the quantities of all other goods being consumed, and given a person's tastes, successive additions of equal units of a good to the process of consumption eventually yield ever smaller additions to total utility.*

Thus Jevons distinguished between the total utility associated with a given level of consumption and the **marginal utility**, or the change in total utility produced by a unit change in consumption (or any other activity). Jevons, in short, discovered a special case of the general principle of declining marginal benefit, which we have already met in Chapter 1. Indeed, Jevons did more than that.

The best combination of goods among all those attainable by a consumer, the one that would maximize *total* utility, argued Jevons, was the one that equated the *marginal* utilities of a dollar's worth of every good. Consider a consumer at position *A* in Figure 3.1. Such a consumer would be consuming 120 pounds of apples per week, receiving a high *total* utility, as represented, perhaps, by a point such as *P* in the upper graph of Figure 1.4 "Declining Marginal Benefit" (see p. 14). Yet this person's *marginal* utility would be low, represented by the height of block *e* in that graph. On the other hand, this consumer would be consuming no butter at all. Hence the consumer's total utility from butter consumption would be 0 (as at point *O* in the upper graph of Figure 1.4), but the marginal utility would be high (as the height of block *a*). Surely, Jevons would argue, the consumer's combined total utility from apple and butter consumption could be increased by a $1 reduction in apple consumption (a loss of 1 pound at our assumed price of $1/pound) and a $1 increase in butter consumption (a gain of 1/4 pound at our assumed price of $4/pound). While the former would reduce total utility by an amount equal to *e* (the marginal cost), the latter would raise total utility by a larger amount equal to *a* (the marginal benefit). Thus a move, along the budget line, from point *A* in Figure 3.1 toward point *B* would raise total utility. Jevons used the optimization principle to show that consumers could reach maximum total utility only by selecting a bundle

of consumption goods such that the marginal utility (MU) per dollar of any one good was equal to that of any other good:

Condition for maximum total utility:
MU *per dollar of apples* = MU *per dollar of butter* = MU *per dollar of any other good*

Yet, for all its brilliance, the work of Jevons still rested on the belief that utility, whether total or marginal, was a quantity that could somehow be *measured*. The first step away from this belief was taken at the time of Jevons' death.

BIOGRAPHY 3.2:

William S. Jevons

William Stanley Jevons (1835–1882) was born in Liverpool, England, the son of an iron merchant. He studied mathematics, the natural sciences, and metallurgy at University College, London, and then became an assayer at the Royal Mint in Sidney, Australia. After he returned to London, his interest turned to logic, philosophy, and political economy. In later years, he taught political economy at Owens College, Manchester, and at University College, London.

His writings covered a wide range of subjects, reflecting his training and life history. Uniformly, these works were exact, lucid, original. He wrote on gold mining in Australia (where he lived from 1853–59) and on Britain's dwindling coal reserves (a book that is useful even today). He wrote on money and finance (in particular, the effect of gold discoveries on the general price level). He developed the sunspot theory of business cycles, tracing periodic sunspot activity to the weather and from there to agricultural production and economic activity in general. (Later, he incorporated other causes of the cycle as well.) And he wrote a famous treatise on logic and the scientific method.

Yet his immortality was achieved by his pioneering application of mathematics to economics.

In a paper read to the British Association for the Advancement of Science in 1862, he introduced the concept of the "final degree of utility," now known as *marginal utility*. This single decisive achievement made scientific history. His subsequent *Theory of Political Economy* (1871) contains a systematic exposition of the theory of consumer optimization based on the marginal utility concept.

The achievement of Jevons was genuinely original, although he had three forerunners of whom he was unaware. W. F. Lloyd of England in 1834, J. Dupuit of France in 1844, and H. H. Gossen of Germany in 1854 had each developed the notion of marginal utility, but no one had paid attention at the time. And even after Jevons, the concept was independently derived by Carl Menger of Austria in 1871 and by Léon Walras of France in 1874 (see Biography 16.1). At that point, the "marginal revolution" in economics was irreversible. In Britain and the Commonwealth, for a period of half a century, practically all elementary students both of logic and of political economy were brought up on Jevons. We can still learn much from him today (see Analytical Example 3.3, "Chicken Little in America").

BIOGRAPHY 3.3:

Francis Y. Edgeworth

Francis Ysidro Edgeworth (1845–1926), son of a British father and Spanish mother, was born in Edgeworthstown, Ireland, on an estate where his ancestors established themselves at the time of Queen Elizabeth. He studied classics and mathematics at Trinity College, Dublin, and later at Oxford. He was steeped in Milton, Pope, Virgil, and Homer and would quote them on numerous occasions throughout his life.

He spent early years in London, first as a barrister, then as a teacher of logic and political economy at King's College. In 1891, he was appointed professor of political economy at Oxford, and there he stayed for the rest of his life, teaching, writing, and editing the prestigious *Economic Journal*.

For decades, he was a prolific exponent of the application of mathematics to the social sciences. *Mathematical Psychics: An Essay on the Application of Mathematics to the Moral Sciences* (1881) was his first contribution to economics. This book contains two of his most enduring achievements, the discoveries of the indifference curve (discussed in this chapter) and of the contract curve (to be discussed in Chapter 15). Practically all of his other work on economic theory has been collected in *Papers Relating to Political Economy*, 3 vols. (1925).

As a mathematician, Edgeworth devoted much effort to measurement—of ethical value (or utility), of belief (or probability), of evidence (or statistics), and of economic value (or index numbers). Yet at times he also entertained the possibility of mathematical reasoning without numerical data.[1] "We cannot *count* the golden sands of life," he said, "we cannot *number* the 'innumerable' smiles of seas of love; but we seem to be capable of observing that there is here a *greater*, there a *less*, multitude of pleasure units, mass of happiness; and that is enough."

Thus Edgeworth, speaking like a true prophet, clearly pointed the way beyond the cardinal and toward the ordinal labeling of his indifference curves. His words, although dressed in poetic garb, say precisely what this chapter says: the theory of consumer choice does not depend on our ability to label each indifference curve with cardinal numbers (17 utils, 33 utils, and the like); ordinal numbers (such as 1st, 2nd, and 3rd), which tell us whether the utility of one set of goods is equal to, greater than, or less than that of another, will serve the purpose just as well.

[1]Francis Y. Edgeworth, *Mathematical Psychics* (London: C. Kegan Paul, 1881), Part I.

The Discovery of the Consumption-Indifference Curve

Another Englishman, Francis Ysidro Edgeworth (see Biography 3.3) visualized Figure 3.1 as the unseen base of a mountain. He imagined a third dimension, rising above the plane of paper, in which one might measure the utility total associated with any given combination of our two goods.

Figure 3.3 depicts Edgeworth's vision of the utility mountain (luckily, it is the only three-dimensional graph in this book). Because the consumer has neither apples nor butter to consume at point O, the mountain has a zero elevation above this point. Now consider segment OC. As the consumer acquires more and more butter, the quantity of apples remaining at zero, total utility rises, and the mountain begins to take shape. In accordance with the insight of Jevons, Edgeworth imagined total utility rising at a decreasing rate. This was pictured earlier in the upper part of Figure 1.4, "Declining Marginal Benefit," and it is pictured here as the utility mountain rising along curved line $ODEF$.

Similarly, as the consumer acquires more

FIGURE 3.3 The Utility Mountain

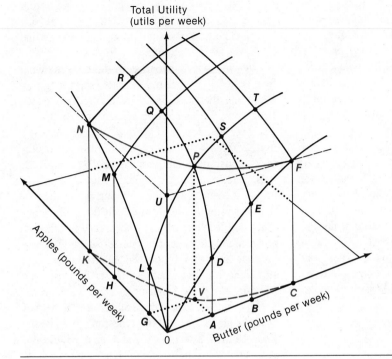

The British economist Edgeworth imagined a utility mountain rising above the plane that is the field of choice. Each point on the mountain's surface (such as *P*) indicates the utility total (such as *OU* = *VP*) that is associated with the consumption of the set of goods directly underneath (such as *V* consisting of *OG* of apples and *OA* of butter). A succession of horizontal planes (such as *NUF*) parallel to the field of choice (*KOC*) contain curves (such as *NPF*) that outline the mountain and along which total utility is constant. When these curves are projected unto the field of choice, they become utility contours (such as *KVC*).

and more apples, but the quantity of butter remains at zero (a process that can be pictured by moving along segment *OK*), total utility rises by less and less, along *OLMN*.

Finally, Edgeworth imagined the elevation of his mountain to increase as quantities of one good were added to any initial *positive* quantity of the other good. Holding apple consumption constant at *G*, *H*, or *K*, respectively, increased butter consumption raises total utility along *LP*, *MQ*, or *NR*. Holding butter consumption constant at *A*, *B*, or *C*, respectively, increased apple consumption raises total utility along *DP*, *ES*, or *FT*. Thus the utility mountain looks like the end of a loaf of French bread!

Fortunately, having once visited the third dimension, we need not stay there. Edgeworth had a wonderful idea: He imagined cutting into the mountain at a given level of utility, such as *OU*, and doing so along a horizontal plane (such as *NUF*) precisely parallel to the base of the mountain (*KOC*). Such a cut touches the mountain along a curved line (such as *NPF*) in the same way as would a horizontal cut into a loaf of French bread. This curved line, noted Edgeworth, can be projected onto the base of the mountain: *Plumb* vertical lines from *N*, *P*, and *F* yield *K*, *V*, and *C*, respectively. Thus the cut along *NPF* is reproduced as dashed line *KVC*. Edgeworth called this projection a **utility contour** or **consumption-indifference curve**. He argued, correctly, that it shows all the alternative combinations of two consumption goods that yield the same total of utility; all points on the curve correspond to the same height (*OU* in our case) in the third dimension. Because all combinations on the curve have the same total of utility, a utility-maximizing consumer would be indifferent about choosing among them.

Such an indifference curve is very much like

the contour line of a real mountain, which a mapmaker might draw to connect all the points of equal elevation. Indeed, just as a mapmaker labels a contour line with a cardinal number (such as 20 feet above sea level), so Edgeworth placed a cardinal utility number (such as 20 *utils*, or units of utility) next to the indifference curve. Note line *KVC* in Figure 3.4. It is a reproduction of line *KVC* of Figure 3.3 and a projection onto the field of choice of all the 20-util total-utility points on the imaginary utility mountain.

Note: Just as mapmakers draw many contours on their maps (for elevations of 10 feet, 20 feet, 30 feet, and so on), Edgeworth was aware that one could draw a whole family of utility contours, each one corresponding to a different utility total. If we cut the utility mountain successively at levels below or above *U*, we could derive the utility contours lying to the left or right of line *KVC* in Figure 3.4. They correspond, as their labels show, to lower or higher utility totals.

FIGURE 3.4 Utility Contours

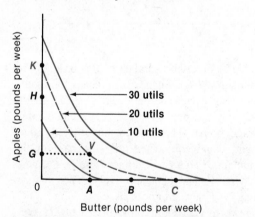

A utility contour, derived from Edgeworth's utility mountain, contains all the points of equal elevation on the imaginary utility mountain. Line *KVC*, for instance, corresponds to the projected curve so labelled in Figure 3.3. It shows all the alternative combinations of apples and butter that yield to the consumer the same total utility (of 20 utils). The curve to the right of *KVC* would be higher in the third dimension than *KVC* and would have a higher total of utility. Similarly the curve to the left of *KVC* would be lower on the mountain and would have a lower total of utility.

Caution: Point *V* does *not* indicate that the consumer is indifferent between *OG* apples and *OA* butter. Rather, the consumer is indifferent among *OG* apples plus *OA* butter, on the one hand, and all other combinations depicted by line *KVC*, on the other hand.

It was but a short step, taken somewhat inconsistently by Vilfredo Pareto (see Biography 14.1) and then decisively by Irving Fisher (see Biography 9.2) and John Hicks (see Biography 4.2), to abandon the *cardinal measurement* (1 unit, 2 units, 5 units, 15 units) of utility altogether. A consumer's preferences can be described, these later economists argued, without resort to utility measurement and without knowledge of the utility mountain from which the utility contours are derived. It is not necessary to tell *how much* a consumer values one set of goods compared to another (10 utils vs. 20 utils), it is quite sufficient to know whether one set is considered inferior, equal, or superior to another. An *ordinal ranking* (1st, 2nd, 5th, 15th), with the help of any arbitary scale, will do. One can eliminate the word ''utils'' after 10, 20, and 30 in Figure 3.4 and will still know enough, as long as it is understood that any curve labeled 10 simply refers to sets of goods all of which provide less total utility than sets found on a curve labeled with a higher number, be it 20, 30, or 566.

Analysis of the Consumption-Indifference Curve

Modern economists map the preferences of consumers with the help of consumption-indifference curves, and they construct these curves on the basis of four simple assumptions that do not require any utility measurement. These assumptions are good approximations of people's actual behavior, exceptions being rare.

1. Consumers are able to rank bundles of goods. It is assumed, first, that consumers can rank, on a scale of better or worse, all conceivable combinations of goods. When comparing two bundles of goods, they can tell whether they prefer one to the other or find them equally desirable. If preference is indicated, it is not necessary to gauge its intensity.

2. *Consumers prefer more of any good to less.* It is assumed that consumers always prefer a larger to a smaller quantity of any good because they have not yet reached the point of satiation. This implies that larger quantities of a good are associated with rising total utility (or positive marginal utility). Because there are so many goods in the world, this assumption is likely to be satisfied. As our Chapter 1 discussion of the optimization principle has shown, consuming so much of one good that satiation is reached is unlikely to be optimal. As a result of our second assumption, indifference curves must be *nega-*

tively sloped. Consider Panel (a) of Figure 3.5, and focus on the combination of goods represented by point A. As long as people are not satiated with any good, any set of goods above and to the right of A will be preferred to A itself. This is true of point B because it contains more pounds of apples and as much butter as A. It is true of C because it contains more of both goods. It is true of D because it contains more butter and as many pounds of apples as A. Since an indifference curve is the locus of points that are *equally* desirable, such a curve cannot possibly connect A with any of the *preferred* points contained in segment DAB.

For analogous reasons, such a curve cannot

FIGURE 3.5 The Indifference Curve Analyzed

(a) Assumptions 1 and 2

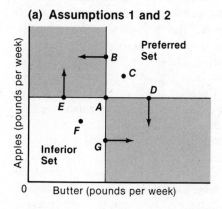

(c) Assumption 4

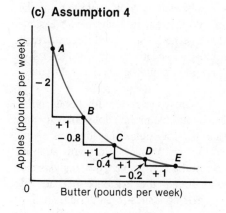

(b) Assumption 3

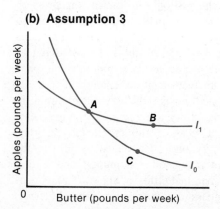

This set of graphs illustrates three major characteristics of a normal indifference curve: it must be negatively sloped when more is preferred to less (a); it cannot intersect other indifference curves when choices are transitive (b); it is subject to a diminishing marginal rate of substitution and thus bowed out toward the origin (c).

possibly connect *A* with any of the *inferior* points in segment *EAG*. All points in this segment are inferior because they contain less of one or both goods than does *A*. As a result, an indifference curve conforming to our second assumption cannot be positively sloped, nor can it be vertical or horizontal. An indifference curve containing set *A* must necessarily go through the shaded segments of our graph; that is, be negatively sloped.

There is another way of seeing why indifference curves must be negatively sloped: A move from *A* to *D* would raise a consumer's total utility because of an increase in butter consumption, all else being equal. Once at *D*, the consumer could be made to sacrifice an amount of apples just sufficient to offset the utility gained by the move from *A* to *D*. The set of goods so found would be equally desirable as *A* and, as the arrow at *D* indicates, it would lie in the shaded segment below D. Similarly, moves from *A* to *B*, *E*, or *G* could be compensated by additional moves in the direction of the arrows; in each case, the same conclusion emerges: an indifference curve through *A* must be negatively sloped. Naturally, the same argument could be made for any other point.

Note: We are concerned with goods only, not with bads. Our assumption does not deny that people want less of things that they hate and cannot instantly and costlessly discard, such as garbage or pollution. However, our analysis can easily accommodate the existence of bads by considering their opposites to be goods, such as garbage removal or pollution abatement.

3. Consumers rank bundles of goods in a consistent manner. It is assumed that consumers are consistent when they rank bundles of goods in order of preference. If set *A* is preferred to *B* and *B* is preferred to *C*, consistency requires that *A* is also preferred to *C*. When choices are made in such a noncontradictory fashion, **transitivity** in choice is said to prevail.

As a result of this assumption, it is impossible for indifference curves to meet or intersect. Consider panel (b) of Figure 3.5. According to indifference curve I_1, set *A* is as desirable as set *B*; according to curve I_0, *A* is as good as *C*. Logic

then requires for *B* to be valued as much as *C*. Yet the graph tells us that *B* contains more of both goods than *C*; so it must be preferred to *C* (by assumption 2).

Indifference curves that intersect and meet always lead to such inconsistencies. They are just as impossible as intersecting contour lines on a geographer's map. A given point on a mountain surface cannot be 500 feet and 800 feet above sea level at the same time. In the same way, point *A* in Panel (*b*) of Figure 3.5 cannot correspond simultaneously to the total utility level implied by I_0 and to the higher level implied by I_1.

4. Consumers insist on a diminishing marginal rate of substitution. It is assumed, finally, that consumers who acquire successive additional units of one good at the expense of another good will remain indifferent about such substitution only if they have to sacrifice ever smaller quantities of the second good. This is likely to be so because the relative importance people attach to different goods changes with the relative quantities available to them. Typically, the scarcer a good becomes, the greater is its marginal utility relative to that of a good that is becoming more plentiful. Consider panel (c) of Figure 3.5. A person who consumes the set of goods depicted by *A* might feel equally well off if 2 pounds of apples were sacrificed for an additional 1 pound of butter. Therefore, *B* is on the same indifference curve as *A*. Yet this subjective exchange ratio in the consumer's mind is likely to change with circumstances. Once at *B*, total utility might remain unchanged only if a much smaller sacrifice of apples were made to gain another pound of butter yet. And so on, at *C*, *D*, and *E*. As a result, the indifference curve is bowed out or *convex* with respect to the origin of the graph.

A nonmathematical explanation (admittedly oversimplified) invokes the principle of diminishing marginal utility without relying on the measurability of marginal utility: If the marginal utility of any one good depends only on the quantity of that good, the move from *A* to *B* raises the marginal utility of apples (and reduces the willingness to give them up at the old terms) because there is less of them. The same move lowers the marginal utility of butter (and reduces the eagerness to get more of it) because there is more of it. This could explain the decline in the subjective indifferent exchange ratio, which is, of course, our old friend from Chapter 2, the *marginal rate of substitution (MRS)*. In our graph, this rate is pictured as the amount of apples the consumer is willing to sacrifice indifferently for an extra unit of butter. We will denote it as $MRS_{a/b}$. This everchanging $MRS_{a/b}$ is in fact the *slope* of the indifference curve. Between points A and B, its absolute value is 2/1, on the average.

Note: If it takes *one* pound of butter to raise total utility enough to compensate precisely for the total utility decline caused by the loss of *two* pounds of apples (and this is what the consumer's indifference implies), we can write $MU_{1b} = MU_{2a}$. Knowing full well that marginal utility cannot be measured, we can, nevertheless, set each of these equivalences equal to *x utils*, or units of satisfaction, calling $MU_{1b} = x$ and also $MU_{2a} = x$. It follows logically, that $MU_{1a} = 0.5x$ and that $MU_{1b}/MU_{1a} = x/0.5x = 2/1$. Thus the absolute value of the slope is seen to equal also the ratio of the unmeasurable marginal utility of a pound of butter to that of a pound of apples.

$$|\text{Indifference curve slope}| = MRS_{a/b} = \frac{MU_b}{MU_a}$$

It is but a short step now to find the answer to our original question about the way utility-maximizing consumers divide their expenditure.

The Optimum of the Consumer

Figure 3.6 brings together the various aspects of the consumer's optimum. Panel (a) depicts the field of choice, constrained by prices and budget. Panel (b) depicts a consumer's tastes with the help of a family of indifference curves. Logically, but not practically, one can draw such a curve through every point in the field of choice, thereby relating the consumer's subjective evaluation of any one combination of goods to every other one in the field. Five curves, labelled I_0 to I_4, have

been drawn. Their labels, unlike those of Edgeworth in Figure 3.4, have no cardinal significance. (Bundles of goods on curve I_4 do not necessarily yield *twice* the utility of bundles on curve I_2.) The labels do, however, have an ordinal meaning (Bundles of goods on curve I_4 do yield *higher* utility, of whatever size, than those on curve I_2). Thus the labels remind us that all sets of goods above a given curve yield higher utility totals, and all sets below it lower ones, than do the sets on the curve. Combination A, therefore, is preferred to B, C, and D; A is considered inferior to E and F, but just as good as G.

Panel (c) of Figure 3.6 combines the other two graphs, and the solution becomes obvious. Given the constraints implied by the budget line, the consumer reaches maximum utility by choosing combination A; that is, by purchasing OD pounds of apples and OE pounds of butter per week.

Note: This combination lies on the highest indifference curve that can be reached along the budget line. A is found where the budget line just touches an indifference curve. At optimum point A, therefore, the slopes of budget line and indifference curve are the same.

Condition for Consumer's Optimum:

Slope of budget line = Slope of indifference curve

$$\frac{P_b}{P_a} = MRS_{a/b} = \frac{MU_b}{MU_a}$$

Therefore, $\quad \dfrac{MU_a}{P_a} = \dfrac{MU_b}{P_b}.$

Indifference-curve analysis thus confirms the conclusion reached by Jevons and discussed above. The condition for consumer's optimum can easily be expanded to any number of goods so that

$$\frac{MU_a}{P_a} = \frac{MU_b}{P_b} = \frac{MU_c}{P_c} = \cdots = \frac{MU_n}{P_n}.$$

FIGURE 3.6 The Consumer's Optimum

(a) Opportunities

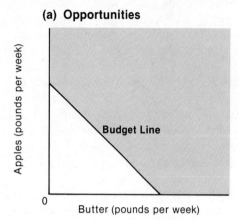

(c) The Consumer's Optimum

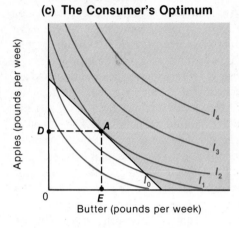

(b) Preferences

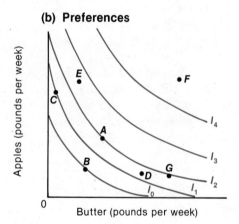

This set of graphs summarizes how utility-maximizing consumers divide their expenditures among different goods. Panel (a) depicts opportunities. It shows how prices and budget define what can be bought. Panel (b) depicts preferences. It shows the subjective value the consumer places on every set of goods relative to every other set. Panel (c) shows the best set of goods (point A) that the consumer can buy within the unshaded realm of the possible. This set lies on the highest indifference curve, I_2, that can be reached along the consumption-possibilities frontier.

This analysis, furthermore, has a great number of important applications. We will consider four of them.

Applications of Indifference-Curve Analysis

Application 1: Lump-Sum Vs. Selective Sales Tax

Governments can raise revenue in many ways. Consider the choice between a **lump-sum tax**, a fixed dollar levy imposed on people regardless of what they do, and a **selective sales tax** levied on the purchase of a particular good only (but in a way that yields the same revenue). Figure 3.7 on page 66 shows why the lump-sum tax is more efficient. Picture a consumer with budget line AB and indifference curves I_0, I_1, and I_2. The optimum position is C. Government imposes a selective sales tax on butter consumption only. This raises the price of butter only; the budget line becomes AD. The consumer finds a new optimum at E; utility falls from I_2 to I_0. The government's tax revenue can be depicted by dotted line EF. (It is measured in terms of the quantity of additional butter the consumer could buy if the

ANALYTICAL EXAMPLE 3.1:
The Derivation of Indifference Curves:
Revealed Preference

Economists have used several approaches to derive actual indifference curves. The **revealed-preference approach,** which was introduced by Paul Samuelson (see Biography 19.1), relies on observing the actual market behavior of people. Consider Figure 3A. Suppose a person is observed choosing combination *D* when relative prices are given by the slope of line *AB*. By assumption 2, found in the section on "The Analysis of The Consumption Indifference Curve," this choice reveals as *superior* all bundles of goods in shaded rectangle *CDE*. From what we know about a consumer's optimum, this choice also reveals that all other points on line *AB* and below it are *inferior* to *D*. (All bundles of goods in the shaded triangle were available to the consumer and cost as much as *D* or less but were not chosen.) An indifference curve through *D* must, therefore, go through the remaining unshaded areas.

This area can be narrowed by further observations. Consider Figure 3B, which elaborates upon Figure 3A. Suppose the consumer is observed choosing combination *F* (which we know to be inferior to *D*) when relative prices are given by the slope of line *GH*. By reasoning analogous to the above, the unshaded area can be reduced by the dotted area *BFH*. Or suppose combination *K* is chosen when relative prices are given by the slope of line *LM*. Since *D* is available, *K* must be preferred to *D*, and so must be all bundles of goods in the crosshatched area above and to the right of *K*. In this way, repeated observations narrow the zone of ignorance until the exact indifference curve through *D* is found, looking, perhaps, like line I_0. All this assumes, of course, that the consumer's tastes have not changed during the period of observation.

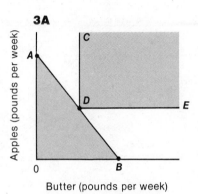

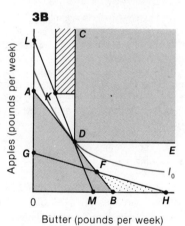

tax were removed and the same quantity of apples were bought as at *E*.)

Now consider the alternative. Let the government impose an equivalent lump-sum tax of *EF* = *GB*. Prices are unaffected; the budget line makes a parallel shift from *AB* to *HG*. The consumer buys combination *K*; utility drops from I_2 to I_1 only. The difference in utility between I_1 and I_0 is the **excess burden** of the selective butter tax, a drop in utility that is unnecessary in order to collect tax revenue *GB* and that could be avoided by the use of a different type of tax.

Application 2:   Cash or In-Kind Subsidy

Governments that wish to provide a given amount of subsidy can do so in many ways. Consider the choice between a *subsidy in kind* (for example, vouchers for specific goods), usually preferred by taxpayers, and a *subsidy in cash*. Figure 3.8 shows why a cash subsidy may be better (and certainly will not be worse) *for recipients* than a subsidy in kind. Picture a consumer with budget line *AB* and indifference curves I_0, I_1, and I_2. The optimum position is *C*.

FIGURE 3.7
Lump-Sum vs. Selective Sales Tax

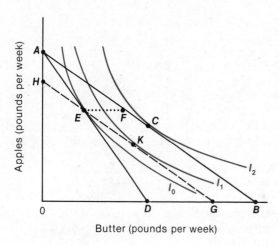

Butter (pounds per week)

On efficiency grounds, a lump-sum tax on consumers is better than a selective sales tax on a particular good: A move from a selective sales tax to a lump-sum tax that collects the same amount of revenue leaves government equally well off but raises the welfare of consumers (who move from C to K rather than from C to E). Note: An analogous argument can be made in favor of lump-sum subsidies rather than subsidies for particular goods.

Let government provide free vouchers that permit the purchase of $AD = BE$ of butter only. The budget line becomes ADE. The consumer finds a new optimum at D; utility rises from I_0 to I_1.

Now consider the alternative. Let the government provide an amount of cash sufficient to purchase BE of butter but with no strings attached. The budget line shifts to FE, leaving intact all the opportunities along DE but providing additional ones along DF. (The latter, of course, is what taxpayers often dislike.) In our case, the consumer buys combination G, containing less butter than at C but bringing utility to an even higher level, I_2 instead of I_1. This shows the possible inefficiency of the voucher approach (as long as we focus only on the recipients' utility).

Note: What if the consumer's preferences were depicted by lines I_0 and i_1 (and I_1, I_2 didn't

exist)? The consumer would go to position H regardless of the form of the subsidy.

Application 3:
Rationing and Mandated Purchases

Governments often set maximum purchase limits on particular goods or on all goods. (Consider the wartime rationing of food or gasoline.) Governments also require minimum purchases of particular goods. (Consider requirements to buy automobile safety features, social security, or trash collection services.) All these regulations may or may not affect any particular consumer. Consider Figure 3.9. Picture a consumer with budget line AB and indifference curves I_0 and I_1. The optimum position is C. Let government

FIGURE 3.8 Cash or In-Kind Subsidy

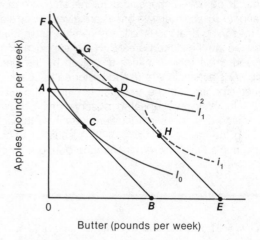

Butter (pounds per week)

On efficiency grounds, a cash subsidy given to consumers may be better for them (and it will not be worse) than an equivalent subsidy in kind: As long as taxpayers do not derive utility from seeing others consume specific quantities of goods, a move from an in-kind subsidy to a cash subsidy of equal value leaves donors equally well off but may raise the welfare of recipients (who may move from C to G rather than C to D). Note: An analogous argument can be made with respect to taxes in cash rather than taxes in kind (which collect a number of physical units of a good of equal cash value).

impose rationing of butter only. If the maximum allowed were *OD* per week, this particular consumer would not be affected at all. (Low-income people often are in this position.) If the ration were *OE* per week, it would be *potentially* binding: Purchase opportunities in triangle *BEH* would be eliminated by the ration limit (depicted by dashed line *EH*). In fact, however, this consumer's preferences are such that all of these opportunities are considered inferior compared to *C*, which could still be purchased. A binding limit is depicted by dotted line *FG*. Legally, the consumer could not reach a higher utility than that implied by point *G*, namely, I_0, which is lower than I_1. Preferring point *C*, the consumer may well move from *G* toward *C* by entering the black market for butter.

The case is analogous for mandated purchases. If government *required* the purchase of not less than *OF* butter per week, our consumer, already purchasing the larger quantity of butter corresponding to *C*, would not be affected at all. (High-income people often are in this position.) A required minimum purchase of *OE*, however, would be binding. Legally, the consumer could not reach a higher utility than that implied by point *H*, namely I_0. Preferring point *C*, the consumer may well move from *H* toward *C* by

ANALYTICAL EXAMPLE 3.2:

The Derivation of Indifference Curves: Experiment

Instead of relying on repeated observations of the market behavior of a *single* person *over time* (and assuming stability of this person's tastes), a second approach to the derivation of indifference curves experiments with *many* persons at a *given time* (and assumes that all have identical tastes). In a 1967 experiment at UCLA, students were asked to rank bundles of money ($0–$25) and ball point pens (0–180).

To find the indifference curve going through point *A* in Figure 3C, all combinations both above and to the right of *A* were ruled out as impossibly equivalent to *A* by the "more-is-preferred-to-less principle" (note the shading). Then subjects were asked to rank *A* versus *B*, *A* versus *C*, and so on. If *A* was preferred to *B*, combination *B* and all others to the left and below it were eliminated as inferior to *A*. If *C* was preferred to *A*, all points above and to the right of it were likewise eliminated. In this way, the zone of ignorance about the location of the indifference curve through *A* was successively narrowed.

Subjects were motivated to tell the truth by a payoff: after making their choice, a point *X* in the field of choice was selected at random, and subjects received the bundle of goods corresponding to *X* or *A*, whichever was preferred.

Figure 3D shows one of the indifference maps so derived.

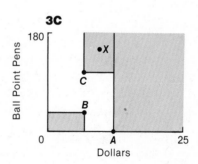

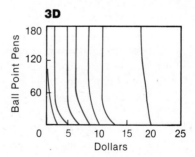

Source: K. R. MacCrimmon and M. Toda, "The Experimental Determination of Indifference Curves," *Review of Economic Studies*, October 1969, pp. 433–51. (Note also the literature about other experiments cited there.)

FIGURE 3.9
Rationing and Mandated Purchases

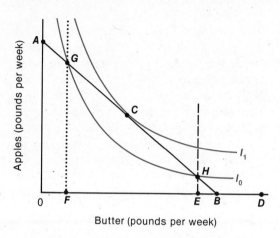

Rationing and mandated purchases alike, if effectively binding for a particular consumer, are bound to lower utility. Note: The argument made here for a single good can be extended to cover more goods than one.

cheating on mandated purchases (as by failing to maintain auto safety features or trading them away).

Application 4:
Measuring the Cost of Living

Almost everyone wants to know what is happening to the cost of living. Payments of wages, pensions, welfare benefits, alimony, rents, and much more are often adjusted with the Consumer Price Index. Few people realize the inevitable problems of index construction. If all prices moved in the same direction and proportion, no problem would exist at all. However, when some prices fall, others stay constant, and still others rise, and changing prices do so to varying degrees, one must agree on some kind of method to *weight* these divergent changes. To measure the change in the overall level of prices from year 0 to year 1, for example, one typically weights individual price changes in accordance with the

quantities of goods bought at these prices. With equal logic, one can use the quantities purchased in year 0 as those purchased in year 1, but this is likely to give rise to the **index-number problem**: If relative quantities change from year 0 to year 1, an index of prices takes on a different value depending on whether year 0 or year 1 quantities are used as weights in the construction of the index. Indifference curve analysis helps to highlight the problem.

The Laspeyres Price Index. The Consumer Price Index, for example, is a **Laspeyres-type index**, which always measures price (or quantity) change from year 0 to year 1 by using quantity (or price) weights *of year 0*. Suppose we wanted to measure the cost-of-living change for a consumer of two goods whose preferences are depicted by I_0 and I_1 in panel (a) of Figure 3.10. In year 0, let us imagine, the budget line is AB, and the consumer chooses to consume combination C, containing a year 0 quantity of apples of q_a^0 and a year 0 quantity of butter of q_b^0. If the respective year 0 prices (which are reflected in the slope of this budget line) are labelled p_a^0 and p_b^0, we can calculate the consumer's year 0 *actual expenditures*, E_A^0, as

$$E_A^0 = (q_a^0 \cdot p_a^0) + (q_b^0 \cdot p_b^0).$$

Now let us define year 1 *necessary expenditures*, E_N^1, as those that would enable the consumer to buy the year 0 quantities of goods (point C) at year 1 prices (p_a^1 and p_b^1):

$$E_N^1 = (q_a^0 \cdot p_a^1) + (q_b^0 \cdot p_b^1).$$

The Laspeyres price index (L_p) is simply

$$L_p = \frac{E_N^1}{E_A^0} \cdot 100.$$

If year 1 necessary expenditures were $1,000 and year 0 actual expenditures were $800, the index would come to 125, indicating an increase in the cost of living of 25 percent.

Yet this would be a *maximum* estimate of the

FIGURE 3.10 Measuring the Cost of Living

(a) The Laspeyres Price Index

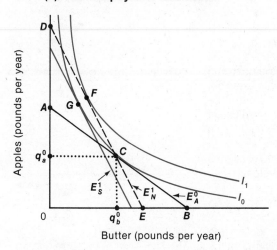

(b) The Paasche Price Index

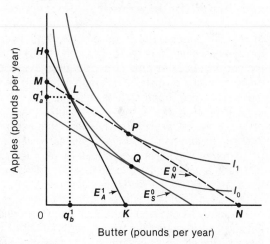

Indifference-curve analysis is useful in the interpretation of index numbers. A Laspeyres price index, the ratio of expenditures E_N^1 to E_A^0 in panel (a), is likely to overstate cost-of-living increases. A Paasche price index, the ratio of expenditures E_A^1 to E_N^0 in panel (b), is likely to understate them.

---

consumer's actual cost-of-living increase. If, as is likely, all prices did not rise in the same proportion, a year 1 budget line would have a different slope, such as line DE in panel (a) of Figure 3.10. A consumer would need in year 1 the purchasing power depicted by this dashed line in order to continue buying the year 0 *bundle of goods* at point C (and receive utility level I_0). Yet a consumer who was able to buy year 0 combination C, but was faced with such different year 1 relative prices, would in fact choose combination F in year 1 (and receive higher utility level I_1). A year 1 expenditure level sufficient to maintain the lower year 0 *utility level*, E_S^1, is lower than E_N^1. It is depicted by the color budget line and would enable the consumer at G to maintain in year 1 the year 0 utility level, I_0.

Note: What happens to the actual welfare of our consumer in year 1 relative to year 0 depends also on the actual expenditure, E_A^1, not shown in panel (a). If E_A^1 is larger than E_N^1 or equal to it, the consumer's year 1 welfare will certainly be

higher. If E_A^1 is smaller than E_N^1, the consumer's welfare may still be higher (contrary to what almost everyone believes) *as long as E_A^1 exceeds E_S^1.*

The Paasche Price Index. It is also logical to construct a **Paasche-type index**, which always measures price (or quantity) change from year 0 to year 1 by using quantity (or price) weights *of year 1*. Consider panel (b) of Figure 3.10. A consumer in year 1, we imagine, has a budget line HK and chooses combination L, containing a year 1 quantity of apples of q_a^1 and a year 1 quantity of butter of q_b^1. If the respective year 1 prices, reflected in this budget line, are labeled p_a^1 and p_b^1, we can calculate the consumer's year 1 actual expenditures, E_A^1, as

$$E_A^1 = (q_a^1 \cdot p_a^1) + (q_b^1 \cdot p_b^1).$$

Now let us define year 0 necessary expenditures, E_N^0, as those which would have enabled the

ANALYTICAL EXAMPLE 3.3:

Chicken Little in America

In recent years, the U.S. government has become extremely safety-conscious on behalf of consumers. Agencies have mush-roomed that seek to protect people from the food they eat and drink, from their own habits (too much smoking, too little exercise, too fast driving), from hazards at work, and above all from the thousands of gadgets they buy. Since there are insufficient resources to reduce to zero all conceivable risks, one might wish that the government would allocate its limited resources as a utility-maximizing private consumer would. Jevons' rule tells us that such a consumer would be foolish to divide expenditures so as to get 200 utils per dollar of apples and 10 utils per dollar of butter. Such a consumer could spend $1 less on butter and $1 more on apples and end up with an extra net benefit of 190 utils. Optimization requires the same marginal utility per dollar (the same marginal benefit-cost ratio) in all lines of expenditure. Yet the U. S. government is continually violating this principle. It rarely looks at marginal magnitudes at all; it ignores even the most obvious lessons taught us by total benefit-cost ratios.

Consider the accompanying table with 1977 data on total benefit-cost ratios for regulatory actions taken by the Consumer Products Safety Commission. Ratios less than one indicate that the benefits of government safety standards were lower than the costs (lower, that is, than other benefits forgone). Yet the actions were taken, nevertheless. In addition, if data on marginal benefits per dollar were available for the projects cited here, we would almost certainly find that governmental resources could have been spent more effectively. For example, the government could have forgotten about safety standards for ladders, chainsaws, matches, and pajamas in order to focus on totally different types of safety projects. The elimination of auto accidents and smoking would save 50,000 and 200,000 lives per year, respectively—considerably more per dollar spent than any of the programs shown in the table. A better division of governmental resources might also have been made possible within the agency—as by shifting standard-setting efforts from drain cleaners to bathtubs and showers or even from antihistamines to extension cords—depending, in each case, on the relative magnitudes of *marginal* benefits per dollar spent (not shown).

Project	Benefit-Cost Ratio
Bathtubs and Showers	2.70
Over-the-Counter Antihistamines	2.52
Public Playground Equipment	2.02
Gas Space Heaters	1.85
Drain Cleaners	1.08
Ladders	0.94
Glazing Materials	0.91
Ranges and Ovens	0.87
Trouble Lights	0.75
Chain Saws	0.67
Upholstered Furniture	0.48
Power Saws (portable)	0.40
Power Mowers	0.40
Matches	0.37
Rust Remover	0.34
Petroleum Distillates	0.25
Power Saws (nonportable)	0.16
Ammonia	0.11
Extension Cords	0.10
Television Sets	0.09
Wearing Apparel	0.02

Sources: Steven E. Rhoads, "How Much Should We Spend to Save a Life?" and Max Singer, "How to Reduce Risks Rationally," *Public Interest*, Spring 1978, pp. 74–112; Henry G. Grabowski and John M. Vernon, "Consumer Product Safety Regulation," *The American Economic Review*, May 1978, Vol. 68, No. 2, pp. 284-289.

ANALYTICAL EXAMPLE 3.4:
Measuring Soviet Economic Growth

The index-number problem emerges whenever an attempt is made to compare, over time or space, heterogeneous aggregates of prices or output. The section of this chapter on "Measuring the Cost of Living" noted the difficulties associated with comparing price levels over time; consider the similar difficulty of comparing output levels over time. Heterogeneous outputs of apples, blast furnaces, medical care, and steel, for example, cannot be compared directly; they have to be added together using the common denominator of money. To yield meaningful results, the same price weights must be applied to the lists of quantities produced in two different periods, but one can use the prices of one year just as much as those of another. If (as is likely) relative prices come to differ over time, different results can emerge.

Raymond P. Powell attempted to measure the growth of Soviet GNP from 1928–37, a time during which the Soviets industrialized their economy.[1] Measured in 1928 prices, the average annual growth rate was 11.9 percent, but measured in 1937 prices, it was 6.2 percent. Neither answer is more correct than the other. The hypothetical example in the accompanying table highlights the problem. Evaluate each year's physical output at earlier 1928 prices (as a Laspeyres *quantity* index would) and aggregate output is seen to have risen from $(100 \cdot 1) + (50 \cdot 1) = 150$ rubles to $(90 \cdot 1) + (300 \cdot 1) = 390$ rubles—at an average rate of more than 11 percent per year. Now evaluate each year's physical output at later 1937 prices (as a Paasche quantity index would), and aggregate output can be seen to have risen from $(100 \cdot 2) + (50 \cdot 0.5) = 225$ rubles to $(90 \cdot 2) + (300 \cdot 0.5) = 330$ rubles—at an average rate of less than 5 percent per year. There is no logical way to escape the problem.

Type of Output	1928		1937	
	Quantity	Price	Quantity	Price
Food	100	1	90	2
Machinery	50	1	300	0.5

[1]Raymond P. Powell, "Economic Growth in the U.S.S.R.," *Scientific American*, December 1968, pp. 17–23. Reprinted in Heinz Kohler, *Readings in Economics*, 2nd ed. (New York: Holt, Rinehart, & Winston, 1969), pp. 629–39.

consumer to buy the year 1 quantities of goods (point L) at year 0 prices (p_a^0 and p_b^0):

$$E_N^0 = (q_a^1 \cdot p_a^0) + (q_b^1 \cdot p_b^0).$$

The Paasche price index (P_p) is simply

$$P_p = \frac{E_A^1}{E_N^0} \cdot 100.$$

If year 1 actual expenditures were $952 and year 0 necessary expenditures were $850, the index would come to 112, indicating an increase in the cost of living of 12 percent.

Yet this would be a *minimum* estimate (in contrast to the *maximum* Laspeyres estimate) of the consumer's actual cost-of-living increase. If, as is likely, all prices did not rise in the same proportion, a year 0 budget line would have had a different slope, such as line MN in panel (b) of Figure 3.10. A consumer would have needed in year 0 the purchasing power depicted by this dashed line in order to have bought the year 1 bundle of goods at point L (and have received utility level I_0). Yet a consumer who would have been able to buy year 1 combination L, but who would have been faced with different year 0 relative prices, would in fact have chosen combination P in year 0 (and have received higher utility level I_1). A year 0 expenditure level, E_S^0, just sufficient to produce the lower year 0 utility level I_0 could have been lower than E_N^0. It is depicted by the color budget line and would have enabled the consumer at Q to maintain in year 0 the year 1 utility level I_0.

Note: What happens to the actual welfare of our consumer in year 1 relative to year 0 depends also on actual expenditures, E_A^0, not shown in panel (b). If E_A^0 was equal to or larger than E_N^0, the consumer's year 1 welfare will certainly be smaller. If E_A^0 was smaller than E_N^0, the consumer's year 1 welfare may still be smaller. This is true as long as E_A^0 exceeds E_S^0.

A true price index will forever escape us. But the forgoing analysis tells us that it lies somewhere between the lower limit of the Paasche index and the upper limit of the Laspeyres index.

SUMMARY

1. All conceivable consumption choices can be depicted graphically as a field of choice. However, a consumer's actual choices are always constrained by positive prices and a limited budget. The budget line (or consumption-possibilities frontier) is a graphical device that separates attainable from unattainable combinations of goods. Its slope reflects relative prices of goods; its position reflects the size of the budget.

2. A utility-maximizing consumer must somehow evaluate and compare the utility derivable from the alternative combinations of goods that are attainable. Bentham, who focussed on total utility, was not very helpful. Jevons defined the solution in principle: total utility is maximized when the marginal utilities per dollar of every good consumed are equalized.

3. Edgeworth went a step further and showed that utility totals associated with various combinations of goods can be depicted on the field of choice as utility contours or consumption-indifference curves.

4. Edgeworth-type indifference curves can, however, be constructed without resort to utility measurement, on the basis of four simple assumptions: Consumers are able to rank bundles of goods in order of preference; they prefer more of any good to less; they rank bundles of goods in a consistent manner; and they insist on a diminishing marginal rate of substitution (MRS). The MRS reflects the relative marginal utilities of goods and equals the changing slope of the indifference curve.

5. The optimum division of a utility-maximizing consumer's expenditures can be made evident by combining the budget line (depicting the consumer's opportunities) with a family of consumption-indifference curves (depicting the consumer's preferences). The optimum is found on the highest indifference curve that can be reached along the budget line.

6. The theory of the consumer's optimum has a great number of important applications. Discussed are the choice between a lump-sum and selective sales tax, the choice between a subsidy in cash and one in kind, the effect of rationing and mandated purchases, and the measurement of the cost of living.

KEY TERMS

budget line
consumption-indifference curve
consumption-possibilities frontier
excess burden
field of choice
index-number problem
Laspeyres-type index

lump-sum tax

marginal utility (*MU*)

Paasche-type index

principle of diminishing marginal utility

revealed-preference approach

selective sales tax

transitivity

utility

utility contour

QUESTIONS AND PROBLEMS

1. Draw the budget line for a consumer with a monthly budget of $500, which is to be allocated between goods *a* and *b*, priced at $10 and $20 per unit, respectively.

    a. Show the effect on this budget line if, simultaneously, the budget and the price of *a* halved, while the price of *b* doubled.

    b. If only the price of *a* halved, could the consumer buy more of *b*? Explain.

    c. Starting with the original budget line, show the effect on the consumer if government, simultaneously, rationed good *a* at 20 units and good *b* at 10 units per month. What if the rations were 40*a* and 20*b*?

    d. Starting with the original budget line, show the effect on the consumer if government handed out 300 ration points per month and required the consumer to pay 5 points per unit of good *a* and 20 points per unit of good *b*, in addition to money.

    e. Starting with the original budget line, show the effect on the consumer if consumption required 10 hours of time per unit of *a* and 1 hour per unit of *b*, but the consumer had a total of only 150 hours to spend.

2. Consider the effect on your answer to 1.d. if ration points could be traded for money in "white" markets; consider the effect on your answer to 1.e. if time could be traded for money (as by working more or less outside the home in income-earning activities or inside the home in activities that substitute for the spending of income).

3. Again consider the consumer described in the opening paragraph of Question 1. Imagine that the consumer's marginal utility of each good is shown in the table and is dependent only on the amount consumed of that good. Use the rule of Jevons to determine the optimum quantities to be consumed of each good.

Units Consumed (in pounds)	Marginal utility (in utils/pound)	
	Good a	Good b
5	60	50
10	55	45
15	50	40
20	45	35
25	40	30
30	35	25
35	30	20
40	25	15

4. *Mr. A*: All of the assumptions about indifference curves in this chapter are wrong:

    a. Consumers are able to rank bundles of goods? Then why do they say: "These goods are so different, I can't choose" or "I don't care, you choose for me" or "Whichever I choose, I know I'll be sorry"?

    b. Consumers prefer more of any good to less? What about *complementary* goods, such as bacon and eggs, cars and roads, cars and gasoline, French fries and ketchup, knives and forks, peanut butter and jelly, rifles and ammunition, right shoes and left shoes, tea and lemon, TV sets and electricity, vermouth and gin? Given an amount of one item of these pairs, an increased amount of the other item will be considered a nuisance at worst and a matter of indifference at best. Or what about goods some people can't stand, such as lipstick, hated foods, pornographic books? I can easily imagine indifference curves that are horizontal, vertical, and even positively sloped. In fact, I think they might be circular.

c. Consumers rank bundles of goods in a consistent manner? I observe people making inconsistent choices all the time, probably because comparing pairs of goods one at a time is not the same thing as making rank orderings of many goods simultaneously. This problem is worse when we turn from individual choices to group choices.

d. Consumers insist on a diminishing marginal rate of substitution? What about *perfect substitutes*, such as two nickels and one dime, a gallon of Amoco gas and a similar gallon of Mobil, and (for some people) a glass of Coors and a glass of Budweiser? What about the phenomenon of *addiction*, whether to alcohol, cigarettes, classical music, gambling, heroin, mountain climbing, rock and roll, or stamp collecting? I can easily imagine indifference curves that are negatively sloped, but are straight lines or concave with respect to the origin.

Ms. B: I am speechless.

What about you? What response would you make to each of Mr. A's points?

5. Consider the diagram below of a person's budget line and three indifference curves.

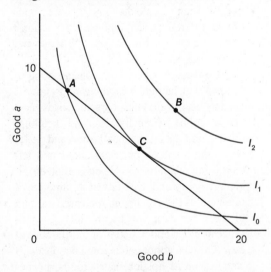

a. If the price of good *a* were $15, what would be the size of the consumer's budget?

b. Given your answer to question 5a, what would be the price of good *b*?

c. What is the consumer's *MRS* at the optimum?

d. Why is point *A* not the optimum? Why not *B*?

e. If utility-maximizing consumers in another city paid half as much for good *a* and twice as much for good *b*, what would their *MRS* be?

6. Consider the graph in Question 5. Let good *a* stand for food and good *b* for all other goods.

a. Show the effect on the consumer's optimum if the government provided free food stamps for 5 units of food.

b. What if the government made people buy each $2 worth of those food stamps for $1 worth of money?

c. Show that a cash grant smaller than the value of the in-kind subsidy might be able to raise the recipients' welfare just as much.

d. Make an analogous argument about in-kind fringe benefits often provided by employers (such as life insurance, medical care, or recreational facilities).

7. The index-number problem has been illustrated in this chapter by comparisons of price or output levels over *time*. It is just as serious for *spatial* comparisons at a given time. Invent numerical examples (similar to the one in Analytical Example 3.4, "Measuring Soviet Economic Growth") to illustrate the problem of comparing

a. price levels between New York and Los Angeles.

b. output levels between the United States and Russia.

8. A family of indifference curves depicts a person's tastes, but, surely, these tastes are not determined by genes and fixed forever: people are born with few tastes (a liking for warmth and mother's milk, a dislike of falling, loud noises, and being wet). Thereafter, tastes are learned (from parents and peers, teachers and preachers, business advertising and government propaganda). Tastes, therefore, change with age and also with the cycles of fashion—whether in art, cars, dress, food, or even scientific doctrines.

a. How might one depict a change in a person's tastes?

b. How would one account for interdependencies in people's tastes, such as the desire to be like others (bandwagon effect), to be unlike others (snob effect), to see others well off (benevolence), or to see them in misery (malevolence)?

c. Can a person's tastes ever be wrong? (*Hint*: Consider arsonists, dope addicts, the feeble-minded or immature, neurotics, psychotics. If your answer is yes, ask yourself who can be trusted to have the correct tastes and how these tastes could be made effective in people's choices).

SELECTED READINGS

Black, R. D. Collison, and Könekamp, Rosamond. *Papers and Correspondence of William Stanley Jevons*, vol. 1. Clifton, N.J.: Augustus M. Kelley, 1972.

Discusses the life and work of Jevons. *See also* Harriet W. Jevons, "William Stanley Jevons." *Econometrica*, July 1934, pp. 225-37.

Galbraith, John K. *The Affluent Society*. Boston: Houghton Mifflin, 1958; *The New Industrial State*. Boston: Houghton Mifflin, 1971.

Argues that people's tastes are artificial creations of business advertising and therefore, not worth respecting. For a contrary view, *see* F. A. von Hayek. "The Non Sequitur of the Dependence Effect." *Southern Economic Journal*, April 1961, pp. 346-48.

Keynes, John M. *Essays in Biography*. New York: Harcourt, Brace and Co., 1933, pp. 267-93.

Discusses the life and work of Edgeworth. *See also* Arthur L. Bowley. "Francis Ysidro Edgeworth." *Econometrica*, April 1934, pp. 113-24.

Leibenstein, Harvey. *Beyond Economic Man: A New Foundation for Microeconomics*, chaps. 4 and 11. Cambridge: Harvard University Press, 1976.

Discusses interdependencies in people's tastes and the process of decision making *within* multiperson households.

Linder, Staffan B. *The Harried Leisure Class*. New York: Columbia University Press, 1970.

Discusses time as an important constraint to people's consumption choices.

Scott, Robert H. "Avarice, Altruism, and Second Party Preferences." *The Quarterly Journal of Economics*, February 1972, pp. 1-18.

A discussion of interdependent utilities.

Seligman, Benjamin B. *The Reaffirmation of Tradition. Main Currents in Modern Economics, vol. 2*. Chicago: Quadrangle, 1962.

A critical review of the work of Jevons.

Weinstein, Arnold A. "Transitivity of Preference: A Comparison Among Age Groups." *Journal of Political Economy*, March-April 1968, pp. 307-11.

Reports on an experiment to test the consistency of people's choices; concludes that transitivity is an acquired skill (it increases with age).

CHAPTER 4

The Demand for Consumption Goods

In the previous chapter, we isolated the major elements that explain the division of a consumer's expenditures among different consumption goods. The elements consisted of objective factors on the one hand, notably the prices of goods and the size of the consumer's budget, and of subjective factors on the other hand, notably the consumer's preferences. Figure 3.6, ''The Consumer's Optimum'' (p. 64), brought these elements together and depicted the consumption choices of a consumer who cared to maximize utility. In Chapter 4, we will test the validity of our theory of consumer choice by developing some of its behavioral implications and comparing them with the observed behavior of real-world consumers.

The first of these implications is the famous **''law'' of downward-sloping demand**, referring to the tendency of people normally to buy larger quantities of something when its price is lower, all else being equal. Note the careful wording. The term ''law'' has been placed in quotation marks because it is not in fact a rigid law (although traditionally referred to as such) but a tendency normally observed.

Also note: As every beginning student in economics learns rather quickly, **demand** never refers to a single quantity number but rather to the alternative amounts of an item a person (or group of persons) would buy during a given

period at all conceivable prices of this item, all else being equal. We can now appreciate the meaning of this. Let us denote a person's demand for a consumption good x by D_x. As we have shown, D_x depends on (or is a function of) the price of this good, P_x; the prices of any other good, P_y, P_z, and so on; the consumer's budget, B; and the consumer's tastes, T. All of this can be written as

$$D_x = f(P_x, P_y, P_z, \ldots, B, T).$$

If we assume that P_y, P_z, . . . , B and T do not vary, then the demand for x depends on its own price alone.

$$D_x = f(P_x)$$

Every conceivable price of x will thus be associated with a particular (and probably different) quantity demanded of x; hence *demand* refers to a set of many price-quantity combinations. Our earlier analysis of the consumer's optimum can help us derive such a relationship.

The Demand for a Good as a Function of Its Own Price

Picture a consumer whose tastes are summarized by indifference curves I_0 to I_3 in panel (a) of Figure 4.1. Imagine an initial optimum at a, corresponding to a weekly budget of $120 and prices of $2.50 per pound of apples and $6 per pound of butter. (Hence distance *0A* measures $120 per week divided by $2.50 per pound, or 48 pounds per week. Distance *0B* measures $120 per week divided by $6 per pound, or 20 pounds per week.) The actual quantity of butter purchased at point *a* is graphed in panel (b) as point *e*.

Now let the consumer's tastes and budget remain unchanged, along with the apple price. Let the price of butter fall, successively, to $3, $2, and $1.50 per pound. The budget line will swing around point *A* from *AB* to *AC, AD,* and *AE,* respectively. (Distance *0C* measures 40 pounds per week, *0D* 60 pounds per week, and

0E 80 pounds per week, as implied by the lower prices of butter.) The consumer's optimum will move from point *a* to *b, c,* and *d,* respectively, along a path called the **price-consumption line**. This line indicates how the optimum quantities of two consumption goods change in response to a change in the price of one of these goods, all else being equal.

Now consider panel (b). The quantities of butter consumed at the various optima have been plotted separately there, along with the corresponding butter prices. The points so derived, labeled *e* through *h*, trace out the familiar downward-sloping demand curve. Naturally, if initially we had assumed different tastes (had drawn different indifference curves), had as-

FIGURE 4.1 The Price-Consumption Line

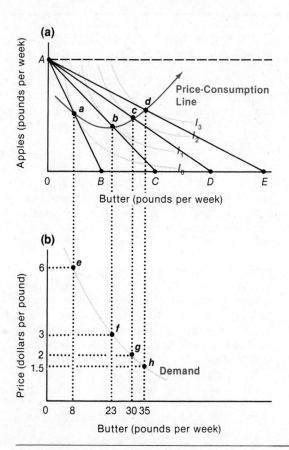

The decreasing price of a consumption good, here butter, is pictured by budget line *AB* swinging to the right to become *AC, AD,* and then *AE*. This decrease in butter price gives rise to an increased quantity of butter demanded, all else being equal. (Tastes throughout are depicted by indifference curves I_0 to I_3; the weekly budget remains $120; the apple price stays at $2.50 per pound.) The price-consumption line in panel (a) traces the alternative optima selected by a utility-maximizing consumer; the implied demand curve for butter, pictured in panel (b), is downward-sloping.

sumed a different budget size or apple price (and had thus started from a budget line unlike *AB*), we would have derived a different demand curve. That is why a change in tastes, budget, or the price of any other good *shifts* a given demand curve to the right or left and is referred to as a **change in demand**. In contrast, a change in the good's own price, while tastes, budget, and other prices are unchanged, causes a *movement along* a given demand curve (as between *e* and *f*) and is referred to as a **change in quantity demanded**.

Three things should be noted. First, as long as the price-consumption line, in response to lowered prices of the good measured along the horizontal axis (here butter), follows a path toward the right, the demand curve of this good will be downward-sloping. This will be so regardless of whether the consumption of the other

good (here apples) falls (as it does between *a* and *b*) or rises (as it does between *b* and *d*).

Second, the price-consumption line can never cross the dashed horizontal line drawn through point *A*. That line would depict the budget line if the price of butter were to become zero. The consumer could then spend the entire budget on apples, buying the maximum possible quantity of *0A*, while picking up for nothing any desired quantity of butter. Such a combination would lie on the dashed line. Any combination above that line would remain unavailable because the limited budget, along with the positive apple price, would not allow the acquisition of any apple quantity larger than *0A*.

Third, a hypothetical case could be made for an upward-sloping demand curve: Imagine indifference curve I_1 touching budget line *AC* above

CLOSE-UP 4.1:

The Demand for Alcoholism, Hijacking, and Homicide

The "law" of downward-sloping demand has wide applicability, far beyond the world of markets in which things are bought for money. Consider three cases in point: alcoholism, hijacking, and homicide.

Although alcoholism is widely regarded as a disease over which victims have no control, it turns out that alcoholics, too, respond to price signals. Dr. George Bigelow set up an experiment in which chronic alcoholics had to pull on a one-pound lever in order to get a drink. The more they had to pull (or the higher the "price" in terms of number of pulls), the less they drank.

He also varied the time the alcoholics had to wait between drinks to get another drink. When they did not have to wait, they drank all the alcohol available. When they had to wait longer between drinks, they drank less—even though the same amount of alcohol was available. (For example, those who had to wait 90 minutes between drinks drank half the amount they would drink without waiting.)

In another test, alcoholics could have 24 drinks a day if they wanted, but if they took more than five, other privileges were taken away. These privileges (the "price" for drinking) included socializing, recreation, and regular food (the same food pureed in a blender was provided to those who took more than five drinks). The alcoholics stopped at five drinks 80 percent of the time.

The first U.S. airliner was hijacked to Cuba on May 1, 1961 during a Miami-Key West flight. From 1961–67, there were 7 more such episodes; then, from 1968–72, there were 124 hijackings. In 1973, the course of this national epidemic was sharply reversed; there were only 11 hijackings from 1973–76. A simple explanation is: the price for the crime had been increased steeply.

In January, 1973, a system of mandatory preboard screening of passengers and carry-on baggage was put into effect; in February, 1973, a U.S.-Cuba treaty instituted extradition or punishment of hijackers. As a result, rates of apprehension of hijackers (and the likelihood of their incarceration) rose sharply. (In 1968, 15 percent of hijackers were caught; from 1973 on, 100 percent.) In addition, sentences handed out changed from mild to severe. (The average sen-

and to the left of point *a*. The lower butter price would then be associated, at a new optimum *b'* (not shown), with a *lower* butter quantity purchased. Point *f*, in panel (b), would be below and to the left of point *e*. Such a situation, in which consumers buy less of an item when its price is lower and more when it is higher, all else being equal, is called **Giffen's paradox**. This situation is named after a British statistician, Sir Robert Giffen (1837–1910), and has been observed only on the rarest of occasions. A possible explanation is given later in this chapter.

The Demand for a Good as a Function of Income

A mental experiment analogous to the one in the previous section reveals the likely effect on quantity demanded of changes in income. Consider Figure 4.2. Imagine a consumer, whose tastes are depicted by indifference curves I_0 to I_3 in panel (a), who neither borrows nor saves and whose budget, therefore, equals income. Picture an initial optimum at *a*, corresponding to a weekly income of $40 and prices of $4 per pound of apples and $2 per pound of butter. (Hence distance *0A* measures $40 per week divided by $4 per pound, or 10 pounds per week. Distance *0B* measures $40 per week divided by $2 per pound, or 20 pounds per week.) The actual quantity of butter purchased at point *a* is graphed in panel (b) as point *e*.

Now let the consumer's tastes and both prices remain unchanged. Let income rise, successively, to $80, $120, and $160 per week. The budget line will shift out from *AB* to *CD, EF,* and

---

tence in 1968 was 1.5 years; in 1973, it was 23 years.) Hijackers responded to this increased price. A demand equation calculated from the relevant data reveals that without the higher price, 1973–76 hijackings would have numbered not 11, but between 52 and 71.

It is often argued that murderers are unlikely to engage in rational comparisons of costs and benefits prior to their crime. Hence, it is said, a higher price for murder (in the form of greater probability of arrest and conviction, followed by long prison terms or execution) will have no effect on the quantity demanded (the number of such crimes committed). A 1929–68 time-series study of England and Wales provides a test.

Before 1957, all convicted murderers in England and Wales were subject to execution, unless they received Royal Mercy. More than 50 percent were in fact executed. A 1957 Homicide Act limited crimes subject to execution to murders in furtherance of theft, murder by shooting, and murder of police officers. Only 10 percent of those convicted were in fact executed. The rest received life imprisonment, but were typically set free after 10–15 years.

The homicide rate after 1957 soared. A de-

mand equation calculated from the relevant data reveals that every extra execution, all else being equal, would prevent more than 4 additional murders.

Note: A similar study for the United States and for the 1935–69 period argued that each additional execution might have saved between 7 and 8 potential murder victims.

Sources: "Deterrence," *The Public Interest*, Summer 1973, pp. 119–20 (on alcoholism); William M. Landes, "An Economic Study of U.S. Aircraft Hijacking, 1961–76," *The Journal of Law and Economics*, April 1978, pp. 1–31; Kenneth I. Wolpin, "Capital Punishment and Homicide in England: A Summary of Results," *The American Economic Review*, May 1978, pp. 422–27; Isaac Ehrlich, "The Deterrent Effect of Capital Punishment: A Question of Life and Death," *The American Economic Review*, June 1975, pp. 397–417. (For the ensuing controversy on that study, see *The American Economic Review*, June 1977, pp. 445–58; and Kenneth L. Avio, "Capital Punishment in Canada: A Time-Series Analysis of the Deterrent Hypothesis," *The Canadian Journal of Economics*, November 1979, pp. 647–76.

GH, respectively. The consumer's optimum will move from point *a* to *b, c,* and *d,* along a path called the **income-consumption line**. This line indicates how the optimum quantities of two consumption goods change in response to a change in income, all else being equal.

FIGURE 4.2   The Income-Consumption Line

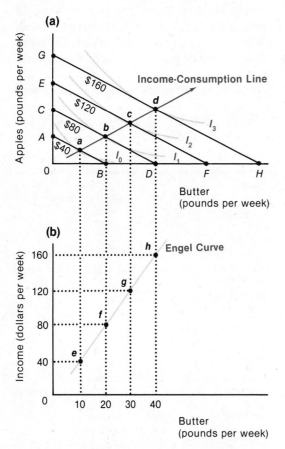

(a)

Apples (pounds per week)

G
E
C
A

$160
$120
$80
$40

Income-Consumption Line

d
c
b
a

I_3
I_2
I_1
I_0

0   B   D   F   H

Butter
(pounds per week)

(b)

Income (dollars per week)

160 .... h   Engel Curve
120 .... g
80 .... f
40 .... e

0   10   20   30   40

Butter
(pounds per week)

Increasing income is pictured by parallel shifts of budget line *AB* to *CD, EF,* and then *GH*. This increase in income gives rise to an increased quantity of butter demanded, all else being equal. (Tastes throughout are depicted by indifference curves I_0 to I_3; the prices of apples and butter remain at $4 and $2 per pound, respectively.) The income-consumption line in panel (a) traces the alternative optima selected by a utility-maximizing consumer; the implied Engel curve for butter, pictured in panel (b), is upward-sloping.

Now consider panel (b). The quantities of butter consumed at the various optima have been plotted separately there, along with the corresponding incomes. The points so derived, labeled *e* through *h,* trace out an upward-sloping **Engel curve**. Such a curve always shows the alternative amounts of an item a person (or group of persons) would buy during a given period at all conceivable incomes, all else being equal. The curve is named after a German statistician, Ernst Engel (1821–96), who should not be confused with Friedrich Engels, the friend of Karl Marx. Ernst Engel studied the budgets and expenditures of large numbers of families. In 1857, he pronounced what is now known as **Engel's Law**, that food expenditures take a smaller percentage of income the larger income is. This tendency has been confirmed ever since throughout the world, not only for families, but also for nations. Engel also noted that clothing and housing tended to take a constant percentage of family incomes, while luxuries (such as education, health care, transportation, recreation, and saving) took increasing percentages of higher incomes.

Two things should be noted about the Engel curve in Figure 4.2. First, while Engel himself related income to various types of money expenditures, our curve relates income to physical quantities bought. As long as prices are given, money expenditures and physical quantities move, of course, together, and one magnitude can always be calculated from the other. (At our assumed price of $2 per pound, the 10 pounds of butter per week at point *e* correspond to $20 of butter *expenditures*, and so on for points *f* to *h.*)

Note, second, that an upward-sloping Engel curve is typical but not inevitable. As long as the income-consumption line, in response to higher income, follows a path toward the right, an upward-sloping Engel curve is implied. At higher incomes, all else being equal, the consumer is then consuming larger physical quantities. Goods of which larger physical quantities are consumed at higher than at lower incomes are called **normal goods**. However, an upward-sloping Engel curve need not be a straight line. To the extent that quantities bought rise *less rapidly* than income, the normal goods involved are called **necessities**, and the Engel curve has an *ever-increasing* slope to the right of point *e*. (As income doubled from $40 to $80, for instance, butter consumption would less than double from 10 to, say, only 15 pounds per week.) To the extent that quantities bought rise *more rapidly* than income, the normal goods involved are called **luxuries**, and the Engel curve has an *ever-decreasing* slope to the right of point *e*. (As income doubled from $40 to $80, for instance, butter consumption would more than double from 10 to, say, 28 pounds per week.) Not all goods are normal, however. Imagine a set of indifference curves that are vertical displacements of each other (such that their slopes are identical at any given quantity measured on the horizontal axis). In that case, tangency points *b, c,* and *d* would be vertically above *a*, and the Engel curve would be a vertical line, too. No matter what the income, the consumer would consume the identical physical quantity. (Salt might be an example.) Indeed, it is possible for curves I_1 through I_3 to be tangent on higher budget lines above and to the *left* of *a*. The income-consumption line through *a* would then be pointing upwards to the left, and the corresponding Engel curve would be likewise sloping upwards and left from point *e*. At higher incomes, all else being equal, the consumer would then be consuming smaller physical quantities. Goods of which smaller physical quantities are consumed at higher incomes are called **inferior goods**. Examples might be bulky, but not necessarily nutritious and palatable foods (bread, pasta, potatoes, rice, turnips, pigs' feet), as well as all kinds of low-quality goods that people abandon the moment their income rises (second-hand clothes, reconditioned tires, long-distance bus rides, routine tooth extractions, and, some think, even having children.) As it turns out, Giffen's paradox is always associated with inferior goods, although the reverse is not true. Not all inferior goods produce the paradox. To solve the paradox, we must come to understand the distinction between *substitution* and *income effects*.

Substitution and Income Effects

Even a simple price change, all else remaining equal, gives rise to two different effects. This discovery was made by the Russian mathematician Evgeny Slutsky (see Biography 4.1), but it was developed fully by a British economist, Sir John Hicks (see Biography 4.2). Any price change, all else being equal, gives rise, first of all, to a **substitution effect**, in that the consumer substitutes, in the optimal bundle of consumption goods, more of the now relatively cheaper good for less of the now relatively more expensive good.

A price change also gives rise to an **income effect**, which results from the change in real income implied by the price change. If, for example, the price of a good has fallen, all else being equal, the consumer's real income has in fact risen. Hence the consumer will buy more of the good if it is a normal good but less if it is an inferior good. The income effect, therefore, reinforces the substitution effect (that makes people buy a larger quantity at a lower price) in the case of normal goods but counteracts the substitution effect in the case of inferior goods. If the income effect occurs in the opposite direction of the substitution effect, it can offset it partially, exactly, or more than fully; only the last of these three contingencies produces Giffen's paradox.

Consider Figure 4.3. Panel (a) illustrates the case of a normal good (butter). A consumer with tastes depicted by I_0 and I_1 and budget line *AB* has chosen to consume combination *a*. The price of butter falls, as shown by the budget line's swing to *AC*, all other factors relevant to butter demand remaining equal. The consumer chooses combination *b*. Conceptually, the horizontal movement from *a* to *b* can be divided with the help of artificial budget line *DE*, the slope of which reflects the new relative prices depicted by line *AC*. The consumer could have remained equally well off by moving from *a* to *c*, substituting more butter for less apples to this extent. (Note how both *a* and *c* are found on indifference curve I_0.) This portion of the increased butter demand is the substitution effect. It doesn't tell the whole story

BIOGRAPHY 4.1:

Evgeny E. Slutsky

Evgeny Evgenievich Slutsky (1880–1948) was born in Novoe, Russia. He studied physics and mathematics at the University of Kiev but was expelled from the university in 1901 because of participation in student revolts. After spending three years at the Institute of Technology in Munich, Germany, he was allowed to return to Kiev, where he graduated with a gold medal in 1911. Near the time of the Soviet Revolution, he received a degree in political economy from the University of Moscow. By 1920, he was a full professor at the Kiev Institute of Commerce; later he worked at the Central Statistical Board in Moscow and the University of Moscow. He was a member of the Mathematical Institute of the Academy of Sciences of the U.S.S.R.

Two of Slutsky's many articles have had the most lasting influence, but, in each case, the article remained unknown to most economists and mathematicians for many years. Slutsky's great contribution to the theory of consumer behavior, for instance, appeared under the title "Sulla teoria del bilancio del consumatore" in the Italian journal *Giornale degli Economisti*, July 1915, pp. 1–26. Publication in Italian, in wartime, and in highly mathematical form helped keep the article out of the limelight. Slutsky's achievement was to show that any change in price has two effects. The *substitution effect* refers to the change in quantity as a result of changed relative prices with real (not money) income fixed. This substitution effect is measured while the consumer maintains a given level of welfare. The *income effect* refers to the change in quantity as a result of changed real income. This income effect shifts the consumer from one welfare level to another.

The two effects are independent and additive. Slutsky defined them, however, somewhat differently than did Hicks, whose approach is illustrated in Figure 4.3. Consider panel (a). While Hicks viewed a given level of welfare as a given total of utility (represented, for example, by indifference curve I_0), Slutsky thought of a given level of welfare as an original set of goods consumed (such as that shown by point a). To find Slutsky's substitution and income effects, one would have to draw dashed line *DE* through point a. It would indicate the budget line enabling the consumer to buy the original set of goods (point a) at the new prices. This budget line would be tangent to some indifference curve lying between I_0 and I_1; and the horizontal difference between point a and this tangency point is Slutsky's measure of the substitution effect. The horizontal difference between this tangency point and point b is, in turn, his measure of the income effect.

The second major contribution of Slutsky was his business cycle theory. His basic article on the analysis of time series appeared in Russian (with an English summary) as "The Summation of Random Causes as the Source of Cyclic Processes."[1] Slutsky demonstrated that an oscillatory series could be generated from a random series by taking a moving sum or difference. This oscillatory series displayed approximate regularity, with varying length and amplitude of oscillation, very similar to many economic time series.

[1]Evgeny E. Slutsky, "The Summation of Random Causes as the Source of Cyclic Processes," *Problems of Economic Conditions* (Moscow: The Conjuncture Institute, 1927), pp. 34–64 and 156–60.

because the consumer in effect received a real income increase that can be depicted by a parallel shift of *DE* to *AC*. The consumer chose to buy a butter quantity corresponding to *b*, not *c*. This portion of the increased butter demand is the income effect. In the case of normal goods, it always reinforces the substitution effect. The demand curve for butter is certainly downward-sloping.

Panel (b) illustrates the case of an inferior good (pigs' feet) that does not exhibit Giffen's paradox. A consumer with tastes depicted by I_0

FIGURE 4.3 Substitution and Income Effects

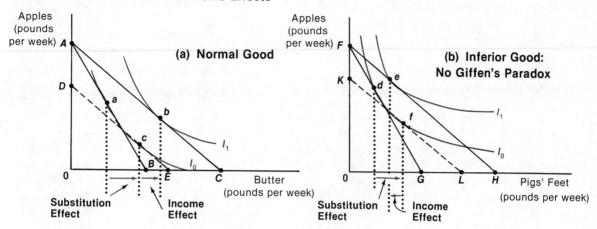

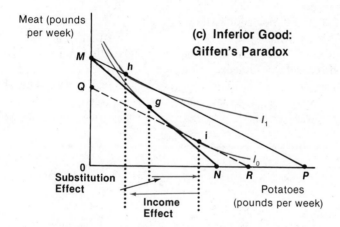

These three graphs illustrate the two effects on quantity demanded of lower price: 1. The *substitution effect* of lower price increases quantity demanded. (The horizontal arrows so labeled consistently point to the right.) 2. The *income effect* of lower price reinforces the substitution effect in the case of normal goods, as shown in panel (a). In the case of inferior goods, the income effect works to offset the substitution effect, either partially, as in panel (b), exactly (not shown), or more than fully, as in panel (c). Except in the last case, which produces Giffen's paradox and is extremely rare, the theory of consumer behavior thus points to downward-sloping demand curves for consumption goods.

and I_1 and budget line FG has chosen to consume combination d. The price of pigs' feet falls, as shown by the budget line's swing to FH, all other factors relevant to the demand for pigs' feet remaining the same. The consumer chooses combination e. Our conceptual subdivision shows a substitution effect equal to the horizontal distance between d and f, partially offset by an income effect equal to the horizontal distance between f and e. Still, the net effect is an *increased* quantity of pigs' feet demanded (measured by the horizontal distance between d and e), hence a downward-sloping demand curve for pigs' feet is involved.

Panel (c), finally, illustrates the case of an inferior good (potatoes) that does give rise to Giffen's paradox. A consumer with tastes depicted by I_0 and I_1 and budget line MN has chosen to consume combination g. The price of potatoes falls, as shown by the budget line's swing to MP, all other factors relevant to the demand for potatoes remaining the same. The consumer chooses combination h. The substitution effect, equal to the horizontal distance between g and i, is swamped by the offsetting income effect equal to the horizontal distance between i and h. The net effect is a *decreased* quantity of potatoes demanded (measured by the horizontal distance between g and h), hence an upward-sloping demand curve for potatoes is implied.

Indeed, Giffen himself noted this paradox when studying the Irish famine of 1846–49. In that case, the price of potatoes went up because of blight, rather than down as in the example above. The Irish found that buying the same amount of potatoes cost more money and left less for other goods, such as meat. The resultant combination of goods provided insufficient calories for sheer survival. Yet, by spending even less on meat and buying more potatoes, the calorie count could be raised. Thus the higher price of potatoes gave rise to a larger quantity of potatoes demanded. In Asiatic countries, a relationship similar to that between potatoes and meat has been observed between rice and fish. Apparently, inferior goods that take a small part of the family budget, as our pigs' feet in panel (b), have only a trivial income effect, and in such cases the substitution effect cannot be overpowered by the income effect. In the rare instances in which inferior goods make up a large part of the family budget, however, as when a country's main staple of food is involved, the income effect can overpower the substitution effect. A price fall (or rise) in this good makes people very much richer (or poorer); so they buy a lot less (or more) of the inferior good.

The Demand for a Good as a Function of Another Good's Price

We can learn even more about the nature of demand from another mental experiment in which we vary neither the price of the good in

BIOGRAPHY 4.2:

John R. Hicks

John Richard Hicks (1904–   ) was born in Leamington Spa, England. Educated at Oxford, where he studied mathematics, philosophy, politics, and economics, he later became a lecturer at the London School of Economics, a fellow at Cambridge, and a professor, first at Manchester and then at Oxford. While at Oxford in 1964 he was knighted, and in 1972 he was awarded the Nobel Memorial Prize in Economic Science (jointly with Kenneth Arrow—see Biography 19.2).

His major works include *The Theory of Wages* (1932, revised 1963), *Value and Capital* (1939, revised 1946), *A Contribution to the Theory of the Trade Cycle* (1950), *A Revision of Demand Theory* (1956), *Capital and Growth* (1965), and *Capital and Time* (1973).

His major achievements are the skillful refine-ment and application of three theories: the economic theory of the consumer (indifference curve analysis, the concept of the marginal rate of substitution, classification of the effect of price changes into substitution and income effects); the theory of general equilibrium among a multitude of markets; and dynamic theory (about combinations of accelerator, multiplier, and lagged linear functions producing oscillations overlaid on patterns of growth).

Much of the content of this chapter (and other chapters) owes its prominent place in modern economic theory to the work of Hicks. Readers may wish to review, in particular, how the Hicksian interpretation of substitution and income effects differs from that of Slutsky who first introduced these concepts (see Biography 4.1).

CLOSE-UP 4.2:

Substitution and Income Effects in the World of White Rats

Sometimes even economists manage to devise controlled experiments. Consider the following one. Two white rats were placed in cages that contained levers to activate dipper cups. When its lever was depressed, one dipper cup provided a measured quantity of root beer; the other one provided collins mix. Each rat was given a fixed "income" of so many pushes on the levers per day, and experimenters set the "price" per unit of root beer and collins mix as the number of pushes the rats had to "spend" to get a unit.

Initially, the rats were given an income of 300 pushes per day; both liquids were priced at 20 pushes per unit. Rat 1 settled down to a pattern of drinking about 11 units of root beer per day and about 4 of collins mix. Rat 2 chose more than 14 units of root beer and less than 1 unit of collins mix per day.

Experimenters then doubled the "price" of root beer to 40 pushes and halved the price of collins mix to 10. At the same time, Slutsky-like, they adjusted the income of each rat so it could afford to continue its old consumption pattern if it so chose. This eliminated any possible income effect of the price change. Would the pure substitution effect work as the theory of human consumer behavior predicts? Would the rats consume more of the cheaper collins mix and less of the dearer root beer, even though they could afford to drink as much of both goods as previously?

The answer was yes. Rat 1 changed its consumption to about 8 units of root beer and 17 of collins mix per day. Rat 2 ended up consuming about 9 units of root beer and 25 of collins mix per day. Even rats have downward-sloping demand curves.

Source: John H. Kagel, Raymond C. Battalio, Howard Rachlin, Leonard Green, Robert L. Basemann, W. R. Klemm, "Experimental Studies of Consumer Demand Behavior," *Economic Inquiry*, March 1975, pp. 22–38. See also Tom Alexander, "Economics According to the Rats," *Fortune*, December 1, 1980, pp. 127–32, for a discussion of other experiments.

---

question nor income or tastes, but in which we vary the price of another good. Consider Figure 4.4, which illustrates the concepts of independent, complementary, and substitute goods.

First, imagine a consumer of salt and tea whose tastes are depicted by indifference curves I_0 and I_1 in panel (a). With an initial budget line of AB, the optimum is found at a. Consumption of tea equals OD when the price of salt is $1 per pound (point c). How will the quantity of tea vary, not with the price of tea, but with the price of salt? Let the price of salt fall from $1 per pound to 50¢ per pound, all other relevant factors (tastes, budget, and other prices) remaining unchanged. The budget line swings around B to BC, and a new optimum is found at b. The quantity of tea demanded remains unchanged and is plotted, at the new price, at d in the lower graph. When the quantity demanded of one good *does not respond to a changed price of another good*, all else being equal, the goods are said to be **independent goods**. Surely, many pairs of goods—ranging from salt and tea to men's shoes and women's shoes to baby rattles and oil filters—are of this nature.

Now consider panel (b). We imagine a consumer of lemons and tea whose tastes are depicted by I_2 and I_3. With an initial budget line of EF, the optimum is found at e. Consumption of tea equals OH when the price of lemons is $2 per pound (point g). We let this price fall to $1, all else remaining equal. The budget line swings around F to FG, and a new optimum is found at f. The quantity of tea rises to OK and is plotted, at the new price, at h in the lower graph. When the quantity demanded of one good *varies inversely with the price of another good*, all else being equal, the goods are said to be **complementary goods**. These are goods that "go together," that cooperate with each other in the process of

FIGURE 4.4 Independent, Complementary, and Substitute Goods

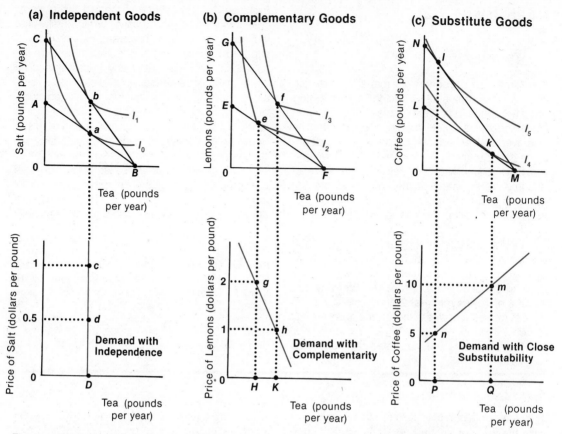

The quantity demanded of a consumption good, such as tea, might be *independent* of the price of another good, such as salt, pictured in panel (a). The quantity might vary *inversely* with the price of another good such as lemons, pictured in panel (b). Finally, the quantity might vary *in the same direction* as the price of another good such as coffee, pictured in panel (c).

---

consumption. When the price of one falls and people buy more of it, they buy more of the other good as well. Besides lemons and tea, other examples are autos and gasoline, fishing licenses and fishing poles, hamburgers and ketchup, hot dogs and buns, knives and forks, shoes and laces, strawberries and shortcake, trousers and belts, turkeys and cranberry sauce.

Finally, consider panel (c). We imagine a consumer of coffee and tea whose tastes are depicted by I_4 and I_5. With an initial budget line of LM, the optimum is found at k. Consumption of tea equals $0Q$ when the price of coffee is $10 per pound (point m). We let this price fall to $5,

all else remaining equal. The budget line swings around M to MN, and a new optimum is found at *1*. The quantity of tea falls to $0P$ and is plotted, at the new price, at n in the lower graph. When the quantity demanded of one good *varies in the same direction as the price of another good*, all else being equal, the goods are said to be **substitute goods**. These are "either-or" goods that are rivals in consumption. When the price of one falls and people buy more of it, they buy less of the other good because it fulfills the same basic want. Besides coffee and tea, examples are beef and pork, butter and margarine, ice cream and ice milk, motorcycles and bicycles, new houses and old ones, oil and coal, truck and rail freight, tuna and salmon.

Note: The above distinctions among independent, complementary, and substitute goods, although commonly used, are not the only possible ones. Our analysis did not separate out the substitution and income effects. One could argue, for instance, that a fall in the price of salt or lemons or coffee, all else being equal, constitutes a rise in real income, and this by itself would lead, in each case, to increased purchases of tea (assuming it is a normal good). One could deduct this income effect on tea purchases from the total effect observed in Figure 4.4 and classify goods as independents, complements, or substitutes only after adjusting for this income effect, on the basis of the pure relative price effect alone.

From Individual Demand to Market Demand

We have seen how the quantity demanded of a good can be related to any one of a number of factors that influence it. Economists are, however, particularly interested in the relationship between the quantity demanded of a good and its own price, as illustrated in panel (b) of Figure 4.1. Moreover, they tend to focus attention not so much on the demand of one individual, but on **market demand**, the sum of the demands of all potential market participants. This sum can be derived quite easily in most instances.

As long as all individuals who demand a given good face identical market prices (and this we assume in the perfect markets we study in Part Two), individual demands will differ due to differences in budgets and tastes, but they can be added together at each price. Table 4.1 shows the derivation of a market demand schedule. Although we believe that thousands, perhaps millions, of buyers would appear in any perfect market, we need not concern ourselves with such large numbers. For a moment, and only to simplify the arithmetic, we can imagine only three buyers to exist in the market for apples. Their respective demand schedules might be those shown in columns (2) through (4) of Table 4.1. Their combined market demand is shown in column (5). Naturally, all this information can be graphed, as in Figure 4.5.

Note that the market demand line will shift to the right (or left) as the number of consumers increases (or decreases). It will also shift with any of the factors that shift an individual consumer's demand, such as changes in income, the prices of complementary or substitute goods, and tastes. Because of the large numbers of buyers in

TABLE 4.1 Deriving the Market Demand Schedule

Price (dollars per bushel)	Quantity of Apples Demanded (bushels per year)			
	Household A	Household B	Household C	All Three Households
(1)	(2)	(3)	(4)	(5) = (2) + (3) + (4)
21	0	5	0	5
18	1	6	0	7
15	2	7	1	10
12	3	8	2	13
9	4	9	3	16
6	5	10	4	19
3	6	11	5	22
0	7	12	6	25

A market demand schedule can be derived by adding, at each conceivable price, the quantities demanded by all potential market participants, all else, of course, being held equal.

FIGURE 4.5 Deriving Market Demand

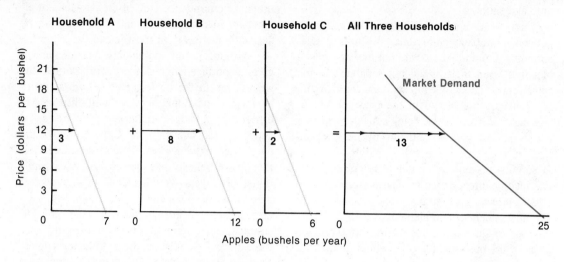

This set of graphs is based on Table 4.1. It shows how, all else being equal, market demand can be derived by adding horizontally, at each conceivable price, the quantities demanded by all potential market participants.

a perfect market, shifts in a single individual's demand will affect market demand only imperceptibly, but widespread changes in individual demands will shift market demand noticeably. (Imagine what would happen to Figure 4.5 if everyone's income rose, if the price of oranges fell, or if it was reported that apples cure cancer.)

While the story told so far is likely to be correct in most instances, we should note a number of exceptions. These exceptions occur when the tastes of people are interdependent in such a way that the quantity demanded by one individual rises or falls with the quantities others are seen to demand (bandwagon or snob effects) or when people try to impress each other by the conspicuous consumption of expensive goods, such as diamonds, mink coats, and Rolls Royces (Veblen effect).

The Bandwagon Effect

Sometimes people like to conform, behave like others, join the crowd, keep up with the Joneses. They want to be fashionable and stylish. When the demand for a good by each individual varies directly with the quantity others are seen to demand, a **bandwagon effect** is said to occur. It is by no means difficult to find examples. Consider how women are swept by the "need" for long skirts, then pant suits, then mini-skirts or how men must have first white shirts, then colored shirts, then turtlenecks. Consider how some cannot live without their pet rocks or automobile air conditioners or tape players; how youngsters first crave, and later disdain, hoola hoops, skate boards, crew cuts, and long hair.

In situations such as these, our simple horizontal addition of individual demand curves will not do, for the position of each consumer's demand will vary with market demand. Consider Figure 4.6, which depicts the bandwagon effect. Let D_A represent a market demand line derived by the horizontal summation of the demands of all individuals each one of whom believes that the actual quantity of long skirts purchased in the market will be $0A$. Let D_B, D_C, and D_D, similarly, represent hypothetical market demand lines built on the expectation by all individuals of market sales equal to *0B, 0C,* and *0D,* respectively. Then only one point on each of these curves (points *a* through *d,* respectively) represents a situation in which these quantity expectations are realized. The color line connecting these points is the true market demand line.

If the price is $60 per skirt, point *a* on this true market demand line tells us, people buy quantity *0A.* This is the only price at which the expectations embodied in line *D_A* are realized. Let price fall to $24 per skirt. Line *D_A* tells us that substitution and income effects will lead to an increase in quantity demanded from *a* toward *e.* Yet the quantity demanded corresponding to point *e* exceeds *0A.* People would find market sales greater than expected; they would "get on the bandwagon"; line *D_A* would begin to shift right. As long as price remained at $24, this shift of demand would cease only at *D_D.* People would then base their own purchases on expected market sales of *0D* and, as point *d* indicates, this is exactly what market sales would be. Thus a downward-sloping market demand line can still be derived in the presence of the bandwagon effect, but the slope of this line is flatter than it would otherwise be.

The Snob Effect

People do not always conform to behavioral norms. At times, they search for exclusiveness. They seek dignity, prestige, and status through being different. Instead of "being one of the gang," they like to set themselves off from the mass. When the demand for a good by each individual varies inversely with the quantity others are seen to demand, a **snob effect** is said to occur. Consider how people often buy things just because others are *not*—distinctive cars, clothes, food, and houses, for instance.

In such cases, the market demand curve must be derived in a fashion analogous to that shown in the previous section. Consider Figure 4.7, which graphically depicts the snob effect. Let *D_A* represent a market demand line derived by the horizontal summation of the demands of all individuals each of whom believes that the actual quantity of frogs' legs purchased in the market will be *0A.* Let *D_B, D_C,* and *D_D,* similarly, represent hypothetical market demand lines built on the expectation by all individuals of market sales equal to *0B, 0C,* and *0D,* respectively. Unlike before, at any given price, people now

FIGURE 4.6 Market Demand with Bandwagon Effect

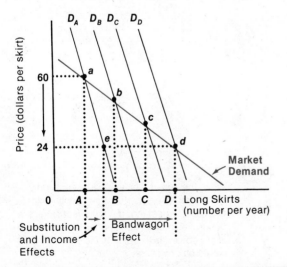

When the demand for a good by each individual varies directly with the quantity others are seen to demand, a *bandwagon effect* is said to occur. The market demand curve in this case is still downward-sloping but is flatter than it would otherwise be.

demand less rather than more when market sales are high. As before, only points *a* through *d* represent situations in which these quantity expectations are realized. The color line connecting them is the true market demand line.

If the price is $20 per pound, point *a* on this true market line tells us, people buy quantity *0A*. This is the only price at which the expectations embodied in line D_A are realized. Let price fall to $9 per pound. Line D_A tells us that substitution and income effects will lead to an increase in quantity demanded from *a* toward *e*. Yet the quantity demanded corresponding to point *e* exceeds *0A*. People would find market sales greater than expected; they would snobbishly withdraw from the market; line D_A would begin to shift left. As long as price remained at $9, this shift of demand would cease only at D_C. People would then base their own purchases on expected market sales of *0C* and, as point *c* indicates, this is exactly what market sales would be. Thus a downward-sloping demand line can still be derived in the presence of the snob effect, but the slope of this line is steeper than it would otherwise be.

Note: The snob effect could never overpower the combined substitution and income effects because this would require quantity demanded at the lower price to be less than at the higher price (point *c* would have to be below and to the left of *a*), and such low market sales would encourage all the snobs to buy more!

The Veblen Effect

Some people allow their decision to buy a consumption good to be influenced not so much by their desire to buy (or not to buy) what others are buying, but by a wish to impress others with the high price they can afford to pay. When the demand for a good by each individual varies directly with the prevailing market price, a **Veblen effect** is said to occur. It is named after the American economist Thorstein Veblen (1857–1929), who wrote about this type of "conspicuous consumption" by people who tried to advertise their wealth. We are not likely to meet many people who drive around in diamond-studded Rolls Royces, but let us consider the argument. To the extent that this effect occurs, the market

FIGURE 4.7   Market Demand with Snob Effect

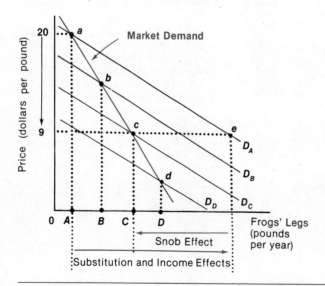

When the demand for a good by each individual varies inversely with the quantity others are seen to demand, a *snob effect* is said to occur. The market demand curve in this case is still downward-sloping but is steeper than it would otherwise be.

demand curve could have an upward-sloping section in it. Consider Figure 4.8, which depicts the Veblen effect. Let D_A represent a market demand line derived by the horizontal summation of the demands of all individuals each of whom believes that the actual market price of mink coats will be $0A$. Let D_B, D_C, and D_D, similarly, represent hypothetical market demand lines built on the expectation by all individuals of market prices equal to $0B$, $0C$, and $0D$, respectively. Note how people's demand shifts right with higher expected prices (because of the enhanced possibility of impressing others). Only points a through d represent situations in which these price expectations are realized. The color line connecting them is the true market demand line.

If the price is $0C$, point c on this true market line tells us, people buy 340 mink coats per year. This is the only quantity at which the expectations embodied in line D_C are realized. Let price fall to $0A$. Line D_C tells us that substitution and income effects will lead to an increase in quantity demanded from c toward e. Yet the price corresponding to point e falls short of $0C$. People would find market price smaller than expected; they would want to buy less now that mink coats are not expensive enough to impress people; line D_C would begin to shift left. As long as price remained at $0A$, this shift of demand would cease only at D_A. People would then base their purchases on an expected market price of $0A$ and, as point a indicates, this is exactly what market price would be. Thus the Veblen effect can overpower the normal substitution and income effects and produce an upward-sloping market demand line.

Note, however, that market demand is still likely to be downward-sloping at very high and very low prices, producing the line's backward S shape. At some high price people run into their budget limits and will be unable to buy any mink coats. Thus market demand cannot possibly run upwards and to the right forever. At some low price, on the other hand, almost everyone can afford mink coats. Their value for purposes of conspicuous consumption then disappears and so does our entire argument.

FIGURE 4.8
Market Demand with Veblen Effect

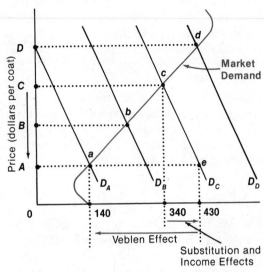

When the demand for a good by each individual varies directly with the prevailing market price, a *Veblen effect* is said to occur. At least a section of the market demand curve in this case can be upward-sloping.

Empirical Studies of Market Demand

Economists have tested their notions about market demand by engaging in a wide variety of empirical studies. Five types of approaches have been used: consumer interviews, consumer clinics, market experiments, time-series studies, and cross-section studies.

Consumer Interviews

Some investigators have simply collared consumers on the street and in shopping centers and asked them how much they would buy of a good at various conceivable prices of this good. In this way, they have amassed data such as those in columns (2) to (4) of Table 4.1. Such data, however, are nonsensical, unless the consumers interviewed represent a carefully selected sample of the population. Even when this was the case, economists have often been less than happy with the results. Consumers so interviewed tend to make snap judgments that may not reflect their actual behavior in a real rather than a hypothetical market situation. Consumers may also be unwilling to tell the truth, especially if true answers would reveal socially deprecating character traits. To avoid embarrassment, they might give acceptable but untrue answers. Rather than *ask* consumers, other investigators have preferred to *observe* them. This can be done in a variety of direct and indirect ways.

Consumer Clinics

One direct way of observing consumers is to study consumer behavior in consumer clinics or laboratories. Consumers are placed in a simulated market situation, such as an artificial store with goods packaged, displayed, and priced by the experimenter. Consumers are given a fixed amount of money and asked to spend it in this "store." Experimenters vary budgets and prices and note the subsequent behavior of consumers. Once again, however, general confidence in the results is lacking. For one thing, the consumers so tested may be too small a sample of the whole population to allow valid conclusions about all consumers. In addition, consumers so tested know the artificiality of the situation. Would they spend their own hard-earned money in reality in the same way as they spend this manna from heaven? Considering what we know about business people living on expense accounts and about politicians spending the taxpayers' money, one can have doubts. Finally, this type of study is very expensive to undertake.

Market Experiments

A second direct way of observing consumers is to conduct experiments in real markets. A firm may increase the price of a consumption good by 5 percent in one store or city, by 10 percent in another, and reduce it by 5 percent in a third.

(The Parker Pen Company once tested the demand for its ink, called Quink, by raising prices in 4 cities from 15 cents to 25 cents.) Mail-order merchants sometimes print two different prices in a given issue of a national magazine, every even-numbered copy containing, perhaps, a low price; every odd-numbered one a high price. Half the copies distributed in every town will then make one offer, half another. The different mail orders are then tabulated, and the totals are considered to represent two dots on the demand line.

Once more, this approach can yield ambivalent results. It tends to be costly to the experimenter because customers faced with higher temporary prices may be lost permanently. Alternatively, the effects observed in the short run (such as a negligible loss of customers during the test period) may be quite inapplicable to the long run (if the price change were to be made permanent). In addition, the experimenter has no control over all the other factors that also affect demand. Coincidentally with the experiment, people's tastes and incomes may change, as may other prices, and even the weather and local strikes may affect demand.

Time-Series Studies

One indirect way of observing consumers is to study the statistical record of their past behavior. **Time-series studies** investigate economic data pertaining to a given population during different past periods of time. Suppose that a study of the U.S. potato market for the years 1978–81 revealed average annual prices of $3, $1, $5, and $2 per pound, respectively, for each of the four years, while corresponding potato purchases in these four years were found to have been 8 million, 11 million, 2 million, and 7 million pounds. One could plot these data as in panel (a) of Figure 4.9. One might be tempted to draw a line that would be as close as possible to the four data plots and call it the market demand for the 1978–81 period. This approach, however, is not necessarily legitimate. Each set of historical price-quantity data reveals only one of the many data combinations that might have occurred during the period in question (and that constitute that period's market demand). It is quite possible that the potato market demand in 1978 looked like line D_1 in panel (b). While it shows the various quantities people would then have demanded at all conceivable prices, only one of these quantities (8 million tons) was realized because only one of these prices ($3 per pound) actually materialized as a result of the position (not shown) of that year's supply. Thus we know with certainty only a single dot on the 1978 market demand line, the one labeled 1978. Market demands for subsequent years might, similarly, have looked like lines D_2, D_3, and D_4 in panel (b), indicating continual changes in demand during this four-year period. This might have happened in response to changes in the number of consumers, in their incomes and tastes, in the prices of other goods, and so on.

One can, however, overcome this **identification problem**, the difficulty of identifying a large number of potential data (such as those on a market demand line) from a few historical data, each of which may belong to a different set of potential data. By also gathering historical data on all the other likely influences on demand and then employing the *least-squares multiple regression technique*, a careful statistician can actually make a fairly good estimate of market demand. This technique yields estimates of some variable, such as market demand, in such a way that the sum of the squared differences between each estimate and the associated magnitude actually observed is minimized. Each estimate conforms to an equation such as

$$D_x = a + bP_x + cY + dP_y + \text{other terms,}$$

where a, b, c, and d are positive or negative constants,
D_x is the quantity of x demanded,
P_x is its price,
Y is income,
and P_y is the price of some other good, y.

Once this relationship is estimated, one can hold all terms other than P_x constant and examine the partial relationship between P_x and D_x (which is market demand). We should note that this technique is not foolproof. The statistician will grind out nonsense if an important explanatory variable is forgotten or if several such variables are included that are highly correlated.

FIGURE 4.9 The Identification Problem

(a) False Market Demand

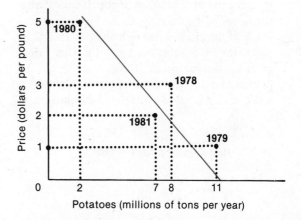

(b) True Market Demands

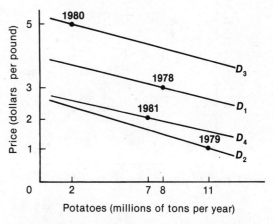

A time-series study might reveal price and quantity data about the U.S. potato market as plotted in panel (a). It is not necessarily legitimate, however, to identify as the likely market demand for the given period some line like the one drawn in panel (a). True market demands may have looked very different, as shown in panel (b). Each set of actual price-quantity data reveals only one of the many data combinations that might have occurred during the period in question.

Figure 4.10 summarizes an actual time-series study of the potato market in the United States.

Cross-Section Studies

Instead of looking at the past behavior of a *given* population during *different* periods of time, one can use **cross-section studies** to analyze economic data pertaining to *different* populations during the *same* past period of time. Suppose that a study of the electric power market in four U.S. cities in 1981 revealed four different price-quantity combinations. These, too, might be plotted like the data in panel (a) of Figure 4.9, and a market demand line might be estimated on

the assumption that the people in any one city, if faced with the prices actually prevailing in the other cities, would consume the quantities actually consumed in the other cities. Again, however, possible differences among cities in income and the like could vitiate the result, but once more, careful multiple regression analysis can help overcome this problem.

Figure 4.11 summarizes actual cross-section studies of urban residential water markets in six regions of the United States. The studies were based on a survey of the 1960 water markets of 218 cities.

Market Demand Examined: Elasticity

The study of market demand relationships allows economists to answer a multitude of important questions. All kinds of people in business—ranging from producers of cars, electric power, fountain pens, records, and wheat to providers of educational services, rail transport, spectator sports, and telephone services—want to know what would happen to their sales if their prices changed or people's incomes changed or the prices of other goods changed. All kinds of government officials, concerned with their tax revenues or the (''excessive'' or ''insufficient'') quantities of various goods people buy, want to know what would happen if they took actions that affected prices or incomes. Thus local officials worry about the use of taxis and bridges and about property taxes; state officials worry about gambling and liquor; federal officials are concerned about air fares, the consumption of cigarettes and gasoline, the design of a national health insurance, and the plight of public transit. Sometimes these decision makers receive bad advice: They are told that nothing can be done to discourage ''excessive'' numbers of directory assistance calls or ''excessive'' consumption of gasoline because people *need* the phone numbers and because they *must* drive their cars to work and shop. Such advice, almost always, is incorrect. As the previous sections have shown, the

FIGURE 4.10
The Market Demand for Potatoes:
A Time-Series Study

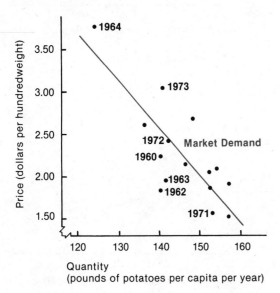

The market demand line shown in this graph was calculated by the *least-squares multiple regression technique* as $Q = 1.636 - 0.177P + 0.093Y$, where Q measures per capita consumption of potatoes, P their price, and Y is per capita income at 1958 prices.
Source: Daniel B. Suits, ''Agriculture'' in Walter Adams, ed., *The Structure of American Industry,* 5th edition (New York: Macmillan, 1977), pp. 3-4.

**FIGURE 4.11 The Market Demand for Water:
A Cross-Section Study**

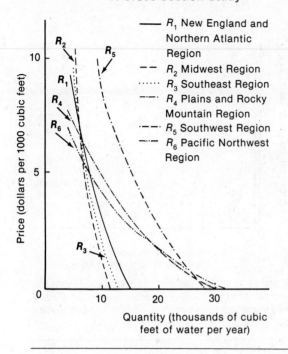

The market demand lines shown in this graph were calculated by the least-squares multiple regression technique. Each demand equation relates the quantity of water demanded per urban household to the average price of water, median household income, precipitation during the growing season (a factor that influences water demand for horticultural purposes), and the average number of residents per water meter.
Source: Henry S. Foster and Bruce R. Beattie, "Urban Residential Demand for Water in the United States," *Land Economics,* February 1979, p. 53. Copyright © 1979 by The Board of Regents of the University of Wisconsin System.

quantities of goods demanded by people are responsive to the prices of these goods, to income, and to the prices of other goods. Changes in these variables will change the quantities demanded. This section will discuss various **elasticities of demand**, exact measures of the responsiveness of quantity demanded to other variables. Because several types of variables can affect quantity demanded, several types of elasticity can be calculated, including own-price elasticity, income elasticity, and cross-price elasticity.

The Own-Price Elasticity of Demand

Consider Figure 4.12, which shows the market demand for apples. Imagine an original price-quantity combination at E, corresponding to an original apple price, P_a, of $0A$ and an original apple quantity, Q_a, of $0B$. Let there be a price change, ΔP_a, of EG, all other factors influencing

quantity remaining equal. Quantity demanded will then change by ΔQ_a, or GF.

Now it is tempting, indeed, to designate the reciprocal of the *slope* between E and F, or $\Delta Q_a/\Delta P_a$ as a measure of the responsiveness of the good's quantity demanded to its own price. Let P_a measure 30 cents per pound and ΔP_a equal -10 cents per pound. Let Q_a measure 15 million tons per year and ΔQ_a equal $+10$ million tons per year. Then $\Delta Q_a/\Delta P_a$ equals $+10$ million tons/-10 cents per pound. Such a measure, however, suffers from a major problem.

The ratio of quantity change to price change is not a pure number and, therefore, cannot be compared with similar measures of responsiveness for, say, gasoline (measured in gallons) or cloth (measured in yards). Which is bigger: $+10$ million tons of apples/-10 cents per pound or $+100,000$ gallons of gasoline/$-\$0.02$ per gallon? Yet one may wish to know whether consumers are more or less responsive to a change in the price of apples than they are to a change in the price of gasoline. Fortunately, the problem can be overcome by turning the absolute changes in quantity and price into relative (or percentage) changes. These relative changes can be determined by dividing the change in quantity by the original quantity and by dividing the change in price by the original price. Economists, in turn, relate these relative changes to one another and measure the responsiveness of quantity demanded to a good's *own* price as follows:

Own-price elasticity of demand, $\epsilon_D^{q \cdot p}$ = $\dfrac{\dfrac{\Delta Q_a}{Q_a}}{\dfrac{\Delta P_a}{P_a}}$

Using the above numbers, this formula yields

$$\frac{\dfrac{+10 \text{ million tons}}{15 \text{ million tons}}}{\dfrac{-10\cancel{c} \text{ per pound}}{30\cancel{c} \text{ per pound}}} = \frac{+0.666}{-0.333} = -2$$

Both numerator and denominator could be multiplied by 100 to yield percentage changes: a 66.6 percent increase in quantity demanded resulted from a 33.3 percent decrease in the good's own price, all other relevant factors remaining equal. Thus the **own-price elasticity of demand** equals the percentage change in quantity demanded of a good divided by the percentage change in the good's own price, all else being equal.[1]

A minor problem is that as long as the law of downward-sloping demand prevails (and that is mostly the case, excepting instances of Giffen's paradox and Veblen effects), any measure of own-price elasticity will be a negative number. When people's responsiveness to a price change

[1]After a change in quantity and price, there is, of course an original quantity, Q_0 (equal to OB in Figure 4.12), and a new quantity, Q_1 (equal to OD). There is, similarly, an original price, P_0 (equal to OA), and a new price, P_1 (equal to OC). Some economists prefer to divide ΔQ by an average of Q_0 and Q_1 rather than by Q_0 and to divide ΔP by an average of P_0 and P_1 rather than by P_0. The following section on arc elasticity vs. point elasticity will return to this matter.

FIGURE 4.12

The Market Demand for Apples

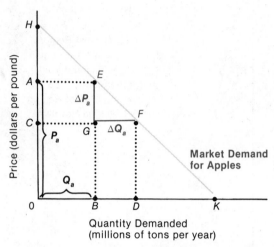

A good's own-price elasticity of demand is measured as the percentage change in quantity demanded divided by the percentage change in the good's price, all else being equal.

is high, as in the above example, the calculated elasticity number may be -2. When people's responsiveness to a price change is low, the calculated number may be -0.02, which is a *larger* number than -2. Many economists prefer to avoid the likely confusion resulting from smaller numbers (such as -2) designating high responsiveness and larger numbers (such as -0.02) designating low responsiveness. So they ignore the minus sign and simply look at the *absolute values* involved. The absolute value of -2 is $|2|$, which designates high elasticity; the absolute value of -0.02 is $|0.02|$, which designates low elasticity. (The vertical lines warn us that minus signs are being ignored.)

Arc Elasticity vs. Point Elasticity. The elasticity number calculated above was derived using rather large changes in price and quantity. It measures, strictly speaking, the responsiveness of demand in the *EF range* on Figure 4.12 rather than at point E only. An elasticity measure that refers in this way to a finite section of a demand (or supply) line is called **arc elasticity**. More often than not, however, economists are interested in the effects of very small changes in price and quantity. Take another look at Figure 4.12 and imagine that ΔP_a shrank and shrank until G was just barely below E. Naturally, ΔQ_a would shrink too; and point F would move very close to E. If we made ΔP_a and, therefore, ΔQ_a infinitesimal, our formula would measure elasticity in the immediate vicinity of point E itself (and the kind of problem noted in footnote 1 would disappear). An elasticity measure that refers in this way to a point on a demand (or supply) line is called **point elasticity**. It so happens that the size of point elasticity can be determined almost instantly at any point on any demand (or supply) line, whether it is straight or curved or sloping to the right or to the left, by using three simple steps:

1. Place a tangent—a straight line that *just touches* (but does not intersect) the demand (or supply) line—on the point at which elasticity is to be measured.

2. Along this tangent, measure the distance (in any convenient units of length) from this point to the horizontal axis (or abscissa) and also the distance from this point to the vertical axis (or ordinate).

3. The elasticity at the point in question equals the distance from the point to the abscissa ($P{\rightarrow}A$), divided by the distance from the point to the ordinate ($P{\rightarrow}O$). *PAPO* is a key word to remember!

We will prove the *PAPO* rule by measuring elasticity at point E in Figure 4.12. Because the demand line in question is a straight line, step 1 above has already been performed. A tangent placed at point E coincides with demand line HK. The distance along the tangent from our point to the abscissa equals EK; the distance along the tangent from our point to the ordinate is EH (step 2). Hence elasticity at E equals EK/EH (step 3).

Rewriting the elasticity definition, we get

$$\epsilon_D^{o\text{-}p} = \frac{\Delta Q_a}{Q_a} \cdot \frac{P_a}{\Delta P_a} = \frac{\Delta Q_a}{\Delta P_a} \cdot \frac{P_a}{Q_a}.$$

Inserting the appropriate values from Figure 4.12, this

$\epsilon_D^{o\text{-}p}$ becomes $\dfrac{GF}{EG} \cdot \dfrac{EB}{BO}$.

Because EGF and EBK are similar triangles, $\dfrac{GF}{EG} = \dfrac{BK}{EB}$ and

$$\epsilon_D^{o\text{-}p} = \frac{BK}{EB} \cdot \frac{EB}{BO} = \frac{BK}{BO} = \frac{EK}{EH}.$$

Elasticity Is Not Slope. It is important to keep the concepts of elasticity and slope separate. Consider again Figure 4.12. At every point on demand line HK, the slope is the same and equals the ratio EG/GF. Yet the *PAPO* rule tells us that elasticity at H equals HK divided by zero, or (what economists call) infinity. Elasticity at F equals FK/FH; and at K, it equals zero divided by KH, or zero. Elasticity changes from point to point! Figure 4.13 illustrates how elasticity can vary.

The variability of elasticity explains why it is usually nonsensical to talk about "*the elasticity of a demand line.*" Every point on most market demand lines has a different elasticity. Exceptions are extremely rare. Among these would be:

1. a vertical demand line (elasticity of zero at every point),

2. a horizontal one (elasticity of infinity at every point),

3. one shaped like a rectangular hyperbola, or

4. a straight, upward-sloping line (exhibiting Giffen's paradox or the Veblen effect) that also passes through the origin.

The latter two exceptions have an elasticity of unity at every point. Can you confirm the four statements about elasticity just made with the help of the *PAPO* rule?

Elasticity, Expenditure, Revenue. What we have just learned about elasticity has important implications: Whenever the own-price elasticity of demand exceeds unity, a decrease in price increases the total expenditures of consumers and

FIGURE 4.13 How Elasticity Can Vary

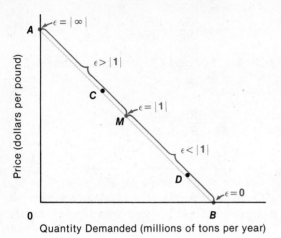

Quantity Demanded (millions of tons per year)

Along a straight, downward-sloping demand line, the own-price elasticity of demand takes on a different value at every point. With the help of the *PAPO* rule, derived from the definition of this type of elasticity, the absolute values of the elasticity can be shown always to produce the same pattern: Elasticity equals infinity (and demand is said to be "perfectly elastic") where demand intercepts the ordinate (point *A*). Elasticity equals zero (and demand is said to be "perfectly inelastic") where demand intercepts the abscissa (point *B*). Elasticity equals unity at midpoint *M*. (By definition, at the midpoint, *MB = MA*, hence *MB/MA* equals one.) Between *M* and *A*, the absolute value of elasticity always exceeds unity. (This must be so because the *PAPO* rule makes us divide one distance, such as *CB*, by a smaller distance, such as *CA*.) Demand in this region is said to be "relatively elastic," and elasticity rises increasingly above unity as one moves from *M* toward *A*. Between *M* and *B*, the absolute value of elasticity always falls short of unity. (This must be so because the *PAPO* rule makes us divide one distance, such as *DB*, by a larger distance, such as *DA*.) Demand in this region is said to be "relatively inelastic," and elasticity falls increasingly below unity as one moves from *M* toward *B*. All of the above holds true regardless of the slope of the demand line.

(what is the same thing) the total revenues of firms. Whenever this elasticity falls short of unity, a decrease in price decreases the total expenditures of consumers and the total revenues of firms. An increase in price has the opposite effects in each case.

Consider Figure 4.14. Panels (a) and (b)

feature the identical market demand line. Panel (a) pictures the effect of a price cut in the region of relatively elastic demand. A 28 percent cut in price, from *0A* to *0B*, produces a 128 percent rise in quantity demanded, from *0C* to *0D*. As a result, the total expenditures of consumers (which equal price multiplied by quantity) rise from *0AEC* to *0BFD*. As firms see it, the revenue loss shown by the dotted rectangle is more than offset by the gain of the cross hatched region.

Panel (b), in contrast, pictures the effect of a price cut in the region of relatively inelastic demand. Even a 62 percent cut in price, from *0a* to *0b*, produces only a 35 percent rise in quantity demanded, from *0c* to *0d*. As a result, the total expenditures of consumers fall from *0aec* to *0bfd*. As firms see it, the revenue loss shown by the dotted rectangle is not made up by the gain of the cross hatched one. In each situation, obviously, a price rise would have the opposite effect, which is why businesses and governments are so interested in estimates of elasticity.

The Income Elasticity of Demand

Decision makers are equally interested in measuring how changes in income affect quantities demanded of a good. Economists make such measurements as well. They define the **income elasticity of demand** as the percentage change in quantity demanded of a good divided by the percentage change in the income of consumers, all else being equal. Labeling income as *Y*, we say

$$\textit{Income of elasticity of demand, } \epsilon_D^Y = \frac{\dfrac{\Delta Q_a}{Q_a}}{\dfrac{\Delta Y}{Y}}$$

Estimates of income elasticity are positive for normal goods (less than unity for "necessities" and greater than unity for "luxuries"); they are negative for inferior goods. The *PAPO* rule can be used to read off elasticity at any point on an Engel curve.

FIGURE 4.14 Elasticity, Expenditure, and Revenue

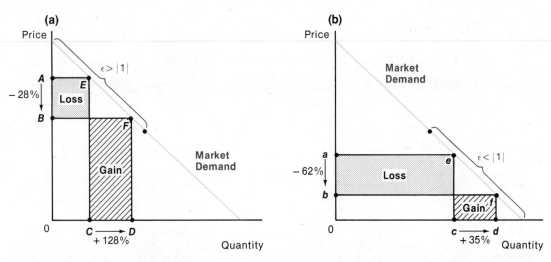

When market demand is relatively (own-price) elastic, as shown in panel (a), a price cut of any size produces increased consumer expenditures and a net gain in the revenues of firms. When market demand is relatively (own-price) inelastic, as shown in panel (b), a price cut of any size produces decreased consumer expenditures and a net loss in the revenues of firms. Increases in price have the opposite effects.

The Cross-Price Elasticity of Demand

A third important elasticity concept, finally, relates the quantities demanded of one good to changes in the price of another good. Economists define the **cross-price elasticity of demand** as the percentage change in quantity demanded of one good, a, divided by the percentage change in the price of another good, b, all else being equal.

$$\textit{Cross-price elasticity of demand, } \epsilon_D^{c\text{-}p} = \frac{\dfrac{\Delta Q_a}{Q_a}}{\dfrac{\Delta P_b}{P_b}}$$

Estimates of such cross-price elasticity are zero for independent goods, positive for substitutes, and negative for complements.

Empirical Measures of Elasticities

Economics literature contains an abundance of empirical elasticity estimates. Tables 4.2 to 4.5 provide a small sample of elasticity estimates

from the study of U.S. markets. As a look at the sources indicates, these studies were made at different times and places, and the estimates reflect, of course, the price-quantity relationships observed then and there. At other times or places, different results could well have been obtained. It is important, therefore, not to look upon these elasticity data as if they indicated some inherent and permanent characteristic of the goods involved.

Consider Table 4.2, which shows own-price elasticities. As is usual, one finds high elasticities for goods that have good substitutes, and low elasticities for those that do not. There are many substitutes for cottonseed oil; there are few for gasoline. Two other matters should be noted.

First, the narrowness with which a good is defined influences the number of substitutes it has and, therefore, the elasticity estimate. There may be few substitutes for gasoline in general, but there are many for Esso gasoline and even more for Esso gasoline sold at a particular station.

Second, the length of time under considera-

ANALYTICAL EXAMPLE 4.1:
Designing a National Dental Health Insurance

Designers of National Health Insurance proposals have been greatly concerned with a number of questions. What would happen to the quantity of various services demanded if prices to patients were cut to zero or were cut 75 percent? What would be the cost to government? Knowledge of elasticities is crucial to answering these questions. A 1970 national cross-sectional survey of the demand for dental care in 1970 revealed the ranges of elasticities (actual values) shown in the table below, which were calculated separately for (white) children, adult females, and adult males:

Service	Own-Price Elasticities	Income Elasticities
Examinations	−0.59 to −0.03	+0.73 to +0.51
Cleanings	−1.34 to −0.14	+0.80 to +0.74
Fillings	−0.95 to −0.58	+0.88 to +0.28
Crowns	−1.70 to +0.89	−0.08 to +0.93
Extractions	−1.51 to +0.21	−0.13 to +0.47
Dentures	−0.59 to +2.20	−0.08 to +0.26
Orthodontia	−0.08	+1.24

Extractions and dentures were found to be inferior goods for adults (poor person's dentistry); preventive care, fillings, and such exotic care as orthodontia being preferred at higher incomes. Most importantly, the researchers found that, due to relatively high price elasticities, visits to dentists would more than double for adults and more than triple for children if prices to patients were cut to zero. Quantity demanded would still increase considerably with patients paying 25 percent and the government paying 75 percent. It would be impossible to meet such demand with the current number of dentists in the population. To avoid long waiting periods before patients could see doctors, patients would have to pay rather high percentages of the payments until the supply of dental services was adjusted. Alternatively, because price elasticity was generally highest for children, the likely shortage could be alleviated if dental insurance was phased in slowly for children. (Such a strategy was followed in 1974 when Sweden inaugurated its national dental insurance plan.)

Source: Willard G. Manning, Jr. and Charles E. Phelps, "The Demand for Dental Care," *The Bell Journal of Economics*, Autumn 1979, pp. 503–25. Table (p. 512) copyright © 1979, American Telephone and Telegraph Company.

tion also influences the number of substitutes available. A doubling of the price of gasoline this year may cut back gasoline consumption by only 14 percent, but over a period of five, ten, or fifty years, the response would be much stronger. Given enough time, people can change their lifestyles and walk and bicycle more or take fewer and shorter trips. They can change the location of their residences and jobs. They can produce smaller and more efficient cars that use less gasoline per mile. They can discover new types of energy, and much more. Indeed, economists often make short-run and long-run estimates of elasticity, and these confirm that elasticity tends to be higher for longer periods, often dramatically so. Consider Table 4.3, which com-

TABLE 4.2   Selected Estimates of Own-Price Elasticities of Demand in the United States (absolute values)

Good	Elasticity	Source	Good	Elasticity	Source
Cottonseed oil	6.92	B	Shoes	0.70	H
Tomatoes (fresh)	4.60	H	Household appliances	0.67	H
Green peas (fresh)	2.80	H	Legal services	0.61	H
Scrod	2.20	A	Physicians' services	0.58	H
Legal gambling	1.91	N	Rail travel (commuter)	0.54	H
Lamb	1.90	E,M	Jewelry, watches	0.54	H
Restaurant meals	1.63	H	Water	0.52	D
Marijuana	1.51	K	Cigarettes	0.51	J
Peaches	1.50	E	Stationery	0.47	H
Butter	1.40	L	Radio, TV repair	0.47	H
Automobiles	1.35	P	Sea scallops	0.46	A
China, glassware	1.34	H	Toilet articles	0.44	H
Apples	1.30	E	Cabbage	0.40	H
Taxi service	1.24	H	Auto repair	0.36	H
Chicken	1.20	E	Medical insurance	0.31	H
Radios, TV sets	1.19	H	Margarine	0.30	L
Beer	1.13	G	Potatoes	0.30	C
Furniture	1.01	H	Coffee	0.25	C
Housing	1.00	H	Eggs	0.23	B
Alcohol	0.92	H	Spectator sports	0.21	H
Beef	0.92	R	Bus travel (intercity)	0.20	H
Sports equipment, boats, etc.	0.88	H	Theatre, opera	0.18	H
Movies	0.87	H	Natural gas (residential)	0.15	H
Flowers, seeds	0.82	H	Gasoline and oil	0.14	H
Citrus fruit	0.80	E	Milk	0.14	B
Bus travel (local)	0.77	H	Electricity (residential)	0.13	H
Air travel (foreign)	0.70	H	Newspapers, magazines	0.10	H

TABLE 4.3   Long-Run VS. Short-Run Elasticities[a]

Good	Elasticity Short-Run	Elasticity Long-Run	Good	Elasticity Short-Run	Elasticity Long-Run
China, glassware	1.34	8.80	Radio, TV repair	0.47	3.84
Alcohol	0.92	3.63	Toilet articles	0.44	2.42
Sports equipment, boats, etc	0.88	2.39	Medical insurance	0.31	0.92
Movies	0.87	3.67	Bus travel (intercity)	0.20	2.17
Flowers, seeds	0.82	2.65	Theatre, opera	0.18	0.31
Bus travel (local)	0.77	3.54	Natural gas (residential)	0.15	10.74
Air travel (foreign)	0.70	4.00	Gasoline, oil	0.14	0.48
Shoes	0.70	1.20	Electricity (residential)	0.13	1.90
Rail travel (commuter)	0.54	1.70	Newspapers, magazines	0.10	0.52
Jewelry, watches	0.54	0.67			

[a]Own-price elasticities of demand, United States, absolute values, SOURCE for each item is the source for the same item in Table 4.2

CLOSE-UP 4.3:

Cross-Price Elasticity and the Cellophane Case

The U.S. Department of Justice brought suit against the du Pont Company (which sold 75 percent of the cellophane used in the United States) for having monopolized the sale of cellophane. In its defense, du Pont claimed that the relevant market was wider than that of cellophane and should include all flexible wrapping materials (of which du Pont sold less than 20 percent). To prove its point, du Pont produced cross-price elasticities between cellophane and close substitutes, such as aluminum foils, wax paper, and polyethylene. In a 1956 landmark decision, the U.S. Supreme Court agreed with du Pont.

Source: *U.S. Reports*, vol. 351 (Washington, D.C.: U.S. Government Printing Office, 1956), p. 400.

pares long-run and short-run elasticities. Then turn to Table 4.4, which shows estimates of income elasticities. It differentiates between inferior goods (with negative elasticities) and normal goods. Among normal goods, it differentiates between necessities (with positive elasticities below unity) and luxuries (with elasticities above unity).

Finally, Table 4.5 presents cross-price elasticity data on a number of substitute goods. Note that similar estimates for complements would produce negative elasticities; cross-price elasticity estimates for independent goods would produce zero elasticities.

The Manifold Uses of Elasticity Estimates

The British economist Gregory King (1648–1712) noted that bumper crops always seemed to spell bad times for farmers and that poor crops spelled good times. Anyone with a knowledge of the low own-price and income elasticities for farm products can easily solve the puzzle. Indeed, recognition of this fact led American farmers during this century, with the help of their government, to *restrict* output and *raise* their revenues. Take another look at panel (b) of Figure 4.14. Mentally reverse the arrows shown

TABLE 4.4   Selected Estimates of Income Elasticities of Demand in the United States

Good	Elasticity	Source	Good	Elasticity	Source
Automobiles	2.46	H	Tobacco	0.64	H
Alcohol	1.54	H	Gasoline, oil	0.48	H
Housing, owner-occupied	1.49	H	Housing, rental	0.43	H
Furniture	1.48	H	Butter	0.42	Q
Books	1.44	H	Eggs	0.37	Q
Dental services	1.42	H	Electricity, residential	0.20	O
Restaurant meals	1.40	H	Coffee	0	I
Shoes	1.10	H	Margarine	−0.20	Q
Clothing	1.02	H	Starchy roots	−0.20	I
Water	1.02	H	Pig products	−0.20	I
Medical insurance	0.92	H	Flour	−0.36	Q
Physicians' services	0.75	H	Whole milk	−0.50	I

TABLE 4.5 Selected Estimates of Cross-Price Elasticities of Demand in the United States

Good with Quantity Change	Good with Price Change	Elasticity	Source
Florida Interior oranges	Florida Indian River oranges	+1.56	F
Margarine	Butter	+0.81	Q
Butter	Margarine	+0.67	Q
Natural gas	Fuel oil	+0.44	O
Beef	Pork	+0.28	Q
Electricity	Natural gas	+0.20	O
Pork	Beef	+0.14	Q
California oranges	Florida Interior oranges	+0.14	F

SOURCES TO TABLES 4.2 TO 4.5:
A. Frederick W. Bell, "The Pope and the Price of Fish," *The American Economic Review*, December 1968.
B. G. E. Brandow, "Interrelations Among Demands for Farm Products and Implications for Control of Market Supply," *Bulletin 680* (University Park: Pennsylvania State University Agricultural Experiment Station, 1961).
C. Rex F. Daly, "Coffee Consumption and Prices in the United States," *Agricultural Economic Research* (Washington, D.C.: U.S. Department of Agriculture, Economic Research Service, July 1958).
D. Henry S. Foster, Jr., and Bruce R. Beattie, "Urban Residential Demand for Water in the United States," *Land Economics*, February 1979.
E. Karl A. Fox, *The Analysis of Demand for Farm Products, Technical Bulletin 1081* (Washington, D.C.: U.S. Department of Agriculture, September 1953).
F. Marshall B. Godwin, W. Fred Chapman, Jr., and William T. Hanley, *Competition Between Florida and California Valencia Oranges in the Fruit Market, Bulletin 704* (Washington, D.C.: U.S. Department of Agriculture, Economic Research Service, December 1965).
G. T. F. Hogarty and K. G. Elsinger, "The Demand for Beer," *The Review of Economics and Statistics*, May 1972.
H. H. S. Houthakker and Lester D. Taylor, *Consumer Demand in the United States: Analyses and Projections*, 2nd ed. (Cambridge: Harvard University Press, 1970).
I. Richard G. Lipsey, and Peter O. Steiner, *Microeconomics*, 5th ed. (New York: Harper and Row, 1979), p. 133.
J. Herbert L. Lyon, Julian L. Simon, "Price Elasticity of the Demand for Cigarettes in the United States," *American Journal of Agricultural Economics*, November 1968.
K. Charles T. Nisbet, and Firouz Vakil, "Some Estimates of Price and Expenditure Elasticities of Demand for Marijuana Among UCLA Students," *The Review of Economics and Statistics*, November 1972.
L. A. S. Rojko, *The Demand and Price Structure for Dairy Products, Technical Bulletin 1168* (Washington, D.C.: U.S. Department of Agriculture, 1957).
M. Henry Schultz, *The Theory and Measurement of Demand* (Chicago: Chicago University Press, 1938).
N. Daniel B. Suits, "The Elasticity of Demand for Gambling, " *The Quarterly Journal of Economics*, February 1979.
O. L. Taylor, R. Halvorsen, "Energy Substitution in U.S. Manufacturing," *The Review of Economics and Statistics*, November 1977.
P. U.S. Senate, Subcommittee on Antitrust and Monopoly, *Administered Prices: Automobiles* (Washington, D.C.: U.S. Government Printing Office, 1958).
Q. H. Wold and L. Jureen, *Demand Analysis* (New York: Wiley, 1953).
R. Elmer Working, *The Demand for Meat* (Chicago: University of Chicago Press, 1951).

there, and interchange the "gain" and "loss" labels. When demand is own-price inelastic, a relatively small cut in quantity allows price to be raised so much that consumers spend, and producers receive, more money than before. In addition, the lower quantity lowers the producers' costs. The Parker Pen Company followed this strategy in the 1950s when it realized the low own-price elasticity for its ink (called Quink). Various telephone companies in 1977 followed this strategy when they became aware of the low own-price elasticity for directory assistance calls and started charging for such calls. The owners of ball parks who are aware of the low own-price elasticity for spectator sports know what they are doing when they do *not* lower price to fill the empty seats [as from 0c to 0d in panel (b) of Figure 4.14].

On the other hand, consider panel (a) of Figure 4.14. When demand is own-price elastic, a cut in price causes consumers to buy so much more that their expenditures, and the revenues of

ANALYTICAL EXAMPLE 4.2:

The Demand Elasticity of Animal Consumers

Biologists and psychologists have shown that the study of animal behavior can provide important insights for the study of human behavior. Economists are just beginning to realize that much can be learned from the similarities of the *economic* behavior of different species. The insights of the Slutsky-Hicks theory of (human) consumer choice, for example, have been duplicated by biologists while studying such diverse species as protozoa, bumblebees, sunfish, and deer mice. If one characterizes changes in the natural environment of such animals as changes in the relative prices of goods available to the animals, one can show that their changes in consumption patterns correspond precisely to the changes that economic theory would predict for human consumers under similar circumstances. Economists, therefore, should be able to study animals, as psychologists do, and derive conclusions about people.

The types of rat experiments described in Close-Up 4.2 have, for example, yielded estimates of demand elasticities that make a lot of sense for human consumers as well. Consider the accompanying table. Part (A) lists own-price elasticities and cross-price elasticities of demand by rats implied by so-called *income-compensated demand curves* (which only show the substitution effect of any price changes on the quantity demanded). Note that the own-price elasticity is lower for an essential good (food) than it is for a nonessential one (root beer), which is just what one would expect for people as well. Or consider the *cross-price* elasticities in part (B) in which all numbers are based on *ordinary* or *uncompensated* demand curves that show the substitution as well as income effect of any price changes on quantity demanded. The cross-price elasticities for essential goods (food and water) are negative, implying that these goods are complements. The cross-price elasticities of nonessential goods (root beer, collins mix, etc.), however, are positive or near zero, implying that these goods are substitutes or independents. Finally note that the *own-price* elasticities in part (B) are generally higher than in part (A), which is also as one would expect if the consumers were human and the goods involved were normal goods. The income effect, included in part (B) but not in (A), reinforces the substitution effect of any price change; hence the effect of any price change on quantity demanded (and measured own-price elasticity) is stronger.

producers, rise. Henry Ford I followed this strategy in the early decades of the auto company. So did the Columbia Record Company in the 1930s and AT&T's long-distance department in the 1960s.

Government officials find knowledge of elasticities to be just as crucial in their decision making. A tax hike that raises the price of a product with inelastic demand (such as alcohol, movies, cigarettes, water, coffee, or gasoline) will raise lots of extra revenue but may not cut quantity demanded very much. If a large cut in quantity is desired (to cure cancer from cigarettes or conserve water or gasoline) only a very large hike in the tax will do the trick. On the other hand, a tax hike that raises the price of a product with elastic demand (such as restaurant meals and legal gambling), will decrease government revenues and also cut quantity demanded very much, as people turn to substitutes (such as cooking at home and illegal gambling).

Business and government leaders who do not

(A) Based on Income-Compensated Demand (measures substitution effect of price changes only)				
	Good	**Own-Price Elasticity**	**Goods**	**Cross-Price Elasticity**
Essential	{ Food	|0.04|to|0.18|	Water/food	0.03 to 0.13
			Saccharin solution/food	0.06 to 0.18
Non-essential	{ Root beer	|0.31| to |2.22|	Collins mix/ root beer	0.76 to 4.12
			Cherry cola/ root beer	0.72

(B) Based on Ordinary Demand (measures substitution and income effect of price changes)				
	Good	**Own-Price Elasticity**	**Goods**	**Cross-Price Elasticity**
Essential	{ Food	|0.12| to |0.20|	Water/food	−0.13 to −0.55
	{ Water	|0.90|	Food/water	−0.32
Non-essential	{ Root beer	|1.03| to |6.39|	Collins mix/ root beer	0.15
			Cherry cola/ root beer	2.27
	Cherry cola	|1.05| to |3.98|	Root beer/ cherry cola	0.83
			Saccharin solution/ cherry cola	0.01
	Saccharin solution	|1.02|	Cherry cola/ saccharin solution	−0.01

Source: John H. Kagel, Raymond C. Battalio, Howard Rachlin, and Leonard Green, "Demand Curves for Animal Consumers," *The Quarterly Journal of Economics*, Vol. XCVI, No. 1, February 1981, pp. 1–15. Table (from p. 6 and 12) © 1981 by the President and Fellows of Harvard College. Published by John Wiley & Sons, Inc.

heed the crucial information embodied in elasticity estimates can make serious mistakes. When the railroads of the 1930s raised their fares (in the face of price-elastic demand), their revenues plummeted. When city governments in the 1950s raised property tax rates (in the face of price-elastic demand), many businesses and households abandoned the cities, producing lowered city-property values and tax collections, as well as suburban sprawl, road congestion, and air pollution.

SUMMARY

1. A person's demand for a consumption good is a function of many variables, such as the good's own price, the prices of other goods, and the consumer's budget and tastes. With the help of indifference curve analysis, one can derive the demand for a good as a function of its own price alone. Normally, such demand curves follow the "law" of downward-sloping demand. A rare exception is Giffen's paradox.

2. Demand for a good can also be derived as a function of income alone. This demand is pictured by an Engel curve. Engel curves for normal goods are upward-sloping; those for inferior goods are downward-sloping.

3. Even a simple price change, all else being equal, can have two different effects: the substitution effect and the income effect. The substitution effect of lowered price, for example, always increases quantity demanded. The income effect of lowered price reinforces the substitution effect in the case of normal goods but works against it in the case of inferior goods. This may (but need not) produce Giffen's paradox.

4. Indifference curve analysis can also be used to derive the demand for a consumption good as a function of another good's price. This analysis will reveal whether any two goods are independents, complements, or substitutes.

5. The individual demands of all potential market participants can be added together to derive market demand. This procedure becomes complicated in the presence of bandwagon, snob, or Veblen effects. The Veblen effect is capable of producing an upward-sloping section in the market demand line.

6. Empirical studies of market demand have used a number of approaches, including consumer interviews, consumer clinics, market experiments. time-series studies, and cross-section studies.

7. The study of market demand relationships allows economists to answer a multitude of important questions posed by decision makers in business and government.

8. Particularly important in answering such questions is the calculation of exact measures of the responsiveness of quantity demanded to other variables. Such measures include the own-price elasticity of demand, the income elasticity of demand, and the cross-price elasticity of demand.

9. Empirical measures of these elasticities have many uses in business and government.

KEY TERMS

arc elasticity
bandwagon effect
change in demand
change in quantity demanded
complementary goods
cross-price elasticity of demand
cross-section studies
demand
elasticities of demand
Engel curve
Engel's law
Giffen's paradox
identification problem
income-consumption line
income effect
income elasticity of demand
independent goods
inferior goods
"law" of downward-sloping demand
luxuries
market demand
necessities
normal goods
own-price elasticity of demand
point elasticity
price-consumption line
snob effect
substitute goods
substitution effect
time-series studies
Veblen effect

QUESTIONS AND PROBLEMS

1. Consider Figure 4.1, panel (a), but imagine that the vertical axis measures *money* spent on all goods other than butter. In that case, a demand curve for butter must exhibit an own-price elasticity of greater than unity when the price-consumption line is sloping downwards to the right and an own-price elasticity of less than unity when it is sloping upwards to the right. Explain.

2. "The 'law' of downward-sloping demand is universally applicable and not just to things traded for money in the market: The longer the lines at the ski lift, the less often do people come back to ski; the more unpleasant are our neighbors, the less often do we visit them; the muddier the short cut across the lawn, the less often do we use it; the lower a professor's grades, the fewer the students who take the course; the higher are market wages, the less time do we give to friends, spouses, children, parents, and even to genuine reflection by ourselves; the more parking tickets are issued, the fewer the violations." Explain. Then make a list of your own examples of the "law" of downward-sloping demand outside the realm of money and markets.

3. What do you think are the own-price and income elasticities of demand for the following: beer, Coca Cola, Diet Pepsi, gasoline, Levi jeans, required textbooks, safety pins, sports cars. Give reasons for your answers.

4. Which of the following are likely to have positive cross-price elasticities of demand: automobiles and oil, gin and tonic, a Harvard education and a Yale education, ham and cheese, men's shoes and women's shoes. Give reasons for your answers.

5. In the graph below, consider the two demand curves (D_1 and D_2) and the three Engel curves (E_1, E_2, and E_3). Determine the own-price elastic-

ity of demand on D_1 at points a, c, g, and h, and on D_2 at points c and e. Then determine income elasticity at b, d, and f.

6. Assuming all other things are equal, calculate in each case below the magnitude of the own-price elasticity of demand:

a. In 1975, New York City's Taxi and Limousine Commission authorized a 17.5 percent increase in fares. Taxi company revenues went up by 10.5 percent.

b. In 1975, New York City's Metropolitan Transportation Authority raised tolls for 7 bridges and 2 tunnels with these results:

Facility	Toll Increase	Traffic Count[2]
Bronx Whitestone Bridge	50¢ to 75¢	1.791 to 1.765
Cross Bay Bridge	50¢ to 75¢	0.381 to 0.328
Henry Hudson Bridge	50¢ to 75¢	0.777 to 0.616
Marine Parkway Bridge	50¢ to 75¢	0.486 to 0.421
Throgs Neck Bridge	50¢ to 75¢	2.125 to 2.016
Triborough Bridge	50¢ to 75¢	3.400 to 3.000
Verrazano Narrows Bridge	75¢ to $1	2.390 to 2.328
Brooklyn Battery Tunnel	70¢ to 75¢	0.904 to 0.838
Queens Midtown Tunnel	50¢ to 75¢	1.360 to 1.240

Can you explain the differences in your results?

7. a. Consider the own-price elasticities of U.S. airline travel in the table below calculated separately for different lengths of trip.[3] Could the Civil Aeronautics Board have helped airlines by authorizing an "across-the-board" increase in fares? Explain.

Distance in Miles	Elasticity
28	0.76
400	1.02
650	1.07
1500	1.14
2500	1.17

[2]Million vehicles, Sept. 1–21, 1975, compared to same period in 1974.

[3]Arthur de Vany, "The Revealed Value of Time in Air Travel," *The Review of Economics and Statistics*, February 1974, p. 80.

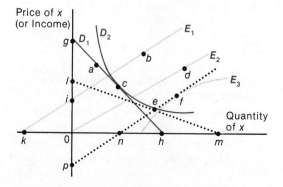

b. In recent years, economists have calculated own-price elasticities for gasoline to be much higher than in the 1960s (see the earlier and lower elasticities indicated in Table 4.3). These new estimates range from 0.2 in the short run (1 year) to 0.4 for 5 years and 0.8 for 10 years.[4] On that basis, President Carter's advisers in late 1979 urged an increase in the federal gasoline tax from 4¢ to 50¢ per gallon. They argued that the new price of $1.50 per gallon would cut gasoline consumption by 7 million barrels per day within a year. (A barrel holds 42 gallons.) What must have been the daily consumption at the time of this advice? What gasoline savings could one expect in future years?

8. Determine whether each of the following statements is true or false:

a. In a world of two goods, both cannot be inferior; both cannot be luxury goods.

b. All inferior goods produce Giffen's paradox.

c. An indifference curve between perfect substitutes (of which one is as good as the other, as two nickels vs. one dime) would be straight like a budget line.

d. An indifference curve between perfect complements (that must be consumed in fixed proportions to be any good at all, as right shoes and left shoes) would be right-angled like the two axes of a graph.

e. The snob effect makes the market demand curve less (own-price) elastic at any given price.

f. The bandwagon effect makes the market demand curve less (own-price) elastic at any given quantity.

g. Any demand curve that intersects both axes cannot have constant own-price elasticity throughout.

h. The demand curve for the output of a single firm in a perfect market must be horizontal (and exhibit an infinite own-price elasticity at every point).

i. On two parallel, downward-sloping demand curves, the own-price elasticity of demand is the same at any given price.

j. On two parallel, downward-sloping demand curves, the own-price elasticity of demand is the same at any given quantity.

k. Luxuries, unlike necessities, have an income elasticity of less than unity.

l. Positive cross-price elasticity denotes Giffen's paradox.

m. If your college has doubled its tuition in the last decade, but the number of student applications and enrollments remained the same, this indicates a zero own-price elasticity of demand.

SELECTED READINGS

Allen, R. G. D. "The Work of Eugen Slutsky." *Econometrica*, July 1950, pp. 209–16.

Hicks, John R., and Allen, R. G. D. "A Reconsideration of the Theory of Value." *Economica*, February 1934, pp. 52–76 and May 1934, pp. 196–219.

A crucial article in value theory.

Houthakker, H. S., and Taylor, Lester D. *Consumer Demand in the United States: Analyses and Projections*. Cambridge: Harvard University Press, 1970.

Estimation of demand equations for 82 expenditure categories, of Engel curves, price and income elasticities, etc.

Leibenstein, Harvey. *Beyond Economic Man: A New Foundation for Microeconomics*. Cambridge: Harvard University Press, 1976, chap. 4.

A discussion of bandwagon, snob, and Veblen effects.

Samuelson, Paul A. "Complementarity—An Essay on the 40th Anniversary of the Hicks-Allen Revolution in Demand Theory." *Journal of Economic Literature*, December 1974, pp. 1255–89.

An important survey article on the concepts of substitutability and complementarity.

Seligman, Ben B. *The Reaffirmation of Tradition*. Main Currents in Modern Economics, vol. 2. Chicago: Quadrangle Books, 1971, pp. 403–21.

A critical discussion of the work of John R. Hicks.

Slutsky, Eugen. "On the Theory of the Budget of the Consumer." American Economic Association, *Readings in Price Theory*. Chicago: Irwin, 1952, pp. 27–56.

A translation of the famous 1915 article.

---

[4]*The New York Times*, November 25, 1979, pp. F1 and 18; Robert S. Pindyck, *The Structure of World Energy Demand* (Cambridge: MIT Press, 1979).

CHAPTER 5

The Technology of the Firm

Chapters 3 and 4 explored the factors that determine the *demand* for consumption goods; Chapters 5 and 6 will turn to those factors that determine the *supply* of consumption goods. Chapter 5 will focus on the *physical* aspects of the productive process by which firms make goods available to people when and where they are wanted; Chapter 6 will consider the *monetary* aspects as well. The discussion of scarcity in Chapter 1 noted that in any given period a society's ability to produce goods is limited by the quantities of resources available and by the current state of its technology (the set of production methods known to people). Every single firm, we must now add, is similarly constrained by resources and technology—whether it is large or small, whether it produces airplane rides, apples, or medical care, whether it is run by a genius, a moron, or a group of either type. With the inevitably limited inputs chosen by it, the firm cannot produce a larger quantity of any given type of output than current technology allows. This physical constraint on the producer of every good can be summarized by a **production function**. The production function is the technical relationship, stated in physical and not in value terms, between all conceivable combinations of inputs used during a period and the associated *maximum* quantities of some type of

output, given the state of technology. This relationship can be expressed in the form of an equation, a table, or a graph.

If we denote, respectively, the quantities of human, capital, and natural resource services used in a given period by L, K, and T; the state of technology by t, and the maximum possible outputs obtainable from combinations of the above by Q, we can write a production function as

$$Q = f(L, K, T), \text{ given } t.$$

Naturally, any change in technology, t, will change the relationship between physical input combinations *(L, K, and T)* and the associated maximum output quantities, Q. That, however, is a matter to be discussed in Chapter 10. This chapter focuses on the production function under a *given* state of technology. Even with this restriction, the production function is a complicated relationship.

Consider the production of apples. Current technical knowledge allows firms to produce apples with a near-infinite variety of input combinations. Orchards can be located in many places —in Oregon or Michigan, in Maine or Virginia, at sea level or at high elevations. Accordingly, such natural resources as the inherent fertility of the soil, the amount of annual rainfall or sunshine, and the length of the growing season can be varied widely. A similar story can be told about capital resources. Orchards can be established on 1-acre lots or on 5,000-acre lots; they can be placed in the open (and usually are), but they can also be set up under glass. They can be planted with trees bred to resist disease or with ordinary ones that are sprayed with pesticides—by hand, tank car, or even by plane. Orchards can be equipped with bee hives (to assist fertilization) or sprinkler systems (to prevent damage from frost), with irrigation equipment, rodent control, or cold-storage barns. The quantity of human resources used can, similarly, be adjusted almost without limit. People can be used to plant trees and fertilize them, to prune trees and harvest the crop, to store and market the crop, to run and repair equipment, to supervise operations, and much more.

Given enough time, a firm engaged in apple production can vary all of these inputs. Economists have a special name for this situation. A time period so long that a firm can vary the quantities of *all* of its inputs is called the **long run**. In contrast, a time period so short that the quantity of at least one of the firm's inputs cannot be varied is called the **short run**. Obviously, the length involved differs for firms in different industries. For example, an apple producer would require a minimum of five years to increase the number of fruit-bearing trees (they cannot be grown overnight); yet a street vendor selling apples might be able to increase all relevant inputs in a day. We will begin our study of the production function with a discussion of the short run. In the simplest possible case, a firm may be able to vary the quantity of only one of its inputs.

The Case of a Single Variable Input

Imagine an apple producer who was limited, during a given period, not only by the current state of technology, but also by fixed quantities of

capital and natural resources, $\overline{K}$ and $\overline{T}$. During a given year, for instance, this producer may have available (and be unable to vary in quantity) 1,000 mature apple trees (on a 5-acre hilltop in Oregon), 3 tons of fertilizer, 2 orchard-spraying machines, and so on. The number of full-time laborers, L, may, however, be freely variable; by varying the number of workers, the firm may be able to vary its output. The production function of this firm can be written as

$$Q = f(L), \text{ given } \overline{K}, \overline{T}, t.$$

Alternatively, this relationship can be expressed by the type of data in columns (1) to (3) of Table 5.1. Rows (A) to (J) list ten of many more conceivable combinations of fixed and variable inputs and the maximum total output associated with each. Consider row (A). The use for a year of 1,000 apple trees, 3 tons of fertilizer, etc. is designated in column (1) as the use of 1 unit of fixed input. If no labor at all were performed, as shown by the 0 in column (2), the firm would end up producing no apples at all, as column (3) shows. An unholy alliance of winter storms, spring frost, summer drought, and various pests would ruin the unprotected trees. Even if apples grew on them, there would be no one to do the harvesting. Yet the firm has many alternatives. Some of them are shown in rows (B) through (J). If the firm used the work of even one person for a year—row (B)—the picture would be altered drastically. Sprinkling blossoms against frost and watering roots during the drought, perhaps, would reward the firm, eventually, with an apple harvest of 1,000 bushels.

There are other possibilities, of course. The use of two workers for a year would bring even better results. Two workers—row (C)—would be able to do what one alone could not accomplish: prune the tops of trees, fertilize their roots, and wrap their trunks to keep the rodents away. As a result, the trees would grow more and larger apples; total product would rise to 2,700 bushels a year. The hiring of three workers—row (D)—instead of two would yield even more spectacular

TABLE 5.1   A Simple Production Function

	Inputs Per Year			Output Per Year	
	Fixed (1,000 apple trees, 3 tons of fertilizer, etc.) (1)	**Variable (workers)** (2)	**Maximum Total Product (bushels of apples)** (3)	**Marginal Product of Labor (bushels of apples per extra worker)** (4) = $\Delta(3)/\Delta(2)$	**Average Product of Labor (bushels of apples per worker)** (5) = (3)/(2)
(A)	1	0	0		—
(B)	1	1	1,000	1,000 ⎫	1,000
(C)	1	2	2,700	1,700 ⎬ Increasing returns to labor	1,350
(D)	1	3	5,000	2,300 ⎭	1,667
(E)	1	4	7,000	2,000	1,750
(F)	1	5	8,300	1,300	1,660
(G)	1	6	9,000	700 ⎫ Decreasing returns to labor	1,500
(H)	1	7	9,300	300 ⎬	1,329
(I)	1	8	9,300	0	1,163
(J)	1	9	9,000	−300 ⎭	1,000

Each row of this table shows a conceivable combination of inputs used per year, columns (1) and (2), and the associated maximum total product, column (3), given the state of technology. Column (4) depicts the *law of eventually diminishing returns to a variable input:* Given technical knowledge and a fixed quantity of some input, such as the natural and capital resources listed in column (1), equal successive additions of another input, such as the labor listed in column (2), eventually yield declining additions to total output, such as the apple crop in column (3). As this example indicates, the law in question may operate only after a range of increasing returns has been passed. The returns involved refer to the variable input's *marginal product* and should not be confused with its *average product,* column (5). Note: As the pointers between columns (3) and (4) indicate, the marginal products shown refer to the intervals between rows.

success. There would now be time to fix and run the spraying machines, to harvest more of the apples, to take care of the cold-storage barn. Fewer apples would be eaten by worms, remain unharvested, or spoil before reaching the market. Total product would rise to 5,000 bushels a year.

And so it would go, but not forever. Proceeding on the path of hiring more labor, an orchardist would soon come face to face with a technological fact of life: Given fixed quantities of capital and natural resources, illustrated by the unchanging entries in column (1), equal successive additions of labor would be bound to yield, eventually, ever smaller additions to the crop, followed by zero additions or even negative ones,

as shown by column (4). Sooner or later, there would be too many workers relative to the fixed number of trees and quantity of equipment. Once trees were saturated with fertilizer, water, and tender loving care, additional workers would have nothing to do except eat apples and get into each other's way! Inevitably, the principle of declining marginal benefit (first noted in Chapter 1) would come into play. When the benefit that is declining refers to physical product rather than utility, the principle is usually referred to as the **law of variable proportions** or the **law of diminishing returns**. Strictly speaking, it should be given the awkward name of *the law of eventually diminishing returns to a variable input.*

The Law of Diminishing Returns

The nature of the law of diminishing returns, which can be observed in all production functions, can be most clearly understood with the help of a new concept: **Marginal product** is the physical change in the total product attributable to a unit change in some input in the productive process, all else being equal. (In later chapters, when there is danger of confusing physical product with its market value, we will refer to this concept as **marginal physical product**. In this chapter, however, all units are measured in physical terms.) The marginal product of labor in Table 5.1 can be calculated by noting the change in the total product evidenced by the difference between any two adjacent numbers in column (3), a difference that is always associated in our example with a unit change in labor input in column (2). The results are shown directly in column (4). As the brackets indicate, **diminishing returns to a variable input** always refer to declines in that input's *marginal* product as a larger quantity of the input is used. These declines should not be confused with possible declines of total product—column (3)—or of **average product**—column (5). Average product is the ratio of total product to the total quantity of an input used. The average product of the variable labor input is shown in column (5).

Table 5.1 also highlights the fact that the eventual inevitability of diminishing returns, as a variable input is added to a fixed input, does not preclude the existence of a limited range of **increasing returns to a variable input**, in which use of a larger quantity of the input is associated with *increases* in its marginal product. Note how labor's marginal product in our orchard declines when 3 or more workers are employed but rises prior to this point. Similarly (though not shown in Table 5.1), there might exist a range of **constant returns to a variable input**, in which use of a larger quantity of the input is associated with constancy in its marginal product. This, too, would have to be a transitory stage, or it would be possible to add more and more workers to our 5-acre orchard (and receive ever-constant amounts of extra output in return) until the entire world's apple crop was being produced there. The mental image of a thousand, a million, and, finally, a billion workers being crammed into our 5-acre piece of land should be enough to convince us that increasing and constant returns must *eventually* give way to diminishing returns. Because increasing or constant returns are a limited possibility, however, economists who do not wish to be misunderstood talk of the law of *eventually* diminishing returns.

Note: While the concepts of increasing, constant, or diminishing returns to a variable input refer to the behavior of the marginal product of a particular type of input (such as labor), it is not a good idea to link the marginal product of an input type to any particular unit of that input (such as a particular worker). In Table 5.1, each of the persons employed can be assumed to be an *equally good* worker. The sixth person hired should not be viewed as any weaker, lazier, or less intelligent than the first five, even though he or she would add so much less to the total crop. Nor need the ninth person be any different from the sixth. The different performances of workers would stem from the different *circumstances* existing when these workers arrived on the scene. If worker number 9 were hired first, he or she, too, would produce a marginal product of +1,000 rather than −300 bushels. If worker number 1 were hired in eighth place, he or she, too, would produce a marginal product of zero rather than of 1,000 bushels. By the same token, if our orchardist were to fire any one of eight workers laboring in the orchard, no matter whether he or she was hired as the first, fourth, or eighth one, the total produced would not change at all, since the product associated with seven workers is the same as that for eight workers, as shown in column (3). This may seem surprising, but it is really little more than common sense. People by themselves produce nothing. How productive they are depends on the world into which they are placed. Their productivity depends on the quantity and quality of the natural, capital, and other human resources they find in this world. Ask yourself this: What would *your* marginal product be if you were to join the productive process—just as you now are—in

ANALYTICAL EXAMPLE 5.1:
Marginal Products in Professional Basketball

Production functions can be estimated not only for orchards and steel plants but for more unusual types of producers, such as professional basketball teams. A Cobb-Douglas production function was calculated for the 1976–77 season of the National Basketball Association. Output was measured as the ratio of final scores of games; ten types of inputs were entered in the production function, from the ratio of field-goal-shooting percentages to the ratio of turnovers, from play at home or in the opponent's court to the difference in the number of blocked shots. The accompanying table shows the estimated marginal products of all of these basketball inputs.

Inputs	League	Boston	Buffalo	N.Y. Knicks	N.Y. Nets
Field-goal-shooting percentage	0.6245	0.5445	0.6637	0.5262	0.5858
Free-throw-shooting percentage	0.1132	0.0733	0.1600	0.0943	0.1238
Offensive rebounds	0.0737	0.0636	0.0792	0.0565	0.0734
Defensive rebounds	0.0553	0.0753	0.0428	0.1169	−0.0036
Assists	0.0121	0.0326	−0.0100	0.0185	0.0398
Personal fouls	−0.1178	−0.1590	−0.1033	−0.1182	−0.1182
Steals	0.0160	0.0156	0.0093	0.0408	0.0211
Turnovers	−0.1094	−0.0702	−0.1129	−0.1329	−0.0739
Home court	0.0135	0.0147	0.0071	0.0298	−0.0025
Blocked shots	0.0008	0.0022	−0.0005	0.0011	0.0009

The first entry indicates, for the league as a whole, a 0.6245 increase in the ratio of final scores for a 1 unit increase in that of field-goal-shooting percentages. Note how personal fouls and turnovers had negative marginal products, while the advantage of the home court was much smaller than usually supposed.

Source: Thomas A. Zak, Cliff J. Huang, John J. Siegfried, "Production Efficiency: The Case of Professional Basketball," *Journal of Business*, July 1979, pp. 379–92. Table adapted by permission of the University of Chicago Press. Copyright 1979 by the University of Chicago.

Central Africa or in fourth-century Tibet rather than in the present-day United States?

A Graphical Exposition

Figure 5.1 is a graphical illustration of a simple production function. The heavy dots in panel (a) depict the data from columns (2) and (3) of Table 5.1; the heavy dots in panel (b) graph data from columns (2) and (4) and from columns (2) and

(5). Note that the marginal products of labor have been plotted at the midpoints of the ranges to which they apply and that all the heavy dots have been connected by smooth curves. These curves give us additional information (about points between the heavy dots), which was not contained in Table 5.1; all of our subsequent discussions will be based on this more detailed information now available in the graph.

It is important to understand the nature of the

FIGURE 5.1 Total, Marginal, and Average Product

This is a graphical picture of a production function, which is based on the data in Table 5.1 and assumes, of course, a given technology and fixed quantities of nonlabor inputs. Note: The marginal products of labor have been plotted at the midpoints of the ranges to which they apply.

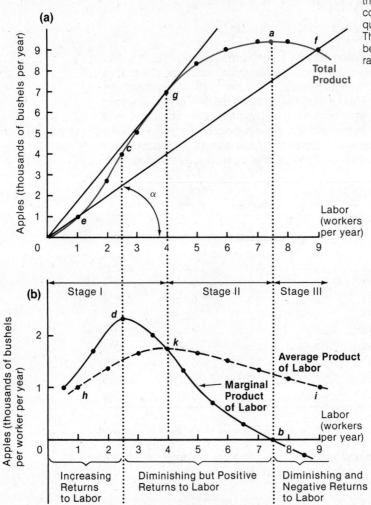

relationships between 1. total product and marginal product, 2. total product and average product, 3. marginal product and average product, and finally 4. the average products of different inputs.

First, note that the *height* of labor's marginal-product curve measures nothing else but the *slope* of the total-product curve. As long as total product is rising with increased use of labor, all else being equal, the slope of the total-product curve is positive (as between 0 and

a). Correspondingly, in panel (b), labor's marginal product is positive (as between 0 and *b*). You may wish to review Figure 1.4, ''Declining Marginal Benefit,'' which illustrates this relationship in a different way (see p. 14).

Observe how the total product is rising at an increasing rate between 0 and *c* (the point of inflexion on the curve), but rising at a decreasing rate between *c* and *a*. Correspondingly, in panel (b), labor's marginal product is positive and rising up to point *d* (which is directly below *c*), but positive and falling between *d* and *b* (which is found directly below *a*). The input quantity corresponding to *d*, at which marginal product is maximized and beyond which it falls, is called the **point of diminishing returns**. Thus labor's marginal-product curve shows directly two ranges of labor inputs: the one producing increasing returns and the one producing diminishing but positive returns in terms of output. Finally, there exists, of course, a third range in which (excessive) labor inputs yield negative marginal products (to the right of *b*) and, therefore, cause total product to decline (to the right of *a*). These three *ranges* are indicated by the brackets underneath panel (b). They should not be confused with the three *stages* underneath panel (a), to be discussed below.

Second, consider the relationship between labor's total and average product. Because labor's average product always equals total product divided by corresponding labor input, its size can be gauged in panel (a) by the slope of a ray originating at 0 and going to any desired point on the total-product curve. Thus the average product of one worker (at point *e*) is 1,000 bushels (the height of *e*) divided by 1 worker, or 1,000 bushels. This average product of one worker is shown by point *h* in panel (b), but it can also be read as the slope of straight line 0*ef* in panel (a) or, mathematically, as tangent α. Because the ray through 0*e* also passes through *f*, the average product of nine workers must also be 1,000 bushels; indeed, 9,000 bushels (the height of *f*) divided by 9 workers does equal 1,000 bushels. The average product of 9 workers is shown by point *i* in panel (b) and, again, by tangent α in panel (a). Once this is understood, it is easy to imagine a series of rays emanating from point 0 in panel (a) and aiming, successively, at points further and further to the right along the total-product curve. These rays would cut the total-product curve at *e*, then *c*, then *g*, *a*, and *f*; the ever-changing angle α (formed by the rays and the abscissa of the graph) would trace out the size of labor's average product. Can you show how angle α (and labor's average product) would rise, with increasing use of labor, to a maximum for

ray 0*g*, but would decline once more than 4 workers were employed? Note how, in panel (b), labor's average product reflects this behavior of angle α. The average product rises to point *k* (directly below *g*) and then declines.

Third, consider the relationship between labor's marginal and average products. As it turns out, the behavior of average "anything" (be it product or even a student's grades) is always related in the following way to the behavior of marginal "anything": When marginal is above average, it pulls up the average. When marginal is below average, it pulls down the average. As long as marginal is equal to average, average does not change.

You can verify this behavior by looking at Figure 5.1. Note that while marginal product exceeds average product, average product is rising (from *h* toward *k*). While marginal product falls short of average product, average product is falling (from *k* toward *i*). Average product reaches a maximum when it equals the marginal product (as it does at point *k*).

Students are apt to be quite familiar with this phenomenon without realizing it. Anyone receiving a new grade (which we might call a *marginal* grade) knows how it can pull down or up one's grade *average*. A marginal grade below average will pull down the average; one above average will pull up the average. This is true, furthermore, regardless of what the marginal grade itself is doing. Each new grade can be better than the last one (marginal grades are rising); yet if these new (and improving) grades are below the average, the average will still go down. Each new grade, on the other hand, can be worse than the last one (marginal grades are falling); yet if these new (and deteriorating) grades are above the average, the average will still go up. Observe this phenomenon in Figure 5.1: marginal product is falling between *d* and *k*, but because it is above average, it still pulls the average up.

Finally, the three stages of the production function, labeled I, II, and III, tell us something about the **productivity** of each type of input, which is the ratio of output produced to input quantity used, or the average product. Throughout stage I, while the use of labor is increased from 0 to 4 workers per year and the quantities of nonlabor inputs are held fixed, the productivities of both types of inputs increase. The increase in labor's productivity is obvious from the stage I segment of the average-product curve in panel (b). The average product of labor rises up to maximum k at the dotted borderline between stages I and II. The increase in the average product of nonlabor inputs is not graphed directly, but it can be seen indirectly in panel (a). Because the quantity of nonlabor inputs is constant throughout, the increase in total product from 0 toward g must be associated with a corresponding increase in the ratio of total product to this constant amount of nonlabor inputs.

Now consider stage II, wherein the use of labor is increased further from 4 to between 7 and 8 units. The productivity of labor obviously declines to the right of k in panel (b). The productivity of nonlabor inputs, on the other hand, continues to rise to its maximum at the borderline between stages II and III. Again, this can be seen indirectly in panel (a). Because total product rises from g toward a, the ratio of total product to the constant amount of nonlabor inputs must also rise.

Note: Given the kind of production function introduced here, it is impossible to maximize simultaneously the productivity of *both* labor and nonlabor resources. (Whether anyone would ever *want* to do such a thing is another question to which we will turn in the next chapter.)

Consider stage III. The productivities of both types of inputs decline. The average-product-of-labor curve in panel (b) tells us directly that labor productivity is declining. The declining total-product curve in panel (a) to the right of point a tells us indirectly that the productivity of nonlabor inputs is declining. Presumably, no firm will ever utilize input combinations such as those in stage III where greater use of variable inputs yields lower total product. Stage III is characterized by **technical inefficiency** because it is now possible, within a given firm, to produce a given output with less of one or more inputs without increasing the amount of other

inputs. Economists usually assume (perhaps wrongly) that each firm by itself achieves **technical efficiency**, a situation in which it is impossible for a given firm to produce a given output with less of one or more inputs without increasing other inputs. Note: *Technical* efficiency should not be confused with *economic* efficiency (discussed in Chapter 14). Unlike technical efficiency, economic efficiency always involves the *comparison* of the circumstances of two or more firms or households.

The Case of Two Variable Inputs

We are now ready to study a more complicated case in which two inputs vary. Consider a producer of wheat who is limited, during a given period, by the current state of technology, t, and by fixed natural resources, $\bar{T}$, but who can freely vary the quantities of both labor and capital, L and K. The firm's production function can be written as

$$Q = f(L, K), \text{ given } \bar{T} \text{ and } t.$$

This production function can be expressed by numerical data such as those in Table 5.2. The table can be read like a mileage chart. The use of 2 units of capital plus 5 units of labor, it tells us, would yield 892 bushels of wheat per year; 6 units of capital used with 3 units of labor would yield 1,196 bushels instead, and so on for all other combinations. Note: The production function shown here is subject to diminishing returns to either input. Holding capital constant at any level and increasing labor by equal units will raise output by ever-decreasing amounts. (Moving from left to right along any row, you might verify this fact by calculating the marginal products of labor). Similarly, holding labor constant at any given level while capital is increased will also raise output by ever-decreasing amounts. (Moving along any column from the bottom to the top, you may wish to calculate the marginal products of capital.)

A complex production function can be illus-

TABLE 5.2 A Complex Production Function

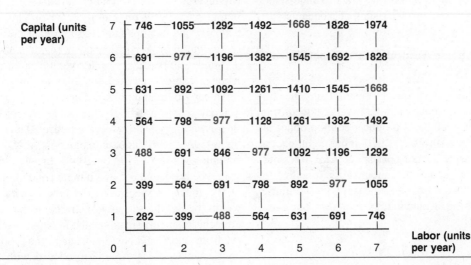

Maximum Total Product
(bushels of wheat per year)

Capital (units per year)							
7	746 — 1055 — 1292 — 1492 — 1668 — 1828 — 1974						
6	691 — 977 — 1196 — 1382 — 1545 — 1692 — 1828						
5	631 — 892 — 1092 — 1261 — 1410 — 1545 — 1668						
4	564 — 798 — 977 — 1128 — 1261 — 1382 — 1492						
3	488 — 691 — 846 — 977 — 1092 — 1196 — 1292						
2	399 — 564 — 691 — 798 — 892 — 977 — 1055						
1	282 — 399 — 488 — 564 — 631 — 691 — 746						
0	1	2	3	4	5	6	7

Labor (units per year)

Given technical knowledge and a fixed quantity of some input (such as natural resources not shown here), different combinations of two variable inputs (such as labor and capital) may yield the alternative total products shown in this grid. The production function shown here is subject throughout to diminishing returns to either labor (given capital) or capital (given labor). Its equation is $Q = 282 \sqrt{K \cdot L}$.

trated graphically in a number of ways. One way is to use a three-dimensional graph like the graph of the utility mountain in Figure 3.3 (see p. 59). Our firm could be viewed very much like the consumer in Chapter 3. Instead of consuming apples and butter to produce utility, it consumes the services of labor and capital to produce wheat. Table 5.2 could be treated like the firm's field of choice. A total-product mountain could be erected above this table in a third dimension, indicating by its height above each input combination the total quantity of wheat that this combination would yield. As the numbers in Table 5.2 indicate, this total-product mountain would start at a zero elevation in the lower left corner and rise to its highest point in the upper right one. Unlike in the case of total utility, furthermore, there would be no problem at all with *measuring* the total product involved because we do know how to measure such physical quantities as bushels, gallons, and tons of output. Thus each number in Table 5.2 can be considered a mea-

surement of the height of the total-product mountain above that number.

Yet it is not necessary to construct such a mountain. Just as the utility mountain could be collapsed to a two-dimensional set of consumption-indifference curves, so the total-product mountain can be reduced to a set of **production-indifference curves**. Each of these curves shows all the alternative combinations of two inputs that yield the same maximum total product and among which a producer would be indifferent from a purely technical point of view. As we shall see later, this does not mean indifference from an economic, profit-maximizing point of view. That is why it is probably wiser to call the production-indifference curve by one of its other names, such as **equal-product curve** or **isoquant**. The technical information highlighted in color in Table 5.2 has been transferred to Figure 5.2, which illustrates how a more complex production function can be presented graphically.

Isoquants Analyzed

To understand what isoquants reveal about the production function, it is important to understand a number of the characteristics of isoquants.

Horizontal and Vertical Slopes Denote Zero Marginal Products

The right-angled isoquants pictured in panel (a) of Figure 5.3 are far from impossible, but consider what they tell us: A producer could produce at most 50 units of product with input combination A. If the same quantity of capital were used, but more labor (such as the amount corresponding to B), output would remain unchanged at 50 units. This unchanged output implies a zero marginal

FIGURE 5.2 Isoquants

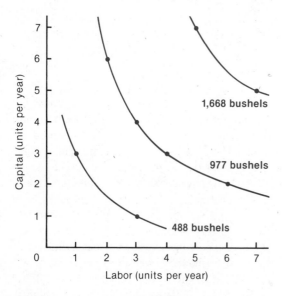

A set of isoquants is a graphic picture of a complex production function. Any given isoquant shows all the alternative combinations of two inputs (such as the services of labor and capital) that yield the same maximum total product (such as bushels of wheat). This set of isoquants assumes, of course, a given technology and fixed quantities of any other inputs.

product of *labor* on the horizontal isoquant segment to the right of A. Similarly, if the same quantity of labor were used as in A, but more capital (such as the amount corresponding to C), output would still remain at 50 units. This unchanged output implies a zero marginal product of *capital* on the vertical isoquant segment above A. Surely, no producer would ever use additional labor or capital that added nothing to output. A producer would avoid the implied technical inefficiency (corresponding to the stage III borderline in Figure 5.1) and would produce 50 units of output *only* with input combination A. Correspondingly, 100, 150, or 200 units of output would be produced only with input combinations D, E, and F, respectively. All levels of output would be produced only with the technically efficient input combinations that lie on the dotted ray from 0 to F and beyond. That is, the product concerned would always be produced with the same capital-to-labor ratio (the one given by the slope of the dotted ray).

Positive Slope Denotes Negative Marginal Products

Consider the positively sloped isoquant segments found in the shaded area of panel (b) of Figure 5.3. If such isoquants existed, no producer would ever select an input combination in the shaded area for this reason: If a producer could produce 30 units of product with input combination *a*, the use of extra labor with capital unchanged (implied by a move from *a* to *b*) would *reduce* total output (*b* lies below the 30-unit isoquant). In region *ab*, labor's marginal product is, therefore, negative. Output could be kept unchanged only if, along with the counterproductive extra labor, extra capital were added, too (by a move from *b* to *c*). But what producer, who could produce 30 units of some output with capital-labor combination *a*, would ever wish to produce the same output with combination *c*, which used more of both inputs? All other input combinations below the dotted line from 0 to *a* and beyond, similarly, denote the presence of negative marginal products of labor.

FIGURE 5.3 Isoquants Analyzed

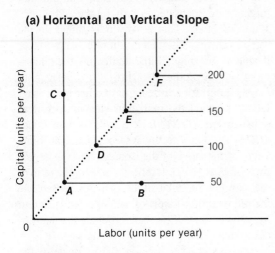

(a) Horizontal and Vertical Slope

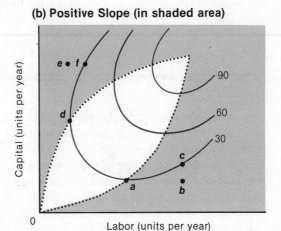

(b) Positive Slope (in shaded area)

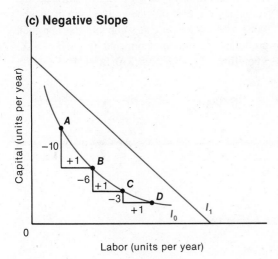

(c) Negative Slope

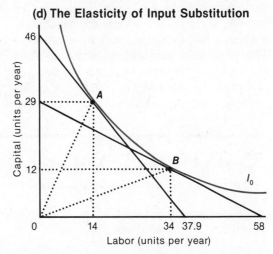

(d) The Elasticity of Input Substitution

This set of graphs illustrates major features of isoquants: Horizontal and vertical segments of isoquants—panel (a)—and isoquant segments with positive slope—panel (b)—denote regions of technical inefficiency. Technically efficient segments of isoquants must be negatively sloped—panel (c). The ease or difficulty with which producers can switch among known techniques of production can be measured by the elasticity of input substitution—panel (d).

An analogous story can be told for the area above the dotted line from 0 to *d* and beyond. In that region, capital, rather than labor, has negative marginal products: If a producer could produce 30 units of product with input combination *d*, the use of extra capital, with labor unchanged

(as implied by a move from *d* to *e*) would *reduce* total output (*e* lies below the 30-unit isoquant). Output could be kept unchanged only if, along with the counterproductive capital, extra labor were added, too (by a move from *e* to *f*). At *f*, a producer would end up using more of *both* inputs than at d but would be getting the same output. All the technically efficient input combinations are, therefore, found in the unshaded lens-shaped area within which isoquants are negatively sloped.

Negative Slope Denotes Positive Marginal Products

We can assume that producers are interested in using inputs only as long as they yield positive marginal products. This implies that producers will focus on negatively sloped segments of isoquants when making input choices. Isoquant I_0 in panel (c) of Figure 5.3 illustrates one possibility.

Isoquant I_0 is analogous to the consumption-indifference curve analyzed in Chapter 3 (see p. 60-63). This time, it is not apples and butter that are consumed to produce invisible utility; the services of capital and workers are consumed to produce a visible product, such as wheat. Consider a producer who was producing the given output level represented by I_0 and was doing so with input combination A. If 10 units of capital were now removed from the process of produc-

tion (and assuming capital's marginal product was positive), output would fall, but this fall might be compensated exactly by the addition of 1 unit of labor. That is why B is found on the same isoquant as A. The rate at which a producer is able to exchange, without affecting the quantity of output produced, a little bit of one input (say, capital) for a little bit of another input (say, labor) is called the **marginal rate of technical substitution (MRTS).** We will denote it as $MRTS_{K/L}$. This rate always equals the absolute value of the slope of the isoquant. In region AB, this comes to $|10/1|$. It reflects, in turn, the ratio of the marginal products of the two inputs. Because the removal of 10 units of capital reduces output by some amount X, we can so denote the marginal product of 10 units of capital and say $MP_{10K} = X$. It follows that $MP_{1K} = 0.1X$. Because the addition of 1 unit of labor raises output by the same amount X, we can so denote the marginal product of 1 unit of labor and say $MP_{1L} = X$. Therefore, $MP_{1L}/MP_{1K} = X/0.1X = 10/1$.

$$|\text{Isoquant slope}| = MRTS_{K/L} = \frac{MP_L}{MP_K}$$

ANALYTICAL EXAMPLE 5.2:

Empirical Estimates of Isoquants

The accompanying graph shows empirical estimates of isoquants, based on U.S. and Japanese data.

The isoquants can cross because five graphs have been superimposed on each other. Each isoquant refers to a different set of industries:

    A = textiles, wood products, grain milling
    B = agriculture, mining, paper, nonferrous metals
    C = steel, rubber, transport equipment
    D = apparel, personal services
    E = electric power
    Can you guess why isoquant E has such a different shape?

Source: K. J. Arrow, H. B. Chenery, B. S. Minhas, R. M. Solow, "Capital-Labor Substitution and Economic Efficiency," *The Review of Economics and Statistics*, August 1961, p. 240. Copyright, 1961, by the President and Fellows of Harvard College.

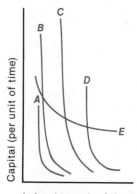

Note: Just as consumption-indifference curves in Chapter 3 were depicted as subject to a diminishing marginal rate of substitution, so isoquant I_0 in panel (c) depicts a frequently observed characteristic of production functions: a diminishing marginal rate of technical substitution. If our producer, having moved from A to B, wanted to substitute ever more labor for capital, output could be kept unchanged only if equal increases in labor went hand in hand with *ever smaller* sacrifices of capital (or equal sacrifices of capital were compensated by *ever larger* increases of labor).

Consider, in contrast, the meaning of straight-line isoquant I_1. I_1 depicts a constant marginal rate of technical substitution, which implies that the two inputs are perfect substitutes for each other. In such a case, we might as well treat them as a single input.

Finally, note one other analogy to the theory of the consumer: Like consumption-indifference curves, isoquants cannot intersect. Any given input combination cannot, simultaneously, yield two different maximum output quantities.

The Elasticity of Input Substitution

Economists like to measure the ease or difficulty with which inputs can be substituted for each other and with which producers can switch, therefore, from one known technique of production to another. The **elasticity of input substitution**, usually denoted by σ, is a measure of this substitutability. It is the percentage change in the ratio of two inputs used in producing a given output quantity, divided by the associated percentage change in the marginal rate of technical substitution between these inputs.

Consider panel (d) of Figure 5.3. Let us calculate the elasticity between A and B on isoquant I_0. Because the inputs involved are labor, L, and capital, K, we can write:

$$\text{Elasticity of input substitution, } \sigma = \frac{\dfrac{\Delta(K/L)}{K/L} \cdot 100}{\dfrac{\Delta MRTS_{K/L}}{MRTS_{K/L}} \cdot 100}$$

The capital-to-labor ratio at A is 29/14, or 2.07. It becomes 12/34 or 0.35 at B, making for a change of -83 percent. The $MRTS_{K/L}$ at A equals the slope of the isoquant at A and is given by the slope of the tangent at that point. Its absolute value is 46/37.9 or 1.21. The $MRTS_{K/L}$ becomes 29/58 or 0.5 at B, making for a change of -59 percent. Hence $\sigma = -83/-59 = 1.41$. Because the input ratio and the marginal rate of technical substitution always move in the same direction, the elasticity of input substitution is always positive for isoquants that allow input substitution. The magnitude of σ is zero, for example, in the extreme case of right-angled isoquants, as in panel (a), Figure 5.3, because, as we noted, input substitution is then ruled out. In that case, only one capital-to-labor ratio exists that is technically efficient (the one given by the slope of line $0F$) and the numerator in the above formula equals zero. In contrast, σ is infinite for straight-line isoquants, such as I_1 in panel (c), because the "two" inputs related in this way are perfect substitutes. In that case, only one MRTS exists, and the denominator of the above formula equals zero.

The value of σ lies, therefore, between zero and infinity for normal convex isoquants, and it is larger the easier input substitution is. Hence σ roughly indicates which firms or industries, in the face of rising relative input prices, will be able to hold their costs down and which will incur increases in production costs that must ultimately increase output prices or reduce profits. A large σ indicates that the rising price of one input can be easily escaped by switching to a different technique of production that favors the use of another input that is relatively cheaper. In contrast, a low or even zero value of σ indicates that, for technological reasons, the producer is almost or completely unable to change the mix of inputs used.

The Case of Nothing but Variable Inputs

We now turn to the long run, in which all inputs can be varied at the same time. Economists have been particularly interested in the effects on output of variations in the *scale* of the productive process. Scale is said to vary when all inputs are not only changed at the same time, but are changed in the same proportion as well. Three types of consequences occur when all inputs are changed simultaneously and in the same proportion: constant, increasing, or decreasing returns to scale.

Constant Returns to Scale

If a simultaneous and equal percentage change in the use of all physical inputs leads to an *identical* percentage change in physical output, a firm's production function is said to exhibit **constant returns to scale**. Ordinarily, this is the kind of result one would expect. If a firm can combine, for example, 1,000 apple trees, 3 tons of fertilizer, 2 orchard-spraying machines, etc., with 4 workers to produce 7,000 bushels of apples in a year, why shouldn't it be able to combine 2,000 apple trees, 6 tons of fertilizer, 4 orchard-spraying machines, and 2 etc. with 8 workers to produce 14,000 bushels of apples in a year? Indeed, it might, as Table 5.3 illustrates. The data in columns (1) to (3) have been taken from Table 5.1. They might represent the original technical alternatives open to the firm, with the formerly fixed inputs in column (1) denoting 1,000 apple trees, 3 tons of fertilizer, and the like. The data in columns (4) to (6) then represent a different set of technical alternatives that would prevail if the firm doubled all inputs, including the previously fixed ones. Obviously, these data are only illustrative. Inputs can be changed by *any* percentage; there is nothing magic about *doubling* all inputs (an increase of 100 percent.) For example, under constant returns to scale, a 5.2 percent increase (or decrease) in all inputs would increase (or decrease) output by 5.2 percent as well. Such constant returns to scale, however, do not always occur.

Increasing Returns to Scale

If a simultaneous and equal percentage change in the use of all physical inputs leads to a *larger* percentage change in physical output, a firm's production function is said to exhibit **increasing returns to scale**, which are also called **economies of mass production** or simply **economies of scale**. Why should the average products of all inputs rise when scale is increased and, therefore, fall when scale is reduced? A number of possible reasons can be cited. Most important among these are the advantages inherent in a specialization of inputs (a subject first introduced in Chapter 2) and the operation of certain physical laws.

As the scale of production becomes larger, the process of production can be broken down into a multitude of ever-narrower tasks, and more and more people and machines can specialize in performing these different tasks. As a result, people who have different inherent talents can concentrate on what they can do best. The person with a knack for mechanics can work full-time fixing orchard-spraying machines when there are 300 of them but could hardly make a full-time job out of fixing just one. At the same time, other people can specialize in accounting, financing, marketing, apple picking, bee keeping, research, or perhaps even in worker dental care. Even when talents are not inherent, it is easier to create and then maintain skills in people when each person's work is reduced to a simple and repetitive operation: "practice makes perfect." This advantage is lost to the Jack-of-all-trades who must pass from operation to operation, moving, possibly, among many different locations of work, using ever-different sets of tools, and all the while losing valuable time in-between tasks or while "warming up" for a new one.

The very simplicity and repetitiveness of narrowly specialized, large-scale operations encourages, in turn, the invention and use of machines. When only 900 bushels of apples are produced per year, who would think of installing an assembly line to sort and wash them? The introduction of all kinds of specialized capital equipment, from electric turbines and internal combustion engines to computers and servo-mechanisms, testifies to the endless possibilities of increasing' productivity through the use of specialization.

TABLE 5.3   Constant Returns to Scale Illustrated

	Scale 1			Scale 2		
	Inputs (respective units per year)		Output (bushels per year)	Inputs (respective units per year)		Output (bushels per year)
	Capital and Land (1)	Labor (2)	Apples (3)	Capital and Land (4)	Labor (5)	Apples (6)
(A)	1	0	0	2	0	0
(B)	1	1	1,000	2	2	2,000
(C)	1	2	2,700	2	4	5,400
(D)	1	3	5,000	2	6	10,000
(E)	1	4	7,000 →	2	8	14,000
(F)	1	5	8,300	2	10	16,600
(G)	1	6	9,000	2	12	18,000
(H)	1	7	9,300	2	14	18,600

If a simultaneous and equal percentage change in the use of all its physical inputs leads to an identical percentage change in its physical output, a firm's production function is said to exhibit *constant returns to scale*. Note how, in this example, the doubling of all inputs also doubles the return they bring; that is, total output. When columns (1) and (2) become columns (4) and (5), column (3) becomes column (6). The same process would, of course, work in reverse: If constant returns to scale existed, the halving of all inputs would halve the associated outputs.

The operation of certain physical laws is also responsible for increasing returns to scale. Consider a box that is 1 foot long, 1 foot wide, and 1 foot high. It has a surface area of 6 square feet and a volume of 1 cubic foot. If one quadruples the length, width, and height, the surface area becomes 96 square feet, and the volume grows to 64 cubic feet. A 16-fold increase in surface area produces a 64-fold increase in volume! Frequently, the input quantities needed to construct "containers," such as cargo ships, office buildings, or pipelines, depend on their surface area, but their output depends on their volume. Larger scale, therefore, yields more output per unit of input. Many similar examples can be cited: A 20-ton stamping machine can be more effective than 500 hammers made with the same inputs; high-temperature processes often work better on a larger scale; a 1,000-horsepower motor may take fewer inputs to build than two 500-horsepower motors do; firms may need fewer administrators or pieces of standby equipment per unit of output and fewer inventories per dollar of sales the larger are output and sales.

Decreasing Returns to Scale

If a simultaneous and equal percentage change in the use of all physical inputs leads to a *smaller* percentage change in physical output, a firm's production function is said to exhibit **decreasing returns to scale**, which are also called **diseconomies of scale**. Why should the average products of all inputs fall when scale is increased and, therefore, rise when scale is reduced? Specialization, as we noted in Chapter 2, carries with it the cost of coordination. Within firms, managerial coordination rules; it becomes more difficult on a larger scale.

The most important reason for decreasing returns to scale is the increasing inability of management to make right things go right and keep wrong things from going wrong! Recall the knowledge problem, first discussed in Chapter 2 (see pp. 28-30). We then focused on the whole economy, but in the case of a single firm the problem still arises: How can each employee know at all times what he or she must do if the goal of the firm is to be achieved? Once more, a

ANALYTICAL EXAMPLE 5.3:
The Energy Crisis and Input Substitution in U.S. Agriculture

American agriculture during this century has experienced sizable increases in productivity, many of them related to increased use of energy. In 1979, U.S. farms were using more than 4 million tractors, 3 million trucks, and half a million combines. Some 35 million acres were irrigated; 20 million tons of fertilizer and almost half a million tons of pesticides were used. Because all of these inputs require energy for their manufacture or operation, U.S. agriculture seems very susceptible to disruptions in energy supplies. This seems all the more true because the biological nature of agriculture is such that serious output loss occurs unless operations are performed regularly or during critical periods. (Consider the importance of regularity in the environmental control of poultry housing or the importance of timing in the planting of corn and the harvesting of wheat).

In order to gauge possibilities for input substitution that would make agriculture less dependent on regular and sufficient energy supplies, an agricultural production function was estimated. Agricultural output was taken to be a function of land, hired labor, mechanical energy (in the form of farm machinery and fuels), and chemical energy (fertilizers and pesticides). The accompanying table lists the elasticities of substitution derived from this function.

As the frequency of rather high elasticity estimates indicates, there is a surprising degree of flexibility in the use of agricultural inputs. If energy supplies were seriously reduced, U.S. agricultural output could be maintained by substituting land or labor for mechanical energy, as in columns (1) and (3). It would be much harder to substitute them for chemical energy, as in columns (2) and (4). In the short run, it would, of course, be easiest to substitute one form of energy (say, tractor cultivation) for another (say, chemical weed control), as column (5) indicates.

multitude of knowledge fragments, dispersed in the minds of separate individuals and not available to a single mind in its totality, have to be used jointly. There are only two methods of doing this. First, one can convey to a single mind (or that of a very small group of persons) all the knowledge that should be used but is, in the first instance, given to others. That mind can then digest the knowledge, formulate a plan of action, and issue appropriate orders that tell everyone else what to do. Second, one can convey to each person whatever additional knowledge is needed to dovetail independent individual actions with those of all others.

While the market economy as a whole uses the second method to coordinate the actions of households and firms, each individual firm inter-

nally uses the first method instead. The employees of a firm do not make their own decisions on the basis of price signals. Rather, they are being paid for their willingness to obey the authority of central planners! A supervisor does not *induce* a worker to oil machine X in shop Y by offering to pay more for this task than for another one. Rather, he *orders* the oiling to be done and that's that! Thus a large firm may be viewed as countless people placed in an administrative hierarchy (reaching from the top echelon of executives down to the lowliest of night watchguards). They are all tied together by an elaborate system of communications channels through which information flows up and orders flow down.

This observation brings us to the main point: Since the decision-making power of top manage-

Region	Elasticities of Substitution Between:				
	Land and Mechanical Energy (1)	Land and Chemical Energy (2)	Hired Labor and Mechanical Energy (3)	Hired Labor and Chemical Energy (4)	Mechanical Energy and Chemical Energy (5)
United States	1.36	0.78	1.91	0.27	1.19
Northeast	1.35	0.84	2.12	0.23	1.48
Appalachian	1.35	0.87	1.99	0.25	1.31
Southeast	1.33	0.92	1.97	0.26	1.38
Lake states	1.37	0.80	1.98	0.23	1.16
Corn belt	1.39	0.80	2.26	0.05	1.16
Delta states	1.35	0.85	2.00	0.25	1.33
Northern plains	1.37	0.72	2.05	0.60	0.96
Southern plains	1.35	0.76	1.79	0.31	1.06
Mountain	1.34	0.65	1.67	0.36	0.99
Pacific	1.35	0.72	1.98	0.18	1.42

Note the regional elasticity differences for any given policy. A policy maker would be well advised to take account of them. Consider the substitution of labor for machinery in column (3). This is considerably easier in the Corn Belt ($\sigma = 2.26$), where large-scale corn and soybean production takes place, than in the Mountain Region ($\sigma = 1.67$), where small-scale operations produce specialized crops on irrigated plots of land.

Source: Kerry Webb and Marvin Duncan, "Energy Alternatives in U.S. Crop Production," *Federal Reserve Bank of Kansas City Economic Review*, February 1979, pp. 14–23.

ment would be paralyzed by any attempt to give it *all* the information that is contained in the minds of all employees and that is relevant to the joint productive enterprise, the function of the firm's hierarchy is to *prevent* information from reaching the upper ranks of management except in highly condensed and abstract form! Important as it is to know that machine X in shop Y needs oiling, top management must be spared the knowledge of this fact. The upward-bound information channels must operate like a stratified sieve. As information possessed by any employee travels up the hierarchy (such as worker A's knowledge about squeaky machine X in shop Y), it must be acted upon at the lowest available executive rank (as by a supervisor's order that the machine be oiled). Thus all infor-

mation, wherever it originates, must be stopped at the next highest level and translated into instructions. But it must also be translated into more abstract and condensed form and passed on up the hierarchy. Our supervisor, for instance, must eventually order another 100 gallons of oil from the purchasing department. And the purchasing department must eventually report to the accounting department monthly costs of $10 million for all kinds of supplies, one of which was a 100-gallon drum of oil (which would be a detail of no interest to top management at all). But the accountants must eventually report figures on overall annual revenue and production cost to top management. Thus the squeaky machine, in totally unrecognizable fashion, makes itself known at the top!

Communications flowing in the reverse direction must have a corresponding fate. General orders from the top (say, to cut costs) must eventually be translated into specific orders further down (such as to throw out that oil-guzzling machine X in shop Y and replace it with a brand-new machine Z).

Now imagine what happens when a firm grows and grows and grows. Some 76 employees turn into 760, and 760 turn into 7,600, and they, in turn, become 760,000. The channels of communication become longer and longer. And the chances that essential information will not get through become greater and greater! There are so many workers and supervisors and Vice-Presidents In Charge Of This-and-That! It becomes difficult to determine who is responsible for what. Some things are done ten times; some not at all. Perhaps 50 different people waste a total of 10 valuable hours reporting and fixing that one squeaky machine. Perhaps no one at all

bothers about the machine, since everyone expects someone else to be responsible. So a $50,000 machine turns into a $325 piece of scrap for lack of $7.16 worth of oil. Would you be surprised if that firm's average product went down?

Indeed, this incident may give rise to a new Office for Scientific Management. Reams of paper and hundreds of hours of labor may be devoted to producing exact job descriptions for every position in the firm that tell what each person must and must not do. Yet all this red tape may not help at all. Even though worker number 39,373 is supposed to oil machine X in shop Y (according to page 291 of *the* booklet), the next time machine X needs oil, worker number 39,373 may just happen to be ill, to be giving birth to a baby, or to be away on jury duty. The machine-destroying accident may happen all over again because it is impossible to lay down iron-clad rules for all conceivable contingencies.

CLOSE-UP 5.1:

The Optimum Size of Cargo Ships

In recent years, the average size of cargo ships has been increasing rapidly, but a limit to this trend is in sight. The output of a ship can be viewed as the *quantity of cargo it hauls per mile*. Because the quantity of labor and materials required to build a container is a function of its surface area, while holding and hauling capacity is a function of the volume enclosed, the hauling operations of a ship tend to be subject to increasing returns to scale. The hauling cost per ton tends to *decrease* with larger ship size.

A ship in port, however, is a different matter from a ship at sea. The output of a ship in port is better viewed as the *quantity of cargo it loads or unloads per day*. The capacity to handle cargo in port tends to be a function of the length of ship because length determines the number of possible hatches and cranes. Because length cannot grow in proportion to volume, the handling operations of a ship tend to be subject to decreasing

returns to scale. The handling cost per ton tends to *increase* with larger ship size.

Economies of scale in *hauling* cargo must, therefore, be traded off against diseconomies in *handling* it. This yields an optimum ship size where the marginal benefit of large size (lower hauling cost per ton) just equals the associated marginal cost (higher handling cost per ton).

In 1980, the Chevron Shipping Company subjected four of its supertankers to "downsizing," a process akin to removing the center leaf of a dining room table and shoving the table back together again. Four 200,000-ton ships were sliced apart, a 100-foot section was removed from the middle of each, and the remainder was rewelded together. The result was a set of four 150,000 ton tankers capable of operating in ports that were previously inaccessible.

Sources: Jan Owen Jansson and Dan Shneerson, "Economies of Scale of General Cargo Ships," *The Review of Economics and Statistics*, May 1978, pp. 287–93; "Shrinking the Oversized Supertanker," *The New York Times*, July 18, 1980, pp. D1 and 6.

Would you be surprised if that firm's average product went down?

This new incident may cause a lot of bad blood. There may be charges and countercharges. Who was responsible? Nobody, according to the rule book, of course, but this doesn't make sense to anybody. Before long, workers will feel caught up in and overwhelmed by a vast impersonal bureaucracy. Their morale will sag. Work will slow down. Absenteeism will rise. There will be careless work. Would you be surprised if that firm's average product went down?

There may also be trouble at the top. Information essential to the prosperity or even survival of the firm may be lost or garbled during its tortuous travels along ever-longer communication routes. Or even this condensed information may become so voluminous as to be impossible to handle. As a result, top management may make wrong decisions: they may fail to be responsive to new opportunities or they may act at the wrong time—and mistakes at that level may cost billions of dollars! Indeed, at its worst, management may completely lose contact with reality. It may become the victim of a sort of organizational mental illness: Top people may come to be surrounded by aides eager to please their superiors, always ready to confirm their ideas. These aides may deliberately filter out information contradicting the top people's image of the world they guide. As a result, that image may become unshakable. Top management may become incapable of learning anything new. Thinking themselves to be looking out of a window, they may actually be looking at a mirror! Would you be surprised if that firm's average product went down?

Our earlier discussion of physical laws provides another way of thinking about decreasing returns to scale. It may in fact be impossible to make true scale changes in a firm. Recall the above discussion of the geometric properties of a box. When length, width, and height are scaled up from 1 to 4, surface area rises from 1 to 16, volume from 1 to 64. In what sense then is a larger box a scaled-up version of a smaller one? Something like scaling up a box may happen

during the growth of a firm. When some of its dimensions (such as the numbers of workers and machines) are increased a thousandfold, other dimensions (such as the required length of communication channels and the required number of messages) may increase by a millionfold. If management increases a thousandfold, too, disaster may be close at hand. Perhaps the forgoing story about decreasing returns to scale simply reflects old-fashioned diminishing returns to variable inputs in the presence of the *relatively* fixed input of management.

Note: The forgoing speculation notwithstanding, one should not confuse constant, increasing, and decreasing returns *to scale* with constant, increasing, and decreasing returns *to a single variable input*. Returns to scale occur when all inputs change and do so in the same proportion. When all inputs are increased in this way, they yield, respectively, constant, increasing, or decreasing *average* products. Returns to a single variable input, on the other hand, occur while some other inputs are fixed. When this variable input is increased, it yields, respectively, constant, increasing, or decreasing *marginal* products.

Returns to Scale and Isoquants

Each of the three types of returns to scale produces a distinctive pattern on an isoquant map. Consider Figure 5.4. Panel (a) pictures a family of isoquants for a production function subject to *constant* returns to scale. Note how 50 units of output are produced by 3 units of capital and 1 unit of labor (point A). Double both inputs, and output doubles as well (point B). Triple them, and output triples (point C). When constant returns to scale prevail, distance $0A = AB = BC$ along any ray from the origin, indicating that any given percentage change in output requires an *identical* percentage change in all inputs.

Panel (b) pictures isoquants for a production function subject to *increasing* returns to scale. Note how 50 units of output are produced by 3 units of capital and 1 unit of labor (point D).

FIGURE 5.4 The Spacing of Isoquants

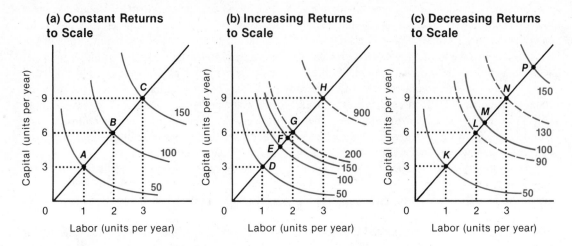

The presence of constant, increasing, or decreasing returns to scale, as in panels (a) to (c), respectively, can be recognized by looking at the spacing of isoquants.

Double both inputs, and output quadruples (point *G*); triple them, and it rises 18 fold (point *H*). The isoquant (now dashed) for 100 units of output in panel (a) is labeled 200 units now; the one for 150 units in (a) carries a 900-unit label in (b). When increasing returns to scale prevail, successively numbered isoquants get ever closer along any ray from the origin. In our case, although the difference between the relevant isoquants remains at 50 units of output, distance $0D > DE > EF$, indicating that any given percentage change in output requires a *smaller* percentage change in all inputs.

Panel (c), finally, pictures isoquants for a production function subject to *decreasing* returns to scale. Note how 50 units of output are produced by 3 units of capital and 1 unit of labor (point *K*). Double both inputs, and output fails to double (point *L*); triple them, and it fails to triple (point *N*). The isoquant (now dashed) for 100 units of output in panel (a) is labeled 90 units now; the one for 150 units in (a) carries a 130-unit label in (c). When decreasing returns to scale prevail, successively numbered isoquants lie farther and farther apart along any ray from the origin. In our case, although the difference

between the relevant isoquants remains at 50 units of output, distance $0K < KM < MP$, indicating that any given percentage change in output requires a *larger* percentage change in all inputs.

Empirical Studies of Production Functions

Economists derive their ideas about production functions in a variety of ways, including engineering estimates, market observations, time-series studies, and cross-section studies.

Engineering Estimates

Chapter 4 noted how consumer interviews and consumer clinics might be used to study demand. In an analogous approach, the economist turns to technical experts, such as engineers and agricultural scientists, to study production functions. Based on their day-to-day experience with the productive process or on the deliberate performance of controlled experiments, such experts may supply information about physical input-output

ANALYTICAL EXAMPLE 5.4:
The Production of Culture

One economist recently estimated production functions for five of the "fine arts": Theater, opera, symphony, ballet, and modern dance. Using 1966–74 Ford Foundation data for 164 performing arts companies, James Gapinski measured output by the number of cultural experiences enjoyed by patrons and then related it to three types of inputs: labor services of artists, labor services of "adjuvants" (administrators, box office and maintenance help, parking lot attendants, promotional personnel, stage hands, ushers, and the like), and capital services (of structures, musical instruments, stage sets, costumes, scores, scripts, and the like).

The accompanying table shows excerpts from a multitude of fascinating implications of the estimated production functions.

	Theater	Opera	Symphony	Ballet
Part A				
Scale Coefficient				
$\lambda = 0.25$	0.2823	0.2802	0.3079	0.1315
$\lambda = 0.75$	0.7610	0.7640	0.7741	0.7309
$\lambda = 1.25$	1.2398	1.2359	1.2263	1.2036
$\lambda = 2.00$	1.9438	1.9517	1.9129	1.4531
$\lambda = 3.00$	2.7445	2.9391	2.8260	1.3347
$\lambda = 4.00$	3.2361	3.9701	3.6750	1.1139
Part B				
Elasticity of Input Substitution				
1. Artists, capital	0.7533	0.7198	0.8510	0.7223
2. Adjuvants, capital	1.1225	1.3308	1.1189	1.7114
3. Artists, adjuvants	1.4134	3.6444	2.1612	1.5506

Part (A) shows what happened to output when all inputs were simultaneously multiplied by some coefficient, such as 0.25 or 4.00. Theater, opera, and symphony showed decreasing returns to scale for all scalar adjustments. (For example, the reduction of all theater inputs to 25 percent reduced theater output to only 28.23 percent; a 4-fold increase of all theater inputs raised theater output only 3.2361-fold.) Ballet, however, was a maverick, showing increasing returns to scale for input decreases and extreme decreasing returns to scale for input increases. (For example, a reduction of all ballet inputs to 25 percent reduced ballet output to 13.15 percent; a 4-fold increase of all ballet inputs raised ballet output only 1.1139-fold.)

Part (B) shows estimates of the elasticity of substitution for different input pairs. Note that this elasticity is uniformly low for artists and capital (1), indicating that they cannot very easily be substituted for one another. Elasticity is not as low for adjuvants and capital (2). Finally, the elasticity is fairly high for artists and adjuvants (3): one type of labor can easily be substituted for another type.

Source: James H. Gapinski, "The Production of Culture," *The Review of Economics and Statistics*, November 1980, p. 584. Copyright © 1980 by the President and Fellows of Harvard College.

relationships. The German agricultural scientist Johann Heinrich von Thünen, (see Biography 5.1), for example, was a pioneer in exploring the nature of production functions by careful experiment. He collected the kinds of data found in Table 5.1 by applying, in a given locale and year, different amounts of variable inputs to various plots of identical land. Each of the rows, labeled (A) through (J) in Table 5.1, might represent one of his experiments. In that fashion, Thünen independently discovered the law of first increasing, but eventually diminishing returns, which had been first stated (in 1767) by the French statesman, M. de Turgot (1727–81).

Market Observations

A second approach to the study of production functions, somewhat analogous to the market experiments described in Chapter 4, is to observe the fate of firms in their respective markets. University of Chicago economist George Stigler has suggested the **survivor principle** as a method of making inferences about the production function in an industry.[1] The fundamental postulate of this principle is that competition among differently sized firms in an industry will, in the long run, allow only the technically most efficient firms to survive. Hence, the characteristics of these survivors reveal those of the industry's production function.

If firms of many different sizes survive in an industry in the long run, Stigler argues, we can conclude that technical efficiency is not a function of the size of firms and that constant returns to scale exist. If, over time, firms of small size are supplanted by larger ones, we can suspect the presence of increasing returns to scale in small firms. On the other hand, if large firms eventually give way to smaller ones, the presence of decreasing returns to scale can be assumed.

Stigler studied firms in a number of indus-

tries, among them those making steel ingots by open-hearth or Bessemer processes. He classified the firms involved by size, calculated the share of each class in industry output, and observed the historical trend of these shares. Table 5.4 is taken from his study. Stigler noted the persistent and rapid decline in the number of firms and their output shares in class (A), as well as the less spectacular decline in classes (B), (C), and (G). Similarly, the growth in number and output shares of firms in classes (D) to (F), suggested to him constant returns to scale in this industry over a wide range of sizes of firms (from 2.5 to 25 percent of industry capacity).

Time-Series Studies

A third approach to the study of production functions is to gather statistical data for one firm or group of firms on inputs used and outputs produced in various past periods and assume that the different input-output relationships observed for these past periods can be considered alternatives available in the present. The major problem associated with this approach is *the identification problem*, the difficulty of identifying a large number of potential data from a few historical data each of which may belong to a different set of potential data. This problem has already been discussed in Chapter 4 in connection with demand functions. In the case of production-function measurement, additional problems arise. Apart from the possible unwillingness of firms to disclose the relevant data, economists often find themselves unable to measure physical inputs and outputs. How does one measure and add together labor services when so many different types are being performed with varying degrees of skill? How is one to measure and add together capital services that come from a multitude of structures, machines, and the like, each unit of which, furthermore, is at a different stage in its life cycle? How is one to measure the output of a college, a hospital, a law firm, or a police department? How about that of the Equal Employment Opportunities Commission or the Department of Defense? Even the seemingly obvious output of an apple orchard might be difficult

[1]George J. Stigler, "The Economies of Scale," *The Journal of Law and Economics*, October 1958, pp. 54–71. For an appraisal, *see* William G. Shepherd, "What Does the Survivor Technique Show About Economies of Scale?" *The Southern Economic Journal*, July 1967, pp. 113–22.

TABLE 5.4 The Survivor Principle and the U.S. Steel Ingot Industry

Class	Each Firm in Class	Percentage of Industry Output Produced by:			Number of Firms in Class		
		All Firms in Class					
		1930	1938	1951	1930	1938	1951
(A)	Under 0.5	7.16	6.11	4.65	39	29	22
(B)	0.5 to 1	5.94	5.08	5.37	9	7	7
(C)	1 to 2.5	13.17	8.30	9.07	9	6	6
(D)	2.5 to 5	10.64	16.59	22.21	3	4	5
(E)	5 to 10	11.18	14.03	8.12	2	2	1
(F)	10 to 25	13.24	13.99	16.10	1	1	1
(G)	25 and over	38.67	35.91	34.50	1	1	1

SOURCE: George J. Stigler, "The Economies of Scale," *The Journal of Law and Economics,* October 1958, pp. 54–71. Reprinted by permission of the University of Chicago Press. Copyright 1958 by the University of Chicago.

to measure, if not only apples, but also cider and jelly are produced, along with such by-products as hay and honey in the summer and sleigh rides in the winter. Economists, of course, do make such measurements, but these measurements are rarely immune to criticism.

Paul H. Douglas, an economist who later became a distinguished U.S. Senator, and Charles W. Cobb, a mathematician, were among the pioneers of the time-series approach to production-function measurement. Using U.S. 1899–1922 data on labor services, L, capital services, K, and aggregate real output, Q, they calculated an economywide production function for all firms in manufacturing. Their regression equation took the form $Q = AL^a K^b$, wherein A, a,

and b were positive constants. This so-called **Cobb-Douglas production function** is a special type of constant-elasticity-of-substitution, or **CES production function**. Its elasticity of input substitution is always equal to unity. The sum of $a + b$, furthermore, is a returns-to-scale parameter. When there are constant returns to scale, the sum equals unity; $a + b$ exceeds unity for increasing returns to scale; $a + b$ falls short of unity in the presence of decreasing returns to scale.

The crucial parameters of the Cobb and Douglas study are given in row (A) of Table 5.5. The results of comparable studies by Douglas and other researchers are given in rows (B) through (E). Note that the size of a indicates the percent-

TABLE 5.5 Production Function Parameters: Time-Series Estimates

Country	Period	a	b	a +b
(A) United States	1899–1922	0.73	0.25	0.98
(B) Victoria	1907–29	0.84	0.23	1.07
(C) New South Wales	1901–27	0.78	0.20	0.98
(D) Norway	1900–55	0.76	0.20	0.96
(E) New Zealand	1915–35*	0.42	0.49	0.91

For aggregates of manufacturing firms, time-series regression studies (based on Cobb-Douglas functions of $Q = AL^a K^b$) consistently produce results close to constant returns to scale, shown by the fact that the sum of coefficients a and b approximates unity.
*excluding 1917.
SOURCE: Paul H. Douglas, "Are There Laws of Production?" *The American Economic Review,* March 1948, pp. 1–41; A.A. Walters, "Production and Cost Functions: An Econometric Survey," *Econometrica,* January–April 1963, pp. 1–66.

TABLE 5.6   Production Function Parameters: Cross-Section Estimates

Country	Year	Industry	a	b	a+b
(A) United States	1957	Furniture	0.90	0.20	1.10
		Chemicals	0.89	0.20	1.09
		Printing	0.62	0.46	1.08
		Food, beverages	0.51	0.56	1.07
	1909	Foods	0.72	0.35	1.07
	1957	Rubber, plastics	0.58	0.48	1.06
		Instruments	0.83	0.21	1.04
		Lumber	0.65	0.39	1.04
		Apparel	0.91	0.13	1.04
		Leather	0.96	0.08	1.04
		Stone, clay	0.40	0.63	1.03
		Fabricated metals	0.88	0.15	1.03
		Electrical machinery	0.66	0.38	1.03
		Nonelectrical machinery	0.62	0.40	1.02
		Transport equipment	0.79	0.23	1.02
	1919	Manufacturing	0.76	0.25	1.01
	1957	Textiles	0.88	0.12	1.00
		Paper, pulp	0.56	0.42	0.98
	1909	Metals, machinery	0.71	0.26	0.97
	1957	Primary metals	0.59	0.37	0.96
		Petroleum	0.64	0.31	0.95
(B) Canada	1952/67	Telephone	0.71	0.41	1.11
	1937	Manufacturing	0.43	0.58	1.01
(C) France	1945	Gas	0.80	0.14	0.94
(D) United Kingdom	1950	Coal	0.79	0.29	1.08
(E) South Africa	1937/38	Manufacturing	0.66	0.32	0.98
(F) India	1951	Basic chemicals	0.80	0.37	1.17
		Coal	0.71	0.44	1.15
		Paper	0.64	0.45	1.09
		Cotton	0.92	0.12	1.04
		Jute	0.84	0.14	0.98
		Sugar	0.59	0.33	0.92
		Electricity	0.20	0.67	0.87
(G) Australia	1912	Manufacturing	0.52	0.47	0.99

For firms in various industries and countries, cross-section regression studies (based on Cobb-Douglas functions of $Q = AL^a K^b$) consistently produce results suggesting the existence of close-to-constant returns to scale. This is shown by the fact that the sum of coefficients a and b approximates unity.

SOURCES: Same as Table 5.5; also A. Rodney Dobell et al., "Telephone Communications in Canada: Demand, Production, and Investment Decisions," *The Bell Journal of Economics and Management Science,* Spring 1972, pp. 175–219; John R. Moroney, "Cobb-Douglas Production Functions and Returns to Scale in U.S. Manufacturing Industry," *Western Economic Journal,* December 1967, pp. 39–51.

age increase in aggregate manufacturing output that could be expected from a 1 percent increase in labor services, all else being equal. The size of *b* indicates the increase in output expected from a 1 percent increase in capital services. Thus the Cobb and Douglas study, row (A), predicts a .98 percent increase in manufacturing output from a 1 percent increase in both labor and capital inputs—almost constant returns to scale.

Cross-section studies

A fourth approach to the study of production functions is to gather statistical data for a given year on inputs used and outputs produced by different firms or groups of firms and assume that the different input-output relationships observed among these firms or groups can be considered present alternatives available to each of them. This approach has also been discussed in Chapter 4 in connection with the statistical measurement of demand. Table 5.6 brings together the results from a wide variety of cross-section studies.

Cross-section studies have also yielded important information about the elasticity of input substitution. While the mathematical property of the Cobb-Douglas function is such that the elasticity of substitution is always a constant equal to unity, some researchers have calculated CES production functions that allow the elasticity constant to be different from unity (or even **VES production functions** that allow for the possibility of a *variable elasticity of substitution*). Consider Table 5.7, which shows estimates of elasticities of capital-labor substitution. In general, the results indicate that capital-labor substitution is easier in primary production than in manufacturing.

Second Thoughts: The Matter of X-Inefficiency

In recent years, an admittedly controversial theory has become a subject of debate. If you take another look at the definition of the production function, you will notice that it is about the relationship of inputs to the *maximum* output obtainable from them. Statistical studies, however, look at *actual* output obtained. Unless we can

TABLE 5.7 Selected Estimates of Elasticities of Capital–Labor Substitution

(A) Primary Production

Petroleum, natural gas	1.71
Metal mining	1.41
Agriculture	1.20
Nonmetallic minerals	1.18
Fishing	0.94
Coal mining	0.93

(B) Manufacturing

Coal	1.35
Publishing, printing	1.21
Paper	1.14
Nonferrous metals	1.10
Nonmetallic mineral production	1.08
Transport equipment	1.04
Petroleum products	1.04
Iron and steel	1.00
Rubber	0.98
Shipbuilding	0.97
Processed food	0.93
Machinery	0.93
Chemicals	0.90
Lumber and wood products	0.84
Grain milling production	0.81
Textiles	0.80
Leather products	0.72
Apparel	0.42

(C) Utilities and Services

Transport	1.74
Trade	1.12
Electric power	0.82

The elasticities shown above were estimated from CES-production functions calculated from U.S. and Japanese data.
SOURCE: Adapted from K. J. Arrow, H. B. Chenery, B. S. Minhas, R. M. Solow, "Capital-Labor Substitution and Economic Efficiency," *The Review of Economics and Statistics*, August 1961, p. 240. Copyright, 1961, by the President and Fellows of Harvard College.

BIOGRAPHY 5.1:

Johann H. von Thünen

Johann Heinrich von Thünen (1783–1850) was born into an old feudal family in the Grand Duchy of Oldenburg, Germany. On his father's estate, Kanarienhausen, he developed an early interest in agriculture and mathematics. He attended an agricultural college near Hamburg, and later the University of Göttingen but never graduated; he preferred the career of a practical farmer. Nevertheless, he had many insights of genius. Above all else, these insights concerned the production function, the location of economic activities, and the distribution of income. His thoughts are preserved in his single major book, *The Isolated State in Relation to Agriculture and Political Economy*, which appeared in four installments between 1826 and 1863.

Unlike any of his contemporaries except Cournot (see Biography 11.1) and Gossen, von Thünen applied mathematics to economic analysis. On his estate in Mecklenburg, he kept meticulous farm accounts from 1810–20, costing every plot of land, every bushel of rye, every cow and goose. By doing so, von Thünen became the first investigator who put his occupational life into the service of scientific economic research. He thus became the patron saint of *econometrics* (the application of statistical methods to the study of economics). The data he collected served as the empirical basis for his discovery of the law of eventually diminishing marginal products.

His agricultural activities also led von Thünen to a brilliant and original vision, which many consider his peak achievement. He envisioned an extended domain, of circular form and uniform fertility, isolated from the rest of the world, free from all obstacles to or special facilities for transport (such as mountains or rivers), with a single source of demand for agricultural products—a town in its center. He demonstrated how the uniform variation of transport costs with distance, which follows from his assumptions, would bring about a regional specialization among different products and different techniques of producing the same product. This specialization would reveal itself in the establishment of a series of concentric rings around the town, each being the optimal location for a different type of activity. Products that were perishable, imposed heavy transport costs, or had to be cultivated intensively would be produced near the population center; others would be produced farther away. (He pictured seven rings of activities outwards from the town: horticulture, forestry for building and fuel, cereal production by crop rotation, cereal production by alternating crops and pasture, cereal production via the three-field system, stock farming, and hunting.) Von Thünen showed that differential rent would arise to reflect differential advantage of location. He later introduced differential fertility and additional towns as well. He thus anticipated the location theories of Alfred Weber and August Lösch and proved himself superior to his British contemporary, David Ricardo, whose rent theory was based on fertility differences alone, a single product (corn), and zero transport costs. (That theory is discussed in Figure 8.13, "Ricardo's Differential Rents," on page 235.)

In a third major accomplishment, von Thünen developed a theory of income distribution based on the concept of marginal productivity. He stated clearly and explicitly that the (real) wage of all workers, in a large firm employing many workers, would tend to equal the marginal product of the last worker employed. Consider Table 5.1, row (G): If a 6th worker raises annual output by 700

assume that firms always get the maximum output from any given set of inputs they use, all statistical measurements of production functions are seriously flawed. In 1966, Harvey Leibenstein (see Biography 5.2) challenged economists to examine the possibility that firms do not always obtain the maximum possible output. For a century, he argued, economists have focused on the removal of *economic* inefficiency but have ignored another kind of inefficiency, which he

bushels of apples per year, no employer would pay more than 700 bushels as a wage. If all workers are alike and 6 are hired, all get this wage regardless of the chronological order in which they are hired. Von Thünen applied this thinking to capital as well, suggesting that the profit of capital would equal the marginal product of the last small portion of capital employed. Von Thünen was, however, baffled by these results: If his theory of actual wage (or profit) determination was correct, all units, except for the labor (or capital) unit hired last, would be receiving less than the marginal products associated with the chronological order of their hiring. See Table 5.1, column (4). This seemed unfair. Such thoughts led von Thünen into the realm of normative statements. Living in the stormy days when social revolution, incited by the misery of workers, seemed imminent, he looked for an *ethical principle* that would reconcile the claims of workers (demanding "the whole produce of labor") with those of the owners of capital and land (offering "bare subsistence" to the workers). Von Thünen suggested a compromise, a "natural wage," w, equal to the geometric mean between a worker's subsistence requirements, a, and total product, p. In his own eyes, the formula $w = \sqrt{ap}$ was his highest achievement. He had it engraved on his tombstone to indicate not how wages actually were determined, but how they ought to be determined in a just society.

Indeed, von Thünen exhibited great concern for his own workers. At a time when most employers treated farm hands like cattle, he supported a doctor, nurse, and cottage-hospital on his estate for the free treatment of all workers and their families. He provided sick pay and retirement pensions. In return, however, he required punctili-ous performance of duty, paying workers by piece rates whenever possible. In his book, von Thünen also introduced the concept of human capital:

> The reluctance to view a man as capital is especially ruinous of mankind in wartime; here capital is protected, but not man, and in time of war we have no hesitation in sacrificing one hundred men in the bloom of their years to save one cannon. In a hundred men at least twenty times as much capital is lost as is lost in one cannon. But the production of the cannon is the cause of an expenditure of the state treasury, while human beings are again available for nothing by means of a simple conscription order. . . . When the statement was made to Napoleon, the founder of the conscription system, that a planned operation would cost too many men, he replied: "That is nothing. The women produce more of them than I can use."

Unfortunately for economic science, von Thünen's many original ideas never had the influence they deserved. He was a prophet with little honor in any country. In Germany, economic theorists and political liberals were equally despised; von Thünen was both, and his lack of academic status didn't help. In Britain, Ricardo's brilliant advocacy of policies eclipsed the German thinker's superior theoretical ability. It took nearly a century after Ricardo before a British economist of like stature, Alfred Marshall (see Biography 7.1), would say: "I loved von Thünen above all my other masters."[1]

[1]A. C. Pigou, ed., *Memorials of Alfred Marshall* (London: Macmillan, 1925), p. 360.

called *X-inefficiency*. Although both of these concepts will be discussed in detail in Chapter 14, we can quickly establish what Leibenstein had in mind.

Economic inefficiency is a situation in which it is possible, through some reallocation of resources or goods among different firms or households, to make some or all people better off without making others worse off. Consider this example: Imagine two firms (Alpha and Beta) producing the same (or different) products with identical types of inputs (capital, K, and labor, L). If the marginal rate of technical substitution were $5K$ for $1L$ in Alpha but $1K$ for $1L$ in Beta, economic inefficiency would prevail. One could remove, for example, $5K$ from Alpha and give $1K$ to Beta in return for $1L$ that would have to go to Alpha. This would leave Alpha's and Beta's outputs unchanged, while freeing $4K$. These additional units of capital, when used by Alpha, Beta, or any other firm, could then raise output somewhere in the economy. Because the removal of such economic inefficiency always involves a reallocation of resources or goods among different firms or households, this type of inefficiency is also called **allocative inefficiency**.

Leibenstein, in contrast, wanted economists to focus on a matter *internal* to a firm (and long studied in departments of business administration)—namely, the possibility that Alpha and Beta, regardless of the existence or absence of allocative inefficiency, and for reasons internal to each, might be getting less output from the resources at their disposal than was possible. Consider again our example. When Alpha's MRTS was $5K$ for $1L$, its total output was, perhaps, 5,000 bushels of apples per year. Yet a better internal administration of given input quantities might have produced, let us suppose, 6,000 bushels per year. Similarly, when Beta's MRTS was $1K$ for $1L$, its total output, perhaps, was 900 bushels of apples per year (or 500 bicycles per year). Yet the maximum output of Beta might have been 1,100 bushels (or 590 bicycles) instead. Naturally, this kind of situation might prevail even after the removal of allocative inefficiency, when, perhaps, Alpha's and Beta's marginal rates of technical substitution had been equalized at, say, $3K$ for $1L$. Whenever the actual output a firm gets from given resources falls short of the maximum output it *could* get if it administered its resources better, **X-inefficiency** exists. It is measured by the gap between maximum and actual output and can be removed not by a reallocation of resources among different firms, but by a better administration of unchanged quantities of resources *within* each firm.

The Possible Cause of X-Inefficiency

Leibenstein suggested that the kind of slack or technical inefficiency just discussed was most likely to occur as firms grew beyond the stage at which a single owner could keep a watchful eye on everything. He focused on the distinction between *principals* (owners) and *agents* (people working for others). He argued that in multiperson firms exceeding, perhaps, ten persons, agents are free to make many decisions. This is so because employment contracts clearly specify rates of pay in advance but cannot possibly specify every task workers must perform in return. These contracts are necessarily vague and incomplete on all matters relating to worker effort. As a result, workers have a lot of discretion as to the type of activities they perform, the pace of these activities, and their quality (Leibenstein called this area of worker discretion the *APQ bundle*—in reference to *activity type, pace,* and *quality*).

Consider a group of workers in any firm. Unless the group is small and the owner at all times works right along with the rest, the owner has limited control over what workers do. The larger the firm, the more owners there are likely to be, the farther removed from actual operations they must necessarily be, and the more vague must be their instructions. Consider what operating instructions can possibly be given by the owners of General Motors. Even in a much smaller firm, such as the orchard discussed early in the chapter, agents have a lot of discretion. A supervisor may send out workers to root-feed the trees, to prune, spray, or water them, to pick apples, to fix the truck, or to put a new roof on the storage barn. Or workers may be sent out to select their own activities. In either case, the activity types selected may not be the best ones for maximizing output; workers may do their work at a pace unreasonably slow; they may do a sloppy job. The effect on output can be disastrous. Trees improperly fertilized, pruned, sprayed, or watered may yield half their potential crop. Apples carelessly picked may rot in a week.

In most firms, the problem just discussed

ANALYTICAL EXAMPLE 5.5:

Capital-Labor Substitution in Soviet Economic Growth

In 1950, a 10 percent increase in capital by itself would have increased the output of Soviet industry (mining, manufacturing, power) by almost 9 percent; by 1969, the output response to a 10 percent increase in capital had dropped to only 4 percent. This phenomenon has been explained with the help of a CES-production function for Soviet industry for the 1950–69 period. The accompanying graph shows the estimated production isoquant between the services of capital, K, and labor, L. An elasticity of capital-labor substitution significantly less than unity was calculated. The low elasticity estimate ($\sigma = 0.403$) was interpreted as foreshadowing future difficulties with the traditional Soviet growth strategy of capital-labor substitution.

From 1950–69, Soviet capital inputs grew rapidly (at annual rates between 7.9 and 12.6 percent); labor inputs grew much more slowly, if at all (at annual rates from -1.3 to $+5.8$ percent). As one input rose relative to the other, the effect was the same as if it had risen while the other was constant: diminishing returns set in. Output increases based on further capital accumulation decreased.

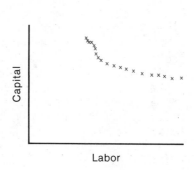

Source: Martin L. Weitzman, "Soviet Postwar Economic Growth and Capital-Labor Substitution," *The American Economic Review*, September 1970, pp. 676–92.

---

cannot possibly be removed by assuring that a single boss knows all, sees all, controls all. The production process is too complex to eliminate all the discretion workers have over their effort. Yet, Leibenstein contends, X-inefficiency can be reduced—for example, by motivating workers better. In contrast to his critics, furthermore, Leibenstein argues that X-inefficiency that can be profitably removed is widespread.

Evidence on X-Inefficiency

When a firm produces less output than is possible, using a given set of inputs, the firm's profit is lower than it could be. The profit is lower because inputs translate into costs, and output becomes revenue. If one could find two firms

exactly alike, except for Leibenstein's X-factor, the one with X-inefficiency should have a lower profit. Recently, an opportunity arose to test this X-inefficiency hypothesis under well-controlled conditions.[2] Investigators studied a string of restaurants operated by one company on a franchise basis. Because of the franchisor's desire to have a uniformly good reputation that would be associated with every eating place despite the fact that each was operated by a different owner, the parent company provided a great deal of direction. It prescribed the restaurant's architecture, each item on the menu, and all prices. Its head

[2]This example is based on John P. Shelton, "Allocative Efficiency vs. 'X-Efficiency': Comment," *The American Economic Review*, December 1967, pp. 1252–58.

BIOGRAPHY 5.2:

Harvey Leibenstein

Harvey Leibenstein (1922-   ) was born in Russia but came to Canada at an early age. He studied at Northwestern University and Princeton and became professor of economics first at the University of California (Berkeley) and in 1967 at Harvard.

The titles of his works reflect his major interests in population economics and X-efficiency theory: *A Theory of Economic Demographic Development*, (1954), *Economic Backwardness and Economic Growth*, (1957), *Economic Theory and Organizational Analysis*, (1960), *Beyond Economic Man: A New Foundation for Microeconomics*, (1976), *General X-Efficiency Theory and Economic Development*, (1978), *Inflation, Income Distribution, and X-Efficiency Theory* (1980).

In the Preface to his *Beyond Economic Man*, Leibenstein introduces his thoughts on X-efficiency with a quotation from Tolstoy's *War and Peace*:

> . . . military science assumes the strength of an army to be identical with its numbers. Military science says that the more troops the greater the strength. *Les gros battaillons ont toujours raison* (Large battalions are always victorious) . . .
>
> In military affairs the strength of an army is the product of its mass and some unknown x . . .
>
> That unknown quantity is the spirit of the army, . . .
>
> The spirit of an army is the factor which multiplied by the mass gives the resulting force. To define and express the significance of this unknown factor—the spirit of an army—is a problem for science.
>
> This problem is only solvable if we cease arbitrarily to substitute for the unknown x itself the conditions under which that force becomes apparent—such as the commands of the general, the equipment employed, and so on—mistaking these for the real significance of the factor, and if we recognize this unknown quantity in its entirety as being the greater or lesser desire to fight and to face danger.

Leibenstein expands:

> Without straining his meaning too much, Tolstoy's argument is similar to one of the central theses of this volume, despite the fact that his concern is the art of war, and mine economics, one of the arts of peace. To shift to the common language of economics, what Tolstoy is saying is that merely knowing the observable *inputs* (the number of guns, men, the commands of the generals, and so on) does not tell you the outcome, contrary to the claims of the "military scientists." Something else is involved, an X-factor that Tolstoy equates with "spirit". Similarly, in . . . this volume I argue that knowing the allocation of inputs and the state of the arts of production is not enough, there is also something else involved—what I have called the X-efficiency element.

Leibenstein's critics, such as George Stigler (see Biography 17.1 and the "Selected Readings" section of this chapter), are apt to dismiss the very concept of X-inefficiency as nonsensical. They tend to view Leibenstein's "missed opportunities within firms" for utilizing existing resources as effectively as they might be used as uncontrollable. In most cases, they contend, the alleged gap between a firm's actual and potential output can in fact not be closed, except at an inordinate cost (such as placing an overseer next to every worker). Therefore, it is not worthwhile to get the extra output. Why spend an extra $5 in better resource administration only to get an extra $1 of output? Leibenstein, of course, disagrees. He thinks firms miss plenty of opportunities to raise output in a cost-effective way.

chef determined optimum recipes so that each franchisee would know exactly how many pounds of coffee to use in the coffee-making equipment, how many slices of bacon to use with an order of eggs, and how many ounces of meat to put in an entree. All ingredients, down to napkins and tableware, were supplied by the parent company, which, also handled the ac-counting centrally. A service manual standard-ized service at each restaurant.

On 22 occasions, a franchisee quit, and the parent company assigned a company manager until a new franchisee could be found. These managers were invariably experienced, having worked with the parent company for many years. The investigators took such opportunities to com-

ANALYTICAL EXAMPLE 5.6:
Evidence on X-Inefficiency Abroad

The International Labor Organization has sent productivity missions to a number of countries. These missions examined the productive process in many firms and suggested simple reorganizations, involving plant layout, materials handling, waste controls, work methods, and payment by results. The increases in output, without any increases in labor or capital inputs, were often spectacular. As the table shows, this was true for technically backward countries, such as Burma, as well as for advanced ones, such as Israel.

Place	Increase in Labor Productivity (percent)	Place	Increase in Labor Productivity (percent)
Burma		**Israel**	
Molding railroad brake shoes	100	Orange picking	91
Chair assembly	100	Refrigerator assembly	75
Smithy	40	Diamond cutting, polishing	45
Match manufacture	24	Locomotive repair	30
Greece		**Malaya**	
Pharmaceutical	20	Pottery	20
India		Furniture	10
Seven textile mills	5-250	Engineering workshop	10
Engineering firms		**Pakistan**	
All operations	102	Weaving	10–141
One operation	385	Bleaching	59
One operation	500	**Thailand**	
Indonesia		Saucepan polishing	50
Radio assembly	40	Locomotive maintenance	44
Printing	30	Saucepan assembly	42
Enamel ware	30	Cigarettes	5
Knitting	15		

Source: Peter Kilby, "Organization and Productivity in Backward Economies," *Quarterly Journal of Economics*, May 1962, Vol. LXXVI, p. 306. Copyright 1962 by Harvard University.

pare the performance of identical restaurants when run by franchise-owners and when run by company managers. The results were clear cut: Establishments run by owners made a profit of 9.5 percent on the average; those run by company managers made a profit of only 1.8 percent. Said a company executive: "When a restaurant is operated by a franchise-owner instead of a company manager . . . profits go up. This is because franchise-owners just watch the little things closer; they utilize the cooks and waitresses better; they reduce waste."

A note of caution: By itself, anecdotal evidence such as the above proves nothing about the overall importance of X-inefficiency. A more systematic evaluation will be undertaken in Chapter 14. In the meantime, however, we are warned of this important challenge to traditional production-function measurements.

SUMMARY

1. The technical relationship between inputs and output, which is called *the production function*, is a crucial factor in determining the supply of goods. The production function can be expressed in the form of an equation, a table, or a graph. It can refer to the short run or the long run. A simple, short-run production function, in which a single input only can vary, illustrates the *law of eventually diminishing returns* to increases in a variable input. Such diminishing returns might be preceded by a limited range of increasing or constant returns and always refer to the input's *marginal product*. A graphical exposition of the simple, short-run production function highlights a number of important relationships, including those between total product and marginal product, between total and average product, between marginal and average product, and between the average products of different inputs.

2. A more complex, short-run production function, in which two inputs can vary, shows diminishing returns to either input. It can be presented graphically by a set of isoquants.

3. An analysis of isoquants reveals *technical*

inefficiency in segments with horizontal, vertical, or positive slope and *technical efficiency* in negatively sloped segments. Isoquants that are convex with respect to the origin are likely to be typical of real-world production functions. The slopes of isoquants equal the marginal rate of technical substitution of inputs and also the ratio of their marginal products. The ease and difficulty with which producers can switch among known techniques of production is measured by the *elasticity of input substitution*.

4. A long-run production function, in which all inputs are variable, can be subject to constant, increasing, or decreasing *returns to scale* (which must not be confused with constant, increasing, or decreasing *returns to a single variable input*). While the appearance of increasing returns to scale is usually associated with advantages from specialization and the operation of certain physical laws, decreasing returns to scale are generally attributed to the difficulties of managerial coordination. The presence of constant, increasing, or decreasing returns to scale is reflected in the spacing of isoquants.

5. Empirical investigations of production functions rely on engineering estimates, market observations (the survivor principle), time-series studies, and cross-section studies.

6. While the production function pertains to the relationship between inputs and the *maximum* output obtainable from them, statistical studies use data on actual output. Unless we can assume that firms always get the maximum output from any given set of inputs they use, all empirical measurements of production functions are seriously flawed. The theory of X-inefficiency addresses this issue.

KEY TERMS

allocative inefficiency
average product
CES production function
Cobb-Douglas production function
constant returns to a variable input

constant returns to scale

decreasing returns to scale

diminishing returns to a variable input

diseconomies of scale

economic inefficiency

economies of scale

economies of mass production

elasticity of input substitution

equal-product curve

increasing returns to a variable input

increasing returns to scale

isoquant

law of diminishing returns

law of variable proportions

long run

marginal (physical) product

marginal rate of technical substitution (MRTS)

point of diminishing returns

production function

production-indifference curve

productivity

short run

survivor principle

technical efficiency

technical inefficiency

VES production function

X-inefficiency

QUESTIONS AND PROBLEMS

1. Consider the data below. Assume other inputs and technology are fixed. Calculate the marginal and average products of labor.

Labor (hours per year)	Total Product (tons per year)
0	0
10	500
20	800
30	900

2. Take another look at Figure 5.1, "Total, Marginal, and Average Product." What do you think is the marginal product of *nonlabor* inputs in Stages I, II, and III?

3. *Mr. A:* If one increased the scale of a flea by a factor of 1,000, one would increase its strength by a million (strength of wings and muscles is proportional to their cross section) but would increase its weight by a billion (weight is proportional to volume). Such a scaled-up flea, therefore, couldn't jump at all. There is a lesson in this for the large firm.

Ms. B: Of course. And there is another lesson in the fate of the dinosaurs. They died out because their nervous systems and pea-sized brains couldn't keep up with their overgrown bodies.

Explain, using the concepts of returns to scale.

4. John R. Moroney's cross-section study of U.S. manufacturing yielded the 1958 data given in the accompanying table.[3] Applying Stigler's survivor principle, the author concluded that the wide variation in plant sizes evidenced by these data provided independent confirmation of the existence in U.S. manufacturing of constant returns to scale (this story was also told by Table 5.1). Do you agree? Why or why not?

Industry	Value Added (in thousands of dollars)	
	In Smallest Plant	In Largest Plant
Furniture	85.1	726.9
Chemicals	365.7	6,414.3
Printing	134.7	321.5
Food, beverages	191.5	774.6
Rubber, plastics	203.7	6,452.7
Instruments	148.0	1,528.5
Lumber	40.6	201.1
Apparel	88.6	1,013.9
Leather	202.0	1,475.9
Stone, clay	156.2	575.5
Fabricated metals	167.1	645.0
Transport equipment	194.0	5,196.4
Textiles	203.4	2,277.9
Paper, pulp	360.7	5,156.9
Primary metals	344.3	9,349.2
Petroleum	299.1	5,046.7

[3]John R. Moroney, "Cobb-Douglas Production Functions and Returns to Scale in U.S. Manufacturing Industry," *Western Economic Journal*, December 1967, pp. 39–51.

5. Consider Table 5.6, "Production Function Parameters: Cross-Section Estimates." What would happen to British coal output if labor and capital inputs each were increased by 1 percent? What if capital only was increased by 1 percent? What if capital was decreased by 1 percent?

6. To the extent that its existence can be traced to insufficient worker motivation, how, if at all, could one ever *eliminate* X-inefficiency? (*Hints:* Consider the possible role of external incentives, such as monetary rewards or public praise, or of internal incentives, such as feelings of joy or guilt. Consider the possible role of worker participation in management. If you know anything about them, drawn on the Swedish, Soviet, or Yugoslav experiences.)

7. Are the following statements true or false?

a. In the presence of diminishing returns, a firm can do nothing to increase the marginal product of its variable input.

b. When marginal product rises, average product rises.

c. When marginal product falls, average product falls.

d. If the law of diminishing returns did not hold, one could grow the annual world crop of wheat in a single flower pot.

e. The elasticity of input substitution equals the slope of an isoquant.

8. Are the following statements true or false?

a. The existence of increasing returns to scale refutes the law of diminishing returns.

b. In the presence of decreasing returns to scale, a firm can do nothing to increase the average product of its inputs.

c. If one constructed a total-product mountain, as suggested in the section on "The Case of Two Variable Inputs," the mountain would be very steep in the presence of increasing returns to scale and very flat in the presence of decreasing returns to scale.

d. In the presence of increasing returns to scale, a decrease in scale reduces the average products of all inputs.

e. In the presence of decreasing returns to scale, an increase in scale reduces the average products of all inputs.

f. X-inefficiency might be discovered by studying the operations of a single firm.

g. Allocative inefficiency can never be found by studying the operations of a single firm.

SELECTED READINGS

Cobb, Charles W. and Douglas, Paul H. "A Theory of Production." *The American Economic Review*, March 1928, pp. 139–65.

The original article on what is now called the Cobb-Douglas production function.

Dempsey, Bernard W. *The Frontier Wage*. Chicago: Loyola University Press, 1960.

A complete translation of volume II, section 1 of Thünen's work on income distribution by marginal products, originally published in 1850.

Dickinson, H. D. "Von Thünen's Economics." *Economic Journal*, December 1969, pp. 894–902.

Douglas, Paul H. *The Theory of Wages*. New York: Macmillian, 1934.

A pathbreaking statistical study of U.S. production functions. *See also* idem, "Are There Laws of Production?" *The American Economic Review*, March 1948, pp. 1–41. The author's presidential address to the American Economic Association.

Hall, Peter, ed. *Von Thünen's Isolated State*. Oxford: Pergamon Press, 1966.

A translation of volume I of Thünen's work on location theory and rent, originally published in 1826, plus excerpts from volume II, section 1 (1850) and section 2 (1863).

Leibenstein, Harvey. "Allocative Efficiency vs. 'X-Efficiency.'" *The American Economic Review*, June 1966, pp. 392–415.

The original article on X-efficiency theory. It is reprinted in *idem. Beyond Economic Man: A New Foundation for Microeconomics*. Cambridge: Harvard University Press, 1976, chap. 3. For elaborations, see the Appendix to this book ("Toward a Mathematical Formalization of X-Efficiency Theory"), as well as idem. "Aspects of the X-Efficiency Theory of the Firm." *The Bell Journal of Economics and Management Science*, Autumn 1975, pp. 580–606; "On the Basic Proposition of X-Efficiency Theory." *The American Economic Review*, May 1978, pp. 328–34; and "A Branch of Economics is Missing: Micro-Micro Theory." *Journal of Economic Literature*, June 1979, pp. 477–502.

Lovell, C. A. Knox. "Estimation and Prediction with CES and VES Production Functions." *International Economic Review*, October 1973, pp. 676–92.

Schneider, Erich. "Johann Heinrich von Thünen." *Econometrica*, January 1934, pp. 1–12.

Stigler, George J. "The Xistence of X-Efficiency." *The American Economic Review*, March 1976, pp. 213–16.

A critique of the Leibenstein theory. For a reply, see Harvey Leibenstein. "X-Inefficiency Xists—Reply to an Xorcist." *The American Economic Review*, March 1978, pp. 203–11; and "Microeconomics and X-Efficiency Theory: If There Is No Crisis, There Ought to be." *The Public Interest, Special Issue 1980: The Crisis in Economic Theory*, pp. 97–110.

CHAPTER 6

The Supply of Consumption Goods

The technology of firms, discussed in the previous chapter, is only one of the factors that determine the supply of consumption goods (and of other goods as well). This chapter will consider what other factors are involved in determining supply. We will continue to imagine an economy with perfect markets in which no individual household or firm, acting alone, can influence prices. Under such circumstances, the manager of a firm can easily translate the physical units of input and output that are found in the production function into monetary units. Given the market prices of inputs, physical input quantities can be translated into costs of production. Given the market price of output, physical output quantities can be translated into revenues. As a result, the output quantity that maximizes the difference between total revenue and total cost can be identified, and, economists postulate, this is the output quantity a profit-maximizing firm will supply. Given technology, its fixed inputs, and all input prices, such a firm will, of course, supply different output quantities at different output prices. The concept of **supply**, like *demand*, thus refers to a set of many price-quantity combinations. *Supply* denotes the alternative amounts of an item that would be offered for sale during a given period at all conceivable prices of this item, all else being equal.

Accounting Cost Vs. Opportunity Cost

Cost plays a very important role in the supply of goods, but cost means many things to many people. The proverbial person in the street, if asked to list costs of production, would most likely mention current expenditures, especially cash expenditures (like, perhaps, for wages or raw materials). Business accountants are more careful, recognizing as costs of production also items that may require neither current nor cash expenditures (such as periodic insurance premiums, property taxes, or depreciation allowances). Yet the accountant's concept remains far less sophisticated than the economist's notion of *opportunity cost*, which will be utilized here.

The accountant focuses on **explicit costs**. These are highly visible costs that the owners of firms incur when acquiring resource services from other households or when acquiring intermediate goods from other firms. These visible expenditures include wages and salaries paid for the use of other people's labor, rental payments for the use of other people's natural or capital resources, interest payments for the use of other people's money, payments for raw materials or services supplied by other firms, and payments of taxes. With the exception of depreciation allowances (which return to the owners of firms, over the lifetime of their plant and equipment, an amount of tax-free revenue equal to the historical cost of their assets), the accountant ignores a whole range of **implicit costs**. These are hidden costs that the owners of firms incur when using the services of their own resources in their own firms instead of hiring them out to collect the maximum income available elsewhere. When owners work in their firms or when they use their own land, equipment, and money in their firms, they forgo the wages, rent, and interest they might have earned in their best outside alternatives. The economist insists that such forgone incomes should be added to explicit costs whenever the costs of production are to be determined.

The economist, as we first learned in Chapter 1, always pictures costs in terms of forgone alternatives. When resources are used to produce one good, these resources cannot be used to make other goods; the lost opportunity of having these other goods represents *cost* in the economist's sense. Surely, economists argue, such opportunity cost is incurred regardless of whether the resources that make one good instead of another happen to be owned by outsiders or by the owners of the firm in which they are used and whether the right to their use is acquired for cash or cash plays no role at all. Indeed, picture the case of a Robinson Crusoe who produces goods by applying only his own labor to natural resources owned by no one. Accounting cost would be zero, but opportunity cost would be all too real. Economists, therefore, prefer measuring the cost of one good as the value of other goods that could have been made instead. They estimate such cost always as the *sum* of explicit and implicit ones, or as the minimum payment necessary to keep all resources (regardless of ownership) in their present employment. This minimum payment equals, of course, the maximum payment these resources could get elsewhere. It measures, therefore, the value of output they could produce in their best alternative employment.

Costs in the Short Run

Let us return to the orchard discussed in the previous chapter. Table 5.1, "A Simple Production Function," depicted the orchard's operations in the short run when the firm was saddled with some productive inputs the quantities of which it could not vary (see p. 111). The number of trees, the quantity of fertilizer, the set of equipment, and the size of the management team, perhaps, were the fixed inputs; the number of hired workers was the only variable input. The potential levels of production associated with all the technically efficient input combinations, formerly listed in rows (A) to (H) of Table 5.1, have been reproduced as column (1) of Table 6.1. This table also shows the various types of cost associated with each of these potential crops.

Fixed, Variable, and Total Costs

Columns (2) to (4) of Table 6.1 show the overall levels of three types of cost. **Fixed cost**, in column (2), does not vary with the level of production. It arises from the use of inputs the quantity of which is fixed during the period in question. In general, these costs are fixed because of long-term contractual agreements that cannot be cancelled without stiff penalties or because of the presence of resources so specialized that they are of no use anywhere else (such as buildings or machines made for a narrowly defined task). In the short run, a firm cannot escape its fixed cost, not even by shutting down and cutting production to zero. **Variable cost**, in column (3), in contrast, does vary with the level of production. It is associated with the use of inputs the quantity of which can be varied and the variation of which changes the level of production during a given period. **Total cost**, in column (4), is simply the sum of fixed and variable costs.

In principle, any particular type of cost can be fixed or variable. Consider labor cost. If the owner of a firm signed a ten-year employment contract with a worker, promising a $10,000 annual salary, the $10,000 would become a fixed

TABLE 6.1   Short-Run Cost Alternatives

Total Product (bushels of apples per year)	Fixed Cost	Variable Cost	Total Cost	Average Variable Cost	Average Total Cost	Marginal Cost
		(dollars per year)			(dollars per bushel)	
(1)	(2)	(3)	(4)=(2)+(3)	$(5)=\frac{(3)}{(1)}$	$(6)=\frac{(4)}{(1)}$	$(7)=\frac{\Delta(4)}{\Delta(1)}$
(A) 0	25,000	0	25,000	?	?	
						10.00
(B) 1,000	25,000	10,000	35,000	10.00	35.00	
						5.88
(C) 2,700	25,000	20,000	45,000	7.41	16.67	
						4.35
(D) 5,000	25,000	30,000	55,000	6.00	11.00	
						5.00
(E) 7,000	25,000	40,000	65,000	5.71	9.29	
						7.69
(F) 8,300	25,000	50,000	75,000	6.02	9.04	
						14.29
(G) 9,000	25,000	60,000	85,000	6.67	9.44	
						33.33
(H) 9,300	25,000	70,000	95,000	7.53	10.22	

As long as a firm has at least one input it cannot vary (let us assume it operates an orchard with a given number of trees, quantity of fertilizer, set of equipment, and management team), that firm operates in the short run. In the short run, it is saddled with a fixed cost—column (2)—for these fixed inputs. Yet the firm might be able to vary other inputs (for example, hired labor). By varying such other inputs—and the associated costs represented by column (3)—the firm can vary its total cost (4), as well as the level of its production (1) and other types of cost dependent on the level of production (5-7). Note: As the pointers between columns (6) and (7) indicate, the marginal costs shown refer to the intervals between rows (A) through (H).

cost *for those ten years*. Regardless of whether the firm ended up producing 100 bushels of apples in a year, 100,000 bushels, or none at all, it would still have to pay out $10,000 a year. In the long run, of course, this cost could be escaped. After the contract period had elapsed, the salary contract would not have to be renewed. Thus the same labor cost, looked upon over a longer period, would be a variable cost.

Note: The economist's distinction between fixed and variable costs should not be confused with the accountant's distinction between indirect and direct costs. While the economist asks whether cost is variable with respect to the overall level of output in a given period, the accountant asks whether cost is attributable to the production of a particular unit of output. The use of labor, raw materials, and machine time is often attributable to the production of a specific unit of output, and the costs are then called **direct** or **prime costs**. Because administrative or heating expenses and the depreciation of buildings are usually not attributable to producing a specific unit of output, such costs are called **indirect** or **overhead costs**.

Table 6.2 explains how the fixed cost in column (2) of Table 6.1 could conceivably be calculated in the case of the orchard business. Our orchard might be owned and run by a married couple that is being billed each year for $3,000 of property taxes. Because these taxes have to be paid regardless of the level of production, they represent a fixed cost. They are an explicit cost, too, and every accountant would take note of them. Yet accountants would ignore the three implicit-cost entries in Table 6.2. They represent the maximum incomes our couple could receive if they quit the orchard business and turned to their best alternatives. They might be able to sell the orchard and all its equipment and lend out the proceeds to someone else for $4,000 a year. They might take up the best jobs they could get in a nearby town, one as a substitute teacher ($5,000 a year) and the other as a newspaper reporter ($13,000 a year). Thus the very fact of their being in business initially burdens our two owner-managers with $25,000 a year in disadvantages. If they didn't own and run the orchard, they would take in $22,000 per year in other income and spend $3,000 per year less because someone else would have to worry about the property taxes. Because every conceivable level of output is thus burdened with this $25,000 cost, the $25,000 entry is found in every row of column (2) of Table 6.1.

The story is different, of course, for column (3). Because hired workers, by assumption, are the only input our orchardists can vary, their variable cost depends entirely on the number of workers hired and the prevailing annual wage for this type of work. Assuming the annual wage to equal $10,000, and considering (from a glance at Table 5.1, "A Simple Production Function") how many workers are needed to produce any of the crops listed in column (1) of Table 6.1, we can calculate the variable cost associated with different potential crops (3). Thus a 1,000 bushel-per-year crop, requiring one worker for a year, would cost $10,000, and so on down the column. We can now calculate total cost in column (4) as the sum of the fixed and variable costs in columns (2) and (3).

Average-Variable, Average-Total, and Marginal Costs

From the information in columns (1), (3), and (4) of Table 6.1, we can calculate three other types of cost. **Average variable cost** equals variable cost divided by total product. Thus, in row (B), as long as our orchardists hire only one worker for a year and wages are the only variable cost, this comes to $10,000 per year divided by 1,000 bushels per year, or $10 per bushel (5). **Average total cost** equals total cost divided by total product. Thus, in row (B), as long as our orchardists hire only one worker for a year, this comes to $35,000 per year divided by 1,000 bushels per year, or $35 per bushel (6). **Marginal cost**, finally, is the *change* in total cost, as from $25,000 per year in row (A) to $35,000 per year in row (B) of column (4) divided by the corresponding *change* in total product, as from 0 to 1,000 bushels per year from rows (A) to (B) in

TABLE 6.2   Calculating Fixed Cost

	Dollars Per Year
Explicit:	
Property taxes	$ 3,000
Implicit:	
Forgone potential income from selling the orchard and lending out the proceeds	4,000
Forgone potential salary as substitute teacher (spouse 1)	5,000
Forgone potential salary as newspaper reporter (spouse 2)	13,000
Total	$25,000

The opportunity cost of running a firm includes explicit costs as well as implicit ones, as shown here with reference to the fixed cost of an orchard. Taking account of implicit costs as well as explicit ones allows the owners of firms to make the best decisions on the long-run desirability of being in business.

column (1). In this case, it comes to +$10,000 per year divided by +1,000 bushels per year, or $10 per bushel. This figure is an average for the range of output between 0 and 1,000 bushels a year; hence, it appears between rows (A) and (B) in column (7).

Note: Marginal cost can also be calculated by dividing the change in *variable* cost by the corresponding change in total product. Because

fixed cost does not change, the change in total cost always equals that in variable cost.

The Cost Curves

For purposes of analyzing the alternatives before our firm, it is useful to plot the data from Table 6.1 in a graph (see Figure 6.1). In panel (a), the fixed-cost and variable-cost data of columns (2)

ANALYTICAL EXAMPLE 6.1:
The Marginal Cost of Highways

Governments are often interested in developing cost functions for the goods they provide in order to collect appropriate revenues from the beneficiaries of these goods. Highways are an example of such a good. Although a large fraction of the cost of constructing and operating highways is insensitive to vehicle characteristics, various types of marginal costs can be attributed to particular classes of vehicles. The presence of heavy truck traffic, for example, influences the number and width of lanes required, the type and thickness of pavement, curvature and gradient standards, the design of bridges, and so on. With the appropriate information in hand, government can treat different vehicle classes differently when assigning tax burdens or determining toll schedules.

A 1952 study of Virginia highways concerned itself with this issue. The accompanying table summarizes its results. Note how more than half of Virginia's highway costs could be attributed to passenger cars.

		Summary Allocation of Cost Responsibility (thousands of dollars)			
Class and Gross Weight of Vehicles	**Pavement Costs** (1)	**Grading and Drainage Costs** (2)	**Structure Costs** (3)	**Joint Costs** (4)	**Total Cost Responsibility** (5)
1. Passenger cars	$11,056	$6,499	$2,111	$31,600	$51,265
Trucks					
2. Up to 10,000	1,196	703	228	3,418	5,546
3. 10,001–16,000	2,137	816	260	1,100	4,324
4. 16,001–24,000	4,692	1,386	794	1,905	8,777
5. 24,001–35,000	882	261	207	362	1,712
6. 35,001–40,000	2,670	676	537	937	4,821
7. 40,001–50,000	2,649	670	533	930	4,783
Totals	$25,284	$11,010	$4,671	$40,265	$81,230

Source: Allen R. Ferguson, "A Marginal Cost Function for Highway Construction and Operation," *The American Economic Review*, May 1958, pp. 223–34.

FIGURE 6.1   Short-Run Cost Curves

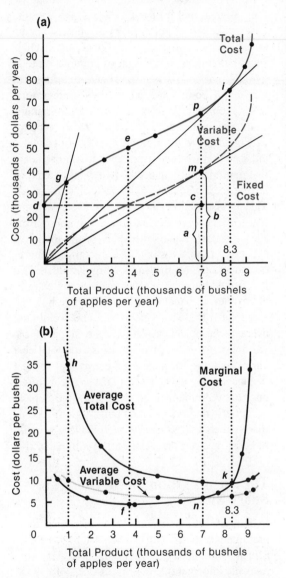

These graphs, based on Table 6.1, summarize the cost alternatives of a firm operating in the short run. Given technology and input prices, any firm can predict in this way the minimum levels of various types of cost associated with each potential level of production. Note: Marginal costs have been plotted at the midpoints of the ranges to which they apply, and all data plots have been connected by smooth curves. These curves give us additional information (about points between the heavy dots) that was not contained in Table 6.1. All of our subsequent discussions will be based on this more detailed information now available in this graph.

and (3) are plotted against total product from column (1). Note the horizontal (fixed cost) and upward-sloping (variable cost) dashed lines. The solid total-cost line is the vertical addition of the two dashed lines. Consider, for example, how a 7,000 bushel-a-year total product can be produced with $25,000 of fixed cost (distance *a*) plus $40,000 of variable cost (distance *b*). Dis-

tance *mp*, of course, equals distance *a*. Alternatively, distance *cp* equals distance *b*.

In panel (b), the average-variable, average-total, and marginal-cost data are similarly plotted against total product. The heavy dots represent the data in columns (5) to (7) of Table 6.1. The relationships between the total curves in panel (a) and the average or marginal curves in panel (b) are analogous to those noted when discussing total, marginal, and average product graphed in Figure 5.1 (see p. 114).

The slope of the total-cost curve equals marginal cost. Therefore, the *height* of the marginal-cost curve measures the *slope* of the total-cost curve. Because the slope of the total-cost curve is positive throughout, marginal cost is always positive as well. As long as increased production raises total cost at a decreasing rate (as between *d* and *e*, the point of inflexion on the curve), marginal cost is falling to its minimum at *f* (point *f* is directly below *e*). On the other hand, once increased production raises total cost at an increasing rate (as it does to the right of *e*), marginal cost is rising (to the right of *f*). This increase of marginal cost reflects the appearance of diminishing returns to the variable input.

The relationship between total cost and average total cost can be gauged by the slope of a ray originating at 0 in panel (a) and going to any desired point on the total-cost curve. Thus the average total cost of 1,000 bushels is $35,000 per year divided by 1,000 bushels per year, or the slope of ray *0g*. This $35-per-bushel value is shown by point *h* in panel (b). We can imagine a series of similar rays emanating from point 0 in panel (a) and aiming, successively, at points further and further to the right along the total-cost curve. The everchanging angle formed by this ray and the abscissa of the graph, would trace out the behavior of average total cost. Can you show how this angle (and average total cost) would fall, with increasing production, to a minimum for ray *0i* and would then rise? Note how, in panel (b), average total cost falls to point *k* (directly below *i*) and then rises.

We can also imagine a series of rays from 0 in panel (a) toward the dashed curve of variable cost; the everchanging slopes of these rays would trace out the size of average variable cost. Can you show how this slope (and average variable cost) would decline with increasing production, to a minimum for ray *0m*, and would then rise? Note how in panel (b), average variable cost falls to point *n* (directly below *m*) and then rises.

Note how panel (b) also confirms our discus-

sion, in the previous chapter, of the characteristic relationship between average and marginal. As long as marginal cost is below average variable cost (to the left of point *n*), it pulls down average variable cost (even when marginal cost itself is rising, as it does to the right of point *f*). As long as marginal cost is below average total cost (to the left of point *k*), it pulls down average total cost (even when marginal cost itself is rising). Similarly, marginal cost above either type of average cost (to the right of *n* or *k*, respectively) pulls up that average cost. Thus it is no accident that marginal cost equals the two types of average cost at their respective minima (points *n* and *k*). This is also visible in panel (a). Note how the slope of ray *0i* (which measures minimum average total cost) equals the slope of the total-cost curve at *i* (and the slope of the total-cost curve, of course, always measures marginal cost). This is reflected by average total cost meeting marginal cost at *k* in panel (b). Similarly, note how the slope of ray *0m* (which measures minimum average variable cost) equals the slope of the variable-cost curve at *m*. Because the total-cost curve and the variable-cost curve are vertical displacements of each other (the vertical difference between them being fixed cost), the slope at *m* equals that at *p* and thus, again, equals marginal cost. This is reflected by average variable cost meeting marginal cost at *n* in panel (b).

The Firm's Optimum in the Short Run

It is easy to show how the graphical tools presented as Figure 6.1 can be used to determine a firm's optimum rate of production. The only relevant information missing in our story is the market price of the product. Given costs (which depend, as we just learned, on the production function and input prices), the outcome of any business venture depends entirely on the size of that price. A firm can maximize its **profit**, or the difference between its total revenue and the total (explicit and implicit) cost associated with producing that revenue, by following the optimization principle explained in Chapter 1:

The firm must adjust its rate of production until the given price of its output, which is the marginal benefit of production, equals its marginal cost of production.

The orchard business can provide examples of a number of possible outcomes that will illustrate this profit-maximizing rule.

A Profitable Business

Figure 6.2 illustrates what would happen if our orchardists could sell apples at $12 per bushel. If the price were $12 per bushel, they could maximize their profit by choosing an 8,625 bushel-per-year production level.

Consider panel (a). If apples sold at $12 per bushel, 1,000 bushels would sell for $12,000 (point *a*), 3,000 bushels for $36,000 (point *b*), and so on along a straight line of total revenue. Because this line is not only straight, but also goes through the origin of the graph, its slope simultaneously measures the ratio of total revenue to total product—that is, **average revenue** or product price—and the ratio of any change in total revenue to the corresponding change in total product—that is, **marginal revenue**. The graph shows that all potential output levels to the left of point *c* would yield a negative profit or **loss**, because total cost would exceed total revenue by various amounts. (Such losses can be measured, for any given output level, as the vertical difference between the total-cost and total-revenue lines in the shaded area.) As far as we can see in our graph, output levels to the right of point *c*, however, would yield profits because total revenue would exceed total cost. This difference would again vary, the maximum profit being associated with an output of 8,625 bushels of apples per year. At that output level, total revenue would equal $103,500 per year (distance *ef*), total cost $79,695 per year (distance *df*). Thus profit would equal $23,805 per year (distance *ed*). Distance *ed* represents the maximum possible profit because the total-revenue and total-cost lines diverge along *ce* and *cd*, respectively, but they converge to the right of points *e* and *d*. At

FIGURE 6.2 A Profitable Business

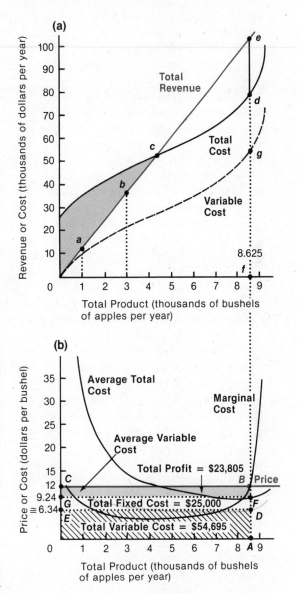

If product price were $12 per bushel, this firm would find its optimal rate of production at 8,625 bushels per year. Point *B*, therefore, is one point on its short-run supply curve.

these two points, their respective slopes are equal.

Because the slope of the total-revenue line

equals marginal revenue as well as price and because the slope of the total-cost curve equals marginal cost, our orchardists could turn to panel (b) and search for an equality of price and marginal cost. Such equality can be found at point *B*, which indicates the same optimum output level of 8,625 bushels per year. Note how, in panel (b), rectangle *0ABC* represents the total revenue associated with this optimum output: 8,625 bushels per year (distance *0A*) times a price of $12 per bushel (distance *AB*), or $103,500 per year.

The graph in panel (b) provides a variety of other information. The orchard's variable cost, measured by distance *gf* in panel (a) equals the crosshatched rectangle *0ADE*, or 8,625 bushels per year (distance *0A*) times an average variable cost of slightly over $6.34 per bushel (distance *AD*), or $54,695 per year. The orchard's total cost, measured by distance *df* in panel (a), can be seen to equal rectangle *0AFG*, or 8,625 bushels per year (distance *0A*) times an average total cost of $9.24 per bushel (distance *AF*), or $79,695 per year. Because total cost is the sum of fixed and variable costs, total fixed cost, measured by distance *dg* in panel (a), equals white rectangle *EDFG*, or 8,625 bushels per year (distance *ED*) times slightly under $2.90 per bushel (distance *DF*), or $25,000 per year. Distance *DF*, of course, equals **average fixed cost**—total fixed cost divided by total product or, more simply, the difference between average total and average variable cost.

At a price of $12 per bushel (distance *AB*) but an average total cost of $9.24 per bushel (distance *AF*), **average profit**—that is, total profit divided by total product (or price minus average total cost)—equals $2.76 per bushel (distance *FB*). Hence total profit, measured by distance *ed* in panel (a), equals shaded rectangle *GFBC*, or 8,625 bushels per year (distance *GF*) times an average profit of $2.76 per bushel (distance *FB*), or $23,805 per year.

If our orchardists did face a price of $12 per bushel and, therefore, did produce 8,625 bushels per year, they would be doing well, indeed. They would take in revenue of $103,500 a year, while

paying out $54,695 to hired workers and $3,000 in property taxes (as noted in Table 6.2). They would keep the remaining $45,805, and this amount, given our assumptions, would be the firm's taxable *accounting* profit. Only $23,805 of this amount, however, would represent *economic* profit, a gain over and above our orchardists' best alternative income of $22,000 (which is the sum of the implicit fixed-cost items in Table 6.2).

A Zero-Profit Business

Figure 6.3 depicts a zero-profit business. Our perfectly competitive orchardists (who would have no control over the market price of their product) might be less lucky than in Figure 6.2. Suppose the price of apples were only $9.04 per bushel, all else remaining equal. Under these circumstances, the total-revenue line has a lower slope than in Figure 6.2. In fact, it just touches the total-cost curve at a single point, *a*. Any output level other than 8,300 bushels per year would result in losses. As panel (a) indicates, this output level would yield total revenue of $75,032 per year (distance *ac*), an identical total cost, and zero profit. Note how the obvious equality of the slopes of the total-revenue and total-cost lines at point *a* once more confirms the optimization principle: The total net benefit of an activity (the profit from producing apples, in our case) is maximized when marginal benefit (the slope of our total-revenue line) just equals marginal cost (the slope of our total-cost curve).

Panel (b) tells the same story. Price equals marginal cost at point *I*, suggesting the same optimal output of 8,300 bushels per year. Rectangle *0HIK* represents the associated total revenue of 8,300 bushels per year times a price of $9.04 per bushel (distance *HI*), or $75,032 per year. The orchard's variable cost, measured by distance *bc* in panel (a), equals crosshatched rectangle *0HLM*, or 8,300 bushels per year times an average variable cost of slightly under $6.03 per bushel (distance *HL*), or $50,032 per year. The orchard's total cost, measured by distance *ac* in panel (a), can be seen to equal rectangle *0HIK*, or 8,300 bushels per year times an average total cost of $9.04 per bushel (distance *HI*), or $75,032 per year. Thus total fixed cost, measured

FIGURE 6.3 A Zero-Profit Business

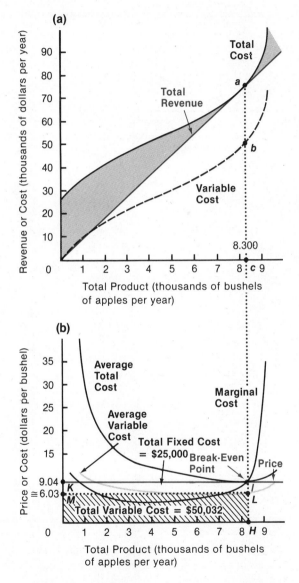

If product price were $9.04 per bushel, this firm would find its optimal rate of production at 8,300 bushels per year. Point *I*, therefore, is one point on its short-run supply curve.

by distance *ab* in panel (a), equals the area of the white rectangle *MLIK*, or 8,300 bushels per year times an average fixed cost of slightly more than $3.01 per bushel (distance *LI*), or $25,000 per year.

At a price of $9.04 per bushel, the business would make no profit at all. Our orchardists could do no better than just break even. Indeed, an output level at which total revenue equals total cost (a) and at which price equals average total cost *(I)* is called a **break-even point**. When price also equals *minimum* average total cost (point *I*), a firm cannot escape choosing the break-even level of production. Under the circumstances, producing at zero profit, however, is preferable to closing down. If our friends closed down, they would lose all their revenue and would save their variable cost, but they would still be saddled with $25,000 per year of fixed cost, and hence a loss equal to this amount. Surely, it would be better to have a zero profit: If they produced 8,300 bushels per year, they would take in revenue of $75,032 per year, while paying out $50,032 to hired workers and $3,000 in property taxes. They would keep $22,000 and be just as well off as they could have been with their best alternative.

A Losing Business

In the short run, it could even be rational for the orchardists to stay in business while making a loss. Suppose the price of apples were $7.25 per bushel, all else remaining the same, as depicted in Figure 6.4. As the shaded gap between total cost and total revenue indicates in panel (a), the orchardists could then find no output level at all at which total revenue would be sufficient to cover total cost. Operating this business would mean operating it with a loss. But note: There exists a range of output levels (between point *a* and point *b*) that would yield total revenue more than sufficient to cover *variable* cost. Producing any one of these outputs would leave some revenue to cover a portion of fixed cost. As a result, the firm's loss (which would equal fixed cost, if it shut down at once) could be reduced to a figure below fixed cost. As long as fixed cost

ANALYTICAL EXAMPLE 6.2:

Break-Even Analysis: The Case of the Flying Professor

The owners of existing or potential firms often use a simplified version of Panel (a), Figures 6.2–6.5, to determine the minimum sales volume required to make a new type of business activity worthwhile. Consider the case of a professor who had saved $50,000 and was thinking of spending it on a small airplane. What were the prospects for entering the air charter business—the business of carrying freight or taking people to major air terminals, other small airports, or simply for scenic rides? The prospective 1980 finances of such a venture are shown in the accompanying table.

Fixed Cost (dollars per year)		Average Variable Cost (dollars per flight hour)		Average Revenue
Explicit				
Hangar rent	$ 1,000	Aircraft repairs	$10.--	$75.--
Insurance	600	Gasoline	9.--	
Telephone	150	Avionics repairs	3.--	
Taxes, licenses	100	Miscellaneous	3.--	
Aeronautical charts	100	(long-distance		
Miscellaneous supplies	100	phone, landing fees)		
Implicit		Total	$25.--	
Salary forgone (college teaching)	$30,000			
Interest forgone (on $50,000 investment)	5,000			
Depreciation (on $50,000 plane)	2,500			
Other income forgone (writing college texts)	2,000			
Total	$41,550			

Using the data in the table and assuming that hourly variable cost and revenue would be unaffected by the number of hours flown per year, the professor drew the accompanying graph.

could not be escaped (the orchard could not be sold to escape property taxes, to cash in and lend out the owners' equity, and to free the owners for their alternative jobs), it would be wise to pursue a policy of loss minimization. Note how the shaded gap of loss could be narrowed the most (and the excess of total revenue over variable cost could be widened the most) by producing 7,680 bushels of apples per year. Our orchardists would gain total revenue of $55,680 per year (distance *cd*), incur a total cost of $70,000 per year (distance *ed*), and make a loss of $14,320 per year (distance *ec*). This loss would be preferable to that of $25,000 per year at the zero production

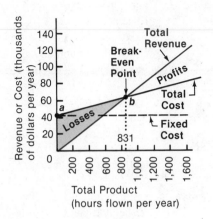

It became immediately obvious that the sale of fewer than 831 flight hours per year would yield losses (compared to the professor's alternatives). The sale of more than 831 flight hours would produce profits. At exactly 831 hours per year, the business would break even. Note how, at the break-even point *(b)*, total revenue of 831 hours times $75 per hour, or $62,325, would be generated. Total cost would be the same: $41,550 (fixed) plus $20,775 (variable), the latter figure being equal to 831 times $25.

In this way, the expected-total-revenue and expected-total-cost lines for any prospective business can be juxtaposed in order to determine the minimum sales volume required to avoid losses. This procedure, called **break-even analysis**, is instantly adaptable to changes in the basic data. Note how any change in annual fixed cost changes the total-cost line's intercept at point *a*. A change in hourly variable cost ($25 per hour in our case) changes the slope of the total-cost line. A change in hourly revenue ($75 per hour in our case) changes the slope of the total-revenue line. In any of these cases, the new break-even output level can be determined at a glance by looking for the new break-even point. In many businesses, average variable cost and average revenue are in fact constant for wide ranges of output. For them, the kind of straight-line analysis used here can be an important decision-making tool.

Note: It does not follow, as the above graph seems to imply, that unlimited output yields infinite profit. Eventually, increases in output are bound to turn down the line of total revenue or turn up the line of total cost.

level (distance 0*g*). This loss would be $10,680 per year lower than fixed cost (*ef* = 0*g*), and this improved performance equals the maximum possible excess of total revenue over variable cost (distance *cf*).

We can quickly check our results in panel (b). Price equals marginal cost at point *P*, con-

firming as optimal an output of 7,680 bushels per year. Rectangle *0NPQ* shows the associated total revenue of 7,680 bushels per year times a price of $7.25 per bushel (distance *NP*), or $55,680 per year. The orchard's variable cost, measured by distance *fd* in panel (a), equals crosshatched rectangle *0NRS*, or 7,680 bushels per year times an average variable cost of slightly under $5.86 per bushel (distance *NR*), or $45,000 per year. The orchard's total cost, measured by distance *ed*

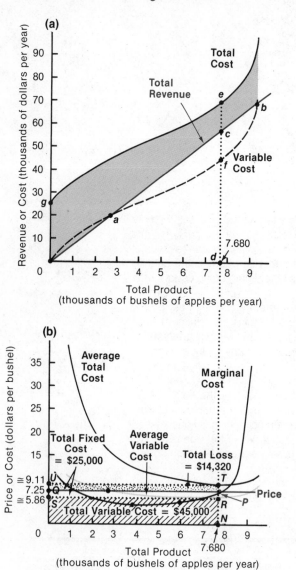

FIGURE 6.4 A Losing Business

(a)

(b)

If product price were $7.25 per bushel, this firm would find its optimal rate of production at 7,680 bushels per year. Point *P*, therefore, is one point on its short-run supply curve.

in panel (a), can be seen to equal rectangle *ONTU*, or 7,680 bushels per year times an average total cost of slightly over $9.11 per bushel (distance *NT*), or $70,000 per year. Thus total fixed cost, measured by distance *ef* in panel (a), equals the combined area of the white and dotted rectangles, *SRTU*, or 7,680 bushels per year times an average fixed cost of slightly under $3.26 per bushel (distance *RT*), or $25,000 per year.

Because, at the optimal production level, price (distance *NP*) would fall short of average total cost (distance *NT*), a negative average profit, or **average loss** would be made, which would come to slightly more than $1.86 per bushel and yield a total loss of $14,320 per year, as shown by the dotted rectangle in panel (b) and by distance *ec* in panel (a). The white rectangle, of course, corresponds to distance *cf* in panel (a), the portion of fixed cost that is covered by revenue.

Note how our friends, if they produced 7,680 bushels per year, would take in $55,680 per year, while paying out $45,000 to hired workers and $3,000 in property taxes. They would keep $7,680, which is $14,320 less than alternatives available to them in the long run (as indicated by the calculated loss). For the time being, though, this would be better than nothing.

A Business on the Fence

The product price can be so low—slightly above $5.71 per bushel in our case—that whether to produce at a loss or to shut down operations at once would become a matter of indifference. The situation of a business on the fence is depicted in Figure 6.5 on p. 158. As the shaded gap between total cost and total revenue indicates in panel (a), our orchardists could find no output level at which total revenue would cover total cost. Indeed, as a comparison of the variable-cost and total-revenue lines indicates, with the single exception of the 7,000 bushels-a-year output level, total revenue would be insufficient even to cover variable cost. In the short run, producing 7,000 bushels a year would not be wrong, however.

Our orchardists would receive total revenue of $40,000 per year (distance *bc*). They would incur variable costs of the same amount. Their total cost (distance *ac*) would equal $65,000 per year. They would make, therefore, a $25,000-per-year loss equal to fixed cost (distance *ab*). An immediate shutdown would produce an identical loss (distance 0*d*).

As always, panel (b) tells the same story. Price equals marginal cost at point *W*. Rectangle 0*VWX* shows total revenue of 7,000 bushels per year times a price slightly above $5.71 per bushel (distance *VW*), or $40,000 per year. Variable cost, equal to distance *bc* in panel (a), equals crosshatched rectangle 0*VWX*, or 7,000 bushels per year times an average variable cost slightly over $5.71 per bushel (distance *VW*), or $40,000 per year. Total cost, measured by distance *ac* in panel (a), equals rectangle 0*VYZ*, or 7,000 bushels per year times an average total cost slightly under $9.29 per bushel (distance *VY*), or $65,000 per year. Total fixed cost, measured by distance *ab* in panel (a), therefore equals rectangle *XWYZ*, or 7,000 bushels per year times average fixed cost of slightly over $3.57 per bushel (distance *WY*), or $25,000 per year. This is also the total loss.

The owners of such a business would be "sitting on the fence." If they shut down, they would lose $25,000 compared to their best alternative. If they operated, at the 7,000-bushel-a-year level, they would take in $40,000 of revenue, pay an equal amount to hired workers, and have nothing left to pay property taxes ($3,000) or to reimburse themselves for their forgone income alternatives. That is why our orchardists would be at the verge of shutting down at once. Indeed, an output level at which total revenue equals variable cost and at which price equals average variable cost (points *b* and *W*, respectively) is called a **shutdown point**. When price also equals *minimum* average variable cost (point *W*), a firm cannot escape choosing the shutdown level of production. Although whether to produce or shut down has become at this point a matter of indifference, even the slightest further deterioration of product price would cause the firm to cease operations immediately.

Supply in the Short Run

From the forgoing discussion, we can conclude that, in the short run, while firms are saddled with fixed cost that they cannot escape,

1. no firm will operate with a loss in excess of fixed cost, because there exists the alternative of closing down and making a loss equal to fixed cost;

2. a firm might operate with a loss equal to fixed cost, because the alternative of closing down would yield an identical loss (see Figure 6.5);

3. a firm will operate with a loss falling short of fixed cost, because the alternative of closing down would yield a bigger loss equal to fixed cost (see Figure 6.4);

4. a firm will operate with zero profit, because implicit costs (counted as part of fixed cost) are then fully covered by revenues; hence owners would earn from their resources in their own firm exactly what they could at best earn elsewhere, and shutting down would deprive them of these earnings (see Figure 6.3);

5. a firm will operate with a positive profit because its presence indicates earnings in excess of the owners' best alternative (see Figure 6.2).

Indeed, we can be more precise. Notice in Figures 6.2 to 6.5 how the optimum level of production in each case corresponds exactly to the intersection (at points *B, I, P,* and *W,* respectively) of the price line with rising marginal cost. From this correspondence, we can conclude:

> *In the short run and in a perfectly competitive market, the rising arm of a firm's marginal-cost curve, above the minimum level of average variable cost, shows how much the firm would produce and offer for sale at alternative product prices. This segment of the rising arm is the firm's short-run supply.*

The color line in Figure 6.6 depicts the **"law" of upward-sloping supply**, the tendency of sellers normally to offer for sale larger quantities of an item when its price is higher, all else being equal.

FIGURE 6.5   A Business on the Fence

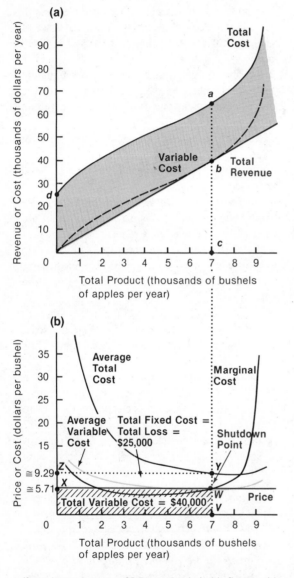

(a)

(b)

If product price were $5.71 per bushel, this firm would be indifferent about producing 7,000 bushels per year or shutting down at once. Point *W*, therefore, is the lowest point on its short-run supply curve.

Note: Had we assumed, in our earlier discussions, a different technology, different amounts of fixed inputs, or different prices of fixed or variable inputs, we would have derived a different supply curve. That is why a change in technology, fixed inputs, and input prices *shifts* a good's short-run supply curve to the right or left and is referred to as a **change in supply**. In contrast, a change in the good's own price, while other factors remain unchanged (a situation we envisioned when moving from Figure 6.2 to 6.5), causes a *movement along* a given supply curve (as from *B* to *W*) and is referred to as a **change in quantity supplied**.

Costs and Supply in the Long Run

A firm operating in the short run, by definition, is operating with at least one input quantity that is fixed. As a result (even if it avoids X-inefficiency), it is not necessarily producing its output at as low a cost as could be achieved in the long run when all inputs are variable. Consider Figure 6.7. Imagine a firm that used only the two types of inputs shown in this graph, capital and labor, and that could produce any given quantity of its output with the help of many different combinations of these inputs. This firm's production possibilities are illustrated by three isoquants for output levels of 100, 150, and 200 bushels of product, respectively. Imagine further that this firm faced input prices of $250 per year for a unit of capital service and of $125 per year for a unit of labor service. We can draw a family of straight **isocost lines** (akin to the budget lines of Chapter 3), each of which shows all the alternative combinations of the two inputs that the firm is able to buy in a given period at current market prices, while incurring the same total cost. The lines are labeled accordingly. Note, for example, how $500 could purchase 2 units of capital or 4 units of labor or any combination of them lying on the isocost line with the $500 label. The absolute value of the slope of every isocost line, therefore, reflects the ratio of the price of a unit

FIGURE 6.6 Short-Run Supply

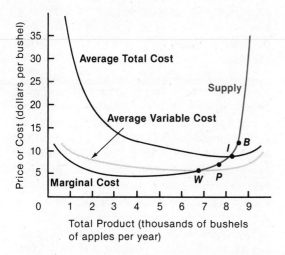

This graph, which is based on panel (b) of Figures 6.2 to 6.5, highlights an important fact: In the short run, the optimum levels of production corresponding to all conceivable product prices are always found on the rising arm, above minimum average variable cost, of the perfectly competitive firm's marginal cost curve. This rising portion of the marginal-cost curve, which appears in color, is the firm's short-run supply.

of labor service, P_L, to that of a unit of capital service, P_K; in our case, \$125/\$250 or 1/2.

$$|\text{Isocost line slope}| = \frac{P_L}{P_K}$$

Now consider this firm in the short run with, perhaps, a fixed quantity of 3 units of capital (note the horizontal line). If it wanted to produce 100 bushels of product per year, it would have to use input combination *a*, and this would cost, as the dashed isocost line shows, \$1,125 per year. Average total cost would equal \$11.25 per bushel. Yet, as point *b* indicates, the same amount of output could be produced at a total cost of \$1,000 per year (and average total cost could be reduced to \$10 per bushel), if less capital and more labor was utilized. A profit-maximizing firm, surely,

would take advantage of this possibility in the long run.

Note: It is no accident that the least costly combination of inputs (or the *firm's optimum*) is found at *b* where isocost line and isoquant are just touching each other. At such a point of equal slopes, the ratio of input prices equals the ratio of the inputs' marginal products, MP, and the result is analogous to the consumer's optimum discussed in Chapter 3:

Condition for Firm's Optimum:
Slope of isocost line = slope of isoquant

$$\frac{P_L}{P_K} = MRTS_{K/L} = \frac{MP_L}{MP_K}.$$

FIGURE 6.7 Isoquants and Isocost Lines

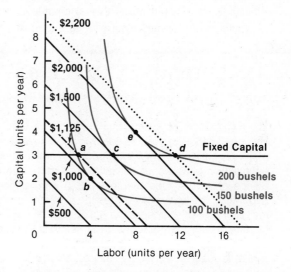

In the long run, when all inputs can be freely varied, a profit maximizing firm would produce all levels of output at minimum possible cost, as by utilizing input combinations *b, c,* or *e*. These represent tangencies of isoquants and isocost lines and, therefore, positions in which the marginal product per dollar of one input equals that of any other input. In the short run, however, a firm may be forced by the fixity of one input to produce many output levels at costs exceeding those achievable in the long run, as illustrated by points *a* and *d*.

Therefore, $\dfrac{MP_L}{P_L} = \dfrac{MP_K}{P_K}$

When this condition is fulfilled, profit is maximized because no further substitution of inputs can reduce the cost of producing a given output (and thus a given revenue). A contrary example can illustrate the point: If MP_L as well as MP_K equaled 50 bushels, the firm could produce the same output with one unit of capital less and one unit of labor more. At $P_L = \$125$ and $P_K = \$250$, this would reduce cost and raise profit by $125.

Point c happens to be an optimum point. If our firm wanted to produce 150 bushels per year, given its 3-unit fixed capital, it would have to use input combination c, and it would spend $1,500 per year. Its average total cost would equal $10 per bushel, and, quite by accident, this would be the lowest figure achievable with the firm's given **plant** or physical production facility, as defined by the set of fixed inputs available to the firm. When a firm in this way produces the output level associated with the minimum average total cost

achievable from a given plant, it is said to have an **optimal rate of plant operation** or to be producing its **capacity output**. Operation at break-even point I in the graph of a zero-profit business in Figure 6.3 also corresponds to this situation.

Yet a firm may have good reasons not to operate at capacity. Just as it may wish to operate below capacity at some product prices (note points P and W in Figures 6.4 and 6.5), so it may wish to operate above capacity at other product prices (note point B in Figure 6.2). Operation below capacity corresponds to point a in Figure 6.7. Operation above capacity corresponds to point d. The implications of operating at point a were noted above; operations at point d can be analyzed similarly. A firm with 3 units of fixed capital, that wanted to produce 200 bushels per year, would have to use input combination d. It would then spend $2,200 per year. The average total cost would equal $11 per bushel. Yet, in the long run, the use of less labor and more capital

ANALYTICAL EXAMPLE 6.3:

Incremental-Profit Analysis: The Case of Continental Air Lines

The owners of existing firms that are saddled with fixed costs often use a simplified version of panel (b), Figures 6.2–6.5, to determine whether they should take on a bit of extra business. Their approach is nothing else but an application of the optimization principle, usually known as **incremental-profit analysis**. Heeding the advice of Jevons (see Biography 3.2) with respect to fixed cost ("Bygones are bygones"), the analyst compares the expected *marginal revenue* with the expected *marginal cost* of a prospective action; the difference between the two is the extra, incremental, or **marginal profit** the action is likely to bring to the business.

Consider the case of Continental Air Lines, Inc. In 1962, it filled only half the available seats on its Boeing 707 jets, a number that was 15 percent worse than the national average. Yet running many half-empty flights *raised* the firm's profit. Here is why: The typical flight's total cost came to $4,500. Of this amount, $2,500 were the flight's share of fixed costs that would be incurred even if no flight were made; $2,000 were "out-of-pocket" costs. The typical flight's revenue came to $3,100. Thus each extra flight added to total revenue (produced a marginal revenue of) $3,100. Each flight added to total cost (produced a marginal cost of) $2,000. The difference between marginal revenue and marginal cost ($3,100–$2,000) was the marginal or incremental profit ($1,100) from running an extra flight.

Source: "Airline Takes the Marginal Route," *Business Week*, April 20, 1963, pp. 111–14.

CLOSE-UP 6.1:

The Price of Sugar and the Supply of Moonshine

This chapter teaches that the supply of any product is affected by the prices of the inputs needed to make it. Consider the case of "moonshine"—illegal whiskey produced in regions of steep mountains and dense forests from Virginia to Georgia. For decades, agents of the Treasury Department's Bureau of Alcohol, Tobacco, and Firearms have been waging a seemingly hopeless battle against the elusive moonshiners. In recent times, the "revenuers" have been using airplane reconnaissance, infrared heat sensors, and dynamite to shut down the stills. The moonshiners, in turn, have abandoned wood and coke as fuel and have substituted propane gas because it produces no telltale smoke. Some of them have even camouflaged their operations against overflights with mock cemeteries, complete with fake tombstones and plastic flowers. In 1973, however, moonshiners were hit by a catastrophe that rivaled the appearance of federal agents: the price of sugar tripled, and it takes 10 pounds of sugar to make a gallon of illegal booze.

Moonshine producers are always in a hurry to finish their batch and move on to another location. Unlike the producers of "government whiskey," they cannot rely on the slow process of drawing natural sugars from grain being distilled. Thus, in 1973, along with the price of sugar, the price of moonshine soared from $6 to $15 per gallon. At that level, its price was close to the price of legal whiskey, and the market for moonshine contracted severely.

In the meantime, precisely the opposite has been happening halfway around the globe. In such places as the hinterlands of *Soviet* Georgia, an estimated quarter million people were processing cheap Cuban sugar into a vodka-like home brew called *samogon*, which was stronger than but selling for much less than state-produced liquor. As a popular ditty put it, "Thank you, thank you, Cuba. All of Russia does proclaim, Ten ounces per kilo of sugar, And it burns with a bright blue flame."

Sources: *The Wall Street Journal*, July 30, 1975; *The New York Times*, January 23, 1980, p. A12; "Russians Make a Big Business of Moonshine," *The New York Times*, March 8, 1981, p. 11.

(at point *e*) could reduce average total cost to $10.

The Planning Curve under Constant Returns to Scale

Imagine the owners of a firm still in its planning stage or, if you prefer, the owners of an existing firm who are contemplating major changes in the long run. They might imagine setting up plants of many different sizes, each one defined by a different-sized set of fixed inputs. Our orchardists, for example, might draw up one blueprint for a 5-acre lot with 1,000 apple trees (and the appropriate equipment to service them). They might draw up other blueprints for 50 acres and 10,000 trees, for 100 acres and 20,000 trees, and many more. And for each of these blueprints,

they might produce a graph like Figure 6.1 to show short-run cost curves.

The short-run average total cost and short-run marginal cost for blueprints 3, 10, and 21, for example, might appear as lines $SRATC$ and $SRMC$ in panel (a) of Figure 6.8. The subscript refers to the number of the hypothetical blueprint; larger numbers refer to plants of larger sizes.

A picture like that found in panel (a) would indicate the presence of constant returns to scale: The owners of our firm might determine that they could produce, at an average total cost of $10 per bushel, 100,000 bushels of apples per year, if they used 50 acres and 10,000 trees and operated this plant at capacity (point *a*). They might find that quadrupling all inputs would quadruple total cost but would quadruple output as well, yielding the same minimum average total cost (point *c*). And they might discover that, given enough time to adjust all inputs appropriately, any other output level could be produced at an equivalent cost (point *b*).

Once fixed inputs corresponding to SRATC₃ were in place, the firm could, of course, produce an output of 200,000 bushels per year, but operating above capacity in this manner would drive short-run average total cost up from *a* to *d*. Given enough time for adjusting the number of trees and other inputs—perhaps by following a blueprint 6 (not shown)—these costs could be reduced to *e*. Under the circumstances, therefore, our firm's average total cost in the long run, *LRATC*, could always be reduced to $10 per bushel for any conceivable level of output. The long-run average-total-cost line is also called the **planning curve**. It helps owners of firms make long-range plans because it is tangent to all the curves of short-run average total cost and is, therefore, the *geometric locus* of the minimum achievable average total costs for all conceivable output levels. When the planning curve is horizontal, long-run marginal cost, *LRMC*, coincides with it. (Marginal above average would pull average up; marginal below average would pull average down.) While the upward-sloping lines of short-run marginal cost indicate our firm's short-run response to changes in product price (given alternative plant sizes), this horizontal *LRMC* is its long-run supply. Given enough time, this line tells us, our firm can supply *any* annual apple crop at $10 per bushel.

The Planning Curve under Increasing and Decreasing Returns to Scale

A firm's long-run supply need not be a horizontal line, however. Consider panel (b) of Figure 6.8. The owners of our single-plant firm might determine that they could produce, at an average total cost of $15 per bushel, 50,000 bushels of apples per year, if they used 25 acres and 5,000 trees and operated this plant at capacity (point *f*). Note: What they could do is not necessarily what they would do. They might find that doubling all

inputs would double costs but triple output, yielding a lower minimum average total cost (point *g*). A further 17 percent increase in all inputs (and total cost) might raise output by 67 percent and also reveal the **optimum plant**, or that plant, among all conceivable ones, with the lowest possible minimum average total cost (point *h*). In our case, this figure would come to $7 per bushel. That, however, would be the end of increasing returns to scale.

Further proportionate increases in all inputs might bring about lesser increases in output. Starting from the optimum plant (29), operated at capacity (point *h*), a doubling of all inputs might raise output by only 40 percent, yielding a higher minimum average total cost of $10 per bushel (point *i*). A further 93 percent increase in all inputs might raise output by a mere 29 percent and raise minimum average total cost to $15 per bushel (point *k*). Decreasing returns to scale might thus follow on the heels of increasing returns to scale.

Once more, the owners of our firm could draw the planning curve. This time, however, this geometric locus of the minimum achievable average total costs for all conceivable output levels would not be a straight line. This line of long-run average total cost *(LRATC)*, like the lines of short-run average total cost *(SRATC)*, would be U-shaped. Because it would envelop all the short-run curves, touching each at only a single point, it is also called an **envelope curve**.

Note: Unlike in the case of constant returns to scale, the long-run average total cost curve in the presence of increasing or decreasing returns to scale does not connect all the *minimum* points of short-run curves, such as *a, b,* or *c* in panel (a) or *f, g, h, i,* or *k* in panel (b). Except for point *h*, the long-run average total cost curve in panel (b) never coincides with the minima of short-run average total cost curves. Point *m* does not coincide with *f*, nor *n* with *g*, nor *p* with *i*, nor *q* with *k*.

A U-shaped curve of long-run average total cost implies the following:

1. When increasing returns to scale exist, it is

FIGURE 6.8 Short-Run vs. Long-Run Costs

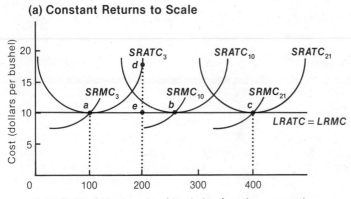

(a) Constant Returns to Scale

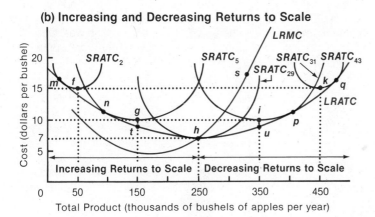

(b) Increasing and Decreasing Returns to Scale

The long-run marginal-cost curve at or above the level of long-run average total cost is the long-run supply curve of an individual firm operating in perfect markets. The *LRMC* is horizontal, as in panel (a), in the presence of constant returns to scale. It is upward-sloping, as in panel (b), when increasing returns to scale at lower output levels give way to decreasing returns to scale at higher ones. In the long run, no firm will continue to operate while making losses; nothing, therefore, is supplied at prices below average total cost—as, for example, below point *h* in panel (b).

cheaper to produce a *given* output (such as that corresponding to point *m* or *n*) by running a larger plant *below* capacity (plant #2 at *m* instead of *f*, plant #5 at *n* instead of *g*) than by putting together an appropriately designed smaller plant (#1 or #3, not shown) that would produce this output when run at its capacity.

2. When decreasing returns to scale exist, it is similarly cheaper to produce a *given* output (such as that corresponding to point *p* or *q*) by running a smaller plant *above* capacity (plant #31 at *p* instead of *i*, plant #43 at *q* instead of *k*) than by putting together an appropriately designed larger plant (#39 or #47, not shown) that would produce this output when run at its capacity.

(If you should find this material difficult to understand, be assured that it is. You may find comfort in reading Biography 6.1 of Jacob Viner, one of this century's great economists. As you will see, he, too, had difficulty!)

Also note: A U-shaped curve of long-run average total cost implies a separate line of long-run marginal cost, such as *LRMC* in panel (b). (Falling average implies marginal below it, rising average implies marginal above it.) Because firms will not stay in business in the long run when making losses, and because every product price below the lowest possible average total cost at *h* would create such losses, the firm's long-run supply curve equals the rising branch of

BIOGRAPHY 6.1:

Jacob Viner

Jacob Viner (1892–1970) was born in Montreal, Canada and studied at McGill and Harvard. For many decades, he taught economics, first at the University of Chicago and later at Princeton. He was also a frequent consultant to the U. S. government. His presidency of the American Economic Association in 1939 was only one of a large number of honors bestowed upon him (among them honorary degrees from thirteen institutions of higher learning).

Viner's major interest was international trade. Consider this partial listing of his works: *Dumping: A Problem in International Trade* (1923), *Canada's Balance of International Indebtedness, 1900–1913* (1924), *Studies in the Theory of International Trade* (1937), *The Customs Union Issue* (1950), *International Economics* (1951), *International Trade and Economic Development* (1952). Viner also wrote on other subjects: *The Long View and the Short* (1958), *The Role of Providence in the Social Order* (1972).

Among microeconomists, Viner is best known for his brilliant article on "Cost Curves and Supply Curves," which appeared in the *Zeitschrift für Nationalökonomie* (September 1931, pp. 23–46). In this article, Viner introduced much of the material contained in this chapter, but he also made a single, though famous, mistake (which should not detract from his achievement). He instructed his draftsman to draw a smooth curve of long-run average total cost, as in panel (b) of Figure 6.8. The curve was to pass through all the minimum points of short-run total cost (such as *f*, *g*, *h*, *i*, and *k*) without ever rising above a short-run curve. His draftsman objected that this couldn't be done. Viner insisted; the result was a rather impossible graph.

Viner had confused the minimum (short-run) average total cost achievable in a given plant (such as *g* for plant #5 or *i* for plant #31) with the minimum (long-run) average total cost achievable for a given rate of production (such as *t* for 150,000 and *u* for 350,000 bushels of apples per year). The latter may well require the underutilization or overutilization of some plant. Two decades later, when his justly famous article was readied for reprinting, Viner declined the opportunity to revise it:[1]

> I do not take advantage of the opportunity [to revise]. . . . The error in Chart IV is left uncorrected so that future teachers and students may share the pleasure of many of their predecessors of pointing out that if I had known what an "envelope" was I would not have given my excellent draftsman the technically impossible and economically inappropriate assignment. . . ."

[1]"Supplementary Note (1950)" in American Economic Association, *Readings in Price Theory* (Chicago: Irwin, 1952), p. 227.

---

its long-run marginal cost above long-run average total cost.

Empirical Studies of Cost and Supply

Empirical studies of costs and supply are plagued by the difficulties, discussed in Chapter 5, of estimating production functions. In addition, as noted earlier in this chapter, problems arise because the economist's notion of cost differs from that of the accountant. Economics researchers, who inevitably must use accounting data, have to correct such data to bring them in line with the economist's idea of opportunity cost. This is a difficult task because accountants ignore most implicit costs and when they don't, as in the case of depreciation, they arrange the relevant numbers with a view to reaping tax advantages and not to reflecting the economic life of the assets in question.

Table 6.3 reports on some of the major

FIGURE 6.9   An Empirical Cost Function

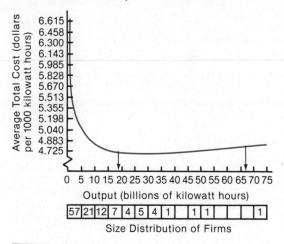

Size Distribution of Firms

This L-shaped cost function for U.S. firms producing electric power was calculated from cross-section data for a 1970 sample of 114 firms. The bulk of electricity output was generated by firms operating in the essentially flat area of the average total cost curve. (The arrows indicate the boundaries of the region of no significant economies or diseconomies of scale.) The replacement of existing firms by a much smaller number of extremely large firms (operating at minimum average total cost) would have reduced total U.S. electricity generating costs by only 3 percent in 1970.

Source: From Laurits R. Christensen and William H. Greene, "Economies of Scale in U.S. Electric Power Generation," *Journal of Political Economy*, August 1976, p. 674. Reprinted by permission of The University of Chicago Press. © 1976 by The University of Chicago.

empirical studies of long-run cost conducted by economists. The table can be studied most profitably after glancing once more at panel (b) of Figure 6.8. The long-run average total cost of a small or medium-sized firm in an industry may be that shown by points *m* or *n*, while larger firms enjoy costs as low as *h*. Column (2) of Table 6.3 shows this relative size for a number of industries studied. Evidence is overwhelming that long-run average total cost curves tend to be L-shaped, with the horizontal portion of the letter *L* covering a rather wide range of output. (This result, of course, reflects the widespread evidence on near-constant returns to scale, which was reported in Chapter 5.)

Figure 6.9 is an example of a typical empirical cost function. There is little evidence of long-run average total cost curves turning up as in section *hpq* of Figure 6.8. This may be the consequence of the fact that many cost studies use input-output data supplied by *engineers*, and engineers may not be very good at picking up diseconomies of scale which, as we argued, are likely to be caused by difficulties of *managerial* coordination. On the other hand, the absence of significant evidence on such diseconomies may instead reflect the fact that firms know when to stop their growth!

From Individual Supply to Market Supply

As in the case of demand, economists focus attention not so much on the supply of an *individual* firm, but on **market supply**, the sum of the supplies of all market participants.

Short-Run Market Supply

As long as all firms supplying a given product face identical market prices for inputs as well as outputs (and this we assume in the perfect markets we study throughout Part Two of this book), individual supplies will differ due to differences in technology or fixed input quantities, but they can be added together at each product price. Table 6.4 demonstrates how the short-run market supply schedule can be derived. Although we believe that thousands, perhaps millions, of sellers would appear in any perfect market, we need not concern ourselves with such large numbers. For the moment, and only to simplify the arithmetic, we can imagine only three sellers to exist in the market for apples. Their respective supply schedules might be those shown in columns (2) through (4) of Table 6.4. Their combined market supply schedule is shown in column (5). Natural-

TABLE 6.3 Summary of Selected Long-Run Cost Studies

Country, Industry (1)	Long-run Average Total Cost of Small Firms as a Percent- age of Minimum Achieved by Large Firms (2)	Source (3)
United States		
Hospitals (a)	130	C
(b)	100	I
Commercial banking		
demand deposits	116	A
installment loans	102	A
Electric power	112	D
Railroads (a) west	107 ⎫	
south	100 ⎬	B
east	83 ⎭	
(b)	100	G
Airlines (local service)	100	E
Trucking	95	H
Canada		
Life insurance	114	F

SOURCES:

A. F. W. Bell and N. B. Murphy, *Costs in Commercial Banking* (Boston: Federal Reserve Bank of Boston, Research Report No. 41, 1968).
B. George H. Borts, "The Estimation of Rail Cost Functions," *Econometrica*, January 1960, pp. 108–31.
C. Harold A. Cohen, "Hospital Cost Curves with Emphasis on Measuring Patient Care Output," in Herbert F. Klarman, ed., *Empirical Studies in Health Economics* (Baltimore: John Hopkins Press, 1970), pp. 279–93.
D. Laurits R. Christensen and William H. Greene, "Economies of Scale in U.S. Electric Power Generation," *Journal of Political Economy*, August 1976, pp. 655–76.
E. George Eads, Marc Nerlove, William Raduchel, "A Long-Run Cost Function for the Local Service Airline Industry: An Experiment in Non-Linear Estimation," *The Review of Economics and Statistics*, August 1969, pp. 258–70.
F. Randall Geehan, "Returns to Scale in the Life Insurance Industry," *The Bell Journal of Economics*, Autumn 1977, pp. 497–514.
G. Zvi Griliches, "Cost Allocation in Railroad Regulation," *The Bell Journal of Economics and Management Science*, Spring 1972, pp. 26–41.
H. Roger Koenker, "Optimal Scale and the Size Distribution of American Trucking Firms," *Journal of Transport Economics and Policy*, January 1977, pp. 54–67.
I. Judith R. Lave and Lester B. Lave, "Hospital Cost Functions," *The American Economic Review*, June 1970, pp. 379–95.
J. Aubrey Silberston, "Economies of Scale in Theory and Practice," *The Economic Journal*, March 1972, pp. 369–91. (In this study, small firms are defined as those producing half the output volume at which minimum average total costs are reached.)

ly, all this information can be graphed, as in Figure 6.10.

We have already noted a number of factors that will shift an individual firm's supply, such as changes in technology, the quantity of fixed inputs, and input prices. Because of the large number of sellers in a perfect market, such shifts in a single firm's supply will affect market supply only imperceptibly, but widespread changes in individual supplies will shift market supply noticeably. (Imagine what would happen to Figure 6.10 if a technical improvement in apple produc-

tion became generally available, if the climate changed, or if the prices of inputs rose sharply.)

Long-Run Market Supply

While the simple horizontal addition of short-run supply curves of individual firms is a tolerably correct procedure for deriving *short-run* market supply, things are much more complicated in the case of *long-run* supply. In the long run, neither the number of firms nor the size of their plants is fixed. As a result, a possible problem emerges

TABLE 6.3   (continued)

Country, Industry (1)	Long-run Average Total Cost of Small Firms as a Percentage of Minimum Achieved by Large Firms (2)	Source (3)
United Kingdom		J
Beer	155	
Dyes	144	
Newspapers	140	
Oil refineries	127	
Bread	130	
Bricks	130	
Ethylene	130	
Aircraft	125+	
Polymer manufacture	123	
Detergents	120	
Electric motors	120	
Sulfuric acid	119	
Cement	117	
Computers	113–116	
Steel	112–117	
Cars	110–113	
Refrigerators, washers	112	
Synthetic yarn extrusion	111	
Iron foundry	110–115	
Diesel engines	110+	
Machine tools	110	
Turbogenerators	110	
Footwear	105	
Bicycles		
Book printing	≈ 100	
Cotton textiles		
Plastics		

with the construction of a long-run market supply curve. Given its production function, the prices of inputs, and the number and size of other firms, the long-run supply of each *individual firm* in an industry may be accurately depicted, as in Figure 6.8, by horizontal *LRMC* in panel (a) or by upward-sloping *LRMC* (above point *h*) in panel (b). Yet the *industry's* long-run supply curve need not necessarily look like either of these lines. If the production functions or input prices available to individual firms were affected by the number and size of other firms operating in the industry, the derivation of long-run market supply would involve the addition of individual market supplies that were changing in the very

process of addition! The number and size of other firms can affect a firm's production function *(technological externalities)* or a firm's input prices *(pecuniary externalities)*.

Technological Externalities. When the *production function* of one firm is affected, favorably or unfavorably, by the operation of other firms, a **technological externality** is said to exist. To illustrate the effect of a favorable externality, let us imagine our apple orchard being operated on swampy soil. Its production function may be that underlying panel (b) of Figure 6.8. Its long-run supply curve may be *LRMC* above point *h* in that graph. Accordingly,

TABLE 6.4   Deriving the Short-Run Market Supply Schedule

Price (dollars per bushel) (1)	Quantity of Apples Supplied (bushels per year)			
	Firm A (2)	Firm B (3)	Firm C (4)	All Three Firms (5) = (2) + (3) + (4)
0	0	0	0	0
3.00	0	1,500	0	1,500
5.71	7,000	2,250	0	9,250
7.25	7,680	2,800	3,320	13,800
9.04	8,300	3,150	3,450	14,900
12.00	8,625	4,000	3,750	16,375
20.00	8,995	4,850	4,750	18,595
30.00	9,125	5,875	6,000	21,000

A short-run market supply schedule can be derived by adding, at each conceivable price, the quantities supplied by all potential market participants, all else being held equal. Note: Column (2) data refer to the firm depicted in Figure 6.6.

an increase in the price of apples from $7 per bushel to $17 per bushel, would, in the long run, increase our firm's annual quantity supplied from 250,000 bushels (point *h*) to 330,000 bushels (point *s*). Yet the simultaneous appearance of many new or larger competitors might falsify this result.

Our orchardists might find that higher product prices were drawing in ever larger numbers of new competitors, who were all draining land to plant new orchards. Our orchardists' own land might be drained indirectly as well. As a consequence, any given set of inputs might yield more apples than before because apple trees flourish in drier soil. This would mean that any given cost yielded more apples than before; all cost curves would shift down as the industry grew in size. Our orchard's individual supply curve would end up below or to the right of its former position. The firm might supply 400,000 rather than 330,000 bushels per year at the $17 price.

The process involved will be discussed in detail in the next chapter, but we can see now that *favorable* technological externalities make a long-run market supply line much flatter than a simple horizontal addition of given upward-sloping *LRMC* curves would suggest. Indeed, the market supply derived from such upward-sloping curves could even be horizontal or downward-

sloping. Favorable technological externalities that caused horizontal individual supplies [corresponding to *LRMC* in panel (a) of Figure 6.8] to shift down during an industry's expansion would, similarly, produce a downward-sloping market supply line.

Note: The presence of *unfavorable* technological externalities associated with industry growth would make the market supply line *steeper* than otherwise. Consider an apple orchard in the desert, relying on irrigation from wells. The appearance, as a result of higher product price, of more or larger firms might drastically reduce the water available to the original firms, leading to less output from otherwise identical inputs. Less output for the same cost would cause individual supply lines to shift above previous ones in the very process of industry expansion. Similar examples of unfavorable technological externalities would be the increasing difficulty of catching fish the more boats are fishing, the increasing difficulty of oil producers to get oil out of the ground the more oil wells there are, and the increasing difficulty of power stations to find cool river water the more firms there are to use rivers for cooling purposes.

Pecuniary Externalities.   When *input prices* paid by our firm are affected, favorably or unfavorably, by the operation of other firms, a **pecuniary externality** is said to exist. Our apple orchard can provide an example of the presence of an unfavorable externality. Imagine that any increase in product price caused additional firms to enter the apple industry or caused existing firms to expand. Their activities might raise the prices of inputs used in the industry: the wages of apple pickers, the rental rates of spraying machines, the prices of fertilizer and pesticides. As a consequence, any given set of inputs would yield the same quantity of apples as before but would cost more. Our orchard's cost curves would shift up as the industry grew in size; its supply curve would end up above or to the left of its former position. If, in panel (b) of Figure 6.8, the apple price rose from $7 per bushel to $17 per bushel, our firm's quantity supplied might rise from 250,000 bushels not to 330,000 bushels per year, but only to 260,000 bushels per year. The market supply line would be steeper than otherwise.

Note: An analogous argument can be made with respect to *favorable* pecuniary externalities. Their presence would make the market supply line flatter than otherwise, possibly even negatively sloped. Consider the possibility of *lowered*

input prices as an industry expanded because, perhaps, the presence of a larger number of firms stimulated the development of more or better resources usable by the industry (see Chapter 7 for further discussion).

Market Supply Examined: Elasticity

As in the case of *quantity demanded*, economists are interested in measuring the responsiveness of a good's *quantity supplied* to the good's price. A good's **price elasticity of supply** is the percentage change in quantity supplied divided by the percentage change in the good's price, all else being equal. Denoting this elasticity by ϵ_s, quantity supplied by Q, price by P, and changes in these variables by Δ, the elasticity formula for any good, a, is analogous to the elasticity formula for demand presented in Chapter 4:

$$\text{Price elasticity of supply, } \epsilon_s = \frac{\dfrac{\Delta Q_a}{Q_a}}{\dfrac{\Delta P_a}{P_a}}.$$

Indeed, the entire discussion of own-price elasticity in Chapter 4 (see pp. 95–98) is relevant

FIGURE 6.10 Deriving Short-Run Market Supply

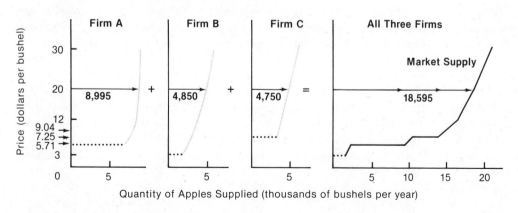

This graph, which is based on Table 6.4, shows how short-run market supply can be derived by adding horizontally, at each conceivable price, the quantities supplied by all market participants, all else being equal.

here. As in the case of demand, the elasticity of supply can be read instantly at any point along a supply curve by applying the *PAPO* rule. (According to the *PAPO* rule, the elasticity at a given point equals the distance from the point to the abscissa, P→A, divided by the distance from the point to the ordinate, P→O, along a tangent to the curve at the point in question.) Consider Figure 6.11, which shows eight different supply lines, labeled S_1 through S_8. To measure the price elasticity of supply at point *a* on S_1, for example, we place a tangent on S_1 at *a*, which is conveniently provided by supply line S_2 and its dotted extension. The price elasticity of supply at *a* then equals distance *ab* (point to abscissa) divided by the distance *ac* (point to ordinate), or about +2. This means that a one-percent change in price will elicit, in the immediate vicinity of *a*, a two-percent change in quantity supplied in the same direction. By placing similar tangents at other points on S_1, similar calculations could be performed.

Now consider the straight supply line S_2. Obviously, at point *a*, the price elasticity of supply is also +2. To the left and below *a*, this elasticity is larger; to the right and above *a*, it is smaller, but it is always larger than unity. (Can you show why elasticity is always larger than unity along any straight supply line that intercepts the ordinate in quadrant I of our coordinates?)

In contrast, the price elasticity of supply at any point on lines S_3 and S_4 equals unity exactly. Elasticity is unity for all points on any straight supply line going through the origin. The distance from any chosen point to the abscissa then always equals that from the point to the ordinate, because both axes are met at origin 0. Now consider the price elasticity of supply at *d*, on either line S_5 or S_6. It equals distance *de* (point to abscissa) divided by distance *df* (point to ordinate), or +0.56. This means that a one-percent change in price will elicit, in the immediate vicinity of *d*, only about a 0.5 percent change in quantity supplied in the same direction. Indeed, along any straight supply line that intercepts the abscissa in quadrant I of our coordi-

FIGURE 6.11 Price Elasticity of Supply

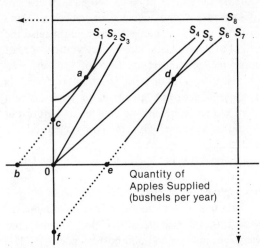

With the help of the *PAPO* rule (see p. 97), the price elasticity of supply can be determined instantly at any point on any supply curve.

nates, the price elasticity of supply, though changing, is less than unity because one quantity (such as *de*) is always divided by a larger one (such as *df*).

Finally, consider vertical supply line, S_7, and horizontal line, S_8. Price elasticity of supply equals zero at all points on the vertical line because point-to-abscissa distances of varying lengths are always divided by infinity (point to ordinate). Common sense tells us that a vertical supply line indicates that no change in price can elicit even the slightest change in quantity supplied. Such may be the situation in the very short run, as when fishing boats return from the sea (or berry pickers return from the forest) and offer a momentarily fixed quantity of perishable products for sale. Given more time, of course, boats can go to sea (or berry pickers to the forest) more or less frequently, hence the quantity they supply will become responsive to price. Not surprisingly, therefore, price elasticities of supply, like those of demand, tend to be larger in the long run

CLOSE-UP 6.2:

The Long-Run Price Elasticity of the Supply of New Housing Construction

The purchase price of a new house is based essentially on two components: the price of the land and the price of the structure. Given that the price elasticity of the supply of land in urban areas is less than infinity, a rising demand for new homes inevitably drives up the price of land and consequently the price of housing. James R. Follain, Jr. wanted to know whether an increased demand for new homes would have a similar effect on the housing price by driving up the price of the structure component.

Using data for the 1947–75 period, he tested the hypothesis that the long-run supply of new residential construction had an elasticity of infinity. This would be true if the building industry, given enough time, could adjust its capabilities without limit at given minimum average total costs. Test results confirmed the hypothesis. The long-run supply curve for new construction was found to be horizontal. This suggested that the portion of recent increases in housing prices attributable to a lethargic response by builders would eventually dissipate. Note: This situation is depicted in panel (a) of Figure 6.8 by the rising short-run supply curves (SRMC) and by the horizontal long-run supply curve (LRMC).

Source: James R. Follain, Jr., "The Price Elasticity of the Long-Run Supply of New Housing Construction," *Land Economics*, May 1979, pp. 190–99.

---

than in the short run. The extreme case is illustrated by line S_8, which has an elasticity of infinity at all points. It corresponds to the constant-returns-to-scale long-run supply line of panel (a) in Figure 6.8.

Note: Supply elasticities can also be defined and calculated with respect to variables other than a good's own price. When goods are produced jointly (wool and mutton) or when goods are competitive in production (wheat and rye), economists calculate *cross-price elasticities* of supply, which show the responsiveness of one good's quantity supplied to the price of another good. Similarly, various *income elasticities* of supply can be calculated—for example, the responsiveness of the supply of a good to incomes earned in the industry could be determined to see whether higher incomes reduce the quantity of inputs supplied to an industry and hence reduce the quantity supplied of the industry's product. In general, though, economists have been less inclined to calculate these other types of elasticities than in the case of demand because such estimates are less useful. Unlike demand elasticities, supply elasticities tell us nothing, for example, about the amount of money spent by buyers or taken in by sellers (see Chapter 4 for a discussion of the types of elasticity of demand).

Table 6.5 brings together the results of supply studies for fresh vegetables during the 1919–55 period. The short-run elasticities were calculated for one growing period. Not surprisingly, long-run elasticities are larger, often considerably so. In the long run, each firm can change the quantities of formerly fixed inputs. In addition, the number of firms in the industry can change. More firms are likely to enter an industry as the price of the industry's product rises because that raises profit (all else being equal), and profit indicates the extra income owners of firms can earn in this industry as compared to other industries. Similarly, existing firms will leave an industry altogether if the price of the industry's product falls sufficiently to create losses. While firms may continue producing while making losses in the short run, they will never do so in the long run because losses (as economists define them) point to extra income the owners of firms could earn in other activities. Thus it is not surprising, as Table 6.5 tells us, that a 1 percent change in the price of spinach causes only a 0.2 percent change, in the same direction, in quantity

TABLE 6.5   Selected Estimates of Price Elasticities of Supply in the United States

Good	Elasticity		Good	Elasticity	
	Short Run	Long Run		Short Run	Long Run
Cantalopes	0.02	0.04	Green snap beans	0.15	∞
Lettuce	0.03	0.16	Eggplant	0.16	0.34
Green peppers	0.07	0.26	Tomatoes	0.16	0.90
Green lima beans	0.10	1.70	Kale	0.20	0.23
Shallots	0.12	0.31	Spinach	0.20	4.70
Beets	0.13	1.00	Watermelons	0.23	0.48
Carrots	0.14	1.00	Green peas	0.31	4.40
Cauliflower	0.14	1.10	Onions	0.34	1.00
Celery	0.14	0.95	Cabbage	0.36	1.20

SOURCE: Adapted from Marc Nerlove and William Addison, "Statistical Estimation of Long-Run Elasticities of Supply and Demand," *Journal of Farm Economics*, November 1958, Vol. XL, p. 872.

supplied when a given growing season is considered. Yet, over a longer period, when the size and number of firms can change, the change in quantity supplied associated with a 1 percent price change rises to 4.7 percent.

SUMMARY

1. Given the prices of output and inputs, production-function data can be translated into prospective revenues and costs. The relationship between revenue and cost, in turn, determines how much of a good a profit-maximizing firm will supply. It is important to distinguish the accountant's concept of cost from that of the economist. With the exception of depreciation allowances, the accountant focuses on *explicit* costs. The economist, in order to derive a measure of opportunity cost, adds *implicit* costs to explicit costs.

2. The *total* cost incurred by a firm in the short run can be divided into *fixed* and *variable* costs (which should not be confused with *indirect* and *direct* costs). Economists use information about variable and total cost to calculate *average variable cost, average total cost*, and *marginal cost*.

3. Graphs of short-run cost curves can be used to depict the optimum rate of production of a

firm in the short run. As long as product price equals or exceeds minimum average variable cost, the optimum output level is always found where product price and rising marginal cost are equal.

4. Analysis of short-run cost curves and product-price information leads to the identification of the rising arm of the marginal-cost curve (above minimum average variable cost) as the firm's short-run supply curve.

5. A firm operating in the short run (even if it avoids X-inefficiency) is not necessarily producing its output at a cost as low as could be achieved in the long run when all conceivable input combinations can be realized. This difference between costs achievable in the short run and in the long run can be illustrated with the help of isoquants and isocost lines. A profit-maximizing firm's optimum input combination for a given output is found at the point where the relevant isoquant just touches an isocost line. The long-run marginal cost at or above the level of long-run average total cost is the long-run supply curve of firms operating in perfect markets. This long-run supply curve is horizontal in the presence of constant returns to scale and upward-sloping when increasing returns to scale at lower output levels give way to decreasing returns to scale at higher levels.

6. Evidence from a number of empirical studies of cost and supply indicates that curves of long-run average total cost tend to be L-shaped, with the horizontal portion of the letter *L* covering a rather wide range of output.

7. The supply curves of individual firms can be added together to yield market supply, although the presence of technological or pecuniary externalities may complicate the procedure.

8. The responsiveness of a good's quantity supplied to its price is measured by the price elasticity of supply. Empirical measures indicate higher elasticities for the long run than the short run.

KEY TERMS

average fixed cost
average loss
average profit
average revenue
average total cost *(ATC)*
average variable cost *(AVC)*
break-even analysis
break-even point
capacity output
change in quantity supplied
change in supply
direct costs
envelope curve
explicit costs
fixed cost
implicit costs
incremental-profit analysis
indirect costs
isocost line
"law" of upward-sloping supply
loss
marginal cost *(MC)*
marginal profit
marginal revenue *(MR)*
market supply

optimal rate of plant operation
optimum plant
overhead costs
pecuniary externality
planning curve
plant
price elasticity of supply
prime costs
profit
shutdown point
supply
technological externality
total cost
variable cost

QUESTIONS AND PROBLEMS

1. "Given the economist's definition of cost as *opportunity cost*, the average total costs of different firms in an industry cannot differ. If one firm, for example, had superior management or land, it would have lower average variable costs than its competitors, but its average fixed costs would be correspondingly higher." Discuss.

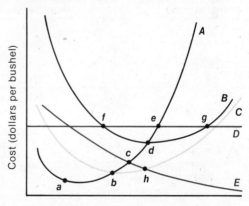

2. Consider the graph above and identify:
  a. the marginal-cost curve.
  b. the average-total-cost curve.
  c. the average-variable-cost curve.
  d. the average-fixed-cost curve.

e. the short-run supply curve.

f. the marginal-revenue curve.

g. the average-revenue curve.

h. the capacity output level.

i. the break-even point on the short-run supply curve.

j. the shutdown point on the short-run supply curve.

3. Consider the profitable business in Figure 6.2.

a. What would happen to the firm's optimum, if government imposed a 50 percent tax on profit?

b. What if the government imposed a $20,000 license fee?

c. A $1 tax per bushel of output?

4. Suppose that each of the input combinations, A to D, in the table below could produce an output of 1,000 bushels of apples per year. Draw the 1,000-bushel isoquant in a graph. Assume that 1 pound of fertilizer sells for one fifth as much as 1 hour of labor, and determine the minimum-cost combination of inputs for this level of output. What would the minimum-cost combination be if the price of labor halved?

	Fertilizer (pounds per year)	Labor (hours per year)
(A)	1,000	200
(B)	640	360
(C)	360	640
(D)	200	1,000

5. In Figures 6.1–6.5, *short-run* total-cost curves appear along with *short-run* average-total-cost and marginal-cost curves. Yet when *long-run* average total cost and marginal cost are depicted in Figure 6.8, no long-run total-cost curve is shown. How would you draw a long-run total-cost curve and why?

6. Review Analytical Example 6.2 "Break-Even Analysis."

a. Suppose the charter business were already a going concern, selling 700 hours a year (at an average total cost of $84.36). Would the ex-professor be wiser to accept or to reject someone's offer to pay $50 for an hour's ride? How about $20?

b. Produce a break-even analysis for the prospective publication of a college textbook.

7. In 1974, a quarter million baby turkeys were killed by turkey hatcheries in Georgia because the cost of raising turkeys (34 cents a pound) far outstripped what farmers could get for them (20 cents a pound). Analyze this event with the help of *incremental-profit analysis* (refer to Analytical Example 6.3).

8. Are each of the following true or false?

a. Direct costs equal prime costs.

b. Prime costs equal variable costs.

c. Indirect costs equal overhead costs.

d. Overhead costs equal fixed costs.

e. If marginal cost were to fall with higher output, average total cost would have to fall.

f. The total variable cost at any output level equals the sum of marginal costs up to that output level.

g. The most profitable level of production for any firm is the one at which average total cost is minimized.

h. If the profitable apple orchard pictured in Figure 6.2 were run by a surgeon, its profit would instantly vanish.

i. The minimum point on a curve of short-run average total cost shows the lowest average total cost of production for a given fixed cost.

j. A rise in a good's price leads to an increase in its supply.

k. The long-run average-total-cost curve shows the lowest possible average cost for producing any given output when the firm has time to make all the adjustments in input combinations it wants to make.

l. The long-run supply curve of a firm is an envelope curve.

m. The lowest point on a firm's long-run supply curve can be found at the capacity output level of the optimum plant.

n. Technological externalities make the market supply curve less price elastic at any given quantity.

o. Pecuniary externalities make the market supply curve less price elastic at any given price.

p. All straight-line supply curves have the same price elasticity at every point on the curve.

q. The slope of a straight total-cost line equals marginal cost.

r. The slope of a straight total-cost line equals average variable cost.

s. The slope of a straight total-cost line equals average total cost.

t. The presence of X-inefficiency would push all cost curves vertically downward.

u. If one drew a curve of average fixed cost in a graph like Figure 6.1, it would decline and never rise, no matter how big production became.

SELECTED READINGS

Johnston, John. *Statistical Cost Analysis*. New York: McGraw-Hill, 1960.

An important work on cost functions and their empirical estimation.

Machlup, Fritz; Samuelson, Paul; and Baumol, William J. "In Memoriam: Jacob Viner (1892–1970)." *Journal of Political Economy*, January/February 1972, pp. i–15.

Viner, Jacob. "Cost Curves and Supply Curves." American Economic Association. *Readings in Price Theory*, Chicago: Irwin, 1952, chap. 10.

A reprint of the famous article of 1931, with the addition of a supplementary note.

Walters, Alan A. "Production and Cost Functions: An Econometric Survey." *Econometrica*, January–April, 1963, pp. 1–66.

Tables VI–VIII summarize a large number of empirical cost studies. Includes an excellent bibliography.

APPENDIX 6A

Linear Programming

The conventional theory of the firm, as presented in Chapters 5 and 6, is rather general. It covers the short run and the long run. It considers relationships between output and other variables (such as inputs, revenue, cost, or profit) that are linear or curvilinear. It extends over any range of output. Many of the day-to-day problems of business managers, however, are concerned with the short run only and with linear relations over fairly narrow ranges of output. The mathematical technique of **linear programming** is ideally suited for solving managerial problems under such circumstances. The technique was developed since World War II: in the Soviet Union by Leonid V. Kantorovich (see Biography 6A.1) and in the United States by George B. Dantzig and Tjalling C. Koopmans. The technique involves the maximization (or minimization) of a linear function of variables, subject to constraints that limit what can be done, as will be explained below.

While the term *programming* simply refers to a systematic type of decision making, the adjective *linear* reminds us that all relevant relationships are those that can be represented by straight lines (as, for example, in Analytical Example 6.2, "Break-Even Analysis"). The fact that relationships are linear implies constant returns to scale and input and output prices that do not vary with a firm's output level. All of this is likely to be true over limited output ranges, even for firms that do not operate in perfect markets. Let us consider a number of typical applications of the technique.

A Minimization Problem

One frequent problem faced by management is finding that input mix among a variety of possible input mixes which *minimizes* the total cost of producing a specified output. Consider the case of a firm that wishes to produce 3 tons of paint per day. Assume all relevant relationships are linear: Up to the desired output quantity, the prices of the firm's inputs (labor and capital) are constant at $600 per unit of labor and $1,800 per unit of capital, and constant returns to scale prevail in the firm's production function. The four different production processes that are available are shown in columns (A) to (D) of Table 6A.1.

The information in Table 6A.1 can be graphed, as in Figure 6A.1. If paint is produced by process (A), labor, L, must be combined with capital, K, in a fixed ratio of 20 to 1, as shown in the graph by the ray labeled "Production Process A." Point A_1 indicates that $20L$ plus $1K$ can produce 1 ton of paint by process (A). Point A_2 indicates that doubling the inputs doubles output, and A_3 tells us that tripling inputs triples output. Output is similarly measured along the other production rays. Using process (B), which combines labor and capital in a fixed ratio of 10 to 2, the input combinations needed to produce one, two, and three tons of paint are shown by points B_1, B_2, and B_3, respectively. Again, constant returns to scale prevail: Distances $0B_1$, B_1B_2, and B_2B_3 are equal to each other, just as $0A_1$ equals A_1A_2 and A_2A_3, in turn.

FIGURE 6A.1
Production-Process Rays and Isoquants

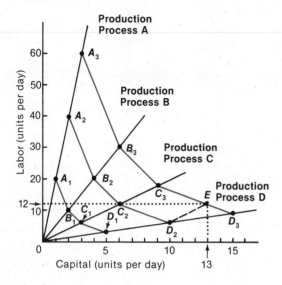

The four straight rays from the origin represent the limited number of production processes available to a firm. Under constant returns to scale, equal distances (such as $0A_1$, A_1A_2, and A_2A_3) along any one ray represent equal output quantities. Isoquants can be constructed by connecting input combinations producing the same output (such as A_1, B_1, C_1, and D_1).

Note: While equal distances along any *one* ray represent equal output quantities, equal distances along *different* rays do not because A_1, B_1, C_1, and D_1 each represent input combinations capable of producing 1 ton of paint per day, and distances $0A_1$, $0B_1$, $0C_1$, and $0D_1$ are clearly different.

We can, however, join points of equal output on the four production rays to give us *isoquants* for various output levels. Line $A_2B_2C_2D_2$, for instance, shows all the combinations of inputs

capable of producing at most 2 tons of paint per day. Any point on a segment between two production process rays, such as E, indicates an output quantity that can be produced by a combination of the two processes represented by the two rays the segment connects. Note how point E indicates the production of 3 tons of paint by use of $12L$ and $13K$, a combination that does not appear in any of the four processes in Table 6A.1. Yet the feat can be accomplished by producing 1 ton by means of process C (using $6L$ plus $3K$) and 2 more tons by means of process D (using $6L$ and $10K$). This can be determined graphically by constructing a line from E parallel to ray C (dashed line) or parallel to ray D (not shown). The dashed line happens to intersect ray D at D_2, indicating that the input combination corresponding to E can produce 3 tons if 2 of them are produced by process D (a line through E parallel to ray D would intersect ray C at C_1, indicating E would also require 1 ton produced by process C).

To solve this minimization problem, we need information not only about possible input combinations but also about *input prices*. The slope of each *isocost line* (Figure 6A.2) reflects the assumed input prices of $600 per unit of labor and $1,800 per unit of capital. When the 3-ton isoquant of Figure 6A.1 ($A_3B_3C_3D_3$) is superimposed upon the isocost lines, the solution to our problem emerges at once: 3 tons of paint per day are produced most cheaply by using production process C. Any other input combination capable of producing 3 tons per day (such as F) would cost more.

Note: The solution to every linear programming problem can always be read at a "corner," such as C_3. (What if the isocost line had had a

TABLE 6A.1 Alternative Ways to Produce a Product

Type of Input	Units of Input Needed for the Production of 1 Ton of Paint per Day, Using Process			
	(A)	(B)	(C)	(D)
Labor	20	10	6	3
Capital	1	2	3	5

TABLE 6A.2 Alternative Ways to Use Given Inputs

Type of Input	Units of Inputs Needed for the Production of		Quantity of Inputs Available (units per day)
	1 Refrigerator (1)	1 Washer (2)	(3)
Labor #1 (hours)	10	0	350
Labor #2 (hours)	0	5	125
Raw materials (pounds)	50	100	3,000
Machine time (hours)	5	4	200

slightly different slope and coincided with an isoquant *segment*, such as B_3C_3? Then corners B_3 and C_3 would have been equally good at giving us the answer, and all points in-between would have been equivalent.)

While the above example is an extremely simple one (that could have been solved without the graphs), many real-world problems are considerably more complex (and cannot be solved with the help of graphs at all). A more complex example follows.

A Maximization Problem

Another typical problem faced by management is finding that product mix which maximizes the value of output produced with the available inputs. Table 6A.2 clearly points to alternative ways to use given inputs. The firm in question could produce either refrigerators or washers (but each with a single production process only.)

The technology embodied in columns (1) and (2) of the table and the fixed quantities of inputs available to the firm in column (3) restrict the production possibilities to the product combinations in the unshaded area of Figure 6A.3. Because there are only 350 units of type #1 labor in a day and 10 units of such labor are needed to make one refrigerator, a maximum of 35 refrigerators can be produced in a day. The vertical line limits refrigerator production but not the production of washers, which does not require this type of labor at all. The availability of only 125 units of labor #2, similarly, only limits the production

of washers (to a maximum of 25 per day); hence the horizontal line. Because raw materials and machine time must be used for either product, these inputs limit the production of both. Some 3,000 units of raw materials can make 60 refrigerators *or* 30 washers; some 200 hours of machine time can make 40 refrigerators *or* 50 washers; hence the sloped lines. Note how the combination of these constraint lines produces a production possibilities frontier for our firm (color line). Given its present technology, the firm's inputs are insufficient to produce any of the product mixes lying in the shaded area of the graph.

FIGURE 6A.2 Cost Minimization

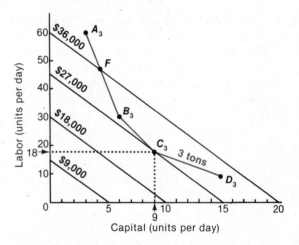

The cost of producing 3 tons of product per day can be minimized (at $27,000 per day), if production process C is utilized. The optimum combination of inputs at C_3 uses 18 units of labor and 9 units of capital.

As in the minimization example, a graphical solution can be found easily. Figure 6A.4 shows a family of **isorevenue lines** that are akin to isocost lines. Instead of showing input combinations that cost the same amount, each of these lines shows all the alternative combinations of two outputs that the firm is able to sell in a given period at current market prices, *while receiving the same total revenue*. The lines in Figure 6A.4 have been drawn on the assumption that the firm can sell each washer at $280 and each refrigerator at $200. When the production-possibilities fron-tier of Figure 6A.3 is superimposed upon the isorevenue lines, the solution to our problem is immediately apparent: Revenue is maximized when $16\frac{2}{3}$ washers and $26\frac{2}{3}$ refrigerators are produced per day. Any other feasible output combination (such as *P, Q* or *N*) would bring in less revenue. As in the minimization problem, the solution emerges at a ''corner'' (point *M*).

Naturally, in more complicated problems (involving, perhaps, hundreds of products, each one producible by a variety of processes), graphical solutions are out of the question. George B.

BIOGRAPHY 6A.1:

Leonid V. Kantorovich

Leonid Vitalyevich Kantorovich (1912–   ) was born in St. Petersburg, Russia. His career as a mathematical genius advanced rapidly. At the age of 14, he enrolled at Leningrad University; by the time he was 22, he was a full professor of mathematics. During World War II, he worked at Leningrad's Naval Engineering School; in 1949, he received the Stalin Prize for his work in pure mathematics on functional analysis and computer development. In 1958, he was elected to the prestigious Soviet Academy of Sciences and re-ceived the 1965 Lenin Prize for his work in mathematical economics (shared with the chief architects of the mathematical revolution in So-viet economics, V. S. Nemchinov and V. V. Novozhilov). In the 1970s, Kantorovich headed the Moscow Institute for the Management of the National Economy. While there, in 1975, he re-ceived the Nobel Memorial Prize in Economic Science (jointly with T. C. Koopmans). He is now working at the All-Union Scientific Research Insti-tute for Systems Research.

In the 1930s, the Central Plywood Trust ap-proached Kantorovich with a problem. The pro-ducers of plywood were rotating logs in stripping machines that cut off a continuous thin sheet of material. These sheets were then laminated to make plywood. There were many types of logs and many machines with different productivities.

How could one match logs to machines so as to process the largest possible volume per unit of time? Kantorovich responded by inventing linear programming. His 1939 Leningrad paper, "Math-ematical Methods of Organizing and Planning Production," was the first publication ever to appear on the subject.

By 1943, Kantorovich realized that the nation-al economic plan itself could be viewed as a grandiose linear programming problem. He ex-tended linear programming from a tool for solv-ing short-run planning problems of the firm to one for solving the short-run planning problems of the nation. He noted that the optimum solution of the national planning problem revealed shadow prices for all goods and resources, which could be used to make crucial decisions. His calcula-tion of positive prices for the use of scarce capital and natural resources, however, clashed with Stalinist ideology (which insisted that such re-sources be priced at zero under socialism to reflect their common ownership by all the people). As a result of this clash, Kantorovich's book on *The Best Use of Economic Resources* was not published until 1959, well after Stalin's death. Since then, Kantorovich has extended his earlier model of optimal short-run national planning to long-run planning as well.

FIGURE 6A.3 Input Constraints and Production Possibilities

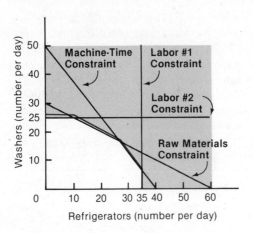

Given technology and fixed input quantities, a firm's production possibilities (indicated by the unshaded area) can be determined.

Dantzig was the first to develop a mathematical routine for solving such complicated problems called the **simplex method**. The simplex method does not get its name, however, because it is simple, but because *simplex* refers to the *n*-dimensional analogue of a triangle, and a computer can be programmed to search the "corners" of such triangles for the optimum solution to linear programming problems.

The Simplex Method and Shadow Prices

Our product-mix problem is simple enough to lend itself to a demonstration of the algebraic solution that would normally be performed by a computer. For this purpose, it is useful to expand the data of Table 6A.2 in Table 6A.3, "Activity Analysis." Our firm is engaged in six "activities" defined in such a way that as a group they must utilize completely the inputs available. These activities include the production of refrigerators, the production of washers, and the "production" of unemployment of each one of the

four inputs. Columns (1)–(6) show how much of each type of input must be utilized to perform each of the six activities at the level of 1 unit: The production of 1 refrigerator *(R)*, column (1) tells us, uses up 10 hours of labor #1, zero hours of labor #2, 50 pounds of raw materials, and 5 hours of machine time. Similarly, the production of 1 washer *(W)* uses up zero hours of labor #1, 5 hours of labor #2, 100 pounds of raw materials, and 4 hours of machine time. The "production" of 1 unit of unemployment of labor #1 (U_{L1}) uses up 1 hour of labor #1 and none of the other inputs. Finally, the "production" of 1 unit of unemployment of labor #2 (U_{L2}), of raw materials (U_{RM}), or of machine time (U_M) each uses only one unit of the respective inputs. Altogether, of course, only the input quantities shown in column (7), listing the constraints *(C)*, can be used.

The information contained in each of the table columns can be written as a column vector, such as

$$R = \begin{bmatrix} 10 \\ 0 \\ 50 \\ 5 \end{bmatrix} \text{ or } U_M = \begin{bmatrix} 0 \\ 0 \\ 0 \\ 1 \end{bmatrix} \text{ or } C = \begin{bmatrix} 350 \\ 125 \\ 3,000 \\ 200 \end{bmatrix}$$

Correspondingly, the performance of any one of these activities at a higher rate raises the input utilization in proportion:

$$3R = 3\begin{bmatrix} 10 \\ 0 \\ 50 \\ 5 \end{bmatrix} = \begin{bmatrix} 3 \times 10 \\ 3 \times 0 \\ 3 \times 50 \\ 3 \times 5 \end{bmatrix} = \begin{bmatrix} 30 \\ 0 \\ 150 \\ 15 \end{bmatrix}$$

This indicates that the production of 3 refrigerators uses 30 hours of labor #1, zero hours of labor #2, 150 pounds of raw materials, and 15 hours of machine time.

To determine the optimal levels of each of the six activities, we need, first, the firm's **objective function**, a statement of the goal (or objective) that is to be achieved. Since we assumed that the firm will seek a maximum value

(V) of output produced from its given resources in column (7), and since output prices were assumed to be $200 per refrigerator and $280 per washer, we can state the firm's objective as the *maximization* of

$$V = 200a + 280b, \tag{6A.1}$$

where *a* and *b*, respectively, denote the numbers of refrigerators and washers produced.

We can, second, designate the firm's production possibilities by a single equation, in which the letters *a* through *f* refer to the unknown levels of the six possible activities:

$$aR + bW + cU_{L1} + dU_{L2} + eU_{RM} + fU_M = C. \tag{6A.2}$$

According to this equation, producing *a* units of refrigerators plus *b* units of washers, while keeping *c, d, e,* and *f* units, respectively, of labor #1, labor #2, raw materials, and machine time unemployed, must exactly meet the constraint of available inputs. The capital letters are, of course, short-hand ways of writing down columns (1)–(7) of Table 6A.3. Equation (6A.2), therefore, should be envisioned to imply the following:

$$a\begin{bmatrix} 10 \\ 0 \\ 50 \\ 5 \end{bmatrix} + b\begin{bmatrix} 0 \\ 5 \\ 100 \\ 4 \end{bmatrix} + c\begin{bmatrix} 1 \\ 0 \\ 0 \\ 0 \end{bmatrix} + d\begin{bmatrix} 0 \\ 1 \\ 0 \\ 0 \end{bmatrix}$$
$$+ e\begin{bmatrix} 0 \\ 0 \\ 1 \\ 0 \end{bmatrix} + f\begin{bmatrix} 0 \\ 0 \\ 0 \\ 1 \end{bmatrix} = \begin{bmatrix} 350 \\ 125 \\ 3,000 \\ 200 \end{bmatrix}$$

This can be expanded into four equations, one for each of the table rows:

$$10a + 0b + 1c + 0d + 0e + 0f = 350 \tag{6A.3}$$

$$0a + 5b + 0c + 1d + 0e + 0f = 125 \tag{6A.4}$$

FIGURE 6A.4 Revenue Maximization

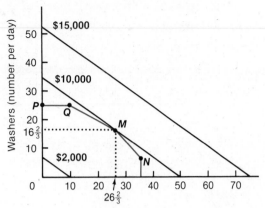

The revenue from using the given inputs underlying the production possibilities frontier shown here can be maximized (at $10,000 per day) by producing output combination *M*. This optimum combines the production of $16\frac{2}{3}$ washers and $26\frac{2}{3}$ refrigerators per day.

$$50a + 100b + 0c + 0d + 1e + 0f = 3,000 \tag{6A.5}$$

$$5a + 4b + 0c + 0d + 0e + 1f = 200 \tag{6A.6}$$

These equations are easy to interpret. For example, equation (6A.3) refers to hours of labor #1: 10 hours times the unknown quantity *a* of refrigerators, plus 1 hour times the unknown quantity *c* of unemployed labor #1, must equal the 350 hours of labor #1 available. Equations (6A.4) through (6A.6) make similar statements about the other 3 types of input.

Our firm's optimum production program can be found by solving equations (6A.3)–(6A.6), subject to the goal stated in equation (6A.1). But note that the *four* equations (6A.3)–(6A.6) contain *six* unknowns; hence a large number of answers are possible. Some of these answers (namely all those providing negative values for *a* to *f*) can be ruled out as economic nonsense: One cannot produce negative refrigerators or negative washers, and the "production" of negative unemployment for inputs would, in effect, amount to using greater input quantities than are availa-

TABLE 6A.3 Activity Analysis

Type of Input	Units of Inputs Needed for the Production of						Constraints (Units of inputs available per day)
	1 Refrigerator	1 Washer	1 Unit of Unemployment of				
			Labor #1	Labor #2	Raw Materials	Machine Time	
	(1)	(2)	(3)	(4)	(5)	(6)	(7)
(A) Labor #1 (hours)	10	0	1	0	0	0	350
(B) Labor #2 (hours)	0	5	0	1	0	0	125
(C) Raw materials (pounds)	50	100	0	0	1	0	3,000
(D) Machine time (hours)	5	4	0	0	0	1	200

ble. The *simplex method* provides a systematic procedure for finding the best solution among all the remaining combinations of zero or positive unknowns.

Finding the Basic Feasible Solution

The simplex method begins by establishing a "basic feasible solution"; that is, *any* solution of *n* equations and *n* unknowns that does not violate the constraints. If, for example, we arbitrarily set *a* and *b* equal to zero, we are left with four equations and four unknowns, summarized by

Basic feasible solution.
$$cU_{L1} + dU_{L2} + eU_{RM} + fU_M = C \qquad (6A.7)$$

In this case, as an inspection of equations (6A.3)–(6A.6) immediately reveals, $c = 350$, $d = 125$, $e = 3,000$, and $f = 200$. The firm "produces" nothing but unemployment; no refrigerators or washers are produced; the value of output equals zero.

Improving Upon the Basic Solution

Step 2 of the simplex method (see Table 6A.4) tests for possible changes in this basic solution. The simplex method, in effect, applies the optimization principle. *Any activity not included in a given solution*, the simplex method suggests, *should be added, and other activities requiring equivalent resources should be deleted, if the net effect is to improve upon the achievement of the goal.* That goal, in our case, is to maximize *V*.

Consider, for example, adding the produc-

tion of refrigerators to the four activities contained in equation (6A.7). To find the amounts of other activities that are equivalent to the production of 1 refrigerator, we write

$$R = wU_{L1} + xU_{L2} + yU_{RM} + zU_M. \qquad (6A.8)$$

This, of course, is shorthand for four equations:

$$\begin{bmatrix} 10 \\ 0 \\ 50 \\ 5 \end{bmatrix} = w \begin{bmatrix} 1 \\ 0 \\ 0 \\ 0 \end{bmatrix} + x \begin{bmatrix} 0 \\ 1 \\ 0 \\ 0 \end{bmatrix} + y \begin{bmatrix} 0 \\ 0 \\ 1 \\ 0 \end{bmatrix} + z \begin{bmatrix} 0 \\ 0 \\ 0 \\ 1 \end{bmatrix}$$

It follows that $w = 10$, $x = 0$, $y = 50$, and $z = 5$. Therefore,

$$R = 10U_{L1} + 0U_{L2} + 50U_{RM} + 5U_M. \qquad (6A.9)$$

If the firm wants to add 1R to its operations, it must reduce labor #1 unemployment by 10 units, raw material unemployment by 50 units and machine-time unemployment by 5 units. As the first line of Table 6A.4 shows, the addition would raise total revenue by $200 (the price of a refrigerator); the deletion would have no effect on revenue; the net benefit of this move would equal $200. The remaining lines show analogous equivalences for the other 5 activities.

Because the net benefit from producing washers is largest, the simplex method recommends adding the maximum possible amount of washers (αW) to the firm's original production program in equation (6A.7) and, of course, deducting amounts of present activities that make equivalent demands on inputs, or $\alpha(5U_{L2}$

$+ 100U_{RM} + 4U_M)$. The solution then changes from equation (6A.7) to read

$$\alpha W - \alpha(5U_{L2} + 100U_{RM} + 4U_M) + 350U_{L1} \\ + 125U_{L2} + 3000U_{RM} + 200U_M = C \quad \textbf{(6A.10)}$$

or

$$\alpha W + 350U_{L1} + (125 - 5\alpha)U_{L2} + (3000 \\ - 100\alpha)U_{RM} + (200 - 4\alpha)U_M = C. \quad \textbf{(6A.11)}$$

Since no activity can occur at a negative level, the maximum possible value for α is 25, a value that completely eliminates the unemployment of labor #2. The new program becomes

> *Second feasible solution.*
> $25W + 350U_{L1} + 500U_{RM} + 100U_M = C$
>
> **(6A.12)**

By producing 25 washers, and leaving 350 units of labor #1, 500 units of raw materials, and 100 units of machine time unemployed, the firm would exactly "utilize" all available inputs. The value of this program, compared to the original one in equation (6A.7), equals 25 × $280, or $7,000. In Figure 6A.4, this computational step has moved the firm from point O to point P.

Looking for Further Improvement

Once more, the simplex method recommends a test of the net benefit to be gained from adding to any of the six types of activities. Table 6A.5 shows Step 3 of the simplex method.

Table 6A.5 tells us that we could further improve upon our goal by adding the production of as many refrigerators as possible (βR) to the latest production program in equation (6A.12), while deducting amounts of present activities that make equivalent demands on inputs, or $\beta(10U_{L1} + 50U_{RM} + 5U_M)$. The solution then changes from equation (6A.12) to read

$$\beta R - \beta(10U_{L1} + 50U_{RM} + 5U_M) + 25W \\ + 350U_{L1} + 500U_{RM} + 100U_M = C \quad \textbf{(6A.13)}$$

or

$$\beta R + 25W + (350 - 10\beta)U_{L1} + (500 \\ - 50\beta)U_{RM} + (100 - 5\beta)U_M = C. \quad \textbf{(6A.14)}$$

The maximum possible value for β (that preserves nonnegative parameters) is 10, a value that completely eliminates the unemployment of raw materials. The new program becomes

> *Third feasible solution.*
> $10R + 25W + 250U_{L1} + 50\ U_M = C$
>
> **(6A.15)**

Once more, the firm would exactly utilize available inputs; its output would be worth (10 × $200) + (25 × $280), or $9,000. In Figure 6A.4, this computational step has moved the firm from Point P to point Q.

TABLE 6A.4   Simplex Method: Step 2

Activity That Might be Added to Program (1)	Equivalent Activities in Present Program (2)	Marginal Benefit of Addition (value of 1) (3)	Marginal Cost of Addition (value of 2) (4)	Marginal Net Benefit of Addition (5) = (3) − (4)
R	$10U_{L1} + 50U_{RM} + 5U_M$	$200	0	+$200
W	$5U_{L2} + 100U_{RM} + 4U_M$	$280	0	+$280
U_{L1}	U_{LI}	0	0	0
U_{L2}	U_{L2}	0	0	0
U_{RM}	U_{RM}	0	0	0
U_M	U_M	0	0	0

TABLE 6A.5   Simplex Method: Step 3

Activity That Might be Added to Program (1)	Equivalent Activities in Present Program (2)	Marginal Benefit of Addition (value of 1) (3)	Marginal Cost of Addition (value of 2) (4)	Marginal Net Benefit of Addition (5) = (3) − (4)
R	$10U_{L1} + 50U_{RM} + 5U_M$	$200	0	+$200
W	W	$280	$280	0
U_{L1}	U_{L1}	0	0	0
U_{L2}	$0.2W - 20U_{RM} - 0.8U_M$	0	$56	−$56
U_{RM}	U_{RM}	0	0	0
U_M	U_M	0	0	0

Further Improvement Still

The next test of possible further gain is provided by Table 6A.6, which shows step 4 of the method.

Surprisingly, this table tells our firm that it could do even better by keeping more of its labor #2 unemployed. If we add the maximum possible amount of labor #2 unemployment (γU_{L2}) to the last production program (equation 6A.15), while deducting amounts of present activities that make equivalent demands on inputs, or $\gamma(-0.4R + 0.2W + 4U_{L1} + 1.2U_M)$, the solution changes to

$$\gamma U_{L2} - \gamma(-0.4R + 0.2W + 4U_{L1} + 1.2U_M) + 10R + 25W + 250U_{L1} + 50U_M = C \quad \textbf{(6A.16)}$$

or

$$(10 + 0.4\gamma)R + (25 - 0.2\gamma)W + (250 - 4\gamma)U_{L1} + \gamma U_{L2} + (50 - 1.2\gamma)U_M = C. \quad \textbf{(6A.17)}$$

The maximum possible value for γ is 41.67, a value that completely eliminates the unemployment of machine time. The new program becomes

Fourth feasible solution.
$$26.67R + 16.67W + 83.33U_{L1} + 41.67U_{L2} = C. \quad \textbf{(6A.18)}$$

The firm's output now is worth (26.67 × $200) + (16.67 × $280), or $10,000. In Figure 6A.4, this computational step has moved the firm from point Q to the optimum at M. The simplex method provides a way of testing this fact.

Confirming the Optimum Solution

Consider Table 6A.7, constructed by the same procedure as the last three tables. Column (5) of this table indicates that no marginal net benefits can be reaped by any further changing of the

TABLE 6A.6   Simplex Method: Step 4

Activity That Might be Added to Program (1)	Equivalent Activities in Present Program (2)	Marginal Benefit of Addition (value of 1) (3)	Marginal Cost of Addition (value of 2) (4)	Marginal Net Benefit of Addition (5) = (3) − (4)
R	R	$200	$200	0
W	W	$280	$280	0
U_{L1}	U_{L1}	0	0	0
U_{L2}	$-0.4R + 0.2W + 4U_{L1} + 1.2U_M$	0	−$24	+$24
U_{RM}	$0.02R - 0.2U_{L1} - 0.1U_M$	0	$4	− $4
U_M	U_M	0	0	0

TABLE 6A.7   Simplex Method: Step 5

Activity That Might be Added to Program (1)	Equivalent Activities in Present Program (2)	Marginal Benefit of Addition (value of 1) (3)	Marginal Cost of Addition (value of 2) (4)	Marginal Net Benefit of Addition (5) = (3) − (4)
R	R	$200	$200	0
W	W	$280	$280	0
U_{L1}	U_{L1}	0	0	0
U_{L2}	U_{L2}	0	0	0
U_{RM}	$-0.01\overline{33}R+0.0166W+0.1\overline{33}U_{L1}-0.08\overline{33}U_{L2}$	0	$2	−$2
U_M	$0.\overline{33}R-0.1\overline{66}W-3.\overline{33}U_{L1}+0.8\overline{33}U_{L2}$	0	$20	−$20

Shadow prices of inputs

firm's production program. Just as our graphical analysis did earlier, the algebraic procedure points to the production of 26.67 refrigerators and 16.67 washers as the revenue-maximizing program. Any other conceivable program would produce less revenue. Given the fixed inputs and, therefore, costs, any other program would produce lower profit.

Indeed, equation (6A.18) tells us that our firm would be wise to leave 83.33 units of labor #1 and 41.67 units of labor #2 totally unused. These are, of course, the amounts left when 26.67 × 10, or 266.67, units of labor #1 (needed for refrigerator production) are subtracted from 350 total units available and when 16.67 × 5, or 83.33, units of labor #2 (needed for washer production) are subtracted from the 125 unit total available. (Can you show that, under the optimum program, the totals of raw materials and machine time are fully utilized and how they are distributed between the production of the two products?)

Shadow Prices

The boxed numbers in column (4) of Table 6A.7 provide crucial information about the value to our firm of additional units of input. The numbers highlighted there are called **shadow prices**; these are the implicit valuations that always emerge as a by-product of solving a linear programming problem algebraically. Note that an extra unit of labor #1, as well as of labor #2, is

designated as worthless to the firm (because the firm already has more of each than it can profitably use). On the other hand, the firm's production is now limited by the full use of all available raw materials and machine time, and these bottleneck inputs have positive shadow prices of $2 and $20, respectively. These shadow prices indicate that the firm could raise the value of its output by $2 (or $20) if it could get another unit of raw materials (or machine time). Such shadow prices are extremely important pieces of information for economic decision makers because they indicate the true scarcity of inputs or outputs (which may not be indicated by their actual market prices).

Note: The value of inputs used, calculated at their shadow prices, always equals the value of the output they produce. In our case, the shadow price of both types of labor is zero, but the total value of raw materials comes to 3,000 units × $2, or $6,000, and the total value of machine time comes to 200 units × $20, or $4,000. These values, of course, add to the $10,000 value of output.

The Manifold Uses of Linear Programming

Any reader who has worked through the forgoing example with pencil and paper will appreciate the help computers can provide to linear programming. Indeed, the advent of the computer has made linear programming a highly effective management tool with wide applicability.

Determining the Best Product Mix

Oil companies with limited crude oil supplies and refinery capacity use the technique to determine their product mix among diesel fuel, heating oil, kerosene, lubricants, and gasoline with different octane ratings. Forest product companies employ linear programming to determine the best combination of lumber, plywood, and paper that can be made from given supplies of logs and a fixed milling capacity. Tomato processors use it to determine their output mix among canned whole tomatoes, chili sauce, ketchup, stewed tomatoes, tomato juice, tomato paste, and soup. Police departments, law firms, and the Internal Revenue Service use linear programming to figure out the most efficient allocation of their staffs.

Determining the Best Input Mix

The technique is often directed toward achieving a *given* goal with the best combination of inputs. Producers of cake use linear programming to determine the ideal makeup of their ingredient lists; farmers use it to select the best combinations of cows in their herds in order to produce a given quality of milk. Hospitals want to supply their patients with minimum quantities of required calories, minerals, proteins, and vitamins (contained in different quantities in different foods), and linear programming helps them to do so at minimum cost. Directors of college dining halls have the same goal, as do managers of cattle feedlots! All kinds of firms use the technique to split their advertising budgets among such media as billboards, newspapers, magazines, radio, and TV in order to reach, with minimum cost, a specified number of customers of given age and income.

Determining the Best Transportation System

Innumerable users of the linear programming technique are concerned with the most efficient routing of products over space. In the United States, the technique was first developed to help with the complicated transportation tasks of the U.S. Air Force. Yet the procedure is just as useful for the efficient scheduling of everyday deliveries by private firms that may have many production, warehousing, and sales facilities in different parts of the country and wish to achieve a given set of deliveries at minimum cost.

Other uses

The technique has found uses far beyond the management problems of individual firms or government departments. Scientists have used linear programming to model the movements of seasonal labor forces in Africa, the flood control, power production, and irrigation aspects of the Ganges-Brahmaputra river system in India, the national economic planning of the Soviet Union, and even the survival and diffusion of insect colonies.

KEY TERMS

isorevenue line
linear programming
objective function
shadow prices
simplex method

SELECTED READINGS

Baumol, William J. "Activity Analysis in One Lesson." *The American Economic Review*, December 1958, pp. 837–73; and *Economic Theory and Operations Analysis*, 4th ed. Englewood Cliffs, N.J.: Prentice-Hall, 1977.

Bland, Robert G. "The Allocation of Resources by Linear Programming," *Scientific American,* June 1981, pp. 126–44.

A superb exposition of the current state of the art.

Dantzig, George M. *A Procedure for Maximizing a Linear Function Subject to Linear Inequalities*. Washington, D.C.: Headquarters U.S. Air Force, 1948.

The original statement of the simplex method.

Dantzig, George M. *Linear Programming and Extensions*. Princeton: Princeton University Press, 1963.

Dorfman, Robert. "Mathematical, or Linear, Programming: A Nonmathematical Exposition." *The American Economic Review*, December 1953, pp. 797–825.

Dorfman, Robert; Samuelson; Paul A.; and Solow, Robert M. *Linear Programming and Economic Analysis*. New York: McGraw-Hill, 1958.

Kantorovich, Leonid V. "Mathematical Methods of Organizing and Planning Production." *Management Science,* July 1960, pp. 366–422; idem. *The Best Use of Economic Resources*. Cambridge: Harvard University Press, 1965; idem. "Essays in Optimal Planning." *Problems of Economics*, August–September–October 1976, pp. 3–251.

> Translations of the original 1939 article; of his 1943 work not published until 1959; and of 18 essays, with an introduction on the life and work of Kantorovich by Leon Smolinski.

Koopmans, Tjalling C. *Activity Analysis of Production and Allocation*. Chicago: Cowles Commission, 1951; idem. *Three Essays on the State of Economic Science*. New York: McGraw-Hill, 1957; idem. *Scientific Papers of Tjalling C. Koopmans*. New York: Springer, 1970.

> Major works by the American co-winner of the 1975 Nobel Prize honoring the developers of linear programming.

Stigler, George J. "The Cost of Subsistence." *Journal of Farm Economics*, May 1945, pp. 303–14.

> A paper famous as a forerunner of the linear programming technique.

Ward, Benjamin. "Linear Programming and Soviet Planning." In John P. Hardt, ed. *Mathematics and Computers in Soviet Economic Planning*. New Haven: Yale University Press, 1967, chap. 3.

Wilson, Edward O. "The Ergonomics of Caste in the Social Insects." *The American Economic Review*, December 1978, pp. 25–35.

> A fascinating application of linear programming to the survival of insect colonies.

CHAPTER 7

Market Equilibrium: Consumption Goods

Chapters 4 and 6 showed why households and firms, respectively, will demand or supply different quantities of consumption goods at different potential prices. This chapter brings together our previous analysis of market demand and that of market supply. We will study the process by which, in a perfect market, only one of the many potential prices emerges as the actual market price. The British economist, Alfred Marshall (see Biography 7.1), defined **market equilibrium** as a situation in which there is no innate tendency for price or quantity to change. In order to apply this definition, however, it is important to specify the time period. Marshall suggested a threefold classification of equilibrium: *momentary, short-run,* and *long-run* equilibrium.

Momentary equilibrium refers to market equilibrium in a period so short that the quantity supplied is absolutely fixed. **Short-run equilibrium** refers to a market equilibrium during a somewhat longer period in which a given number of firms can vary quantity supplied by changing the utilization rate of given plants. **Long-run equilibrium** refers to market equilibrium in a period so long that new firms can enter the industry and old ones can leave it or change the size of their plants. The exact length of each period, of course, will vary with the industry in question.

Momentary Equilibrium

To analyze momentary equilibrium, imagine a situation in which a given amount of a good already exists, in which the good in question cannot be stored, and in which time is too short to produce additional units. In such a situation, market supply is equal to a fixed quantity regardless of price. (The price elasticity of supply is zero.) This situation is illustrated by the vertical supply line in Figure 7.1. The supply shown there refers to 2,000 pounds of perishable fish that have just been landed by a number of fishing boats. Until their next trip out, the fishers cannot supply more. If the fish cannot be stored (and that we assume), the fishers might as well sell it for whatever it will bring. Given the market demand shown in the graph, point *e* denotes the equilibrium price and quantity. Only a price of $2.50 per pound can "clear" the market by balancing the quantities demanded and supplied.

If price were higher, such as $3.50 per pound, the market would have a **surplus**. A surplus always denotes an amount by which the quantity demanded at a given price falls short of the quantity supplied. In this case, quantity demanded would equal 1,000 pounds per day (point *a*) and quantity supplied would be 2,000 pounds per day (point *b*). Trying to unload their wares, frustrated would-be sellers would under-bid each other to attract customers. Price would fall, and quantity demanded would rise. (Note arrows *A* and *B*.)

If price were lower than $2.50 per pound, such as $1.50 per pound, the market would have a **shortage**. A shortage always denotes an amount by which the quantity demanded at a given price exceeds the quantity supplied. In this case, quantity demanded would equal 3,000 pounds per day (point *d*) and quantity supplied would be 2,000 pounds per day (point *c*). This time, frustrated would-be buyers would outbid each other, trying to buy what doesn't exist. Price would rise, and quantity demanded would fall (as indicated by arrows *C* and *D*).

Note: One must be careful not to apply the preceding analysis too freely. Many goods exist in absolutely fixed amounts, such as the paintings of old masters, back issues of *Time* magazine, or antique pieces of furniture. Yet the relevant market supply curves can still be upward-sloping

FIGURE 7.1 Momentary Equilibrium

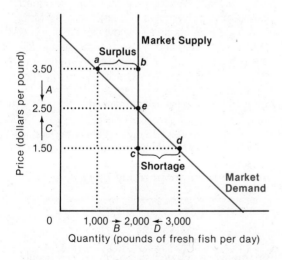

In a period so short that quantity supplied is absolutely fixed, momentary equilibrium is reached where vertical market supply intersects downward-sloping market demand (point *e*).

FIGURE 7.2 Short-Run Equilibrium

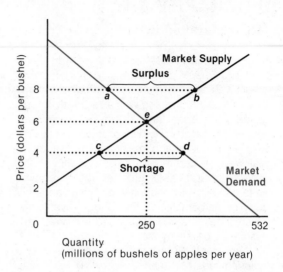

Quantity
(millions of bushels of apples per year)

In a perfect market, short-run equilibrium is reached where upward-sloping market supply intersects downward-sloping market demand (point *e*). At any higher price, there would be surpluses, tending to depress price. At any lower price, there would be shortages, tending to raise price. Note: Figure 7.2 is a visual illustration of the story told in Chapter 1. Apples are *scarce* because, at a zero price, people's desire for this good (532 million bushels per year) exceeds the amount then available (zero). Yet, at a sufficiently high price, a scarce good can be in surplus, too.

because these items (unlike fresh fish, fresh strawberries, or fresh mushrooms) can easily be stored. Thus owners are likely to vary the quantities put on the market with the prevailing price. (Fish, strawberries, or mushrooms can, of course, be preserved, but canned fish, frozen strawberries, and dried mushrooms are hardly the same products as their fresh counterparts.)

Short-Run Equilibrium

The analysis of equilibrium is similar when we lengthen our time horizon to include the short run. In the short run, a given number of firms is

BIOGRAPHY 7.1:

Alfred Marshall

Alfred Marshall (1842–1924) was born in Clapham, a suburb of London, England. His tyrannical father, a Bank of England cashier who wrote a tract on *Man's Rights and Woman's Duties*, forced him to study Hebrew and the classics in preparation for the ministry. He also ordered him to stay away from chess and mathematics, but to no avail. When Alfred received a scholarship for the study of theology at Oxford, he rebelled against his father. A kindly uncle helped him finance his study of mathematics at Cambridge; eventually, Marshall became one of Cambridge's great professors of political economy.

Very much like Adam Smith, Marshall was a profoundly learned man, overflowing with ideas covering such diverse fields as biology, economics, history, mathematics, and philosophy. But Marshall's father had left his mark. Alfred was always afraid of speaking too soon and was never in a hurry to rush into print. He took infinite care and insisted on the highest standards of accuracy and truth and on the full mastery of his material. The bulk of his work is contained in his *Principles of Economics* (1890), *Industry and Trade* (1919), and *Money, Credit, and Commerce* (1923).

By 1890, when he published his *Principles* (fully 20 years after first sharing its contents with his students), he had already laid the foundation, through years of teaching, for what is now called the neoclassical school. His book's success was instant and complete. In the English-speaking world, it was the leading text for decades, going through eight editions in Marshall's lifetime. Generations of economists were brought up under the pervasive influence of his thought.

Even today, many copies of Marshall's *Principles* are sold every year. This is not surprising because almost the entire corpus of modern microeconomics can be traced to some suggestion by Marshall. He introduced such concepts as the short run and the long run; he was a master of *partial analysis*, the analysis of phenomena in relatively small sectors of the economy within which events can be assumed not to call forth repercussions in social aggregates. He made *consumers'* and *producers' surplus* (first found in Dupuit), *price elasticity of demand* (found in embryonic form in Cournot), the *marginal productivity theory of distribution* (found in von Thünen), and *external* (pecuniary and technological) and *internal* (returns to scale) *economies* permanent additions to the economist's set of tools. Marshall laid the groundwork for the statistical measurement of demand and cost functions. He introduced diagrammatic analysis into the discipline, the impact of which any comparison of modern economics texts with pre-Marshallian ones can quickly show. (Marshall himself, however, buried his diagrams in footnotes and appendices.) Most of all, of course, Marshall is known for his analysis of supply and demand. While Ricardo had elucidated the cost side of market phenomena and Jevons the utility side, Marshall put them together in his famous "scissors diagram" (Figure 7.2). About the old controversy, he writes:[1]

> We might as reasonably dispute whether it is the upper or the under blade of a pair of scissors that cuts a piece of paper, as whether value is governed by utility or cost of

able to respond to market prices by varying output within given plants. The market supply line in Figure 7.2, therefore, is upward-sloping. In perfect analogy to our earlier discussion, point *e* alone depicts the equilibrium price and quantity. At the $6-per-bushel price, every buyer can find a seller, and every seller can find a buyer, for just the quantity each of them wishes to trade. Any higher price, such as $8 per bushel, would produce a surplus (and pressure for price to fall). Any lower price, such as $4 per bushel, would produce a shortage (and pressure for price to rise).

Note: Firms in the short run can adjust the

production. It is true that when one blade is held still, and the cutting is effected by moving the other, we may say with careless brevity that the cutting is done by the second; but the statement is not strictly accurate, and it is to be excused only so long as it claims to be merely a popular and not a strictly scientific account of what happens.

Marshall hoped that all the manifold tools which he had developed would be put to work in the great task of conquering scarcity: "Political economy follows the actions of individuals and of nations as they seek, by separate or collective endeavour, to increase the material means of their well-being and to turn their resources to the best account."[2] But, like Adam Smith, he was also aware of the costs of economic growth:

> When the necessaries of life are once provided, everyone should seek to increase the beauty of things in his possession rather than their number. . . . An improvement in the artistic character of furniture and clothing train the higher faculties of those who make them, and is a source of growing happiness to those who use them. . . . The world would go much better if everyone would buy fewer and simpler things, and would take trouble in selecting them for their real beauty.

[1]Alfred Marshall, *Principles of Economics*, 8th ed. (London: Macmillan, 1922), p. 348.

[2]Alfred Marshall, *Elements of Economics of Industry* (London: Macmillan, 1920), pp. 1, 83, and 84.

utilization rate of their fixed plants. As a result, surpluses and shortages are eliminated not only by adjustments on the part of buyers (as in the momentary run), but also by adjustments on the part of sellers. Thus a price fall from $8 per bushel to $6 per bushel would raise quantity demanded (from *a* to *e*), but it would also lower quantity supplied (from *b* to *e*). Similarly, a price rise from $4 per bushel to $6 per bushel would lower quantity demanded (from *d* to *e*), but it would also raise quantity supplied (from *c* to *e*). All of these adjustments, of course, would occur for the reasons already discussed in Chapters 4 and 6.

In a perfect market, the equilibrium price and quantity is established by the collective action of large numbers of market participants. Yet, as Chapter 2 pointed out, no individual, acting alone, has the power to affect the equilibrium price.

Once equilibrium is reached, any one seller who simply announced a price above equilibrium would immediately lose all customers; they would know that they could find identical units being sold (at the equilibrium price) by thousands of other sellers. Once equilibrium is reached, any one buyer who simply announced a price below equilibrium would immediately drive away all sellers; they would know that they could find thousands of other buyers willing to pay the equilibrium price.

Nor can any one seller or buyer cause a shift of the equilibrium price by some positive *action*, like dropping out of the market entirely. Because the kind of market demand line illustrated in Figure 7.2 would be the summation of thousands or millions of individual demand lines, the loss of any one of these components would shift the market demand line to the left (and hence the intersection point down), but imperceptibly so. The boycotting of the market (in protest of too high a price) by any one of 70 million household-buyers of apples, for example, just would not make a big enough dent. Perhaps this buyer could cause a surplus of 20 bushels a year at the $6-per-bushel price, but given the 250-million-bushel-per-year market volume, this might drop the equilibrium price only to $5.9999999 per bushel—that is, leave it unchanged! You are in this position yourself when it comes to buying apples. Do you think you could make the price of apples come down if you (and you alone) decided not to buy any?

Similarly, the market supply line of Figure

CLOSE-UP 7.1:

Finding the Equilibrium Price: Egg Clearinghouse, Inc.

Nestled among the large, stately houses of the University of New Hampshire's fraternity row sits a new building with a public television station in its basement and a dentist's office on the main floor. In a sunny, paneled room on the second floor, millions of eggs are auctioned every day. This second-floor office is the site of Egg Clearinghouse, Inc., but there aren't any shouting and waving people, nor are there any eggs. Buyers and sellers of about 1 percent of the 190 million U.S. eggs laid every day meet here, but not in person. A computer matches their offers. Because buyers and sellers of the other 99 percent of the eggs use clearinghouse transactions as a barometer of where demand can be matched with supply, the computer clearinghouse helps to set prices throughout the egg industry.

Source: Meg Cox, "Egg Clearinghouse, Inc., Despite Its Size, Plays a Big Role in Determining Prices," *The Wall Street Journal*, March 6, 1978.

7.2 is the summation of thousands upon thousands of individual supply lines. The loss of any one of these components would shift the market supply line to the left (and hence the intersection point up), but imperceptibly so. If there were 60,000 competitors, the single orchardist who dropped out entirely (in protest of too low a price) might cause a shortage of 7,000 bushels per year at the $6-per-bushel price, but given the 250-million-bushel-per-year market volume, this might raise the equilibrium price only to $6.0011 per bushel—that is, leave it unchanged as well. This is why economists talk of **atomistic competition** in perfect markets. The power of each market participant, like that of an atom in a vast ocean, is too insignificant to affect the equilibrium price.

Long-Run Equilibrium

Once we extend our time horizon even further to include the long run, we may discover forces for inevitable change that are hidden in the short run. Given the conditions of a perfect market, which allow firms freely to enter or exit industries, the existence of *profits* in the short run would induce existing firms to expand their capacities, and induce new firms to enter the industry. Profit, after all, measures income to the owners of firms for the services of their own resources that exceeds the amount available from their best outside alternatives. Similarly, the existence of *losses* in the short run would induce existing firms to contract their capacities and even to leave their industry altogether. It would also discourage outsiders from establishing new firms in the industry. Losses, after all, measure the extent to which the owners of firms could get higher income for the services of their own resources in alternative pursuits. A perfect market will be in long-run equilibrium only when the producers in the industry make neither profits nor losses. In such a zero-profit situation, the owners of firms are, of course, earning from their own resources used in their own firms exactly as much income as they would earn in their best alternatives. They have, therefore, no reason to leave the industry for those alternatives. Nor have outsiders any reason to enter this industry and abandon those alternative pursuits.

A Profitable Industry Expands

Panels (a) and (b) of Figure 7.3 picture a short-run equilibrium that harbors within it the seeds for long-run change. Panel (a) shows market demand, D, market supply, S, and the equilibrium price and quantity corresponding to point e. Panel (b) illustrates the situation of a typical firm in this industry, very much like that in Figure 6.2, "A Profitable Business" (see p. 151). Faced with a market price of $8 per bushel, the firm produces 3,500 bushels of apples per year, a tiny fraction of the 170-million-bushel total supplied by all firms as a group. This particular level of the firm's output is, of course, selected because it equates (at point *a*) the marginal benefit of production (which is the apple price, *P*) with the marginal cost of production, *MC*. Note how point *a* is one point on the firm's supply curve, *s*, and how *s* is one of many components of market supply, *S*, and equals the rising branch of *MC* above the minimum point of average variable cost, *AVC*.

Note also: At the optimal output level, average total cost, *ATC*, equals $6.50 per bushel (point *b*). Hence an average profit of $8−$6.50, or $1.50 per bushel is being made (distance *ab*); total profit equals $1.50 per bushel times 3,500 bushels per year, or $5,250 per year (the shaded area). It is not difficult to see why the owners of such a firm would be tempted to enlarge their productive capacity so as to reap even larger profits. Nor is it hard to see why all kinds of other people, not currently in the apple business at all, would also be planting new apple trees, building apple storage barns, and ordering orchard spraying machines. These others may be producers of bobby pins (making a loss on their investment) or enterprising taxi drivers (with houses on three-acre lots).

Over the years, as it enlarged its capacity, our firm's supply line, *s* (along with all the other cost lines) would, therefore, appear farther to the right (note the arrows). Market supply, *S*, would also shift right because there would be more

---

ANALYTICAL EXAMPLE 7.1:
The Pope and the Price of Fish

For more than 1000 years, the Catholic Church required its members to abstain from meat on Friday in the spirit of penance. In December of 1966, however, the American Catholic bishops, following prior authorization from Pope Paul VI, terminated obligatory meatless Fridays (except during Lent). One economist decided to test the impact of this decision on the fish market. Using data for New England, where a large quantity of fish is regularly landed and consumed and where 45 percent of the population is Catholic, Frederick W. Bell estimated two demand equations for a variety of fish: one for January, 1957 to November, 1966 (prior to the Church decree) and another one for December, 1966 to August, 1967. He isolated the effect on the price of each type of fish of such influences as the quantity landed, personal income, cold storage holdings, imports, meat and poultry prices, Lenten demand, other fish prices, and the Church decree. In accordance with theoretical expectations (that a fall in demand reduces price, all else being equal), he discovered a 12.5 percent average decline in fish prices *attributable to the decree*. The accompanying table shows some of his results.

Species	Percentage Change in Price Due to Church Decree
Sea scallops	−17
Yellowtail flounder	−14
Large haddock	−21
Scrod	−2
Cod	−10
Ocean perch	−10
Whiting	−20

Source: Frederick W. Bell, "The Pope and the Price of Fish," *The American Economic Review*, December 1968, pp. 1346–50.

FIGURE 7.3   A Profitable Industry Expands

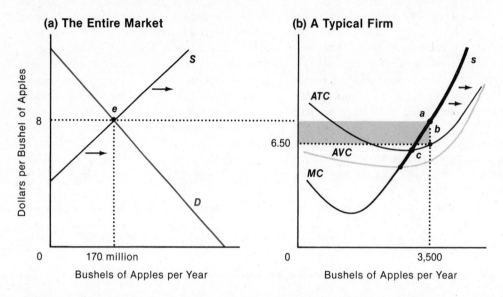

When markets are perfect, a short-run equilibrium—panel (a)—in which the typical firm makes a profit—panel (b)—harbors within it the seeds for long-run change. The number and size of firms in the industry will grow, and this process will cease precisely when product price (now at e) has fallen to equal the minimum average total cost (ATC) of producing the product (now at c). Caution: The level of minimum ATC itself may change in the process of industry expansion.

firms and larger ones. As a result, given demand, intersection *e* would move, and the equilibrium price would fall. This process would continue until its ultimate cause (the existence of profits) was eliminated. Profits would be eliminated when the equilibrium price, then at intersection *e** (not shown) below and to the right of *e*, was just equal to the minimum average total cost of production (now at *c*).

Caution: During the process of industry expansion, the minimum level of *ATC* itself might change. This change in minimum *ATC* might be due to **external economies**—that is, favorable technological or pecuniary externalities associated with industry growth—or it might be the result of **external diseconomies**—that is, unfavorable technological or pecuniary externalities associated with industry growth. These concepts must not be confused with **internal economies** (increasing returns to scale) or **internal**

diseconomies (decreasing returns to scale), which determine the shape of the individual firm's long-run supply curves. (See Figure 6.8, "Short-Run Vs. Long-Run Costs," on page 163.)

An Unprofitable Industry Contracts

Whether we have profits in the industry initially (as assumed in the preceding section) or whether we have losses in the industry (as about to be discussed), the end result is the same: zero profits. Panel (a) of Figure 7.4 shows market demand, *D*, market supply, *S*, and the equilibrium price and quantity, corresponding to point *e*. Panel (b) illustrates the unprofitable situation of a typical firm in this industry, very much like that in Figure 6.4, "A Losing Business" (see p. 156). Faced with a market price of $5 per bushel, the firm produces 2,700 bushels of apples per year, a tiny fraction of the 280-million-bushel total supplied by all firms as a group. This output level equates (at point *a*) product price, *P*, and marginal cost, *MC*.

At this optimal output level, average total cost, *ATC*, equals $6.10 per bushel (point *b*). Hence an average loss of $6.10–$5, or $1.10 per bushel is being incurred (distance *ab*); total loss equals $1.10 per bushel times 2,700 bushels per year, or $2,970 per year (dotted area). Clearly, the owners of such a firm would wish to escape the loss by contracting their productive capacity and eventually leaving the industry altogether. And outsiders would have no desire to enter this field of activity.

After a number of years, the firm pictured in panel (b) may have disappeared—along, perhaps, with thousands of others—or its capacity may have been severely cut. In the latter case, its supply line, *s* (along with all the other cost lines) would appear further to the left (note the arrows). Market supply, *S*, would also shift left because there would be fewer and smaller firms. As a result, intersection *e* would move, given demand, and the equilibrium price would rise. This process would continue until its ultimate cause (the existence of losses) was eliminated. Losses would be eliminated when the equilibrium price, then at intersection *e** (not shown) above and to the left of *e*, was just equal to minimum average total cost of production (now at *c*).

Note again that during the process of industry contraction the minimum level of *ATC* itself might change, depending on the existence or absence of external economies or diseconomies.

The Normal Price

As we have just seen, in an economy with perfect markets, profits or losses invite an expansion or contraction, respectively, of the affected industry. Because this process comes to a halt precisely when profits or losses have been eliminated,

CLOSE-UP 7.2:

Profit and Industry Expansion: Department Store Dentistry

In 1979, 10 percent of the U.S. population had never seen a dentist; 50 percent hadn't seen one for more than a year; only 5 percent saw one regularly. Prices and profits in the industry were high. This situation induced a number of dental entrepreneurs to make sweeping changes, getting out of their low-volume, single-chair practices and setting up (with the increased use of technicians) high-volume, lower-priced operations in department stores.

Montgomery Ward first leased space in several West Coast stores to such dental centers. Sears, Roebuck and Co. soon did the same on the west coast, while Korvettes and Times Square Stores Corporation opened similar centers in New York. Before long, the idea spread throughout the nation. Following store hours and relying on the huge potential market (some 100,000 people walk through a single department store in a month), the average department store dentist handled more than 750 patients a month (compared to 240 patients for the single-chair practitioner). Patients could usually see dentists at a moment's notice and at 20 to 40 percent lower fees. (Note: At some Montgomery Ward stores, lawyers have joined the move to department stores. Shoppers can go into the Law Store, pay $10, pick up a telephone in a private booth, and talk with a lawyer. Offering such services at a low price, which can be known in advance, has opened up a huge market of people who fear being hit by an unknown amount.)

Sources: Elizabeth Bailey, "The Department Store Dentist," *Forbes*, March 19, 1979, pp. 112 and 114; Anton Rupert, "Shopping-Center Shingles," *The Wall Street Journal*, October 16, 1979, p. 48; "Moving the Dentist's Chair to Retail Stores," *Business Week*, January 19, 1981, pp. 56 and 58.

FIGURE 7.4   An Unprofitable Industry Contracts

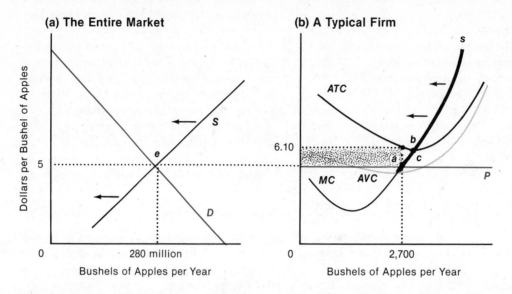

When markets are perfect, a short-run equilibrium—panel (a)—in which the typical firm makes a loss—panel (b)—harbors within it the seeds for long-run change. The number and size of firms in the industry will decline, and this process will cease precisely when product price (now at e) has risen to equal the minimum average total cost (*ATC*) of producing the product (now at c). Caution: The level of minimum *ATC* itself may change in the process of industry contraction.

---

there exists the ever-present tendency for equilibrium price to change until the volume of a good that is demanded is sold at a price equal to the lowest possible average total cost of producing it. This level of price is called the **normal price**. Once the normal price is reached, the owners of firms earn, from their own resources used in their own firms, neither more nor less than they could earn in their best outside alternatives. As was shown in Figure 6.3, "A Zero-Profit Business" (p. 153), the revenue of firms then just covers their total cost, variable and fixed, including, of course, implicit cost. Figure 7.5 illustrates the nature of long-run equilibrium as well as a variety of ways in which it might be restored once it is upset.

A Constant-Cost Industry.   Consider panel (a) in Figure 7.5. Imagine market demand, *D*, and market supply, *S*, to prevail. According to inter-

section *a*, when apples sell at $6 per bushel and 250 million bushels are traded per year, we have a short-run equilibrium. We now assume that the typical firm's short-run and long-run cost curves look like those in panel (a) of Figure 6.8, "Short-Run Vs. Long-Run Costs." Thus the typical firm, before industry growth, finds itself in long-run equilibrium as well: Faced with a $6-per-bushel price, such a firm equates price, *P*, with short-run and long-run marginal cost, *SRMC* and *LRMC*, at *b* and produces 3,000 bushels per year. Because short-run and long-run average total cost (*SRATC* and *LRATC*) equal *P* at *b*, the firm makes zero profit. There is no reason for new firms to enter the industry or for old ones to expand or contract. Because *a* and *b* are found at the same level, $6 is not only the short-run equilibrium price but also the long-run normal price.

Now imagine that demand rose to *D**. A new

FIGURE 7.5 Long-Run Industry Supply Curves

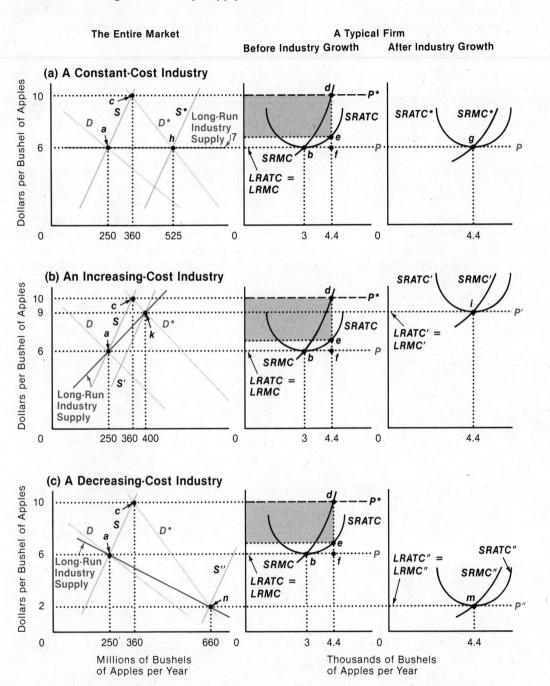

Long-run *industry* supply curves can be horizontal as in panel (a), upward-sloping as in panel (b), or downward-sloping as in panel (c). This is true even if the long-run supply of every *firm* is a horizontal line (as is assumed here).

short-run equilibrium at *c* would be established, with price at $10 per bushel and quantity at 360 million bushels per year. The long-run equilibrium would be gone: the typical firm would now equate higher price, *P** (shown by the horizontal dashed line), with SRMC at *d*, and produce 4,400 bushels per year. (The movement by the typical firm from *b* to *d* corresponds to the movement by all firms from *a* to *c*). Yet short-run average total cost for the new optimal output volume would equal only $7 per bushel (point *e*). Thus the firm would make a profit of $3 per bushel (distance *de*) and a total profit of $13,200 per year (shaded). Indeed, the firm would notice that the long-run average total cost of producing the new output volume was only $6 per bushel (point *f*), and the firm would wish to acquire a larger plant with minimum *SRATC* at *f*. At the same time, new firms would be attracted into the industry by all the profit being made. The industry would begin to expand; supply curve, *S*, would shift to the right.

Panel (a) pictures the case of a **constant-cost industry**, so called because the normal price of its product is unchanged after the industry has ceased to expand or contract. This situation arises whenever technological or pecuniary externalities are absent. Under such circumstances, our expanding firm's cost curves simply shift to the right, as from SRATC and SRMC to SRATC* and SRMC*. (Note that point *g* on the graph after industry growth corresponds to point *f* on that picturing the firm before industry growth.) The shift of SRMC to SRMC* on the right-hand side of our graph, is depicted, along with the entry of new firms, by the rightward shift of *S* to *S**. At the new equilibrium at *h*, product price has returned to $6 per bushel; larger and more numerous firms supply 525 million bushels per year. The typical firm, now larger, supplies 4,400 bushels per year, according to the new equality of *P* with SRMC* = LRMC (at *g=f*). Zero profit has returned; the equilibrium price equals the normal price.

Note how an increase in market demand from *D* to *D** has, in the long run, called forth such an increase in supply that market price

remained unchanged. A constant-cost industry's long-run supply, therefore, is a horizontal line, such as the color line through *a* and *h*.

An Increasing-Cost Industry. Panel (b) of Figure 7.5 depicts the same initial situation as in panel (a), and the same intermediate position, caused by the increase in demand. Accordingly, identical curves and points have been given the same labels as in panel (a).

Panel (b), however, depicts the case of an **increasing-cost industry,** so called because the normal price of its product is higher after the industry has ceased to expand or is lower after it has ceased to contract. This situation arises whenever unfavorable technological or pecuniary externalities are associated with industry expansion. Under such circumstances, the cost curves of all firms shift up. Thus an expanding firm's cost curves are not only shifted right, but also up, as from short-run or long-run *ATC* and *MC* to *ATC'* and *MC'*. The shift of *SRMC* to *SRMC'*, on the right-hand side of the graph, is again depicted, along with the entry of new firms, by the rightward shift of *S*, but this shift is weaker than in panel (a), halting at *S'* and equilibrium point *k*. This weaker shift of *S* to *S'* reflects the fact that the adjustment process is faster when profits are squeezed away not only by falling product price (as in panel *a*), but also by rising costs. In panel (b), therefore, the industry's expansion comes to a halt by the time product price has fallen to $9 per bushel and larger and more numerous firms supply 400 million bushels per year (point *k*). The typical firm, now larger, supplies 4,400 bushels per year, according to the equality of *P'* with *SRMC'=LRMC'* (at *i*). Zero profit has returned; the equilibrium price equals the normal price.

This time, however, an increase in market demand from *D* to *D** has, in the long run, called forth an increase in supply so weak that market price rose. An increasing-cost industry's long-run supply, therefore, is an upward-sloping line, like the color line through *a* and *k*.

A Decreasing-Cost Industry. Panel (c), finally, depicts the same initial situation as in panel (a), and the same intermediate position, caused by the increase in demand. Accordingly, identical curves and points have been given the same labels as in panel (a).

Panel (c) now depicts the case of a **decreasing-cost industry**, so called because the normal price of its product is lower after the industry has ceased to expand or is higher after it has ceased to contract. This situation arises whenever favorable technological or pecuniary externalities are associated with industry expansion. Under such circumstances, the cost curves of all firms shift down. Thus an expanding firm's cost curves are not only shifted right, but also down, as from short-run or long-run ATC and MC to ATC'' and MC''. The shift of SRMC to SRMC'' on the right-hand side of the graph is again depicted, along with the entry of new firms, by the rightward shift of S, but this shift is now stronger than in either panel (a) or (b), halting at S'' and equilibrium point n. This stronger shift from S to S'' reflects the fact that the adjustment process is slower when profits are squeezed away by falling product price but are enlarged by falling costs. In panel (c), therefore, the industry's expansion comes to a halt only by the time product price has fallen to $2 per bushel and larger and more numerous firms supply 660 million bushels per year (point n). The typical firm, now larger, supplies 4,400 bushels per year, according to the new equality of P'' with SRMC''=LRMC'' (at m). Zero profit has returned; the equilibrium price equals the normal price.

This time, however, an increase in market demand from D to D* has, in the long run, called forth an increase in supply so strong that market price fell. A decreasing-cost industry's long-run supply, therefore, is a downward-sloping line, such as the color line through a and n.

Two Ageless Debates

When Alfred Marshall introduced the preceding analysis, he effectively put an end to a seemingly eternal debate about the forces that determine the prices of goods in perfect markets.

Subjective-Utility Vs. Objective-Cost Theories

For thousands of years, there have been those who argued that the price of a good is determined by *subjective factors*; that is, by the usefulness or utility the good has for people, which is reflected in demand. According to this argument, a pound of meat fetches a high price compared to a pound of mud because meat has greater usefulness. Unfortunately, this theory left too many questions unanswered: Don't people derive much greater satisfaction from water than from diamonds? Isn't life itself impossible without the former but quite tolerable without the latter? Why then does a pound of water fetch such a low price compared to a pound of diamonds?

Questions such as these gave rise to an alternative theory, according to which the price of a good is determined by *objective factors*; that is, by the cost of producing the good, which is reflected in supply. Because it costs so much more to produce a pound of meat than to produce a pound of mud, the argument went, meat has the higher price. Similarly, diamonds have a higher price than water because diamonds cost more to produce. Yet, again, there were counterexamples.

Alfred Marshall put an end to this fruitless debate by noting that demand and supply (subjective and objective factors) were *both* responsible for the level of a good's price. He likened the two forces to the blades on a pair of scissors. Just as it is pointless to say that a piece of paper is cut by the moving blade when the other is held stationary, Marshall argued, it is also pointless to claim that either demand or supply alone determines price.

Thus the principle of mutual determination of prices permanently superseded the idea of a single determinant. The Marshallian analysis did little, however, to end another debate about the morality of prices.

Just Price vs. Scarcity Price

For as long as there have been buyers, they have wished for lower prices. For as long as there have been sellers, they have wished for higher ones. Philosophers since Aristotle have argued about the "morally just" level of prices. Governments of all ages have attempted to define and impose such prices. The Roman emperor Diocletian prescribed "just prices" for all goods and executed sellers who overcharged buyers. A millenium later, St. Thomas Aquinas drew up rules of his own, and he assured violators of eternal damnation. Modern governments in all countries continue to follow their lead, although punishment tends to be less drastic.

Economists, of course, are quite bewildered by this debate. They look upon the equilibrium prices discussed earlier in this chapter not as something to be moralized about, but as crucial bits of information about the degree of scarcity prevailing, information that allows vast numbers of people to work together in an orderly way. Consider the $6-per-bushel apple price depicted in Figure 7.2. It summarizes for all concerned a vast amount of dispersed knowledge. A household looking at this price is told, indirectly of course, that apples can be had for $6 a bushel because there happen to be another 90 million would-be apple buyers who value apples in millions of different ways, all of which is reflected in market demand which, for purposes of consistency, must equal market supply. In turn, the market supply reflects the different circumstances of some 60,000 orchardists who happen to be endowed with so many apple trees, who happen to possess certain kinds of technical knowledge, who happen to face certain weather conditions, who happen to be confronted with certain wage levels that must be paid to get people to pick apples rather than produce cars . . . *and much more*! Of course, no household really wants to be told all these things. That is why perfect markets eliminate the infinite detail and just provide, to each consumer, the most necessary information in capsule form: *"If you*

are willing to pay $6 per bushel, you can buy all the apples you like."

This price implies, of course, that there are good reasons (not given to the household) why it could *not* have all the apples it wanted for $4 per bushel. The reason might be that many orchardists would then make losses and go out of business, and thus there would be fewer apples. Or perhaps other people would then want so many more apples (and would so quickly snap up available stores of them) that this household couldn't find any, even if orchardists did supply the same amount as before. A million and one reasons might be given. But our household would have neither the inclination nor the time to listen. Thus the market economy saves the household the trouble of wasting its time hearing lengthy explanations. It just sends out its broadcast message!

The same message, of course, goes to all other households at the same time, and a similar message goes to each and every firm: *"If you are willing to accept $6 per bushel, you can sell all the apples you like."* This message, too, takes the place of lengthy detailed explanations. If a firm were unable to produce apples at anything less than $20 per bushel, it would quickly get the point: There are lots of other producers around who are smarter or more fortunate! They know more about putting together fertilizer, trees, and tender loving care, or they enjoy a better climate, or whatever. This price tells the firm: "The apple business is not for you!"

Naturally, any well-intentioned government, which wanted to establish a "just price" of $8 (to help sellers) or of $4 (to help buyers), would upset the intricate mechanism that determines a proper indicator of scarcity in the $6-per-bushel equilibrium price. When establishing a "just price" other than the equilibrium price, such government would inevitably create a surplus or a shortage and thus open a Pandora's box of problems. These problems would, ultimately, force the government to abandon its intervention or to replace the spontaneous market coordination of people's activities with a managerial coordination of its own. These are matters to which we will return in later chapters. The remainder of this chapter will describe a few of the manifold uses of the tools of analysis just discussed.

Applications of Marshallian Analysis

Application 1:   Cobweb Cycles

For centuries, interested observers have noted a curious phenomenon in many markets: In one period, quantity traded is small and price high. In the next period, quantity is high and price is low. Again and again this cycle repeats itself. This phenomenon applies to a wide variety of goods— from cattle, corn, and hogs to lumber, ships, and wine and even to new economics Ph.D.s. All these goods have in common a considerable time lag between the decision to produce them and their final availability for sale in the market.

Marshall's analysis of market equilibrium provides a simple explanation—by pointing out that while movement to equilibrium is an ever-present tendency, equilibrium is *not* a continuous state of affairs. More often than not, the world is not settled down nicely at an equilibrium, but *is in the process of moving toward one*. This movement can take many forms, including that of an *eternal cycle*, a *damped cycle*, or an *explosive cycle*, among others.

An Eternal Cycle.   In panel (a) of Figure 7.6, the market demand for pork is represented by D; we assume the market supply to be fixed in an initial period at 2 million tons per year, represented by dashed line S_1. Point a, therefore, depicts a momentary equilibrium. Price equals $4,000 per ton. Compared with their past experience, hog producers may find this price very attractive. Accordingly, they may wish to increase quantity supplied, *but they cannot do it overnight*. In fact, there is a biologically determined lag of about one year between breeding and slaughter: Hogs have a gestation period of

four months; it takes two months after birth before they can be weaned, and another four to six months before they have reached marketable weight. Hog producers, therefore, inevitably make production decisions in the present that affect supply with a considerable lag. Once the future arrives, supply is again momentarily fixed. The decision in period 1 to supply not 2 million but 5 million tons of pork per year, for instance, yields market supply S_2 in period 2. If market demand has not changed (and that we assume), the increased supply cannot be sold at the $4,000 price (point b). A new momentary equilibrium is reached at c. Price plummets to $1,500 per ton. Almost certainly, hog producers will then contract their operations so as to supply, perhaps, only 2 million tons of pork per year. Period 3 supply, S_3, once more momentarily fixed, equals S_1, but it doesn't sell at $1,500 per ton (point d). Given demand, price soars to $4,000 per ton in period 3 (point a). From here, the cycle continues: from a not to b (as producers expect), but to c; from c not to d, but to a, and so on forever more—unless, of course, producers learn from their experience and change their ways of adjusting quantity supplied to price. Their present behavior is summarized by supply line S^*. Unlike the supply lines we have met before, this one indicates the quantity supplied in one period as a function of the price prevailing in an earlier period: Point b shows the quantity supplied in period 2 when price is $4,000 per ton in period 1; point d shows the quantity supplied in period 3 when price is $1,500 per ton in period 2. As long as producers continue to make decisions according to lagged supply line S^*, the potential equilibrium at e cannot be reached.

A Damped Cycle.   In panel (b) of Figure 7.6, the cycle begins again at a momentary equilibrium with a price of $4,000 per ton and a quantity of 2 million tons, fixed for the year (point f). The producers' reaction to the high price, however, is not as strong as in panel (a): Distance fg is less than distance ab; the slope of S^{**} is larger than that of S^*. As a result, the price-quantity cycle

FIGURE 7.6 Cobweb Cycles

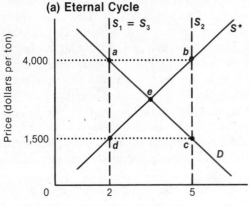

(a) Eternal Cycle

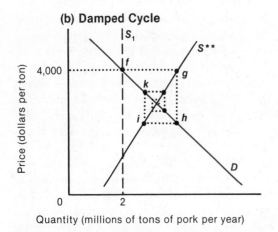

(b) Damped Cycle

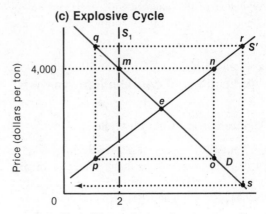

(c) Explosive Cycle

The tendency of the prices and quantities of some goods to rise above and then fall below some intermediate level in alternate periods produces patterns like cobwebs on demand and supply diagrams. Note: The slopes of the three demand lines are identical. In (a), the slope of supply line S^* equals the absolute value of the slope of D, providing the basis for an eternal cycle. In panel (b), the slope of S^{**} exceeds that of S^* (distance $fg < ab$), forming the basis for a damped cycle (all else being equal). In panel (c), the slope of S' is below that of S^* (distance $mn > ab$); this is the basis for an explosive cycle (all else being equal).

dampens over time. Momentary equilibrium moves from f not to g (as producers expect), but to h; from h not to i, but to k; and from there along the dotted lines to an equilibrium at the intersection of D and S^{**} in the center of the graph. We can see from the pattern in the graph why the tendency of the prices and quantities of some goods to rise above and then fall below some intermediate level in alternate periods is referred to as a **cobweb cycle**.

An Explosive Cycle. Finally, consider panel (c) of Figure 7.6. The cycle starts again at a momentary equilibrium with a price of $4,000 per ton and a quantity of 2 million tons, fixed for the year (point m). This time the producers' reaction to the high price is *stronger* than in panel (a): Distance mn exceeds distance ab, the slope of S' is smaller than that of S^*. As a result, the price-quantity cycle *explodes* over time. Momentary equilibrium moves from m not to n (as producers expect), but to o; from o not to p, but to q; from q not to r, but to s . . . Clearly, such a cycle cannot be maintained much longer than that! Its continued life would require negative prices and negative quantities; that is, economic nonsense. Sooner or later, therefore, an explosive cycle must cease, perhaps because the hog-raising industry disappears from the scene or because hog producers and consumers change the behavior depicted by D and S' in the graph.

Note: In all three cycles discussed, point e is a potential equilibrium. If the price-quantity combination at e ever prevailed, it could be maintained over time.

The real-world cattle cycles depicted in Figure 7.7 are a mixture of the three types of cycles just discussed; they are superimposed upon an upward secular trend in the total number of cattle.

Application 2:   Consumers' Surplus and Producers' Surplus

People often misunderstand the nature of the competitive process by which equilibrium is reached in perfect markets. From their own experience with competitive sports, they are apt to visualize competition as personal rivalry, as a situation of strife and conflict in which one party endeavors to gain what another endeavors to gain at the same time. Hence the success of one party is believed to involve the failure of the other. Yet this view is quite inapplicable to the process of competition in perfect markets. This process is an *impersonal* one; it serves to ferret out possibilities that allow everyone to win at the same time.

Personal rivalry requires that rivals know each other and have the power to affect each other. But in perfect markets there are so many market participants that few of them know each other, and no one participant has the power to affect any other specific participant. Market participants are personally impotent (and know others to be equally impotent) concerning market prices because they are set by the collective actions of so many. Each buyer and seller rather looks upon other buyers and sellers the way you would look at other buyers when shopping, say, for apples. Would you know those millions of others who compete for apples with you? Even if you met one of your ''competitors'' in the store, would you view him or her as a personal enemy?

More important, the impersonal competition in perfect markets, far from creating a win-or-

FIGURE 7.7   Cattle Cycles

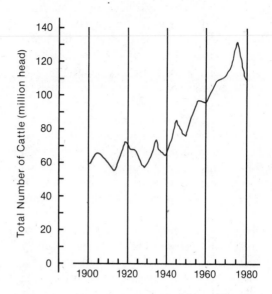

Since 1900, there have been seven complete cattle cycles in the United States. The typical cycle has lasted about 11 years, but no two cycles have been alike.
Source: John Rosine, ''Cattle Cycles—Past and Present,'' *Ninth District Quarterly* (Federal Reserve Bank of Minneapolis, November 1974), pp. 13–20; U.S. Bureau of the Census, *Statistical Abstract of the United States 1979* (Washington, D.C.: U.S. Government Printing Office, 1979), p. 720.

lose situation, allows large numbers of people to provide each other with mutual benefits. Obviously, in a world of scarcity, such provision with mutual benefits cannot possibly mean that everyone can have everything—as sellers could by charging infinite prices and buyers could by paying zero prices. Perfect competition helps people make deals—and only those deals from which one party benefits while simultaneously benefiting the other. The equilibrium price identifies these mutually beneficial possibilities. All who could gain from trading at this price are assured that they can so trade, that they are not reaching for the impossible, that their wishes are consistent with those of others who would also gain. The establishment of the equilibrium price, furthermore, also determines how the common gain is shared.

Figure 7.8, which illustrates the gains from trade, is based on Figure 7.2. Imagine all potentially traded bushels of apples as tokens in a game called *Exchange*. We line up, on the horizontal axis, each one of the bushels demanded according to the *maximum* price someone would be willing to pay for it (line *D*). A bushel for which someone most eager for apples would be willing to pay $11 is first in line, next to the vertical axis. A bushel for which someone else (or the same person) is only willing to pay $8 (or $2) is placed further to the right (at *a* or *b*, respectively). Similarly, we line up horizontally bushels potentially supplied according to the *minimum* price someone would be willing to accept for them (line *S*). A bushel someone is willing to supply for the least amount, say $2, is first in line for trading (*c*). A bushel someone else (or the same firm) would be willing to supply for a higher price (say $7) appears further to the right (at *d*) with less of a chance to be traded. The game is played by making all mutually beneficial trades and rejecting all trades that would cause one party to lose. Interestingly, a *vertical* line drawn through equilibrium point *e* discriminates between the trades that would be made and those that would be rejected. A *horizontal* line drawn through point *e* shows us how the traders split their joint gain (note the two dotted lines).

The Consumers' Surplus.   Those bushels that would have been bought for the equilibrium price or more (such as *a*) are traded (at the equilibrium price). As Alfred Marshall saw it, however, to the extent that buyers are willing to pay more than they do pay, they each reap a little bit of a "consumer's surplus." Marshall measured the sum of these surpluses by the white triangle *fge*. He defined this **consumers' surplus** as the difference between the sum of money consumers actually pay for a given quantity (here rectangle *Ogei*) and the maximum they could have been made to pay on an all-or-nothing basis (here *Ofei*).

FIGURE 7.8   The Gains from Trade

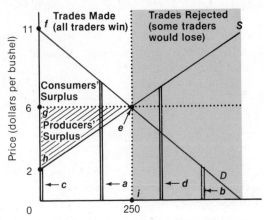

Quantity (millions of bushels of apples per year)

An age-old conflict between buyers and sellers must be resolved in any market. Buyers always want lower prices; sellers always want higher ones. Competition becomes the arbiter, setting price at the only level (here $6) that can be maintained. In the process, potential trades that involve a clear gain to both buyer and seller are, in fact, made (unshaded). Trades that would bring loss to either buyer or seller are rejected (shaded). Those who trade do so at a clear gain to themselves (note triangle *fhe*). The level of the equilibrium price determines how that gain is split among them (the white portion goes to buyers, and the crosshatched one goes to sellers).

The Producers' Surplus.   Those bushels that would have been sold for the equilibrium price or less (such as *c*) are traded too (at the equilibrium price). To the extent that sellers are willing to accept less than they do receive, they each reap a little bit of a "producer's surplus." The sum of these surpluses is measured by the crosshatched triangle *ghe*. This **producers' surplus** is defined as the difference between the sum of money producers actually receive for a given quantity (here rectangle *Ogei*) and the minimum they could have been made to accept on an all-or-nothing basis (here *Ohei*).

Conclusion.   All bushels lined up in the unshaded area are traded at a clear gain to all buyers and sellers involved. The equilibrium price determines how buyers and sellers share the total gain from trade (triangle *fhe*).

On the other hand, all potential bushels (such as *b*) that would have been bought only below the equilibrium price are not traded. The same holds for potential bushels (such as *d*) that would have been produced only if sale for more than the equilibrium price had been possible. All the bushels lined up in the shaded area are not traded at all, because such trade would require one of the trading parties to lose. In a world of scarcity, such discrimination concerning who can and cannot participate in an economic activity is inevitable. The higher-cost suppliers and less-eager demanders alike must be left out to avoid the chaos that would result if everyone tried to do what cannot possibly be done. Among the potential traders in the shaded area, there is not a single supplier who could cover marginal cost, even when getting paid the highest price an excluded demander offered to pay. No *voluntary* exchange, therefore, can bring these people together.

Second Thoughts. The preceding analysis of consumers' and producers' surplus can be traced back to 1844, when a French engineer, Jules Dupuit, attempted to measure the social benefit of such public goods as roads, canals, and bridges. Alfred Marshall popularized these notions, and he entertained high hopes for their use as a tool for public policy. (As will be shown in the next sections, one can analyze the effects of excise taxes or import quotas by studying how they change the consumers' and producers' surpluses in the affected markets.) Yet the concepts quickly became controversial and have remained so ever since. We can illustrate this controversy by focusing on the consumers' surplus.

Marshall himself had noted that the measurement of the consumers' surplus by a triangular area under demand curve, *D*, was correct only if certain assumptions held. One of these assumptions was the absence of an income effect for any change in the good's price. To the extent that a fall in price, for example, raised consumers' real income and, therefore (depending on whether the good was a normal or inferior one), added to or subtracted from the substitution effect, the white triangle in Figure 7.8 would not provide a correct measure of consumers' surplus (but would overstate or understate its magnitude, respectively). Marshall defended himself against such possible error by confining his own discussions to changes of consumers' surplus resulting from small changes in prices and to such goods as matches, newspapers, postage stamps, salt, and tea (which are unimportant in the budgets of most consumers and might have zero income elasticities of demand). Yet such restriction made a wide use of the concept impossible, and many economists

CLOSE-UP 7.3:

Consumers' Surplus and the March on Washington

On November 15, 1969, the largest assembly of dissenters in U.S. history gathered in Washington, D.C. to urge an end to the Vietnam War. The intensity of their feeling was indicated by the fact that they came from every state, and they traveled long distances and spent much time and money in the process. A group of economists estimated a demand curve for this mass demonstration, plotting various prices of participation (calculated at $1 per hour of travel time plus 5.5¢ per person per mile) against the number of participants from different states. This enabled them to calculate the average price paid per marcher, as well as the total market value of the march ($7.1 million). From this information the researchers also calculated the consumers' surplus (from the area under the demand curve and above the price): $10.1 million.

Source: Charles J. Cicchetti, A. Myrick Freeman, III, Robert H. Haveman, and Jack Knetsch, "On the Economics of Mass Demonstrations: A Case Study of the November 1969 March on Washington," *The American Economic Review*, September 1971, pp. 719–24.

have called it "worse than useless" (P. A. Samuelson) and "no more than a theoretical toy" (I. M. D. Little).

Yet the notion that the sum actually paid for a quantity of a good understates the satisfaction this quantity provides has proven too important to be abandoned because of measurement problems. John Hicks (see Biography 4.2) has tried to rescue the concept, at least at the level of the individual consumer.

The Hicksian Consumer Surpluses. John Hicks defined four possible measures of the consumer's surplus, each being a sum of money which, if taken from (or given to) a consumer, would offset the gain from a price fall (or substitute for the loss from a price rise). These four measures are illustrated, for the case of a price fall, in Figure 7.9. The horizontal axis measures the quantity of apples consumed by an individual; the vertical axis measures the consumer's income (or the quantities of "all other goods" consumed, at fixed prices). The consumer's income is assumed to equal $0A$. Given the initial price of apples, the budget line is AB. The consumer's initial optimum is at C, on indifference curve I_0. Then the price of apples falls, all else being equal. The budget line becomes AD, and the consumer's optimum shifts to E, on to higher indifference curve I_1.

The first of the Hicksian measures is the **price-compensating variation**, the *maximum* amount of income the consumer would *pay* for the privilege of buying (any desired quantity of) a good at a lower price. In our example, this measure equals AF because the consumer would, with only $0F$ of income left, reach income-apple combination G at the new price (dashed line FH parallels AD); G provides as much satisfaction as initial C (both are on indifference curve I_0).

An alternative measure is the **price-equivalent variation**, the *minimum* amount of income the consumer would *accept* for relinquishing the opportunity of buying (any desired quantity of) a good at a lower price. In our example, this measure equals AK because the consumer could, with total income of $0K$, reach income-apple

combination L at the old price (dashed line KJ parallels AB); L provides as much satisfaction as E (both are on indifference curve I_1).

The third Hicksian measure is the **quantity-compensating variation**, the *maximum* amount of income the consumer would *pay* for the privilege of buying a good at a lower price, *while being constrained to buying the quantity (here $0Q$) that the consumer would buy at the lower price in the absence of compensation.* In our example, this measure equals EM, because the consumer could, after paying this amount, reach income-apple combination M, which provides as much satisfaction as the initial position C (both are on indifference curve I_0).

Finally, there is the **quantity-equivalent**

Figure 7.9 Four Versions of the Consumer's Surplus

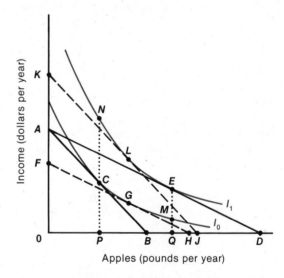

John Hicks expanded Alfred Marshall's notion of the consumer's surplus. Here a consumer moves from C to E in response to a decreased price of apples. The surplus might be measured by either a price-compensating or a quantity-compensating variation (by AF or EM). Each leaves the consumer in the initial welfare position (G and M are found on indifference curve I_0, as is initial position C). This surplus might also be measured by either a price-equivalent or a quantity-equivalent variation (by AK or CN). Each of these leaves the consumer in the new welfare position (L and N are found on indifference curve I_1, as is new position E).

variation, the *minimum* amount of income the consumer would *accept* for relinquishing the opportunity of buying a good at a lower price, *while being constrained to buying the quantity (here* 0*P) that the consumer would buy at a higher price in the absence of compensation.* In our example, this measure equals *CN*, because the consumer could, after receiving this amount, reach income-apple combination *N*, which provides as much satisfaction as the new position *E* (both are on indifference curve *I₁*).

Unfortunately, the Hicksian measurements of the consumer's surplus remain nonoperational. No one knows how to go about measuring the amounts involved for even a single consumer, let alone millions of them. Yet economists do make statistical measurements of market demand curves. And many of them do continue to use the theoretically suspect Marshallian triangle on their policy evaluations, at least as a rough approximation of the theoretically purer Hicksian measures. Excise taxation and import quotas are two types of policies evaluated using Marshallian rather than the Hicksian analysis.

Application 3: Excise Taxation

The Marshallian analysis of demand and supply allows economists to predict the effects of government intervention in markets. Consider the imposition of an **excise tax**, a tax per unit of product equal to, say, $3 per bushel of apples sold.

Figure 7.10 is based on the diagram of short-run equilibrium in Figure 7.2. It shows an initial equilibrium at *e*, with price at $6 per bushel and quantity at 250 million bushels of apples traded per year. What would happen if sellers were asked to deliver $3 to the government for every bushel of apples sold?

The Short Run. Given the short-run market demand and market supply pictured in Figure 7.10, price to buyers surely could not rise by $3 to $9 per bushel. If it did, quantity demanded would fall to 110 million bushels per year (point *a*), but sellers (who would collect $9 per bushel,

pay $3 to the tax collector, and keep $6) would continue to supply 250 million bushels (point *e*). Thus a surplus of 250 − 110, or 140 million bushels per year, would develop (distance *ab*). Price to buyers would then fall below $9.

Nor could sellers bear the entire tax. If price to sellers fell by $3 to $3 per bushel, quantity supplied would fall to 75 million bushels per year (point *c*), but buyers (who would continue to be charged $6 per bushel, $3 of which would go to the tax collector) would continue to demand 250 million bushels per year (point *e*). Thus a shortage of 250 − 75, or 175 million bushels per year, would develop (distance *cd*). Price to sellers would then rise above $3.

We can find the solution by fitting a vertical wedge (*fg*) that is equal to the $3-per-bushel tax between the supply and demand curves to the left of equilibrium point *e*. The points where such a wedge meets the demand and supply curves indicate that the price to the buyer must rise from the original $6 to $7.75 per bushel, while the price kept by the seller (after paying the tax) must fall to $4.75. In our example, this is the only equilibrium possible, equating quantity demanded (point *f*) with quantity supplied (point *g*) at 170 million bushels per year.

Government would collect a tax of 170 million bushels per year times $3 per bushel, or $510 million per year (rectangle *fghi*). The consumers' surplus would decrease by dotted area *kefi* and the producers' surplus by crosshatched area *kegh*. Note: The loss of consumers' and producers' surplus that results from the excise tax can be divided into two parts. A portion of this loss is offset by the government's gain (or that of the beneficiaries of governmental spending). This **transfer loss** equals the government's tax receipts and is shown by the unshaded rectangle *fghi*. Another portion of the loss, however, is *not offset by anybody else's gain*. It is called the **deadweight loss** and is shown by shaded triangle *feg*.

A final note: If demand had been perfectly inelastic with respect to price (a vertical line), the excise tax would have been shifted entirely onto buyers. Similarly, it would have been shifted

FIGURE 7.10   Imposing an Excise Tax

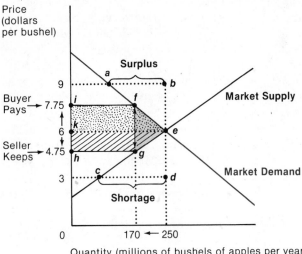

In the short run, the imposition of an excise tax (here of $3 per bushel) raises the price to buyers (here from $6 to $7.75 per bushel) and lowers the price to sellers (here from $6 to $4.75 per bushel). The trading volume falls (here from 250 million to 170 million bushels per year). As a result, the consumers' and producers' surpluses decline (by amounts equal to the dotted and crosshatched areas). A portion of this loss is a transfer loss to government (unshaded); another portion is a deadweight loss (shaded).

entirely onto sellers if supply had been perfectly price-inelastic.

The Long Run.   Our analysis has to be modified with respect to the long run. Imagine that the apple industry had been in long-run equilibrium prior to the imposition of the tax. Because the tax lowers the net price to sellers, the typical firm would be making losses after the imposition of the tax. The industry's position would be precisely that of the unprofitable and therefore contracting industry pictured in Figure 7.4. This contraction would have to continue until the price to sellers was again equal to minimum average total cost (ATC). Another glance at Figure 7.5 shows three possible outcomes.

If the industry was one of constant cost, its contraction would not change the level of minimum ATC; hence price to sellers would ultimately return to $6 per bushel (given our example of Figure 7.10). In the long run, consumers would be paying $9 per bushel (and market supply would intersect line ke below a).

If the industry was one of increasing cost, its contraction would lower the level of minimum

ATC; hence price to sellers would, ultimately, remain below $6 per bushel.

If the industry was one of decreasing cost, its contraction would raise the level of minimum ATC; hence price to sellers would, ultimately, have to *exceed* $6 per bushel. Because price to buyers would be even $3 higher than the sellers' above-$6 price, quantity demanded might then fall to zero. If it did, the entire industry would disappear. The power to tax is, indeed, the power to destroy!

Application 4:   Import Quotas

The Marshallian tools also help economists predict the effects of *quantitative* market restrictions imposed by government. Consider the imposition of an **import quota**, a maximum physical limit on the amount of a good that may be imported.

The diagram of short-run equilibrium in Figure 7.11 is based on Figure 7.2. It shows an initial equilibrium at *e*, with price at $200 per ton and quantity at 13 million tons of sugar traded per year. Of this amount, 5 million tons are supplied by domestic sources (distance *ab*) and another 8 million tons are imported (distance *be*). What would happen if the government imposed an import quota limiting sugar imports, regardless of price, to 4 million tons per year (distance *bd*)?

The Short Run. A shortage of *de* at the $200-per-ton price would drive the price up to $242 per ton (point *g*); quantity traded would fall to 10 million tons per year. (The straight line through points *d* and *g*, which parallels the U.S.-sources supply line by the amount of the quota *bd*, would be the new market supply). Note how U.S. suppliers would increase quantity supplied by 1 million tons per year (from *b* to *h*). Together with quota imports of *hg* (equal to *bd*), quantity supplied at the new price would equal quantity demanded (point *g*).

There would, therefore, be a loss of consumers' surplus equal to area *igea*. U.S. producers would gain *ihba* of this amount in added producers' surplus (dotted). Foreign producers would gain crosshatched area *hgfc* because the identical 4 million tons (*hg* = *cf*) were imported before at the lower price of $200 per ton. That, however, would not be the whole story. Foreign producers also used to sell the 1 million tons now sold by U.S. producers (distance *bc*) and the 3 million tons now sold not at all (distance *fe*). On these accounts, foreigners would *lose* producers' surplus; and additional losses would occur if the quota was assigned not to those (low-marginal-cost) foreign producers who used to supply the 6 to 9 millionth tons, but to those others (with higher marginal costs) who supplied the 10 to 13 millionth tons.

So far as the United States is concerned, the effect is clear: Producers would gain, consumers would lose a much larger amount. The two shaded triangles, furthermore, would represent deadweight losses; area *bhc* being frittered away in higher-than-necessary production costs (because expensive domestic production would be substituted for cheaper foreign production), area *fge* reflecting the surplus forgone as a result of the decline in the volume of trade.

FIGURE 7.11 Imposing an Import Quota

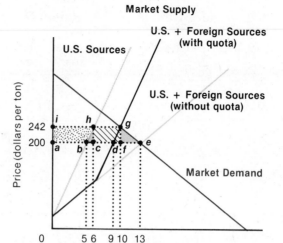

In the short run, the imposition of an import quota (here equal to *hg*) raises the market price (here from $200 to $242 per ton). The trading volume falls (here from 13 million to 10 million tons per year). As a result the consumers' surplus declines (by area *igea*). A portion of this loss is transferred to domestic producers (dotted), another portion to foreign producers (crosshatched), and the rest is deadweight loss (shaded).

The Long Run. The long-run effects would be analogous to those discussed in the section on excise taxation. This time, however, the effects would work in the opposite direction. If the domestic sugar industry was in long-run equilibrium prior to the quota imposition, the typical firm would find itself making profits after the quota had raised the price. The industry's position would be that of the profitable and therefore expanding industry pictured in Figure 7.3. This expansion would have to continue until the price was again equal to minimum average total cost. Figure 7.5 shows three possible outcomes.

In the case of a constant-cost industry, price would ultimately return to $200 per ton. Domestic supply plus the quota would intersect market

ANALYTICAL EXAMPLE 7.2:
The Welfare Effects of U.S. Sugar Quotas

Ever since 1948, the U.S. government has imposed quotas on sugar imports. As a result, the U.S. price of sugar has exceeded the world market price, by 40 percent in 1970. One economist has calculated the effects of this policy, using 1970 data. The total loss of consumers' surplus (equivalent to area *igea* in Figure 7.11) equalled $585.96 million. Of this amount, domestic producers gained $228.73 million (the dotted area in Figure 7.11), foreign producers gained $267.28 (the crosshatched area). The deadweight loss due to lower trade volume (area *fge*) was $10.28 million; the deadweight loss due to increased production cost (area *bhc*) was $79.67 million.

Source: Ilse Mintz, *U.S. Import Quotas: Costs and Consequences* (Washington, D.C.: American Enterprise Institute for Public Policy Research, February 1973).

demand at *e*. In the case of an increasing-cost industry, minimum *ATC* would rise with the industry's expansion, which would cease when domestic supply plus quota intersected market demand somewhere between *g* and *e*. In the case of a decreasing-cost industry, minimum *ATC* would fall with the industry's expansion, which would cease when domestic supply plus quota intersected market demand somewhere to the right and below *e*. Then consumers would be getting more sugar than before the quota, and at a lower price. (This possible outcome is often cited by those making the so-called ''infant industry'' argument in favor of quotas.)

SUMMARY

1. This chapter joins the analysis of market demand to that of market supply. It studies the nature of momentary, short-run, and long-run equilibrium in a perfect market. *Momentary equilibrium* is the equilibrium reached in a period so short that the quantity supplied is absolutely fixed. Price is reduced by surpluses and raised by shortages, until quantity demanded equals that which is supplied.

2. *Short-run equilibrium* is the equilibrium reached in a period sufficiently long for a given

number of firms to be able to vary quantity supplied by changing the utilization rate of given plants.

3. *Long-run equilibrium* is the equilibrium reached in a period so long that new firms can enter the industry and old ones can leave it or change the size of their plants. When markets are perfect, firms make zero economic profits in the long run because profitable industries expand, depressing product price, and unprofitable industries contract, raising product price, until product price equals *minimum average total cost*; that is, normal price. In the process of industry expansion or contraction, the normal price itself may change. Accordingly, the long-run industry supply curve can be horizontal, upward-sloping, or downward-sloping; the industry can be one of constant cost, increasing cost, or decreasing cost.

4. The Marshallian analysis of equilibrium-price determination put an effective end to the eternal conflict between the subjective-utility and objective-cost theories of price. It did not, however, hinder the ageless attempts by the powerful to replace the market equilibrium price, which properly reflects the degree of scarcity prevailing, with a ''just'' price, which is considered morally acceptable.

5. Applications of the Marshallian apparatus include explanations of cobweb cycles, the gains from trade with the help of the consumers' and producers' surpluses, the effects of excise taxation, and the effects of import quotas.

KEY TERMS

atomistic competition
cobweb cycle
constant-cost industry
consumers' surplus
deadweight loss
decreasing-cost industry
excise tax
external diseconomies
external economies
import quota
increasing-cost industry
internal diseconomies
internal economies
long-run equilibrium
market equilibrium
momentary equilibrium
normal price
price-compensating variation
price-equivalent variation
producers' surplus
quantity-compensating variation
quantity-equivalent variation
shortage
short-run equilibrium
surplus
transfer loss

QUESTIONS AND PROBLEMS

1. In 1979, a 5-foot by 9-foot painting by Frederic Church, entitled "Icebergs," was sold for $2.5 million at a New York auction. At the time, only two paintings had ever commanded more at auction: a Velazquez (*Portrait of Juan de Pareja*), which sold for $5.54 million in 1970 and a Titian (*Diana and Actaeon*), which sold for 4.07 million in 1971. Can you explain these prices with the help of the Marshallian tools of supply and demand?

2. All available tickets to athletic or artistic events are often sold out prior to the season. As the season progresses, these tickets are sometimes resold at higher-than-original prices (a phenomenon called "scalping") but at other times are sold at lower-than-original prices. Explain.

3. In mid-1972, the U.S. wheat price was $1.70 per bushel. Then the Russians entered the market, buying up 19 million metric tons of wheat (one quarter of the U.S. crop). By the end of the summer, the price of wheat was $5 per bushel. Even the per-bushel price of rye (which the Russians did not buy) jumped from $1.01 to $3.86, that of oats from 80¢ to $2.06, and that of soybeans from $3.50 to $12. Can you explain these events?

4. When markets are perfect, what do you think would happen to an industry, given market demand for its product, if its inputs were gradually becoming exhausted? Explain.

5. Many observers have decried as immoral the existence of markets for babies, corneas, blood, or kidneys, in which the supply comes from paid donors and thus adds to the nonmarket supply from unpaid donors. What do you think about this "commercialism"? (*Hint:* Consider, for example, the effect of such a commercial delivery system on the price paid for blood and on the quantity available to those needing transfusions. What if you were told that the frequency of transfusion hepatitis among recipients of blood from paid donors was ten times greater than among those receiving blood from unpaid donors?)

6. The equilibrium price depicted in Figure 7.2 is *stable*; that is, it would be reestablished through competition if, inadvertently, it ever rose above or fell below this level. What would competition do, however, if market demand had the peculiar position given in the graph shown on the next page and if the price moved away from its equilibrium at *e*?

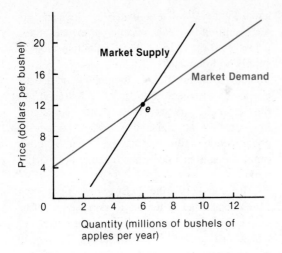

7. A society wishing to reduce the consumption of illegal drugs has two available strategies: a. reducing demand by harassing buyers or b. reducing supply by harassing sellers. Considering the fact that higher drug prices impose heavy costs on innocent bystanders (as addicts turn to robbery and murder to acquire additional funds), which is the better strategy? Explain.

8. Analyze the effect, in terms of consumers' and producers' surplus, of a governmentally imposed below-equilibrium limit on the quantity demanded.

SELECTED READINGS

Dupuit, Jules. "On the Measurement of the Utility of Public Works." In American Economic Association, *Readings in Welfare Economics*. Homewood, Illinois: Irwin, 1969, pp. 255–83.

> A translation of the famous article of 1844 on consumers' surplus.

Hicks, John R. "The Rehabilitation of Consumer's Surplus." *Review of Economic Studies*, February 1941, pp. 108–16; idem. "The Four Consumer's Surpluses." *Review of Economic Studies*, no. 1, 1943, pp. 31–41; idem. "The Generalized Theory of Consumer's Surplus." *Review of Economic Studies*, no. 2, 1946, pp. 68–74.

Marshall, Alfred. *Principles of Economics*, 9th ed., with annotations by C. W. Guillebaud, vols. I and II. London: Macmillan, 1961.

Mishan, E. J. *Welfare Economics: Five Introductory Essays*. New York: Random House, 1964, pp. 184–98.

> On realism and relevance in the theory of consumer's surplus.

Pigou, A. C. *Memorials of Alfred Marshall*. London: Macmillan, 1925.

> Memorials by Edgeworth, Keynes, Pigou and others; selections from Marshall's writings and letters; a complete bibliography of his works.

Smith, Vernon L. "An Experimental Study of Competitive Market Behavior." *The Journal of Political Economy*, April 1962, pp. 111–37.

> Reports on a six-year experiment designed to study the process by which a competitive equilibrium of demand and supply is attained.

Schumpeter, Joseph A. *Ten Great Economists*. New York: Oxford University Press, 1951, chap. 4.

> On Alfred Marshall.

Shove, G. F., et al. "The Centenary of the Birth of Alfred Marshall." *The Economic Journal*, December 1942, pp. 289–349.

CHAPTER 8

Market Equilibrium: Resource Services

In the previous chapters, we have discussed the demand for and the supply of *consumption goods* and the interaction of these forces in perfect markets. In the present chapter, we turn to markets in which the *services of resources* are traded. As was illustrated by the lower loop of Part A in Figure 2.2, "Circular Flows" (p. 37), firms rather than households appear as demanders in markets for resource services; households rather than firms appear as suppliers. Note: The markets discussed in this chapter are markets for the *flows* of resource services, not the *stocks* of resources themselves. In this chapter we will discuss how people hire themselves out to firms for limited periods of time and how they hire out the natural and capital resources they own for similarly limited periods, *without relinquishing their ownership* in the resources involved. Thus we are not discussing markets in which people are traded (as might happen in a system of slavery), nor are we discussing markets in which ownership rights to capital or natural resource stocks are being bought and sold.[1] We will, furthermore, continue to assume the existence of perfect markets for the flows of resource

services and for the outputs firms produce with their help.

Demand: A Single Variable Input

The demand for resource services is invariably a **derived demand**—derived, that is, from the demand for goods. Unless there was a demand for apples, no firm would demand the services of human apple pickers or orchard-spraying machines, nor would it be interested in acquiring the right to use acres of land on which to plant apple trees. Indeed, firms can be expected to follow the optimization principle and always hire that quantity of any resource service which equates the marginal benefit of resource use with the associated marginal cost. As a result, the demand for the services of a resource, just like that for a consumer good, turns out to be not a single quantity, but a whole set of alternative price-quantity combinations. All this can be shown most easily in the case of a firm that can vary only a single input.

A Numerical Example

Consider a firm in the short run, subject to the production function given in Table 8.1. Given its technical know-how and fixed quantities of natur-

---

[1] "Markets for Bonds and Stocks," the appendix to Chapter 9 of the *Workbook* that accompanies this text, discusses markets in which ownership rights to resource stocks are traded.

al and capital resource services (1), the firm can vary labor services (2) and, therefore, its output (3). The marginal product of labor (4) is, in fact, the marginal benefit to the firm of using extra workers. When this benefit is measured in physical terms (as so many bushels of apples) it is called the marginal *physical* product of the variable input, MPP_i. The marginal benefit, however, can also be measured in dollars. Because the firm is assumed to operate in perfect markets, the volume of its activities will not affect the price of its output, P_o, of, say, $12 per bushel of apples. Thus each marginal physical product can be multiplied by the same product price of $12 to yield the **marginal value product** of the variable input, MVP_i (5). As long as it operates in perfect markets, the firm's volume of activities does not affect input prices either. Thus the price of the variable input, P_i, assumed at $10,000 per worker per year, is, in fact, the marginal cost (6) to the firm of using extra workers. The firm can always get another worker for a year for another $10,000.

Columns (5) and (6), clearly, contain all the information necessary for an optimal input decision. As long as the marginal value product of the variable input exceeds the input price, as in rows (A) to (F), the firm can raise its profit by hiring more units of the variable input. Thus the first worker hired raises the firm's revenue by $12,000 (because 1,000 bushels are added to output and sell for $12 each), but the firm's cost only rises by $10,000 (because that is the worker's wage). Thus the firm's profit rises (or its loss falls) by the $2,000 difference. Similarly, once the marginal value product falls short of the input price, the firm can raise its profit by hiring fewer units of the variable input, as in rows (G) to (I). Profit maximization calls for equating MVP_i with P_i: At some input combination between rows (F) and (G)—involving, perhaps, the hiring of five full-time workers and one part-time worker—both magnitudes will equal $10,000.

A Graphical Exposition

Figure 8.1 is a graphical illustration of how to derive the demand curve for a single variable input. In this graph, the data from columns (5) and (6) of Table 8.1 are plotted against those of column (2). At the assumed price of $10,000 per worker per year, the firm can equate labor's marginal value product with labor's price by hiring 5.4 workers per year (point *a*). Note: At a higher price of, say, $27,600 per worker per year, the firm would maximize profit by hiring only 2.5 workers per year (point *b*); at a lower price of, say, $3,600 per worker per year, it would hire 6.5 workers instead (point *c*). Thus the downward-sloping branch of labor's marginal-value-product curve is, in fact, the competitive firm's demand curve for labor if labor is the firm's only variable input. Similar demand curves can be derived, in analogous fashion, for all other inputs.

Before proceeding to the more complex case in which several inputs are variable, it is important to understand the relationship between change in quantity demanded and change in demand and the relationship between input decision and output decision.

Change in Quantity Demanded Vs. Change in Demand

As we have just shown, the *quantity demanded* of any resource service varies with its price (and this is always illustrated by a *movement along* the demand curve, as from *a* to *b* or to *c*). In addition, the *demand* for resource services changes (and the entire demand curve *shifts*) if there is a change in the underlying conditions determining the marginal value product of an input. Any change in technical knowledge, in the quantities of other inputs used, or in product price shifts the marginal-value-product curve of an input. This causes the firm to demand more or less of an input even at any given input price. Consider, for instance, a technical improvement that doubled all the entries in column (3) of Table 8.1, while leaving unaffected the inputs in columns (1) and (2). This doubling of maximum total product would double all the entries in column (4) and, therefore, all those in column (5) as well. Accordingly, a new marginal-value-product curve would appear in Figure 8.1. This

TABLE 8.1 The Input Decision

Inputs Per Year		Output Per Year		Marginal Benefit and Marginal Cost of Input Use	
Fixed (1,000 apple trees, 3 tons of fertilizer, etc.)	Variable (workers)	Maximum Total Product (bushels of apples)	Marginal Physical Product of Variable Input, MPP_i (bushels of apples per extra worker)	Marginal Benefit = Marginal Value Product of Variable Input, $MVP_i = MPP_i \cdot P_o$ (dollars per extra worker per year)	Marginal Cost = Price of Variable Input, P_i
(1)	(2)	(3)	$(4) = \dfrac{\Delta(3)}{\Delta(2)}$	$(5) = (4) \cdot \$12$	(6)
(A) 1	0	0			
			1,000	$12,000	$10,000
(B) 1	1	1,000			
			1,700	20,400	10,000
(C) 1	2	2,700			
			2,300	27,600	10,000
(D) 1	3	5,000			
			2,000	24,000	10,000
(E) 1	4	7,000			
			1,300	15,600	10,000
(F) 1	5	8,300			
			700	8,400	10,000
(G) 1	6	9,000			
			300	3,600	10,000
(H) 1	7	9,300			
			0	0	10,000
(I) 1	8	9,300			

The data in columns (1) to (4), taken from Table 5.1, "A Simple Production Function," depict the technical possibilities open to a firm in the short run. Given the assumed price of output, P_o ($12 per bushel of apples), the firm can translate the variable input's marginal product from physical into value terms; column (4) becomes column (5). This marginal benefit of input use, MVP_i, can be compared with the associated marginal cost, which is the price of the input, P_i, in column (6). As long as MVP_i exceeds P_i, as in rows (A) to (F), the firm's profit can be increased by using more of the variable input. Once MVP_i falls short of P_i, as in rows (G) to (I), the firm's profit can be increased by using less of the variable input. The optimum variable-input quantity is found between rows (F) and (G), where MVP_i equals P_i and where both equal $10,000 (not shown). Note: As the pointers between columns (3) and (4) indicate, the entries in columns (4) to (6) refer to the intervals between rows (A) through (I).

**FIGURE 8.1 A Firm's Demand for Labor:
The Simple Case**

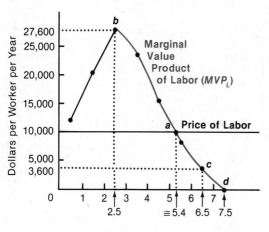

Labor (workers per year)

In the case of a single variable input, the downward-sloping branch of the input's marginal-value-product curve is, in fact, the competitive firm's demand curve for the input involved. Given technology, fixed quantities of other inputs, and product price, the firm pictured here demands the services of 5.4 workers per year if the price of labor is $10,000 per worker per year (point a). All else being equal, the firm would, however, demand the services of 2.5 or 6.5 or 7.5 workers per year, if the annual wage were $27,600 or $3,600 or zero, respectively (points b, c and d). Note: Using data from Table 8.1, marginal value products have been plotted at the midpoints of the ranges to which they apply, and all data plots have been connected by smooth curves. These curves give us additional information (about points between the heavy dots) that was not contained in Table 8.1; all of our subsequent discussions will be based on the more detailed information now available in this graph.

new curve would lie above the one presently shown (except for point d). At the $10,000 price of labor, the profit-maximizing input quantity would change to more than 6 workers per year.

An increase in the quantity of nonlabor inputs in column (1) of Table 8.1 or a doubling of product price from $12 to $24 per bushel would have identical results. The effect of doubling product price illustrates clearly how an increase in the demand for a good, by raising the good's price, translates itself into an increased demand for the inputs producing the good. Naturally, all

of these effects can work in the direction of decreasing demand as well.

Input Decision Vs. Output Decision

A firm's input decision is inextricably linked with its output decision. The profit-maximizing input decision depicted in Figure 8.1 corresponds exactly to the output decision depicted in Figure 6.2, "A Profitable Business" (p. 151) because both examples are based on identical assumptions concerning the production function and market prices (of $12 per bushel of apples and $10,000 per year per worker employed). The firm discussed in Figure 6.2 chose to produce 8,625 bushels of apples per year, and this output *implied* the use of about 5.4 workers per year. (Note the total variable cost of $54,695 given in Figure 6.2.) The firm discussed in Figure 8.1 chose to use about 5.4 workers per year, and this input *implied* the production of 8,625 bushels of apples per year.

Indeed, the profit-maximizing rule of the present chapter (under perfect competition, equate the declining marginal value product of an input, MVP_i, with input price, P_i) can be shown to be identical to the profit-maximizing rule of Chapter 6 (under perfect competition, equate the rising marginal cost of an output, MC_o, with output price, P_o).

The best input decision requires

$$MVP_i = P_i \qquad \qquad (8.1)$$

and this comes to $10,000 = $10,000 at *a* in Figure 8.1. Equation (8.1) can be rewritten as

$$MPP_i \cdot P_o = P_i \qquad \qquad (8.2)$$

or $833\frac{1}{3}$ bushels · $12/bushel = $10,000, in our example. Rearranging terms, equation (8.2) becomes

$$P_o = \frac{P_i}{MPP_i} \qquad \qquad (8.3)$$

or $12/bushel = $10,000/$833\frac{1}{3}$ bushels.

ANALYTICAL EXAMPLE 8.1:
Input Demand and Nonprofit Firms

Analytical Example 5.4, "The Production of Culture," reported on a recent estimate of production functions for various branches of the arts. The same study can be used to test whether performing arts companies use profit-maximizing input quantities as suggested by point a of Figure 8.1. If they did, we should expect the marginal value product of any input to equal its price (or the marginal physical product to equal the ratio of input price to output price). Yet the accompanying table shows a consistent divergence between MPP_i and the ratio of P_i to P_o in the 164 companies studied.

	Theater	Opera	Symphony	Ballet
(A)				
Input: Artists				
Marginal Physical product *(MPP)*	0.5943	0.2909	0.0870	0.5899
Ratio of input price to output price (P_i/P_o)	1.057	0.735	1.431	0.855
(B)				
Input: Capital				
Marginal physical product *(MPP)*	0.2051	0.0849	0.0347	0.1136
Ratio of input price to output price (P_i/P_o)	0.285	0.201	0.390	0.231

The marginal physical product was consistently below the relevant ratio of prices, implying marginal value product below input price. This implies an excessive use of these inputs from a profit-maximizing point of view, as would be the case if the firm depicted in Figure 8.1 used labor according to point c rather than a. Yet all this should not surprise us. Performing arts companies are frequently nonprofit organizations, heavily subsidized by private and public gifts, which augment revenues from ticket sales. If the price of labor depicted in Figure 8.1 were subsidized to the tune of $6,400 (the vertical difference between a and c), it would be perfectly rational to utilize a labor quantity corresponding to c (because the subsidy would effectively lower the price of labor to the $3,600 level shown there). The same, of course, holds true for capital as well.

Source: James H. Gapinski, "The Production of Culture," *The Review of Economics and Statistics*, November 1980, pp. 578–86.

Yet the price of an input, divided by the input's marginal physical product, is nothing else but the marginal cost of producing a unit of output with the help of this input. If labor is the only variable input, costs $10,000 a unit, and has a marginal product of $833\frac{1}{3}$ bushels, the marginal cost of producing one bushel comes to $12. Hence it follows that

$$P_0 = MC_0 \qquad \textbf{(8.4)}$$

which, of course, is the best output decision of $12/bushel = $12/bushel at B in Figure 6.2. Thus the two profit-maximizing rules of equations (8.1) and (8.4) are one and the same.

Demand: Several Variable Inputs

If we assume the simultaneous variability of more than one input, a downward-sloping demand curve can still be derived for each input. The procedure, however, involves more than deriving individual curves for each input by the method discussed in the previous section. This added complexity results because few inputs are **independent inputs** such that a change in the quantity of one has no effect on the marginal physical products of other inputs. (Mass-production machines and artisans who work with their hands and simple tools may be an example of independent inputs.) Normally, inputs are **complementary inputs** such that a change in the quantity of one changes the marginal physical products of other inputs in the same direction. (Consider workers in an apple orchard. The more apple trees there are, the greater is the marginal productivity of any given number of workers likely to be; the more workers there are, the greater is the marginal productivity of any given number of trees likely to be.) Figure 8.2 depicts the demand for labor of a firm with two such complementary inputs, both of which are variable. Let the firm use capital as well as labor services. As long as it uses 3 units of the former ($K=3$), the marginal value product of labor, MVP_L, may vary with the quantity of labor employed in accordance with the line going through points a and b. At a price of $17,000 per worker per year, the firm would demand the services of 10 workers (point a). All else being equal, it would demand the services of 18 workers if labor's price dropped to $10,000 (point b). Yet line ab would not be the firm's demand curve for labor, if it always hired additional capital with additional labor. If the lower price of labor caused it to hire 6 units of capital services ($K=6$) and labor's marginal value product of any given quantity of labor rose accordingly, the MVP_L line would shift up and right as indicated. The firm would demand 45 workers at the $10,000 price (point c). Thus its demand for labor would be the flatter line going through points a and c.

The demand for one input when several inputs are variable, can, however, also be derived more directly by a procedure akin to the derivation, in Figure 4.1 ''The Price-Consump-

tion Line'' (p. 77), of a household's demand for a good. Turn to panel (a) of Figure 4.1 and imagine that capital services are measured on the vertical axis, that labor services are measured on the horizontal one, and that lines I_0 to I_3 represented the capital-labor isoquants of a firm. An isocost line might swing around point A from AB to AC, to AD, and to AE, indicating successively lower prices of labor. A profit-maximizing firm would select the alternative optima shown by points a through d, and the implied demand curve for labor would appear exactly as in panel (b) of Figure 4.1. Indeed, this analogy to the theory of the household can be carried further.

Take another look at panel (a) of Figure 4.3, ''Substitution and Income Effects'' (p. 83). Once more imagine that capital services are on the vertical axis, that labor services are on the horizontal one, and that lines I_0 and I_1 are isoquants. With isocost line AB, a firm would choose an initial optimum at a but a new one at b once labor's price fell to produce isocost line AC. The increased quantity of labor demanded (the horizontal distance between a and b) could then be separated into two parts. As in the case of the household, the horizontal move from a to c is called the **substitution effect**, but the move from c to b is called the **scale effect** or the **output effect** (rather than the income effect).

The substitution effect makes a firm buy more of an input with a lowered price because the change in relative prices makes the firm substitute, in the optimal bundle of inputs used, more of the relatively cheaper input for less of the relatively more expensive one. Note how, in our imagined version of Figure 4.3, an unchanged output, represented by isoquant I_0, would be produced with input combination c rather than a, using less capital and more labor.

The scale or output effect, depicted by a move from c to b in Figure 4.3, on the other hand, makes the firm buy more of both inputs and produce a larger output after the price of one input has fallen. This increase in output occurs because the fall in the price of one input, here labor, effectively reduces the firm's marginal

FIGURE 8.2 A Firm's Demand for Labor: A Complex Case

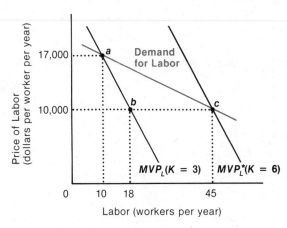

If a lower price of one input (here labor) causes a firm to hire additional amounts not only of this input but of complementary inputs as well (here capital services), the first input's marginal value product curve shifts up or to the right, as from MVP_L to MVP_L^*. The firm's demand curve for the input (here line ac) is, therefore, flatter than any given marginal-value-product (MVP) curve.

cost curve. Given the price of output, this raises the profit-maximizing level of output. (As a glance at Figure 6.2, ''A Profitable Business'' on p. 151 can quickly confirm, a downward shift of the marginal cost curve moves the profit-maximizing output level to the right of point B.)

Note: While the substitution effect always increases the quantity demanded of an input with lowered price, and while the output effect usually reinforces this result, the output effect could also operate in the *opposite* direction from the substitution effect. This counter movement would be analogous to the cases of inferior goods, illustrated in panels (b) and (c) of Figure 4.3. Those inputs for which the output effect works counter to the substitution effect are called **regressive inputs**.

From Individual Demand to Market Demand

As was the case regarding the demand for consumer goods illustrated in Figure 4.5, ''Deriving Market Demand'' (p. 88), the demands of individual firms for inputs can be added together to derive market demand. The derivation of market demand for an input is slightly more complicated than for a consumer good, however. The input demand curve of each firm is based on the assumption of a given product price (such as $12 per bushel in our example above). Given this product price, the firm pictured in Figure 8.1 would, indeed, increase quantity demanded from 2.5 to 6.5 workers per year if the annual price of labor fell from $27,600 to $3,600. Yet a simultaneous hiring of more labor by 100,000 other firms would raise industry output substantially and would almost certainly reduce product price from $12 to, say, $2.77 per bushel. This would shift our firm's marginal-value-product-of-labor curve down and to the left. The firm would hire, perhaps, only 4.5 workers at the $3,600 price. As a result, the *market* demand for labor is steeper than suggested by a horizontal summation of *given* marginal-value-product curves of individual firms (see Figure 8.3).

Note: As in the case of demand for goods, economists are intensely interested in the *price elasticity* of demand for resource services. This type of price elasticity, as defined in Chapter 4, is the percentage change in quantity demanded divided by the percentage change in price, all else being equal. This elasticity can be measured at various points along a resource demand curve exactly as indicated in Chapter 4. As in the case of goods, the magnitude of this elasticity is likely to be higher when substitutes are readily available (which, in turn, is the more likely the longer the time period under consideration). In addition, the demand for resource services being derived demand, their price elasticity is influenced by the price elasticity of the products they make. One might think, for example, that an increased price for a type of labor for which no substitutes exist

FIGURE 8.3 Deriving the Market Demand for Labor

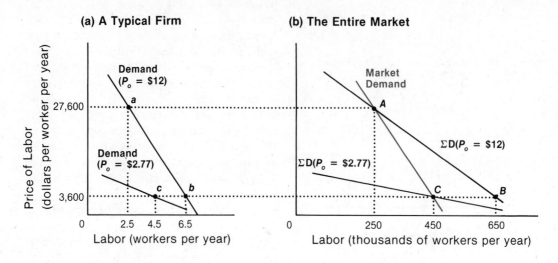

This graph illustrates how the market demand for labor (or any other input) can be derived from the individual demands of firms. Line *ab* in panel (a) represents a typical firm's demand for labor when the price of output equals $12 per bushel. The horizontal summation of this demand line for 100,000 similar firms is shown by line *AB* in panel (b). A similar individual demand line (and its summation for all firms) is shown for an output price of $2.77 per bushel. If labor's price is $27,600 a year initially, the typical firm demands 2.5 workers (point *a*); firms as a group demand 250,000 workers (point *A*). When labor's price falls to $3,600 a year, the individual firm would demand 6.5 workers, all else being equal. But if all firms hire more labor and raise output so much as to lower its price (to $2.77 per bushel as shown), the individual firm's demand line shifts. The firm then only demands 4.5 workers (point *c*), and firms as a group demand 450,000 of them (point *C*). Thus market demand is the steep line going through points *A* and *C*.

would give rise to a zero change in labor quantity demanded. Yet this conclusion would be wrong if there existed perfect substitutes for the *product* of this labor. The higher labor cost, which would drive up the price of its product, would in this instance reduce to zero the product quantity demanded and would, therefore, eliminate all of the demand for this type of labor as well.

Supply: The Case of Labor

What factors determine the supply of resource services? To answer this question we will focus on labor initially. Each individual, every day, has exactly 24 hours available, but obviously nobody can supply this much labor in a day on a regular basis. People have **reservation demands** for resources; that is, demands for purposes other than the sale of their services in the market. People certainly have reservation demands for their time. For want of a better term, economists refer to such nonmarket uses of time as the consumption of **leisure**, but this term is used to describe more than sleeping, eating, going to the beach, and being with family and friends. It can also include study and hard work in the home. When analyzing a person's allocation of time between leisure so defined and work for pay, economists make use of the indifference curve analysis introduced in Chapter 3. The individual is once more viewed as making a choice between two goods. This time, the choice is not between two specific consumer goods (such as apples and butter), but between income (or the set of *all* consumer goods that can be bought with that income) and leisure. Figure 8.4, which is analogous to Figure 3.6, "The Consumer's Optimum" (p. 64), shows that the individual is constrained by budget line *AB*. It divides the field of choice into attainable combinations (unshaded) of income and leisure and unattainable ones (shaded). The maximum amount of leisure available is obviously 24 hours per day (point *B*). The maximum income, however, depends on the prevailing wage. If it were $5 per hour (and that we assume), the individual could earn at most $120 per day, but that would require working 24 hours a day (point *A*). Note: The absolute value of the budget line's slope equals the prevailing wage; $120 per day divided by 24 hours per day comes to $5 per hour:

|Budget line slope| = wage

Any change in the wage would tilt the budget line around point *B* as an anchor point. A rise in the wage would tilt it upwards (point *A* would move up along the vertical axis); any fall in the wage would tilt it downwards (point *A* would move down toward 0). Correspondingly, the shaded world of the impossible would shrink or expand.

Figure 8.4 also includes a set of indifference curves, labelled I_0 to I_4. These curves display the characteristics discussed in Figure 3.5, "The Indifference Curve Analyzed" (p. 61). Each curve shows income-leisure combinations among which the individual is indifferent, but any combination on a higher-numbered curve is always preferred to one on a lower-numbered curve. The curvature of each indifference curve reflects the familiar diminishing marginal rate of substitution, now between income, *y*, and leisure, *l*. Thus the absolute value of an indifference curve's slope at any point also equals the ratio of marginal utilities of leisure to income.

FIGURE 8.4   An Individual's Income-Leisure Choice

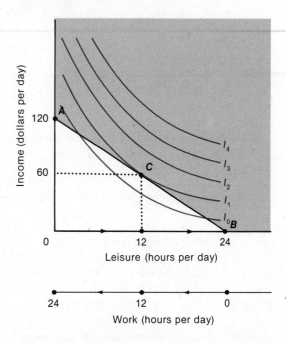

This graph brings together the elements involved when a utility-maximizing individual decides on the allocation of time between leisure and income-producing work. Budget line *AB* separates possible income-leisure choices (unshaded) from impossible ones (shaded). Indifference curves I_0 to I_4 depict the individual's preferences. Point *C* indicates the optimum income-leisure combination because, among all the possible combinations in triangle *0AB*, it yields the highest total utility.

|Indifference curve slope|

$$= MRS_{y/l} = \frac{MU_l}{MU_y}$$

Given the individual's opportunities and preferences (shown by the budget line and the indifference curves, respectively), the individual's optimum is found at point *C*. The consumption of 12 hours of leisure per day, which implies the supplying of 12 hours of labor per day and the receipt of $60 of income per day, maximizes the person's overall utility. At point C, the budget line is just tangent to the highest-numbered indifference curve that can be reached. Therefore, we have:

The Condition for the Labor Supplier's Optimum:

Slope of budget line = slope of indifference curve

$$\text{Wage} = MRS_{y/l} = \frac{MU_l}{MU_y}.$$

At point C, our individual receives $5 per hour and is indifferent about exchanging, at the margin, $5 of income for 1 hour of leisure. Thus an hour of leisure is valued at the margin five times as highly as a dollar of income (or a dollar's worth of consumer goods). The preceding indifference curve analysis can now be expanded to illustrate how the individual would vary the quantity of labor supplied with changes in a variety of factors—such as the wage rate or the amount of nonlabor income.

The Price-Consumption Line

Panel (a) of Figure 8.5 depicts a set of indifference curves identical to those in Figure 8.4, but Figure 8.5 illustrates the individual's behavior when confronted by different wage rates. If the hourly wage is $3, the lowest budget line is relevant and the maximum daily income is $72. The individual's optimum is then at point a where this budget line is tangent to the highest indifference curve (I_0) that can be reached with this budget. At point a the person chooses 17 hours of leisure and 7 hours of work per day; this labor quantity is indicated separately in panel (b) of our graph at point A.

If the hourly wage rises to $5, a new budget line that yields a maximum daily income of $120

FIGURE 8.5 The Price-Consumption Line

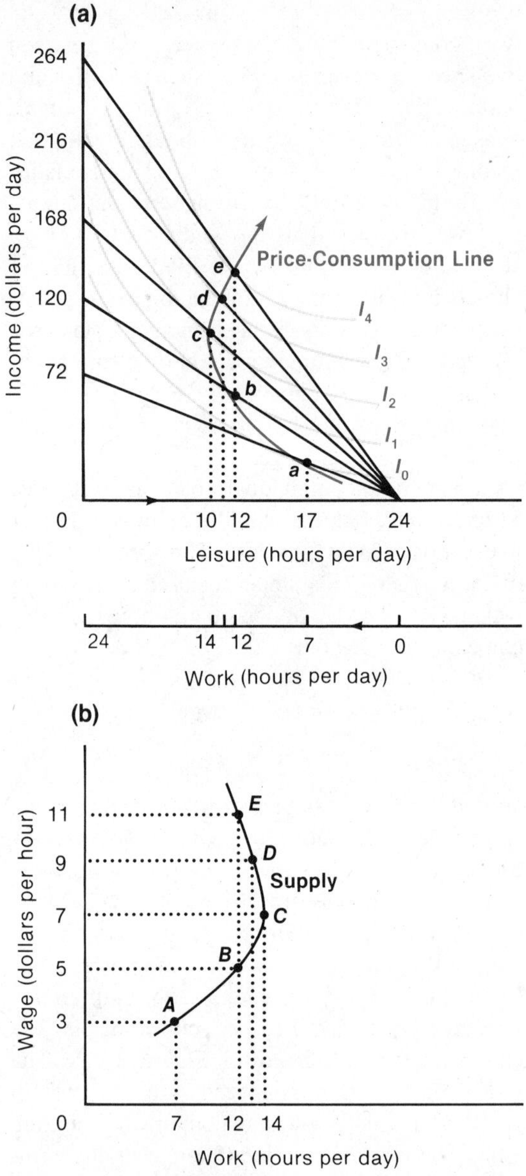

An increasing *wage* (which can also be viewed as the *price of leisure*) is pictured by a budget line swinging upwards in panel (a). This wage increase gives rise at first to lower and later to higher quantities of leisure demanded, all else being equal. Note how the optima move from *a* to *e* along the price-consumption line. All this translates, in panel (b), to first higher and later lower quantities of labor supplied as labor's hourly wage rises from $3 to $11.

FIGURE 8.6   The Income-Consumption Line

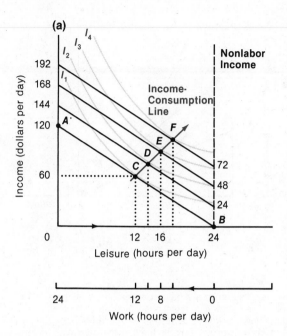

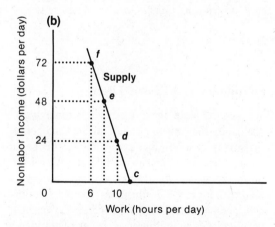

The receipt of increasing amounts of nonlabor income is pictured in panel (a) by parallel upward shifts of budget line *AB*. This increase in nonlabor income gives rise to an increased quantity of leisure demanded, all else being equal. Note how the optima move from *C* to *F* along the income-consumption line. All this translates, in panel (b), to a lower quantity of labor supplied as nonlabor income rises from zero to $72 per day.

becomes relevant. The individual's optimum moves to point *b* (which corresponds to point *C* in Figure 8.4). This choice is shown by point *B* in panel (b).

Successively higher wage rates of $7, $9, and $11 per hour keep moving the budget line up in panel (a) and yield new optima at *c, d,* and *e*. Once more, these choices are shown by points *C, D,* and *E* in panel (b).

In panel (a), the color line that connects the various optima is the price-consumption line, already familiar to us from Chapter 4. The two consumption goods between which the individual chooses are in this case not apples and butter, but leisure on the one hand and all other consumption goods (represented by income) on the other hand. The price, of course, is the wage, which can also be viewed as the price of leisure: For every leisure hour that the individual chooses to consume, a price has to be paid equal to the wage that might have been earned instead.

Because the leisure-consumption choice implies a choice about hours worked a labor supply line can be derived as in panel (b). The particular supply curve is backward-bending, indicating that this individual would supply smaller quantities of labor at higher wages once the wage exceeded a certain level ($7 per hour). Such a phenomenon is frequently observed in labor markets, but it is not a logical necessity.

The Income-Consumption Line

We can, similarly, isolate the effect on the quantity of labor supplied of changes in other variables. Consider Figure 8.6. Indifference curves I_1 to I_4 in panel (a) depict once more a person's preferences concerning income and leisure. Point *C* represents an original optimum where nonlabor income is zero and the wage rate is $5 per hour. Figure 8.6 shows the individual's behavior when confronted with different levels of nonlabor income, such as income from the sale of capital or natural resource services or a government grant.

FIGURE 8.7 Substitution and Income Effects

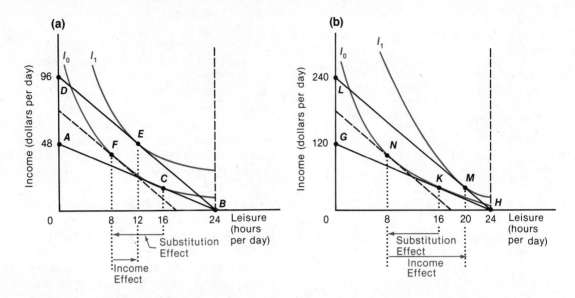

These two graphs illustrate the two effects on the quantity of leisure demanded (and, therefore, the quantity of labor supplied) of a higher price of leisure (that is, of a higher wage): The *substitution effect* of a higher wage decreases the quantity of leisure demanded and increases labor supplied. (Note the horizontal arrows so labeled in both graphs. They consistently point to the left.) The *income effect* of higher price works counter to the substitution effect and can offset it partially, as shown in panel (a), offset it exactly (not shown), or offset it more than fully, as shown in panel (b). Therefore, it is possible for a supply-of-labor curve (not shown) to have positively as well as negatively sloped segments.

When such income is zero, the individual works 12 hours a day—point *C* in panel (a), point *c* in panel (b). When such income equals $24 per day, budget line *AB* makes a parallel upward shift to this extent; the individual's new optimum is at *D*, implying more leisure and less work. This choice is shown at *d* in panel (b). Nonlabor incomes of $48 and $72 per day, similarly, shift the optimum to *E* and *F* in panel (a), and the quantity of labor supplied drops further to *e* and *f* in panel (b).

In panel (a), the color line that connects the various optima is the income-consumption line, already familiar to us from Chapter 4. This line indicates increased consumption of leisure with rising income; leisure must then be a normal good for the individual concerned.

Substitution and Income Effects

We can separate the effect of a simple wage change on the consumption of leisure (and hence the supply of work) into a substitution effect and an income effect—just as we did in Chapter 4 for ordinary consumption goods that are bought in markets. Figure 8.7 illustrates the substitution and income effects of a wage increase. Consider panel (a). Given indifference curves I_0 and I_1 and an initial wage rate of $2 per hour, an individual's optimum is found at *C* on budget line *AB*. Sixteen hours of leisure are consumed; 8 hours of labor, therefore, are supplied. When the wage rate doubles, the budget line swings to *BD*; the new optimum is at *E*. Leisure falls to 12 hours a day and labor supplied rises to 12 hours also.

ANALYTICAL EXAMPLE 8.2:

Empirical Indifference Curves for Income and Leisure

Empirical indifference curves for income-leisure choices have been derived for a sample of 200 low-income textile workers in the southeastern United States. In oral interviews, workers were asked: 1. What is the maximum amount of money per week they would be willing to pay in order to have on their jobs a specified nonpecuniary benefit currently not available (such as a rest period, less lint dust, a grievance system, air conditioning, less noise, paid sick leave, a pension plan, a nurse at the plant, and health insurance) and 2. What is the maximum amount of overtime per week they would be willing to work without pay in order to receive this same benefit. The workers' marginal rates of substitution between wage income and leisure were deduced from the equivalence of these two evaluations. The results are reproduced in panel (a) of the accompanying graph. Note: While these indifference curves obey the usual axioms of transitivity and convexity, they also yield labor supply curves that are negatively sloped throughout the range of realistic wage rates, as shown in panel (b). The workers in question desired to maintain approximately a given level of wage income irrespective of the wage rate. (Point X in both graphs corresponds to their actual wage income and hours worked.)

Source: L. F. Dunn, "An Empirical Indifference Function for Income and Leisure," *Review of Economics and Statistics*, November 1978, pp. 533–40. *See also* her "Measurement of Internal Income-Leisure Tradeoffs," *The Quarterly Journal of Economics*, August 1979, pp. 373–93.

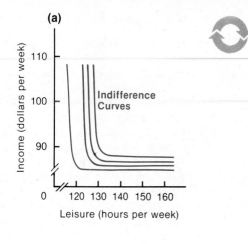

(a)

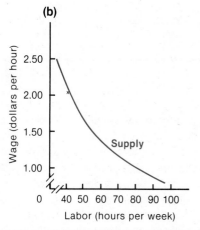

(b)

This pattern of movement implies an upward-sloping supply curve of labor.

With the help of the dashed artificial budget line, the slope of which reflects the higher wage, the move from C to E can be analyzed.

The individual could have remained equally well off by moving from C to F, substituting more labor and income (and other consumption goods) for leisure to this extent. (Note how both C and F are found on indifference curve I_0.) This potential move represents the substitution effect, which always makes a person consume less of a good with higher price. In this case, the price of

leisure has risen, and the individual is tempted to consume only 8 instead of 16 hours of it. Yet this is not the whole story. The wage hike has also given the individual a rise in real income, depicted by a parallel shift of the artificial dashed budget to the actual one labeled BD. The income effect makes people buy more of normal goods if income rises. In this case, the individual buys extra leisure, moving from 8 to 12 hours per day. Thus the income effect partially offsets the substitution effect, and the final choice falls on E.

Indeed, it is possible for the income effect to overwhelm the substitution effect, as shown in

CLOSE-UP 8.1:

Economics According to the Rats

The kinds of labor supply curves found in panel (b) of Figure 8.5 and panel (b) of Figure 8.6 have been verified by experiments with rats and pigeons. Experimenters made these animals push levers (or peck at buttons) a certain number of times before they could obtain food. When the number of pushes or pecks was decreased for a given unit of food (that is, when the "wage" was increased per unit of effort), the hungry animals pushed and pecked faster and more diligently at first. The quantity of labor supplied rose, as from *A* to *C* in Figure 8.5. Further increases in the "wage", however, produced a slowing down of effort, a substitution of leisure for food income (as between *C* and *E* in Figure 8.5).

While holding the "wage" constant, the same animals were also supplied intermittently with various quantities of *free* food. As pictured in Figure 8.6, the rats and pigeons reduced their work output when they received free food while they worked. Interestingly, low-wage rats (who had to push a lot for a given amount of food) reduced their work more than high-wage rats. Did high-wage rats love working for the sake of working?

Source: These and other experiments are noted in Tom Alexander, "Economics According to the Rats," *Fortune*, December 1, 1980, pp. 127–32. *See also* Close-Up 4.2, "Substitution and Income Effects in the World of White Rats" (p. 85) and Analytical Example 4.2, "The Demand Elasticity of Animal Consumers" (p. 104-105).

---

panel (b). Given indifference curves I_0 and I_1, and an initial wage rate of $5 per hour, an individual's optimum is found at *K* on budget line *GH*. Sixteen hours of leisure are consumed, 8 hours of labor performed. Once more, the wage rate doubles, the budget line swings to *HL*; the new optimum is at *M*. Leisure rises to 20 hours a day, and labor supplied falls to 4 hours. This time, the supply of labor is backward-bending. Although the individual could have remained equally well off by moving from *K* to *N* (and would thus have supplied more labor), the income effect overwhelms the substitution effect.

   Note: The income effect for ordinary consumption goods that are also normal goods *reinforces* the substitution effect (as noted in Chapter 4) because a higher price of those goods makes people poorer and thus makes them buy less on that account as well. The income effect for leisure always *works counter to* the substitution effect because a higher price of leisure (which is the wage) makes people richer, not poorer and thus makes them "buy" more leisure (assuming it is a normal good). The possibility of the income effect overpowering the substitution ef-

fect (which is rare for ordinary consumption goods because it requires the presence of Giffen's paradox) is fairly high in the case of leisure for the following reasons. Individuals are usually highly diversified when consuming ordinary goods. They consume small quantities of many types of goods. Thus a change in the price of any one of them (be it butter, pigs' feet, or potatoes) affects the consumer's real income but usually to a minor degree. Individuals are, on the other hand, highly specialized when it comes to supplying resource services. Most of them supply relatively large quantities of services of a single resource only, usually labor. Thus a change in the price of labor is likely to have a substantial impact on the person's real income; hence a powerful income effect occurs.

Supply: Natural and Capital Resource Services

The crucial difference between the supply of labor services and that of nonlabor services is that resource owners must be present when their labor services are being used, but they can be absent when their natural or capital resources are being put to work. The supply of nonlabor services, therefore, does not require the painful sacrifice of leisure on the part of resource owners. One is tempted to conclude that the individual supply curves of natural and capital resource services must be vertical lines, as in panel (a) of Figure 8.8. That is, each individual may simply supply, regardless of price, whatever maximum quantity of services (such as $0A$ in panel (a)) his or her nonhuman resources can yield. In the very short run, supply could be a vertical line, as in panel (a). It is also conceivable, however, that resource owners have reservation demands even for their nonhuman resources. Rather than rent

out a plot of land for anything less than $0B$ dollars per acre per year, its owner may use it as a garden or let it grow wild and enjoy the animals it attracts. Or rather than rent it for less than $0B$, the owner might turn the land into a private air strip and golf course. In such a case, the individual supply curve would look like the one in panel (b) of Figure 8.8.

Most nonhuman resources, furthermore, can be augmented or diminished in quantity in the long run. Arable land can be created by filling in bays, draining swamps, irrigating deserts, terracing hillsides, and fertilization—and it can easily be destroyed by mismanagement and neglect. (Consider the Kansas dust bowl, the many North African deserts that once were fertile plains, and

CLOSE-UP 8.2:

Negative Income Tax and Labor Supply

In the late 1960s, the U.S. Congress debated the introduction of a negative-income-tax system designed to help the poor. Under such a program, families whose income falls below a given figure would receive cash grants from the government, and these grants would be reduced as the families' earned income rose. One thought has haunted the program's sponsors: Would the beneficiaries of such a program simply take the money and withdraw from the labor force? Would the rest of society then have to support these people permanently? Economists predicted two outcomes: 1. the receipt of nonlabor income in itself would tend to reduce work performed (consider Figure 8.6). 2. on the other hand, the reduction of the grant as *earned* income rose would in effect lower the recipients' wage rate. (If they took a job at $5 per hour, but then the original government grant was reduced by $3, the effective wage would fall to $2.) This lowered wage would produce both a substitution effect (less work) and an income effect (more work), a matter illustrated in Figure 8.7. What would be the *net* effect of all these forces? To answer these questions, the U.S. Con-

gress funded a number of large-scale experiments—beginning in 1968—in New Jersey's six largest cities; in Gary, Indiana; in Seattle, Washington; in Denver, Colorado; and in rural Iowa and North Carolina.

The New Jersey results indicated that the labor supply effects of such a program are small, involving a 5- to 10-percent reduction in the amount of work done by program participants. Even this reduction did not take the form of total withdrawal from work. Instead, recipients worked fewer hours, did less moonlighting, and took more time to search for jobs during periods of unemployment. Also, secondary workers in a family reduced their supply more than primary ones; English-speaking whites reduced their supply more than blacks or Spanish-speaking workers.

Source: Joseph A. Pechman, Michael Timpane, editors, *Work Incentives and Income Guarantees: The New Jersey Negative Income Tax Experiment* (Washington, D.C.: Brookings Institution, 1975). See also Robert A. Moffitt, "The Labor Supply Response in the Gary Experiment," *The Journal of Human Resources*, Fall 1979, pp. 477–87. (In Gary, the work-reducing response of female household heads was found to be as high as 30 percent). Reports on still other experiments can be found in "The Seattle and Denver Income Maintenance Experiments," *The Journal of Human Resources*, Fall 1980, entire issue.

the many now-barren mountainsides throughout the world that once supported a prosperous agriculture.) Similarly, gas, oil, and minerals can be newly discovered, but known sites of deposit can also be abandoned. Apartment dwellings, blast furnaces, milling machines, and oil tankers, in turn, can be newly produced, as well as be destroyed through wear and tear or abandonment. For these reasons, the quantity supplied of most nonhuman resources is in the long run highly responsive to the price for their services. In the long run, even an individual's supply curve of nonhuman resource services is likely to have the familiar upward slope.

From Individual Supply to Market Supply

Individual labor supplies, like the one shown in panel (b) of Figure 8.5, can be added together horizontally to derive market supply. The market supply line could have the same shape as the individual line shown in our graph; it could also be upward-sloping throughout. Indeed, market supply is likely to be upward-sloping because not all individuals have backward-bending supply curves, and, for those who do, the bend points will appear at difference wage levels.

The market supplies of the services of natural and capital resources, like those for labor services, can be derived by horizontal summation and are best viewed as upward-sloping lines. Such lines would be upward-sloping, even in the short run, as long as different owners had different minimum prices (such as $0B$ in Figure 8.8) at which they began to supply the services of their resources.

Note: Economists calculate the elasticity of *supply* of resource services (as for the supply of goods) as a measure of the responsiveness of quantity supplied to price (see Chapter 6 for a discussion of how elasticity of supply is calculated for goods).

The Interaction of Demand and Supply

As in the markets for goods, equilibrium is established in the markets for resource services through the interaction of the forces of demand and supply.

FIGURE 8.8   An Individual's Supply of Nonlabor Resource Services

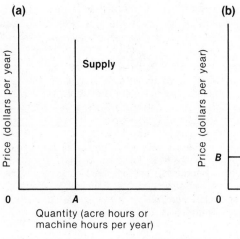

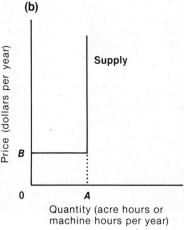

In the short run, an individual's supply of nonlabor services may be completely unresponsive to price, as illustrated in panel (a). Supply may respond to price, however, if the owner has a reservation demand for the resource, as shown in panel (b). In the case of reproducible and destructible resources, long-run supply is certain to be upward-sloping (not shown).

The Short Run

Figure 8.9 illustrates how equilibrium is established in the labor market in the short run, in which the number of people is fixed.

The Long Run

In the long run, the same principle of equating demand with supply applies, but demand and supply are likely to differ from their short-run counterparts. Until the markets for outputs are in long-run equilibrium (a matter discussed in Chapter 7), the demand for inputs will change. And, as we have noted above, the sellers of resource services have plenty of ways to change the supply of many inputs in the long run, too.

The British economist Thomas Robert Malthus (1766–1834) developed a simple theory of the labor market, often called the **iron law of wages**.

Malthus argued that as long as workers earn more than a subsistence wage (a wage that allows them to perpetuate their numbers precisely because it is just sufficient to ensure the survival of worker, spouse, and enough children to replace the parents), population will grow. More than two children per family will survive because there will be enough goods to ensure their survival. As long as workers earn less than subsistence, on the other hand, population will fall. Many children will be born, but there won't be enough goods even to rear the parental replacements. Because population and labor supply go hand in hand, actual wages above subsistence will invite greater labor supply and a fall in wages. Actual wages below subsistence will invite lower labor supply and a rise in wages. Hence wages in the long run will come to equal the subsistence wage. Workers will just earn their normal price—what it costs to reproduce them! Figure 8.10 illustrates this iron law of wages.

Nowadays, of course, economists do not subscribe to the simple Malthusian dynamics of population change. Yet they note that in perfect markets the long-run supply of many reproducible resources (including human-capital, real-capital, and natural ones) is fairly well described

FIGURE 8.9
The Market for Labor: The Short Run

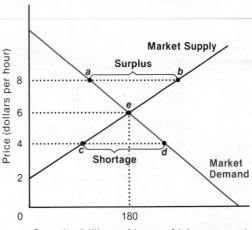

In a perfect market for the services of a resource, equilibrium is reached where market supply intersects market demand (point *e*). At any higher price, there would be surpluses, tending to depress price. At any lower price, there would be shortages, tending to raise price. This is true not only for the services of this unspecified type of labor, but for the services of other resources as well.

by Malthusian dynamics: The supply is infinitely elastic at a price that covers the cost of reproducing these resources. (See Chapters 9 and 15 for further discussion.)

Applications

Application 1:   Wage Differentials

When we look at the world around us, one thing is easily perceived: People earn vastly different wages in different occupations. Is this because real-world labor markets are far from perfect (a matter to be discussed in Chapter 13), or can such differentials exist even in perfect markets?

In the short run, certainly, such differentials

can exist even in perfect labor markets. Market demand and market supply for janitors and truck drivers, for example, might just happen to intersect at different wage levels, as in panels (a) and (b) of Figure 8.11. Yet if people were alike and jobs were alike, the free mobility found in perfect markets would eliminate such differentials eventually. Janitors would leave their occupations; supply, S, in panel (a) of our graph would shift to the left. Given demand, D, janitorial wages would rise. As exjanitors turned into truck drivers, supply, S^*, in panel (b) of our graph would shift to the right. Given demand, D^*, truck driver wages would fall. These changes would continue until the wage differential had disappeared.

Yet people are not alike; nor are jobs. That is why wage differentials could persist even in a world of perfect labor markets.

Differences in People.   There exist certain biological differences among people. People differ in physical strength, in size, and in intelligence. Some have a natural talent for athletics, music, or science; others are utterly inept in these fields. To the extent that these personal qualities cannot be acquired after birth, low-priced janitors cannot enter the occupations making use of these talents, and wage differentials can persist even in the long run.

Differences in Jobs.   While people can sell the services of their natural and capital resources without being present when they are used, a seller of labor power must personally accompany what is being sold. For this reason, nonmonetary aspects of jobs become a crucial consideration. Jobs differ in a million ways: Some have to be performed in harsh northern climates; others in the humid South. Some must be done in urban areas; others in the countryside. Some can be carried out in small firms; others only in giant ones. Some jobs have regular hours; others require overtime, work on weekends and holidays or even at night. Some provide opportunities for advancement, responsibility, prestige, and power. Some are physically tiring, dirty, smelly,

FIGURE 8.10   The Iron Law of Wages

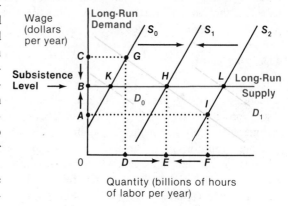

Quantity (billions of hours of labor per year)

As Malthus saw it, the long-run supply of labor was infinitely elastic at the subsistence wage, here equal to OB. Given the long-run demand for labor as shown by the solid line, and given short-run supply S_0, labor's wage might temporarily settle at OC, and OD hours might be supplied (corresponding to intersection G). This level, however, would encourage population growth. Labor supply would gradually rise to S_1. At the new equilibrium at H, hours supplied would equal OE, the wage would be at subsistence, and population would cease to grow. By the same token, a short-run supply S_2 might temporarily push labor's wage below subsistence to OA, and OF hours might be supplied (corresponding to intersection I). This, however, would force starvation and death upon people. Labor supply would gradually fall back to S_1. In the end, as if in obedience to an iron law of wages, labor's wage would always come to equal the level of subsistence. Population size, and the amount of labor supplied, would depend entirely on the demand for labor. If that demand fell to dashed line D_0, labor supplied would eventually correspond to intersection K. If that demand rose to dashed line D_1, labor supplied would eventually correspond to intersection L.

and noisy; others are boring, dull, and lonely. Some must be preceded by long periods of training and income forgone; others involve risks to health and life.

The list could be lengthened, but this much is clear: People have different preferences with respect to job characteristics. Some people like the northern climate, others hate it. Some love cities, others abhor them. Some seek out responsibility, others run from it. To the extent that monetary wage differentials only offset nonmonetary differences in the perceived attractiveness

FIGURE 8.11   Wage Differentials

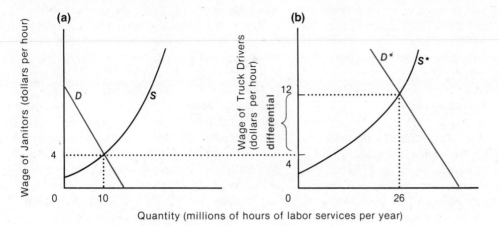

Quantity (millions of hours of labor services per year)

In perfect labor markets, the wage differential depicted here could not persist if all people and all jobs were alike. By the same token, biological differences in people and differences in the attractiveness of jobs can produce permanent wage differentials even when labor markets are perfect.

---

of jobs, the differentials can persist. Such wage differentials are then called **equalizing wage differentials** or **compensating wage differentials**. If all the janitors depicted in Figure 8.11 believed that they would rather lead a peaceful life than get paid $8 per hour more risking their lives on the highways, no shifts of supplies would occur in the two markets. Indeed, this sort of analysis has given rise to an interesting study about the value people place on a human life.

Wage Differentials and the Value of Life. R. Thaler and S. Rosen examined 1967 U.S. wage differentials among a number of occupations, along with differentials in occupational death rates. Some of their results are shown in Table 8.2. The authors of this study concluded that workers were accepting, on the average, $176 in extra annual wages for the added risk that 1 out of 1,000 workers in their occupation would die at work during the year. This means that people put an implicit value of $176,000 on their own lives.[2]

[2]Another study involving 496 blue-collar workers in 1969 calculated premiums for job hazards of $400 per year and an implicit value of life as high as $1 million. *See* W. Kip Viscusi, *Employment Hazards: An Investigation of Market Performance* (Cambridge: Harvard University Press, 1979).

Application 2:   Pure Rent and Quasi Rent

In everyday usage, the term *rent* refers to payment for the use of apartments, cars, land, and similar items that are used by one person but owned by someone else. Economists, however, use the term in a different sense. They give the name **rent** to that portion of a payment for the services of any resource (human, natural or capital) which exceeds the minimum amount necessary to bring forth the quantity that is in fact supplied. (Rent is thus analogous to *producer surplus* in the markets for goods.)

Consider Figure 8.12. Panels (a) through (c) picture three rather different market supplies of the services of three unspecified types of resources. Given demand, the price per hour of service turns out to be 0A in every case. The quantities actually supplied equal 0B, 0C, and 0D, respectively. Note: Given the vertical supply line in panel (a), which intersects the horizontal axis at B, the entire shaded area is rent as defined above because quantity 0B would be supplied even at a zero price. The situation is different in panel (b). The payment represented by the dotted rectangle is necessary to bring forth quantity 0C.

The shaded area above it is rent. Finally, in panel (c), the necessary payments equal the dotted area: A first unit of resource service would be supplied for as little as $0E$, a last unit for only DF. In fact, every unit is paid the price of $0A$. The roughly triangular shaded area, therefore, measures the amount of rent.

Economists are careful, however, to distinguish *pure rent* from *quasi rent*.

Pure Rent.   The excess payment called rent is a **pure rent** when the quantity supplied *is totally unresponsive to its price in the long run* because the resource in question can neither be destroyed nor produced by people. The classical economists pointed to the "original and indestructible powers of the soil" as an example of such a resource. The British economist David Ricardo (1772–1823), in a famous debate about the high price of "corn" (a term then referring to grain), argued against those who blamed high corn prices on high rents charged tenant farmers by

"greedy" landlords. Consider Figure 8.13. Because the Napoleonic Wars had interrupted foreign trade, argued Ricardo, England's supply of corn was unusually low, as at S. Given market demand, D, the price of corn was high ($0a$). Production was profitable on many farms. Farm A was producing quantity $0b$, Farm B quantity $0c$, and Farm C quantity $0d$, and each equated high market price with marginal cost. Now consider, Ricardo urged, each tenant farmer's position *prior* to the payment of rent to the owners of land. Because different plots of land have different fertility (an example of what Ricardo viewed as the "original and indestructible powers of the soil"), equal human effort applied to different plots of land is unequally rewarded: On Farm A, fertility is highest; output per unit of input is highest; the curve of average total cost (excluding rent) is lowest (ATC_x). On Farm C, fertility is lowest; output per unit of input is lowest; the curve of average total cost (excluding rent) is highest. Farm B's position is somewhere between

TABLE 8.2   Differential Wages and Death Rates

Occupation	Occupational Annual Deaths per 100,000	Extra Annual Wage
Fishers	19	$ 33
Fire fighters	44	77
Police officers, detectives	78	137
Electricians	93	164
Teamsters	114	201
Sawyers	133	234
Crane or derrick operators	147	259
Sailors	163	287
Bartenders	176	310
Mine operatives	176	310
Taxicab drivers	182	320
Locomotive stokers	186	327
Structural ironworkers	204	359
Boilermakers	230	405
Lumberjacks	256	451
Guards, doorkeepers	267	470

SOURCE: Adapted from Richard Thaler and Sherwin Rosen, *The Value of Saving a Life: Evidence from the Labor Market* (Rochester, N.Y.: University of Rochester, Department of Economics, December 1973). Reprinted in Nestor E. Terleckyj, ed., *Household Production and Consumption* (New York: National Bureau of Economic Research, 1975), pp. 265–98.

the two. For Farm *A*, revenue minus cost (excluding rent), therefore, equals the shaded area; for Farm *B*, revenue minus cost (excluding rent) equals the crosshatched area; for Farm *C*, revenue minus cost (excluding rent) equals zero.

Who will collect the net revenue shown by the shaded and crosshatched areas? The landlords will collect this revenue in the form of rents, said Ricardo. Tenant farmer *A* will have no choice but to hand over the money represented by the shaded area, for the alternative is to farm inferior land, like *C*, which provides no net revenue. The tenant of Farm *B* will be in a similar position. Landlords, therefore, will pocket *differential* rent, reflecting precisely the different fertilities of their soil.

Would taxing the rents reduce the price of corn? Of course not, said Ricardo. Abolishing tariffs and allowing the free import of corn, however, *would* reduce the price. Supply would rise to *S**, and the price of corn would fall to *0e*. Domestic production would drop from *0g* to *0f*, and imports would equal *fh*. Production on Farms *B* and *C* would cease, that on Farm *A*

would contract to *0i*. Rents would be gone. Although the supply of the ''powers of the soil'' would be unchanged, like the vertical line in panel (a) of Figure 8.12, the decreased price of corn would so reduce the derived demand for corn-growing land that landlords would not be able to collect a penny of rent.

Modern economists are less likely to think of the fertility of the soil as conducive to payments of pure rent. They are too aware of humanity's ability to destroy as well as produce this fertility. They point instead to such nonreproducible and unique aspects as the *location* of a plot of land or the special talents of famous athletes, models, movie actors, scientists, singers, or TV personalities. These special talents or unique features are best represented by the type of supply curve shown in panels (a) and (b) of Figure 8.12. Panel (a), for instance, might refer to the services provided by the parcel of land at the corner of New York City's 5th Avenue and 50th Street (site of Rockefeller Center and Saks Fifth Avenue). Or it might refer to an oil field or mineral deposit. Panel (b) might depict the supply of labor ser-

FIGURE 8.12   Rents

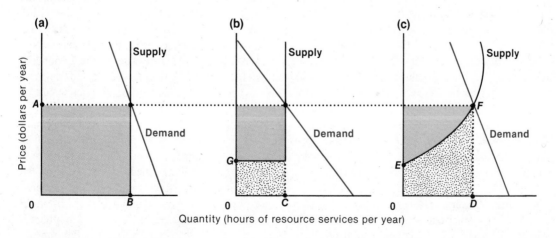

Economists give the name *rent* to that portion of a payment for the services of any resource (human, natural, or capital) which exceeds the minimum amount necessary to bring forth the quantity that is in fact supplied. Given the differently shaped supply and demand curves shown in the three markets pictured here, price (*0A*) is the same in all markets, but rents (shaded areas) and minimum necessary payments (dotted areas) differ in each market.

CLOSE-UP 8.3:

The Price of Beauty

"God makes models," it has been said, "and He doesn't make many of them." As a result, the market for models is depicted well by panel (b) of Figure 8.12. In 1980, four leading agencies—Ford Models, Inc., Wilhelmina Models, Inc., Elite Model Management, and Zoli—were battling each other for the limited supply of this gift of nature. Advertisers complained that the cost of buying status in the form of pretty faces had become outrageous. But the prices kept rising. New York's top three agencies each listed 15 to 20 models grossing over $100,000 a year. Most coveted were the exclusive contracts to represent cosmetic products. These contracts ranged from $50,000 to $300,000 annually and lasted up to 5 years, while requiring only 15 to 30 days of work a year. In 1979, Clotilde, a model representing Shiseido's flagship cosmetic line, was earning $190,000 a year. Lauren Hutton, representing Revlon's Ultima II cosmetics, was working under a $250,000 annual contract. And Cheryl Tiegs was earning $300,000 a year, selling her lips, eyes, and face to Cover Girl makeup (Noxell Corporation). Even then, Noxell didn't get the rights to her hair or legs; they belonged to Bristol-Myers Clairesse hair coloring and, more recently, to Sears, Roebuck and Co. which paid a "seven figure" sum to get Ms. Tiegs to promote its "personality jeans." Unfortunately for the models, nature that giveth also taketh away. Beauty is perishable; a female model's career averages only 6 years. (Male models, such as William Loock, may work into their sixties but earn much less than women).

Source: Gwen Kinkead, "The Price of Beauty is Getting Beyond Compare," *Fortune*, December 3, 1979, pp. 60–66; Dave Lindorff, "$125 an Hour: The Male Models," *The New York Times*, May 18, 1980, p. F3; "Cheryl Tiegs and Sears, Roebuck," *ibid.*, December 7, 1980, p. F19.

vices by Muhammed Ali, Lauren Hutton, Marilyn Monroe, Albert Einstein, Joan Baez, or Walter Cronkite. As long as demand for such services is high enough—the quantity demanded exceeding $0B$ at a zero price in panel (a) and exceeding $0C$ at a price of $0G$ in panel (b)—their sellers receive pure rent. Pure rent serves the function, of course, of allocating the resource in question to the highest-valued use. Except by a fortuitous act of nature, even a huge pure rent will not call forth increased supply in the long run. On the other hand, even the complete elimination of pure rent will not reduce supply. The realization of this fact gave rise to the **single-tax movement** of Henry George.

The Single-Taxers. Henry George (1837–1897) was an American seaman, journalist, and printer who argued for the finance of all governmental activities by a single tax on the ever-rising incomes of the owners of land. He viewed these incomes as pure rents, land being absolutely fixed in supply, but subject to ever-rising demand associated with population growth and its westward expansion. Landowners, he argued, contributed nothing to deserve such "windfall gains." George's ideas were popular among the poor, and his book, *Progress and Poverty*, became the all-time best-seller in economics. It sold millions of copies and brought him international fame. Indeed, as a candidate of the Labor and Socialist parties, he was almost elected mayor of New York in 1886, outpolling another would-be politician, Theodore Roosevelt.

In the end, George's ideas proved unacceptable. For one thing, pure rents accrue to others besides the owners of land. Thus equity would call for taxing Muhammed Ali as much as the owner of a Wall Street parcel of land. Indeed, one might argue, the original owners of high-rent land are likely to have long sold it to others at a correspondingly high price, leaving current owners with nothing more than a normal interest return on their investment in the land. Real-world "rents," therefore, are a mixture of many types of payments, including implicit interest for the money owners have invested in land, buildings, and other improvements on their land, implicit wages for the work of landowners, reimbursement for air conditioning, heating, and general maintenance expenses, and, finally, pure rent. It is next to impossible to separate these elements. Furthermore, even the taxation of all pure rents would provide insufficient revenue to finance government.

Still, Henry George's ideas linger on. New York City's Henry George School of Social Science and a handful of George's supporters at the University of Missouri still promote these ideas. Some cities, such as Pittsburgh, place a higher tax on the assessed value of land than on the assessed value of buildings standing on it. And many cities, confusing real world ''rent'' with pure rent, impose rent controls with disastrous results. Similar disaster awaits those who confuse quasi rent with pure rent.

Quasi Rent.   The excess payment defined by economists as rent is called a **quasi rent** when the quantity supplied *is responsive to its price in the long run* because the resource in question can

be destroyed and produced by people. For such resources, the elimination of rent does not change the quantity supplied in the short run but does change quantity supplied in the long run. All returns to human and real capital made by people are quasi rents as long as these resources are temporarily fixed in supply. While we cannot produce at will more parcels of land with the unique location of Wall Street, we can produce more apartment houses, oil tankers, and orchards planted with apple trees. While we cannot produce at will more people with the unique talents of Muhammed Ali or Albert Einstein, we can produce quite ordinary dentists and economics professors. Let panel (a) of Figure 8.12 represent the temporarily fixed supply, with no alternative uses, of the services of apartment houses, oil tankers, and apple orchards. Let panels (b) and (c) represent the supply of services, with some alternative uses, of dentists or economics professors. Imagine a tax eliminated all of the rents. Surely, unlike in the pure rent case, supply would change in the long run. If the price for their services was cut to zero now, apartment houses, oil tankers, and apple orchards would eventually

FIGURE 8.13   Ricardo's Differential Rents

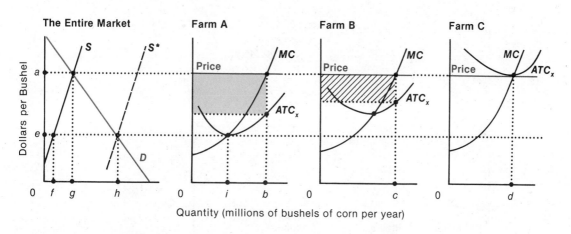

When the price of a product is high enough to generate strong demand for inputs in fixed supply (such as fertile plots of land), the owners of those inputs are able to collect rent. Plots of land with different fertility, argued Ricardo, will yield differential rent (equal to the shaded area for Farm A, the crosshatched area for Farm B, and zero for Farm C). These modern concepts and graphs illustrate Ricardo's verbal argument.

disappear because nobody would make the costly investment in their maintenance and replacement. Similarly, if the price for the services of dentists and professors was cut to eliminate rent and equal that of their best alternative employment, dentists and professors would eventually disappear because nobody would make the costly investment in the acquisition of the requisite type of human capital. By the same token, the payment of quasi rents so high that owners of apartment dwellings, oil tankers, or dental skills receive an unusually high return on their investment will eventually increase the stocks of these resources and the services supplied by them. The test of quasi rent vs. pure rent is this: If the change in rent has no effect on long-run supply or has no predictable effect (because nature does the supplying), the rent is a pure rent. If the change in rent does affect long-run supply (because people do the supplying), the rent is a quasi rent.

Application 3:
The Functional Distribution of Income

The classical economists saw society as split into three distinct classes:

ANALYTICAL EXAMPLE 8.3:

The Cost of the Draft

In 1980, when Congress debated the renewal of the military draft, many argued that the draft would avoid the high budgetary cost of the volunteer army. Yet a draft army is also costly; the costs are simply borne by different people. Consider the 1965 cross-section study by Walter Oi, which is summarized (and simplified) in the accompanying graph. From geographic differences in enlistments, civilian incomes, and unemployment rates, Oi estimated the supply curve of military personnel shown here and juxtaposed it with demand. Under a volunteer army, the actual

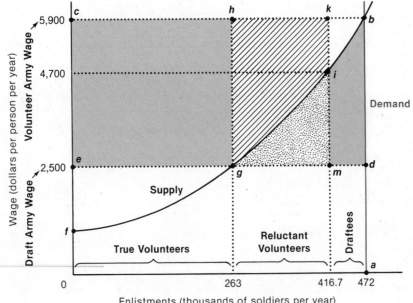

1. the *workers* (or proletariat), who supplied the services of human resources only (and received wages);

2. the *landlords* (or aristocrats), who supplied the services of natural resources only (and received rents); and

3. the *capitalists* (or bourgeoisie), who supplied the services of capital resources only (and received interest).

As the classical economists saw it, each of these classes of people performed a different function in society. These economists were interested, therefore, in the **functional distribution of income**; that is, the apportionment of national income among the owners of human resources, natural resources, and capital resources. Nowadays it is not appropriate to equate this functional income distribution with a distribution among distinct social classes because any given individual can and often does own and supply the services of more than one type of resource. Thus any given individual is likely to be a member of more than one of the classical economist's classes of income recipients. Modern economists, therefore, tend to pay more attention to the

1965 enlistments of 472,000 soldiers would have cost the taxpayers $5,900 per enlistee, or a total of $2.7848 billion (area *0abc*). In fact, only $2,500 per enlistee was paid, or a total of $1.18 billion (area *0ade*), an apparent saving of $1.6048 billion.

Yet an implicit tax on enlistees was being substituted for an explicit tax on all citizens: At the lower draft-army wage, only 263,000 of enlistees were true volunteers. Under the volunteer army, they would have received rent equal to area *fghc*; in the draft army they received only *fge* of rent, hence they lost *eghc* (shaded), or $894.2 million.

Another 153,700 enlistees were "reluctant volunteers," who enlisted only to avoid being drafted. They lost rent equal to *gikh* (crosshatched). They also lost an additional amount: One can always assume that the minimum price at which any unit of a resource is voluntarily supplied to a specific use—the height of the supply curve—equals that resource's next best income opportunity, adjusted for compensating wage differentials. Thus the first enlistee in the graph is willing to enlist for as little as *0f* and the last one only for *ab* because their alternative incomes or aversions to army life differ to this extent. It follows that reluctant volunteers also lost *gmi* (dotted), which represents pay these people require to volunteer for the army and be fully compensated for 1. the forgone alternative of the best civilian jobs they could get plus 2. any aversion they might have to army life. The total implicit tax on reluctant volunteers thus came to area *gmkh*, or $522.58 million.

There were, finally, 55,300 involuntary draftees. They lost rent of *ibk*, plus forgone civilian income or wage differentials of at least *mdbi* (shaded), or no less than $188.02 million. (Because the actual draftees probably were not the same people who would have volunteered at the $5,900 wage, but people on the supply curve to the right of point *b*, the implicit tax on them may have been much higher than *mdbi*).

Thus annual total losses to enlistees (area *edbc*) came to at least $1.6048 billion, easily matching the taxpayers' gain. Indeed, there were added losses, such as the costs to those taking less preferred, but draft-exempt jobs, to those staying in school to escape the draft, and to those engaging in illegal draft evasion, and to others.

Source: Walter Y. Oi, "The Economic Cost of the Draft," *The American Economic Review*, May 1967, pp. 39–62.

personal distribution of income, which is the apportionment of national income *among persons* (each of whom is likely to receive several types of income).

Nevertheless, the analysis of resource markets presented in this chapter has led to a remarkable discovery about the functional distribution of income. The American economist John Bates Clark (see Biography 8.1) noted that perfect markets produce the following results: every unit of every type of labor employed is paid the marginal value product associated with the employed quantity of that type of labor. (See, for instance, equilibrium point *a* in Figure 8.1.) Every unit of every type of natural resource employed is paid the marginal value product associated with the employed quantity of that type of natural resource. Every unit of every type of capital resource employed is paid the marginal value product associated with the employed quantity of that type of capital resource. The total income of the owners of any type of resource, therefore, equals the resource quantity employed multiplied by the marginal value product of the resource. Thus we can calculate the *total* wages, rents, and interest paid for the services of human, natural, and capital resources during a period. Let us call this sum *X*.

In perfect markets in the long run, Clark observed, this sum is exactly equal to the value, *Y*, of all goods produced during the same period, when these goods are evaluated at their market prices.

Note: In long-run competitive equilibrium, as we noted in Chapter 7, economic profit is zero; hence the market prices of goods just cover average total cost. Indeed, product prices equal the minimum *ATC* on the lowest possible *ATC* curve. Thus firms in the immediate vicinity of long-run equilibrium are operating neither under increasing returns to scale (which would induce them to expand in order to lower cost), nor under decreasing returns to scale (which would induce them to contract in order to lower cost). The implied operation under constant returns to scale is crucial for Clark's finding, for (as more advanced texts show) under increasing returns to

scale *X* exceeds *Y*, and under decreasing returns to scale *Y* exceeds *X*.

From his observations, Clark formulated the **marginal productivity theory of distribution**: In long-run competitive equilibrium, total money income, *X*, exactly equals the market value of total production, *Y*, if each employed unit of each resource is paid the marginal value product associated with the total employed quantity of this resource (see Figure 8.14).

Figure 8.14 is based on a constant-returns-to-scale production function for apples, produced only by labor, *L*, and capital, *K*, and such that output equals $\sqrt{L \cdot K}$. In panel (a), the average and marginal products of labor (*APL* and *MPL*) have been plotted on the assumption of a fixed input of 800 hours of capital service. If 1,250 hours of labor are used, for example, total product equals $\sqrt{1,250 \cdot 800} = 1,000$ bushels. Thus the average product of labor equals 1,000 bushels divided by 1,250 labor hours, or 0.8 bushels (point *b*), and area 0*ebf* represents the 1,000-bushel total of output. (This 1,000-bushel figure can be multiplied by any assumed market price to obtain the *value* of total output.) Substituting 1,251 in the above square root (so that the equation reads $\sqrt{1,251 \cdot 800} = 1,000.4$ bushels), the marginal product of labor can be calculated as 0.4 bushels (point *a*). If each hour of labor receives this amount, labor's share of output equals the 500-bushel area 0*eag* (or the equivalent value in cash). This implies that capital's share must equal the shaded residual, which also happens to be 500 bushels.

The test comes in panel (b). We plot the average and marginal products of capital (*APK* and *MPK*), assuming a fixed input of 1,250 hours of labor. By our formula, if 800 hours of capital are used, total product again equals 1,000 bushels. Thus the average product of capital equals 1,000 bushels divided by 800 capital hours, or 1.25 bushels (point *d*), and area 0*hdi* represents total output. Substituting 801 in the original square root (so that the equation reads $\sqrt{1,250 \cdot 801} = 1,000.625$ bushels), the marginal product of capital can be calculated as 0.625 bushels (point *c*). If each hour of capital receives

BIOGRAPHY 8.1:
John B. Clark

John Bates Clark (1847–1938) was born in Providence, Rhode Island. Coming from a family of strict Puritans, he studied ethics, philosophy, and economics first at Amherst College and later at Heidelberg and Zürich. He taught economics at Carleton College (where Thorstein Veblen was his pupil), then briefly at Smith and Amherst, but mostly at Columbia University. He was a cofounder of the American Economic Association and its third president. Active in pacifist causes, he became the first director of the Carnegie Endowment for International Peace.

His works include *The Philosophy of Wealth* (1887), *The Distribution of Wealth: A Theory of Wages, Interest, and Profits* (1899), *The Control of Trusts* (1901), and *Essentials of Economic Theory* (1907).

Clark was the first genuinely original theorist to emerge in the New World. Driven by a deep moral concern about distributive justice, he turned his attention to an ancient riddle: How does one allocate, among two or more cooperating inputs, the total product which they jointly produce? This problem had long been viewed as unsolvable, akin to deciding whether the father or the mother was responsible for the baby. (Indeed, Sir William Petty once called labor the father of production and land the mother.) In the process, Clark discovered the *marginal productivity principle of distribution*. His pioneering work quickly gained him a wide international reputation.

His writings were filled, however, with ethical overtones that annoyed many. Writing, as he did, at a time of emerging labor unions, increasing industrial concentration, and attacks against the economic order by Marxists and the followers of Henry George, he was concerned about the fate of his new-found principle of "just" distribution. He feared labor unions would exploit capitalists by forcing wages above the marginal value product of labor and that trusts would exploit workers by forcing wages below labor's *MVP*. He believed that competition ought to be enforced in all markets and that henceforth all questions of distributive justice might be settled with reference to the marginal productivity principle of distribution. Clark writes:[1]

> There is working, if we will see it, a law that makes for peace founded on justice. It tends in the direction of a fair division of products between employers and employed, and if it could work entirely without hindrances, would actually give to every laborer substantially what he produces. In the midst of all prevalent abuses, this basic law asserts itself like a law of gravitation, and so long as monopoly is excluded and competition is free—so long as both labor and capital can move without hindrance to the points at which they can create the largest products and get the largest rewards—its action cannot be stopped. . . . In this is the most inspiriting fact for the social reformer. If there are "inspiration points" on the mountaintops of science, as well as on those of nature, this is one of them, and it is reached whenever a man discovers that in a highly imperfect society the fundamental law makes for justice, that it is impossible to prevent it from working. . . . Nature is behind the reformer, often unseen, always efficient, and, in the end, resistless. To get a glimpse of what it can do and what man can help it do is to get a vision of the kingdoms of the earth, and the glory of them—a glory that may come from a moral redemption of the economic system. . . . Till recently American workmen have lived with their employers without hating them; and if wages can be fixed now by some appeal to the principle of justice, they can live with them in that way again.

The American Economic Association honors his memory by presenting, every two years, the J. B. Clark medal to an economist under the age of 40 who has made a significant contribution to economic theory.

[1]John B. Clark, *Social Justice Without Socialism* (Boston: Houghton Mifflin, 1914) pp. 34–37.

this amount, capital's share of output equals the 500-bushel shaded area *Ohck*. This implies that labor's share equals the unshaded residual. Either way, incomes exactly exhaust product.

Clark, however, went beyond these positive conclusions to make normative statements suggesting that this type of income distribution was *just*. After all, he argued, under this system of distribution, the withdrawal of any unit of resource service reduces the value of national product precisely by the associated marginal value product. Thus every unit is getting paid exactly what it contributes to production. To Clark, the profit-maximizing equality of input price and the input's marginal value product denoted fairness and the absence of **exploitation.** Karl Marx would have disagreed. To him the payment of *any* rent and interest points to exploitation because such payment enables owners of natural and capital resources to buy a portion of the national product. Even if each worker receives the portion of national product that would be lost if that worker alone withdrew from the labor force (the Clarkian result), Marx would charge exploitation because workers as a group did not receive the *entire* national product.

Application 4:
Wider Uses of the Time-Allocation Model

Under the leadership of Gary S. Becker (see Biography 8.2), economists have recently moved to apply economic theory to the whole spectrum of human behavior outside the marketplace. The

FIGURE 8.14 The Product Exhaustion Theorem

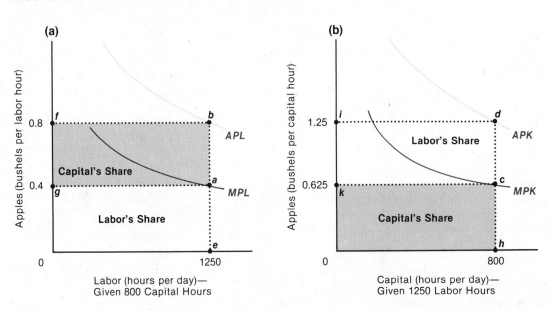

According to the product exhaustion theorem, in long-run competitive equilibrium, the total product jointly produced by various resources (here 1,000 bushels of apples produced by 1,250 hours of labor and 800 hours of capital service per day) will precisely be exhausted if each unit of resources is paid the marginal product associated with the employed quantity of this type of resource. In this example, labor's marginal product so calculated comes to 0.4 bushels per hour (point *a*); hence labor's share equals this amount multiplied by 1,250, or 500 bushels, which is the white rectangle in panel (a). Capital's marginal product so calculated comes to 0.625 bushels per hour (point *c*); hence capital's share equals this amount multiplied by 800, or 500 bushels as well, which is the shaded rectangle in panel (b). The equality of shares is pure coincidence; the fact that they add up to equal total product is not.

time-allocation model introduced in Figure 8.4 has been the starting point for many of these endeavors. Becker argues that a household can be viewed as something like a firm, with a **household production function** that relates household inputs to household outputs. The household inputs are consumer and human capital goods bought in markets, on the one hand, and the *time* of household members on the other. Within the household, these "raw materials" are then turned into "finished goods"—such as children, health, love, meals, and recreation—from which utility is derived. According to this view, the household's opportunity cost of any activity always involves a combination of goods and time.

This model of household-as-factory has been used to explain the form households take, the behavior of household members, the changes in behavior over time, and the differences in behavior over space. This model is used to explore questions such as the following: Why are many households based on monogamy, and what explains the appearance of polygamy? What explains matriarchy, patriarchy, or the observed mixture of traditional marriages, consensual marriages, extended families, communes, and single-member households? Why do people marry when they do and how do they pick the mate they choose? Why is there divorce? How do people decide on the number of children to have (and on the time they spend with them)? What determines the labor force decisions of husbands and wives (the hours of work, the occupations—including, perhaps, criminal activity—even the mode of transport for getting to work)? What accounts for household investment activity; that is, for behavior in matters of health (exercise, nutrition, medical care), education, migration, suicide? How do people decide on how much time to devote to search (for a mate, for a job, for the best deal on consumer goods, for information on political candidates prior to a vote)? What determines the time household members devote to cocktail parties, extramarital affairs, religion, sex, and sleep? The list could be lengthened.

The Becker approach has yielded a myriad of testable hypotheses about human behavior. Viewing the household as a factory that processes inputs of consumer goods and time leads, inevitably, to this conclusion: Over time, as real income rises, people end up having more consumer goods per day, but because they still have only 24 hours in a day, people do not experience a corresponding increase in their leisure time. (Between 1890 and 1980 in the United States, for instance, real income per head has risen about fivefold, but the portion of the day available for leisure activities has not even doubled.) This reduces the marginal product of goods relative to the marginal product of leisure time. (In Table 8.1, leisure time might be seen as the fixed input and consumer goods as the variable input. Thus an increase in consumer goods is less and less capable of raising output—now seen as the utility produced by the household-as-factory.) This in-

---

BIOGRAPHY 8.2:

Gary S. Becker

Gary Stanley Becker (1930–   ) was born in Pottsville, Pennsylvania. He studied at Princeton and the University of Chicago and then turned to teaching economics—first at Columbia University and now at the University of Chicago.

He is best known for his ingenious application of economic theory to areas long considered outside the realm of economic decision making. These areas include racial and sexual discrimination, crime and punishment, marriage and the family, human capital formation, and social interactions. Becker's interests are reflected in his books, including *The Economics of Discrimination* (1957; 2nd ed. 1971), *Human Capital* (1964; 2nd ed. 1975), *Essays in the Economics of Crime and Punishment* (1974, with W. M. Landes), and *The Economic Approach to Human Behavior* (1976). Application 4, "Wider Uses of the Time-Allocation Model," affords a glimpse of Becker's thoughts.

In 1967, the American Economic Association awarded Becker the J. B. Clark medal in recognition of his outstanding work.

creased relative scarcity of leisure time induces households to do everything possible to conserve time and to cram an ever-higher consumption of goods into a unit of time. Is it surprising then if people feel harried? Is it surprising that they have no time for being shaved by barbers (a common practice not so long ago), for making elaborate meals, for being with children (or having any), for caring for elderly family members, for traveling on transatlantic luxury liners, for visiting museums, for taking leisurely walks in the country, for going to worship, for reading books? Is it surprising then that people consume time-saving goods, such as electric shavers, frozen foods, the services of nursery schools and nursing homes, the services of supersonic transport planes, and, above all, the television set?

Becker's model can be used to compare different population groups at a given time as well. Consider high-income versus low-income people. Can you see why Americans in general (high-income people) are superconscious of time and seem wasteful of goods and why just the opposite is true for the residents of poor countries? Can you also see why the young (low-income people) might spend a lot of time waiting for buses and hitchhiking and *walking* around in search of jobs, while their harried (but richer) elders choose modes of transport (the private car) and of job search (advertisements and employment agencies) that minimize the use of their time?

SUMMARY

1. This chapter discusses markets for the *flows* of resource services, not for the *stocks* of resources. The demand for these inputs (derived from the demand for output) is exercised by firms. Firms can be expected to hire that quantity of any resource service which equates the marginal benefit of resource use with the associated marginal cost. In perfect markets, the marginal benefit is an input's *marginal value product*; the marginal cost is its price. The downward-sloping branch of an input's marginal-value-product curve becomes the competitive firm's demand for a single variable input.

2. When a firm can vary several inputs simultaneously, the derivation of the demand curve for any one input is only slightly more complex. The effect of a change in input price on quantity demanded can be divided into the *substitution effect* and *output effect*.

3. The demands of individual firms for any input can be added together to derive market demand. The procedure is slightly more complicated than the procedure for determining the market demand for consumer goods. As for consumer goods, a price elasticity of demand can be calculated for inputs.

4. The individual's supply of labor can be derived from an analysis of the income-leisure choice (which leads a utility-maximizing person to equate the wage with the marginal rate of substitution between income and leisure). The supply can be derived with respect to the wage or any other variable, such as nonlabor income. The effect of any wage change can be separated into the familiar substitution and income effects. While the income effect for ordinary (and normal) consumption goods reinforces the substitution effect, the income effect works counter to the substitution effect in the case of leisure.

5. Unlike in the case of labor, the supply of *nonlabor* resource services does not involve the sacrifice of leisure on the part of resource owners. Nevertheless, nonlabor resource supply is likely to be responsive to price, particularly in the long run.

6. The supplies of services by individual resource owners can be added together to derive market supply. Once again, the price elasticity of supply can be calculated for inputs in the same manner as for goods.

7. Equilibrium is established in the markets for resource services through the interaction of demand and supply. The equilibrium in the short run can differ from that in the long run. While not subscribing to the Malthusian theory of the labor market, economists note that in perfect markets the long-run supply of many reproducible resources can be described by Malthusian dynamics: the supply is infinitely elastic at a price that covers the cost of reproducing these resources.

8. The theoretical tools discussed in this chapter can be applied to the analysis of wage differentials and the implicit value people place on their own lives when making occupational choices; the concepts of pure rent and quasi rent; the functional distribution of income; and the whole spectrum of human behavior outside the marketplace.

KEY TERMS

compensating wage differentials
complementary inputs
derived demand
equalizing wage differentials
exploitation
functional distribution of income
household production function
independent inputs
iron law of wages
leisure
marginal productivity theory of distribution
marginal value product *(MVP)*
output effect
personal distribution of income
product-exhaustion theorem
pure rent
quasi rent
regressive inputs
rent
reservation demands
scale effect
single-tax movement
substitution effect

QUESTIONS AND PROBLEMS

1. Figure 8.2 explains why the demand for an input would be flatter when two complementary inputs vary simultaneously than when a single input alone varies. Show why the demand line would also be flatter (and not steeper) if inputs were *anti-complementary* such that the increased use of one decreased the marginal physical product of the other.

2. In the Yugoslav worker-managed firm, workers receive wages but also share the firm's profit among themselves. At any given wage, they tend to hire fewer workers than the capitalist profit-maximizing firms depicted in Figure 8.1. Can you explain why? [*Hint*: You may wish to review panel (b) of Figure 5.1, "Total, Marginal, and Average Product" (p. 114), and add a curve of labor's *average* value product to Figure 8.1.]

3. Figure 8.4 indicates the hours of work a person would choose if free to choose. How would one have to modify this analysis to account for such phenomena as moonlighting (holding two or more jobs) and overtime pay? (*Hints:* Imagine the workday in Figure 8.4 was inflexibly set at 8 hours. Then imagine that the workday was flexible, but the employer wanted the worker to work 16 hours.)

4. Cobweb cycles, first discussed in Chapter 7, have been observed in the markets for accountants, engineers, and other types of college-trained labor. Can you explain why?

5. Individuals with special talents frequently receive huge salaries. Consider Joe Namath of the New York Jets football team ($450,000 in 1976), Barbara Walters of ABC television ($1 million for each of 5 years), or Dan Rather of CBS ($8 million over a 5-year period).

    a. Show why a large portion of such salaries can be described as pure economic rent.

    b. Show why the individuals involved might nevertheless be exploited (if exploitation is defined as payment of a wage below marginal value product).

    c. Indicate under what circumstances such

exploitation, if present, would disappear.

d. Illustrate the following graphically: Some individuals with special talents have felt uncomfortable about the pure rent element in their earnings.. Joan Baez and Muhammed Ali have wanted ticket prices to their performances kept low so that their poorer fans could see them. Yet these lower prices caused severe shortages and ticket scalping. (Many who bought the cheap tickets resold them at much higher prices, in effect pocketing the pure rent the performers would otherwise have collected). When Ali noticed that his poor fans still did not see him, he agreed to charging market-clearing prices and collecting the rent and gave donations to charity instead.

6. *Mr. A:* There exists a serious problem of labor exploitation, .right here in the United States.[3] In hundreds of so-called ''sheltered workshops'' around the country, physically and mentally handicapped persons are working for as little as 10 cents an hour. This is perfectly legal: Under federal law, a handicapped worker's productivity is to be measured against the average output of ''normal'' workers, and pay is set accordingly. If ''normal'' workers produce 100 widgets and earn $5 an hour, a handicapped worker who produces 10 widgets can get paid 50¢. But it is exploitation nevertheless.

Ms. B: Nonsense, they get paid for what they produce, don't they? In fact, *exploitation* is no more than a word, without any reality behind it. Sort of like *leprechaun, unicorn,* or *witch.*

What do you think?

7. Using the concept of a household production function, explain the following phenomena:

a. When the ratio of women's to men's wages rises, more wives enter the labor force and husbands work fewer hours.

b. As wages rise over time, the size of families declines.

8. Are each of the following true or false?

a. In a competitive industry, any firm that collects revenue in excess of its variable cost in the short run is earning a quasi rent.

b. After including rents paid to landlords, all of Ricardo's farms of differential fertility would have identical cost curves.

c. The presence of X-inefficiency would shift down the demand for inputs.

d. The construction of a superhighway might create pure rents for the owners of land near the highway.

e. If 100 percent of quasi rents was taxed, the quantity supplied would not change in the long run.

f. If 100 percent of pure rents was taxed, the quantity supplied would not change in the long run.

g. If the market supply of labor was backward-bending, two different equilibrium points might exist.

h. If the wage ever wandered from one of the two equilibrium points resulting from a backward-bending labor supply curve, this equilibrium would not be re-established.

i. The fact that the price elasticity of the supply of doctors is -0.91[4] proves the American Medical Association's claim that lower medical fees would reduce the quantity of medical services.

j. The deterioration and ultimate abandonment of the housing stock in many cities has been traced to the imposition of rent control.

k. The policy of rent control, in turn, can be traced to a tragic confusion of pure rent with quasi rent.

SELECTED READINGS

Bailey, Martin J. *Reducing Risks to Life: Measurement of the Benefits.* Washington, D. C.: American Enterprise Institute, 1980.

---

[3]Jonathan Kwitny and Jerry Landauer, ''Minimal Wage,'' *The Wall Street Journal,* October 17, 1979, pp. 1 and 24.

[4]Martin S. Feldstein, ''The Rising Price of Physicians' Services,'' *Review of Economics and Statistics,* May 1970, pp. 121–33.

A review of studies that estimate the value of human lives on the basis of people's willingness to accept riskier jobs at appropriately higher wages or to buy safety crash helmets, nonflammable pajamas, seat belts, smoke detectors, sprinkler systems, and the like. (*See also* Analytical Example 10.2, "Smoke Detectors as Insurance".)

Becker, Gary S. "A Theory of the Allocation of Time." *Economic Journal*, September 1965, pp. 493–517.

The original article on the new theory of consumer behavior. Reprinted as Chapter 5 in *idem. The Economic Approach to Human Behavior*. Chicago: University of Chicago Press, 1976. For further applications, including some frivolous, but amusing ones, *see* Becker, Gary S.; Landes, Elisabeth M.; and Michael, Robert T. "An Economic Analysis of Marital Instability." *Journal of Political Economy*, December 1977, pp. 1141–87; Bergstrom, T.C. "Toward a Deeper Economics of Sleeping." *Journal of Political Economy*, April 1976, pp. 411–12; Blinder, Alan S. "The Economics of Brushing Teeth." *Journal of Political Economy*, July–August 1974, pp. 887–91; Fair, Ray C. "A Theory of Extramarital Affairs." *Journal of Political Economy*, February 1978, pp. 45–61; and Hoffman, Emily P. "The Deeper Economics of Sleeping: Important Clues toward the Discovery of Activity X." *Journal of Political Economy*, June 1977, pp. 647–49.

Clark, John B. "Distribution as Determined by a Law of Rent." *Quarterly Journal of Economics*, April 1891, pp. 289–318.

The original article on distribution and marginal productivity.

Douglas, Paul H. *The Theory of Wages*. New York: Macmillan, 1934.

A pioneering study of econometric measurement concerning the demand for and supply of inputs.

Everett, John R. *Religion in Economics*. Morningside Heights, N.Y.: King's Crown Press, 1946.

A study of John B. Clark.

Ferber, Robert and Hirsch, Werner Z. "Social Experimentation and Economic Policy: A Survey." *Journal of Economic Literature*, December 1978, pp. 1379–1414.

A discussion of income-maintenance and other social experiments, such as Close-Up 8.2, "Negative Income Tax and Labor Supply."

Freeman, Richard B. *The Market for College-Trained Manpower*. Cambridge: Harvard University Press, 1971.

A study of career choice and cobweb adjustment patterns in markets for college-trained labor.

Linder, Staffan B. *The Harried Leisure Class*. New York: Columbia University Press, 1970.

An important and amusing discussion of the increasing scarcity of time. *See also* the symposium on this book in *Quarterly Journal of Economics*, November 1973, pp. 628–75.

Mishan, E. J. *Welfare Economics: Five Introductory Essays*. New York: Random House, 1964, pp. 199–213.

A discussion of four measures of rent, analogous to the four measures of consumer's surplus discussed in Chapter 7.

Seligman, Ben B. *Main Currents in Modern Economics*, vol. 2. Chicago: Quadrangle, 1962, pp. 311–28.

A critical review of the work of John B. Clark.

Watts, Harold W., and Rees, Albert. *The New Jersey Income-Maintenance Experiment, vol. 2: Labor-Supply Responses*. New York: Academic Press, 1977.

PART 3

The Complexity of the Market Economy

CHAPTER 9

Coping with Time:
Interest and Capital

This chapter is the first in a series that extends the discussion of Part Two to issues of greater complexity. In Part Two, decisions of households and firms were treated as if they only involved a comparison of present benefits with present costs. Yet we know that consumers and producers routinely make decisions involving the passage of time. Consider households that exchange present consumption for future consumption by saving part of their income now and spending it in the future. Consider firms that similarly transform present consumption goods into future consumption goods by diverting resources now from the production of consumption goods to that of investment goods (which help produce future consumption goods, in turn). As a result of such intertemporal decision making, **capital markets** arise, sometimes also referred to as **asset markets**. In these markets, certificates of indebtedness are traded, along with ownership claims to the stocks of natural resources and of physical capital goods. (In a slave society, claims to people would be traded in such markets as well.) The existence of capital markets was noted briefly in Part (b) of Figure 2.2, "Circular Flows" (see p. 37). In the present chapter, we will discuss these markets at length.

We will continue to assume that markets are perfect (in the sense discussed in Chapter 2).

Indeed, we now extend the condition of full knowledge on the part of traders to cover not only the present but also the future. We thereby assume away *uncertainty*, a complication to be discussed in the next chapter. Until then, we will analyze how people would act in a world of certainty in which even the future outcomes of their decisions are known in advance. Just as people without parachutes know that they *will* be killed if they jump out of an airplane at 20,000 feet, so the households and firms in our world are imagined to anticipate the future perfectly.

Households as Savers

Members of households typically save part of their incomes during their peak working years, as between the ages of 25 and 65. They often dissave during earlier years when they establish their families or during later years when they have entered retirement. We will focus on positive saving.

Households can save in a variety of ways; the simplest one is nothing else but the accumulation of coins, paper bills, and checking account balances that do not bear interest. Such money assets have **perfect liquidity**, an ability to be transformed without loss of value and at a moment's notice into any other asset. Yet households usually part with money savings and supply such funds to others. They can do so in the **loanable-funds market,** a market in which the money of some people is traded for **certificates of indebtedness** (or IOUs) issued by other people. These certificates are promises by the issuer to make future payments of money to the holder. Households act as suppliers in this market whenever they deposit money in savings accounts, buy corporate and government bonds, or acquire certificates of deposit, endowment life insurance, or pension claims. All of these actions amount to acquiring IOUs. Invariably, these IOUs are less liquid than money, but, unlike money, they provide an interest return so that more than one future dollar is received for every dollar given up now. However, households can and often do convert their money savings not into IOUs, but into **ownership claims**. These ownership claims are rights to the exclusive use of assets—assets that are often less liquid even than certificates of indebtedness. Such rights also yield streams of future income, in money or in kind. Consider corporate shares, deeds to natural resources and to physical capital goods, or even consumer durables and human capital (such as health, education, and training).

Regardless of whether households save in the form of money, IOUs, or ownership claims, the act of saving enables them to trade current consumption for future consumption: The money now not spent on restaurant meals, vacation trips, and apartment rentals (current consumption) can be set aside in a mattress and spent on these things later (future consumption). Or this money can be converted into such assets as bonds, skills, and furnished homes—assets that yield future interest, salaries, and income in kind (and thus future restaurant meals, vacation trips, and housing services). Indeed, the household saving decision can be analyzed in a way analogous to Figure 3.6 "The Consumer's Optimum" (see p. 64). Instead of considering a choice, at a given time, between two different consumption goods (such as apples and butter), we now consider a choice between identical sets of con-

sumption goods at two different times. The time difference, however, makes these goods as different from each other as the apples and butter of our earlier example.

Time Preference

Panel (a) of Figure 9.1 depicts three types of indifference curves between combinations of current consumption goods, C_c, and future consumption goods, C_f. (To eliminate any possible confusion because of changes in the general price level, we evaluate present and future sets of goods in *constant dollars*.) Which one of the three curves, labeled I_0, I_1, and I_2, best describes a person's preferences between current and future consumption goods? When Eugen von Böhm-Bawerk (see Biography 9.1) first studied intertemporal decision making, he opted for the behavioral implications here described by I_0, and he rejected those implied by I_1 and I_2. Typical consumers, he argued, were *impatient* to consume now rather than later. They did not want to undertake the unpleasant task of abstinence and waiting. They subjectively valued present goods more highly than future goods of like kind and number. Böhm-Bawerk thought this was so for two reasons: 1. People oftentimes expected a more ample provision of goods in the future than in the present, and 2. people systematically underestimated their future wants (a matter Böhm-Bawerk attributed to "incomplete imagination" or a "defect of will," which gave imagined future wants not the same sharp reality as those presently felt). We can picture all this by reviewing Figure 1.1, "The Scarcity Problem" on page 5. As Böhm-Bawerk saw it, in people's imaginations future scarcity was usually less than present scarcity because the right-hand circle in our earlier graph was imagined as larger in the future and the left-hand one as smaller. As a result, people's marginal utility of future income and consumption goods was lower than that of present ones, and, Böhm-Bawerk argued, they would indifferently trade a given set of present consumption goods only for a *larger* set of future ones.

FIGURE 9.1 The Impatient Consumer

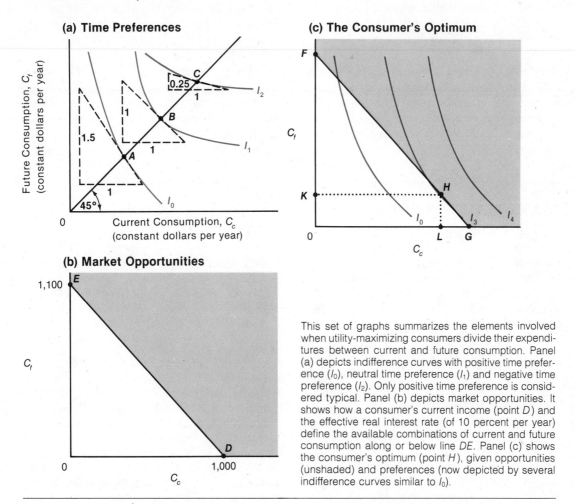

This set of graphs summarizes the elements involved when utility-maximizing consumers divide their expenditures between current and future consumption. Panel (a) depicts indifference curves with positive time preference (I_0), neutral time preference (I_1) and negative time preference (I_2). Only positive time preference is considered typical. Panel (b) depicts market opportunities. It shows how a consumer's current income (point D) and the effective real interest rate (of 10 percent per year) define the available combinations of current and future consumption along or below line DE. Panel (c) shows the consumer's optimum (point H), given opportunities (unshaded) and preferences (now depicted by several indifference curves similar to I_0).

This, of course, is exactly what is shown by indifference curve I_0, in contrast to I_1 and I_2. Consider, for instance, the slope of our three indifference curves along the 45-degree ray $0C$. At point A on curve I_0, a consumer is willing to trade, indifferently, 1 unit of current consumption goods for 1.5 units of future ones. (Note the dashed triangle constructed underneath point A.) Indifference curve I_0, which has an absolute slope of greater than one at all points, is said to depict a consumer with **positive time preference**, a high preference for current over future

consumption that leads lenders to exact more than one unit of future consumption for the sacrifice of one unit of present consumption. Note: Even this high price is increasing as more and more current consumption is sacrificed in return for more future consumption. Notice how the slope of indifference curve I_0 rises as one moves along it from right to left. The slope of an indifference curve relating current consumption to future consumption is the marginal rate of substitution between current and future consumption, also known as the **marginal time preference**.

If consumers were less impatient than Böhm-Bawerk saw them, they might, of course, have the kind of preferences depicted by line I_1 or I_2. Line I_2, which has an absolute slope of less than one at all points, depicts a consumer with **negative time preference**, a high preference for future over current consumption that implies a lender's willingness to accept less than one unit of future consumption for the sacrifice of one unit of current consumption. (Note the dashed triangle underneath point C.) Such behavior is not impossible but is likely to be rare (especially under conditions of certainty about the future). Examples of persons with negative time preference might include extraordinarily miserly individuals or those whose present circumstances of abundance are believed to give way to future scarcity. (Consider a farmer's time preference for water if the farm land is flooded in the spring but subject to drought in the summer. Consider a consumer's time preference for bananas if a large quantity possessed now is certain to spoil fast.

BIOGRAPHY 9.1:

Eugen von Böhm-Bawerk

Eugen von Böhm-Bawerk (1851–1914) was born in Brünn, Moravia. His father was vice-governor of Moravia—the descendant of a long line of civil servants. Although Eugen was more interested in physical science, family tradition won out. He studied law at the University of Vienna, then political science at Heidelberg, Leipzig, Jena.

At the age of 30, he was made a professor at the University of Innsbruck. Along with Carl Menger and Friedrich von Wieser, he became the founder of a special brand of economic theory, called the Austrian School. On three occasions (in 1895, 1897, and from 1900–1904), Böhm-Bawerk served the Austro-Hungarian Empire as Minister of Finance. During the last decade of his life, while a professor of political economy at the University of Vienna, he gave a series of famous seminars and became the inspiring teacher of many, including Joseph A. Schumpeter (see Biography 10.2). In those days, Böhm-Bawerk displayed a formidable talent as a debater; he was always quick to concede his opponents' good points but ever-ready to destroy their errors with irrefutable logic.

Böhm-Bawerk, the theorist, focused on the role of *time* in economic life and, thus, on the role of interest and capital. Indeed, his major work is *Capital and Interest*, which appeared in two volumes: The *History and Critique of Interest Theories* (1884) provided a painstaking review of explanations for interest that had been proffered since ancient times. The *Positive Theory of Capital* (1889) presented Böhm-Bawerk's own exposition. (*Further Essays on Capital and Interest* appeared as an appendix to this volume in 1909.)

Schumpeter called his teacher the "bourgeois Marx," for like Marx (see Biography 15.1) who wrote *Capital*, Böhm-Bawerk held a grand vision of the economic process in which interest and capital played crucial roles. Yet Böhm-Bawerk thoroughly disagreed with Marx and even wrote *Karl Marx and the Close of His System* (1896). Marx, for example, viewed interest as a form of exploitation that arose in the *process of production*. According to Marx, exploitation resulted when a small number of capitalists had a monopoly in the ownership of physical capital goods badly needed by workers. Hence capitalists could force workers to hand over part of the "workers'" output. Böhm-Bawerk instead viewed interest as arising in the *process of exchange*, as a phenomenon linked with barter across time of present for future goods. Karl Marx, the revolutionary, saw capital as a historical concept, as physical goods about which class conflict arose. Böhm-Bawerk, the scientist, viewed capital as a theoretical concept, as the present value of future income streams. Unlike Marx, Böhm-Bawerk viewed interest and capital as concepts that would manifest themselves in any economic system, regardless of time and place—even in a socialist system.

Finally, turn to line I_1, drawn symmetrically around the 45° line. It pictures a **neutral time preference**, the lack of any intrinsic preference between current and future consumption. (Note the consumer's willingness, at point B, to trade indifferently 1 unit of current for 1 unit of future consumption, while positive time preference is found to the left of B and negative time preference to the right of it.)

Market Opportunities

We now turn, in panel (b) of Figure 9.1, to a consumer's objective opportunities for exchanging current consumption for future consumption. To facilitate the exposition, we first assume that current income and potential consumption can be transformed into future income and potential consumption in only one way: by the purchase of risk-free bonds that yield effective real interest of 10 percent per year. Our consumer's market opportunities are then defined by present income and this 10 percent interest rate. The consumer could consume $1,000 of goods now (distance $0D$) or lend $1,000 now (by purchasing a bond) and then consume $1,100 of goods in a year (distance $0E$). Or any combination of current and future consumption goods lying on (or below) budget line ED could be consumed. As usual, combinations in the shaded area are unattainable.

The absolute value of the slope of line ED (which is $\frac{\$1,100}{\$1,000} = 1.1$) equals the value of $1 + r$ (which is $1 + \frac{10}{100} = 1.1$, where r is the assumed effective real rate of interest of 10 percent per year). Note: It is crucial to distinguish between nominal, real, and effective rates of interest. The interest rate referred to in everyday usage is the **nominal rate of interest**, which indicates the percentage by which the dollar amount returned to a lender exceeds the dollar amount lent. Because of widespread inflation, an adjustment must be made to find the **real rate of interest**, which indicates the percentage by which the *purchasing power* (or actual quantity of consumption goods) returned to a lender exceeds the purchasing power lent. The real rate always equals the nominal rate minus the rate of infla-

tion. Imagine, for example, that you lent $1,000 at a nominal rate of 20 percent per year. You would receive $1,200 worth of money a year hence. If the general price level was unchanged, you could actually buy 20 percent more goods; the real rate of interest would be 20 percent $-$ 0 percent $=$ 20 percent as well. If the general price level rose by 12 percent, 20 percent, or 30 percent, however, the real rate would equal, respectively, 8 percent, 0 percent, or -10 percent. In the case of a real rate of -10 percent, your purchasing power would actually have been reduced. *Throughout this chapter, we will consider real rather than nominal rates of interest.* Surely, people with a positive time preference who operate under certainty, as we assume, cannot be expected to surrender current purchasing power for the promise of a positive nominal rate of interest alone; they must be assured of a positive real rate.

We further assume that people are not fooled by any particular way in which nominal interest contracts are expressed. We always refer to the **effective rate of interest**, which is the rate that is in effect paid per year. An interest contract, for example, may offer to pay "10 percent, compounded quarterly." This amounts to the payment of interest on the interest after the first quarter of the year and implies an effective *annual* rate of 10.19 percent. Similarly, nominal interest, which is paid less often than annually, implies lower-than-stated effective rates.

The Optimum

Panel (c) of Figure 9.1, finally, brings preferences and opportunities together to depict the consumer's optimum. Given positive time preference (depicted by indifference curves I_0, I_3, and I_4), given an initial income $0G$, and an effective real interest rate of 10 percent per year (implied by the slope of FG), this consumer maximizes utility at H. This optimum point implies current consumption of $0L$ and current lending of LG, hence future consumption of HL. At point H, as usual, the budget line and an indifference curve are tangent to each other. At that point, $1 + r$

equals the consumer's marginal rate of time preference.

Households as Lenders

Changes in time preference and market opportunities will change a consumer's optimum. Consider, for instance, successive increases in the time premiums of real interest offered to the consumer, as depicted in Figure 9.2. Indifference curves I_0 to I_2 in panel (a) depict a consumer's time preference. The consumer's income is $1,000 per year (point A); an effective real interest rate of 10 percent per year establishes budget line AB. Thus an initial optimum is found at point a. Current consumption then equals $600 per year and saving $400 per year. If all saving is lent (and this we assume), the 10 percent rate of interest calls forth a $400 per year supply of loanable funds, as shown by point d in panel (b).

Let the interest rate rise first to 30 percent per year, and then to 50 percent, all else being equal. In panel (a) new optima are found at points b and then c. Correspondingly, the quantity of loanable funds supplied rises in panel (b) from d to e and then to f. By summing such supply curves for all individuals, a similar market supply curve can be derived.

Note: An individual's supply of loanable funds could also be backward-sloping, similar to the supply of labor, depicted in panel (b) of Figure 8.5 "The Price-Consumption Line" (p. 222), because the income effect of higher real interest rates works counter to the substitution effect. Whenever the real interest rate goes up, more future consumption can be had for a given sacrifice of current consumption. This increased interest rate implies a fall in the price of a unit of future consumption (measured in terms of the required sacrifice of current consumption). Thus the substitution effect makes the consumer "buy" more future consumption and less current consumption. Saving and lending rise. At the same time, however, the lowered price of future consumption makes the consumer richer. This income effect induces more future as well as

more current consumption (hence less saving and lending). Unlike in Figure 9.2 here, the net effect might be a reduction in saving and lending. (This would be the case, for example, if indifference curve I_2 were tangent to budget line AD to the right of b.)

Firms as Investors

When Böhm-Bawerk wrote about interest, he gave a second reason for its existence besides the impatience of consumers who want to consume now rather than wait for future consumption. Present goods, he said, have a *technical superiority* over future goods. When current consumption goods are sacrificed to make current capital goods, future labor and natural resources, together with these capital goods, can produce a larger quantity of consumption goods, and can do so permanently.

Indirect, time-consuming, roundabout methods of production—methods that are capitalistic (in the literal sense of being capital-using)—Böhm-Bawerk argued, are superior to direct ones (that simply apply raw labor to natural resources). Consider Robinson Crusoe. Surrounded by nothing but natural resources, and using his bare hands only, he might catch 5 fishes a day. Over time, his daily food production would equal the series 5 . . . 5 . . . 5 . . . 5 . . . and so on, forever. Now suppose that Crusoe went hungry for a day and sacrificed the five fishes he might have caught. He might use his time to make a net and even build a canoe. Starting the next day, he might catch 10 fishes per day, and he might do so in half the time previously spent. He might spend the remainder of the time each day repairing net and canoe, thereby making his capital goods last as long as he lives. As a result, his daily food production would equal the series 0 . . . 10 . . . 10 . . . 10 and so on, forever. A 5-fish sacrifice on day 1 would thus yield a 5-fish increase in output on all future days—a real interest return of 100 percent per day! In this way, Böhm-Bawerk noted, the sacrifice of present consumption goods (like the 5 fishes sacrificed by Crusoe on day 1)

FIGURE 9.2 The Supply of Loanable Funds

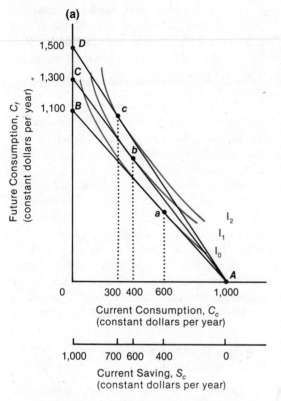

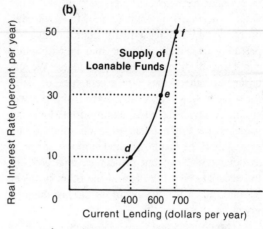

An increase in the real interest rate from 10 percent to 30 percent to 50 percent per year is pictured in panel (a) by budget line AB swinging to the right to become AC, then AD. All else being equal (time preference being depicted by indifference curves I_0 to I_2 and current income being $1,000 per year), the consumer's optimum changes from a to b and to c. Correspondingly, current consumption drops from $600 to $400 and $300, while saving rises from $400 to $600 to $700 per year. When lent, these savings become the supply of loanable funds shown in panel (b).

can be productively transformed in every society through capital formation (like Crusoe's production and subsequent maintenance of net and canoe) into a *permanently* larger flow of future consumption goods. Present consumption goods thus have a **time productivity**: they have the ability, when sacrificed now for the sake of creating capital goods, to yield permanently more future consumption goods. This productivity, Böhm-Bawerk argued, is not only a physical productivity (as shown by the production of a permanently greater *quantity* of fish), but is also a value productivity. (Crusoe's investment would, in a market economy, yield a greater *value* of fish because his impatience to consume now rather than later would limit the sacrifice of current consumption. This would limit the production of current capital and future consumption

goods long before the price of these future consumption goods had fallen sufficiently to turn the positive physical productivity of time into a negative value productivity.) Indeed, firms in our modern economy, similar to Robinson Crusoe and the planners of socialist economies, are continually engaged in the process of **capital budgeting**: identifying available investment opportunities, selecting investment projects to be carried out, and, finally, arranging for their financing.

Identifying Investment Opportunities

Robinson Crusoe's net-canoe investment project enabled him to get more fish (or "revenue") with a given effort (or "cost"). Put differently, it allowed him to get the same amount of fish with less effort. The managers of modern-day firms, similarly, can think of many investment projects that would raise revenue, given cost (or which would lower cost, given revenue). In either case, profit would be increased. Consider the case of a privately owned airport, the manager of which can think of five investment projects. We can describe each of these by a sequence of dated (positive or negative) cash flows. To keep things simple, we will make two assumptions. First, the projects are independent of each other in the sense that the outflows and inflows of cash associated with any one project are unaffected by the acceptance or rejection of the other projects. Second, all cash flows occur on the last day of a given year.

The projects and their associated cash flows (excluding the cost of financing) are listed in rows (A) through (E) of Table 9.1.

Project (A) is the acquisition of three new airplanes at a cost of $300,000, their operation for five years in charter flights and teaching, and their subsequent sale. The positive numbers listed in the year 1 through 5 columns indicate revenues after annual costs of operation (fuel, maintenance, depreciation, taxes, and the like), and the last entry includes the salvage value.

Project (B) is the construction of a new hangar at a cost of $100,000, the receipt of various annual net operating revenues in subsequent years (rental fees minus taxes, mainte-

nance, depreciation, and the like), and the sale of the hangar at the end of year 5.

Project (C) is the purchase for $33,000 of a flight simulator and various audiovisual aids used in flight training. Net revenues are expected to rise as indicated from year 1 to year 4, to remain level at $10,000 through year 10, and then to cease.

Project (D) is the construction of a new runway at a total cost of $550,000. Net revenues (landing fees minus repair, snowplowing costs, taxes, and the like) of $50,000 a year are expected subsequently for 20 years.

Project (E), finally, is the construction of a restaurant at a cost of $65,000. The restaurant is expected to yield net revenues of $20,000 for 4 years and to be sold for $50,000 at the end of year 5.

The listing of all possible investment projects is, however, only the first step in drawing up a capital budget. The next step is to select worthwhile projects from among possible ones.

Selecting Investment Projects to Be Carried Out

Our manager must now decide which of the possible investment projects are worth undertaking. If the firm's goal is to maximize profit (and this we still assume), each project's total revenue must somehow be compared with its total cost.

TABLE 9.1   A Firm's Investment Opportunities

Project	Net Cash Flows, Excluding Financing Cost (in thousands of dollars) at End of Year:					
	0	1	2	3	4	5
(A) Airplanes	−300	+50	+60	+70	+80	+210
(B) Hangar	−100	+10	+12	+15	+20	+50
(C) Teaching Aids	−33	+2	+5	+8	+10	+10→through year 10
(D) Runway	−550	+50	+50	+50	+50	+50→through year 20
(E) Restaurant	−65	+20	+20	+20	+20	+50

A firm's investment opportunities can be described by sequences of dated cash flows.

This, however, can hardly be as simple as adding up all the numbers found in any one row and concluding, for instance, that project (A) is worthwhile because it produces an overall profit of $170,000. This figure would be correct only if the market rate of interest and, therefore, financing costs, were zero.

Financing costs are excluded from Table 9.1, but they are unlikely to be zero. Indeed, they equal forgone interest income if the firm finances its investment projects with its own funds (such as past depreciation allowances and retained profits), which could have been lent to others. And these costs equal the interest that must be paid to others if the firm borrows other people's funds. If the relevant interest rate were 10 percent per year, the $300,000 expenditure on project (A) would impose a $30,000 annual interest cost on the firm, regardless of whether it used own funds or borrowed funds. Yet one should not now conclude that project (A) makes a profit of $20,000; that is, the $170,000 sum of all entries in row (A) minus the $150,000 interest cost over five years.

Dollars spent or received at different times are not of equal value in a world in which interest exists (for one or the other of Böhm-Bawerk's reasons). If the interest rate were 10 percent per year, a single dollar in year 0 could be lent and turned into $1.10 in year 1, into $1.21 in year 2, into $1.331 in year 3, into $1.4641 in year 4, and into $1.61051 in year 5. And the process can be reversed as well: Anyone expecting to receive with certainty $1.61051 in year 5 (and we assume certainty throughout this chapter) might just as well accept $1 now as an exact equivalent. (When lent at 10 percent per year, this present $1 would turn into $1.61051 five years hence). Similarly, of course, $1.4641, due to be received or spent in year 4, can be treated as $1 in year 0, as can $1.331 due in year 3, $1.21 due in year 2, and $1.10 due in year 1.

The process of making dollars of different dates comparable is called **compounding** when the interest rate is used to compute the *future value of present dollars*. The process of making dollars of different dates comparable is called **discounting** when the interest rate is used to compute the *present value of future dollars* (and the interest rate itself is then often referred to as the **discount rate**).

If the interest rate is r, the future value in year t (or FV_t) of any present value in year 0 (or PV_0) is thus given by the compound interest formula.

The Compound Interest Formula:
$$FV_t = PV_0 (1 + r)^t$$

Note how $1 in year 0 was shown above to turn into $1.331 in year 3 at an interest rate of 10 percent per year. Our formula confirms this:

$$FV_3 = \$1\left(1 + \frac{10}{100}\right)^3 = \$1(1.1)^3 = \$1(1.331)$$
$$= \$1.331.$$

The above formula implies, of course, the discounting formula.

The Discounting Formula:
$$PV_0 = \frac{FV_t}{(1 + r)^t}$$

Note how $1.61051 in year 5 was shown above to be the equivalent, at an interest rate of 10 percent per year, of $1 in year 0. The discounting formula confirms this result:

$$PV_0 = \frac{\$1.61051}{\left(1 + \dfrac{10}{100}\right)^5} = \frac{\$1.61051}{(1.1)^5} = \frac{\$1.61051}{1.61051}$$
$$= \$1$$

Table 9.2 shows the future equivalences of $1 for a variety of years and interest rates. By implication, it shows the discount factors by which future amounts must be divided to arrive at present-value equivalents. This table can be used to find the present value of each of the entries listed in Table 9.1.

Consider row (A) of Table 9.1 and apply to it, as the discounting formula demands, the discount factors of, say, the 10 percent column of Table 9.2. The −$300,000 in year 0 ("the present") must be divided by 1, which yields the

TABLE 9.2   Compound Interest and Discount Factors

| Year | Interest Rate per Year | | | | |
	5 percent	10 percent	15 percent	20 percent	25 percent
0	1	1	1	1	1
1	1.0500	1.1000	1.1500	1.2000	1.2500
2	1.1025	1.2100	1.3225	1.4400	1.5625
3	1.1576	1.3310	1.5209	1.7280	1.9531
4	1.2155	1.4641	1.7490	2.0736	2.4414
5	1.2763	1.6105	2.0114	2.4883	3.0518

A single dollar will turn into various larger amounts when compounded at interest. (Note how $1 turns into $1.44 in 2 years at 20 percent interest per year.) Conversely, any given future amount can be discounted to find its earlier-period equivalent. (Note how, at 15 percent interest per year, $1.75 equals $1 four years earlier or $1.32 two years earlier.)

present equivalent of −$300,000. The $50,000 of year 1, however, must be divided by 1.1, which yields a present equivalent of $45,454.55. (This sum, if available now and invested at 10 percent per year, would turn into $50,000 a year hence.) The $60,000 of year 2 must be divided by 1.21, and this yields $49,586.78. (This sum, if available now and invested at 10 percent per year, would turn into $60,000 two years hence.) The remaining entries in row (A), Table 9.1, are analogously divided by the remaining entries in the 10 percent column of Table 9.2, yielding present values, respectively, of $52,592.04, $54,641.08, and $130,394.28. These *comparable* dollars can, of course, be added together.

The addition of the present values of the negative and positive components of an investment project yields its **net present value**. The net present value for project (A) comes to −$300,000 + $332,668.73, which equals $32,668.73. This value implies that it is worthwhile to undertake project (A) at the assumed rate of interest of 10 percent per year. If the firm used its own funds to finance the project, it would earn, in terms of present dollars, $32,668.73 more than if it lent these funds to someone else. If it used borrowed funds, the firm would earn, in terms of present dollars, $32,668.73, even after paying others 10 percent per year on the borrowed funds.

The 10 percent column of Table 9.3 shows the net present values, similarly calculated, for

TABLE 9.3   Net Present Values of Investment Projects (in thousands of dollars)

| Project | Rate of Interest per Year | | | | | |
	0 percent	5 percent	10 percent	15 percent	20 percent	25 percent
(A) Airplanes	170.0	92.9	32.7	−15.0	−53.2	−84.2
(B) Hangar	7.0	−11.0	−25.0	−36.1	−44.9	−52.1
(C) Teaching aids	52.0	30.3	15.5	5.1	−2.4	−7.9
(D) Runway	450.0	73.0	−124.0	−237.0	−307.0	−352.0
(E) Restaurant	65.0	45.1	29.4	17.0	6.9	−1.4

This table shows, for various rates of interest, the (year-zero) net present values of the investment projects listed in Table 9.1. Note how, at an interest rate of 10 percent per year, the $32,668.73 net present value of Project (A) (here rounded) would, together with the $300,000 initial cost of the project, produce exactly the stream of payments shown in row (A), Table 9.1: $332,668.73 invested at 10 percent per year, would turn into $365,935.60 in year 1. Taking out the $50,000 net revenue of year 1 (shown in Table 9.1) and investing the remainder would yield $347,529.16 in year 2. Taking out the $60,000 net revenue of year 2 and investing the remainder would yield $316,282.07 in year 3. Taking out the $70,000 net revenue of year 3 and investing the remainder would yield $270,910.27 in year 4. Taking out the $80,000 net revenue of year 4 and investing the remainder would yield $210,000 in year 5, the net revenue of that year. At a 10 percent per year rate of interest, therefore, project (A) is equivalent in year 0 to spending $300,000 and getting $332,668.73. Hence it is equivalent to a year 0 profit of $32,668.73, which is the net present value of project (A).

FIGURE 9.3 The Demand for Loanable Funds

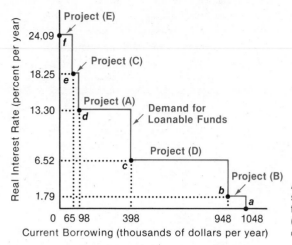

A firm's demand for loanable funds is downward-sloping. This shape reflects the increasing likelihood that the firm's investment projects are profitable (have positive net present values) as the market rate of interest declines.

all the projects of Table 9.1. The remaining columns of this table show what the net present values would be at alternative rates of interest. Note how the profitability of each investment project varies with the prevailing rate of interest —the rate the firm could earn by lending its own funds to others or the rate it must pay to borrow other people's funds. If the market rate of interest were zero (the firm could neither earn a cent by lending its funds nor would have to pay a cent for borrowing all the funds it could use), all five investment projects would be worthwhile to undertake. They would then yield the profits indicated in the 0 percent column of Table 9.3. At the other extreme, a market rate of 25 percent per year would make all projects unprofitable. After counting in as costs the interest forgone on own funds or paid out on borrowed funds, the projects would yield the losses shown in the 25 percent column of Table 9.3. Other market rates imply other investment decisions that lie between these two extremes. At a market rate of 10 percent per year, projects (A), (C), and (E) would be worthwhile; projects (B) and (D) would be equivalent to losing, respectively, 25,000 and 124,000 presently available dollars.

Firms as Borrowers

If our firm were interested in maximizing profit, it would include in its capital budget all investment projects with a positive net present value. It would be indifferent about undertaking those with a zero net present value. It would reject those with a negative net present value.

Under certain circumstances, one can also say that the firm would undertake all those projects that yielded an **internal rate of return** in excess of the current market rate of interest.[1] The internal rate of return is that interest rate which makes the net present value of an investment project just equal to zero. Hence it would be a matter of indifference to undertake or reject the project. Note in Table 9.3 that the internal rate of return for project (A) must lie somewhere between 10 percent and 15 percent, a range in which positive net present values give way to negative ones. In fact, the internal rate of return for project (A) equals 13.3 percent per year. The corresponding rates for projects (B) through (E)

[1] A reservation to this statement will be noted below in Application 1: Conflicting Investment Criteria (pp. 266).

equal, respectively, 1.79 percent, 18.25 percent, 6.52 percent, and 24.09 percent per year.

Let us now assume, for the sake of illustration, that our firm uses borrowed funds exclusively. We can easily derive its demand for loanable funds from the forgoing data. At a zero rate of interest, Table 9.3 tells us, all projects are worthwhile; hence the firm borrows $1,048,000 (the sum of the year 0 data in Table 9.1) to carry out all the projects. This amount is shown by point *a* in Figure 9.3.

Once the market rate of interest exceeds 1.79 percent per year—the internal rate of return for project (B)—that project's net present value is negative. So the project is rejected and the quantity of funds demanded drops to $948,000 (point *b*). Again, once the market rate of interest exceeds 6.52 percent per year—the internal rate of return for project (D)—the quantity of funds demanded drops to $398,000 (point *c*). When the market rate exceeds 13.3 percent per year, project (A) is eliminated; the quantity of funds demanded drops to $98,000 (point *d*). Similarly,

market rates above 18.25 percent per year eliminate project (C) and reduce the quantity of funds demanded to $65,000 (point *e*). Finally, even project (E) cannot survive market rates above 24.09 percent per year, and the quantity of funds demanded by our firm vanishes altogether (point *f*). The firm's capital budget becomes zero.

A market demand line can, of course, be derived in the usual fashion. More likely than not, if the demands of many individual firms were added horizontally at each rate of interest, the stairstep shape of the demand line shown here would give way to the usual smooth appearance.

The Pure Rate of Interest

The forgoing analysis of households as savers and lenders and firms as investors and borrowers can be used to explain the determination of the **pure rate of interest**, the interest rate that emerges in a perfect market for loanable funds when there is certainty (and, therefore, no risk).

CLOSE-UP 9.1:

Owning vs. Leasing Government Buildings

The calculation of present value can help government officials decide which is more advantageous: owning or leasing public buildings. Such a choice had to be made in the mid-1970s, when the federal government wanted to acquire a complex of buildings at the University of Virginia for use as the Civil Service Commission's Federal Executive Institute and Managerial Training Center. The General Services Administration (GSA), following guidelines issued by the Office of Management and Budget, used a 7 percent discount rate to calculate the net present value of construction and ownership costs at $27.2 million and then a 9 percent discount rate to calculate the net present value of lease payments at $17.2 million. The GSA recommended leasing the buildings.

The General Accounting Office (GAO), however, argued that a single discount rate should be used—namely, one based on the Treasury's borrowing costs over a 30-year period. On that basis, the GAO calculated the net present value of ownership costs at $15.6 million and that of leasing at $16.0 million and recommended ownership of the buildings (As the discussion of benefit-cost analysis in Chapter 19 will show, there exists much controversy on what constitutes the proper discount rate to evaluate public projects. Some argue that it should equal the rate of return that resources used in the public sector could earn in the private one instead. Others disagree. There is general agreement, however, that a *uniform* rate should be used for all government projects.)

Source: Charles J. Stokes, *Economics For Managers* (New York: McGraw-Hill, 1979), pp. 471–74.

Consider the market for loanable funds depicted in Figure 9.4. Imagine the market supply line is derived from a multitude of individual ones, such as the one shown in panel (b) of Figure 9.2. Imagine, similarly, the market demand line is derived from the summation, for many firms, of demand lines such as the one depicted by Figure 9.3. Because demand exceeds supply at a zero rate of interest, a positive rate emerges. This rate settles, in our example, at 10 percent per year because there are shortages at lower rates and surpluses at higher ones. Corresponding to equilibrium point *e*, $900 million worth of funds are traded per year.

At this equilibrium, all households with marginal rates of time preference of 10 percent per year or less (and, therefore, willing to lend at 10 percent) are able to lend their funds and to improve their lot. (Consider the lender of the dollar labeled *a* who would have been indifferent about lending it at 5 percent but who receives 10 percent.) All firms with marginal rates of time productivity of 10 percent per year or more (and, therefore, willing to borrow at 10 percent) are able to borrow all they wish and to profit as a result. (Consider the borrower of the dollar labeled *b* who would have been indifferent about borrowing it at 20 percent but who receives it at 10 percent.) Thus the marginal lender and borrower (of the 900 millionth dollar in our example) have, respectively, rates of time preference or time productivity just equal to the pure rate of interest. All those potential lenders (to the right and above *e*) who would sacrifice current consumption only at rates of interest above 10 percent per year are excluded from the market. So are all potential borrowers (to the right and below *e*) whose investment projects would yield returns of less than 10 percent per year. Thus the market brings together those who have funds (and thus control over resources) with those who have no funds (but are skilled in the use of resources) but only to the extent that the freeing of resources from current consumption and using them for investment (and the production of future consumption) is considered advantageous by all concerned. The establishment of the pure rate of

FIGURE 9.4   The Market for Loanable Funds

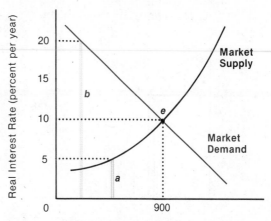

The pure rate of interest (here 10 percent per year) is determined by the interaction of supply and demand in a perfect market for loanable funds under conditions of certainty.

interest can also be illustrated with the help of a famous diagram introduced by Irving Fisher (see Biography 9.2).

Panel (a) of Figure 9.5 depicts a society's intertemporal production-possibilities frontier. Given their current resources and technology, the people in this society could produce only current consumption (point *A*). By sacrificing 1 unit of current consumption, people could carry out their most productive investment projects and produce, eventually, 3.25 units of future consumption goods (point *B*). They could, similarly, move to points *C* or *D* by carrying out increasingly less productive investment projects. Note the absolute value of the slope of our intertemporal production-possibilities frontier. It declines from 3.25 in region *AB* (implying 3.25 future units − 1 current unit = 2.25 units return on the unit of consumption sacrificed) to 1 in region *BC* (implying a zero return) and to 0.5 in region *CD* (implying a negative return). This slope measures the **marginal time productivity** of present goods, or the additional future goods producers are able to create for a unit sacrifice of present

FIGURE 9.5 Fisher's Interest Diagram

(a) Marginal Time Productivity

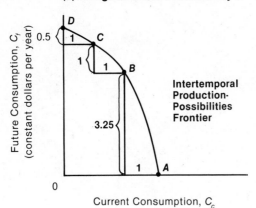

(b) Marginal Time Preference

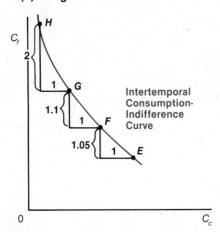

(c) Optimum: Pure Rate of Interest

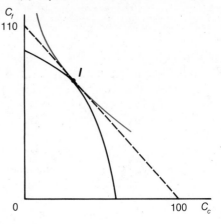

This set of diagrams illustrates how the people of a community are able—panel (a)—and willing—panel (b)—to swap current consumption goods for future ones. At optimum point *I* in panel (c), marginal time preference is perfectly matched with marginal time productivity. The slope of the dashed line simultaneously equals the marginal time preference at *I* (measured by the slope of the intertemporal consumption-indifference curve) and the marginal time productivity at *I* (measured by the slope of the intertemporal production-possibilities frontier). The dashed line's slope (absolute value 1.1) implies a pure rate of interest of 10 percent per year.

ones. In our example, moving from *A* to *D*, this productivity declines progressively.

Yet long before profitable investment opportunities were exhausted in this way, Fisher argued, the impatience of consumers to consume now would put an end to sacrifices of current consumption goods. Panel (b) of Figure 9.5 depicts a communitywide intertemporal consumption-indifference curve. It illustrates, starting at *E* and moving toward *H*, how consumers as a group insist (in order to remain indiffer-

ent) on ever-higher rewards of future consumption goods for successive equal sacrifices of current ones. The rise in their marginal time preference is shown by the changing slope of the indifference curve. Its absolute value rises from 1.05 in region *EF* to 1.1 in region *FG* to 2 in region *GH*.

Panel (c) shows Irving Fisher's way of illustrating Böhm-Bawerk's reasons for the emergence of interest. Superimposing panels (a) and (b), we find the community's optimum at point *I*,

FIGURE 9.6 How to Capitalize an Income Stream

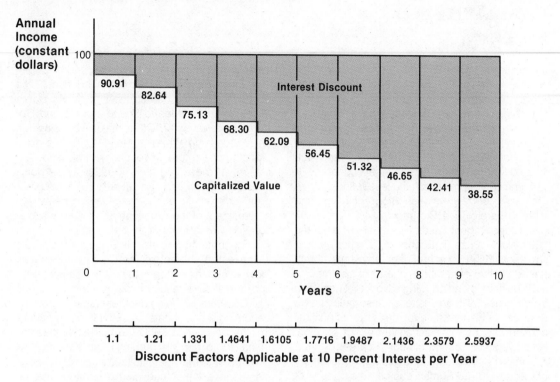

An income stream (represented here by 10 columns of $100) has a *present* or *capitalized value* that can be found by discounting separately each component part at the applicable rate of interest and then summing the results. In this example, the present value is given by the expression

$$PV_0 = \frac{FV_1}{(1 + r)} + \frac{FV_2}{(1 + r)^2} + \frac{FV_3}{(1 + r)^3} + \cdots + \frac{FV_{10}}{(1 + r)^{10}},$$

wherein each future value equals $100, r = 10 percent, and the 10 parts in the equation correspond to the white portions of the columns in the graph. Their sum is the capitalized value of $614.45 given by the lower white area. The upper shaded area of $385.55 has been discounted away. Note how later dollars shrink more than earlier ones as the time perspective of interest is applied (just as farther objects shrink more than nearer ones in spatial perspective).

where the highest possible welfare is reached, given preferences and production possibilities. (Indifference curves below the one shown would imply lower welfare; curves above the one shown would be out of reach of the community's production possibilities.) At point *I*, the two curves are just touching each other, and their slopes equal that of the dashed line. This slope reflects a pure rate of interest of 10 percent per year, simultaneously equal to marginal time productivity and marginal time preference.

Fisher's Concept of Capital

Having focused on the essential nature of interest (as a phenomenon arising from time preference and time productivity), we now turn to the nature of capital. Irving Fisher generalized the concept to include more than physical capital goods, more than the structures, machines, and stocks of raw materials usually referred to as "capital resources." He viewed **capital** as the stock of all useful things or assets that yield streams of

BIOGRAPHY 9.2:

Irving Fisher

Irving Fisher (1867–1947) was born at Saugerties, New York, the son of a Congregational minister. As did his father, Fisher studied at Yale. Mathematics was his favorite subject. He won first prize in a math contest even as a freshman; his doctoral dissertation, *Mathematical Investigations in the Theory of Value and Prices* (1892) was a landmark in the development of mathematical economics. It won immediate praise from no lesser figures than Francis Y. Edgeworth (see Biography 3.3) and Vilfredo Pareto (see Biography 14.1). Some 55 years later, Ragnar Frisch (eventual winner of the 1969 Nobel Prize in Economic Science) would say about Fisher: "He has been anywhere from a decade to two generations ahead of his time . . . it will be hard to find any single work that has been more influential than Fisher's dissertation."[1] No wonder that Fisher was a full professor of political economy at Yale within seven years of graduation. He stayed there during his entire career.

Fisher's main contributions lay in the theory of utility and consumer choice, the theory of interest and capital, and the theory of statistics (index numbers, distributed lags). These contributions are reflected in such works as *The Nature of Capital and Income* (1906) and *The Theory of Interest* (1930), a revision of a 1907 book. "Dedi-cated to the memory of John Rae and of Eugen von Böhm-Bawerk who laid the foundations," *The Theory of Interest* carries the subtitle *As Determined by Impatience to Spend Income and Opportunity to Invest It.* Other major works include *The Purchasing Power of Money* (1911), a great pioneering venture in econometrics, and *The Making of Index Numbers* (1922). These works established Fisher's reputation as the country's greatest scientific economist. As such, he served as president of the American Economic Association and was a founder and the first president of the Econometric Society. He played a major role in the establishment of the Cowles Foundation (now at Yale) as a means to nurture mathematical and quantitative research in economics.

But there was also another side to Fisher. By becoming a passionate crusader in many causes that he believed essential to human welfare, he managed to dim his reputation as an important contributor to the scientific foundation of economics. Fisher's father had died of tuberculosis; he himself had a three-year bout with the disease. Subsequently, he became compulsive about fresh air and promoting the health of his family, his country, and then the world. Fisher campaigned for "biologic living," diet and exercise programs,

income over time. And these assets can be *valued*, Fisher argued, with the help of the discounting process. **Capitalized value** can be derived by applying the pure rate of interest to the income stream produced by each asset. Capitalized value is nothing else but *the present value of the income stream.* Figure 9.6 on page 263 provides a visual illustration of this process of **capitalization** (or deriving capitalized or present value).

Consider any income-producing asset (it is significant that it can be any asset at all): a bond, a share of common stock, an acre of land, a deposit of coal, a machine, a house, a car, even a skill embodied in a person. Let the asset produce, with certainty, a net income stream of $100 at the end of each of 10 years (after which the asset disappears). If the pure rate of interest is 10 percent per year, and people can lend and borrow all the money they wish at this rate in a perfect market, the capitalized value of the asset at the end of year 0 is precisely $614.45. Figure 9.6 tells us why: The height of each column represents $100 received at the end of the stated year. But $100 at the end of year 1 is equivalent to only $90.91 now. (At 10 percent interest per year, it will grow by a factor of 1.1 into $100 in a year.) Similarly, for all the other future receipts. Note how $100 to be received in 10 years is equivalent to only $38.55 now. (At 10 percent interest per

eugenics research, the conservation of racial vigor, and abstention from alcohol and tobacco.

Fisher was also an inventor, taking out patents on the internal mechanisms of the piano, a tent for tuberculosis patients, and a visible-card index system. The index system was very successful and eventually gave rise to Remington Rand, bringing him a fortune. Fisher then campaigned for "the compensated dollar" (the gold content of which would be changed in accordance with the price index) and "100 percent money" (which would be based on a 100 percent reserve requirement). He pictured depressions as merely "dances of the dollar," easily avoidable by sound money. He spent more than $100,000 of his own funds seeking to develop support for his monetary proposals; his ill-timed belief in the 1920s that prosperity would stay forever cost him between $8 million and $10 million during the Great Depression. Before long, he was ridiculed as a health faddist and monetary crank. Yet Fisher's scientific work has stood the test of time. The theory of interest and capital discussed in this chapter is a major part of his work.

[1]Ragnar Frisch, "Irving Fisher at Eighty," *Econometrica*, April 1947, pp. 71–72.

year, it will grow by a factor of 2.5937 into $100 in 10 years.)

Figure 9.6 clearly shows why an increase in the interest rate instantly reduces the capitalized value of an income stream. It expands the shaded area of interest discount. A fall in the interest rate, for analogous reasons, raises capitalized value. The most dramatic example of how a change in the interest rate changes capitalized value is provided by the constant and perpetual income stream associated with government bonds (such as British "consols" and Canadian "perps") that are never repaid but pay a fixed sum of annual interest forever. The discount formula in this case simplifies to

$$PV = \frac{FV}{r}.$$

If interest of $100 per year is paid forever, the bond's capitalized value is $100/0.10 at an interest rate of 10 percent per year, or $1,000. Raise this interest rate to 20 percent (or reduce it to 5 percent), and the bond's value instantly changes to $500 (or $2,000). Note: The values just computed, permanently invested at the respective interest rates, would yield the $100 annual stream forever.

We are now ready to take Fisher's ideas a step further: In perfect markets and under conditions of certainty, the price of each asset will come to equal the asset's capitalized value and, in the case of reproducible assets in the long run, will come to equal the average cost of producing the asset as well.

Asset Prices in the Short Run

Asset prices will come to equal their capitalized values for a simple reason: Competition will bid asset prices up or down until they equal capitalized values. If the price of an asset exceeded its capitalized value, everyone would want to sell it, nobody would want to buy it, and its price would fall. Consider the asset depicted in Figure 9.6. If it were priced at $1,000, everyone holding this asset would want to sell it because $1,000, invested at the assumed going rate of interest of 10 percent per year, would yield a *permanent* income stream of $100 a year, not just a limited stream of $100 a year for a decade. Nobody, however, would want to buy the asset because $1,000, invested to bring $100 for only 10 years would yield considerably less than the going rate of 10 percent per year.

Similarly, if the price of an asset fell short of its capitalized value (and equaled, perhaps, $500 in our example), everyone would want to buy it, nobody would want to sell it, and its price would rise. Note: When all asset prices equal the capitalized value of income streams derived from these assets, all assets yield the same annual percentage return. This return is the interest rate used to calculate the capitalized value.

ANALYTICAL EXAMPLE 9.1:

Time is Money

In spite of the well-known saying, people often forget the time value of money. Such was the case in 1972 when *Consumer Reports* gave advice to home buyers. Builders of new homes, the magazine said, frequently offer to sell many appliances with the house: from clothes dryers, dishwashers, and garbage disposals to refrigerators, trash compactors, and washing machines. One such builder, said the magazine, offered appliances for $450, the cost of which could be added to a 27-year mortgage, increasing monthly payments by $3.32. Yet these appliances could be bought in the store for $675 and paid off in 2 years, by monthly payments of $32.71. Was the builder offering a good deal? No, said the magazine, one would be paying an extra $1,075.68 on one's mortgage (324 months × $3.32) if appliances were included on the mortgage but only $785.04 to the store (24 months × $32.71) if appliances were purchased separately.

   The magazine's advice was surely wrong! Assume the homebuyer could easily have put money into a savings account at 5 percent interest per year. As Figure 9.6 so clearly shows, in the presence of interest, future dollars are less important than present ones, and this is more true the farther away the future is. When 5 percent annual interest is available, $1 payable in a year is equivalent to only $1/1.05 or about 95¢ now, $1 in 2 years to $1/1.05^2 or about 91¢ now, and $1 in 27 years to

Asset Prices in the Long Run

The prices of reproducible assets will come to equal their average costs of production in the long run because it will be profitable to change the rate of production whenever this equality does not hold. Consider again Figure 9.6. Imagine the asset was a machine priced (as expected) at $614.45. If someone could produce such machines for $500, more of them would be produced. This increase in production would eventually increase the supply of services of such machines and decrease the price of such services. Thus the annual income derivable from the use of these machines would fall below the $100 shown in our graph. Accordingly, the capitalized value and, as we have argued, the price of the machine, would fall. This price decline would continue until the price equaled production cost.

   Similarly, if such machines could only be produced for $1,000, no one would produce them while their price was $614.45. This decline in production would eventually decrease the supply of services of such machines (as existing ones

wore out) and would increase the price of such services. Thus the annual income derivable from the use of these machines would rise above the $100 shown in the graph. Accordingly, the capitalized value and, therefore, the price of the machine, would rise. This price increase would continue until the price equaled production cost.

Applications

We now turn to a number of applications of the tools of interest and capital analysis developed so far.

Application 1:
Conflicting Investment Criteria

Our earlier discussion yielded the "golden rule" of capital budgeting:

   If you care to maximize the profit of your firm, carry out all investment projects that have a positive net present value at the

$1/1.05^{27}$ or about 27¢ now. If we calculate the present value of the above 2-year payment stream (assuming for convenience that one half of $785.04 is paid at the end of each year), it comes to

$$\frac{\$392.52}{1.05} + \frac{\$392.52}{1.05^2} = \$373.83 + \$356.03 = \$729.86.$$

If we, similarly, calculate the present value of the 27-year payment stream (assuming for convenience that $\frac{1}{27}$ of $1,075.68 is paid at the end of each year), it comes to

$$\frac{\$39.84}{1.05} + \frac{\$39.84}{1.05^2} + \ldots \frac{\$39.84}{1.05^{27}} = \$37.94 + \$36.14 + \ldots + \$10.67 = \$583.38.$$

This means that someone could have put $583.38 at 5 percent interest per year into a savings account and taken out $39.84 at the end of each of 27 years and would have exactly exhausted the account. On the other hand, such a person would have had to place $729.86 into such an account in order to make the two near-term payments of $392.52. Thus the builder's deal was better after all. Note: Had we taken account of inflation, as we have not, our argument could have been strengthened.

Source: "Notes to Homebuyers on Financing Future Schlock," *Consumer Reports*, April 1972.

current market rate of interest (or that have an internal rate of return in excess of this market rate).

Whenever a firm 1. is able to lend or borrow all the funds it wants at the current market rate of interest and 2. faces investment projects that are independent of each other and produce streams of returns that are first negative and then positive, a firm is well served by either of the criteria in the above rule. On occasions when these two conditions are not met, however, it is wise to ignore the parenthetical portion of the above rule because it conflicts with the positive-net-present-value criterion.

Net Present Value Vs. Internal Rate of Return. The present-value criterion will appear to contradict the internal-rate-of-return criterion when a firm's investment funds are rationed by some device other than the equilibrium market rate of interest. Consider again Figure 9.3. Let the market rate of interest be 10 percent

per year. The firm would then demand, as we noted earlier, $398,000 worth of funds in order to carry out projects (A), (C), and (E). (These projects alone would then have positive present values; these projects alone also have internal rates of return in excess of 10 percent per year.) Now let the firm's funds be restricted to $100,000. It would now be important to *rank* acceptable projects according to their profitability in order to pursue the most profitable ones first. Here a problem arises: A ranking by net present value changes with the market rate of interest; a ranking by internal rate of return is invariant with respect to that rate (see Table 9.4). According to the internal-rate-of-return criterion, the limited $100,000 are best spent on project (E), then (C), then (A). A consideration of project costs (shown in Table 9.1) effectively eliminates project (A). Yet the net-present-value criterion (at the 10 percent rate) counsels an ordering of projects (A), then (E), then (C).

Worse yet, in some instances, a meaningful internal rate of return cannot be calculated. The annual cash flow pattern of +$16,000, −$20,000, and +$6,000, for example, has two negative internal rates of return of −25 percent and −50 percent per year, yet its net present value (at a market rate of 10 percent per year) equals *positive* $2,776.86.

It is also possible for an investment project to have *several* positive internal rates of return. The annual cash flow pattern of −$8,000, +$17,900, and −$10,000, for example, produces internal rates of return of 7.87 percent and 15.88 percent per year. At 10 percent, the net present value is $8.26.

As advanced treatises show, all these problems can be overcome by using only the net-present-value criterion. If unlimited funds are available at the current market rate of interest, all investment projects with positive net present values should be carried out. If funds are rationed (and because different projects involve different initial costs), profit is maximized by selecting that financially feasible subset of all profitable projects that maximizes net present value. In the example with the $100,000 spending limit, the projects that maximize net present value are project (E) which costs $65,000 and project (C) which costs $33,000, rather than *one-third* of project (A) which costs $300,000. At 10 percent per year, the net present value of one-third of project (A), according to Table 9.3, would be one-third of $32,700, or $10,900, while the net present value of the combination of projects (E) and (C) would equal $46,900 (the sum of $29,400 plus $15,500 plus $2,000 of unspent funds).

Net Present Value Vs. Payback Method. Many firms make investment decisions on the basis of the **payback method**, which rejects all investment projects the returns of which require more than a predetermined length of time to repay the initial investment outlay. Consider the projects in Table 9.1. If the payback period was set at 4 years, all projects but (E), which returns $80 on $65, would be rejected.

Note: This criterion is extremely crude. It completely ignores possible returns to the initial investment outlay in years after the payback period (such as in year 5 and later). The criterion also ignores the existence of interest. All payments and receipts within the payback period are treated as equivalent, regardless of their timing. Thus the method is almost certain to produce incorrect results for a profit-maximizing firm. As is evident from Figure 9.3, the choice of project (E) alone is correct only at market rates of interest in excess of 18.25 percent per year. At lower rates, other projects are worthwhile, too.

The only possible advantage of the payback method is that it might be used to select projects yielding a quick return and from which a hasty exit can be made. Such a focus on a quick return may be desirable under conditions of uncertainty (assumed away in the present chapter) when late returns might be ignored because it is believed that they will be eroded by political upheaval, technological obsolescence, or competitive imitation. Otherwise the golden rule of capital budgeting remains most useful: Carry out all projects with positive net present value.

Application 2:   Investing in Human Capital

When studying economic growth, economists have become increasingly aware of an awkward "residual": The growth of real national output (in the United States, at an average rate of 3.12 percent per year from 1900–1960) could be explained only in part by the growth of inputs, as these were conventionally measured. (In the United States for the 1900–1960 period, labor hours accounted for 34.8 percent, the services of natural resources for 2.5 percent, and those of physical capital goods for 18.6 percent of the observed output growth.) What explained the remaining increase in output (or some 44.1 percent of the observed rate of growth)? Economists called it an "increase in productivity," but this only gave a name to their ignorance; it did not dispel it. Theodore W. Schultz (see Biography 9.3) took strong hints provided by Smith, von Thünen, and Fisher and argued that there was another, although invisible input at work. This input, distinct from raw labor, was **human capital**—the health care, education, and training embodied in people. The very existence of this invisible capital could be deduced from the existence of an unexplained income stream, and the value of this human capital could be calculated with the help of Fisher's discounting technique. Schultz argued (and later studies by Edward F. Denison confirmed) that human capital had become an increasingly important input in the productive process. While owning little physical capital, most people owned a great deal of human capital and were thus capitalists. While it was customary to value physical capital and list it on balance sheets, Schultz noted, economists were hesitant to capitalize the income stream emanating from people and list it in a similar fashion. Capitalizing the income stream emanating from people smacked of valuing people like slaves and went counter to deep moral values. Yet Schultz urged his colleagues to overcome this reluctance and to study the investments *free people* were obviously making in themselves in order to enhance their welfare.

Physical Vs. Human Capital. Indeed, there are many similarities between investing in physical goods and investing in people. Take another look at Table 9.1. Now imagine that the numbers referred to *household* investment projects instead. Such projects could include not airplanes,

CLOSE-UP 9.2:

Investing in Wine

It is often claimed that buying wine young, storing it for a number of years (while it appreciates in gastronomic quality and market price), and then selling it, yields a return out of all proportion to other investments. This result, however, is quite incompatible with the way economic theory predicts assets will be priced. One economist recently tested the assertion.

Using 1973–77 Heublein wine auction price data for red Bordeaux and California Cabernet Sauvignon, he established that the return on investments in wine equalled that available on Treasury Bills.

Now ask yourself this: What would happen to the rates of return on wine, Treasury Bills, and a host of other assets if they were not equal to each other, assuming all relevant factors (such as risk) were the same?

Source: William S. Krasker, "The Rate of Return to Storing Wines," *Journal of Political Economy*, December 1979, pp. 1363–67. Note: Elizabeth Jaeger, in "To Save or Savor: The Rate of Return to Storing Wine," *Journal of Political Economy*, June 1981, pp. 584–92, argues that wine is a risky asset and accordingly outperforms riskless Treasury bills by a 16.6 percent risk premium. Krasker's results are rejected because he underestimated wine prices and because his estimate of storage costs was inflated.

TABLE 9.4 Alternative Rankings of Acceptable Investment Projects

Project	Internal Rate of Return (percent per year)	Ranking according to					
		Internal Rate of Return	Net Present Value, Given an Annual Market Rate of Interest of				
			0 percent	5 percent	10 percent	15 percent	20 percent
(A) Airplanes	13.30	3	2	1	1	—	—
(B) Hangar	1.79	5	5	—	—	—	—
(C) Teaching aids	18.25	2	4	4	3	2	—
(D) Runway	6.52	4	1	2	—	—	—
(E) Restaurant	24.09	1	3	3	2	1	1

This table, which is based on Table 9.3, shows that rankings by internal rate of return do not vary with the market rate of interest but that rankings by present value do vary with market interest.

hangars, runways, and the like, but apprenticeship and on-the-job training, formal education (elementary school, high school, college), informal education (such as home-study courses), health maintenance or improvement, migration for better job opportunities. In each case, there would be a cost (such as the tuition, fees, and transportation expenses incurred and the labor income forgone while going to college). In each case, there would also be a later payoff (such as the higher lifetime income earned with a college degree, even after deducting health and education maintenance expenses). Thus human investments can be analyzed in precisely the same fashion as physical ones: Whenever the net present value of (negative and positive) cash flows is positive when the appropriate market rate of interest is applied, the investment is worth undertaking.

While the similarities are striking, it should be noted that human investments do differ from physical ones in a number of ways: A person's health, skills, and knowledge (unlike a machine) cannot easily be transferred to someone else.

Thus human capital cannot be confiscated or stolen, nor can it ordinarily be sold or bequeathed. (Even here there are exceptions: Consider how athletes sell the rights to their services to sports teams. Consider how parents with much human capital find it easier than parents without it to help their children acquire their own human capital.) Human capital is also portable and can usually be moved more easily than many types of physical capital. Human capital often provides a number of nonpecuniary benefits to its holder in addition to monetary ones. (Studies show, for example, that college graduates have happier marriages, less mental illness, and more enjoyable jobs than high-school graduates only. However, college graduates also work more hours and experience more pressure on the job.) Finally, human capital is subject to quite sudden and unexpected depreciation in the case of a person's death.

Returns on Human Capital. Statistical studies indicate that returns on investment in human capital are often substantial. Such studies begin with the type of data on schooling and lifetime income listed in Table 9.5 (p. 274). These studies must then tackle a number of statistical problems, such as the question of whether all educational expenditures are investments or some of them are consumption and whether all of the extra ob-

CLOSE-UP 9.3:

The Present Value of the Past

The past is normally viewed as concluded, done, inert. A hundred years ago, William Stanley Jevons (see Biography 3.2) urged economic decision makers to ignore the past and look to the future. "Bygones are bygones," he said. More recently, we have been urged to recognize the present importance of the past. Might present action not be influenced by the memory of the past just as much as by the anticipation of the future? And might the memory of the past not be subject to a backward-looking discount rate similar to the one that shrinks the present importance of the future, and the more so the farther away it is?

If this is so, people might not automatically choose the course of action with the highest present value of future net benefits. They might also look at the present value of past net benefits, and they might do so all the more the older they are (the longer is their past and the shorter is their future).

Consider how firms persist in research projects just because they have spent a lot of resources on them in the past (and how countries persist in wars just because they have already lost many lives). Consider how social unrest persists even though its causes are disappearing (but because past injustice is still recalled). Ask yourself why the young sometimes won't trust anyone over 30 and why the old can't agree with the young.

Source: Charles Wolf, Jr., "The Present Value of the Past," *Journal of Political Economy*, August 1970, pp. 783–92.

BIOGRAPHY 9.3:
Theodore W. Schultz

Theodore William Schultz (1902–   ) was born among German settlers on a farm near Arlington, South Dakota. He studied agricultural economics first at South Dakota State College and then at the University of Wisconsin. He taught the same subject at Iowa State, then moved on to a distinguished career at the University of Chicago, where he has remained. In 1960, he served as president of the American Economic Association.

Throughout his career, Schultz has focused on the role of the agricultural sector in the economy. He has written a number of books on U.S. agricultural policy and others on the process of economic development in poor countries, including *The Economic Organization of Agriculture* (1953), *Economic Growth and Agriculture* (1968), and *Distortions of Agricultural Incentives* (1978).

His interest in economic growth led Schultz to discover the crucial role of human capital, not only in the poor countries he studied, but also in rich ones. Having served in post-World War II Germany, with its physical capital in ruins, Schultz was struck by the extraordinary speed of recovery. He attributed this rate of recovery to human capital, which, like a ghost, was still there. Because people had the skills to rebuild their physical capital stock and had the knowledge to operate it, they quickly regained their former levels of output. Indeed, their invisible human capital had gone on growing even while bridges, factories, and houses were being destroyed. Prewar output levels were soon surpassed with the help of a larger stock of human capital. In his *Transforming Traditional Agriculture* (1976), Schultz drew parallels between the experience of war-torn Europe and that of poor countries, such as India, where investments in health care and education produced extraordinary increases in productivity. But he also pointed out how misguided governmental policies that fix prices below equilibrium levels can easily counteract the potential benefits derivable from human capital accumulation. (In the mid-1960s, when the Indian government held down the prices of wheat and rice to aid industrialization, the government destroyed farmers' incentives and produced stagnating output levels, just when new knowledge might have achieved the opposite.)

Schultz's work on human capital, including *The Economic Value of Education* (1963) and *Investment in Education: The Equity-Efficiency Quandary* (1972), has, however, inspired applications far beyond the ones cited here. These applications have already been noted in Chapter 8 and are explored in a selection of articles edited by Schultz on the *Economics of the Family: Marriage, Children, and Human Capital* (1974). In 1979, Schultz was awarded the Nobel Memorial Prize in Economic Science (jointly with Sir Arthur Lewis) for his work on human capital.

served income can be attributed to extra schooling. (Perhaps those with more schooling are also more talented and more hardworking and would, therefore, have earned more income even without the extra schooling.) In addition, analysts must take into account, of course, the timing of extra income and of the investment expenditures made to achieve it. In the 1950s and 1960s, such studies calculated rates of return of 10–15 percent per year, showing investments in college education as very profitable indeed. In the 1970s and early 1980s, however (with college fees higher and many starting salaries relatively lower), net present values of college education projects plummeted, implying much lower rates of return of about 7.5 percent per year.

A final note: Even though the term itself may not be used, the concept of human capital is routinely employed the world over. Consider how juries determine damages in injury and death cases on the basis of the net present value of the victims' future income streams. Consider how governments of poor countries complain about the ''brain drain''; that is, the migration, by choice, of their healthier and more educated citizens to richer countries. These governments are aware of the fact that the emigrants take with them invisible capital and thus a stream of future output. Indeed, some governments argue that emigrants should *pay* for the invisible capital they take, especially if it was put in place by public expenditures. (Note how the Soviets demanded such payments from emigrating Jews; how the East Germans, from 1962–1979, sold 14,000 political prisoners to West Germany for $15,000 a head; and how the Cubans sold 1,113 men, prisoners from the Bay of Pigs invasion, to the United States for $55,950 each.) Consider

how Mao Tse Tung's Red Guards, during the Great Proletarian Cultural Revolution in the late 1960s, attempted to create the classless society. All differences in income and status, they said, had to be eliminated: differences between males and females, the old and the young, leaders and followers, experts and lay persons, the skilled and the unskilled, mental and physical work, workers and managers, urban workers and peasants, the rich and the poor, teachers and students. As they moved through the countryside, the Red Guards turned student into teacher, teacher into worker, worker into manager, manager into peasant, and peasant into doctor. The common own-

ANALYTICAL EXAMPLE 9.2:

Is There Interest under Socialism?

Throughout history, there have been those who looked upon interest as something immoral. These include Moses and Aristotle, Mohammed and medieval scholastics, Karl Marx, and, more recently, the Ayatollah Khomeini. Marx taught socialists to associate interest with the idle rich; that is, with bloated bondholders, who were getting income for nothing. The Soviets, accordingly, claimed for decades that interest played no role in their system.

Yet, under socialism no less than under capitalism, there exist near-infinite opportunities to invest, and many of these must be forgone because people are impatient to consume now. Thus a pure rate of interest exists regardless of whether anyone is willing to admit it! As Soviet planners soon discovered, the basic truths depicted by Figure 9.5 are not confined to capitalism. Marxist ideology, however, prevented the Soviets from identifying, with the help of their economy's pure interest rate, the most productive investment projects. Planners, therefore, had no way to direct the limited resources released from present consumption to the most productive projects first. They added outlays to receipts without regard to their timing, and calculated, in effect, the net present values of investment projects at a zero interest rate (akin to the zero-interest column of Table 9.3). As a result, planners found many more projects worthwhile than could possibly be carried out with the resources that could be spared from current consumption.

To choose among all these "worthwhile" investment projects, the planners calculated for each project a **payback period**, the number of years it takes for initial investment outlays to be paid back by (undiscounted) future receipts. (Thus a project with annual cash flows of −100, +30, +30, +30, +30 has a payback period of 3.33 years.) The planners then compared actual payback periods with an *arbitrary norm* (such as "4 years or sooner") and thereby reduced the potential number of projects to a feasible one.

As was noted in Application 1: Conflicting Investment Criteria, the payback method involves, of course, the crude application of an interest rate without

ership of natural resources and physical capital was not enough to create socialism; they wanted to equalize the ownership of human capital as well.[2]

Application 3:   The Exhaustion of Nonrenewable Natural Resources

In the 1970s, predictions of doomsday became

[2]For a more thorough discussion, *see* Heinz Kohler, *Scarcity and Freedom: An Introduction to Economics* (Lexington, Mass.: D.C. Heath, 1977), chap. 37 and Steven N. S. Cheung, "Irving Fisher and the Red Guards," *Journal of Political Economy*, May/June 1969, pp. 430–33.

popular. Because the world has finite stocks of nonrenewable natural resources (such as coal, metallic ores, natural gas, and oil) and because demand for them is positive and even growing, the argument went, one could confidently predict the complete exhaustion of these resources (and, it was implied, the collapse of modern civilization). The dates for this exhaustion and collapse were typically shown to be within the next 100 years. Table 9.6 illustrates some of these doomsday predictions. The logic behind the table is impeccable: If the stocks of certain natural resources are finite (at whatever level), any positive rate of consumption (whether constant or grow-

mentioning the term. (In medieval times, people similarly talked of making a "4-year purchase," instead of lending a sum at 25 percent interest per year, because four annual 25-unit payments of money returned an initial 100-unit sum.)

Indeed, Soviet planners have at times also calculated the *reciprocal* of the payback period (1/3.33 in our earlier example, or 0.30), and they have called this reciprocal the **coefficient of relative effectiveness**. Planners compared it to an arbitrary **norm of relative effectiveness** (such as "0.25 or more") to weed out investment projects. Note: These planners were, in effect, comparing something like an internal rate of return (of, say, 30 percent per year) with an interest rate (of, say, 25 percent per year).

Yet the Soviets utilized *different* norms of relative effectiveness for different industries. As a result, they rejected investment projects in some industries in favor of those in others, although the former could have contributed much more to net present value and hence economic growth. (Consider Table 9.3. Let the economy's pure rate of interest be 10 percent per year. Now imagine applying a "norm of relative effectiveness" of 0.05 to projects (A) and (B), of 0.15 to projects (C) and (D), and of 0.25 to project (E). If you recognize the given "norms" as code words for interest rates of 5 percent, 15 percent, and 25 percent per year, you see from Table 9.3 that projects (A) and (C) will be accepted but that projects (B), (D), and (E) will be rejected. Yet this is not the correct decision, as the 10 percent column reveals.) According to Soviet Nobel Prize winner L. V. Kantorovich (see Biography 6A.1), the Soviet Union could have gotten, around 1960, from 30 percent to 50 percent more output from its existing resources. He attributed this fact in part to the planners' failure to make investment decisions with the help of an undisguised and uniform equilibrium interest rate. Perhaps his numbers were exaggerated to emphasize the importance of finally recognizing the crucial role of interest, even under socialism.[1]

[1]See Judith Thornton, "Differential Capital Charges and Resource Allocation in Soviet Industry," *Journal of Political Economy*, May/June 1971, pp. 545–61. Her calculations were confined to Soviet industry for 1960–64. They suggested possible increases in value added of 3–4 percent if differential capital charges were eliminated.

TABLE 9.5 Schooling and Lifetime Incomes

Years of School Completed	Lifetime Income of Males from Age 18 to Death	Extra Lifetime Income Over Previous Category
Fewer than 8 years	$280,000	—
8 years	344,000	$ 64,000
High school, 1–3 years	389,000	45,000
High school, 4 years	479,000	90,000
College, 1–3 years	543,000	64,000
College, 4 years or more	758,000	215,000

Data such as these (referring to 1972) are only some of those needed to determine the worthwhileness of educational investments. Also needed are data on the cost of these investments, the exact timing of costs and receipts, and the appropriate interest rate for calculating net present value. Thus (ignoring nonmonetary benefits) a 1972 youngster may have been well advised *not* to finish high school if the discounted value of the $90,000 of extra income shown in the last column fell short of the cost of the last high-school year. Under such circumstances the same money, invested at interest, would have generated more than $90,000 over the youngster's lifetime.

SOURCE: U.S. Bureau of the Census, *Statistical Abstract of the United States: 1978* (Washington, D.C.: U.S. Government Printing Office, 1978) p. 144.

ing) will exhaust the stocks.[3] This conclusion follows from the assumption. Yet, with one voice, economists have characterized the doomsday models as utterly worthless because such models have one glaring defect: They completely ignore people's adaptive behavior in response to the workings of the price system.

The Role of the Price System. In the absence of government intervention to prevent such an adjustment, economic analysis predicts, the gradual depletion of a nonrenewable natural resource will raise its price. This price increase will lead consumers to reduce the quantity demanded and will slow down the rate of depletion. The higher price will also encourage producers to initiate production from known stocks of resources that have higher extraction costs, to step up exploration, and to develop substitutes.

Consider how, in recent years, sharply higher prices of crude oil have led consumers to substitute small cars for large ones, buses for

[3]This line of argument can be found in Jay W. Forrester, *World Dynamics* (Cambridge, Mass.: Wright-Allen Press, 1971); Donella H. Meadows et al., *The Limits to Growth: A Report for the Club of Rome's Project on the Predicament of Mankind* (New York: Universe Books, 1972); and Mihajlo Mesarovic and Eduard Pestel, *Mankind at the Turning Point: The Second Report to the Club of Rome* (New York: New American Library, 1974).

private cars, insulation for heating or air conditioning, short trips for long trips. Consider how producers have found it profitable, because of higher prices, to find and extract natural resources that cost more to extract. (In the case of oil, producers have achieved "enhanced recovery" of oil from old reservoirs via the injection of water, steam, soap suds, and explosives or the replacement of rotary drills with jackhammers. Oil producers are extracting "synthetic" oil from coal, shale rock, and tar sands. Producers are discovering and developing major new oil fields in faraway and forbidding places, such as Alaska's frigid North Slope, the Gulf of Mexico, and the stormy North Sea.)

The preceding examples show that the quantities of "known global reserves," which are given in Table 9.6, are themselves a variable. Indeed, studies of *crustal abundance* of resources (their availability in the top 1 mile of the earth's crust) typically indicate quantities a million times the size of "known global reserves." Raise the price (or improve technology) and previously known but "subeconomic" deposits become worthwhile candidates for extraction; previously unknown but "speculative" deposits are found. The appearance of these additional supplies explains the fact that for many natural resources the ratio of known global reserves to consumption has remained constant over the decades, in spite

TABLE 9.6   Doomsday Predictions

Resource	Known Global Reserves	Number of Years Known Global Reserves Will Last		
		at 1970 Global Consumption Rates	if Global Consumption Rates Grew as in the Past	if Global Consumption Rates Grew as in the Past and Reserves Were 5 Times Known Amounts
Coal	5×10^{12} tons	2,300	111	150
Aluminum	1.17×10^9 tons	100	31	55
Chromium	7.75×10^8 tons	420	95	154
Cobalt	4.8×10^9 pounds	110	60	148
Copper	308×10^6 tons	36	21	48
Gold	353×10^6 troy ounces	11	9	29
Iron	1×10^{11} tons	240	93	173
Lead	91×10^6 tons	26	21	64
Manganese	8×10^8 tons	97	46	94
Mercury	3.34×10^6 flasks	13	13	41
Molybdenum	10.8×10^9 pounds	79	34	65
Nickel	147×10^9 pounds	150	53	96
Platinum	429×10^6 troy ounces	130	47	85
Silver	5.5×10^9 troy ounces	16	13	42
Tin	4.3×10^6 long tons	17	15	61
Tungsten	2.9×10^9 pounds	40	28	72
Zinc	123×10^6 tons	23	18	50
Natural gas	1.14×10^{15} cubic feet	38	22	49
Petroleum	455×10^9 barrels	31	20	50

Doomsday modelers base their predictions on data such as those found in this table.

SOURCE: Adapted from Donella H. Meadows et al., *The Limits to Growth: A Report for the Club of Rome's Project on the Predicament of Mankind.* A Potomac Associates book published by Universe Books, New York, 1972. Graphics by Potomac Associates.

of ever-increasing rates of consumption. The reserve-consumption ratios in Table 9.7, which refers to non-Communist countries only, are typical.

Consider, finally, how the search for substitutes is accelerated by higher resource prices. Nothing can illustrate this accelerated search for substitutes more dramatically than the recent whirlwind of activity set off by higher crude oil prices, including: the construction of nuclear power plants (the fission of one gram of U^{235} produces energy equivalent to 14 barrels of oil); the production of biofuels (ethyl alcohol from cattails, corn, desert plants, seaweed, sugar beets, and wheat can be used to make gasohol); the burning of plant and animal wastes (from peanut shells and garbage to cow manure); the

harnessing of waterfalls, wind, and the sea (tides, waves, temperature gradients); research on solar cells, power stations in outer space, geothermal energy, and nuclear fusion.

Applying Our Tools.   We can utilize the tools developed earlier in this chapter to illustrate why the prices of nonrenewable natural resources would, in fact, increase over time as depletion progressed, would thereby promote the adaptive behavior just discussed, and would prevent the type of sudden and unexpected resource exhaustion routinely pictured by the prophets of world cataclysm.

It is easiest to analyze the case of an identical annual demand for a resource, say copper ore, the stock of which is *not* increased as a result of

TABLE 9.7   Reserve-Consumption Ratios

Resource	1950	1960	1969
Aluminum	—	252	279
Copper	63	49	59
Iron	527	686	>1,000
Lead	18	16	26
Nickel	140	195	135
Tin	25	25	25
Zinc	26	26	22
Petroleum	25	39	32

This table (applicable to non-Communist countries) shows that reserve-consumption ratios for natural resources are not declining over time.

SOURCE: Roy W. Wright, "Ferrous and Non-Ferrous Metal Resources," *Centennial Volume, American Institute of Mining, Metallurgical and Petroleum Engineers* (New York: American Institute of Mining, Metallurgical, and Petroleum Engineers, 1971), p. 18. Copyright © 1971 American Institute of Mining, Metallurgical, and Petroleum Engineers (Incorporated).

higher output price and can be mined at a constant average-total and marginal cost (see Figure 9.7). The average-total and marginal cost of extracting a ton of copper ore, assumed constant at $0A$, is shown by the solid horizontal line in panel (a); the annual demand (assumed equal every year) is shown in panel (b). Now consider the fact that the copper ore deposit is viewed by its owner as an asset (very much like a building, machine, or skill) that is capable of producing a stream of net benefits.

These net benefits are the difference (such as AB at time 0) between the price per ton of copper ore and the assumed average and marginal cost of extracting it. And these net benefits can be received, at the owner's discretion, at any point in time. That is, the owner can mine the entire deposit now, can mine part of it, or can leave it in the ground indefinitely (without incurring storage costs or having to worry about deterioration). Note: Every ton that is mined now yields the net price AB, which can be invested at the pure rate of interest (still assuming perfect capital markets and certainty). If the net price per ton were $100 in year 0 (distance AB) and if funds could be lent at a pure rate of interest of 10 percent per year, any ton mined and sold now could in fact be turned into $110 in year 1, into $121 in year 2, and so on. To make the owner indifferent about mining this ton now or mining it later, *the net price must appreciate over time at a rate equal to the pure rate of interest.*

Given an interest rate of r, the schedule of net prices (N) from year 0 to year n (the year of resource exhaustion) must, therefore, be

$$N_0 \ldots N_0 (1 + r) \ldots N_0 (1 + r)^2 \ldots N_0 (1 + r)^3 \ldots \text{ and, finally, } N_0 (1 + r)^n.$$

Such a schedule of rising net prices (shown in our graph by a rise of AB to ED) equalizes the present values of all net prices. This schedule, therefore, equalizes the present value of all tons regardless of when they are mined; it maximizes the present value of the entire deposit.

Now consider this: Given market demand, a different gross price (measured by the height of line BCD) calls forth a different quantity demanded. If the price per ton of ore is B, quantity demanded is F. At higher price C, quantity demanded drops to G; at price D, nothing at all is demanded. Thus the rate of extraction can be expected to decline over time. Indeed, an owner will exhaust the deposit precisely at the moment at which price becomes so high (here D) as to eliminate demand.

The Timing of Exhaustion. How do we know that time t_n coincides with resource exhaustion? Suppose it didn't. If exhaustion had occurred

FIGURE 9.7 The Exhaustion of a Nonrenewable Natural Resource

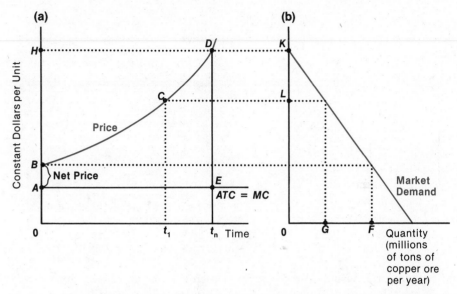

Under certain assumptions (such as perfect markets, certainty, constant average-total and marginal costs of extraction, and constant market demand), the price of a nonrenewable resource rises over time at a rate equal to the pure rate of interest, as depicted by line BD in panel (a). Correspondingly, the annual quantity demanded (and mined) falls over time. Eventually, at time t_n, the last ton mined is also the last ton demanded. Resource exhaustion becomes a foreseen event, not an unexpected catastrophe.

earlier, as at time t_1, price thereafter (because of positive demand, zero supply) would have risen more rapidly than postulated by line segment CD. In our assumed world of certainty, owners would have foreseen this future rate of price rise exceeding the rate of interest. They would have reduced earlier supply—sacrificing, say, $100 = N_0$ in year 0, or $133.10 = N_0 (1 + r)^3$ in year 3, in order to reap in year n a higher-valued net price in excess of $N_0 (1 + r)^n$. The earlier conservation would have assured later availability and pushed the time of exhaustion from t_1 to t_n.

Correspondingly, if exhaustion had not yet occurred at time t_n, price thereafter (because of zero demand, positive supply) would have risen less rapidly than postulated by the line segment to the right of D. Owners would have foreseen this future rate of price rise falling short of the rate of interest. They would have reduced later supply—sacrificing in year $n + 1$, perhaps, an amount

falling short of $N_0 (1 + r)^{n+1}$ in order to reap a higher-valued net price of $100 = N_0$ in year 0 or of $133.10 = N_0 (1 + r)^3$ in year 3. The later cut and earlier increase in supply would have pushed forward the time of exhaustion from t_{n+1} to t_n.

Extensions of the Analysis. The forgoing analysis can be extended in many ways. For example:

What would be the effect of a higher rate of interest? Net price would have to rise at a faster rate, of course. With initial gross price B, the price line in panel (a) of Figure 9.7 would lie above line BCD to the right of B. Thus quantity demanded and mined would be lower in all but the initial period. Long before period t_n, the price line would cross dotted line HK, and demand would vanish. Yet some of the resource stock would then be unused! It would be in the interest of owners to charge an initial price lower than B

FIGURE 9.8   The Natural Growth Curve

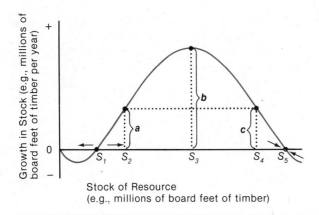

Stock of Resource
(e.g., millions of board feet of timber)

Any given biomass grows at a rate depending on the density of the biomass in the environment. Below a critical population size, here S_1, growth is negative, and the population becomes extinct. Above this value, each unit of the population has great opportunities for extracting nourishment from the environment, and the population grows. (Note the arrows pointing away from S_1.) Absolute growth just beyond the population's minimum viable size, S_1, is at first small because the population is small. As the population grows, absolute growth rises to a maximum at S_3. Then, as units compete with each other for food, growth declines until a natural equilibrium is reached at S_5. (As the arrows indicate, small disturbances from S_5 reestablish this population size.)

(and sell more than F initially). This would make it impossible to sell as much later as in Figure 9.7. Later prices would have to be higher than in Figure 9.7. Indeed, as the smaller net price grew at the faster pace of the higher interest rate, the new price line in panel (a) would cross the old one and reach dotted line HK to the left of D. Once more, the last ton mined would become the last ton demanded, but the time of exhaustion would come earlier. (This makes intuitive sense: the higher pure rate of interest reflects greater impatience to consume now, which implies less conservation as well.)

What would be the effect of a constant extraction cost lower than A? An unchanged initial gross price of B would then produce a larger net price, and as it rose at the unchanged rate of interest, the price line would lie above BD. As above, this would lead to premature elimination of demand. Owners would, therefore, charge an initial price lower than B (and sell more than F initially). Thus they would have to sell less later; once more later prices would have to be above those in Figure 9.7. These higher later prices could occur only if the initial net price was larger than in Figure 9.7; that is, if not all of the decrease in cost was reflected in the lower gross price. The initially higher net price

would then grow at the unchanged rate of interest, and the price line in panel (a) would start below B, cross line BD and reach dotted line HK to the left of D. Once more, the time of exhaustion would come earlier.

In addition, one may, of course, wish to drop some of the assumptions made earlier and analyze situations in which demand and resource stock change. These changes might occur as higher output price stimulates the invention of substitutes or the discovery of new deposits.

Application 4:   The Management of Renewable Natural Resources

Whenever they are used at all, nonrenewable natural resources are inevitably depleted. Renewable ones needn't be. Consider such natural resources as fertile land, fish, and forests. To the extent that such resources are properly managed, they can be preserved forever. This section will indicate what the proper management of renewable resources is likely to involve. We assume that the stocks of resources in question are completely appropriated; that is, they are the property of someone who can and does exclude all others from their use. (In Chapter 18, we will discuss the opposite case in which such resources are not appropriated, are common property, and provide services that are freely available to all.)

Figure 9.8 summarizes typical features of biological populations in a constant environment. The absolute rate of population growth depends on the density of the population in the environment and hence its ability to get food and deal with predators. If population size is below a critical number, S_1, the population dies out (due to interspecies competition). Between sizes S_1 and S_5, the population grows. The annual addition to the stock is, however, a variable. For population sizes S_1 to S_3, growth itself is increasing. Between sizes S_3 and S_5, growth is decreasing (due to crowding and insufficient food). Size S_5 is the population's **natural equilibrium**, or the population size that would be achieved (in the absence of harvesting) once the population exceeded its minimum viable size S_1; and it is the size that would be reestablished after disturbances that did not push population below S_1 (note the arrows). The height of the natural growth curve at each conceivable resource stock indicates the **sustainable yield**; that is, the maximum amount that can be harvested without depleting the given stock. Thus it is possible to keep the population permanently at size S_2 by annually harvesting quantity a. The same harvest ($c = a$) can be accomplished from a permanent population of S_4.

Note that the maximum sustainable yield (equal to b) occurs at population size S_3. It is often suggested that proper management of a renewable natural resource calls for the achievement of the maximum sustainable yield. This is, however, unlikely to be true.

Imagine that the resource in question were a stand of trees at its natural equilibrium S_5. This equilibrium level might correspond to 10 million board feet of timber. An exclusive owner could pursue a number of strategies. These strategies can be most easily explored with the help of Figure 9.9. The lower part of the graph reproduces the natural growth curve of Figure 9.8, but it now lies on its side. The upper part shows that for any given stock of the natural resource population, average total harvesting cost varies with the size of the harvest (just as, in Table 6.1, ''Short-Run Cost Alternatives,'' (p. 146) the average total cost of producing apples was seen to vary with the size of the apple crop, given the number of apple trees). Yet average total harvesting cost also varies with the size of the natural resource stock, given the size of a particular harvest. Such cost tends to be lower at higher resource stocks. As tree density increases, for example, logging costs often decline; at a harvest of 0.3 million board feet, average total harvesting cost declines perhaps, from 90¢ per board foot when the stock is 3 million (point A) to 30¢ per board foot when the stock is 9 million (point B).

Now imagine an owner incurring the costs of harvesting the entire population S_5 at once and selling it at the going market price (of, say, $1 per board foot), or for $10 million. The owner would then have a one-time net receipt of $10 million minus the cost of harvesting S_5 (not shown in our graph).

The owner might instead pursue a sustainable-yield strategy, reducing the initial population to a level such as S_2, S_3, or S_4 and then forever harvesting a quantity such as a, b, or c per year. If the chosen stock level were S_4 or, perhaps, 9 million board feet, this strategy would yield $S_5 - S_4$ or 1 million board feet initially, or $1 million minus the cost of harvesting $S_5 - S_4$. This strategy would, in addition, yield c or, perhaps, 0.3 million board feet per year; thus an additional and perpetual stream (at our assumed price) of $300,000 per year minus the annual harvesting cost of 0.3 million times 30¢ (point B), or $90,000.

It is obvious that we are dealing once again with a classic investment decision that requires the calculation and comparison of net present values. The choice is between $2 million now (if harvesting the *entire* stock should cost $8 million) and a series of net receipts, such as $850,000 now (if harvesting 1 million board feet from a stock of 10 million should cost $150,000, as suggested by point C) plus $210,000 per year forever (equal to the $300,000 − $90,000 noted above).

Which one of these two (or many other)

FIGURE 9.9 Harvesting Costs and Sustainable-Yield Strategies

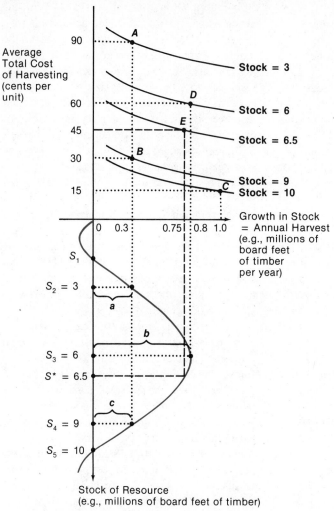

The average total cost of harvesting a renewable natural resource varies with the size of the resource stock. Note: The average total cost curves shown in the upper part of this graph can be expected to turn up at higher annual harvests and thus take on the typical U-shape.

strategies is best for the owner depends clearly on the appropriate interest rate that must be used to discount future net benefits to the present. Because the present value of a perpetual series of $210,000 per year equals that amount divided by the interest rate, an annual interest rate of about 18.26 percent or 0.1826 produces a present value of $1.15 million. Together with the assumed $850,000 receipt from reducing population from S_5 to S_4, this would make for a $2 million present

value of sustainable-yield strategy S_4—a value equal to the present value of instantly reducing the entire population to zero.

It follows that any interest rate lower than 18.26 percent per year would make our particular sustainable-yield strategy (S_4) more attractive than eliminating the entire population, while any interest rate higher than 18.26 percent per year would induce a profit-maximizing owner to favor the latter one of the two strategies discussed.

ANALYTICAL EXAMPLE 9.3:

Are You Worth Your Weight in Gold?

Let us suppose you are 25 years old and have just graduated from college. Your lifetime income (in present dollars) may come to $800,000 (see Table 9.5). Yet this money will not be earned all at once. Suppose it comes to you in 40 annual installments of $20,000 each. If the pure rate of interest were 10 percent per year, you could calculate the present value of yourself as

$$\frac{20{,}000}{1.10} + \frac{\$20{,}000}{1.10^2} + \ldots + \frac{\$20{,}000}{1.10^{40}} = \$195{,}581.$$

Now suppose yours is one of the weights shown in column (1) below. Because 1 pound *avoirdupois* (in which humans are usually weighed) equals 14.58333 troy ounces (in which gold is weighed), your weight can be converted as shown in column (2). Let the present price of gold be $554 per troy ounce. Then column (3) indicates the gold value of your weight.

Weight (pounds) (1)	Weight (troy ounces) (2)	Gold Value of Weight (3)
125	1822.92	$1,009,898
150	2187.50	1,211,875
175	2552.08	1,413,852
200	2916.67	1,615,835

A comparison of any number in column (3) with your present value calculated above indicates that you are *not* worth your weight in gold. But this can be remedied. If you went on a diet and brought your weight down to 353.03 troy ounces, or about 24 pounds, you would be worth your weight in gold!

Source: Adapted from Harry G. Johnson, "Are You Worth Your Weight in Gold?" in Harry G. Johnson and Burton A. Weisbrod, eds., *The Daily Economist* (Englewood Cliffs, N.J.: Prentice-Hall, 1973), pp. 30–33.

Thus it is not inconceivable that a renewable resource would, nevertheless, be deliberately destroyed even by an exclusive owner.

There are, of course, many different sustainable-yield strategies besides the particular one discussed above, as illustrated by Figure 9.8. Our owner would naturally wish to compare the present value of the resource-destroying strategy (our assumed $2 million) not with the present value of just *any* sustainable-yield strategy chosen at random (such as our S_4 strategy), but with the highest present value produced by the best-of-all-possible sustainable-yield strategies. Consider two additional strategies, namely the maintenance of resource stock S_3 and the maintenance of S_2. Compared to the S_4 strategy, both of these new ones seem to be better. As the lower part of Figure 9.9 indicates, both allow a larger initial reduction in the resource stock while permitting larger or equal annual harvests thereafter (b or a).

Yet, as the upper part of Figure 9.9 reminds us, we must consider the altered cost picture as well. The *initial* gain from reducing the tree population from S_5 to S_3 (or S_2) equals 4 (or 7) million board feet, hence $4 (or 7) million in revenue. The per unit harvesting costs, consistent with the lowest of the (presumably) U-shaped *ATC* curves in our graph, might be 12¢ (or 32¢), making for a total cost of $480,000 (or $2.24 million); hence an initial net gain of $3.52 (or $4.76) million.

Now consider the *annual* harvesting picture: A permanent stock of S_3 (or S_2) would allow a permanent annual harvest shown by b (or a) in Figure 9.9, equal to 0.8 (or 0.3) million board feet per year and worth $800,000 (or $300,000) per year. Annual harvesting costs, which must be deducted from this revenue, would equal 60¢ (or 90¢) per unit at point D (or A); hence total costs would be $480,000=0.8 million times 60¢ (or $270,000=0.3 million times 90¢). Thus the S_3 and S_2 strategies would yield permanent streams of net receipts of $320,000 and $30,000, respectively, per year. At the 18.26 percent interest rate noted above, the present values of these income streams would come to $1,752,464 and $164,294, respectively. Hence the overall present value of sustainable-yield strategy S_3 (or S_2) would equal $3.52 million plus $1.752464 million = $5.272464 million (or $4.76 million plus $0.164294 million = $4.924294 million). Under our assumptions, the maximum sustainable yield strategy S_3 clearly emerges as best among the four strategies now considered (reduction of the resource stock to zero, to S_2, to S_3, or to S_4).

Note: It does not follow from the above that the maximum sustainable-yield strategy is the best of all possible strategies at an interest rate of 18.26 percent per year. Consider a final possibility, the reduction of the resource stock to S^* or to 6.5 million board feet. This strategy initially yields 3.5 million board feet and, therefore, $3.5 million, minus harvesting costs of, say, 11¢ per unit and $385,000 overall, or a net receipt of $3.115 million. It also allows a perpetual annual harvest of slightly less than b, equal, perhaps, to 0.75 million board feet per year. This means

annual receipts of $750,000 minus harvesting costs of, say, 45¢ per board foot (point E), totaling $337,500. This strategy produces a perpetual annual stream of net receipts of $412,500. At an interest rate of 18.26 percent per year, this stream has a present value of $2,259,036. Overall, strategy S^* thus has a present value of $5,374,036, clearly *higher* than that of maximum sustainable-yield strategy S_3. (Can you figure out which interest rate would equate the present value of strategy S^* with the resource-destroying strategy?[4])

SUMMARY

1. As a result of intertemporal decision making, capital markets arise in which certificates of indebtedness are traded, along with ownership claims to the stocks of natural resources and of physical capital goods. This chapter studies perfect capital markets under conditions of certainty. The household saving decision, a choice between present and future consumption goods, can be analyzed just like the choice between two present consumption goods by contrasting preferences with market opportunities. The preferences reflect impatience to consume now rather than later; the opportunities reflect the ability to earn interest by delaying consumption. The household's optimum combination of current and future consumption is found by equating the marginal rate of time preference with $1 + r$, where r is the effective real rate of interest.

2. The saving of households contributes to the supply of loanable funds. The quantity supplied changes with the interest rate, and the change can be separated into the substitution effect and the income effect.

3. While households have to balance their impatience to consume now with their ability to

---

[4]The answer appears in the *Student Workbook to Accompany Intermediate Microeconomics*, Chapter 9, Problem 11.

earn interest by consuming later, firms must balance their urge to take advantage of investment opportunities with their need to pay interest or forgo interest income. Their capital budgeting identifies available investment opportunities, selects investment projects to be carried out, and arranges for their financing. Given the prevailing interest rate (at which outside funds can be borrowed and the firm's own funds can be lent), a firm's investment projects can be evaluated on the basis of their *net present value*.

4. It is profitable for firms to undertake all investment projects with positive net present values. Because these values vary with the prevailing rate of interest, the quantity of loanable funds demanded by firms varies with the interest rate as well.

5. The interest rate that equates supply and demand in a perfect market for loanable funds under conditions of certainty is called the *pure rate of interest*. Its determination can also be depicted by Irving Fisher's famous diagram, contrasting a society's impatience to consume with its opportunities to invest.

6. While the essence of interest can be found by studying time preference and time productivity, the essence of capital can be found by studying income streams produced over time. With the help of the discounting process, such income streams can be used to establish the capitalized value of assets. In perfect markets and under conditions of certainty, the price of each asset will come to equal the asset's capitalized value. Each asset, therefore, will yield the same return as any other asset. In the case of reproducible assets, an asset's price will in the long run also come to equal the average total cost of producing the asset.

7. The tools developed in this chapter can be applied to the analyses of different investment criteria (net present value vs. internal rate of return, net present value vs. payback method), of investments in human capital, of doomsday models (predicting the sudden exhaustion of nonrenewable natural resources) and of the proper management of renewable natural resources.

KEY TERMS

asset markets
capital
capital budgeting
capitalization
capitalized value
capital markets
certificates of indebtedness
coefficient of relative effectiveness
compounding
discounting
discount rate
effective rate of interest
human capital
internal rate of return
loanable-funds market
marginal time preference
marginal time productivity
natural equilibrium
negative time preference
net present value
neutral time preference
nominal rate of interest
norm of relative effectiveness
ownership claims
payback method
payback period
perfect liquidity
positive time preference
pure rate of interest
real rate of interest
sustainable yield
time productivity

QUESTIONS AND PROBLEMS

1. Consider panel (c) of Figure 9.1. Let the consumer's initial position be at F_j. Where is the consumer's optimum? How can it be reached?

2. Consider this 2-year investment project: -100, $+125$. What is the net present value at interest rates of 10 percent, 20 percent, and 30 percent? What is the highest interest rate at which it would be worth carrying out the project? Does your answer differ depending on whether you already have the funds or must borrow them?

3. Assuming a general level of interest of 5 percent per year, which is preferable:

    a. a $250 gift now or a $1,000 loan without interest for six years?

    b. a $1,000 gift now or a monthly salary increase of $50?

    c. a year's work in return for being paid $10,000 now or $1 million in 50 years?

    d. a lottery prize of $20,000 now or $1,000 per year for 30 years?

    e. buying a $5,000 car for cash now but at a discount of 5 percent or on credit with full payment required in 1 year?

4. "The pure rate of interest influences the length of time meat animals or trees are allowed to grow, the time wine or cheese are allowed to age, and the time durable goods are likely to last." Try to figure out why.

5. Compared to a decade earlier, the early 1980s brought a dramatic increase in the market price of medallions (government licenses) needed to run New York City taxicabs and in the market price of used-car rental firms (such as Rent-A-Wreck, Lease-A-Lemon, and Ugly-Duckling-Rent-A-Car). In Martin County, Kentucky, coal mine operators became instant millionaires, and even the prices of car dealerships, mining supply stores, and houses soared. Simultaneously, hefty decreases occurred in the market price of seats on the New York Stock Exchange. Can you explain why? (*Hint:* Consider OPEC.)

6. The Passamaquoddy tidal power project has long been viewed as a promising joint venture by the United States and Canada. Both parties agreed that the investment project would require heavy initial costs and would yield a flow of benefits stretching for decades into the future. Using the same figures for costs and benefits, the Canadians calculated a negative present value for the project and rejected it while the Americans calculated a positive present value and recommended carrying out the project. Can you explain the different results?

7. Comment on whether the following statements about *nonrenewable* natural resources make sense:

    a. "Conservation means the greatest good of the greatest number, and that for the longest time." (Gifford Pinchot, father of the American conservation movement).

    b. "Any divergence between the rate of increase over time of the net price of such a resource and the rate of interest quickly leads to a retardation or speeding up of resource extraction (and an equalization of the two rates)."

8. Suppose that a campaign was mounted to recycle paper "in order to save the trees." In the long run, would an increase in recycling save trees? (*Hint:* What would happen to the demand for and price of trees? To the value of tree lots?)

SELECTED READINGS

Bogachev, V. and Kantorovich, L. "The Price of Time." *Problems of Economics*, February 1970, pp. 3–27.

> Translation of a 1969 article in *Kommunist*, indicating the Soviet discovery of interest.

Denison, Edward F. *The Sources of Economic Growth in the United States and the Alternatives Before Us.* New York: Committee for Economic Development, 1962; idem. *Why Growth Rates Differ: Postwar Experience in Nine Western Countries.* Washington, D.C.: Brookings Institution, 1967, and idem. *Accounting for United States Economic Growth, 1929–1969,* Washington, D.C.: Brookings Institution, 1974.

> Three of the original studies measuring the impact of human capital on growth. For a follow-up see idem, *Accounting for Slower Economic Growth: The United States in the 1970s.* Washington, D.C.: Brookings Institution, 1979.

Fellner, William, et al. *Ten Economic Studies in the Tradition of Irving Fisher.* New York: Wiley, 1967.

> Essays honoring the memory of Fisher, written at the centennial of his birth.

Fisher, Irving Norton. *My Father Irving Fisher.* New York: Comet Press, 1956.

> The story of Fisher's life and work.

Freeman, Richard B. *The Over-Educated American*. New York: Academic Press, 1976; idem. "The Decline in the Economic Rewards to College Education." *The Review of Economics and Statistics*, February 1977, pp. 18–29.

> A discussion of recent decreases in the returns to human investment; note the ensuing controversy in the *Journal of Human Resources*, Winter 1980.

Goeller, H. E., and Weinberg, Alvin M. "The Age of Substitutability." *The American Economic Review*, December 1978, pp. 1–11.

> A discussion of the principle of infinite substitutability, derived from a study of the crustal abundance of all elements, according to which humanity has almost inexhaustible natural resources for an infinite length of time.

Herfindahl, Orris C., and Kneese, Allen V. *Economic Theory of Natural Resources*. Columbus: Merrill, 1974.

> An advanced text.

Hotelling, Harold. "The Economics of Exhaustible Resources." *The Journal of Political Economy*, April 1931, pp. 137–75.

> A classic article in the field.

Kuenne, Robert E. *Eugen von Böhm-Bawerk*. New York: Columbia University Press, 1971.

> The story of Böhm-Bawerk's life and work.

Lecomber, Richard. *The Economics of Natural Resources*. New York: Wiley, 1979.

> A superb text.

Nordhaus, William D. "World Dynamics: Measurement Without Data." *Economic Journal*, December 1973, pp. 1156–83.

> A discussion of doomsday models.

Schultz, Theodore W. "Investment in Human Capital." *The American Economic Review*, March 1961, pp. 1–17; idem. "Nobel Lecture: The Economics of Being Poor." *Journal of Political Economy*, August 1980, pp. 639–51.

> The first of these is the presidential address to the American Economic Association.

Schumpeter, Joseph A. *Ten Great Economists: From Marx to Keynes*. New York: Oxford University Press, 1951.

> Chapters 6 and 8 discuss the lives and works of Böhm-Bawerk and Fisher.

Seligman, Ben B. *Main Currents in Modern Economics*. Chicago: Quadrangle, 1962, vol. 2, pp. 294–310, and vol. 3, pp. 637–46.

> A critical review of the work of Böhm-Bawerk and Fisher.

Stigler, George J., and Becker, Gary S. "De Gustibus Non Est Disputandum." *The American Economic Review*, March 1977, pp. 76–90.

> An extension of the human capital concept to investments serving production in households rather than in firms. The capacity to appreciate music (or heroin) is shown to be increased (or decreased) by prior consumption thereof, which is seen to increase "music capital" (or decrease "euphoria capital").

CHAPTER 10

Coping with Uncertainty: Insurance and Gambling, Search and Futures Markets

Chapter 9 extended the analysis of decision making from the present to the future. We continued to assume, however, that people compared benefits and costs under conditions of certainty. In the present chapter, we will study situations of **uncertainty** in which people possess less than complete knowledge on matters relevant to their decision making.

Types of Uncertainty

There are two types of uncertainty. **Primary uncertainty**, or **event uncertainty**, exists when certain future events, which are bound to affect the outcome of present decisions, have not yet occurred and no one can possibly know what they will be like. Consider a farmer who can control all productive inputs except the weather. The size of the farmer's crop—depending, as it is, on nature—is inevitably uncertain. Consider a manufacturer who can control physical inputs as well as outputs perfectly but who cannot know about future changes in the preferences of customers, in technology, or in government policies —all of which are certain to affect the eventual outcome of present decisions.

Secondary uncertainty, or **market uncertainty**, exists when certain facts about the present or future are known to some people but not to

other people. Consider the consumer who wishes to buy a given type of car at the cheapest possible price but who does not know (as potential sellers do) at which places and prices it is presently available. Consider the manufacturer who plans to supply a commodity in the future but who does not know at which future price it can be sold. (If the present plans of all future buyers and suppliers could be revealed, the future equilibrium price could be known now.)

In the following sections, we will study how people deal with these two types of uncertainty. We will note how people enter **contingent-claim markets** in which they trade rights to variable quantities of particular goods—the quantities being dependent on the occurrence of specified "states of the world." In such markets, people can reduce **risk**—or the uncertainty-induced chance of variation in their welfare—through *insurance*, or they can increase risk through *gambling*. In addition to buying insurance, people who dislike uncertainty can also mitigate it by searching for added information or entering **futures markets**, in which they commit themselves now to trade, at specified dates in the future, specified quantities and qualities of goods at specified prices. (These markets contrast with **spot markets**, in which people agree to trade specified quantities and qualities of goods at specified prices and do it now.)

Note: In the following sections we will *not* make the distinction between uncertainty and risk that was introduced by Frank H. Knight (see Biography 10.1). This distinction, although once followed by many economists, has largely been abandoned. Knight reserved the term *risk* for situations in which people cannot foretell the specific outcome of an action because two or more outcomes are possible but in which people do know the types of outcomes and the associated objective probability distribution. The **objective probability** of an event is the relative frequency with which it occurs in a series of trials repeated under identical conditions. Thus we do not know whether the toss of a single coin will produce heads or tails. But we do know that one and only one of these two events must occur (the events are collectively exhaustive and mutually exclusive) and that the probability of each equals one-half. (When tossed a large enough number of times, each of the two sides will show up half the time.) In the same way, we do not know whether the use of a particular house or car will be terminated by fire or accident this year, but we do know (from statistics on large numbers of similar cases) that, say, 1 out of 250 like objects will suffer this fate.

Knight suggested, on the other hand, that the term *uncertainty* be reserved for situations in which people cannot foretell the specific outcome of an action because two or more outcomes are possible and in which people neither know the types of outcomes nor the associated objective probability distribution. Research directed toward technical change provides a fitting example. Will such efforts lead to the discovery of a new source of abundant energy? Or to new strains of wheat? And if the former, will it lead to the availability of cheap solar cells, of fusion power, or of as-yet-undreamed-of other energy sources? No one can know even the types of all outcomes, much less the objective probabilities of their occurrence. The uniqueness of the contemplated events makes the very concept of objective probability an inappropriate one. Under such circumstances, no two individuals may agree, but each person can still attach a **subjective probability**

BIOGRAPHY 10.1:
Frank H. Knight

Frank Hyneman Knight (1885–1972) was born in rural McLean County, Illinois. He studied philosophy, theology, and social science at Tennessee's Milligan College and later at Cornell University. He was a professor of economics at the University of Iowa and, from 1927 to his death, at the University of Chicago. Together with Friedrich von Hayek (see Biography 2.1) and Henry Simons, he established a tradition known as the Chicago School of Economics, later to be carried on by Milton Friedman (see Biography 2.2) and George Stigler (see Biography 17.1). The School's advocacy of free enterprise and its rejection of government interference in markets are well reflected in two of Knight's books: *The Ethics of Competition and Other Essays* (1935) and *Freedom and Reform: Essays in Economics and Social Philosophy* (1947). In these collections of essays, Knight identifies the greatest enemies of the free market as those who argue for the free market only in order to defend their own special interests. He laments the destruction of religion by science and the fact that nothing has replaced this moral force. As people turn to government to solve their problems, Knight argues, the free enterprise system is being corrupted, with loss of freedom and dictatorship as the inevitable consequence.

Knight's most famous book, however, is *Risk, Uncertainty and Profit* (1921). This work stimulated rich advances in the study of uncertainty and earned Knight, in 1950, the presidency and, in 1957, the Walker medal of the American Economic Association.

In this book, Knight distinguishes decisions involving risk from those involving uncertainty. Risk decisions, he argues, are insurable (because the nature and probabilities of various future outcomes are objectively known); uncertainty decisions are not insurable (because the nature and probabilities of various future outcomes can only be estimated subjectively). Knight argues that *profit* is a reward for those who are willing to act in the face of uncertainty (as he defines it) and who are lucky enough to avoid loss.

to every imaginable outcome—can attach, that is, to each outcome a measure of personal belief in the likelihood of its occurrence.

We will ignore Knight's distinction because it has proved sterile. All decision makers must somehow forecast the future, must assign probabilities to the possible outcomes of their actions. It matters little whether these probabilities are agreed upon by everyone and, therefore, *objective* (as in situations of **Knightian risk** or whether they are controversial and *subjective* (as in situations of **Knightian uncertainty**).

The Maximization of Expected Utility

With the help of Table 10.1, we can illustrate how modern economists imagine choices are made when primary uncertainty exists.

Human Actions Vs. States of the World

An individual farmer is faced with a choice between two actions (A_1 and A_2). Nature, in turn, is "choosing" between two possible "states of the world" (S_1 and S_2). Four possible consequences emerge in the body of the table and might represent the net income of the farm under the given combinations of actions and events.

Our farmer's belief about the likelihood of rain during the growing season can be indicated by a probability number between 0 and 1, which can be assigned to each possible event such that zero indicates belief in a zero chance of the event happening and unity indicates belief that the event is going to happen with certainty. Let our

farmer believe in a 50-50 chance of "much" or "little" rain. These subjective probabilities are shown at the bottom of the table. Their sum equals unity because we assume that "much" or "little" rain (however defined) are the only possible states of the world and that they are mutually exclusive.

Expected Value

The **mathematical expectation** or the (subjectively) **expected monetary value** *(EMV)* of each possible action equals the sum of the action's possible monetary outcomes, each outcome being weighted by its subjective probability. Thus, we get for action A_1 an expected monetary value, EMV_1, of $25(0.5) + 5(0.5) = 15$, and for action A_2 we get an expected monetary value, EMV_2, of $15(0.5) + 15(0.5) = 15$ as well.

It is tempting to predict that people acting under primary uncertainty will simply maximize the subjectively expected monetary value of their actions. If this were so, our farmer would be indifferent about the two possible actions shown in Table 10.1. Yet this is not necessarily so.

While the expected monetary values of both actions are alike (and equal to $15,000 per year), action A_2 provides this amount with certainty, no matter which state of the world pertains. Action A_1 involves risk. It provides a 50-50 chance of a larger income (of $25,000 per year) or a smaller one (of $5,000 per year). Choosing action A_1 over action A_2 thus amounts to taking a gamble: Our farmer would be giving up the certainty of $15,000 a year for the uncertain prospect of getting either $25,000 or $5,000 a year. Many

TABLE 10.1   A Payoff Matrix

Individual Actions	States of the World	
	S_1 = Much Rain	S_2 = Little Rain
A_1 = Fertilizing	25	5
A_2 = Not fertilizing	15	15
	Subjective probabilities:	
	0.5	0.5

This payoff matrix shows a farm's net income (in thousands of dollars per year) dependent on the farmer's decision to fertilize or not to fertilize the land and on nature's provision of much or little rain during the growing season.

TABLE 10.2 The St. Petersburg Game

Number of Toss	Payoff if Heads First Appears at Given Toss (1)	Probability of Heads First Appearing at Given Toss (2)	Expected value = payoff × probability (3) = (1) × (2)
1	$ 1	0.5	50¢
2	2	$(0.5)^2$	50¢
3	4	$(0.5)^3$	50¢
4	8	$(0.5)^4$	50¢
5	16	$(0.5)^5$	50¢
.	.	.	.
.	.	.	.
.	.	.	.

The St. Petersburg game has an expected monetary value of infinity (equal to the sum of the last column of this table).

people do not like to take such a gamble, not even when it is a **fair gamble**—that is, when its mathematical expectation is zero. The choice of A_1 over A_2 is in fact such a fair gamble. The expected monetary value of loss ($15,000 by not taking action A_2) exactly equals that of gain ($15,000 by taking action A_1). The apparent paradox of people refusing to make fair gambles was first solved some 250 years ago.

The St. Petersburg Paradox

A Swiss mathematician, Daniel Bernoulli (1700–1782) studied gamblers at the casinos of St. Petersburg. He considered the following game between two persons, X and Y:

A fair coin is tossed until heads appears; if heads appears on the first toss, X pays Y $1; if heads appears for the first time on the second toss, X pays Y $2; if heads appears first on the third toss, X pays Y $4; and so on, with X always paying 2^{n-1} at the nth toss if heads appears. If it is to be a fair gamble, what fee, Bernoulli asked, should Y be willing to pay X for the privilege of playing this game? Because the player of a fair game is never asked to pay more than the mathematical expectation of gain, this value can be calculated easily. Consider Table 10.2. Given a probability of 0.5 for heads to appear on the first toss, the mathematical expectation of gain is $1(0.5) = 50¢ if the game ends after the first toss. Given a probability of $(0.5)^2$ for heads to

appear first on the second toss, the mathematical expectation of gain is $2(0.5)^2 = 50¢ if the game ends after the second toss. And so it goes. Thus the mathematical expectation of the entire game is the sum of the expected values of all possible outcomes, or the infinite series 50¢ + 50¢ + . . . = ∞. Yet people are clearly not willing to pay such an infinite sum of money for this fair gamble.

One could probably solve the paradox by postulating that gamblers cannot possibly be convinced to take this game seriously. How could they be so gullible as to believe that payoff would actually be made should they be lucky enough to win a large sum? (If heads did not appear until the 42nd toss, the required payoff would equal more than the entire U.S. gross national product!) Bernoulli, however, had a different idea. He argued that people making decisions under uncertainty were not attempting to maximize expected *monetary* values but maximized expected *utilities* instead. He thought that the marginal utility of money declines the more money people have. Any person starting with $500, for example, would, therefore, place a smaller subjective value on gaining an extra sum than on losing an equal amount. Any game with an equal probability of gaining and winning a given amount is, therefore, fair in *monetary* terms but unfair in *utility* terms. The game's expected utility is negative. No wonder people refuse to play it!

In Figure 10.1, it is assumed, in accordance with Bernoulli's postulate, that the total utility of money rises with greater amounts of it, while its marginal utility (shown by the slope of the total utility curve) declines. In this graph, the total utility of money, U, is related to the amount of money, \$, by the equation $U = \sqrt{\$}$. Thus a person with \$500 is assumed to receive $\sqrt{500}$ or 22.36 utils from it (point A). The same person would, however, receive only 5.92 extra utils from an added \$300 (when moving from A to C), while losing 8.22 utils by a loss of \$300 (when moving from A to B). Given this type of utility function, the St. Petersburg paradox is easily solved. While the expected monetary value of the game equals infinity, its expected utility equals

$$\sqrt{1} \ (0.5) + \sqrt{2} \ (0.5)^2 + \sqrt{4} \ (0.5)^3$$
$$+ \sqrt{8} \ (0.5)^4 + \sqrt{16} \ (0.5)^5 + \ldots$$
$$= 1(1/2) + \sqrt{2} \ (1/4) + 2(1/8) + 2\sqrt{2} \ 1/16 +$$
$$4(1/32) + \ldots$$
$$= 1/2 + \sqrt{2} \ 1/4 + 1/4 + \sqrt{2} \ 1/8$$
$$+ 1/8 + \ldots$$
$$= 1 + \sqrt{2} \ (1/2)$$
$$= 1.707.$$

By the above equation, an expected utility of 1.707 translates into a dollar equivalent of $(1.707)^2 = \$2.91$. This then is the far-less-than-infinite amount that a person who maximized expected utility and possessed the above utility function would pay for the privilege of playing the St. Petersburg game.

Note: Someone else who also maximized expected utility but possessed a different utility function would act quite differently. Even if people, as is likely, maximize the expected utility rather than the expected monetary value of their actions when facing uncertainty, *we cannot predict their behavior without a knowledge of their utility functions*. Indeed, the shape of these functions reveals important information about people's attitudes concerning the spread of possible outcomes of their action around the action's expected value. The extent of such spread in fact measures the **risk** of an action. People's attitudes toward such a spread, therefore, reveal their attitudes toward risk.

FIGURE 10.1   The Utility of Money

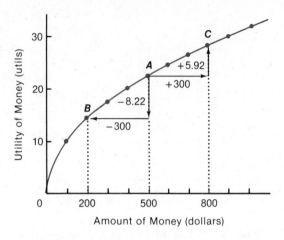

This graph illustrates declining marginal utility of money. The total utility of money, U, here is related to the amount of money, \$, by the equation $U = \sqrt{\$}$. Other relationships are, of course, also possible.

Attitudes Toward Risk

People can view risk in one of three ways. They can be averse to it, they can be neutral toward it, or they can seek it out.

Risk Aversion

Imagine for a moment that the farmer whose choices are pictured in Table 10.1 possessed the type of utility function postulated by Bernoulli (see panel (a) of Figure 10.2). Action A_2, as we noted earlier, would bring the farmer a net income of \$15,000 a year, regardless of the weather. This amount of money is associated, according to point B on the utility function, with a total utility of $0b$. Action A_1, on the other hand, would bring the farmer, with equal probability, a net income of \$5,000 a year or of \$25,000 a year. As we can see from points A and C, respectively, the associated utilities equal $0a$ and $0c$. The

FIGURE 10.2 Attitudes Toward Risk

(a) Risk Aversion

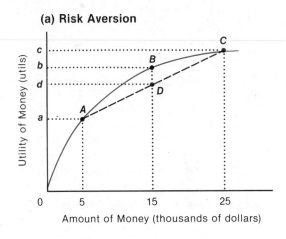

(b) Risk Neutrality

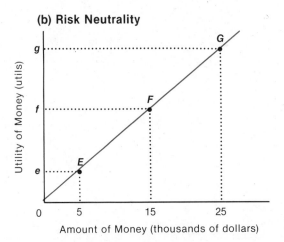

(c) Risk Seeking

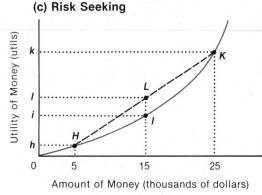

This set of graphs illustrates three basic attitudes toward risk: risk aversion in panel (a), risk neutrality in panel (b), and risk seeking in panel (c). These attitudes correspond, respectively, to declining, constant, and increasing marginal utilities of money.

expected utility from an equally weighted $5,000 or $25,000 a year, however, equals the sum of half of 0*a* plus half of 0*c*. This utility is shown in the graph by 0*d* and corresponds to point *D*, located on the dashed line connecting *A* and *C* and above the $15,000 expected monetary value of the $5,000 or $25,000 gamble. (Note: The expected utility of receiving $5,000 with a probability of 0.2 or $25,000 with a probability of 0.8 could similarly be read off on line *AC*, but at a point above the $5,000(0.2) + $25,000(0.8) = $21,000 expected monetary value of this different gamble.)

Whenever a person in this way considers the utility (as at point *B*) of a certain prospect of money to be higher than the expected utility (as at point *D*) of an uncertain prospect of equal expected monetary value, the person is said to hold an attitude of **risk aversion**. This is always the case when a person's marginal utility of money (shown here by the slope of utility function 0*ABC*) declines with larger amounts of money.

Risk aversion is, indeed, quite common. Consider how people do all kinds of things, small and large, to escape gambles: they place person-to-person calls instead of station-to-station calls;

at airports, banks, and post offices, they prefer single lines feeding to many clerks to the chance of getting into a slow or fast line; they diversify their assets and do not "place all eggs in one basket"; they reject fair gambles (as our risk-averse farmer would by taking action A_2 to gain utility $0b$ rather than action A_1 with equal expected monetary value but smaller expected utility $0d$); and, as we shall see, people buy insurance.

Risk Neutrality

Let us imagine instead that our farmer's utility function is illustrated by panel (b) of Figure 10.2. In this case, the utility of action A_2, with its certain payoff of $15,000 a year, would equal $0f$, corresponding to point F. Action A_1 would bring, according to points E and G, utility of $0e$ or $0g$, and with equal probability. The expected utility of this gamble, however, would also equal $0f$. (A straight line between E and G leads us to point F above the $15,000 expected monetary value of the $5,000 or $25,000 gamble.)

Whenever a person in this way considers the utility (as at point F) of a certain prospect of money to be equal to the expected utility (as at

ANALYTICAL EXAMPLE 10.1:

Risk and Investment in Education

Any one person who invests in human capital through education can only guess at the rate of return because there are many uncertainties: the length of the person's life, future market conditions that determine average incomes, and the spread of actual incomes around the average. A person with a B.A. degree who is about to enter the Ph.D. program, for example, will have to compare the (discounted) expected monetary values of these alternatives. A different spread of expected incomes (as, perhaps, among private industry, government, or university employment) will produce a different expected value (and rate of return). In addition, any given expected monetary value of future income will mean less to a person the more risk-averse the person is.

Using 1966 data, an economist recently calculated average rates of return from the Ph.D. program for 200,000 U.S. scientists. As the accompanying table shows, rates of return differed markedly, depending on where an individual was employed and what the degree of risk aversion was (calculated on a scale from 0 to 1). While a risk-neutral person in private industry received a 7.8 percent rate of return from the Ph.D., for example, a rather risk-averse person earned only 0.7 percent (circled numbers).

Employer	Average rates of return from Ph.D. over B.A. Degree, if Degree of Risk Aversion Equals			
	0	**0.2**	**0.4**	**0.6**
Private industry	0.078	0.057	0.034	0.007
Government	0.081	0.058	0.035	0.009
Educational institution	0.156	0.118	0.080	0.040

Source: Yoram Weiss, "The Risk Element in Occupational and Educational Choices," *Journal of Political Economy*, November–December, 1972, pp. 1203–13. Adapted by permission of the University of Chicago Press. © 1972 by the University of Chicago.

point *F*) of an uncertain prospect of equal expected monetary value, the person is said to hold an attitude of **risk neutrality**. This is always the case when a person's marginal utility of money (shown here by the slope of utility function 0*EFG*) remains constant with larger amounts of money.

Risk neutrality is not very common. If all people were risk neutral, our farmer would be truly indifferent between actions A_1 and A_2 because, as we saw, their expected monetary values are equal. By the same token, you would have to be willing to pay $100 for the privilege of taking each of the following fair gambles, for the expected monetary value of each of these is also $100:

1. a 99 percent chance of getting $101.01 and a 1 percent chance of getting nothing.
2. a 50 percent chance of getting $101 and a 50 percent chance of getting $99.
3. a 1 percent chance of getting $10,000 and a 99 percent chance of getting nothing.
4. a 1 percent chance of getting $1 million, a 1 percent chance of losing $990,000, and a 98 percent chance of getting nothing.

After thinking about it, you might pay the price for 1 and 2 or something close to it, but do you have the sweepstakes mentality to go after 3? Are you ready for the Russian roulette of 4?

Risk Seeking

We now imagine that our farmer's utility function is illustrated by panel (c) of Figure 10.2. In this case, the utility of action A_2, with its certain payoff of $15,000 a year, would equal 0*i*, corresponding to point *I*. Action A_1 would bring, according to points *H* and *K*, utility of 0*h* or 0*k*, and with equal probability. By the now-familiar procedure, we can establish the expected utility of this gamble as 0*l*, corresponding to point *L* on dashed line *HK*.

Whenever a person in this way considers the utility (as at point *I*) of a certain prospect of money to be lower than the expected utility (as at point *L*) of an uncertain prospect of equal expected monetary value, the person is said to hold an attitude of **risk seeking**. This is always the case when a person's marginal utility of money (shown here by the slope of utility function 0*HIK*) rises with larger amounts of money.

Risk seeking, like risk neutrality, is not very common. If all people were risk seekers, our farmer would, of course, prefer action A_1 to A_2. And all of us would constantly seek out and accept huge riches-or-ruin gambles. In fact, of course, most of us have the opposite inclination and seek out insurance.

From Risk Aversion to Insurance

The existence of risk aversion gives rise to a market for insurance.

The Demand Side

Consider Figure 10.3. The utility function shown there is that of the risk averter first pictured in panel (a) of Figure 10.2. Suppose that this person was assured of a $25,000 income but also saw a 50-50 chance of losing a $20,000 house through fire in a given year. (This rather unrealistic number has been chosen in order to produce an easily readable graph.) This person would, in fact, face a gamble between $25,000 (and its associated utility 0*a*) and $5,000 (and its lower utility 0*b*), both cases being considered of equal subjective probability. The expected monetary value of this gamble would equal $15,000 and, as point *C* tells us, provide an expected utility of 0*c*.

Note: The risk-averse person would derive equal expected utility from $11,000 to be received with certainty because point *D* on this person's utility function is found at the same level as *C*. Such a person, therefore, would be willing to pay up to $14,000 for a contingent claim according to which someone would contract to pay $20,000 if the house burned down.

The Supply Side

When risk averters, seeking to replace uncertainty with certainty, in this way offer to buy

FIGURE 10.3 Risk Aversion and Insurance

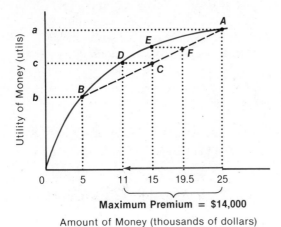

A risk-averse person can reduce risk (or the spread of possible outcomes around an expected value) by buying insurance. In this example, an equally probable $5,000 or $25,000 (with a $15,000 expected monetary value) could be escaped, without a change in welfare, by purchasing $20,000 of insurance for a premium of $14,000. (The resultant certain utility of $11,000, corresponding to point *D*, would then just equal the utility expected under uncertainty, corresponding to point *C*.) Any lower insurance premium would, of course, raise welfare in comparison with the situation of uncertainty.

contingent claims, others may well supply them. An insurance company might notice that the objective probability of someone's house burning down in a given year is in fact not 0.5, but 0.004. In order to make good on claims, it would, therefore, have to collect $20,000 from every 250 home-owners like our risk-averse friend plus, let us say, an added 20 percent to cover operating costs. It could, therefore, offer to sell the contingent claim sought by our friend for as little as $24,000 per year divided by 250, or $96 per year—a far cry from the $14,000-a-year maximum premium our friend was willing to pay.

Indeed, even if the company's estimate of probability agreed with our home-owner's (and it would have to collect $20,000 plus expenses from every 2 persons), the premium could be as low as $12,000 per year. In either case, therefore, there would be room for a mutually profitable deal. Such a deal would leave our friend somewhere on the utility function to the right of *D* and to the left of *A*, and such a position would yield, with certainty, a utility greater than 0*c*, the utility expected in an uncertain world.

No wonder that insurance has been big business ever since ancient times. Even the Babylonians insured their caravans, the Greeks their sea trade. And in 1688, Lloyd's of London was formed—now the world's most famous insurance company. It was named after a coffee house where merchants and shippers met to negotiate marine insurance. Now the venerable company sells policies worldwide, ranging from the expected to the highly unusual. Among the expected, one finds auto, aviation, burglary, fire, health, liability, and life insurance. But Lloyd's has also insured dancers, movie stars, and soccer players against damage to their legs; ball teams, ski resorts, and vacationers against bad weather; international businesses against nationalization or contract cancellations after *coups d'état*; and even a Texan against death from the uncontrolled reentry of Skylab (that $1 million policy cost $250). In 1979, Lloyd's had 18,500 broker-members and collected $4 billion in premiums.

At the same time, plans were underway in many insurance companies to compete more effectively for Lloyd's business. In what was billed as "the most important change in the international insurance business in decades," a New York Insurance Exchange was opened in 1980. Modeled after Lloyd's, it was scheduled to become primarily a marketplace for high-risk

FIGURE 10.4   Risk Seeking and Gambling

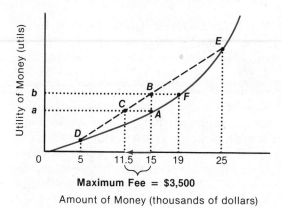

Amount of Money (thousands of dollars)

A risk-seeking person can increase risk (or the spread of possible outcomes around an expected value) by gambling. In this example, a certain prospect of $15,000 could be escaped, without a change in welfare, by paying a fee of $3,500 for the privilege of gambling for an equally probable loss or gain of $10,000. (The resultant expected utility of the gamble, corresponding to point C, would then just equal the utility received under certainty and corresponding to point A.) Any lower gambling fee would, of course, raise welfare in comparison with the situation of certainty.

insurance, covering such things as offshore oil rigs and satellites. The exchange was designed to let insurance companies that had taken on such huge risks sell off smaller pieces of it to many others and to attract to this type of reinsurance a multitude of individual investors.

From Risk Seeking to Gambling

Just as risk aversion gives rise to insurance, so risk seeking leads to a market for gambling.

The Demand Side

Consider Figure 10.4. The utility function shown there is that of the risk seeker first pictured in panel (c) of Figure 10.2.

Suppose that this person was assured of a $15,000 income but was also offered a bet to win or lose, with equal probability, $10,000 in a year. This person would compare utility $0a$, associated with the $15,000 certain income, with higher utility $0b$, associated with the $15,000 mathematical expectation of the gamble. This person, therefore, would be willing to take the gamble. Indeed, the person would pay up to $3,500 for the privilege of taking the gamble.

After having paid the $3,500 fee, any

$10,000 win would reduce to $6,500, and any $10,000 loss would increase to $13,500. Thus the odds of winning would worsen from 1:1 (the $10,000 to $10,000 ratio, equivalent to ratio DB/BE in our graph) to 1:2.0769 (the $6,500 to $13,500 ratio, equivalent to ratio DC/CE in the graph). These odds also indicate that the probability of winning $10,000 would lower from 1 chance in 2 (or 0.5) to 1 chance in 3.0769 or (0.325). The mathematical expectation of $25,000 (now with a probability of 0.325) and of $5,000 (now with a probability of 0.675) equals $11,500, which (as point C indicates) has an expected utility of $0a$, just equal to the utility (at point A) of the $15,000 certain income.

Such a person, therefore, would be willing to pay up to $3,500 for the mere privilege of winning or losing $10,000 contingent upon an uncertain event, such as the performance of a race horse, the roll of a die, or the drawing of a lottery number.

The Supply Side

When risk seekers, seeking to replace certainty with uncertainty, in this way offer to buy contingent claims, others may well supply them. No wonder that all types of gambling have flourished for centuries and in many cultures. Like insurance, gambling is big business, too. Apart from betting on horse races and lotteries, which are legal in many states, Las Vegas long held a U.S. monopoly in casino gambling (1979 taxable casino profit equalled $2 billion). Recently, Atlantic City established two casinos (with a taxable casino profit of $220 million in 1979); eight more casinos were scheduled to operate by 1985. Indeed, as New Jersey was contemplating an extension of such gambling to the Meadowlands, a stone's throw from Manhattan, New York's Casino Gambling Study Panel in 1979 recommended setting up some 40 casinos, from Niagara Falls and the Catskills to Manhattan and Coney Island. (The panel projected a taxable casino profit of $3 billion.) Similar panels made similar suggestions from Pennsylvania to Massachusetts to Quebec.

Simultaneous Insuring and Gambling

It does not follow from the forgoing analysis that risk averters always buy insurance and never gamble. Nor does it follow that risk seekers always gamble and never buy insurance. What each group will do depends very much on whether the insurance or gambles they confront are more-than-fair, fair, or unfair.

Insurance and Gambles: From More-than-Fair to Unfair

We already noted that a gamble is called *fair* when its expected monetary value is zero, any expectation of gain being exactly offset by that of loss. The same definition applies to **fair insurance**. Accordingly, insurance contracts and gambles are called *more than fair* when their expected monetary value is positive, when the expectation of gain exceeds that of loss. Similarly, insurance contracts and gambles are *unfair* when their expected monetary value is negative and the expectation of gain falls short of that of loss. An analysis of our earlier examples can quickly establish how people with different attitudes toward risk will act when confronted with

these three different types of insurance contracts or gambles.

The Risk Averter's Attitude toward Insurance. Consider once more Figure 10.3, in which our house owner was willing to replace the $5,000 vs. $25,000 gamble with a $25,000 certainty minus a premium of up to $14,000 a year. Because the $20,000 house was believed to have a 50 percent chance of burning down in a year, its owner had a mathematical expectation of gain from insurance of $10,000 a year (the owner could expect to collect from the insurance company $20,000 every second year). The insured owner's expectation of loss, on the other hand, was nothing else but the insurance premium.

If the premium were smaller than $10,000 a year (and the insurance, therefore, was more than fair), our owner would end up with a certain amount of money in excess of $15,000 and a utility corresponding to some point to the right of E. Surely, such would be better than the expected utility without insurance (corresponding to C). Risk averters, therefore, do buy insurance that is more than fair.

If the premium were exactly $10,000 a year (and the insurance, therefore, was fair), our owner would end up with exactly $15,000 and a utility corresponding to point E. This, too, would be better than the expected utility without insurance (corresponding to C). Risk averters, therefore, do buy insurance that is fair.

If the premium were larger than $10,000 a year (and the insurance, therefore, was unfair), premiums between $10,001 and $14,000 a year would leave the owner with $14,999 to $11,000 of money a year and a utility corresponding to some point between D and just to the left of E. Such would be as good or better than the expected utility without insurance (corresponding to C). Risk averters, therefore, buy *some* insurance that is unfair. They won't buy it, however, if it is *too* unfair. Any premium above $14,000 a year would reduce the person's money to below $11,000 a year and reduce utility below 0c (below what it would be without insurance). Risk averters would not buy such insurance.

ANALYTICAL EXAMPLE 10.2:

Smoke Detectors as Insurance

People can and often do reduce the risk of death and injury by the voluntary purchase of safety devices. One economist recently studied people's behavior with respect to the purchase of smoke detectors. She estimated that in the United States in 1976 there would have been 6,492 deaths and 6,759 injuries from residential fires in the absence of smoke detectors. In fact, however, 13 percent of households voluntarily installed smoke detectors, 80 percent of which were operational and provided 45 percent protection against death and 30 percent protection against injury. (These suprisingly low numbers are explained by people's inability to escape in spite of being warned or by their failure to respond correctly to alarms.) As a result, actual fire deaths were reduced to 6,200 and injuries to 6,750 in 1976. (If all households had had detectors, the numbers of deaths and injuries would have been 4,155 and 5,089, respectively.)

It was also estimated how much people paid for this reduction in the fire hazard. The average purchase price of a smoke detector in 1976, for example, was $39.65, while the annual operating cost was $1.57 (for batteries). Present values for the stream of operating costs were determined for discount rates of 5 and 10 percent.

All these data were then used to estimate the implicit value the purchasers of smoke detectors had placed upon their lives. The results are shown (in part) in the accompanying table for a variety of assumptions. These include the two discount rates noted above, as well as alternative weights people might attach to the relative importance of reducing the probability of death or injury.

Weighting Scheme (importance attached to reducing death, *D*, versus injury, *I*)		Implicit Value of Life, Given a Discount Rate of	
D	*I*	**5 percent**	**10 percent**
1.0	0.5	$227,273	$271,562
1.0	0.1	287,611	343,658
1.0	0	308,544	368,671

Note: Readers may wish to compare these results with those noted in the section of Chapter 8 on "Wage Differentials and the Value of Life."

Source: Rachel Dardis, "The Value of a Life: New Evidence from the Martketplace," *The American Economic Review*, December 1980, pp. 1077–82.

The Risk Seeker's Attitude toward Insurance. Assume all circumstances to be the same as in the previous section, except that the home-owner is risk-seeking, and the utility function is depicted by Figure 10.4. Even the person depicted there would replace the $5,000 vs. $25,000 gamble with a $25,000 certain amount, minus insurance premium, as long as the premium was no more than $6,000 a year (such insurance would be more than fair). The amount of money available with certainty would then lie between $19,000 and $25,000 a year, and the associated utility (corresponding to some point between F and E) would exceed the expected utility of the gamble (corresponding to B). Risk seekers, therefore, do buy *some* insurance that is more than fair.

By the same token, however, they reject other insurance contracts that are more than fair, and they reject all that are fair or less than fair. In our example, premiums between $6,001 and $9,999 (still leaving the insurance more than fair), of $10,000 (making the insurance fair), and in excess of $10,000 (making the insurance unfair) would all produce remaining money amounts below $19,000 a year. They would, therefore, produce utilities corresponding to points along the line from 0 to just left of F, always lower than the expected utility of the gamble (corresponding to B).

The Risk Averter's Attitude toward Gambling. Just as risk seekers can be persuaded to buy insurance when it is considerably more than fair, so risk averters would take gambles if they were considerably more than fair. Consider, again, Figure 10.3. This time, a risk averter with

a certain sum of $15,000 would reject the $5,000 vs. $25,000 equally probable and, therefore, fair gamble because E lies above C.

Since even this fair gamble would be rejected by the risk averter, obviously an unfair one, with an expected utility corresponding to some point between B and C, would be rejected all the more. These positions would also bring lower utility than E.

Indeed, *some* more-than-fair gambles, with expected utilities corresponding to points between C and F, would be rejected as well. Even these positions would bring lower utilities than E. Yet other more-than-fair gambles would be acceptable, even to the risk averter. In our example, these gambles are those with mathematical expectations between $19,500 and $25,000 a year, all of which produce expected utilities (on segment FA) as large or larger than the utility of the $15,000 a year certain sum assumed available initially.

The Risk Seeker's Attitude toward Gambling. Just as risk averters will reject insurance when it

---

CLOSE-UP 10.1:

California Pyramids

In 1980, "pyramid parties" became a fad that swept California with a revival-meeting intensity. Even 300 arrests and $250 fines for violating a state ban on "endless chain schemes" didn't cool the pyramid fever. The pyramid parties were an extension of the endless-chain-letter idea. A player paid $1,000 to enter the bottom of the pyramid. If two other players could be induced to do likewise, the initial outlay was recouped; if they, in turn, recruited enough others, the original player could rise to the top of a 64-person pyramid and collect $16,000. Party goers proselytized relatives, friends, neighbors, and anyone else interested in making a fast buck. And the Federal Reserve in Los Angeles noted double the normal demand for $50 and $100 denomination bills. Said the head of the fraud and forgery unit of the

state's department of justice: "I've never seen anything like this, and nothing seems to end it. Arrests and publicity don't have the impact they normally would."

Note: Pyramid schemes were being investigated by New York police as well. In one Long Island raid, a former district attorney was discovered among the crowd. Upon his arrest, he promptly called the persecution of gamblers a misplaced priority of law enforcement agencies. "Everyone there fully realized the risk involved," he said. "They were there to socialize, have some fun, and hopefully win some money. There was no fraud involved. The people there knew what they were doing."

Sources: G. Christian Hill, "California Pyramids: Modern Wonders of Western World." *The Wall Street Journal*, May 29, 1980, pp. 1 and 29; Shawn G. Kennedy, "Pyramid Game on L.I. Raided," *The New York Times*, July 2, 1980, p. 81.

TABLE 10.3   Risk: Attitudes and Behavior

Person's Attitude Toward Risk	Person's View of					
	Insurance, if Contract Is			Gambling, if Contract Is		
	More than Fair	Fair	Unfair	More than Fair	Fair	Unfair
Risk aversion	Desirable	Desirable	Sometimes desirable	Sometimes desirable	Undesirable	Undesirable
Risk neutrality	Desirable	Indifferent	Undesirable	Desirable	Indifferent	Undesirable
Risk seeking	Sometimes desirable	Undesirable	Undesirable	Desirable	Desirable	Sometimes desirable

Regardless of their attitudes toward risk, people may find insurance or gambling desirable or undesirable depending on the type of contract offered them.

is extremely unfair, so risk seekers reject gambles that are considerably unfair, as implied in Figure 10.4. We already know why the person pictured there would reject the certainty of $15,000 in favor of a fair gamble—an equally probable $5,000 or $25,000: Point *B* lies above point *A*.

Since a fair gamble would be accepted, obviously a more-than-fair one, with an expected utility corresponding to some point between *B* and *E*, would be accepted all the more. These positions would also bring higher utility than *A*.

Indeed, as we have seen, *some* unfair gambles, with expected utilities corresponding to points between *B* and *C*, would be accepted as well. Even these positions would bring higher utilities than *A*. Yet other unfair gambles would not be acceptable, even to the risk seeker. In our example, these gambles are those with mathematical expectations between $5,000 and $11,499 a year, all of which produce expected utilities (on segment *DC*) smaller than the utility of the $15,000 a year certain sum assumed available initially.

The attitudes of risk seekers and risk averters toward both gambling and insurance are summarized in Table 10.3, along with the attitudes of risk-neutral persons.

A Paradox

We now must face a paradox. Our analysis leads us to conclude that a risk averter will buy a fair insurance contract, and even a not-too-unfair one but will never take a fair or unfair gamble. Similarly, a risk seeker will never buy a fair or unfair insurance contract but will take a fair and not-too-unfair gamble. Yet real-world people do buy fair and unfair insurance and take fair and unfair gambles at the same time! How can they possibly be risk averters and risk seekers simultaneously?

A possible explanation for the paradox that most people are risk averters yet *do* take fair and not-too-unfair gambles, contrary to what Table 10.3 tells us, is that people gamble not only in order to change their wealth, but also for the very fun of it. The very activity of being at the races or visiting the casinos, perhaps, is recreational for them, like playing tennis or going to the beach. Thus there are consumption aspects to gambling that create additional utility not considered above. This explanation rings true when one considers the high frequency of repetitive small-stakes gambling at casinos (which can hardly have significant impact on people's wealth). It doesn't ring true when one considers the purchase of state lottery tickets.

The most famous answer to this paradox, however, is provided by Milton Friedman and L. J. Savage. They suggest that people's utility functions may not look at all like those found in Figure 10.2 but may look like the one in Figure 10.5. The marginal utility of money declines, the hypothesis says, when the amount of money is below a certain level (such as *A*), rises between that level and a higher one (as between *A* and *B*), and falls again above that higher level.

Now consider a person with an amount of money equal to A. That person may face the possibility of a large loss of AC, as did our house owner in Figure 10.3. For reasons indicated then, that person would buy insurance, trading in the gamble between C and A for the certainty of some intermediate amount, such as D. The utility of this certain amount, corresponding to point d,

ANALYTICAL EXAMPLE 10.3:
Sweepstakes Contests

Each year, advertising agencies hold hundreds of sweepstakes contests—random drawings that differ from lotteries in that no explicit entry fee is required. Millions of people participate. Edward B. Selby, Jr. and William Beranek decided to investigate the participants' attitudes toward risk. They focused on contests in the *Reader's Digest* during 1976 and 1977. They argued (as Table 10.3 confirms) that risk-averse people would enter only more-than-fair gambles, that risk-neutral persons would also enter fair gambles, and that risk seekers alone would even enter unfair gambles. In order to determine the degree of fairness of the contests, the investigators then calculated the expected winnings from a single entry as in the table below and compared them with the certain cost of entry of 20 cents. (This cost includes postage, stationery, and the participant's time cost. The time of absorbing the rules, of estimating the value of "African safaris" or "nights on the town," and of filling out the forms was priced at the then existing minimum wage.). The comparison of 20 cents with the expected winnings showed most contests not worth entering. Except for the first three contests in the table, most contests were unfair gambles.

Were most sweepstakes participants, therefore, risk seekers? Not necessarily. It is also possible that these people looked beyond the expected pecuniary gain and received direct utility from the "pleasures of gambling" or the "wiling away of otherwise idle time."

Sweepstake	Expected Winnings from Single Entry (in cents)
Lysol products	30.000
The Great Meow Mix	29.814
G.E. New Car and Bike	20.686
Miss America	19.875
Help Young America Save Energy	17.857
Glass Plus	10.337
Miss Clairol Silver Anniversary	10.023
Feetstakes	9.195
Breakfast Shopper	8.335
Help Young America	2.544
Superstar Vacation	2.017

Source: Edward B. Selby, Jr. and William Beranek, "Sweepstakes Contests: Analysis, Strategies, and Survey," *The American Economic Review*, March 1981, vol. 71, no. 1 pp. 189–95.

would exceed the utility expected from the gamble, corresponding to some point, such as *b*, on the dashed line between *c* and *a*. This is why the utility function from 0 to *a* is said to lie in the region of insurance.

The same person, on the other hand, may be attracted by a lottery, offering a large chance of losing a small sum (the ticket price *AD*) and a small chance of winning a large sum (a lottery price of *AE*). The expected monetary value of this gamble between *D* and *E* may equal the amount *F*. As can be seen in our graph, the expected utility derived from the gamble, corresponding to *f*, exceeds the utility at *a* of the certain amount of money held initially. The person will take the gamble; thus, a given person may be found simultaneously in the first and last row of Table 10.3 (note the encircled portions).

Market Uncertainty and Search

When people are confronted by uncertainty of the market, rather than uncertainty of events, they can try to overcome their ignorance of the facts by engaging in **search**, an activity designed to discover information already possessed by other people. Like all activities, the search for information absorbs resources and time, and there is, therefore, an optimum point beyond which a wise decision maker does not carry the effort. *Pigheadedness* (looking forever for that needle in the haystack) is sure to violate the optimization principle, but so is *faintheartedness* (not looking at all). Consider, for example, the search for the terms at which exchange can be carried out.

The Search for Price

George J. Stigler was among the first to emphasize how buyers and sellers alike must inevitably act before they have perfect knowledge of the best available price. Someone about to buy a new car, for example, can visit any number of dealers; each additional visit will bring with it not only an ever-increasing total cost of the search, but also an ever-declining probability of finding a lower price. Consider Table 10.4. A buyer who had to spend an extra $150 to visit the fourth dealer, for example, would not find the added search worthwhile: The $150 marginal cost would exceed the $125 marginal benefit.

The phenomenon just described is, of course, widely applicable, and not only to buyers. Consider how people often engage in lengthy searches for the highest possible price when selling their homes or their labor. The fact that a wide dispersion of prices persists in such markets is an indicator of ignorance in these markets. This ignorance can be overcome in part by direct search of the type just described but also by the purchase of second-hand information (expert advice) and the monitoring of free information disseminated by others (which might be misinformation). Note: When markets are completely centralized, such as those for securities traded at major stock exchanges, everyone can know all the prices quoted by all traders at a given time. In that rare case, price dispersion disappears.

FIGURE 10.5
The Friedman-Savage Hypothesis

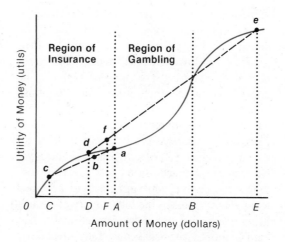

A person whose utility function looks like the one pictured here may buy fair and not-too-unfair insurance while simultaneously taking fair and not-too-unfair gambles.

The Search for Quality

An even more interesting problem, highlighted by George A. Akerlof, is people's ignorance about the *quality* of things traded in markets. Consider the market for *used* cars. Why is it, Akerlof asked, that brand-new cars fetch such a low price when resold on the used-car market? The answer is fairly simple:

The buyer of a new car faces a (low) probability of x that the new car is a "lemon." Once the car has been bought and used, the buyer knows the car's quality with certainty. Surely, buyers are more likely to resell their cars when they are lemons. Buyers of used cars, in turn, assume this to be so. They cannot differentiate good used cars (for which they would gladly pay a fairly high price) from bad used cars (for which they would pay almost nothing). As a result, they offer an average price that seems unreasonably low to the seller of a good used car and delightfully high to the seller of a bad used car. No wonder that good cars disappear from the used-car market, while lemons abound. The abundance of lemons, of course, only strengthens the determination of people to pay little for used cars.

Sellers who know the (high) quality of what they have to sell try to dispel the ignorance on the buyers' side by engaging in a variety of activities that would be irrational if the quality of their products was low. Such sellers engage in informational advertising (the citing of facts and the drawing of valid conclusions). They establish brand names whereby they make themselves vulnerable to loss of repeat sales if quality is low. They offer prepurchase inspection by experts of the buyer's choosing, money-back guarantees, or free service contracts. In the labor market, too, sellers engage in **signaling**, an activity designed to convince buyers of the high quality of what is being sold. Consider how workers advertise their high quality by acquiring educational credentials (which low-quality workers would find it difficult or impossible to get). Buyers, in turn, engage in **screening**, an activity designed to select high-quality sellers. Consider how employers select high-quality workers from an applicant pool with the help of educational credentials, even though the education itself may be totally unrelated to the immediate tasks to be performed. (Screening based on indices that cannot be altered at the discretion of individual workers, such as age, race, or sex, is typically illegal.)

Market Uncertainty and Futures Markets

When market uncertainty involves ignorance not about present facts, but about the future, people can sometimes dispel it with the help of futures markets. Note that unconditional rather than contingent claims are being traded in these markets. In futures markets, people commit themselves now to trade, at specified dates in the future, specified quantities and qualities of goods at specified prices; these agreements are not contingent on the occurrence of unforeseeable events, such as a house burning down or lottery number 97,531 being drawn. Futures markets balance demand and supply *in advance*; on the basis of the combined information available to traders now, they produce the best possible estimates of future prices. Futures markets are windows on the future. They serve to redistribute uncertainty over the population, from hedgers who wish to minimize price risk to speculators who wish to assume it.

The Role of Hedging

Hedging is the taking of equal and opposite positions in the spot and futures markets, with the hope that this will prevent a loss due to price fluctuations. A hedger attempts to have neither a net asset or **long position** (in which more of something is owned than owed) nor a net liability or **short position** (in which more of something is owed than owned). A successful hedger's net worth is, therefore, unaffected by price changes.

The Selling Hedge or Short Hedge. Consider a farmer who wishes to fix the value, at the

TABLE 10.4 Searching for the Lowest Price

Number of sellers canvassed	Probability of Finding Minimum Price Equal to		Expected Minimum Price
	$4,000	$6,000	
1	0.5	0.5	$5,000
2	0.75	0.25	4,500
3	0.875	0.125	4,250
4	0.9375	0.0625	4,125
.	.	.	
.	.	.	
.	.	.	
∞	1.0	0	$4,000

If sellers of a given type of car are equally divided between prices of $4,000 and $6,000, a buyer searching for the lowest possible price is ever more likely to find it the more sellers are canvassed.
SOURCE: Based on George J. Stigler, "The Economics of Information," *The Journal of Political Economy*, June 1961, p. 214. Reprinted by permission of the University of Chicago Press. © 1970 by the University of Chicago.

current spot price, of a 10,000 bushel wheat crop just before the harvest. This farmer is in a long position in the spot market, owning wheat and owing none at all. The farmer can protect the value of this existing inventory (at the spot price of, say, $2.77 per bushel) by selling in the futures market, thereby gaining a short position in it. The farmer's initial moves, we assume, are made on September 5, as indicated at the top of Table 10.5. Various consequences are possible, but we will consider only two:

Case I indicates what would happen if spot and futures prices both fell by equal amounts. While the farmer would lose 12¢ per bushel on the actual wheat (compared to the September 5 price), there would be a gain of 12¢ per bushel on the futures contracts. Thus the farmer in fact would receive $2.77 per bushel.

TABLE 10.5 The Selling Hedge

Spot Market		Futures Market
September 5 Spot price is $2.77 per bushel; farmer owns 10,000 bushels of not-yet-harvested wheat		December futures price is $2.87 per bushel; farmer sells two contracts of December wheat futures (a single grain contract is 5,000 bushels)
Case I		
November 20 Spot price is $2.65 per bushel; farmer sells 10,000 bushels of wheat		December futures price is $2.75 per bushel; farmer buys two contracts of December wheat
Loss: 12¢ per bushel		Gain: 12¢ per bushel
	Net result: 0	
Case II		
November 20 Spot price is $2.87 per bushel; farmer sells 10,000 bushels of wheat		December futures price is $2.97 per bushel; farmer buys two contracts of December wheat
Gain: 10¢ per bushel		Loss: 10¢ per bushel
	Net result: 0	

The **selling hedge** or **short hedge** aims to provide price protection for producers, merchants, and warehousers while they hold inventories of commodities, as they inevitably must.

Case II is analogous to I. It indicates what would happen if spot and futures prices both rose by equal amounts. Once more, the farmer would be successful in "locking in" the pre-harvest price.

Note: If the farmer hadn't hedged at all, the farmer would have lost $1,200 in Case I (compared to September 5) and would have gained $1,000 in Case II. A risk-averse individual may prefer the results of Table 10.5.

The Buying Hedge or Long Hedge. Just as sellers try to assure their revenues, so buyers who need a continuing supply of raw materials can attempt through hedging to assure their costs. Consider a builder who has just contracted to deliver a number of houses a year hence. The contract is based on the current spot prices of raw materials, including 10 carloads of plywood. The builder has, in effect, just sold plywood that isn't owned (and won't have to be bought until construction begins seven months hence). The builder is in a short position in the spot market. The builder could, of course, buy the plywood (and all other materials) right now. But buying now would incur storage, insurance, and interest costs. The builder can instead "lock in" the current spot price by buying a futures contract and taking a long position in that market. Table 10.6 shows the initial moves and two possible consequences:

Case I indicates what would happen if spot and futures prices both rose by equal amounts. While the builder would lose $32 per thousand square feet (MSF) on the actual plywood (compared to the September 5 price), there would be a gain of $32 per MSF on the futures contracts. Thus the builder would, in fact, have "locked in" the plywood at $137 per MSF, a price on which the building contract was based.

Case II indicates what would happen if spot and futures prices both fell by equal amounts. Once again the builder's initial cost estimate would effectively be maintained.

If the builder hadn't hedged at all, the builder's housing construction cost would have been much higher and the profit margin much lower (compared to September 5) in Case I. The opposites would have been true in Case II. Presumably, a risk-averse builder does not desire

TABLE 10.6 The Buying Hedge

	Spot Market	Futures Market
September 5	Spot price is $137 per MSF (1,000 square feet); builder in effect sells 10 carloads of plywood (when signing the building contract)	May futures price is $142 per MSF; builder buys 10 contracts of May plywood futures
Case I		
April 5	Spot price is $169 per MSF; builder buys 10 carloads of plywood (to carry out the construction contract)	May futures price is $174 per MSF; builder sells 10 contracts of May plywood futures
	Loss: $32 per MSF	Gain: $32 per MSF
	Net result: 0	
Case II		
April 5	Spot price is $117 per MSF; builder buys 10 carloads of plywood	May futures price is $122 per MSF; builder sells 10 contracts of May plywood futures
	Gain: $20 per MSF	Loss: $20 per MSF
	Net result: 0	

The **buying hedge** or **long hedge** aims to provide price protection for buyers who plan to buy materials in the future and have already contracted to make future delivery to others of these materials (or of goods made with them).

to speculate in this way on plywood price fluctuations but only wants to protect the projected margin of profit from the building activity, which is what hedging allows.

The Role of Speculation

Speculating is the deliberate taking of long or short positions in spot or futures markets, with the hope that this will lead to profit from price fluctuations. Unlike hedgers, speculators do want price changes to affect their net worth.

Speculators, like hedgers, can work the short or the long side of the market. The speculator anticipating a decline in prices will sell futures at today's levels hoping to follow up this action with a later purchase of futures at a lower price, thus making a profit. The speculator anticipating a rise in prices will buy futures, aiming at a later sale at a higher price and also making a profit. Consider these actual examples:

1. On January 7, 1974, a speculator sold one October, 1974 soybean meal futures contract (100 tons) at $180 per ton. The commodity exchange required a **margin deposit** (a good-faith payment to assure performance on the contract) of 8.33 percent of the full value of the contract; that is, $1,500. On June 14, 1974, the speculator bought an October, 1974 soybean meal futures contract at $101.50 per ton, realizing a gain of $78.50 per ton. The speculator made a profit, in just 5 months, of $7,850 on the invested $1,500.

2. On January 2, 1973, a speculator bought one December, 1973 soybean futures contract at $113.75 per ton. On August 13, 1973, the same contract could be sold at $284.20, at a gain of $170.45 per ton or $17,045 for the contract.

Note: First, gains such as these are far from automatic. Large losses are equally likely. Second, speculators, although often maligned as greedy gamblers, perform an extremely useful social function. Price fluctuations in a market economy are inevitable, and the associated risk must be borne by someone. Speculation permits these risks to be shifted from the producers and merchants of goods to others. Speculators are

willing to assume the risk of price changes for the opportunity of making a profit. Their speculation in commodities is distinguishable from gambling because the risks assumed exist as an inevitable part of marketing commodities, whereas the risks in gambling are created for their own sake.

Besides taking risks off the shoulders of others, speculators normally help smooth out price fluctuations over time. When they buy in times of low prices, they tend to raise prices; when they sell in times of high prices, they tend to lower them—compared, in each case, to what prices would otherwise have been. Nevertheless, speculators are always denounced as "scalpers" who rip off people at times of intense scarcity by selling at high prices. Those critics do not realize that without speculators prices would be higher still. (On rare occasions, speculators do aggravate price fluctuations. The most famous recent example is discussed in Close-Up 10.3, "The Great Silver Squeeze of 1980." An equally

---

CLOSE-UP 10.2:
The Value of Common Cents

In February 1980, the price of May 1980 copper futures at New York's Commodity Exchange reached an all-time high of $1.48 a pound. This worried one buyer of high-grade copper bars, the U.S. Mint. In 1979, the mint had produced 7 billion pennies, each bright new cent weighing 3.11 grams. There are 453.6 grams to the pound, which works out to 145.85 new (unworn) pennies to a pound, or 2.15 cents less than the futures price. When the intrinsic value of the common copper cent exceeds 1¢, people begin to melt down the coins. (Melting down pennies is relatively easy and doesn't require the high temperatures necessary to reduce gold or silver.) While the U.S. Mint was contemplating a ban on unlicensed melting, the Canadian Mint quickly moved to make its 1¢ coins thinner instead.

Source: H. J. Maidenberg, "The Value of Common Cents," *The New York Times*, February 18, 1980, p. D4.

famous ancient example occurred in Holland in the 1630s when new tulip varieties were developed and tulip trading was introduced by the Amsterdam and Rotterdam stock exchanges. For a brief period, a rare type of bulb sold for $10,000 apiece, but the price fell precipitously thereafter.)

The Role of Organized Commodities Exchanges

To facilitate the trading of futures contracts by hedgers and speculators, organized commodities exchanges have been established. The first of these, the Chicago Board of Trade, came into existence in 1848. By now, there are many others, including the Chicago Mercantile Exchange, the Kansas City Board of Trade, the Minneapolis Grain Exchange, the Winnipeg Commodity Exchange, and a number of others in New York: the Amex Commodities Exchange, the Comex or Commodity Exchange, the Coffee, Sugar, and Cocoa Exchange, the Cotton Exchange, the Mercantile Exchange, and, since 1980, the Futures Exchange.

On the floor of these exchanges, exchange members trade, in **open-outcry auctions** (using shouts and hand signals), more than 70 commodities, including: *primary commodities* (such as barley, cattle, cocoa, coffee, corn, cotton, eggs, flax seed, hogs, lumber, oats, pepper, potatoes, rubber, sorghum, soybeans, sugar, wheat, aluminum, copper, gold, lead, platinum, silver, tin, and zinc) and *processed commodities* (such as cottonseed and soybean oil, hides, iced broilers, lard, orange juice, plywood, pork bellies, and wool). Most recently, interest rate futures have been introduced with spectacular success, including U.S. Treasury bills, notes, and bonds; commercial paper; Ginnie Mae (Government National Mortgage Association) contracts; and Eurodollar CDs (certificates of deposit). Plans are underway to create futures markets for many other goods as well, including energy products (such as coal, crude oil, electricity, gasoline, heating oil, and uranium), ocean freight rates, and even whiskey and wine.

Each exchange standardizes the commodities in which it conducts futures trading with the help of detailed contract specifications. At the Chicago Board of Trade, for example, a plywood futures contract calls for a boxcar of 36 banded units of 66 pieces each (2,376 pieces), sized 48″ by 96″ (76,032 square feet total), four or five ply, half-inch thick, exterior glue 32/16, free on board, Portland, Oregon.

The volume of futures trading on all U.S. exchanges has increased rapidly in recent years, from 12 million contracts worth $145 billion in 1970 to 90 million contracts worth $5 trillion in 1980. The ever-changing prices established through this trading reflect the ever-changing knowledge, jointly possessed by all traders, about trends in demand and supply. Every bit of relevant news is immediately reflected in futures prices, whether it is news about a coming recession in U.S. home building, a Congressional defeat of sugar price supports, a drought in Thailand's sugar cane fields, the slow germination of cotton planted in Alabama, the introduction of cocoa stockpiles on the Ivory Coast, labor troubles at El Salvador's coffee-drying plants, Mugabe's victory in platinum-rich Zimbabwe, a political shake-up and transportation breakdown in Uganda, Chinese cotton buying, the disappearance of anchovies from the coast of Peru, a planned orange-juice promotion campaign by a major producer, or Coca Cola's decision to replace sugar with corn sweeteners.

The resulting prices are continually reported in major newspapers around the world. Table 10.7 is an example of a typical futures market page.

Applications

Application 1: Adverse Selection and Moral Hazard

We have seen how risk-averse individuals can improve their welfare with the help of insurance. What about insurance companies? Are they gambling? Not at all. The **law of large numbers** tells

TABLE 10.7 The Futures Market Page

GRAINS & OILS

WHEAT (CBT) 5,000 bu.; $ per bu.

Season High	Season Low	Month	High	Low	Close	Chg.	Open Interest
4.96	3.84½	Jul	4.18	4.14½	4.16½	-.04	19716
5.06	3.98	Sep	4.31	4.27¾	4.29¼	-.03½	10340
5.23½	4.18½	Dec	4.50	4.46	4.47¾	-.04	7912
5.37½	4.33	Mar	4.64	4.62	4.62½	-.04	3254
4.96	4.40½	May	4.70½	4.68	4.68½	-.03½	378
4.75	4.62	Jul	4.63	4.62	4.63	-.05	9

Est. sales 12,112; sales Thur. 14,749.
Total open interest Thur. 41,658, off 285 from Wed.

SOYBEANS (CBT) 5,000 bu.; $ per bu.

Season High	Season Low	Month	High	Low	Close	Chg.	Open Interest
8.57	5.95	Jul	6.33	6.26¾	6.32	+.01¾	37345
8.01½	6.06	Aug	6.39	6.34½	6.38¾	+.00¼	10297
7.95	6.15	Sep	6.47½	6.42¼	6.47	+.00½	4146
7.91	6.31	Nov	6.61	6.55¾	6.60½	-.00¼	22797
7.84½	6.49	Jan	6.74½	6.70½	6.74¼	-.01¾	12064
7.87	6.67½	Mar	6.89	6.85	6.88¾	-.01	8662
7.41½	6.81	May	6.99½	6.96	6.99½	-.01¼	4082
7.12	7.06	Jul	7.08	7.05	7.08	-.01½	154

Est. sales 18,358; sales Thur. 21,878.
Total open interest Thur. 99,584, up 83 from Wed.

SOYBEAN OIL (CBT) 60,000 lb.; ¢ per lb.

Season High	Season Low	Month	High	Low	Close	Chg.	Open Interest
28.80	20.12	Jul	22.25	21.92	22.23	+ .06	25080
28.60	20.40	Aug	22.45	22.14	22.45	+ .08	8078
27.90	20.70	Sep	22.65	22.40	22.65	+ .08	5808
27.65	20.98	Oct	22.85	22.60	22.82	+ .07	5066
27.15	21.37	Dec	23.15	22.90	23.12	+ .05	7320
26.65	21.55	Jan	23.20	23.05	23.20	+ .07	4425
26.95	21.90	Mar	23.50	23.35	23.47	......	2287
27.00	22.35	May	23.65	23.60	23.65	- .10	1131
25.35	22.72	Jul	24.05	23.90	24.05	+ .12	524

Est. sales 8,015; sales Thur. 11,999.
Total open interest Thur. 59,778, up 201 from Wed.

LIVESTOCK

CATTLE, Feeder (CME)
42,000 lb.; ¢ per lb.

Season High	Season Low	Month	High	Low	Close	Chg.	Open Interest
88.00	65.45	Aug	71.30	70.90	71.22	- .05	6689
87.25	65.17	Sep	71.25	70.80	71.25	+ .05	1548
86.80	64.55	Oct	71.10	70.75	70.97	- .08	2817
87.00	65.15	Nov	72.15	1.80	71.97	- .03	1026
75.00	69.10	Jan	.....	.....	73.25	......	43
75.00	72.00	Mar	73.75	73.75	73.75	......	22
75.25	70.00	Apr	.....	.....	74.55	+ .05	48

Est. sales 2,025; sales Fri. 3,687.
Total open interest Fri. 12,215, off 65 from Thur.

PORK BELLIES (CME)
38,000 lb; ¢ per lb.

Season High	Season Low	Month	High	Low	Close	Chg.	Open Interest
58.85	30.90	Jul	32.75	32.00	32.25	- .35	12118
57.80	30.80	Aug	32.45	31.90	32.17	- .18	10662
57.15	45.80	Feb	47.25	46.55	46.85	+ .03	2033
57.50	38.75	Mar	47.00	46.65	46.90	+ .10	236
57.75	46.15	May	47.60	47.30	47.30	- .20	49
49.90	48.00	Jul	48.60	48.00	48.00	+ .05	13
48.90	47.30	Aug	47.85	47.45	47.45	......	19

Est. sales 4,836; sales Thur. 7,149.
Total open interest Thur. 25,245, up 961 from Wed.

ICED BROILERS (CME)
30,000 lb.; ¢ per lb.

Season High	Season Low	Month	High	Low	Close	Chg.	Open Interest
48.00	40.65	Jun	43.10	43.00	43.10	- .25	268
47.50	41.65	Jul	44.60	44.35	44.40	......	246
46.60	41.70	Aug	43.90	43.75	43.90	+ .10	224
44.25	42.00	Oct	42.75	42.75	42.75	+ .20	175
43.95	42.87	Dec	42.90	42.90	42.90	- .10	82

Est. sales 36; sales Thur. 40.
Total open interest Thur. 1,000, off 14 from Wed.

FOODS

COFFEE (NYCSE) 37,500 lb. ¢ per lb.

Season High	Season Low	Month	High	Low	Close	Chg.	Open Interest
215.65	149.25	Jul	203.00	200.0.	200.65	- 1.09	4943
214.78	168.50	Sep	210.40	207.25	208.07	- 1.35	6933
204.50	168.25	Dec	204.50	201.10	201.36	- 1.57	2049
199.00	165.50	Mar	196.95	194.00	194.37	- 1.13	1111
196.50	168.00	May	195.00	193.50	193.86	- 1.39	318
195.50	175.46	Jul	195.50	193.02	193.02	- 1.98	72
195.50	180.25	Sep	195.50	195.25	193.88	- 1.85	28

Est. sales 3,637; sales Thur. 3,190.
Total open interest Thur. 15,454 up 90 from Wed.
Spot 1.85.

EGGS, Shell (CME) 22,500 doz.; ¢ per doz.

Season High	Season Low	Month	High	Low	Close	Chg.	Open Interest
53.95	41.25	Jun	.....	.....	45.00	......	6
51.00	48.00	Jul	.....	.....	48.00	......	1
60.90	54.50	Sep	58.50	58.00	58.50	+ .50	46
56.00	55.45	Oct	.....	.....	55.60	......	1
60.50	59.50	Dec	.....	.....	61.25	......	2
58.20	58.20	Jan	.....	.....	58.20	......	1

Est. sales 1; sales Thur. nil.
Total open interest Thur. 58, off 2 from Wed.

ORANGE JUICE (NYCTN, CA)
15,000 lb.; ¢ per lb.

Season High	Season Low	Month	High	Low	Close	Chg.	Open Interest
113.75	83.70	May	94.55	94.55	94.60	+0.15	263
111.50	83.25	Jul	89.70	89.40	89.50	+0.25	2336
109.30	86.50	Sep	90.55	90.25	90.20	+0.05	1493
105.25	87.80	Nov	91.00	91.00	91.0+	......	618
107.75	87.30	Jan	92.80	92.65	92.80	+0.50	879
107.75	88.00	Mar	93.60	93.60	93.70	+0.20	572
107.90	89.25	May	.....	.....	95.50	+0 15	314
107.50	102.00	Jul	.....	.....	96.10	+0.15	5

Est. sales 120; sales Thur. 103.
Total open interest Thur. 6,480 up 3 from Wed.

SUGAR, World (NYCSE) 112,000 lb.; ¢ per lb.

Season High	Season Low	Month	High	Low	Close	Chg.	Open Interest
36.65	7.60	Jul	36.65	35.60	36.58	+ 1.77	16078
35.65	7.85	Sep	34.99	34.99	34.99	+ 1.00	7553
35.79	10.03	Oct		35.62	35.62	+ 1.00	18720
6.45	17.05	Jan	36.45	36.45	36.45	+ 1.00	158
36.53	13.73	Mar	.....	.....	36.54	+ 1.00	17515
36.33	15.55	May	.....	.....	36.30	+ 1.00	6094
36.09	21.85	Jul	36.00	36.00	36.00	+ 1.00	2978
35.75	27.20	Sep	.....	.....	35.70	+ 1.00	426
35.45	28.75	Oct	.....	.....	35.48	+ 1.00	855

Est. sales 12,550; sales Thur. 14,452.
Total open interest Thur. 70,377 up 838 from Wed.
Sugar No. 11 spot 34.89.

WOOD

LUMBER (CME) 100,000 bd. ft.; $ per 1,000 bd. ft.

Season High	Season Low	Month	High	Low	Close	Chg.	Open Interest
243.60	164.80	Jul	197.80	195.30	197.80	+5.00	3779
245.20	175.00	Sep	205.90	203.00	205.90	+5.00	2672
238.90	172.00	Nov	206.70	202.20	206.70	+5.00	1586
new contracts							
130,00 bd. ft.							
226.50	156.50	Jan	198.40	195.00	198.40	+5.00	1867
228.10	160.00	Mar	211.40	207.50	211.30	+4.80	789
233.50	164.00	May	217.00	214.50	216.40	+4.10	397
225.00	169.00	Jul	221.00	219.50	220.50	+3.00	264
228.00	221.50	Sep	.....	.....	224.20	+2.70	5

PLYWOOD (CBT) 76,032 sq. ft.; $ per 1,000 sq. ft

Season High	Season Low	Month	High	Low	Close	Chg.	Open Interest
209.00	160.20	Jul	193.50	190.20	191.40	+1.70	1771
211.20	164.70	Sep	197.00	194.50	195.00	g-1.70	1236
212.40	166.80	Nov	198.70	196.50	196.80	+1.80	575
214.00	170.50	Jan	203.00	201.50	201.50	+2.20	467
219.00	174.50	Mar	207.00	205.50	205.50	+2.50	584
223.00	178.50	May	211.00	208.50	210.50	+4.00	271
215.00	183.00	Jul	......	......	213.00	+3.50	99
211.00	189.00	Sep	......	......	212.00	+ .5	3

Est. sales 721; sales Thur. 1,022.
Total open interest Thur. 5,006, up 73 from Wed.

METALS

PLATINUM (NYM)
50 troy oz.; $ per troy oz.

Season High	Season Low	Month	High	Low	Close	Chg.	Open Interest
763.5	501.00	May	551.50	551.50	543.80	- 0.50	9
1071.5	315.40	Jul	565.00	547.00	550.80	- 1.50	3224
1113.5	375.50	Oct	569.50	556.00	558.80	- 1.20	1526
1148.5	388.00	Jan	573.50	71.00	569.80	- 1.70	644
1189.5	579.00	Apr	......	......	581.00	.. 2.00	539
655.5	595.00	Jul	......	......	593.00	- 1.00	21

Est. sales 1,012; sales Thur. 865.
Total open interest Thur. 5,973 up 122 from Tues.

SILVER (NYCX) 5,000 troy oz.; ¢ per troy oz.

Season High	Season Low	Month	High	Low	Close	Chg.	Open Interest
4100.00	610.50	May	1195.0	1125.0	1196.0	+036.0	395
1290.00	110.00	Jun	......	......	1198.0	+035.0	14
4240.00	642.40	Jul	1206.0	1135.0	1205.0	+038.0	6748
4280.00	666.00	Sep	1230.0	1170.0	1225.0	+037.0	4532
4437.00	796.00	Dec	1260.0	1200.0	1255.0	+036.0	3001
4183.00	843.50	Jan	1265.0	1250.0	1265.0	+035.0	1654
4493.50	924.00	Mar	1290.0	1265.0	1286.0	+035.0	3523
4530.50	1006.00	•May	1306.0	1305.0	1306.0	+034.0	2154
4357.00	1229.00	Jul	1327.0	1273.0	1327.0	+034.0	1449
4200.00	1254.00	Sep	......	......	1348.0	+034.0	436
4140.00	1340.00	Dec	......	......	1379.0	+034.0	81
4164.00	4164.00	Jan	......	......	1390.0	+034.0	21
1468.00	1328.00	Mar	......	......	1411.0	+034.0	1

Est. sales 2,000; sales Thur. 2,754.
Total open interest Thur. 24,009 off 491 from Wed.

GOLD (IMM) 100 troy oz.; $ per troy oz.

Season High	Season Low	Month	High	Low	Close	Chg.	Open Interest
914.50	226.00	Jun	515.30	509.00	510.30	- 3.90	5085
532.00	507.20	Jul	......	......	514.00	- 4.50	30
938.00	231.70	Sep	527.90	520.00	521.00	- 5.50	4622
550.00	528.00	Oct	......	......	525.00	- 5.50	10
957.50	262.50	Dec	541.00	534.50	535.30	- 3.70	3837
976.00	282.20	Mar	553.00	547.00	549.20	- 2.60	2664
578.00	551.00	Apr	555.80	553.20	553.20	- 2.60	12
993.90	351.70	Jun	566.50	560.00	563.20	- 1.20	3071
1011.20	455.90	Sep	580.00	573.00	577.20	- .20	1933
1031.90	559.10	Dec	592.00	589.00	591.20	+ .50	970
732.00	608.00	Mar	609.00	605.20	605. 0	+ .90	6

Est. sales 3,739; sales Thur. 6,015.
Total open interest Thur. 22,240, off 634 from Wed.

FIBERS

COTTON (NYCTN) 50,000 lb.; ¢ per lb.

Season High	Season Low	Month	High	Low	Close	Chg.	Open Interest
90.67	64.00	Jul	78.45	77.40	77.59	-0.31	12214
90.50	64.25	Oct	76.30	75.30	75.55	-0.04	3753
90.75	66.00	Dec	74.15	73.15	73.46	+0.09	13323
91.00	70.00	Mar	75.25	74.30	74.75	+0.35	5149
92.10	74.80	May	.....	.....	75.55	+0.05	415
81.60	75.50	Jul	77.10	77.00	76.75	+0.55	125
79.95	76.50	Oct	78.00	77.00	77.50	......	4

st. sales 5,550; sales Thur. 10,098.
Total open interest Thur 34,983 off 711 from Wed.

FINANCIAL

LONG-TERM TREAS. BONDS (CBT)
8%–$100,000 prin.; pts. and 32d's of 100%

Season High	Season Low	Month	High	Low	Close	Chg.	Open Interest
95-31	63-15	Jun	81-30	81-04	81-29	+63	9099
95-22	64-05	Sep	81-30	81-03	81-29	+63	16660
95-27	64-24	Dec	81-23	80-26	81-22	+62	11543
95-27	65-14	Mar	81-17	80-19	81-17	+64	8828
94-20	65-04	Jun	81-10	80-08	81-07	+61	7546
92-15	65-25	Sep	81-02	80-08	81-00	g-62	6670
91-18	65-19	Dec	80-28	80-04	80-28	+64	6248
91-15	65-23	Mar	80-23	79-25	80-23	+64	5562
88-08	65-23	Jun	80-19	80-05	80-19	+64	5525
83-09	65-24	Sep	80-16	80-02	80-16	+64	3354
82-16	69-25	Dec	80-13	79-31	80-13	+63	406

Est. sales 22,304; sales Thur. 19,117.
Total open interest Thur. 81,441, up 70 from Wed.

This table shows excerpts from newspaper reports on the May 23, 1980 trading in U.S. futures markets. Next to each commodity is a key to the exchange: CBT = Chicago Board of Trade, CME = Chicago Mercantile Exchange, NYCSE = New York Coffee and Sugar Exchange, NYCTN, CA = New York Cotton Exchange, Citrus Associates, NYCX = Comex or Commodity Exchange in New York, IMM = International Monetary Market of the CME. Then follows the contract size (5,000 bushels in the case of wheat) and the monetary units represented by the figures in the table (dollars per bushel in the case of wheat). Each row then gives, for the stated *future* month, the highest and lowest price contracted during the season and then the highest and lowest price contracted on the Friday of May 23, 1980, the closing price on that day, and the change from the previous trading day's closing price. **Open interest** is the number of contracts outstanding for the stated month and not yet liquidated by delivery of the commodity or by an offsetting contract.

them that what is unpredictable and subject to chance for the individual is predictable and uniform in a mass of like individuals: Nobody knows whether John Doe's house will burn down this year. But if statistics tell us that only 1 of 250 like houses have burned down in the country in each of the past 50 years (and have done so for unrelated reasons), an insurance company that insures a sufficiently large random sample of the population can be virtually certain of the sample's behavior. All else being equal (no nuclear war, no invasion from outer space, no volcanic eruptions), the sample's behavior will be like that of the population at large. The company can, therefore, set premiums in such a way as to cover or more than cover benefits paid out.

Or can it? First, an insurance company must deal with two ageless problems: adverse selection and moral hazard.

Adverse Selection. An insurance company faces the problem of **adverse selection** when those who buy insurance make up a biased sample such that their probability of loss differs markedly and, from the point of view of the insurance company, adversely from the population at large. This problem can arise because of differential access to information similar to the used-car market discussed above. The would-be insured know their own riskiness: whether they are accident prone, subject to hereditary disease, thinking of suicide. The insurance company only knows what is true *on the average* for the population as a whole. If the company offers fair insurance, high-risk people will look upon the premiums as more than fair; low-risk people will see them as less than fair and *may* not buy insurance at all. As a result, it is quite possible for only "lemons" to seek out insurance!

Figure 10.6 graphically illustrates the insurance company's problem of adverse selection. Imagine that all people had the utility function shown in this graph and also owned an identical amount of $25,000 initially. All people also face the same potential loss of $20,000, but two equal-sized classes of people exist when it comes to probabilities. Class I people are low-risk; their

probability of loss is only 0.2. Class II people are high-risk; their probability of loss is 0.8.

An uninsured class I person, therefore, faces a gamble between $5,000 (with a probability of 0.2) and $25,000 (with a probability of 0.8). The expected monetary value of the gamble equals $21,000. Such a person's expected utility corresponds to point C on dashed line AB. Such a person would be delighted to buy fair insurance; that is, pay a premium of $4,000 and have a certain utility corresponding to point D (which exceeds C).

An uninsured class II person, on the other hand, faces a gamble between $5,000 (with a probability of 0.8) and $25,000 (with a probability of 0.2). The expected monetary value of this gamble equals $9,000. Such a person's expected utility corresponds to point E, and such a person

FIGURE 10.6 Adverse Selection

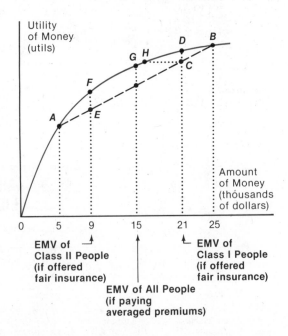

EMV of Class II People (if offered fair insurance)

EMV of All People (if paying averaged premiums)

EMV of Class I People (if offered fair insurance)

Under some conditions, it is quite possible for low-risk people *not* to insure and for high-risk people only to insure. Such an adversely selected population sample leads to insurance company losses.

would gladly pay a premium of $16,000 for fair insurance, thereby gaining certain utility corresponding to *F*.

The insurance company, unfortunately, may not be able to tell who is class I and who is class II. If it issued fair insurance, it would charge everyone the *average* premium of $10,000, thereby giving everyone an expected monetary value of $15,000. This would delight class II people. They would be getting more-than-fair insurance. They would buy insurance, getting utility corresponding to *G* instead of *F* (and, as we saw, *F* already was preferred to uninsured utility at *E*). All this would, however, dismay

---

CLOSE-UP 10.3:

The Great Silver Squeeze of 1980

The most dramatic series of events ever to happen on the commodities exchanges reached a climax in 1980. Speculators bought large numbers of futures contracts for silver, gradually running up the futures price from $6 per ounce in the spring of 1979 to a peak of more than $50 per ounce in January, 1980. These speculators included the oil-rich Hunt brothers of Texas (Nelson Bunker, William Herbert, and Lamar), but they were not alone. Conticommodity Services (the brokerage arm of the Continental Grain Company), Kuwaiti "oil interests," and Hong Kong "elements" were playing the same game.

Normally, only a small percentage of futures trading leads to delivery of a commodity. Rather, the majority of contracts are matched up on the exchange floor before their expiration date: Speculators with long positions, for example, liquidate their rights to receive commodities by selling their contracts (hopefully at a higher price), while hedgers with short positions close out their positions by buying contracts, as illustrated in Table 10.5. In January, 1980, when open interest amounted to 105,187 contracts, or about 526 million ounces of silver, and when merchants had registered the availability of only 77 million ounces, however, speculators gave every impression of planning to take actual delivery of the metal. They had *cornered* the market: Because the holders of short positions couldn't deliver what didn't exist, the speculators could insist on astronomical prices for giving up their contracts.

The directors of New York's Comex and Chicago's Board of Trade, where silver futures are traded, however, intervened. They limited each trader's allowable futures position to 600 contracts, restricted trading to the liquidation of contracts, raised margin deposits, and even suspended silver trading altogether. After its January peak, the price of silver futures plunged to about $10 per ounce in March. (Can you find evidence for this in Table 10.7?)

Brokers made **margin calls** requiring their speculating customers (the value of whose contract holdings was declining) to make additional good-faith cash deposits. This was bad for the Hunts, who at one point held more than $1 *billion* in silver contracts. By March, they couldn't meet a margin call, but by May 1980, they arranged a credit line of $1.1 billion with a group of 13 major U.S. banks to pay off their silver debts. In return for the favor, they had to sell 63 million ounces of silver and coal properties in North Dakota and Montana; they had to mortgage everything—from cotton plantations in Mississippi, parking lots in downtown Anchorage, Alaska, and the family jewel (the Placid Oil Company) to a bowling alley and shopping center in Dallas, interests in World Championship Tennis, 500 thoroughbred horses, and 75,000 heads of cattle. Even personal items had to be put in hock, from the furniture in Bunker's Kentucky farm house to Herbert's Greek and Roman statues to Lamar's Rolex watch and Mercedes-Benz!

Note: The Hunts themselves vehemently denied that they had ever intended to corner the silver market.

Sources: *The New York Times*, January 22, 1980, pp. D1 and 7; March 29, 1980, pp. 29 and 32; April 22, 1980, pp. D1 and 10; May 28, 1980, pp. D1 and 7; *The Wall Street Journal*, May 27, 1980, pp. 1 and 35. For the Hunts' side of the story, *see* Roy Rowan, "A Talkfest With the Hunts," *Fortune*, August 11, 1980, pp. 163–68.

class I people. They would be getting less-than-fair insurance. In *this* example, they would not buy it, for the utility corresponding to G is below H (which corresponds to that received without insurance at C).

As a result, the insurance company will get all the lemons (class II people), and it will make losses. It will raise premiums but thereby drive low-risk people away all the more!

One possible solution is this: Low-risk people might *signal* to the company that they are low-risk people by offering to accept high deductibles in their policies, a type of behavior irrational for high-risk people. (A **deductible** is a fixed dollar amount by which any insurance company benefit payment falls short of a loss suffered by an insured.) Or the low-risk people might offer to buy **coinsurance**, an arrangement whereby they commit themselves to shoulder a fixed percentage (rather than a fixed dollar amount) of any loss. In either case, the insurance company could *screen* applicants by their willingness to accept deductibles and coinsurance, and it could offer lower premiums to these people.

Moral Hazard.   An insurance company faces the problem of **moral hazard** when those who have bought insurance subsequently change their behavior in such a way as to increase the probability of the occurrence of any loss or of a larger loss. Once insured, people might relax protective measures and be less careful about their lives, health, and physical wealth. Insurance companies look upon this as something akin to fraud, but economists are more likely to view this ''unwillingness to uphold moral values'' as the simple result of the law of downward-sloping demand: Once having bought health insurance, for example, a person will view medical services as being offered at a low or zero price and will naturally demand a larger quantity.

Insurance companies attempt to counteract moral hazard by increasing people's incentive to avoid claims. They can do this, again, by using deductibles and coinsurance. They can include cancellation provisions, as when life insurance becomes invalid in the case of suicide or when fire insurance becomes invalid in the case of arson. They can reward people for loss-prevention behavior, as when premiums for burglary, flood, or life insurance are reduced when people, respectively, install alarm systems, build dikes, or refrain from smoking.

Application 2:
Technical Advance and the Entrepreneur

As we noted earlier, Frank H. Knight stimulated many of the advances that led to our current understanding of behavior under uncertainty. His notion that profit was somehow a reward for the way a special type of person acts in the face of uncertainty is another case in point. Joseph A. Schumpeter (see Biography 10.2) called such a person an **entrepreneur**, and he attributed the capitalist economy's remarkable rate of technical advance to this type of person.

Economic Growth and Technical Advance. Consider the fact that the U.S. real gross national product has grown more than 11-fold during this century. Measured at 1958 prices, the nation's output has grown from a mere $72 billion in 1900 to $826 billion in 1976. This comes to an average annual rate of growth of almost 3.3 percent. Economists have studied the reasons for this performance. They have found that it cannot be explained merely by similar increases in inputs, such as labor hours, human capital, or physical capital. The *ratio* of total output to total inputs has risen over time. Economists have attributed the difference between the observed increase in total output and the smaller hypothetical increase that could have been expected as a result of observed increases in inputs to **technical advance**, an improvement in known methods of production. Table 10.8 summarizes the results of one major study of the sources of U.S. economic growth.

Technical Advance and the Production Function. Technical advance makes it possible to meet old wants in entirely new ways, either with

TABLE 10.8   The Sources of U.S. Economic Growth

Factors Responsible for Observed Growth	Percentage of Growth Rate Explained by Given Factor	
	1909-1929	1929-1969
Increased labor hours	39	27
Increased human capital (education)	13	12
Increased physical capital	26	15
Technical advance	(12)	(28)
Others	10	18

As the encircled numbers indicate, technical advance during this century explains a significant (and increasing) proportion of the U.S. rate of economic growth.

SOURCE: Derived from information in Edward F. Denison, *The Sources of Economic Growth in the United States and the Alternatives Before Us* (New York: Committee for Economic Development, 1962) and idem, *Accounting for United States Economic Growth 1929-1969* (Washington, D.C.: Brookings Institution, 1974).

the help of new products or by producing old products in new ways. The appearance of new products can be viewed as the birth of a new production function; producing an old product in a new way can be viewed as a fundamental change in a pre-existing production function. In Table 5.1, "A Simple Production Function" (p. 111), technical advance can be depicted as an event that left all data in columns (1) and (2) unchanged but raised those in column (3). This increase in column (3) data, of course, is equivalent to a decrease in column (1) and (2) data while column (3) data remain unchanged. Again, in Figure 5.2, "Isoquants" (p. 118), technical advance can be viewed as a relabeling, with larger output numbers, of all isoquants. The 488-bushel, 977-bushel, and 1,668-bushel figures might, for example, be replaced with 977-bushel, 1,954-bushel, and 3,337-bushel labels. Note: Such technical advance makes it possible to produce any given output at lower cost, all else being equal.

Invention Vs. Innovation. The birth of new production functions or the change of old ones should not, however, be confused with **invention**, the intellectual act of generating a new idea. An act of invention may be the random result of hard work by gifted individuals who, driven by curiosity, work with little assistance and few resources. That's how the incandescent light bulb, the reaper, and the telegraph were invent-

ed. Yet invention today is less likely to emerge from the long, slow process of unsystematic trial and error engaged in by independent tinkerers. The first industrial research laboratory in the United States was established as late as 1876 by Thomas Edison. Nowadays, there are thousands of such laboratories, each one engaged in the *systematic* derivation of new knowledge. These laboratories carry on **basic research**, scientific inquiry not directed toward any specific "useful" discovery. Biologists may study why cells proliferate; physicists may study the laws of motion. Such laboratories also carry on **applied research**, the application to a particular problem of the knowledge gained in basic research. Biological principles may now be applied to the creation of new varieties of plants or animals, physical principles to the design of new computers and communications via satellites.

Yet all this research has no effect on economic growth! Another step is needed: Someone must be the first to put new ideas to practical use; this person must move, so to speak, from the laboratory to the field or factory bench and translate inventions into new products, new qualities of old products, or new processes of production. Such an act of **innovation** is carried out by Schumpeter's **entrepreneur**. An entrepreneur is not like a manager-bureaucrat who keeps an established firm running in routine ways. Such a person rather employs imagination and daring, introduces commercially something that has

BIOGRAPHY 10.2:

Joseph A. Schumpeter

Joseph Alois Schumpeter (1883–1950) was born in Triesch, Moravia. His study of law and economics at the University of Vienna was followed by a varied career as banker, jurist, Austrian Minister of Finance (1919–20), and professor at the Universities of Czernowitz, Graz, and Bonn. When Hitler came to power, he emigrated and became a professor at Harvard University. Just before his death, he was honored with the presidency of the American Economic Association.

Schumpeter was well versed not only in economics, but in history, linguistics, mathematics, philosophy, and sociology. His writings have a broad scope, which is rare in this century. This scope is most evident in his last book, *History of Economic Analysis* (1954), a truly monumental scholarly achievement. Schumpeter is best known, however, for his views on the entrepreneur (noted in this chapter) and for his grand vision of capitalism. In *The Theory of Economic Development* (1912) and in the two-volume *Business Cycles: A Theoretical, Historical, and Statistical Analysis of the Capitalist Process* (1939) he assigns a key role to risk-taking entrepreneurs. Their innovations, along with imitations, Schumpeter argues, produce bursts of investment at irregular intervals, and hence business cycles. They also produce, in the long run, an ever-growing stream of new products at decreasing cost and thus a progressive increase in the economic welfare of the masses. Says Schumpeter:

> The capitalist engine is first and last an engine of mass production which unavoidably means also production for the masses. . . . Queen Elizabeth owned silk stockings. The capitalist achievement does not typically consist in providing more silk stockings for queens but in bringing them within the reach of factory girls in return for steadily decreasing amounts of effort.[1]

Yet Schumpeter also believed that capitalism harbored within itself the seeds for its own destruction. Unlike Marx, he did not think that it would break down under its failures (and by violent revolution), but rather because of its success (and by peaceful evolution). In his *Capitalism, Socialism and Democracy* (1942), Schumpeter predicts that capitalism would fall victim to the very organizations to which it gave birth: In large corporations, the daring entrepreneur will be replaced by the "organization man" (a bureaucrat)

never been tried before, and, in the process, deliberately accepts great risk.

The "Gale of Creative Destruction." As Schumpeter saw it, risk-taking entrepreneurs, who introduce successful innovations, temporarily become single sellers, or monopolists. They introduce products that never existed before, or they produce old products at reduced cost, making it impossible for established firms to compete. Yet over time, the monopoly is ended as a swarm of imitators also introduces the new product or process. Thus, in a "gale of creative destruction," old products and processes disappear, and technical advance is diffused throughout the economy. And the innovating entrepreneurs, if their innovations prove a success, are rewarded for their risk bearing with economic profit, at least temporarily.

Thus Schumpeter viewed competition in the capitalist economy as the sequential creation and destruction of monopolies: the stagecoach being replaced by the railroad, the railroad by the automobile, the automobile by airplanes, and airplanes, perhaps, by rocketships.

Application 3:
Marketing Weather Forecasts

As we noted earlier, people might deal with uncertainty by searching for information. Such search might involve the purchase of information

or by the committee, which will dampen the innovative zeal. In addition, rising affluence will support a large class of intellectuals who will not appreciate the system. The argument for capitalism, Schumpeter says, is long-run' and rational. The system is capable of generating impressive economic growth and pouring out an avalanche of consumption goods. Most people, however, are concerned with the short-run and emotional. They focus not on long-run material progress (from which they themselves benefit so much), but on short-run instabilities and inequalities in income (which are an inevitable by-product of the perennial "gale of creative destruction" brought about by technology-advancing entrepreneurs). Before long, a coalition of anti-business intellectuals, government bureaucrats, and labor unions—intent on taming the business cycle and eliminating income inequalities—will smother the capitalist engine with interventionist policies that will discourage the innovator once and for all.

[1]Joseph A. Schumpeter, *Capitalism, Socialism, and Democracy*, 3rd ed. (New York: Harper & Row, 1962), p. 67.

from others. For example, the farmer's dilemma, illustrated in Table 10.1, could be resolved with a perfect weather forecast. If such a forecast could be produced and it predicted much rain, the farmer would take action A_1 (and collect $25,000). If the forecast predicted little rain, the farmer would take action A_2 (and collect $15,000). A private producer of such a forecast would, however, not divulge the content of the forecast without first being paid for it. How much would the farmer be willing to pay in advance of being told?

The Demand Side. The farmer would have to replace the subjective probabilities about the states of the world (given as 0.5 each in the

earlier table) with different probabilities relating to the likely content of the forecast. Suppose the farmer judged the probability of a "heavy rain" forecast to be 0.9 and the probability of a "light rain" forecast to be 0.1. The expected monetary value of the farmer's actions would then be $24,000 or the sum of (0.9)$25,000 (the farmer's net income from action A_1, which would be taken after a "heavy rain" forecast) plus (0.1)$15,000 (the farmer's net income from action A_2, which would be taken after a "light rain" forecast).

Presumably, the farmer would pay a maximum of $9,000 for a perfect forecast because $9,000 is the difference between the expected monetary values of the farmer's actions with a perfect forecast ($24,000) and without a perfect forecast ($15,000).

The Supply Side. Suppose someone could produce such a perfect forecast for $9,000 or less and offer it to our farmer: What if there were lots of farmers like our friend? Could a producer of weather information collect a maximum of $9,000 from each? This is unlikely. Because each farmer would know that he or she could get the information from any one of the others, no farmer would buy it; therefore, it probably wouldn't be produced!

Why *probably*? A producer of forecasts who could not sell the information directly might still be able to appropriate the value of the forecast by suppressing the information and taking actions such as the following:

a. If the future weather (known as yet only to the forecaster) promised a large crop and very low future spot prices, the forecaster could become a speculator and sell futures contracts for this crop at their presently still-high prices and liquidate the contracts by later buying at the lower prices.

b. If the future weather (known as yet only to the forecaster) promised a small crop and very high future spot prices, the forecaster could buy futures contracts at the presently still-low prices and liquidate the contracts by later selling at the higher prices.

Note: The very activity of selling futures

CLOSE-UP 10.4:

The Commodity Futures Trading Commission

The Commodity Futures Trading Commission was established in 1975. Its task, similar to that of the Securities and Exchange Commission (founded in 1934), was the surveillance of futures markets in order to avert fraudulent practices. In the wake of the Great Silver Squeeze of 1980 (see Close-Up 10.3) the Commission asked Congress for power to regulate the size of margin deposits for futures contracts. As the accompanying table shows, these deposits, as set by the exchanges, were rather low. The exchanges opposed such regulation, arguing that a margin deposit was not a cash down payment but merely good-faith money to bind a contract.

Commodity	Contract Size	Initial Margin Deposit for Speculators[a]
Cattle (feeder)	42,000 pounds	$ 2,000
Coffee "C"	37,500 pounds	15,000
Copper	25,000 pounds	4,000
Cotton No. 2	50,000 pounds	3,500
Gold	100 troy ounces	12,000
Silver	5,000 troy ounces	40,000
Sugar	112,000 pounds	8,000
Treasury bills	$1 million face value	5,000
Treasury bonds	$100,000 face value	6,000

[a]Margin deposits for hedgers were much lower.

Source: "Margins for Selected Futures Contracts," May 26, 1980. © 1980 by the New York Times Company. Reprinted by permission.

short (or buying them long) would immediately tend to depress (or raise) the futures prices of this crop. In this way, the weather forecaster's private knowledge would be revealed to the world! Although they would not be given the reason, millions of others who were interested in this crop would be told to expect lower (or higher) prices in the future. Futures markets truly are windows on the future!

SUMMARY

1. When people possess less than complete knowledge relevant to their decision making, they operate under uncertainty. One must distinguish *primary* or *event uncertainty* from *secondary* or *market uncertainty*. People can cope with uncertainty by entering contingent claim markets, searching for information, or operating in futures markets.

2. Economists assume that people seek to maximize not the expected *monetary value* but the expected *utility* of their actions, as explained in the discussion of the St. Petersburg paradox.

3. People will have one of three different attitudes toward risk: risk aversion, risk neutrality, or risk seeking.

4. The existence of risk aversion gives rise to a demand for and supply of insurance.

5. The existence of risk seeking, in contrast, gives rise to a demand for and supply of gambling.

6. Risk averters do not always buy insurance, while they avoid gambling. Risk seekers do not always gamble, while they avoid buying insurance. What either will do depends on whether the insurance or gambles they confront are more than fair, fair, or unfair. As the Friedman-Savage hypothesis indicates, some people may even buy insurance and gamble simultaneously.

7. When people are confronted by uncertainty of the market rather than uncertainty of events, they can try to overcome their ignorance of the facts by searching for information already possessed by other people. They may engage in the search for price, the search for quality, signaling, or screening.

8. When market uncertainty is caused by ignorance not about present facts, but about the future, people can sometimes dispel the uncertainty with the help of futures markets. These markets serve to redistribute uncertainty over the population, from hedgers who wish to minimize price risk to speculators who wish to assume it. Because price fluctuations in a market economy are inevitable, speculators perform extremely useful functions in shouldering price risks and (normally) smoothing out price fluctuations over time. Organized commodities exchanges facilitate the trading of futures contracts by hedgers and speculators.

9. The analysis of uncertainty has a number of wider applications, including: the problems of adverse selection and moral hazard, the role of risk-taking entrepreneurs in economic growth, and the marketing of information.

KEY TERMS

adverse selection
applied research
basic research
buying hedge
coinsurance
contingent-claim markets
deductible
entrepreneur
event uncertainty
expected monetary value *(EMV)*
fair gamble
fair insurance
futures markets
hedging
innovation
invention
Knightian risk
Knightian uncertainty
law of large numbers
long hedge
long position
margin calls
margin deposit
market uncertainty
mathematical expectation
moral hazard
objective probability
open interest

open-outcry auctions
primary uncertainty
risk
risk aversion
risk neutrality
risk seeking
screening
search
secondary uncertainty
selling hedge
short hedge
short position
signaling
speculating
spot markets
subjective probability
technical advance
uncertainty

QUESTIONS AND PROBLEMS

1. Calculate the expected monetary value for each of these games from your point of view:

    a. We flip a coin; if heads appears, I get $1 from you; if tails appears, you get $1 from me.

    b. We flip a coin; if heads appears, I get $1 from you; if tails appears, you get $10 from me.

How much would you pay me for the privilege of playing either game?

2. Psychiatrists distinguish calculated risk taking from neurotic risk taking. The former, they say, involves conscious deliberation, planning and training, the positive goal of personal achievement, and the taking of responsibility for the outcome (at least in part). The latter, they say, involves no deliberation, no planning and preparation, but the negative goal of escaping from something and letting pure chance determine the outcome. Which of these types of risk taking (if either) fits the astronaut, the cigarette smoker, the drug addict, the entrepreneur, the gambler, the hedger, the insurance company, the speculator?

3. Consider Figure 10.2.

    a. Prove that the risk averter pictured in panel (a) would be even more averse to an equally probable $3,000 or $27,000 prospect than to the $5,000 or $25,000 one shown there.

    b. How would this person value an equally probable $3,000 or $16,000 prospect? A prospect providing a probability of 0.2 for $3,000 and of 0.8 for $16,000?

    c. Prove that the risk seeker pictured in panel (c) would be even more thrilled about an equally probable $3,000 or $27,000 prospect than about the $5,000 or $25,000 one shown there.

4. Take another look at Figure 10.5, which involved an insurance purchase that replaced a gamble between C and A with the certainty of D, as well as a gamble that replaced the certainty of A with a gamble between D and E. Reread the discussion and determine whether

    a. the insurance was fair or unfair.

    b. the gamble was fair or unfair.

5. Consider Table 10.5. Work out the consequences for two other cases and prove that hedging need not be foolproof.

    a. Imagine a Case III in which (on November 20) the spot price equals $2.82 and the December futures price equals $2.85 per bushel.

    b. Imagine a Case IV in which (on November 20) the spot price equals $2.71 and the December futures price equals $2.94 per bushel.

6. Some economists have suggested that one might take notice of uncertain future *preferences* by creating markets for claims contingent on tastes. Suppose you were contemplating a trip at some time in your life to a scenic wonder similar to Yellowstone Park. If you were sure of going, you might wish to make sure that the scenic wonder was still there in the future (and wasn't going to be destroyed in the meantime by, say, uranium strip mining). Then you might be willing to pay, say, $100 for the option to purchase

an entrance ticket in 20 years at a price specified now. Yet you might judge the probability of going to be 0.2 and that of not going to be 0.8. In the case of not going you wouldn't want to pay a cent for the option. Do you think one could set up a market here in which the owners of Scenic Wonder could sell contingency claims to potential future visitors now, thereby allowing the voice of future generations to speak and to provide enough money to resist would-be uranium miners? (*Hint*: think of moral hazard.)

7. In the 1860s, Gilbert, Henry, and Maxwell developed the theory of electromagnetism. In the 1880s, Hertz conducted laboratory demonstrations of the production and detection of wireless waves. In 1897, Marconi introduced the radio, based on the former work. Which one of these was an entrepreneur? Explain.

8. Consider a perfectly competitive industry in long-run equilibrium. With the help of graphs, similar to Figure 7.5, ''Long-Run Industry Supply Curves'' (p. 197), illustrate the ''gale of creative destruction'' that might be unleashed by a Schumpeterian entrepreneur.

SELECTED READINGS

Akerlof, George A. ''The Market for 'Lemons': Quality Uncertainty and the Market Mechanism.'' *The Quarterly Journal of Economics*, August 1970, pp. 488–500.

    A seminal article on which this chapter's discussion of quality uncertainty is based.

Arrow, Kenneth J. *Essays in the Theory of Risk-Bearing*. Chicago: Markham, 1971.

    Twelve essays from the intermediate to the advanced level. *See also* Arrow's presidential address to the American Economic Association: ''Limited Knowledge and Economic Analysis.'' *The American Economic Review*, March 1974, pp. 1–10.

Bernoulli, Daniel. ''Exposition of a New Theory on the Measurement of Risk.'' *Econometrica*, January 1954, pp. 23–36.

    A translation of Bernoulli's original solution (1738) of the St. Petersburg paradox.

Fellner, William. *The Economics of Technical Advance*. New York: General Learning Press, 1971.

A superb discussion of the meaning, measurement, and implications of technical progress.

Friedman, Milton and Savage, L. J. "The Utility Analysis of Choices Involving Risk." *Journal of Political Economy*, August 1948, 279–304. Reprinted in George J. Stigler and Kenneth E. Boulding, eds. *Readings in Price Theory*. Homewood, Ill.: Irwin, 1952, chap. 3.

The source of this chapter's discussion of the Friedman-Savage hypothesis. For recent empirical evidence in support of the hypothesis, see Gregory G. Brunk, "A Test of the Friedman-Savage Gambling Model," *The Quarterly Journal of Economics,* May 1981, pp. 341–48.

Harris, Seymour E., ed. *Schumpeter: Social Scientist.* Cambridge: Harvard University Press, 1951.

A collection of 20 essays on the life and work of Schumpeter.

Hirshleifer, Jack. "Speculation and Equilibrium: Information, Risk, and Markets." *The Quarterly Journal of Economics*, November 1975, pp. 519–42.

Argues that the literature on uncertainty is preoccupied with price risks while ignoring quantity risks. *See also* the discussion of this article in the November 1976 issue of the same journal, pp. 667–96.

Hirshleifer, Jack and Riley, John G. "The Analytics of Uncertainty and Information—An Expository Survey." *Journal of Economic Literature*, December 1979, pp. 1375–1421.

An excellent summary of the literature.

Meade, James E. *The Theory of Indicative Planning.* Manchester, England: Manchester University Press, 1970; idem. *The Controlled Economy.* London: Allen and Unwin, 1971.

Superb discussions of uncertainty and of reducing it via national economic planning.

Samuelson, Paul A. "St. Petersburg Paradoxes: Defanged, Dissected, and Historically Described." *Journal of Economic Literature*, March 1977, pp. 24–55.

Seligman, Ben B. *Main Currents in Modern Economics*, vol. 3. Chicago: Quadrangle, 1962, pp. 646–65 and 694–713.

Critical reviews of the work of Knight and Schumpeter.

Spence, Michael. "Job Market Signaling." *The Quarterly Journal of Economics*. August 1973, pp. 355–74.

The first article on the subject.

Stigler, George. "The Economics of Information." *Journal of Political Economy*, June 1961, pp. 213–25; idem. "Information in the Labor Market." *Journal of Political Economy*, October 1962, pp. 94–105.

The first articles on search.

CHAPTER 11

Monopoly and Cartels

Barring gifts or loans from other societies, the people of any society (as a group) can increase the yearly flow of goods available to them in only one of three ways:

1. People can utilize the existing stocks of their resources at a higher rate. That is, they can opt for less leisure and less conservation of capital and natural resources.

2. People can increase the size of their resource stocks and then use them at the accustomed rate. For example, they can trade in lowered current consumption for greater investment in human and physical capital.

3. People can increase their productivity. Risk-bearing entrepreneurs, for example, can make innovative changes that coax a larger flow of goods from identical resource flows.

In an economy with perfect markets, what is true for people as a group is also true for every individual. Barring the receipt of gifts or loans from other people, every individual who wishes to have an increased command over goods must do one of the three things just mentioned. In an economy with perfect markets, every individual who wishes to have a larger piece of the pie and who cannot get it through gifts or loans must engage in an activity that enlarges the pie itself. In the absence of perfect markets, on the other

hand, there is another way for individuals to increase their command over goods.

Regardless of the type of market prevailing, all individuals as a group can never get more goods unless the overall quantity of goods is larger. When markets are imperfect, however, a subset of all people can get more even from a constant or shrinking pie—at the expense of other people. In imperfect markets, some people can get more goods at others' expense through a cunning alteration of the prices at which exchanges take place. To the extent that individuals can raise the prices of things being sold or reduce the prices of things being bought purchasing power can be transferred to these manipulators of prices.

When all markets are perfect, no person, of course, has the power to manipulate prices in such a manner because trading partners have plenty of alternatives open to them. If any one seller, for example, tried to dictate a price above the competitive equilibrium level, all buyers would disappear. Buyers could find many other sellers able and willing to supply, at the competitive equilibrium price, as much as they wanted of any good. But now consider this: What if a seller were able to kill off competition in whatever was for sale (and in its close substitutes as well)? What if there were no other sellers or at least no other independently acting ones? In this situation, buyers would be trapped. Instead of finding innumerable sellers, buyers would find only a single seller (or a group of sellers acting as one). Buyers would be confronted by a **monopoly**, an industry that has only a single seller and the product of which has no close substitutes, or by a **cartel**, a group of conspiring sellers acting as one and making joint price-quantity decisions with a view toward earning a larger profit than competition would allow. This chapter will consider the effects of monopolies and cartels in the markets for goods; Chapter 13 will consider imperfectly competitive markets for resource services.

The Sources of Monopoly Power

Monopoly power is the ability of a seller to raise the price of something that is for sale above the perfectly competitive level. This power can originate from a number of technological and legal sources, including increasing returns to scale, exclusive ownership of key resources, patents and copyrights, and exclusive franchises.

Increasing Returns to Scale

Consider an industry subject to increasing returns to scale. As noted in Chapter 5, under such conditions, a simultaneous and equal percentage change in the use of all physical inputs leads to a larger percentage change in physical output. Chapter 6 showed how an increase in scale under such conditions of increasing returns shifts average-total (and marginal) cost curves not only to the right, but also down (see Figure 6.8, "Short-Run Vs. Long-Run Costs" on p. 163). This shift is now illustrated, with respect to a hypothetical producer of electric power, in Figure 11.1 which depicts a producer who is capable of setting up a multitude of different-sized power plants. Design number 41, for example, yields short-run average-total-cost curve $SRATC_{41}$, design number 71 yields curve $SRATC_{71}$, and so on, until design number 112 produces the optimum plant, the one that has taken advantage of all available economies of scale and yields the low-

est possible minimum average total cost (at point m). The firm's long-run average-total-cost curve $LRATC$, therefore, is the color envelope curve labeled $LRATC$. Whenever long-run average total cost is in this way declining throughout the range of possible quantities demanded in the market (as shown here by market demand line AB), the situation is one of **natural monopoly**.

The assumed technical facts—not uncommon for producers of electric power, gas, water, and telephone service—enable a single firm to produce more cheaply than two or more firms. The first firm to recognize and take advantage of such increasing returns to scale can profitably supply the entire market (instead of a negligible fraction thereof), while keeping additional firms out of the market by the certain prospect of losses. Consider how such a firm might design and construct plant number 71, produce 300 million kilowatt hours at 4.4 cents each (point a) and sell them at 7 cents each (point b). Any potential rival, in order to meet the 7 cents per kilowatt hour price, would have to construct a

FIGURE 11.1 The Natural Monopoly

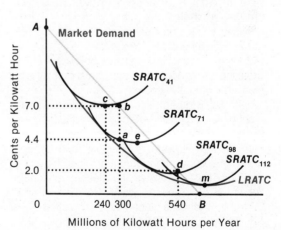

Whenever long-run average total cost is declining throughout the range of possible quantities demanded in the market, the first firm expanding its scale sufficiently to supply the entire market may secure for itself a natural monopoly.

plant of size number 41 at least and run it at its optimal rate (point c). All else being equal, such extra output of 240 million kilowatt hours would raise total quantity supplied to 540 million kilowatt hours, a quantity that could not be sold for more than 2 cents per kilowatt hour (point d). This price would inevitably engulf the new and the old firm in losses. (Both c and e, the minimum average total costs associated with plants 41 and 71, respectively, clearly exceed 2 cents.) These losses would be even larger should the potential newcomer build a plant as large as or larger than number 71, for the resultant market supply could not even be sold at the lowest of all possible average total costs, corresponding to point m. This sort of analysis would keep newcomers at bay, or this sort of scenario would, eventually, allow only one firm to survive. Monopoly need not, however, be the result of technical factors.

Exclusive Ownership of Key Resources

Sometimes firms become the only sellers in their industry because they have exclusive ownership of a key resource without which the industry's product cannot be produced. The Aluminum Company of America (Alcoa) once controlled most domestic bauxite deposits (from which aluminum is made), and it also controlled many strategic water power sites capable of generating the massive electric power needed for aluminum ingot production. American Metal Climax once controlled 90 percent of the world's molybdenum (all of it in one Colorado mountain); the International Nickel Company once owned a similar percentage of the world's nickel. And the de Beers Company of South Africa (see Close-Up 11.2) owns or leases most of the diamond mines in the world.

The exclusive ownership conducive to monoply need not necessarily involve natural resources, however. Consider why New York's Met long held a monopoly in American opera: all the experienced singers available were under long-run contracts to the Met. Professional baseball and football clubs, similarly, sign up all the talented players, making life rather impossible for potential competitors. The same kind of advantage would also accrue to any firm that could sign up all the possessors of some secret production recipe similar, perhaps, to that of making a genuine Stradivarius violin. On that account, however, government nowadays provides a helping hand.

Patents and Copyrights

Government frequently promotes the establishment of monopoly when it issues patents and copyrights. A **patent** is an exclusive right to the

---

CLOSE-UP 11.1:

Monopoly in "Monopoly"

Around 1900, Elizabeth Magee of Virginia devised "The Landlord's Game." Many versions of it were played for years. Eventually, Parker Brothers acquired the rights to the game, called it "Monopoly", and sold more than 80 million copies worldwide. In 1973, the monopoly in "Monopoly" was challenged. Ralph Anspach, professor of economics at San Francisco State, invented a new game, which he called "Anti-Monopoly". The object of the game was not the building but the breaking of monopolies. The game quickly sold more than 400,000 copies.

Parker Brothers filed suit, claiming infringement of its trademark. Anspach, Inc. filed a countersuit, claiming that the Parker Brothers trademark was invalid, that "Monopoly" had become part of the English language, and that the use of this word was free to all, like Kleenex or aspirin. Yet, in 1977, a court ruled in favor of Parker Brothers. Under the gleeful eyes of its officials, all remaining 7,000 "Anti-Monopoly" games were buried in a Minnesota landfill.

Source: *The New York Times*, June 12, 1976, p. 33 and July 6, 1977, p. D9.

use of an invention. It is limited to a period of 17 years and permits the holder to prevent all others from producing a specified product or using a specified process. Patents are, of course, granted in order to encourage the production and disclosure of inventions and to stimulate innovation that is often risky and expensive to undertake but all too easy and cheap for others to copy. Many monopolies in the past have been based on patents, including patents for such products or processes as aluminum, cash registers, cellophane, instant photographic pictures, rayon, scotch tape, shoe machinery, and xerography. Monopolies can, similarly, be created with the help of a **copyright**, the exclusive right to the reproduction, publishing, or sale of a literary, musical, or artistic work. Although patents and copyrights are only granted for limited periods, the seller so favored often acquires an impregnable market position by the time this protection expires.

Exclusive Franchises

The most ancient source of monopoly, and one that often has the most enduring effect, is the **exclusive franchise**, a governmental grant to a single seller of the exclusive right to produce and sell a good. Kings throughout history have granted this special privilege to their favored subjects, presumably because it provided a way to enrich them (by enabling them to charge their fellow citizens above-competitive prices) without any drain whatever from the royal purse. For Americans, the monopoly of the British East India Company is, perhaps, of the greatest significance. That monopoly gave rise to the Boston Tea Party.

This type of contrived barrier to competition is common everywhere. Consider the exclusive franchises granted by the federal government to the U.S. Postal Service, by state governments to single restaurant chains operating along their turnpikes, and by city governments to cable television companies, garbage collectors, taxi companies, and various concessions (from airport car rentals to food service and parking at sports events).

The Profit-Maximizing Monopoly: The Short Run

Just as we analyzed in Chapter 6 the likely behavior of a profit-maximizing firm under perfect competition, we can predict the probable behavior of a profit-maximizing monopoly. Contrary to what many people think, no monopoly

---

CLOSE-UP 11.2:

De Beers: Diamonds are Forever

De Beers Consolidated Mines, Ltd. of South Africa has run a worldwide diamond cartel for more than a century. It handles about 80 percent of the world's uncut diamonds, the only competitor being the Soviet Union. In 1978, de Beers netted $852 million, an impressive 44 percent on its stockholders' equity. Unlike OPEC's dealings, those of de Beers are secretive. The key to market control are the "sights," diamond sales to wholesalers and cutters that occur every five weeks in London, Kimberley, and Lucerne. Attendance is by invitation only, and invitations are issued to some 300 persons. They must follow de Beers policies on pricing and sales or they will be barred from the "sights"—and that means no access to diamonds anywhere. As a result, no one speaks ill of the Central Selling Organization or the Syndicate. Nobody wants to offend the hand that feeds.

The company gets its diamonds for about $10 a carat; its selling price averages $80 a carat. (A *carat* equals 200 milligrams or 1/142 of an ounce. It was named for a carob seed, noted for its consistency in weight.)

Source: Paul Gibson, "De Beers: Can a Cartel be Forever?" *Forbes*, May 28, 1979, pp. 45–56; "How de Beers Dominates the Diamonds," *The Economist*, February 23, 1980, pp. 101–102.

ever charges the highest possible price or "what the traffic will bear," which is easily seen by following the route of thought taken by A. A. Cournot, who developed the theory of monopoly (see Biography 11.1).

The Demand Function and Total Revenue

A monopoly traps buyers in the sense that they cannot buy the given product from any other firm. Even a good substitute is unavailable. In another sense, however, buyers are free. They can always buy smaller quantities if prices are raised and even refuse to buy the product at all should the monopoly raise price by too much. A monopoly, therefore, has to reckon with the "law" of downward-sloping demand. Being the only seller in its industry, it is confronted, furthermore, with the entire market demand, which might consist of the data in columns (1) and (2) of Table 11.1. Unlike the firm in perfect competition (which is a price taker), a monopoly can set price at whatever level it wishes. The monopoly is a price setter, but it must also live with the consequences: Given price, buyers decide what quantity they will take; this price-quantity combination determines the monopoly's total revenue and, by implication, its marginal revenue as well. Note: If our monopoly charged "the highest possible price" (an outrageous 50 cents per kilowatt hour, perhaps), it would sell

nothing at all. Thus its total revenue would be zero, and it would soon go out of business!

The data of Table 11.1 can be plotted, as in Figure 11.2. In panel (b), for example, price-quantity combinations A to F have been plotted as the fat dots so labeled on the market demand line. The demand line's midpoint M has also been indicated. The total and marginal revenue data of Table 11.1 have been similarly plotted. (Note the fat dots on the respective curves.)

As we learned from Figure 4.13, "How Elasticity Can Vary" (p. 98), the absolute value of the price elasticity of demand in segment AM exceeds unity; it equals unity at M; and it falls short of unity in segment MF. These elasticities imply that price reductions that start from the 50-cents-per-kilowatt-hour/no-sales combination at A and stop just shy of the 25-cents-per-kilowatt-hour/25-million-kilowatt-hours-per-day sales combination corresponding to point M will increase quantity demanded so much as to raise total revenue. Panel (a) shows that total revenue rises from 0 toward m. On the other hand, price reductions starting just below 25 cents per kilowatt hour do not lead to a proportionate increase in quantity demanded. Total revenue, therefore, falls, as from m toward f in panel (a). Maximum total revenue, found at point m, therefore, corresponds to the unitary price elasticity of demand that is found at midpoint M on our straight-line demand function. (Can you see why Cournot,

TABLE 11.1   A Monopoly's Demand and Revenue

	Market Demand		Revenue	
	Price (cents per kilowatt hour)	Quantity (million kilowatt hours per day)	Total Revenue (million dollars per day)	Marginal Revenue (cents per kilowatt hour)
	(1)	(2)	(3) = (1) × (2)	(4) = $\dfrac{\Delta 3}{\Delta 2}$
(A)	50	0	0	
				40
(B)	40	10	4	
				20
(C)	30	20	6	
				0
(D)	20	30	6	
				−20
(E)	10	40	4	
				−40
(F)	0	50	0	

A monopoly is confronted with the entire market demand, in columns (1) and (2). It can set price, in column (1), at whatever level it wishes but must then take the consequences, in columns (2)–(4).

who investigated the behavior of a profit-maximizing monopoly selling mineral water wanted for its healing power, argued that the monopoly would choose a price corresponding to midpoint M on its straight-line demand if any amount of water could be produced at zero cost from a natural spring?)

The Demand Function and Marginal Revenue

Note in Figure 11.2 that a monopoly's total-revenue line ceases to be a ray from the origin as is true for a firm under perfect competition (see Figure 6.2, "A Profitable Business" on pg. 151). Correspondingly, a monopoly's marginal revenue ceases to be equal to the market price; marginal revenue for a monopoly cannot be depicted by a horizontal line. Our monopoly does not face, helplessly, a market-determined price. It sets its own price, but knows that quantity sold varies accordingly. If it charges 40 cents per kilowatt hour, for instance, it sells 10 million kilowatt hours per day (point B in our graph), and its total revenue is $4 million a day (point b). If it instead charges 30 cents per kilowatt hour, it sells 20 million kilowatt hours per day (point C), and its total revenue is $6 million a day (point c). Thus **marginal revenue**, or the change in total revenue divided by the associated change in total product, equals +$2 million per day divided by +10 million kilowatt hours per day, or 20 cents per kilowatt hour, as shown by "triangle" abc underneath the total-revenue curve in panel (a) of Figure 11.2 and by point G in panel (b). Marginal revenue is thus considerably smaller than either the old price of 40 cents or the new one of 30 cents per kilowatt hour. The reason is simple.

While the extra sales bring in extra revenue of $3 million per day (+10 million kilowatt hours per day at 30 cents each), these extra sales, we assumed, can be made only by lowering the price from 40 cents to 30 cents per kilowatt hour. Thus 10 cents are also lost for each of the 10 million kilowatt hours that would have been sold had the price remained at 40 cents per kilowatt hour. This loss from lower price comes to $1 million

FIGURE 11.2
Monopoly: Total and Marginal Revenue

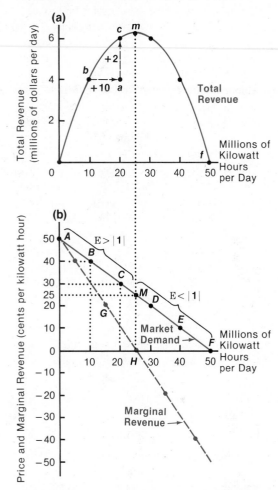

A monopoly is confronted with the entire market demand (line AF). It can set price at whatever level it wishes but must then live with the consequences: Quantity demanded varies with price; depending on the price elasticity of demand, any price reduction will raise, leave unchanged, or reduce total revenue and will thus be associated with positive, zero, or negative marginal revenue. This graph shows analagous implications for any price increase.

per day. When offset against the $3 million gain from larger sales, a net gain is made of only $2 million, or 20 cents per kilowatt hour, indicated, respectively, by distance ac in panel (a) and by point G in panel (b).

Indeed, when the price elasticity of demand is absolutely less than unity (as in section *MF* of our demand line), any revenue loss from lowered price exceeds any gain from larger sales. Then total revenue (to the right of *m*) declines; marginal revenue (to the right of *H*) is negative. (The reader may wish to review Figure 4.14 "Elasticity, Expenditure, Revenue" on page 99.)

Note: It is no accident that marginal revenue is zero (point *H*) exactly when the absolute value of the price elasticity of demand is unity (point *M*) and when total revenue is maximized (point *m*). The marginal revenue line associated with a straight-line demand function always connects the demand function's intercept on the vertical axis (point *A*) with a point such as *H*, midway between the origin 0 of the graph and the demand function's intercept on the horizontal axis (point *F*). This is why Cournot's advice to the producer of costless mineral water could also be phrased as selecting a price that reduced marginal revenue to zero. Most monopolies, of course, do not have zero costs. Because profit maximization is then more complicated than maximizing total revenue or setting marginal revenue to zero, we must turn to costs.

Cost Curves

Our analysis in Chapter 6 of the perfectly competitive firm can now be extended: A monopoly, just like a perfectly competitive firm, faces a production function, must pay for its inputs, and can calculate the costs of producing various levels of output. These costs can be depicted by the types of curves shown in Figure 6.1, "Short-Run Cost Curves" (p. 149). The costs of producing any given quantity of any given product, however, will not necessarily be identical regardless of whether the producing firm is a perfect competitor or a monopoly. As we have seen, a monopoly's production costs may be lower due to economies of scale. On the other hand, these costs may also be higher due to a greater likelihood of X-inefficiency when the fear of competitors is absent (see Chapter 14 for further discussion). At the moment, we need accept only the

FIGURE 11.3   A Profit-Making Monopoly

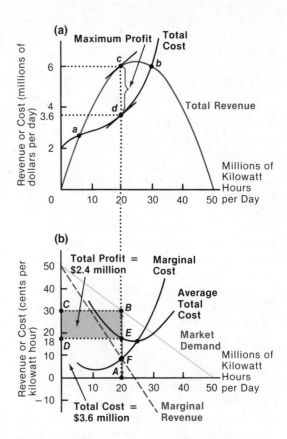

A profit-maximizing monopoly finds its optimal rate of production where constant or rising marginal cost equals constant or falling marginal revenue. Given the short-run revenue and cost functions shown here, this equality occurs at points *c* and *d* in panel (a) and at *F* in panel (b). The corresponding optimal rate of production equals 20 million kilowatt hours per day; therefore, a price of 30¢ per kilowatt hour is set. In this example, total revenue exceeds total cost; thus a positive profit is made that is equal to $2.4 million per day (distance *cd* in the top panel; the shaded rectangle in the bottom panel).

fact that a monopoly's cost curves will have the same *general* shape as those of any other firm.

Profit Maximization

Just like any other firm, a monopoly will maximize its profit by selecting an output volume that

FIGURE 11.4 A Zero-Profit Monopoly

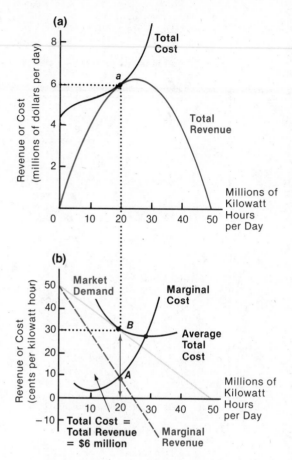

A profit-maximizing monopoly finds its optimal rate of production where constant or rising marginal cost equals constant or falling marginal revenue. Given the short-run revenue and cost functions shown here, this equality occurs at point a in panel (a) and at A in panel (b). The corresponding optimal rate of production equals 20 million kilowatt hours per day; therefore, a price of 30¢ per kilowatt hour is set, but zero profit is made: total cost just equals total revenue (point a); average cost just equals average revenue or price (point B). Any other production volume would yield losses.

maximizes the difference between total revenue and total cost (and, therefore, equates constant or rising marginal cost with constant or falling marginal revenue). Figure 11.3 is a copy of Figure 11.2, but with various cost curves super-

imposed upon it. Given the assumed conditions of revenue and cost, this monopoly would maximize profit by producing an output volume of 20 million kilowatt hours per day.

Consider panel (a) of Figure 11.3. It is obvious that any output volume to the left of point *a* or to the right of point *b* would yield losses because total cost would exceed total revenue. All intermediate output levels would yield positive profits, but to varying degrees. The maximum possible profit would be $2.4 million per day (distance *cd*), corresponding to the 20-million-kilowatt-hour total noted above. It is no accident that the slope of the total-revenue curve at *c* exactly equals that of the total-cost curve at *d*. Between *a* on the one hand and *c* or *d* on the other, total revenue and total cost increasingly diverge from each other; so total profit grows. Between *c* or *d* on the one hand and *b* on the other, total revenue and total cost converge; so total profit declines.

Panel (b) of Figure 11.3 leads to the same conclusion, of course. The ever-changing slope, at various potential output volumes, of the total-revenue curve is now reflected by the height of the marginal-revenue curve. The ever-changing slope of the total-cost curve, similarly, shows up as the height of the marginal cost curve. The equality of marginal cost and marginal revenue at *F* signifies maximum profit. Consider what would happen if the firm produced the associated 20 million kilowatt hours per day and set a 30-cents-per-kilowatt-hour price to make people demand just this (20-million-kilowatt-hour) quantity (point *B*). Total revenue would then equal rectangle *0ABC*; that is, 20 million kilowatt hours times the 30-cents-per-kilowatt-hour price, or $6 million per day, also shown by point *c* in panel (a). Total cost would equal rectangle *0AED*; that is, 20 million kilowatt hours times the 18-cents-per-kilowatt-hour average total cost, or $3.6 million per day, also shown by point *d* in panel (a). Total profit, therefore, would equal shaded rectangle *EBCD*; that is, 20 million kilowatt hours times the 12-cents-per-kilowatt-hour average profit *BE*, or $2.4 million per day, also shown by distance *cd* in panel (a).

Note: The making of positive profit is not inevitable. Given identical demand but less favorable cost conditions, our monopoly could just as well be making zero profit, as illustrated in Figure 11.4, or even a loss, as illustrated by Figure 11.5.

The Profit-Maximizing Monopoly: The Long Run

A major difference between a perfectly competitive firm and a monopoly is evident in the long run. While both types of firms *will* go out of business rather than make losses in the long run, and while both *may* make zero profit permanently, the difference between the two concerns the possibility of making positive profit. As was illustrated in Figure 7.3, "A Profitable Industry Expands" (p. 194), competitive firms cannot expect to make positive profits in the long run. Quite the contrary is true for a monopoly. Its profit, if positive, may well be permanent because entry into the industry is blocked to other firms for one of the reasons already mentioned.

Figure 11.3, however, does not necessarily depict long-run equilibrium. (Figure 11.3 would represent long-run equilibrium only if all the curves shown there pertained to the long run.) Suppose, however, that the demand and marginal revenue in panel (b) were long-run curves, while the cost curves were short-run curves. The implications are analyzed in Figure 11.6, which is a copy of Figure 11.3, but the earlier curves of marginal and average total cost are now labeled $SRMC_1$ and $SRATC_1$. The short-run profit-maximizing output level (corresponding to point F and equal to 20 million kilowatt hours per day) is still shown, along with the associated profit of $2.4 million per day (rectangle $EBCD$).

We now postulate long-run curves of marginal and average total cost, such as color lines $LRMC$ and $LRATC$. Under such conditions, our monopoly would wish to change its scale. (Note how the initial output volume could be produced, in a larger plant, at a lower average total cost shown by point M, which lies below E.) Given

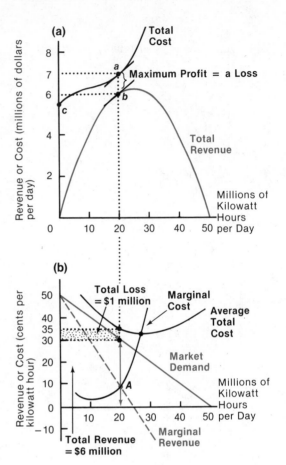

FIGURE 11.5   A Loss-Incurring Monopoly

A profit-maximizing monopoly finds its optimal rate of production where constant or rising marginal cost equals constant or falling marginal revenue. Given the short-run revenue and cost functions shown here, this equality occurs at points a and b in panel (a) and at A in panel (b). The corresponding optimal rate of production equals 20 million kilowatt hours per day; therefore, a price of 30¢ per kilowatt hour is set, but a loss is incurred: total cost exceeds total revenue by $1 million per day (distance ab in the top panel; the dotted rectangle in the lower panel). Any other production volume would yield larger losses. Note: This monopoly would cease to exist in the long run and would produce at the indicated output level in the short run only as long as its loss fell short of fixed cost, as is the case here. (Remember that fixed cost can be read off at the point where the total cost curve intercepts the vertical axis, as at c.)

FIGURE 11.6 The Monopoly in the Long Run

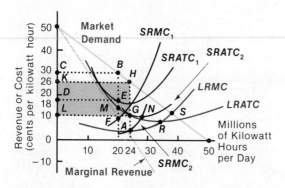

In the long run, a monopoly produces an output volume (here 23.5 million kilowatt hours per day) that equates long-run marginal cost with long-run marginal revenue (here at point A). Because entry into the industry is blocked to other firms, the resultant profit (shaded rectangle GHKL) is permanent.

Now consider a monopoly that faces the same type of downward-sloping market demand that perfectly competitive firms face as a group:

1. Such a monopoly, as we have just seen, may well earn positive profit in the long run.

2. In addition, because its marginal revenue always falls short of price and its profit is maximized when marginal revenue is equated to marginal cost, this monopoly will always choose to produce an output volume at which price exceeds marginal cost. (Note how H exceeds A in Figure 11.6 and how the firm would have to produce a quantity and charge a price corresponding to point S if it were to act like a perfect competitor, equating price with marginal cost.)

3. Finally, a monopoly is very unlikely to produce at minimum average total cost. (Note how, in Figure 11.6, G exceeds short-run minimum average total cost N as well as the long-run minimum at R.)

Of these three characteristics of monopoly, the second one will always be present. For this reason, Abba P. Lerner, in 1934, suggested that the gap between price, P, and marginal cost, MC, could be used to measure *the degree of monopoly power exercised by a firm*. This **Lerner index** is usually calculated as the ratio of

$$\frac{P - MC}{P}$$

Consider Figure 11.6. The final equilibrium price is 26 cents per kilowatt hour (point H). Long-run marginal cost at the chosen output volume equals 2.5 cents per kilowatt hour (point A). Thus the index comes to

$$\frac{26\cancel{c} - 2.5\cancel{c}}{26\cancel{c}} = 0.9.$$

This contrasts with a maximum of 1 (for Cournot's zero-marginal-cost producer of mineral water) and a minimum of 0 (for the perfectly competitive firm that equates price and marginal cost).

Note: Because every profit-maximizing firm

enough time, our monopoly would equate (at point A) long-run marginal cost with long-run marginal revenue. It would produce 24 million kilowatt hours per day, sell them at 26 cents each (point H), and take in a total revenue of $6.24 million per day. All this output would be produced in the cheapest possible way, at an average total cost of 10 cents per kilowatt hour (point G), utilizing a larger plant with short-run curves of average and marginal cost, SRATC₂ and SRMC₂. Thus a profit of 16 cents per kilowatt hour (distance GH) would yield total profit of $3.84 million per day (shaded rectangle GHKL). In the absence of changes in demand or costs, this profit would be permanent.

An Index of Monopoly Power

Figure 7.5, "Long-Run Industry Supply Curves" (p. 197), demonstrated that the perfectly competitive firm in the long run will always produce an output volume at which economic profit is zero, at which price equals marginal cost, and at which price also equals minimum average total cost.

equates marginal cost, *MC*, and marginal revenue, *MR*, the Lerner index can be rewritten as

$$\frac{P - MR}{P}.$$

In addition, marginal revenue is always related to the (absolute value of the) price elasticity of demand, ϵ, such that

$$MR = P - \frac{P}{|\epsilon|}.$$

(This will not be proven here, but consider that the price elasticity of demand facing a perfectly competitive firm is infinite. In that case, P/ϵ becomes zero, and, as we know, $MR = P$.) It follows that the Lerner index also equals

$$\frac{1}{|\epsilon|},$$

which makes intuitive sense. A firm facing an infinite price elasticity of demand (as perfect competitors do) would have zero power to raise price. A firm facing a very low elasticity would have a high degree of such power. (In Chapter 14, we will pursue further the significance of the gap between marginal cost and price.)

The Nature of Cartels

It is not difficult to see why firms in an otherwise competitive industry might be tempted to form a cartel. If such firms were lucky enough to imitate the behavior of a profit-making monopoly, their efforts would yield an important prize: permanent economic profit instead of the ever-present tendency toward zero profit.

In principle, the formation of a cartel is easy. All it takes is an agreement among all the existing sellers to charge an identical and higher price and to restrict supply until it equals market demand at the cartel price. In practice, however, such would-be monopolists often run afoul of one or more of three obstacles: organizational difficulties, a high price elasticity of demand, or a high price elasticity of supply.

Organizational difficulties include the problem of getting all or most existing sellers to join the cartel in the first place. When there are many sellers, this may be a hopeless task. Even when there are few, but they do not get along with each other (because of political differences, for example), the original formation of the cartel may not be possible. But organizational difficulties occur beyond this initial stage. Cartel members must frequently meet and agree on a common price to be charged; they must allocate among themselves the necessary reductions in quantity supplied; they must keep each other from cheating on the agreement. It takes a strong and lasting spirit of cooperation to achieve all this. Even when it is present, the cartel may fail.

No degree of organizational success can overcome a *high price elasticity of market demand*. Consider the extreme case of an infinite elasticity where buyers have plenty of good substitutes available for the cartel's product. Under such circumstances, any increase in price by the cartel leads to the total disappearance of quantity demanded. Selling nothing at a very high price will satisfy few sellers, indeed.

Finally, a cartel may be wrecked by a *high price elasticity of supply*. Even if cartel members are loyal and reduce quantity supplied in response to the higher price, newcomers who have no inclination to join the conspiracy may enter the industry, attracted, of course, by the very price rise engineered by the cartel. These new suppliers may offset or more than offset the supply reduction by the cartel. Then a glut will develop on the market, and buyers will find it easy to be supplied below the cartel price.

In spite of these likely difficulties, cartels have been formed throughout history through private efforts, with the help of government, and even as a result of international agreements. Not surprisingly, successful cartels have been rare.

Private Cartels

Consider the formation of a private price-fixing and output-restricting agreement among hundreds of thousands of wheat farmers. Their initial circumstances might be those depicted by point *e* in Figure 11.7. Some 2.5 billion bushels of wheat might be traded in the year prior to the cartel's formation, and wheat might sell at a competitive equilibrium price of $2 per bushel. Yet, a bright organizer might note, a slight restriction of the yearly supply to 2.1875 billion bushels could raise price to $3 per bushel and benefit all the farmers. How could the organizer persuade all the wheat farmers in the nation to join and to agree on cutting next year's output by 12.5 percent below this year's crop so as to raise price from the old equilibrium level of $2 to an estimated new level of $3 per bushel? (In 1968, when the National Farmers' Organization tried to organize a cattle cartel, only 10 percent of the farmers joined.)

Even if the initial step could be taken, buyers could surely find farmers cheating on the agreement. Imagine yourself to be one of the farmers who has just voted on the above scheme. You used to produce, say, 5,000 bushels, getting $10,000 of gross revenue at the old $2-per-bushel price. Now you know that you will have to cut output by 12.5 percent (as everyone else has to). Then you will sell 4,375 bushels. If the price rises to $3, this will gross $13,125, a clear gain of $3,125. But you know something else. You know that you play an insignificant part in this whole scheme. Nobody would ever notice if you,

BIOGRAPHY 11.1:

Antoine A. Cournot

Antoine Augustin Cournot (1801–1877) was born at Gray, France. He studied mathematics at the École Normale Supérieure in Paris. While a student, he worked as a secretary for one of Napoleon's generals. Later, he became a professor of mathematics at the University of Lyons and Rector, first at the Academy of Grenoble and then at the Academy of Dijon. The works that brought him widespread recognition are concerned with probability theory and epistemology. His wider interests, however, led him to become the founder of mathematical economics, through the publication, in 1838, of his greatest book, *Researches into the Mathematical Principles of the Theory of Wealth*. At the time, the book had no impact at all. Not a single copy was sold! This was, of course, disappointing to the author, who proceeded to simplify the presentation and produce two less mathematical versions of the book in 1863 (*Principles of the Theory of Wealth*) and 1876 (*Summary View of Economic Doctrines*) but to no avail. Not until William Jevons (see Biography 3.2) paid glowing tribute to Cournot two years after his death were his pioneering qualities recognized.

Cournot's great book has few equals in eco-

nomics for sheer originality and boldness of conception. It contained the nucleus of Alfred Marshall's economics. Unlike any previous book, it developed a theory of monopoly, introducing for the first time demand, marginal-revenue, and total-revenue functions, contrasting these with total and marginal costs, and deriving clearly the profit-maximizing principle of marginal-revenue-equal-to-marginal-cost. Starting from monopoly, Cournot similarly explored the economics of two sellers (duopoly), few sellers (oligopoly) and, eventually, innumerable sellers. While Cournot took the partial-equilibrium approach to analysis, he was not blind to the desirability of studying the entire economic system at once, but he thought that such a general-equilibrium approach was beyond the reach even of mathematical analysis. Even so, he influenced Léon Walras, inventor of general equilibrium analysis (see Biography 16.1), no less than Alfred Marshall (see Biography 7.1). And Cournot produced his work in defiance of dispiriting conditions. During many years, he was troubled by an infirmity of the eyes that made continuous work impossible and eventually led to blindness.

FIGURE 11.7 The Cartel

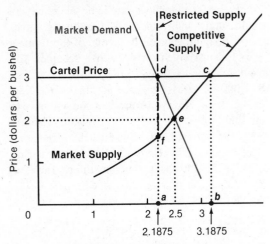

Quantity (billions of bushels of wheat per year)

Competitive sellers of a good may improve their welfare at the expense of buyers by conspiring to raise price and by restricting the quantity supplied. If wheat farmers, for example, could agree to restrict supply so that the line going through *f, e,* and *c* was shifted to dashed line *fd,* they could escape the $2-per-bushel competitive equilibrium price (corresponding to *e*) and enjoy the $3-per-bushel cartel price (corresponding to *d*). In the process, they would replace, just as a monopoly does, a price equal to marginal cost (at *e*) with a price (at *d*) above marginal cost (at *f*).

just you, did not cut your output. Total supply would then be cut, you might figure, from 2.5 billion bushels to only 2.187500625 billion bushels (instead of the agreed upon 2.1875 billion bushels). That would surely make no difference. As long as the others stuck to the agreement, price would still rise to $3, or almost that. And then your gross income would rise to almost $15,000, not just to $13,125. Even if you were caught (which would be unlikely), nobody could fine you or throw you in jail. Under the English common law (unwritten law), private conspiracies to fix output and market shares and prices cannot be enforced. It would pay you to cheat!

(In 1968, some cattle farmers blew up cattle scales and sat on the roads obstructing cattle shipments by the "chiselers." But many more of them were marketing their cattle; some even used house trailers to conceal their shipments.)

As you might expect, there would be others who would have the same bright idea of cheating as you. There would even be some who were brighter than that. They would *raise* their output in the hope of making a killing when all others cut theirs and caused price to go up. And even if the original conspirators were totally loyal to each other and honestly abided by the agreement, the scheme might fail: *New* sellers might appear on the scene, because of the new and higher price. Former potato farmers might grow wheat to get a piece of the loot. And foreign farmers might ship in huge quantities. Before long, a surplus of *dc* might appear in the market, putting strong pressure on price to fall. Thus a privately arranged price-fixing agreement has an excellent chance of breaking down.

Government-Sponsored National Cartels

It is not surprising that would-be cartel-makers turn to government for help against reluctant joiners, argumentative members, chiselers and outsiders. More often than not, this government help is provided and takes the form of *legislating*, separately or in combination, the setting of a higher price, a cutback in supply, or even an increase in demand.

Legislatures that desire to fix prices above competitive equilibrium levels either enact special price laws or grant broad powers to specially designed departments of the executive to do such price fixing. Among such executive departments are the multitude of federal "alphabet agencies": the CAB, the FCC, the FMC, the FPC, the FTC, and the ICC, to name just a few! The Civil Aeronautics Board (CAB) has long been responsible for regulating interstate airline service. It set fares at notoriously high levels to accommodate even the higher-cost producers. On identical routes served by CAB-regulated interstate and by nonregulated *intrastate* airlines, the fares of the intrastate lines (such as California's *Pacific Southwest* and Texas's *Southwest*) were about 50 percent below the rates of CAB carriers. The Federal Communications Commission (FCC) has performed a similar role for telephone and telegraph companies and radio and television broadcasters. The Federal Maritime Commission (FMC) has done the same thing with respect to ocean shipping, and the Federal Power Commission (FPC) with respect to natural gas and electric power producers. The Federal Trade Commission (FTC) has long kept retail prices high enough to allow high-cost outlets to live side by side with lower-cost chain stores. The Interstate Commerce Commission (ICC) has promoted high prices for interstate barge and ship companies, buses, railroads, and (nonagricultural) truckers. (Chapter 17 will describe how some of these practices were being stopped in the early 1980s.)

The federal laws setting minimum prices of goods above competitive equilibrium levels have included, most notably, laws fixing prices for agricultural products. These products have ranged from almonds, barley, beans, butter, cheese, corn, cotton, dates, flax seed, honey, milk, lemons, mohair, raisins, sorghum, and oats to peanuts, potatoes, rice, rye, soybeans, sugar beets and cane, tung nuts, tobacco, walnuts, wheat, and wool.

Many state and local governments, in addition, protect sellers beyond the reach of federal laws from the supposed ravages of competition. State liquor commissions set liquor prices; state public utility commissions set electric power and telephone rates. State insurance commissions set insurance rates; city transport commissions set rates on buses, subways, and taxis. For some 38 years prior to 1976 (when a federal law repealed them), states as well as cities promoted minimum retail prices for almost everything. Their so-called **fair-trade laws** allowed any manufacturer to fix a minimum price for a product and, if a single retailer agreed to it, to bind all retailers to it, even those who refused to sign an agreement

with the manufacturer. Those selling for less could be enjoined, fined, and even jailed. As recently as 1974, 36 states, from California to New York, still had such laws.

Initial price-fixing moves have to be reinforced by further decrees or laws, as Figure 11.7 illustrates. When price is raised above its equilibrium level (and kept there by law), a surplus develops because quantity demanded drops (along *ed* in the graph), while quantity supplied rises (along *ec*). To avoid the surplus, a govern-

---

CLOSE-UP 11.3:

Supporting the Price of Sugar

As the rain pelted the leaky old warehouse one summer day in 1978, a mysterious substance as viscous as lava and as dark as motor oil oozed under the doors and into a street of Riviera Beach, Florida, attracting swarms of flies and bees. The warehouse was filled with raw sugar acquired by the federal government under its new 1977 price support program; the scene was repeated in many places all over the United States.

Under the new program, sugar growers could borrow money (at 14.73¢ a pound) from the government but had to turn over their crops as collateral. If later market prices were higher, they could reclaim the sugar; if they were not, they forfeited their crops; taxpayers, through the government, became the reluctant owners of the sugar. The stakes were large. At a time when the world price of sugar was less than 8¢ a pound, each penny increase in price added $224 million to the American sugar growers' revenue, but (as they said) this would "only" cost the average American one extra dollar per year.

Sources: William Robbins, "Conflicting Interests Over Sugar Create Unwanted U.S. Surpluses," *The New York Times*, January 14, 1979, pp. 1 and 48; *idem*, "Lobbyists Worked Off Stage to Shape Sugar Laws," *The New York Times*, January 15, 1979, pp. A1 and D4; and *idem*, "Powerful Rivals Clash Over Sugar Price Supports," *The New York Times*, January 16, 1979, pp. A1 and D11. .

ment unwilling to let the price fall must either cut the supply or raise the demand; that is, it must bend the market supply line left until it goes through point *d* or shift the market demand line right until it goes through point *c*.

Supply has often been cut by denying or restricting market entry to new sellers and by forcing existing sellers to reduce their own supply. From its inception in 1938 until recently, for example, the CAB has not allowed the creation of a single new interstate airline, finding such a move "not required by the public interest, convenience, and necessity." The CAB also enforced market sharing or output restrictions among the existing ten domestic airlines in order to give them "route security" and to avoid "excessive, destructive, and cut-throat competition." The other federal alphabet agencies, as well as their brethren at the lower levels of government, have performed identical supply-restricting functions.

Similarly, agricultural price legislation has been buttressed by restrictions on domestic output and on imports. Domestic farmers have been issued **acreage allotments** that restrict the total acreage that can be planted with particular crops to or below that achieved at a given date in the past. Farmers have also been given **marketing quotas** that set a maximum amount of a product that particular farmers can legally sell. (Marketing quotas were set when farmers with acreage allotments responded by, nevertheless, producing *more*, due to their flooding of the restricted acreage with fertilizer, pesticides, high-yield seeds, and tender, loving care). In addition, under the old Soil Bank Program and more recent land-set-asides, farmers have been paid subsidies for taking land entirely out of production. This program has been reinforced by controls on agricultural imports that take the form of either high **tariffs** (import taxes) or low **import quotas** (maximum physical limits on the amounts of goods that may be imported).

The federal government has also helped nonagricultural sellers of goods by such "protective" foreign trade legislation. Even though, in many cases, minimum prices have not been legislated, such restrictions to the domestic mar-

ket supply raise prices indirectly above the level that would otherwise pertain. Thus we have tariffs on cars, steel, and textiles; we have import quotas on baseball mitts, bicycles, and umbrellas; and we have persuaded foreign governments to impose, "voluntarily," export quotas on their firms (as in the case of Japanese steel and television sets). The list could easily be lengthened. Indeed, a whole range of other *nontariff* barriers (usually in the form of red tape that discourages foreign trade) serves to accomplish the same goal of reducing alternative sources of supply to the domestic buyer and thus enabling favored domestic sellers to charge more.

State governments, similarly, have pushed up the prices of many goods by placing restrictions on the output produced or the number of producers. Under the Prorationing Program in Oklahoma and Texas, for instance, the number of days per month during which existing oil wells may pump is restricted by law (with the exception of offshore wells that are under federal jurisdiction). Every state in the union also requires the licensing of a multitude of "professions," broadly defined to include not just architects, doctors, dentists, lawyers, and psychologists, but also astrologers, barbers, bartenders, dancing instructors, egg graders, morticians, television aerial erectors, and yacht sellers!

In addition to reinforcing high prices with cuts in supply, governments can do something for sellers that even the most perfectly organized private cartel would find impossible to do: a government can actually force buyers to buy the same quantity (or even more) at the very time that price is raised. The most common approach is to tax people and then use the money to make purchases from or give outright gifts to the favored sellers. Under the agricultural programs in effect prior to 1974 and again since 1977, for instance, the federal government stands ready to purchase, at the prices officially legislated, butter, peanuts, sugar, wheat, and other products. In Figure 11.7, the government might set the price at $3 per bushel, while letting farmers produce what they like (point *c*) and letting them sell privately what they can (point *d*). The government might then buy the difference (*dc*), spending the taxpayers' money (equal to *abcd*). Taxes finance such purchases as well as the cost of their subsequent storage, destruction, or give-away (be it in the form of school lunches or aid to India). A host of other producers, such as airlines, bus companies, ocean shippers, railroads, and subways, are also subsidized by various levels of government. Thus taxpayers in all parts of the country who help finance subsidies to airlines or railroads or farmers are, in fact, being forced to "buy" airplane rides and railroad trips and butter without even realizing it. In this way, they are helping to maintain the government-sponsored high prices of air travel or railroad shipping or butter, which, of course, is the object of the monopoly game: for some people to gain at the expense of other people, without making an effort to reduce overall scarcity.

International Cartels

Often governments join with other governments to form cartels. The practice goes back to at least 1470 when the Vatican under Pope Paul II joined with King Ferdinand of Naples to form an *alum* cartel that lasted 30 years. (Alum is an astringent, crystalline double sulfate of aluminum and potassium that was used in medicine, leather tanning, cloth dyeing, and the arts. At the time, the Turks also supplied it, but the use of Turkish alum was declared un-Christian by the Pope.) In more recent times, OPEC (the Organization of Petroleum Exporting Countries) has, of course, provided an example of spectacular success; it is discussed in detail in Analytical Example 11.2, "OPEC—the World's Most Successful Cartel."

Similar success is not impossible, perhaps, for bauxite and uranium producers. Indeed, at the time of this writing, an International Bauxite Association (IBA) had succeeded in tripling the price of bauxite. The group was formed in 1974 by Australia, the Dominican Republic, Ghana, Guinea, Guyana, Haiti, Indonesia, Jamaica, Sierra Leone, Surinam, and Yugoslavia.

There has been much speculation about other international cartels, actual and potential, ranging from bananas (Central America, Ecuador), coffee (Brazil, Colombia), and grain (Australia, Canada, the United States) to natural rubber (Indonesia, Malaysia, Sri Lanka, Thailand), phosphate rock (Morocco, Tunisia), and tea (India, Sri Lanka). In general, though, the prospects for other international cartels are dim:

First, more often than not, some sellers in an industry do not wish to cooperate. (Consider the political differences between the Soviet Union and South Africa, both of which would have to join cartels for chromium, gold, or manganese. Consider how Iceland refused to join IATA, the International Air Transport Association, and how, as a consequence, until 1978 Icelandic

CLOSE-UP 11.4:

Orange Uprising

To Jacques Giddens, grower of navel oranges in Orange Cove, California, the federal marketing quotas were "crazy." Each year, he said, they forced him to throw away perfectly good food merely to hold up prices. In 1976, he rebelled.

After selling 3,441 cartons of oranges above his Department of Agriculture quota, Mr. Giddens was fined $12,620 by the government. He declined to pay, sued the government, and lost. He was broke but not broken. In fact, after his revolt, the rancher managed to exceed his marketing quota by leasing some of his trees directly to consumers at $16 apiece. He guaranteed each lessee 120 pounds of fruit. His ranch did the picking and packing; the lessee paid the shipping.

"This is exempt from the marketing order," Mr. Giddens explained, "because when you lease a tree from me, that's your tree, and all I do is ship you the fruit from it. I take care of it for you. It's not covered by the quota."

At the time, he said, he was the only orange grower in the country who leased trees.

Source: Richard Haitch, "Orange Uprising," *The New York Times*, May 11, 1980, p. 37.

ANALYTICAL EXAMPLE 11.1:

Dental Cartels

Dental practitioners in the United States must be licensed by state boards. 35 states do not honor licenses granted in other jurisdictions. Consequently, dentists seeking to practice in those states must pass local examinations regardless of their previous experience. Large percentages of out-of-state applicants are typically denied licenses; most in-state graduates successfully complete dental board exams. This discriminating procedure has the effect of insulating practitioners from competition from nonresident dentists who might otherwise migrate. This competition-avoiding effect, however, is absent in the 15 states that have reciprocity agreements binding them to endorse each other's licenses. Do dentists in the "protected" states manage to charge higher prices? A study of 1970 prices based on a survey of 10,000 dental practitioners indicates that prices in protected states are higher:

Service	Average Price in Reciprocity States	Average Price in Nonreciprocity States	Percentage Difference
Periodic oral exam	$ 3.44	$ 3.75	+9.0
Complete series of X-rays	5.47	5.65	+3.3
Dental prophylaxis	7.61	8.26	+8.5
Simple tooth removal	6.32	7.45	+17.9
Root canal extirpation and filling	51.37	56.42	+9.8
Amalgam filling (1 surface)	6.33	6.52	+3.0
Amalgam filling (2 surfaces)	10.05	10.35	+3.0
Gold inlay (2 surfaces)	47.00	50.73	+7.9
Cast gold crown	70.38	74.72	+6.2
Bridge (2 units)	143.23	154.19	+7.7
Acrylic-base denture	147.50	150.33	+1.9
Denture repair	16.41	16.38	−0.2

Source: Lawrence Shepard, "Licensing Restrictions and the Cost of Dental Care," *The Journal of Law and Economics*, April 1978, pp. 187–201. Table reprinted by permission of the University of Chicago Press. Copyright 1973 by the University of Chicago Law School.

Airlines provided the only low-priced scheduled service across the Atlantic but was also denied landing rights in Europe, except in Iceland and Luxembourg.)

Second, the price elasticity of demand is often high because substitutes are available. The availability of substitutes has blocked the success of a copper cartel, the Conseil Intergouvernemental des Pays Exportateurs de Cuivre (CIPEC), formed by Chile, Peru, Zaire, and Zambia.

Finally, the price elasticity of supply is often high because the product can easily be produced in many places (consider grain). Therefore, it is not surprising that only about one third of all the international cartels formed in the past have ever managed to raise price at all, and very few of these have managed to last more than five years.

A Final Note

Often governments aid the formation of cartels for reasons unrelated to the monopolistic consequences here discussed. Federal government programs relating to agriculture, for example, have been enacted for purposes of equity in order to maintain **parity**, defined as the 1910–14 relationship between the prices received by farmers for agricultural goods and the prices paid by them for nonagricultural goods. But regardless of the "good" intent, such policies have promoted monopoly, and that alone is our concern in this chapter. (The wisdom of the parity program can be questioned on other grounds. In 1910–14, the bushels-per-acre yields of U.S. farmers equaled, for example, 14.3 in wheat, 26 in corn, 200.3 in cotton. By 1972–76, these yields were 30.6, 86.7, and 477.2, respectively, Thus even substantial reductions in prices per bushel need not imply reduced farm income.)

State programs that have promoted monopoly, similarly, have often been enacted for other reasons. Consider the Texas restrictions on oil production. They emerged because oil is *fugacious*; it will migrate underground heedless of surface boundary lines. Prior to the state's prorationing law, landowners would produce as fast as possible, especially along the boundaries of their tracts, lest their neighbors drain away their oil. This runaway production dissipated underground pressure too rapidly; oil was bypassed by water and permanently lost. Thus the law was enacted to prevent this physical waste.

State and local licensing provisions, finally, have the admirable goal of certifying the competency of sellers to buyers. But they also restrict the number of practitioners unnecessarily. Examples abound, but here is just one: Of 2,149 aspiring general contractors who took the Florida construction industry licensing board exam in 1973, all failed. Another reason why licensing can be seen as a device to restrict trade rather than to protect the public from unscrupulous charlatans is that state licensing usually evaluates novices only at the start of their careers. Short of outright criminality, they are rarely unlicensed,

even if they turn out to be undependable, incompetent, or senile! As the saying goes, the road to hell is paved with good intentions.

Applications

Application 1:
The Author-Publisher Conflict

Authors, it is said, usually prefer a lower sales price for their books than do their publishers. If authors are paid a fixed percentage of list price, which is often the case, it is not difficult to see why. Consider Figure 11.8. Panel (b) shows a hypothetical market demand function for a book, along with the implied marginal revenue line; panel (a) shows the total revenue function. Assume that the book is produced at a total fixed cost of $100,000 (point E) but at a constant marginal (and average-variable) cost of $9.50 per copy. The implied cost curves are shown in the graph. The profit-maximizing publisher's best choice now becomes obvious: marginal cost and marginal revenue are equated at a, if 15,000 copies are produced. This quantity will be demanded at only one price, $17.50 per copy (point b). The publisher can look forward to an average profit of $1.33 (distance bc) or a total profit of $20,000 per year, as shown by the shaded rectangle in panel (b) and distance AB in panel (a).

Note: Any other output volume would reduce total profit, as is implied by the configuration of marginal revenue and marginal cost in panel (b). Every single book produced in excess of 15,000 copies a year would add more to total cost than to total revenue (to the right of point a, marginal cost exceeds marginal revenue). Every single book subtracted from the 15,000 annual quantity would reduce total revenue by more than total cost (to the left of point a, marginal revenue exceeds marginal cost).

Now think of the author. Having written the book, the author's marginal cost of production is zero. Being in the position of Cournot's owner of the costless mineral spring, the author, therefore, wants to maximize total revenue at M or, if you

FIGURE 11.8   Author Vs. Publisher

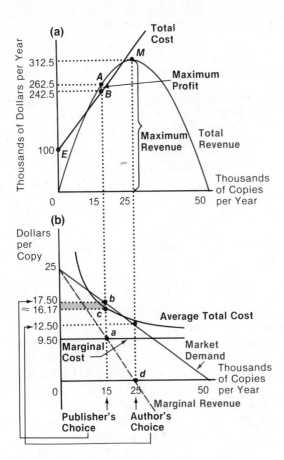

Authors who receive royalties equal to a fixed percentage of the list price of their books—contrary to what one might guess—prefer a lower price than their publishers do.

prefer, equate zero marginal cost with zero marginal revenue at point d (where the price elasticity of demand equals unity). For the author, getting annual royalties equal to x percent of $312,500 (point M) is preferable to getting x percent of $262,500 (point A). Thus the author wishes for a larger number of copies being sold and a lower price per copy. Naturally, the publisher wins.

Application 2:   Price Discrimination

In the above discussion of profit-maximization, we implicitly assumed that monopolies, like perfect competitors, charge all customers identical prices, but often they do not. Whenever a seller charges a given buyer or different buyers different prices for identical units of a good— even though such price differences cannot be justified by differences in the cost of serving these buyers—**price discrimination** is said to exist. Price discrimination can enhance a monopoly's possibilities for profit making.

Firms with the power to set prices (such firms need not necessarily be pure monopolies) can engage in price discrimination whenever they face customers with different price elasticities of demand and are able to segregate these customers accordingly. Obviously, sellers would not be successful in charging some people higher prices than other people, if those favored with the offer of low prices could resell their acquisitions to the less fortunate would-be buyers. The British economist A. C. Pigou (see Biography 18.1), who first examined price discrimination in detail identified three types of price discrimination: first-degree, second-degree, and third-degree.

First-Degree Price Discrimination.   One refers to **first-degree price discrimination** or **perfect price discrimination** when a seller charges each buyer for each unit bought the maximum price the buyer is willing to pay for that unit. As a result, the seller can appropriate the entire consumer surplus and leave the buyer indifferent about buying or not buying. The demand and cost conditions of the firm pictured in Figure 11.9 are identical to those given in panel (b) of Figure 11.3 for a profit-making monopoly. Yet we now assume that this firm is able to practice perfect price discrimination. It charges 50 cents for the first kilowatt hour sold (represented by the thin column next to the vertical axis). It charges the same customer or a different one slightly less than 50 cents for the second kilowatt hour, and so on along the downward slope of market demand until the 10 million th kilowatt hour is sold for 40 cents and the 28 millionth one for 22 cents. As a result of this procedure, the divergence between price and marginal revenue disappears; the market demand line becomes the marginal revenue line as well.

As is true for all firms, our price-discriminating monopoly finds its profit-maximizing output volume by equating marginal cost and marginal revenue (point *B*). Thus it produces 28 million kilowatt hours per day, at an average total cost of 18 cents (point *a*). The graph clearly shows the division of our firm's total revenue (*0ABC*) between total cost (unshaded) and total profit (shaded). And there can be little doubt that the profit so achieved exceeds that of the identical firm in the absence of price discrimination, shown in panel (b) of Figure 11.3.

The achievement of such perfect price discrimination is, however, extremely difficult (and confined, perhaps, to the haggling that tourists experience in foreign bazaars), which is why would-be price discriminators usually turn to a cruder alternative.

Second-Degree Price Discrimination. One refers to **second-degree price discrimination** when a seller partitions market demand into fairly large blocks of product units and charges a given buyer or different buyers different prices for these blocks but uniform prices within the blocks. As a result, the firm captures only a portion of the consumer surplus (see Figure 11.10). Once more, the demand and cost conditions of the firm pictured in Figure 11.10 are identical to those in Figure 11.3. We now assume that this firm is able to practice second-degree price discrimination. Thus it announces a rate schedule according to which it charges 40 cents per kilowatt hour for the first 10 million kilowatt hours bought, 30 cents per kilowatt hour for the next 10 million, 20 cents per kilowatt hour for the next 10 million, and so on. As a result of this procedure, the firm's marginal revenue line takes on a stair-step appearance.

Once more, the firm maximizes profit by

choosing the output volume that equates marginal cost and marginal revenue (point *a*). Thus it produces 27 million kilowatt hours per day at an average total cost of 17.5 cents (point *b*). The graph again shows the division of the firm's total revenue (the *sum* of blocks *A, B,* and *C* up to the chosen quantity) between total cost (unshaded) and total profit (shaded). Clearly, the profit so achieved exceeds that of the identical firm in the absence of price discrimination, shown in panel (b) of Figure 11.3.

It is fairly easy to find examples of second-degree price discrimination. Consider how electricity, natural gas, water, telephone, Xeroxing services, and even credit card loans are routinely sold in this way. People pay so much for the first 500 kilowatt hours, 1,000 cubic feet, 3 minutes of talking, 100 Xerox copies, or $500 of credit; they pay ever less for additional similar blocks. The same principle operates when drug stores sell vitamins at 100 for $1 and 200 for $1.01; when restaurants sell lunches at $1.25 per person and $2 per couple; when grocers sell cans of peas

FIGURE 11.9
First-Degree Price Discrimination

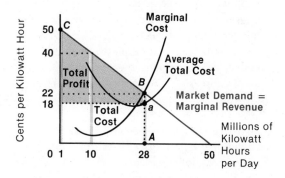

A seller practices *first-degree* or *perfect price discrimination* when each buyer is charged for each unit bought the maximum price the buyer is willing to pay for that unit. As a result, the seller appropriates the entire consumer surplus. The firm shown here, if it could practice such price discrimination, would produce 28 million kilowatt hours per day and reap a profit equal to the shaded area.

FIGURE 11.10
Second-Degree Price Discrimination

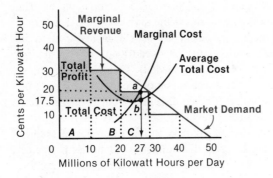

A seller practices *second-degree price discrimination* when market demand is partitioned into fairly large blocks of product units and a given buyer or different buyers are charged different prices for these blocks but uniform prices within the blocks. As a result, the seller captures a portion of the consumer surplus. The firm shown here, if it could practice such price discrimination, would produce 27 million kilowatt hours per day and reap a profit equal to the shaded area.

at 30¢ for 1, 55¢ for 2, and 75¢ for 3; and when magazines offer subscriptions at $10 for a year, $18 for 2 years, and $24 for 3 years.

Note: Car dealers make no similar offers because it would be worthwhile for people to reject the offer of 1 car for $5,000 in favor of 2 cars for $8,000, only to resell the second car for less than $5,000 and thus to wreck the $5,000 car market entirely. In the case of canned peas, it isn't worth the trouble for the buyer to resell.

Third-Degree Price Discrimination. One refers to **third-degree price discrimination** when a seller partitions market demand into two or more groups of customers and charges different prices among, but uniform prices within, these groups. The firm pictured in Figure 11.11 is assumed to sell television sets at home and abroad but to face markets in which the price elasticity of demand differs at any given price. At a price of $125 per set, for example, the elasticity in the domestic market (at point *a*) equals |0.38| and that in the foreign market (at point *b*) equals

|1.79|. (The reader may wish to review the PAPO rule for calculating elasticity in Chapter 4.)

If the firm charged an identical price in both markets, it would not be getting as much profit as it could get through price discrimination: uniform prices imply diverging marginal revenues when price elasticities differ. Note how, in panel (a) of Figure 11.11, the marginal revenue corresponding to a $125 price is negative (as measured by the intersection, not shown, of the dashed marginal-revenue line and a vertical line going through point *a*). In panel (b) of our graph, on the other hand, the marginal revenue corresponding to a $125 price is still positive (point *c*). Under such circumstances, the firm could increase profit by switching a unit from the market with the lower elasticity (and marginal revenue) to that with the higher elasticity (and marginal revenue). Profit maximization, therefore, requires identical marginal revenues in all markets served by a firm.

Profit maximization also requires, of course, an identity between marginal revenue and marginal cost, which is determined in panel (c) of our graph where the *horizontal sum* of marginal revenues is compared with marginal cost. The profit-maximizing output is thus found to be 14 million television sets per year. This output implies a marginal cost of $125 per set and, following the horizontal dotted line left from point *d*, sales of 5 and 9 million sets, respectively, in the foreign and domestic markets. As points *e* and *f* indicate, these sales volumes alone assure for both markets identical marginal revenues, which, in turn, are identical with marginal cost.

The final solution is that 5 and 9 million sets per year can be sold in the two markets, respectively, at prices of $165 and $295 per set (points *h* and *i*). Thus a profit-maximizing price discriminator will charge a higher price in the market that has a lower price elasticity of demand at any given price. This strategy, of course, makes intuitive sense; examples abound.

The very example just utilized is not farfetched. In 1980, SONY of Japan was accused of making a profit by dumping television sets in the

United States below cost. This was an unlikely story, for no one can ever make a profit by selling below (average total) cost. It was true, however, that SONY sold TVs at $180 in the United States and identical ones at $333 in Japan. Figure 11.11 can explain these facts. As we assumed in the hypothetical graph, SONY faced much more competition abroad (and thus a higher price elasticity of demand) than at home.

The separation of markets on the basis of geography need not, however, involve international frontiers. Consider how state universities charge different fees to in-state and out-of-state students, how airport managers charge different gasoline prices to transient planes and those based on their field, how supermarket chains charge different prices in suburbs and central cities (and to a degree not justified by differences

in cost). Nor is geography the only basis for price discrimination of the third degree.

Equally common is market separation on the basis of people's age, sex, and income. Think how children or the elderly are offered lower prices by airlines, banks, barbers, and cinemas. Consider ''ladies' day'' at the golf and tennis club, on the ski slopes; consider the lower prices some doctors and lawyers charge the poor and that journals and newspapers charge students or members of the armed forces.

Market separation on the basis of time is another favorite. New books and films are sold early to the most eager at high prices and much later to others at lower prices. Movie theaters have matinees, twilight hours, and regular showings; prices of electricity, telephone service, and vacation resorts vary by time of day or year.

FIGURE 11.11 Third-Degree Price Discrimination

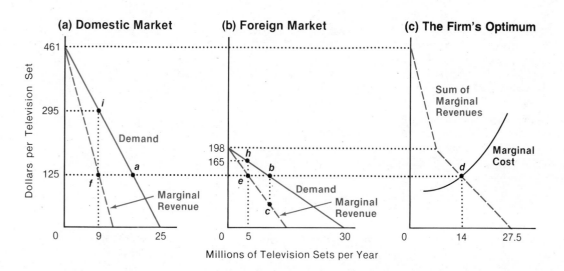

A seller practices *third-degree price discrimination* when market demand is partitioned into two or more groups of customers and different prices are charged for different groups, but uniform prices are charged within these groups. The firm shown here, if it could practice such price discrimination, would sell a total of 14 million television sets: 9 million for $295 each in the domestic market and 5 million for $165 each in the foreign market.

Caution: The horizontally combined marginal revenue only serves the purpose of helping the firm find the best output volume and hence the marginal cost (here $125) with which the price-discriminating firm then separately equates the marginal revenues of the two markets (at f and e). The kinked line of the combined marginal revenues should not be confused with the kinked demand curves (and their implied *discontinuous* marginal revenue curves) to be discussed in the next chapter. Those kinked demand curves refer to oligopolists who do *not* engage in price discrimination, but charge uniform prices.

ANALYTICAL EXAMPLE 11.2:
OPEC—the World's Most Successful Cartel

In 1960 at Baghdad, the governments of five major oil-exporting countries (Iran, Iraq, Kuwait, Saudi Arabia, and Venezuela) formed OPEC, the Organization of Petroleum Exporting Countries. By 1980, there were eight additional members: Algeria, Ecuador, Gabon, Indonesia, Libya, Nigeria, Qatar, and the United Arab Emirates. After having wielded little power for more than a decade, the organization demanded and received a higher price for oil and a greater share of profit from the oil companies in 1973. On January 1, 1973, the price of oil was $2.12 a barrel. By year's end (following an Arab-led embargo of oil exports to the United States that was seen to aid Israel in that year's Yom Kippur War), the price was $11.65 a barrel. By mid-1980, it ranged from $28 to $37 a barrel. An unprecedented transfer of income was occurring from oil-consuming to oil-producing nations. (By 1980, OPEC was producing 26.5 million barrels a day, at an average total cost of about 25 cents a barrel. OPEC's total revenue exceeded $300 billion a year, which would have been sufficient to buy up, in about three years, 100 percent of the shares of all companies listed on the New York Stock Exchange. The market value of these shares, on September 30, 1979, was $961.3 billion.)

Are the consuming nations helpless in the face of this stranglehold? Not really, although they are acting as if they were. Consider a suggestion by M. A. Adelman. His idea is illustrated by the graph below. Let world market demand for oil be represented by line *AB* and the associated marginal revenue by dashed line *AM*. Let the marginal cost of producing oil be zero (for it is almost that). Then the profit-maximizing position of the OPEC cartel is given by the marginal-cost and marginal-revenue intersection at *M*. Like Cournot's producer of mineral water, OPEC maximizes profit by maximizing revenue. Since average total cost of production is very low as well (*MF*), the maximum monopoly profit (shaded area *GFEK*) is just slightly lower than maximum revenue (*OMEK*).

In fact, however, OPEC hasn't yet reached this position, having gradually moved from output-price combination *C* in 1970 to combination *D* in 1980. Output-price combination *E*, however, is likely to be the eventual outcome.

Indeed, every possible way in which people can be grouped by eagerness of demand might be used for price discrimination: Milk producers charge different prices to households and to butter or cheese manufacturers. Electric companies discriminate between residential and industrial customers; periodicals discriminate between new and old subscribers. Railroads transport goods with low *value density* (such as coal) for less than goods with high value per cubic foot; they charge more per mile on short hauls than on long hauls. The U.S. Postal Service charges more for first class mail than for equally heavy advertisements, books, or newspapers. Manufac-

turers sell branded gasoline and tires for more than physically identical unbranded ones. Airlines charge more for first-class seats on daytime trips than for night coach, group charters, or "no frills" flights (and the differences cannot be fully explained by differences in services rendered). At the stadium, box seats, grandstand seats, and bleachers do not cost the same.

Application 3: Markup Pricing

Firms frequently set their prices by simply adding a percentage markup to their average varia-

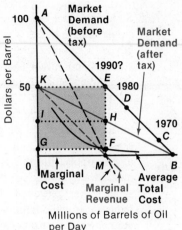

Millions of Barrels of Oil
per Day

Now consider what would happen if consuming nations imposed a tax equal to a fixed percentage of market price. The market demand line facing OPEC would swing left around point *B*; in the case of a 50 percent tax, it would swing from *BA* to *BK*. Whatever the price paid by consumers, such as *EM*, the consumers' government would collect half of it, such as *EH*. Accordingly, the marginal revenue line facing OPEC would change from *AM* to *KM*, but the profit-maximizing output would remain at *M*!

Consumers would pay *EM* per barrel, the consumers' government would collect *EH* per barrel, and OPEC would earn *HM* per barrel. OPEC's profit would be cut from *GFEK* (shaded), to *GFHI*. Indeed, a steeper proportional tax, equal to the ratio *EF/EM*, or 91 percent in our example, would eliminate OPEC's profit entirely, and the transfer of income would be ended.

Sources: Based on *The New York Times*, June 11, 1980, pp. 1 and D4 and October 29, 1979, p. D3; M. A. Adelman, "Constraints on the World Oil Monopoly Price," *Resources and Energy* 1(1978), pp. 3–19.

ble cost of production. Is this procedure inconsistent with Cournot's theory of monopoly, according to which firms maximize their profit only if they choose an output volume that equates marginal revenue with marginal cost? Not necessarily. As we noted in the section on "An Index of Monopoly Power,"

$$MR = P - \frac{P}{|\epsilon|}$$

Equating marginal revenue with marginal cost, therefore, implies that

$$MC = P - \frac{P}{|\epsilon|}$$

This, in turn, can be written as

$$MC = P - \frac{P}{|\epsilon|} = P \left(1 - \frac{1}{|\epsilon|}\right).$$

Dividing by the parenthetical expression, we get

$$\frac{MC}{\left(1 - \frac{1}{|\epsilon|}\right)} = P;$$

hence

$$\frac{MC}{\frac{|\epsilon|}{|\epsilon|} - \frac{1}{|\epsilon|}} = P,$$

and

$$\frac{MC}{\frac{|\epsilon| - 1}{|\epsilon|}} = P.$$

Thus equating marginal revenue with marginal cost implies

$$P = MC\left(\frac{|\epsilon|}{|\epsilon| - 1}\right)$$

To the extent that a firm's marginal cost is constant over a wide range of output (as pictured, for example, in Figure 11.8), marginal cost equals average variable cost. Hence our equation comes to

$$P = AVC\left(\frac{|\epsilon|}{|\epsilon| - 1}\right),$$

which is precisely the formula for a percentage markup!

Let the price elasticity of demand equal $|4|$. Then

$$P = AVC\left(\frac{4}{4 - 1}\right) = AVC\left(\frac{4}{3}\right) = AVC\ (1.33)$$

If this firm sets price 33 percent above average variable cost, it, in effect, equates marginal revenue with marginal cost.

Note: As we have seen when discussing the author-publisher conflict, a firm with monopoly power and positive marginal cost will always choose an output volume at which price elasticity exceeds $|1|$. The optimal markup, from the point of view of a monopoly with positive and also constant marginal cost, is, therefore, the higher the less price-elastic demand is. Let $|\epsilon| = 1.1$ in the above formula. Then

$$P = AVC\left(\frac{1.1}{1.1 - 1}\right) = AVC\left(\frac{1.1}{0.1}\right)$$

$$= AVC\ (11),$$

calling for a markup of 1,000 percent.

Application 4:   Bilateral Monopoly

Sometimes not only does an industry contain a single seller, but this seller also faces a single buyer. Examples are: the producers of space vehicles and military hardware facing the federal government; the manufacture (until recently) of all telephones by Western Electric and their purchase by a single firm, AT&T; or a cartel of tobacco producers facing a single tobacco processing firm. Such a situation is termed a **bilateral monopoly**, but this is somewhat of a misnomer. Strictly speaking, *monopoly* means ''single seller''; the existence of a single buyer in an industry is called **monopsony**. Assuming that neither trading partner can practice price discrimination, how will output and price be determined in such a situation? As Cournot noted almost 150 years ago, the outcome is theoretically indeterminate and depends entirely on the bargaining skills of the two trading partners. We can, however, determine broad limits within which the final price or quantity are bound to settle.

Figure 11.12 contains an imagined marginal-value-product curve of a monopsony processor of tobacco. This curve is also the market demand faced by the monopoly seller of tobacco. The tobacco seller can derive the associated marginal-revenue curve as indicated. If the single tobacco seller's marginal-cost curve looks as shown, this monopoly will maximize profit by equating (at point *a*) marginal cost and marginal revenue. Thus the monopoly will wish to supply 2.6 million tons of tobacco per year at a price of $2,800 per ton (point *b*).

The monopsony, however, will resist this choice. The tobacco processor will view the monopoly's marginal-cost curve as its market-supply curve (which is what it would be under perfect competition when sellers do not have monopoly power). It will figure that it could get, for example, 3.3 million tons of tobacco for $1,357 each (point *d*), at a price that would just cover the supplier's marginal cost of production. It will figure that it could, similarly, get 5 million tons for $1,871 each (point *e*), and so on. Because of its power to push up price through larger purchases, the monopsonist's **marginal outlay**, or its change in total outlay divided by the corresponding change in the total quantity purchased, will actually exceed the price it pays. As the above example shows, a 1.7-million-ton increase in annual purchases (from 3.3 to 5 million tons per year) would raise total outlay by $4.8769 billion per year (from $1,357 per ton times 3.3 million tons per year, or $4.4781 billion per year, to $1,871 per ton times 5 million tons per year, or $9.355 billion per year). Thus marginal outlay would equal $4.8769 billion per year divided by 1.7 million tons per year, or almost $2,869 per ton. This amount is, indeed, the average height of the marginal-outlay curve in the corresponding quantity range (between points c and f).

To maximize its profit the monopsony will wish to equate (at point c) its marginal value product with its marginal outlay. (The reader may wish to review Figure 8.1, "A Firm's Demand for Labor: The Simple Case" (p. 216), where the same rule was employed. In that earlier example, of course, the input bought was labor rather than tobacco, and the input's price was unaffected by the amount bought. Thus the firm's marginal outlay was constant and equal to the market price of labor.) Thus our monopsony will wish to purchase 3.3 million tons of tobacco per year and offer a price of $1,357 per ton (point d). As our graph shows, the two trading partners' choices are irreconcilable. In order to establish a price and trading volume, one or the other or both must compromise.

Application 5: The "Captured" State

Some people argue that government officials are inevitably "captured" by would-be monopolists who want to be aided in securing monopoly power. We have seen plenty of examples above. Why does government help people acquire power over prices to gain income? Why doesn't it insist that people gain income only through productive contributions?

We all like to think of government as the impartial servant of the public good. We like to

FIGURE 11.12   Bilateral Monopoly

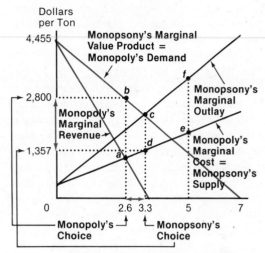

When a single seller in an industry *(monopoly)* also faces a single buyer *(monopsony)*, a *bilateral monopoly* is said to exist. The price-quantity combination that will emerge from this situation is theoretically indeterminate but will lie within a predictable range (note the arrows).

see government as the instrumentality by which the nation achieves *the national interest*— meaning, perhaps, an overall reduction in the realm of scarcity. But the nation does not talk to government officials; individuals do. Within the nation, there are many individuals whose interests conflict with those of other individuals. For each of these individuals, income can be gained more easily by taking it away from other people —given the overall degree of scarcity prevailing —than by making genuine contributions toward reducing the realm of scarcity by working harder, saving more, or making cost-reducing innovations. Is it surprising that some of these individuals want the government to intercede for their *special interest* (which is to gain power to raise the prices of whatever they sell in order to raise their income in the easiest way)? To the extent that government responds to such requests, it does not govern in the national interest; it promotes a coalition of special interests. Sellers use many devices to get government to promote their special interest in above-equilibrium minimum prices, reduced supply, or increased demand for whatever they have to sell.

The "Capture" of Legislators. Sellers can induce legislators at all levels of government to rig markets directly—or to set up appropriate agencies to do the rigging—by channeling a number of rewards to them. Perhaps the most important reward is campaign contributions.

All legislators must be elected. Those with the "proper" attitude—toward minimum prices (for airplane trips, electricity, insurance, labor, liquor, milk, taxi rides, telephone service, or wheat), toward supply-restricting laws (ranging widely from those concerning cartels, copyrights, exclusive franchising, and immigration to others on import and marketing quotas, mergers, patents, professional licensing, tariffs, and union affairs), and toward demand-raising laws (awarding government contracts or subsidies for anything from peanuts to railroads to the unemployed)—can be rewarded by the beneficiaries of this "proper" attitude. Early rewards come in the form of votes and in the form of funds to finance expensive radio and TV campaigns designed to gather other people's votes. (A federal campaign cost a minimum of $100,000 in 1980.) During the early 1970s, major corporations as well as other organizations—ranging from dairy farmers, dentists, and doctors to seafarers, teachers, and truckers—spent more than $100 million

ANALYTICAL EXAMPLE 11.3:
The Market Value of Monopoly Power

As was shown in the section of Chapter 9 on "Fisher's Concept of Capital," the present value of any future income stream can be calculated by a process called *capitalization*, which yields the likely market value of the asset from which the income stream is derived. *Monopoly power*, which enables its holder to collect a stream of future economic profits, is such an asset. The table below indicates recent market prices people have paid in order to acquire the source of such power.

Sources of Monopoly Power	Market Price	Year
Boston taxicab licenses	$23,000	1967
Chicago taxicab licenses	$10,000–18,000	1968
New York taxicab licenses	$68,000	1980
American Baseball League franchises	$20–25.3 million	1981
National Baseball League franchises	$6–11 million	1971
National Basketball League franchises	$1–3 million	1971
Commodity Futures Exchange seats	$200,000–325,000	1980
New York Stock Exchange seats	$82,000–212,000	1979
Television station licenses	$2–50 million	1979
Tobacco growing rights (per acre)	$1,500–3,000	1960
Trucking operating rights (per route)	$5,000–2.5 million	1979

Note: If the government were to auction off monopoly rights at the time of their creation at the kind of prices indicated in the above table, government would thereby recoup for its citizens as a group the present value of money to be taken from them in the future through the exercise of monopoly power. If government fails to do this

on federal election campaigns alone. Following rather aggressive solicitation of funds by top officials in the Nixon Administration, many corporations made illegal contributions. Among those who eventually admitted to such contributions publicly were American Airlines, Ashland Oil, Braniff Airlines, Goodyear Tire and Rubber, Gulf Oil, Minnesota Mining and Manufacturing (3M), and Phillips Petroleum.

Once elected, these officials are, of course, expected to show proper gratitude toward their beneficiaries. They are expected to vote in the "right" way and to lend a ready and sympathetic ear to professional lobbyists who will point out the "national interest" in all types of legislation under consideration, which is really the special interest of those who lobby and whose income position is being advanced by the legislation. Meanwhile, the voices of those whose income position is being eroded by the very same legislation go unheard. The interests of the organized special pleaders are visible and concentrated: their gain may be $100 million worth of extra revenues that would come to a single firm, or a small group of them, as a result of higher legal prices, a subsidy, or a government contract. On the contrary, the interest of their unorganized victims is invisible and diffuse; their loss may be 50 cents from each of 200 million consumers or taxpayers. The special-interest groups can afford to hire full-time professional lobbyists (together with large staffs of lawyers, public relations people, and so on). They can easily inundate the overworked staffs of every single legislator with

---

initially (as is usually the case), it cannot easily do it later. Once the initial recipient of a monopoly right has sold it to someone else, the purchaser of this right will not make economic profits because cost will be so much higher. In New York City, for example, someone may pay $78,000 for a taxi, only $10,000 of which is for the physical car, the remainder going for the medallion needed to run it. If the present value of future monopoly profits equals the medallion's $68,000 market value, extra profit and extra cost just offset each other. Secondary owners of monopoly rights, therefore, would justifiably resent it if they suddenly had to pay the government for these rights.

The same facts make it difficult to deregulate an industry that was government-regulated in the past. Thus the impact of the Motor Carrier Act of 1980 on the balance sheets of trucking firms was swift and massive. The size of suddenly worthless monopoly-route privileges, carried as intangible "operating rights" assets on the books, ranged from a low of $3 million (Cooper-Jarrett) to a high of $34.9 million (Yellow Freight System).

Sources: Edmund W. Kitch et al., "The Regulation of Taxicabs in Chicago," *The Journal of Law and Economics*, October 1971, pp. 285–350; David A. Andelman, "New York's Taxi Industry Thriving on Some Controversial Economics," *The New York Times*, March 13, 1980, pp. A1 and B8; R. G. Noll, ed., *Government and the Sports Business* (Washington D.C.: Brookings, 1974); Laurel Sorenson, "Seats on Major Exchanges These Days Are Bringing Sellers Some Record Sums," *The Wall Street Journal*, September 3, 1980, p. 38; Karen W. Arenson, "New York Stock Exchange Faces Challenge," *The New York Times*, October 29, 1979, pp. A1 and D3; R. G. Noll et al., *Economic Aspects of Television Regulation* (Washington, D.C.: Brookings, 1973); Ronald Alsop, "Once-Shaky UHF Stations Lure Viewers, and Surging Profits Attract Eager Buyers," *The Wall Street Journal*, January 8, 1980, p. 46; F. H. Maier et al., "The Sale Value of Flue-Cured Tobacco Allotments," *Technical Bulletin* 148 (Agricultural Experiment Station, VPI, April 1960); M. Kafoglis, "A Paradox of Regulated Trucking," *Regulation*, September-October, 1977, pp. 27–32; Thomas Baker, "Reality Takes the Wheel," *Forbes*, October 27, 1980, pp. 133–34; *The New York Times,* June 17, 1981, p. 1.

good advice on the meaning of "sound public policy." They can orchestrate, if necessary, a letter campaign by thousands who have a lot to gain. The millions who lose are silent. Thus legislators get a nicely biased view of things. By following the "national interest" as represented by special-interest groups the compliant legislators can gather further rewards: more campaign funds in the future, more votes from those with new jobs in new plants built in their home districts by beneficiaries grateful for their help, job offers in case of a lost election, all-expenses-paid vacations, and, perhaps, even gifts of fur coats. Much of this, incidentally, is perfectly legal if financed from people's personal incomes (as in the case of a gift from a high-salaried corporate officer); it is quite illegal if it is financed by corporate funds.

The "Capture" of Regulators.   Now consider the regulatory bodies set up by the legislative branch of government (and discussed in more detail in Chapter 17). Their officials, too, are systematically influenced by those they are supposed to "regulate." They, too, receive rewards for being compliant when approached by the special interests.

Many regulators have strong bonds with the regulated. For example, it is not at all unusual to put doctors on a professional licensing board for practitioners of medicine, to put airline industry officials on the CAB, to place electric power company executives on the FPC. Even when such choices are not dictated by the need for expert knowledge, lobbyists will see to it that this is exactly what happens. (No wonder that regulators are frequently found to own securities and thus have a personal financial interest in companies they regulate. In 1974, for example, 19 officials of the FPC, which had raised natural gas prices, held natural gas company stock.)

Even when members of a regulated industry are not the regulators, chummy relations quickly develop. Regulators necessarily have frequent contact with the regulated at formal public hearings before the various commissions involved or at the more than 100,000 nonpublic meetings a year in which specific issues are "informally adjudicated."

The federal alphabet agencies, for instance, employ so-called administrative law judges. They gather evidence, conduct hearings, and make decisions on the government-sponsored cartels about rates charged, the number of firms allowed, and so on. This procedure is typically lengthy and even then any decision can be appealed to the full regulatory commission or challenged in court or both. A recent railroad merger case took 3 years and 275 days of hearings to decide. It produced a veritable paper nightmare of 50,000 pages of transcripts and 100,000 pages of exhibits. There is plenty of occasion for regulators and the regulated to get to know each other not just during hearings, but also during informal contacts over lunch, at business conventions, and at social gatherings. Naturally, the CAB members (who awarded that new route bringing in $100 million in annual revenues) will be invited to the airline's inaugural flight. Naturally, the ICC members (who approved that railroad merger cutting costs by $100 million a year) will go on the inaugural ride, complete with fancy food, liquor, and entertainment. Before long, government officials and industry executives are personal friends. In 1974, the chairman of the CAB was taken on an all-expenses-paid golfing trip to Bermuda by Boeing and United Aircraft Company officials and journeyed through Europe with a TWA vice president—all while issues vital to these firms were being decided by the CAB.

Sooner or later, it becomes obvious that friendly regulators (like friendly legislators whose reelection bids fail) can expect future jobs from those they now regulate. In 1971, for example, 12 of 24 former CAB members were employed by the firms they used to regulate. Could it be any clearer why government underwrites the monopoly game?

SUMMARY

1.   If people as a group wish to increase their command over goods (barring the receipt of gifts or loans from other such groups), they must engage in some activity that enlarges the overall quantity of goods available. Any subset of all people can, however, always gain additional goods even if the total quantity thereof is unchanged. They can do so at the expense of other people, by forming *monopolies* or *cartels*. Monopolies and cartels have the ability to raise the price of something that is for sale above the perfectly competitive level. This *monopoly power* originates from technological or legal sources, including increasing returns to scale, exclusive ownership of key resources, patents and copyrights, and exclusive franchises.

2. Contrary to what many people think, a profit-maximizing monopoly does not charge the highest possible price, but one that corresponds to the quantity that equates (constant or rising) marginal cost with (constant or falling) marginal revenue. Equating marginal cost and marginal revenue leads to maximum possible profit, but in the short run such profit can be positive, zero, or even negative.

3. A major difference between a perfectly competitive firm and a monopoly is that the monopoly may reap positive profit *even in the long run* when it equates long-run marginal cost and long-run marginal revenue.

4. There are other differences between a perfectly competitive firm and a monopoly: A monopoly will always choose an output volume at which price exceeds marginal cost; a monopoly is unlikely to produce at minimum average total cost. The gap between price and marginal cost (which is always present when firms are able to exercise monopoly power) provides the basis for constructing the Lerner index of monopoly power.

5. Firms also establish cartels in the hope of reaping permanent economic profit. The success of cartels, however, is often elusive because of organizational difficulties, a high price elasticity of demand, or a high price elasticity of supply. Yet firms try to overcome these obstacles—by private efforts, with the help of various levels of government, and even via international agreements.

6. Some applications of the theory of monopoly include the author-publisher conflict, price discrimination (of the first, second, and third degree), markup pricing, bilateral monopoly, and the notion of the "captured" state.

KEY TERMS

acreage allotments
bilateral monopoly
cartel
copyright
exclusive franchise
fair-trade laws
first-degree price discrimination
import quotas
Lerner index
marginal outlay (*MO*)
marginal revenue (*MR*)
marketing quotas
monopoly
monopoly power
monopsony
natural monopoly
parity
patent
perfect price discrimination
price discrimination
second-degree price discrimination
tariffs
third-degree price discrimination

QUESTIONS AND PROBLEMS

1. The text lists technological and legal sources of monopoly power. Can you think of illegal ones?

2. Consider the zero-profit monopoly in Figure 11.4. Could the firm pictured there make a positive profit with the help of first- or second-degree price discrimination? Explain.

3. Consider the profit-making monopoly depicted in Figure 11.3.

a. At which point, to the left of E, must average total cost intersect market demand?

b. To which point on the marginal-cost curve does the total-cost curve's point of inflexion (between a and d) correspond?

Explain your answers.

4. Consider the following data for a monopoly and determine its profit-maximizing price.

Price	Quantity	Total Cost
8	5	30
7	6	32
6	7	34
5	8	36
4	9	38
3	10	48

5. The monopoly pictured in Figure 11.6 in the long run is not producing its output at the lowest of all possible average total costs (shown by point R). What would make a monopoly produce at a point such as R?

6. The section on third-degree price discrimination gives many examples. Examine them and try to determine in each case *why* such price discrimination is possible. (*Hint #1:* Children are more apt than adults to get homemade haircuts; thus their price elasticity of demand is relatively high and the price is lower than for adults. Barbers need not fear that children will resell their cheap haircuts to adults who are being charged more. *Hint #2:* Bulky books may not be mailed at all if the charge is high; thus the shipper's price elasticity of demand is high and the price is lower than for first-class mail. Those who mail books cannot resell these cheap postal services to others who are charged so much more per pound of first class mail. *Hint #3:* Executives traveling on expense accounts are unlikely to switch from first-class air transportation to third-rate buses; thus their price elasticity of demand is relatively low, and the price is higher—out of all proportion to any increased leg room and food consumption. Such executives, furthermore, cannot obtain this service more cheaply by buying a night coach passenger's ticket.)

7. Do you think price discrimination could ever be practiced by *buyers*? Explain.

8. Are each of the following true or false?

a. A monopoly that faces a price-inelastic demand at its chosen price cannot be maximizing profit.

b. The author of a book who received a fixed percentage of the publisher's profit would wish to price the book in such a way that price elasticity of demand was greater than $|1|$.

c. In situations of bilateral monopoly, the monopsony will always opt for a higher price and lower quantity than the monopoly.

SELECTED READINGS

Brozen, Yale. "Is the Government the Source of Monopoly?" *Intercollegiate Review*, Winter 1968–69. Reprinted in Tibor R. Machan, ed. *The Libertarian Alternative: Essays in Social and Political Philosophy.* Chicago: Nelson-Hall, 1974, chap. 9.

Horvitz, Paul M. "The Pricing of Textbooks and the Remuneration of Authors." *The American Economic Review,* May 1966, pp. 812–20. Reprinted in Harry G. Johnson and Burton A. Weisbrod. *The Daily Economist.* Englewood Cliffs, N.J.: Prentice-Hall, 1973, pp. 22–29. *See also* idem, "A Note on Textbook Pricing." *The American Economic Review*, September 1965, pp. 844–48, which explores the possibilities of intertemporal price discrimination in the textbook market.

Kessel, Reuben A. "Price Discrimination in Medicine." *The Journal of Law and Economics*, October 1958, pp. 20–53.

A discussion of the cartel sponsored by the American Medical Association.

Leffler, Keith B. "Physician Licensure: Competition and Monopoly in American Medicine." *The Journal of Law and Economics*, April 1978, pp. 165–86.

A further discussion in light of Akerlof's "lemons" model, cited in Chapter 10, of Kessel's article, cited above.

Lerner, Abba P. "The Concept of Monopoly and the

Measurement of Monopoly Power.'' *Review of Economic Studies*, June 1934, pp. 157–75.

> The original proposal of the Lerner index of monopoly power.

Moore, Henry L. ''The Personality of Antoine Augustin Cournot.'' *The Quarterly Journal of Economics*, May 1905, pp. 370–99.

Nichol, A. J. ''Tragedies in the Life of Cournot.'' *Econometrica*, July 1938, pp. 193–97.

Pigou, A. C. *The Economics of Welfare*, 4th ed. London: Macmillan, 1950.

> The first systematic discussion of the three degrees of price discrimination.

Silberman, Jonathan, and Yochum, Gilbert. ''The Market for Special Interest Campaign Funds: An Exploratory Approach.'' *Public Choice*, 1980, pp. 75–83.

Stocking, George W. *Cartels in Action: Case Studies of International Diplomacy*. New York: Twentieth Century Fund, 1946.

Vernon, Raymond, ed. *The Oil Crisis*. New York: Norton, 1976.

> An excellent narrative of the events leading to the 1973–74 OPEC victory.

CHAPTER 12

Oligopoly and Monopolistic Competition

Chapter 11 explained why sellers of goods, seeking to gain economic profit on a permanent basis, may wish to eliminate all other sellers in their industry or at least to collude with them. We also noted the technological and legal foundations on which some firms manage to build successful monopolies or cartels. For many other firms, however, complete success remains elusive in this monopoly game, although they may succeed in part. As a result, most firms come to inhabit a "twilight zone," lying somewhere between monopoly or cartel on the one hand and perfect competition on the other. In all market economies, this middle ground, in which features of monopoly blend with those of competition, is of major importance. Although Cournot clearly pointed to it in 1838, it took another century before economists paid serious attention to it. In 1933, under the leadership of Edward H. Chamberlin of Cambridge, Massachusetts (see Biography 12.1) and Joan V. Robinson of Cambridge, England (see Biography 13.1), a major revolution was launched in microeconomic theory, similar in importance to the macroeconomic one initiated by J. M. Keynes in 1936. Economists began to focus on **imperfect competition**; that is, market situations, other than pure monopoly and cartel, in which individual sellers nevertheless face downward-sloping demand curves and thus have some measure of control over price.

The Coca Cola Company, for example, because of its trademark, has a legal monopoly in this drink. No one else may produce it, and the firm can charge any price it likes for it. But when it does, it better be aware of its obvious rivals, from the makers of Pepsi Cola to those of orange juice. Because these rivals produce a whole range of fairly good substitutes, the Coca Cola Company does not enjoy a pure monopoly. The suburban corner drugstore, similarly, because of its location, has a local monopoly of sorts. It, too, can charge any price it wishes for its drugs. But it better be aware that if its prices get too much out of line, customers will trade in the advantage of short trips to the neighborhood store for lower prices at competing drugstores downtown. This chapter will discuss the types of situations illustrated by the Coca Cola Company and the corner drugstore.

In this chapter we will first consider **oligopoly**, a market structure in which the entry of new firms is difficult and relatively few sellers compete with one another, offering either homogeneous products (cement, steel, rail transportation) or differentiated ones (cars, cigarettes, soap). Later in the chapter, we will turn to **monopolistic competition**, a market structure in which the entry of new firms is easy and large number of sellers compete with one another, offering differentiated products.

Oligopoly and Strategic Behavior

In situations of oligopoly, one encounters **strategic behavior**—the type of behavior arising among a small number of actors who have conflicting interests and are mutually conscious of the interdependence of their decisions. There being so few sellers, each one of them has identifiable rivals, the actions of whom become known almost at once; every seller is intensely aware that the actions of any one significantly affect the fortunes of all others. Because collusion at the expense of buyers is either absent or so informal as to be imperfect, the decisions of any one seller on such matters as product quantity, price, quality, or advertising are bound to be viewed by the other sellers as attempts to gain at their expense. These decisions, therefore, are bound to call forth some sort of reaction, the type and extent of which is hard to predict. When any one move is likely to call forth a countermove, what will be the end result? Nobody knows! Economists have developed dozens of theories to capture this interdependence. As a group, these theories reflect the rich array of actual behavior patterns, but no single one is universally accepted as *the* theory of oligopoly. We will resist a Teutonic compulsion to list all the competing theories, but we will consider a few of the more important ones.

Decision Making Under Oligopoly: Output Quantity

Cournot himself considered the case of two competitors whose decision making focused on the *quantity* of output produced. Each of them was making output decisions on the assumption that its rival was supplying a fixed quantity that would not be adjusted in response to any output decision made by itself. Panel (a) of Figure 12.1 pictures a hypothetical market demand line AB, which is based on the equation $Q = 100 - P$, where Q and P are quantity and price in the market as a whole. At a price of $100, therefore, quantity demanded is zero (point A); at a zero price, quantity is 100 units per year (point B). Our graph also shows the implied marginal revenue as dashed line AC. Now let fixed cost as well as the marginal cost of production be zero (only to keep the graph uncluttered); marginal cost is shown by line OB. A pure monopolist would choose a quantity of 50 units per year (point C), charge a price of $50 per unit (point D), and make a profit of $2,500 per year (rectangle $OCDE$). Not so our two competitors.

Let Firm X believe that Firm Y is going to supply $q_Y = 60$. Then the demand facing X will be seen by X as market demand Q minus 60 or as $Q = 100 - P - 60 = 40 - P$. This demand line and its marginal revenue line is shown in panel (b) as lines FG and FH, respectively. At zero marginal cost, Firm X would supply 20 units (point H), charge $20 each (point I), and (still assuming zero fixed cost) make a profit of $400 (rectangle $OHIK$). Note: At a price of $20, market demand would equal 80, leaving exactly 60 units to be supplied by Firm Y, as we assumed.

In a similar fashion, one can calculate how much output X would supply for various other assumed quantities supplied by Y, and this output is shown by X's **reaction curve** in panel (c) of our graph, which shows the best quantity supplied from X's point of view for every possible quantity supplied by Y. The quantity combination calculated above (if $q_Y = 60$, then $q_X = 20$) is shown as point L.

When X supplies 20 units, firm Y, however, may not supply 60 units at all. Suppose, as Cournot assumed, that Y also believed that any quantity decision of its own would call forth no reaction from X. Noting X's decision to supply 20 units, Firm Y would then, by an analogous procedure, calculate its demand as $Q - 20 = 100 - P - 20 = 80 - P$ and would end up supplying 40 units instead; this output is shown by point M

FIGURE 12.1 Cournot's Model

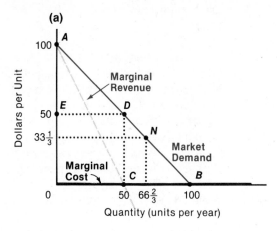

(a)

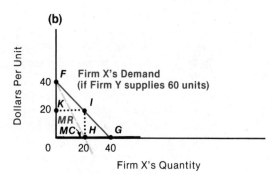

(b)

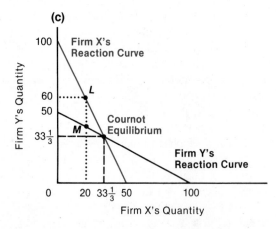

(c)

When each of two firms in an industry makes output decisions on the assumption that its rival is supplying a fixed quantity that will not be adjusted in response to any output decision made by itself, a Cournot equilibrium emerges.

on Y's reaction curve. Analogously, Y would supply nothing if X supplied 100; 50 units if X supplied nothing, and so on. (The equations of the reaction curves are $q_X = 50 - 0.5q_Y$ and $q_Y = 50 - 0.5q_X$, respectively.)

As panel (c) of our graph shows, the only quantity combination that would not elicit further reactions from the two rivals is the **Cournot equilibrium**, which is found at the intersection of the two reaction curves. The Cournot equilibrium point reflects the decision, on the part of both firms, to supply $33\frac{1}{3}$ units. Note: If a total of $66\frac{2}{3}$ units were thus supplied, market price would equal $33.33, as seen clearly by point N in panel (a). Total revenue and (in this example) profit would come to $2,222.22, clearly less than the potential monopoly profit of $2,500 calculated above. Indeed, Cournot reckoned, a gradual increase in the number of competitors would in this way eventually reduce the price to marginal cost (to zero in our case). The case also shows, however, the "price" these firms are paying for not colluding with each other and the incentive that exists to form a cartel, cut production, and raise price.

Note: It is fairly easy to find fault with almost all existing theories of oligopoly, including Cournot's. Consider what it takes for his equilibrium to be attained. No matter how stupidly wrong Firm X is (when counting on its rival to supply a fixed quantity $\bar{q}_Y$ but finding instead a quantity adjustment being made by Firm Y), it will continue to be steadily stupid to the end! The implied inability of each firm to learn from experience is not exactly credible. Next, we will turn to other models that focus attention not on adjustments in quantity, but on adjustments in price.

Decision Making Under Oligopoly: Price

In a situation of oligopoly, any seller's change in price in the downward direction can easily be interpreted by rivals as an attempt to eliminate them by luring away their customers. Rivals are unlikely to take this lying down. They will answer such "predatory price cutting" with price cuts of their own. This may give rise to a further price cut by the original firm, and so on in an endless chain. There are plenty of precedents for such a chain of price cuts. A **price war** in which rival firms successively cut their prices below those of competitors (and perhaps even below their own cost) occurred in the 1870s among railroads hauling freight between New York and Chicago. A price war raged among oil producers in the 1880s, among the makers of cigarettes in the 1930s, and among the makers of heavy electrical equipment in the 1950s. And in

---

BIOGRAPHY 12.1:

Edward H. Chamberlin

Edward Hastings Chamberlin (1899–1967) was born at La Conner, Washington. He studied at the Universities of Iowa, Michigan, and Harvard. He taught at Harvard during his entire career, where he was also editor of the *Quarterly Journal of Economics*.

Chamberlin's 1927 Ph.D. thesis, in which he fused the hitherto separate theories of monopoly and perfect competition, became his first book as *The Theory of Monopolistic Competition: A Reorientation of the Theory of Value* (1933). Its brilliant exposition and original contributions quickly swept the profession, which soon talked of the Chamberlinian revolution. Note: As Chamberlin used the term "monopolistic competition," it included what is now generally termed (differentiated) oligopoly as well as what is now called monopolistic competition. All these sellers have, of course, an absolute monopoly of their differentiated product but are subject to the competition of imperfect substitutes. Hence the title of the book.

As fate would have it, and as has happened before in the history of science, Joan Robinson of Cambridge, England, published a similar book six months later. Rather grieved, Chamberlin (who in fact had stressed all along such aspects as product differentiation and advertising, neglected by Robinson) spent much of his life trying to differentiate his product from Robinson's and defending his work against critics. While bringing out ever new editions of his book, he also edited *Monopoly and Competition and Their Regulation* (1954), and he wrote *Towards a More General Theory of Value* (1957) and *The Economic Analysis of Labor Union Power* (1958).

Says Chamberlin in the 8th edition of *The Theory of Monopolistic Competition*:

Monopolistic competition is a challenge to the traditional viewpoint of economics that competition and monopoly are alternatives and that individual prices are to be explained in terms of either the one or the other. By contrast, it is held that most economic situations are composites of both competition and monopoly and that, wherever this is the case, a false view is given by neglecting either one of the two forces. . . . This seems to be a very simple idea. . . . Its inherent reasonableness was never better expressed than by a student who observed to me . . . . "Chapter IV is easy—you don't say anything in it."

My own observation of Chapter IV, however, would be quite different. . . . It contains not a technique, but a way of looking at the economic system; and changing one's economic Weltanschauung is something very different from . . . adding new tools to one's kit. . . . This concept of a blending of competition and monopoly is quite lacking in Mrs. Robinson's *Imperfect Competition*. . . . Imperfect and monopolistic competition have been commonly linked as different names for the same thing. Their elements of . . . dissimilarities [seem to be] hardly recognized. I submit . . . that there is no evidence . . . that Mrs. Robinson thinks of monopoly . . . and competition in any other way but as mutually exclusive. This difference in conception between us is in fact the key to an understanding of many other differences in treatment. (pp. 204–207).

the 1970s, price wars have raged among New England banks (with respect to NOW accounts), transatlantic airlines and rent-a-car companies.

Sometimes the participants in such struggles end up pricing their product below cost and go bankrupt, leaving the field to their luckier competitors whose longer staying power may be the result of lower cost, greater financial reserves, or profitable lines of business in other industries. As all wars, price wars are bitter experiences for the firms involved. They see their profits disappear and their very existence threatened, all the while knowing that monopoly profits could be assured with the proper degree of cooperation.

On the other hand, any seller's change of price in the upward direction can be suicidal as well. If the rivals simply sit back and do nothing, the seller who raises prices is likely to lose a lot of customers to those rivals—and again there may be red ink as a result.

Some theorists, therefore, have argued that oligopolistic firms will have "sticky" prices, which they will be very reluctant to change.

The Kinked Demand Curve

Paul M. Sweezy, in 1939, developed the theory of the **kinked demand curve** to account for this expected price rigidity (see Figure 12.2). An oligopolistic firm is imagined to be selling 800 million packs of cigarettes per year at a price of $1 per pack (point *a*). It sees itself as facing two subjectively estimated demand lines. One of these, extending from *b* to *d* and beyond, indicates how much this firm expects to sell at various prices if its rivals exactly match any price change it cares to initiate. The other demand line, extending from *c* to *f* and beyond, indicates how much this firm expects to sell at various prices if its rivals do not react to any price change it cares to initiate. Note how a hypothetical price increase from $1 to $1.25 per pack would reduce quantity demanded from *a* to *d* if rivals raised their prices equally, while the same price hike would reduce quantity demanded from *a* to *c* if rivals held the line on their prices and thus lured

customers away from our firm. Note how, similarly, a hypothetical price cut from $1 to 75 cents per pack would increase quantity demanded from *a* to *e* if rivals lowered their prices equally, while the same price cut would increase quantity demanded from *a* to *f* if rivals did not match the cut and thus allowed our firm to lure customers away from them.

As Sweezy saw it, any one firm is likely to reason as follows: If it raised its price, rivals could increase their market share by doing nothing, and that is exactly what the rivals would do. Thus the demand line relevant to our firm for any increase in price is color segment *ac* and not dashed segment *ad*. On the other hand, if the firm lowered its price, rivals would decrease their market share by doing nothing, and that is exactly what rivals would *not* do. Thus the demand line relevant to our firm for any decrease in price is color segment *ab* and not dashed segment *af*.

Our firm's entire demand line, therefore, is found when the irrelevant segments (dashed) are deleted. It is the kinked color line *cab*, with the kink occurring at the level of the present price (point *a*). Corresponding to this kinked line of demand, a strangely-shaped marginal-revenue line, going from *c* to *g, h,* and *i,* can be derived:

As was shown with the help of Figure 11.2, "Monopoly: Total and Marginal Revenue" (p. 323), the marginal-revenue line corresponding to any straight demand line can always be found half-way between that demand line and the vertical axis. Thus the marginal revenue corresponding to demand segment *ca* equals *cg* (distance *kg,* for instance, being equal to *gf*). Because the pessimistic assumptions of our firm about the behavior of its rivals make demand line *caf* inapplicable to the right of point *a,* its marginal-revenue line becomes similarly irrelevant to the right of point *g,* and this segment hasn't even been drawn. Analogously, the marginal revenue corresponding to demand segment *ab* goes from *h* to *i* and beyond (distance *0i,* for instance, being equal to *ib,* distance *mh* equalling *hn,* and so on). Again, because demand line *bd* is inapplicable to the left of point *a,* its marginal-revenue line is

FIGURE 12.2   Sweezy's Model

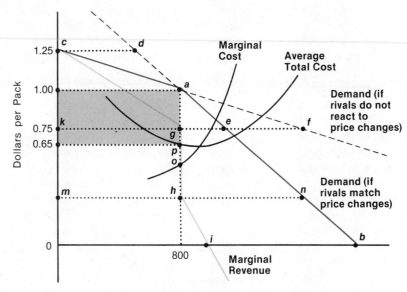

An oligopolistic firm that assumes the worst of its rivals (they will not match price increases; they will promptly match price decreases) ends up with a kinked demand line, such as color line *cab* shown here. Such a firm also has a discontinuous marginal-revenue line, as evidenced by line *cghi*.

irrelevant to the left of *h*, and this segment also has not been drawn.

We can now view our firm's profit picture by introducing cost curves. Because the firm has chosen to produce 800 million packs of cigarettes per year, marginal cost must equal marginal revenue at this quantity, and it does (point *o*). The average total cost corresponding to this output level (point *p*) is seen to equal 65 cents a pack. Thus a profit per pack of 35¢ is made (distance *ap*), and total profit equals $280 million per year (shaded rectangle).

Implications of the Kinked Demand Curve. The existence of a kinked demand curve implies, among other things, that oligopolistic firms, quite unlike perfect competitors or monopolists, may not change price even in the face of moder-

ate changes in 1. marginal cost or 2. demand. These two implications are illustrated, respectively, in panels (a) and (b) of Figure 12.3. Panel (a) shows an original profit-maximizing equilibrium corresponding to the intersection, at point *c*, of marginal revenue, *MR*, and marginal cost, MC_0. The firm produces 800 million packs of cigarettes per year and sells each for $1. Let marginal cost rise as high as MC_1, or let if fall as low as MC_2. The *MR-MC* intersection changes (to *b* or *d*, respectively), but the profit-maximizing output and price remain the same.

Panel (b) pictures an identical initial equilibrium, corresponding to intersection *e* of original MC_0 and MR_0. Now let demand fall from D_0 to D_1, which changes marginal revenue from MR_0 to MR_1. A new equilibrium corresponds to the *MC-MR* intersection at *f*. Quantity produced is down to 525 million packs a year, but price (now corresponding to point h on D_1 rather than i on D_0) is the same.

Criticisms of the Sweezy Model. As they did with Cournot's model, economists have found much in the Sweezy model with which to quarrel. Consider how the model does not explain how the initial price is derived in the first place. The model suggests that prices should be more rigid in oligopolistic industries than in those dominated by monopoly. Yet empirical studies by George J. Stigler, by Julian Simon, by Walter J. Primeaux, Jr. and Mark R. Bomball, and by others have shown exactly the opposite to be true.[1] No wonder that many economists prefer to explain oligopolistic pricing by means other than the Sweezy model.

Gentlemen's Agreements

Some economists argue that oligopolists who cannot manage to build a cartel, but recognize the inevitable interdependence of their actions, are most likely to construct some kind of communications network among themselves. (Consider the political analogies of NATO joining the Warsaw Pact vs. détente and telephone hotlines.) As a result, oligopolists can, perhaps, make output and price decisions that are not instantly interpreted by their rivals as signs of aggression, but rather serve the purpose of mutual accommodation. Such communications may be overt, as in the case of **gentlemen's agreements** (sorry about that, ladies), informal oral understandings among oligopolists in the same industry that they will maintain a certain minimum price. These agreements are apt to be ratified by nothing more than a handshake over lunch, and they have in fact been made on many occasions. (When such overt communications are illegal, as is often the case, communications may be covert instead).

In the 1880s, gentlemen's agreements involved the coal, cordage, rail transport, salt, and whiskey industries. Later, it was the cement and steel companies' turn. Between 1907 and 1911, for example, all the important steel industry executives regularly attended the celebrated dinners given by Judge Elbert H. Gary, then chairman of the board of directors of U.S. Steel. And for many years later, their **basing-point system**, called *Pittsburgh plus*, worked like a charm. Until 1948, all steel companies, regardless of their location, would quote prices equal to those charged by U.S. Steel at its Pittsburgh mills (the basing point) plus rail freight from the basing point to the buyer's location. No wonder that the U.S. Navy Department, when it opened 31 secret bids for a quantity of rolled steel on May 26, 1936, found 31 identical prices of $20,727.26 each. And in the same year, the U.S. Engineer's Office at Tucumari, New Mexico, received 11 sealed bids for the delivery of 6,000 barrels of cement. Each one of them was identical, right up to the sixth decimal point: $3.286854 per barrel.[2] How often, do you think, is this going to happen by pure chance?

Nowadays, Gary-style understandings are quite illegal in the United States, but this does not mean that they are uncommon. People of the same industry do meet at trade association conventions, and as Adam Smith himself taught us long ago, "people of the same trade seldom meet together, even for merriment and diversion, but the conversation ends in a conspiracy against the public, or in some contrivance to raise prices."

[1]George J. Stigler, "The Kinky Oligopoly Demand Curve and Rigid Prices," *Journal of Political Economy*, October 1947, pp. 432–49; Julian L. Simon, "A Further Test of the Kinky Oligopoly Demand Curve," *The American Economic Review*, December 1969, pp. 971–75; Walter J. Primeaux, Jr., and Mark R. Bomball, "A Reexamination of the Kinky Oligopoly Demand Curve," *Journal of Political Economy*, July/August 1974, pp. 851–62; Walter J. Primeaux, Jr., and Mickey C. Smith, "Pricing Patterns and the Kinky Demand Curve," *The Journal of Law and Economics*, April 1976, pp. 189–99.

[2]These charming examples are cited in Max E. Fletcher, *Economics and Social Problems* (Boston: Houghton Mifflin, 1979), pp. 172–73.

FIGURE 12.3   Implications of Kinked Oligopoly Demand

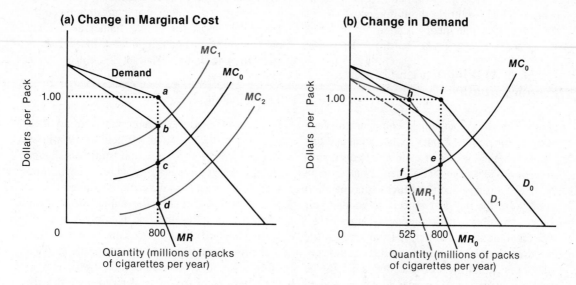

(a) Change in Marginal Cost

(b) Change in Demand

The existence of kinked oligopoly demand implies price rigidity even in the face of moderate changes in marginal cost (a) or demand (b).

In fact, the U.S. Department of Justice has estimated that a third of U.S. firms were involved in private, informal price-fixing activities in 1974. Food producers engaged in price fixing included the makers of beef, beer, bread and bakery products, eggs, milk and milk products, seafood, sugar, and soft drinks. Price fixing, however, was not confined to commodities. The professional societies of accountants, architects, doctors, engineers, lawyers and real estate brokers routinely circulated schedules on minimum fees that no "ethical" member was supposed to violate. Yet oligopolistic price fixing can and does occur in even more subtle ways.

Price Leadership

According to a set of industry practices called **price leadership**, one firm, the price leader, announces and occasionally changes list prices, which the other firms immediately adopt as well. The whole process works tacitly, as if by telepa-

thy. There is no written agreement, not even a handshake over lunch. Yet a clearly observable parallelism of action emerges. Examples of this practice abound. Industries (and their usual price leaders) involved have included those making aluminum (Alcoa), automobiles (General Motors), banking (Chase Manhattan), cigarettes (Reynolds), ready-to-eat cereals (Kellogg), turbogenerators (General Electric), steel (U.S. Steel), and many more.

Note: As is true for all other theories of oligopoly pricing, those concerning gentlemen's agreements and their unspoken counterpart, price leadership, are far from complete. It is unclear, for example, how a price leader is selected (indeed, the position often changes hands, as it has among Kellogg, General Mills, and Post in the cereals industry). Nor is it clear how a particular price is determined. Is the monopoly price chosen? Is it a much lower **limit price** that prevents the entry into the industry of new rivals? Is it a matter of finding a **focal-point price**, one that has a compelling prominence for reasons of aesthetics, precedent, symmetry (round numbers, $199.95, splitting the difference)? On all these questions, the theory is silent.

Decision Making Under Oligopoly: Product Quality

Some oligopolists (but not all) compete with each other on still another front. To the extent that this is possible, they go out of their way to differentiate their product from that of their competitors in the same industry. Such **product differentiation** can involve the physical aspects of goods (their color, durability, flavor, octane rating, size, style, and the like), the purely legal aspects (the introduction of a trademark), or the conditions of sale. These conditions of sale, indeed, must be very broadly defined. Consider how firms seek to be pleasantly different (and thus gain a degree of monopoly power) by building a new store closer to your home, providing free convenient parking, more business hours per week, attractive reusable containers, more and friendlier clerks, music while you shop, carpeted floors, more trading stamps, easier credit terms, prompter delivery, better warranties, faster repair and maintenance —the list goes on.

Not all product differentiation, of course, involves genuine improvements in quality. New brand names, designs, or packaging may simply serve the purpose of making people believe in differences that do not exist. But even when higher quality is a fiction, when the belief in fiction is fact, sellers have a greater power over price.

Product differentiation, whether fact or fiction, involves complex decisions that are even more difficult to analyze than decisions about output quantity and price. Quantity and price, after all, can only move in two directions—up or down—but, as the above list indicates, product quality can take on innumerable dimensions. It is not surprising, perhaps, that economic theorists have advanced little beyond Chamberlin, who pointed them to this important and hitherto neglected aspect of competition.

Indeed, one of the most interesting pieces of theoretical apparatus in this field precedes the publication of Chamberlin's book by four years and comes to us from Harold Hotelling.

The Hotelling Paradox

Panel (a) of Figure 12.4 represents a group of 19 buyers (but we can think of them as 19 million just as well). They are uniformly distributed along a straight line of geographic distance, from west *(W)* to east *(E)*. We can think of this line as Main Street or a transcontinental railroad or even a beach. Now let us imagine that only two sellers exist. They sell equally priced products, identical in the minds of all buyers except for the location of sale. No buyer, therefore, prefers one seller to the other except for one reason: to minimize the cost, in time or money, of transportation (and that cost is assumed uniform per unit of distance everywhere). We have thus reduced the enormously complex issue of product quality to one dimension only: product differentiation on the basis of seller location.

If one wanted to minimize the total cost, in time or money, of transportation, if all buyers wished to contact a seller once but could not pool their trips, Hotelling asked, where should the two sellers be located? The answer is shown in panel (a). Sellers should locate symmetrically at the quartile points of our line, seller A's position coinciding with the location of buyer #5 and seller B's with the location of buyer #15. Under these circumstances, buyers 1–9 would buy from A, because it would be costlier for each one of them to go to B. Buyers 11–19 would buy from B, because it would be costlier for each one of these to go to A. Buyer #10, located on the line of indifference that would divide the market between the two sellers, would find it equally costly to go to A or B and would thus be indifferent between the two sources of supply. If one represented the transportation cost from one buyer's location to the next location by $1, the

FIGURE 12.4 The Hotelling Paradox

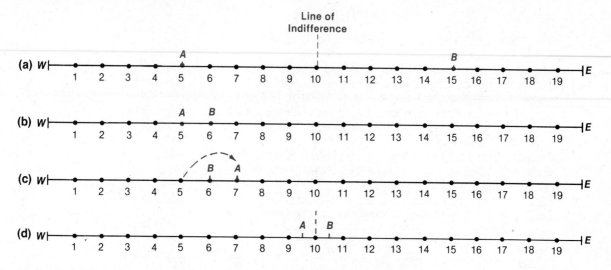

Under certain conditions, competition by means of product differentiation leads to products that are hardly differentiated at all. Similar "adjacencies" abound outside the area of economics proper.

total cost of transportation for all buyers would equal $45. (Buyers 5 and 15 would spend nothing; buyers 4, 6, 14, and 16 would spend $1 each; buyers 3, 7, 13, and 17 $2 each, and so on.) The locational product differentiation given in panel (a) would thus be ideal for minimizing the total cost of all buyers, but the sellers would not choose these locations.

Imagine that seller A (a restaurant on Main Street, perhaps, or an ice cream vendor on a beach) first appeared and in fact located at location #5. Where would B locate? The answer is given in panel (b). Seller B would locate at location #6, between A and the mass of customers, as close to A as possible without erasing the (locational) difference between the two. As a result, only buyers 1–5 would buy from A, while buyers 6–19 would buy from B. Society's transportation cost would by far exceed the $45 minimum calculated above; it would equal $101 instead. (Can you show how this figure is derived?)

Yet this result would be unstable if relocation

costs were zero (and this we will assume). As shown in panel (c), seller A could use the same strategy as B did. By now jumping over B and locating at #7, A could gain all the customers from 7–19, while B would be left with only 1–6. So far as total transportation costs are concerned, this would be an improvement (they would decline to $93), but the situation would still be unstable because B could, in turn, jump over A and locate at #8, thereby gaining a larger share of the market.

Where will it all end? Look at panel (d). Both sellers will end up in the geographic center of the market, near the line of indifference and only imperceptibly differentiated from each other. Total transportation cost will not be minimized (and will equal $81.50 in this example).

Hotelling's paradox is that competition by means of product differentiation may lead to products that are hardly differentiated at all. Hotelling was the first to realize that this theory had much wider applicability than has been indicated so far.

ANALYTICAL EXAMPLE 12.1:
The Cost of Automobile Model Changes

The efforts by some firms to differentiate their product from those of competitors are very costly, indeed. Some people argue that this product differentiation represents a waste of resources that could better be used to produce other goods. Others maintain that the ability to choose among many versions of a basic product makes people better off. Three economists decided to investigate the factual side of the issue. They estimated the annual cost of auto model changes from 1950–1960 compared to the 1949 model. As the table below shows, these extra costs reached a figure as high as $5.6 billion (in 1957). In many years, they amounted to almost a quarter of the total cost of a car.

Year (1)	Millions of Extra Dollars Compared to 1949 Model Cars				Extra Dollars per Car (6)
	Retooling Cost (2)	Producer's Direct Cost[a] (3)	Consumer's Gasoline Cost (4)	Total (5)=(2)+(3)+(4)	
1950	20	−27	13	6	1
1951	45	267	36	348	65
1952	82	460	102	644	148
1953	246	436	161	844	138
1954	264	1,072	240	1,576	362
1955	469	2,425	372	3,266	527
1956	336	3,040	590	3,966	630
1957	772	4,048	806	5,626	905
1958	626	2,354	949	3,924	922
1959	532	3,675	1,147	5,354	962
1960	537	3,456	1,346	5,339	888

[a]Extra factory and selling costs due to the production of larger and heavier cars with automatic transmissions, increased horsepower, power steering, power brakes.

Source: Franklin M. Fisher, Zvi Griliches, Carl Kaysen, "The Cost of Automobile Model Changes Since 1949," *The Journal of Political Economy*, October 1962, pp. 433–51. Table adapted by permission of the University of Chicago Press. Copyright 1962 by the University of Chicago.

Wider Applications of Hotelling's Paradox

When one considers "distance" figuratively instead of literally, the above technique of analysis can be applied to competing sellers whose products are separated not geographically, but by any one of a host of other dimensions of quality. *W* in our graph, for example, might denote not the western edge of a market, but the extreme degree of blandness of a beer or sweetness of cider. *E*, correspondingly, might not denote the eastern edge of the market, but the extreme degree of bitterness of a beer or of sourness of cider. Consumers might then be viewed not as uniformly distributed along a *geographic* line, but as distributed along a line of "characteristics space," differentiated from one another by tastes that indicate different degrees of preference for a characteristic such as bitterness, sourness, or the like. Thus buyer #1 might prefer the sweetest of all possible ciders (or the blandest of all possible beers) over all others, while buyer #19 would prefer the most sour cider (and the most bitter beer). Other buyers would have preferences between these two extremes. Again we could ask: Where would sellers "locate"? Which one of 19 possible varieties of cider (or beer) would each of them produce and offer for sale? Again the answer would follow our earlier analysis.

Society's cost (now measured in terms of the dissatisfaction buyers feel when they cannot get exactly the quality of product that is most preferred) would be minimized if seller A produced the product quality most preferred by buyer #5 and if seller B produced the product quality that was first choice for buyer #15. As we learned from panel (a) before, dissatisfaction would then equal 45 units. No single buyer would have to buy a product quality more than 5 gradations away from the one that was most preferred; many buyers would get product qualities much closer to their first choice.

Yet the end result once more would not be the one pictured in panel (a). If seller A produced the product most liked by buyer #5, seller B would produce the product most liked by buyer #6, thereby getting buyers 7–19 to buy from B as well. Although none of them would rank B's product as their first choice, all of them would prefer B's to A's, for the latter would still be one notch further away from their ideal. As panel (b) of our graph shows, #7 would almost get first choice when buying from B, while #19, extremely unhappy with B's product as well as A's, would still prefer B's. B's product characteristics would be a little bit closer to nonexistent product quality 19 than would be A's.

The end result, of course, would be the same old sameness depicted in panel (d). This undue tendency of competitors to imitate each other in product quality, Hotelling argued, explains a lot about the real world of economics and beyond. It explains why all shoes are so much alike but also why political parties and religions are so much alike. Anyone who takes a sharply contrasting position from a competitor (as when the Republicans or the Baptists locate at 5 in the belief that the Democrats or the Methodists will locate at 15) will find the competitor getting between this position and as many "customers" as possible (as when the Democrats or the Methodists locate at 6 instead).

Decision Making Under Oligopoly: Advertising

Unlike individual firms under perfect competition, for whom it would make no sense to advertise, imperfect competitors do advertise, with a vengeance. In 1980 imperfect competitors spent several hundred dollars for every man, woman, and child in the United States on advertising. As used here, the term *advertising* includes not only newspaper and magazine ads, radio and television announcements, direct mail solicitations, roadside billboards, and Goodyear blimps, but also store window displays, the distribution of free samples and trading stamps, a variety of contests and games, the efforts of salespeople, and much more. All this activity, of course, is designed to increase the demand for a firm's product at the expense of that for the products of competitors or even entirely different products. Regardless of whether a firm's attempt to shift its demand curve to the right is successful or not, advertising raises that firm's costs. As Chamberlin envisioned it, **selling cost**—that is, cost designed to alter a firm's demand curve—can be added to the familiar curves of (average or marginal) production cost. Depending on the degree to which the demand curve is shifted at the same time, the firm's profit is or is not increased as a result. Advertising, accordingly, will be continued or abandoned.

Advertising, it is often claimed, comes in two forms, but the two types are difficult to disentangle in practice. Some advertising is clearly **informative advertising**, which provides genuine information to buyers about the very existence of products or sellers, about price, and about quality. Because people are by nature less than omniscient, such advertising plays an important role in that it reduces people's ignorance and helps them make choices. As noted in Chapter 10, information can be a very valuable

CLOSE-UP 12.1:

Brand Loyalty:
The Case of Turkey Meat

In 1965, an experiment was conducted to test the reaction of consumers to brand names. In Part I of the experiment, subjects from Detroit were handed two plates, each with a slice of turkey meat. The slices were in fact from the same turkey, but they were labeled differently. One label was that of a heavily advertised brand well known in Detroit; the other was given an unfamiliar name. The results: 10 percent thought the slices tasted alike; 34 percent preferred the unknown brand; 56 percent preferred the known brand. In Part II of the experiment, subjects were handed two plates with tender and tough turkey meat, respectively. There were no brand labels. The results: 13 percent thought the slices tasted alike; 7 percent preferred the tough meat; 80 percent preferred the tender meat. In Part III of the experiment, subjects were asked to guess which brand the Part II samples belonged to. Some 64 percent thought that the sample they had preferred must have been the familiar brand.

Many similar experiments have shown that people can perceive actual differences in product quality in the *absence* of brand names, but that they perceive identical goods as different in the *presence* of brand names—and then prefer the familiar brand.

Source: James C. Makens, "Effect of Brand Preference Upon Consumers' Perceived Taste of Turkey Meat," *Journal of Applied Psychology*, August 1965, pp. 261–63.

commodity, indeed. Other types of advertising, however, are of more questionable value.

Persuasive advertising is designed to divert people's attention from facts to images and make them buy more as a result of imagined advantages. This persuasion occurs, perhaps, when products are associated with beautiful women, hand-some men, gracious living, and the like and when people are gradually turned into Pavlovian dogs. In a thousand different ways, people are "brainwashed" into being loyal to a particular firm's particular product until they are ready to shout "We'd rather fight than switch." People get precious little information when they are told that "blondes have more fun," that a cigarette "has the honest taste," or that they can now "put a tiger in their tank." Yet even in advertisements like these, people do get some information; if nothing else, they learn about the existence of the product concerned. Those, therefore, who would ban persuasive advertising on the grounds that the resources devoted to it represent a social waste would have a hard time sorting out informative from persuasive statements.

This is not to say that there is no room for improvement. Along with government agencies, such as the Federal Trade Commission or the Food and Drug Administration, a business-sponsored National Advertising Review Board seeks to eliminate blatant deception from advertisements. In 1981, for example, one ad showed a picture of a slim actress and the words, "California Avocados. Only 17 calories a slice. Would this body lie to you?" Apparently it would, because the ad also promised consumers specified quantities of vitamins plus potassium, but the size portion that would justify that claim would contain 132 calories. The ad was challenged and withdrawn. Yet subtle deception, half-truths, and "little white lies" persist. Thus we are told that "Anacin contains 23 percent more pain reliever than other leading headache remedies," but we are not told that Anacin equals 400 mg of plain aspirin (plus some caffeine) as compared with the 325 mg content of the standard (and so much cheaper) aspirin tablet. Banks promise us "the highest interest rate allowed by law" but invariably fail to mention that almost all other banks offer identical rates. Even cleverly chosen brand names can deceive: ReaLemon sounds like the genuine article, yet all other brands of such (reconstituted) lemon juice are indistinguishable from it.

Monopolistic Competition

Much of what has been said so far about product differentiation and advertising applies to *monopolistic competitors* as well as oligopolists. Yet monopolistic competitors are distinguished from oligopolists by the absence of strategic behavior. Entry into a monopolistically competitive "industry" is easy; large numbers of firms compete in it; and no single firm need fear any noticeable impact of its actions on any one competitor (of whom there are so many). No single firm, therefore, need fear any reaction by these others. The retail trade and service sectors of the economy are prime examples of monopolistic competition.

Note: In the above paragraph, the term *industry* appears in quotation marks and for a good reason. Traditionally, economists have considered an *industry* as composed of all firms producing an identical product. To the extent that the product of each firm is differentiated in a multitude of ways from that of every other firm, an obvious difficulty arises with this industry concept. Chamberlin attempted to overcome this problem by distinguishing **product groups**— groups of closely related but differentiated products that serve the same wants—and then treating all firms producing such products as if they belonged to an "industry." Such product groups, he thought, are distinguishable from each other by obvious gaps in the endless chain of substitutes such that the similar products of any two firms within a Chamberlinian group are related by a high cross-price elasticity of demand, while the more dissimilar products of any two firms placed in different groups are related by a very low or zero cross-price elasticity.

Profit Maximization

The behavior of the monopolistically competitive firm can be analyzed very much like that of the pure monopoly, but there is a difference in the long run. Entry into the "industry" being easy, zero economic profit is the inevitable long-run result for a monopolistic competitor, as shown in Figure 12.5. Panel (a) depicts a barbershop's downward-sloping demand line. Unlike wheat farmers, barbers do have their own identifiable products that cannot be duplicated perfectly. As a result, they have a group of more or less loyal patrons who prefer a particular firm's service, location, or whatever. Unlike wheat farmers, barbers, therefore, do have some measure of control over price. When they raise price, sales do not instantly fall to zero (as they would for the wheat farmer who insisted on getting more than the going price set at the Chicago Board of Trade). Yet our barber cannot raise price to infinity either. At $9.50 per haircut in our example, even the most loyal patrons will vanish for cheaper competitors. By the same token, monopolistically competitive barbers (unlike wheat farmers) will not gain all the world's customers by lowering price even a bit. Many people would continue to rely on their familiar (and now more expensive) shops.

Given our barber's demand, the implied marginal revenue-line (dashed), and the cost curves shown in panel (a) of Figure 12.5, profit is maximized (as it would be for a pure monopoly) according to intersection *a*. Every day, 48 haircuts are produced at an average total cost of $4.30 (point *b*) and for a price of $6.50 (point *c*). Thus the barber makes a profit of $105.60 per day (shaded rectangle).

Yet this profit will not continue into the long run. When economic profit is being made and entry into the industry is easy, others enter the industry—in this case opening up other barbershops. These other barbers would also like to earn $105.60 a day over and above their next best alternative (which, be it remembered, is what economic profit indicates). Gradually, some of our barber's customers (who may discover these new stores and prefer their work or location) will drift away. Our friend's demand will shrink, as from the demand line in panel (a) to the lower one in panel (b). In the end, this barber will produce only 30 haircuts per day (point *d*), at a price and average total cost of $5 (point *e*).

FIGURE 12.5 The Monopolistic Competitor

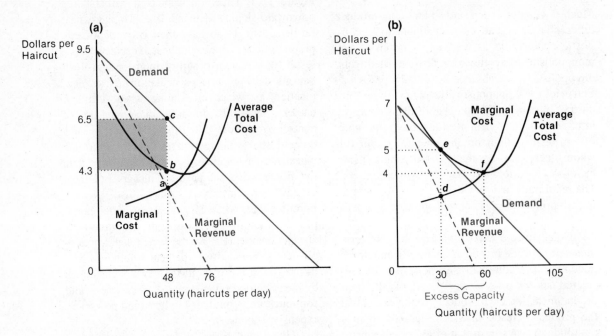

If monopolistically competitive firms make economic profit, as shown by the shaded rectangle in panel (a), entry of new firms into their "industry" will occur. This entry of new firms will reduce the demand for each firm and eliminate economic profit, as shown in panel (b). The inducement for entry being gone, entry into the "industry" will then cease.

Economic profit will have disappeared, just as it would have in perfect competition. But monopolistic competition is distinguished from perfect competition by the occurrence of *excess capacity.*

Excess Capacity

As was shown in Chapter 6, in long-run equilibrium, perfectly competitive firms are producing at minimum average total cost. They operate their plants at the optimal rate; they produce capacity output. Not so for monopolistic competitors. Note how our firm, depicted in panel (b), produces 30 haircuts at an average total cost of $5 (point *e*), while its average total cost could be as low as $4 if it produced twice as much (point *f*). This difference between a monopolistically competitive firm's capacity output and its profit-maximizing lower actual output is called its **excess capacity**.

This excess capacity can be seen in many places. Consider how hotels, movie houses, and restaurants are rarely filled, how gas station attendants and retail store clerks mostly have plenty of spare time left to serve other customers. But beware: the occurrence of excess capacity does not imply that the higher-than-minimum cost of production found in monopolistically competitive "industries" is a pure waste. What if, in our example, half the barbershops closed down? As panel (b) of Figure 12.5 shows, the other half could make up for this shutdown by producing twice as many haircuts each for $1 less on the average. But there would be a cost to buyers: Barbershops would be less conveniently

CLOSE-UP 12.2:

Advertising and the Price of Legal Services

Advertising, it is often claimed, only raises costs and, therefore, prices, but this is decidedly too simplistic a view. Until recently, for example, there was no advertising in the market for legal services. Bar associations routinely threw out members who were so "unethical" as to compete with their colleagues by advertising their fees or the nature of their services. They argued that such ads encouraged "extravagant self-laudatory brashness" and "unscrupulous solicitation" that was not designed to uphold the dignity of the profession. The object of lawyers, it was argued, was to provide service, not to make profit (a fine distinction surely lost on consumers).

Along came John Bates and Van O'Steen, law partners in Phoenix, Arizona, who defied the advertising ban. They were promptly taken to court, but eventually, on June 27, 1977, the U.S. Supreme Court agreed with them, citing the First Amendment guarantee of free speech.

The results have been amazing. In Phoenix, the fee for an uncontested divorce has dropped from $350 to $150. Similar price reductions have resulted all over the country for the preparation of wills, title searches, and much more. And many innovative types of services are being offered as well, from do-it-yourself divorce kits at $16.95 (instructions and forms included) to telephone consultations at $9.95.

Source: Warren Weaver, Jr., "Court Rules Lawyer May Advertise Fee For Routine Service," *The New York Times*, June 28, 1977, pp. 1 and 14; "Publicizing Fees," *ibid.*, July 1, 1977, p. 22; "Lawyers May Now Advertise," *ibid.*, July 3, 1977, p. E5; and Carol H. Falk, "Lawyers Are Facing Surge in Competition As Courts Drop Curbs," *The Wall Street Journal*, October 18, 1978, pp. 1 and 21.

---

located; customers would have to wait longer to be served; they would have a smaller selection of work quality to choose from. The opposite of this cost, of course, is the *benefit* buyers get when many firms operate permanently at a fraction of their capacity. Given people's genuine preference for diversity, this advantage may well make producing at higher-than-minimum average total cost worthwhile. Barbers, as you know, are not all alike. Would you rather have 10 barbers in your neighborhood, 2 of whom cut your hair just the way you like it and are always ready to serve you instantly because they are always underemployed; or would you prefer 5 who charge less, but none of whom ever manages to do the perfect job you crave and all of whom are always crowded? The answer, undoubtedly, will vary from product group to product group. This answer will depend on the extent to which an elimination of excess capacity can cut average total cost and prices (this will be the more likely, for example, the higher total fixed costs are); it will also depend on the degree to which products within their class can be substituted for one another (whether you think, for example, that all barbers are pretty much alike or that they differ as night does from day).

Applications

Application 1: Mergers

An obvious way for oligopolistic firms to escape the uncertainty of rival reactions—if they cannot establish a formal çartel and if they do not wish to rely on such informal and inevitably imperfect means of collusion as price leadership—is to eliminate their rivals by merging with them. Merging is the direct purchase of the assets of one firm by another. Such **mergers** can be **horizontal mergers**, among firms that sell closely related products in the same geographic market —as when one of two electric power companies in a city merges with the other. Mergers can also be **vertical mergers**, in which the merging units are related as suppliers and users of each other's products—as when an electric power company merges, on the one hand, with the crude oil refiners and railroads that supply it with fuel oil and, on the other hand, with the aluminum producers that use electric power. Mergers can also be **conglomerate mergers** among firms that have neither competititve nor buyer-seller relations but operate in many industries and, perhaps, even countries. In the United States three distinct waves of merger activity can be identified.

The First Wave. A first wave of mergers, totaling 2,890, occurred during 1896–1903. These mergers were mostly horizontal ones. For example, the Standard Oil Company ended up with 90 percent of the U.S. petroleum refining capacity, U.S. Steel with 65 percent of U.S. steel-making capacity, the American Can Company with 90 percent of the tin can market, and American Tobacco with 90 percent of the tobacco products market. Similar successes were achieved by Allis-Chalmers, the Corn Products Refining Company (now CPC International), Du Pont, Eastman Kodak, International Harvester, International Paper, International Salt, National Lead (now NL Industries), Pittsburgh Plate Glass (now PPG Industries), Standard Sanitary (now American Standard), United Fruit (now United Brands), United Shoe Machinery, U.S. Gypsum, U. S. Rubber (now Uniroyal), and more.

The Second Wave. A second wave of 6,848 mergers occurred during 1923–33. These mergers were predominantly vertical ones and involved firms in such industries as automobiles, chemicals, food, metals, and petroleum.

The Third Wave. A third wave of mergers, totaling 17,307, occurred during 1950–69. Many of these mergers were conglomerate ones. Such mergers were not necessarily designed to gain monopoly, but served to reduce risk by diversifying operations. Sometimes, such diversification is achieved through **product-extension mergers**, as when the merging firms do not directly compete but use related production processes or marketing channels. (Consider how Procter and Gamble produced detergents and once tried to move into the liquid bleach market by merging with Clorox.) At other times, diversification is achieved through **market-extension mergers**, involving firms in the same line of business but in different geographic areas. (Consider how Kroger acquired more supermarkets in new geographic areas.) Other conglomerate mergers, however, cannot be classified as either of these two types. A classic example is the International Telephone and Telegraph Company (ITT). It started out as a communications company and still operates as such in 123 countries. As a natural move, it branched into the manufacture of telephone equipment. But before long it also rented cars (Avis); it built homes (Levitt and Sons); it baked bread (Continental); it operated hotels and motor inns (Sheraton); it made consumer loans; it produced glass and sand; it processed data; it sold insurance, ran secretarial schools, rented billboards, was active in publishing (Bobbs-Merrill, Putnam's), and much more! By 1980, ITT had sales of $18.5 billion and employed close to 350,000 workers, worldwide.

It is instructive to look at the annual listing in *Fortune* of the 500 largest industrial corporations. Ranked by sales in 1980, Exxon was first (with $103.1 billion in sales) and was followed (in this order) by Mobil, General Motors, Texaco, Standard Oil of California, Ford, Gulf Oil, IBM, Standard Oil of Indiana, and General Electric (with $25.0 billion in sales). In many recent years, the sales of each of the 10 largest corporations have exceeded the revenues of each of the 50 states. And the top corporations have had sales exceeding the national income of most of the world's nations! In 1975, while corporations as a group made 87 percent of private business sales in the United States, the 100 largest industrial corporations alone accounted for more than 15 percent, and the 500 largest for more than 23 percent. Just 2,000 firms like them could have supplied *everything* all types of private firms were supplying.

ANALYTICAL EXAMPLE 12.2:

Advertising and the Price of Eyeglasses

It is often claimed that advertising, by creating loyalty to brand names, supports the positions of would-be monopolists. Yet the fact that advertising can also be seen as an important weapon for those who want to challenge established firms by competing with them through lower prices was suggested recently by a study of the market for eyeglasses. The data of the accompanying table are based on a 1963 national sample of 634 individuals who obtained eyeglasses, had eye examinations, or both. The prices paid were compared for states in which professional societies of opticians and optometrists forbade their members to advertise (and in which this prohibition was even written into law) and for states that allowed such advertising—see rows (1) and (3). In every case, advertising went hand in hand with lower prices. This result showed even more strongly when comparing prices only in the most extreme states—rows (2) and (4)—in which the ban on advertising was strictest (North Carolina) or the freedom to advertise was of longest standing (Texas, District of Columbia).

Population Group	Average Prices in States with Complete Advertising Restrictions	Average Prices in States with No Advertising Restrictions	Difference
Eyeglasses Alone			
(1) All individuals	$33.04	$26.34	$ 6.70
(2) Individuals in Texas, North Carolina, and the District of Columbia only	$37.48	$17.98	$19.50
Eyeglasses and Eye Examinations Combined			
(3) All individuals	$40.96	$37.10	$ 3.86
(4) Individuals in Texas, North Carolina, and the District of Columbia only	$50.73	$29.97	$20.76

Postscript: In 1978, in the wake of a 1977 U.S. Supreme Court decision on advertising by lawyers (see Close-Up 12.2), the Federal Trade Commission ruled restrictions on eyeglass advertising illegal. The result was a widespread drop in eyeglass prices. In 1980, a federal appeals court opened the way for physicians to advertise fees and services.

Source: Lee Benham, "The Effect of Advertising on the Price of Eyeglasses," *The Journal of Law and Economics*," October 1972, pp. 337–52. Table adapted by permission of the University of Chicago Press. Copyright 1972 by the University of Chicago.

Application 2:
"False" Wants Vs. "True" Needs

In recent years, some economists have moved the subject of advertising from the realm of *positive* theory (which, as we noted in Chapter 2, seeks to explain what *is*) into the realm of *normative statements* (which seek to teach us what *ought to be*). Harvard's John Kenneth Galbraith, groups of "radical" economists, and others have argued that advertising is bad for us. As they see it, advertising largely misinforms people; it manipulates them into wanting products they do not really need. Thus people buy white bread, we are told, and soft drinks and TV dinners, the nutritional values of which are pure fantasy. People waste money on deodorants, electric toothbrushes, liquor, and tobacco. And they suffocate themselves in machinery: airplanes, boats, cars, dishwashers, lawnmowers, snowmobiles, and vacuum cleaners. Such is the power of Madison Avenue! Indeed, without it, these critics assert, scarcity would be a thing of the past. (In terms of Figure 1.1, "The Scarcity Problem" on page 5, without advertising the left-hand circle would presumably shrink to be equal to or smaller than the right-hand one.)

The Creation of "False" Wants. Advertising critics admit that people do, of course, have certain legitimate material wants. They need enough food, clothing, shelter, and medical care to keep the body safe and sound. But, essentially, these "true" needs are simple and minimal. What then is the origin of "false" wants? That is a long story, according to these critics:

People are born with few innate desires, with wants that are *theirs* in the ultimate sense of being fixed in their genes. Beyond the liking of mother's milk and the disliking of loud noises and such, it is inevitable that most preferences are learned from other people. Unfortunately, it is asserted, people are brought up to like and dislike the wrong things in our society. People are not being informed; they are being deformed. They are not taught what is good for them and then set free to be agents of their own will. Instead they are made into sheep that follow the interests of a host of hidden and not so hidden persuaders. Parents and playmates, neighbors and teachers, businesses and governments all join in a ceaseless effort to brainwash the young into "needing" a multitude of material things. Before they are grown up, such wants have become as natural as the very air they breathe. Yet most of these wants are false.

Consider, critics say, the sad example set by parents: They dare not reject the materialistic goals sought by their neighbors. The social isolation resulting from being "different" is considered worse than death itself. So they do what the majority does, wasting day after day, year after year, in the pursuit of gadgets to "keep up with the Joneses." Getting no support from their parents, children naturally cave in to a similar fear of ostracism. They keep up with their peers, accumulating lollipops and tricycles today, clothes and sportscars tomorrow. The drive to acquire things becomes an addiction before they even reach school. And teachers, it is said, lovingly nourish the poisonous seed that has been planted. They do not really care to take children on exciting adventures in human enlightenment or even to teach them cognitive abilities. Note, we are told, how often the natural curiosity of children is met with insincere answers, subtle condescension, and even open disrespect; note how original thinking is discouraged in favor of learning "the facts." Note how children in school are taught the very traits that will allow them to make money later in life to satisfy their "needs": they must be punctual and disciplined; they must patiently wait for rewards; above all, they must conform.

All this conditioning is further reinforced, we are told, by ceaseless advertising on the part of firms and by propaganda on the part of government. Business and government leaders join in exploiting for their own ends the materialist cravings instilled in people. Corporate executives or generals, seeking to build new empires for themselves, easily persuade people to spend their incomes on a new type of car today or to tax themselves for new types of weaponry tomorrow. And crippled by their inability to think for themselves and to make decisions for their own good, people succumb to the deception of professional persuaders. Consumer sovereignty in the marketplace becomes a farce. Rather than calling the tune on what is produced, households dance to the siren song of Madison Avenue. Democracy becomes a mockery too. The whole process is *reversed*: At the ballot box, sovereign citizens do not instruct their government, but officials tell voters how to behave in a way the officials have already determined.

Thus, advertising critics conclude, people end up being automatons, helpless puppets moved by strings behind their backs. They veritably sleepwalk through life, dominated by false wants and falsely believing that their satisfaction will lead to happiness. How much better life would be, they say, if we would silence the intrusive, raucous, ugly voices of the advertisers!

Criticizing the Critics. Other observers of contemporary life, however, are disturbed by claims that advertisers create "false" wants. Sure enough, they say, firms and governments do advertise and propagandize, but they do not create "false" wants. They merely identify wants that already exist, and they try to persuade people to satisfy them in particular ways. For example, all people at all times and in all places want food. Although the "manipulators" have nothing to do with this fact, they might try to channel such a basic desire toward ice cream— and Baskin-Robbins ice cream at that. Similarly, all people want clothing, but they might be induced to satisfy this basic want with long skirts today, short ones tomorrow, and pants thereafter —Robert Hall pants at that. People want beauty, cleanliness, excitement, mobility, shelter, and sex. The "manipulators" do not create these desires either, we are told, but they do their best to direct them: toward RCA Beethoven records, Sweet Life herbal essence shampoo, and scenic rides in Schweizer sailplanes; toward Ford Fiestas, American Barn homes, and *Playboy* magazines. Indeed, it is argued, the *limited* power of the alleged manipulators is evidenced by their preoccupation with market surveys, by their failure to launch 80 to 90 percent of all technically successful new products at all (because they do not survive market research) and by their withdrawal of a third to a half of those products that are launched (because they fail to sell sufficiently during the first year). At the same time, the *thoughtful* appraisal of their own choices by households is evidenced by their refusal to make repeat purchases where their basic desires have

not been satisfied by a specific product, by their purchase of disinterested advice (an appraiser's, before buying a house and a mechanic's before buying a used car), and by their subscription to consumer magazines. The manipulation of votes is, similarly, highly exaggerated. Therefore, it is concluded, we better accept people's spending decisions and political votes as expressions of their "true" wants. Those who would deny the value of these decisions are simply would-be dictators who would love to impose their own tastes on others. These tastes are usually those of an arrogant cultural élite that claims to *know* that Beaujolais is better than Budweiser, camping in the High Sierras is preferable to snowmobiling in Iowa, and a visit to the Louvre is more tasteful than one to Miami Beach.

There is simply no way, the critics' critics conclude, to separate "false" wants from "true" needs. Who among the billions of people on earth could possibly be trusted to do so? So we must, in the end, accept people's own words and consider every expression of material wants as an expression of true material need. There is simply no objective way of making moral judgments about the material wants people express, ranking material wants on a scale of better or worse, approving of some and disapproving of others. Certainly, their professional skills do not endow economists with any special ability to decide for others which goods are truly good for them and which are "bads" in disguise.

Application 3:   Industrial Organization

Market structures that fall between the polar cases of perfect competition and pure monopoly are of obviously great importance. By pointing to this crucial middle area, Chamberlin revised microeconomic theory drastically and permanently. But he also set in motion a blending of abstract price theory with empirical research that gave rise to a new specialization within economic science: **industrial organization**. While microeconomic theorists thrive on simplicity and rigor and like best models focusing on the barest of essentials, the practitioners of industrial organization lean toward explanations of market structure, behavior, and performance that are rich in institutional and quantitative detail. Let us consider some of the institutional and quantitative detail that industrial organization economists would add to the theoretical apparatus discussed earlier in this chapter.

Indexes of Industrial Concentration. To study the exact extent to which particular markets are dominated by a few large firms, one can construct **concentration ratios**, each one of

which equals the percentage of industry sales attributable to a given number of largest firms, usually the 4, 8, 20, and 50 largest companies. Thus a 4-firm concentration ratio of 62 would indicate that the 4 largest firms in the industry accounted for 62 percent of industry sales in a given year.

A 1972 study of 450 U.S. industries revealed that this 4-firm concentration ratio was between 0 and 19 for 87 industries, between 20 and 39 for 168 of them, between 40 and 59 for another 118, and at 60 or above for the remaining

TABLE 12.1 Concentration Ratios in the United States, 1972

Industry	4-Firm Ratio	8-Firm Ratio	Number of Firms
Electron receiving tubes	95	99	21
Motor vehicles, car bodies	93	99	165
Primary lead	93	99	12
Cereal breakfast foods	90	98	34
Electric lamps	90	94	103
Turbines and generators	90	96	59
Household refrigerators/freezers	85	98	30
Cigarettes	84	n.a.	13
Cathode-ray (TV) tubes	83	97	69
Household laundry equipment	83	98	20
Carbon/graphite products	80	91	58
Primary aluminum	79	92	12
Household vacuum cleaners	75	91	34
Chocolate, cocoa products	74	88	39
Calculating/accounting machines	73	89	74
Tires, inner tubes	73	90	136
Aircraft	66	86	141
Metal cans	66	79	134
Roasted coffee	65	79	162
Sanitary paper products	63	82	72
Soap and detergents	62	74	577
Storage batteries	57	85	138
Glass containers	55	76	27
Wine, brandy	53	68	183
Malt beverages	52	70	108
Pet food	51	71	147

In many U.S. industries, concentration ratios are high and the number of firms is small.
SOURCE: U.S. Bureau of the Census, Census of Manufactures, 1972 *Special Report Series: Concentration Ratios in Manufacturing,* MC72(SR)-2 (Washington, D.C.: U.S. Government Printing Office, 1975).

77 industries. Table 12.1 contains much richer detail.

To some extent, large concentration ratios, such as those of Table 12.1, may even *understate* the market power of firms, for the ratios refer to the nation as a whole. Many markets, however, are effectively limited to a much smaller area because of such factors as prohibitive transportation costs, perishable products, and so on. Suppose there were in a hypothetical industry 1,000 producers, all of equal size. Then the 4 "largest" companies would ship 4/1,000 of output, or 0.4 percent. If producers competed on a national scale, buyers everywhere would have 1,000 sellers to choose from, and the low concentration ratio might correctly indicate, at least so far as *numbers* are concerned, that perfect competition exists in the industry. Yet, if each firm was the sole supplier in a three-county area and transportation beyond that area was impossible or difficult, each firm would have something close to a monopoly. Yet, because the concentration ratio is calculated on a national basis, it would not reflect this monopoly situation.

On the other hand, a high concentration ratio does not necessarily denote imperfect competition. Imports from abroad (of great importance in the case of motor vehicles, for example) may substantially alter the picture. Thus, the 4 largest firms may account for 100 percent of domestic shipments, yet they may supply only 1 percent of the total sold, if imports are of overwhelming importance. Other perfect substitutes may also be available in large quantities domestically (such as recycled aluminum).

Finally, the meaning of the industry classification must be carefully assessed. "Calculating/accounting machines" (see Table 12.1), for instance, is a broad category. Although the 4 largest firms supply 73 percent of shipments, we might want to know what these shipments are. It may turn out that each of the four firms supplies 100 percent of *particular* machines that have no good substitutes; then the ratio understates what it is supposed to test. Vice versa, "cereal breakfast foods" may be too narrow a category. There are undoubtedly excellent breakfast-food substitutes. Even though 4 companies make 90 percent of shipments, their market power may be much less than the concentration ratio seems to indicate.

The Structure of the U.S. Economy. Industrial organization economists can also tell us much about the U.S. economy as a whole. Table 12.2 shows a breakdown of the gross domestic product (GDP) by major sectors of the economy. In a rather crude fashion, these data have been juxtaposed with likely market structures. Note how the goods supplied by government (such as national defense, police protection, postal service, and public schooling) are classified as produced by monopoly (1). The typical buyer looking for any type of transportation service (2), whether by air, pipeline, rail, road, or water, was likely to face monopolies or government-sponsored cartels. Monopolies or cartels also dominated the fields of finance and insurance (3), of telephone, telegraph, radio, and television services (4), and of electricity, gas, and sanitation services (5). Although many agricultural markets come closest to perfect competition in the real world, other agricultural markets are heavily rigged with the help of government. Thus the contribution of the agriculture-forestry-fishing sector has been split into rows (6) and (14) to reflect these divergent situations.

With minor exceptions (for example, clothing and shoe manufacturing), the products of the manufacturing industries—be they aircraft, breakfast foods, cars, cement, cigarettes, gasoline, heavy machinery, steel, or soap—were supplied by oligopoly. These facts are reflected in rows (7) and (13). Equally oligopolistic were wholesale trade, construction, and mining product markets (coal, crude oil, metal, natural gas, and nonmetallic minerals) in rows (8) to (10).

Much of the remainder of the economy operated under monopolistic competition, which held for most services (11), ranging widely from auto repair, barbering, and domestic service to entertainment, hotel, and legal services, medical care, real estate, and restaurant services. Also

ANALYTICAL EXAMPLE 12.3:

Industrial Concentration by Pure Chance

Among many other things, industrial-organization economists study the reasons for observed degrees of concentration. They find, of course, the expected reasons: economies of scale, legal barriers to entry. Yet one economist has pointed to an unusual possibility, the operation of sheer luck:

F. M. Scherer conducted a computer-simulation experiment for an imaginary industry containing 50 identical firms and having neither economies of scale nor legal entry barriers. Each firm initially held a market share of 2 percent. Scherer instructed his computer to let the industry grow at 6 percent per year but to give each individual firm a random probability of growing somewhat faster or slower than this average. (This average growth rate and the variability of individual firms' growth around the average were set equal to 1954–60 figures actually observed among *Fortune's* list of 500 top industrial corporations.) The computer followed the fortunes of each firm through 140 years of simulated history; this experiment was repeated sixteen times. The result, shown in the accompanying table, is truly amazing.

Simulation	4-Firm Concentration Ratio at Year:							
	1	20	40	60	80	100	120	140
Run 1	8.0	19.5	29.3	36.3	40.7	44.9	38.8	41.3
Run 2	8.0	20.3	21.4	28.1	37.5	41.6	50.8	55.6
Run 3	8.0	18.8	28.9	44.6	43.1	47.1	56.5	45.0
Run 4	8.0	20.9	26.7	31.8	41.9	41.0	64.5	59.8
Run 5	8.0	23.5	33.2	43.8	60.5	60.5	71.9	63.6
Run 6	8.0	21.3	26.6	29.7	35.8	51.2	59.1	72.9
Run 7	8.0	21.1	31.4	29.0	42.8	52.8	50.3	53.1
Run 8	8.0	21.6	23.5	42.2	47.3	64.4	73.1	76.6
Run 9	8.0	18.4	29.3	38.0	45.3	42.5	43.9	52.4
Run 10	8.0	20.0	29.7	43.7	40.1	43.1	42.9	42.9
Run 11	8.0	23.9	29.1	29.5	43.2	50.1	57.1	71.7
Run 12	8.0	15.7	23.3	24.1	34.5	41.1	42.9	53.1
Run 13	8.0	23.8	31.3	44.8	43.5	42.8	57.3	65.2
Run 14	8.0	17.8	23.3	29.3	54.2	51.4	56.0	64.7
Run 15	8.0	21.8	18.3	23.9	31.9	33.5	43.9	65.7
Run 16	8.0	17.5	27.1	28.3	30.7	39.9	37.7	35.3
Average	8.0	20.4	27.0	33.8	42.1	46.7	52.9	57.4

Within a few decades, the imaginary industry ended up with the very degree of concentration observed for real-world U.S. manufacturing industries—in spite of the assumed absence of the usual causes of concentration. After a simulated century had elapsed, it was not uncommon to find a single leading firm holding 25-35 percent of the market, while its former equals held 0.1 percent! How did Scherer explain it? By pure chance: Some firms got an early run of luck and grew faster than the average for several years in a row. Once they led the pack, it was harder for the other firms to catch up because everybody had an equal chance to grow by a given percentage in every year.

Source: F. M. Scherer, *Industrial Market Structure and Economic Performance*, 2nd ed. p. 146. Copyright © 1980 Houghton Mifflin Company. Used by permission.

TABLE 12.2 The U.S. Economy in 1978

Sector	Contribution to Gross Domestic Product (GDP) (billions of dollars)	(percent)	Likely Market Structure
(1) Government	258.9		
(2) Transportation	81.4		
(3) Finance, insurance	76.4		Monopoly
(4) Communications	55.9	26.5	or
(5) Electricity, gas, sanitation	53.5		cartel
(6) Part of agriculture, forestry, fishing	31.6		
(7) Part of manufacturing	471.4		
(8) Wholesale trade	153.0	36.8	Oligopoly
(9) Construction	95.3		
(10) Mining	55.1		
(11) Services	491.0		Monopolistic
(12) Retail trade	207.5	35.0	competition
(13) Part of manufacturing	37.7		
(14) Part of agriculture, forestry, fishing	35.0	1.7	Perfect competition
Total	2,103.7	100.0	

Goods in the United States are supplied largely under conditions of imperfect competition.
SOURCE: U.S. Department of Commerce, Bureau of Economic Analysis, *Survey of Current Business,* July 1979, pp. 51–52.

operating under monopolistic competition were retail trade (12) and, as noted, small segments of manufacturing (13). The only candidates for perfect competition remaining, in row (14), were found in agriculture, forestry, and fishing.

Note: Over time, the relative magnitudes found in Table 12.2 change very slowly, if at all. More recent data are almost certain to show the same percentage breakdown.

SUMMARY

1. This chapter focuses on *imperfect competition*; that is, market situations other than pure monopoly and cartel in which individual sellers, nevertheless, face downward-sloping demand curves and thus have some measure of control over price. Two market structures can be distinguished: a. oligopoly, in which the entry of new firms is difficult and relatively few sellers com-

pete with one another, offering either homogeneous or differentiated products, and b. monopolistic competition, in which the entry of new firms is easy and large numbers of sellers compete with one another, offering differentiated products. In situations of oligopoly, strategic behavior takes on crucial importance. Because the number of actors is so small and because they have conflicting interests, they are mutually conscious of the interdependence of their decisions. Economists have developed dozens of theories to capture this interdependence.

2. In Cournot's model decisions focus on output. Each oligopolistic firm assumes that its rivals supply a fixed quantity regardless of its own decisions. The Cournot equilibrium identifies a possible outcome in which the separate output decisions of firms are consistent with one another and with market demand.

3. In Sweezy's kinked-demand curve model, decisions focus on price and on the avoidance of price wars. The Sweezy model has a number of implications, including the likelihood of rigid oligopoly prices, even in the face of moderate changes in marginal cost or demand. Because the Sweezy model does not stand up well to empirical verification, rival models of oligopolistic pricing abound. These rival models include those stressing the importance of gentlemen's agreements and of price leadership; these models, too, are far from perfect.

4. Some oligopolists compete with each other on still another front, that of product differentiation. This, too, gives them a degree of monopoly power—even when actual differences do not exist, but buyers only imagine them. Product differentiation is difficult to analyze because of its complexity; one theoretical attempt leads to the Hotelling paradox.

5. Oligopolists, finally, compete with each other by incurring selling costs, designed to alter the demand they face. Advertising can be informative as well as persuasive, but it is next to impossible to disentangle these two.

6. *Monopolistic competitors* also compete on the basis of product differentiation and advertising; they are distinguished from oligopolists by the absence of strategic behavior. The behavior of the monopolistically competitive firm can be analyzed very much like that of the pure monopoly, but there is a difference in the long run: zero long-run profit is inevitable for the monopolistic competitor. The long-run equilibrium of monopolistic competition is also different from that of perfect competition in that *excess capacity* occurs in monopolistic competition.

7. Some of the wider applications of the tools developed here include the story of business mergers, the debate on ''false'' wants vs. ''true'' needs, and the birth and nature of a new field of specialization in economics: industrial organization.

KEY TERMS

basing-point system
concentration ratios

conglomerate mergers
Cournot equilibrium
excess capacity
focal-point price
gentlemen's agreements
horizontal mergers
Hotelling's paradox
imperfect competition
industrial organization
informative advertising
kinked demand curve
limit price
market-extension mergers
mergers
monopolistic competition
oligopoly
persuasive advertising
price leadership
price war
product differentiation
product-extension mergers
product groups
reaction curve
selling cost
strategic behavior
vertical mergers

QUESTIONS AND PROBLEMS

1. In the section on Cournot's model, ''Decision Making Under Oligopoly: Output Quantity,'' it is claimed that the two firms discussed there have an incentive to form a cartel, cut production, and raise price. Write the perfect cartel agreement for this case: the quantity each firm must produce, the price it must charge, the increase in profit it can expect.

2. Figure 12.2, ''Sweezy's Model,'' shows the conventional kinked demand curve for a timid, pessimistic oligopolist. Now draw a different kinked demand curve (and the associated curve of marginal revenue) for an aggressive, optimistic oligopolist.

3. Figure 12.3, "Implications of Kinked Oligopoly Demand," illustrates that price can be rigid even in the face of moderate changes in marginal cost or demand. Show the price and quantity effects for:

    a. a profit-maximizing *oligopoly* of *major* changes in marginal cost and demand.

    b. a profit-maximizing *monopoly* of *any* changes in marginal cost and demand.

    c. a profit-maximizing *perfect competitor* of *any* changes in marginal cost and demand.

4. Consider Figure 12.4, "Hotelling's Paradox."

    a. What would be the ideal and actual locations of a third firm, C, that appeared on the scene?

    b. How would you modify the entire analysis if the customers were not distributed uniformly over geographic space or along the continuum for any other characteristic?

    c. Do you think there are "product-characteristics leaders" as there are price leaders?

5. Can you think of other examples besides the ones mentioned in the text where Hotelling's paradox is at work? (*Hints:* Consider Goldwater's presidential campaign, then McGovern's. Consider the sameness of automobiles, economics texts, and television programs; consider why bars, barbershops, and gas stations locate right next to each other.)

6. *Mr. A:* Advertising, besides supporting product variety, provides another major benefit not mentioned in this chapter's text: it subsidizes the mass communications media. In recent years, it has provided 50 percent of periodical, 70 percent of newspaper, and almost 100 percent of (noneducational) radio and television station revenue.

    Ms. B: You call that a benefit? Advertisers want to reach the largest possible audience; the media make sure to reach it by appealing to the lowest

possible denominator. So we get scandal sheets and television's wasteland.

What do you think?

7. The accompanying graph shows a monopolistically competitive firm in short-run equilibrium.

    a. Why is it in short-run equilibrium?

    b. What will happen in the long run?

    c. Given long-run equilibrium, how would advertising alter the picture? (Consider both successful and unsuccessful advertising.)

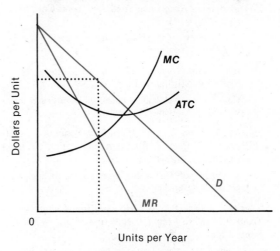

8. In 1972, the 4-firm concentration ratio in the ready-mixed concrete industry was 6, the 8-firm ratio was 10, and the number of firms was 3,978. The corresponding three numbers for bread and cake were 29, 39, 2,800; for fluid milk, 18, 26, and 2,024; for newspapers, 17, 28, and 7,461. Do you think these figures understate or overstate monopoly power? Why?

SELECTED READINGS

Adams, Walter, ed. *The Structure of American Industry*, 5th ed. New York: Macmillan, 1977.

    An example of industrial organization economics at its best; contains studies of the structure, conduct, and performance of 13 industries.

Archibald, G. C. "Chamberlin vs. Chicago." *Review of Economic Studies*, October 1961, pp. 2–28.

    Contrasts Chamberlin's views on imperfect competition with those of the Chicago school (see Stigler below).

Bain, J. S. *Barriers to New Competition*, Cambridge: Harvard University Press, 1956.

An important work in industrial organization.

Chamberlin, Edward H. *The Theory of Monopolistic Competition: A Reorientation of the Theory of Value*, 8th ed. Cambridge: Harvard University Press, 1965.

This edition of the work also contains a bibliography of some 1,500 articles about Chamberlin's work.

Comanor, William S. and Wilson, Thomas. *Advertising and Market Power*. Cambridge: Harvard University Press, 1975.

Dewey, Donald. *The Theory of Imperfect Competition: A Radical Reconstruction*. New York: Columbia University Press, 1969.

A critical review of the now widely accepted Chamberlin-Robinson achievement.

Galbraith, John Kenneth. *The Affluent Society*. Boston: Houghton Mifflin, 1958.

Contains the well-known attack on advertising as a violation of consumer sovereignty.

Hayek, Friedrich A. von. "The Non-Sequitur of the 'Dependence Effect.'" *Southern Economic Journal*, April 1961, pp. 346–48.

A critique of Galbraith's view on advertising and consumer sovereignty.

Kuenne, Robert E., ed. *Monopolistic Competition Theory: Studies in Impact*. New York: John Wiley & Sons, 1967.

Contains 17 essays written by major scholars in honor of Chamberlin.

Lindbeck, Assar. *The Political Economy of the New Left*, 2nd ed. New York: Harper and Row, 1977.

Contains a superb discussion of the debate on "false" wants vs. "true" needs.

Meade, James E. "The Optimal Balance Between Economies of Scale and Variety of Products: an Illustrative Model." *Economica*, August 1974, pp. 359–67.

Discusses the trade-off, in a monopolistically competitive industry, between excess capacity and product variety on the one hand and lower average cost but less variety on the other.

Nicholls, William. *Price Policies in the Cigarette Industry*. Nashville: Vanderbilt University Press, 1951.

One of many excellent case studies of price leadership.

Robinson, Joan V. *The Economics of Imperfect Competition*. London: Macmillan, 1933.

Schelling, Thomas C. *The Strategy of Conflict*. Cambridge: Harvard University Press, 1960.

On the theory of focal points.

Seligman, Ben B. *The Thrust Toward Technique*, vol. 3 of *Main Currents in Modern Economics*. Chicago: Quadrangle Books, 1962, pp. 716–29.

A discussion of the work of J. Robinson and E. H. Chamberlin.

Stackelberg, Heinrich von. *The Theory of the Market Economy*. New York: Oxford University Press, 1952.

Presents yet another model of oligopolistic behavior (pp. 195 ff.).

Stigler, George J. "Monopolistic Competition in Retrospect." In *Five Lectures on Economic Problems*. New York: Macmillan, 1949.

A severe criticism of the Chamberlinian revolution.

Stigler, George J. "The Literature of Economics: The Case of the Kinked Oligopoly Demand Curve." *Economic Inquiry*, April 1978, pp. 185–204.

A superb summary with an excellent bibliography.

Stigler, George J. and Boulding, Kenneth E. *AEA Readings in Price Theory*. Chicago: Irwin, 1952.

See especially chap. 20 (Sweezy's model), chap. 21 (Stigler's criticism of Sweezy), and chap. 23 (Hotelling's paradox).

Stigler, George J., and Kindahl, James K. *The Behavior of Industrial Prices*. New York: National Bureau of Economic Research and Columbia University Press, 1970.

Shows oligopolistic actual transactions prices are much more flexible than officially quoted prices.

APPENDIX 12A

Game Theory

More often than not, economic theorists describe the behavior of decision makers in terms of *maximization* (as of utility or profit) or *minimization* (as of disutility or cost). Yet, as the study of oligopoly has shown, this type of decision making gets to be very complex when the results achieved by one economic agent depend not only on this agent's own actions, but also on those of identifiable others who are conscious of this fact and may or may not be willing to cooperate. Thus one firm's desire to maximize profit may be opposed by other firms seeking to maximize their profits, and this conscious conflict of wills gives rise to a peculiar and disconcerting mixture of several interlocking maximization problems.

When people interact with other people (rather than with nature—a matter discussed in Chapter 10) and when these other people can actively seek to thwart the attainment of the first people's goals, all those involved must base their decisions on what they expect others to do and, therefore, on what they think others expect them to do, and perhaps even on what they think the others think they expect them to do . . . Under such circumstances, when no actor is in complete control of the factors influencing the outcome, how can one even talk of an *individual's* rational behavior, much less predict its results?

No wonder that to this day there exists no satisfactory theory of oligopoly. There are bits and pieces, as Chapter 12 attests, but they do not make for a unified whole. There is, however, hope, based on a development that originated in 1944. In that year, two Princeton professors, a mathematician and an economist, joined forces to suggest a new approach to the problem of inter-locking decision making. One of them was John von Neumann (1903–1957), Hungarian-born mathematical genius and one of three co-inventors of the U.S. hydrogen bomb. The other one was Oskar Morgenstern (see Biography 12A.1). They looked upon any decision-making situation in which the payoff to people's choices depends not only on them (and nature), but also on other people's choices as a **game**. They developed a highly novel analytical apparatus, called **game theory**, which is a method for studying decision making in situations of conflict when the fates of those who seek different goals are interlocked. Game theory is a method with universal applicability—useful not only for analyzing the behavior of oligopolistic firms but also that of chess and poker players, cops and robbers, diplomats, military strategists, and politicians fighting for nomination. This appendix can do no more than provide a brief introduction to this fascinating subject.

The Two-Person Zero-Sum Game

The simplest of all possible games (and inevitably also the dullest) is one between two persons and in which the winnings of one person are exactly matched by the losses of the other. Because the sum of (positive) winnings and (negative) losses equals zero, this game is called a **zero-sum game**. Table 12A.1 shows the major elements involved in every game: players, control variables, and payoffs. Consider Part (I) first. The "players" are two firms that compete with each other by introducing newly differentiated products. Each firm has three "control variables." Each can introduce one of three products; Products A, B, or C in the case of Firm 1; Products D, E, or F in the case of Firm 2. The resultant "payoffs," in terms of market share gained or lost by Firm 1, are shown in the body of the table. Because this is a zero-sum game, any gain to Firm 1 is a loss to Firm 2 and the opposite. Consider the first row. If Firm 1 introduced Product A and Firm 2 responded with Product D, it tells us, Firm 1 would gain (and Firm 2 lose) 3 percent of the market. On the other hand, if Firm 1 introduced Product A, while Firm 2 responded with Product E or F, Firm 1 would gain 0 or 4 percent of the market, respectively (and Firm 2 would lose identical shares). The entries in the next two rows of Table 12A.1 are similarly interpreted.

How should a player act, given the likelihood of several different outcomes for any one action?

Pessimistic Assumptions

Von Neumann and Morgenstern suggested that each party would imagine itself in the place of its rival and ask: "What would I do in response to my own strategy if I was my own rival?" They also suggested this pessimistic answer: "If I was my rival, I would do what was best for this rival and worst for me; that is, I would choose the most damaging counterstrategy."

Thus, if Firm 1 chose A, Firm 2 would choose E (giving Firm 1 a zero increase in market share). If Firm 1 chose B, Firm 2 would choose D (giving Firm 1 a 4 percent loss in market share and itself a 4 percent gain). And if Firm 1 chose C, Firm 2 would choose F (giving Firm 1 a 3 percent loss in market share and itself a 3 percent gain). All these terrible outcomes (terrible, that is, from the point of view of Firm 1) are shown in the last column of our table, labeled "row minimum."

We can, however, also look at all this from the point of view of Firm 2. Thus, if Firm 2 chose to introduce Products D, E, or F, Firm 1 would choose Products C, A, or B, respectively,

each time giving itself the best possible result and, by implication, handing the worst possible outcome to Firm 2. All these worst outcomes (worst from the point of view of Firm 2) are shown in the last row of our table, labeled "column maximum." Note: In this zero-sum game, these maxima for Firm 1 imply, of course, minima of −4, 0, and −8 for Firm 2.

Maximin and Minimax Strategies

Von Neumann and Morgenstern suggested that each firm (always expecting the worst) would now choose that strategy which made the worst possible outcome as good as possible. For Firm 1, as we have just seen, these worst possible outcomes are given in the last column. Thus Firm 1 would choose the encircled maximum of these minima (the *maximum minimorum*). According to this **maximin strategy**, it would introduce Product A. As you can see from Table 12A.1, the worst that could then happen to Firm 1 would be a zero increase in market share.

In this zero-sum game, the worst possible outcomes for Firm 2 are, of course, the best possible ones for Firm 1. Firm 2, therefore, would choose the encircled minimum of the maxima (the *minimum maximorum*) shown in the last row. According to this **minimax strategy**, Firm 2 would introduce Product E. The worst that could then happen to Firm 2 would be a zero increase in Firm 1's market share and, therefore, a zero decrease in its own market share.

We can now easily see the result, which is shown by the boxed number in table 12A.1, Part (I). Firm 1 would choose A and Firm 2 would choose E; neither firm would gain or lose any share of the market.

Review

We can quickly review what we have learned by now examining Part (II) of Table 12A.1. This time we imagine a group of smugglers who can brashly take their load by truck over the freeway or can sneakily take a smaller amount via a circuitous mountain road. The border patrol, on

TABLE 12A.1   Zero-Sum Games

(I) Market-share Game:		Matrix of Firm 1's Gain (+) or Loss (−) of Market Share (in percent)			
		Firm 2			
		Product D	Product E	Product F	Row Minimum
Firm 1	Product A	+3	0	+4	0 ←Maximin
	Product B	−4	−2	+8	−4
	Product C	+4	−1	−3	−3
Column Maximum		+4	0	+8	

Minimax

(II) Smuggling Game:		Matrix of Smuggler's Gain (+) or Loss (−), in million dollars			
		Border Patrol			
		Guards Freeway Only	Guards Mountain Road Only	Guards Both Lightly	Row Minimum
Smugglers	Take freeway	−10 A	+10 B	−4 C	−10
	Take mountain road	+4 D	+2 E	+2 F	+2 ←Maximin
Column Maximum		+4	+10	+2	

Minimax

Both of the zero-sum games pictured here have a saddle point. Players, therefore, do best by pursuing a pure maximin or minimax strategy. These strategies lead to the results shown by the two boxed numbers.

the other hand, can concentrate their forces on the freeway or on the mountain road or they can split them up between the two.

Here are the possible outcomes if the smugglers take the freeway: If they run into a heavy freeway guard (box A), they will be caught, lose their entire load, and be out of $10 million. If the patrol only guards the mountain road, the smugglers will get through and gain $10 million (box B). If the smugglers find a light freeway guard, they will not be caught, but will not get through, and so they will be out of $4 million in expenses (box C).

What if the smugglers take the mountain road? If the freeway is guarded heavily, the smugglers will get through, but their load will be smaller because of the terrain, so they gain only $4 million (box D). If the patrol guards the mountain road heavily or lightly the smugglers will get through , but they will also have to share their loot with the mountain people who help them (box E and F).

Let us assume that any gain (or loss) to the

smugglers can be regarded as an equal loss (or gain) to the border patrol. Then our previous analysis applies fully. The smugglers will consider the worst that can happen to them (last column) and "maximin" by taking the mountain road. The border patrol will consider the best that can happen to the smugglers (last row) and "minimax" by guarding both roads lightly. The result: The smugglers will get through, but only with a small load and by paying heavy bribes. Their net gain will be $2 million (box F).

Saddle Point

A game in which the maximin equals the minimax is said to have a **saddle point**. Note the zero in the last column of Part (I) and the +2 in that column of Part (II) versus the zero in the last row of Part (I) and the +2 in that column of Part (II). Such games end up being rather dull. Even if one player knows the other player's choice in advance (if Firm 1 knows that Firm 2 will introduce Product E or if Firm 2 knows that Firm 1 will

BIOGRAPHY 12A.1:

Oskar Morgenstern

Oskar Morgenstern (1902–1977) was born in Görlitz, Germany. He studied at Vienna, where he earned his doctorate, at the Universities of London, Paris, and Rome, as well as at Harvard and Columbia. He became a professor of economics at the University of Vienna, where he also edited the famous *Zeitschrift für Nationalökonomie*, and was director of the Austrian Institute for Business Cycle Research. In 1938, like so many other European scholars, Morgenstern moved to the United States where he joined the faculty at Princeton University.

At the time, Morgenstern had already published a steady stream of papers, on business cycle theory, monetary policy, and international trade. His first major book, *Wirtschaftsprognose* (1928) was a study of the theory and applications of economic forecasting. It was never translated, unlike his second work, on economic policy, *The Limits of Economics* (1937). Early on, Morgenstern showed a great ability to suggest important overlooked problems, as well as new ways to approach them. His most imaginative and ambitious contribution to economics grew out of his collaboration with John von Neumann: the *Theory of Games and Economic Behavior* (1944). The two authors adopted a thoroughly mathematical approach, using a kind of mathematics seldom seen in economics, with concepts drawn from set theory, group theory, and mathematical logic. The present appendix does no more than convey the flavor of their contribution, which extends to much more than two-person games and has spawned innumerable studies of both conflict and cooperation.

Morgenstern's work, however, did not cease with the theory of games. Other major books of his include *On the Accuracy of Economic Observations* (1950, revised 1963), a brilliant critique of the common types of statistics used in economic discourse and a "must" reading for every economist. This work was followed by the editing of *Economic Activity Analysis* (1954) and the writing of *International Financial Transactions and Business Cycles* (1959) and *The Question of National Defense* (1959). In his last book, written with Gerald Thompson, Morgenstern returned to his early interest in business cycle theory: *Mathematical Theory of Expanding and Contracting Economies* (1976).

Morgenstern was active in a large number of diverse undertakings which ranged from the Econometric Research Program at Princeton, the Rand Corporation, and Mathematica to the

introduce product A), the first player's own choice will not change. Neither can do better than making the saddle-point choice. Under such circumstances, neither has an incentive ever to change strategy. Each chooses the same strategy over and over again. Not all games, however, have a saddle point. Imagine interchanging the +3 and 0 in the first row of the market-share game. This change would not affect the maximin, which would still be zero, but it would affect the minimax, which would then be +3. Under such circumstances, Firm 1 would still introduce Product A; Firm 2 would still introduce Product E; but Firm 1 would gain (and Firm 2 lose) 3 percent of the market.

Note: Because there would be no saddle point in this example, one firm (namely, Firm 2) would then change its strategy if it knew the other's strategy in advance. If Firm 2 knew that Firm 1 will introduce Product A, Firm 2 could do better with Product D (which would then yield a zero market-share increase for Firm 1). But if Firm 1 knew that Firm 2 will introduce Product D, it would introduce Product C; and if Firm 2 knew *that* it would bring out F and that wouldn't be the end of the story yet!

When there is no saddle point, therefore, sticking to a given strategy does not work. Such rigidity in behavior would reveal precious information to the other player and upset the stability

League of Nations' study on *Economic Stability in the Postwar World* to the Atomic Energy Commission and consultations at the White House.

Throughout his life, Morgenstern offered deep, but constructive criticism of economists. This criticism is illustrated in one of his last articles in which he commented on the inadequacy of textbooks on which young economists were being brought up.[1] "What these books have in common . . .," he says, "is that few, if any unsolved theoretical (as distinct from applied) problems in economics are mentioned. . . . It is, therefore, all the more surprising that anyone should want to go into a science that seems to have no open theoretical problems left—a vastly different situation from that of physics or biology where even the layman knows that those worlds are filled with riddles. . . . however, the world of social phenomena . . . holds such a plenitude of difficult, important and unsolved theoretical problems."

Morgenstern mentioned 13 such problems, but this author won't spoil the fun for those readers who want to find out for themselves!

[1]Oskar Morgenstern, "Thirteen Critical Points in Contemporary Economic Theory: An Interpretation," *Journal of Economic Literature*, December 1972, pp. 1163–89.

of the game. A no-saddle-point game, by introducing security aspects into the game, becomes much more interesting. As von Neumann and Morgenstern have shown (but which cannot be shown in this brief Appendix), under such circumstances players can still employ an unbeatable **mixed strategy** that alternates at random between the available pure strategies and thereby avoids patterns of behavior that would reveal important information to the other players. (Why, do you think, border patrols make their rounds at random instead of using a discernable pattern? Why do night watchguards and postal inspectors do the same? Why do professors pick quiz questions at random from a book?)

The Two-Person Nonzero-Sum Game

People can also play a **nonzero-sum game** in which the winnings and losses of all players add to a positive or negative number. The most famous game of this type is, perhaps, illustrated in Table 12A.2. The police, it is imagined, have arrested two men suspected of robbery. The District Attorney locks the men up in separate rooms, then tells each man that the following deal is being offered to both of them:

If the man confesses, while his partner keeps quiet, the "cooperative" partner will be allowed to plead guilty to a lesser charge and get off with 1 year in jail, but the other partner will get 10 years (box B or C). They have one hour to decide.

The two men also know this: If they both confess, they will both get 10 years, but 2 years off for being so helpful. Thus they will both end up spending 8 years in jail (box A). If they both keep quiet, the D.A.'s evidence being less than perfect, they can only be nailed on the lesser charge (of possessing stolen goods), and both will get 2 years (box D).

What will they do? Consider the point of view of Suspect 1: If Suspect 2 kept quiet, then, by confessing, Suspect 1 could get 1 year (box B) instead of 2 years (box D). If Suspect 2 confessed, then, by confessing, Suspect 1 could get 8 years (box A) instead of 10 years (box C).

An analogous argument, of course, can be made for Suspect 2. Thus each will realize that he will be better off confessing no matter what his partner does. Both will "maximin"—that is, both will confess—and both will get 8 years!

From the prisoners' point of view, of course, box D would be a much better choice. Yet, while Suspect 1 tries for B, Suspect 2 tries for C; both get A. Thus are the wages of selfishness. Note: This type of game is being played every day, in a million different ways.

Consider Table 12A.3 Part (I) pictures a situation common before the outbreak of a price war. Two competing firms are charging identical prices and would neither gain nor lose if they maintained the *status quo* (box D). Yet if Firm 1 maintained its price, but Firm 2 cut its price by

TABLE 12A.2 The Prisoners' Dilemma

Interrogation Game:			Matrix of Each Suspect's Loss of Free Time via Jail Sentence		
			Suspect 2		Row Minimum (for suspect 1)
			Confess	Keep Quiet	
Suspect 1	Confess		A −8 years / −8 years	B −10 years / −1 year	−8 years Maximin
	Keep Quiet		C −1 year / −10 years	D −2 years / −2 years	−10 years
Column Minimum (for suspect 2)			(−8 years) Maximin	−10 years	

The **prisoners' dilemma** illustrates game situations in which the best common choice of strategies (block D in this example) is unstable, offers great incentives to cheat, and leads to the worst choice possible (block A).

10 percent, Firm 1 would lose $8 million, while Firm 2 would gain $6 million (box C). An analogous result would emerge, if Firm 2 maintained its price, but Firm 1 made the price cut (box B). A simultaneous price cut, on the other hand, would bring equal $6 million losses to both firms (box A). Again, we have a prisoners' dilemma. Seeking to assure the best of the worst that can happen (note the encircled number in the last column), Firm 1 will cut its price. Seeking to achieve the same goal (note the encircled number in the last row), Firm 2 will cut its price as well. They will end up in box A, while box D would have been so much better for them.

Part (II) pictures a similar story. Each of two competing firms is assumed to be spending $1 million per year on advertising. The extra revenue received by each as a result of advertising is $1 million; so the net effect is zero (box A). If Firm 2 now "disarmed" by spending only $200,000, while Firm 1 continued to spend $1 million, customers would abandon 2 for 1. Firm 1 would gain $1.2 million in sales; Firm 2 lose $400,000, its $1.2 million loss in sales being partially offset by the $800,000 cut in advertising expenditures (box B). An analogous result would occur if only Firm 1 cut its advertising, while

Firm 2 did not (box C). Yet if both firms "disarmed" at the same time and spent $200,000 only on advertising, neither would gain or lose customers and revenue, but both would have lowered costs and thus a gain of $800,000 (box D).

With each firm going after the best of the worst, they end up in box A, spending $1 million each. Yet each could be so much better off by a simultaneous agreement to "disarm" and go after box D. (Can you see why U.S. tobacco companies were delighted, not grieved, when the government some years ago banned cigarette ads from television?)

Wide Applicability

Games abound in which selfishness, uncooperativeness, hate, and suspicion put everyone in the worst possible spot (box A), while a dose of altruism, cooperation, love, and trust could make everyone better off (box D). Yet the great gains to be had from collusion (2 years' jail instead of 8, zero loss instead of $6 million, a $800,000 gain instead of none) again and again remain unrealized because each player has an incentive to cheat and make an even greater gain (1 year's

TABLE 12A.3 Nonzero-Sum Games

(I) Price War Game:

Matrix of Each Firm's Annual Gain (+) or Loss (−) Compared to
Original Position (in million dollars)

		Firm 2		Row Minimum
		Cut Price 10 Percent	Maintain Price	(for Firm 1)
Firm 1	Cut Price 10 percent	A −6 / −6	B −8 / +6	−6 Maximin
	Maintain Price	C +6 / −8	D 0 / 0	−8
Column minimum (for Firm 2)		Ⓐ−6 Maximin	−8	

(II) Advertising War Game:

Matrix of Each Firm's Annual Gain (+) or Loss (−) Compared to
Original Position (in million dollars)

		Firm 2		Row Minimum
		Spend $1 million	Spend $200,000	(for Firm 1)
Firm 1	Spend $1 million	A 0 / 0	B −0.4 / +1.2	0 Maximin
	Spend $200,000	C +1.2 / −0.4	D +0.8 / +0.8	−0.4
Column Minimum (for Firm 2)		Ⓞ 0 Maximin	−0.4	

The games pictured here also are prisoners'-dilemma games. In Part (I) as well as (II), the best common strategy is found in box D, but the worst one (box A) is chosen.

jail instead of 2 years', $6 million gained instead of zero lost, $1.2 million gained instead of $800,000). Thus prisoners who could form an unspoken cartel and improve their common lot turn into stool pigeons, and firms that could form a cartel and raise profit by maintaining price (or by advertising less) end up with a price or advertising war instead (that is, with lowering prices and advertising as much as ever). People who could form a "cartel" and raise welfare by polluting less end up polluting more. And governments that could form a "cartel" and raise welfare by disarming end up in an arms race instead.

It is fairly easy to see what it would take to escape such prisoners'-dilemma games.

Escaping the Dilemma

There are at least three steps people could take to escape the dilemma. One is to open up communications. If our prisoners could only have talked with one another! They could have reasoned together and ended up in situation D instead of A. The prisoners' dilemma feeds on uncertainty and distrust. Consider the international arms race. Early warning systems, telephone hot lines, and policies of détente, by opening up communications between the "prisoners" in separate rooms, have so far helped avoid nuclear holocaust. On the other hand, nobody knows what goes on in foreign-weapons labs, and on that account suspicion thrives. We have not avoided the development of ever-new weapons. Military leaders fear the worst. (Are "they" developing weapons to deliver poison gas? Deadly germs? The neutron bomb?) And thus is born the irresistible momentum to the arms race.

A second step toward escaping the dilemma is the institution of swift and certain punishment for those not choosing the best joint strategy. Betrayal and double cross must do more harm than good. Consider how rat finks are assassinated in the streets, how price cutters are threatened with even larger cuts, how the recipients of payola are fired on the spot, and how nuclear attackers are promised instant annihilation in turn. Consider, on the other hand, how those who know themselves to be immune from detection and punishment go ahead and do as they please. The secret developers of new weapons are a case in point. Once their weapons are revealed, they can count on years of undisturbed advantage. (Note: The certainty of swift punishment would worsen the entries in block A of our prisoners' dilemma tables above, perhaps to -8 years plus death in Table 12A.2 and to $-\$9$ million in both Parts (I) and (II) of Table 12A.3. The outcome would be a new game, called Chicken, and its solution would be quite a different one. Can you show why?)

A third step toward escape from the dilemma is to repeat the game. People can then *learn* to cooperate and to trust, which does not happen if the game is played only once. Consider how the same nuclear deterrence game is played anew on every single day, while the develop-a-new-weapon game is different every time.

Criticisms

Game theory has not brought permanent relief from the complexities of imperfect competition. Not everyone is happy with the kind of theory just introduced. Some would rather substitute less pessimistic assumptions about people's behavior. Do typical players of "games," they ask, really choose the best of the worst for themselves or the worst of the best for their opponents? Do people fear the worst more than they hope for the best? Might they not fear regret more than disaster? Might the glittering prize of cooperative bliss not attract them more than the skeletons of earlier aspirants repel? If so, might one not do better by substituting still different strategies for those suggested by von Neumann and Morgenstern?

Of course one could. A wealth of alternative approaches exists. So far, no one of them has been universally accepted as the best theory for explaining the games people play.

KEY TERMS

game
game theory
maximin strategy
minimax strategy
mixed strategy
nonzero-sum game
prisoners' dilemma
saddle point
zero-sum game

SELECTED READINGS

Boulding, Kenneth E. *Conflict and Defense: A General Theory*. New York: Harper and Row, 1962.

Cross, John G. *The Economics of Bargaining*. New York: Basic Books, 1969.

Friedman, James W. *Oligopoly and the Theory of Games*. Amsterdam: North Holland, 1977.

Leibenstein, Harvey. *Beyond Economic Man: A New Foundation for Microeconomics*. Cambridge: Harvard University Press, 1976, esp. chap. 9.

Applies game theory to the analysis of X-inefficiency.

Luce, R. Duncan, and Raiffa, Howard. *Games and Decisions*. New York: Wiley, 1954.

McDonald, John. *Strategy in Poker, Business, and War*. New York: Norton, 1950.

Neumann, John von, and Morgenstern, Oskar. *Theory of Games and Economic Behavior*. 3rd ed. Princeton: Princeton University Press, 1953.

Rapoport, A. *Fights, Games, and Debates*. Ann Arbor: University of Michigan Press, 1960.

Schelling, T. C. *The Strategy of Conflict*. Cambridge: Harvard University Press, 1960.

Schotter, Andrew, and Schwödiauer, Gerhard. "Economics and the Theory of Games: A Survey." *Journal of Economic Literature*, June 1980, pp. 479–527.

Shackle, G. L. S. *Expectations in Economics*. Cambridge, England: Cambridge University Press, 1949.

> Postulates that decision makers in conflict situations compare two "focus outcomes" (hope for the best and fear of the worst) and make a choice between the two (instead of focusing on the latter alone).

Shubik, Martin. *Strategy and Market Structure*. New York: Wiley, 1959.

> The most ambitious application of game theory to the analysis of oligopoly.

Shubik, Martin. *Essays in Mathematical Economics: In Honor of Oskar Morgenstern*. Princeton: Princeton University Press, 1967.

> Contains a 175-item bibliography of Morgenstern's work (through 1964) plus 27 essays on game theory, mathematical programming, decision theory, and more.

Telser, Lester G. *Competition, Collusion, and Game Theory*. Chicago: Aldine-Atherton, 1972.

Williams, J. D. *The Compleat Strategyst*. New York: McGraw-Hill, 1954.

CHAPTER 13

Imperfect Markets for Resource Services

When we examined the markets for resource services in Chapter 8, we were looking at a world of perfect competition. The present chapter, however, will consider how the results obtained earlier must be modified in the presence of imperfect competition. This time, we will concentrate on markets in which the services of human resources are traded, but much of what we find is applicable not only to labor, but to other types of resource services as well.

It would be possible to consider a great multitude of market imperfections; this chapter will focus on only four:

1. perfectly competitive sellers of labor confronting perfectly competitive buyers of labor, all of which buyers exert monopoly power in their respective product markets;
2. perfectly competitive sellers of labor confronting a single buyer only—a monopsony in the labor market—that is a perfectly competitive seller in the product market;
3. a single seller of labor confronting perfectly competitive buyers of labor; and
4. a single seller of labor confronting a monopsonistic buyer of labor.

Monopoly power on the selling side of a labor market is usually exercised by workers who have formed a cartel for the joint sale of their labor; that is, a **labor union**.

Competition in the Labor Market, Modified by Monopoly Power in the Product Market

Consider a firm with any degree of monopoly power. It may be an electric power company and a pure monopoly. It may be an oligopolistic automobile manufacturer or a monopolistically competitive restaurant. As we have learned in Chapters 11 and 12, one thing clearly differentiates such sellers from perfectly competitive ones: they face downward-sloping demand curves; and their marginal revenue, therefore, is lower than their product price.

When such firms enter the labor market, they often find themselves among innumerable buyers, however, and face just as many sellers. Consider how the producers of many different goods frequently compete with each other for the same labor, whether unskilled or skilled, such as secretarial help. The monopoly power of such firms in their respective product markets has, however, a definite impact on their behavior in the labor market. The quantity of labor demanded by such firms will not be one that equates the given wage with labor's marginal value product, but a lower quantity that equates this wage with labor's **marginal revenue product** (*MRP*), which is its marginal physical product multiplied by marginal revenue (rather than by product price), as shown in Table 13.1. The marginal physical products associated with alternative numbers of workers are given in column (2). The data in column (3) indicate the firm's assumed monopoly power in the product market: Hiring extra workers, even though associated with declining *marginal* products in column (2), raises *total* product (not shown). In order to sell this larger output, the firm pictured here must lower its product price. By implication, marginal revenue is below that price, in column (4). We can calculate labor's marginal value product (column 5) or its marginal revenue product (column 6) by simple multiplication.

Note: The marginal benefit for such a firm of using labor does not equal labor's marginal value product, as it would if the firm could sell any amount of its product at a given price. (For a discussion of that case, the reader may wish to review Table 8.1, "The Input Decision" on p. 215.) The marginal benefit relevant for the input decision now equals the marginal revenue product; as more workers are hired, marginal revenue product declines much more rapidly than the marginal value product because a larger number of workers now brings not only a decline in

marginal physical product, but also a decline in product price (without which the extra output could not be sold).

Now assume that our firm faces a market wage of $225 per worker per week no matter how many workers it hires, as in column (7). This wage is our firm's constant marginal cost of acquiring labor. The profit-maximizing input decision is then indicated by the boxed numbers in our table. The firm does best for itself by hiring 2 workers. (A third worker would add only $68 to total weekly revenue, while adding $225 to cost. Larger numbers of workers, as the negative numbers in column 6 indicate, would even *reduce* total revenue, while adding to cost, because their extra physical output would depress price so much as to produce negative marginal revenue.)

A firm that is a perfect competitor in the labor market but has monopoly power in the product market maximizes profit by hiring that quantity of labor which results in labor's marginal revenue product being equal to its wage:

$$MRP_L = W$$

TABLE 13.1   The Labor Input Decision: Product Market Monopoly

Workers (number per week) (1)	Marginal Physical Product of Labor, MPP_L (product units per extra worker) (2)	Product Price, P (3)	Marginal Revenue, MR (4)	Marginal Value Product of Labor, $MVP_L = MPP_L \cdot P$ (5) = (2) × (3)	Marginal Revenue Product of Labor $MRP_L = MPP_L \cdot MR$ (6) = (2) × (4)	Labor's Wage, W (7)
1	500	1.00	0.80	500	400	225
2	450	0.86	0.50	387	225	225
3	400	0.69	0.17	276	68	225
4	350	0.56	−0.10	196	−35	225
5	300	0.45	−0.34	135	−102	225
6	250	0.36	−0.52	90	−130	225

For a firm with monopoly power in the product market, product price, in column (3), exceeds marginal revenue, in column (4). As a result, the marginal benefit for such a firm of using labor does not equal labor's marginal value product, in column (5), but its lower marginal revenue product, in column (6). Such a firm hires extra workers as long as the marginal revenue product of labor does not fall short of the marginal cost of acquiring labor (which in this example equals the wage). Given the conditions pictured here, a profit-maximizing firm hires 2 workers and thereby sets MRP_L equal to W at $225 per worker per week (boxed numbers).

A Graphical Exposition

This rule can be demonstrated graphically as well. Figure 13.1 is a graph of Table 13.1, column (1) against columns (5)–(7). The 2-worker profit-maximizing input quantity corresponds to intersection *b* of the two lines of labor's marginal-revenue product and labor's wage. As a quick review of Figure 8.1, "A Firm's Demand for Labor: The Simple Case" (p. 216) can show, in the absence of product market monopoly power, the firm would demand the 3.7 workers corresponding to intersection *f*. The lower quantity demanded in the present case of a competitive buyer of labor whose labor market behavior is modified by its product market monopoly power should not surprise us.

Just as a firm with monopoly power restricts *output* below the level at which output price equals marginal cost (and thus raises output price above marginal cost), it also restricts *input* use below the level at which input price equals marginal value product (point *f*). Thus the gap between output price and marginal cost of production (which, we noted in Chapter 11, is the basis for Lerner's index of monopoly power) now reappears in the input market as a gap (*bd* in our graph) between input price and marginal

value product. Economists have a special name for this gap.

Monopolistic Exploitation

When discussing Clark's marginal productivity theory of distribution in Chapter 8, we already noted how some (but not all) economists view the equality of an input's price with its marginal value product as the *absence* of exploitation. Correspondingly, such economists view a situation in which input price and marginal value product differ as one in which exploitation is present. When, as in our case, an input's marginal value product exceeds its price because the input's user possesses monopoly power in the product market (which makes the input's marginal revenue product fall short of its marginal value product), such economists talk of **monopolistic exploitation** of the input.

In the case of labor, we can write

Monopolistic exploitation of labor:

$$MVP > W \text{ because } MRP < MVP$$

The extent of labor's monopolistic exploitation is shown by the shaded area in our graph.

FIGURE 13.1
The Demand for Labor Reconsidered

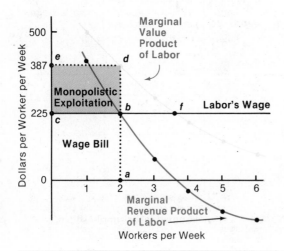

This graph is a modification of Figure 8.1, "A Firm's Demand For Labor: The Simple Case." It shows how a firm facing a market-determined wage in the labor market (here $225 per worker per week) but having monopoly power in its product market will demand labor according to its curve of labor's marginal *revenue* product, not marginal *value* product. Marginal revenue product, not marginal value product measures such a firm's marginal benefit of using labor; the market-determined wage shows such a firm's marginal cost of acquiring labor. The optimum labor quantity hired by such a profit-maximizing firm, therefore, corresponds to intersection *b* and equals 2 workers in this example). Note: When labor's marginal value product exceeds its wage because marginal revenue product falls short of marginal value product, labor is said to be subject to *monopolistic exploitation*.

Even though the weekly marginal product of 2 workers is worth \$387 (point *d*), they each receive only \$225. Thus they are said to be exploited by the \$162 difference. Such a difference would not exist if our firm's product-market monopoly power did not exist and it hired the 3.7 workers corresponding to point *f*.

Note: Many economists are not very happy with this use of the emotionally laden term *exploitation*, popularized mainly by British economists like Joan Robinson and A. C. Pigou (see Biography 13.1 and Biography 18.1, respectively). As Figure 13.1 clearly shows (and as Table 13.1 attests as well), if our firm (positioned at optimum point *b*) were to fire any one of its two workers, it would lose revenue of \$225, not of \$387. Thus the firm is paying the marginal worker exactly what this worker is worth to the firm. So who is exploiting whom? Who is pocketing something that rightfully belongs to someone else? The consumers of our firm's product are really the ones to blame because they will take the extra output produced by a second worker only if product price is reduced from \$1 per unit to 86¢ (note Table 13.1), which is why labor's marginal revenue product lies below its marginal value product. It would not be impossible for the consumers of the firm's product to be poorer than the workers who make it; in that case the poor would be exploiting the "rich." Clearly this situation is not what most people have in mind when hearing the word *exploitation*. Unfortunately, this use of the term is so entrenched in the literature of economics that it is impossible to change it now.

Monopsony in the Labor Market, but Competition in the Product Market

Consider a firm that sells its product in a competitive market but is the only buyer in a labor market in which a multitude of sellers compete with one another. Such a situation is far from unusual. A typical example given is the "company town," dominated by a single employer. Think of Seattle and the Boeing Company;

Butte, Montana and the Anaconda Copper Mining Company; Hershey, Pennsylvania and the Hershey Chocolate Company; Barstow, California and the Santa Fe Railway. Such dominant employers have "captured" work forces to the extent that such places are inhabited by workers who cannot or will not leave the area (being ignorant of alternatives, unable to find transportation, or reluctant to leave pretty scenery or good friends).

Monopsony need not necessarily be based on the geographic concentration of immobile resources, however. It can also arise out of an extreme degree of occupational immobility. Consider the options open to someone with specialized training, such as an astronaut, general, or designer of nuclear submarines. There is likely to be only a single employer for such sellers of labor. Finally, monopsony in the labor market is often the result of employers who agree to act jointly in the hiring of labor and not to compete with each other for workers. Such **antipirating agreements** have been reached on a national basis by major league sports clubs and different departments of the federal government; on a regional basis by coal mining firms and by those manufacturing furniture and garments; and on a local basis by colleges, construction firms, hospitals, hotels, newspapers, and restaurants.

As was noted in Chapter 11, one thing clearly differentiates monopsonies from perfectly competitive buyers: monopsonies face upward-sloping supply curves; their marginal outlay, therefore, exceeds the price they pay for their input.

This fact has a noticeable impact on the labor market, even when the firms involved have no monopoly power whatever in their product markets. The quantity of labor demanded by such firms will not be one that equates any given wage with labor's marginal value product, but a lower quantity that equates the firm's marginal outlay on labor (implied by a wage the firm has set) with labor's marginal value product, as shown by Table 13.2. An assumed labor supply schedule is given in columns (1) and (2). Because our firm is the only buyer of labor in the market, it can set

TABLE 13.2 The Labor Input Decision: Monopsony

Workers (number per week)	Labor's Wage, W	Marginal Cost and Marginal Benefit of Using Labor:	
		Marginal Outlay on Labor, MO_L	Marginal Value Product of Labor, MVP_L
		(dollars per extra worker per week)	
(1)	(2)	(3)	(4)
100	50	100	700
200	100	200	600
300	150	300	500
400	200	400	400
500	250	500	300
600	300	600	200

For a firm with monopsony power in the labor market, labor's wage, in column (2), falls short of the marginal outlay on labor, in column (3). The latter is the marginal cost for such a firm of using labor. Such a firm hires extra workers as long as the marginal outlay on labor does not exceed the marginal benefit from using labor (which in this example equals labor's marginal value product). Given the conditions pictured here, a profit-maximizing firm hires 400 workers and thereby sets MO_L equal to MVP_L at $400 per worker per week (boxed numbers).

any wage it desires but must then take whatever number of workers present themselves. Because we assume that the firm can coax out a larger number of workers only by offering a higher wage to everyone, the firm's marginal outlay on labor, in column (3), exceeds the wage. (Example: If the firm set a wage of $50 per worker per week, it would get 100 workers and spend $5,000 per week. If the firm wanted 200 workers, it would have to offer $100 per week to all of them. Thus it would spend $20,000 instead. An extra outlay of $15,000 would bring forth 100 extra workers; thus a marginal outlay of $150 per worker per week would bring forth workers in the 100–200 worker range, and this number clearly exceeds the $100 wage paid to any one worker.)

Note: The marginal outlay on labor (which exceeds the wage) is clearly the marginal cost to such a firm of using labor. Unlike in earlier examples, this marginal cost is no longer a market-determined wage beyond the control of our firm.

If our firm, however, is a price taker in its product market, its marginal benefit of using labor is still labor's marginal value product, or

labor's marginal physical product multiplied by a given market-determined product price. The profit-maximizing input decision is again indicated by the boxed numbers in our table. The firm does best for itself by hiring 400 workers. (If it hired fewer of them, it would forgo profit unnecessarily because extra workers would then add less to the firm's total cost than to its total revenue. The reverse would be true if it hired more than the optimum number.)

A firm that is a perfect competitor in the product market but has monopsony power in the labor market maximizes profit by hiring that quantity of labor which results in labor's marginal value product being equal to the marginal outlay on labor:

$$MVP_L = MO_L$$

A Graphical Exposition

This rule can be demonstrated graphically as well. Figure 13.2 is a graph of Table 13.2, column (1) against columns (2)–(4)—and all points between those in the table. The 400-worker profit-maximizing input quantity corresponds to intersection *d* of the two lines of marginal value product of labor and marginal outlay on labor. In the absence of monopsony power, the firm would, of course, demand the 533 workers corresponding to intersection *f* (and would do so at a market-determined wage of $267 per worker per week). As in the earlier example, we thus note a gap between labor's wage ($200 measured at *b*) and its marginal value product ($400 measured at *d*). This gap has a special name.

Monopsonistic Exploitation

Whenever an input's marginal value product exceeds its price because the input's user possesses monopsony power in the input market (which makes the marginal outlay on the input exceed its price), economists talk of **monopsonistic exploitation** of the input.

In the case of labor, we can write

Monopsonistic exploitation of labor:

$$MVP > W \text{ because } MO > W$$

The extent of labor's monopsonistic exploitation is shown by the shaded area in our example. Even though the weekly marginal value product of 400 workers equals $400 (point *d*), they each receive only $200. Once more, such a difference would not exist if our firm's labor market monopsony power did not exist and it hired the 533 workers corresponding to point *f*.

Note: In this instance, as in the previous one, the term "exploitation" can easily be mislead-

FIGURE 13.2 Monopsony in the Labor Market

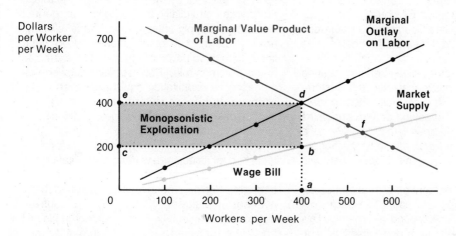

This graph is a modification of Figure 8.1, "A Firm's Demand For Labor: The Simple Case." It shows how a firm facing a market-determined price in the product market but having monopsony power in the labor market will demand labor according to its curve of labor's marginal value product. The firm's marginal cost of acquiring labor, however, is not a horizontal line at a market-determined wage, but rather a rising line of marginal outlays that exceed the wages this firm can set. The optimum quantity hired by such a profit-maximizing firm, therefore, corresponds to intersection *d* (and equals 400 workers in this example). Note: When labor's marginal value product exceeds its wage because marginal outlay exceeds wage, labor is said to be subject to *monopsonistic exploitation.*

ing. The "exploited" workers need not be migrant farm workers or teenage waitresses; they may very well be star athletes or five-star generals, among the richest people in the country.

Cartels in the Labor Market: The Emergence of Labor Unions

By forming cartels, the sellers of inputs—just like the sellers of output— can possibly improve their incomes at the expense of other people. Until not so long ago, it has been particularly difficult, however, for the sellers of labor to form cartels.

Imagine that a few electricians in a city got together and plotted to form a union of the members of their craft who would agree to work only at a certain wage and to perform no more than a specified amount of work. Their price-raising conspiracy would not work unless all existing electricians agreed to it, remained loyal to it, and succeeded in keeping out newcomers or in forcing them to join.

Just suppose their initial organizational efforts were a success. Assume they agreed on demanding double the hourly wages for half the hours worked. How could they enforce such a demand? What if employers just laughed at them? They could threaten the employers with work slowdowns or even strikes. But what if employers called the workers' bluff and just locked them out of their plants until a lack of income brought them all to their senses? Even if

BIOGRAPHY 13.1:

Joan V. Robinson

Joan Violet Robinson (1903–   ) was born in England, was educated at London and Cambridge, and has taught at Cambridge University since 1931. As Augustin Cournot (see Biography 11.1) before her and Edward Chamberlin (see Biography 12.1) in her own time, Joan Robinson was a pioneer in the study of the behavior of firms in imperfectly competitive markets. "It is customary," she writes in *The Economics of Imperfect Competition* (1933), "in setting out the principles of economic theory, to open with the analysis of a perfectly competitive world, and to treat monopoly as a special case. . . . This process can with advantage be reversed. . . . It is more proper to set out the analysis of monopoly, treating perfect competition as a special case." The book covered some of the same ground as Chamberlin's but also other matters, from price discrimination to monopolistic and monopsonistic exploitation.

"The fundamental cause of exploitation," says Robinson, "will be found to be the lack of perfect elasticity in the supply of labor or in the demand for commodities. . . . Thus the function of a trade union or a minimum wage law in removing exploitation lies not so much in the fact that it improves the bargaining strength of the workers as in the fact that by means of a 'common rule' it reproduces artificially the condition of perfect elasticity of supply of labor to individual employers."[1] [Note the horizontal, union-imposed wage lines in the three parts of Figure 13.4 as examples of this common rule.] Robinson also showed that *monopolistic* exploitation could exist even in the absence of monopsony (see Figure 13.1), and that unions and minimum wages could not remove it.

The Economics of Imperfect Competition established for its author a worldwide reputation at a young age; this renown has been maintained through a lifelong penchant for travel, debate, and social criticism. (Chamberlin, in contrast, abstained from social criticism, except in his last book, which painted a frightful picture of industry domination by labor unions.) Early on, Joan Robinson became a vehement Marxian critic of the market economy, denouncing the system of private property on which it rests and the great evils of unemployment and injustice that she attributed to it. These "heretical" ideas have found expression in such books as *Private Enterprise and*

employers succumbed and paid the same amount of money for half the hours worked, how could the union keep any one electrician from trying to work, at the new wage of $16 per hour, say, *twice* the allowable time? And if one tried it, how could the union keep all the workers from trying it at the same time? If all the workers tried to work double the allowable time, employers would have the power to nudge the wage down to $14 and $13 and, finally, to $8 per hour where it was before. Even if members were totally loyal to each other and did not cheat, how could the union prevent the electricians of other cities from appearing on the scene and offering to work for $8? How could it keep employers from then firing union workers and hiring those others? Or how could it prevent employers from closing shop and

---

Public Control (1945), *An Essay on Marxian Economics* (1942), *Economic Philosophy* (1962), *Freedom and Necessity* (1970), and *Aspects of Development and Underdevelopment* (1979).

While promoting her own revolution in microeconomics, Robinson worked tirelessly to expound that of her colleague, John M. Keynes, in macroeconomics and to extend his theory to long-run questions of capital accumulation and growth. Thus she came to write *Introduction to the Theory of Employment* (1937), *The Rate of Interest and Other Essays* (1952), *The Accumulation of Capital* (1956), *Essays in the Theory of Economic Growth* (1962), and (with John Eatwell) *An Introduction to Modern Economics* (1973). Her *Collected Economic Papers*, which appeared in five volumes between 1951 and 1979, show how thoroughly the land of economics is crisscrossed with the footprints of this prolific scholar. Of Chamberlin's long quest (noted in Chapter 12) to have his product recognized as different from hers, she once said, "I'm sorry I ruined his life."

[1]Joan V. Robinson, *The Economics of Imperfect Competition* (London: Macmillan, 1933), pp. 281–82.

---

moving to other cities? Workers could form a national union, including, perhaps, hundreds of thousands of people.

But what if other regional unions existed who had no desire to lay down their lives? The presence of regional unions might lead to a series of **jurisdictional strikes**, wherein workers belonging to one union, in an attempt to force the recognition of a single union, walked off the job to interrupt the work being done by fellow workers belonging to another union. But even if a national union were formed, and even if cheaters were still absent among the larger number of workers in this national union (which is a highly improbable case), what would prevent foreign electricians from immigrating and working for $8? Or what would prevent employers from shifting electrical work to foreign subsidiaries? An international union? Even that would not be good enough! New technical-school graduates might appear on the scene and offer to work for $8. Or employers might come up with a compliant labor-replacing device that could do the work of recalcitrant people for $8. Or firms might decide to produce different products that require no electricians at all.

For all these reasons, unions long have had a tough time. They were always concerned about their "security" and rightly so. In the United States about 50 years ago, however, unions acquired a trump card in the form of government aid. A brief look at history will help us see what happened.

The Early Unions

Labor unions have existed in the United States almost since the days of independence. In Boston, New York, and Philadelphia, carpenters, shoemakers, and printers banded together as early as 1791. These organizations of workers, however, were weak and short-lived. Not only did they face the militant opposition of employers, but there were legal impediments. The first labor unions faced the **conspiracy doctrine**, according to which U.S. courts, just like those in France, Germany, and Great Britain, looked at workers who "conspired" to raise wages as common criminals. Not until 1842 did the Massachusetts Supreme Court establish the legality of unions. Still, they had no general impact for many decades thereafter.

The Labor Movement Comes to Stay

The Knights of Labor, founded in 1869, was the first national union of importance, but it vanished quickly after reaching its peak of influence in 1886. In that very year, the American Federation of Labor (AFL) was founded. Like the unions of a century earlier, those belonging to this federation were **craft unions**, each being a union of workers possessing a common set of skills but possibly being employed by different firms. Under the leadership of Samuel Gompers, such

unions of plumbers, carpenters, and the like developed a practical-minded philosophy. Unlike the Knights of Labor, who had called for the establishment of a cooperative, noncapitalist order, the AFL had no aspirations to revolutionize society. It was concerned with bread and butter for its members as long as it was *more* and *now*. Membership in the AFL and other unions grew to 5 million by 1920 (then 13 percent of the labor force), but then declined until, in the 1930s, government intervened. Public opinion blamed big business for the Great Depression and began to favor the self-protection of workers by means of unions. This public support was reflected in legislation helpful to union organization.

Helpful Laws

The Norris-La Guardia Act of 1932 took a first and giant step toward protecting labor unions. It outlawed one of the most powerful weapons employers had used against union activities: the **injunction**, a court decree, enforceable by arrest and jail, forbidding certain actions. Although unions as such had been legalized in 1842, many of their actions could still be blocked by this device. Employers found it easy to obtain injunctions against strikes, peaceful picketing, and even membership drives. Such injunctions, once obtained, automatically made a union a wrongdoer in the eyes of the law if it persisted in actions that were vital to its functioning.

President Roosevelt's New Deal quickly broadened the new freedoms granted to labor. The National Labor Relations Act, or Wagner Act, of 1935 affirmed the right of unions to organize and to bargain collectively. The act made collective bargaining contracts legally enforceable but went even further than that. First, it guaranteed unions recognition by employers by ordering employers to bargain with the duly elected representatives of their workers if a majority of them wanted to bargain collectively. Second, the law outlawed a number of *antiunion practices*, such as firing workers for joining a union, refusing to hire them if sympathetic to unions, threatening to close the firm if workers

CLOSE-UP 13.1:

The Public School Monopsony

Two economists, John H. Landon and Robert N. Baird, recently investigated the monopsony power school teachers have to confront. They studied first-year teacher salaries in 136 local U.S. school districts during 1966–67. They found the number of independent (and, therefore, competing) districts in an area to be an important determinant of entry-level salaries. The fewer and larger were the districts in a given metropolitan area, the lower were teacher salaries. Teachers who were facing a single large school district had only unpalatable alternatives to low salaries: move to another city (and leave behind a favored area and friends), commute for long distances, take nonteaching jobs, engage in a lengthy search for private teaching positions. They usually accepted lower, monopsonistically-set salaries instead.

Source: John H. Landon and Robert N. Baird, "Monopsony in the Market for Public School Teachers," *The American Economic Review*, December 1971, pp. 966–71.

join a union, interfering with or dominating the administration of a union, and refusing to bargain with a union. In effect, these rules made it illegal for an employer to make individual bargains with workers who were willing to ignore union policy and, say, accept a job at a lower wage.

A Change in Strategy

As government threw its support to labor, the labor movement itself underwent a significant change. Some labor leaders abandoned the principle that union membership should be limited to specific skills. Instead, workers were to be organized in **industrial unions**, each being a union of workers employed in the same industry, without regard to particular skills. As a result, millions in the mass-production industries (autos, electrical products, steel) qualified for membership in the new Congress of Industrial Organizations (CIO). Under the leadership of John L. Lewis, the CIO engaged in massive organization drives in the 1930s. Often there was violence. In famous sit-down strikes, the new unions seized the auto plants. Labor leaders, such as Walter Reuther, were beaten up by the hired strongmen of the Ford Motor Company. Still, one by one, the industrial giants—Ford, General Motors, U.S. Steel—succumbed, recognizing a CIO union as their workers' bargaining agent. Union membership soared from below 3 million in 1933 to 15 million by 1945 (then 23 percent of the labor force).

Labor Union Vs. Competitive Buyers of Labor

How a union emerging in a previously competitive labor market will act depends, of course, on the goal the union wants to pursue. Labor unions pursue many goals, such as better working conditions, clear-cut grievance procedures, job security, and a host of fringe benefits, ranging from health and life insurance to paid vacations and pension plans. In the United States, however, their dominant goal has always been the achieve-

ment of higher money income for those employed.

One must not confuse labor's wage (a rate per unit of time) with labor's income (the wage multiplied by the number of time units worked). It is not at all obvious, therefore, how a union is to act when seeking to promote the best interests of workers. Can it hope to raise labor's income by increasing its wage and keeping employment unchanged? Must it accept a cut in employment when pushing wages up? If it must accept an employment cut, what is the ideal wage level from labor's point of view? To answer these questions we now turn to Figure 13.3. We assume that market demand and market supply equilibrate at a weekly wage of $250 per worker in the absence of a union (point *a*) and that 4,000 workers are then employed. Now let them form a union and threaten employers with a strike unless their wage is raised.

Pushing Up the Wage

As the market demand line indicates, employers demand smaller quantities of labor as the wage rises above its competitive equilibrium level. At a weekly wage of $375 per worker, they demand only 3,000 workers (point *b*); at a weekly wage of $460, they demand 2,320 workers (point *c*), and so on. All else being equal, a union that pushes the wage up, therefore, is bound to lower the employment opportunities of workers. And the union has essentially three courses of action open to it: letting employers ration jobs, raising demand, and reducing supply.

Letting Employers Ration Jobs. First, the union can insist on a given above-equilibrium wage of, say, $460 per week and then let employers decide who is and who is not lucky enough to remain employed. In our example, employment would fall from 4,000 workers (point *a*) to 2,320 workers (point *c*). Those who would remain employed would clearly be better off; their unemployed fellow workers would be worse off. Indeed, unemployment would exceed the 1,680 workers thrown out of work (distance

FIGURE 13.3 Labor Union vs. Competitive Labor Market

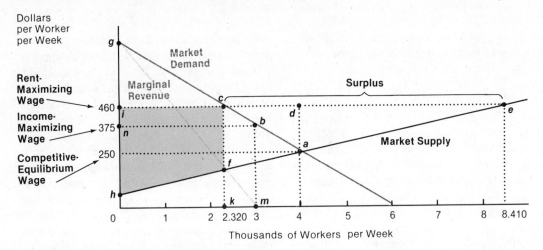

All else being equal, if a labor union is formed in a previously competitive market and pushes the wage above its equilibrium level ($250 per week in this example), the level of employment will fall. Beyond that, one can only speculate: The union might ignore the resultant labor surplus. It might also attempt to remove the labor surplus using policies designed to raise the demand for labor or reduce its supply. Nor can one predict which particular wage the union will set. The union may wish to maximize the total income of workers, given market demand (area *0mbn*). It may wish instead to maximize the workers' economic rent (shaded); that is, seek the maximum possible excess of the workers' actual income (area *0kci*) over their next best alternatives (area *0kfh*). Or the union may pursue altogether different goals.

---

cd). As the upward-sloping market supply curve indicates, the higher wage would attract 4,410 additional workers into the market (distance *de*). Thus a labor surplus (or unemployment) of 1,680 + 4,410 = 6,090 workers would occur (distance *ce*).

Note: Unions have been instrumental in supporting either government programs of unemployment insurance and welfare assistance for the unemployed (represented by distance *ce* in our graph) or programs of public-service jobs. Such programs are equivalent, respectively, to subsidies paid farmers for *not* producing crops "supported" by governmentally set above-equilibrium prices or to government crop purchase plans. In either the labor or farmer case, taxpayers are made to protect members of cartels from undesirable consequences that follow upon their price-raising conspiracy.

Raising Demand. Our union's second option is to insist on a wage of, say, $460 per week but also to take measures to assure that none of its present members lose their jobs. This happy result would occur if the union could manage to

1. bring about a rightward shift in the demand for labor until the demand line went through point *d* in our graph and
2. force employers never to use anyone but union members (while the union, of course, refused to admit to its rosters the 4,410 potential new workers represented by distance *de*).

Examples of policy 1 include: union support of government-mandated consumer purchases, regardless of whether consumers wish to buy the goods involved (automobile safety belts, aircraft emergency locator transmitters, household fire alarms); union-instigated governmental import restrictions, wage subsidies to employers, or tax cuts to consumers who buy the products of labor; and (as in the case of the International Ladies Garment Workers Union) cooperation with management to raise the productivity of labor or raise product price by advertising. (Remember that labor's marginal physical product and product price are the factors behind the market demand for labor.) Union attempts to shift the demand curve for labor to the right also include a whole range of practices that force employers to continue paying workers who are not really needed because their work is being done, or could be done, by fewer workers or by machines. Thus musicians have forced minimum orchestra sizes on film and opera producers regardless of the size actually needed and have forced broadcasters to employ "standby orchestras" while records were being played; stokers who used to feed steam boilers have forced railroads to keep them on, riding along on diesel locomotives that don't have steam boilers. Printers have insisted on setting "dummy type" for advertising copy, which newspapers never use when advertisers submit ready-to-print copy, and electricians have torn apart and rewired prewired equipment. Airline pilots have insisted on a third licensed pilot in the cockpit (where a flight engineer would do just fine), and bricklayers have restricted the number of bricks that can be laid in an hour. Textile workers have similarly limited the number of looms attended and painters the width of brushes. Such workers, who do not work or do unnecessary work, may as well take along a featherbed and sleep on the job, which is why this practice is called **featherbedding**.

Examples of policy 2 (forcing employers to use only union members) include the establishment of **closed shops** (in which only union members are hired) or of **union shops** (in which all employees, within 30 days after hiring, have to become union members or at least pay union dues as a condition of continued employment). Such policy is often reinforced by the restriction of union membership to a few (4,000 in our

case), by insisting on lengthy apprenticeships, charging high initiation fees, administering impossible entrance tests, or simply denying access to blacks, females, Jews, or any other easily identifiable group.

Reducing Supply. The union's third option is to insist on a wage of, say, $460 per week, but also take measures to assure that no more than the appropriate number of workers (2,320 of them in our example) apply for the job. This strategy would be equivalent to bending the market supply curve at point f to coincide with line fc, which could be accomplished by restricting union membership even more severely by any of the aforementioned measures. Here, too, governmental support comes in handy. Consider how government (with the enthusiastic support of many unions) has restricted the supply of labor by setting maximum basic hours, prohibiting child labor, and severely limiting immigration.

Other laws have reduced the supply of labor in particular occupations: Until 1971, when the U.S. Supreme Court voided them, many so-called state protective laws barred designated persons from specified jobs. Females, for instance, were often barred from jobs requiring lifting of weights in excess of 25 pounds (but they were apparently free to lift heavier children at home) as well as from such "dangerous" occupations as bar tending, bellhopping, coal mining, meter reading, pinsetting, shoe shining, and truck driving.

A Final Note

A union that pushes labor's wage above its competitive level will, of course, have to decide on the exact level it prefers, somewhere between points a and g in our graph. Many possibilities exist, but two of the more interesting ones have been indicated in Figure 13.3. A union may push the wage to $375 per week where the market demand for labor (point b) has a price elasticity of $|1|$ and the marginal revenue to the union from selling labor is zero (point m). In this way, the union maximizes the total income of its members (area $0mbn$). Given the assumed market demand, no other wage-employment combination can produce an income total as large as \$1,125,000 per week (or \$375 per week times 3,000 workers).

Or a union may push the wage to \$460 per week (point c) where the union's marginal revenue of selling labor just equals the marginal cost of supplying it (point f). Note that the height of point f on the supply curve represents the lowest wage (\$170) that worker #2,320 would accept for this type of work and thus, presumably, the highest wage that worker could get elsewhere. This worker's best alternative income is, therefore, the marginal cost of supplying his or her labor in this particular market. By implication, shaded area $cfhi$ represents the maximum possible excess of workers' actual income over their next best alternatives. It represents the maximum possible economic rent workers can earn in this market. (The reader may wish to review the discussion of rent in Chapter 8.)

Labor Union vs. Labor Monopsony

What if a labor union emerges not in an otherwise competitive labor market, but in response to a labor monopsony? Just as no definite outcome could be predicted in the case of a bilateral monopoly in a goods market (see Figure 11.12 on p. 343), when a union has monopoly power over the supply of labor and a firm has monopsony power over the demand for it, no definite outcome can be predicted. What happens depends on the personalities involved and their bargaining skills. (Not surprisingly, game theory, discussed in Appendix 12A, has been fruitfully applied in this area.) We can, however, imagine a number of possible outcomes, in response to a wage hike, including higher employment, unchanged employment, and lower employment.

Higher Employment

Panel (a) of Figure 13.4 is basically a copy of Figure 13.2. The upward-sloping line going

through points b and e represents the competitive market supply faced by our monopsonist before the advent of the union. The upward-sloping line going through points a and h, accordingly, represents the monopsonist's marginal outlay on labor when there is no union. And the monopsonist's profit-maximizing position, before the union appears, corresponds to intersection a: At \$400 per worker per week, the monopsonist equates the marginal value product of labor (marginal benefit) with the marginal outlay on labor (marginal cost), hires 400 workers, and pays each one \$200 a week (point b). The resulting monopsonistic exploitation is the sum of the dotted and shaded rectangles (area $abcd$).

Now let a union appear and enforce a minimum wage of \$300 per worker. The firm may pay more but never less, and, as the (old and new) supply line to the right of point e indicates, the firm will have to pay more if it wishes to hire more than 600 workers. The firm can, however, get up to 600 workers for \$300 per worker per week (line fe is its new supply up to that quantity). After all, each one of these workers, as the old supply indicates to the *left* of point e, was willing to work for less than \$300 before the union was formed. The union has effectively repealed the original market supply line to the left of point e. Our monopsony faces a new market supply consisting of two parts: line fe and line eg and beyond.

Accordingly, our monopsony's marginal outlay on labor is different, too. The repeal of the old market supply to the left of e (the refusal of 600 workers to work for less than \$300 a week, even though they were once willing to do so) has repealed the original line of marginal outlay to the left of h. Up to a quantity of 600 workers per week, the old cause for the divergence between market supply and marginal outlay is gone. The monopsony once had to pay ever-higher wages to get extra workers. Now it can get any number up to 600 workers at exactly the same wage of \$300 a week. Line fe is not only its new market supply, but its new marginal outlay as well! Until 600 workers are hired, each additional worker adds only \$300 a week to the firm's total outlay on

FIGURE 13.4   Labor Union vs. Labor Monopsony

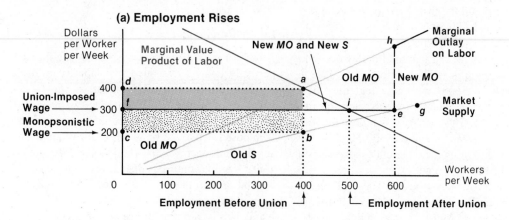

(a) Employment Rises

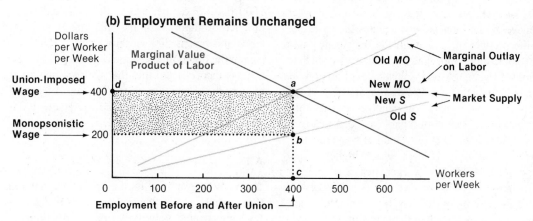

(b) Employment Remains Unchanged

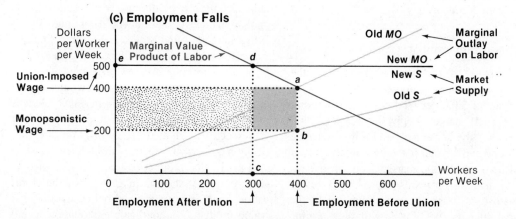

(c) Employment Falls

All else being equal, if a labor union is formed to face a monopsony and pushes the wage above its original level ($200 per week in this example), the effect on the level of employment cannot be predicted. Depending on the extent of the wage hike, employment may rise (a), remain unchanged (b), or fall (c).

labor, an amount exactly equal to the union-imposed wage.

Note: Should the firm wish to hire even one worker beyond 600, it would have to pay that worker (and all workers) a little more than $300 per week. Thus the old marginal outlay curve to right of point *h* is still in effect. (Because *h* corresponds to $600, we know that the 601st worker hired would impose roughly such an extra cost on the firm. This extra cost would be the sum of that new worker's wage of $300.50 plus tiny raises of 50¢ to bring the other 600 workers up to the level of the newcomer.)

We are now ready to see the end result: Given the new conditions imposed by the union, our monopsony's profit-maximizing position corresponds to intersection *i*. At $300 per worker per week, the monopsonist equates the marginal value product of labor with the marginal outlay on labor, hires 500 workers, and pays each one $300 a week. Monopsonistic exploitation is gone. The shaded part has disappeared as a result of labor's lower marginal value product (point *i* instead of *a*). The dotted part has been incorporated into the workers' new total of wage income. Indeed, not only is their wage higher ($300 instead of $200 per worker per week); their employment has *risen* as well (500 instead of 400 workers are employed). This higher employment, however, is not an inevitable result of a labor union facing a monopsony.

Unchanged Employment

Consider panel (b) of Figure 13.4. Suppose the union were greedier and imposed a weekly minimum wage of $400 per worker. Up to the point where the old market supply line reaches $400 (not shown), the horizontal, union-imposed line from *d* to *a* and beyond is the monopsony's new line of both supply and marginal outlay. Therefore, the firm maximizes its profit at intersection *a*, equating, at $400 per worker per week, the marginal value product of labor with the marginal outlay on labor and hiring 400 workers just as before. This time, all of the old monopsonistic

exploitation (dotted area) is incorporated into the workers' new total of wage income (area *0cad*).

Lower Employment

A union facing a monopsony, just as one facing perfectly competitive buyers of labor, can also *decrease* the level of employment, as shown in panel (c) of Figure 13.4. This time, we imagine that a weekly minimum wage of $500 per worker is imposed. Up to the point where the old market supply line reaches $500 (not shown), the horizontal, union-imposed line from *e* to *d* and beyond is the monopsony's new line of both supply and marginal outlay. Therefore, the firm maximizes its profit at intersection *d*, equating, at $500 per worker per week, the marginal value product of labor with the marginal outlay on labor and hiring 300 workers only. This time, part of the old monopsonistic exploitation (dotted area) is incorporated into the workers' new total of wage income (area *0cde*); the remainder (shaded) is eliminated because the 301st to 400th workers are now unemployed.

A Final Note

As the three graphs of Figure 13.4 show, a union that pushes labor's wage above the level a monopsony would voluntarily pay can eliminate monopsonistic exploitation. Yet, should it exist, monopolistic exploitation would continue. To see why, in your mind, relabel the three lines of labor's marginal value product in Figure 13.4 as "marginal revenue product of labor." The monopsony's optimum input choices would then be quite unaffected. The optimum input choices would correspond, as before, to points *i*, *a*, and *d*, respectively, in the three graphs. Yet as Figure 13.1 has shown, there would then exist a marginal-value-product-of-labor curve *above* the ones presently shown. In each case, therefore, labor would receive a wage below its marginal value product. Monopolistic exploitation would persist because while the union can eliminate the divergence between wage and marginal outlay, it

ANALYTICAL EXAMPLE 13.1:
Fire Fighters Fight Monopsony

Using a large cross section of union and nonunion cities during 1960–66, Orley Ashenfelter followed the efforts of one of the largest unions in the public sector to counter the monopsony power of local governments. The table summarizes his observations about the International Association of Fire Fighters. Considering all cities studied, the author concluded that the 1966 average hourly wage of unionized firefighters had been raised from 6–16 percent above that of nonunion firefighters as a result of a 3–9 percent relative reduction of average annual duty hours of unionized firefighters and a 0–10 percent relative increase in their average annual salary.

	Percentage Difference Between Union and Nonunion Cities, 1966	
	Small-Size Cities	Moderate-Size Cities
Average hourly wage	+16.0	+9.4
Average weekly duty hours	−5.8	−8.5
Average annual salary	+10.1	+1.0

Source: Orley Ashenfelter, "The Effect of Unionization on Wages in the Public Sector: The Case of Fire Fighters," *Industrial and Labor Relations Review*, January 1971, pp. 191–202.

has no power to eliminate any divergence between product price and the marginal cost of production. The former divergence causes monopsonistic exploitation; the latter divergence, monopolistic exploitation.

Empirical Studies of Labor Union Effects

Economic theory, as we have just seen, helps economists predict certain effects of labor unions: for example, unions that push for wage increases in otherwise competitive labor markets or that press for substantial increases in monopsonistic labor markets will decrease employment opportunities for workers.

Workers who lose or are unable to find employment in unionized firms will presumably swell the supply to nonunionized firms and will depress wages in these nonunion firms below what they would otherwise be. (In 1980, only 22 percent of the U.S. labor force was unionized, down from an all-time high of 26 percent in the mid-1950s.) One would expect, therefore, that any significant amount of union activity is reflected in wage differentials between unionized and nonunionized workers.

Unions and Relative Wages

Empirical estimates of union-caused wage differentials are, however, tricky business because wage differentials actually found to exist need not be union-caused. What if unions tend to form in large firms that use lots of skilled labor and would pay their workers more than other firms even in the absence of unions? What if unions tend to form in growing, profitable industries in which competitive pressures would have raised wages in any case? On the other hand, the absence of wage differentials does not prove the ineffectiveness of unions, either. What if nonunionized firms simply follow the wage hikes won by unions in nearby plants, thereby raising the wages of unorganized workers as much as those of union workers?

There are, happily, statistical procedures for isolating the relative wage effect of unions alone. Careful studies noted in this chapter's "Selected Readings" by R. B. Freeman, H. G. Lewis, A. Rees, and others have concluded that about one-third of unions have increased their members' wages from 15–20 percent above what they would otherwise have been (airline pilots and teamsters being examples). Another one-third of unions have raised wages from 5–10 percent

(auto and steel workers). A final one-third of unions have had no effect at all (retail clerks, textile workers).

The effects of unions on wages, furthermore, have varied over time. At the bottom of the depression, in 1933, union wages exceeded those of nonunion workers by as much as 25 percent, mainly because unions resisted cuts in wages, while wages did fall in competitive labor markets. In periods of inflationary boom, as in the late 1940s, union wages exceeded those of nonunion workers by only 5 percent, mainly because long-term union contracts slowed down the kinds of wage hikes that were occurring in tight competitive labor markets. More recently, in the

---

CLOSE-UP 13.2:

Hospital Interns and Residents Revolt

Graduates of medical schools become physicians the moment they receive their degrees. After graduation, however, they must undergo from three to six years of additional training in hospitals, depending on the specialty they have chosen. As first-year interns, physicians care for patients under the supervision of second- and third-year residents. Residents, in turn, provide the bulk of medical care in hospitals, particularly at nights and on weekends when senior attending physicians usually are not present. Because housestaff physicians are paid far less than senior staff members, the young doctors have long contended that they were being exploited. On the other hand, hospital administrators have argued that interns and residents are performing what the administrators regard as on-the-job training.

In 1979, young interns and resident physicians in hospitals around the country organized a new collective bargaining drive as a result of a U.S. Court of Appeals decision that upheld their contention that they were professional hospital employees rather than students completing their medical education. Dr. Jay Dobkin, president of

the Physicians National Housestaff Association, which represented 13,000 of the 60,000 interns and residents practicing in hospitals in the country, called the court's decision "a victory for the cause of fair treatment for young doctors and their patients." In New York City, where state labor regulations allowed hospital staff physicians to bargain collectively, Dr. Jonathan House, president of the Committee of Interns and Residents (the local affiliate of the National Housestaff Association), said: "For a doctor who is working 80 or 100 or more hours a week caring for patients to be told that he or she is not a doctor, but just a student is an insult. It is very exciting to know that this will no longer be the case, that we no longer will be treated with contempt by some hospitals."

As a result of the decision, House, a third-year resident in internal medicine at the Harlem Hospital Center, said that young housestaff physicians would begin organizing drives at such hospitals as the Columbia-Presbyterian Medical Center, Mt. Sinai, and other private voluntary institutions that have refused to extend collective bargaining rights to residents and interns.

Source: Ronald Sullivan, "Interns and Residents Begin New Bargaining Drive," *The New York Times,* April 15, 1979, p. 18.

1960s, union wages were 10–15 percent above nonunion ones. (The same was true of fringe benefits. Even the employment effects were similar: 10–15 percent *below* the experience of nonunion industries.)

A variety of other union effects have been targets of investigation, including, among others,

1. a possible union-caused reduction in productivity (as a result of featherbedding, strikes, and closed shops that prevent employers from hiring the best people available unless they happen to be union members),
2. the possibility of widespread racketeering (as a result of the inevitable monopoly power of unions), and
3. the possible emergence of various forms of racial discrimination (as a result of union attempts to ration a lower number of available jobs).

Unions and Productivity

At the end of World War II, the then giant unions, for the first time, learned to use their strength. Paralyzing strikes in steel, coal, and shipping brought production to a halt and alarmed the public. Jurisdictional strikes, resulting from two unions fighting each other for jurisdiction over a group of workers, were another source of alarm. Labor, it was argued, had been given on overdose of power. To counter this power, Congress passed the Taft-Hartley Act of 1947.

The new act outlawed the closed shop but not the union shop. In so doing, Congress favored the view of employers that a fundamental principle of freedom was violated if people were forced to join an organization, that they, as employers, found it difficult to hire the best workers for a job (because they were restricted to taking those whom the union admitted to its membership), and that union leaders, having an assured membership, were likely to become irresponsible and deal dishonestly with their members. Many states have since passed so-called **right-to-work laws,** outlawing the union shop.

The new act also banned "unfair union practices," including refusal of a union to bargain with an employer, featherbedding, striking without 60 days' notice, and striking to force the recognition of one union where another has already been certified. In addition, unions were required not to charge excessive initiation fees, to make financial reports to their members, disclose their officers' salaries, and refrain from using dues for political contributions. The act also empowered employers to sue unions for breach of contract and to engage (without coercion) in antiunion activities. Finally, it allowed the President to ask for 80-day court suspensions of strikes or lockouts that "imperil the national health and safety."

Yet recent studies by R. B. Freeman reveal that unions cannot be blamed for any reduction in productivity. These studies show, for example, that unions by themselves (as opposed to other factors) have raised productivity from 20–25 percent in U.S. manufacturing industries. (Exceptions, such as the underground bituminous coal industry, are noted.) The favorable productivity effect is attributed by Freeman to greater worker morale under unionized conditions and to a shock effect on management: Workers who need not fear arbitrary actions against them and who have a large measure of control over their working conditions are likely to quit less often and are more likely to cooperate with management on changes designed to raise productivity. Managers, on the other hand, are galvanized into seeking such changes in order to maintain profit in the face of union wage demands. What about strikes? In the past two decades, they have cost the U.S. economy only 0.2 percent of working time, much less than coffee breaks.

Unions and Racketeering

In 1959, the Landrum-Griffin Act was passed against a background of hearings of the McClellan committee into labor racketeering. The hearings had exposed "gangsterism, bribery, and hoodlumism" in the affairs of some unions. Some union leaders had diverted union funds for personal use, had taken payoffs from employers for union protection, and were even involved in blackmail, arson, and murder. In retaliation against such labor racketeers who fattened themselves by extortion from both workers and employers, the act put still more curbs on union power. The act was particularly concerned with the misuse of union funds. Members of unions were guaranteed the right to vote in secret. The list of unfair practices was lengthened.

The strong federal sanctions provided by the act have, in fact, nipped corruption inside unions in the bud. In the 1970s only a tiny fraction of 1 percent of union elections violated the federal law, and a survey of union members revealed that 99 percent of them saw no signs of union leaders turning into bosses who engaged in graft and extortion.

Unions and Racial Discrimination

Additional laws in the 1960s and 1970s have severely curbed union power to deny membership on the basis of age, ethnic background, race, religion, sex, or other arbitrary differences. (The use of a like power of employers was also made illegal.) The most important legislation in this connection was certain sections of the Civil Rights Act of 1964, which outlawed racial and sex discrimination and set up an Equal Employment Opportunities Commission. Originally, this commission could receive complaints concerning union and employer discrimination, attempt a reconciliation of the parties involved, and help them go to court. Since the passage of the Equal Employment Opportunities Act of 1972, the commission can also issue cease-and-desist orders and initiate suits of its own. In addition, the federal government has pressured unions to set up **affirmative-action plans** designed not only to end discriminatory practices based on ethnic background, race, sex, and the like, but also to make deliberate efforts at overcoming the present effects of past discrimination (as in admission to membership or to union apprenticeship programs). Similar pressure on employers, notably federal agencies and their suppliers, has been aimed at preventing discrimination in hiring, in on-the-job training, in compensation, in promotion, in layoffs, in recall, and in discharge.

Without doubt, craft unions in particular have in the past discriminated against racial minorities, and even now union seniority rules conflict with affirmative-action programs. Yet, empirical evidence collected by Freeman suggests that unionism has on the average raised the income of black workers relative to whites. Because a larger percentage of black workers than white workers is unionized, blacks gain relatively more from union-caused increases in wages and fringe benefits. In addition, because everyone within a unionized firm is paid the standard union rate and is promoted by seniority, discrimination by race is impeded.

Applications

Application 1: The Baseball Players' Market

Baseball was the first sport to be organized professionally in the United States.[1] From the start, team owners recognized a common interest in preventing competition for players that would drive up salaries. Accordingly, the baseball players' market came to provide a perfect example of monopsony in action. Talented athletes who wanted to play professional baseball with a major league team found that the teams were not competing for the services of players. A player who wanted a first contract with a team had to sign a **reserve clause** handing over to the team's owners all rights to his future services. Thereafter, no other team would tamper with the player thusly "reserved" by the original team that signed him on. In future years, the owners of the original team could dispose of the player's ser-

---

[1]This section is based in part on Simon Rottenberg, "The Baseball Players' Labor Market," *Journal of Political Economy*, June 1956, pp. 242–58; and Gerald W. Scully, "Pay and Performance in Major League Baseball," *The American Economic Review*, December 1974, pp. 915–30.

vices as they saw fit: they could keep the player on (and either raise his salary, keep it unchanged, or cut it by a prearranged maximum percentage below that of the previous season); they could sell the contract to another team (and then the player had to report to the new owners within 3 days); they could terminate the contract (but even that was not certain to let the player off the hook because each team in the league, in inverse order of season standings, then had the opportunity to purchase the player's contract, and if any team did, the player was again bound to it). As long as a player was hooked (and that was the usual case), he could only play for the current owners of his contract and at whatever salary they offered him. His only alternative was not to play baseball at all. (Naturally, the contract owners' ability to depress player salaries was constrained by the need to maintain team morale.)

The Reserve Clause Challenged.   Not surprisingly, the reserve clause was challenged on several occasions. The Federal League before World War I tried to become a third major league but couldn't get players. Its challenge was defeated in court. In the 1940s, the Mexican League was dealt a similar blow. Curt Flood, star outfielder for the St. Louis Cardinals, didn't like being traded to Philadelphia. His court fight against the reserve clause was lost, too; he retired to Majorca. But in 1975, following a favorable arbitrator's ruling won by pitchers Andy Messersmith and Dave McNally, Jim "Catfish" Hunter, ace pitcher for the Oakland As, won a similar fight. The court invalidated his contract with the As; he became a free agent. Thus a new age dawned for professional athletes—the age of free agency.

Star Players' Salaries Explode.   Before long, more than 100 players had changed uniforms. The average player's salary doubled to $100,000 a year. Jim Hunter landed a 5-year $3.5 million contract with the New York Yankees. By 1978, Pete Rose left the Cincinnati Reds to get $800,000 a year from the Philadelphia Phillies. And in 1979, Bill Walton signed up with the San Diego Clippers (National Basketball Association) for $850,000 a year.

It is easy to see why a single player may be worth that much to a team. If Pete Rose could draw even 10 percent more fans for home games alone (and he could), some 200,000 extra tickets per season would be sold for an average $4. In addition, the Phillies would get 40 percent of extra gate receipts from games on the road and extra broadcast fees as well.

Measuring Monopsonistic Exploitation.   Gerald W. Scully estimated the extent of monopsonistic exploitation of baseball players while the reserve clause was in effect. Some of his results are reproduced in Table 13.3. For players with different talents, in columns (1) and (2), Scully calculated first their contribution to the team's gross revenues (3), such as gate receipts, broadcast fees, and the like. He then figured the player's contribution to net revenue (4) by subtracting player training and development costs (which averaged $300,000 per player) as well as other costs, such as nonplayer salaries, transportation for away games, equipment and sales expenses, stadium rental, and imputed interest on the baseball franchise (worth $8.4 million for the average team).

As a comparison of columns (4) and (5) indicates, because average and star players received as salaries considerably less than their contribution to the team's net revenue, they were monopsonistically exploited. Mediocre players, however, exploited their teams instead!

Application 2:
Discrimination in the Labor Market

> And the Lord spake unto Moses, saying, Speak unto the children of Israel and say unto them, When a man shall make a singular vow, the persons shall be for the Lord by thy estimation. And thy estimation shall be of the male from twenty years old even unto sixty years old, even thy estimation shall be fifty shekels of silver, after the shekel of the sanctuary. And if it be a female, then thy estimation shall be thirty shekels. (Leviticus 27:1–4)

TABLE 13.3 The Monopsonistic Exploitation of Baseball Players, 1968–69

| Type of Player (1) | Career Performance (2) | Marginal Revenue Product | | Salary (5) |
		Gross (3)	Net (4)	
Mediocre hitters	**Lifetime Slugging Average** 255	$121,200	$−39,100	$ 9,700
	283	135,000	−25,300	20,000
Average hitters	338	256,600	128,300	29,100
	375	285,100	156,800	39,000
Star hitters	427	405,800	290,500	42,200
	525	499,000	383,700	68,000
Mediocre pitchers	**Lifetime Strikeout-to-Walk Ratio** 1.50	139,500	−20,800	9,000
	1.66	154,300	−6,000	18,100
Average pitchers	2.07	269,600	141,300	23,300
	2.46	316,000	187,700	43,700
Star pitchers	2.79	464,900	349,600	47,200
	3.54	595,000	479,700	86,300

When the reserve clause was in effect, all but mediocre U.S. baseball players were monopsonistically exploited. Note how, for average and star players, the data in column (5) fall short of those in column (4).

SOURCE: Adapted from Gerald W. Scully, "Pay and Performance in Major League Baseball," *The American Economic Review*, December 1974, vol. 64, no. 6, pp. 915–30.

This passage put the worth of a female at 60 percent of that of a male. In today's labor markets, females and various ethnic or racial minorities suffer the same fate, and, it is often claimed, they do so only because people engage in **discrimination**, a term used to designate the making of irrelevant distinctions. Statistical data on people's median incomes seem to bear this out. Such data show consistently, for example, how the income of white males in the United States exceeds that of black males and how the income of males (white or black) exceeds that of females.

Yet it is exceedingly difficult to analyze such data. It surely is not sufficient to point to the "obvious" presence of discrimination throughout the world, affecting not only Puerto Ricans in New York, females in Washington, or blacks in Detroit, but also "coloreds" in England or South Africa, "untouchables" in India, aborigines in New Zealand, Laplanders in Sweden, Jews in the Soviet Union, Palestinians in Israel, Basques in Spain, Chinese in Indonesia, the French in Canada, and many more. Invariably, serious studies show that a significant portion of income differences by sex or race can be explained by factors other than discrimination pure and simple.[2] A 1977 study by Ronald Oaxaca attributed at least a quarter of an observed 67 percent income gap between U.S. males and females to other factors;

[2] The following discussion is based in part on Ronald Oaxaca, "Theory and Measurement in the Economics of Discrimination," *Equal Rights and Industrial Relations* (Madison, Wis.: Industrial Relations Research Association, 1977); Robert H. Frank, "Why Women Earn Less: The Theory and Estimation of Differential Overqualification," *The American Economic Review*, June 1978, pp. 360–73; and Walter E. Williams, "Preference, Prejudice, and Difference—Racial Reasoning in Unfree Markets," *Regulation*, March/April 1979, pp. 39–48.

he explained by other factors as much as 40 percent of a similar (55 percent) gap between whites and blacks. Other researchers find different numbers, and the subject remains charged with considerable controversy as well as emotion. Most agree, however, that income differentials as such prove nothing about discrimination at all. Income differences can, for example, reflect differences in worker job preferences or in worker productivities, as well as genuine discrimination.

Worker Job Preferences.   Some income differences arise because the affected workers themselves "discriminate" among jobs. All jobs are not equally attractive to people. As a result, all types of jobs can be filled only with the help of equalizing wage differentials (see Chapter 8 for further discussion).

Worker Productivities.   As Chapter 8 noted, differences exist not only among jobs, but among people as well. Not all people, for example, are equally productive. Employers may clearly recognize such personal differences and either employ the less productive people less often or pay them lower wages in accordance with the actual differences in productivity. The resultant "discrimination" is no more malevolent than that of a consumer who gets more satisfaction from Burgundy wine than from Bordeaux and, therefore, either buys the former only or pays less for a given amount of the latter than of the former. An employer who gets more output out of worker A than B will, similarly, hire A only or tend to pay B less than A. Women and the members of various minorities may possess less human capital, having received less formal education or on-the-job training in the past (possibly, but not necessarily, because of malevolent discrimination elsewhere in society). They may be less firmly attached to the labor force. Women, especially mothers, enter and leave the labor force more often than men; even when employed, they are more likely to demand free time to care for children. To the extent that employers recognize such personal differences and that these are seen to affect productivity, employers are bound to be selective among particular workers.

Genuine Discrimination.   Finally, a source of income differences that cannot be attributed to any of the factors noted above is discrimination pure and simple, as the term was defined above. Discriminatory employers—either as a result of their own malevolent tastes or of pressure from consumers or even employees—may turn pretty women into TV announcers, while relegating unattractive ones to the radio. They may put men on the high-paid assembly line, while placing women into the lower-paid typing pool. They may let male pilots fly the passengers, and female pilots the freight. At the same time, black workers may refuse to work next to white ones; white clients may refuse to be served by black sales clerks, doctors, or lawyers. As a result of such inexplicable tastes, workers who differ from one

---

CLOSE-UP 13.3:

Discrimination at the University?

A group of economists recently studied faculty salaries at a large urban university. Among other things, they wanted to determine whether discrimination by race or sex was evident. The result: Three quarters of observed salary differences could be explained by such factors as age, years employed, level of education, rank, and department. The researchers attributed the remainder of the salary differences to sex and racial discrimination.

Note: According to this study, while women received on the average 11 percent less pay than men of apparently identical characteristics, blacks received on the average 13 percent *more* pay than comparable whites.

Source: Nancy M. Gordon, Thomas E. Morton, and Ina C. Braden, "Faculty Salaries: Is There Discrimination by Sex, Race, and Discipline?" *The American Economic Review*, June 1974, pp. 419–27.

CLOSE-UP 13.4:

Bakke:
Fighting Reverse Discrimination

When people talk of discrimination in the labor market, they generally refer to the making of irrelevant distinctions based on race, sex, and the like in such matters as hiring, wages, and promotion. And they usually think of discrimination *against* a particular group of people, such as women or minorities. The opposite side of the discrimination coin, of course, is the showing of favoritism. Such favoritism is widespread, too. Consider how a boss may appoint his son vice-president of the company, how the governor may make her brother a state commissioner. Consider how government often encourages or even mandates favoritism—which is usually called **reverse discrimination** or affirmative action—and justifies favoring previously disadvantaged groups on the grounds of righting past wrongs.

Still, reverse discrimination in favor of one group (say, women or blacks) implies discrimination against another group (say, men or whites). This implication has given rise to one of the most heated court battles in recent times.

In the early 1970s, Allan Bakke, a white male engineer, twice sought admission to the medical school at the University of California at Davis. Twice he was rejected. Yet minority applicants with substantially inferior grades and test scores were admitted under the university's affirmative-action program. (This program reserved 16 of 100 places of the entering class to minority students.) Bakke sued for having been denied admittance solely because of his race; a violation, he claimed, of the 14th Amendment to the U.S. Constitution as well as of the Civil Rights Act of 1964.

In mid-1978, the U.S. Supreme Court agreed with Bakke. It ordered him admitted on the grounds that the university's rigid quota deprived him of his civil rights. But the court also noted that race may be used as one of many criteria of admission and that an affirmative-action program without rigid quotas (as that of Harvard) was not illegal.

Note: In 1979, the U.S. Supreme Court rejected a reverse discrimination charge brought by Brian Weber, a white employee of the Kaiser Aluminum and Chemical Company. The court ruled that employers can voluntarily give preferences to women and minorities in hiring and promotion for traditionally segregated job categories.[1]

[1] Urban C. Lehner and Carol H. Falk, "Beyond Bakke: High Court Approves Affirmative Action in Hiring, Promotion," *The Wall Street Journal*, June 28, 1979, pp. 1 and 30. For a detailed analysis of the case, *see* Bernard D. Meltzer, "The Weber Case: Double Talk and Double Standards," *Regulation*, September/October 1979, pp. 34–43.

another in no relevant fashion whatsoever may be segregated into separate labor markets and earn different wages for identical work. Although lay people are often ready to ascribe any and all observed income differences among groups of people to discrimination, many economists are far from certain about the extent to which such differences can be so attributed.

Note: One further complication is that some employers do not discriminate out of malevolence, but because they believe, from a narrow profit-maximizing stance, that it makes sense for them to discriminate. There is an information cost associated with careful hiring: the careful evaluation of potential employees costs an employer time and money. Many employers who hope to retain their employees for many years are willing to incur this cost. Many other employers, however, reduce this cost by quick, short-hand decisions that are discriminatory. Their decision to discriminate is similar to a decision to pollute: costs to the firm are reduced, even though heavy costs may be imposed on the rest of society.

An employer may, for example, prefer worker A to worker B because the employer knows that A workers *as a group* have more desirable characteristics than do B workers as a group. On the average, A workers may possess more human capital than do B workers, they may have longer life spans, or they may be more dependable (in the sense of being less tardy or less liable to quit). The employer, however, may find it extremely costly to check out every *individual* A or B applicant to determine whether the particular worker in fact possesses the known characteristics of his or her group. In order to save this high cost of investigating, the employer may take a short-cut and *prejudge* every A or B applicant as if he or she in fact possessed the known average features of the relevant group. As far as the employer was concerned, it wouldn't matter by which irrelevant feature people were identified as members of their group—whether the feature was sex or color of skin, foreign accent or physical stature, unkempt appearance or vulgar speech, red hair or cross-eyes. As long as the important but hard-to-observe characteristics of people were highly correlated with such superficial but easily observable ones, the employer might use the latter as a proxy for the former. If the crucial group characteristics of A workers and B workers (human capital, life span, dependability, and the like) were fact rather than fiction, the employer would, on the average, come out ahead by judging before all the returns are in, even though many individuals would be judged incorrectly.

The term **prejudice**, as commonly understood, denotes preconceived irrational opinion that leads to unfair partiality toward some people and bias against others. As such, it is an attitude of mind that interferes with fair judgment. On the other hand, some people believe that prejudice can facilitate rational behavior *in the face of imperfect and costly information*. Prejudice in this second sense can exist even in the complete absence of malevolent feelings about any particular type of person. When complete information can be gotten only at a high cost, some decision makers rely on stereotypes to reap personal benefits. Because these benefits come at the cost of many individuals who are incorrectly stereotyped, discrimination, even for the costly-

information reason here discussed, is often made illegal. In addition, this kind of cost-reducing prejudice makes sense, from the narrow perspective of the employer, only when there is *certainty* of worker group characteristics, but *uncertainty* about their individual characteristics. Oftentimes, however, undesirable group characteristics are imaginary rather than real.

Application 3:   Teenage Unemployment and the Minimum Wage

As we have seen above, labor unions have acquired the power to push up money wages and have received much support from government. Government, however, can and does achieve wage increases even more directly by legislating above-equilibrium minimum wages. Thus a federal minimum wage was set at 25¢ per hour under the Fair Labor Standards Act of 1938; this minimum wage had risen to $3.35 per hour by 1981. The original law did not by any means apply to all workers; employees of state and local governments, farm workers, and household workers, for example, were excluded. Over the years, as Congress has raised the minimum with clocklike regularity, however, it has also extended the coverage of the law.

Economic theory predicts employment effects as a result of minimum-wage legislation precisely like those discussed above in connection with union-imposed wage hikes. If the labor markets affected by the imposition or increase of a minimum wage are competitive, the number of jobs declines (see Figure 13.3). If, on the other hand, the affected labor markets are monopsonistic, the job effect is less certain. Employment may rise, remain unchanged, or fall (see Figure 13.4).

By now, U.S. economists have had plenty of experience with actual minimum-wage impositions or increases at both the federal and state levels. Subsequent to its enactment in 1938, the federal minimum wage, for example, has been increased 15 times between 1939 and 1981; it has been extended to new groups of workers 16 times. One economist, Yale Brozen, conducted a careful study of the actual employment effects of these minimum-wage changes.[3]

Brozen found that, because the overwhelming majority of workers have always enjoyed wages exceeding the legislated minimum, most people's wages and jobs have not been affected by changes in the statutory minima. The effects of minimum-wage laws have been primarily on the wages and employment of low-skilled work-

[3]Yale Brozen, ''The Effect of Statutory Minimum Wage Increases on Teen-Age Employment,'' *The Journal of Law and Economics*, April 1969, pp. 109–22.

CLOSE-UP 13.5:
Fast-Food Chains and the Minimum Wage

In the late 1970s, the $16-billion-a-year fast-food industry, which employs many teenagers, tried its best to forestall an increase in the federal minimum wage from $2.30 to $2.65 an hour. Unions that supported the increase predicted that no layoffs would occur and that employees would come to enjoy a well-deserved 15 percent increase in income. Neither side was successful.

The wage increase did occur, but the income increase failed to materialize. The food-chains lowered their employees' weekly hours (by opening later and closing earlier). They hired more adults (who were more skilled and experienced and had lower turnover rates and thus reduced company training costs). They also introduced automation to save labor (computerized cash registers, overnight slow cookers). And some firms selectively raised prices (for late-night hamburgers). When all was said and done, fewer teenagers were employed, and those who were worked fewer hours and earned just about the same as before.

Source: Paul Ingrassia, ''Quick Adjustment: Fast-Food Chains Act to Offset the Effects of Minimum-Pay Rise,'' *The Wall Street Journal*, December 22, 1977, p. 1.

ers. The largest single category of such workers are teenagers. Brozen noted that the monthly change in teenage unemployment, for some 20 years covered by his data, was down 123 times, up 111 times, zero 6 times. Yet, each time the minimum rose, teenage unemployment rose as well. Brozen was unable to attribute this relationship to coincidence.

In addition to these immediate increases in teenage unemployment, Brozen found a long-term upward trend in teenage unemployment relative to that of other people. This trend occurred despite a rising average level of education in this group and a declining rate of labor-force participation. For example, before the $1.15 per hour minimum wage went into effect, unemployment among teenagers was 2.5 times the unemployment rate of the total labor force. In the year following the increase, it was 2.7 times as large. When the minimum wage rose further to $1.25 per hour, the teenage unemployment rate rose further to 3.1 times the general incidence of unemployment; by the time the minimum stood at $1.60 per hour, the multiple had risen to 3.6.

The minimum wage has affected employment opportunities more adversely even for nonwhite teenagers than for teenagers in general. For example, while the ratio of the incidence of general teenage unemployment to the unemployment of all workers rose by 64 percent from 1949–68, that for nonwhite teenage unemployment rose by 154 percent.

Brozen concluded that minimum-wage statutes, at the time of their imposition, have increased the incomes of some workers—namely, those who did not lose their jobs. These increases would, however, have come anyway within two to five years, as evidenced by studying the wage rates of noncovered workers, such as private household and agricultural workers. These rates have been rising 4 percent per year since 1949 despite the wage-depressing effects of additional workers looking for jobs in this sector after having been forced out of jobs covered by minimum wages. Apparently, successive amendments to the minimum-wage statute have raised wages particularly rapidly in the first year in the affected occupations, with very slow rises occurring thereafter. The total increase in the long run has differed little in covered and not-covered occupations. According to Brozen:

> If all that happened as a result of the minimum-wage statute was a change in the timing of wage rate increases, there would be little to concern us. However, in the interval between the time that the minimum wage is raised and the time that productivity and inflation catch up with the increase, thousands of people are jobless, many businesses fail which are never revived, people are forced to migrate who would prefer not to, cities find their slums deteriorating and becoming overpopulated, teenagers are barred from obtaining the opportunity to learn skills which would make them more productive, and permanent damage is done to their attitudes and their ambitions. This is a large price to pay for impatience.

Brozen's study does not stand alone. Numerous later ones have confirmed significant adverse effects of minimum wages on teenage employment.[4] Apparently, the attempt to help the working poor has proven to be the most effective way yet to keep teenagers idle. Because of their healthy propensity to test their abilities and opportunities, teenagers have always switched jobs more often than adults and, therefore, have always experienced higher rates of unemployment. Laws that have legislated teenage wages above teenagers' productivity, however, have

given their jobs to more productive adults or to machines. Such laws have thus eliminated many traditional **entry-level jobs** that require little training or experience and allow untrained and inexperienced job seekers to find employment, gain experience, and depart these stepping-stones for better jobs.

SUMMARY

1. This chapter examines imperfectly competitive markets for resource services by concentrating on the case of labor. In the case of an otherwise competitive labor market in which buyers appear who have monopoly power in the product markets, the buyers determine the best input quantity not by equating a given wage with labor's marginal *value* product, but with labor's marginal *revenue* product. As a result, they employ less labor than otherwise, and labor is *monopolistically exploited*.

2. Another case of labor market imperfection arises when a perfectly competitive seller of products is the only buyer of a given type of labor but confronts a multitude of competitive sellers of it. Such monopsony can arise as a result of geographic isolation, extreme occupational specialization, or antipirating agreements among employers. Such firms determine the best input quantity not by equating a given wage with labor's marginal value product, but by equating marginal outlay on labor (implied by a wage the firm itself has set) with labor's marginal value product. As a result, these firms employ less labor than otherwise, and labor is *monopsonistically exploited*.

3. The sellers of labor, just as those of products, can form cartels, which take the form of labor unions. Labor unions are difficult to establish; U.S. unions, however, have enjoyed a great deal of government help with the task.

4. Labor unions pursue many goals, chief among them being higher money income for those employed. The effects of union-imposed increases in wages differ with the type of market.

[4]As a partial listing only *see* Thomas G. Moore, "The Effect of Minimum Wages on Teenage Unemployment Rates," *Journal of Political Economy*, July/August 1971, pp. 897–902; Douglas K. Adie, "Teen-Age Unemployment and Real Federal Minimum Wages," *Journal of Political Economy*, March/April 1973, pp. 435–41; Finis Welch, "Minimum Wage Legislation in the United States," *Economic Inquiry*, September 1974, pp. 285–318; Jacob Mincer, "Unemployment Effects of Minimum Wages," *Journal of Political Economy*, August 1976, pp. S87–S104; James F. Ragan, "Minimum Wages and the Youth Labor Market," *The Review of Economics and Statistics*, May 1977, pp. 129–36; and Robert Swidinsky, "Minimum Wages and Teenage Unemployment," *Canadian Journal of Economics*, February 1980, pp. 158–71.

If the market is previously competitive, wage increases cause employment to fall; unions can respond to the resulting unemployment by ignoring it or by various attempts to raise the demand for or reduce the supply of labor.

5. If a union imposes wage increases on a monopsony, the effect on the level of employment cannot be predicted. Depending on the extent of the wage hike, employment may rise, remain unchanged, or fall.

6. A number of empirical studies have been conducted concerning the effects of labor unions on relative wages, on productivity, and on the incidence of racketeering and racial discrimination.

7. A number of wider applications of the new theoretical tools include discussions of the baseball players' market, of discrimination in the labor market, and of minimum-wage effects on teenagers.

KEY TERMS

affirmative-action plans

antipirating agreements

closed shops

conspiracy doctrine

craft unions

discrimination

entry-level jobs

featherbedding

industrial unions

injunction

jurisdictional strikes

labor union

marginal revenue product (*MRP*)

monopolistic exploitation

monopsonistic exploitation

prejudice

reserve clause

reverse discrimination

right-to-work laws

union shops

QUESTIONS AND PROBLEMS

1. Part (A) of the following table shows the total number of sandwiches that can be produced by a snack bar when employing different numbers of workers.

	Part (A)	Part (B)
Number of Workers	Number of Sandwiches per Day	Wage per Day
1	80	$10
2	150	15
3	200	20
4	240	25
5	250	30
6	230	40

a. Assuming sandwiches brought in 50¢ each after ingredient costs are deducted, determine the schedule of labor's net marginal value product.

b. If workers were paid $20 per day, how many would be employed? How many at $35 per day?

c. What if sandwiches brought in 10¢ each and the daily wage were $10?

2. Now consider Part (B) as well:

a. How many workers would be employed, and at what wage, if sandwiches brought in 50¢ each and the snack bar were a monopsony?

b. What if a union were organized to fight the monopsony and it insisted on a wage of $30 per day?

3. Consider panels (a) through (c) of Figure 13.4, "Labor Union vs. Monopsony." In each case, determine whether any involuntary unemployment would exist at the union-imposed wage. Explain.

4. During a 1974 players' strike, the owners of National Football League teams rejected the charge of exploiting players and making excessive profits ($945,000 per team in 1973). Teams were then selling for $16 million, they said, which indicated a profit of only 5.9 percent per year. What do you think? (*Hints:* Remember what you learned about the capitalization of assets in Chapter 10. Consider the fact that a competing World Football League was being formed in 1973 and that many cities, including Seattle and Tampa, petitioned NFL owners for an expansion of franchises.)

5. Babe Ruth is often called the greatest baseball player of all times. (He hit 714 home runs in his career, had a 0.342 lifetime batting average and an earned-run average of 2.28 as a pitcher.) He received a salary of $80,000 in 1930, equivalent at the consumer price index to $347,840 in 1979. Do you think he was exploited? Explain. (*Hint:* Pete Rose, not generally considered in the same category as Babe Ruth, earned $800,000 with the Phillies in 1979.)

6. Various forms of price discrimination by monopolies were discussed in Chapter 11. Do you think monopsonies could practice equivalent forms of first-, second-, and third-degree price discrimination? In particular, might not such price discrimination explain the tendency of different groups of people to become segregated into different occupations (such as males vs. females) and to receive different wages?

7. The AFL-CIO, formed in 1955 by the federation of the two previously independent labor groups, has consistently supported increases in the governmentally set minimum wage. Given the disemployment effect actually observed as a result of such increases, why do you think the AFL-CIO supports them? (*Hint:* Members of the AFL-CIO tend to be skilled and experienced).

8. This chapter discussed the consequences of *minimum wages*—wage rates legislated above the level that would otherwise prevail. What, do you think, would be the consequences of *maximum wages*—wage rates legislated below the level that would otherwise prevail? (*Hints:* Consider why people are *drafted* to perform jury duty or military service and ask yourself what it would take to have all-volunteer systems. According to Donald L. Martin, jurors received fees of $89.8 million in 1962, but their forgone income was $232.9 million, all measured in 1958 dollars.[5])

⁵Donald L. Martin, "The Economics of Jury Conscription" *Journal of Political Economy*, July/August 1972, pp. 680–702.

SELECTED READINGS

Becker, Gary S. *The Economics of Discrimination, 2nd ed.* Chicago: University of Chicago Press, 1971.

Argues that hiring discrimination harms both the majority and minority groups.

Dunlop, John T. *Wage Determination Under Trade Unions*. New York: Augustus Kelley, 1966.

Freeman, Richard B., and Medoff, James L. "The Two Faces of Unionism." *The Public Interest*, Fall 1979, pp. 69–93.

Kreps, Juanita. *Women and the American Economy: A Look to the 1980s*. Englewood Cliffs, N.J.: Prentice-Hall, 1976.

Lewis, H. Gregg. *Unionism and Relative Wages in the United States: An Empirical Inquiry*. Chicago: University of Chicago Press, 1963. Idem. "Relative Employment Effects of Unionism." *The American Economic Review*, May 1964, pp. 123–32.

Marshall, Ray. "The Economics of Racial Discrimination: A Survey." *Journal of Economic Literature*, September 1974, pp. 849–71.

Includes an excellent bibliography.

Noll, Roger G. "Major League Team Sports." In Walter Adams, ed. *The Structure of American Industry*, 5th ed. New York: Macmillan, 1977, chap. 11.

A superb discussion of all aspects of this industry.

Posner, Richard A. "The Economics of Privacy," *The American Economic Review*, May 1981, pp. 405–409.

Argues that privacy legislation, by helping prospective employees conceal relevant information from employers, can contribute to labor market inefficiency.

Rees, Albert. *Wage Inflation*. New York: National Industrial Conference Board, 1967. Idem. *The Economics of Work and Pay*. New York: Harper and Row, 1973.

Samuelson, Paul A. "Understanding the Marxian Notion of Exploitation: A Summary of the So-Called Transformation Problem Between Marxian Values and Competitive Prices." *Journal of Economic Literature*, June 1971, pp. 399–431.

A discussion of the Marxian concept of exploitation, which differs significantly from the concepts discussed in this chapter. *See also* the subsequent discussion of Samuelson's article in the same publication, March 1972, pp. 50–57; March 1973, pp. 58–68; and March 1974, pp. 51–77.

PART 4

The Performance of the Market Economy

CHAPTER 14

Efficiency

Scarcity, as noted in Chapter 1, affects all present-day societies. Everywhere, resources and technical knowledge are insufficient to produce all of the goods people want. Under such circumstances, some desires for goods must remain unsatisfied even if no resources or goods are ever wasted by anyone.

This chapter will focus on an important implication of that early lesson: People who dislike scarcity should use their resources as carefully as possible; they should *economize* resources. Yet people are quite capable of making foolish choices with the resources and goods at their disposal. When they do, scarcity is more intense than necessary. Economists, therefore, have long been interested in developing criteria capable of judging the performance of economies and of highlighting the existence of avoidable scarcity. Most important among these criteria is *efficiency*.

In one way or another, the concept of efficiency is always concerned with the possibility of getting more output from given inputs. When the criterion of efficiency is applied, for instance, to the operations of a single firm, economists compare physical output with physical inputs. **Technical efficiency** or **X-efficiency** exists within a firm when it is impossible, with given technical knowledge, to produce a larger output from a given set of inputs (or, as expressed in Chapter 5, when it is impossible to produce a given output with less of one or more inputs without increasing the amount of other inputs).

When the yardstick of efficiency, however, is applied to an entire economy economists compare the *total economic welfare* of all people (which is the ultimate output of the economy) with the *total of resource services utilized* (or the economy's inputs). **Economic efficiency** exists within an economy when it is impossible, with given technology, to produce a larger welfare total from given stocks of resources.

Note: The concept of economic efficiency is also referred to as **allocative efficiency** (because it is about the best allocation of given resources and the goods made with their help) and as **static efficiency** (because it is applied to a short time period (called ''the present'') in which the economy's stocks of resources and technical knowledge are fixed). A third and still broader approach is to survey the relationship between output and inputs not only economywide but also over an extended period, reaching far into the future, in which resource stocks and technology can vary. This measure of performance is called **dynamic efficiency** and exists within an economy when it is impossible to produce a larger welfare total by improving technology or the size and quality of resource stocks. However, economists for many decades have focused their attention on the static notion of economic efficiency.

Defining Economic Efficiency

In principle, it would seem easy to test a society on the degree of economic efficiency it is achieving. Economists, one might think, could simply apply the optimization principle to the economy's present allocation of resources and goods: they could ask themselves whether the marginal benefit of any potential reallocation of resources or goods just equaled the marginal cost. If this marginal benefit did not equal this marginal cost, the present allocation would not be the best one. Total economic welfare could then be increased by doing more of those things found to have marginal benefits in excess of their marginal costs and less of others found to have marginal costs in excess of marginal benefits. This is easier said than done.

The Slippery Concept of a Change in Total Economic Welfare

If total economic welfare is defined as the sum of the welfares of all individuals, a reallocation of resources or goods that affects more than one person may well affect total economic welfare in an ambiguous fashion. Some potential changes, to be sure, would raise total economic welfare with certainty because they would bring to *each* person affected a marginal benefit that, in the judgment of that person, exceeded the associated marginal cost. Other potential changes, however, would affect total economic welfare in an ambiguous way, since they would bring a marginal benefit in excess of marginal cost to only some persons, while imposing a marginal cost in excess of the marginal benefit on other persons.

In the case where changes brought to *each* person a marginal benefit in excess of marginal cost, harmony would reign supreme. Each of the affected persons would agree to the potential change. If a vote were taken, it would be unanimous, because every single person affected by the change would expect to gain from it. Thus total economic welfare would rise with certainty.

In the case where some of the people affected by the change expected to experience a net gain and others a net loss, a unanimous vote would be inconceivable. Conflict rather than harmony would reign. Those people who would get a marginal benefit in excess of marginal cost would vote for the change. Others who would get a marginal cost exceeding the marginal benefit would vote against it. The effect of the change on total economic welfare would be ambiguous. Would the gainers gain more than the losers would lose or the opposite? Would gains just balance losses in welfare? Unless we found a way of measuring each person's welfare and of then comparing it with that of other people (and, contrary to Bentham's hope, no one has found one yet), we could not tell what happened to the magnitude of total economic welfare.

Escaping the Ambiguity

The sort of situation in which the effect of a reallocation of resources or goods on total economic welfare *was ambiguous* would cause confrontation and struggle and, ultimately, victory for some and defeat for others. Economists have little to say about such ambiguous situations. Indeed, economists have decided to focus attention on those contrasting situations in which appropriate changes would raise total economic welfare with certainty. In such situations of **economic inefficiency**, it is possible, through some reallocation of resources or goods, to make some or all people better off (in their own judgment) *without* making others worse off (in *their* own judgment). By rewriting this definition of economic inefficiency, we can also define **economic efficiency** as a situation in which it is *impossible*, through some reallocation of resources or goods, to make some or all people better off (in their own judgment) without making others worse off (in *their* own judgment).

Economists have long wondered how situations of economic inefficiency could be identified so that people's energies could be channeled away from conflicts (from which some people would be certain to lose) and towards agreeable changes (from which no one would lose and some or all would gain).

At the turn of the century, the Italian economist Vilfredo Pareto (see Biography 14.1) spelled out a number of so-called **marginal conditions** that must be met if economic inefficiency is to be avoided and if economic efficiency is to be achieved. By testing the degree to which any society fulfills these marginal conditions, economists can determine whether that society has managed to exhaust all *unambiguous* possibilities for increasing the total economic welfare of its people.

Pareto's Marginal Conditions of Economic Efficiency

Condition 1: The Optimum Allocation of a Resource Among Producers of the Same Good

One marginal condition of economic efficiency deals with the optimum allocation of a resource among producers of the same good:

1. Economic efficiency requires that the marginal rate of transformation (MRT) *between any resource* x *and any good* a *be the same for any two producers,* α *and* β, *producing this good with that resource.*

$$MRT^{\alpha}_{x,a} = MRT^{\beta}_{x,a}$$

Suppose we picked, from among millions of producers, α and β (who might be orchardists in Vermont) and who were using an identical resource x (a type of unskilled labor, perhaps) to produce an identical good a (a type of apple, called Golden Delicious). We might find our two producers in the initial situation shown in part (A) of Table 14.1.

Initial Position.   Producer α is using in a year 20 units of labor to produce 50 units of apples. Producer β is using in a year 10 units of identical labor to produce 80 units of identical apples. Both producers must, of course, also be using various amounts of other resources. These other resources (not shown in the table) will almost certainly differ in type and quantity between the two producers. Thus α's workers may be working with 500 apple trees, 1 ton of fertilizer, and a season of bad weather, while β's workers may be

TABLE 14.1   The Optimum Allocation of a Resource Among Producers of the Same Good

	Input and Output per Year	MRT	Assessment
(A) Initial Situation			
Producer α	20x make 50a	1x for 2a	Inefficiency exists; it is advisable to move a unit of the resource from producer α to producer β
Producer β	10x make 80a	1x for 5a	
	30x make 130a		
(B) New Situation			
Producer α	19x make 48a	1x for 2.1a	
Producer β	11x make 85a	1x for 4.9a	
	30x make 133a		
(C) Final Situation			
Producer α	9x make 22a	1x for 3.1a	Efficiency has been reached; no further changes are desirable
Producer β	21x make 128a	1x for 3.1a	
	30x make 150a		

working with 1,000 apple trees, 20 tons of fertilizer, 2 orchard-spraying machines, plenty of pesticides, and a season of perfect weather. Note in part (A) how our two producers are using initially a total of 30 units of labor, while producing 130 units of apples. Is the allocation of labor between them efficient?

We cannot answer this question, argued Vilfredo Pareto, until we consider how small (or marginal) changes in resource allocation would transform present circumstances. The **marginal rate of transformation**, or *MRT* (first noted in chapter 2) is the rate at which a producer is technically able to exchange, in the process of production, a little bit of one variable (say, labor) for a little bit of another variable (say, apples produced with the help of that labor). The data contained in the top circle in Table 14.1 indicate that α is technically able to exchange, in the initial circumstances just postulated, 1x for 2a, which means that α could produce an extra 2 units of apples per year with an extra 1 unit of labor—assuming all of α's other inputs remained the same. This *MRT* also tells us that α's production would fall by 2 units of apples per year if 1 unit of its labor input were to be lost—again assuming that all of α's other inputs remained the same. Thus the *MRT* of 1x for 2a indicates α's capability to move from the initial position of using 20x and making 50a each year to a new position, *either* using 21x and making 52a *or* using 19x and making 48a each year.

The top circle also indicates that β's *MRT* differs from α's *MRT* and equals 1x for 5a, which means that β could move from its initial position of using 10x and making 80a each year to either using 11x and making 85a or using 9x and making 75a each year. (Caution: As these examples show, the *MRT* must never be confused with the ratio of *total* output to input, such as α's initial 50a/20x or β's 80a/10x.)

The reason β's *MRT* might differ from α's is that producer β's endowment with natural and capital resources, as postulated above, might be so superior as to make its workers more productive than are identical workers employed by α. Thus an additional worker would add more to

output at β than at α, while loss of a worker would reduce output more at β than at α.

Worthwhile Change. The situation depicted by the data in the top circle clearly violates Pareto's first marginal condition stated above. This violation of an efficiency condition implies that economic inefficiency exists, which means it is possible to reorganize matters to make some people better off without making others worse off. Table 14.1 indicates what kind of change is required to escape inefficiency here: If we abstract from transportation cost (and this let us do in this initial presentation), it clearly pays to move a unit of labor from where it is less productive (presently at α) to where it is more productive (presently at β). The resulting new situation is shown in part (B) of Table 14.1. After a unit of labor has been moved from α to β, α's output is lower by 2 units of apples per year (just as α's initial *MRT* predicted) and β's output is higher by 5 units of apples per year (just as β's initial *MRT* predicted). But the sums reveal that output in society *as a whole* has risen from 130 to 133 units of apples per year, even though resource inputs have remained unchanged (at 30 units of labor plus unspecified amounts of other resources).

Clearly, someone in society can now receive an additional 3 units of apples per year, and no one need receive less because of it! The initial situation shown in Table 14.1 was inefficient because people were getting a smaller quantity of goods from their resources than was necessary. Their *actual* production did not equal their *potential* production, depicted by the right-hand circle of Figure 1.1, "The Scarcity Problem" (p. 5).

But isn't the new situation depicted in part (B) still inefficient? Shouldn't one continue to move labor from α to β until all labor is employed by β? Not necessarily, Pareto tells us. If the marginal rates of transformation *in the new situation* continue to diverge, as they do in part (B), inefficiency still exists, and a further reallocation of labor is in order. But continuing along this route, the *MRTs* will eventually come to be equal, as they are in part (C) of Table 14.1, at which point economic efficiency will have been attained and a further reallocation of labor will serve no purpose. Such further reallocation would make the output of one producer rise exactly as much (by 3.1 units of apples per year) as it would reduce the output of the other producer.

Converging *MRTs*. *Why should the* MRTs *eventually come to equal each other?* The key to answering that question is found in the famous **law of diminishing returns**: "Given the quantities of all other inputs being used, and given technical knowledge, successive additions of equal units of a resource to the process of production eventually yield ever smaller additions to total output." This law (already noted in Table 5.1, "A Simple Production Function")

teaches us that our *MRT* of resource *x* for good *a* cannot be expected to remain unchanged as circumstances change. The data in the circles of Table 14.1 indicate what is bound to happen as labor is moved from α to β:

Initially an extra unit of labor is capable of adding 5 units to β's output (A), but subsequent extra units of labor can only add 4.9 units to output (B), then 4.8 units (not shown), and, eventually, 3.1 units (C). This progression reflects the fact that β's initially superior endowment with nonlabor resources is gradually eroding as it employs more labor. As more workers are used with unchanged natural and capital resources, less and less of the natural and capital resources are available *per worker*; hence the addition or loss of a worker has successively smaller impact on total output.

BIOGRAPHY 14.1:

Vilfredo Pareto

Vilfredo Pareto (1848–1923) was born in Paris to an Italian father and a French mother. He studied in Italy, received a doctoral degree in engineering, and eventually became manager general of the Italian Iron Works. After years of industrial practice, he turned to economics. In 1893, he was appointed to succeed Léon Walras (see Biography 16.1) at the University of Lausanne, but he resigned that chair in 1906 and retired to Céligny on Lake Geneva. He devoted most of his later years to the study of sociology.

His major books on economics include *Cours d'Économie Politique*, vols. 1 and 2 (1896–97) and *Manuel d'Économie Politique* (1910). An Italian version of the latter work had appeared in 1906, and an English translation was published in 1971. Although he devoted no more than two decades of his long life to economics, Pareto has become one of the patron saints of the discipline. From its early beginnings, thinkers in the field had attempted to specify the meaning of social welfare and the kind of allocation of resources and goods that would maximize it. Pareto broke away

decisively from traditional practice, most recently exemplified by Bentham (see Biography 3.1). Pareto rejected the cardinal measurement of utility and any interpersonal comparisons thereof. He restricted economic science to welfare comparisons that require only intrapersonal comparisons (in which affected individuals themselves testified to the direction of change in their welfare). He insisted that economic science should make pronouncements only about unambiguous changes in social welfare. If a reallocation of resources or goods left some individuals, in their own estimation, equally well off but others better off, social welfare had increased. If some felt equally well off but others worse off, social welfare had decreased. If some were better off and others worse off, the situation could not be evaluated by economic science—unless, that is, the gainers actually compensated the losers to the losers' full satisfaction and were still better off. Such a case would, of course, be indistinguishable from one in which no one was worse off, but some people were better off.

The very act of reallocating labor changes α's marginal rate of transformation, too. Initially the loss of a unit of labor costs α only 2 units of output (A), but subsequent equal reductions in labor input reduce output by 2.1 units (B), then by 2.2 units (not shown), and, eventually, by 3.1 units (C). This progression reflects the fact that α's initially inferior endowment with nonlabor resources is gradually being overcome as α employs less labor. As fewer workers are used with unchanged natural and capital resources, more and more of the natural and capital resources are available *per worker*; hence the addition or loss of a worker has a successively greater impact on total output.

The reallocation of resources in the face of inefficiency, therefore, changes circumstances in such a way as to limit the desirable degree of reallocation. Compare parts (A) and (C) of Table 14.1 and note how, in the end, only 11 of α's 20 labor units have been reallocated to β. Note also how, as a result, output from given resources, now differently employed, has risen by 15 percent from 130 to 150 units of apples per year. This increase in output shows the extent to which human desires were unnecessarily frustrated by the inefficient allocation of resources depicted in part (A).

Wide Applicability.   Although this example involved labor and apples, the first marginal condition is applicable to literally billions of situations. Resource *x* can be labor, but it can also be fertilizer or steel or turret lathes. Good *a* can be apples, but it can also be airplanes, haircuts, or residential houses. Even the term "producer" can refer to more than the ordinary business firm; it might refer to a region or even a country! Suppose α meant "Oregon" (or even "China"), while β stood for "Vermont" (or the "United States"). It is easy to imagine circumstances under which the shift of at least some units of labor (or any resource) from Oregon to Vermont (or from China to the United States) would increase the world's output of goods. Artificial political boundaries that prevent such shifts make scarcity more severe than it has to be. The

abolition of such boundaries (as within the United States or within a Common Market) helps raise the material welfare of people.

Condition 2:   The Optimum Specialization of Production Among Producers of the Same Goods

A second marginal condition of economic efficiency concerns the optimum specialization of production among producers of the same goods:

> 2.   *Economic efficiency requires that the marginal rate of transformation* (**MRT**) *between any two goods* **a** *and* **b**, *be the same for any two producers,* α *and* β, *producing both goods.*

$$MRT^{\alpha}_{a,b} = MRT^{\beta}_{a,b}$$

Consider Table 14.2 and imagine that producers α and β were farmers in Vermont who were both producing apples (good *a*) as well as butter (good *b*).

Initial Position.   Initially, we find α using unspecified amounts of resources to produce 20 units of apples as well as 30 units of butter per year. Producer β produces 50 units of apples and 60 units of butter per year with similarly unspecified, but undoubtedly different, amounts of resources. Is the total annual production—of 70 units of apples and 90 units of butter—the largest possible output we can get from the resources employed by α and β?

The marginal rates of transformation given in the top circle of Table 14.2 help us answer this question in the negative: Under present circumstances, producer α is technically able to produce 1*a* less and, with the resources so released, to produce 2*b* more or to produce 1*a* more and 2*b* less. Producer β, on the other hand, endowed with different resources or different know-how, can presently exchange 1*a* for 5*b* in the process of production. Clearly, this violation of the second marginal condition stated above spells economic inefficiency.

TABLE 14.2   The Optimum Specialization of Production Among Producers of the Same Goods

	Outputs per Year	MRT	Assessment
(A) Initial Situation			
Producer α	20a and 30b	1a for 2b	Inefficiency exists; it is advisable for α to produce more a (and less b) and for β to produce more b (and less a)
Producer β	50a and 60b	1a for 5b	
	70a and 90b		
(B) New Situation			
Producer α	21a and 28b	1a for 2.1b	
Producer β	49a and 65b	1a for 4.9b	
	70a and 93b		
(C) Final Situation			
Producer α	27a and 11b	1a for 3.6b	Efficiency has been reached; no further changes are desirable
Producer β	43a and 91b	1a for 3.6b	
	70a and 102b		

Note how α is relatively better at producing apples, an extra unit of which can be had for the mere sacrifice of 2 units of butter, while β has to sacrifice 5 units of butter to produce another 1 unit of apples. Note also how β is relatively better at producing butter, 5 extra units of which can be had for the mere sacrifice of 1 unit of apples—as opposed to the gain of only 2 extra units of butter that α could achieve for an identical sacrifice of apples. Accordingly, it is advisable for α to produce more apples and for β to produce more butter.

Worthwhile Change.   Part (B) of Table 14.2 shows the effect of an initial reallocation of resources within each producing unit from the production of one good to the other. Note how this reallocation leaves overall apple production unchanged, while raising the overall production of butter by 3 units from 90 to 93 units per year. Thus, this reallocation makes it possible for someone to be better off without anyone else being worse off. Indeed, this process of specialization (of α producing more apples and of β more butter) should be carried further as long as the MRTs continue to diverge, as they do in part (B) of our table. Eventually, though, these MRTs are also going to become equal as shown in part (C).

Converging MRTs.   As α switches resources out of butter production to the production of apples, it is likely to switch first those resources least suitable for making butter and most suitable for making apples. As this process continues, it may have to switch into apple-production resources less suitable for making apples and more suitable for making butter, which will cause the sacrifice per extra unit of apples to rise from 2b in (A) to 2.1b in (B) to 2.9b (not shown) and, eventually, to 3.6b in (C). Producer β's experience is bound to be similar. As β takes successively out of apple production resources that are ever less suited to making butter, the gains per extra unit of apples sacrificed will decline from 5b in (A) to 4.9b in (B) to 4.3b (not shown) and, eventually, to 3.6b in (C). At that point, in our example, efficiency is reached. In the meantime, output from given resources, differently employed within each firm, has risen by 13 percent from 90 to 102 units of butter per year.

Wide Applicability.   As was true for the first marginal condition, so this second one is applicable to billions of situations. Not only can goods a and b represent any two goods, but α and β can again refer to any two "producers," including regions or countries. Consider how international trading in goods might substitute for the international movement of resources should the latter prove impossible. If, in Table 14.2, α stood for China and β for the United States, an *internal* shift of resources from the initial situation in part (A) to the final one in part (C) could be followed by trade: Given the new production volumes shown in part (C), China (α) could export $7a$ to the United States (β) in return for $25b$, which would leave the Chinese with $27a$ (their production) minus $7a$ (their export), or $20a$ (as in the initial situation). This exchange would leave Americans with $43a$ (their production) plus $7a$ (their import), or $50a$ (as in the initial situation). This arrangement would also give the Chinese $11b$ (their production) plus $25b$ (their import), or $36b$ (a clear gain over their initial position in part (A) and would leave Americans with $91b$ (their production) minus $25b$ (their export), or $66b$ (also a clear gain over initial circumstances). Thus the overall gain in output between the initial and final situations ($102b - 90b = 12b$) might be shared equally between the Chinese and the Americans (both of whom would gain $6b$).

Condition 3: The Optimum Composition of Production and Consumption

Other Pareto conditions of economic efficiency are more subtle than the two just discussed. Economic welfare can possibly be increased, not because a greater quantity of goods could be made available, but because a different and preferred set of goods could be produced:

> 3. *Economic efficiency requires that the marginal rate of transformation* (MRT) *between any two goods,* a *and* b, *produced by any producer,* α, *be equal to the marginal rate of substitution* (MRS) *between these two goods for any consumer,* X, *who consumes both.*

$$MRT^{\alpha}_{a,b} = MRS^{X}_{a,b}$$

Imagine picking, from among many millions of producers and consumers, α and X who have in common only that they produce and consume, respectively, apples (good a) and butter (good b).

Initial Position. In part (A) of Table 14.3, we find α producing 20 units of apples and 30 units of butter per year, while X is consuming 10 units of apples and 20 units of butter per year. In the top circle, the marginal rate of transformation is assumed to be $1a$ for $2b$ for α. We must now use another concept first met in Chapter 2 and discussed in detail in Chapter 3: A consumer's **marginal rate of substitution**, or *MRS*, is the rate at which a consumer is willing to exchange, *as a matter of indifference*, a little bit of one variable (say, the consumption of apples) for a little bit of another variable (say, the consumption of butter). Thus consumer X's *MRS* of $1a$ for $5b$ in the top circle indicates that person's willingness to move, as a matter of indifference, from the initial position of consuming each year $10a$ and $20b$ to a new position, consuming each year *either* $11a$ and $15b$ *or* $9a$ and $25b$. The fact that the consumer is indifferent about this change implies that consumer X would feel *better off* if *more* than $5b$ could be procured for the sacrifice of $1a$ or if *more* than $1a$ could be procured for the sacrifice of $5b$. The indicated *MRS* also implies that consumer X would feel *worse off* if *less* than $5b$ were to be received for the sacrifice of $1a$ or if less than $1a$ were received for the sacrifice of $5b$.

The data inside the top circle of Table 14.3 show Pareto's third marginal condition to be violated because the producer's *MRT* does not equal the consumer's *MRS*. Consumer X is seen to value an extra unit of apples much more highly than such extra unit objectively costs. Note how X is *willing* to sacrifice 5 units of butter for a unit of apples that α is *able* to produce with resources released by sacrificing only 2 units of butter. Thus it is possible to make someone better off without making anyone worse off.

Worthwhile Change. It is a matter of indifference (costing the same resources) for α to produce 2 units of butter less per year and 1 unit of apples more. As a result of this change in the composition of production, consumer X can

TABLE 14.3   The Optimum Composition of Production and Consumption

	Outputs Produced or Consumed per Year	MRT or MRS	Assessment
(A) Initial Situation			
Producer α	20a and 30b	1a for 2b	Inefficiency exists; it is advisable for α to produce, and for X to consume, more a (and less b)
Consumer X	10a and 20b	1a for 5b	
(B) New Situation			
Producer α	21a and 28b	1a for 2.1b	
Consumer X	11a and 18b	1a for 4.9b	
(C) Final Situation			
Producer α	27a and 11b	1a for 3.6b	Efficiency has been reached; no further changes are desirable
Consumer X	17a and 1b	1a for 3.6b	

consume 1 more unit of apples per year but must consume 2 less units of butter per year. *Since X would have been indifferent about sacrificing 5 units of butter for 1 unit of additional apples, X is now in fact better off.* Thus the new situation in part (B) implies that a greater economic welfare is being received than in the initial situation in part (A).

Converging *MRT* and *MRS*.   As in our previous example, this reallocation of resources should be continued as long as the marginal condition continues to be violated, as is the case in part (B). And as before, the marginal rates of transformation and substitution will converge as a result of the gradual shift in the composition of production and consumption: we noted above why producer α's *MRT* might change from 1a for 2b to 1a for 2.1b, 2.9b and, eventually, 3.6b. The consumer's *MRS* will also change with the consumer's circumstances (see Chapter 3). As the consumer consumes more and more apples per year, consumption of additional units will be less and less capable of raising the consumer's welfare and will thus seem less and less urgent. At the same time, and for analogous reasons, as the consumer consumes less and less butter per year, sacrifices of additional units will be more and more capable of lowering the consumer's welfare and will thus seem less and less advisable. Hence the amount of (ever-more-precious)

butter the consumer will be willing to sacrifice for an extra unit of (ever-less-precious) apples will decline; from 5b in (A) to 4.9b in (B) to 4.1b (not shown) and, eventually, to 3.6b in (C). At that point, economic efficiency will have been reached, and further changes in the composition of production and consumption will not be desirable.

Condition 4: The Optimum Allocation of Goods Among Consumers of the Same Goods

Given the overall quantity of production and even each person's share in this total, another important requirement of economic efficiency is that each person has the best combination of specific goods. According to Pareto:

> *4.   Economic efficiency requires that the marginal rate of substitution (MRS) between any two goods, a and b, be the same for any two consumers, X and Y, consuming both goods.*
>
> $$MRS_{a,b}^X = MRS_{a,b}^Y$$

Consider Table 14.4. Imagine that we picked, from among millions of consumers, X and Y who had in common that they consumed apples (good *a*) and butter (good *b*).

TABLE 14.4   The Optimum Allocation of Goods Among Consumers of the Same Goods

	Goods Consumed per Year	MRS	Assessment
(A) Initial Situation			Inefficiency exists; it is advisable for X to consume more a (and less b) and for Y to consume more b (and less a)
Consumer X	10a and 20b	1a for 5b	
Consumer Y	200a and 50b	1a for 2b	
	210a and 70b		
(B) New Situation			
Consumer X	11a and 17b	1a for 4.8b	
Consumer Y	199a and 53b	1a for 2.1b	
	210a and 70b		
(C) Final Situation			Efficiency has been reached; no further changes are desirable
Consumer X	20a and 2b	1a for 2.9b	
Consumer Y	190a and 68b	1a for 2.9b	
	210a and 70b		

Initial Position. In part (A), we find consumer X consuming 10 units of apples and 20 units of butter per year, while Y is consuming 200a and 50b per year. The data inside the top circle indicate that Pareto's condition of efficiency is violated. There must be a way to squeeze a greater satisfaction from the 210 units of apples plus 70 units of butter being consumed per year by X and Y.

At the moment, X values the consumption of 1 unit of apples more highly than Y because X is willing—as a matter of indifference—to sacrifice 5 units of butter per year to get another unit of apples, while Y is indifferent about sacrificing 2b for 1a. Accordingly, it is advisable for X to consume more apples and for Y to consume more butter.

Worthwhile Change. Part (B) of Table 14.4 shows the effect of an initial exchange of 1a for 3b between our two consumers. Both are better off because X, who would have been indifferent about giving up 5b, gave up only 3b for 1a. Y, who would have been indifferent about receiving only 2b, received 3b for 1a. Thus this reallocation of an unchanged total of goods has clearly raised total economic welfare.

Converging MRSs. This reallocation of goods, for reasons discussed in the previous section, has also changed the marginal rates of substitution. Note the first signs of their convergence inside the second circle. Having more apples and less butter than before, X now values another unit of apples somewhat less (at 4.8 rather than 5 units of butter). Having fewer apples and more butter than before, Y values another unit of apples somewhat more (at 2.1 rather than 2 units of butter).

However, 4.8 is still different from 2.1; hence situation (B) is still inefficient. Further reallocation is desirable until, as in situation (C), the two consumers' marginal rates of substitution have become equal. At that point of equality, the total utility derived by X and Y from the available set of goods is, of course, vastly higher than in the initial situation. Further changes in their consumption patterns would serve no purpose.

The Pareto Optimum: Summary and Criticisms

When all the marginal conditions of economic efficiency are fulfilled simultaneously, a society

CLOSE-UP 14.1:

Stalin and Comecon

Stalin's changing attitudes towards foreign trade provide an illustration of the second Pareto condition discussed in Table 14.2. Until the end of World War II, Stalin viewed foreign trade with suspicion. He looked upon it as a "safety valve" that would assure the fulfillment of the national economic plan. Foreign trade allowed the import of essential items that could not be produced at home; exports were a necessary evil to pay for these imports. Ideally, though, a zero volume of foreign trade would assure total independence from a hostile world surrounding the Soviet Union, while Stalin built "socialism in one country."

After 1945, other socialist countries emerged: Poland, Rumania, Bulgaria, Albania, Yugoslavia, Hungary, Czechoslovakia, East Germany—and in Asia others still. There is nothing wrong, argued Stalin's economists, with being dependent on friends. These economists urged abandonment of the old policy of minimizing foreign trade in favor of a grand international division of labor in "the socialist camp." Starting in 1949, the above-named countries joined the Soviet Union in a Council for Mutual Economic Aid (frequently abbreviated as Comecon or CMEA). They attempted to specialize in production in accordance with differences in their technical circumstances. The *MRT* data in parts (A) and (B) of Table 14.2 are an indication of such differences. For example, Albania would specialize in early potatoes, Bulgaria in industrial sewing machines, Czechoslovakia in sugar beet combines, East Germany in plastics, Hungary in aluminum products, Poland in horticultural tractors, Rumania in reed cellulose, and the Soviet Union in fishing vessels. In this way, given resources would yield higher output than a policy of national self-sufficiency could provide.[1]

---

[1]For a detailed listing of specialization decisions, see Heinz Kohler, *Economic Integration in the Soviet Bloc* (New York: Praeger, 1965), pp. 127–40.

---

is said to have reached its **Pareto optimum**. One can, however, find efficiency conditions other than the four described above; as Pareto noted, a near-infinite number exists. All such efficiency conditions, however, can be summarized by the following two propositions:

1. Whenever one can technically transform a little bit of one variable into a little bit of another, the marginal rate of technical transformation (the amount of one variable one can obtain objectively by sacrificing a unit of the other) must equal the marginal rate of indifferent substitution (the amount of one variable a person could substitute for a unit of the other without a feeling of gain or loss). That is, any *MRT* must equal any corresponding *MRS*.

2. All equivalent marginal rates of technical transformation or of indifferent substitution must be equal. That is, any *MRT* must equal anybody

else's corresponding *MRT*; any *MRS* must equal anybody else's corresponding *MRS*.

Note how the third Pareto condition discussed above is described perfectly by proposition 1, while the first, second, and fourth conditions are covered by proposition 2.

As long as these two propositions are not fulfilled and marginal inequalities persist, Pareto tells us, a reallocation of resources or goods is possible that raises total economic welfare with certainty. Although most present-day economists would agree, Pareto is not without his critics.

The Pareto definition of economic efficiency is based on a number of value judgments. Some economists do not share these values. They do not consider economic efficiency, as defined by Pareto, to be a worthy goal to pursue.

First, Pareto defines total economic welfare in terms of the welfare of all the individuals comprising society. Total economic welfare is somehow the sum of individual welfares; it is not a separate concept independent of these individual building blocks. Pareto's critics often look upon, society as an entity independent of the individuals comprising it, and they talk of "the social good" as separate from the sum of individual welfares.

Second, Pareto assumes that adult individuals (with the rarest of exceptions) are the best judges of their own welfares. An increase or decrease in the welfare of an individual is counted as such only when the affected individual so testifies. Pareto's critics often believe that the preferences of some people are superior to those of others and that everybody's welfare should be judged on the basis of these superior tastes.

Third, Pareto assumes, contrary to Bentham (see Chapter 3), that the welfare of one individual cannot be compared with that of another. As a result, Pareto is willing to make pronouncements about changes in total economic welfare only when the welfare of all individuals (in their own judgments) have remained unchanged or moved in the same direction. Pareto remains silent on all other comparisons. Even if a million people said they were better off as a result of a reallocation of resources or goods, a single statement to the contrary would lead Pareto to claim ignorance about the effect on total economic welfare.

As a consequence, the Pareto optimum, unlike Bentham's welfare maximum, is not a unique situation. Many possible situations would be considered optimal by the Pareto criterion. For example, the situation in part (C) of Table 14.4 is efficient because the Pareto condition concerning equality of the marginal rates of substitution is satisfied. According to Pareto, no further changes could be recommended by economists because such changes would not increase total economic welfare *with certainty*. But now consider a situation in which the two individuals consumed completely different shares of the total quantities of the goods available. Suppose X as well as Y each consumed $105a$ and $35b$. If the marginal rates of substitution were still equal (at whatever rate), this situation would be equally efficient as the one depicted in part (C). Again, the Pareto criterion would not endorse any change because, again, such change would not raise total economic welfare *unambiguously*.

Yet the two situations would almost surely differ by a Benthamite measure of welfare (which measured and added together each person's welfare with the help of a cardinal number). Quite possibly, Pareto's critics assert, making poor X richer at the expense of rich Y would raise the total of economic welfare by giving, say, 300 units of extra satisfaction to poor X, while taking 20 units from rich Y. Yet Pareto, crippled by his

CLOSE-UP 14.2:

The POW Camp

World War II prisoner-of-war camps provide an illustration of the fourth Pareto condition of economic efficiency—the optimum allocation of goods among consumers of the same goods—discussed in Table 14.4. In these POW camps, almost no production occurred. Yet prisoners received many products, ranging from canned milk, beef, biscuits, butter, and jam to cigarettes, chocolate, sugar, clothing, razor blades, and writing paper. Like manna from heaven, these products came in the form of rations handed out by the detaining power, through Red Cross packages and private parcels. More often than not, everyone received almost identical quantities of all items. Yet within seconds of receipt, widespread and spontaneous exchange of products occurred. People placed different personal evaluations on the items in their possession. The *MRS* data in parts (A) and (B) of Table 14.4 are an indication of such differences. Through exchange, the prisoners reallocated a given quantity of goods in such a way that the comfort of everyone was increased at the same time.

Source: R. A. Radford, "The Economic Organization of a POW Camp," *Economica*, November 1945, pp. 189–201.

own assumptions, would support the status quo and refuse to endorse any change in the (legitimate) fear that poor X might gain 300 and rich Y lose 800 units of satisfaction in the process. Since we cannot measure these changes in satisfaction but can only speculate about them, Pareto refuses to make a judgment. Any distribution of goods among consumers that is associated with equal marginal rates of substitution is, therefore, considered equally acceptable by his efficiency criterion, which exasperates Pareto's critics.

The next chapter will discuss various criteria of *equity* that can be used to make the kinds of moral judgments Pareto's critics demand and to distinguish among the many situations that cannot be ranked on a scale of better or worse by the Pareto criterion.

The Economic Efficiency of Perfect Markets

Pareto noted a close link between perfect markets and the achievement of economic efficiency. Indeed, every conceivable Pareto condition of economic efficiency would tend to be fulfilled if profit-maximizing firms and utility-maximizing households were to determine the optimum quantities they wished to trade with the help of equilibrium prices established in perfect markets. A consideration of two of the marginal conditions discussed above will illustrate why the behavior of firms and households in perfect markets is linked to economic efficiency.

The First Pareto Condition

Numerical Example.   Consider again our two orchardists from Table 14.1. Their technical circumstances differed greatly, but both were using unskilled labor (along with other inputs) to produce apples. More than that: in perfect markets, both would face identical prices of labor and apples—prices that neither firm could influence by its own actions. Thus market forces might establish an equilibrium price of labor of

$3.10 per unit and an equilibrium price of apples of $1 per unit. Yet if such equilibrium prices were established, producer α would never be content being in the kind of situation depicted in part (A) of our table. Given α's *MRT* of $1x$ for $2a$, the owner of α could clearly increase profit or reduce loss (by $1.10) through releasing a unit of labor (lowering cost by $3.10) and then producing and selling 2 units of apples less (lowering revenue by 2 times $1, or $2). Thus self-interest would drive α to do just what Table 14.1 demanded: release labor.

Firm β, on the other hand, would not be any more content. Given its initial *MRT* of $1x$ for $5a$, it could increase profit or reduce loss (by $1.90) through hiring an additional unit of labor (raising cost by $3.10) and producing and selling 5 units of apples more (raising revenue by 5×1 or $5). Thus self-interest would drive β as well to do what Table 14.1 demanded: use more labor.

Each firm would continue in this effort until a unit of labor released (in α's case) or a unit of labor added (in β's case) changed cost precisely as much as the resultant change in output was worth. In our case, once loss of a unit of labor at α reduced output by 3.1 units and once gain of a unit of labor at β raised output by 3.1 units (and hence by 3.1 times $1, or $3.10), further changes would be of no interest to either firm. They would end up exactly in the position depicted in part (C) of Table 14.1. Both firms would thus cooperate with each other in a task that was in the social interest: they would help reallocate resources in a fashion that yielded greater output than before and thus reduced overall scarcity.

Note: They would be reallocating resources and reducing overall scarcity out of pure self-interest (to get a higher profit or a reduced loss for themselves); they would not even be aware of each other's existence, much less of what they were doing for society!

Graphic Exposition.   Panel (a) of Figure 14.1 depicts a competitive labor market that has established a wage of $3.10 per unit of labor. This wage would become the marginal cost of acquiring labor that would be a given to all firms, including α and β, depicted in panels (b) and (c). According to the input rule first illustrated in Figure 8.1, "A Firm's Demand for Labor: The Simple Case" (p. 216), each firm would maximize profit by buying that input quantity at which the input's declining marginal value product, MVP_i, just equaled the input's price, P_i. Thus firm α would choose to employ 9 units of labor (in accordance with intersection a); firm β would choose 21 units of labor (intersection b). As a result, the marginal value product of labor in one firm (distance A) would exactly equal that in the other firm (distance B).

$$MVP_i^\alpha = \$3.10 = MVP_i^\beta$$

Because an input's marginal value product equals its marginal physical product, MPP_i, multiplied by output price, P_o, the above equality implies that

$$MPP_i^\alpha \cdot P_o = \$3.10 = MPP_i^\beta \cdot P_o$$

Because, furthermore, the output price is the same for all perfectly competitive firms (and assumed here to equal \$1 per unit of apples), it also follows that labor's marginal physical product would be the same in the two firms.

$$MPP_i^\alpha = 3.1 \text{ units of apples} = MPP_i^\beta$$

Yet the marginal physical product of an input is nothing else but Pareto's marginal rate of transformation between this input and the output it makes. Thus

$$MRT_{x,a}^\alpha = 3.1 \text{ units of apples} = MRT_{x,a}^\beta$$

Profit maximization under perfect competition, therefore, would keep α and β away from the kind of choices that spell economic inefficiency for the economy, which are depicted in part (A)

FIGURE 14.1   Perfect Competition and Pareto's First Condition

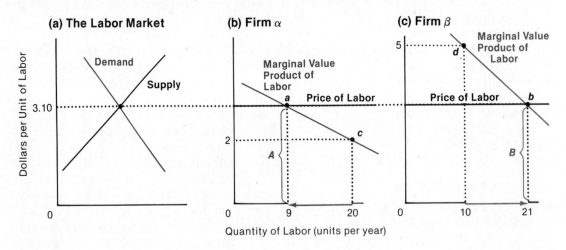

Perfectly competitive firms maximize profit by buying input quantities at which an input's declining marginal value product, MVP_i, just equals the input's price, P_i (points a and b). Because all firms face the identical input price, any input's marginal value product comes to be the same in all firms ($A = B$). Because an input's marginal value product, in turn, equals its marginal physical product, MPP_i, multiplied by output price, P_o and because output price is the same for all firms, any input's marginal physical product comes to be the same in all firms as well. This equality fulfills Pareto's first condition because the marginal physical product of an input is the marginal rate of transformation of the input into output.

of Table 14.1 and by points c and d in Figure 14.1.

The Second Pareto Condition

Numerical Example. Now consider our two producers from Table 14.2. Both were producing apples and butter. In perfect markets, both would face identical prices of apples and butter—prices that neither firm could influence. Let these market equilibrium prices equal $1 per unit of apples and 27.8¢ per unit of butter. Given these equilibrium prices, producer α would never be content being in the kind of situation depicted in part (A) of our table. Given α's *MRT* of $1a$ for $2b$, the owner of α could clearly increase profit or reduce loss (by 44.4¢) by producing and selling a unit of apples more (gaining revenue of $1) while producing and selling 2 units of butter less (losing revenue of 55.6¢). Because 1 unit of apples, by assumption, employed the same resources as 2 units of butter, α's costs would be unaffected. Thus self-interest would drive α to do just what Table 14.2 demanded: produce more apples and less butter.

Firm β, on the other hand, would not be content either. Given its initial *MRT* of $1a$ for $5b$, it could increase profit or reduce loss (by 39¢) though producing and selling a unit of apples less (lowering revenue by $1), while producing and selling 5 units of butter more (raising revenue by 5 times 27.8¢, or $1.39). Because 1 unit of apples, by assumption, employed the same resources as 5 units of butter, β's costs would be unaffected. Thus self-interest would also drive β to do just what Table 14.2 demanded: produce more butter and fewer apples.

Each firm would continue in this effort until an extra unit of apple production changed revenue precisely as much as did the accompanying change in butter production. In our case, once each firm's *MRT* was $1a$ for $3.6b$ (both quantities of which would be worth $1), further changes would be of no interest to either firm. They would end up exactly in the position depicted in part (C) of Table 14.2. Once more, as economists used to put it, "private vice" (the pursuit of profit) would yield "public virtue" (a reduction in overall scarcity).

Graphic Exposition. Panels (a) and (d), respectively, of Figure 14.2 depict competitive markets for apples and butter in which prices of $1 per unit of apples and 27.8¢ per unit of butter have been established. These prices would become the marginal benefit of selling these products for all firms, including α and β, depicted in panels (b) and (e) or (c) and (f), respectively. According to the output rule first illustrated in Figure 6.2, "A Profitable Business," (p. 151) each firm would maximize profit by producing and selling that output quantity at which the output's rising marginal cost, *MC*, just equaled its price, *P*. Thus firm α would choose to produce 27 units of apples (intersection a) and 11 units of butter (intersection b). Firm β would choose to produce 43 units of apples (intersection c) and 91 units of butter (intersection d). As a result, the marginal cost of producing apples in one firm (distance A) would exactly equal that in the other firm (distance B).

$$MC_a^\alpha = \$1 = MC_a^\beta$$

The same would be true with respect to the marginal cost of butter (distance $C = D$).

$$MC_b^\alpha = 27.8¢ = MC_b^\beta$$

By implication, one firm's marginal cost ratio (A/C) would also equal that of the other (B/D), each being equated with the identical ratio of market prices.

$$\left(\frac{MC_a}{MC_b}\right)^\alpha = \frac{\$1}{27.8¢} = \frac{3.6}{1} = \left(\frac{MC_a}{MC_b}\right)^\beta$$

Yet the reciprocal of the marginal cost ratio of two goods is nothing else but Pareto's marginal rate of transformation between them. If, at the margin, it costs 3.6 times as much to produce a unit of apples as to produce a unit of butter, one can transform 1 unit of apples into 3.6 units of butter. Thus the above implies

$$MRT_{a,b}^\alpha = 1a \text{ for } 3.6b = MRT_{a,b}^\beta$$

FIGURE 14.2   Perfect Compeition and Pareto's Second Condition

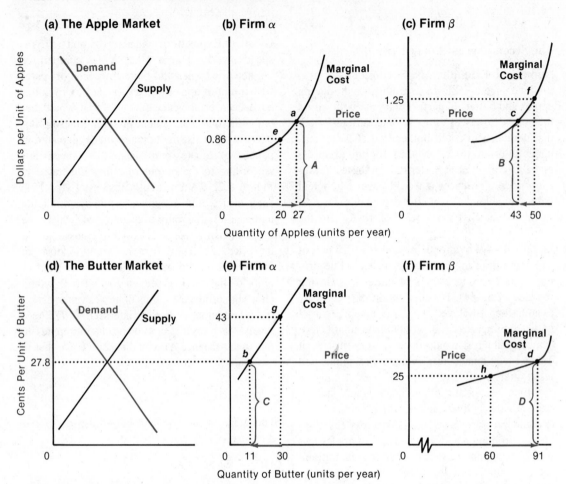

Perfectly competitive firms maximize profit by producing output quantities at which rising marginal cost, MC, just equals output price, P (points a through d). Because they face the identical output prices in any given market, all firms in effect equate each other's marginal costs of producing any good (A = B and C = D). As a result, firms equate the marginal cost ratio of any two goods $\frac{A}{C} = \frac{B}{D}$. This equality fulfills Pareto's second condition because each marginal cost ratio is a marginal rate of transformation of one good into another.

Profit maximization under perfect competition, therefore, would keep α and β away from the kind of choices that spell economic inefficiency for the economy, which are depicted in part (A) of Table 14.2 and by points e through h in Figure 14.2.

All Other Pareto Conditions

It can be shown that all other Pareto conditions would similarly be fulfilled in a world in which all decision makers faced identical equilibrium prices of resources and goods and were given the freedom to pursue their own self-interest. Thus Pareto's third condition would be fulfilled for two reasons: 1. As we have just seen, profit-maximizing firms would equate marginal costs of production with product prices and, therefore, would equate marginal cost ratios (or marginal rates of transformation between any two goods) with the price ratios of these goods. 2. As we learned in Chapter 3, utility-maximizing households would equate marginal rates of substitution between any two goods with their price ratios as well and with the very ratios of prices faced by firms. Thus any firm's *MRT* between goods would equal any household's *MRS*:

$$MRT^{\alpha}_{a,b} = MRS^{X}_{a,b}$$

because each would be equated with the identical ratio of $\dfrac{P_a}{P_b}$.

Pareto's fourth condition would also be fulfilled in perfect markets because all households would face identical prices for any given good. Thus any household who maximized utility by equating the marginal rate of substitution between goods with their price ratio would by that very fact equate its marginal rate of substitution with that of any other household that would act in the same way:

$$MRS^{X}_{a,b} = MRS^{Y}_{a,b}$$

because each would be equated with the identical ratio of $\dfrac{P_a}{P_b}$.

All other Pareto conditions would be fulfilled in a similar fashion. Not surprisingly, this way of achieving economic efficiency is seen as an enormous advantage of an economic system with perfect markets. Such a system would not require saints to run it; ordinary mortals would do quite well! As Adam Smith described such

[1]Adam Smith, *An Inquiry into the Nature and Causes of the Wealth of Nations*, vol. 2 (Homewood, Ill.: Richard D. Irwin, 1963), pp. 22–23.

a system,[1] "Every individual . . . endeavours . . . to employ his [resources] . . . that [their] produce may be of the greatest value. . . . He generally . . . neither intends to promote the public interest, nor knows how much he is promoting it. . . . He intends only his own security, . . . only his own gain. And he is in this . . . led by an Invisible Hand to promote an end which was no part of his intention. . . . By pursuing his own interest he frequently promotes that of the society more effectually than when he really intends to promote it."

The Economic Inefficiency of Imperfect Markets

In the presence of monopoly, cartels, oligopoly, and all other forms of imperfect competition, economic efficiency would *not* emerge automatically as the happy by-product of self-interested behavior. Economic efficiency would occur only by sheer accident, if at all. Consider the Pareto conditions just discussed.

The First Pareto Condition

Figure 14.3 pictures the profit-maximizing behavior of two firms that are perfect competitors in the product market but have monopsony power in the labor market. For reasons discussed in Chapter 13, each would equate its marginal outlay on labor with labor's marginal value product. Firm α would do so at intersection *a*; firm β at intersection *d*. Accordingly, α would hire 6,150 units of labor (at a wage of $1.95); β would hire 7,000 units (at a wage of $2.80).

Note: Unlike in Figure 14.1, which depicts the fulfillment of the first condition in the case of perfect competition, labor's marginal value product would now diverge between the two firms *(A ≠ B)*. At α, the marginal unit of labor would add $3 to revenue and—given a competitive product price of, say, $1 per unit—3 units to output. At β, the marginal unit of labor would add $5 to revenue and—given the same product price—5 units to output. Call labor x and product a, and a clear violation of Pareto's first condition emerges:

$$MRT^\alpha_{x,a} \ (=1x \text{ for } 3a) \neq MRT^\beta_{x,a} \ (=1x \text{ for } 5a)$$

Despite the inefficiency neither firm would have any incentive to change its behavior because each would be maximizing profit. Thus economic inefficiency would persist.

The Second Pareto Condition

Figure 14.4 represents the profit-maximizing behavior of two firms that are imperfect competitors in the markets for two goods. For reasons discussed in Chapters 11–12, such firms would equate their marginal costs of production with marginal revenue. Firm α would do so at intersections a and g; firm β at intersections d and k. Accordingly, α would produce 10,000 refrigera-

tors and 16,000 washers per year, while β would produce 18,000 and 26,000 units, respectively.

Note: Unlike in Figure 14.2, which illustrates the fulfillment of the second condition in the case of perfect competition, the two firms' marginal costs, as well as their ratios would now diverge ($A \neq B$, $C \neq D$, and $A/C \neq B/D$). Realizing that these ratios are closely linked to the marginal rates of transformation between the two goods (and denoting refrigerators by r and washers by w), a clear violation of Pareto's second condition can be observed:

$$\left(\frac{MC_r}{MC_w}\right)^\alpha = \frac{\$150}{\$150}, \text{ hence } MRT^\alpha_{r,w} \text{ is } 1r \text{ for } 1w.$$

$$\left(\frac{MC_r}{MC_w}\right)^\beta = \frac{\$50}{\$100}, \text{ hence } MRT^\beta_{r,w} \text{ is } 1r \text{ for } 0.5w.$$

Therefore, $MRT^\alpha_{r,w} \neq MRT^\beta_{r,w}$. In spite of this violation, neither firm would have any incentive to change its behavior because each would be

FIGURE 14.3 Imperfect Competition and Pareto's First Condition

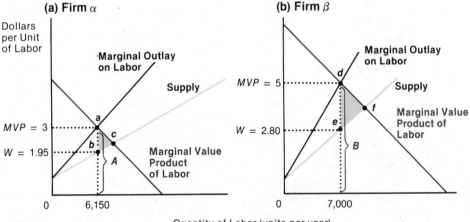

Input buyers that have monopsony power but act as perfect competitors in the output market maximize profit by buying input quantities at which an input's declining marginal value product just equals the marginal outlay on the input (points a and d). Under such circumstances, firms are unlikely to equate the input's marginal value products. Note how, in this example, $A \neq B$. Because an input's marginal value product, in turn, equals its marginal physical product multiplied by output price (and because output price is the same for all) the input's marginal physical products also differ between the firms. This inequality of the marginal physical products violates Pareto's first condition.

FIGURE 14.4   Imperfect Competition and Pareto's Second Condition

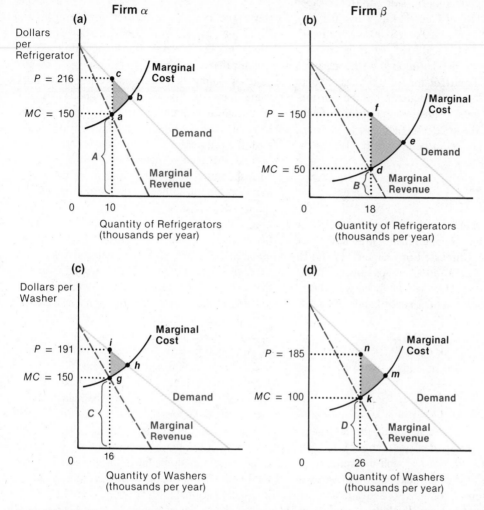

Sellers that have monopoly power maximize profit on the goods they sell by producing output quantities at which rising marginal cost just equals falling marginal revenue (points *a*, *d*, *g*, *k*). Under such circumstances, firms are unlikely to equate their marginal costs. Note how, in this example, $A \neq B$ and $C \neq D$. Because the marginal rate of transformation between any two goods is, in turn, closely linked to the ratio of marginal production costs, the *MRTs* are also unlikely to be the same for any two firms producing the same goods. This inequality of the *MRTs* violates Pareto's second condition.

---

maximizing profit. Thus economic inefficiency would persist.

All Other Pareto Conditions

It can be shown that all other Pareto conditions would similarly be fulfilled only by accident if

decision makers pursued their self-interest in a world of imperfect competition.

Pareto's third condition might not be fulfilled even if consumers equated the price ratio of any two goods with their marginal rate of substitution. This inefficiency might occur because the corresponding marginal rate of transformation of producers might deviate from the exchange ratio implied by the market prices of goods. Consider panels (b) and (d) of Figure 14.4. While firm β's marginal costs equal $50 and $100, respectively, its prices equal $150 and $185. Thus the marginal rate of transformation (implied by the marginal costs) equals 1 refrigerator for 0.5 washer (both being worth $50 in the factory). Yet the consumers' marginal rate of substitution (which is equated by them to the price ratio) equals 1 refrigerator for 0.81 washer (both being worth $150 in the market). Thus

$$MRT^{\alpha}_{r,w} \neq MRS^{X}_{r,w}.$$

Pareto's fourth condition could similarly be violated if, for example, firms practiced price discrimination (discussed in Chapter 11). Under such circumstances, different consumers buying identical goods could easily be faced with different prices. As a result, it could happen that

$$MRS^{X}_{a,b} \neq MRS^{Y}_{a,b} .$$

because each would be equated with a different ratio of $\dfrac{P_a}{P_b}$.

Analogous problems can arise with all other Pareto conditions as well. Given the prevalence of imperfect competition (see Table 12.2, "The U.S. Economy in 1978"), such theoretical conclusions are, of course, disturbing. Not surprisingly, therefore, economists have attempted to measure in our economy the extent of unnecessary scarcity that economic inefficiency implies.

Measuring the Welfare Loss from Economic Inefficiency

Arnold Harberger, about 30 years ago, made the first attempt to measure the welfare loss implied by economic inefficiency.[2]

[2]Arnold C. Harberger, "Monopoly and Resource Allocation," *The American Economic Review*, May 1954, pp. 77–87. *Note also* the discussion on pp. 88–92.

Harberger's Measure

Harberger focused on the fact, visible in Figure 14.4, that firms with monopoly power in the goods market always choose output levels at which price exceeds marginal cost. As a result, units of output that potential consumers would value more highly than other goods are not produced, and potential welfare is unnecessarily forgone. Note in Figure 14.4 how firm α could push the production of refrigerators and washers beyond the chosen quantities to higher levels corresponding to points *b* and *h*, respectively. Each one of these extra units would be valued (along demand-line segments *cb* or *ih*) more highly than the resources needed to make them (as measured along marginal-cost line segments *ab* or *gh*). The height of marginal cost reflects, in turn, the most highly valued alternative goods that could be produced with the resources involved. The shaded "triangles" thus measure the loss of potential consumer welfare. They are a measure of the inefficiency caused by monopoly power. (For firm β, of course, "triangles" *def* and *kmn* can be similarly interpreted.)

When Harberger set out to measure the extent of inefficiency, however, he made a number of special assumptions, which are illustrated in Figure 14.5. Harberger assumed that demand was unit-elastic, that producers did not engage in price discrimination, and that long-run average total cost was constant (and, therefore, equal to long-run marginal cost) for both firms and industries. (The reader may wish to review the discussion of such a case in Figure 6.8, "Short-Run Vs. Long-Run Costs" on p. 163).

Using data for 1924–28, Harberger calculated the deadweight welfare loss imposed by monopoly power (and shown by the shaded "triangle" in Figure 14.5) for each of 73 U.S. manufacturing industries. He summed the results to $26.5 million. Expanding his sample result to all of manufacturing, he reached an estimate of $59 million, equal to about 0.1 percent of the gross national product (GNP).

An equivalent loss in 1980 would have come to $2.5 billion; that is, to $11.34 for every person

FIGURE 14.5 Harberger's Measure of Welfare Loss

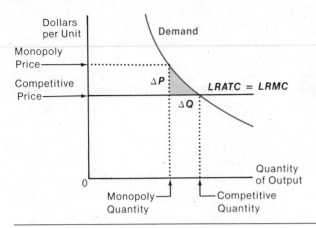

Because the area of a triangle equals its base times its height, divided by 2, the welfare loss of the roughly triangular shaded area in this graph can be approximated by $L = \dfrac{\Delta P \cdot \Delta Q}{2}$. Harberger assumed that firms that received his sample's average rate of return on invested capital were receiving zero *economic* profits and were charging a competitive price equal to long-run average total cost. He assumed that firms with greater returns were charging a monopoly price that exceeded the competitive price by ΔP. Assuming a price elasticity of demand equal to 1, Harberger used the elasticity formula $(\varepsilon = \dfrac{\Delta Q}{Q} : \dfrac{\Delta P}{P})$, along with his estimate of ΔP and industry data on P and Q, to calculate the monopoly output restriction ΔQ, and thus L.

in the United States or just about enough to take everyone to a restaurant once a year. If the size of this loss does not seem very impressive, be assured that the initial impact of Harberger's research was similar: the results of his research seemed to suggest that economists who concerned themselves with economic inefficiency were wasting their time with trivia.

Harberger Confirmed

A number of scholars followed in Harberger's footsteps and subsequently derived similarly trivial estimates of the extent of economic inefficiency. Some of them focused on goods markets as Harberger had done.[3] Others approached the matter by studying input markets[4] and the effects

[3]*See,* for instance, David Schwartzman, "The Burden of Monopoly," *Journal of Political Economy,* December 1960, pp. 627–30; idem, "The Effect of Monopoly: A Correction," *Journal of Political Economy,* October 1961, p. 494; Dean A. Worcester, Jr., "New Estimates of the Welfare Loss to Monopoly, United States, 1956–1969," *Southern Economic Journal,* October 1973, pp. 234–45; John J. Siegfried and Thomas K. Tiemann, "The Welfare Cost of Monopoly: An Inter-Industry Analysis," *Economic Inquiry,* June 1974, pp. 190–202.

[4]*See,* for instance, Albert Rees, "The Effects of Unions on Resource Allocation," *The Journal of Law and Economics,* October 1963, pp. 69–78.

of trade barriers.[5] They, too, calculated minute welfare losses, usually below 1 percent of GNP.

Figure 14.3 can be used to illustrate the input-market approach to estimating economic inefficiency. Note how firms with monopsony power in the input market always choose input levels at which an input's marginal value product exceeds the wage paid to the input *(a > b* and *d > e).* As a result, units of input that could produce output valued more highly than alternatives (such as leisure or other goods) are not used, and potential welfare is unnecessarily forgone. Note how firm α could push the use of labor beyond the chosen quantity to the higher level corresponding to point *c.* Each of these extra units would produce output valued more highly (along line segment *ac*) than alternatives (measured along line segment *bc,* which indicates the minimum wages people are willing to accept in this market and thus the best alternatives they must have available elsewhere). The shaded triangle *abc* thus measures the welfare

[5]A summary of such studies can be found in Charles P. Kindleberger and Peter H. Lindert, *International Economics,* 6th ed. (Homewood, Ill.: Irwin, 1978), p. 120. For a graphic illustration of the loss involved *see* "Application 4: Import Quotas" in Chapter 7 and Analytical Example 7.2, "The Welfare Effects of U.S. Sugar Quotas."

loss. (A similar interpretation can be made of firm β's triangle *def*.)

Harberger Criticized

While some researchers confirmed Harberger's estimate, other scholars seriously disagreed.[6] Three of the many criticisms of Harberger's estimate were: 1. Harberger understated the monopoly price distortion ΔP; 2. his assumption of unitary elasticity was too low and brought down the calculated quantity distortion, ΔQ; 3. manufacturing accounts for only a quarter of the GNP, and monopoly power is exercised in other sectors as well.

First, critics argued that Harberger had understated the monopoly price distortion, ΔP, for two reasons: He had used the average rate of return on invested capital in manufacturing as a proxy for the normal interest return on invested capital that competitive conditions would produce. Quite possibly the typically lower average rate of return on invested capital in such sectors as agriculture and services should have been used to approximate implicit interest costs. Harberger had also insufficiently accounted for the fact that monopoly power is a valuable asset (recall Analytical Example 11.3, "The Market Value of Monopoly Power"). More often than not, this asset is not acquired for nothing, and it has to be continually defended against would-be competitors. Thus firms spend money on campaign contributions, legislative lobbying, even outright bribes (recall, "Application 5: The 'Captured' State" in Chapter 11). Firms also spend large sums on persuasive advertising, antitrust and patent lawyers, and government licenses. Firms invest in deliberate excess capacity to deter new

[6]*See*, for instance, George J. Stigler, "The Statistics of Monopoly and Merger," *Journal of Political Economy*, February 1956, pp. 33–40; Charles K. Rowley, *Antitrust and Economic Efficiency* (London: Macmillan, 1973); Abram Bergson, "On Monopoly Welfare Losses," *The American Economic Review*, December 1973, pp. 853–70 (but note the subsequent discussion in the December 1975 issue, pp. 1008–31); Richard Hartman, "On Monopoly Welfare Losses, Once Again," *Economic Inquiry*, April 1978, pp. 293–301.

entrants into the industry or to secure higher cartel quotas (a practice once common among U.S. cement and oil producers). In addition, critics said, firms engage in a great deal of useless product differentiation. Note: It does not matter whether such expenditures are successful in attaining or defending monopoly power. What matters is the fact that such costs would not exist under perfect competition and should be deducted from observed accounting costs before competitive costs are estimated. Barring such adjustments, the costs of an imperfectly competitive firm may appear so high as to make its profit look merely like a competitive return on invested capital.

For example, consider a person buying a New York taxi for $10,000. Such a person would also have to buy the $68,000 medallion (license) to run it. Let annual revenues equal $50,000 and explicit costs (wages, fuel, repairs, insurance, and the like) $42,200. The $7,800 difference between annual revenues and explicit costs will then appear as a mere 10 percent return on the $78,000 capital investment—just equal, perhaps, to the implicit return on capital a competitive market might require in the long run. Yet, instead of adding $7,800 of implicit cost to $42,200 of explicit costs (and thus deriving a $50,000 estimate of long-run cost), one may wish to treat only $1,000 as legitimate implicit interest on the $10,000 taxi. Adding this $1,000 to the explicit costs of $42,200 would yield a long-run cost estimate of $43,200 and reveal not a competitive firm's zero economic profit (and a zero price distortion ΔP), but a monopolistic profit of $6,800 (and a significant ΔP).

Second, Harberger's critics argued that his assumption of unitary elasticity was too low and biased downward the calculated quantity distortion, ΔQ. This criticism can be appreciated by recalling that imperfectly competitive firms face downward-sloping demand curves, hence downward-sloping marginal revenue curves. As long as the price elasticity of demand exceeds $|1|$, marginal revenue (although declining with higher output) is positive; marginal revenue reaches zero precisely at an output volume that corresponds to

CLOSE-UP 14.3:

The Economics of Rent Seeking

From the individual point of view, it is perfectly rational to expend resources for the purpose of gaining an asset that produces economic rent. Monopoly power created by government (in the form of a limited number of import licenses, off-shore oil-drilling rights, taxi medallions, and the like) is an example of such an asset; this power enables its holder to gain higher income than otherwise. From the point of view of society, resources expended on rent seeking, however, are wasted. Such resources do not contribute to an increase in social welfare; they merely help transfer welfare from some people to other people. In his *Cours d'Économie Politique*, Pareto says:

> Let us suppose that in a country of thirty million inhabitants it is proposed, under some pretext or other, to get each citizen to pay out one franc a year, and to distribute the total amount amongst thirty persons. Every one of the donors will give up one franc a year; every one of the beneficiaries will receive one million francs a year. The two groups will differ very greatly in their response to this situation. Those who hope to gain a million a year . . . will win newspapers over to their interest by financial inducements and drum up support from all quarters. A discreet hand will warm the palms of needy legislators, even of ministers. . . . Those who hope to gain a million apiece have agents everywhere, who descend in swarms on the electorate, urging the voters that sound and enlightened patriotism calls for the success of their modest proposal. . . . In contrast, the individual who is threatened with losing one franc a year—even if he is fully aware of what is afoot—will not for so small a thing forgo a picnic in the country, or fall out with useful or congenial friends. . . . In these circumstances the outcome is not in doubt: the spoliators will win hands down.

More recently, Jeffrey Brennen, an economist at the Virginia Polytechnic Institute, devised a classroom game to demonstrate the social waste created by rent seeking.[1] In the game the instructor offers a prize of, say, $2 for which students in the class can bid. The students are told to write the amount of money they are willing to pay on a signed piece of paper and hand it in. They are also told that the highest bidder will take the prize, that they must pay the instructor the amount of their bid regardless of whether they are the highest bidder, and that they are free not to participate at all. The prize can, of course, be viewed as the classroom equivalent of the net present value of a stream of monopoly profits offered by government and sought by rent seekers. The bids students make can be viewed as the value of resources expended in efforts to acquire monopoly power.

The results of the game say much about the real world: The total of bids submitted tends to rise with the size of the class (the number of competitors seeking to gain monopoly). In classes of more than 40 students, the high bid tends to be close to $2, and the sum of bids is often several times the value of the prize. In one instance, this sum came to $24.37.

[1]As reported in Richard B. McKenzie, *Economic Issues in Public Policies* (New York: McGraw-Hill, 1980), pp. 70–71.

---

unitary price elasticity. A profit-maximizing firm, however, will choose an output volume that equates marginal cost (which will typically be positive) with marginal revenue (which will, therefore, be positive as well). As a result, a profit-maximizing firm will choose an output volume at which not only is marginal revenue positive, but price elasticity of demand is also greater than $|1|$. By estimating this elasticity as equal to $|1|$, Harberger implicitly assumed zero marginal revenue—a situation profit-maximizing firms would choose only in the unusual case of their having zero marginal costs.

Third, Harberger's critics maintained that

manufacturing accounts for only a quarter of the GNP and that monopoly power is surely exercised in other sectors as well. (A look at Table 12.2, "The U.S. Economy in 1978" on page 373 will confirm both of these facts.) Because Harberger focused on manufacturing in calculating his estimate, his calculation of the welfare loss was considered to be too low.

Harberger Corrected

Not surprisingly, some of Harberger's critics have calculated welfare losses as high as 4–8 percent of the GNP. Their calculations, however, have also remained controversial.[7] Figure 14.6 summarizes the arguments just reviewed. Harberger estimated the competitive price at the level of *LRATC* by using accounting data of cost and adding a competitive return on capital equal to the average return earned by his sample. Using a lower estimate of the proper rate of return based on other sectors in the economy, might yield *LRATC'* instead. Applying this lower rate of return to a lower total of invested capital (that excluded the capitalized value of monopoly power itself) might yield *LRATC** as the likeliest level of long-run average total cost and price

under perfect competition. Finally, replacing demand line *DD* by *D*D** (which is more elastic in the relevant range) raises the loss triangle from the shaded area to the shaded-plus-dotted one.

X-Efficiency vs. Economic Efficiency

The preceding section described controversial estimates of economic welfare unnecessarily lost because of economic inefficiency. Much less controversial are estimates of welfare losses due to technical inefficiency within the boundaries of individual firms. As a result of the persuasive work of Harvey Leibenstein and his imitators, many economists have come to view X-inefficiency as all-pervasive and as much more significant in scope than economic inefficiency.[8]

Firms with monopoly power, it is believed, not only incur considerable expenses to obtain, strengthen, and defend that power (as discussed in the previous section), but they are generally lax on cost control because they do not face intense competitive pressure. Before long, such extravagances as lavish offices, high entertainment budgets, and long coffee breaks push costs to unnecessary levels.

The kinds of examples of X-inefficiency given in Chapter 5 have been confirmed in innumerable investigations. One recent study investigated electric power producers.[9] In 49 U.S. cities that had two or more competing companies, average total cost was 11 percent lower, all else being equal, than in cities without such competition. Another study focused on banks.[10] In 34 U.S. metropolitan areas, banks

---

[7]*See*, for instance, David R. Kamerschen, "An Estimation of the 'Welfare Losses' from Monopoly in the American Economy," *Western Economic Journal*, Summer 1966, pp. 221–36 (with critical comments by Dean A. Worcester, Jr., "Innovations in the Calculation of Welfare Loss to Monopoly," *Western Economic Journal*, September 1969, pp. 234–43, and Victor P. Goldberg, "Welfare Loss and Monopoly: The Unmaking of an Estimate," *Economic Inquiry*, April 1978, pp. 310–312); Gordon Tullock, "The Welfare Costs of Tariffs, Monopolies, and Theft," *Western Economic Journal*, June 1967, pp. 224–32 (with comments by E. J. Mishan, "A Note on the Costs of Tariffs, Monopolies, and Thefts" in the September 1969 issue, pp. 230–33); David R. Kamerschen and Richard L. Wallace, "The Costs of Monopoly," *Antitrust Bulletin*, Summer 1972, pp. 485–96; Anne O. Krueger, "The Political Economy of the Rent-Seeking Society," *The American Economic Review*, June 1974, pp. 291–303; Richard A. Posner, "The Social Costs of Monopoly and Regulation," *Journal of Political Economy*, August 1975, pp. 807–27; Keith Cowling and Dennis C. Mueller, "The Social Costs of Monopoly Power," *The Economic Journal*, December 1978, pp. 727–48.

[8]Note the discussion of X-inefficiency in "Second Thoughts: The Matter of X-Inefficiency" in Chapter 5 as well as the writings by Leibenstein and Stigler cited at the end of Chapter 5.

[9]Walter J. Primeaux, "An Assessment of X-Efficiency Gained Through Competition," *Review of Economics and Statistics*, February 1977, pp. 105–108.

[10]Franklin R. Edwards, "Managerial Objectives in Regulated Industries: Expense-Preference Behavior in Banking," *Journal of Political Economy*, February 1977, pp. 147–62.

FIGURE 14.6   Correcting Harberger's Estimate

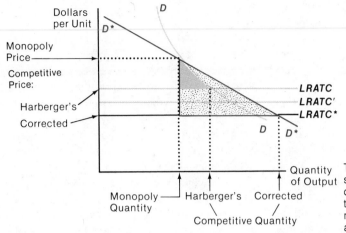

This graph is a copy of Figure 14.5, with some of the corrections suggested by critics indicated as well. The result of these corrections is a larger loss estimate, consisting not only of the shaded area, but the dotted one as well.

with little competition had larger staffs and higher labor costs, all else being equal, than banks located in places with competition. Indeed, business newspapers, magazines, and trade journals —from the *Wall Street Journal, Barron's, Business Week, Forbes,* and *Fortune* to *Computerworld* and *Iron Age*—fill their pages with sad stories of sleeping giants, stuck in old modes of operation, lacking new ideas, lethargic, and inbred.

Note: The waste of resources due to X-inefficiency is likely to be much more significant than that from economic inefficiency. Comanor and Leibenstein believe that if half of national production were produced by firms with monopoly power (a conservative estimate), if their long-run average total and marginal cost were on the average 6 percent below price, and if the price elasticity of demand were |2|, a Harberger-type estimate of welfare loss would equal 0.18 percent of national product.[11] If the actual costs of these firms, however, were inflated by X-inefficiency so that true costs were 18 percent

below price, a corrected Harberger-type loss estimate would equal 3 percent of national product. At the same time, the pure waste of resources from X-inefficiency would come to another 9 percent of national product. The overall waste of 12 percent of national product would have come, in 1980, to a quite respectable $1,350 for every person in the United States (see Figure 14.7).

Static vs. Dynamic Efficiency

Some economists argue that all the fuss about X-efficiency and economic efficiency is out of place. What matters, they say, is not *static efficiency* (squeezing the greatest possible welfare from the resources and technical knowledge given to a firm or economy at the present), but *dynamic efficiency* (raising the ratio of total output to total inputs over time by *changing* resources and technology). As was noted in "Application 2: Technical Advance and the Entrepreneur" in Chapter 10, Joseph Schumpeter (see Biography 10.2) was foremost among those who argued for dynamic efficiency. Schumpeter firmly believed that monopolies more so than

[11]William S. Comanor and Harvey Leibenstein, "Allocative Efficiency, X-Efficiency, and the Measurement of Welfare Losses," *Economica,* August 1969, pp. 304–309.

perfect competitors would be the ones best suited to promote dynamic efficiency. In more recent years, John Kenneth Galbraith has expressed similar thoughts with respect to large oligopolistic firms.

The Hypothetical Argument

Imagine an economy that at every moment in time wasted 12 percent of its resources by incurring unnecessary costs (X-inefficiency) and by violating Pareto's conditions of economic efficiency. If that economy's output, because of the very circumstances that produced X-inefficiency and economic inefficiency grew at a rate of 6 percent per year, while it would grow at only 3 percent per year if it managed to avoid the aforementioned inefficiencies, one would be well advised to embrace static inefficiency as the price of superior dynamic performance. That economy's output would not grow at 3 percent a year, as the series

100—103—106.09—109.27—112.55
—115.93 . . .

It would grow instead from its lower inefficient base at a rate of 6 percent a year, such as the series

88—93.28—98.88—104.81—111.10
—117.76 . . .

Note: After a mere 5 years, the people in the latter economy would have overcome their output handicap. Forevermore, they would be better off than the people in the former economy (which would always avoid Leibenstein's and Pareto's inefficiency alike).

As Schumpeter put it, "A system . . . that at every given point of time fully utilizes its possibilities to the best advantage may yet in the long run be inferior to a system that does so at *no* given point of time, because the latter's failure to do so may be a condition for the level or speed of long-run performance."[12]

---

[12]Joseph A. Schumpeter, *Capitalism, Socialism, and Democracy*, 3rd ed. (New York: Harper & Row, 1950), p. 83.

FIGURE 14.7 X-Inefficiency and Economic Inefficiency

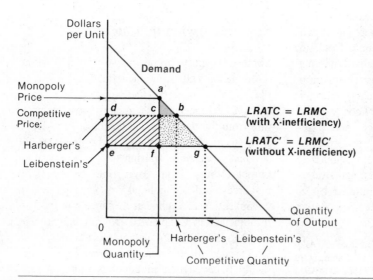

Given demand and observed costs *LRATC*, Harberger's procedure would identify shaded rectangle *abc* as the welfare loss due to economic inefficiency. Acceptance of Leibenstein's argument that monopoly power allows firms not only to raise price, but also to raise cost (as from *LRATC'* to *LRATC*) raises the estimate of economic inefficiency to include dotted area *bcfg*; an added welfare loss of pure X-inefficiency appears (crosshatched area *cdef*).

Market Structure and Dynamic Efficiency

Schumpeter thought that the two scenarios above represented economies under perfect and imperfect markets, respectively. He claimed that firms that are large and hold monopoly power are likely to have a larger cash flow and more borrowing ability than smaller and competitive firms. Because the large firms with monopoly power would be able to count on a broader and more durable market, they would engage in more research and product development (R&D). They would innovate more, introducing the assembly line today and computers and robots to run it tomorrow; giving consumers ballpoint pens or instant photos today and space settlements or doubled lifetimes tomorrow. Competitive firms, on the other hand, even if they could find the funds, would shy away from R&D and entrepreneurial innovation. If their R&D were a technical failure (and much money sunk into research and experimenting did not yield that more productive type of apple tree, let us say), the investors alone would have to bear all the cost. If it were a technical success (and a phenomenally more productive apple tree were bred), the investors would have to share the gain with the world at large: Production costs would be reduced and some profit would be made—*in the short run*. But before long, new firms would enter the field imitating the new; they would help raise industry supply greatly and would reduce the product's equilibrium price—eliminating profit. Thus any long-range, high-cost investment in research and innovation on the part of such firms would be discouraged.

The argument, however, can also be reversed. Might monopolistic giants not be lethargic? Might they not be run by "abominable no-men" who veto every innovative move because there are no competitors who pose a threat? Might not a multitude of important innovations occur precisely under perfect competition, as the result of random tinkering by a multitude of individuals engaged in the productive process? With very little monetary investment, such people might raise the yield of apple trees today by applying fertilizer to their roots (rather than spreading it on the ground). They might raise it tomorrow by sprinkling water on apple blossoms when the spring frost is about to kill the year's crop in its infancy. And when other firms imitated their methods and competed away the profit associated with their temporary headstart, they might find another way yet to get more apples still from the same resources! Thus they might once more lower their cost and recreate their profit. By always being a step ahead of everyone else, such successful innovators could enjoy a permanent profit even when free entry into their field was guaranteed to all. Such innovators would just have to come up with *repeated* innovations to accomplish the feat, but that very necessity would produce a better performance on the dynamic efficiency front than imperfect competition ever could. Who is right? Is imperfect or perfect competition more conducive to dynamic efficiency?

Empirical Evidence

Economists have amassed a great deal of empirical evidence, which does not clearly corroborate either of the two hypotheses just discussed. Data show that the major force promoting R&D and subsequent innovation is not to be found in the absolute size of firms nor in the degree of firm concentration in their industry. The research and development expenditures of U.S. firms, for instance, when measured per dollar of sales, rise up to a point with the size of firms, then level off, and even decline. The output resulting from R&D, as measured by inventions, is clearly not concentrated in the hands of giant firms, nor in those operating in highly concentrated industries. The majority of inventions are in fact made by individuals and small firms. Innovations, in turn, are often made by small and competitive firms (but then frequently imitated by larger ones). The secret seems to be this: Dynamic efficiency is advanced by the existence of moderately high barriers to entry into an industry. Where the entry of new firms is very easy, fear of rapid imitation seems to discourage significant R&D

ANALYTICAL EXAMPLE 14.1:
The Cost of Monopoly Power of Large U.S. and British Firms

Two economists recently measured the social cost of the monopoly power of large firms in the United States and Great Britain. Their U.S. sample contained 734 firms during 1963–66; the British sample included 102 firms during 1968/69. The authors estimated welfare losses in four ways: according to Harberger's procedure—column (1) of the table below; after making corrections typically suggested by Harberger's critics—in column (2); after assuming advertising expenditures to be a social waste

Monopoly Welfare Losses by Firm

Company	Harberger Methodology (1)	Harberger Corrected (2)	Harberger Corrected plus Advertising Expenditures (3)	Harberger Corrected plus Advertising Expenditures plus After-Tax Monopoly Profit (4)
(A) United States, 1963–66 (in millions of dollars per year)				
1. General Motors	$123.4	$1,060.5	$ 1,347.8	$ 1,780.3
2. AT&T	—	—	1,025.0	1,025.0
3. Unilever	—	—	490.5	490.5
4. Procter & Gamble	3.3	56.7	427.0	427.0
5. Dupont	36.3	225.1	275.4	375.3
6. Ford Motor	5.2	160.4	331.7	331.7
7. IBM	36.8	251.7	288.7	319.8
8. Genesco	—	—	202.6	292.6
9. R. J. Reynolds	10.8	73.1	269.3	278.8
10. Sears Roebuck	0.5	36.2	272.5	272.5
11. Eastman Kodak	27.7	136.3	201.1	258.5
12. American Cyanamid	1.9	27.6	240.8	240.8
13. Exxon	2.4	115.6	197.8	197.8
14. Colgate-Palmolive	—	3.9	160.3	160.3
15. Chrysler	1.1	39.8	155.5	155.5
16. General Electric	2.6	83.4	148.8	148.8
17. Pan American Airways	0.1	1.1	147.2	147.2
18. Pacific Telephone & Telegraph	—	—	138.1	138.1
19. Gilette	4.7	27.8	112.3	129.2
20. Minnesota Mining & Manufacturing (3M)	8.2	62.5	107.1	129.1
Total for 734 firms	$448.2	$4,527.1	$14,005.4	$14,997.6
Total for 734 firms as percent of these firms' gross corporate product	0.4%	4.0%	12.3%	13.1%

and adding them to the previously estimated loss—column (3); and after assuming monopoly after-tax profits to be an indication of resources wasted in the process of gaining monopoly power and adding them as well—column (4). The results for the top 20 offenders (ranked by the fourth-column estimate) are shown here, along with the results for the entire sample.

Source: Keith Cowling and Dennis C. Mueller, "The Social Costs of Monopoly Power," *The Economic Journal*, December 1978, pp. 740–42. © 1978 by the Royal Economic Society. Published by Cambridge University Press.

Company	Harberger Methodology (1)	Harberger Corrected (2)	Harberger Corrected plus Advertising Expenditures (3)	Harberger Corrected plus Advertising Expenditures plus After-Tax Monopoly Profit (4)
(B) Great Britain, 1968–69 (in millions of pounds per year)				
1. British Petroleum	£5.1	£74.1	£75.1	£82.7
2. Shell Transport and Trading	2.2	49.4	53.6	53.6
3. British American Tobacco	1.0	26.8	27.5	49.1
4. Unilever	—	2.8	28.2	29.0
5. I.C.I.	0.5	17.6	21.1	27.9
6. Rank Xerox	3.4	13.9	14.2	27.5
7. IBM (U.K.)	2.2	11.1	11.3	21.9
8. Great Universal Stores	0.5	9.6	11.0	21.6
9. Beecham	0.6	6.2	14.3	20.4
10. Imperial Group	—	2.8	20.1	20.1
11. Marks & Spencer	0.6	9.8	9.8	18.6
12. Ford	0.2	7.2	8.8	16.6
13. F. W. Woolworth	0.3	7.3	7.8	15.9
14. J. Lyon	—	—	2.8	14.2
15. Burmah	0.2	5.3	5.9	13.9
16. Distillers	0.2	5.6	7.1	13.4
17. Rank Organization	1.2	11.5	12.1	12.5
18. Thorn	0.3	5.6	7.1	12.5
19. Cadbury Schweppes	—	1.8	11.4	12.3
20. Reckitt & Coleman	0.1	2.9	8.3	10.4
Total for 102 firms	£21.4	£385.8	£537.4	£719.3
Total for 102 firms as percent of these firms' gross corporate product	0.2%	3.9%	5.4%	7.2%

ANALYTICAL EXAMPLE 14.2:

The Sources of Invention

A group of researchers considered 70 major inventions for the period since 1880. They wanted to determine whether inventions came mainly from large-scale industrial laboratories, as is often believed. On the contrary, more than 54 percent of the inventions could clearly be attributed to individuals working alone, and more than 11 percent to individuals working with research institutions. The remaining 34 percent did come out of industrial research labs, but many of these belonged to small firms, not large ones.

Major Inventions Since 1880

(A) Inventions by Individuals		(B) Inventions by Mixture of Individuals and Institutions	(C) Inventions by Industrial Research Laboratories
1. Air conditioning	29. Rhesus haemolytic disease treatment	39. Continuous casting of steel	47. Acrylic fibres
2. Air-cushion vehicles	30. Safety razor	40. Electronic digital computers	48. Aldrin, Chlordane, and Dieldrin
3. Automatic transmissions	31. Self-winding wrist watch	41. Long-playing record	49. Cellophane tape
4. Bakelite	32. Streptomycin	42. Radar	50. Continuous hot-strip rolling
5. Ballpoint pen	33. Sulzer loom	43. Rockets	51. Crease-resisting fabrics
6. Catalytic cracking of petroleum	34. Synthetic light polarizer	44. Shell moulding	52. DDT
7. Cellophane	35. Titanium	45. Stainless steels	53. Diesel-electric locomotive
8. Chromium plating	36. Wankel engine	46. Tungsten carbide tools	54. Duco lacquers
9. Cinerama	37. Xerography		55. Float glass
10. Cotton picker	38. Zip fastener		56. Fluorescent lighting
11. Cyclotron			57. Freon refrigerants
12. Domestic gas refrigeration			58. Methyl Methacrylate polymers
13. Electric precipitation			59. Modern artificial lighting
14. Electron microscope			60. Neoprene
15. Gyro compass			61. Nylon, perlon
16. Hardening of liquid fats			62. Oxygen steel making
17. Helicopter			63. Polyethylene
18. Insulin			64. Semisynthentic penicillins
19. Jet engine			65. Silicones
20. Kodachrome			66. Synthetic detergents
21. Magnetic recording			67. Television
22. Moulton bicycle			68. Terylene polyester fibre
23. Penicillin			69. Tetraethyl lead
24. Phototypesetting			70. Transistor
25. Polaroid camera			
26. Power steering			
27. Quick freezing			
28. Radio			

A study of 27 major inventions for the period 1946–55 confirmed that independent individuals and small firms play a prominent role in generating new ideas. The development of these ideas for commercial utilization, however, was typically undertaken by medium-sized firms. Large firms were aggressive followers.

Source: John Jewkes, David Sawers, Richard Stillerman, *The Sources of Invention*, 2nd ed. (New York: Norton, 1969), chap. 4. Daniel Hamberg, "Invention in the Industrial Research Laboratory," *Journal of Political Economy*, April 1963, pp. 95–115.

and innovation, regardless of the prevailing size or number of firms. Where entry is next to impossible, the lack of any competitive threat seems to dull the incentive of existing firms to push technical advance. Yet where entry barriers are moderate, strong R&D and innovative activity is observed—carried out either by newcomers or by existing firms wishing to keep out newcomers. Thus a *blend* of small and large firms (which are neither perfect competitors nor monopolies) seems most conducive to technical progress.

SUMMARY

1. Scarcity may be unavoidable, but people who make foolish choices with the resources and goods at their disposal can make scarcity more intense than necessary. Economists measure the existence of avoidable scarcity with the help of efficiency criteria, including *technical efficiency*, which applies to the firm, and either *static* or *dynamic efficiency*, both of which apply to the whole economy. In principle, one could test the degree of economic efficiency a society is achieving by applying the optimization principle to any given allocation of resources or goods and asking whether a reallocation would raise total economic welfare. When a reallocation affects more than one person, however, it is not always possible to ascertain what happens to that welfare total. Following Pareto, economists escape this problem by focusing on situations of economic inefficiency. Such situations have room for changes that would raise total economic welfare with certainty because no one would lose and some or all people would gain.

2. Economic inefficiency can be eliminated, and economic efficiency be attained, by fulfilling certain marginal conditions first stated by Pareto, including those concerning:

   a. the optimum allocation of a resource among producers of the same good;

   b. the optimum specialization of production among producers of the same good;

   c. the optimum composition of production and consumption;

   d. the optimum allocation of goods among consumers of the same goods.

3. A general requirement for the achievement of the Pareto optimum is: Whenever one can technically transform a little bit of one variable into a little bit of another, the marginal rate of technical transformation must equal the marginal rate of indifferent substitution. All equivalent marginal rates of technical transformation or of indifferent substitution must be equal. Pareto's efficiency criterion for judging the desirability of any given allocation of resources or goods enjoys wide assent among economists, but there are critics who do not accept the value judgments from which Pareto's criterion is derived.

4. A close relationship exists between market structure and the extent of economic efficiency achieved. When profit-maximizing firms and utility-maximizing households, *with the help of equilibrium prices established in perfect markets*, determine the optimum quantities they wish to trade, all conceivable Pareto conditions of economic efficiency come to be fulfilled.

5. *In imperfect markets*, on the other hand, the pursuit by firms and households of identical goals has no such beneficial effect. Indeed, economic efficiency then occurs only by accident, if at all.

6. Starting more than three decades ago, economists made their first attempts to measure the welfare loss implied by the prevalence of imperfect markets in the economy. An early measurement by Harberger put the loss at 0.1 percent of GNP, but a number of critics disagreed with this trivial estimate and supplied larger ones.

7. While exact measurements of economic inefficiency remain controversial, Leibenstein's work has persuaded many economists that X-inefficiency is all-pervasive and much more significant in scope than economic inefficiency.

8. Some economists argue that all the fuss about X-efficiency and economic efficiency is equally out of place and that an economy's *dynamic efficiency* is more important than either of these two. While it is obvious that a dynamically more efficient economy can in time overcome any output handicap imposed by static inefficiency, it is not obvious, as Schumpeter and Galbraith have argued, that monopolies and oligopolists are bound to produce superior dynamic efficiency. Empirical evidence suggests that technical advance is fastest in industries that have moderate barriers to entry and contain a blend of small and large firms that are neither monopolies nor perfect competitors.

KEY TERMS

allocative efficiency
dynamic efficiency
economic efficiency
economic inefficiency
law of diminishing returns
marginal conditions
marginal rate of substitution *(MRS)*
marginal rate of transformation *(MRT)*
Pareto optimum
static efficiency
technical efficiency
X-efficiency

QUESTIONS AND PROBLEMS

1. *Ms. A:* When Pareto advocates a move towards economic efficiency, he is urging us to get a marginal benefit at a zero marginal cost.
Mr. B: Right. And he wants us to forgo any change in which a marginal benefit comes at a positive marginal cost because we can't measure the size of the marginal cost.
Evaluate these statements.
2. Invent a marginal rate of transformation between fishing vessels and sewing machines for the Soviet Union and another such *MRT* for Bulgaria so that it would pay the Soviet Union to specialize in producing fishing vessels, while Bulgaria specialized in sewing machines. Using

your numbers, prove that specialization and trade could make everyone better off at the same time. Review Close-Up 14.1 and ask yourself what kind of data economic planners in Comecon would need to determine marginal rates of transformation.
3. Suppose a gasoline shortage developed this winter and the U.S. government ("in the interest of fairness") were to allocate equal quantities of gasoline to each driver. Would this allocation be economically efficient? What difference would it make whether the government allowed or forbade people to trade its rations?
4. "If one family consumed, each month, ten times as much of each and every good as another family, the situation would be very unjust, even though it would be economically efficient." Comment on the validity of this statement.
5. The following is another marginal condition of economic efficiency: *Economic efficiency requires that the marginal rate of transformation between any two resources,* x *and* y, *be the same for any two producers,* α *and* β, *using both resources (to produce identical or different goods).*
   a. Explain this condition. (*Hints:* The *MRT* in this case refers to the rate at which a little bit of, say, labor can be exchanged for a little bit of, say, machine time in the process of production while output remains unaffected. This *MRT* is equivalent to the marginal rate of technical substitution discussed in Chapter 5. You might adapt Table 14.4 for your answer, imagining producers to "eat up" labor and machine time to produce visible products, just as consumers eat apples and butter to produce invisible satisfaction.)
   b. Show why this condition would be fulfilled under perfect competition but probably not under imperfect competition.
6. *Ms. A:* All that glitters is not gold. I can see a real problem with *implementing* moves away from economic inefficiency: Even if two parties wanted to get together and make themselves better off, third parties (who would become no worse off by objective standards) would interfere because these

third parties would *feel* worse off. After all, most people look at their own welfare *relative to* that of others. They rejoice when others get worse off, and they resent it when others get better off. Hence they will do their best to obstruct any changes that improve the lot of others.

Mr. B: You are much too cynical. People aren't as malevolent as you depict them. Most people rejoice when others rejoice.

What do you think? Does the existence of malevolence or benevolence destroy the applicability of the Pareto criterion?

7. *Ms. A:* There is nothing impossible about interpersonal comparisons of utility. When there is one orange left at the end of a long hike, I know exactly which family member needs it the most. When some people have mink coats and others starve, I know exactly who should be helped at the expense of whom. It just takes a little bit of imaginative empathy, of which Pareto seems to have none.

Discuss. (*Hint:* Consider the difference between making scientific statements and moral judgments.)

8. *Mr. A:* The argument that large firms with monopoly power are likely to tolerate X-inefficiency is absurd. The lower-than-possible profits would depress stock prices below their potential value; outsiders would put in a bid for a controlling interest; these outsiders would oust the old management and then redirect the firm's behavior to eliminate all traces of X-inefficiency.

Mr. B: Of course. Or the existing management would eliminate X-inefficiency for fear of such takeover bids.

What do you think?

SELECTED READINGS

Amoroso, Luigi. "Vilfredo Pareto." *Econometrica*, January 1938, pp. 1–21.

An expanded story of Pareto's life and work.

Boulding, Kenneth E. "Welfare Economics." In *Collected Papers*, vol. 1. Boulder: Colorado Associated University Press, 1971, chap. 24; *Also available in* Bernard F. Haley, ed. *A Survey of Contemporary Economics*, vol. 2. Homewood, Ill.: Irwin, 1952, chap. 1.

A more advanced treatment of Pareto's ideas.

Buchanan, James M. et al., eds. *Toward a Theory of the Rent-Seeking Society*. College Station: Texas A & M University Press, 1981.

A collection of 18 essays on the resource-wasting activities by which people seek transfers of wealth through the aegis of the state.

Drucker, Peter F. *Management: Tasks, Responsibilities, Practices*. New York: Harper and Row, 1974.

Galbraith, John Kenneth. *American Capitalism: The Theory of Countervailing Power*, rev. ed. Boston: Houghton Mifflin, 1956.

Includes the thesis that imperfect competition among oligopolistic giants promotes dynamic efficiency.

Harberger, Arnold C. "Three Basic Postulates for Applied Welfare Economics: An Interpretive Essay." *Journal of Economic Literature*, September 1971, pp. 785–97.

A vigorous defense of the much criticized consumer surplus approach to measuring welfare effects.

Kamien, Morton I. and Schwartz, Nancy L. "Market Structure and Innovation: A Survey." *Journal of Economic Literature*, March 1975, pp. 1–38.

Kohler, Heinz. *Scarcity and Freedom: An Introduction to Economics*. Lexington, Mass.: D.C. Heath, 1977, chap. 5.

A graphical exposition of some of the Pareto conditions.

Leibenstein, Harvey. *Beyond Economic Man: A New Foundation for Microeconomics*. Cambridge: Harvard University Press, 1976.

An expanded discussion of X-efficiency.

Mansfield, Edwin, et al. *The Production and Application of New Industrial Technology*. New York: Norton, 1977.

A superb discussion of empirical research.

Mishan, E. J. *Welfare Economics: Five Introductory Essays*. New York: Random House, 1964.

A more advanced treatment of Pareto's ideas.

Pareto, Vilfredo. *Manual of Political Economy*. New York: Augustus M. Kelley, 1971.

This is the only one of Pareto's works available in English. Note William Jaffé. "Pareto Translated: A Review Article." *Journal of Economic Literature*, December 1972 as well as the controversy elicited by this review (same journal, March 1974).

Rowley, Charles K. and Peacock, Alan T. *Welfare Economics: A Liberal Restatement*. New York: Wiley, 1975.

   An advanced discussion of the relationship between Pareto's ideas and liberalism.

Scherer, F. M. *Industrial Market Structure and Economic Performance*, 2nd ed. Chicago: Rand McNally, 1980, chap. 15.

   A superb discussion of the relationship between market structure and technological innovation.

Schumpeter, Joseph A. *Ten Great Economists: From Marx to Keynes*. New York: Oxford University Press, 1951, chap. 5 on Vilfredo Pareto.

Seligman, Ben B. *Main Currents in Modern Economics*. Chicago: Quadrangle, 1962, pp. 386–403.

   A critical review of the work of Pareto.

Williamson, Oliver. *The Economics of Discretionary Behavior: Managerial Objectives in a Theory of the Firm*. Englewood Cliffs: Prentice-Hall, 1964.

   On managers' ability to let costs drift up at the expense of profit to finance their own objectives.

CHAPTER 15

Equity

Even in the absence of technical inefficiency, scarcity can be more severe than necessary. As the previous chapter noted, such a situation can arise when there is *economic* inefficiency, when it is possible to reallocate resources or goods in such a way that some people would consider themselves better off, while nobody would feel worse off than before. Total economic welfare, defined as the sum of individual welfares, can then be increased with certainty by abandoning economic inefficiency and embracing economic efficiency. Once economic efficiency has been achieved, total economic welfare cannot be raised further by increasing the welfare of some people *without* decreasing that of others. Some claim, however, that total economic welfare can often be raised even in such circumstances, namely by increasing the welfare of some people *at the expense of* that of others. Inevitably, such an increase in the welfare of some at the expense of others requires moral judgments about the very situations among which Pareto would not choose. Because Pareto wanted to be an objective scientist, he would not rank, on a scale of better or worse, alternative allocations of resources or goods if such ranking required comparison of the welfare gains of some people with the welfare losses of others. Prophets and poets, philosophers and politicians, on the other hand, rarely exercise Pareto's restraint. They urge us to pur-

sue **economic equity** or **economic justice,** a situation in which the apportionment of resources or goods among people is considered *fair*.

The Efficiency-Equity Distinction

The mapping of preferences with the help of indifference curves (see Chapter 3) allows us to highlight the crucial distinction between economic efficiency and economic equity. Panel (a) of Figure 15.1 depicts the circumstances of Mr. Jones, who is consuming 6 pounds of apples and 45 pounds of butter per year (point *A*). The single indifference curve going through *A* shows the marginal rate of substitution to be 0.5/1 in the vicinity of *A*. Panel (b) presents similar information for Ms. Smith. She consumes 44 pounds of apples and 35 pounds of butter per year (point *B*), but her *MRS* equals 3/1. The inequality of the two *MRS*s spells inefficiency (see "Condition 4: The Optimum Allocation of Goods Among Consumers of the Same Goods" in Chapter 14).

The diagram in panel (c), called the **Edgeworth box,** depicts the same situation in a novel way. Jones's situation in panel (a) has been reproduced in the lower left-hand corner of the box, the origin of which is labeled 0_J. The position of Jones is again shown at point *A*, but a whole family of Jones's indifference curves has

FIGURE 15.1 The Edgeworth Box

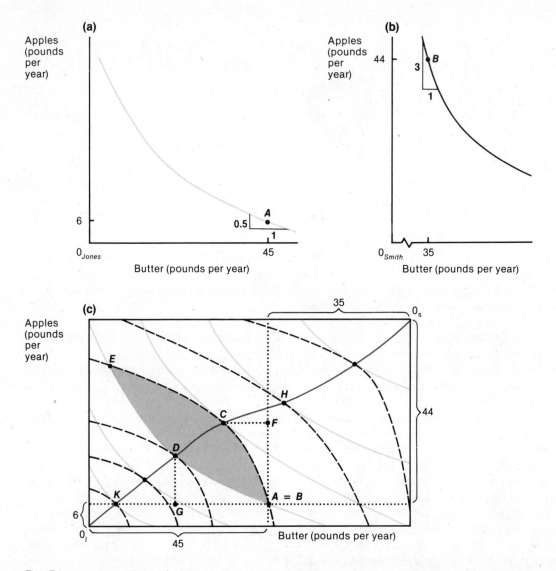

The Edgeworth box diagram[1] highlights the crucial distinctions between economic efficiency and economic inefficiency, and between economic efficiency and economic equity. Situations of inefficiency, shown in panels (a) and (b), can be depicted as lying off a contract curve, as at point A (which equals B) in panel (c). Such situations of inefficiency can be removed through peaceful trading that can make everyone better off at one of the many efficient positions on the contract curve. Moves *along* this curve, however, affect the equity of the situation and inevitably cause conflict.

---

[1]Although it is named after him, this box diagram does not appear in any of Edgeworth's writings; it was first used by Pareto in 1893. *See* Vincent J. Tarascio, "A Correction: On the Genealogy of the So-called Edgeworth-Bowley Diagram," *Western Economic Journal*, June 1972, pp. 193–97; and William Jaffé, "Edgeworth's Contract Curve," Parts I and II, *History of Political Economy*, Fall and Winter 1974, pp. 343–59 and 381–404.

been added to the curve going through point *A* (see the solid lines convex with respect to O_J).

Smith's situation in panel (b) has also been reproduced in panel (c) but panel (b) has been rotated 180 degrees, and point *B* of that graph has been positioned to coincide with point *A*. As a result, the origin of panel (b) now appears at the upper right-hand corner of the box, labeled O_S. The position of Smith is now also seen at *A*, but with respect to origin O_S; a whole family of Smith's indifference curves has been added to the one going through point *A* (see the dashed lines convex with respect to O_S).

The dimensions of the box, it should be noted, correspond exactly to the total annual quantities consumed by the two people. The vertical distance measures 50 pounds of apples per year. As the brackets indicate, Jones consumes 6 of these (measured up from O_J), and Smith consumes 44 (measured down from O_S). The horizontal distance measures 80 pounds of butter per year. Jones consumes 45 of these (measured right from O_J); Smith consumes 35 (measured left from O_S).

The inefficiency of the situation is immediately evidenced by the obviously different slopes, at point *A*, of the two people's indifference curves. (Recall that the slope of an indifference curve equals the *MRS*.) Now notice the manifold possibilities for improvement: If Smith gave up, in favor of Jones, an amount of apples equal to *AF* and received an amount of butter equal to *FC* in return, both people would end up at point *C*. Smith would be equally well off (as evidenced by the fact that *C* is found on the same dashed indifference curve as *A*), but Jones would be better off. (With respect to O_J, the solid indifference curve going through *C* is higher than the one going through *A*). At point *C*, the slopes of the two people's indifference curves are equal: therefore, their *MRS*s would be equal and efficiency would prevail.

Another alternative to *A* is found at point *D*: If Jones gave up, in favor of Smith, an amount of butter equal to *AG* and received an amount of apples equal to *GD* in return, both people would end up at point *D*. Jones would be equally well

off (as evidenced by the fact that *D* is found on the same solid indifference curve as *A*), but Smith would be better off. (With respect to O_S, the dashed indifference curve going through *D* is higher than the one going through *A*.) At point *D*, the slopes of the two people's indifference curves are equal, therefore, their *MRS*s would again be equal and efficiency would prevail.

As a matter of fact, if Jones and Smith traded with each other in such a way as to arrive at any point within the lens-shaped shaded area *ADEC*, both would reach a higher indifference curve at the same time! As Pareto taught us, however, economic efficiency requires *equality* of the *MRS*s of different people. In the Edgeworth box, the two *MRS*s are equal wherever the two persons' indifference curves have the same slope. All such efficient points (including *K, D, C,* or *H*) have been linked by a color line, which economists call the **contract curve**. They use this term because people who find themselves in inefficient positions not on the curve (as at point *A*) can *contract* to trade with each other so that one or both can become better off at a position on the contract curve (as between *C* and *D* in our example). All positions that are not on the contract curve are inefficient; they make it possible for people to play a **positive-sum game**, in which no one wins utility at someone else's expense and the sum of (positive) winnings and (nonexisting negative) losses is positive.

The Edgeworth box diagram in panel (c) illustrates an important matter: Efficiency does not depict a single position, but a whole range of them. Any position on the contract curve is equally efficient. Once the *MRS*s are equalized, possibilities for simultaneous mutual gain are exhausted, regardless of the *total* quantities of goods consumed by the two individuals. Point *K* is efficient, as is *D, C,* and *H*.

Note: Once efficiency has been achieved by moving from positions off the contract curve to positions on it, any one person can become better off *only at the expense of another*. Quite possibly, people can then play only a **zero-sum game**, in which the winnings of utility of some are exactly matched by the losses of others and the sum of (positive) winnings and (negative) losses is zero. As long as we cannot measure and compare utilities, we can never be sure if winnings balance losses, of course, but we can be sure of conflict all *along* the contract curve. The contract curve, therefore, can also be called a **conflict curve**. People who find themselves in positions on the curve (as at point *C*) find themselves *fighting* with one another about moving (as from *C* to *H* or *C* to *K*) because in such a case one person becomes better off only at the expense of the other. Note how at *H*, Jones's indifference curve is so much higher than at *C*, but that of Smith is so much lower. The opposite is the case at *K*. A move along the conflict curve raises the issue of *equity*.

The importance of the efficiency-equity distinction, which is brought out so clearly in the box diagram, cannot be overemphasized. In many potential conflict situations, which might give rise to divorces or strikes or even wars, there exist in fact possibilities for peaceful accommodation, for mutually beneficial trade, akin to a move from point *A* not on the contract curve to a point between *C* and *D* lying on it. Awareness of such possibilities can avoid many an unnecessary conflict because conflict is inevitable only if one is already on the contract curve and determined to move. Note: The advocates of equity do not agree among themselves on the meaning of their goal. Two major arguments dominate their debate about the proper slice of the ''pie'' that should go to any one person. One group seeks to promote *distributive* economic justice; another group pursues *commutative* economic justice.

Notions of Distributive Justice

The advocates of **distributive justice** argue that goods should be apportioned among people by some authority seeking to act justly. Such an authority is said to be acting justly whenever the percentage of all goods going to any one person is determined by this authority with reference to some personal characteristic that establishes the recipient as meritorious.

There is little agreement, however, as to who that authority should be or what characteristic it should consult. Should the characteristic be a person's IQ, race, color of hair? Would a person's needs, humanity, or working time be more appropriate?

Apportioning Goods According to Need

Some argue that equity is served best when all people receive goods in accordance with their needs. No one, probably, has popularized this idea more than Karl Marx (see Biography 15.1). He argued that goods would be apportioned according to need after the establishment of communism, an event he predicted to occur at the end of a long period of historical development and after the demise of both capitalism and socialism. At that future time, Marx argued, scarcity will not exist because a new and selfless kind of person will have emerged (with a greatly reduced desire for goods), while a new and much more productive economy will have developed (with a greatly expanded ability to produce goods). In terms of Figure 1.1, ''The Scarcity Problem'' (p. 5), by the time communism will have been established the left-hand circle will have shrunk and the right-hand circle will have expanded to eliminate the scarcity problem.

Many of Marx's followers, however, argue that need could and should become the principle of apportioning goods *now*. The satisfaction of ''true material needs,'' they say, requires minimal amounts and simple types of food, clothing, and shelter, some medical care, and relatively little else. These amounts, it is argued, may differ among individuals: a sick person will require more drugs and medical care than a healthy one, a hardworking adult more food and clothing than a newborn infant, any person in Maine more fuel than any person in Florida. However, assert many of Marx's followers, all people can get exactly what they need the moment they learn to identify and reject material desires that are ''false.'' Who needs fancy cameras, private airplanes, houses on islands in the middle of the sea, jet trips to the far corners of the globe?

BIOGRAPHY 15.1:

Karl Marx

Karl Marx (1818–1883) was born in Trier, Germany. He studied history, law, and philosophy at the universities of Bonn, Berlin, and Jena. He earned a doctoral degree in philosophy, then worked as a newspaper editor. His newspaper work brought trouble with the Prussian authorities and forced him to emigrate to France, then Belgium, and, finally, England. In London, he was part-time correspondent for *The New York Daily Tribune* for a decade; his meager earnings were supplemented by Friedrich Engels, who owned factories in Germany and England and was a lifelong friend and collaborator. Marx spent much time in the British Museum studying and writing. Through his writings, he came to influence the thought of generations; today, over a third of the world's population lives in countries calling themselves Marxist. Many espouse his teachings with religious fervor.

The major works of Marx include: *Economic and Philosophical Manuscripts* (1844), *The Communist Manifesto* (1848), *The Grundrisse* (1857–58), *Theories of Surplus-Value* (1861–63), and *Capital: A Critique of Political Economy* (vols. 1–3, 1867–80, edited by Engels 1883–94).

Marx provided a grandiose vision of historical evolution. As he saw it, *economic conditions* (the ways in which resources are owned and used and newly produced goods are apportioned) shape people's attitudes and actions and, ultimately, history. Capitalism, for example, is characterized by the crucial fact that natural and capital resources are owned by a small minority of the population—the capitalist class, or *bourgeoisie*. The vast majority of people own only their bodies, and have only their labor to sell. They are the working class, or *proletariat*. By virtue of their economic position, and independent of individual volition, argued Marx, these classes are antagonistic to each other. Inevitably, they struggle over the *economic surplus*, the difference between the total of goods produced and the portion needed to maintain and reproduce the capital and human resources who helped produce that total. To the extent that the bourgeoisie keeps the economic

surplus, said Marx, it *exploits* the proletariat. This exploitation does not arise from individual circumstances, occasionally and accidentally, but from the logic of the capitalist system—unavoidably and independently of individual intention.

Equally unavoidable is revolution. Workers will expropriate the bourgeois expropriators and seize political power. A new era of *socialism* will be ushered in; workers will enjoy ownership of nonhuman resources and will be the masters of the productive process rather than its slaves. "Let the ruling classes tremble. . . . The proletarians have nothing to lose but their chains. They have a world to win. WORKING MEN OF ALL COUNTRIES, UNITE!"[1]

But socialism will still have a defect, said Marx: the attitudes of workers will still be influenced by their experiences in the old society. Thus workers cannot be expected to work without material incentives or harsh commands. Because they will still have to be rewarded according to their contribution to production (such as hours worked) there will still be income inequality. Eventually though, socialism will turn into *communism*, which will have no defects at all. Communism will be an industrialized, classless, and nonexploitative society. Above all, the socialist transition stage will have produced a dramatic change in the outlook of people. A "new person" unlike the present ones will emerge, who will contribute freely and gladly to the well-being of all, being neither coaxed by material incentives nor by bureaucratic commands. The abundance created by economic growth and the lack of egoism exhibited by the new type of human being will make possible a new principle of production and distribution: "From each according to his ability, to each according to his need."[2]

[1] Karl Marx and Friedrich Engels, *Manifesto of the Communist Party*, in Robert C. Tucker, ed., *The Marx-Engels Reader*, 2nd ed. (New York: W. W. Norton, 1978), p. 500.
[2] Karl Marx, *Critique of the Gotha Program*, in Robert C. Tucker, ed., *The Marx-Engels Reader*, 2nd ed. (New York: W. W. Norton, 1978), p. 531.

People may think they need these things as long as parents and teachers, friends and neighbors, businesses and governments all conspire to enslave them to such "false material desires." But if people are made conscious of this propaganda, it is said, if they are inspired to shed false desires, scarcity will vanish, allowing all people to get exactly what they truly need. (See "Application 2: 'False' Wants Vs. 'True' Needs" in Chapter 12.) Figure 15.2 illustrates how rejecting false material desires is thought to lead to abundance.

Note: those who would apportion goods according to need leave unclear who is to define "true" material needs and "false" material desires. Is bread, for example, always a "true material need" while a jet trip to Paris is always a "false material desire"? Could the answer differ with circumstances? Who among the billions of people on earth can be trusted to give the correct answer? We clearly cannot let all persons decide for themselves, because if we did, we would return to the dilemma of scarcity illustrated in Chapter 1. Some people do consider cameras or

jet trips to Paris to be true needs; all true needs, as defined by all people for themselves, add up, in the left-hand part of Figure 15.2, to the outer broken circle, not to the inner solid one. The proposal summarized in Figure 15.2, therefore, requires that some authority (who allegedly knows better) decides—contrary to their opinions—what all other people "truly need" and apportions available goods accordingly.

Note also: When all people are assured of getting what they "truly need" (as defined by someone else), they have no incentive to either contribute to the process of production at all or to contribute in such a way as to produce just the types of goods that are "truly needed." Thus it will also be necessary for someone—perhaps the same authority who gives people what they "truly need"—to draft people into the labor force and to tell them what kinds of goods they must produce. Otherwise, people might just go on an endless vacation, trusting that they will get in any case whatever someone else has decided they need. Even if the recipients of goods should feel impelled by conscience to work and to work hard (and if these people didn't have to be threatened with punishment for loafing), only if someone told them exactly what to produce would the composition of the set of goods produced equal the composition required for the satisfaction of what someone has defined as "true needs." Otherwise the people who were working might be producing cars or satin sheets or television sets at the very time at which these had been defined as "false material desires." Under these circumstances, this production would be akin, in the eyes of authority, to producing totally useless things, such as cans of steamed cherry pits, jars of shredded bees' wings, or kegs of frozen glass splinters. Apportioning goods "according to needs" almost certainly implies a centralized definition of needs as well as a centralized direction of labor.

FIGURE 15.2   One Path to Abundance: Rejecting Material Desires that Are "False"

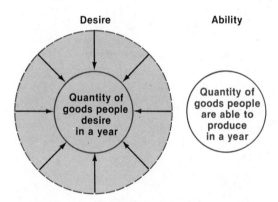

Some thinkers urge that people should abandon their "false material desires" and seek satisfaction of only their "true material needs" (note the shrinking of the left-hand circle). Abandoning "false" material desires would eliminate scarcity, it is said, because the goods people are able to produce (right-hand circle) are sufficient to satisfy the "true material needs" of everyone. Thus output could be apportioned according to need.

Apportioning Goods Equally to All

Some advocates of distributive justice would give all people, as a basic human right, an exactly equal share of the total set of goods produced in any one year. When the argument is presented as a matter of moral judgment, little can be said about it. However, two of the more complex arguments for the equal apportionment of goods were presented by an economist, Abba P. Lerner, and by a philosopher, John Rawls.

Abba Lerner. In order to illustrate Lerner's argument, let us suppose that a society's annual output of a multitude of goods were to be apportioned among 200 million persons. If the goods involved had freely flexible prices, one could distribute them most easily by apportioning among people an amount of, say, 2 trillion *dollars* and letting each person buy whatever quantities of whatever goods he or she could afford at whatever equilibrium prices emerged. Clearly, this method of distributing the available goods would work regardless of how much money income was given to any one person.

However, argues Lerner, it would surely be desirable to apportion the dollars (and hence the goods they can buy) in such a way as to maximize the total satisfaction people *as a group* derived from the goods available. For the sake of this desirable goal, says Lerner, one would have to give every person an exactly equal dollar amount (of $2 trillion divided by 200 million people, or of $10,000 per person in our example). This conclusion is based on Lerner's use of the principle of diminishing marginal utility, first discussed in the section on "The Concept of Utility: A Historic Note" in Chapter 3. Consider the effect of giving money income to any one person: Presumably, the first dollar received would be spent to satisfy that person's most urgent material desire (as defined by that person), the second dollar would be spent on the next urgent desire, and so on. Each additional dollar of income would thus raise the person's overall satisfaction (or utility) but by less and less. In other words, while the person's *total* utility derived from income would rise with higher income, the person's *marginal* utility of income would fall with higher income.

For any one person, A, the declining marginal utility of income is illustrated by line MU_A in Figure 15.3.

The first dollar received by person A would bring utility represented by the thin column *la*. Additional dollars would bring smaller *extra* or marginal utility, even though total utility would rise. Thus the 8,000th dollar received in a year would bring marginal utility of *mb* (which is smaller than *la*), but it would bring the total utility of all 8,000 dollars received up to area *lmba*, the *sum* of all those thin columns of marginal utility associated with the 1st, 2nd, 3rd, and, eventually, the 8,000th dollar received. Similarly, if person A were to receive 20,000 dollars per year, the 20,000th dollar would bring still lower marginal utility of *qf*, which would be but the last addition to a utility total then equalling *lqfa*.

According to Lerner, a similar story could be told about any other person, B. The first dollar given to B would bring utility represented by thin column *qg*. If B received a 5,000th dollar (measured from right to left in the graph), B's marginal utility of income would be only *pe*, but B's total utility would then equal *qgep*. And if B received 20,000 dollars, marginal utility would be only *lk*, but total utility *qgkl*.

How then, asks Lerner, can one possibly conclude that A and B and all others in this 200-million-person population should get an exactly equal $10,000 annual share of the 2 trillion dollars available (and of the goods they represent)? Surely, to squeeze the greatest possible amount of human welfare from the available goods would require, *in principle*, giving more income to those who could enjoy it more than to others who would enjoy it less. In our example, this principle seems to lead to a clear-cut conclusion: Because B's enjoyment at any given income level is always below A's, the total utility of $20,000 of income would be maximized if A (a more efficient pleasure machine) received $15,000 of income and B received only $5,000. (Note: if A and B received these amounts, their marginal utilities would be *pe* and equal to each other. Thus no reallocation of income could raise total utility.)

FIGURE 15.3 The Equal Income Argument

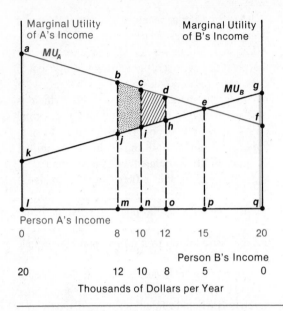

Person A's Income

| 0 | | 8 | 10 | 12 | 15 | 20 |

Person B's Income

| 20 | | 12 | 10 | 8 | 5 | 0 |

Thousands of Dollars per Year

All agree that one could hypothetically maximize the total welfare derived from a society's annual production of goods by apportioning the money income that can buy those goods in such a way (point *p*) as to equalize the marginal utility of money income among all persons (point *e*). Since one cannot in fact measure and compare people's marginal utility of income, however, it is argued by some that an absolutely equal income distri-bution (point *n*) is preferable to unequal distributions: In the face of uncertainty about the location of point *e*, it is said, equal dollar deviations from equality raise total welfare as often as they lower it, but each time total welfare is raised, it is raised by less (crosshatched area) than it is reduced (dotted area) when the total is lowered. This entire argument rests on the operation of the principle of diminishing marginal utility.

In real-life situations, however, we do not know people's marginal-utility-of-income lines, continues the argument. There exists no way to measure the satisfaction a person receives from the goods acquired by means of the spending of money income. One can measure a person's weight (as so many pounds), a person's height (as so many inches), and a person's temperature (as so many degrees), but one cannot measure a person's satisfaction (as so many "utils"?). Hence a graph such as Figure 15.3 must forever remain hypothetical. One can only *imagine* measuring A's marginal utilities for a 1st, 8,000th, and 20,000th dollar, plotting them as distances *la*, *mb*, and *qf*, and comparing them with similar data for B (such as *qg*, *oh*, and *lk*). Hence, one cannot know whether B's marginal utility line intersects A's marginal utility line at *e*, as in our example, or at some other point. One cannot know the true social-utility-maximizing apportionment of income.

If, however, each person received an identical income (of $10,000 in our example) corresponding to midpoint *n*, there would be a 50–50

chance that the distribution of income that would maximize utility in society (because A's and B's marginal utilities were equal to each other) was in fact to the right or to the left of our chosen point *n*. Every time the actual distribution of income deviated from the equal income distribution point *n* in the direction of the true (but unknown) point of equality of marginal utilities, total utility in society would go up. Thus moving income distribution from *n* to *o* (closer to ideal point *p*) would give A $2000 of additional income at the expense of B. As a result, A's total utility would rise by *ncdo*, but B's total utility would fall by *niho*, resulting in a social net gain in utility equal to crosshatched area *icdh*.

On the other hand, every time the actual distribution of income deviated from the equal income distribution point *n* in a direction away from the true but unknown point of equality of marginal utilities, total utility in society would go down. Thus, moving income distribution from *n* to *m* (farther from ideal point *p*) would give B $2000 of additional income at the expense of A. As a result, B's total utility would rise by *mjin*, but A's total utility would fall by more, namely *mbcn*, resulting in a social net loss in utility equal to dotted area *jbci*.

The argument concludes by noting that the *size* of the loss associated with an incorrect deviation from equality (the dotted area) would exceed the size of the gain associated with an equal correct deviation from equality (the cross-hatched area). Since, in a large population, frequent deviations from equality can be expected to result in the same frequency of losses as of gains, such deviations would create a decline in social welfare *with certainty*: 100 million cross-hatched-area gains would be overpowered by 100 million dotted-area losses. Thus, in the face of our inability to measure people's ability to enjoy income, a policy of absolute income equality is preferable to a policy of inequality.

Note: The validity of the Lerner argument is by no means universally accepted. To name just one criticism, many economists have been troubled by the thought that different people's marginal-utility-of-income schedules may be interdependent and that the lines drawn in Figure 15.3 may shift during the very process of income redistribution.

John Rawls.   Rawls asks us to imagine people "in a state of nature" in which they all rely, individually, on their own efforts. Because these people realize that social cooperation could give everyone a better life, they decide to form a society. They meet in an assembly for the purpose of drawing up a "social contract" that is to govern their relations with one another, including the way the benefits of their cooperation are to be apportioned among them. What rule of division will they agree upon?

People in this "original position," Rawls argues, cannot know what kind of personal position they will have in the new society about to be formed. They cannot know whether they will end up as butchers, coal miners, deep sea divers, cleaners of sewers, judges, tax assessors, captains of industry, inventors of life-saving drugs, or pilots of jets. Therefore, they will consider the matter impartially, and they will reject income inequality. Each person will fear ending up with the lowest-paying job and will want to press for a "maximin" rule that makes as large as possible the lowest income any person can get.

Rawls concludes that impartial people who do not have an ax to grind (because they do not know what their position in society will be) would come to agree unanimously on income equality. According to Rawls, income equality would, therefore, be the proper rule for our society in which such a unanimous agreement cannot be reached because real people do know their actual positions in society. Those with above-average incomes will defend inequality because it is in their interest to do so. (Rawls recognizes, however, that everyone might agree on inequality of income, if, in comparison to an egalitarian division, it made possible an improvement of everyone's position at the same time, as will be illustrated in Figure 15.5.)

Conclusion.   Any policy that divides incomes equally among all people would have identical implications for incentives as a policy of apportionment according to need. If everyone were assured of the same income as everyone else no matter what, someone would have to make sure that people worked at all and also that they produced the types of goods people wanted. Income differentials (for example, between those who worked hard and others who loafed or between those who produced what people wanted and others who produced what people did not want) that could provide these incentives would be outlawed. Therefore, some human authority, some type of economic commander-in-chief, would have to make people work and tell them what to make.

Apportioning Goods According to Hours Worked

A third variant of distributive justice demands that each person receive a share of society's total output corresponding to the number of hours that person worked. This policy requires that someone keeps track of hours of labor performed. If a janitor, a farmer, and a surgeon each worked 40 hours a week, it would only be fair according to this view to give the same income to each. Someone who worked 20 hours should then get half the amount given to the former three.

Unlike the previous two cases discussed above, this approach clearly has the advantage of providing a strong incentive to work, but it has at least two drawbacks. First, if strictly followed, unlike the "needs" and equality criteria, this criterion would give a zero share of goods to those who didn't work—even the very young, the disabled, or the very old who could not perform labor. Thus exceptions would surely have to be made, requiring someone's definition of "inability to work."

Second, as in the other instances above, there would exist no incentive for people to produce the right kinds of goods. If the hours-worked criterion were to be strictly followed, a person working 40 hours producing apples would get the same share of society's output as would someone else spending 40 hours packing Mississippi river-bottom mud that nobody wanted. Don't assume either that the apple producer would be more meritorious than the mud packer! What if people didn't want apples either, but preferred refrigerators? If refrigerator making, compared with apple growing, was risky (as to life and health), dirty, dull, and tiring, involved great and unwanted responsibilities, and had to be performed at night and on holidays, no one might volunteer for such work. Consumers would have no way to encourage refrigerator making and discourage apple producing with the help of income differentials: if any apple producer spent 40 hours instead in refrigerator making, the same income share would be assigned as before, so why should he or she switch?

Once more, this method of creating distributive justice implies the need for a central human

CLOSE-UP 15.1:

Income Equality in Cuba

In the 1960s, Che Guevara and Castro were eager to accomplish egalitarian income goals. The Cuban government introduced free food service at all places of work. It provided equal rations of food, clothing, and other goods in state stores. It made education and medical care and even buses and public phones available free of charge (and housing almost free). It provided all Cubans with free vacations at beach resorts.

The rate of absenteeism on the job soared. Productivity on the job and the quality of work plummeted. Said Castro rather sadly: "Perhaps our greatest idealism lies in having believed that a society . . . could, all of a sudden, be turned into a society in which everybody behaved in an ethical, moral way."

So Castro postponed the realization of some of his dreams. He provided every adult citizen with a "work force control card." A "labor history file" was set up by all enterprises for every worker. Students and housewives and workers and peasants were organized along military lines into "battalions" and "brigades" and *assigned* to jobs. They could not leave their jobs without government approval. All infractions of labor discipline (coming late to work, disobeying a superior, damaging the means of production, doing shoddy work, and even showing the wrong political attitude) were recorded in the person's file. People absent from work without a valid excuse for more than 15 days were sent to labor farms. Finally, a 1971 "antiloafing law" promised two years of labor camp to all able-bodied men (aged 17 to 60) who were not on a job or did not stay there. As a result, 100,000 *mongollones* (lazy birds) straggled forward to take jobs.

Source: Heinz Kohler, *Scarcity and Freedom: An Introduction to Economics* (Lexington, Mass.: D. C. Heath, 1977), pp. 501–502.

planner who would tell people what they should produce during the hours they worked.

The Notion of Commutative Justice

All the advocates of distributive justice focus on some *human authority acting justly* to establish a tight link between the output shares the authority allots to people and some personal characteristic of these people—their needs, their humanity, their industry. The advocates of **commutative justice** instead focus on the *just nature of an impersonal process* that generates any given apportionment of output. To them, the output shares ultimately received by people would be fair (even if they should be highly unequal) as long as these shares had been determined by the free choices of all people, all of whom enjoyed *equal opportunities* to influence the process of allocating resources to the production of goods.

For example, the advocates of commutative justice would be happy with a world in which all persons were given the chance, as far as possible, to own equal quantities of all resources and were given an equal freedom to use these resources to produce goods and to trade resources and goods with others. However, the advocates of commutative justice hasten to add, people so privileged should also be held responsible for the consequences of their choices.

Being given the chance to own the same amount of resources might require, first, a society that made free health care, general education, and vocational training available to all. These opportunities would serve the purpose of equalizing human resources owned insofar as it was possible and reasonable. (Any differences remaining among people's ability to sell labor services would then be traceable to such factors as their genetic makeup or their own choices. Presumably, one would not wish to equalize the skills of people by barring books from the intelligent until the retarded can catch up, or by dismembering the healthy until the crippled can be cured, or by forcing everyone to lead identical

lives as a result of making identical choices on everything.)

Being given a chance to own the same amount of resources might require, second, a society that redistributed, at the time of each person's death, any accumulations of natural and capital resources so as to keep their ownership as equal as possible. Differences might then be allowed only to the extent that people acted differently during their lifetimes, as by being thriftier or more hardworking than others.

Finally, an equal freedom to use resources might imply a world in which no one was allowed to do anything with resources that all others were not also allowed to do, and an equal freedom to trade resources and goods might imply that everyone was allowed to trade with anyone else at whatever terms were agreeable to the parties involved.

In short, the advocates of commutative justice conceive of economic activity as something like a card game, and they intend to make it fair. As long as one distributes cards at the beginning of the game fairly (equal quantities of resources to all) and as long as one follows rules equally applicable to all (equal freedom to use resources, to trade resources and goods), the end result is seen as just. But in a fair card game, some win and others lose! Similarly, in a society aspiring to commutative justice the incomes of people (and thus their share of output) can be expected to differ in the end.

Person A may decide to be a hermit, to have nothing to do with the rest of the world, and to live on whatever goods her resources can produce in isolation. Person B may earn $10,000 a year for work as a baker of bread (even though he could have gone to school and made music his career); he may also take in $5,000 a year in rent for 100 acres of his land used by someone else to grow asparagus. Person C may forgo income for a while, study music, and finally play in an orchestra for $30,000 a year, all the while growing lettuce on 100 acres of her land for a profit of $2,000 a year. Person D may go into the business of giving airplane rides, using owned resources as well as those hired from others—and incurring a $20,000 annual loss. And so it would go . . .

Would the distribution of income be fair? Decidely yes—the advocates of commutative justice would say—as long as each one of our friends could have done whatever any one of them did in fact do!

Note: A society that is commutatively just would not require any central planner defining "true needs" or making sure that people contributed to the process of production and did so by producing the right kinds of goods. Income recipients would decide for themselves what their needs were. If they spent money on symphony concerts and asparagus (rather than on bread, lettuce, and airplane rides), people producing the former would end up with higher incomes than others producing the latter. Thus the system here contemplated would automatically see to it that high incomes (and large shares of output) would go only to those people who had allocated resources in ways pleasing to people. And it would give low incomes (and small shares of output) to those others who had allocated resources in ways not conducive to satisfying people's most urgent needs—*as defined by these people themselves*. This apportionment of income would happen regardless of how hard producers had worked or how good their intentions had been. The objective fact that people preferred concerts over airplane rides would show itself in higher income in the former than in the latter activity. Given equal opportunities, higher incomes for concert performers would be regarded as perfectly fair, for the producer of unwanted airplane rides (or any other low-income person) would be free to overcome his or her low income by redirecting resources from what people wanted less to what they obviously wanted more eagerly.

Naturally, there would be some people in any society who could not take advantage of opportunities even if they were available (the retarded) or who might become victims of unfortunate accidents (an earthquake). Here the advocates of commutative justice—just like the advocates of the labor-hour variant of distributive

justice—suggest a humanitarian redistribution through government of some income from the more to the less fortunate.

The Personal Distribution of Income in the United States

People who have embraced one or another of the notions of economic equity discussed above usually cite statistics to prove how badly the world falls short of their standards of equity. Table 15.1 contains typical data on the personal distribution of income (which should not be confused with the functional distribution of income discussed in Chapter 8, Application 3). The table shows a highly unequal distribution of income. Note how the poorest 14.7 percent of all households (with 1978 incomes under $5,000) received only 2.4 percent of that year's aggregate household income, while the richest 3 percent of households (with incomes above $50,000) received 11.6 percent of the total.

The Lorenz Curve

The Lorenz curve is a graphical device that shows the way in which income (or wealth) is apportioned among the members of any group and highlights the extent of equality or inequality among them. Figure 15.4 shows how to graph the data in Table 15.1 by drawing a square measuring percentage of total money income received on the vertical axis and the percentage of households on the horizontal axis. Households are arranged from left to right from the one with the lowest to the one with the highest income.

The straight line that has been drawn from the bottom left corner at 0 to the top right corner at *e* is the **line of perfect equality**, because it represents the hypothetical position of the Lorenz curve if the same amount of money income went to each household. If all households in the country shared total income equally, 20 percent of the households would share 20 percent of total income (at *a*), 40 percent of all households would share 40 percent of total income (at *b*), and so on,

TABLE 15.1   The Distribution of Money Income Before Taxes Among U.S. Households in 1978

Income Class (1)	Percent of Households in Class (2)	Percent of Total Income Received by Households in Class (3)	Percent of Households in Class or Lower Ones (4)	Percent of Total Income Received by Households in Class or Lower Ones (5)
Under $5,000	14.7	2.4	14.7	2.4
$ 5,000–$ 9,999	18.4	7.7	33.1	10.1
$10,000–$14,999	16.7	11.5	49.8	21.6
$15,000–$19,999	15.3	14.9	65.1	36.5
$20,000–$24,999	12.2	15.4	77.3	51.9
$25,000–$49,999	19.8	36.5	97.1	88.4
$50,000 and over	3.0	11.6	100.0	100.0

In 1978, some $1,371.1 billion of aggregate household income was distributed in a highly uneven fashion among 73.33 million U.S. households.
SOURCE: U.S. Bureau of the Census, *Current Population Reports*, Series, P–60, No. 121, "Money Income in 1978 of Households in the United States" (Washington, D.C.: U.S. Government Printing Office, 1980), p. 3.

until 100 percent of all households shared 100 percent of total income (at *e*).

Note: This line of perfect equality should not be called one of perfect *equity*, or *justice*, for there is no objective way of defining what apportionment of income is perfectly just. One can, however, determine objectively whether income is apportioned perfectly equally, be that considered just or not.

At the other extreme, if one household received all the money income while all the others received none of it, what would the Lorenz curve look like? If we arranged the households on the horizontal axis as before on the basis of income, we would find that the poorest 20 percent of all households received 0 percent of total income (at *g* rather than at *a*), that the poorest 40 percent of all households similarly shared 0 percent of total income (at *h* rather than *b*), and so on. Even 99 percent of all households would still share 0 percent of total income (just a little bit to the left of *f* rather than to the left and below *e*). Yet when we considered all households, including the one having all the income, we would find that 100 percent of households had 100 percent of income

(at *e*). Thus we could call the line 0*fe* a **line of perfect inequality,** because it represents the

FIGURE 15.4   The Lorenz Curve

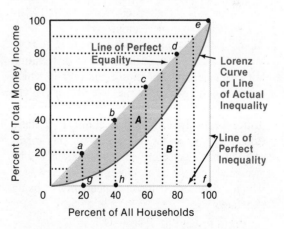

This Lorenz curve is a representation of the way in which money income was apportioned among U.S. households in 1978. The ratio of area *A* to *A+B* is the *Gini coefficient*. (The data used to plot this graph were taken from the fourth and fifth columns of Table 15.1.)

hypothetical position of the Lorenz curve if all the income went to one household and none of it to all the others.

In reality, 1978 money income in the United States was distributed neither perfectly equally (as would be shown by the line of perfect equality) nor perfectly unequally (as shown by the line of perfect inequality). Plotting the data of columns (4) and (5) of Table 15.1 reveals the actual Lorenz curve or the **line of actual inequality**. Like a loose string fastened to points 0 and *e*, this line hanging below the line of perfect equality (0*e*), and above that of perfect inequality (0*fe*), provides a visual representation of actual income inequality in the United States. Any increase in equality would shift it toward 0*e*, any decrease toward 0*fe*. In fact, the extent of income inequality has been unchanged for many decades.

The Gini Coefficient

Economists often summarize the extent of personal income inequality with the help of the **Gini coefficient**, the ratio of shaded area *A* (between the lines of perfect equality and actual inequality) to areas *A* + *B* (between the lines of perfect equality and perfect inequality). Thus the Gini coefficient can hypothetically range from 0 (perfect equality) to 1 (perfect inequality), but in the United States it typically lies in the 0.35 to 0.45 range. Whether one considers such a distribution fair or not depends, of course, entirely on which criterion of equity one wishes to embrace. Advocates of the absolute-equality type of distributive justice certainly cannot find comfort in these statistics. Whether the proponents of other forms of economic justice are able to do so cannot be answered until we take a closer look at the way in which the observed income inequality is being generated.

How Income Inequality Is Generated

Except for any possible redistribution of income through government, households in the U.S.

economy receive money income in return for supplying to the process of production the services of human, natural, and capital resources that they own. Thus the money income earned by any one household (and the share of output it can claim) depends on three things: 1. on the (size and quality of the) stocks of resources owned, 2. on the rate at which these stocks are placed in the process of production, and 3. on the prices that are established in the resource markets for the use of the resources involved. Thus the principle of income distribution that the market economy follows is: *"From each according to his or her ability and willingness to contribute resources to the process of production, to each according to the market's objective evaluation of the output produced by these resources."*

The Ability to Contribute

Differences clearly exist with respect to the ability of different households to contribute resources to the process of production. Households own vastly different quantities and qualities of human, natural, and capital resources and not only because different households contain different numbers of people. As a result of differences in biological inheritance and differential rates of resource acquisition after birth (due, in turn, to differences in effort or luck), people come to own different stocks of human capital and of physical capital and natural resources as well. Those advocates of commutative justice who would endow people with as nearly equal stocks of resources as possible will find little to cheer about here.

The Willingness to Contribute

There is a second reason why household money incomes differ. Households often exhibit differential willingness to contribute resource services to the process of production. Not only do some household members stay out of the labor force entirely, but even those who do work do so for varying numbers of hours per year, simply because they differ from other people when it comes to choosing between leisure and the goods its sacrifice can bring. Similar differences in voluntary choice occur with respect to nonhuman resources. The advocates of commutative justice would find nothing to worry here.

Rates of Pay

Finally, a third reason for income differences is that households receive differential rates of pay for the resource services they do offer both in perfect and imperfect markets.

Perfect Markets.   As was noted in "Application 1: Wage Differentials" in Chapter 8, people who are free to move among jobs may fail to do so in spite of permanent wage differentials. Such wage differentials may be seen to equalize nonmonetary aspects of jobs, and such differentials cause income differences for the same number of hours worked. Similar differential returns can arise when people exhibit different attitudes toward risk taking with their nonhuman resources. Consider how some people will operate in the stock market, gamble in casinos, speculate in futures markets, and undertake risky innovations, while others will not (see Chapters 9 and 10). Inevitably, differences in monetary returns will arise as a result. Consider, finally, how perfect markets are not always in equilibrium. Multitudes of people who are engaged in similar activities jointly determine the values of the activities involved, and these values can change. Today, all the people demanding apples (or beef) and all the people supplying these goods may jointly determine that apples are worth $12 per bushel (and beef is worth $5 per pound). All the people demanding the services of apple pickers (or pasture land) and all the people supplying these resource services may jointly determine that such service is worth $4 per hour per apple picker (and $100 per year per acre of pasture land). Now consider how a sudden change in taste could raise the demand for apples and lower that for beef, how the wages of apple pickers and the rents of orchard land would suddenly rise (together with the price of apples), while the

wages of butchers and the rents of pastures would plummet (together with the price of beef). Through no fault of their own, those contributing resources to the apple industry would suddenly find a pot of gold in their laps. Those contributing resources to the beef industry (and working just as hard as ever before) would suddenly find themselves being punished. This scenario illustrates the price system's way to encourage people to reallocate resources: to make butchers become apple pickers, to make pastureland owners grow apple trees. Temporarily, though, their rates of return would surely differ. The advocates of commutative justice wouldn't mind. They would, however, object to differential rates of pay arising from the use of monopoly power.

Imperfect Markets.   In the presence of imperfect markets, otherwise temporary differences in returns to resources can become permanent ones and can then contribute to permanent differences in income, which people cannot escape by appropriate resource reallocations. The market price of beef may turn out to be $10 per pound (instead of $5 per pound) if government helps beef producers form a cartel and helps defend the cartel against would-be intruders by restricting imports, along with new domestic production. The market price of butchers may turn out to be $20 per hour (instead of $4 per hour) if government helps these workers restrict their numbers (with the help of labor unions or "professional" licensing boards) and thus prevents other workers who earn less from becoming butchers and thereby eliminating the artificial wage differentials.

Indeed, economists have in recent years spent much effort trying to determine how successful monopoly power has been in restricting resource mobility, in raising the prices of favored resources, and thus in redistributing income towards the holders of such power. Table 15.2 summarizes the results obtained by two researchers. As the table shows, monopoly power (as measured by concentration ratios and entry barriers) has indeed raised profit rates. Consider how, in the 1936–40 study, high concentration always produced higher profit rates than moderate concentration, while higher entry barriers, given concentration, did the same.

Note: These results are controversial.[2] Other economists have attributed the apparent correlation between profitability and monopoly power in Table 15.2 to a number of errors: the use of accounting instead of economic profit, the failure to account for the absolute size of firms studied (large ones being more prevalent in concentrated industries and earning high profit for being technically more efficient), the subjective definitions of "high" and "moderate" concentration, the subjective classification of entry barriers, the use of too small a sample of industries, the use of time periods in which profits were abnormally high, and more.

[2]*See*, for instance, Yale Brozen, "Bain's Concentration and Rates of Return Revisited," *Journal of Law and Economics*, October 1971, pp. 351–69, and "Concentration and Profits: Does Concentration Matter?" *Antitrust Bulletin*, Summer 1974, pp. 381–99; and Harold Demsetz, "Are Large Corporations Inefficient?" in M. Bruce Johnson, ed., *The Attack on Corporate America* (New York: McGraw-Hill, 1978), pp. 245–51.

Conclusion

The observed inequality of income in the U.S. market economy is clearly not the result of any deliberate distribution according to need or hours worked, and it directly contradicts the ideal of absolute income equality. Thus the advocates of all three types of distributive justice discussed above are bound to see economic injustice. The same disillusionment is likely to descend upon the advocates of commutative justice. Their ideal of equal opportunity remains unrealized when resource stocks are not equally distributed and when permanent price differences for resource services are allowed to emerge solely because of monopolistic market restrictions.

Creating Economic Justice

It is hardly surprising that proposals abound for turning perceived economic injustice into economic justice. Nor is it surprising that two basic approaches are recommended: promoting com-

TABLE 15.2   Profit Rates vs. Concentration and Entry Barriers: U.S. Manufacturing

| | Entry Barriers | | |
Concentration	Low to Moderate	Substantial	Very High
1936–40 (20 industries)			
High	10.5	10.2	19.0
Moderate	5.3	7.0	—
1947–51 (20 industries)			
High	15.4	14.0	19.0
Moderate	10.1	12.5	—
1950–60 (30 industries)			
High	11.9	11.1	16.4
Moderate	8.6	12.2	—

Studies by Bain and Mann related average profit rates on stockholders' equity to industrial concentration and entry barriers. An 8-firm concentration ratio of 70 or more was considered "high," a lower one "moderate." Entry barriers were defined as "very high" when firms could hold prices 10 percent or more above minimum average total cost without inducing new entry. Bain included industries making automobiles, cigarettes, high-quality fountain pens, liquor, tractors, and typewriters in this group. Barriers were defined as "substantial" when prices could be held 5–9 percent above minimum ATC; such industries included copper, complex farm machines, petroleum refining, high-quality men's and specialty shoes, soap, and steel. Industries that could keep price only 1–4 percent above minimum ATC had "low to moderate" barriers and included producers of canned fruits and vegetables, cement, simple farm machinery, flour, low-quality fountain pens, gypsum products, meat packing, metal containers, rayon, women's and low-quality men's shoes, tires, and tubes.
SOURCES: Joe S. Bain, *Barriers to New Competition* (Cambridge: Harvard University Press, 1956), pp. 192–200; H. Michael Mann, "Seller Concentration, Barriers to Entry, and Rates of Return in Thirty Industries," *Review of Economics and Statistics,* August 1966, pp. 296–307.

mutative justice and promoting distributive justice.

Promoting Commutative Justice

Some people argue for government intervention to promote equal opportunity. To enhance a more equal distribution of resource stocks, they support measures such as public education, job training, and health care. They also support any and all measures to eliminate monopolistic practices (by private individuals and groups as well as by government) that differentially restrict people's opportunities to utilize their resources.

Promoting Distributive Justice

Other people argue for government intervention to promote not equal *opportunity*, but equal or less unequal *end results*. They usually support some kind of "Robin Hood scheme," taxing the rich and subsidizing the poor. They are not willing to rely on private charity to redress the inequality they observe. Rejecting private handouts to beggars as well as soup kitchens, church missions, and even the extended family, they opt for governmental aid in kind (commodity distributions, medical clinics, public housing) or in cash (agricultural subsidies, negative income taxes, rent supplements, welfare payments, and the like). Schemes of this sort, if pushed vigorously enough, can, however, pose a problem.

A significant amount of governmental redistribution can destroy the important incentives the price system creates as we already noted in Chapter 8 when discussing Close-Up 8.1 "Economics According to the Rats," and Close-Up 8.2 "Negative Income Tax and Labor Supply." Consider the example earlier in the present chapter of a change in demand from beef to apples. If one taxed suddenly rich apple pickers and orchardland owners and subsidized suddenly poor butchers and pastureland owners, why should butchers still move to become apple pickers? Why should pastureland owners bother about planting apple trees? The attempt to be "fair" would take the heart out of the price system's

message. Instead of telling people that they could recapture their once higher incomes only by doing what sovereign dollar-voting consumers had decreed (taking resources out of the beef industry and putting them into the apple industry instead), people would be getting quite a different message: *"No matter whether you produce apples or beef, your income will be, more or less, the same."* Of course, people would then have little reason to change their behavior; resources would *not* be used efficiently for the purposes most wanted by households.

In short, as long as the payment of income is tied to contributions made to society's output, *differential* payments are necessary based not on effort put in, but on the objective result achieved; that is, based on whether the right kind of output is produced. Without differential payments, there couldn't be rewards and penalties to entice required changes in behavior.

The incentive problem is even greater if the tie between income received and contribution is broken entirely. Suppose all persons were guaranteed, through an appropriate program of government taxation and subsidies, an exactly identical income, independent of their contribution to production. Such a policy would effectively countermand *all* the orders of the price system with this single message: *"No matter what you do, your income will, ultimately, be the same!"* Under such circumstances, people may wonder about working only three hours a day, if at all. The nation's production-possibilities frontier would suddenly collapse on itself. Everyone would be contributing fewer resources for use in the process of production. Society's output and, therefore, society's total money income would fall. Like children fighting over a pie and spilling half of it on the floor, our egalitarian crusaders would have destroyed the very thing they wanted to distribute. The latest message to all, printed above in italics, would turn out to have been a classic Delphic oracle indeed. Everyone's income would ultimately be *the same* all right, but the same *as everyone else's* (and close to zero), not the same *as before!*

Many thoughtful economists, therefore, are

ANALYTICAL EXAMPLE 15.1:

Monopoly and the Distribution of Wealth

As was noted in the section on "Fisher's Concept of Capital" in Chapter 9 (p. 263), a future stream of income can be capitalized to yield its present market value. This procedure was applied in Analytical Example 11.3, "The Market Value of Monopoly Power" (p. 344) to calculate the market values of such income-producing assets as taxi and TV-station licenses, baseball franchises, stock-exchange seats, truck operating rights, and more. The very first owners of such assets usually get them for nothing; at that very moment these owners receive great wealth because the expectation of greater-than-competitive returns from these assets capitalizes into a high market value.

In a pathbreaking study, two economists recently estimated the effect of such sudden wealth creation since 1890 on the 1962 distribution of wealth in the United States. The results, some of which appear in the accompanying table, are striking: In the absence of past monopoly (which has channeled a stream of above-competitive payments from consumers to holders of monopoly power), the 1962 wealth distribution might have looked like column (4), (5), (6), or (7) rather than column (3). The wealthiest would have been less wealthy and the poorest less poor, the extent of the difference depending on the indicated assumptions about the probable size of monopoly profits and their distribution over time.

Thus the 93.3 percent of households that in fact held 44.5 percent of total wealth in 1962 (subtotal A) would have held anywhere from 54.1 to 79.6 percent of total wealth in the absence of past monopoly. The wealthiest 6.7 percent of households, on the other hand (subtotal B), would have been relatively worse off in the absence of past monopoly, holding not 55.5 percent, but only 20.4 to 45.9 percent of total wealth.

hesitant to recommend creating perfect income equality and breaking the link between income and productive contribution. They recognize that people generally must be given rewards in order to contribute to the process of production at all. Without such rewards, the world's work simply would not get done. They also recognize that people must be given differential rewards if the right things are to be done. Most economists do not rule out, of course, a *limited* redistribution to offset income differences arising from factors beyond people's control, such as inheritance or monopolistic practices.

Figure 15.5 illustrates the fairness-incentive problem graphically. Consider the case of two persons (or groups of persons), P and R. Let P be poor and have no earning capacity at all (or a low one). Let R earn $20 per hour and be rich. In

accordance with our analysis in Figure 8.4 "An Individual's Income-Leisure Choice" (p. 221), we would not be surprised if R, when taxed to support P (and when thus receiving an effectively lower wage), were 1. to reduce hours worked and 2. to reduce hours worked all the more the higher was the tax. Some of the possibilities are shown in Table 15.3. In this example, society's income is maximized (at $160) if R is not taxed at all and P receives nothing, as in row (A). In row (D), society's income is cut in half (to $80) if a tax rate of 50 percent is introduced and P and R are given identical incomes (of $40 each). Yet in row (C) a less strict goal that maintains some income inequality enables P as well as R to be better off (with $48 and $72, respectively). Note that Figure 15.5 is based on columns (4) and (5) of Table 15.3.

| | Actual 1962 Wealth Distribution | | Hypothetical 1962 Wealth Distribution Without Past Monopoly If After-Tax Monopoly Profits since 1890 Equaled | | | |
| | | | 2 percent of GNP and were spread over | | 3 percent of GNP and were spread over | |
Wealth Class (1)	**Percent of Households in Class** (2)	**Percent of Total Wealth Held by Households in Class** (3)	**10 years** (4)	**40 years** (5)	**10 years** (6)	**40 years** (7)
Under $1,000	28.3	—	0.8	0.7	2.0	1.4
$1,000–$4,999	17.3	2.4	4.5	3.8	7.3	5.0
$5,000–$9,999	14.6	5.3	8.5	7.3	12.9	9.2
$10,000–$24,999	22.3	17.7	26.2	23.0	37.9	27.6
$25,000–$49,999	10.8	19.1	19.3	19.4	19.5	19.7
Subtotal A	93.3	44.5	59.2	54.1	79.6	62.8
$50,000–$99,999	4.3	14.8	10.2	12.1	3.7	9.7
$100,000–$199,999	1.2	8.1	7.0	7.3	5.4	6.7
$200,000–$499,999	1.0	14.1	11.6	12.3	8.1	10.7
$500,000 and over	0.3	18.5	12.1	14.1	3.1	10.2
Subtotal B	6.7	55.5	40.8	45.9	20.4	37.2

Source: William S. Comanor and Robert H. Smiley, "Monopoly and the Distribution of Wealth," *The Quarterly Journal of Economics*, 89 (May 1975): 190–92. Copyright 1975 Harvard University. (Note subsequent discussion in the February 1980 issue, pp. 185–98.)

FIGURE 15.5 The Limits to Redistribution

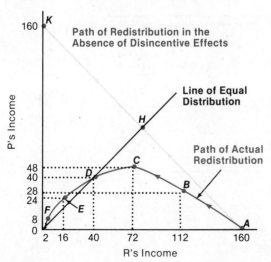

It may be impossible to redistribute income from rich R to poor P along line *AHK* (which implies an unchanged income total). It may only be possible to redistribute along line *ACF* (because the very act of redistribution has disincentive effects that reduce the income total). Under the circumstances, any attempt to redistribute a *given* income from a position of extreme inequality (*A*) to absolute equality (*H*) is bound to fail; an equal distribution of a *lower* income is possible (*D*), but this makes all people worse off than would be possible while maintaining some degree of inequality (*C*). The difference between *C* and *D* illustrates the exception to the Rawlsian absolute-equality rule.

TABLE 15.3   Hypothetical Income Redistribution

	Tax Rate on R (1)	Hours Worked by R (2)	Pre-Tax Income of R (3) = (2) × $20	Tax Revenue and Transfer to P (4) = (1) × (3)	After-Tax Income of R (5) = (3) − (4)
(A)	0%	8	$160	$ 0	$160
(B)	20%	7	140	28	112
(C)	40%	6	120	48	72
(D)	50%	4	80	40	40
(E)	60%	2	40	24	16
(F)	80%	0.5	10	8	2
(G)	100%	0	0	0	0

Redistributive taxation that changes extreme income inequality, in row (A), to absolute equality, in row (D), may well produce disincentive effects so strong that all people are worse off than would be possible under some degree of inequality, as in row (C).

ANALYTICAL EXAMPLE 15.2:
Private Charity in the United States

Do Americans redistribute their unequal incomes voluntarily? One economist investigated American behavior with respect to charitable donations. He analyzed the $2.1 billion worth of gifts claimed on 8.7 million individual tax returns in 1950. Of the $244 average gift, some 54 percent went for person-to-person support, 31 percent to religious organizations, and the remaining 15 percent to community chests, etc.

    Also analyzed, over several decades, were changes in such donations with respect to their "price" and the donors' income. (The "price" of donations is defined as 1 minus the donor's marginal tax rate; the higher the marginal tax rate, the greater is the tax saving associated with donations and thus the lower is their price.) As the table below indicates, the extent of donations was negatively related to price and positively related to donor income, which is just what one would expect for any normal good.

Year	(A) Percentage of Income Given as Donations (by income classes)			(B) The Price of Donations (by income classes)		
	Below $10,000	$10,000–$100,000	Above $100,000	Below $10,000	$10,000–$100,000	Above $100,000
1930	1.87	2.86	5.75	0.986	0.872	0.750
1936	1.80	2.44	10.40	0.946	0.767	0.318
1940	2.07	3.33	14.93	0.954	0.697	0.280
1946	5.12	4.90	13.51	0.794	0.481	0.150
1950	4.84	4.48	10.07	0.818	0.618	0.239
1956	4.44	4.74	16.07	0.802	0.561	0.146
1960	4.20	4.45	17.14	0.790	0.608	0.148
1966	3.56	3.49	16.38	0.820	0.671	0.285

Source: Robert A. Schwartz, "Personal Philanthropic Contributions," *Journal of Political Economy*, November/December 1970, pp. 1264–91. Table adapted by permission of the University of Chicago Press. © 1970 by the University of Chicago.

SUMMARY

1. The advocates of economic *efficiency* aim to raise total economic welfare by reallocating resources or goods whenever this results in some people feeling better off while nobody feels worse off. The advocates of economic *equity* (who do not accept the taboo against interpersonal comparisons of welfare) aim to raise total economic welfare by reallocating resources or goods whenever this results in some people feeling better off, while others are judged to feel worse off *to a lesser degree*. The crucial distinction between economic efficiency and economic equity can most clearly be seen with the help of the Edgeworth box diagram. Movements to its *contract curve* illustrate moves toward economic efficiency from which all can gain at the same time. Movements along its *conflict curve* illustrate alleged moves toward economic equity from which some people gain, while others lose.

2. The advocates of equity do not agree among themselves. Some urge the creation of *distributive justice*, a situation in which goods are apportioned among people by some authority seeking to act justly, preferably by consulting some personal characteristic that measures the recipient's merit. This personal characteristic could be a person's "needs," a person's "basic human right to an equal output share," or the number of hours a person works. The use of "needs" or "basic human rights" as criteria of apportionment produces serious problems with incentives. Using the criterion of hours worked overcomes incentive problems only in part.

3. The incentive problems disappear when equity is viewed as *fairness of the process* that produces and distributes goods rather than as *fairness of the end result* of that process. The advocates of *commutative justice* aim to create a situation in which goods are apportioned among people as a result of free choices by all people, all of whom enjoy as nearly equal opportunities as possible in the process of resource allocation.

4. The actual distribution of money income among households in the United States is highly unequal. This inequality can be illustrated in tabular form but also with the help of the *Lorenz curve* or the *Gini coefficient*. Excepting advocates of absolute income equality, proponents of economic equity cannot tell whether their goal has been fulfilled by looking solely at actual inequality without looking at how actual inequality is being generated.

5. Income inequality among households is generated by differences in ability or willingness to contribute resources to the process of production and by the receipt of differential rates of pay for the resource services they do offer. Differential rates of pay can arise in perfect markets; contributing causes include equalizing wage differentials, differing attitudes toward risk, and disequilibrium situations. Differential rates can also arise as a result of monopoly power exercised in imperfect markets. Given the causes of observed income inequality in the United States, neither the proponents of distributive justice nor those of commutative justice are likely to approve of the observed inequality.

6. It is hardly surprising that proposals abound for turning perceived economic injustice into economic justice. The proponents of commutative justice seek to achieve equal opportunity; those of distributive justice seek equal or less unequal end results. The latter approach, if pursued vigorously enough with the help of government, however, runs into the fairness-incentive dilemma.

KEY TERMS

commutative justice
conflict curve
contract curve
distributive justice
economic equity
economic justice
Edgeworth box
Gini coefficient
line of actual inequality
line of perfect equality
line of perfect inequality

Lorenz curve
positive-sum game
zero-sum game

QUESTIONS AND PROBLEMS

1. Consider panel (c) of Figure 15.1, "The Edgeworth Box."

a. Indicate the positions to which Jones and Smith might move, without either of them becoming worse off, if their initial position was at E. What if their initial position was at F or G?

b. Imagine that one could measure total utility in the third dimension above the diagram. What would the utility mountain look like above the contract curve?

c. Imagine that Jones and Smith had identical tastes and, therefore, identical sets of indifference curves. Would mutually beneficial trade between them still be possible? Explain.

d. Change "Jones" to "labor union" and "Smith" to "employer." Change "apples" to "wages" and "butter" to "vacations." Re-interpret the diagram as a model of collective bargaining. What would happen if union and employer *started out* at a position on the contract curve?

e. Some diplomats like to "trade" with their counterparts; others call this "appeasement" and cry: "Millions for defense, not a penny for tribute!" Illustrate these attitudes with the help of the Edgeworth box.

f. Draw a new Edgeworth box to depict the following: "Jack Sprat can eat no fat, his wife can eat no lean."

2. *Mr. A:* Interpersonal comparisons of utility are impossible. No one can say with confidence: "Your headache is worse than mine," or "I enjoy apple pie more than you." Therefore, no one can ever tell which apportionment of goods among people is fair.

Ms. B: I can. When some people can afford private planes and yachts, while others lack insulin or milk, economic injustice prevails. Evaluate these two positions.

3. "People are socially conditioned to desire many things. Honest self-examination, objective observation of others, as well as all the sacred texts of humanity teach us the same thing: People are better off, if they don't get all they want. The government should decide what people truly need and ought to get." Evaluate this position.

4. "Putting it bluntly, the Marxists are telling us that '*need* creates *right*': need creates the right of the hungry to an adequate diet, of the homeless to housing, of the sick to medical care, of the freezing to fuel, and so on, without end. But that is absurd. Such a philosophy implies that someone has the duty to provide and that there can be rights without responsibilities." Evaluate this position.

5. *Mr. A:* People should not get differential rewards. I am for *equality*. That is why I think that everyone should get the same money income no matter what. It would only be fair. We are all humans, after all.

Ms. B: You hypocrite! Would you really want to live in a society where you'd have a zero chance of being rich? I doubt it. Why are you so interested in good grades, accumulating credits, making the Dean's list, getting that scholarship, winning that best-thesis prize, and taking home that *magna cum laude* degree? If you were interested in equality, you would be content with being indistinguishable from all other students. In fact, you would leave college without that sheepskin and be equal with everyone else who never went to college.

Evaluate these two positions.

6. *Mr. A:* Lerner's income-equality argument is a farce. He argues for equality allegedly because we can't measure people's capacity to enjoy income, hence cannot justify departures from equality. Do you seriously think he would argue against equality, if we could make such measurement? Suppose we could prove some day that one person was an extremely efficient pleasure machine (was so much better than all other people at deriving utility from the consumption of goods). Suppose social welfare would be maximized if this person received 99 percent of output. Would Lerner agree with such inequality? *Ms. B:* There are other problems with his argument, too: Why can't the marginal utility of income (unlike that of apples) *rise* with higher income? Why must the utility each person derives from income be dependent only on that person's income, and not on other people's?

Evaluate these two criticisms.

7. *Mr. A:* Rawls is wrong. What makes him think people are unwilling to gamble? Instead of being fearful lest they end up with the smallest income (which makes them favor equality), most people I know are attracted by the chance of getting a higher income than anyone else (which makes them favor inequality).

Ms. B: So true; I think all those income-equality arguments are nothing but rationalizations for envy. Note how the advocates of equality usually offer their advice to "society" in the sense of the United States. Why not to the world at large? Because that would give everyone (in 1975 purchasing power) a mere $1,250 a year share of world output.

Evaluate these two criticisms.

8. Consider the efficient situation depicted in part (C) of Table 14.4. Is this allocation of goods also equitable? (*Hint:* Apply each of the criteria for equity discussed in this chapter.)

SELECTED READINGS

Boulding, Kenneth E. "The Grants Economy." In *Collected Papers*, vol. 2. Boulder: Colorado Associated University Press, 1971, pp. 477–85.

Urges economists to study not only two-way exchanges, but also the ever-increasing importance of one-way transfers (coerced and voluntary) of exchangeables. *See also* his *The Economy of Love and Fear: A Preface to Grants Economics*. Belmont, Calif.: Wadsworth, 1973.

Boulding, Kenneth E., and Pfaff, Martin. *Redistribution to the Rich and the Poor: The Grants Economics of Income Distribution*. Belmont, Calif.: Wadsworth, 1972.

A fascinating discussion of explicit and implicit grants that sometimes increase and at other times decrease income equality.

Hayek, Friedrich von. *The Constitution of Liberty*. Chicago: University of Chicago Press, 1960; *Studies in Philosophy, Politics, and Economics*. Chicago: University of Chicago Press, 1967; and *Law, Legislation, and Liberty, vol. 2: The Mirage of Social Justice*. Chicago: University of Chicago Press, 1976.

Von Hayek discusses many concepts of economic justice and argues in favor of commutative justice.

Kohler, Heinz. *Scarcity and Freedom: An Introduction to Economics*. Lexington, Mass.: D. C. Heath, 1977, chaps. 36 and 37.

Discusses experiments with income equality in communes (Bruderhof, kibbutz), China (under Mao), and Cuba (under Castro).

Kohler, Heinz. *Welfare and Planning: An Analysis of Capitalism Vs. Socialism*. 2nd ed. Huntington, N.Y.: Krieger, 1979, chaps. 6–13.

Discusses models and cases of economic systems and the equity issue.

Lerner, Abba P. *The Economics of Control: Principles of Welfare Economics*. New York: Macmillan, 1944, chap. 3.

Presents the argument noted in the text. For a particularly interesting criticism, see John Bennett, "The Probable Gain from Egalitarian Redistribution," *Oxford Economic Papers*, March 1981, pp. 165–69.

Louis, Arthur. "America's Centimillionaires." *Fortune*, May 1968; and "The New Rich." *Fortune*, September 1973.

These articles show how the wealthiest individuals in the United States frequently do not reach this position through inheritance, but almost instantly at the moment monopoly power is generated and capitalized.

Rawls, John. *A Theory of Justice*. Cambridge, Mass.: Harvard University Press, 1971.

Presents the argument described in the text. *See also* Norman Daniels, ed. *Reading Rawls: Critical Studies on Rawls' "A Theory of Justice"*. New York: Basic Books [1975].

Sahota, Gian Singh. "Theories of Personal Income Distribution: A Survey. *Journal of Economic Literature*, March 1978, pp. 1–55.

Schumpeter, Joseph A. *Ten Great Economists: From*

Marx to Keynes. New York: Oxford University Press, 1951, chap. 1.

>A discussion of Marx and his work.

Thurow, Lester C. *Generating Inequality: Mechanisms of Distribution in the U.S. Economy*. New York: Basic Books, 1975.

Tucker, Robert C., ed. *The Marx-Engels Reader*, 2nd ed. New York: Norton, 1978.

>Lengthy excerpts from most of the writings of Marx.

Vernon, John M. *Market Structure and Industrial Performance: A Review of Statistical Findings* (Boston: Allyn and Bacon, 1974).

>Chaps. 3 and 4 survey recent studies of the profit consequences of market structure.

CHAPTER 16

General Equilibrium

Modern economies, as noted in Chapter 2, are characterized by an incredible degree of interdependence because millions of households and firms participate in an intricate system of specialization and exchange. The activities of such multitudes of separate decision makers must be carefully coordinated; this coordination can be accomplished deliberately, with the help of central managers, or spontaneously, with the help of markets. In the intervening chapters, we have studied only pieces of the market economy. One at a time, as if they existed in isolation from all the rest, we studied households in their dual roles as demanders of consumption goods (Chapters 3 and 4) and suppliers of resource services (Chapter 8). We studied firms in their dual roles as suppliers of consumption goods (Chapters 5 and 6) and demanders of resource services (Chapter 8). We also studied markets for individual consumption goods (Chapter 7) and individual resource services (Chapter 8), both in the short run and in the long run. Even in our subsequent recognition in Part Three (Chapters 9–13) of the many complexities of the market economy, the basic approach was to focus on one decision maker or one market at a time and to ignore the many interrelationships among them.

Ceteris paribus, "all else being equal," became a key phrase as we studied, again and again, a **partial equilibrium**, a situation in one part of the economy that contained no innate tendency to change because, for example, an individual household had maximized utility, an individual firm maximized profit, or an individual market equated supply and demand—given, in each case, assumed data concerning the rest of the economy. Recall, for example, how the consumer's optimum was derived, *given* money income, the prices of goods, and preferences. Recall how the competitive producer's optimum was derived, *given* the price of output, the prices of inputs, and technology. Or recall how equilibrium in the market for a consumption good was derived, *given* market supply and demand and, therefore, the numbers of producers and consumers and all the factors that determine their individual supplies and demands.

For a wide range of problems, this partial equilibrium approach is, in fact, quite sufficient. Ignoring interrelationships often incurs only a small loss of predictive accuracy. The previous chapters have provided a multitude of examples. But the time has come to return to the point of overview from which we departed and to recognize that each partial equilibrium is part of a vast interdependent process. The economic problem of scarcity is not being tackled by a multitude of different processes occurring independently of each other, side by side, each one proceeding in its own track and being careful not to get in the way of the others. Nor are these processes occurring sequentially, with households deciding on the supply of resource services on Mondays, firms on their input demands on Tuesdays, market equilibrium being established on Wednesdays, the incomes then earned giving rise to the demand for goods on Thursdays, which, perhaps, is satisfied by production and supply on Fridays. Instead, the price system is always busy fitting all these activities together, arranging a *simultaneous and mutual* determination of all prices and quantities. Economists wonder: Does the price system also produce a **general equilibrium**, a state of the economy in which billions of optimizing decisions by millions of decision makers are compatible with each other because all input and output markets are in equilibrium at the same time?

A Verbal-Graphical Approach

Nothing in economics is more difficult than the analysis of general equilibrium. This nonmathematical book cannot possibly do justice to this analysis, but two familiar tools—words and graphs—can help provide a basic understanding of what is involved.

Imagine a perfectly competitive economy that was, in fact, in a state of general equilibrium, as defined above. When this state of affairs is upset, three types of effects can be observed: the **impact effect** is the effect of an initial change in supply or demand on the market concerned; the **spillout effect** is the effect of this change on other markets; and the **feedback effect** is the effect of these secondary changes in other markets on the market in which the initial change occurred. Consider these effects of a change in demand from beef to apples.

Impact Effects

A Lower Demand for Beef. Panels (a) to (c) of Figure 16.1 depict an original long-run equilibrium in the beef market. The sample house-

hold shown in panel (a) consumes 3 pounds of beef per week at the $2.50-per-pound price. That price, at which market demand D and market supply S are just equal in panel (b), is the equilibrium price. This equilibrium price equals the normal price, as shown in panel (c). Our sample firm, which, as always, produces where marginal cost of production equals marginal benefit (or product price), has a minimum average total cost just equal to price.

Note what would happen if this household's demand for beef fell, as suggested in panel (d), from the dashed to the solid line. As long as price remained unchanged (at $2.50), the household would cut purchases from the old quantity at point a to the new one at b, which illustrates its fall in demand. If, however, other households were cutting purchases too (and this we assume), market demand for beef would fall, as in panel (e), from D (now dashed) to D'. If the flow of beef from the market to households fell, while the flow of beef from producers to the market continued unabated, a *surplus* would develop at the old 2.50-per-pound price (shown by distance de). Storage facilities in the marketplace would fill up and overflow. Competition among sellers would reduce the price to $1.67 per pound (corresponding to intersection f). This lower price would be a signal to all involved to change their behavior.

Beef-eating households would, as households always do when the price of a good falls, increase their quantity demanded, as from b to c in panel (d). Beef-producing firms would, as firms always do when the price of a good falls, decrease their quantity supplied, as from g to h in panel (f). However, inherent in the situation would be a tendency for further change, because the new $1.67-per-pound equilibrium price would no longer equal the $2.50-per-pound normal price. Consider how the typical firm would have turned from a zero-profit business into a losing business: Its price would have fallen (from point g to h), its average total cost would have risen (from point g to i), and it would then make losses, shown by the dotted rectangle in panel

FIGURE 16.1 A Fall in the Demand for Beef

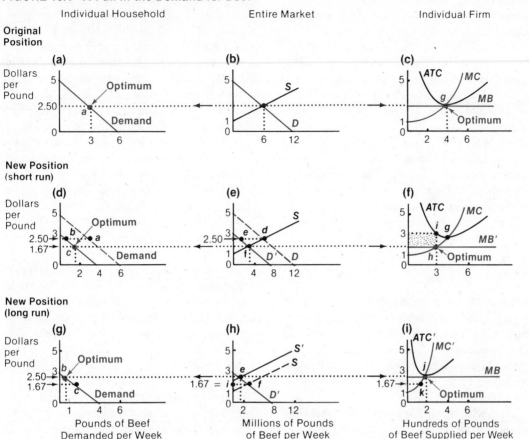

This set of graphs shows some of the adjustments, in a perfectly competitive market economy, to a fall in the demand for beef. If the industry involved is a constant-cost industry, as is assumed, the normal price of the product is unchanged after the industry has ceased to contract.

(f). The process described in Figure 7.4, "An Unprofitable Industry Contracts" (p. 196), would begin.

As soon as they could, firms would reduce their capacities or shut down completely. The particular firm illustrated here is assumed to reduce its capacity (a move akin to shifting from scale 2 to scale 1 in Table 5.3, "Constant Returns to Scale Illustrated" on p. 123), which is why panel (i) cost curves are to the *left* of their original position in panel (f). Compare *ATC'* and *MC'* with *ATC* and *MC*. Other firms, in ever-increasing numbers, would also reduce capacity

or even shut down entirely. As they did, market supply would fall as from *S* (now dashed) to *S'* in panel (h). But if the flow of beef from the producers to the market fell, while the flow of beef from the market to the households continued unchanged, a *shortage* would develop at the new $1.67-per-pound price (shown by distance *fi*). Storage facilities in the marketplace would empty out and, finally, be insufficient to meet demand. Competition among buyers would raise the price to $2.50 per pound (corresponding to intersection *e*). This higher price would be a new signal to all involved to change their behavior.

Beef-eating households would, as households always do when the price of a good rises, decrease their quantity demanded, as from c to b in panel (g). Beef-producing firms would, as firms always do when the price of a good rises, increase their quantity supplied, as from k to j in panel (i). Ignoring feedback effects, a final equilibrium would be reached when the firms remaining in the industry, as in panel (i), were again just covering cost with revenue. Their losses would have disappeared because the product price would be back at its old level, while average total cost (which had earlier risen to i above its minimum) would in this constant-cost industry again have fallen to that minimum at j. In the end, beef producers would have done exactly what households had asked of them: produce less beef.

A Higher Demand for Apples. Panels (a) to (c) of Figure 16.2 again picture an original long-run equilibrium. The household shown in panel (a) consumes 3 bushels of apples per year at the $12-per-bushel price. That price is the equilibrium price, in panel (b), and is also the normal price, in panel (c).

Note what would happen if this household's demand for apples rose, as suggested in panel (d), from the dashed to the solid line. As long as price remained unchanged (at $12), the household's higher demand would increase purchases from the old quantity at point a to the new one at b. If, however, other households were increasing purchases too (and this we assume), market demand for apples would rise, as in panel (e), from D (now dashed) to D'. And if the flow of apples from the market to households rose, while the flow of apples from producers to the market continued unchanged, a *shortage* would develop at the old $12-per-bushel price (shown by distance de). Apple storage facilities would empty out in no time, and demand would not be met. Competition among buyers would raise the price to $16 per bushel (corresponding to intersection f). This higher price would be a signal to all involved to change their behavior.

Apple-eating households would, as house-holds always do when the price of a good rises, decrease their quantity demanded, as from b to c in panel (d). Apple-producing firms would, as firms always do when the price of a good rises, increase their quantity supplied, as from g to h in panel (f). However, inherent in the situation would be a tendency for further change, because the new $16-per-bushel price would no longer equal the $12-per-bushel normal price. Consider how the typical firm would have turned from a zero-profit business into a profitable business: Its price would have risen (from point g to h), its average total cost would have risen less (from point g to i), and it would now make a profit, shown by the shaded rectangle in panel (f). The process described in Figure 7.3, "A Profitable Industry Expands" (p. 194), would begin.

As soon as they could, existing firms would expand their capacities and new firms would enter the industry. The particular firm shown here is assumed to expand its capacity (a move akin to going from scale 1 to scale 2 in Table 5.3, "Constant Returns to Scale Illustrated"), which is why panel (i) cost curves are to the *right* of their original position in panel (f). Compare ATC' and MC' with ATC and MC. Other existing firms, in ever-increasing numbers, would do the same, and new ones would enter the industry. As they did, market supply would rise as from S (now dashed) to S' in panel (h). But if the flow of apples from the producers to the market rose, while the flow of apples from the market to the households continued unchanged, a *surplus* would develop at the new $16-per-bushel price (shown by distance fi). Storage facilities would fill up and overflow. Competition among sellers would lower the price to $12 per bushel (corresponding to intersection e). This lower price would be a new signal to all involved to change their behavior.

Apple-eating households would, as house-holds always do when the price of a good falls, increase their quantity demanded, as from c to b in panel (g). Apple-producing firms would, as firms always do when the price of a good falls, decrease their quantity supplied, as from k to j in panel (i). Ignoring feedback effects, a final equi-

FIGURE 16.2 A Rise in the Demand for Apples

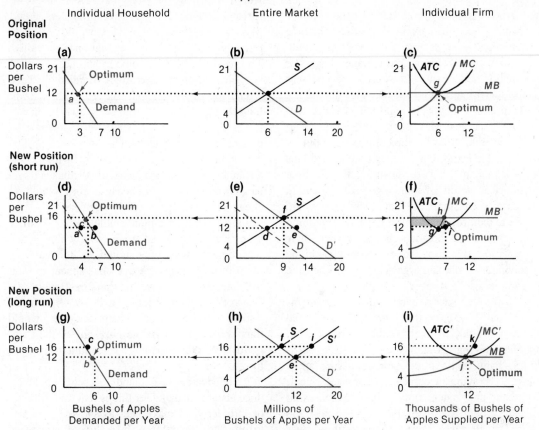

This set of graphs shows some of the adjustments, in a perfectly competitive market economy, to a rise in the demand for apples. If the industry involved is a constant-cost industry, as is assumed, the normal price of the product is unchanged after the industry has ceased to expand.

librium would be reached when the firms in the industry, as in panel (i), were again just covering cost with revenue. Their profits would have disappeared because the product price would be back at its old level, while average total cost (which had earlier risen to *i* above its minimum) would in this constant-cost industry again have fallen to that minimum at *j*. In the end, apple producers would have done exactly what households had asked of them: produce more apples.

Spillout Effects

Impact effects like those just described are only a tiny portion of the price system's work. The many firms that would reduce output or entirely leave the beef business, for instance, would, by their simultaneous actions, reduce the market demand for steers, butchers, ranch hands, veterinarians, pastures, feed lots, hay, corn, silos, harvesters, and much more. These reductions of demand would, by themselves, tend to lower the prices of all these things and send out clear signals to all involved to change their behavior too in ways consistent with the households' desire to have less beef. Thus cattle breeders and owners of pastureland and makers of harvesters and all the rest would find their incomes falling, and they would have the incentive to put their resources into other, more remunerative fields.

To be sure, each individual would be free to buck the trend. Individuals could do just the opposite of what price changes (and resultant income differentials) were asking of them. People could go *into* cattle breeding, pastureland, harvester production, and so on, just when the reverse was in the social interest; if they did, they should not be surprised if they were punished by exceptionally low incomes. Most people, therefore, could be expected to go in the direction pointed out by the Invisible Hand. Once enough inputs had thus been taken out of these declining fields, these input prices would, of course, go back up, and in the case of constant-cost industries, they would return to their original levels. Then the remaining (and fewer) cattle breeders, pasture owners, harvester producers, and so on, would again be receiving their old and higher incomes. The time of famine would be over.

In the same way, many old and new firms that would increase the output of the apple industry would, by their simultaneous actions, *increase* the market demand for fertilizer, pesticides, baby apple trees, storage barns, apple pickers, spraying machines, rubber, steel, coal, iron ore, and much more. These increases in demand would, by themselves, tend to raise the prices of all these things and constitute clear signals to all involved to change their behavior too in ways consistent with the households' desire to have more apples. Thus producers of fertilizer, human apple pickers, makers of iron ore, and all the rest would find their incomes rising, and they would have the incentive to place more of their resources into such remunerative fields. To be sure, each individual would be free to go against the trend, but those who did go out of fertilizer manufacture, apple picking, iron ore mining, and so on, just when the reverse was in the social interest, would be punished by losing what, at least for a while, would be exceptionally high incomes. Most people, therefore, could be expected to go in the direction pointed out by the Invisible Hand. Once enough new inputs had thus been put into these expanding fields, these input prices would, of course, go back down, and in the case of constant-cost industries, they

would return to their original levels. Then the (greater number) of fertilizer producers, apple pickers, and iron ore miners would again be receiving the lower incomes that once prevailed. The feast would have come to an end.

Finally, many seemingly unrelated effects would occur throughout the economy. Some households, such as the unlucky owners of pastureland, might react to their fall in income by demanding fewer yachts. The owners of profitable orchards might demand more furniture and airplane rides. The producers of cornflakes might supply more of them, because corn would be cheaper once there were fewer steers to be fed. Thus, in a billion unpredictable ways, the price system would tell just those from whom action was required what they should do. It would tell them in unmistakable ways (that appeal to their self-interests) to move in the direction of the "carrot" (higher income) and away from the "stick" (lower income). The price system would thus become the invisible *governor* of the competitive market economy, spreading its signals throughout.

The decreased demand for beef would reduce also the demand for things required, directly or indirectly, to make beef as shown, in panels (a) to (c) of Figure 16.3, by a shift of the dashed lines to the solid ones. In the same way, the increased demand for apples would increase also the demand for things required to make apples, as shown in panels (d) to (f). In addition, all kinds of seemingly unrelated effects would occur, as shown in panels (g) to (i). Thus the original change in household demand, akin to the ripple effect in a pond into which a stone has been thrown, would spread throughout the economy. The arrows in Figure 16.3 highlight the movements of the equilibrium points and the resultant price changes.

Feedback Effects

Figure 16.3 suggests why owners of iron ore mines, producers of tree fertilizer, human apple pickers, and people giving airplane rides would have higher incomes and would, therefore

FIGURE 16.3 How Price Signals Would Spread

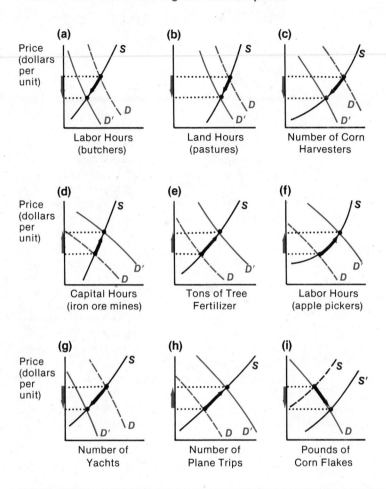

This set of graphs depicts some of the *spillout effects* of a lower demand for beef and a higher demand for apples.

(among many other things) demand more beef. This increase in the demand for beef forces us to reconsider the new long-run position shown in Figure 16.1 (which was based on the assumption of a *decreased* demand for beef by other people).

On the other hand, it is also possible that unlucky butchers, pastureland owners, and producers of corn harvesters or yachts or cornflakes would demand fewer apples. This decrease in demand forces us to reconsider Figure 16.2, which was based on the assumption of an initial *rise* in the demand for apples. All these new and offsetting changes in demand would, in turn, have spillout and feedback effects of their own!

Words and graphs can help illustrate the complexity of establishing a general equilibrium in the economy, but they cannot take us beyond this point. Because the full analysis of general equilibrium is an incredibly complex problem the solution of which is bound to escape the grasp of words and graphs, economists have turned to mathematics.

The Equations of Walras

In 1874, the French economist Léon Walras (the *s* is sounded) was the first to provide a precise formulation of the web of interconnections discussed and graphed in the preceding section. Walras (see Biography 16.1) viewed the economic system as a vast set of simultaneous equations. He described each household's demand for each good by a separate equation. He likewise described each household's supply of each resource service, each firm's supply of each good, and each firm's demand for each resource service using equations. He also formulated a market-clearing equation for the market of each good and of each resource service. Walras then showed, for a world of perfect competition, that it was theoretically possible to solve the resultant set of equations simultaneously for the prices and quantities of all inputs and outputs because *the number of independent equations equaled the number of the unknowns.*

The theoretical solution of Walras was, of course, nothing else but a general equilibrium of his hypothetical economy. When prices and quantities in all markets were thus in equilibrium simultaneously, short-run general equilibrium existed. When all firms in addition earned zero economic profit and no reproducible resources earned quasi-rent, long-run general equilibrium existed as well. Even though Walras' math was clumsy, he thus provided, as Joseph Schumpeter later put it, nothing less than "the Magna Carta of exact economics."

Walras was content with showing the theoretical possibility of a general equilibrium; he doubted the empirical usefulness of the analysis. Given the millions of equations involved, he saw no chance for filling them with numerical content. Yet his theory of *tâtonnement* or "groping" did provide a poetic vision of how an economy could solve the equations. He imagined price-taking buyers and sellers announcing the quantities they wanted to trade at prices "criés au hasard" (cried at random) by a price-making auctioneer. As long as the aggregate plans of buyers and sellers were in conflict, new prices would be "cried" and quantities would be adjusted. Only when an equilibrium set of prices was found would actual trading take place. Walras's theory, alas, hardly provided an accurate

BIOGRAPHY 16.1:
Marie Esprit Léon Walras

Marie Esprit Léon Walras (1834–1910) was born in Évreux, France. At a young age, he studied classics, literature, and science but then failed twice to be admitted to the prestigious École Polytechnique in Paris because of his poor math. He studied briefly at the École des Mines and then began to drift, writing an unsuccessful novel, engaging in free-lance journalism, lecturing on social reform, and managing a bank for cooperatives (which failed). His father, Auguste, who was an economist (and classmate of Cournot), urged him to study economics. Walras did study economics—not formally, but on his own. By 1860, when he published a polemic against Proudhon *(L'Économie Politique et La Justice: Examen Critique et Réfutation des Doctrines Économiques de M. P.-J. Proudhon),* he knew he wanted to unite mathematics with economic theory. His opportunity to pursue this area of study came after he read a paper at an international congress on taxation at Lausanne (where, ironically, Proudhon's essay won 1st prize). In the audience was a man who later founded a chair of political economy at the University of Lausanne. In 1870, Walras was the first to be appointed to that chair, even though he lacked formal training; there he stayed till he retired and his student Pareto (see Biography 14.1) replaced him.

description of the real world. In addition, subsequent generations of economists were not satisfied with the Walrasian counting of equations and unknowns or for that matter, with his assumption of universal perfect competition. Consequently, general equilibrium analysis remained a difficult challenge.

Walrasian Economics Since Walras

Mathematical economists were not convinced by the Walrasian claim that a general equilibrium was possible because a solution "in principle" of

Schumpeter (see Biography 10.2) called Walras the greatest of all economists; certainly the Walrasian analysis of general equilibrium (which is introduced in this chapter) is an outstanding landmark on the road economics has traveled to the status of an exact science. In addition, Walras became the third independent discoverer of the principle of diminishing marginal utility, besides Menger and Jevons (see Biography 3.2). Both of these great achievements appeared in *Éléments d'Économie Politique Pure* (1874–77), which was followed by two supplements, *Études d'Économie Sociale* (1896) and *Études d'Économie Politique Appliquée* (1898).

Although Walras's work is now recognized as a great achievement second to none, his efforts at the time were viewed with indifference or hostility by students and most colleagues alike, with Enrico Barone, Irving Fisher (Biography 9.2), and Vilfredo Pareto being the most notable exceptions. In addition, Walras alienated many by attaching as much importance to his questionable ideas about social justice, land nationalization schemes, sound monetary management, and the like as to his superb achievement in pure theory. Thus Walras found himself isolated, but he was a prolific letter writer. The copies he kept of his own correspondence and the letters he received show how Walras walked a solitary path, with little encouragement other than what he found in himself. In one letter he says to a friend: "If one wants to harvest quickly, one must plant carrots and salads; if one has the ambition to plant oaks, one must have the sense to tell oneself: my grandchildren will owe me this shade."[1]

Walras writes in his *Notice Autobiographique* (1904):

> On the afternoon of June 23, 1903, I met again at the door of my office the young professor, Henry L. Moore, of Columbia University of New York, who, after having explained to me the difficulties he himself had encountered in America, said: "You must recognize, my dear M. Walras, that for a scientific revolution such as you wish to make in economics, it requires 50 years."
>
> "That is the exact period," I responded.

There is a monument to Walras now at the University of Lausanne. Rightly, it bears no other inscription but *"Équilibre Économique."*

[1]Cited in Joseph A. Schumpeter, *History of Economic Analysis* (New York: Oxford University Press, 1954), p. 829.

his system of equations for a perfectly competitive economy was conceivable. Later economists argued that an equality of the numbers of independent equations and unknowns was neither a sufficient nor even a necessary condition for the existence of such a general equilibrium. To appreciate why an equal number of independent equations and unknowns may not be a *sufficient* condition for the existence of general equilibrium, consider the following two equations with two unknowns:

$$x^2 + y^2 = 0$$
$$x^2 - y^2 = 1$$

These equations have no solution in the realm of real numbers, the only realm that has any economic meaning. The solution is $x = \sqrt{1/2}$ and $y = i\sqrt{1/2}$, where the imaginary number i satisfies $i^2 = -1$. How can we be sure, critics asked, that the Walrasian "solution in principle" wasn't a solution such as this one? Maybe his solution contained all sorts of imaginary or negative numbers that grossly violated economic reality. (In general, negative prices and quantities lack economic meaning.)

Now focus on the first of the two equations above. Even though we have one equation with *two* unknowns, it does have a solution in the realm of real numbers (x = y = 0); hence the Walrasian equation-and-unknown counting is not even a *necessary* condition for the existence of a general economic equilibrium.

In addition, economists wondered about the uniqueness or lack thereof of any general equilibrium. Might it not be possible, they asked, that many different sets of all prices and quantities equally satisfied the Walrasian equations? Consider how many different resource allocations can be economically efficient (as noted in the opening section of Chapter 15). Thus economists set out to analyze the problem with rigor. Using topology and set theory, it was finally proved beyond doubt by Wald, von Neumann, Arrow, Debreu, and McKenzie that a general economic equilibrium can be achieved given a fairly wide set of assumptions (barring only a few conditions, such as increasing returns to scale, joint products, externalities, satiation of wants).[1]

Economists also investigated the stability of this general equilibrium: Would such an equilibrium, they asked, be reestablished once disturbed? This line of research originated in Walras's theory of groping, was revived by Hicks, and was pursued by Samuelson, Arrow, Hurwicz, and others.[2]

More recently the theory of the whole economy has been developed on many fronts, incorporating the introduction of uncertainty,[3] a method for actually calculating general equilibrium prices,[4] and consideration of imperfectly competitive markets.[5] (Given the nature of the mathematics involved, all these matters go beyond the level of this book.)

Leontief's Input-Output Analysis

A major new departure in general equilibrium analysis was made in 1941 by Wassily Leontief (see Biography 16.2). He brought the Walrasian theory from the level of supreme abstraction down to a level that allowed the numerical specification of economic interdependencies in the U.S. economy. He invented the **input-output table**, which lists the flows of all newly produced goods and of resource services between all their suppliers and recipients, to illustrate the web of interrelationships in an economy.

The Input-Output Table

Leontief's new tool shows how the decisions of any one economic actor are intricately bound up

[1]Abraham Wald, "On Some Systems of Equations of Mathematical Economics," *Econometrica*, October, 1951, pp. 368–403 (the translation of a 1936 paper); John von Neumann, "A Model of General Economic Equilibrium," *Review of Economic Studies* 1, (1945): 1–9 (translation of a 1937 article); Kenneth J. Arrow and Gerard Debreu, "Existence of an Equilibrium for a Competitive Economy," *Econometrica*, July 1954, pp. 265–90; Gerard Debreu, *Theory of Value: An Axiomatic Analysis of Economic Equilibrium* (New York: John Wiley & Sons, 1959); Lionel W. McKenzie, "On the Existence of General Equilibrium for a Competitive Market," *Econometrica*, January 1959, pp. 54–71.

[2]John R. Hicks, *Value and Capital* (Oxford: Clarendon Press, 1939); Paul A. Samuelson, "The Stability of Equilibrium: Comparative Statics and Dynamics," *Econometrica*, April 1941, pp. 97–120; *idem*, "The Stability of Equilibrium: Linear and Nonlinear Systems," *Econometrica*, January 1942, pp. 1–25; and *idem*, "The Relation between Hicksian Stability and True Dynamic Stability," *Econometrica*, July-October 1944, pp. 256–57; Kenneth J. Arrow and Leo Hurwicz, "On the Stability of the Competitive Equilibrium,

Part I," *Econometrica*, October 1958, pp. 522–52; Kenneth J. Arrow, H. D. Block, Leo Hurwicz, "On the Stability of the Competitive Equilibrium, Part II," *Econometrica*, January 1959, pp. 82–109.

[3]Roy Radner, "Competitive Equilibrium Under Uncertainty," *Econometrica*, January 1968, pp. 31–58.

[4]Herbert Scarf, "An Example of an Algorithm for Calculating General Equilibrium Prices," *The American Economic Review*, September 1969, pp. 669–77.

[5]Jean Jaskold-Gabszewicz and Jean-Philippe Vial, "Oligopoly 'a la Cournot' in a General Equilibrium Analysis," *Journal of Economic Theory*, June 1972, pp. 381–400; Thomas Marschak and Reinhard Selten, *General Equilibrium With Price-Making Firms* (New York: Springer Verlag, 1974); Donald J. Roberts and Hugo Sonnenschein, "On the Foundations of the Theory of Monopolistic Competition," *Econometrica*, January 1977, pp. 101–13; William Novshek and Hugo Sonnenschein, "Cournot and Walras Equilibrium," *Journal of Economic Theory*, December 1978, pp. 223–66.

BIOGRAPHY 16.2:

Wassily W. Leontief

Wassily W. Leontief (1906–   ) was born in Petrograd, Russia, the son of an economist. He studied at the universities of Leningrad and Berlin, subsequently did research at the University of Kiel, and advised the Chinese government in Nanking. In 1931, he joined the National Bureau of Economic Research and the faculty of Harvard. He stayed at Harvard until his retirement and subsequent move to New York University. While at Harvard, in 1970, he served as president of the American Economic Association. In 1973, "for his input-output methods of quantifying interdependencies in an economy and using them to predict large-scale trends," he was awarded the Nobel Memorial Prize in Economic Science.

Even though Leontief had experimented with primitive chessboard balances of the Soviet economy in the 1920s while at Leningrad, his major work on input-output analysis appeared much later as *The Structure of [the] American Economy: 1919–1939: An Empirical Application of Equilibrium Analysis* (1941). Other important works include *Studies in the Structure of the American Economy: Theoretical and Empirical Explorations in Input-Output Analysis* (1953); *Input-Output Economics* (1966); *Essays in Economics, vol. 1: Theories and Theorizing* (1966), *vol. 2: Theories, Facts, and Policies* (1977); and *The Future of the World Economy: A United Nations Study* (1977).

During World War II, the U.S. government was the first to develop input-output tables; nowadays, such tables are commonly used around the world. But everywhere, analysts have run into the problem of having insufficient data that advancing theoretical knowledge and high-speed computers are ready to use. Said Leontief in his presidential address to the American Economic Association:

> Economics today rides the crest of intellectual respectability and popular acclaim. . . . But I submit that the consistently indifferent performance in practical applications is in fact a symptom of a fundamental imbalance in the present state of our discipline. The weak and all too slowly growing empirical foundation clearly cannot support the proliferating superstructure of pure, or should I say, speculative economic theory. . . . The task of securing a massive flow of primary economic data can be compared to that of providing the high energy physicists with a gigantic accelerator. The scientists have their machines while the economists are still waiting for their data. In our case not only must the society be willing to provide year after year the millions of dollars required for maintenance of a vast statistical machine, but a large number of citizens must be prepared to play, at least, a passive and occasionally even an active part in actual fact-finding operations. It is as if the electrons and protons had to be persuaded to cooperate with the physicist. . . . Economists should be prepared to take a leading role in shaping this major social enterprise. . . . [The] public has amply demonstrated its readiness to back the pursuit of knowledge. It will lend its generous support to our venture, too, if we take the trouble to explain what it is all about.[1]

[1]Wassily Leontief, "Theoretical Assumptions and Nonobserved Facts," *The American Economic Review*, March 1971, pp. 1–7.

with all other decisions. In general equilibrium, the decision to produce any one good, for instance, requires decisions to produce many other goods as well, because any one output, by requiring inputs, affects other outputs, and so on in an infinite chain. Table 16.1 represents a highly simplified version of such a table, depicting a hypothetical economy's interrelationships during a given past year. The table *columns* show *inputs* (that is, flows of newly produced goods and of resource services) received during the year by the parties listed on top from the parties listed on the left. The *rows* show *outputs*; each row shows how the total flow, in column (8), of any newly produced good or resource service (which came from the party listed on the left), was distributed during the year among the various recipients listed on top.

Obviously, any input-output table that is to be used for serious analysis or even centralized economic planning would have to contain millions of rows and columns. Besides the electric power, steel, and corn listed in rows (A) to (C) of our table, there would have to be separate rows

for all other newly produced goods—from milk and shoes and electric motors to turret lathes and government office buildings and superhighways! Indeed, different types of any one product would have to be listed separately, too, right down to such detail as boys' tennis shoes size 10 and color blue. A complete table, similarly, would have to specify in detail the types of resource services required. The large categories listed in rows (D) to (F) would have to be broken down into all their different components. The quality of any worker, for instance, clearly varies with age, skill, and

TABLE 16.1 The Input-Output Table

Recipients / Suppliers	Of Intermediate Goods and Primary Resources			Of Final Goods and Primary Resources				Total
	Electric power producers (1)	Steel producers (2)	Corn producers (3)	Domestic house-holds (4)	Domestic producers (5)	Domestic govern-ment (6)	Foreigners (7)	(8)
(A) Electric power producers (millions of kilowatt hours)	40	120	20	160		50	10	400
(B) Steel producers (millions of tons)	80	200	5	0	400	0	115	800
(C) Corn producers (millions of tons)	40	80	100	500	−120	200	−300	500
(D) Owners of human resources (millions of labor hours)	4	800	500	50		400	96	1,850
(E) Owners of natural resources (millions of acre hours)	4	200	2,500	200		600	0	3,504
(F) Owners of capital resources (millions of machine hours)	100	400	100	0		100	0	700

An input-output table is like a map of an economy. It gives an overview of the flows of commodities and services during a period between their suppliers (listed on the left) and their recipients (listed on top).

health; the quality of any piece of land varies with its location and the weather; and the quality of a machine varies with its wear and tear. All of these factors would have to be accounted for.

Nevertheless, for purposes of illustration only, we shall assume that the oversimplified picture of Table 16.1 represents a complete picture of an economy in which only three goods were produced—rows (A) to (C)—and in which only three types of homogeneous resources were utilized—rows (D) to (F).

The Rows.　It is easy to interpret the meaning of each row of our table. Row (A), column (8), indicates that electric power producers were producing, during the year in question, some 400 million kilowatt hours. Some 180 million of these kilowatt hours were delivered to domestic producers, in columns (1) to (3), and *completely used up* in the making of other goods. This portion of electric power output, therefore, is placed in the category of **intermediate goods**, or goods produced by domestic producers during a period and then used up by the same or other domestic producers during the same period in the making of other goods. Another 220 million kilowatt hours, however, listed in columns (4), (6), and (7), were not used up domestically in the making of other goods. These goods are placed among **final goods**, or goods produced by domestic producers during a period but not used up by the same or other domestic producers during the same period in the making of other goods.

Note: Final goods may well have been used up (by households, government, or foreigners) or they may even have been sold to other producers in the country (and been added by them to their capital stock for *future* use). But goods can never be called final goods if they have been used up by *domestic producers* during the *same period* they were produced because that would make them intermediate goods.

Row (B), column (8) shows that 800 million tons of steel were produced this year. Of this total, some 285 million tons were completely used up by the makers of electric power (1), steel (2), and corn (3), leaving 515 million tons for

final recipients. Of these 515 million tons, 400 million tons were received by domestic producers but not yet used up in the making of other goods (5), and 115 million tons were exported (7).

Row (C), column (8) shows that 500 million tons of corn were produced this year. However, another 300 million tons were imported from abroad—the negative entry in column (7)—while 120 million more tons were taken out of storage by domestic producers—the negative entry in column (5). Thus domestic supplies came to 500 + 300 + 120 = 920 million tons. Of this total, 220 million tons were completely used up by the makers of electric power (1), steel (2), and corn (3), perhaps in the production of plastic parts used in electric generators and blast furnaces and, of course, as seed. The remaining 700 million tons were delivered to domestic households (4) and government agencies (6).

Row (D) shows that 1,850 million labor hours were performed during the year. Some 1,304 million of these were used in the making of electric power (1), steel (2), and corn (3). The remaining 546 million hours were directly used by domestic households (4), government agencies (6), and foreigners (7), perhaps in the form of services provided by barbers, typists, or technical advisers, respectively. Note: It is no accident that an X appears in row (D), column (5). Labor hours delivered to domestic producers must have been used up by them during the year in question in the making of goods; hence they appear in columns (1) to (3). Unlike steel or corn received (which might be used up or stored for future use), labor hours (just like acre hours, machine hours, and kilowatt hours) cannot be stored for future use.

Rows (E) and (F), similarly, list the totals of acre hours and machine hours used during the year as well as the purposes to which they were put.

The Columns.　The columns of our table have, of course, been discussed by implication. Columns (1) to (3) show all the inputs used by our three types of producers while producing the output totals given in column (8) of rows (A) to

(C). Electric power producers, for instance, produced this year 400 million kilowatt hours—row (A), column (8)—by completely using up the newly produced goods and primary resource services listed in column (1): 40 million kilowatt hours (electric power used to run electric generators), 80 million tons of steel (to build transmission towers), 40 million tons of corn (to make plastic parts used in generators), 4 million labor hours (which might have involved 1,515 workers working 8 hours a day for slightly over 11 months), 4 million acre hours (which might have involved using slightly under 457 acres year round as sites for electric power stations and transmission facilities); and 100 million machine hours (which might have involved using 11,416 machines year round to generate electricity). Columns (2) and (3) can be similarly interpreted.

Column (4) lists all the goods received for private consumption by households (electricity, corn, services of barbers and of private garden plots). Column (5) shows the change in the country's capital stock, or its annual investment (inventories of steel went up, inventories of corn went down). Column (6) lists goods received by government agencies and thus by people for collective consumption (electric light and heat for government offices, public schools, and hospitals; corn for the meals of soldiers; the services of clerks, doctors, and police officers; land used for parks and highways, and so on). Column (7), finally, lists the country's foreign trade (exports of electric power, steel, and labor services; imports of corn).

The input-output table can show us the effects of any disturbance of an initial equilibrium. Consider the effects of changes in the demands listed in columns (4) to (7).

Changes in Final Demands

Let households demand 80 million kilowatt hours of electric power *less* next year, but let government agencies (in charge of street lighting and important research) demand some 120 million kilowatt hours *more*. Let foreigners demand 55 million fewer tons of steel per year, while government agencies (in charge of a new space program) demand 95 million additional tons. Let domestic producers stop importing corn, while increasing corn inventories by 100 million tons per year (instead of drawing them down at a rate of 120 million tons). And let government demand 400 million fewer acre hours of natural resources, while private households (eager to set up garden plots) demand 400 million acre hours more.

All the changes to Table 16.1 are incorporated in columns (4) to (7) of Table 16.2. To understand how Leontief would figure the effects of our contemplated changes in demand, the reader should now imagine this table to be completely blank—except, of course, for the new compositions of final demand which we have just assumed in columns (4)–(7). The assumed changes in demand (compared to Table 16.1) have been highlighted by the encircled numbers in Table 16.2. Obviously each of these changes requires other changes in the original data of Table 16.1.

The increase by 40 million kilowatt hours a year of the row (A) entries in columns (4) to (7) from 220 to 260, for instance, requires at the very least a corresponding increase from 400 to 440 in the total output of electric power in column (8) of row (A). That increase in total electric power output, in turn, requires increases in all the inputs used by electric power producers in column (1), which raises all the totals in column (8) and all the other entries in due course! This chain reaction illustrates why Leontief would quickly examine the technical facts of life.

Technical Coefficients

Leontief would use the type of information found in columns (1) to (3) of Table 16.1 to calculate **technical coefficients** for all goods. Technical coefficients are numbers showing the quantities of inputs producers in an industry require on the average per unit of output. The technical coefficients in Table 16.3 have been derived from

TABLE 16.2   A New Input-Output Table

Recipients	Of Intermediate Goods and Primary Resources			Of Final Goods and Primary Resources				Total
Suppliers	Electric power producers (1)	Steel producers (2)	Corn producers (3)	Domestic households (4)	Domestic producers (5)	Domestic government (6)	Foreigners (7)	(8)
(A) Electric power producers (millions of kilowatt hours)	48.862	132.889	46.873	⑧⓪		①⑦⓪	10	304.685 134.638 49.301 488.624
(B) Steel producers (millions of tons)	97.725	221.481	11.718	0	400	⑨⑤	⑥⓪	81.894 777.423 26.607 885.924
(C) Corn producers (millions of tons)	48.862	88.592	234.364	500	①⓪⓪	200	⓪	48.322 · 114.008 1,009.488 1,171.818
(D) Owners of human resources (millions of labor hours)	4.886	885.924	1,171.818	50		400	96	2,608.628
(E) Owners of natural resources (millions of acre hours)	4.886	221.481	5,859.09	⑥⓪⓪		②⓪⓪	0	6,885.457
(F) Owners of capital resources (millions of machine hours)	122.156	442.962	234.364	0		100	0	899.482

This new input-output table shows the effects, throughout our hypothetical economy, of the changes in final demand highlighted by the encircled numbers. As a comparison with Table 16.1 indicates, the *impact, spillout,* and *feedback effects* leave no part of the economy untouched.

Table 16.1. Every entry in column (1) of Table 16.1, for instance, has been divided by the 400-million-kilowatt-hour total of electric power output shown in row (A), column (8). This division yielded column (1) of the new table: Because it took 40 million kilowatt hours to produce 400 million kilowatt hours, it took on

the average 0.10 kilowatt hour to produce 1 kilowatt hour. Because it took 80 million tons of steel to produce 400 million kilowatt hours, it took on the average 0.20 ton to produce 1 kilowatt hour. And so on. Columns (2) and (3) of Table 16.3 have been similarly derived.

Armed with technical coefficients, Leontief

TABLE 16.3   Technical Coefficients

	Inputs Required on the Average to Make		
	1 Kilowatt Hour of Electric Power (1)	1 Ton of Steel (2)	1 Ton of Corn (3)
(A) Electric power (kilowatt hours)	$\frac{40}{400} = 0.10$	$\frac{120}{800} = 0.15$	$\frac{20}{500} = 0.04$
(B) Steel (tons)	$\frac{80}{400} = 0.20$	$\frac{200}{800} = 0.25$	$\frac{5}{500} = 0.01$
(C) Corn (tons)	$\frac{40}{400} = 0.10$	$\frac{80}{800} = 0.10$	$\frac{100}{500} = 0.20$
(D) Human resources (labor hours)	$\frac{4}{400} = 0.01$	$\frac{800}{800} = 1.00$	$\frac{500}{500} = 1.00$
(E) Natural resources (acre hours)	$\frac{4}{400} = 0.01$	$\frac{200}{800} = 0.25$	$\frac{2500}{500} = 5.00$
(F) Capital resources (machine hours)	$\frac{100}{400} = 0.25$	$\frac{400}{800} = 0.50$	$\frac{100}{500} = 0.20$

Technical coefficients can be calculated from an input-output table. The figures shown here are based on Table 16.1, columns (1)–(3) and (8).

would figure, to begin with, that increasing annual electric power output by 40 million kilowatt hours to accommodate the changes contemplated in row (A), columns (4) to (7) requires extra inputs equal to 40 million times all the entries in column (1) of Table 16.3. But increasing inputs in this way would only be a first approximation of the truth. As one can see in the very first entry in column (1) of Table 16.3, in this economy electric power requires electric power for its production! Thus any 40-million-kilowatt-hour increase in electric power output requires *another* 40 million times 0.10, or another 4-million-kilowatt-hour increase in electric power production; this, in turn, requires another 4 million times 0.10, or a 0.4-million-kilowatt-hour increase; and so on in an ever-dwindling chain. Even *further* electric power is needed to help produce the additional steel and corn!

It is easy to see how this sort of computation would quickly get out of hand if it were to be pursued by mentally following chains of reasoning such as the one above. Fortunately, however, the mathematical technique of *matrix inversion* is a tool that enables analysts to calculate speedily all the effects, direct and indirect, of the types of changes envisioned in the example above. Matrix inversion produces, from the technical coefficients for intermediate goods (the top half of our Table 16.3) the so-called **Leontief inverse matrix**, a table showing, for those goods of which a portion of output is used up in the process of production itself (electric power, steel, and corn in our example), the total outputs ultimately required if one unit of such a good is to be delivered to final users. For serious analysis of general equilibrium, the Leontief inverse matrix is an indispensable tool. (The derivation of the Leontief inverse matrix is discussed in an Appendix to this chapter in the *Student Workbook* that accompanies this text.)

Interpreting the Leontief Inverse Matrix

Column (1) of Table 16.4 indicates that the recipients of final goods in our hypothetical economy could get 1 kilowatt hour of electric power provided total electric power output equaled 1.1718673 kilowatt hours, total steel output equaled 0.314976 tons, and total corn output equaled 0.1858554 tons. These production levels would assure sufficient raw materials throughout the economy to accommodate the ultimate delivery of 1 kilowatt hour to a final user. In addition, of course, the services of human, natural, and capital resources would also be needed.

Note how easily an analyst or central planner, looking only at the technical coefficients table, could have come to incorrect conclusions. Providing some final user with 1 extra kilowatt hour of power, such a planner might have figured, would *directly* require the production of 1 extra kilowatt hour (a matter of common sense), and would *indirectly* require the raw material production of another 0.10 kilowatt hour of power, 0.20 ton of steel, and 0.10 ton of corn, as the entries in column (1) of Table 16.3 seem to indicate. Yet this conclusion would be quite wrong! As column (1) of the Leontief inverse tells us, providing some final user with 1 extra kilowatt hour of power requires extra total output of not 1.1 but 1.1718673 kilowatt hours of power; of not 0.20 but 0.314976 ton of steel; and of not 0.10 but 0.1858554 ton of corn! The inverse makes us aware not only of the direct extra output requirements (which common sense indicates) and not only of the most obvious

indirect ones (which the technical coefficients point out), but also of those that are far from obvious (and which are too complex to be grasped by any human mind).

Completing the New Input-Output Table

Total Output Requirements.   Armed with the Leontief inverse, it is easy to work out the total output requirements implied by our hypothetical new set of final demands. Imagine in Table 16.2 that columns (1) to (3) plus (8) were still empty. Using the Leontief inverse, we can now fill in the top three cells in column (8):

Noting in columns (4) to (7) of row (A) how final users now demand $80 + 170 + 10 = 260$ million kilowatt hours, multiplying each of the column (1) entries in Table 16.4 by 260 million yields the total production levels of electric power, steel, and corn that accommodate this goal. The resultant figures, rounded to three decimals, are shown in column (8) of Table 16.2: 304.68549 million kilowatt hours of power, 81.89376 million tons of steel, and 48.322404 million tons of corn.

Final demanders also seek to obtain $400 + 95 + 60 = 555$ million tons of steel. Multiplying each of the column (2) entries in Table 16.4 by 555 million yields the *additional* total output of electric power, steel, and corn required to ac-

TABLE 16.4   The Leontief Inverse Matrix

	Total Output Required if Delivery to Final Users is to Equal		
	1 Kilowatt Hour of Electric Power (1)	1 Ton of Steel (2)	1 Ton of Corn (3)
(A) Electric power (kilowatt hours)	1.1718673	0.2425902	0.0616257
(B) Steel (tons)	0.314976	1.4007629	0.0332583
(C) Corn (tons)	0.1858554	0.2054191	1.2618605

The Leontief inverse can be calculated from a table of technical coefficients with the help of matrix algebra. This table is based on Table 16.3 and, ultimately, on Table 16.1. All figures are rounded.

commodate this additional goal. The resultant figures—134.63756 million kilowatt hours of power, 777.4234 million tons of steel, and 114.0076 million tons of corn—are also shown in Table 16.2.

Finally, final demanders also seek to acquire 500 + 100 + 200 = 800 million tons of corn. Multiplying each of the column (3) entries in Table 16.4 by 800 million reveals further total output requirements for the three goods put out by this economy. The results—49.30056 million kilowatt hours of power, 26.60664 million tons of steel, and 1,009.4884 million tons of corn—are shown in column (8) of Table 16.2, along with the totals of the entries we have just imagined making in the top three rows.

Input Requirements of Intermediate Goods. At this point, we must imagine that columns (1) to (3) of Table 16.2, as well as the lower half of column (8), are still blank. Knowing the total output requirements of all goods produced by the economy from rows (A) to (C) of column (8), we can simply use the technical coefficients in Table 16.3 to calculate all the inputs required by each type of producer—assuming, of course, that the technical relationships between inputs and outputs that were observed in the past also hold in the future (even if the volume of production, and thus perhaps even the number of producers, should be different). Leontief's method does, in fact, assume such constant returns to scale.

Multiplying the 488.624-million-kilowatt-hour total output of electric power by all the entries in column (1) of Table 16.3 yields the entries in column (1) of Table 16.2. Similar multiplications—of the 885.924-million-ton total output of steel by the column (2) entries in Table 16.3 and of the 1,171.818-million-ton total output of corn by the column (3) entries in Table 16.3—yields all the data for columns (2) and (3) of Table 16.2.

At this point, a quick accuracy check can be made. Do the column (8) totals of rows (A) to (C), which were independently derived with the help of the Leontief inverse, equal the sum of all the entries in their respective rows? They do.

Input Requirements of Primary Resource Services. At this point, only three cells in our table remain blank: the column (8) totals of rows (D) to (F) can be calculated by simple addition of all the entries in these three rows, yielding the three boxed numbers in column (8). If the economy can come up with the flows of resource services represented by these boxes, Table 16.2 can provide a feasible as well as a well-coordinated outline of economic activities that must be performed to accommodate the imagined set of new demands.

Wider Applications

The above example provides only the barest outline of Leontief's innovation, but it is sufficient to suggest why economists the world over have embraced the new technique with considerable success. Economic analysts in advanced economies have used input-output tables to estimate the consequences for different economic sectors of disarmament agreements or price hikes by the OPEC cartel. They have made such estimates by working through, as we have, the implications of changes in final demands likely to be brought about by these events. Economists in poor countries have used the technique to plan strategies of economic development; those in centrally planned economies have used the technique to formulate coordinated sets of commands likely to guide households and firms toward producing politically determined sets of final goods. Thus economic science, in the past few decades, has made giant steps beyond earlier approaches to general economic equilibrium. These earlier approaches included the famous *Tableau Économique* of François Quesnay (1694–1774), which mapped the flows of goods and money among economic sectors (and was inspired by physician Quesnay's study of the circulation of blood in the human body), the reproduction schema of Karl Marx (1818–83), and the equations of Walras (1834–1910). Yet none of these theoretical tools enabled analysts to handle the empirical content of general equilibrium as Leontief's technique does.

ANALYTICAL EXAMPLE 16.1:
The Economic Effects of Disarmament

Input-output analysis has been used to predict the major economic effects certain to follow an international agreement to disarm. The accompanying table, based on 1958 U.S. data, shows some of the predicted results. For example, the 1958 military expenditures on food and kindred products in fact equalled $536 million (at 1947 prices). Yet a complete cessation of military spending would have reduced demand in that industry by $1,513 million because other industries, depending on military demand, would also reduce their demands for food and kindred products. All other entries can be similarly interpreted.

Industry	Military Demand (millions of 1947 dollars)	
	Direct	Direct and Indirect
(1)	(2)	(3)
Food and kindred products	536	1,513
Apparel and textile-mill products	143	575
Leather products	24	116
Paper and allied products	–	788
Chemicals and allied products	85	877
Fuel and power	991	2,633
Rubber and rubber products	6	244
Lumber and wood products	19	451
Nonmetallic minerals and products	–	337
Primary metals	–	3,384
Fabricated metal products	106	1,281
Machinery (except electrical)	166	823
Electrical machinery	915	3,110
Transportation equipment and ordnance	9,478	10,609
Instruments and allied products	22	370
Miscellaneous manufacturing industries	–	119
Transportation	730	1,486
Trade	78	735
Service and finance	705	1,886
Construction	967	967
Unallocated and waste products	742	2,144

Clearly, disarmament by itself would produce massive but differential cuts in industry sales, as indicated in column (3), and thus cuts in output and employment. Yet the same analysis can be used to indicate the opposite effects of any increase in nonmilitary demands and can help guide policy makers toward actions that minimize adjustment effects.

Source: Wassily W. Leontief and Marvin Hoffenberg, "The Economic Effects of Disarmament," *Scientific American*, April 1961, pp. 47–55. Copyright © 1961 by Scientific American, Inc. All rights reserved.

ANALYTICAL EXAMPLE 16.2:

The Structure of Development

Input-output analysis, by facilitating comparisons of the internal structures of developed and undeveloped economies, can help map out paths to economic development. The accompanying input-output tables indicate internal structures of model economies symbolically. Each number (at the head of a column or row) represents a different economic sector, O stands for "output," I for "input," D for "final demand," T for "total output," and H for "household-supplied resource services." The color squares represent numerical entries in the various cells of the table.

Table (a) shows a completely interdependent economy. Each sector supplies outputs to all others and draws inputs from all others. Table (b), on the other hand, shows a random pattern of interindustry transactions. Some boxes are empty because no transactions occur between the affected sectors. In table (c), table (b) reappears with sectors rearranged (note the sequence of sector "call numbers"). This rearrangement, called "triangulation" reveals a hierarchical pattern of interindustry transactions. Note how sector 9 delivers its entire output to itself or to final demand but absorbs inputs from all sectors. Sector 8, on the other hand, delivers output to everyone, but uses as inputs only its own output and household-supplied resource services. Thus the sectors above a given row in table (c) are that row's customers; the sectors below a given row are suppliers. Thus any increase in final demand for a sector generates indirect demands that cascade down the diagonal slope of the matrix and leave the sectors above unaffected.

Table (d), finally, shows a "block triangular" economy with interdependence of industries within blocks and hierarchical relationships among them. The analysis of such tables shows development planners in economically less developed countries which "working parts" typically found in developed economies are lacking in their country and also the sequence in which sectors must be developed.

Source: Wassily W. Leontief, "The Structure of Development," *Scientific American*, September 1963, pp. 148–66. Copyright © 1963 by Scientific American, Inc. All rights reserved. Recently, Leontief has developed the first input-output model of the world economy. Interested readers may wish to study his associated discussion of the economic prospects of the less developed nations. *See* "The World Economy of the Year 2000," *Scientific American*, September 1980, pp. 207–31.

SUMMARY

1.   Modern economies are characterized by an incredible degree of interdependence because millions of households and firms participate in an intricate system of specialization and exchange. This interdependence is easily forgotten in the study of partial equilibrium situations that involve only one part of the economy. This chapter focuses on the attainment of *general equilibrium*, a state of the economy in which billions of optimizing decisions by millions of decision makers are compatible with each other because all input and output markets are in equilibrium at the same time. The nature of general equilibrium analysis is first explored by following, verbally and graphically, the *impact, spillout*, and *feedback effects* of a change in the composition of demand. This exploration illustrates that the "Invisible Hand" notion of Adam Smith was in fact a po-

(a) Interdependent Pattern

(b) Random Pattern

(c) Hierarchical Pattern

(d) Block Triangular Pattern

etic expression of general equilibrium analysis.

2. Because words and graphs ultimately cannot express the complex interrelationships in an economy, economists turn to mathematics. Léon Walras was a brilliant pioneer in developing a mathematical theory of general economic equilibrium.

3. By now, mathematical economists have carried general equilibrium analysis far beyond Walras. They have investigated various properties of the general equilibrium, ranging from its existence and economic meaningfulness to its uniqueness and stability. Mathematical economists have also extended the analysis to encompass uncertainty and imperfect markets.

4. Wassily Leontief's input-output analysis is a major new departure in general equilibrium theory. Unlike the Walrasian equations, input-output analysis allows the numerical specification of an economy's interdependencies.

KEY TERMS

feedback effect

final goods

general equilibrium

impact effect

input-output table

intermediate goods

Leontief inverse matrix

partial equilibrium

spillout effect

technical coefficients

QUESTIONS AND PROBLEMS

1. "Everything in a market economy depends on everything else! One can't even stir a flower without troubling a star. That's why a change in the demand for fish might well affect the wages of carpenters, and a change in the supply of crude oil might well affect the price of cereal." Explain.

2. *Mr. A:* The price system is like a vast computer. It continually selects those sets of prices that are closer to general equilibrium while rejecting others further away.

Ms. B: It is impossible to prove this beyond a doubt.

What do you think?

3. Consider an input-output table (refer to Tables 16.1 or 16.2).

    a. Could a column (4) entry be negative? What would a negative entry there mean?

    b. If all entries were in monetary terms, what would be the meaning of the sums of the various rows and columns?

4. "General equilibrium economics is undoubtedly a splendid intellectual achievement. But it is not by any means on the level of Newtonian mechanics. In a world with large complicated corporations, selling thousands of goods and services . . . the way we stick to our simple models (which at best cover one simple limiting case) is ludicrous. I am reminded of . . . the drunk who had lost his keys at night and spent his time searching for them under a streetlamp fifty yards from where he had lost them because that was the only place where he could see anything."[6] Do you agree or disagree with Shubik? Why?

5. Respond to the following question posed by a central planner: "What is wrong with taking account only of *direct* input requirements when planning an output target? After all, if each car requires five tires (including one spare) and if I want one more car, I need only plan for five more tires. If I produced six or seven more tires, I would have a surplus."

6. "I am confused. The caption to Table 16.3 says that the figures are based on Table 16.1, columns (1) to (3) and (8). Yet when I calculate technical coefficients from Table 16.2, I get the same answer." Explain why.

7. Explain what would happen with input-output analysis if constant returns to scale did *not* prevail.

8. Explain the meaning of column (3), Table 16.4.

SELECTED READINGS

Hicks, John R. "Léon Walras." *Econometrica*, October 1934, pp. 338–48.

    On the life and work of Walras.

Jaffé, William, ed. *Correspondence of Léon Walras and Related Papers*, 3 vols. Amsterdam: North-Holland, 1965.

Jaffé, William. "Walras's Economics As Others See It." *Journal of Economic Literature*, June 1980, pp. 528–49.

    In this article, the translator of Walras opposes the common view that Walras constructed a model by the use of which we can examine how the capitalist system works. Instead, he claims, Walras's *Eléments* were intended to be a *realistic utopia*, a delineation of a state of affairs nowhere to be found in the actual world, independent of time and place, ideally perfect in certain respects and yet composed of realistic psychological and material ingredients.

    [6]Martin Shubik, "A Curmudgeon's Guide to Microeconomics," *Journal of Economic Literature*, June 1970, p. 415.

Kohler, Heinz. *Welfare and Planning: An Analysis of Capitalism Vs. Socialism,* 2nd ed. Huntington, N.Y.: Krieger, 1979, chaps. 9 and 10.

> An application of input-output techniques to Soviet central economic planning.

Kuenne, Robert E. *The Theory of General Equilibrium.* Princeton: Princeton University Press, 1963.

> A thorough discussion of the neoclassical construction of the theory, as well as recent extensions into static linear systems, spatial models, and dynamic ones.

Kuenne, Robert E. *Microeconomic Theory of the Market Mechanism: A General Equilibrium Approach.* New York: Macmillan, 1968.

> A study, from the point of view of general equilibrium analysis, of the theory of the consumer, of the firm (under perfect and imperfect competition), and of the complete market mechanism.

Leontief, Wassily W. *The Structure of [the] American Economy, 1919–1939: An Empirical Application of Equilibrium Analysis,* 2nd ed. New York: Oxford University Press, 1951.

Leontief, Wassily W. *Essays in Economics, vol. 1: Theories and Theorizing.* New York: Oxford University Press, 1966; *vol. 2: Theories, Facts, and Policies.* New York: Sharpe, 1977.

> Essays on a variety of subjects from history to mathematical economics; from the economics of Marx to that of Keynes; from international trade, economic development, and growth to Soviet economic science; from dynamic input-output analysis to national economic planning.

Leontief, Wassily W. et al. *Studies in the Structure of the American Economy: Theoretical and Empirical Explorations in Input-Output Analysis,* 2nd ed. New York: Oxford University Press, 1977.

> Essays by Leontief and others.

Morishima, Michio. *Walras' Economics: A Pure Theory of Capital and Money.* Cambridge: Cambridge University Press, 1977.

> The author of *Marx's Economics* argues that Marx should be ranked as high as Walras in the history of mathematical economics and that Walrasian economists have misunderstood Walras just as Marxists often misunderstood Marx.

Morishima, Michio. "W. Jaffé on Léon Walras: A Comment," *Journal of Economic Literature*, June 1980, pp. 550–58.

> A strong critique of Jaffé's interpretation of Walras's work.

The Public Interest, Special Issue 1980. Articles by Kirzner, Hahn, and Arrow on "General Equilibrium and Beyond."

Schumpeter, Joseph A. *Ten Great Economists: From Marx to Keynes.* New York: Oxford University Press, 1951, chap. 2.

> On Walras.

Seligman, Ben B. *Main Currents in Modern Economics, vol. 2: The Reaffirmation of Tradition.* Chicago: Quadrangle, 1962, pp. 367–86 and pp. 434–41.

> A discussion of Walras's work and a discussion of Leontief's work.

U.S. Bureau of the Census. "The Input-Output Structure of the U.S. Economy: 1967." *Survey of Current Business*, February 1974, pp. 24–56.

> An actual input-output table, complete with technical coefficients and inverse.

Walker, Donald A. "Léon Walras in the Light of His Correspondence and Related Papers." *Journal of Political Economy*, July/August 1970, pp. 685–701.

Walras, Léon. *Elements of Pure Economics.* Translated by William Jaffé. Homewood, Ill.: Irwin, 1954.

PART 5

Government Intervention in the Market Economy

CHAPTER 17

Antitrust Policy and Regulation

Government is bound to play a role in any market economy. As Chapter 2 noted, government must, at the very least, establish transferable property rights in all things that are scarce. If it does not, markets in the scarce things so affected fail to spring up. But government *can* also assure that the exchange of scarce things, at terms freely agreed upon by the parties involved, is equally open to all. If exchange at freely agreed-upon terms is not open to all, some people, unlike others, are coerced into uses of property rights they do not consider optimal or are prevented from uses that they do prefer.

A number of the preceding chapters have, of course, noted how government is quite capable of performing an altogether different role. Chapter 11, for instance, discussed government-sponsored cartels and the "captured" state. In such earlier discussions, however, the role of government in the market economy was touched upon as incidental to analyzing the behavior of private households and firms. The remaining three chapters of the book, in contrast, will focus primarily on government. The present chapter examines governmental policy on monopoly and competition. Frequently, but far from consistently, that policy favors competition over monopoly. In part, this bias arises from political arguments concerning the desirability of dispersing economic power and providing equal opportuni-

ties for all. In part, the procompetitive stance reflects economic arguments, including the belief noted in Chapters 14 and 15 that imperfect competition is the source of inefficiency and inequity. Chapter 14 discussed the likely, but quite unnecessary loss of economic welfare under imperfect competition through economic inefficiency and X-inefficiency; Chapter 14 also showed that dynamic efficiency is unlikely to be served best by pure monopoly and most likely to be promoted by a blend of small and large firms. Chapter 15 noted that there are many who judge the income-distribution consequences of imperfect markets to be adverse to their idea of equity.

In the past 100 years, arguments such as these have given rise to a series of **antitrust laws** designed to restrain monopoly and foster competition and thereby to increase the likelihood that product prices will reflect marginal costs (economic efficiency), will equal lowest possible average total costs (technical efficiency), will leave no room for long-run economic profits (economic equity), but will always pressure firms to innovate (dynamic efficiency).

The Impetus to Antitrust Legislation

Late in the last century, private firms in the United States used a number of innovative devices in attempts to replace competition with monopoly. One of these was the horizontal merger, already discussed in Chapter 12, "Application 1: Mergers." A second method of eliminating competition was the formation of a **holding company**, a corporation established for the sole purpose of acquiring a controlling stock interest in two or more competing corporations in an industry and then jointly running their affairs. Holding companies were made possible by an 1888 New Jersey law permitting one corporation to buy stock in another, which was supplemented by a later law permitting a New Jersey corporation to do business anywhere. As a result of this legislation, a New Jersey corporation could be formed for the sole purpose of buying a controlling share of stock in a variety of other corporations. The holding company did not have to own any productive assets directly, but with a minimum of financial investment and some luck its owners could control a vast industrial empire.

Consider the example of an oil company with real estate and equipment of $1 billion. Assume the company has acquired its assets with the cash received from selling $500 million worth of bonds and $500 million worth of stock certificates. Suppose further that half the stock is nonvoting preferred stock (The holders of a corporation's preferred stock, compared to the holders of common stock, receive preferential treatment—as to the payment of dividends, for example—but in return may give up their right to vote on corporate affairs. Further detail may be found in the *Workbook* accompanying this text, in Appendix 9A, "Markets for Bonds and Stocks"). Someone can control the corporation with certainty by owning just a little bit more than half of the *common* stock that alone carries the right to vote. That is, that person can control all of the $1 billion worth of assets by owning just a little more than $125 million worth of common stock. Because in fact most stockholders do not bother to vote, especially if the common stock ownership is widely dispersed, someone can probably control the company by owning a much smaller block of common stock. Suppose instead of owning a fraction above 50

percent, a person can get away with owning as little as 10 percent and still control the firm. That person can control the $1 billion worth of assets with only $25 million worth of common stock and, similarly, can control 10 companies that have $10 billion worth of assets with only $250 million worth of common stock.

Next, let a holding company A own those $250 million worth of common stock. A person who is smart and lucky can endow company A with the 250 million *dollars* needed to buy that much common stock of the 10 operating companies by again selling bonds (worth, say, $125 million), nonvoting preferred stock (worth, say, $62.5 million), and voting common stock (worth, say, the remaining $62.5 million). Making the same assumptions as above, such a person can control company A (and indirectly all 10 oil companies) with as little as 10 percent of its common stock, or $6.25 million.

One can, in fact, go further and pyramid holding company upon holding company. For example, let holding company B hold those $6.25 million worth of common stock. By the same procedure used above, a person can control company B (and hence A and hence all 10 oil producers) with as little as $156,250. Or the person can let holding company C own those $156,250 worth of common stock of B, and then control C, *and ultimately $10 billion worth of oil companies*, with no more than $3,906.25.

Fantastic as it may seem, many actual holding companies (including such well-known companies as American Can, American Tobacco, U.S. Rubber, and U.S. Steel) vastly exceeded the above example in complexity. The $1 billion Associated Gas and Electric Company was controlled by a man holding $100,000 worth of voting stock.

A third device employed in the late 1800s to escape competition was the **trust**, a combination of several corporations under the trusteeship of a single board of directors that manages their affairs jointly. Stockholders of competing companies would surrender their stock certificates (and the right to run enterprise affairs) to a group of "trustees" in return for **trust certificates**, or nonvoting ownership shares in the trust. The trustees would then run all the companies as if they were a single enterprise. Holders of trust certificates would, as before, be entitled to all the profits made. Because most stockholders were more interested in earning something on their financial investment than in running a business, and because the elimination of competition through the device of the trust was expected to raise profits, the number of trusts grew rapidly. Most famous was the oil trust under John D. Rockefeller. Other large ones existed in whiskey, cordage, lead, and sugar. The first laws designed to save competition got their name—*antitrust laws*—from the trust, but these laws were designed to counter forms of anticompetitive behavior other than trusts as well.

Antitrust Laws and Their Applications

The first antitrust law, passed in 1890, is probably one of the shortest pieces of legislation on record.

The Sherman Act

Section 1. Every contract, combination in the form of trust or otherwise, or conspiracy, in restraint of trade or commerce among the several States, or with foreign nations, is hereby declared to be illegal. Every person who shall make any such contract or engage in any such combination or conspiracy, shall be deemed guilty of a misdemeanor, and, on conviction thereof, shall be punished by fine not exceeding five thousand dollars, or by imprisonment not exceeding one year, or by both said punishments, in the discretion of the court.

Section 2. Every person who shall monopolize, or attempt to monopolize, or combine or conspire with any other person or persons, to monopolize any part of the trade or commerce among the several States, or with foreign nations, shall be deemed guilty of a misdemeanor, and, on conviction thereof, shall be punished by fine not exceeding five thousand dollars, or by imprisonment not exceeding one year, or by both said punishments, in the discretion of the court.

Without defining its terms, the Sherman Act thus forbade individual or joint efforts to restrain trade and to "monopolize." The act did not make clear, however, whether it outlawed already *existing* monopolies (that is, certain *market structures*) or only the attempt or only the *successful* attempt to establish monopoly (that is, certain types of business *conduct*). This uncertainty about the law's intent has haunted antitrust policy ever since. Certainly, the act's vague language gave wide latitude of interpretation to the courts.

The Rule of Reason

Not until 1911 did the U.S. Supreme Court enunciate its famous **rule of reason**, according to which only deliberate and unreasonable restraint of trade was illegal under the Sherman Act, not *bigness* per se. To be guilty of monopolization, the court said, a firm must have the *intent* to exercise monopoly power and on that basis engage in actions that restrain trade *unreasonably*. Both the Rockefeller family's Standard Oil Company (then owning 91 percent of refining industry capacity) and the Duke family's American Tobacco Company (supplying 90 percent of the market for most tobacco products) were found guilty under this rule (and were dissolved into several independent firms). These companies were guilty by virtue of the vicious tactics used to dispose of smaller competitors. This interpretation by the court narrowed the scope of the Sherman Act considerably. Subsequently, International Harvester, United Shoe Machinery Corporation, Eastman Kodak, and U.S. Steel were found *not* guilty, precisely because they held near-monopolies which had been "thrust upon them"; that is, without their having made predatory attacks on competitors. Mere size or the existence of unexerted power, the court held in 1920, was no offense.

Market Dominance Illegal Per Se

In 1945, in a case involving Alcoa (then supplying 90 percent of new aluminum production), the court reversed tradition. Alcoa was found guilty because of bigness alone, even though its conduct had not been offensive. Under this new interpretation, du Pont was found innocent in 1956, but the United Shoe Machinery Corporation was forced, in 1969, to set up two rival companies.

With court decisions aimed at shaping *market structure* (that is, the number and size of competing firms in the market), certain difficult problems have inevitably emerged. One of these problems has been the definition of the relevant market in which the accused firm is supposedly exercising monopoly power. For example, Alcoa believed it had a 33 percent share of the aluminum ingot market because it considered the market to include production for sale from new ore and from scrap plus imports, but the government calculated that Alcoa had a 90 percent market share because it considered the market to include only production from new ore, regardless of whether it was for sale or for Alcoa's internal use. Similarly, du Pont was accused of having a monopoly in cellophane (which, given its patent, was strictly-speaking true), but the company argued successfully that the relevant market included other flexible wrapping materials as well and that its share of this larger market was less than 20 percent (see Close-Up 4.3, "Cross-Price Elasticity and the Cellophane Case"). Such problems have come up again and again. Was the 1963 market relevant to the Philadelphia National Bank national banking (4 percent share) or Philadelphia banking (36 percent)? Was the 1975 market relevant to Xerox that for all copying equipment (65 percent share) or that for plain-paper copiers (90 percent)?

Explicit Collusion Illegal Per Se

The courts have been less uncertain about the Sherman Act's intent on matters of collusion. They have consistently held explicit collusive agreements on prices, output, or market shares to be illegal *per se*; that is, they have been considered illegal regardless of motives or consequences. Such have been the rulings by the U.S. Supreme Court on price fixing in the Trans-Missouri Freight Association case of 1897, the Addyston Pipe and Steel Co. case of 1899, the Trenton Potteries case of 1927, the Socony-Vacuum Oil Co. case of 1940, and many more. (The court has been less consistent on pricing behavior that is consciously parallel but involves no direct communication. The accused were found guilty in the Interstate Circuit case of 1939, the American Tobacco case of 1946, the Cement Institute case of 1948, the General Electric-Westinghouse case of 1976, but most cases of tacit collusion since the 1950s have been viewed as exempt.) The courts, finally, have ruled illegal any joint venture by competitors (in the Penn-Olin Chemical Co. case of 1964) and any territorial allocations among them (in the Topco Associates case of 1972).

The Clayton Act

In the years following the enactment of the Sherman Act, powerful new business combinations came into being in many industries (steel, farm machinery, tin cans, etc.). Again and again, practices used to achieve these combinations were held not to violate the act. So Congress enacted another law that focused on conduct rather than market structure and spelled out certain illegal acts. The Clayton Act of 1914 forbade sellers "to discriminate in price between different purchasers of commodities" but permitted such discrimination if differential prices were due to "differences in the grade, quality, or quantity of the commodity sold," if lower prices made "only due allowance for differences in the cost of selling or transportation," or if lower prices were offered "in good faith to meet competition" (see Chapter 11, "Application 2: Price Discrimination"). This prohibition was designed to protect small firms from larger rivals who frequently slashed prices on particular goods in particular markets only for the purpose of eliminating small competitors.

The Clayton Act also outlawed **exclusive contracts** by which sellers agree to "lease or make a sale or contract for sale of . . . commodities . . . on the condition that the lessee or purchaser thereof shall not use or deal in the . . . commodity . . . of a competitor." Such contracts were common, for instance, in automobile retailing and soft-drink bottling. The Clayton Act similarly outlawed **requirements contracts**, according to which buyers agreed to purchase all of their requirements of a commodity from a given seller only. Gas stations often had to sign such a contract with suppliers of gasoline, batteries, tires; electric utilities had to sign such contracts with suppliers of coal or oil. Also outlawed were **tying contracts**, according to which buyers of one good agreed to purchase another good from the same seller as well. Under such contracts, for example, buyers of IBM card-sorting machines might be made to purchase IBM tabulating cards; buyers of tin-can closing machines to buy tin cans; buyers of TV antennas to buy antenna servicing; buyers of electrostatic copying machines to buy specially coated paper; buyers of a popular movie, *Gone With the Wind*, also to buy a terrible one, *Getting Gertie's Garter*; buyers of land to buy the services of a railroad to ship all products produced on the land.

The Clayton Act also forbade any corporation engaged in commerce to acquire the shares of a competing corporation or to purchase the stocks of two or more corporations that were competitors. The act enjoined large, directly competing firms from having **interlocking directorates**, an arrangement under which two or more competing corporations have in common some of the members of their boards of directors.

None of these specific prohibitions, however, were absolute. They applied where the stated conduct would "substantially lessen competition or tend to create a monopoly."

The Federal Trade Commission Act

Also in 1914, the Federal Trade Commission Act was passed, forbidding all "unfair methods of competition." The commission newly created was empowered to issue "cease and desist" orders against violators. (The Wheeler-Lea Act of 1938, in addition to "unfair methods of competition," also outlawed "unfair or deceptive acts or practices" in and of themselves, even if they did not hurt competitors. This later act enabled the Federal Trade Commission to control deceptive advertising practices.)

The Robinson-Patman Act

As an amendment to the Clayton Act, the Robinson-Patman Act of 1936 was to protect small independent wholesalers and retailers from mass distributors (such as chain stores or mail-order houses). The bargaining strength of mass distributors (argued the smaller independent distributors) enabled them to pay "unjustified" lower prices for their purchases and then to undercut competitors. (In fact, as subsequent developments showed, much of their superior competitive strength came from streamlining internal operations.) The Robinson-Patman Act forbade differential quantity discounts among buyers buying the same quantity. It forbade *any* quantity discounts and the charging in one locality of lower prices than elsewhere if they helped to create monopoly.

Not surprisingly, this law created great uncertainty for firms ready to engage in vigorous price competition. Court decisions have since determined that price discrimination is illegal when practiced by dominant firms (United Shoe Machinery case of 1953), but it is allowed when practiced sporadically by smaller firms.

The Celler-Kefauver Act

The Celler-Kefauver Act of 1950, designed to discourage mergers, returned to the control of market structure rather than business conduct. It closed a loophole in the Clayton Act, forbidding not only the acquisition, for purposes of monopolization, of competitors' shares of stock, but also the use of such stock by proxy and the direct acquisition of the assets of a competitive firm.

The Celler-Kefauver Act has been used to challenge all types of mergers, ranging from horizontal ones (Bethlehem-Youngstown Steel case of 1956) to vertical ones (Brown and Kinney Shoe case of 1962) to conglomerate ones (Procter and Gamble/Clorox case of 1967).

Antitrust Policy Assessed

Have antitrust laws effectively promoted competition and restrained the growth of monopoly power? Many critics doubt it.

The Government's Critics

First, these critics argue that the Antitrust Division of the U.S. Department of Justice has been traditionally starved of funds. Until the 1930s, funds were sufficient to go after only a dozen cases per year. Since then, fewer than 50 cases per year have undergone intensive investigation and litigation—still an insignificant number. Why should most firms worry about being indicted?

Furthermore, many of the big cases against monopoly take an incredibly long time (5.5 years on the average) and create an impossible volume of evidence (hundreds of thousands of pages). Conviction, therefore, follows indictment only after a considerable lag and is far from certain. (After 5 years, the jury in the Memorex vs. IBM case couldn't reach a verdict. Given the complexities, said the judge, no jury could have made a rational decision.)

Even when cases are carried through the courts to their ultimate conclusion, penalties imposed upon conviction have traditionally been negligible and have rarely taken the form of imprisonment. (In a 1961 electrical equipment industry case, executives were sentenced to 30 days in jail, but 9 of those days were remitted for good behavior. The defendents were viewed as martyrs by their peers!) Most penalties have taken the form of fines, but they have been incredibly insignificant. A 1950 *Study of Monopoly Power* by the House Committee on the

CLOSE-UP 17.1:
The United States Vs. IBM

In 1969, the U.S. government initiated an antitrust suit against the giant International Business Machines Corporation. At the time, IBM's stock had the highest aggregate value of any company's in the world, equal to that of all the companies traded on the American Stock Exchange. This fact, however, did not exhaust the superlatives connected with the case, for it promised to be the most complex and lengthy suit of its kind.

Even before the trial began in 1975, the government had collected more than 50 million documents for it. The government spent three years presenting its side, which filled 72,000 pages of trial transcript. It took another three years to present IBM's defense.

The government's argument raised the issue of market structure. In 1972, the government charged, IBM unduly dominated the market for "general-purpose electronic digital computer systems" by holding a 72 percent share. IBM, in turn, calculated a 32 percent market share by also including in the relevant market military computers, programmable hand-held calculators, computer leasing and servicing, and more.

The government also took up matters of business conduct. IBM, it charged, went out of its way to erect obstacles to the entry and growth of rivals: It "bundled" computer hardware with programming and maintenance, selling this combination at a single price and thereby keeping out independent programming and servicing firms. It

Judiciary, for instance, revealed the following facts about a group of 25 major companies: During the preceding 12 years, they had been given fines on 77 occasions for violating the antitrust laws. The total of fines paid by a single firm ranged from $3,500 (Socony-Vacuum Oil Company) to $75,000 (A & P). Relating the total of fines paid over 12 years to the firms' assets as of 1948, the percentages ranged from 0.0002 percent (Socony-Vacuum Oil Company) to 0.05 percent (Bausch and Lomb Optical Company).

stressed leasing rather than sale of machines, thereby imposing heavier capital requirements on potential imitators. When rival leasing companies bought up IBM computers and leased them for less than IBM rentals, IBM introduced "fighting machines," a new family of System 370 computers, which outdated the leasing companies' System 360s overnight. When makers of accessory equipment, such as California Computer Products and Telex, took away 10 percent of IBM's accessories market, IBM changed the design of its computers so that related equipment provided by other firms wouldn't work with IBM hardware. It also introduced new accessories of its own that were cheaper and more difficult to imitate. IBM reinforced its "fighting machine" strategy with price discrimination. It accepted slimmer profit margins and even losses on computers facing effective competition—for example, on the 360/90 superpower machine (in competition with Control Data Corporation) and the 360/67 time-sharing machine (with General Electric as the competitor). IBM sharply reduced prices on peripheral equipment (in competition with Telex and Memorex) if customers accepted 2-year instead of 1-month leases on mainframe computers. When rivals, such as Amdahl Corporation and Itel Corporation, introduced imitation IBM computers, IBM cut its prices substantially and instantly. Before long, IBM introduced new and better-working computers and sold them for less than the imitation machines. Overall, IBM left a trail of badly hurt, complaining rivals.

Not so, said IBM. IBM claimed its foremost position in the market was the result of good performance; of skill, industry, and foresight; of producing excellent and ever-better products, with reliable service, at ever-lower prices. A calculation costing $1.50 in the 1950s now costs a fraction of a penny. So far as the allegedly predatory practices go, said IBM, customers want them. Customers want "bundling" because the closest possible working relationship with IBM is valuable to them. Customers want leasing because they are risk-averse and unwilling to own machines when rapid technological advance in the industry is common.

When the two sides rested their arguments in mid-1981, no one expected a judgment soon; appeals were certain to carry the case into the next century—except that the very court that was to hear such an appeal had just upheld as legal many practices (by AT&T and Eastman Kodak) disputed in the IBM trial. This so weakened the government's case that an out-of-court settlement was being considered. The costs of litigation were tremendous; the government had already spent $10 million and IBM $100 million. The benefits, in turn, were questionable. The Sherman Act, after all, declares *restraint* of trade and *monopolizing* to be illegal. Yet monopolies restrict output and raise price; IBM's output has grown by leaps and bounds, and its prices have fallen steadily. Not even the government contested these two facts. No wonder one law professor (Robert H. Bork) dubbed the case "the antitrust division's Vietnam."

Source: *The New York Times*, various issues.

Relating the total of fines paid over 12 years to the firms' *net* profits of a *single* year (1948), the percentages ranged from 0.002 percent (General Motors) to 2.402 percent (Bausch and Lomb Optical Company).

Since that time, these critics argue, things have not changed. From 1955 to 1965, the average fine handed corporations was $12,778; the average fine for individuals was $3,226. True enough, this does not tell the whole story. Convicted firms incur other costs, which are much more substantial. These other costs range from lawyers' fees, treble damage action by injured parties, and consumer brand switching (due to injury to the firm's "image") to refusal of the government to do business with such firms and sanctions by administrative agencies (such as refusal to renew licenses for broadcasting). Yet such costs are often avoided because not all cases are disposed of by the courts. Frequently, the government prosecutor and the accused reach a **consent agreement**, according to which the suit

CLOSE-UP 17.2:

The Electrical Equipment Industry's Conspiracy

Early in 1961, the newspapers headlined one of the biggest pieces of business news in many years. A federal judge in Philadelphia had imposed fines totaling $2 million on 29 electrical-equipment industry firms and dozens of their employees after they were convicted of conspiracy to fix prices and rig bids. Seven prominent executives of the electrical equipment industry, coming from such renowned firms as General Electric, Westinghouse, and Allen-Bradley, were convicted of the same conspiracy and were sentenced to jail. All defendants had pleaded guilty or no defense.

In addition to such common items as refrigerators, washers, and electric motors, which were sold to millions, these firms were producing gigantic pieces of apparatus, such as power transformers, switchgear assemblies, and turbine-generator units, built to specification for relatively few customers. Such items, understandably, had no common price and were sold, mostly to private electric utility companies and to various levels of government, through sealed bids with the lowest bidder getting the business. The prices involved were gigantic, too. A 500,000-kilowatt turbine generator, producing electricity from steam, cost $16 million, for instance. As a result, the economic position of many a firm in this field was one of feast or famine: either there were large orders for

the giant and expensive pieces of equipment or there were none at all.

Naturally, the executives of the industry were less than enthusiastic about this situation. Their anxiety was reinforced by the marked overcapacity with which the industry had come out of World War II. The industry was equipped to meet peak government demands of the war, but that demand had vanished and was not yet replaced by growing private needs. No wonder they all wanted to appropriate for themselves whatever private demand there was for these products. This urgent desire led in 1955, and again in 1957, to price wars among the firms involved. In a famous "white sale," prices of some equipment were cut in successive rounds by as much as 50 percent; that is, by millions of dollars! As you might expect, such price cutting was no solution. Profits throughout the industry plummeted, resulting in red ink in some cases.

While all this was going on, the executives of the firms involved saw one another frequently. They had common interests. They met at industry association meetings and technical conferences. Some were personal friends and met socially. Naturally, they talked about their mutual desire to ensure their firms' survival.

What each needed was secure minimum prices and a minimum share of the market. They needed not to be told that their past behavior had been mutually destructive. It was not difficult to formulate the idea of a common response to a clearly recognized common danger.

is dropped in exchange for voluntary ameliorative action by the accused party, such as spinning off a subdivision or withdrawing a deceptive advertisement. This kind of agreement short-circuits a long court proceeding and spares the accused open court embarrassment and the other consequences should conviction occur. Needless to say, the possibility of reaching consent agreements also opens up vast possibilities for corruption. The accused parties, who have potentially hundreds of millions of dollars to lose, might engineer a favorable outcome outside of court for

a much smaller sum of campaign contributions or other favors. Three government suits against ITT, including one seeking the divestiture of the Hartford Fire Insurance Company, for instance, was dropped in 1971 on President Nixon's orders after ITT had promised, in repeated secret meetings with top administration officials, to underwrite a planned Republican national convention to the tune of $400,000, as well as to rid itself of Avis, the Canteen Corporation, Levitt and Sons, the fire protection division of the Grinnell Corporation, and two smaller insurance companies.

Before long, beginning in 1956 and continuing into 1959, the executives exchanged information on costs, prices, and intentions. They decided to fix prices and divide markets so that everyone could "get along." Nominally sealed bids were rigged in advance so that each company would be assured a certain percentage of the available business. In order to preserve the secrecy of the operation, the executives referred to their companies by code numbers in their correspondence. They made telephone calls from public booths or their homes, rather than from their offices. They also falsified expense accounts for their meetings to cover up the fact that they had all been in a certain place at the same time.

Yet, as so often happens, there is no honor among thieves. An employee of a small conspirator company told all to federal officials in 1959. As a result, two years later, the American business community had the exhilarating spectacle of watching some of the nation's most highly paid (and impeccably dressed) executives being marched off to jail. Some watched in horror, others with glee. Meanwhile, customers were suing the convicted companies for hundreds of millions of dollars' worth of damages for having paid "artificially high" prices. General Electric alone eventually returned some $197.8 million to its electric company customers.

Source: Reprinted with permission from Heinz Kohler, *Economics: The Science of Scarcity* (Hinsdale, Ill.: The Dryden Press, 1970), pp. 398–99.

Before this agreement was finalized, ITT and the White House tried to prevent a Securities and Exchange Commission subpoena of ITT memos and letters on the above deal; when their attempts failed, the commission joined ITT and the White House in foiling the investigations of the House Commerce Committee and the Senate Judiciary Committee. In the end, top ITT and Administration officials committed perjury before the Senate committee.

Last but not least, critics say, the stress on controlling *conduct* rather than *market structure*

is unfortunate. Aspiring monopolists who have the slightest amount of imagination can always discover new ways of accomplishing their purposes without violating the law. The only effective policy is one that enforces a competitive market structure by assuring free entry into and exit from every market. Such a market structure has not been achieved since the enactment of the Sherman Act. Indeed, critics conclude, present policy can only be described as an utter perversion of the act's intent. Despite the fact that the intent of the Sherman Act was to restrain the output-restricting and price-raising actions of would-be monopolists, firms that *expand* trade by producing more output, by producing new types of output, or by selling it at lower prices (and which gain larger market shares as a result) find themselves indicted for *restraint* of trade. Surely, Alcoa expanded trade in 1945 when it built ingot production capacity ahead of anticipated increases in demand. Surely, du Pont expanded trade in 1978 when it developed a low-cost method for producing titanium dioxide pigments, built a new plant, *lowered* price, and gained 40 percent of the market. Surely, Kellogg, General Foods, and General Mills expanded trade when they gained 75 percent of the market· for ready-to-eat cereals by introducing new varieties, such as bran, high-protein, vitamin-enriched, and pre-sweetened cereals. Yet all of these firms were indicted for restraint of trade. American firms, critics say, are understandably confused. Are they supposed to reduce capacity, cut back production, raise price, reduce product variety?

The Government's Position

Government officials respond to critics by pointing to recent improvements. For example, the 1974 Antitrust Procedures and Penalties Act changed antitrust violations from misdemeanors to felonies and raised the maximum fines to $1 million for corporations and $100,000 and three years in jail for individuals. Also, in order to stem possible government-business collusion, new procedures were established for reaching consent agreements: The accused firm must file with the judge involved in a case a list of all contacts with government officials; the government prosecutor must give the judge (and publish in major newspapers) a 60-day advance notice of any proposed out-of-court settlement, spelling out how the settlement will cure the problems giving rise to the suit in the first place; the judge can accept or reject the settlement proposal after noting public response.

Furthermore, argue government defenders, the ghost of Senator Sherman is an *ex officio* member of every board of directors, which is supposed to mean that business executives think twice before any action on pricing, expansion, and the like in order not to come in conflict with the law. According to this view, the law has primarily preventive effects. Yet there is overwhelming evidence that the laws are continually violated on a large scale. It may well be, however, that they would be violated even more without the threat of jail or fines, without the frequent use of court injunctions halting "undesirable" behavior, and without the fear of the other indirect effects of indictment or conviction.

The Regulation of Natural Monopoly

In some situations, like those first depicted in Figure 11.1, "The Natural Monopoly" (p. 319), the long-run average total cost of producing a good is declining throughout the range of quantities that might be demanded in the market. In situations of such persistent economies of scale, the breakup of monopoly and the promotion of competition is undesirable because the lowest possible production cost can only be achieved by a monopoly. Government often protects such firms from competition, but it also attempts to regulate their behavior in order to achieve economic efficiency and equity.

The Theory

The graph in Figure 17.1 refers to an electric power company but could just as well be applied

to gas distribution, telephone service, pipeline transport, or certain railroads for which the optimum plant equals or exceeds the size of the market. In the absence of government regulation, such a firm would, of course, maximize profit by equating marginal revenue, *MR*, with long-run marginal cost, *LRMC*, as at point *a*. This firm would produce 375 million kilowatt hours per year and sell them at 10 cents each (point *b*). Given long-run average total cost, *LRATC*, this price-output combination would produce an economic profit of 2.5 cents per kilowatt hour (distance *bf*), or a total of $9.375 million per year (crosshatched area). This combination would also imply a deadweight efficiency loss of the roughly triangular area *abe* (shaded).

If government regulators wanted to eliminate this deadweight loss by setting a competitive price equal to marginal cost, they would have to set the price at 1.6 cents per kilowatt hour (point *e*). This price would expand quantity demanded to 900 million kilowatt hours per year; the larger output would reduce long-run average total cost from *f* to *d*. Note: Under conditions of increasing returns to scale, long-run marginal cost lies below long-run average total cost; hence a price set equal to marginal cost produces a loss (here equal to *de*) on every unit of output sold. Thus government regulators could eliminate the shaded efficiency loss (and also the crosshatched monopoly profit) in the fashion just indicated, but if they did, they would drive our firm into bankruptcy. The firm would lose $22.5 million per year (area *degh*).

For this reason, government regulators attempt instead to set a full-cost price that just covers average total cost (point *c*). In our example, this price would be 5.6 cents per kilowatt hour and would lead to the production of 650 million kilowatt hours per year. At this price, total revenue would just equal total cost; monopoly profit would be gone. A portion of economic inefficiency would remain (portion *cei* of the shaded area).

One possibility for removing even the last remnants of economic inefficiency here would be for regulators to permit price discrimination. The

FIGURE 17.1
Regulating the Natural Monopoly

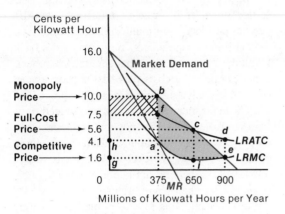

Cents per
Kilowatt Hour

Millions of Kilowatt Hours per Year

In the absence of government regulation, the natural monopoly pictured here maximizes profit by equating at point a the marginal benefit of production (or marginal revenue, MR) with its marginal cost ($LRMC$). It selects a price of 10 cents and produces an output of 375 million kilowatt hours per year, creating monopoly profit (cross-hatched) as well as a deadweight efficiency loss (shaded). If government regulators were to set a 1.6 cent competitive price equal to marginal cost, they would drive the firm into bankruptcy because average total cost (point d) would then exceed price (point e). Regulators can, however, select a compromise, such as the full-cost price of 5.6 cents. This price produces neither profit nor loss but eliminates only a portion of the deadweight loss (area $abci$).

demand and cost curves in Figure 17.2 are identical with those of Figure 17.1, but in Figure 17.2 we assume that regulators would institute a two-tier price structure. They would let the electric company charge 12.78 cents per kilowatt hour for what the market would take, and this quantity (q_1) would equal 201.25 million kilowatt hours per year (point a). In addition, however, a quantity (q_2) of 698.75 million kilowatt hours would be sold at 1.6 cents per kilowatt hour bringing the total to 900 million kilowatt hours per year. Thus marginal buyers would pay a price equal to marginal cost (point c). Average total cost would equal 4.1 cents (point b), and total cost would come to $36.9 million per year. Yet total revenue would add to the same sum: total revenue would equal q_1 times 12.78 cents (or $25.72 million per year) plus q_2 times 1.6 cents (or $11.18 million per year). The practice of price discrimination would avoid the loss (shaded) that marginal-cost pricing would otherwise produce.

Unfortunately, government regulators are not omniscient. They do not possess the complete information about demand and cost conditions given to us in Figures 17.1 and 17.2

Practical Problems

Government regulators who do not have access to all the information implied by the ready-made graphs of the textbook typically seek to set the price charged by a public utility in a way that produces zero economic profit. They attempt to select a price that generates just the revenue needed to attract and keep the resources used by the monopoly firm. This revenue must be sufficient to cover normal operating costs (such as wages, fuel, and depreciation) as well as a "fair" return on the investment made by the firm's owners. Such a policy, of course, makes a lot of sense. An inability to cover the costs mentioned would put an end to the firm. It would be unable to attract workers, buy raw materials, replace its equipment, and keep or expand its capital. Yet the determination of the "fair" return has produced no end of problems.

Regulators must, of course, first determine the desirable *rate* of return, which is not too difficult. If investors can find comparable investments elsewhere in the economy that return 10 percent per year, a similar percentage might be selected. If the return was less than 10 percent,

FIGURE 17.2
A Price-Discriminating Natural Monopoly

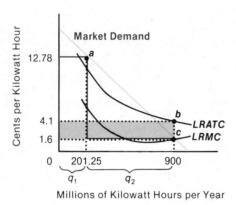

Marginal-cost pricing (point c) inevitably saddles a natural monopoly with a loss (shaded). The loss can be avoided by increasing revenue through price discrimination. In this example, quantity q_1 sold at 12.78 cents per kilowatt hour plus quantity q_2 sold at 1.6 cents per kilowatt hour yields total revenue just equal to total cost (of $36.9 million per year).

present investors would want to withdraw their investment from the firm; the firm would find it impossible to attract additional funds should it ever wish to expand. Much more difficult to determine is the **rate base**, or the value of the investment on which the owners of the regulated firm are to receive a "fair" return and to which the selected rate of return is to be applied. What is the value of the owners' investment? Should it be, regulators have asked, the dollars ever received by the firm through the sale of common stock? Should it be the original cost of the firm's assets, minus depreciation thereon? Should it be the current replacement cost of these assets, given their present conditions? Each of these approaches is likely to yield a different figure; in

times of inflation, current replacement cost is higher, for example, than original cost.

Nor is the determination of the "fair" return the only problem regulators face. Having once settled on a "fair" rate of return of, say, 10 percent per year and on an original cost of, say, $100 million, the regulators might announce their intention to select a price that generates revenues equal to operating costs plus $10 million a year (the "fair" return). Such a cost-plus procedure does little for managerial incentives. Indeed, it is likely to foster X-inefficiency and technical stagnation alike. Why should any manager keep tight control over costs, or even reduce them, when regulators, in the end, are bound to change price so as to keep the owners' returns at exactly $10 million a year? Thus managers may grant large wage increases to unions whenever so asked and assure themselves a quiet life. They may give jobs to incompetent relatives and live lavishly on the company expense account. Any gains in economic efficiency through regulation may thus quickly be eaten up by cost curves that shift up (X-inefficiency) or fail to shift down (lack of dynamic efficiency).

All this inefficiency is conceivably mitigated in the short run by **regulatory lag**, the length of time, sometimes years, that it takes government regulators to review a firm's performance and possibly change its price. The existence of this lag may attenuate the inefficiency effects just noted. If the lag is long, the owners of well-managed regulated firms that reduce costs can earn more than "fair" returns—that is, they will make economic profits—at least until the regulators catch up and lower prices. (Note: Such profits are the very thing many regulators wish to eliminate; hence the restoration of incentives through regulatory lag also implies regulatory failure.) On the other hand, owners of well-managed regulated firms the costs of which are rising (because of inflation, perhaps) will earn less than "fair" returns—that is, they will incur economic losses. Such firms will be unable to attract new funds for expansion, and they are likely to cut costs by reducing the *quality* of the goods they supply.

Regulation is likely to have another undesirable consequence: the **Averch-Johnson effect.** If the return guaranteed by the regulators exceeds the cost of capital, the owners of a natural monopoly will substitute capital for other inputs and will not produce a given output at minimum cost.[1] They will undertake new investment in the firm regardless of whether it increases output. Consider the earlier example of regulators having selected a target rate of return of 10 percent a year. If the cost of capital is only 7 percent, any $1 million addition to the monopoly's capital yields a pure gain of $30,000 a year to investors. (These investors will get $100,000 from the monopoly, they would earn only $70,000 elsewhere.) Indeed, there are other distortions as well. In order to increase the value of the base on which regulators calculate allowable profit, natural monopolies have understated depreciation charges and allowed their suppliers to overcharge them on equipment purchases.

Note: All these problems are compounded when regulators attempt the much more complex task of setting not just one price, but a structure of prices, as a competitive market would in response to fluctuating demand. Consider how the demand for electricity, telephone service, or rail transportation is bound to vary with the time of day, the day of the week, or the season of the year. Proper regulation requires, therefore, appropriately fluctuating prices.

The Regulation of Competition

Ever since 1887, when the Interstate Commerce Commission was set up to regulate the railroads, the number of regulatory bodies at all levels of government and their responsibilities have grown. Consider this partial listing of federal regulatory agencies:

1. The Civil Aeronautics Board (CAB) was set up to regulate airlines;
2. the Federal Communications Commission (FCC) was established to oversee telephone and telegraph companies, radio and television broadcasters, and then cable TV, CB radios and ham operators;
3. the Federal Maritime Commission (FMC) was formed to regulate ocean shipping;
4. the Federal Power Commission (FPC) was set up to regulate natural gas and electric power producers;
5. the Nuclear Regulatory Commission (NRC) functions to regulate the nuclear industry;
6. the Interstate Commerce Commission (ICC) was formed to regulate railroads, inland water and coastal shipping, intercity buses, nonagricultural truckers, and pipelines.

By no stretch of the imagination can all of the above industries be described as natural monopolies. Why then were they subjected to regulation by government? Two competing theories—the public-interest theory and the special-interest theory—attempt to explain the regulation of competitive industries.

The Public-Interest Theory

Some observers believe that government regulates (perfectly or imperfectly) competitive industries "in the public interest." The phrase *the public interest* usually remains undefined, but advocates of this theory often suggest that for reasons of economic equity, government regulators set out to "correct" the distribution of income in favor of buyers by commanding lower than market-clearing prices for goods considered "vital necessities" and "too important" to be priced by the market. Consider the recent federal price ceilings on natural gas and oil or the long-standing state and local controls over interest rates charged by lenders or rents charged by landlords. Oftentimes regulators also promote

[1]Harvey Averch and Leland L. Johnson, "Behavior of the Firm Under Regulatory Constraint," *The American Economic Review*, December 1962, pp. 1052–69. *Note also* Robert M. Spann, "Rate of Return Regulation and Efficiency in Production: An Empirical Test of the Averch-Johnson Thesis," *The Bell Journal of Economics and Management Science*, Spring 1974, pp. 38–52.

price discrimination to subsidize "the worthy," as when railroads are made to carry bulky raw materials at lower rates than finished products or when airlines are made to charge less per passenger mile for short flights or flights to small cities than for longer hauls and flights to large cities.

Not surprisingly, this type of "public interest" regulation causes no end of problems. The below-equilibrium price encourages consumption while discouraging production. As a result, shortages of natural gas and oil occur, students (or veterans) cannot find banks willing to make tuition (or mortgage) loans, and renters cannot find apartments. Shippers of bulky products face a boxcar shortage; short flights to small cities are crammed while long flights are plagued with empty seats. Before long, regulators can find plenty of reasons to expand their bureaucracy: they must now deal with "unexpected" shortages, with "price gouging" and black markets, with sudden deterioration in the quality of products (which is, of course, one way by which regulated firms can raise prices surreptitiously). Why does rent-controlled housing always deteriorate? Why have many operators of price-controlled gas stations ceased to check under the hood, wash windows, offer convenient hours, or accept all credit cards?

The Special Interest Theory

Economist George J. Stigler (see Biography 17.1) proposes another explanation for government regulation of competition.[2] Stigler argues that most of the time, regulation in competitive industries is not thrust upon firms, but procured by them. Firms seek to escape the rigors of competition (see the discussion of government-sponsored cartels and the "captured" state in

[2]George J. Stigler, "The Theory of Economic Regulation," *The Bell Journal of Economics and Management Science*, Spring 1971, pp. 3–21. *See also* Richard A. Posner, "Theories of Economic Regulation," *The Bell Journal*, Autumn 1974, pp. 335–58; and Sam Peltzman, "Toward a More General Theory of Regulation," *The Journal of Law and Economics*, August 1976, pp. 211–40.

BIOGRAPHY 17.1:
George J. Stigler

George Joseph Stigler (1911–   ) was born in Renton, Washington. He studied at the University of Washington, Northwestern, and the University of Chicago. After teaching at Iowa State, the University of Minnesota, and Columbia, he returned to a distinguished career at the University of Chicago. He served in many professional capacities, including the Attorney General's Commission for the Study of Antitrust Laws, the presidency of the American Economic Association, and the editorship of the *Journal of Political Economy*.

Among his many writings are *Production and Distribution Theories: The Formative Period* (1941), *Domestic Servants in the United States: 1900–1940* (1946), *Five Lectures on Economic Problems* (1950), *The Demand and Supply of Scientific Personnel* (1957), *The Theory of Price* (1962), *Capital and Rates of Return in Manufacturing Industries* (1963), *The Intellectual and the Market Place, and Other Essays* (1963), *Essays in the History of Economics* (1965), *The Organization of Industry* (1968), *The Behavior of Industrial Prices* (1970, with James Kindahl), and *The Citizen and the State: Essays on Regulation* (1975).

One theme pervades all his work: his defense of competitive markets. Stigler's research indicates that competitive forces are strong even in our present economy, that they can be kept strong by a moderate amount of antitrust action, and that government regulation, procured by industries wishing to escape competition, is a serious threat to the market economy. He has,

Chapter 11). Firms want entry restrictions and cartel prices. They want subsidies (Airlines, for example, have procured air mail subsidies even when they didn't carry mail). They want to suppress substitutes (Commercial TV stations, for example, want to keep out pay-TV provided by cable companies). They want to promote complements (Airlines, for example, want more and bigger airports; truckers want better high-

therefore, long argued for a reduction in the power of such agencies as the CAB and ICC and against the notion that government can do almost anything, if it really tries. According to Stigler:

> Our faith in the power of the state is a matter of desire rather than demonstration. When the state undertakes to achieve a goal, and fails, we cannot bring ourselves to abandon the goal, nor do we seek alternative means of achieving it, for who is more powerful than a sovereign state? We demand, then, increased efforts of the state, tacitly assuming that where there is a will, there is a governmental way. Yet . . . the sovereign state is not omnipotent. . . .
>
> 1. The state cannot do anything quickly . . .: (Deliberation is intrinsic to large organizations: not only does absolute power corrupt absolutely, it delays fantastically) . . .
>
> 2. When the national state performs detailed economic tasks, the responsible political authorities cannot possibly control the manner in which they are performed, whether directly by governmental agencies or indirectly by regulation of private enterprise. (The lack of control is due to the impossibility of the central authority either to know or to alter the details of a large enterprise) . . .
>
> 3. The democratic state strives to treat all citizens in the same manner; individual differences are ignored if remotely possible. (The striving for uniformity is partly due to a desire

for equality of treatment, but much more to a desire for administrative simplicity. Thus men with a salary of $100,000 must belong to the Social Security System; professors . . . must take a literacy test to vote; . . . the same subsidy per bale of cotton must be given to the hillbilly with two acres and the river valley baron with 5,000 acres. We ought to call him Uncle Same.) . . .

> 4. The ideal public policy, from the viewpoint of the state, is one with identifiable beneficiaries, each of whom is helped appreciably, at the cost of many unidentifiable persons, none of whom is hurt much. (The preference for a well-defined set of beneficiaries has a solid basis in the desire for votes.) . . .
>
> 5. The state never knows when to quit. (One great invention of a private enterprise system is bankruptcy, an institution for putting an eventual stop to costly failure. No such institution has yet been conceived of in the political process, and an unsuccessful policy has no inherent termination. Indeed, political rewards are more closely proportioned to failure than to success, for failure demonstrates the need for larger appropriations and more power.)[1]

[1]George J. Stigler, *A Dialogue on the Proper Economic Role of the State*, Selected Paper No. 7 (University of Chicago: Graduate School of Business, 1963).

ways). From such desires arises the *demand* for regulation.

Firms are also willing to pay a price in campaign contributions, job offers, and votes. In response to this price arises the *supply* of regulation by politicians and bureaucrats. Even when regulation is initiated for other reasons (such as the avoidance of *radio-spectrum* interference), it soon comes to serve the special interests of the

regulated themselves. As long as these special interests are being served, regulation persists, even when officially announced goals are not achieved and a multitude of perverse effects appear.

A Graphical Summary

Panel (a) of Figure 17.3 depicts a hypothetical

competitive market for natural gas, housing space, and the like with a competitive price of 0*A* and quantity 0*D*. Let regulators set a below-equilibrium *price ceiling* of 0*B* "in the public interest," and quantity supplied falls to 0*C*, while quantity demanded rises to 0*E*. Thus a shortage of *CE* occurs. The shaded triangle represents potential welfare unnecessarily forgone.

Panel (b) depicts a hypothetical competitive market for air or truck transport services with a competitive price of 0*F* and quantity 0*I*. This time regulators set an above-equilibrium *price floor* of 0*G* in the special interest of producers. Regulators also command a restricted quantity supplied equal to 0*H*. The efficiency loss is shown by the shaded area, and the monopoly profit is shown by area *GKLM*. Note: The owners of the regulated firms may have to share some of

this profit with others, such as the politicians and regulators who make this gain possible and, perhaps, even with unionized workers, such as airline pilots or teamsters who insist on a piece of the cake. In the presence of such X-inefficiency, line *KL* (representing long-run marginal and average total costs) will shift up, perhaps to dashed line *PQ*. Then a smaller output (0*H* instead of 0*I*) is produced at a higher-than-necessary cost (0*P* instead of 0*K*) and sold at a higher-than-competitive price (0*G* instead of 0*F*).

The Regulation of Health and Safety

A new type of governmental regulation has mushroomed recently that is not tied to specific industries. The regulation of health and safety is

FIGURE 17.3   Regulating Competition

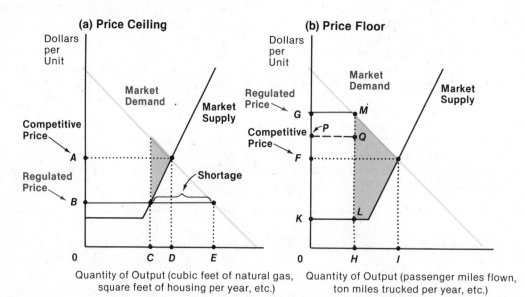

When government regulates competitive markets, it may favor buyers and set a below-equilibrium *price ceiling,* as in panel (a); it may instead favor sellers and set an above-equilibrium *price floor,* as in panel (b). In either case, there are other consequences: In the first case, not all buyers can buy what they wish; in the second case, not all suppliers can be allowed to supply what they wish. In both cases, potential welfare is unnecessarily forgone (shaded areas).

concerned not with the control of prices or market entry, but rather with the control of the types of goods produced and the ways in which they are produced. While concern with health and safety is not new (the Food and Drug Administration was formed in 1906), a large number of new agencies have sprung up since 1970. A partial listing includes the Consumer Products Safety Commission (CPSC), the Environmental Protection Agency (EPA), the National Highway and Traffic Safety Administration (NHTSA), and the Occupational Safety and Health Administration (OSHA).

Much of the work of these agencies is based on the following normative judgments made by self-proclaimed representatives of "the public interest":

1. It is never morally defensible to trade off human health and safety for material goods.
2. Because few private individuals possess the necessary information, governmental experts should determine which trade-offs of this type must be avoided.

Regulation Assessed

In recent years, economists have seriously questioned the worth of many types of regulation. Again and again, they have found the benefits to be low or nonexistent and the costs to be high or unnecessary.

Low Benefits of Regulating Natural Monopolies

George Stigler and Claire Friedland[3] have shown, for instance, that regulators of electric utilities have neither succeeded in changing price (as they might hope with a view toward achieving eco-

nomic efficiency) nor profitability (as they might hope with a view toward achieving equity). Comparing data from states in which electric utilities were regulated with data from states in which electric utilities were unregulated, they found no significant differences in utility rates or stockholder experience. In spite of a professed desire to make a difference, the authors concluded, regulators were in fact regulating nothing.

The Theory of the Second Best

Economists have had second thoughts on theoretical grounds about the desirability of regulating natural monopolies (or pursuing a vigorous antitrust policy). In a celebrated article,[4] Richard G. Lipsey and Kelvin Lancaster showed that if one or more Pareto conditions cannot be satisfied, it is in general not true that the cause of economic efficiency is served by satisfying as many of the other conditions as possible. This **theory of the second best** deals a fatal blow to any policy that attempts to approach the best-of-all-possible worlds by bringing price in line with marginal cost for as many goods as possible and doing so in a piecemeal fashion.

Abram Bergson[5] worked out the implications of the theory for an economy with competitive labor markets in which at least one industry *(A)* always charges a price above marginal cost, but in which government can affect the relation between price and marginal cost in other industries *(B)*. The implications are complex; they will, therefore, only be summarized briefly here. To achieve economic efficiency, government must set the price of B-goods, P_B, to equal marginal cost, MC_B, if goods A and B are

[3]George J. Stigler and Claire Friedland, "What Can Regulators Regulate? The Case of Electricity," *The Journal of Law and Economics*, October 1962, pp. 1–16; reprinted in George J. Stigler, *The Citizen and the State: Essays on Regulation* (Chicago: The University of Chicago Press, 1975), pp. 61–77.

[4]Richard G. Lipsey and Kelvin Lancaster, "The General Theory of the Second Best," *The Review of Economic Studies* 1 (1956): 11–32. For an elegant statement *see also* Edward Foster and Hugo Sonnenschein, "Price Distortion and Economic Welfare," *Econometrica*, March 1970, pp. 281–97; and Kunio Kawamata, "Price Distortion and Potential Welfare," *Econometrica*, May 1974, pp. 435–60.

[5]Abram Bergson, "Optimal Pricing for Public Enterprise," *Quarterly Journal of Economics*, November 1972, pp. 519–44.

independent goods. If *A* and *B* goods are substitutes (or complements), however, P_B must exceed (or fall short of) MC_B. If different industries produce a mixture of independent, substitute, and complementary goods, the proper policy depends on the magnitudes of cross-price elasticities of demand, of the output in industry *A*, and the excess of P_A over MC_A. Therefore, a first-best policy (that simultaneously equates all prices with marginal costs) being out of reach, the equating of price and marginal cost in only some industries is almost surely not the second-best approach. What is second best, however, requires more information than any government is ever likely to possess.

The Theory of the Third Best

To escape the confusion and uncertainty imparted by the theory of the second best, some economists have retreated to a new position.[6] They suggest a **theory of the third best**, according to which policy makers are well advised to eschew *specific* policies (such as bringing prices in line with marginal costs) in favor of *general* policies (such as promoting free-market entry and exit) that on average are likely to have desired effects. Because there is no reason to believe that monopoly promotes efficiency or equity, they say, policies such as those that promote free entry into or exit from markets should be encouraged. This theory does not imply that every existing monopoly must be broken up or regulated.

This new approach is reminiscent of a much earlier suggestion that policy makers be content with promoting **workable competition**, any market structure in which, taking into account structural characteristics and the dynamic factors that shaped them, no clearly indicated change can be effected through public policy that would result in greater social gains than losses.[7]

Because this advice relies so heavily on subjective judgments by policy makers, it is far from universally accepted by economists. George Stigler says with characteristic cynicism:[8]

> To determine whether any industry is workably competitive, therefore, simply have a good graduate student write his dissertation on the industry and render a verdict. It is crucial to this test, of course, that no second graduate student be allowed to study the industry.

Questionable Benefits of Other Types of Regulation

The benefits from regulating competition or health and safety have also been questioned. The regulation of competition redistributes income, the desirability of which depends on one's concept of equity. But one thing is objectively clear: regulation (rather than the tax system) is a poor method of income redistribution. Regulation usually takes several dollars from some people in order to give one dollar to favored recipients. A study of trucking regulation, for example, showed that it had raised freight rates from 10–20 percent above the competitive level and cost shippers an extra $4 billion a year.[9] Yet of this amount truck operators gained only $1.4 billion

[6]*See* F. M. Scherer, *Industrial Market Structure and Economic Performance*, 2nd ed. (Chicago: Rand McNally, 1980), p. 28; L. Athanasiou, "Some Notes on the Theory of Second Best," *Oxford Economic Papers*, March 1966, pp. 83–87; and Yew-Kwang Ng, "Towards a Theory of Third Best," *Public Finance* 1 (1977): 1–15.

[7]*See* John M. Clark, "Toward a Concept of Workable Competition," *The American Economic Review*, June 1940, pp. 241–56; Jesse W. Markham, "An Alternative Approach to the Concept of Workable Competition," *The American Economic Review*, June 1950, pp. 349–61; Stephen H. Sosnick, "A Critique of Concepts of Workable Competition," *Quarterly Journal of Economics*, August 1958, pp. 380–423; and Stephen H. Sosnick, "Toward a Concrete Concept of Effective Competition," *American Journal of Agricultural Economics*, November 1968, pp. 827–53.

[8]George J. Stigler, "Report on Antitrust Policy: Discussion," *The American Economic Review*, May 1956, p. 505.

[9]Thomas Gale Moore, "The Beneficiaries of Trucking Regulation," *The Journal of Law and Economics*, October 1978, pp. 327–44.

per year, or $1 for each $2.86 of increased cost to shippers. The remainder went to members of the teamsters ($1.2 billion) or was dissipated in pure waste ($1.4 billion), which resulted from driving the circuitous routes, from making the empty return trips, and from obeying the other regulations prescribed by the regulators.

The benefits of many health and safety regulations have similarly been questioned. Why shouldn't people be free, some critics have argued, to trade in health and safety for other things? People do it every day. Consider how people travel in private cars even though buses are safer. Consider how they eat cheap food at the Greasy Spoon even though food poisoning is less likely at the Fancy Restaurant. Consider how they take high-paying jobs in smoggy cities, even though lower-paying ones are available in country towns with cleaner air. (See Table 8.2, "Differential Wages and Death Rates" on p. 232 or Analytical Example 10.2, "Smoke Detectors as Insurance" on p. 297.) Why, critics ask, should *government* decide on the trade-offs made? Why not warn people of any and all hazards and let them decide whether they wish to avoid them? Must individual ignorance be used as an excuse for paternalism? Indeed, might individuals not possess *more* information than government bureaucrats whose inevitable ignorance of detailed circumstances is bound to make them treat all people alike even if it makes no sense? (For example, why should a person without children be forced to pay for safety caps on aspirin bottles designed to protect children? Why should a public library be forced to spend twice its annual budget on making itself accessible to the handicapped if there aren't any handicapped persons in town? Why should city subway systems provide elevators to make stations accessible to wheelchairs when it would be vastly cheaper to offer such people free taxi service?)

The High Costs of Regulation

The doubtful benefits of many regulations go hand in hand with very high costs. These costs can be grouped into three categories: 1. the direct costs of administering the regulatory agencies, 2. the direct costs of compliance by the affected parties, and 3. indirect costs. The first two are easiest to quantify.[10] In fiscal 1979, the budgets of the 55 federal regulatory agencies (the 80,000 employees of which managed to fill an equal number of pages of the *Federal Register* with new regulations) came to $4.8 billion. The private sector compliance costs came to a whopping $97.9 billion. This total of compliance costs included 7 cents for every pound of hamburger, $22 for the average hospital bill, $666 for every new car, and $2,000 for every new home. This compliance cost also included the cost to firms— at least $25 billion—of filling out more than 4,400 federal forms. The total of direct costs, almost $103 billion, thus came to about $500 for every person in the country.

The indirect costs of regulation may be more important still. It is impossible to list them all, and they are impossible to quantify. Indirect costs include: the increased likelihood of X-inefficiency from the regulation of natural monopoly; the economic inefficiency created by regulating competition; and a slowdown in technical advance because an ever-larger share of research and development expenditures is devoted to dealing with the governmental approval process. (Particularly affected are the drug and chemical industries. One drug company's application for approval of a muscle relaxant came to 456 volumes, weighed more than a ton, and stood taller than 8 stories. This is not an unusual case.) The indirect costs also include a slowdown in the growth of productivity caused by the rising claim government regulations make on resources available for investments in plant and equipment. Investment is also discouraged by heightened uncertainty regarding future regulations of new processes and products. A study by Edward

---

[10]*See* Murray L. Weidenbaum, "The Costs of Government Regulation of Business," in *The Cost of Government Regulation*, Hearings before the Subcommittee on Economic Growth and Stabilization of the Joint Economic Committee, Congress of the United States (Washington, D.C.: U.S. Government Printing Office, 1978), pp. 31–59.

ANALYTICAL EXAMPLE 17.1:

Regulation and the Price of Cars

Government regulations raise the prices of many products. One study shows the cumulative effect of a decade of federal safety regulations on the price of an American-made car. As the table below indicates, these regulations raised the price by $666, when measured in 1977 dollars.

Year of Regulation	Government-Mandated Equipment	Estimated Increase in Retail Price (in 1977 dollars)
1968	Seat and shoulder belts, standards for exhaust emissions	$ 47.84
1968–69	Windshield defrosting systems, door latches, lamps, etc.	14.53
1969	Head restraints	27.48
1970	Reflective devices and further emission standards	14.77
1968–70	Ignition locking and buzzing systems, interior impact protection	12.75
1971	Fuel evaporative systems	28.33
1972	Improved exhaust emissions and warranty changes; seat-belt warning system	42.37
1972–73	Exterior protection	95.29
1973	Reduced flammability materials, etc.	8.72
1969–73	Improved side-door strength	20.85
1974	Interlock system and improved exhaust emissions	133.50
1975	Additional safety features and catalytic converter	146.66
1976	Hydraulic brakes, improved bumpers, removal of interlock system, etc.	41.54
1977	Leak-resistant fuel system, etc.	21.25
1978	Redesign of emissions controls	9.99
	Total	$665.87

Source: Murray L. Weidenbaum, "The Costs of Government Regulation of Business," in *The Cost of Government Regulation*, Hearings before the Subcommittee on Economic Growth and Stabilization of the Joint Economic Committee, Congress of the United States (Washington, D.C.: U.S. Government Printing Office, 1978), p. 44. Note: Weidenbaum's estimates have been called "inflated" by William K. Tabb, "Government Regulations: Two Sides to the Story," *Challenge*, November–December 1980, pp. 40–48.

Denison shows that pollution and job safety standards alone cut the annual rise in productivity by almost a quarter in the mid-1970s.[11] No wonder that many economists view government regulation with skepticism.

Time for Deregulation

The early 1980s, it seems, is roundup time for runaway regulators—but only for some of them. The number of regulatory agencies, programs,

[11]Edward F. Denison, "Effects of Selected Changes in the Institutional and Human Environment Upon Output Per Unit of Input," *Survey of Current Business*, January 1978, pp. 21–44.

and authorizing statutes, and the size of regulatory budgets, continue on their upward trajectory. Nevertheless, Congress has taken a number of steps—not, generally, to end regulation of natural monopoly or health and safety, but to end regulation of competition.

The Natural Gas Policy Act of 1978, while extending regulation to intrastate gas temporarily, provided for the deregulation of all gas by 1985. Crude oil prices were to be deregulated by 1981. The Airline Deregulation Act of 1978 provided for the gradual removal of all government controls on market entry or exit, routing, fares, and the like; it even mandated the abolition of the CAB by 1985. A 1980 trucking deregulation law, to be fully implemented by 1984, has severely clipped the powers of the ICC. The law

CLOSE-UP 17.3:

Airline Deregulation: The First Effects

Although the process of airline deregulation, begun in 1978, won't be complete until 1985, its early effects can be reviewed now. Deregulation was supported by two Presidents (Ford and Carter), the CAB itself (under economist Alfred E. Kahn), influential members of Congress (such as Senator Edward Kennedy), and most economists. They predicted lower fares, more traffic, and reasonable earnings.

Deregulation was opposed (at least initially) by the major airlines and organized labor. They predicted higher fares, loss of service to small communities, unemployment of airline labor, plummeting profitability, and greater industry concentration.

As of 1979, deregulation supporters turned out to be correct. The average fare per mile rose 5.3 percent, half as much as the consumer price index (adjusting for a doubling of fuel prices in 1979 puts the fare below that of 1978). There were productivity gains unrivaled since the introduction

of jets in the 1950s: average costs fell 32 percent because seating on the typical aircraft rose 5.3 percent, because the number of hours flown rose 12 percent, and because revenue passenger miles rose 10.1 percent. Airline profits (defined by the CAB as net income plus interest paid on long-term debt) averaged 7.9 percent on investment from 1970–78; profits came to 5.8 percent in 1979. (This decline in profits reflects the soaring price of fuel.) Service to small communities was actually up by 21.4 percent (compared to 1976 and when measured in available seat miles), but in many cases small towns had fewer trunk lines and more commuter airlines. Since 1976, employment by trunk lines has risen 14.1 percent. In 1976, the trunk carriers' market share was 90.5 percent; in 1979, their market share was 89.9 percent. Regional carriers raised their share from 8.3 to 9.9 percent. Several new carriers appeared, and intrastate carriers competed on interstate routes.

Source: Based on James C. Miller III, "Is Airline Deregulation Working?" *The Wall Street Journal*, March 26, 1980. *See also* Alfred E. Kahn, "Applications of Economics to an Imperfect World," *The American Economic Review*, May 1979, pp. 1–13.

provides for an end to the antitrust exemption of the industry's rate-setting bureaus. It promotes free market entry and exit, and it returns to truckers the right to set prices, determine routes, and choose the type of cargo they carry. (A railroad deregulation law was enacted as well.) The FCC has similarly moved to end most regulation of radio and television broadcasters, of cable TV companies, and of telecommunications.

SUMMARY

1. In earlier chapters, the role of government in the market economy was touched upon as something incidental to analyzing the behavior of private households and firms, but this chapter focuses on governmental policy on monopoly and competition. Government policy traditionally favors competition. Late in the last century, private firms in the United States used a number of innovative devices in an attempt to replace competition with monopoly. These devices included horizontal mergers, holding companies, and trusts. In response to these devices, antitrust laws were designed to restrain monopoly and foster competition.

2. The Sherman Act of 1890 was the first antitrust law. Its vague language gave the courts wide latitude of interpretation. The courts first established, and later reversed, the "rule of reason," according to which not bigness *per se*, but only deliberate and unreasonable restraint of trade was illegal. The courts, however, have always held explicit collusion to be illegal *per se*. The Clayton Act of 1914 used conduct, rather than market structure, as a criterion and explicitly banned specified acts if they fostered monopoly, including price discrimination; exclusive, requirements, and tying contracts; intercorporate stockholdings; and interlocking directorates. Other antitrust laws (Federal Trade Commission, Wheeler-Lea, Robinson-Patman, Celler-Kefauver) mainly deal with advertising, price discrimination, and mergers.

3. Critics doubt that antitrust laws have effectively promoted competition. They point to the relatively few indictments, the lengthy trials, the few convictions, and the low penalties. They view consent agreements as a cheap escape route for violators of the laws. They believe the government perverts the laws' intent when firms that *expand* trade by producing more, introducing new types of output, or selling for less are nevertheless indicted for *restraint* of trade. Defenders of antitrust policy point to recent increases in penalties and a tightening of procedures for consent agreements. They argue that antitrust laws have, in any case, mainly preventive effects.

4. In situations of natural monopoly, the promotion of competition is undesirable for technical reasons. Government usually seeks to regulate the behavior of such firms. According to economic theory, unless price discrimination is practiced, marginal-cost pricing (for purposes of achieving economic efficiency) produces losses. Full-cost pricing is a likely compromise. Regulation of natural monopoly, however, encounters a number of practical problems: the determination of a "fair" return, the unwitting encouragement of X-inefficiency and dynamic inefficiency (possibly attenuated by regulatory lag), and the Averch-Johnson effect.

5. Government regulation reaches beyond the natural monopolies into the realm of competition. At times, regulation of competitive industries can be explained by the *public interest theory* according to which regulation is thrust upon unwilling firms. According to this view, government intervenes for reasons of economic equity and commands lower-than-equilibrium prices in order to help buyers. (As critics note, such a policy causes no end of problems.) More often, the regulation of competition can be explained by the *special interest theory*, according to which regulation is deliberately procured by firms that want to escape competition.

6. A new kind of regulation—the regulation of health and safety—is often supported by those who argue that trading off health and safety for other things is unjustified no matter what cost.

7. In recent years, economists have seriously questioned the worth of many types of regulation. Empirical study has failed to show benefits from natural monopoly regulation. Theoretical advance has brought into question the desirability of piecemeal policies designed to strengthen competition (the theory of the second best); some economists, therefore, favor less specific general policies (the theory of the third best), which is reminiscent of an older and controversial suggestion to promote "workable competition." The benefits of regulating competition or health and safety are also far from certain. The doubtful benefits of many regulations go hand in hand with very high costs, including the costs of administering regulatory agencies, private sector compliance costs, and such indirect costs as heightened X-inefficiency, economic inefficiency, and dynamic inefficiency.

8. Since the late 1970s, the U.S. government has embarked upon a limited program of deregulation.

KEY TERMS

antitrust laws

Averch-Johnson effect

consent agreement

exclusive contracts

holding company

interlocking directorates

rate base

regulatory lag

requirements contracts

rule of reason

theory of the second best

theory of the third best

trust

trust certificates

tying contracts

workable competition

QUESTIONS AND PROBLEMS

1. "The Clayton Act provisions against exclusive, requirements, and tying contracts are undesirable. Exclusive contracts make it easier for retailers to provide factory-authorized parts and service because they can establish a good working relationship with a single manufacturer. Requirements contracts reduce uncertainty; they enable buyers to count on the receipt of specified quantities at agreed-upon prices. Tying contracts help sellers make sure that their products' reputation is not sullied by breakdowns caused by the use of incompatible raw materials supplied by other firms."
Evaluate this position.

2. "I have a better way for establishing a natural monopoly's rate base: Regulators should simply look at such a firm's actual profit and capitalize it according to Fisher's formula at the chosen fair rate of return. Then they don't have to debate endlessly on whether they should use the original or the reproduction cost of the firm's assets."
Evaluate this position.

3. "If government can regulate a natural monopoly (in order to eliminate economic profit and economic inefficiency), it surely can equally regulate a monopoly that has increasing marginal and average total costs, such as the one depicted in panel (b) of Figure 11.3, 'A Profit-Making Monopoly' (p. 324)."

With the help of Figure 11.3(b), consider the effects on economic profit and on economic efficiency of each of the following types of regulation:

   a. Setting a market-clearing price equal to marginal cost.

   b. Setting a price equal to minimum average total cost.

   c. Providing a per-unit subsidy that encourages an expansion of output equal to *a* above.

   d. Setting a lump-sum tax, in conjunction with *c* above, that reduces economic profit to zero.

4. "The theory of natural-monopoly regulation has a fatal flaw: Even though increasing returns to scale imply that the industry's output can be produced most cheaply by a single firm, it does not follow that such a firm will inevitably charge a monopoly price unless it is regulated. Government can auction off the right to be this single producer to that firm which agrees to sell the good in question at the lowest price. As long as the inputs required for production are available to many potential firms and firms do not collude, there can be vigorous competition among many firms at the bidding stage. More likely than not, such franchising will produce the competitive price, and subsequently no regulation is needed."[12]

Evaluate this position. How would this procedure affect the likelihood of X-efficiency and dynamic efficiency?

5. "The government should adopt *sunset laws* that terminate the life of regulatory agencies after a specified number of years, unless the agency can justify its continued existence by proving that it has in the past produced benefits in excess of costs. Sunset laws would quickly put an end to nit-picking regulations that impose huge costs for tiny benefits."

Evaluate this position for each of the three forms of regulation discussed in this chapter.

6. Certain groups of individuals, by custom or law, are exempted from the antitrust laws. These exempt groups include agricultural cooperatives, defense suppliers, educational institutions, export associations, health-care suppliers, intrastate commerce, labor unions, professional sports, regulated industries. Do you think exemptions are ever justified?

7. "Ralph Nader and all the governmental regulators of health and safety whom he has spawned are best described as fanatics. Fanatics always know what is good for us better than we do, and they always know their duty: make us do what is good for us (with our money of course)."

Evaluate this position.

[12]Based on Harold Demsetz, "Why Regulate Utilities?" *The Journal of Law and Economics*, April 1968, pp. 55–65.

8. "The deregulation of competition hurts many innocent people because the elimination of monopoly power destroys valuable assets. The people who are hurt naturally oppose deregulation. They ought to be compensated."

Evaluate this position. (*Suggestion*: Review Analytical Example 11.3, "The Market Value of Monopoly Power" on p. 344. Then ask yourself: Should the owners of such power be compensated a) if they received it as a gift originally, and b) if they paid for it by purchasing it from the original recipients? Should others who shared the benefits of this power be compensated? Consider airline pilots, teamsters, electricians working for once-regulated firms. Consider owners of restaurants at air and truck terminals positioned on once-mandated and now-abandoned routes. Consider owners of houses with once-limited natural-gas hookups.)

SELECTED READINGS

Bork, Robert H. *The Antitrust Paradox: A Policy at War With Itself*. New York: Basic Books, 1978.

A criticism of antitrust policy by the former Solicitor General of the United States.

Joskow, Paul L. and Noll, Roger G. "Regulation in Theory and Practice: An Overview." *The Economics of Regulation*. New York: National Bureau of Economic Research, 1980.

A survey of latest developments in regulation.

Kahn, Alfred E. *The Economics of Regulation*, 2 vols. New York: Wiley, 1971.

The definitive treatise at the time, written by the later chairman of the CAB and the President's Council on Wage and Price Stability.

Kaysen, Carl, and Turner, Donald F. *Antitrust Policy*. Cambridge: Harvard University Press, 1959.

A superb text.

Kohler, Heinz. *Welfare and Planning: An Analysis of Capitalism Vs. Socialism*, 2nd ed. Huntington, N.Y.: Krieger, 1979, chap. 11.

A study of the ultimate form of regulation: Oskar Lange's socialist market economy.

Miller, James C. III, and Yandle, Bruce. *Benefit-Cost Analysis of Social Regulation*. Washington, D.C.: American Enterprise Institute, 1979.

A selection of case studies on health and safety regulation.

Nelson, James R. *Marginal Cost Pricing in Practice*. Englewood Cliffs, N.J.: Prentice-Hall, 1964.

> A classic book on peak-load pricing by electric utilities, based on the French experience.

Owen, Bruce M. and Braeutigam, Ronald. *The Regulation Game: Strategic Use of the Administrative Process*. Cambridge: Ballinger, 1978.

> Presents the provocative hypothesis that regulation, at the cost of some efficiency, provides substantial benefits by protecting individuals from the risk they would otherwise face from the operation of the efficient but ruthless free market.

Shepherd, William G. and Wilcox, Clair. *Public Policies Toward Business*, 6th ed. Homewood: Richard D. Irwin, 1979.

> A classic text.

Stelzer, Irwin M. *Selected Antitrust Cases*, 5th ed. Homewood: Richard D. Irwin, 1976.

Stigler, George J. *The Citizen and the State: Essays on Regulation*. Chicago: University of Chicago Press, 1975.

CHAPTER 18

Externalities

When discussing the supply curve of a perfectly competitive industry in Chapter 6, we met situations of pecuniary externalities in which the input prices paid by (or the production functions available to) some firms were affected, favorably or unfavorably, by the operation of other firms. This chapter deals exclusively with externalities, but its concern is at once broader and narrower than in Chapter 6. It is broader because we concentrate on interactions involving not only firms, but also households. It is narrower because we do not deal with pecuniary externalities that occur when the behavior of some households or firms affects the *market prices* faced by other households or firms; instead we focus on real or **nonpecuniary externalities**, which include, but are not confined to, the technological ones discussed in Chapter 6.

The Nature of Real Externalities

The **real externalities** discussed in this chapter are direct effects, independent of any price changes, that the actions of some households or firms have on the utility of other households or on the output of other firms, none of whom have invited these effects. Because real externalities occur when the independent actions of some people quite unintentionally spill over onto the lives of their neighbors, economists also call them **spillovers** or **neighborhood effects.** These effects, furthermore, can be of two kinds. They can be detrimental, unfavorable or **negative externalities** that impose costs in the form of decreased utility or output on bystanders who are not being compensated for this injury, to their dismay. Real externalities, however, can also be beneficial, favorable, or **positive externalities** that provide benefits in the form of increased utility or output for bystanders who are not being charged for this favor, to their delight. Examples of both negative and positive externalities abound.

Negative Externalities

Examples of negative externalities include the decrease in utility imposed on some people as a result of economic development, such as the incessant growth of cities, highways, and parking lots—of oil derricks, strip mines, and transmission lines. As the natural beauty, purity, and serenity of mountain valleys, lakes, and woods give way to endless expanses of look-alike tract houses on treeless lots or to the ugly noisy world of blast furnaces, railroad yards, and glass and steel office towers or to commercial strips with garish signs, flapping pennants, and circus colors, some people, at least, will feel worse off.

The ever-present golden arches of McDonald's, the beaming face of Colonel Sanders of Kentucky Fried Chicken, the Dairy Queens, the Burger Chefs, the A & W Root Beer stands, the endless strings of gas stations, motels, shopping malls, and movie theaters could similarly be considered producers of negative externalities.

Another example is the pollution of the air, that yellow-brown dome of hydrocarbons and carbon monoxide, soot, fly ash, and sulfur dioxide covering so many cities, reaching perhaps as high as 10,000 feet. Above that is the crisp blue sky, hidden to people on the ground by thousands of tons of particles suspended in the air. Auto exhausts, industrial smokestacks, heating units, city dumps, and private incinerators continually add to the supply. The trouble with air pollution goes far beyond the obvious, such as eyes that burn, higher cleaning costs, and loss of scenic views. Air pollution also damages property, interferes with the life of plants and animals, has subtle effects on the human life span, and, on occasion, it kills people.

Consider the widespread pollution of water from the raw sewage of millions, along with the insufficiently treated sewage of almost everyone else. Add to this the thermal and organic wastes, the inorganic chemicals, and the long-lived radionuclides dumped by industry. Add the runoff from farms (soil, fertilizer, pesticides) and from livestock feedlots (nitrates). Add the sediment and acid drainage from mines and the petroleum products dumped by accidents or reaching bodies of water via the atmosphere after being vaporized ashore. Add the construction debris and the municipal garbage—and don't forget how millions of watercraft discharge anything from human wastes and oil to ballast and litter. Again, the effects are more than visual. Millions receive inferior drinking water that is safe but bad-tasting, bad-looking, or malodorous. Some receive dangerous water that contains excessive arsenic, fecal bacteria, and lead. Fertilized by various chemicals that are innocuous for humans, algae everywhere grow faster than Jack's beanstalk. They clog city water intakes and strangle boat traffic and, when they die, they do more than ruin waterfront property and recreational facilities: bacteria feed on raw sewage and on dead algae; this bacterial activity consumes dissolved oxygen, which enters the water at the water-air interface or by means of the photosynthesis of water plants. Without dissolved oxygen, the fish population dies, and the number of wild birds sharply declines. Even where animals survive, they ingest dangerous substances, and the possibilities of causing disease in people who eat them are legion. . . .

Finally, people reduce each other's welfare by crowding on beaches, freeways, and ski slopes, while firms reduce each other's *output* by crowding onto grazing lands, oil-bearing lands, and ocean fisheries.

Positive Externalities

Luckily, a similar story can be told about positive externalities. Consider how people provide free benefits to other people by planting beautiful flowers and trees, installing telephones, getting vaccinated, and becoming educated. Lumber companies that plant trees provide recreational benefits and possibly modify the weather favorably for nearby farms; firms that drain mines may also raise the productivity of neighboring ones; beekeepers raise the output of nearby orchards; firms that bury high-tension wires to reduce maintenance costs also remove eyesores to passers-by and increase the safety of aircraft operations at nearby airports.

The Analysis of Pigou

In 1912, British economist A. C. Pigou (see Biography 18.1) became the first to deal with externalities in a systematic way. In the presence of externalities, Pigou argued, perfect competition would not produce a Pareto-type welfare maximum.

Consider, for example, the third Pareto condition discussed in Chapter 14. According to this condition, it is impossible to make someone better off without making someone else worse

BIOGRAPHY 18.1:

Arthur C. Pigou

Arthur Cecil Pigou (1877–1959) was born in Ryde on England's Isle of Wight. He studied at Cambridge, where he became a prize pupil and then the successor of Alfred Marshall (see Biography 7.1). Pigou revered his great teacher and firmly carried on his tradition. But Pigou was also a pioneer in welfare economics. He introduced the distinction (explained in this chapter) between private and social costs and benefits and stressed the need for corrective taxes or subsidies to achieve a Pareto optimum.

Until challenged by Keynes (in the field of macroeconomics), Pigou was Britain's leading economist. His works ranged widely, from his classic *The Economics of Welfare* (which first appeared as *Wealth and Welfare* in 1912) and *A Study in Public Finance* (1928) to *Socialism Vs. Capitalism* (1937) and *Employment and Equilibri-*

um (1941). All his writings reflected his abiding concern with practical matters, with ways in which economics might help improve humanity's condition.

"The social enthusiasm which revolts from the sordidness of mean streets and the joylessness of withered lives . . .," Pigou says in the 1920 edition of *The Economics of Welfare* (p. 5), "is the beginning of economic science." Pigou was always concerned with improving conditions *now* so that life might be better also for the future. He demurred from those of his contemporaries who argued that poverty, after all, could not be inherited: "My reply is that the environment of one generation *can* produce a lasting result, because it can affect the environment of future generations. Environments, in short, as well as people, have children" (p. 98).

off, once the marginal rate of transformation between any two goods, $MRT_{a,b}$, equals the corresponding marginal rate of substitution, $MRS_{a,b}$. According to Pareto, such equality would be brought about under perfect competition because all producers and consumers of a and b would face identical market prices of these two goods, P_a and P_b:

Every profit-maximizing firm would adjust output until marginal cost, MC, equaled that given price. In equilibrium, therefore, MC_a would equal P_a and MC_b would equal P_b. If P_a equaled \$10, so would MC_a; if P_b equaled \$5, so would MC_b; therefore, within a firm producing both goods, $1a$ would be technically exchangeable for $2b$ (because both quantities would be taking \$10 of resources). Thus each firm's MRT would equal $1a$ for $2b$ when profit was maximized.

Similarly, every utility-maximizing household facing the prices just noted would adjust purchases until $1a$ and $2b$ were considered to

provide the same utility at the margin (both quantities costing \$10 in the market). Thus each household's MRS would equal $1a$ for $2b$ when utility was maximized. When externalities are present, however, this grand conclusion about the automatic achievement of Pareto efficiency through perfect competition is upset.

Marginal Private Cost vs. Marginal Social Cost

Each one of the above marginal costs, Pigou noted, was a **marginal private cost** or **marginal internal cost**, which is the marginal cost borne by the firm (or household) actually producing (or consuming) a good. But now suppose that the production of good a involved a negative externality: the production of another unit of a required not only \$10 of additional resources within the firm that produced a (the marginal private cost), but it also forced another firm to spend an additional \$5 to defend itself against a reduction in its output as a result of the first firm's activity. Pigou called such change in the total cost of some firms (or households) that was associated with a unit change in the output (or consumption) of others the **marginal external cost**. And he called the sum of the marginal private cost, MPC, and marginal external cost, MEC, the **marginal social cost**, MSC. The MSC is, in fact, the marginal cost of an activity as seen from the viewpoint of society.

$$MPC + MEC = MSC$$

In our example, MSC_a would thus equal $15, which indicates that it would take $15 of extra resources to produce an extra $1a$ in society—$10 of these resources in the firm producing a and $5 elsewhere. As long as externalities were not involved in the production of good b, this MSC_a implies, of course, that the true marginal rate of transformation would equal not $1a$ for $2b$, but $1a$ for $3b$ (both quantities taking $15 of resources). Because consumers would value $1a$ indifferently with $2b$ (in accordance with the postulated market prices), society's welfare would not be maximized: If $1a$ less were produced, $15 of resources would be released ($10 at the producing firm, $5 elsewhere), and these resources could produce an additional $3b$. Any consumer indifferent about $1a$ and $2b$ could be made better off.

The same argument, Pigou noted, could be made (in analogous fashion) about positive externalities among producers and about (positive or negative) externalities in the realm of consumption.

Marginal Private Benefit vs. Marginal Social Benefit

In the case of externalities in the realm of consumption, a wedge would appear between **marginal private benefit** or **marginal internal benefit** (the marginal benefit enjoyed by a household actually consuming a good) and **marginal social benefit** (the marginal benefit of this activity as seen from the viewpoint of society). This

difference would, of course, be the **marginal external benefit**, the change in the total benefit of some households that was associated with a unit change in the consumption of others.

The marginal external benefit, in turn, could be negative, as when neighbors are harmed by noisy snowmobiles, or it could be positive, as when neighbors benefit from the beautiful flower gardens of others.

The Golden Rule

Having made these observations, Pigou added this golden rule to Pareto's conditions:

> *In order to maximize total economic welfare, all divergences between any activity's marginal social benefit and marginal social cost must be eliminated.*

Pigou thought that government should design appropriate taxes and subsidies to close this gap.

The Role of Taxes on Producers

Panel (a) of Figure 18.1 depicts the market for paper, which, we now assume, involves a negative externality among producers: the producers of paper pollute a river and reduce the output of fishers, who must incur heavy additional costs if they wish to produce as much as before. The competitive paper industry's supply is shown by line S; it represents, of course, the sum (above minimum average variable costs) of the paper companies' marginal private costs, ΣMPC. If we add the fishers' marginal external costs (which vary with the amount of paper produced), we discover the higher marginal social cost of paper production, MSC. Line D represents, in turn, market demand, the sum of marginal private benefits and (we assume) marginal social benefits, $\Sigma MPB = MSB$.

A competitive market would clearly induce production of quantity q_1 at price p_1, corresponding to intersection a. Note: Marginal social cost would exceed marginal social benefit for all units produced beyond q_2, as is indicated by line segments bc and ba. Thus a competitive market would induce production too large for a welfare maximum. The last unit produced, q_1, would, for instance, yield a benefit to a paper consumer of p_1; this last unit would cost an equal amount in the paper factory but would cost an additional amount of ac elsewhere resulting in a net social

FIGURE 18.1 Pigou's Golden Rule

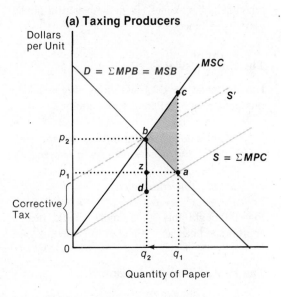

(a) Taxing Producers

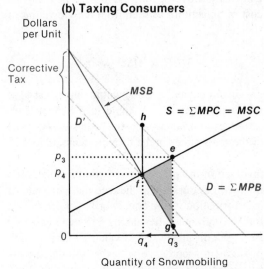

(b) Taxing Consumers

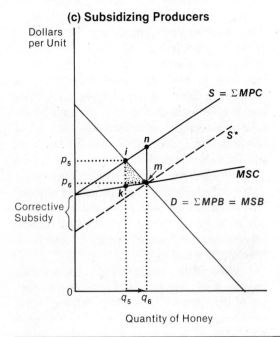

(c) Subsidizing Producers

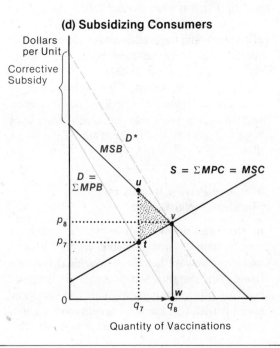

(d) Subsidizing Consumers

loss of ca on that unit. Similar and smaller losses would be made on all units between q_2 and q_1. Neglect of marginal external costs would thus produce a social net benefit from paper production that fell short of its possible maximum (the MSB–MSC difference up to q_2) by shaded area abc.

Government, Pigou would argue, could remove the gap ac between marginal private and marginal social cost by imposing upon paper producers a *per-unit tax* equal to bd, or the MPC–MSC gap at the optimal output volume q_2. This tax would raise the marginal private cost curve to the dashed line, making it the paper producers' new market supply, S'. Paper producers would then produce lower quantity q_2 (note the arrow) and sell it at higher price p_2. Because of the higher price (point b), paper consumers would consume less. Because of the lower net price (point d), paper producers would produce less. Both would have been made aware of the negative aspects of their behavior on other people in society. Marginal social benefit would equal marginal social cost (point b).

The Role of Taxes on Consumers

Panel (b) of Figure 18.1 depicts the market for snowmobiling, which, we assume, involves a negative externality among consumers: The users of snowmobiles create noise and reduce the welfare of many households affected by it. The snowmobilers' demand is shown by D; it represents the sum of the snowmobilers' marginal private benefits, ΣMPB. If we consider their neighbors' negative marginal external benefits (which vary with the amount of snowmobiling), we discover the lower marginal social benefit of snowmobiling, MSB. Line S represents, in turn, market supply, the sum of marginal private costs and (we assume) marginal social costs, $\Sigma MPC = MSC$.

A competitive market would clearly induce production of quantity q_3 at price p_3, corresponding to intersection e. Note: Marginal social cost would exceed marginal social benefit for all units produced beyond q_4, as is indicated by line segments fe and fg. Thus a competitive market would induce consumption too large for a welfare maximum. The last unit consumed, q_3, would, for instance, yield a benefit to a snowmobiler of p_3; this last unit would cost an equal amount to produce, but it would also impose a negative benefit of eg on someone else resulting in a net social loss of eg on that unit. Similar and smaller losses would be made on all units between q_3 and q_4. Neglect of (negative) marginal external benefits would thus produce a social net benefit from snowmobiling that fell short of its possible maximum (the MSB–MSC difference up to q_4) by shaded area efg.

Government, Pigou would argue, could remove the gap eg between marginal private and marginal social benefit by imposing upon snow-

---

Pigou noted that self-interest easily eliminates divergences between marginal private benefits and costs in competitive markets but fails to eliminate divergences between marginal social benefits and costs. As a result, self-interest fails to maximize total economic welfare in the presence of externalities: When producers or consumers impose uncompensated costs on others, competitive markets allow production and consumption to exceed the amount at which marginal social cost just equals marginal social benefit (points b and f). On the other hand, when producers or consumers provide free benefits to others, competitive markets allow production and consumption to fall short of the amount at which marginal social cost just equals marginal social benefit (points m and v). The implied economic inefficiencies (shaded and dotted areas), argued Pigou, can be eliminated through taxation whenever production and consumption are excessive, as in panels (a) and (b), and through subsidies whenever production and consumption are insufficient, as in panels (c) and (d).

Note: In these examples, the divergence between marginal private cost and marginal social cost, in panels (a) and (c), or between marginal private benefit and marginal social benefit, in panels (b) and (d), is itself increasing with the level of activity in question. This particular condition, however, is not the only one possible. Pigou's argument would be just as valid if the divergence in question were the same at all activity levels. Nor does the corrective tax or subsidy have to be a constant per unit, as shown here. Properly designed per-unit taxes or subsidies that vary with the activity level could accomplish the desired correction as well.

mobilers a *per-unit tax* equal to *fh*, or the $MPB-MSB$ gap at the optimal output volume q_4. This tax would lower the marginal private benefit curve to the dashed line, making it the snowmobilers' new market demand, D'. Snowmobile producers would then produce lower quantity q_4 (note the arrow) and sell it at lower price p_4. Snowmobilers, however, would pay more than before, p_4 plus the tax. Marginal social benefit would equal marginal social cost (point f).

The Role of Subsidies for Producers

Panel (c) of Figure 18.1 depicts the market for honey, which, we assume, involves a positive externality among producers: the presence of many bees raises the output of orchardists who can reduce their costs if they wish to produce as much as before. Thus the situation in panel (c) is analogous to that in panel (a), except that marginal social cost now lies *below* marginal private cost. A competitive market would induce production q_5 at p_5, corresponding to intersection i. Marginal social cost would fall short of marginal social benefit not only for all units up to q_5, but also for all units between q_5 and q_6, as is indicated by line segments *km* and *im*. Thus a competitive market would induce production too small for a welfare maximum. The last unit produced, q_5, would, for instance, yield a benefit to a honey consumer of p_5; this last unit would cost an equal amount in the *apiary* (where bee hives are kept) but would *reduce* costs by *ik* in the orchards resulting in a net social gain of *ik* on that unit. Similar and smaller gains would be forgone for all units between q_5 and q_6. Neglect of (negative) marginal external costs would thus produce a social net benefit from honey that fell short of its possible maximum (the $MSB-MSC$ difference up to q_6) by dotted area *ikm*.

Government, Pigou would argue, could remove the gap *ik* between marginal private and marginal social cost by offering to honey producers a *per-unit subsidy* equal to *mn,* or the $MPC-MSC$ gap at the optimal output volume q_6. This subsidy would lower the marginal private cost curve to the dashed line, making it the honey

producers' new market supply, S^*. Honey producers would thus produce larger quantity q_6 (note the arrow) and sell it at lower price p_6. Honey producers, however, would receive more than before, p_6 plus the subsidy. Marginal social benefit would equal marginal social cost (m).

The Role of Subsidies for Consumers

Panel (d) of Figure 18.1 depicts the market for vaccinations, which, we assume, involves a positive externality among consumers: those who get vaccinated are less likely to get sick and, therefore, they raise the welfare of other households who are less likely to catch disease. The situation in panel (d) is analogous to that in panel (b), except that marginal social benefit now lies *above* marginal private benefit. A competitive market would induce production q_7 at p_7, corresponding to intersection t. Marginal social cost would fall short of marginal social benefit not only for all units up to q_7, but also for all units between q_7 and q_8, as is indicated by line segments *tv* and *uv*. Thus a competitive market would induce production too small for a welfare maximum. The last unit produced, q_7, would, for instance, yield a benefit to a vaccinated person of p_7; this last unit would cost an equal amount to produce but would yield an additional benefit of *tu* to other people. There would be a net social gain of *tu* on that unit. Similar and smaller gains would be forgone for all units between q_7 and q_8. Neglect of marginal external benefits would thus produce a social net benefit from vaccinations that fell short of its possible maximum (the $MSB-MSC$ difference up to q_8) by dotted area *tuv*.

Government, Pigou would argue, could remove the gap *tu* between marginal private and marginal social benefit by offering to consumers of vaccinations a *per-unit subsidy* equal to *vw,* or the $MPB-MSB$ gap at the optimal output volume q_8. This subsidy would raise the marginal private benefit curve to the dashed line, making it the vaccination consumers' new market demand, D^*. The producers of vaccinations would then increase quantity to q_8 (note the arrow) and charge price p_8. The consumers involved, however, would pay less than before, p_8 minus the subsidy (or nothing at all in this case). Marginal social benefit would equal marginal social cost (point v).

The Challenge of Coase

For nearly half a century, Pigou's analysis went unchallenged. Then Ronald Coase (see Biography 18.2), in a celebrated 1960 article, pointed out what is quite obvious in retrospect: Pigou's argument about the government's ability to raise social welfare implicitly assumes that the proposed tax-subsidy scheme is costless—which it is unlikely to be. The very costs of administrating the scheme might well exceed the gains to be had from eliminating economic inefficiency (which gains are shown by the shaded and dotted triangles in Figure 18.1).

In addition, Coase pointed out, if government simply assigned unambiguous and transferable property rights, competitive markets might well overcome the externalities problem and achieve economic efficiency without any further government intervention. When formulating his recommendations for government intervention, Pigou had implicitly assumed that the parties affected by externalities could not privately negotiate with one another. In fact, they have plenty of reasons to do just that. Whenever total economic welfare can be raised by reducing the output and consumption of goods with negative externalities, as in panels (a) and (b) of Figure 18.1, and whenever total economic welfare can be raised by increasing the output and consumption of goods with positive externalities, as in panels (c) and (d), the affected parties can negotiate for a change in the allocation of resources that makes everyone better off at the same time.

BIOGRAPHY 18.2:

Ronald H. Coase

Ronald Harry Coase (1910–   ) was born in Willesden, England. He studied and later taught at the London School of Economics. In 1951, he came to the United States, teaching at the Universities of Buffalo, Virginia, and, finally, Chicago. There Coase became the founder of the "new institutional economics," which unifies analytical and institutional economics—two branches that have often been antagonistic toward one another. Again and again, Coase has produced great insights by looking at an economic institution and asking: What are its effects on the allocation of resources? How can one account for its evolution and continued existence in terms of this effect?

This approach produced *British Broadcasting: A Study in Monopoly* (1950) and two of this century's major articles. In "The Nature of the Firm" (1937), referred to in Chapter 2, Coase examined what determines which transactions are conducted within firms and which are conducted in the marketplace.[1] In "The Problem of Social Cost," he challenged Pigou in a way noted at length in this chapter.[2] Through his editorship of *The Journal of Law and Economics*, Coase has rapidly advanced studies in these overlapping fields. He has summed up one result by saying: "It is now generally accepted by all students of the subject that most (perhaps almost all) government regulation is anti-competitive and harmful in its effects." In 1980, the American Economic Association honored Coase by making him one of its Distinguished Fellows.

[1]Ronald H. Coase, "The Nature of the Firm," *Economica*, New Series 4 (November 1937): 386–405.

[2]Ronald H. Coase, "The Problem of Social Cost," *The Journal of Law and Economics* 3 (October 1960): 1–44.

The Possibility of Private Deals

The vertical differences between *MSC* and *MPC* in panel (a) represent the value of extra outputs lost by fishers for various additions to paper production. Thus the production of paper unit q_2 raises the injury to fishers by *db*; the production of paper unit q_1 raises the injury by another *ac*, and increasing paper output all the way from q_2 to q_1 reduces fish output by *bdac*—which is also the value of output fishers would *gain* if paper production was cut from q_1 to q_2. If paper production was so cut, producers of paper would then lose producer surplus of only *adz* (market price being p_1), and consumers of paper would lose consumer surplus of *abz*. Surely, the fisher's potential gain of *bdac* would be more than enough to compensate or overcompensate the losers in a way that made everyone as well off as or better off than before. Unless the transactions costs of finding each other, carrying out the negotiations, signing the contract, and enforcing it were larger than the potential net gain (area *abc*), such a private deal would be made and the welfare-maximizing output mix would be achieved—quite without governmental taxing or subsidizing.

The Coase Theorem

As Coase pointed out, it would make no difference to the allocation of resources how government assigned property rights in a contested resource, such as the river in our example.

Let the government state that fishers had the right not to have fish harmed, that they owned the right to unhindered use of the river. If the river was also wanted by paper companies for purposes of waste dumping, the paper companies would have to pay compensation to fishers for any output losses brought about by paper-company pollution. The production of paper unit number q_2, for example, would cause a fishing loss valued at *db*; the production of paper unit number q_1 would cause a fishing loss valued at *ac*; and so on. Each time, paper producers would have to make a corresponding payment to fishers. The paper producers, therefore, would have to reckon

these damage payments as an explicit cost of doing business. Their marginal private costs would come to equal *MSC*. They would "internalize" the externality; the divergence of private and social cost would disappear. Paper companies would choose to produce the Pareto-optimal quantity q_2 because the production of even one additional unit would bring a price (just below *b* on the demand curve) insufficient to cover the extra production cost, now including damage payments (just *above b* on the *MSC* line).

Amazingly, this resource allocation would not be changed at all if government were to assign property rights in the river to the paper companies and thus gave them the *right* to dump wastes into it and generate harmful externalities affecting fishers. Fishers would then have to *bribe* the paper companies into not exercising their rights. Because the production of paper unit number q_2 would cause a fishing loss valued at *db* (and that of paper unit number q_1 one of *ac*), fishers could make themselves better off by offering bribes up to this magnitude to prevent the production of these units of paper. Paper companies, however, would now have to consider forgone potential bribes as *implicit* costs of doing business. Thus the production of paper unit q_2 would cost them not only an added amount (shown by point *d*) of wages, materials, and the like, but also the loss of *db* that might have been received from fishers had unit q_2 not been produced. Once more, profit-maximizing paper companies would view *MSC* as the relevant indicator of their marginal private cost. Once more they would choose to produce no more than q_2 units. The next unit produced would cost them more (including bribes forgone) than consumers of paper would be willing to pay. Thus paper production would be expanded (and the production of fish restricted) exactly up to the point at which the marginal unit of paper produced just equaled in value the marginal unit of fish sacrificed for its sake. In this way the total value of output would be maximized.

The **Coase theorem** on the allocative neutrality of property rights can be summarized as follows:

ANALYTICAL EXAMPLE 18.1:
The Economics of Bees

The Coasean prediction that externalities are likely to be removed through private bargaining unless transactions costs are prohibitive has recently been confirmed by a study of bees. Beekeepers receive advantages from farmers who grow plants the nectar of which is likely to increase the production of honey. Accordingly, beekeepers pay "apiary rent" for the right to place their hives on the growers' land. But farmers also receive advantages from bees that aid pollination and thereby help increase certain crops, and these farmers pay "pollination fees" for the privilege of having bees on their land.

In the United States, contractual arrangements between the two parties are routine. Sometimes, payments are made in one direction, as in the case of mint that helps yield honey but does not require pollination services. At other times, payments are made in the other direction, as in the case of apples that require pollination services but do not improve honey output. Sometimes payments go both ways, as in the case of alfalfa and red clover.

The accompanying table shows some of the data collected during 1970–71 in this study of Coasean contracts in the state of Washington.

Seasons	Plants	Pollination Fees	Approximate Apiary Rent per Hive
Early spring	Almond (California)	$5–$8	0
	Cherry	$6–$8	0
Late spring (major pollination season)	Apple and soft Fruits	$9–$10	0
	Blueberry (with maple)	$5	0
	Cabbage	$8	0
	Cherry	$9–$10	0
	Cranberry	$9	0
Summer and early fall (major honey season)	Alfalfa	0	13¢–60¢
	Alfalfa (with pollination)	$3–$5	0
	Fireweed	0	25¢–63¢
	Mint	0	15¢–65¢
	Pasture	0	15¢–65¢
	Red clover	0	65¢
	Red clover (with pollination	$3–$6	0
	Sweet clover	0	20¢–25¢

Source: Steven N. S. Cheung, "The Fable of the Bees: An Economic Investigation," *The Journal of Law and Economics*, April 1973, pp. 11–33. Table adapted by permission of the University of Chicago Press. Copyright 1973 by the University of Chicago.

Under perfect competition, and in the absence of income effects and transactions costs, voluntary negotiated agreements among private parties generating or being affected by externalities will lead to the same resource allocation (and output mix) regardless of how property rights are assigned among these parties.

Limitations of the Coase Theorem

Coase recognized that his neutrality theorem might be falsified in the presence of income effects. It would surely make a difference to the distribution of income and wealth whether fishers or paper companies had property rights in our river. The assignment of these rights would determine whether fishers had to be paid damages *by* paper companies or had to pay bribes *to* them. If the income elasticity of demand differed for fishers and paper-company owners, the pattern of demand, and hence of equilibrium prices *and of outputs*, would differ under the two possible assignments of property rights.

Coase also recognized that the presence of high transactions costs might preclude the reaching of voluntary agreements to internalize externalities, especially if the number of parties generating or being affected by externalities was large.

The Large-Numbers Problem: The Case of Pollution

Consider the case of river pollution that involves not a small number of fishers and paper companies who know each other, but literally tens of thousands of people who cannot possibly know each other. Such large numbers of people, all of whom generate wastes or are adversely affected by them, will find voluntary agreements simply too costly to reach. Even identifying all the parties will be prohibitively difficult, as will be the measurement of externalities, the negotiations, and the subsequent policing of agreements.

The production of the welfare-maximizing outputs mix, therefore, is not assured. High transactions costs become the root of all evil; they explain why externalities persist. The recognition of high transactions costs leads directly to the modern post-Pigouvian theory of government intervention, which can be illustrated by considering possible policies for reducing the pollution of a large river.

The Optimum Level of Pollution

It is usually suggested that government should first identify the optimum level of pollution. Although in practice identifying optimum pollution is a costly procedure, the theoretical argument is clear enough (see Figure 18.2). The line labelled *MSB* represents the declining marginal social benefit of waste dumping. Thus the first unit dumped in a year saves society $50 of other goods that would have to be forgone if resources were diverted to treating or recycling that unit of waste (point *a*). By the same token, dumping the 48 millionth, 72 millionth, or 96 millionth unit saves society, respectively, $30, $20, or $10 of other goods (points *b, c,* and *d*). The decline in the dollar figures just cited reflects the fact that it is often very easy to reduce waste emissions by a unit when there is a lot of waste, while it is often very difficult to reduce waste emissions by a unit when there is little waste left. Thus cutting one unit of waste out of 96 million units may cost a mere $10; for this reason the 96 millionth unit, *when dumped*, benefits society to the extent of $10 of other goods (point *d*). Yet cutting out the first unit (which is the last remaining unit of waste) may cost $50; for this reason the first unit, when dumped, benefits society to the extent of $50 of other goods (point *a*). Note: The area under the *MSB* line up to any chosen quantity equals the sum of marginal benefits; thus it shows the total benefit (in terms of other goods *not* sacrificed) of dumping the given quantity. Dumping 72 million units of waste per year saves society 0*acf* of other goods; dumping 120 million units saves society 0*ae* of goods.

The line labeled *MSC* represents the rising

marginal social cost of waste dumping. Thus the first 24 million units dumped in a year have no harmful effect on anything; the natural environment absorbs these wastes easily (and line *MSC* coincides with the horizontal axis). Further dumping begins to cause damages—first to riverfront property perhaps, then to boats and fish, and, finally, to human health. Thus the 48 millionth unit dumped adds $10 to the damage already sustained and brings the total to *ghi*. The 72 millionth unit, in turn, adds $20 to damages and raises the total to *cfi*. The 96 millionth unit adds $30 (point *k*) to the damage total.

The optimum level of pollution equals the dumping of 72 million units of waste per year for the following reason: Up to this quantity, every unit dumped saves society goods valued more highly than those destroyed by pollution damage. Points on line *ac* lie above those on line *0ic*; the optimum amount of dumping brings society a net gain shown by shaded area *0aci*. Dumping *more* than 72 million units a year, however, reduces society's net gain because after that point each additional unit dumped destroys goods valued more highly (along line *ck*) than those saved by dumping rather than abating wastes (and valued along line *ce*). Without government intervention, however, the actual level of pollution will not equal the optimum.

The Actual Level of Pollution

Figure 18.3 is a copy of Figure 18.2, but the line showing the marginal social benefit of dumping is now viewed as the *demand for pollution opportunities*. The change of view is legitimate because the value of other goods that waste dumpers can save by dumping ($50 for the first unit dumped, $20 for the 72 millionth unit, and so on) is also the maximum amount they would pay for the right simply to dump the unit in question.

Now assume that property rights in our river are ill-defined. Anyone who wants to use the river can do so for any purpose whatever. In that case, potential waste dumpers face a *supply of pollution opportunities* that coincides with the

FIGURE 18.2 Optimum Pollution

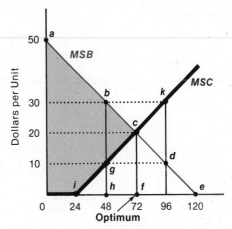

The optimum level of pollution is one at which the declining marginal social benefit from waste dumping just equals its rising marginal social cost (point *c*). This level maximizes society's net gain from dumping wastes (shaded area). Those who insist on zero pollution are asking society to sacrifice this net gain: They are asking to save goods destroyed by pollution and worth *cfi* by sacrificing goods that could be produced if resources were not diverted to pollution abatement and that are worth *0acf*.

horizontal axis: They may do all the dumping they like and at a zero price.

Because demand and supply meet a point *c*, 120 million units will in fact be dumped per year. Each one of these dumped units saves dumpers some resources that would otherwise have had to be spent on treating or recycling wastes and that could not have been spent on producing other goods.

Figure 18.3 also demonstrates that actual pollution in excess of optimal pollution is just as foolish as actual pollution falling short of the optimum. Imagine moving left from point *c* toward *d* by instituting a program of pollution abatement. The line of marginal social *benefit* of waste *dumping* (declining as one moves to the

FIGURE 18.3 Actual Pollution

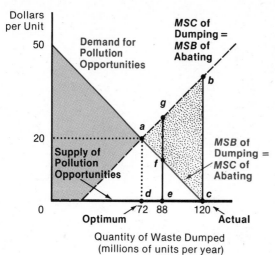

Quantity of Waste Dumped
(millions of units per year)

When property rights are ill-defined, actual pollution may well exceed optimum pollution. Beyond the optimum, society is then losing to pollution goods (area *abcd*) that exceed in value the goods that would have to be sacrificed in order to carry out pollution abatement (area *acd*). The dotted area shows the net loss from excessive pollution (and the net gain from its potential abatement to the optimum level). This net loss offsets in whole or in part the maximum potential net benefit of waste dumping (shaded).

right from the level of zero waste dumping at origin 0) can then be viewed as a line of marginal social *cost* of waste *abating* (rising as one moves to the left from the level of actual waste dumping at point *c*). The line of marginal social cost of waste dumping (rising as one moves to the right from origin 0) can similarly be viewed as a line of marginal social benefit of waste abating (falling as one moves left from point *b*). Abatement of the 120 millionth unit of waste thus would bring a benefit of *bc* (pollution damage avoided), and it would cost nothing (point *c*)—it would be worthwhile. Abating the 88 millionth unit would bring a smaller benefit *(eg)* of pollution damage avoided; it would result in a positive but lower cost *(ef)* of other goods now sacrificed, so it would still be worthwhile (the marginal net gain being *fg*). By

reducing actual pollution from the actual to the optimal level, society would save goods worth *abcd* (because they would not be destroyed by pollution). Society would sacrifice goods worth *acd* (because resources to make them would be diverted to pollution abatement). At the optimum level, there would be a net gain of *abc* (the dotted area). Without government action, however, society is likely to forgo this net gain.

Pollution-Abatement Policies

It is one thing to discuss the optimal level of pollution as if all the relevant information were available. It is quite another matter in the real world. Government frequently has access to only fragmentary data. Many of the data are subjective. (How, for instance, is one to evaluate the effects of waste dumping that offend our aesthetic sensibilities: rivers covered with green, blue, and red iridescent splotches or topped with floating debris, ranging from trash and steel drums to tires and old rubber boots?) In addition, government is more likely to get data on totals and averages than on the marginal quantities our theory demands. Nevertheless, let us consider some of the policy options open to a government that wishes to reduce waste dumping from an excessive level to an optimal one.

Moral Suasion

Government can try voluntarism by appealing to people's consciences and exhort them not to litter or incinerate trash or wear the furs of endangered species. It can urge people to treat their sewage, make less noise, conserve fuel, paper, or water, use unleaded gas and phosphate-free detergents, recycle bottles, and prevent forest fires. Unfortunately, altruism is a notoriously weak force for social change. Asking for large-scale self-restraint is calling for nothing less than an ethical revolution, unlikely to be achieved any time soon.

Even if everyone agreed that all would gain from reducing pollution, few individuals would

ANALYTICAL EXAMPLE 18.2:
Optimizing in Practice: The Delaware

In the 1960s, a government commission studied four proposals to improve the water quality of the Delaware Estuary. The accompanying table shows midpoints of its estimates of costs and benefits for a 20-year time horizon (in millions of dollars and present values, discounted at 3 percent).

In general, conservationists and elected officials supported goal 3; representatives of industry and municipalities, goal 2. The commission voted for a goal between 2 and 3 (circled).

Water Quality Improvement	Total Costs	Total Benefits	Marginal Cost	Marginal Benefit
1 (least)	98	200		
			22	20
2	120	220		
			145	10
3	265	230		
			195	25
4 (most)	460	255		

Based on Allen V. Kneese and Blair T. Bower, *Managing Water Quality: Economics, Technology, Institutions* (Baltimore: The Johns Hopkins Press, 1968), pp. 224–35.

voluntarily act to stop their part in it. In most cases any one producer or consumer contributes an infinitesimal amount to the total damage; therefore, they can be certain that any sacrificial actions of theirs, though costly to themselves, would have no noticeable overall effect. Such actions would appear to be futile, pointless, and akin to holding back a flood with a pail.

By the same logic it follows that individuals would still have the incentive to pollute (and thus to save the cost of abatement) even if they were certain that everyone else would act to stop their dumping of wastes. If only one person were to cheat, the overall result would be indistinguishable from that in which all were complying with antipollution measures. Thus the moral-suasion approach amounts to asking individuals to act against their own interest. Indeed, persons who heeded the call for "responsible citizenship" could hardly expect to be admired as saints by fellow citizens. More likely, they would be looked upon as fools or cranks.

Besides being impractical, the voluntary approach to pollution reduction has another drawback. It contains no mechanism to achieve the optimum amount of pollution. Nevertheless, government tends to use this approach in cases where enforcement is impossible (consider littering in isolated areas of National Parks) or where immediate action is required in brief emergencies (consider a temperature inversion in smoggy Los Angeles).

The Outright Ban

Much more reliable than moral suasion is an outright ban on polluting activities, supported by penalties for noncompliance, such as fines and prison terms. It would, of course, be impractical to ban all polluting activities at once. Consider the extreme chaos that would result if Congress were to outlaw all polluting internal combustion engines (as one of its members once seriously proposed). But limited bans are possible.

In the early 1970s, for example, the federal government banned the use of DDT almost totally and the use of mercury in paints and pesticides. Many states and cities have also tried bans.

Oregon and Vermont banned disposable beverage containers; Connecticut and New York banned phosphates in laundry detergents. Within two miles of the coast, Delaware banned oil refineries, steel plants, paper mills, and off-shore-oil and iron-ore transshipment terminals. Cities such as Boston, Chicago, New York, and Philadelphia banned the spraying of fireproofing asbestos.

Although practical within limits, outright prohibitions are unlikely to achieve optimum pollution—unless, of course, the optimum is at the zero dumping point. Pollution that imposes extreme hazards might have such a zero dumping optimum point. (In that case, the *MSC* line in Figure 18.2 would start above point *a* on the vertical axis). In general, though, risk-averse governments have chosen the ban when the cost of discovering the optimum level was itself prohibitive and they had to choose an arbitrary level between zero and unchecked pollution.

Setting Standards

The most popular approach of governments in the U.S. to pollution abatement has been the setting of standards. Standard setting was first done exclusively at the state and local level. California set the first exhaust emission standards on cars. The first general noise control codes were set in Chicago and New York City. Congress then passed the National Environmental Policy Act, which declared that it is the policy of the U.S. government "to create and maintain conditions under which man and nature can exist in productive harmony." The act created, in the office of the President, a permanent three-member Council of Environmental Quality to recommend environmental policies to the President. The act also gave birth, in 1970, to the Environmental Protection Agency (EPA). The EPA has set a variety of standards concerning many types of pollutants. **Input standards** specify the types of inputs polluters may use (for example, fuel with specified sulfur content). **Emission standards** specify maximum quantities of pollutants that may be released by any one

polluter, and **ambient standards** specify the quantity the environment may contain.

The regulation-by-standards approach has one serious drawback: it is likely to be extremely —and, in part, unnecessarily—costly. First is the administrative cost. The quality of the environment has to be monitored. Standards have to be agreed upon on the basis of scientific evidence concerning emission toxicity and persistence. Pollution has to be traced to its sources, and polluters must be made aware of the standards applying to them. Most expensive, probably, is the enforcement cost. Unlike traffic violations, which can bring harm to the violator (an accident), the violation of input or emission standards brings pure pleasure to the violator (lower costs). People, therefore, are inclined to break such rules; it is extremely difficult for government to catch, prosecute, and convict them.

It is not unlikely that compliance costs are higher than necessary. Because pollution control costs differ among polluters, the overall pollution-avoidance cost can only be minimized if standards are carefully tailored to the special circumstances of each polluter. That is, emission standards must be toughest for those who can avoid pollution at lowest cost. Often this tailoring of standards is also desirable for reasons of equity, because just those polluters who have already avoided some pollution voluntarily are likely to have the highest marginal cost for further reductions in emission. Yet because setting *differentiated* standards for these reasons spells an administrative nightmare, government can almost certainly be relied on to set *uniform* emission standards for all polluters. Such uniform standards are probably inequitable and certainly unnecessarily expensive.

Table 18.1 illustrates why uniform emission standards cannot be expected to minimize the pollution-avoidance cost. Three firms are assumed to exist in an area emitting initial quantities of pollutants given in row (1). Emission standards are set requiring reductions by all firms to 50 percent of former emissions (2). The emissions avoided by following these standards are shown in row (3). Suppose the marginal and average costs of pollution abatement are constant for each firm, as given in row (4). Then the total costs of pollution abatement are those of row (5) of our table. Society is achieving a 50 percent reduction of pollution by incurring an opportunity cost of $480 million a year (circled).

Yet society could have gotten the same result at a much smaller sacrifice of other things. Only rarely is the unit cost of pollution avoidance uniform for all polluters. In our hypothetical case, there are indeed great differences. As shown in row (4), the unit cost of pollution avoidance is exceedingly high for Firm A, less so for Firm C, and least so for Firm B.

Had government known this detail, it could have issued a selective decree, treating different firms differently. For instance, it could have allowed Firm A to dump as much as ever, while forcing Firms B and C to reduce dumping 100 percent. The results are shown in rows (6) through (8). The same 100-million-ton-per-year reduction in pollution could have cost society as little as $260 million of other goods (circled).

Taxing the Dumping of Waste

Government can also use financial incentives, as Pigou taught us long ago, to curb pollution. Figure 18.4 is based on Figure 18.3. As before, optimum pollution equals 72 million units per

TABLE 18.1 Air Pollution Abatement: Uniform vs. Differential Standards

		Firm A	Firm B	Firm C	Total
(1)	Quantity of particulate matter emitted prior to antipollution law (millions of tons per year)	100	20	80	200
(2)	Quantity of particulate matter emitted after 50 percent standards are adopted (millions of tons per year)	50	10	40	100
(3) = (1) − (2)	Quantity of particulate matter emission that is avoided (millions of tons per year)	50	10	40	100
(4)	Unit cost of pollution avoidance (dollars per ton per year)	7	1	3	—
(5) = (3) × (4)	Total cost of pollution avoidance using standards law (millions of dollars per year)	350	10	120	480
(6)	Quantity of particulate matter emitted after selective decree (millions of tons per year)	100	0	0	100
(7) = (1) − (6)	Alternative quantity of particulate matter emission that is avoided (millions of tons per year)	0	20	80	100
(8) = (7) × (4)	Alternative total cost of pollution avoidance using selective decree (millions of dollars per year)	0	20	240	260

If unit costs of pollution avoidance differ among firms, society cannot minimize the opportunity cost of a given amount of pollution avoidance by issuing uniform pollution standards.

year, corresponding to the equality at point *a* of the marginal social benefit and cost of dumping. As before, actual dumping prior to government intervention equals 120 million units per year (point *b*). We now suppose that government imposes a tax of $20 for each unit dumped, equal to the marginal social cost of dumping *(ac)* for the optimal amount of dumping *(0c)*. This action effectively raises the supply of pollution opportunities from the horizontal axis (where it was in Figure 18.3) to the parallel line going through point *a*.

The message to polluters is clear. Instead of being given the right to dump all they want at a zero price, they are now given the right to dump all they want at $20 per unit of wastes. Government has implicitly bestowed a property right in the environment on the public at large, but it stands ready, as the public's agent, to sell this right to individual would-be users.

Polluters, as a result, will reduce dumping to the optimal amount: Units dumped beyond the

optimum save resources *from* abatement uses and *for* the production of other goods, which are valued along line *ab*. The values of these other goods are lower than the tax, which is measured along line *ad*. Polluters would rather lose goods worth *abc* (by diverting the resources that could have made these goods to a reduction in waste dumping from *b* to *c*) than face a tax of *acbd* (for dumping quantity *cb*). On the other hand, polluters would rather pay a tax of *0eac* for dumping *0c* than lose goods worth *0fac* (which the resources capable of abating *0c* can produce).

The most important drawback of this scheme is again the cost of administering it. Nevertheless, government has traveled this route to a limited extent. In 1971, Vermont followed the highly successful system in France, Germany, and Great Britain and introduced fees for waste disposal in waterways if discharges were out of compliance with water quality standards. The

FIGURE 18.4
Pollution Abatement through Taxation

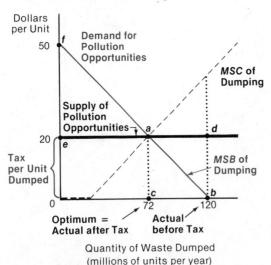

Quantity of Waste Dumped
(millions of units per year)

The imposition of a tax per unit of waste dumped (here of $20) might reduce excessive pollution (point *b*) to the optimal level (point *c*).

FIGURE 18.5
Pollution Abatement through Subsidies

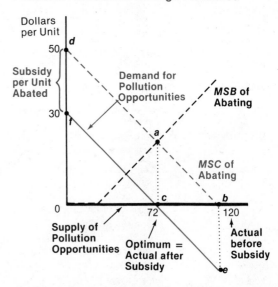

Quantity of Waste Dumped (millions of units per year)

The granting of a subsidy (here, of $20) per unit of waste abated might reduce excessive pollution (point *b*) to the optimal level (point *c*).

fees were to reflect the cost of environmental damage. Fees of somewhat different nature were also charged in Maryland and Michigan for water discharges. The federal government has imposed taxes on the sulfur content of coal, oil, and natural gas, rebated to those who prevent sulfur from escaping during fuel use. The federal government has also imposed a tax on leaded gasoline; Congress has debated other such taxes (on detergents, pesticides, and disposable goods). One proposal urged a 1-cent-per-pound fee for all goods requiring disposal within 10 years of origin. (This fee would come to 5 cents for the Sunday *New York Times* and $35 for a 3,500-pound car.)

Subsidizing Waste Abatement

Pigou's second approach has not escaped notice either. Figure 18.5 is again based on Figure 18.3. Optimum pollution equals 72 million units per year, corresponding to point *a*; actual pollution, prior to government intervention, equals 120 million units (point *b*). We will now suppose that government grants a subsidy of $20 for each unit of abated waste, equal to the marginal social benefit of abating *(ac)* for the optimal amount of abatement *(bc)*. This action effectively lowers the demand for pollution opportunities from where it was (dashed line *db*) to the parallel line going through point *c*.

The message to pollution abaters is clear. As before, they can dump all they want at a zero price (the supply of pollution opportunities again lies on the horizontal axis). But instead of having to bear the marginal social costs of abatement shown on line *bd*, abaters only need bear this cost minus $20 for each unit of abated waste. Government has implicitly bestowed a property right in the environment on the polluters, but it stands ready, as the public's agent, to buy back this right.

Polluters, as a result, will increase abatement from zero (point *b*) to the optimal amount *(bc)*: Abatement from *b* to *c* will bring a subsidy equal to *abec* but will require resources capable of producing goods worth *abc*. Abatement is prefer-

CLOSE-UP 18.1:
Pollution Taxes in the Ruhr

The oldest system of financial incentives to combat pollution goes back to 1904 and is operating in West Germany's Ruhr River basin. In that small area (roughly one-third of the Delaware River watershed) is located 40 percent of the country's industrial capacity, including from 70–90 percent of coal, coke, iron, and steel output. Only five small rivers are available to carry enormous wastes, but there also live 10 million people who need drinking water and desire recreation.

In all but one river (which has been deliberately set aside to carry a disproportionate share of wastes), the water quality is high enough to permit fishing and recreational uses. This achievement is the result of the work of eight authorities which have imposed a combination of water-intake charges and pollution taxes, the latter dependent on both the quantity and quality of wastes dumped. The results have been dramatic, leading, for example, to the recovery of 40 percent of industrial acids used in the area. One steel plant introduced water recirculation, internal treatment, and materials reuse processes that eliminated effluents entirely.

Note: The program concentrates on fighting pollution in the rivers only. Not surprisingly, many polluters have adopted processes, such as the burning of wastes, that have instead generated serious air pollution.

Source: Based on Allen V. Kneese and Blair T. Bower, *Managing Water Quality: Economics, Technology, Institutions* (Baltimore: The Johns Hopkins Press, 1968), pp. 237–53.

able, but abatement of the remaining waste *c0*, on the other hand, is not worthwhile. This further abatement would bring a subsidy equal to *dacf* but require resources capable of producing higher-valued goods worth *Odac*.

This subsidizing scheme is also costly to administer. Government, for instance, will find it difficult to establish original dumping bench-

ANALYTICAL EXAMPLE 18.3:
Estimating a Pollution Tax:
The Reserve Mining Company

At its Silver Bay, Minnesota plant on the north shore of Lake Superior, the Reserve Mining Company processes taconite ore into pellets that contain up to 75 percent iron and are used by the steel industry. During the process, the plant discharges 500 million gallons of water and 60,000 tons of rock tailings into the lake daily. The tailings cause a rapid *eutrophication* (decrease of dissolved oxygen) in the lake, killing aquatic life and reducing its beauty. They also contaminate the lake with asbestos fibers that can cause cancer. While the government has taken Reserve Mining to court, one economist, Jerrold M. Peterson, has calculated a possible pollution tax that might induce the company to alter its waste-discharge procedure. The accompanying table summarizes his calculations of the social costs from the discharge of tailings in 1975. Row (1) shows the current damage to fishing, property values, and tourism. Rows (2) and (3) indicate current costs of filtering asbestos fibers or suffering from additional cancer; row (4) measures (the present value of) various long-run costs. The marginal social cost was found to be 3.9 cents per ton of coarse tailings, 56 cents per ton of fine tailings, and 30.2 cents per ton for all tailings combined.

(1) Lake eutrophication	$3,837,000
(2) Water filtration	1,365,000
(3) Health hazard	532,000
(4) Other	584,000
Total	$6,318,000
Marginal social cost	30.2¢ per ton

Source: Jerrold M. Peterson, "Estimating an Effluent Charge: The Reserve Mining Case," *Land Economics*, August 1977, p. 336. Copyright © 1977 by the Board of Regents of the University of Wisconsin System.

marks for all polluters from which the amounts abated can be calculated. Indeed, governments use a variety of rather imperfect substitutes for the per-unit subsidy. Thus the federal government and various states grant income tax credits, accelerated depreciation privileges, low-interest loans, and exemptions from sales or property taxes to purchasers of pollution abatement equipment. Unfortunately, these are *partial* bribes. As a result, these programs are highly ineffective in encouraging the installation (and continued utilization) of pollution control equipment because they still require a substantial voluntary sacrifice on the part of polluters. They can do better by not controlling pollution at all.

In addition, such programs introduce a bias towards the use of control *equipment* (smokestack scrubbers, catalytic converters, and the like) even when other methods of pollution control may be cheaper. These cheaper methods might include the use of less-polluting fuels, the treatment or recycling of wastes, the use of different production processes (pickling steel with hydrochloric acid rather than sulfuric acid) or the production of different products (unbleached rather than white paper).

Marketing Pollution Rights

Yet another possibility for achieving optimum pollution is illustrated in Figure 18.6. A government that had determined as optimal the dumping of 72 million units of wastes per year could simply outlaw all dumping except by holders of **pollution licenses** or **pollution rights**. The government could then auction off 72 million of these rights, each one being a transferable certificate allowing the holder to dump one unit of specified wastes into a specified environment. As Figure 18.6 shows, the strictly limited supply of rights would assure a reduction of dumping to the optimal level. The demand for pollution opportunities would drive the price per right to $20 (point *a*), and (like a per-unit dumping tax) this price would discourage all dumping beyond the optimum.

Note: Under this scheme, *any* party that wanted rights to nature's capacity to receive wastes and wanted them badly enough to pay the equilibrium price could acquire them. In most cases, these buyers of pollution rights would be polluters. But the purchasers could also be special-interest groups such as conservationists, who—disagreeing with the government's decision to allow *some* pollution—could buy up pollution rights for the purpose of *not* using them, of keeping them out of the hands of potential users.

The use of this rights-selling mechanism would, furthermore, achieve a given pollution avoidance in the most efficient way, as can be illustrated with the help of the numbers contained in Table 18.1. This earlier example would call for the issue by government of 100 million pollution rights per year, and such is the meaning of the vertical *supply* line in Figure 18.7.

What would the demand be for such rights? How many rights would firms want to buy at alternative prices? We already know from row (1), Table 18.1, that firms would dump wastes to the tune of 200 million tons a year if everyone left them alone; that is, charged them nothing. Thus the demand curve for pollution rights would cut the horizontal axis at 200 at a zero price. Demand would be the same up to a price of $1 per right. All of the firms would rather pay $1 or less for the right to pollute than engage in waste abatement, which would cost them, as row (4) in Table 18.1 shows, $1 or more per ton.

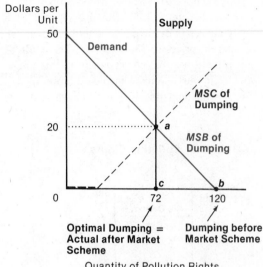

FIGURE 18.6   A Market for Pollution Rights

The introduction of a market for pollution rights might reduce excessive pollution (point *b*) to the optimal level (point *c*).

Once a pollution right cost more than $1 (but less than $3), Firm B would have the incentive to stop dumping. It would rather avoid dumping (at a cost of $1 per ton per year) than pay more than $1 for the right to pollute. Because Firm B's total emissions amounted to 20 million tons per year, the quantity of rights demanded between the $1.01 and $3 prices would drop to 180 million.

Once a pollution right cost more than $3 (but less than $7), Firm C would stop dumping as well. It would rather avoid dumping (at a cost of $3 per ton per year) than pay more than $3 for the right to pollute. Because Firm C's total emissions amounted to 80 million tons per year, the quantity of rights demanded between the $3.01 and $7 prices would drop to 100 million.

Once the pollution rights cost more than $7, Firm A would drop out as well. It would rather avoid dumping (at a cost of $7 per ton per year) than pay more than $7 for the right to pollute.

Because Firm A's total emissions amounted to 100 million tons per year, the quantity of rights demanded above the $7 price would drop to zero.

From the graph it is clear that demand and supply curves in our example would be identical between the prices of $3.01 and $7. The equilibrium price would be indeterminate in this range (ab). Had our example included more firms, however, the demand curve would have taken on

FIGURE 18.7 Pollution Rights in the Air

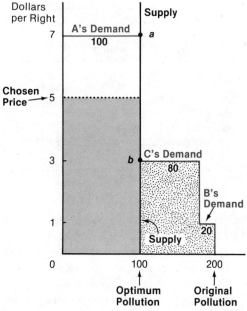

Given the demand for and supply of pollution rights shown here, an auction market would set an equilibrium price anywhere between $3.01 and $7 per right. Each year, 100 million such rights would be bought and sold. In this case, the equilibrium price would cut pollution in half from the 200-million-ton-a-year level that would prevail in the absence of such a market. Furthermore, the opportunity cost of pollution avoidance would be minimized because the firms that could avoid pollution most cheaply (Firms B and C) would be the ones to do so. This opportunity cost equals the dotted area; the shaded area represents government revenue from selling pollution rights.

more of its usual shape, cutting the supply curve at a-unique point. In our case, a government auction might set the price at $5 per right. As a result, Firms B and C would find it cheaper to avoid dumping anything at all than to buy rights and dump wastes. Firm A would continue to dump as much as before. In short, without having had any detailed knowledge of who pollutes, how much, or what the individual firms' avoidance costs would be, without having issued orders to anyone, the government would exactly achieve the efficient result. That is, it would achieve a given amount of pollution avoidance at the minimum opportunity cost shown to be possible in rows (6) to (8) of Table 18.1. Society would give up $260 million of valuable things (dotted area) to avoid half the pollution. No other arrangement could have achieved this at lower cost.

Note the detailed implications of this scheme for prices, profits, and resource allocation. The people who bought electric power from Firms B and C (which now would abate wastes) would pay higher prices, or the owners of Firms B and C would have lower profits, to cover the pollution-avoidance costs. Costs formerly borne by others would now be made visible to customers and owners of polluting enterprises. As a result, they would spend less on other things—perhaps less on furniture and cars. The resources that would have made these other things would be diverted to pollution abatement. Society would thus have reallocated resources from the production of furniture and cars to the production of cleaner air. At the same time, the customers of Firm A would pay more also (or the owners of Firm A would receive lower profits) to cover the pollution rights costing $500 million a year (shaded area in graph). Note that this cost would only be a money transfer from some electric-power consumers and producers to government. The consumers and producers of electric power would have less control over resources; the government would have more control. Although this cost would give Firm A an incentive to find a pollution-avoidance method that cost less than $5 per ton per year (so it could escape the need to spend $500 million a year on pollution rights), at the moment this cost would not affect the degree of pollution by A. The government might use the revenue in any way it pleased, including the policing of the whole arrangement.

In the past, governments have not used this device, but at the time of this writing the Environmental Protection Agency was considering the introduction of auction and even futures markets for air-pollution rights (see Chapter 10 for a discussion of futures markets). First on the agenda was the control by this device of fluorocarbons from refrigeration and air conditioning. (The use of such chemicals as spray-can propellants was banned when scientists first discovered their effects on the ozone layer, a discovery that suggested an increased likelihood of skin cancer from the sun's ultraviolet rays). Futures markets in pollution rights were envisioned mostly to facilitate the planning of big construction projects. Such markets would enable firms to acquire a portion of the atmosphere's limited waste absorption capacity years in advance.

Applications

Application 1:
The Tragedy of the Commons

In Chapter 9, "Application 4: The Management of Renewable Natural Resources," we discussed resources that were completely appropriated. In this section we will consider the opposite case in which such resources are freely accessible to all, are common property, or, we might better say, are nobody's property. In such circumstances, a tragic situation often develops: As more and more individuals make use of the resource, its quality is depleted and it is eventually destroyed. Examples include not only the excessive use of common bodies of air and water as dumping sites, but also the overuse of ocean fisheries, grazing lands, scenic areas, and much more. Before long, whales and tuna, oysters and pearls, sardines and sponges, buffalos and zebras are in danger of becoming extinct. Even national parks

become endangered oases. (On one day in 1980, some 25,000 visitors to the *back country* of Grand Teton National Park vainly looked for solitude among cold blue lakes, deep canyons, and snow-capped peaks.) The problem is again one of divergence between marginal private and social benefit or cost.

The New England Commons. Table 18.2 depicts a situation characteristic of many a New England town commons in the past. (A *commons* was a tract of land considered community property, open to the use of all). All residents were free to put as many cows on the common pasture as they liked. Naturally, the carrying capacity of any pasture is limited; more cows (1) meant less grass per cow and a lower average weight per cow (2). In our example, the grazing of 6 cows maximizes the total weight for the community—see the circled entry in column (3). Additional cows yield negative marginal social benefits (4).

Let the price of meat equal $1 per pound; let the cost of a calf be $64. How many cows would people place on the commons? The answer is "9," because as long as there were fewer animals on the pasture, any individual decision maker would compare the marginal private cost of another cow ($64 for the acquisition of the calf plus *zero* maintenance cost) with the marginal private benefit as perceived by any one individual among many, which is any number in column (2), multiplied by $1. Such an individual would be quite unconcerned with the fact that every added cow made everybody's cows slimmer and that marginal *social* benefit (4) was lower than the private one, perhaps even negative.

How many cows would a sole private owner of the pasture place on it? The answer is "about 5," because that is where our assumed marginal private cost ($64) would just about equal the marginal private benefit as perceived by a sole owner (4) who would care very much about the fact that each added cow made the other cows slimmer (because these wouldn't be the neighbors' cows).

Quite conceivably, the more intensive use of the common pasture would make it less produc-

TABLE 18.2 Cattle on the Commons

Number of Cows (1)	Weight in Pounds Average (2)	Weight in Pounds Total (3)	Weight in Pounds Marginal (4)
1	200	200	
			180
2	190	380	
			154
3	178	534	
			122
4	164	656	
			84
5	148	740	
			40
6	130	(780)	
			−10
7	110	770	
			−66
8	88	704	
			−128
9	64	576	

As more and more cows are added to a common pasture, their average weight declines as, eventually, does the total weight produced.

tive over time. This decrease in productivity would over time reduce all the entries in column (2) and thus in the remainder of Table 18.2 as well. Eventually, the pasture might become totally useless for the grazing of any cows at all. (In perfect analogy, we can, of course, substitute fishing boats on the ocean or visitors in national parks for cows on the commons.) Are there solutions to this tragedy?

First Solution: Private Property Rights. Our discussion has already implied one possible solution: the internalization of externalities through the assignment of property rights to private parties. Common ownership of hunting grounds, for example, was typical among American Indians. Their small numbers in a vast country along with their primitive hunting technology, however, combined to make a tragedy of the commons only a remote possibility. But the arrival of white fur traders and guns vastly increased the incentive and ability of each Indian family to hunt. Before long, beavers were threatened with extinction. In the 1700s, the Iroquois and Montagnais Indians instituted private property rights, assigning to each family a hunting area that could even be inherited. The private owners quickly

practiced conservation, lest next year's "crop" was zero. (In the end, new waves of Europeans made it impossible for the Indians to enforce these property rights, and they joined the white people in taking all the pelts while they could.)

Common property rights to not only land but also livestock and water supplies were similarly converted into private rights on the Great Plains (the Dakotas, Wyoming, Montana, Kansas, Nebraska, Colorado, New Mexico, and Texas). A hundred years ago, when the population on the Great Plains exploded (from 274,000 in 1850 to 7,377,000 in 1900), groups of cattle ranchers combined to restrict entry into common lands on the basis of "customary rights." Lack of trees and rocks made fencing difficult, but the introduction of barbed wire in the 1870s led to widespread land enclosure. Eventually, the transcontinental railroads transferred much of their governmental land grants into private hands. At the same time, the once common ownership of cattle, horses, and sheep came to an end with joint roundups, branding, and central registration. Although the practice of all people having equal rights to water supplies also came to an end, the **riparian doctrine** of the East was not adopted. The riparian doctrine states that each property owner fronting a lake or stream has a right to the unimpaired use of the water but cannot physically use up the water and diminish like rights of others. Instead, the **appropriative doctrine** developed in the West. This doctrine states that the first user of water acquires a right to its use in the original place and manner of use, even to the extent of using up the water (as in irrigation or mining). "First in time means first in right." However, according to the doctrine, such right could be lost if use lapsed, and such a right did not apply to unaccustomed uses. Gold mining associations were among those first enforcing this doctrine.

The conversion of common to private property rights continues in our day as well. See Close-Ups 2.1–2.3 on the birth of property rights concerning the sea, the moon, and the electromagnetic spectrum, and Analytical Example 18.4 on the birth of property rights for lobstering areas.

Second Solution: Restricted Use. When the first solution fails, as often happens, alternatives include agreements on restricted use of the commonly owned resource. For example, the town of Salem, Massachusetts, restricted the use of common forest lands as early as 1669; nowadays governments attempt to introduce property rights through the back door by restricting entry to many a commons. Entry restriction is the purpose of licensing fees ($40,000 for salmon fishing in Bristol Bay, Alaska, in 1979), landing taxes (so much per pound of fish caught), quotas and moratoriums (whales), and all kinds of foolish rules that often do not eliminate overuse but make people spend more resources to achieve it. (Thus "short seasons" give rise to more or larger or speedier vessels that lie idle the rest of the year.)

Application 2:   Highway Congestion

The theory of externalities can also be applied to a problem often faced on a manufactured rather than a natural commons: the rush-hour conges-

tion of highways to which all drivers have free access and for the use of which they are charged nothing at the time of use. (This same analysis could be applied to public airports, beaches, and campgrounds.)

Congestion Illustrated.   The problem of highway congestion is illustrated by Figure 18.8. We will consider traffic on one lane of a one-mile stretch of a road (exactly 5,280 feet). If we assume that cars must travel at a minimum speed of 1 mile per hour, that cars are on the average 16 feet long, and that cars cannot be closer than 1.6 feet to each other at a 1-mile-per-hour speed, it becomes clear that the maximum number of cars that can be on this portion of road at any one moment is 300, because $16 + 1.6 = 17.6$, and 17.6 times 300 = 5,280. This number of cars is represented by the bottom point of the solid vertical line labeled "minimum speed." As indicated at the right-hand edge of Figure 18.8 underneath the horizontal axis, if 300 cars were on this 1-mile stretch of 1-lane road at all times, and if they traveled at 1 mile per hour, only 300 cars would be traversing that stretch of road per hour. A literal case of bumper-to-bumper traffic!

If there were fewer cars on the road at any one time, the situation would look different. At the other extreme, if there were only 30 cars on our 1-mile stretch at any one time, they would cover 30×16, or only 480 feet of the 5,280-foot total length. Thus the distances between cars could be 5,280 feet − 480 feet divided by 30, or 160 feet. Certainly, cars could then travel as fast as 70 miles per hour. Ignoring legal speed limits, 30 cars would get across our 1-mile stretch in 1/70 of an hour, and a total of 30×70, or 2,100 cars could traverse the road in one hour. It is fairly easy to estimate what would happen between these two extremes of 300 and 30 cars. For example, 60 cars on the road could only go at 45 miles per hour because a spacing of only 72 feet would exist between them. Yet a total of 2,700 cars could then traverse the road in 1 hour. The remaining figures have been similarly calculated, always assuming that 1 car-length of distance

ANALYTICAL EXAMPLE 18.4:

Escaping the Commons: Maine Lobsters

In colonial times, it was not unusual to catch lobsters weighing 25 pounds. Those days are long gone, but can the clock be reversed? The Maine lobster fishery has recently provided the data a researcher might seek in a controlled experiment to test the tragedy-of-the-commons thesis. Groups of fishers, stressing the "accustomed rights" of their families, have banded together to keep "outsiders" away from about 10 percent of the lobstering area. In so doing they have effectively appropriated some of the sea's acres. In addition, they have imposed limits on their own catch in order to avoid the tragic depletion of the lobster stock. In this situation it is possible to compare economic data from these controlled-access areas with data from uncontrolled adjacent areas. The differences are highly significant, as shown in the accompanying table. Under private property, productivity and income are higher. In uncontrolled areas, traps are crowded together (just as cows are on the common pasture); as a result, considerably fewer lobsters are caught per trap haul (4). In uncontrolled areas, lobsters are generally caught at a younger age and smaller size; as a result, the weight per trap haul (5) is less.

In the controlled areas, higher income accompanies higher productivity. In addition, the future looks bright. The reproductive stock has been increasing, as indicated by the fact that the probability of catching a *mature* female is now 1.5 times greater in the controlled area than in the uncontrolled one.

	Catch Area	
Features Compared	**Uncontrolled**	**Controlled**
(1) Number of Trap Hauls	4,837	5,896
(2) Number of Lobsters	2,951	5,762
(3) Weight of Lobsters (kg.)	1,568	3,106
(4) Lobsters per Trap Haul	0.61	0.98
(5) Weight per Trap Haul	0.32	0.53
(6) Average Income of Fishers	$16,449	$22,929

Source: Based on James A. Wilson, "A Test of the Tragedy of the Commons," in Garrett Hardin and John Baden, *Managing the Commons* (San Francisco: W. H. Freeman & Co., 1977), pp. 96–111. Copyright © 1977.

between cars allows 10 miles per hour of speed. Interestingly, the greatest number of cars (2,700) could traverse the road if 60 cars were on the stretch at any one moment, traveling at 45 miles per hour.

Yet the number of cars that actually travel on the road is another matter. In deciding whether to use the road, each driver will compare the mar-ginal private cost with the marginal private benefit. The marginal private cost (equal, perhaps, to 20 cents per mile at a 45-mile-per-hour speed) includes such costs as gasoline, oil, depreciation, and the driver's time (for our purposes it does not matter what procedure we use to evaluate the latter). If we now assume a speed limit of 45 miles per hour (note the dashed vertical line), all

FIGURE 18.8 Highway Congestion

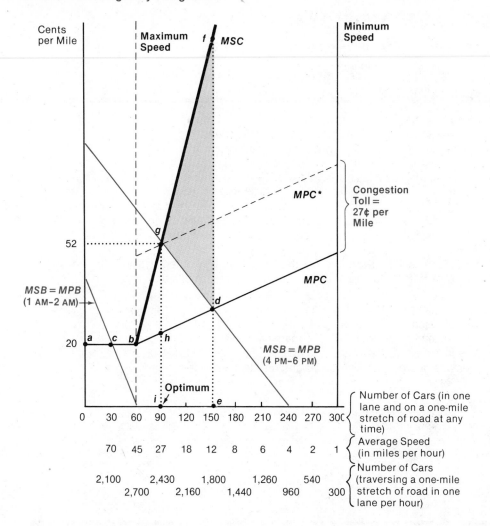

Highway congestion can be depicted as a situation in which the marginal social cost of road use exceeds the marginal private cost. Theoretically, such congestion can be removed by imposing a toll on drivers.

cars can move at this speed as long as only 60 or fewer are on the stretch of road. Each driver's *MPC*, therefore, equals 20 cents per mile (section *ab*). When more than 60 cars are on the road, however, cars cannot go at the speed limit. Each additional driver then helps reduce the average speed of traffic. As a result, the time component

of each driver's marginal private cost rises with the number of cars on the road; this increased time cost explains the rising section of the *MPC* line. Each additional driver, however, imposes delay costs on other drivers as well (just as each additional cow on the commons is not only slimmer itself than cows previously there, but

ANALYTICAL EXAMPLE 18.5:

Estimating the Costs of Traffic Congestion: Toronto

A recent study calculated the time costs of urban road congestion with the help of a traffic simulation model that replicated the queuing of vehicles at traffic lights, the dispersion of platoons of vehicles as they moved from one intersection to another, and the interaction of intersecting traffic flows during the morning rush hour in Toronto. The results are summarized in the first table. Not surprisingly, the table shows higher congestion costs on lanes going *toward* downtown than for those coming *from* it; the reverse is likely for the afternoon rush hour. The results also show substantial marginal external costs. If time is valued at $3.75 per hour, the marginal external costs came to an average of 38 cents per vehicle mile on inbound traffic (weighted by traffic volume). Marginal external costs came to 4 cents per mile on outbound traffic, and to 25 cents per mile on all morning rush-hour traffic combined. Because a simulation model does not have to contend with accidents, rain, snow, and road repair, these costs are likely to be understated at that.

This study indicates that a substantial congestion toll was in order. It also reminds us that an optimal toll would have to vary by street, direction of travel, and time of day.

Another study has simulated the traffic on runways, terminals, and access roads on a summer day at Toronto's International Airport. The results of this study are summarized in the second table. Note how the marginal social cost of using any given facility varies with the time of day and how optimal congestion tolls (which are based on the *difference* between marginal social and private costs) vary accordingly.

Source: Donald N. Dewees, "Estimating the Time Costs of Highway Congestion," *Econometrica*, November 1979, pp. 1499–1512. Copyright 1979 The Econometric Society; Sandford F. Borins, "Pricing and Investment in a Transportation Network: The Case of Toronto Airport," *Canadian Journal of Economics*, November 1978, pp. 686–88. © 1978 The Canadian Economics Association.

imposes a weight reduction on all the other cows also). Thus the marginal social cost lies above *MPC* to the right of point *b*.

To keep things simple, we will ignore other externalities associated with highways, such as air and water pollution (from exhausts and road salts), noise, the disruption of city neighborhoods, and even suburban sprawl. We will also assume that marginal private and social benefits do not diverge. These marginal private and social benefits, however, will surely differ with the time

of day, the day of the week, and even the season of the year. Thus people may not be very eager to travel this stretch of road between 1 AM and 2 AM; they may be much more eager to do so on weekday afternoons between 4 PM and 6 PM when rushing home from work (or on Saturday afternoons when it is time to go to the baseball game or the beach.) Accordingly, two alternative lines of *MSB = MPB* have been drawn in our graph.

Between 1 AM and 2 AM, no problem arises at all. Private decisions will equate simultaneous-

Street	Average Private Time Cost	Marginal External Time Cost
	(hours per vehicle mile)	
Inbound toward downtown		
Sheppard west	0.045	0.000
York Mills west	0.048	0.005
Railside west	0.065	0.074
Lawrence west	0.056	0.120
Victoria Park south	0.071	0.120
Don Mills south	0.086	0.140
Eglinton west	0.055	0.140
Leslie south	0.136	0.380
Outbound from downtown		
Eglinton east	0.037	0.0001
Leslie north	0.036	0.001
Sheppard east	0.042	0.006
York Mills east	0.051	0.006
Victoria Park north	0.056	0.009
Lawrence east	0.052	0.017
Railside east	0.058	0.028
Don Mills north	0.061	0.095

Facility	Marginal Social Cost[a]				Congestion Toll[b]	
	7–9 AM	9AM–4 PM	4–8PM	8–11 PM	9 AM–4 PM	4–8PM
Runway	$6.56	$1.19	$3.18	$2.92	$27–$31	$166–$193
Terminal	6.25	4.31	7.70	6.09	$0.15–$0.50	$0.86–$2.87
Access road	2.61	2.18	2.69	2.47	$0.10–$0.20	$0.37–$0.74

[a]runway: per second; terminal: per overseas passenger; access road: per car.
[b]runway: per landing or takeoff; terminal and access road: per use.

ly marginal private (and social) benefits as well as marginal private (and social) costs (at point *c*). In this case, 30 cars will be on the road, able to go 70 miles per hour but driving at the 45-mile-per-hour speed limit, of course. Certainly, no one will complain about traffic congestion.

Between 4 PM and 6 PM, private decisions will equate *MPB* and *MPC* (at point *d*). Some 150 cars will be on the road, traveling 12 miles per hour. From society's point of view, the benefit received by the marginal driver *(ed)* is not

worth the associated cost *(ef)*, most of which *(df)* is borne by other drivers. Lots of unhappy drivers will do lots of complaining.

Total economic welfare could be increased by reducing cars on the road to the optimum number of 90 (at intersection *g* marginal social benefit and marginal social cost are equalized). Such a reduction by 60 cars would reduce the net welfare of the removed drivers by *dgh*, yet it would reduce the time costs borne by all other drivers by *dfgh* making for a net social gain of *dfg* (shaded). Yet, clearly, no private bargain à la Coase could bring the many parties together.

Imposing a Congestion Toll. Theoretically, the optimum could be achieved with the help of government: Whenever the marginal social cost of road use exceeds marginal private cost, government could impose a toll equal to the difference between the two magnitudes at the optimal volume of traffic. In our case, such a toll would equal 27 cents per mile *(gh)*; this toll would raise *MPC* to the dashed parallel line, *MPC**. As a result, 60 drivers who did not feel that use of this stretch of road gave them benefits of at least 52 cents *(gi)* would stay away. For a perfect achievement of a social optimum, the size of the toll would, of course, have to be varied with the ever-changing intensity of demand (the position of the *MSB* line). This adjustment would not be easy to accomplish; placing a human monitor on every road and issuing millions of invoices every day would not be feasible. The governments of some countries, however, have used a number of imaginative approaches.

The On-Vehicle Point Pricing System. Under a *point pricing system*, motorists incur charges when passing designated points at certain times. Under an *on-vehicle system*, a meter, akin to the electric, water, or gas meters found in people's houses, is attached to each car. This meter can be a solid-state counter, without any moving parts and without any outward sign of counting. At chosen pricing points, electric cables are laid across the road, perhaps in groups of ten. Depending on the price one wants to charge on this road at any one time, the number of cables energized is centrally varied. The number of cables can also be varied at bridges or tunnels, where tolls for these facilities are also imposed by this method. When a car with a meter crosses such a pricing point, the meter counts the electrical impulses generated by the cables.

The On-Vehicle Continuous Pricing System. Sometimes, special pricing zones are designated within which vehicles are charged in accordance with time or distance traveled. If prices are based on time, charges are made from the moment of entry to the moment of exit from a pricing zone (very much as a telephone charge is made from the moment of connection to that of disconnection). Electrical impulses switch meters within cars on or off as the zone borders are crossed. These impulses are varied by time of day, week, or year within any given zone. Drivers (as well as police officers in the street) can ascertain by a light whether the meter has activated. The light might be red for a high price, blue for a low price, and remain off for a zero price. Such meters are run with batteries that have to be purchased at meter stations and inserted.

Off-Vehicle Pricing Systems. Any off-vehicle pricing system requires a method of automatic vehicle identification at certain points or within certain zones, a method of transmitting this information to a central computing station, and a method of analyzing the information received and billing the vehicle owner. One system uses the Link tracer: static electromagnetic elements are embedded in a plastic block attached to each car, requiring no batteries or power connections. An interrogator apparatus, which scans the road with electromagnetic waves is located at pricing points or zone boundaries. The element on the car reacts and identifies the car.

The information so received is transmitted to a computing station that computes the debt of each vehicle in accordance with the places and times traveled.

Whether the costs of such systems are worth the benefits, of course, is another matter!

SUMMARY

1. Nonpecuniary or real externalities are direct effects, independent of any price changes, of the actions of some households or firms on the utility of other households or on the output of other firms, none of whom have invited these effects. Such externalities are said to be negative when costs are imposed in the form of decreased utility or output on bystanders who are not being compensated for this injury. These externalities are said to be positive when benefits are provided in the form of increased utility or output for bystanders who are not being charged for this favor.

2. The British economist A. C. Pigou was the first to deal with externalities in a systematic way. In the presence of externalities, he argued, perfect competition would not produce a Pareto-type welfare maximum. Marginal private cost would diverge from marginal social cost, and marginal private benefit would diverge from marginal social benefit. Pigou argued that government could close the gaps between marginal private and social costs or benefits (and restore the Pareto welfare maximum) by taxing producers and consumers who generated negative externalities and by subsidizing those who generated positive externalities.

3. For nearly half a century, Pigou's analysis went unchallenged. Then Ronald Coase noted two flaws: a. the administration of the tax-subsidy scheme might be too costly to make it worthwhile; b. if government assigned unambiguous and transferable property rights, and as long as transactions costs were low enough, private parties could negotiate among themselves about eliminating externalities—without any further intervention of government. Coase established the theorem that under perfect competition and in the absence of income effects and transactions costs, voluntary negotiated agreements among private parties generating or being affected by externalities will lead to the same resource allocation (and output mix) regardless of how property rights are assigned among these parties.

4. Pollution by and affecting large numbers exemplifies a case in which high transactions costs prevent a negotiated internalization of externalities. In this case, post-Pigouvian theorists also recommend government intervention. The government is urged, first, to determine the optimum level of pollution—which is likely to be smaller than the actual level.

5. Governmental policies to induce pollution abatement to the optimum level include moral suasion, outright prohibition, setting standards, taxing waste dumping, subsidizing waste treatment, and marketing pollution rights.

6. The tools of analysis developed in this chapter can be applied to explain the tragedy of the commons and possible policies to reduce highway congestion.

KEY TERMS

ambient standards
appropriative doctrine
Coase theorem
emission standards
input standards
marginal external benefit *(MEB)*
marginal external cost *(MEC)*
marginal internal benefit
marginal internal cost
marginal private benefit *(MPB)*
marginal private cost *(MPC)*
marginal social benefit *(MSB)*
marginal social cost *(MSC)*
negative externalities
neighborhood effects
nonpecuniary externalities
pollution licenses
pollution rights
positive externalities
real externalities
riparian doctrine
spillovers

QUESTIONS AND PROBLEMS

1. "In the presence of a negative externality, perfect competition cannot be relied upon automatically to produce a Pareto-type welfare maximum." This statement was illustrated numerically in the section on "The Analysis of Pigou." Invent an analogous example for the case of a positive externality.

2. Panel (a) of Figure 18.1 shows how the imposition of a per-unit tax on the output of competitive producers who create negative externalities leads to an increase in total economic welfare (equal to shaded triangle *abc*). Could the same argument be made if the output in question was produced by a monopoly? Explain.

3. "Pigou assumed away a common human trait: altruism. To the extent that people love their neighbors as themselves, they mentally add marginal external costs to marginal private costs and determine the extent of their activities on that basis. In the case of such altruism, any governmental tax on people supposedly creating negative externalities destroys rather than assures a Pareto welfare maximum." Evaluate this position.

4. Coase imagined the following situation: A rancher and wheat farmer operate side by side on unfenced land. Depending on how one looks at it, each is imposing negative externalities on the other. When the farmer grows more wheat, more cultivated fields stand in the way of the cattle, and the production of meat must be restricted. When the rancher increases the size of the herd, more cattle stray onto wheat fields and trample them; thus more meat implies less wheat. The facts, let us suppose, are as follows:

Size of Herd (number of steers)	Crop Loss (tons per year)
1	1
2	3
3	6
4	10

Assume that each steer brings a profit of $30, that each ton of wheat brings a profit of $10, and that transactions costs are zero. Then show that

    a. the externalities will be internalized once property rights are clearly assigned either to the farmer (who now has a right not to have the wheat harmed) or to the rancher (who now has a right to let the cattle roam);

    b. the Coase theorem applies to this case.

5. "When the reserve clause was in effect in organized baseball, people argued that it was needed to prevent wealthy baseball clubs from acquiring too large a share of the good players. This assertion can be refuted with the help of the Coase theorem." Explain. (*Hint*: You may wish to review Chapter 13, "Application 1: The Baseball Players' Market." Then address the question of whether the team for which a player plays would differ with the identity of the owner of his services.)

6. "Coase is wrong. The mere possibility of mutual advantage does not assure its achievement, even in the small-numbers (low-transaction-cost) case. Negotiations will break down because of strategic behavior: Waste-dumping paper companies will threaten to produce more paper (even if they have no such plans), merely in order to extort more bribe money from fishing companies. Or fishing companies will make untrue claims about fish killed in order to extort more damage payments from paper companies." Evaluate this position.

7. One economist has argued that muggers and their victims (muggees) stand in the same predator-prey relationship as fishers and fish, muggees being a common property resource and overmugging being likely for the same reason as overfishing.[1] Do you think the tragedy of the commons can occur in the *muggery* (the geographic place where muggers take wealth from muggees)? Consider the implications.

8. In 1980, governments were worrying about a traffic jam in outer space because 80 satellites were all in the choicest orbit (a narrow region 22,300 miles above the equator where satellites make one revolution every 24 hours and thus remain stationary above the same spot, while being in optical range of nearly half the earth's surface). In order for ground stations to be able to discriminate among signals, these satellites had to be separated by 200–270 miles, and the demand for orbital slots was rising fast. As an economist, can you think of ways to deal with orbital crowding?

---

[1] Philip A. Neher, "The Pure Theory of Muggery," *The American Economic Review*, June 1978, pp. 437–45.

SELECTED READINGS

Coase, Ronald H. "The Problem of Social Cost." *The Journal of Law and Economics*, October 1960, pp. 1–44.

> The seminal article on the Coase theorem. *See also* the "Coase Theory Symposium." In the *Natural Resources Journal*, October 1973 and January 1974.

Council on Environmental Quality. *Environmental Quality - The Tenth Annual Report*. Washington, D.C.: U.S. Government Printing Office, 1979.

> A detailed review of ten years of environmental policy.

Fisher, Anthony C. and Peterson, Frederick M. "The Environment in Economics: A Survey." *Journal of Economic Literature*, March 1976, pp. 1–33.

Furubotn, Eirik and Pejovich, Svetozar. "Property Rights and Economic Theory: A Survey of Recent Literature." *Journal of Economic Literature*, December 1972, pp. 1137–62.

Hardin, Garrett. "The Tragedy of the Commons." *Science*, December 13, 1968, pp. 1243–48. *See also* his "Second Thoughts on 'The Tragedy of the Commons.'" In Herman E. Daly. *Economics, Ecology, Ethics*. San Francisco: Freeman, 1980, pp. 115–20.

> A more detailed discussion of Application 1 in this chapter.

Hardin, Garrett and Baden, John. *Managing the Commons*. San Francisco: Freeman, 1977.

> Twenty-six essays on the consequences of failing to establish private property rights in scarce natural resources.

Leontief, Wassily. "Environmental Repercussions and the Economic Structure: An Input-Output Approach." *Review of Economics and Statistics*, August 1970, pp. 262–71.

> Extends input-output analysis (discussed in Chapter 16) to take into account the flow of materials between the economy and the environment.

Manne, Henry G. *The Economics of Legal Relationships: Readings in the Theory of Property Rights*. St. Paul: West, 1975.

> A superb set of 37 articles.

Mishan, Ezra J. "The Postwar Literature on Externalities: An Interpretative Essay." *Journal of Economic Literature*, March 1971, pp. 1–28.

> See also the controversy about this article in the same publication, March 1972, pp. 57–62.

Pigou, Arthur C. *The Economics of Welfare*, 4th ed. London: Macmillan, 1946.

Roth, Gabriel. *Paying for Roads: The Economics of Traffic Congestion*. Harmondsworth, England: Penguin, 1967.

> A more detailed discussion of Application 2 in this chapter.

Seligman, Ben B. *Main Currents in Modern Economics*, vol. 2: *The Reaffirmation of Tradition*. Chicago: Quadrangle, 1971, pp. 477–96.

> A critical analysis of the work of Pigou.

Staaf, Robert J. and Tannian, Francis X. *Externalities: Theoretical Dimensions of Political Economy*. New York: Dunellen, 1974.

> A collection of 27 major articles on externalities.

CHAPTER 19

Public Goods

As Chapter 18 demonstrated, when private firms or households produce or consume goods, they may well impose unwanted costs on outside parties—or they may enable them to snatch free benefits. Many a good, therefore, is not a **pure private good** in the sense that its producer or consumer alone bears all of the cost and enjoys all of the benefit associated with it. In the presence of externalities, goods have a certain element of "publicness" about them. The present chapter deals with certain extreme cases of goods that have *positive* externalities that affect not only a few people, but literally all members of society. The benefits of such goods lie in the public domain almost entirely.

The Nature of Public Goods

In a number of papers written in the 1950s, Paul Samuelson (see Biography 19.1) formalized the concept of a **pure public good**.[1] He defined it as

a good that provides nonexcludable and nonrival benefits to all people in a given society, be it a locality, state, or nation. **Nonexcludability** is the property of a pure public good that makes it technically impossible or extremely costly to exclude any individual from the enjoyment of the good. Once a given amount of the good is available for anyone, it is available to everyone—simultaneously, automatically, and regardless of whether any payment is made for the privilege by any individual consumer. Should a larger amount of the good be produced, this larger amount is available to everyone as well. The good's benefit always and indivisibly embraces all (which is why economists say that public goods are characterized by **indivisibilities**).

Nonrivalness is the property of a pure public good that prevents rivalry among its consumers because the enjoyment of the good by any one person does not deplete its availability to others. Given the overall quantity of the good, the appearance of new consumers does not lead to a correspondingly diminished consumption by others, as is the case with pure private goods, such as chocolate bars or hamburgers. Given any overall quantity of such private goods, the increased consumption by one person does reduce that of others. A pure public good, in contrast, is nondepletable. One can add extra users, yet previous users will not have less on that account.

[1]Paul A. Samuelson, "The Pure Theory of Public Expenditure," *Review of Economics and Statistics*, November 1954, pp. 387–89; "Diagrammatic Exposition of a Theory of Public Expenditure," *Review of Economics and Statistics*, November 1955, pp. 350–56, and "Aspects of Public Expenditure Theories," *Review of Economics and Statistics*, November 1958, pp. 332–38.

A public good is like the legendary widow's cruse that remains full no matter how many people use its contents. Do such goods really exist?

Examples of such goods on the national level are: an automated air-traffic-control system, a clean natural environment, economic justice (as produced by domestic welfare or foreign aid programs), certain types of knowledge (as of mathematical theorems or weather forecasts), law and order, military security, prestige (as produced by great architecture, national parks, or space exploration), radio and television signals (in the absence of electronic scramblers or cable transmission), and, finally, sound money. Locally, public goods are: flood control, fire and police protection, firework displays, open air concerts, snow removal on public streets, the town hall clock, townwide mosquito spraying, and traffic control (ranging from buoys on the river to lighthouses on the shore to traffic lights at road intersections). All these goods have in common the features of nonexcludability and nonrivalness. Once produced, it is next to impossible to exclude any particular citizen from the benefits: your clean air is my clean air, your weather forecast is mine, your snow-free street is mine as well. Nor does the appearance of additional consumers detract from the consumption of others: when additional citizens make use of a mathematical theorem, others are not prevented from its continued use; when they derive pride from our explorer on the moon, others need not be less proud; when they tune in TV signals or glance at the town's clock, others can do so at the same time.

Pure Public Goods and Market Failure

Chapter 18 showed why goods with positive externalities tend to be produced in quantities insufficient to yield the maximum possible economic welfare. Pigou, therefore, recommended governmental subsidies to stimulate the private provision of such goods (see Figure 18.1, "Pi-

gou's Golden Rule'' on p. 530). In the case of pure public goods, which involve positive externalities to an extreme degree, the Pigouvian problem returns with a vengeance: Unless government intervenes, private firms do not only produce such goods in amounts insufficient to secure maximum economic welfare; they do not produce them at all! The private market fails altogether.

The Free-Rider Problem

Consider a case in which everyone agrees that the collective benefit from a pure public good exceeds its cost. Who is going to produce such a good? A pure private good can be parcelled out to individual buyers and withheld from them unless payment is made, but the very act of producing a pure public good makes it instantly and equally available to all. How then is a private producer going to collect a positive price from all the benefited parties? These beneficiaries can say, ''We won't pay, and if you don't like it, withhold the benefit from us.'' The benefit-producing party must either share the benefit with everyone and bear the cost alone (because this party cannot withhold the good) or must stop producing the good (if this party does not want to give free benefits to others or cannot bear the cost alone).

This unwillingness of individuals voluntarily to help cover the cost of a pure public good, and their eagerness to let others produce the good so they can enjoy its benefits at a zero cost, is called the **free-rider problem**. The name has its origin in the Old West, in the days of cattle rustling. The ranchers of Dodge City banded together to form a vigilante group to catch (and hang) cattle thieves. Everyone contributed to the cost of the security force on horseback—that is, until rustling had been sufficiently discouraged by the existence of this group. Then individual ranchers began to withdraw, realizing that they could benefit just as much if they didn't pay. They became ''free riders'' instead. Before long, the security force collapsed, and cattle rustling resumed. The rational behavior of each rancher

BIOGRAPHY 19.1:

Paul A. Samuelson

Paul Anthony Samuelson (1915–) was born in Gary, Indiana. He studied at the University of Chicago and Harvard before joining the faculty at the Massachusetts Institute of Technology.

While still a graduate student, he wrote 11 major articles, including the now classic analysis of interaction between accelerator and multiplier. At age 23, he prepared a pathbreaking dissertation, which he called nothing less than *Foundations of Economic Analysis*. Using such a title was a rather bold move for such a young man and quite a contrast to the narrow titles of typical dissertations. Samuelson's goal was to cast all of economics in mathematical terms. Thus he showed that the concept of maximization under constraints pervaded all of economic analysis. (Consumers maximized utility, given preferences, incomes, and the prices of goods; firms maximized profit, given technology and the prices of inputs and outputs; governments maximized net social benefits.) He described mathematically the state of an economic system in equilibrium and the process of adjustment from one state to another. He thereby showed that the comparison of equilibrium positions in static states was meaningful only if a dynamic analysis of stability was conducted. Unlike Alfred Marshall (see Biography 7.1), who buried his mathematics in footnotes and appendices, Samuelson was not bashful about his mathematical approach. "The laborious literary working over of essentially mathematical concepts such as is characteristic of much of modern economic theory," he says, "is not only unrewarding from the standpoint of advancing the science, but involves as well gymnastics of a peculiarly depraved type" (p. 6).

Samuelson's sophisticated and oftentimes highly mathematical treatment of advanced economics (ranging from consumer behavior and international trade to business cycles, public finance, and welfare economics) can be sampled in his four-volume *Collected Scientific Papers* (1966–78).

His work has always been supplemented by innovative approaches at the level of the novice. His introductory *Economics* went through 11 editions between 1948 and 1980 and was used by millions. The book presented a "grand neoclassical synthesis," which showed that the time-honored principles of the founding fathers (Smith, Ricardo, and the like) remained valid in a world of full employment brought about with the help of modern national income analysis (as developed by Keynes). Many millions more have followed Samuelson's columns in *Newsweek*, which frequently advocate actively interventionist government policies (in contrast to Milton Friedman—Biography 2.2—the magazine's other economic columnist). Not surprisingly, Samuelson has been showered with many honors. The American Economic Association awarded him its first John Bates Clark medal in 1947 and made him its

---

thus led to the irrational behavior of the entire group, which is where government might have helped.

A Role for Government

Victims of the free-rider problem can agree mutually to coerce themselves: they can instruct their government to use its coercive powers for the purpose of securing the public good's net benefit, which the private market fails to deliver. If cattle rustling cost a group of 100 ranchers $5,000 a month, and if the maintenance of a security force that would prevent this loss cost $1,000 a month, the course of action would be clear: Every rancher could be taxed $10 a month, the security force could be hired with the proceeds, and each rancher would receive a benefit five times the cost.

In the same way, modern-day governments engage in the **public finance** of pure public goods, or the governmental collection of taxes

president in 1961. In 1970, he became the first American to receive the Nobel Memorial Prize for Economic Science. The award committee cited his "outstanding ability to derive important new theorems and to find new applications for existing ones. By his contributions Samuelson has done more than any other contemporary economist to raise the level of scientific analysis in economic theory."

Samuelson resisted urgent requests by Presidents Kennedy and Johnson to join the Council of Economic Advisers. He preferred to remain an economist's economist. As he put it in his presidential address to the American Economic Association, "In the long run, the economic scholar works for the only coin worth having—our own applause. . . . This is not a plea for 'Art for its own sake,' 'Logical elegance for the sake of elegance.' It is not a plea for leaving the real-world problems of political economy to noneconomists. It is not a plea for short-run popularity with members of a narrow in-group. Rather it is a plea for calling shots as they really appear to be (on reflection and after weighing all evidences), even when this means losing popularity with the great audience of men and running against 'the spirit of the times.'"[1]

[1]Paul A. Samuelson, "Economists and the History of Ideas," *The American Economic Review*, March 1962, p. 18.

from all those believed to benefit from the provision of pure public goods and the subsequent channeling of these funds toward the production of such goods, either by government agencies or private firms.

Note: Actual governments often arrange for the tax-financed production of many goods that are hardly pure public ones. These goods, financed by government and supplied free of charge on the grounds that all citizens merit a share of them, are called **merit goods**. Examples

are public education, health care, housing, and social security. In addition, government agencies often produce goods that are sold in markets in competition with private firms, such as electric power, liquor, and sanitation services.

The Optimum Quantity of a Public Good

Imagine a government determined to step in where the private market fails and eager to arrange for the production of a pure public good. What kind of information would such a government have to have to identify the welfare-maximizing quantity to be produced? In principle, Samuelson tells us, the answer is simple enough:

The optimum quantity is the one at which the rising marginal social cost of producing the public good, *MSC*, just equals the good's falling marginal social benefit, *MSB*. The marginal social cost, as always, reflects the opportunity cost of producing the good; that is, the maximum value of other goods that must be forgone to produce it. This marginal social cost is found in the same way for a pure public good as for a pure private one. Nothing new here.

The marginal social benefit of a pure public good, however, is a different sort of thing from that of a pure private good. A given unit of a pure private good (which has no externalities) can only be consumed by one individual; the marginal social benefit of a unit of a pure private good, therefore, equals the marginal private benefit received by a single person only. In contrast, a given unit of a pure public good can be consumed simultaneously by everyone; the marginal social benefit of a unit of a pure public good, therefore, equals the *sum* of the marginal private benefits received by all of its consumers.

The Marginal Social Benefit

Consider Figure 19.1. Panels (a)–(c) refer to a pure private good. Panel (a) depicts the situation for Consumer 1, whose increased consumption is associated with the declining marginal private benefits represented by blocks *a* through *e*. The color line along the top of the blocks thus indicates the maximum prices this consumer would pay in the market for various units of the good and is this consumer's demand curve for the private good. Panel (b) is similarly constructed but for Consumer 2. Given only two consumers (to keep things manageable), the market demand curve is derived in panel (c) in the usual manner: by the *horizontal* summation of the individual demand curves at each price. This procedure was first illustrated in Figure 4.5, "Deriving Market Demand" (p. 88), and it is now highlighted by the labeling and shading of each individual block

of marginal private benefit. The color line in panel (c), therefore, shows the marginal social benefits associated with various quantities of the pure private good.

Panels (d)–(f), refer to a pure public good. Panel (d) shows the situation for Consumer 1; blocks *i* through *m* represent the declining marginal private benefits of various quantities of the public good. The color line along the top of the blocks again indicates the maximum prices this consumer would pay in a market for various units of the good, but it is a *pseudo*–demand curve only because the good is in fact not offered in the market. The color line in panel (e) must be similarly interpreted, with respect to Consumer

ANALYTICAL EXAMPLE 19.1:

Revealed Preference for Public Goods: An Experiment

One economist devised an experiment to test whether people's willingness to reveal their preferences for a public good differed with their knowledge of how they would have to pay for the good. People were asked by the Swedish Radio-TV Company to indicate how much they would pay to see a new program. They were given 50 Krona (Swedish currency) to take part in the test and were told that the program would not be shown unless total receipts (that is, the overall revealed willingness to pay) exceeded the 500-Krona cost. They then had to specify how much they would contribute under different payment structures. The accompanying table shows the results: there were no statistically significant differences. The investigators concluded that misrepresentation of preferences was unlikely unless the payoff to dishonesty was extremely large.

Announced Payment Scheme	Amount Offered (in krona)	
	Median	Mean
(A) The respondent to pay an amount stated by respondent	5	7.61
(B) The respondent to pay a percentage of the amount stated so that total collected = total cost	7	8.84
(C) The respondent to pay an amount determined by a lottery from four possibilities with equal probabilities	5	7.29
(D) The respondent to pay five krona	6.50	7.73
(E) The respondent to pay nothing	7	8.78

Source: Peter Bohm, "Estimating Demand for Public Goods: An Experiment," *European Economic Review* 3 (1972): 121. © 1972 North-Holland Publishing Company.

FIGURE 19.1   Marginal Social Benefit: Pure Private vs. Pure Public Good

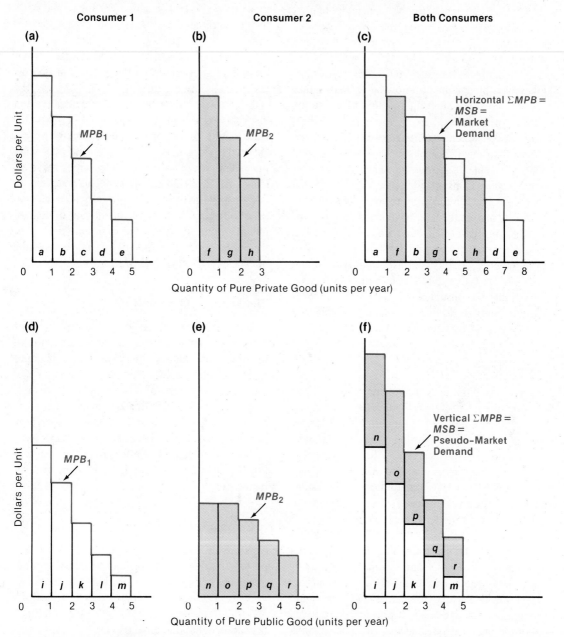

In the case of a pure private good, depicted in panels (a)–(c), the marginal social benefit is derived by the horizontal summation of all consumers' marginal private benefits.

In the case of a pure public good, depicted in panels (d)–(f), a vertical summation of marginal private benefits is in order. Each of the 8 units depicted in panels (a) and (b) is indeed a different unit, consumed privately. In contrast, what appear to be 10 different units in panels (d) and (e) are really 5 units only, each being consumed by both consumers at the same time. Therefore, the total quantity shown in panel (c) is 8, while the total quantity in panel (f) is 5 and not 10.

2. Panel (f) once more combines the two consumers' pseudo–demands into a pseudo–market demand that shows the marginal social benefits associated with various quantities of the pure public good. As the labeling and shading of the individual blocks indicates, the summing of marginal private benefits must now be *vertical* rather than horizontal because the first unit of the public good (ten minutes of a fireworks display, perhaps) is consumed *simultaneously* by Consumer 1 and Consumer 2. Thus it yields a marginal social benefit of *i* plus *n*. The second unit consumed by Consumer 1 is, similarly, identical to the second unit consumed by Consumer 2; hence its marginal social benefit equals *j* plus *o*. And so it goes for all other units as well. The calculation of the marginal social benefit of a pure public good thus contrasts sharply with that of a pure private good. The first unit (perhaps a chocolate bar) consumed by Consumer 1 in panel (a), for example, is a *different* unit from the first unit consumed by Consumer 2 in panel (b).

Identifying the Optimum

Panel (a) of Figure 19.2 contains a streamlined version of panel (f) of Figure 19.1, with the stair-step lines replaced by smooth ones. We now engage in a thought experiment. Let us imagine a fully informed government: This government knows the marginal social cost of producing the public good, line *MSC*. In addition, our consumers have truthfully revealed to government the maximum contributions they would make for added units of the good, reflected in lines *AB* and *CD*. Line *AB* shows the marginal private benefits Consumer 1 derives from various quantities of the public good, and this line corresponds to panel (d) in Figure 19.1. Line *CD* shows the marginal private benefits Consumer 2 derives from the public good, and this line corresponds to panel (e) in the earlier graph. By the vertical addition of these private marginal benefits our omniscient government can derive line *EFD*, which indicates, of course, the position of marginal social benefit, *MSB*.

Note: It is no accident that Consumer 2's

marginal private benefit coincides with the marginal social benefit in range *FD* for public good quantities larger than 0*B*. In that range, Consumer 1's marginal private benefit, we assume, is zero. If it were negative, but added quantities of the public good could be disposed of at no cost (as, perhaps, by the turning off of a TV set), the same result would pertain. If it were negative and disposal costs were prohibitive (as, perhaps, for added units of national defense received by a "dove"), Consumer 1's marginal private benefits would have to be subtracted from those of Consumer 2 to find marginal social benefits.

Possessing the knowledge embodied in panel (a) of our graph, our government can, of course, identify quantity 0*G* as the optimum amount of the public good. That quantity corresponds to the intersection of *MSC* and *MSB* at point *H*.

The Fruits of Omniscience

A government that was benevolent as well as omniscient would arrange for the production of the optimum quantity. In our example, this optimum quantity would yield total social benefits of 0*EHG* at a total social cost of 0*IHG*, and there would be a net benefit of *EHI* (shaded). Because private markets produce zero amounts of pure public goods, this net benefit depicts the potential gain in total economic welfare from the intervention by an omniscient and benevolent government.

A Comparison

This result can be contrasted with that of a perfect market providing a pure private good. Panel (b) of Figure 19.2 contains a streamlined version of panel (c) of Figure 19.1. Lines *MN* and *PQ* represent, respectively, the marginal-private-benefit and demand curves of Consumers 1 and 2, which correspond to panels (a) and (b) of Figure 19.1. The *horizontal* addition of these lines yields line *PRS*, the marginal social benefit as well as the market demand.

Given competitive market supply, an equilibrium price of 0*T* and an equilibrium quantity

**Figure 19.2   The Optimum Quantity of a Pure Public Good
Vs. That of a Pure Private Good**

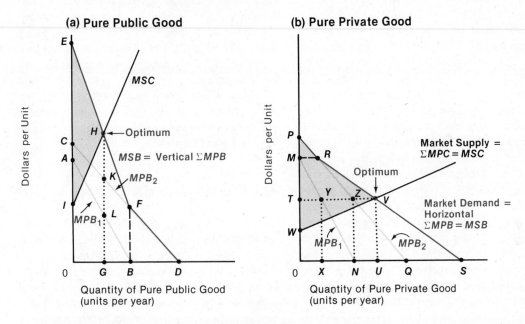

(a) Pure Public Good

(b) Pure Private Good

Quantity of Pure Public Good
(units per year)

Quantity of Pure Private Good
(units per year)

An omniscient government can quickly identify as optimal that amount of a pure public good, $0G$ in panel (a), at which its rising marginal social cost just equals its falling marginal social benefit (point H). Thus the optimum requires that marginal social cost equals the *vertical* sum of marginal private benefits:

$MSC = MPB_1 + MPB_2$. (Note how $GH = GL + GK$.)

In contrast, a competitive market for a pure private good produces an optimum at which marginal social cost separately equals the consumer's marginal private benefit (and thus equals the *horizontal* sum of marginal private benefits):

$MSC = MPB_1 = MPB_2$. (Note how $UV = XY = NZ$.)

Warning: Look closely at the notation in color. In one case, marginal benefits are related by summation; in the other they are related by equality. This difference summarizes the lesson of the previous graph (Figure 19.1) and highlights the distinction between pure public goods, which are consumed jointly by all, and pure private goods, which are consumed separately by each.

---

of $0U$ would emerge. The latter corresponds to the optimum point at which marginal social benefit just equals marginal social cost. Thus the competitive market would yield a total social benefit of $0PRVU$ at a total social cost of $0WVU$, and there would be a net benefit of $WPRV$ (shaded). This net benefit would be achieved without any government action (beyond the initial assignment of transferable property rights and the facilitation of unrestricted exchange).

The Problem of Ignorance

In the real world, governments, no matter how benevolent they are, are far from omniscient. How then are they going to discover people's preferences and identify the marginal social benefit associated with various possible quantities of a public good?

The very necessity to arrange for the provision of public goods by collecting taxes will, in fact, hamper the government's attempt to overcome its ignorance. Consider a government that wanted to imitate the pricing rule of the competitive market. Note how, in panel (b) of Figure 19.2, the competitive market establishes a uniform price of $0T$. While consumers face the same price, different consumers buy different amounts of private goods: Consumer 1 purchases $0X$; Consumer 2 buys $0N$; together, they purchase $0U$. Suppose government wanted to act accordingly and charge each consumer for all units of the public good a uniform tax-price, equal to the marginal private benefit derived by this consumer. Such an attempt would quickly spell trouble because consumers of a pure public good cannot possibly buy different amounts at a given tax-price. By definition, a pure public good is consumed in the same amount by all. Hence, as a result of the above pricing rule, consumers (who by necessity would receive the *identical quantity* of the public good) would enjoy *different marginal private benefits*. (Consider how "hawks" and "doves" are likely to evaluate any given quantity of national defense.) Thus the desire to tax in accordance with marginal private benefit would make it necessary to impose different taxes on different consumers.

Under this scheme, as we can see in panel (a) of Figure 19.2, Consumer 1 would have to be charged GL per unit for quantity $0G$, while Consumer 2 would have to be charged GK per unit for the same amount. (The two charges would add up to the marginal social benefit, GH.) Yet such differential taxation, equitable as it may seem, would lead to a serious problem. Consumers who expected to be taxed in accordance with their marginal private benefit (GL in the case of Consumer 1, GK in the case of Consumer 2) would not reveal the true intensity of their preference to the government. They would understate it, hoping to receive a lower tax bill and be a free rider, at least in part. Hence a government following such a "pricing" rule could not identify the true marginal social benefit, nor the optimum amount of the public good to be provided.

Nor could this problem be solved by pretend-ing, as government officials often do, that public goods were free. If people were convinced that they could get public goods for nothing, they would be apt to *overstate* their true preferences, which is why opinion polls that ask people about new (and allegedly free) government programs never fail to elicit huge majorities in favor of such programs.

How *do* real-world governments, which are not omniscient, in fact find out about people's preferences concerning public goods so that the optimum amounts can be identified?

The Process of Public Choice

In the past three decades, economists have become increasingly interested in the process of *public choice*, by which large groups of people decide on the overall quantity of public goods to be provided, on the particular types of such goods, and on the sharing of the associated tax burdens. The choice of a collective decision-making procedure is in itself an economic choice because every possible procedure has its own advantages and disadvantages, its own benefits and costs.

Decisions about public goods, for example, can be made on the basis of custom, by a dictator, or through democratic voting. If individual preferences are to be channeled into social decisions by voting, people must still choose from among a multitude of possible arrangements. They may favor *direct democracy*, in which all affected citizens vote on every possible governmental action. Or people may prefer a *representative democracy*, in which only a group of representatives, who are elected by all citizens, vote on governmental actions. Indeed, these representatives may turn over many decisions to a permanent group of civil servants, a *bureaucracy*. Real-world governments, of course, use a combination of these arrangements.

What then is the likelihood that people's true preferences for pure public goods will be identified and that optimum amounts will be produced? Many economists now believe that the likelihood is low, indeed. They grant readily that an omniscient government could identify the optimum amounts of pure public goods (as we have done above). They grant also that such a government could then take the necessary actions to raise total economic welfare. But they hesitate to recommend that real-world, less-than-omniscient governments be entrusted with such a task. Such governments, they fear, may fail to raise economic welfare and may lower it instead. Under such circumstances, it would be preferable to have government do nothing and allow people to live with the bad effects of market failure than to have people suffer the worse effects of *government* failure.

Government Failure

Three reasons why the process of public choice may fail to identify and deliver the optimum quantity of pure public goods are: 1. the problem with majority voting, 2. the delegation problem, and 3. the problem of bureaucracy.

The Problem With Majority Voting

In even a direct democracy, in which people make public choices by simple majority voting, it is far from certain that such voting will lead to the satisfaction of people's true preferences for public goods.

Voters in Rational Ignorance. When people vote with dollars in the market, they have every reason to be well informed. A wrong decision will affect them personally and immediately. When it comes to voting at the ballot box, it is quite another matter. In all but very small groups, such voters realize that individual ballots can have only a miniscule effect on the outcome of any vote. One ballot will make a difference only when there is a majority of one (that is, when in its absence all other voters are evenly split), which is likely to happen once in a thousand years. Thus the benefits to any one voter from becoming informed on any public

issue appear questionable, but the costs are not. It takes considerable effort to become so informed. Utility-maximizing voters, therefore, will tend to remain ignorant on matters of public policy, and quite rationally so.

Nevertheless, people may vote. If the costs of voting are low (the weather is fine, the polling place is near) and there are some benefits (a friendly chat with one's neighbors, a feeling of civic duty performed), people may vote in all their ignorance. This kind of voting, of course, can hardly be conducive to procuring optimal amounts of pure public goods. Public goods that have easily identifiable costs but harder-to-comprehend and larger benefits will be voted down without a second thought. Public goods that have obvious benefits but concealed and larger costs will be voted in.

Voter Apathy and Special Interests. When the costs of voting are high (the weather is bad, the polling place is hard to reach) and there are no offsetting benefits, voters will not vote at all. The absence of many voters allows a minority of well-organized voters to provide themselves with large personal benefits at the expense of the members of the majority each one of whom has but little to lose. Given such a redistribution of income, there is no certainty about any increase in social welfare. But the shoe can also be on the other foot. A majority can impose harm on a minority.

The Disadvantaged Minority. When people vote with dollars in the marketplace, everyone's desires are satisfied at the same time—in due proportion to the dollar votes cast. If 92 percent of all dollar votes are spent on trashy magazines, a great many of them will be produced. If 8 percent of dollar votes go for lyrical poetry books, a few of those will be produced as well. Not so in the public domain. If 92 percent of political votes are cast in favor of crime control and 8 percent in favor of flood control, 100 percent of voters will receive protection from crime, and no one will receive protection from floods. Indeed, those expecting to be made worse off by crime control (because the personal benefits they expect fall short of the taxes they will have to pay) will, nevertheless, be made to pay for crime protection. In the political sphere, simple majority voting inevitably suppresses the preferences of the minority. Once more, an increase in total economic welfare is far from certain (see Table 19.1).

Arbitrary Results. Oftentimes people vote on several issues at once. Such tying together of several issues can lead to arbitrary results. Issues that would lose, if considered separately, win in combination—or the opposite (see Table 19.2).

Arbitrary results, however, can also occur for another reason. When there is a choice among three or more alternatives, the outcome of voting will differ depending on the *sequence* in which votes are taken. This **voting paradox** was noted as early as 1785 by Condorcet but has recently been highlighted in the work of Kenneth Arrow (see Biography 19.2). According to the **Arrow impossibility theorem**, there exists no reliable mechanism that can translate complete and transitive individual preference rankings among three or more alternatives into a social preference ranking (for the entire group of individuals), while simultaneously fulfilling the following five conditions generally considered desirable in democratic societies:

1. The social ordering must cover all logically possible sets of individual orderings and be itself internally consistent (that is, it must show transitivity).

2. There must be a positive association between the social ordering and the individual orderings such that society prefers *x* to *y* if all individuals do.

3. The social choice between *x* and *y* must depend only on how individuals rank *x* vs. *y*, not on irrelevant alternatives, such as their rankings of *x* or *y* vs. *z*.

4. All types of preferences must count. That is, the social choice must not be imposed (for example, by custom or religious codes) such that certain preferences are taboo and may not be expressed.

5. Everyone's preferences must count. That is, the social choice must not be dictatorial such that it corresponds to one person's preferences, regardless of everyone else's.

TABLE 19.1 Majority Harms Minority

Voters	Voting on Crime Control			
	Expected Benefit	**Expected Cost (tax)**	**Expected Net Benefit**	**Vote**
(I) A	$ 400	$ 200	$200	for
B	300	200	100	for
C	250	200	50	for
D	100	200	−100	against
E	50	200	−150	against
Total	$1,100	$1,000	$100	for (3:2)
(II) A	$ 280	$ 200	$ 80	for
B	260	200	60	for
C	220	200	20	for
D	100	200	−100	against
E	0	200	−200	against
Total	$ 860	$1,000	−$140	for (3:2)

Under simple majority voting, a majority (voters A, B, and C) often harms a minority (voters D and E). The dollar gain to the majority may exceed the dollar harm to the minority, as in case (I), but the reverse can be true as well, as in case (II).

TABLE 19.2   A Losing Combination

Voters	(I) Voting on Crime Control			(II) Voting on Flood Control			(III) Combined Voting on Crime and Flood Control		
	Benefit	**Cost**	**Vote**	**Benefit**	**Cost**	**Vote**	**Benefit**	**Cost**	**Vote**
A	$ 340	$ 200	for	$ 900	$ 400	for	$1,240	$ 600	for
B	240	200	for	100	400	against	340	600	against
C	240	200	for	500	400	for	740	600	for
D	100	200	against	100	400	against	200	600	against
E	100	200	against	450	400	for	550	600	against
Total	$1,020	$1,000	for (3:2)	$2,050	$2,000	for (3:2)	$3,070	$3,000	against (3:2)

Under simple majority voting, it is not impossible for issues that would win if considered separately—cases (I) and (II)—to lose when considered in combination—case (III).

One of the implications of the Arrow theorem can be illustrated with the example of Table 19.3. The table pictures three voters who seek to establish a social preference ranking among three public goods: the control of crime, floods, and mosquitos. If they vote between crime control and flood control, crime control wins (being favored by Voters A and C). If they vote between flood control and mosquito control, flood control wins (being favored by Voters A and B). Logically, one would now expect this: Crime control being preferred to flood control and flood control being preferred to mosquito control, crime control should be preferred to mosquito control. But such consistency does not occur. In a vote that pits crime control against mosquito control, mosquito control wins (being favored by Voters B and C).

This lack of transitivity in social choice raises the possibility of achieving *any* desired voting result, depending simply on the sequence in which votes are taken. If the first vote taken is between crime control and flood control, crime control wins and flood control is immediately eliminated. If the winning issue (crime control) is then pitted against the remaining one (mosquito control), mosquito control is the final winner. Yet each one of the other two programs could be the final winner, too, if the sequence of voting was changed! (Try to see for yourself by voting a. flood control vs. mosquito control first and then

by voting b. mosquito control vs. crime control first.) This discovery is apt to shake one's faith in democracy.

Possible Remedies.   Possible remedies for the type of government failure just discussed usually take into account the *intensity* of voters' feeling about issues.

For example, the problem of the disadvantaged minority might be solved by imposing a rule that all votes be unanimous, while also allowing the buying and selling of votes. In Case (I) of Table 19.1, the majority of Voters A–C (which would stand to reap a net gain of $350) would have to buy the votes of the minority of Voters D and E (which would stand to incur a net loss of $250). These votes could clearly be purchased for $250 or more. In Case (II), however, the crime-control program would be defeated because the potential gainers (of $160) could not possibly compensate the potential losers (of $300) and still be better off.

Note: Among large numbers of voters, the transactions costs of setting up such a scheme might be prohibitive. In that case, an imperfect substitute, such as simple majority votes combined with **logrolling**, or the trading of votes, might help. In Case (II) of Table 19.1, Voter E has a lot to lose ($200) while C has little to gain ($20). Voter E might secure defeat of the crime-control program by persuading C to vote against

TABLE 19.3   Results Depend on Agenda

Preference Ranking	Voter A	Voter B	Voter C
1st	Crime control	Flood control	Mosquito control
2nd	Flood control	Mosquito control	Crime control
3rd	Mosquito control	Crime control	Flood control

The Arrow impossibility theorem teaches us that it is impossible, under certain reasonable conditions, to translate complete and transitive preference rankings of individual voters into a correspondingly complete and consistent social ranking. One implication can be highlighted with this table's example: Under simple majority voting, the agenda (or order in which votes are taken) can determine the result.

it in return for a similar favor E might render to C on another vote where the shoe is on the other foot.

The problem of voting sequence might be handled by **strategic voting**, a procedure by which people attempt to assure their preferred outcome by misrepresenting their preferences on some votes. Consider Table 19.3 and imagine a voting sequence of crime control vs. flood control (flood control losing), followed by winner vs. mosquito control (the latter winning). Voter A, for whom mosquito control is least preferred, might change this outcome by first voting for flood control, *contrary to* true preferences. As a result, flood control wins. Thus flood control is pitted against mosquito control in the second round, and (if now everyone votes true preferences) flood control wins. This outcome is preferred by A to the previous one. Unfortunately for A, of course, other voters can play this game, too. Thus the outcome of strategic voting is never a certain one.

A determinate outcome can often be assured by **rank-order voting** or **plurality voting**, a procedure in which each voter ranks all of n issues from 1 (most preferred) to n (least preferred) and the lowest number wins. (This procedure yields 6 points for each of the choices in Table 19.3 and, hence, is of little help in this example.) Another possibility is **point voting**, a procedure in which each voter is given x points that can be distributed among issues at the voter's discretion, and the largest number wins.

The Delegation Problem

Delegation is another problem likely to give rise to a very imperfect revelation and satisfaction of people's preferences for pure public goods. Direct democracy inevitably is abandoned in large groups and replaced with representative democracy, in which people do not vote for policies directly, but rather for political candidates.

Economic theorists suggest that elected officials, like all people, are best viewed as engaged in the rational pursuit of self-interest. It would be foolish to assume that they will somehow, miraculously, change their motivation as they move from the realm of private to that of social choice, that they will successfully identify and serve "the common good" rather than maximize their own utility. Elected officials, economists suggest, will follow the optimization principle to maximize votes. They will carry all policies to the point where their extension will cost more votes than are gained. In short, elected officials will pursue policies favored by the median voter (see the discussion of the Hotelling paradox in Chapter 12, which explains an analogous type of behavior in the business world). Because the median voter's preferences might be misinterpreted or suddenly change, political candidates minimize the risk of serious vote loss by adopting ambiguous platforms that are indistinguishable from those of their opponents. When successful, this strategy yields close votes; note the presidential election of 1960 (Kennedy-Nixon), 1968

(Nixon-Humphrey), and 1976 (Carter-Ford). When this policy is spurned (as it was by Goldwater in 1964 and by McGovern in 1972), "landslides" result (leading, in the two instances just noted, to the election of Johnson or Nixon). For our purposes, however, the important lesson is this: Ultimate voters in a representative democracy have all the more reason to remain rationally ignorant or abstain from voting. At best, they will vote for an ill-defined combination of policies; unlike in the market for goods, wherein most individuals cast their dollar votes daily, voting for political candidates occurs only rarely. In the meantime, the elected officials have much leeway to violate the true preferences of the ultimate voters.

The Problem of Bureaucracy

A third reason why the process of public choice may fail to identify and deliver the optimum quantity of pure public goods is that elected officials, wisely or foolishly, allocate dollar amounts to the provision of public goods, but *someone else* implements their decisions. The entire institutional structure through which political decisions are implemented is known as the **bureaucracy**; all the people working for these government agencies (or bureaus) are known as **bureaucrats**. Many economists argue that bureaucrats, too, are best viewed as engaged in the rational pursuit of self-interest. Just like consumers, the owners of firms, voters, and elected officials, bureaucrats are best seen as seeking to use existing institutions to their own advantage. Economists such as James Buchanan (see Biography 19.3) have found that this view of bureaucrats is vastly more productive of explaining their behavior than an alternative view that regards their actions as "impartial service for the common good."

Bureaucrats Maximize Utility. Above all, Buchanan argues, bureaucrats seek to maximize their own utility by preserving and advancing their own careers, which means seeking higher salaries through promotion and seeking lower work loads for a given amount of pay. In hierarchical organizations, both goals can be achieved by multiplying the numbers of subordinates (and titles). Bureaucrats also seek job tenure, prestige, and various fringe benefits (ranging from insurance and pension plans to long coffee breaks, luxurious offices, and trips to important conferences in Rome). The achievement of these and similar goals, invariably, is a function of the agency's budget. As a result, utility maximization translates into budget maximization: "More is always better."

The Iron Triangle. Before long, a bargaining situation develops between bureaucrats on the one hand and legislators on the other. Because few bureaus receive revenue from sales, bureaucrats need legislators to make periodic grants of money. In the background are the "clients" served by the bureaucrats, the special interests for whom the bureaucrats soon become effective in-house lobbyists. Thus the Department of Defense begins to serve defense contractors; the Department of Agriculture serves farmers; the Department of Education serves schools and colleges. Legislators with strong special-interest constituencies (and large numbers of apathetic voters) have, in turn, a powerful incentive to sit on committees that deal with the special-interest groups. These legislators will logroll until they find themselves appointed. Over time, legislative committees will be dominated by legislators who favor the special interests. Thus, an "iron triangle" is formed: special interests, bureaucrats, and legislators, each seeking their own interests, will jointly promote overgenerous budgets for pure public goods. The consequences of the pursuit by government officials of their internal, private goals instead of publicly announced, official goals have been termed **internalities**. Internalities are associated with government failure, just as externalities are associated with market failure.

A Graphical Exposition. Panel (a) of Figure

FIGURE 19.3 **Internalities**

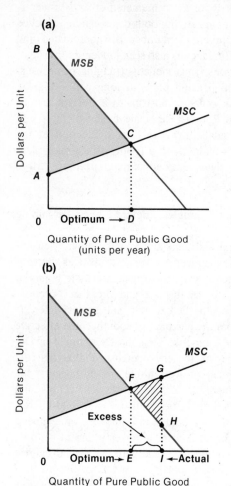

(a)

(b)

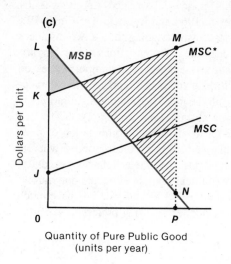

(c)

Government officials may well fail to provide the optimum quantity of a pure public good because they are ill-informed about marginal social benefits and costs. But even if they were omniscient, they might fail to do so as a result of their pursuit of internal, private goals. They might then provide for an excessive amount of such a good, perhaps even at an excessive cost. As a result, the net benefit available to society under ideal conditions or the shaded area in panel (a), might be offset partially by the dotted area in panel (b) or might give way to a net overall loss, represented by the shaded minus the crosshatched area in panel (c).

19.3 depicts the ideal situation that government officials would bring about if they were omniscient, benevolent, and endowed with the strictest sense of public duty. They would identify the optimum quantity of the public good as $0D$ by comparing falling marginal social benefit, *MSB*, with rising marginal social cost, *MSC*. Because the private market would fail to produce any amount of the public good, government officials would impose upon people a total cost of $0ACD$

to procure a total benefit of $0BCD$. The shaded triangle *ABC* depicts the net benefit.

Panel (b) pictures an added element: the provision of an excess amount of the public good because public officials pursue private goals, as noted above. In this case, the total amount provided is not $0E$, the optimum, but $0I$. The difference between $0E$ and $0I$ indicates that people are getting an *added* benefit of *EFHI*, but at an *added* cost of *EFGI*. Thus they are receiving, on the excess quantity, a net loss of crosshatched triangle *FGH*. Overall, people are getting a net benefit of the shaded minus the crosshatched area. They are still better off than without government intervention, but government has now failed to maximize the potential net benefit from the provision of the pure public good.

Panel (c) depicts a situation in which the government's failure to optimize is so extreme that living with market failure, and forgoing the shaded net benefit pictured in panel (a), would be preferable. In this case, government officials present people with a net social loss: As in panel (b), bureaucrats again provide for an above-optimal amount, *0P*. But this time, they also produce it at an excessive cost, pictured by *MSC**. This cost reflects the bureaucrats' tolerance of X-inefficiency: excess staffing, luxury offices, unnecessary trips to Rome. As a result, the public receives total benefits of *0LNP* at a total cost of *0KMP*. The net result is a net loss equal to the shaded minus the crosshatched area. People are worse off than they would be if government had done nothing at all.

Anecdotal Evidence. The word *bureaucrat*, while on the surface merely referring to someone working for a government agency, has pejorative overtones because many people have observed the wasteful expenditure of other people's money by government agencies. As was noted above and depicted in padded cost curve *MSC**, bureaucrats can serve their own ends by endlessly adding to their budgets and spending every cent. According to **Parkinson's law**, pronounced by the British historian in a delightful satirical essay in *The Economist* (November 1955), the number of those employed by government agencies will grow at the same rate regardless of whether the volume of work to be done rises, falls, or even disappears.

A casual look at many a government bureaucracy supports this view of a giant amoeba, endlessly reproducing itself. When Washington was president, one American in 4,000 worked for the federal government; 100 years later, the number was 1 in 400; now it is 1 in 75. In 1980, the Assistant Administrator for Water and Hazardous Materials of the Environmental Protection Agency (note the title) had a staff exceeding Washington's entire first administration.

Increased numbers of bureaucrats can, in turn, make more work for themselves. Consider these true examples from the 1970s:

1. The Postal Service has utilized many labor hours to consider adding four digits to the five-digit ZIP code system. This new system would provide 1 billion ZIP zones, from 000,000,000 to 999,999,999. Thus every man, woman, and child in the country could be given 5 zones—along with, perhaps, a manual the length of a football field.

2. The Bureau of Education for the Handicapped in the Department of Health, Education, and Welfare, after persuading Congress for funds to aid an alleged 12 percent of school children with hearing and vision problems, speech impairments, emotional difficulties, mental retardation, orthopedic defects, and the like, could not find such a percentage of children. Instead of reducing its operations, it declared a "handicapped shortage" and launched "Operation Childfind." A barrage of letters to education officials, grants to university researchers, and media ads followed but failed to reverse the handicapped "shortfall."

3. Each month, Senator Proxmire awards a Golden Fleece to the most ridiculous spending program he can find. Thus he honored the National Institutes of Health for a $102,000 study of whether sunfish drinking gin are more belligerent than sunfish drinking tequila. And the Law Enforcement Assistance Administration got its Fleece for a $27,000 study of why prison inmates would like to escape. Congress itself got the award (in 1979) for an increase of its staff to 18,400 aides (a 57 percent rise over a mere decade).

Where does it all end? The best estimate, perhaps, is summarized in Gordon Tullock's **bureaucratic rule of two**: The removal of an

BIOGRAPHY 19.2:

Kenneth J. Arrow

Kenneth Joseph Arrow (1921–) was born in New York City. He studied at the City College of New York and at Columbia before teaching at the University of Chicago, Harvard, and Stanford.

Arrow made a number of major contributions to economics. The first one, noted in this chapter, lies in the realm of public choice. Using elegant mathematics, he formulated the impossibility theorem in his *Social Choice and Individual Values* (1951). He also noted that voting is more likely to produce economic efficiency when the preferences of people are similar. The net gains to collective action are greatest in a community of like-minded individuals; they are least in political units composed of very diverse groups.

Arrow has also made pathbreaking advances in other areas, notably general equilibrium theory and decision theory. These advances are reflected in his *Essays in the Theory of Risk-Bearing* (1971), *The Limits to Organization* (1974), and *Studies in Resource Allocation Processes* (1977, with Leonid Hurwicz).

In 1957, the American Economic Association awarded Arrow its John Bates Clark medal and later made him its president. In 1972, for "pioneering contributions to general economic equilibrium theory and welfare theory," he was awarded the Nobel Memorial Prize in Economic Science (jointly with John R. Hicks—see Biography 4.2).

In his presidential address to the American Economic Association, Arrow elaborated upon the need to study economic equilibrium and decision making under uncertainty:

The neoclassical model is founded on two concepts. . . . One is the notion of the individual economic agent, whose behavior is governed by a criterion of optimization under constraints which are partly peculiar to the agent, such as production functions, and partly terms of trade with the economic system as a whole. The other is in the market; here . . . the terms of trade [are] adjusted until the decisions of the individuals are mutually consistent in the aggregate, i.e., supply equals demand. . . . The optimization by individual agents has a sense of concreteness about it. . . . They behave in ways whose logic we understand. . . . The market, on the other hand, is a much more ethereal construct. Who exactly is it that is achieving the balancing of supply and demand? Where in fact is the information on bids and offers needed for equilibrium actually collected and stored? Right from the beginning of neoclassical theory, the difficulty of explaining markets in terms of individual self-seeking behavior was perceived. . . . It is Walras's auctioneer which has proved to have had the most enduring effect. . . . What is envisioned is a feedback mechanism in which errors in the price are successively corrected by reference to the disequilibria they generate. This view specifies and makes feasible the operations of the market. . . . One aspect on which we put a great deal of weight . . . is that a market system is informationally econom-

activity from the private to the public sector will double its unit cost of production.

Shaking Up the Bureaucrats

It is difficult to judge the performance of government bureaus. They do not have annual statements of profit and loss. They do not issue stock certificates, the prices of which can be moni-

tored. They do not go bankrupt when competitors do better. Yet there is an obvious need for monitoring performance and improving it where indicated. In recent years, a number of approaches have been much discussed, including 1. benefit-cost analysis, 2. competition among government bureaus, 3. replacing government production with government provision, and 4. introducing direct competition between bureaus and private firms.

ical. . . . The individual agent need not know very much. . . . The economic system, taken as a whole, has vastly more in it than any one individual knows; it contains the utility functions and production possibilities of all individual agents. . . . But clearly this simplification of the individual's decision making is made possible only because the markets have supplied the information economized on, in the form of prices. In equilibrium, at least, the system as a whole gives the impression of great economy in the handling of information, presumably because transmission of prices is . . . much cheaper than transmission of the whole set of production possibilities and utility functions. . . . But . . . production and consumption decisions are in fact made with reference to the future as well as to the present. . . . The information about future commodities needed includes their prices: These prices must be those found on a suitable market, one in which future supply and future demand are equated. . . . Even the futures markets in certain commodities, limited in extent as they are, do not in fact lead to balancing *all* future decisions. . . . The optimizer faces a world of uncertainty.[1]

[1]Kenneth J. Arrow, "Limited Knowledge and Economic Analysis," *The American Economic Review*, March 1974, pp. 1–10.

Benefit-Cost Analysis

According to an old saying, the attitude of bureaucrats is: "If we have the money, let's do it." The optimization principle, introduced in the very first chapter of this book, requires otherwise. Even when a government project produces obvious benefits, they may not be worth the cost; the forgone alternative benefits may be larger. In an attempt to force bureaucrats to examine bene-

fits in relation to costs, the U.S. federal government began introducing Planning-Programming-Budgeting Systems (PPBS) in its agencies in 1965; these systems have now spread to state and local governments as well. These systems require bureaucrats to engage in **benefit-cost analysis**, also referred to as **cost-effectiveness studies**, which is the quantification of the benefits and costs of all contemplated government projects, the rejection of those with benefit-cost ratios below unity, and the apportionment of the budget among those remaining projects that have the highest benefit-cost ratios.

For reasons noted in Chapter 9, benefits and costs that are spread out over time, must, of course, be discounted to the present. So it is the *present* values of streams of benefits and costs that are compared. Projects with negative net present values are rejected (their benefit-cost ratio is below unity); projects with the highest positive net present values are carried out.

In this way, bureaucrats are forced to focus on the three major ingredients of intertemporal choice: benefits, costs, and the discount rate. Unfortunately, this procedure conveys an aura of precision that may not be justified. A benefit-cost ratio of 1.792 looks very precise indeed and seems to suggest that the public project provides public benefits that exceed the forgone private ones by 79.2 percent. Yet this is true only if the benefits and costs have been estimated correctly and the proper discount rate has been applied. Oftentimes, the analyst has much discretion in the estimation of costs, benefits, and discount rates and, therefore, can influence the outcome as well.

Consider estimating the benefits of a flood-control program. Some of the benefits are tangible and not too difficult to calculate: increased farm output, increased generation of electric power, decreased damages to residences and roads. Other benefits, however, are intangible and hard to estimate in dollars and cents: improved recreational opportunities or enhanced scenic beauty.

Similarly, many costs can be difficult to estimate. Estimating the cost of concrete or labor

BIOGRAPHY 19.3:

James M. Buchanan

James McGill Buchanan (1919–   ) was born at Murfreesboro, Tennessee. He studied at the Universities of Tennessee and Chicago, then taught at Florida State, Virginia, and UCLA. He now directs the Center for the Study of Public Choice at the Virginia Polytechnic Institute.

Buchanan is a leader among the new institutional economists; his work has been devoted to exploring the common ground between economics and political science. More than anyone, he has been responsible for the "public choice revolution" of the past two decades, which has taken a radically new look at government. Instead of characterizing government as a superindividual —omniscient, benevolent, and always correcting market failures with precision—scholars influenced by Buchanan are now more apt to look at government from the perspective of individual officials who seek to serve their own purposes. Buchanan developed these ideas in *The Calculus of Consent* (1962, with Gordon Tullock), *Demand and Supply of Public Goods* (1968), *The Limits of Liberty* (1975), *Freedom in Constitutional Contract* (1978), *What Should Economists Do?* (1980), and many other books and articles.

Buchanan has been highly critical of attempts (such as those by Samuelson and Arrow) to build a bridge from theories of maximization (of utility or profit) by individuals to one of maximization by society. Society, Buchanan has argued, is not a thinking and acting being that could possibly maximize its well-being on the basis of a social welfare function that somehow relates different states of the world to social welfare. Hence it is absurd to expect (as Arrow did) that social choices (which in fact are not the choice of a superbeing, but are simply the aggregate result of individual choices) will be internally consistent. Such an expectation should only be held for individual choice. According to Buchanan:

> The object for economists' research is "the economy," which is, by definition, a *social organization*, an interaction among separate choosing entities. . . . "The economy" does not maximize . . . there exists no one person, no single chooser, who maximizes *for* the economy. . . . Paul Samuelson . . . in his *Foundations of Economic Analysis* . . . extended the maximizing construction to welfare economics, extolling the virtues of [a] social welfare function. . . . I have no quarrel with the elaboration and refinements of the maximizing models for individual and firm behavior. . . . My strictures are directed exclusively at the extension of this basic maximizing paradigm to social organization where it does not belong. This is the bridge

going into a dam is one thing; estimating long-run ecological damage is quite another. Even the market prices of concrete and labor may not be the proper ingredients for finding the opportunity cost of providing flood control: What if the price of concrete exceeds the marginal private cost of producing it? What if the marginal social cost of producing concrete falls short of or exceeds the marginal private cost? What if there is massive unemployment of labor, and the use of labor in the flood-control project in no way reduces output anywhere else?

Selecting the proper rate for discounting future benefits and costs is the most difficult task of all. Theoretical considerations, noted in Chapter 9, suggest the *pure rate of interest* is the proper rate for discounting. The pure rate of interest is the rate one would find in perfectly competitive capital markets. This rate would reflect the private sector's marginal time preference and marginal time productivity and would indicate the rate of return that resources used in the public sector could earn in the private one instead. But the real world provides the analyst with a bewildering complexity of rates of return, reflecting differences in risk, in maturity, in

which economists should never have crossed, and which has created major intellectual confusion. "That which emerges" from the . . . exchange process . . . is not the solution to a maximizing problem. . . . "That which emerges" is "that which emerges" and that is that.

My own initial reaction to Arrow's [impossibility theorem] was, and remains, one of nonsurprise. . . . Who would have expected any social process to yield a consistent ordering of results? Only economists who had made the critical methodological error of crossing the bridge from individual to social maximization without having recognized what they were doing would have experienced intellectual-ideological disappointment. . . . What should be the role for the economist . . .? He should neither revert to nihilism nor seek the escapism of social welfare functions. His productivity lies in his ability to search out and to invent social rearrangements which will embody Pareto-superior moves. If an observed position is inefficient, there must be ways of securing agreement on change, agreement which signals mutuality of expected benefits. . . . Yet how many economists do we observe working out such schemes? . . . As persons, both from the streets and the ivory towers, observe modern governmental failures, they can scarcely fail to be turned off by those constructions which require beneficent wisdom on the part of political man. And they can hardly place much credence in the economist consultant whose policy guidelines apply only within institutions that embody such wisdom. Something is amiss, and economists are necessarily being forced to take stock of the social productivity of their efforts. When, as, and if they do, they will, I think, come increasingly to share what I have called the contractarian paradigm. . . .

Economics comes closer to being a "science of contract" than a "science of choice." And with this, the "scientist," as political economist, must assume a different role. The maximizer must be replaced by the arbitrator, the outsider who tries to work out compromises among conflicting claims. The Edgeworth . . . box becomes the first diagram in our elementary textbooks. . . . The unifying principle becomes *gains-from-trade*, not maximization.[1]

[1]James M. Buchanan, "A Contractarian Paradigm for Applying Economic Theory," *The American Economic Review*, May 1975, pp. 225–30.

market imperfections, and in taxation. Thus one can find rates from 0–8 percent a year on short-term liquid assets and from 30–40 percent, perhaps, on investments in the most profitable industries. Which of these is the proper rate of discount, therefore, depends, on the part of the private sector from which the resources to be used on the public project are to be withdrawn. Predicting the sectors from which resources will be withdrawn is next to impossible. A flood-control program may be carried out with resources withdrawn from private consumption, from private investment in low-risk sector A, or from private investment in high-risk sector B. . . . As a result, analysts typically prepare benefit-cost analyses with a range of "plausible" discount rates. And some analysts even argue that government should ignore rates of return in the private sector entirely. They think these rates are "artificial" (influenced by "arbitrary" monetary policy) or "unacceptable" (reflective of people's indifference to the fate of future generations). These analysts favor a conscious value judgment that establishes a "social" rate of discount through which government arbitrates the conflicting claims of present and future generations.

ANALYTICAL EXAMPLE 19.2:

Flooding Hell's Canyon

The Snake River between Idaho and Oregon passes through 200 miles of a geological formation known as Hell's Canyon—the deepest canyon in North America, including the Grand Canyon. From the canyon to the towering Seven Devils Peaks of Idaho and the beautiful Wallowa Mountains of Oregon, the area provides some of the most spectacular scenery in the country. The canyon is also the habitat of large numbers of elk, deer, and bighorn sheep, of huge flocks of redleg partridges, and, in the river itself, of salmon, steelhead, and sturgeon.

Hell's Canyon is also the best remaining site for developing hydroelectric power. Not surprisingly, plans were made in the 1960s to construct either two low dams (at the Mountain Sheep and Pleasant Valley sites) or one high dam (at Mountain Sheep). Conventional benefit-cost analysis, which *ignored* environmental costs, showed the high dam project to be worthwhile. The accompanying table weighs power and flood-control benefits against generating and transmission costs. The Federal Power Commission licensed the construction of the high dam, but the Secretary of the Interior appealed. The U.S. Supreme Court eventually ordered a reconsideration of the entire project that would assess the benefits of *not* developing the canyon.

The initial year's benefits from preserving the canyon for fishing, hunting, and the like were subsequently estimated at $0.895 million. No reliable estimates could be made for the considerable value of the site for scientific research materials and opportunities. (Owing to the great vertical distance between the canyon floor and tops of adjacent rim crags, for example, virtually all of North America's ecological life zones can be found within only half a mile.) Nor was it possible to quantify the value people place on retaining the option (for themselves or future generations) of being able to visit such a remarkable site and not having it irrevocably destroyed. Nor was it possible to evaluate the destruction of the wildlife habitat (for migratory fish, waterfowl, and mammals). It seemed certain, however, that the present value of all

Enough has been said to indicate that benefit-cost analysis, even though seemingly precise, still does not hinder much of the subjective decision making by bureaucrats. The framework of PPBS in no way prevents bureaucrats, who are eager to justify their projects, from exaggerating benefits and understating costs.

Competition Among Government Bureaus

Competition among government bureaus has been suggested as a means of discouraging an unnecessary inflation of cost and of providing legislators with a yardstick by which to judge performance. Thus it has been argued that the competition among Air Force, Army, and Navy (all of which once procured their own planes) produced better-quality products at lower cost. Some believe that government decentralization can achieve the same beneficial result. The police department or school system in one town can be compared with that in another—not only by budget-making legislators, but also by the ultimate consumers of public goods. Legislators can accordingly put pressure on some bureaucrats to emulate the admirable performance of others. Consumers can "vote with their feet" and move to localities where government performs well. Such comparisons are impossible when all public goods are produced by a single government agency.

Interestingly, bureaucrats often oppose de-

	Hell's Canyon Projects (in thousands of dollars per year, rounded)	
	Low Mountain Sheep-Pleasant Valley Complex	High Mountain Sheep Project
1976–80		
Benefits	38,985	40,901
Costs	44,513	39,597
Net benefits	− 5,441	1,304
1981–90		
Benefits	46,133	41,244
Costs	51,074	39,597
Net benefits	− 4,941	1,647
1991–2025		
Benefits	57,758	40,241
Costs	62,335	39,597
Net benefits	− 4,577	644
1976 present value for 1976–2025 period (discounted at 9 percent per year)	−55,042	+13,809

environmental costs would exceed the present value of the high dam, shown in the table. Eventually, Congress passed a law prohibiting construction of the dam.

Source: Based on John V. Krutilla and Anthony C. Fisher, *The Economics of Natural Environments: Studies in the Valuation of Commodity and Amenity Resources* (Baltimore: The Johns Hopkins University Press, 1975), pp. 101–103. Copyright © 1975 by Resources for the Future, Inc. Published by the Johns Hopkins University Press.

centralization and favor consolidation instead. They talk deprecatingly of multiple police departments as "duplication." Yet bureaucrats recommend such "duplication" for the private sector all the time. They never suggest consolidation of all the auto makers but wish to promote as many separate firms as possible.

Government Provision, not Production

While it is true that pure public goods would not be provided by the private market and must be *provided* by government, it does not follow that they must be *produced* by government. Government provision simply requires the collection of taxes and the exercise of demand (because people as individuals would fail to spend money on pure public goods). Yet the *producers* of public goods could well be private firms.

To some extent, government has always been contracting out the production of pure public goods to the private sector. The most notable example is defense—military equipment is produced and research is even conducted by private firms. In the days of the Old West, government contracted out law enforcement in the same way. It collected taxes and then paid bounties to private hunters of criminals. In recent years, many American towns have begun to contract out many of their traditional activities, ranging from fire protection, highway construction, and janitorial services for public buildings to the operation of parking lots and sanitation services. The private production of fire protection has been accomplished at half the original cost and the private production of garbage collection at two thirds the cost.[2]

Government agencies are, of course, involved in the production not only of many pure public goods, but also of other goods. Consider, at the local level, buses, subways, trolleys, cemeteries, electric power, golf courses, libraries, museums, schools, sports stadiums, swimming pools, and zoos. Consider, at the state level, insurance, liquor retailing, gambling, mental institutions, old-age homes, and universities.

---

[2]Roger Ahlbrandt, *Municipal Fire Protection Services: Comparison of Alternative Organizational Forms* (Beverly Hills: Sage, 1973); and E. S. Savas, *The Organization and Efficiency of Solid Waste Collection* (Lexington: Heath, 1977). The latter study, covering 260 cities, noted that private contractors used smaller crews and more productive vehicles than municipal agencies. The former also had fewer absences and used incentive systems to serve more households per hour.

CLOSE-UP 19.1:

New York's Water Crisis

In 1949–50, New York City experienced a severe shortage of water. Three solutions were proposed:

1. Building a dam at Cannonsville, which would cost $1,000 per million gallons of water gained.
2. Plugging leaks in water mains, which would cost $1.61 per million gallons of water gained.
3. Metering customers, which would cost $160 per million gallons of water saved.

The city chose project #1. Benefit-cost analysis had not yet arrived.

Source: Based on George J. Stigler, "Private Vice and Public Virtue," *The Journal of Law and Economics,* October 1961, pp. 1–11.

Consider, at the federal level, commodity stockpiling, lending, postal service, printing, shipbuilding, railroads, and veterans' hospitals. The list could be extended (and even more so in West European countries). Critics of bureaucratic waste suggest that costs could be reduced substantially if government concentrated on pure public goods only and then restricted itself to arranging for their production by the private sector.

Competition Between Bureaus and Private Firms

Finally, placing existing government bureaus in direct competition with private firms is another possible approach to reducing government failure. Two possible candidates for this approach are the U.S. Postal Service and the local public schools.

The operations of the U.S. Postal Service have been described as unbelievably inefficient. Critics believe that private competition could improve matters drastically. United Parcel Service (a private firm) already handles $3\frac{1}{2}$ times as many parcels as the U.S. Postal Service. The Federal Express (another private firm) is handling the high-speed delivery of ever-more small packages. *Better Homes and Gardens, Business Week, Time,* and *The Wall Street Journal* have switched to private delivery of their publications (at an average 10 cents a copy compared to the Postal Service's 16.5 cents). Advertisers have abandoned the mails for the telephone. Many firms are eager to take on the letter business as well, but the Postal Service enjoys a legal monopoly. (No matter who delivers a first-class letter, it must carry U.S. postage.) Some suggest that this monopoly be lifted by Congress. Others believe that technological change will do the trick. The Postal Service, they argue, is employing antediluvian methods to carry the mails. Internal combustion engines and human backs lug around an essentially weightless commodity: information. This information could be transported much better via wire, radio, and satellite. Already an IBM-Comsat-Aetna consortium has

ANALYTICAL EXAMPLE 19.3:

The SST and the Discount Rate

In the 1960s, the U.S. government had to decide whether to support the development of the SST, or supersonic transport plane. Two estimates of likely market size were presented: a pessimistic one by the Institute for Defense Analyses (IDA) and an optimistic one by the Federal Aviation Administration (FAA). Both agencies calculated the net present value of the program at three different discount rates. The results, shown in the accompanying table, indicate the crucial role the choice of discount rate plays in determining a program's desirability. Given the IDA estimate of market size, the program was not worthwhile at any rate above 1.33 percent. Given the FAA's market size projection, the program was undesirable only at rates in excess of 6.85 percent.

Market Estimate	Net Present Values of SST Program (in millions of dollars), Given Annual Discount Rate of		
	5 percent	10 percent	15 percent
By IDA	−344	−528	−579
By FAA	+218	−239	−421

Note: in 1971, the program was abandoned in the United States but not in Europe. The British and French governments had a view of the costs and benefits that was different from the U.S. government's view. Yet in 1979, after spending $500 for every man, woman, and child in the two countries, the production (but not the operation) of the European Concorde was stopped as well. Of the 14 planes ever built, not one had been sold commercially. Operating at a cost four times that of a Boeing 747, the plane's services could not be priced low enough (without subsidies) to elicit sufficient demand. Although the plane crossed the Atlantic in less time than it took its passengers to travel to and from the airport, the time zone difference made it impossible for harried people to travel between America and Europe and return on the same day. The unharried were in no rush!

Source: U.S. Congress, Joint Economic Committee, *Economic Analysis of Public Investment Decisions: Interest Rate Policy and Discounting Analysis* (Washington, D.C.: U.S. Government Printing Office, 1968), pp. 20–21; and *The New York Times,* September 28, 1979.

---

proposed a Satellite Business System to replace interoffice mail communications by electronic means. In 1979, the Postal Service accordingly moved to protect its monopoly by requesting that the definition of ''letters'' be extended to ''orientations of magnetic particles in a manner having a predetermined significance.'' The request was denied.

Many people are also unhappy with the local public schools. Milton Friedman (see Biography 2.2) has suggested a simple solution: that the funds currently collected in taxes be withheld from public school administrators and handed to parents of school children in the form of **education vouchers**.[3] These vouchers would be divisi-

[3]Milton Friedman, *Capitalism and Freedom* (Chicago: University of Chicago Press, 1962), chap. 6; and *Free to Choose* (New York: Harcourt, Brace, Jovanovich, 1980), chap. 6.

ble certificates earmarked for the purchase of educational services only and might be "spent" by their recipients in one or several accredited private or public schools (which could cash them in at the public treasury). As a result of such a voucher system, it is imagined, many different types of schools would emerge: large schools and small ones, schools stressing the arts and schools stressing science, schools stressing general education and others vocational training, morning schools and afternoon schools, segregated schools and integrated ones. Instead of taking whatever a public school board decreed, parents could tailor their children's curriculum to their own tastes! They could spend a part of their certificates on a Monday-morning all-boy art school, another part on a Tuesday-to-Thursday-afternoon coeducational science school, and another part on a Friday all-black vocational school. Parents could buy whatever services they deemed best for their children.

There would be room, too, it is argued, for teachers and administrators to experiment and make greater progress in their fields. Those who had a brand-new idea could open a school and test it out. They would not have to launch a full-scale political campaign to persuade the school board, other civil servants, or legislators of the soundness of their ideas. If successful, they would be swamped with applicants, have big revenues, and expand. Other less successful schools would find their pupils and revenues evaporating and would have to conform to the consumer's choice or go out of business! This important feature of competition is entirely lacking in *public* schools. Because they operate on tax revenue, they can provide bad services and still survive.

Such a voucher system might be used for all goods with positive externalities, resulting in a combination of the best of the public and private sectors. Such goods might be publicly financed (to ensure the provision of an optimum quantity), privately demanded with public money (to ensure that consumers keep as much freedom of choice as possible), and then produced by competing private and public firms (to assure that production occurs in the cheapest way).

SUMMARY

1. This chapter focuses on goods with positive externalities that affect not only a few people, but literally all members of society. Such *pure public goods* provide *nonexcludable* and *nonrival* benefits to all people in a given society.

2. Pigou has shown us that goods with positive externalities tend to be produced in amounts insufficient to secure maximum economic welfare. In the case of pure public goods, which involve positive externalities to an extreme degree, the Pigouvian problem returns with a vengeance: left to themselves, private firms do not produce such goods at all because of *the free-rider problem*; in principle, this problem can be overcome by government intervention.

3. In principle, it is simple enough to determine the quantity of a pure public good that maximizes social welfare. At this optimum quantity the rising marginal social cost of producing the public good just equals the good's falling marginal social benefit, which, in turn, equals the sum of the marginal private benefits received by all of its consumers.

4. In practice, it is next to impossible to get people to reveal their true preferences for pure public goods: If they are taxed according to expected benefits, people will understate their expected benefits. If people are taxed less, they will overstate them.

5. In recent decades, economists have become interested in the process of public choice by which large groups of people decide on the overall quantity of public goods to be provided, on the particular types of such goods, and on the sharing of the associated tax burdens. The study of this process has led economists to conclude that real-world government may well fail to provide optimal amounts of pure public goods.

6. People's individual preferences for pure public goods, for example, are unlikely to be satisfied under a system of direct democracy and majority voting. Contributing factors can include rational voter ignorance, voter apathy and the sway of special interests, the suppression of minority interests, voting on arbitrary combinations of issues, or voting in arbitrary sequences. (The Arrow impossibility theorem elaborates on the role of voting sequence and shows that there exists no reliable mechanism for translating complete and transitive individual preference rankings among three or more alternatives into a social preference ranking, while simultaneously fulfilling certain conditions generally considered desirable in a democracy.) Possible remedies for such problems include the buying and selling of votes, logrolling, strategic voting, rank-order voting, and point voting.

Another reason for the likely imperfect satisfaction of people's preferences for pure public goods is the delegation problem. In a representative democracy, voters have all the more reason to remain rationally ignorant or abstain from voting, and representatives have much leeway to violate voter preferences.

A final reason for government failure is the fact that political decisions are implemented by a bureaucracy; bureaucrats, like all people, are engaged in the rational pursuit of self-interest. An iron triangle develops, consisting of bureaucrats, legislators, and special interests, each of whom seek to promote their own interests. Jointly, they are likely to promote overgenerous budgets for pure public goods. Bureaucrats are likely to produce this excess quantity of public goods at an excess cost as well.

7. Possibilities for improving the performance of government bureaucracy include benefit-cost analysis; competition among government bureaus; government provision, but not production of public goods; and competition between bureaus and private firms.

KEY TERMS

Arrow impossibility theorem

benefit-cost analysis
bureaucracy
bureaucratic rule of two
bureaucrats
cost-effectiveness studies
education vouchers
free-rider problem
indivisibilities
internalities
logrolling
merit goods
nonexcludability
nonrivalness
Parkinson's law
plurality voting
point voting
public finance
pure private good
pure public good
rank-order voting
strategic voting
voting paradox

QUESTIONS AND PROBLEMS

1. "The free-rider problem discussed in this chapter throws new light on the right-to-work vs. union-security debate noted in Chapter 13. The reason that unions insist on union shops or closed shops is that they are producing a public good that affects all employees equally whether they pay union dues or not." Do you agree or disagree with this position? (*Hint*: Consider how unions "produce" working conditions, including rules about safety, lighting, heating, layoffs, promotions, discharge, and pace of work.)

2. "The distinction between pure public goods and merit goods is not a happy one. Quite obviously, the purchase by government of such merit goods as social security or public education, health care, and housing serves the purpose of producing the pure public good of *economic* *justice.* Thus merit goods are seen to be *ingredients* in the production of pure public goods in the same way that courthouses, jails, police cruisers, and polaris submarines are ingredients used in the production of internal or external security.'' Evalute this position.

3. ''In 1976, the city government of New York chose to permit 1,622 murders, 3,400 rapes, 27,456 assaults, 77,940 robberies, and 195,243 burglaries. Today's figures are not any better. These crime rates are outrageous. When there are such obvious added benefits to be derived from additional crime prevention activities, the city ought to produce more of this public good.'' What do you think? (*Hint*: Frame your answer with the help of panel (a) in Figure 19.2).

4. Consider three voters with the following preferences about possible penalties for dope peddling:

Preference Ranking	Voter A	Voter B	Voter C
1st	Small fine	10 years' jail	Death sentence
2nd	10 years' jail	Death sentence	Small fine
3rd	Death sentence	Small fine	10 years' jail

Prove that whoever controls the voting procedure (in a system of simple majority voting) also controls the result.

5. Do you think your college economics department qualifies as a bureau? If so, does it act as the economic theory of bureaucracy predicts? (*Hint*: Ask yourself what would happen if your professor found a way to teach economics effectively with half the number of instructors normally required.)

6. Consider the implications of the following proposed flood protection policies. Which project would you recommend and why?

Plan	Annual Damage	Annual Cost of Project
(A) No protection	$38,000	0
(B) Build levees	32,000	$ 3,000
(C) Build small reservoir	22,000	10,000
(D) Build medium reservoir	13,000	18,000
(E) Build large reservoir	6,000	30,000

7. In 1969, different agencies of the federal government used different discount rates in their respective benefit-cost analyses. Thus the Office of Economic Opportunity used a 3–5 percent rate in evaluating its job corps, ''upward bound,'' and family planning programs; the Department of Agriculture used a 4.875 percent rate for rural conservation and electrification programs. The Department of Defense used a 10 percent rate for air-station and shipyard projects; and the Department of Health, Education, and Welfare used rates between 0 and 10 percent in evaluating programs concerning tuberculosis, cancer, syphilis, arthritis and motor vehicle injury. Evaluate this use of different discount rates.

8. ''The educational voucher plan would be a disaster: most parents wouldn't know how to pick the best schooling for their children; the rich and the poor wouldn't get the same education; education is too important to trust to profit-seeking business; church schools and racially-segregated schools might spring up as a result.'' What do you think?

SELECTED READINGS

Arrow, Kenneth J. *Social Choice and Individual Values*, 2nd ed. New Haven: Yale University Press, 1970.

Presentation of the impossibility theorem.

Arrow, Kenneth J. ''General Economic Equilibrium: Purpose, Analytic Techniques, Collective Choice.'' *The American Economic Review*, June 1974, pp. 253–72.

The 1972 Nobel Prize lecture.

Borcherding, Thomas E., ed. *Budgets and Bureaucrats: The Sources of Government Growth*. Durham: Duke University Press, 1977.

A book of readings.

Buchanan, James M. "An Economic Theory of Clubs." *Economica*, February 1965, pp. 1–14.

A discussion of goods that are neither pure private nor pure public ones because they are excludable but also nonrival. *See also* comments by Y.-K Ng, *Economica*, August 1973 and August 1974.

Buchanan, James M. and Tullock, Gordon. *The Calculus of Consent: Logical Foundations of Constitutional Democracy*. Ann Arbor: University of Michigan Press, 1962.

An analysis of political behavior under different decision rules.

Coase, Ronald H. "The Lighthouse in Economics." *The Journal of Law and Economics*, October 1974, pp. 357–76.

A fascinating discussion of economists' favorite example of a public good—and why their usual conclusion (the need for government intervention) may well be wrong.

Downs, Anthony. *An Economic Theory of Democracy*. New York: Harper and Row, 1957.

Argues that people in the public sector, too, will engage in the rational pursuit of self-interest.

Niskanen, William A. *Bureaucracy and Representative Government*. Chicago: Aldine-Atherton, 1971.

Argues that social gains from government intervention are apt to be consumed by an expansion of the bureaucracy itself.

Proxmire, William. *The Fleecing of America*. Boston: Houghton Mifflin, 1980.

The influential U.S. Senator tells the story of his Golden Fleece Awards.

Sandler, Todd, and Tschirhart, John T. "The Economic Theory of Clubs: An Evaluative Survey." *Journal of Economic Literature*, December 1980, pp. 1481–1521.

A superb discussion of voluntary groups the members of which derive mutual benefit from sharing impure public goods (goods that are characterized by partial rivalry or some excludability of benefits).

U.S. Congress, Joint Economic Committee. *The Analysis and Evaluation of Public Expenditures: The PPB System*, vols. 1–3. Washington, D.C.: U.S. Government Printing Office, 1969.

An important collection of papers on all aspects of PPBS.

U.S. Congress, Joint Economic Committee. *Innovations in Planning, Programming, and Budgeting in State and Local Governments*. Washington, D.C.: U.S. Government Printing Office, 1969.

A discussion of the use of PPBS by states, counties, and cities.

Wilcox, Clair, and Shepherd, William G. *Public Policies Toward Business*, 5th ed. Homewood: Irwin, 1975, part 5.

A detailed discussion of the role of public enterprise.

Wolf, Charles, Jr. "A Theory of Nonmarket Failure: Framework for Implementation Analysis." *The Journal of Law and Economics*, April 1979, pp. 107–39.

An important discussion of government failure.

GLOSSARY

acreage allotments government restrictions of the acreage that farmers may plant with a particular crop (11)

adverse selection a problem faced by insurance companies when those who buy insurance make up a biased sample such that their probability of loss differs markedly and, from the point of view of the company, adversely from the population at large (10)

affirmative-action plan a statement of an organization's intention not only to end discriminatory practices based on ethnic background, race, sex, and the like, but also to make deliberate efforts at overcoming the present effects of past discrimination (13)

allocative efficiency see **economic efficiency** (14)

allocative inefficiency see **economic inefficiency** (5)

ambient standards government rules specifying maximum quantities of pollutants a unit of the environment may contain (18)

antipirating agreements agreements among employers to act jointly in the hiring of labor and not to compete with each other for workers (13)

antitrust laws a series of laws, beginning with the Sherman Act of 1890, designed to restrain monopoly and foster competition (17)

applied research the application to a particular problem of the knowledge gained in basic research (10)

*Chapter numbers appear in parentheses.

appropriative doctrine the notion that the first user of water acquires a right to its use in the original place and manner of use, even to the extent of using up the water (18)

arc elasticity an (average) elasticity measure that refers to a section of a demand (or supply) line rather than a single point (4)

Arrow impossibility theorem the proposition that there exists no reliable mechanism for translating complete and transitive individual preference rankings among three or more alternatives into a social preference ranking, while simultaneously fulfilling certain conditions generally considered desirable in a democracy (19)

asset markets see **capital markets** (9)

atomistic competition the type of competition among buyers or among sellers in perfect markets in which each individual is too insignificant (like an atom in a large universe) to affect the equilibrium price (7)

average fixed cost total fixed cost divided by total product, or the difference between average total and average variable costs (6)

average loss negative average profit (6)

average product the ratio of total product to the total quantity of an input used to produce the product (5)

average profit total profit divided by total product, or price minus average total cost (6)

average revenue total revenue divided by total product; equals product price (6)

average total cost (ATC) total cost divided by total product (6)

average variable cost (AVC) total variable cost divided by total product   (6)

Averch-Johnson effect the production of a given output at higher-than-minimum cost by a regulated firm as a result of wasteful investment whenever the guaranteed return on investment exceeds the cost of capital (17)

bandwagon effect a situation in which the demand for a good by each individual varies directly with the quantity others are seen to demand   (4)

basic research scientific inquiry not directed toward any specific "useful" discovery (10)

basing-point system a system according to which oligopolists, regardless of their location, quote prices equal to those charged by one firm at a given place (the basing point) plus freight from the basing point to the buyer's location   (12)

benefit the advantage derived from an act of choice; an opportunity realized   (1)

benefit-cost analysis the quantification of the benefits and costs of all contemplated government projects, the rejection of those with benefit-cost ratios below unity, and the apportionment of the budget among those remaining projects that have the highest benefit-cost ratios   (19)

bilateral monopoly a situation in which an industry contains not only a single seller (monopoly), but in which this seller also faces a single buyer (monopsony)   (11)

break-even analysis the graphical juxtaposition of expected-total-revenue and expected-total-cost lines for a prospective business, in order to determine the minimum sales volume required to avoid losses   (6)

break-even point a level of output at which total revenue equals total cost and at which price equals average total cost   (6)

budget line a graph of all the alternative combinations of two goods that a consumer is able to buy in a given period at current market prices by fully using a given budget (3)

bureaucracy the entire institutional structure through which political decisions are implemented   (19)

bureaucratic rule of two "The removal of an activity from the private to the public sector will double its unit cost of production." (19)

bureaucrats people working for government agencies   (19)

buying hedge hedging a short position in the spot market by buying futures contracts now and selling them later   (10)

capacity output the output level associated with the minimum average total cost achievable from a given plant   (6)

capital the stock of all useful things or assets that yield streams of income over time   (9); see also **capital resources, financial capital**, and **human capital**

capital budgeting the process of identifying available investment opportunities, selecting investment projects to be carried out, and arranging for their financing   (9)

capitalism an economic system in which most resources are privately owned   (2)

capitalization the process of calculating capitalized value   (9)

capitalized value the present value of an income stream produced by an asset   (9)

capital markets markets in which certificates of indebtedness are traded, along with ownership claims to the stocks of natural resources and of physical capital goods   (9)

capital resources productive ingredients made by people, including structures, equipment, inventories   (1)

cartel a group of conspiring sellers acting as one and making joint price-quantity decisions with a view toward earning a larger profit than competition would allow   (11)

certificate of indebtedness an IOU or promise by the issuer to make future payments of money to the holder   (9)

CES production function   a production function with a constant elasticity of input substitution   (5)

change in demand   a shift in a demand line that indicates a change in the amount of something people wish to buy in a period—in spite of unchanged price and because of other factors, such as a change in the number of buyers or a change in their unique circumstances   (4)

change in quantity demanded   a movement, in response to a change in an item's own price, along a given demand line (that relates the quantity demanded of an item to its own price, all else being equal)   (4)

change in quantity supplied   a movement, in response to a change in an item's own price, along a given supply line (that relates the quantity supplied of an item to its own price, all else being equal)   (6)

change in supply   a shift in a supply line that indicates a change in the amount of something people wish to sell in a period—in spite of unchanged price and because of other factors, such as a change in the number of sellers or a change in their unique circumstances   (6)

closed shops   firms operating under a collective bargaining agreement that forbids the hiring of nonunion workers   (13)

Coase theorem   "Under perfect competition and in the absence of income effects and transactions costs, voluntary negotiated agreements among private parties generating or being affected by externalities will lead to the same resource allocation (and output mix) regardless of how property rights are assigned among these parties."   (18)

Cobb-Douglas production function   a production function relating output, Q, to labor and capital inputs, L and K, in the form of $Q = AL^a K^b$, which has a constant elasticity of input substitution equal to unity and in which the sum of parameters $a + b$, if equal to, greater than, or smaller than unity, indicates the presence of constant, increasing, or decreasing returns to scale, respectively   (5)

cobweb cycle   the tendency of the prices and quantities of some goods to rise above and then fall below some intermediate level in alternate periods   (7)

coefficient of relative effectiveness   the reciprocal of the **payback period**   (9)

coinsurance   an arrangement whereby the insured commit themselves to shoulder a fixed percentage of any loss   (10)

commutative justice   a situation in which goods are apportioned among people as a result of free choices by people all of whom enjoy as nearly equal opportunities as possible in the process of resource allocation   (15)

compensating wage differentials   wage differences that offset nonmonetary differences in the perceived attractiveness of jobs   (8)

complementary goods   two goods such that the quantity demanded of one varies inversely with the price of the other, all else being equal; goods with a negative cross-price elasticity   (4)

complementary inputs   inputs with the characteristic that a change in the quantity of one changes the marginal physical products of other inputs in the same direction   (8)

compounding   the process of computing, with the help of the interest rate, the future value of present dollars   (9)

concentration ratio   the percentage of industry sales attributable to a given number of largest firms, usually the 4, 8, 20, and 50 largest companies   (12)

conflict curve   another name for the **contract curve** in the Edgeworth box diagram, so called because people in efficient positions on the curve can make utility gains only at the expense of other people   (15)

conglomerate mergers   mergers of firms that have neither competitive nor buyer-seller relations   (12)

consent agreement   an agreement between a prosecutor and an accused party according to which a suit is dropped in exchange for voluntary ameliorative action by the accused (17)

conspiracy doctrine a doctrine once held by the courts according to which workers "conspiring" to raise wages were considered common criminals (13)

constant-cost industry an industry in which the product's normal price is unchanged after the industry has ceased to expand or contract (7)

constant returns to a variable input constancy in an input's marginal (physical) product as a larger quantity of the input is used, all else being equal (5)

constant returns to scale a characteristic of the production function such that a simultaneous and equal percentage change in the use of all physical inputs leads to an identical percentage change in physical output (5)

consumers' surplus the difference between the sum of money consumers actually pay for a given quantity and the maximum they could have been made to pay on an all-or-nothing basis (7)

consumption-indifference curve a graph of all the alternative combinations of two consumption goods that yield the same total of utility and among which a utility-maximizing consumer would be indifferent (3)

consumption-possibilities frontier see **budget line** (3)

contingent-claim markets markets in which people trade rights to variable quantities of particular goods—the quantities being dependent on the occurrence of specified "states of the world" (10)

contract curve the locus of all the efficient points in the Edgeworth box diagram, so called because people in inefficient positions not on the curve can make mutually beneficial contracts to achieve efficiency on the curve (15)

copyright the exclusive right to the production, publishing, or sale of a literary, musical, or artistic work (11)

cost the disadvantage associated with an act of choice; the most highly valued alternative benefit forgone; an opportunity lost (1)

cost-effectiveness studies see **benefit-cost analysis** (19)

costs of exchange see **transactions costs** (2)

Cournot equilibrium that output combination between two oligopolists which does not elicit further reactions from either one of them (12)

craft unions unions of workers possessing a common set of skills but possibly being employed by different firms (13)

cross-price elasticity of demand the percentage change in quantity demanded of one good divided by the percentage change in the price of another good, all else being equal (4)

cross-section studies studies that compare economic data pertaining to different populations during the same past period of time (4)

deadweight loss a loss of consumers' or producers' surplus that is not offset by anyone else's gain (7)

decreasing-cost industry an industry in which the product's normal price is lower after the industry has ceased to expand or is higher after it has ceased to contract (7)

decreasing returns to scale a characteristic of the production function such that a simultaneous and equal percentage change in the use of all physical inputs leads to a smaller percentage change in physical output (5)

deductible a fixed dollar amount by which any insurance company benefit payment falls short of a loss suffered by an insured (10)

deliberate coordination see **managerial coordination** (2)

demand a set of price-quantity combinations that represents the alternative amounts of an item that would be bought during a given period at all conceivable prices of this item, all else being equal (4)

derived demand a demand (such as the demand for resource services) that is derived from the demand in other markets (such as the demand for goods)   (8)

desire for goods   the quantities of goods people would take if all goods were available at zero prices   (1)

diminishing returns to a variable input   declines in an input's marginal (physical) product as a larger quantity of the input is used, all else being equal   (5)

direct costs   costs that can be attributed to the production of a particular unit of output   (6)

discounting   the process of computing, with the help of the interest rate, the present value of future dollars   (9)

discount rate   the interest rate used in discounting   (9)

discrimination   the making of irrelevant distinctions, as on the basis of race or sex as a result of malevolent tastes   (13)

diseconomies of scale   see **decreasing returns to scale**   (5)

distributive justice   a situation in which goods are apportioned among people by some authority seeking to act justly, usually by consulting some personal characteristic (such as need or hours worked) that measures the recipient's merit   (15)

dynamic efficiency   a situation within an economy in which it is impossible to produce a larger welfare total by improving technology or the size and quality of resource stocks   (14)

economic efficiency   a situation within an economy in which it is impossible, with given technology, to produce a larger welfare total from given stocks of resources and, therefore, in which it is impossible, through some reallocation of resources or goods among different households or firms, to make some or all people better off (in their own judgment) without making others worse off (in *their* own judgment)   (14)

economic equity   a situation in which the ap-

portionment of resources or goods among people is considered fair   (15)

economic inefficiency   a situation within an economy in which it is possible, with given technology, to produce a larger welfare total from given stocks of resources and, therefore, in which it is possible, through some reallocation of resources or goods among different households or firms, to make some or all people better off (in their own judgment) without making others worse off (in *their* own judgment)   (5, 14)

economic justice   see **commutative justice** and **distributive justice**, or **economic equity**   (15)

economic order   the state of affairs in which the specialized activities of all the people engaged in the division of labor are well coordinated   (2)

economic power   the capacity to make and enforce decisions on the allocation of resources and the apportioning of goods   (2)

economics   the study of how people allocate scarce resources (that usually have many alternative uses) to produce goods and of how they apportion these scarce goods among themselves   (1)

economic system   the social arrangements by which people cooperate with each other in the allocation of resources and the apportionment of goods   (2)

economies of scale   see **increasing returns to scale**   (5)

economies of mass production   see **increasing returns to scale**   (5)

Edgeworth box   a diagram that highlights the crucial distinctions between economic efficiency and inefficiency and between economic efficiency and economic equity   (15)

education vouchers   divisible certificates earmarked for the purchase of educational services   (19)

effective rate of interest   the interest rate that is in effect paid per year   (9)

elasticities of demand   exact measures of the responsiveness of quantity demanded to other variables; see **own-price elasticity of demand**, **income elasticity of demand**, and **cross-price elasticity of demand**   (4)

elasticity of input substitution   the percentage change in the ratio of two inputs used in producing a given output quantity, divided by the associated percentage change in the marginal rate of technical substitution between these inputs   (5)

emission standards   government rules specifying maximum quantities of pollutants that may be released by any one polluter   (18)

Engel curve   a graph of the alternative amounts of an item a person (or group of persons) would buy during a given period at all conceivable incomes, all else being equal   (4)

Engel's law   the observation that food expenditures take a smaller percentage of income the larger income is   (4)

entrepreneur   a special type of person acting in the face of uncertainty; an innovator who first puts new ideas to practical use, translating inventions into new products, new qualities of old products, and new processes of production   (10)

entry-level jobs   jobs that require little training or experience and allow untrained and inexperienced job seekers to find employment, gain experience, and depart these stepping-stones for better jobs   (13)

envelope curve   a curve to which other curves are invariably tangent, such as the **planning curve**, which is tangent to all the curves of short-run average total cost   (6)

equalizing wage differentials   see **compensating wage differentials**   (8)

equal-product curve   see **isoquant**   (5)

equity   see **economic equity**

event uncertainty   uncertainty that exists when certain future events, which are bound to affect the outcome of present decisions, have not yet occurred and no one can possibly know what they will be like   (10)

excess burden   a decrease in utility that is unnecessary in order to collect a given tax revenue and that could be avoided by the use of a different type of tax   (3)

excess capacity   the difference between a monopolistically competitive firm's capacity output and its profit-maximizing lower actual output   (12)

excise tax   a tax per unit of product   (7)

exclusive contracts   contracts by which sellers agree to lease or sell a commodity on the condition that the lessees or purchasers thereof shall not use or deal in the commodity of competitors   (17)

exclusive franchise   a governmental grant to a single seller of the exclusive right to produce and sell a good   (11)

expected monetary value (*EMV*)   the sum of an action's possible monetary outcomes, each outcome being weighted by its subjective probability   (10)

explicit costs   highly visible costs that the owners of firms incur when acquiring resource services from other households or when acquiring intermediate goods from other firms   (6)

exploitation   according to J. B. Clark, a situation in which the price for a unit of resource service falls short of the unit's marginal value product; according to Karl Marx, a situation in which workers as a group do not receive the entire national product   (8)

external diseconomies   unfavorable technological or pecuniary externalities   (7)

external economies   favorable technological or pecuniary externalities   (7)

fair gamble   a gamble with an expected monetary value of zero, any expectation of gain being exactly offset by an expectation of loss   (10)

fair insurance   an insurance with an expected monetary value of zero, any expectation of gain being exactly offset by an expectation of loss   (10)

fair-trade laws   laws allowing manufacturers to fix minimum prices for their products and, if a single retailer agrees to it, to bind all retailers to it   (11)

featherbedding   labor-union practices that force employers to continue paying workers who are not really needed because their work is being done, or could be done, by fewer workers or by machines   (13)

feedback effect   the effect of secondary changes in other markets on the market in which an initial change in supply or demand occurred (16)

field of choice   the set of all the alternative combinations of two goods over which a consumer might conceivably exercise choice (3)

final goods   goods produced by domestic producers during a period but not used up by the same or other domestic producers during the same period in the making of other goods (2, 16)

financial capital   claims (such as money, stocks, deeds, or bonds) against real resources   (1)

first-degree price discrimination   a situation in which a seller charges each buyer for each unit bought the maximum price the buyer is willing to pay for that unit   (11)

fixed cost   cost that does not vary with the level of production during a given period and that is attributable to the use of fixed inputs   (6)

focal-point price   a price that has a compelling prominence for reasons of aesthetics, precedent, or symmetry   (12)

free-rider problem   the unwillingness of individuals voluntarily to help cover the cost of a pure public good and their eagerness to let others produce the good so they can enjoy its benefits at a zero cost   (19)

functional distribution of income   the apportionment of national income among the owners of human, natural, and capital resources (8)

futures markets   markets in which people commit themselves now to trade, at specified dates in the future, specified quantities and qualities of goods at specified prices   (10)

game   any decision-making situation in which the payoff to people's choices depends not only on them (and nature), but also on other people's choices   (12A)

game theory   a method of studying decision making in situations of conflict when the fates of those who seek different goals are interlocked   (12A)

general equilibrium   a state of the economy in which billions of optimizing decisions by millions of decision makers are compatible with each other because all input and output markets are in equilibrium at the same time (16)

gentlemen's agreements   informal oral understandings among oligopolists in the same industry that they will maintain a certain minimum price   (12)

Giffen's paradox   a situation in which consumers buy less of an item when its price is lower and more when it is higher, all else being equal   (4)

Gini coefficient   the ratio of two areas in the Lorenz curve graph that summarizes the extent of income or wealth inequality; the ratio of the area between the line of perfect equality and actual inequality to the area between the line of perfect equality and the line of perfect inequality   (15)

goods   the means by which people satisfy their material wants, including tangible commodities as well as intangible services   (1)

hedging   the taking of equal and opposite positions in the spot and futures markets, with the hope that this will prevent a loss due to price fluctuations   (10)

holding company   a corporation established for the sole purpose of acquiring a controlling stock interest in two or more competing corporations in an industry and then jointly running their affairs   (17)

horizontal mergers   mergers of firms selling closely related products in the same geographic market   (12)

Hotelling's paradox   the fact that, under certain conditions, competition by means of product differentiation leads to products that are hardly differentiated at all   (12)

household production function   a relationship between household inputs (market goods plus time) and household outputs (meals, love, children . . .)   (18)

human capital   the health care, education, and training embodied in people   (1, 9)

human resources   people able and willing to participate in the process of production   (1)

identification problem   the difficulty, encountered in time-series and cross-section studies, of identifying a large number of potential data (such as those on a market demand line) from a few historical data, each of which may belong to a different set of potential data   (4)

impact effect   the effect of an initial change in supply or demand on the market concerned   (16)

imperfect competition   a market situation, other than pure monopoly or cartel, in which individual sellers, nevertheless, face downward-sloping demand curves and thus have some measure of control over price   (12)

implicit costs   hidden costs that the owners of firms incur when using the services of their own resources in their own firm instead of hiring them out to collect the maximum income available elsewhere   (6)

import quota   a maximum physical limit on the amount of a good that may be imported   (7, 11)

impossibility theorem   see **Arrow impossibility theorem**   (19)

income-consumption line   a line indicating how the optimum quantities of two consumption goods change in response to a change in income, all else being equal   (4)

income effect   one of two effects resulting from a price change, all else being equal; the income effect causes a consumer, for example, to buy more of a normal and less of an inferior good when the price change implies an increase in real income   (4)

income elasticity of demand   the percentage change in quantity demanded of a good divided by the percentage change in the income of consumers, all else being equal   (4)

increasing-cost industry   an industry in which the product's normal price is higher after the industry has ceased to expand or is lower after it has ceased to contract   (7)

increasing returns to a variable input   increases in an input's marginal (physical) product as a larger quantity of the input is used, all else being equal   (5)

increasing returns to scale   a characteristic of the production function such that a simultaneous and equal percentage change in the use of all physical inputs leads to a larger percentage change in physical output   (5)

incremental-profit analysis   the comparison of the expected marginal revenue with the expected marginal cost of a prospective action in order to determine the difference between the two (which is the extra, incremental, or marginal profit the action is likely to bring to the business)   (6)

independent goods   two goods such that the quantity demanded of one does not respond to a changed price of the other, all else being equal; goods with zero cross-price elasticity   (4)

independent inputs   inputs with the characteristic that a change in the quantity of one has no effect on the marginal physical products of other inputs   (8)

index-number problem   "If relative quantities (or prices) change from year 0 to year 1, an index of prices (or quantities) takes on a different value depending on whether year 0 or year 1 quantities (or prices) are used as weights in the construction of the index."   (3)

indifference curve   see **consumption-indifference curve**   (3)

indirect costs   costs that cannot be attributed to

the production of a particular unit of output (6)

indivisibilities the characteristic of pure public goods that makes their benefits indivisibly available to all people in society (19)

industrial organization a specialized field of economic study that blends abstract price theory with empirical research (12)

industrial unions unions of workers employed in the same industry, without regard to particular skills (13)

inferior goods goods of which smaller physical quantities are consumed at higher than at lower incomes, all else being equal; goods with a negative income elasticity (4)

informative advertising advertising that provides genuine information to buyers about the very existence of products or sellers, about price, and about quality (12)

injunction a court decree, enforceable by arrest and jail, forbidding certain actions (13)

innovation the activity of an entrepreneur who first puts a new idea to practical use (10)

input-output table a table that lists the flows of all newly produced goods and of resource services between all their suppliers and recipients and thereby illustrates the web of interrelationships in an economy (16)

input standards government rules specifying the types of inputs polluters may use (18)

interlocking directorates an arrangement under which two or more competing corporations have in common some of the members of their boards of directors (17)

intermediate goods goods produced by domestic producers during a period and then used up by the same or other domestic producers during the same period in the making of other goods (2, 16)

internal diseconomies see **decreasing returns to scale** (7)

internal economies see **increasing returns to scale** (7)

internalities the consequences of the pursuit by government officials of their internal, private goals instead of publicly announced, official ones (19)

internal rate of return the interest rate that makes the net present value of an investment project just equal to zero (9)

invention the intellectual act of generating a new idea (10)

Invisible Hand see **market coordination** (2)

iron law of wages the Malthusian notion according to which population changes would assure that wages in the long run equaled the level of subsistence (8)

isocost line a graph of all the alternative combinations of two inputs that a firm is able to buy in a given period at current market prices, while incurring the same total cost (6)

isoquant a graph of all the alternative combinations of two inputs that yield the same maximum total product and among which a producer would be indifferent from a purely technical point of view (5)

isorevenue line a graph of all the alternative combinations of two outputs that a firm is able to sell in a given period at current market prices, while receiving the same total revenue (6A)

jurisdictional strikes strikes wherein workers belonging to one union, in an attempt to force the recognition of a single union, walk off the job to interrupt the work being done by fellow workers belonging to another union (13)

kinked demand curve the demand curve faced by an oligopolist who believes that rivals will not match increases of the present price but will promptly match price decreases (12)

Knightian risk a situation in which people cannot foretell the specific outcome of an action because two or more outcomes are possible but in which people do know the types of outcomes and the associated objective probability distribution (10)

Knightian uncertainty a situation in which people cannot foretell the specific outcome of an action because two or more outcomes are possible and in which people neither know the types of outcomes nor the associated probability distribution (10)

knowledge problem the difficulty of making use jointly of all the knowledge relevant for the most effective division of labor because such knowledge is not available to a single mind in its totality but is found, in billions of dispersed fragments, in the minds of countless separate individuals (2)

labor union a cartel among workers for the joint sale of their labor (13)

Laspeyres-type index an index that measures price (or quantity) change from year 0 to year 1 by using quantity (or price) weights of year 0 (3)

law of diminishing returns "Given technical knowledge and a fixed quantity of some input, equal successive additions of another input to the process of production eventually yield diminishing additions to total output." (5, 14)

"law" of downward-sloping demand the tendency of buyers normally to buy larger quantities of something when its price is lower, all else being equal (4)

law of large numbers the observation that what is unpredictable and subject to chance for the individual is predictable and uniform in a mass of like individuals (10)

"law" of upward-sloping supply the tendency of sellers normally to offer for sale larger quantities of an item when its price is higher, all else being equal (6)

law of variable proportions see **law of diminishing returns** (5)

leisure all nonmarket uses of people's time (8)

Leontief inverse matrix a table showing, for those goods of which a portion of output is used up in the process of production itself, the total outputs ultimately required if one unit of such a good is to be delivered to final users (16)

Lerner index a measure of the degree of monopoly power exercised by a firm, equal to $\frac{P - MC}{P}$ or $\frac{1}{|\epsilon|}$, where P is price, MC is marginal cost, and $|\epsilon|$ is the absolute value of the price elasticity of demand (11)

limit price a price that prevents the entry of new rivals into an oligopolistic industry (12)

linear programming a mathematical technique for the maximization or minimization of a linear function of variables, subject to constraints that limit what can be done (6A)

line of actual inequality see **Lorenz curve** (15)

line of perfect equality the hypothetical position of the Lorenz curve if the same amount of income (or wealth) went to each member of the group in question (15)

line of perfect inequality the hypothetical position of the Lorenz curve if all of income (or wealth) went to one member of a group and none of it to other members (15)

loanable-funds market a market in which the money of some people is traded for certificates of indebtedness (or IOUs) issued by other people (9)

logrolling the trading of votes (19)

long hedge see **buying hedge** (10)

long position a net asset position in which more of something is owned than owed (10)

long run a time period so long that a firm can vary the quantities of all its inputs (5)

long-run equilibrium market equilibrium in a period so long that new firms can enter the industry and old ones can leave it or change the size of their plants (7)

Lorenz curve a graphical device that shows the way in which income (or wealth) is apportioned among the members of any group and highlights the extent of equality or inequality among them (15)

loss   negative profit   (6)

lump-sum tax   a fixed dollar levy imposed on people regardless of what they do   (3)

luxuries   normal goods the consumption of which rises more rapidly than income; goods with a positive income elasticity above unity   (4)

macroeconomics   the study of the aggregate flows of resources and goods and of the overall level of prices   (1)

managerial coordination   the deliberate coordination by a manager or central planner of the separate economic activities of people engaged in a division of labor; also called the system of the **Visible Hand**   (2)

marginal benefit (*MB*)   the increase (or decrease) in an activity's overall benefit, which is attributable to a unit increase (or decrease) in the level of that activity, all else being equal   (1)

marginal conditions   conditions that must be fulfilled to achieve economic efficiency   (14)

marginal cost (*MC*)   an increase (or decrease) in an activity's overall cost, which is attributable to a unit increase (or decrease) in the level of that activity, all else being equal   (1, 6)

marginal external benefit (*MEB*)   the change in the total benefit of some households (or firms) that is associated with a unit change in the consumption (or output) of others   (18)

marginal external cost (*MEC*)   the change in the total cost of some firms (or households) that is associated with a unit change in the output (or consumption) of others   (18)

marginal internal benefit   see **marginal private benefit**   (18)

marginal internal cost   see **marginal private cost**   (18)

marginalist thinking   thinking about the objective possibility and subjective welfare implication of small changes in variables   (1)

marginal outlay (*MO*)   the change in a buyer's total outlay divided by the corresponding change in the total quantity purchased   (11)

marginal (physical) product (*MPP*)   the physical change in the total product attributable to a unit change in some input in the productive process, all else being equal   (5)

marginal private benefit (*MPB*)   the marginal benefit enjoyed by the household (or firm) actually consuming (or producing) a good   (18)

marginal private cost (*MPC*)   the marginal cost borne by the firm (or household) actually producing (or consuming) a good   (18)

marginal productivity theory of distribution   "In long-run competitive equilibrium, total money income exactly equals the market value of total production if each employed unit of each resource is paid the marginal value product associated with the total employed quantity of this resource."   (8)

marginal profit   the difference between marginal revenue and marginal cost   (6)

marginal rate of substitution (*MRS*)   the rate at which a consumer is willing to exchange, as a matter of indifference, a little bit of one variable (say, the consumption of leisure or butter) for a little bit of another variable (say, the consumption of apples received for the sacrifice of leisure or butter)   (2, 14)

marginal rate of technical substitution (*MRTS*)   the rate at which a producer is able to exchange, without affecting the quantity of output produced, a little bit of one input (say, labor) for a little bit of another input (say, capital)   (5)

marginal rate of transformation (*MRT*)   the rate at which a producer is technically able to exchange, in the process of production, a little bit of one variable (say, labor or butter) for a little bit of another variable (say, apples produced with the help of that labor or produced in place of that butter)   (2, 14)

marginal revenue (*MR*)   any change in total revenue divided by the corresponding change in total product (in perfect markets, equal to product price; in imperfect markets, less than product price)   (6, 11)

marginal revenue product (*MRP*) marginal physical product multiplied by marginal revenue (13)

marginal social benefit (*MSB*) the marginal benefit of an activity as seen from the viewpoint of society; the sum of marginal private benefit and marginal external benefit (18)

marginal social cost (*MSC*) the marginal cost of an activity as seen from the viewpoint of society; the sum of marginal private cost and marginal external cost (18)

marginal time preference the slope of an indifference curve relating current consumption to future consumption; the marginal rate of substitution between current and future consumption, or the additional future goods consumers are willing to accept, as a matter of indifference, for a unit sacrifice of present ones (9)

marginal time productivity the slope of a production-possibilities frontier relating current consumption to future consumption; the marginal rate of transformation between current and future consumption or the additional future goods producers are able to create for a unit sacrifice of present ones (9)

marginal utility (*MU*) the increase (or decrease) in an activity's overall utility that is attributable to a unit increase (or decrease) in the level of that activity, all else being equal (3)

marginal value product marginal physical product multiplied by product price (8)

margin calls requests by commodity futures brokers for additional customer margin deposits (10)

margin deposit a good-faith payment to assure performance on a futures contract (10)

market an invisible framework within which owners of property rights can make contact with one another for the purpose of trading something scarce and within which they jointly determine the price of what they are trading (2)

market coordination the spontaneous coordination, by price signals generated in markets, of the separate economic activities of people engaged in a division of labor; also called the system of the **Invisible Hand** (2)

market demand the sum of the demands of all potential market participants (4)

market equilibrium a situation in which there is no innate tendency for price or quantity to change (7)

market-extension merger a type of conglomerate merger involving firms in the same line of business but in different geographic areas (12)

marketing quotas maximum amounts of a product that particular farmers can legally sell (11)

market supply the sum of the supplies of all potential market participants (6)

market uncertainty uncertainty that exists when certain facts about the present or future are known to some people but not to other people (10)

mathematical expectation see **expected monetary value** (10)

maximin strategy a game-theoretic choice of the maximum of all possible minima (choosing the best among a list of worst outcomes) (12A)

merger the direct purchase of the assets of one firm by another (12)

merit goods goods the production of which is financed by government and that are supplied free of charge on the grounds that all citizens merit a share of them (19)

microeconomics the study of the behavior of decision makers in households, firms, and governments who, individually or in groups, make the kinds of choices that determine not only the detailed composition of the aggregate flows of resources and goods, but also the relative prices among individual resources and goods (1)

minimax strategy a game-theoretic choice of the minimum of all possible maxima (choosing the worst among a list of one's opponent's best outcomes) (12A)

mixed strategy a strategy, recommended for

games without saddle points, that shifts at random among the available pure strategies (12A)

momentary equilibrium market equilibrium in a period so short that the quantity supplied is absolutely fixed (7)

monopolisitc competition a market structure in which the entry of new firms is easy and large numbers of sellers compete with one another, offering differentiated products (12)

monopolistic exploitation a situation in which an input's marginal value product exceeds its price because the input's user possesses monopoly power in the product market (which makes the input's marginal revenue product fall short of its marginal value product) (13)

monopoly an industry that has only a single seller the product of which has no close substitutes (11)

monopoly power the ability of a seller to raise the price of something that is for sale above the perfectly competitive level (11)

monopsonistic exploitation a situation in which an input's marginal value product exceeds its price because the input's user possesses monopsony power in the input market (which makes the marginal outlay on the input exceed its price) (13)

monopsony an industry that has only a single buyer (11)

moral hazard a problem faced by insurance companies when those who have bought insurance subsequently change their behavior in such a way as to increase the probability of the occurrence of any loss or of a larger loss (10)

natural equilibrium the size of a biological population that would be achieved (in the absence of harvesting) once the population exceeded its minimum viable size; the size that would be reestablished after disturbances that did not push the population below this minimum size (9)

natural monopoly a situation in which long-run average total cost is declining with higher output throughout the range of possible quantities demanded in the market (11)

natural resources productive ingredients not made by people and as yet untouched by them; gifts of nature in their natural state (1)

necessities normal goods the consumption of which rises less rapidly than income; goods with a positive income elasticity below unity (4)

negative externalities real externalities that impose costs in the form of decreased utility or output on bystanders who are not being compensated for this injury, to their dismay (18)

negative time preference a high preference for future over current consumption that implies a lender's willingness to accept less than one unit of future consumption for the sacrifice of one unit of current consumption (9)

neighborhood effects see **real externalities** (18)

net benefit the difference between the total benefit and total cost of an activity (1)

net present value the sum of the present values of the negative and positive components of an investment project (9)

neutral time preference the lack of any intrinsic preference between current and future consumption (9)

nominal rate of interest the percentage by which the dollar amount returned to a lender exceeds the dollar amount lent (9)

nonexcludability the property of a pure public good that makes it technically impossible or extremely costly to exclude any individual from the enjoyment of the good (19)

nonpecuniary externalities see **real externalities** (18)

nonrivalness the property of pure public goods that prevents rivalry among its consumers because the enjoyment of the good by any one person does not deplete its availability to others (19)

nonzero-sum game   a game in which the winnings and losses of all players add to a positive or negative number   (12A)

normal goods   goods of which larger physical quantities are consumed at higher than at lower incomes, all else being equal; goods with a positive income elasticity   (4)

normal price   a good's price that is equal to the lowest possible average total cost of production   (7)

normative statements   prescriptive statements akin to preaching; value judgments that tell us what ought to be, what is good and what is bad   (2)

norm of relative effectiveness   an arbitrarily selected coefficient of relative effectiveness (9)

objective function   a statement of a goal that is to be achieved   (6A)

objective probability   the relative frequency with which an event occurs in a series of trials repeated under identical conditions (10)

oligopoly   a market structure in which the entry of new firms is difficult and relatively few sellers compete with one another, offering either homogeneous or differentiated products   (12)

open interest   the number of outstanding futures contracts not yet liquidated by delivery of the commodity or by an offsetting contract   (10)

open-outcry auctions   auctions held on the floors of securities and commodities exchanges using shouts and hand signals   (10)

opportunity cost   the disadvantage associated with an act of choice, an opportunity lost; e.g., the forgone quantity of one thing that might have been made possible with the resources that were, in fact, used to do another thing   (1)

optimal rate of plant operation   see **capacity output**   (6)

optimization principle   "People desiring to maximize the welfare they obtain from scarce resources must change the level of any activity as long as they do not value equally its marginal benefit, *MB*, and its marginal cost, *MC*. Whenever they value the marginal benefit more than the marginal cost, an expansion of the activity will raise their total welfare. Whenever they value the marginal benefit less than the marginal cost, a contraction of the activity will raise their total welfare. Whenever they consider the marginal benefit and marginal cost of equal value, the best possible (or optimum) level of the activity has been reached.''   (1)

optimum plant   that plant, among all conceivable ones, with the lowest possible minimum average total cost   (6)

output effect   one of two effects resulting from an input price change, all else being equal; the output effect causes a firm to buy more of a normal and less of a regressive input as a result of a fall in its price (because of the implied decrease in marginal cost that raises the profit-maximizing output level)   (8)

overhead costs   see **indirect costs**   (6)

ownership claims   rights to the exclusive use of assets   (9)

own-price elasticity of demand   the percentage change in quantity demanded of an item divided by the percentage change in its price, all else being equal   (4)

Paasche-type index   an index that measures price (or quantity) change from year 0 to year 1 by using quantity (or price) weights of year 1   (3)

Pareto optimum   a situation in which all marginal conditions of economic efficiency are fulfilled simultaneously   (14)

parity   the 1910-14 relationship between the prices received by U.S. farmers for agricultural goods and the prices paid by them for nonagricultural goods   (11)

Parkinson's law   "The number of those employed by government agencies will grow at the same rate regardless of whether the volume of work to be done rises, falls, or even disappears.''   (19)

partial equilibrium   a situation in one part of

the economy that contains no innate tendency to change because, for example, an individual household has maximized utility, an individual firm maximized profit, or an individual market equated supply and demand—given, in each case, assumed data concerning the rest of the economy (16)

patent an exclusive right to the use of an invention (11)

payback method a criterion for selecting investment projects that rejects all projects the returns of which require more than a predetermined length of time to repay the initial investment outlay (9)

payback period the number of years it takes for initial investment outlays to be paid back by (undiscounted) future receipts (9)

pecuniary externality a situation in which the input prices paid by one firm are affected, favorably or unfavorably, by the operation of other firms (6)

perfect liquidity the ability of an asset to be transformed without loss of value and at a moment's notice into any other asset (9)

perfect market a market in which 1. there is a large number of independent buyers and also of sellers, 2. all units of the traded item are viewed as identical, 3. all buyers and sellers possess full knowledge relevant to trading, and 4. nothing impedes entry into and exit from the market (2)

perfect price discrimination see **first-degree price discrimination** (11)

personal distribution of income the apportionment of national income among persons, each of whom is likely to receive several types of income (8)

persuasive advertising advertising that is designed to divert people's attention from facts to images and make them buy more as a result of imagined advantages (12)

planning curve the curve of long-run average total cost, which is tangent to all the curves of short-run average total cost and which is the geometric locus of the minimum achievable average total costs for all conceivable output levels a firm might produce (6)

plant a physical production facility, as defined by a set of fixed inputs available to a firm (6)

plurality voting see **rank-order voting** (19)

point elasticity an elasticity measure that refers to a point on a demand (or supply) line (4)

point of diminishing returns the input quantity at which marginal product is maximized and beyond which it falls (5)

point voting a procedure in which each voter is given x points that can be distributed among issues at the voter's discretion and in which the largest number wins (19)

pollution licenses see **pollution rights** (18)

pollution rights transferable certificates each of which allow the holder to dump one unit of specified wastes into a specified environment (18)

positive externalities real externalities that provide benefits in the form of increased utility or output for bystanders who are not charged for this favor, to their delight (18)

positive-sum game a game in which no one wins at someone else's expense and the sum of (positive) winnings and (nonexisting negative) losses is positive (15)

positive theory a theory that makes purely descriptive statements and predictions; it explains what is and what causes what (2)

positive time preference a high preference for current over future consumption that leads lenders to exact more than one unit of future consumption for the sacrifice of one unit of present consumption (9)

prejudice preconceived irrational opinion that leads to unfair partiality toward some people and bias against others or, for some, an attitude that facilitates rational behavior in the face of imperfect and costly information (13)

price-compensating variation one of four Hicksian measures of the consumer's surplus, equal to the maximum amount of income the consumer would pay for the privilege of buying any desired quantity of a good at a lower price (7)

price-consumption line a line indicating how the optimum quantities of two consumption goods change in response to a change in the price of one of these goods, all else being equal   (4)

price discrimination   a situation in which a seller charges a given buyer or different buyers different prices for identical units of a good—even though such price differences cannot be justified by differences in the cost of serving these buyers   (11)

price elasticity of demand   see **own-price elasticity of demand** and **cross-price elasticity of demand**   (4)

price elasticity of supply   the percentage change in quantity supplied of an item divided by the percentage change in its price, all else being equal   (6)

price-equivalent variation   one of four Hicksian measures of the consumer's surplus, equal to the minimum amount of income the consumer would accept for relinquishing the opportunity of buying any desired quantity of a good at a lower price   (7)

price leadership   a set of oligopolistic industry practices according to which one firm, the price leader, announces and occasionally changes list prices which the other firms immediately adopt as well   (12)

price system   the set of interdependent prices in all the markets for goods and resources, which changes as long as the independent actions of households and firms are not perfectly coordinated, making households and firms, in turn, change their behavior until coordination is achieved   (2)

price war   a situation in which rival oligopolists successively cut their prices below those of competitors (and perhaps even below their own cost)   (12)

primary uncertainty   see **event uncertainty**   (10)

prime costs   see **direct costs**   (6)

principle of declining marginal benefit   "All other relevant factors being equal, the greater the overall level of any activity during a given period, the smaller will its marginal benefit usually be."   (1)

principle of diminishing marginal utility

"Given the quantities of all other goods being consumed, and given a person's tastes, successive additions of equal units of a good to the process of consumption eventually yield ever smaller additions to total utility."   (3)

prisoners' dilemma   a game situation in which the best common choice of strategies is unstable, offers great incentives to cheat, and leads to the worst choice possible   (12A)

process of production   the set of activities deliberately designed to make goods available to people where and when they are wanted   (1)

producers' surplus   the difference between the sum of money producers actually receive for a given quantity and the minimum they could have been made to accept on an all-or-nothing basis   (7)

product differentiation   the differentiation of products, on the basis of physical aspects, legal matters, or conditions of sale, among all the sellers in an industry   (12)

product-exhaustion theorem   see **marginal productivity theory of distribution**   (8)

product-extension mergers   a type of conglomerate merger in which the merging firms do not directly compete but use related production processes or marketing channels   (12)

product groups   groups of closely related but differentiated products that serve the same wants   (12)

production function   a technical relationship, stated in physical terms, between all conceivable combinations of inputs used during a period and the associated maximum quantities of some type of output, given the state of technology   (5)

production-indifference curve   see **isoquant**   (5)

production-possibilities frontier   all the alternative combinations of two goods or groups of goods that the people in a society are capable of producing in a given period by using their flow of resources fully and in the best possible way, given their present state of technology   (1)

productivity   see **average product**   (5)

profit   the difference between a firm's total revenue and the total (explicit and implicit) cost associated with producing that revenue   (6)

property rights   rights to the exclusive, but perhaps socially circumscribed, use of scarce things   (2)

public finance   the governmental collection of taxes from all those believed to benefit from the provision of pure public goods and the subsequent channeling of these funds toward the production of these goods, either by government agencies or private firms   (19)

pure private good   a good that generates no externalities and the producer or consumer of which alone bears all of the cost and enjoys all of the benefit associated with it   (19)

pure public good   a good that provides nonexcludable and nonrival benefits to all people in a given society   (19)

pure rate of interest   the interest rate that emerges in a perfect market for loanable funds when there is certainty (and, therefore, no risk)   (9)

pure rent   the rent received for the use of a resource the supply of which is totally unresponsive to resource price in the long run because the resource in question can neither be destroyed nor produced by people   (8)

quantity-compensating variation   one of four Hicksian measures of the consumer's surplus, equal to the maximum amount of income the consumer would pay for the privilege of buying any desired good at a lower price, while being constrained to buying the quantity that the consumer would buy at the lower price in the absence of compensation   (7)

quantity-equivalent variation   one of four Hicksian measures of the consumer's surplus, equal to the minimum amount of income the consumer would accept for relinquishing the opportunity of buying any desired good at a lower price, while being constrained to buying the quantity that the consumer would buy at a higher price in the absence of compensation   (7)

quasi rent   the rent received for the use of a resource the supply of which is responsive to resource price in the long run because the resource in question can be destroyed and produced by people   (8)

rank-order voting   a procedure in which each voter ranks all of n issues from 1 (most preferred) to n (least preferred) and in which the lowest number wins   (19)

rate base   the value of the investment on which the owners of a regulated firm are to receive a "fair" return   (17)

reaction curve   a curve showing how much output one oligopolist will supply, given all possible outputs supplied by a second one   (12)

real externalities   direct effects, independent of any price changes, that the actions of some households or firms have on the utility of other households or on the output of other firms, none of whom have invited these effects   (18)

real rate of interest   the percentage by which the purchasing power (or actual quantity of consumption goods) returned to a lender exceeds the purchasing power lent   (9)

regressive inputs   inputs for which the output effect counteracts the substitution effect   (8)

regulatory lag   the length of time, sometimes years, that it takes government regulators to review a firm's performance and possibly change the price of the firm's product   (17)

rent   that portion of a payment for the services of any resource (human, natural, or capital) which exceeds the minimum amount necessary to bring forth the quantity that is in fact supplied   (8)

requirements contracts   contracts according to which buyers agree to purchase all of their requirements of a commodity from given sellers only   (17)

reservation demands demands for resources for purposes other than the sale of their services in the market   (8)

reserve clause a clause in a labor contract that gives all rights to the future services of a worker to the worker's original employer (13)

resources ingredients used in the process of production; resources can be human, natural, or capital   (1)

revealed-preference approach a method of deriving indifference curves by observing the actual market behavior of people   (3)

reverse discrimination see **affirmative-action plans**   (13)

right-to-work laws state laws outlawing the union shop   (13)

riparian doctrine the notion that each property owner fronting a lake or stream has a right to the unimpaired use of the water but cannot physically use up the water and diminish like rights of others   (18)

risk an uncertainty-induced chance of variation in people's welfare; the extent of the spread of possible outcomes of an action around the action's expected value   (10)

risk aversion an attitude according to which a person considers the utility of a certain prospect of money to be *higher than* the expected utility of an uncertain prospect of equal expected monetary value   (10)

risk neutrality an attitude according to which a person considers the utility of a certain prospect of money to be *equal to* the expected utility of an uncertain prospect of equal expected monetary value   (10)

risk seeking an attitude according to which a person considers the utility of a certain prospect of money to be *lower than* the expected utility of an uncertain prospect of equal expected monetary value   (10)

rule of reason a 1911 U.S. Supreme Court interpretation of the Sherman Act, according to which only deliberate and unreasonable restraint of trade was considered illegal   (17)

saddle point the combination of strategies that equates maximin and minimax (in a game) (12A)

satiation that level of any activity at which its marginal benefit equals zero and at which its total benefit is maximized   (1)

scale effect see **output effect**   (8)

scarcity the economic problem, arising from the fact that in all nations on earth today the limited set of goods that can be produced in a period is insufficient to satisfy, simultaneously, the desire for goods by all the people (1)

screening an activity by buyers designed to select high-quality sellers   (10)

search an activity designed to discover information already possessed by other people (10)

secondary uncertainty see **market uncertainty**   (10)

second-degree price discrimination a situation in which a seller partitions market demand into fairly large blocks of product units and charges a given buyer or different buyers different prices for these blocks but uniform prices within the blocks   (11)

selective sales tax a tax levied on the purchase of a particular good only   (3)

selling cost cost designed to alter a firm's demand curve   (12)

selling hedge hedging a long position in the spot market by selling futures contracts now and buying them later   (10)

shadow prices implicit valuations emerging as a by-product of solving a linear programming problem   (6A)

shortage the amount by which the quantity demanded at a given price exceeds the quantity supplied   (7)

short hedge see **selling hedge**   (10)

short position a net liability position in which more of something is owed than owned (10)

short run a time period so short that the quantity of at least one of a firm's inputs cannot be varied   (5)

short-run equilibrium market equilibrium in a period sufficiently long for a given number of firms to be able to vary quantity supplied by changing the utilization rate of given plants   (7)

shutdown point   an output level at which total revenue equals variable cost and at which price equals average variable cost   (6)

signaling   an activity by sellers designed to convince buyers of the high quality of what is being sold   (10)

simplex method   a mathematical routine for solving complicated linear programming problems   (6A)

single-tax movement   a political movement led by Henry George, favoring the finance of all governmental activities by a single tax on land   (8)

snob effect   a situation in which the demand for a good by each individual varies inversely with the quantity others are seen to demand   (4)

speculating   the deliberate taking of long or short positions in spot or futures markets, with the hope that this will lead to profit from price fluctuations   (10)

spillout effect   the effect of a change in supply or demand on markets other than the one in which it occurs   (16)

spillovers   see **real externalities**   (18)

spontaneous coordination   see **market coordination**   (2)

spot markets   markets in which people agree to trade specified quantities and qualities of goods at specified prices and do it now   (10)

static efficiency   see **economic efficiency**   (14)

strategic behavior   behavior arising among a small number of actors who have conflicting interests and are mutually conscious of the interdependence of their decisions   (12)

strategic voting   a procedure by which people attempt to assure their preferred outcome by misrepresenting their preferences on some votes   (19)

subjective probability   a measure of personal belief in the likelihood of an occurrence   (10)

substitute goods   two goods such that the quan-

tity demanded of one varies in the same direction as the price of the other, all else being equal; goods with a positive cross-price elasticity   (4)

substitution effect   one of two effects resulting from a price change, all else being equal; the substitution effect causes a consumer (or a firm) to buy more of a good (or an input) with a lowered price as a result of the change in relative prices   (4, 8)

supply   a set of price-quantity combinations that represents the alternative amounts of an item that would be offered for sale during a given period at all conceivable prices of this item, all else being equal   (6)

surplus   the amount by which the quantity demanded at a given price falls short of the quantity supplied   (7)

survivor principle   a method of making inferences about the production function in an industry that postulates that the technically most efficient production method is revealed by the characteristics of firms surviving competition in that industry in the long run   (5)

sustainable yield   the maximum amount of a biological population that can be harvested without depleting a given stock   (9)

tariff   a tax on imports   (11)

technical advance   an improvement in known methods of production   (10)

technical coefficients   numbers showing the quantity of inputs producers in an industry require on the average per unit of output   (16)

technical efficiency   a situation in which it is impossible for a given firm, with given technical knowledge, to produce a larger output from a given set of inputs (or in which it is impossible to produce a given output with less of one or more inputs without increasing the amount of other inputs)   (5, 14)

technical inefficiency   a situation within a firm in which it is possible, with given technical knowledge, to produce a larger output from a given set of inputs (or to produce a given output with less of one or more inputs without increasing the amount of other inputs)   (5)

technological externality   a situation in which the production function of one firm is affected, favorably or unfavorably, by the operation of other firms   (6)

technology   the set of known methods of production   (1)

theory   a set of propositions intended to serve as an explanation of observed phenomena; a simplified representation of reality   (2)

theory of the second best   if one or more Pareto conditions cannot be satisfied, it is in general not true that the cause of economic efficiency is served by satisfying as many of the other conditions as possible   (17)

theory of the third best   policy makers are well advised to eschew specific policies (such as bringing prices in line with marginal costs) in favor of general policies (such as promoting free market entry and exit) that on average are likely to have desired effects   (17)

third-degree price discrimination   a situation in which a seller partitions market demand into two or more groups of customers and charges different prices among, but uniform prices within, these groups   (11)

time productivity   the ability of present consumption goods, when sacrificed now for the sake of creating capital goods, to yield permanently more future consumption goods   (9)

time-series studies   investigations of economic data pertaining to a given population during different past periods of time   (4)

total cost   the sum of fixed and variable cost   (6)

transactions costs   output sacrificed because resources are used to set up a system of voluntary exchanges and keep it functioning   (2)

transfer costs   output sacrificed because resources are used to transport goods from one point in space or time to another   (2)

transfer loss   a loss of consumers' or producers' surplus that is offset by somebody else's gain   (7)

transitivity   a characteristic of choice denoting consistency or absence of contradiction   (3)

trust   a combination of several corporations under the trusteeship of a single board of directors that manages their affairs jointly   (17)

trust certificates   nonvoting ownership shares in a trust   (17)

tying contracts   contracts according to which buyers of one good agree to purchase another good from the same sellers as well   (17)

uncertainty   a situation in which people possess less than complete knowledge relevant to their decision making   (10)

union shops   firms in which all employees within 30 days after hiring, must become union members or at least pay union dues as a condition of continued employment   (13)

utility   the satisfaction a person derives from an activity   (3)

utility contour   see **consumption-indifference curve**   (3)

variable cost   cost that varies with the level of production during a given period, attributable to the use of variable inputs   (6)

Veblen effect   a situation in which the demand for a good by each individual varies directly with the prevailing market price   (4)

vertical mergers   mergers of firms that are related as suppliers and users of each other's products   (12)

VES production function   a production function with a variable elasticity of input substitution   (5)

Visible Hand   see **managerial coordination**   (2)

voting paradox   the fact that under democratic simple majority voting the choice among three or more alternatives will differ depending on the sequence in which votes are taken   (19)

workable competition   any market structure in which, taking into account structural characteristics and the dynamic factors that shaped them, no clearly indicated change can be effected through public policy that would result in greater social gains than losses (17)

X-efficiency   see **technical efficiency**   (14)
X-inefficiency   a situation in which the actual output a firm gets from given resources falls short of the maximum output it could get, if it administered its resources better; see also **technical inefficiency**   (5)

zero-sum game   a game in which the winnings of some are exactly matched by the losses of others and the sum of (positive) winnings and (negative) losses is zero   (12A, 15)

ANSWERS AND COMMENTS

Odd-Numbered Questions

Chapter 1

1. **a.** *Always*: sand at a beach not yet discovered by people, sunshine, a school of tuna in the ocean. (See the text and glossary definition of natural resources.) *Never*: a highway, a college building, a can of peas. (The first two are capital resources; the can of peas is a capital resource as long as it is part of a firm's inventory and not yet in the possession of a household. Once in the possession of a household, the can of peas is a consumption good.) *Maybe*: 100 cubic feet of coal, if unmined; a cow, if wild; an acre of land, if virgin. (Coal in the factory yard, a domesticated cow, and cultivated land would be capital resources.)

b. *Always*: an automobile-assembly plant, unsold refrigerators held by an appliance dealer, an inventory of groceries held by a food store. (See the text and glossary definition of capital resources.) *Never*: Ford Motor Company stock, a natural waterfall, a truck driver (the first of these may be called *financial* capital, while the last one can be said to embody *human* capital). *Maybe*: a toy truck or a wristwatch, if part of a store's inventory rather than held by a household; a horse, if domesticated rather than wild.

3. **a.** The most highly valued alternative, *b* or *c*.

b. Once more, the most highly valued alternative would be the opportunity cost. It could literally be anything: in the case of foreign aid, perhaps, less aid to the domestic poor, less defense spending, fewer highways (if the foreign aid must be financed from a given government budget) or less housing, less medical care, less investment in new factories (if the aid must be financed by higher taxes on the private sector).

c. If people cared to, they could spend every waking minute working for pay. To the extent that they devote their time to other things, they give up potential money income.

5. Consider Figure 1.4, "Declining Marginal Benefit," and let the horizontal axis measure units of real per capita income. The residents of poor countries may each have available 1 unit of goods per year; the residents of rich countries may enjoy an annual flow of goods corresponding to 5 units. Thus the former will place a high marginal benefit on goods (block *a*);

the latter a low one (block *e*). Therefore, the poor (compared to the rich) will show little eagerness to restrict their wants and give up goods and much eagerness to get more goods.

7. I would vote for Mr. A, with a good deal of sympathy for Ms. B. All the items mentioned have benefits and costs, probably falling marginal benefits and rising marginal costs, just as shown in Figure 1.6. I doubt that either maximization (of total benefit) or minimization (of total cost) produces optimization in any of these instances—a point that was also made more abstractly in Question 6. Consider some of the examples given:

a. *The size of people's wealth.* Few people are extremely wealthy. So most people think "the more wealth the better." Would more wealth be better if they were already very rich?

b. *The size of business organizations.* Owners of small firms often wish them to be larger. But when firms grow really large, people complain about the impersonality of human relationships within them. This is no accident. Due to the complexity of relationships among large numbers of people, these relations must be stripped down to the barest essentials lest the large organization die of communications failure. It cannot survive and also assure the blossoming of full personal relations among all. (This matter is further discussed in the Chapter 5 section on decreasing returns to scale).

c. *Pollution.* The notion of optimum pollution is discussed in detail in Chapter 18.

d. *The length of people's lives.* So far in history, people have lived rather short lives. Thus we naturally consider longer lives better. Would this be so if we lived to be 200? or 500? (Note Boulding's article on The Menace of Methuselah, referred to in the "Selected Readings" of Chapter 1).

Note: James G. March, in "Bounded Rationality, Ambiguity, and the Engineering of Choice," *The Bell Journal of Economics*, Autumn 1978, pp. 587–608, discusses many other types of choice, including such notions as optimal ambition, optimal clarity, optimal sin, and optimal rationality.

Chapter 2

1. The political problems are well-nigh insuperable, but here is a theoretical possibility: An international agreement fixes the quantity of fish that can be "harvested" each year; equal, perhaps, to the annual natural growth of the present stock of fish (if the size of that stock is considered optimal). Fishing rights are then apportioned among nations by any desirable criterion and in such a way that the sum of these rights equals the overall limit previously noted. Everyone, of course, abides by the agreement. If this is not credible, this example clearly shows the important role national governments play not only in defining, but also in enforcing property rights within their zones of sovereignty.

3. True. Licensing for competence promotes—while licensing for restricting numbers hinders—unrestricted voluntary exchanges. The former sets standards and norms; the latter restricts market entry.

5. Under Stalin, central planners decided what households wanted and accordingly determined the production of consumption goods. Yet households received money income, rather than consumption goods directly. They were free to spend their money as they liked, and when they disliked the goods available, they refused to buy them. There was no mechanism to adjust the prices of unsalable goods downward, to create losses among their producers, and to force some producers into bankruptcy. Yet in a well-working market economy this is exactly what would have happened. In such an economy, losses and profits become devices by which the nature and strength of people's wishes are revealed and communicated to producers. In perfect markets, profit (and loss) serves as the inducement for an industry to expand (or contract) when people demand more (or less) of its product. Thus producing for profit *is* producing for people. Higher prices are signals, and resultant profits are inducements, for producers to undertake the very actions desired by people. Thus the price system tackles Hayek's knowledge problem.

7. I vote with Ms. B. Mr. A's statement, incidentally, paraphrases an early book review, in the *Athenaeum*, of Charles Darwin's *On the Origin of Species*. The reviewer could not accept the notion of evolution, which to him meant accepting a universe under the rule of Absolute Ignorance. He preferred belief in a Master Artificer, endowed with Absolute Wisdom, who created and maintained the universe by reason.

Chapter 3

1. The original budget line is solid line *AB*.
  a. The budget line changes to dashed line *AC*.
  b. Yes, for all nonzero quantities of good *a*. The new budget line would then be dotted line *DB*.

Figure A-1

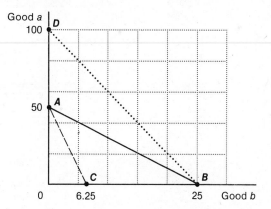

c. The consumer's choices would be legally limited to combinations within the dashed or dotted boxes, respectively. Combinations to the right of line *AB* would, of course, remain financially unattainable.

Figure A-2

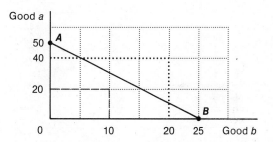

d. The consumer would be restrained, simultaneously, by dollar budget line *AB* and dashed coupon budget line *CD*. Thus only combinations in shaded area 0*AED* would be attainable.

Figure A-3

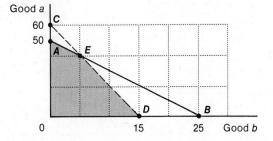

e. The consumer would be restrained, simultaneously, by solid dollar budget line *AB* and dashed time budget line *CD* and beyond. Thus only combinations in shaded area 0*CDB* would be attainable.

Figure A–4

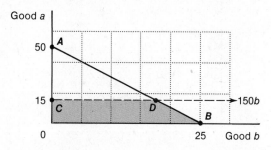

3. In the case of good *a*, the utils per pound convert into utils per $10; in the case of good *b*, they convert into utils per $20. Thus utils per $1 (which Jevons would have us equate) can be calculated as follows:

Units Consumed	Utils per Dollar	
(pounds)	Good *a*	Good *b*
5	6.0	2.5
10	5.5	2.25
15	5.0	2.0
20	4.5	1.75
25	4.0	1.5
30	3.5	1.25
35	3.0	1.0
40	2.5	0.75

Thus it is preferable to buy as many as 40 units of good *a* before the first 5 units of good *b* are bought. Indeed, the answer is: 40*a* (costing $400) plus 5*b* (costing $100) exhaust the budget and also equate marginal utilities per dollar (at 2.5 utils).

5. **a.** $150
  b. $7.50
  c. 1*a* for 2*b* or 0.5*a* for 1*b*
  d. The budget is spent, but utility is less than it could be (corresponding to I_0 rather than I_1). Point *B*, although preferable to optimum *C*, is not attainable.
  e. If the price of *a* were $7.50 and that of *b* were $15, their *MRS* would be 1*a* for 0.5*b* or 2*a* for 1*b* (because *at the optimum* the *MRS* corresponds to the price ratio).

7. **a.**

Good	1982 New York		1982 Los Angeles	
	Quantity	Price	Quantity	Price
Apples	100 pounds	$1/pound	100 pounds	$0.50/pound
Shoes	10 pairs	$50/pair	1 pair	$60/pair

One can use New York quantities to calculate the price index or, with equal logic, one can use Los Angeles quantities instead. The former approach yields $100 + $500 = $600 compared with $50 + $600 = $650. Los Angeles prices appear to be 108.33 percent of New York prices. The latter approach yields $100 + $50 = $150 compared with $50 + $60 = $110. Los Angeles prices appear to be 73.33 percent of New York prices. (Note: This discrepancy in the calculated price index is inevitable as long as *relative* quantities differ).

b.

Good	1982 U.S.	
	Quantity	Price
Apples	100 pounds	$1/pound
Shoes	100 pairs	$50/pair

Good	1982 U.S.S.R.	
	Quantity	Price
Apples	50 pounds	5 rubles/pound
Shoes	10 pairs	50 rubles/pair

One can use U.S. prices to calculate the quantity index, or with equal logic, one can use Soviet prices instead. The former approach yields $100 + $5,000 = $5,100 compared with $50 + $500 = $550. U.S. output appears to be 927.27 percent of Soviet output. The latter approach yields 500 rubles + 5,000 rubles = 5,500 rubles compared with 250 rubles + 500 rubles = 750 rubles. U.S. output appears to be 733.33 percent of Soviet output. (Note: This discrepancy in the calculated quantity index is inevitable as long as *relative* prices differ).

Chapter 4

1. When the price-consumption line is sloping downwards to the right, less money would be spent on all goods other than butter. Hence more money would be spent on butter from the given budget. Given the simultaneous fall in the price of butter, an own-price elasticity of greater than unity is implied.

Similarly, when the price-consumption line is sloping upwards to the right, more money would be spent on all goods other than butter. Hence less money would be spent on butter from the given budget. Given the simultaneous fall in the price of butter, an own-price elasticity of less than unity is implied.

3. Own-price elasticity: relatively high for goods with good substitutes, for goods very narrowly defined, for long time periods. Income elasticity: negative for inferior goods; positive, but below unity for necessities; positive and above unity for luxuries.

See also Tables 4.2-4.4 in the text.

5.   On line D_1 at a: $\dfrac{ah}{ag} > 1$

On line D_1 at c: $\dfrac{ch}{cg} = 1$

On line D_1 at g: $\dfrac{gh}{0} = \infty$

On line D_1 at h: $\dfrac{0}{hg} = 0$

On line D_2 at c: $\dfrac{ch}{cg} = 1$

On line D_2 at e: $\dfrac{em}{el} < 1$

On line E_1 at b: $\dfrac{bk}{bi} > 1$

On line E_2 at d: $\dfrac{d0}{d0} = 1$

On line E_3 at f: $\dfrac{fn}{fp} < 1$

7.   **a.**   No. Given these elasticity estimates, such an increase would raise revenues only for very short trips and would actually lower them in all other cases.

b.   Given the elasticity formula of $\epsilon = \Delta Q/Q : \Delta P/P$, we can calculate $Q = (\Delta Q \cdot P)/(\epsilon \cdot \Delta P)$. We are told that $\epsilon = |0.2|$ in the 1-year case and that $\Delta Q = -7$ million barrels per day. The information also implies an old price of $1.04 per gallon and a price hike of $\Delta P = 46¢$ per gallon. Hence $Q = (-7 \cdot 104)/(-0.2 \cdot 46) = 79.13$ *million barrels per day.*

$\Big[$Check: $\epsilon = \Delta Q/Q : \Delta P/P = -7/79.13 : +46/104 = -8.8\% : 44.2\% = |0.2|\Big]$

Given a 5-year elasticity of $|0.4|$, one can calculate the 5-year savings as $\Delta Q = (\epsilon \cdot Q \cdot \Delta P)/P = [|0.4| (79.13) 46]/104 = 14$ *million barrels per day.*

Similarly, one can calculate the 10-year savings as $\Delta Q = [|0.8| (79.13) 46]/104 = 28$ *million barrels per day.*

Chapter 5

1.   Marginal products of labor (averages for given ranges): 50, 30, 10. Average products of labor: ?, 50, 40, 30

3.   The lesson is, of course, that it may not be possible to make genuine scale changes. The required communication channels in a growing firm may have to grow more than proportionally to the number of cooperating persons lest the kind of diseconomies discussed in the text set in.

5.   If each were increased by 1 percent, coal output would increase by 1.08 percent. If capital only were increased by 1 percent, coal output would increase by 0.29 percent. If capital were decreased by 1 percent, coal output would decrease by 0.29 percent.

7.   **a.**   F
    b.   F
    c.   F
    d.   T
    e.   F

Chapter 6

1.   True, in equilibrium. Review Table 6.1, "Short-Run Cost Alternatives," and Table 6.2, "Calculating Fixed Cost." Suppose a superior manager could reduce the variable inputs for any chosen level of total product so that variable cost was halved. Other firms would bid for this rare talent until our owner—manager's forgone potential salary (included, in this example, as implicit fixed cost) had risen precisely to offset the previously noted cost advantage.

3.   Effect on optimum output quantity:

a.   In the case of a 50 percent profit tax, none. No effect on marginal cost and price.

b.   In the case of a $20,000 license fee, none. A $20,000 increase in fixed cost and an upward parallel shift of the total-cost curve would reduce profit *ed* by this amount in panel (a). A rise in average total cost would move F toward B and reduce the total profit rectangle by $20,000 in panel (b).

c.   In the case of a $1 tax per bushel of output, the optimum output level would fall. The variable and total cost curves in panel (a) would shift up, but not in a parallel fashion. All the cost curves in panel (b) would shift up as well; MC itself would shift up by $1.

5.   The curve of long-run total cost would go through the origin because of the absence of fixed cost in the long run. It would envelop short-run total cost curves based on varying levels of fixed cost as shown below. It would show the lowest total cost of producing any given quantity.

Figure A-5

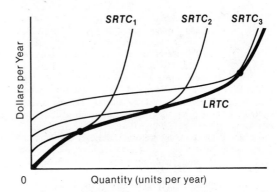

7.   The marginal revenue from killing a baby turkey was 34 cents per pound (a reduction in feed cost). The marginal cost was 20 cents per pound (a reduction in sales revenue). Thus a marginal profit of 14 cents per pound was made.

Chapter 7

1.   Yes, text Figure 7.1, "Momentary Equilibrium," could be used for the explanation, although the supply line would undoubtedly not go down all the way to the horizontal axis in this case. Owners of paintings undoubtedly have a minimum supply price below which they will not sell.

3. Yes, text Figure 7.2, "Short-Run Equilibrium" could be used for the explanation. An increase in Russian demand for wheat raised the wheat price directly. The higher price induced other purchasers to decrease quantity demanded and possibly increase their demand for substitutes, causing the higher prices for rye, oats, soybeans.

5. On a typical demand-supply diagram, if one graphs the quantity demanded at a zero price as a dot on the horizontal axis and if one graphs the quantity supplied by unpaid donors to the left of that demanded, a shortage is seen to exist. Some form of nonprice rationing must be employed. Many will go without babies, corneas, etc.

Now imagine the introduction of a market. Even if the quantity demanded were unchanged at all conceivable positive prices (an unlikely story often imagined by people), higher prices are bound to coax out larger quantities supplied. Equilibrium will be established where positively-sloped supply intersects vertical demand. The price will be positive, but *all* who previously wanted the goods in question (and many of whom did not get them) will now get what they want.

The fear of hepatitis might shift the demand to the left, leading to lower price and quantity.

7. The reduction of demand is the better strategy. All else being equal, this strategy reduces price along with quantity. The reduction in supply raises price, while reducing quantity.

Chapter 8

1. Take the case of two types of labor, *a* and *b*, which interfere with each other. Let the marginal-physical-product to input-price ratio be equalized initially: $MPP_a/P_a = MPP_b/P_b$. Now let the price of *a* fall. All else being equal, the profit-maximizing user will want to use more *a*. But this lowers the marginal physical (and value) product *curve* of *b* (by assumption of anti-complementarity). Given the price of *b*, this leads to the use of less *b*. This, in turn, raises the marginal physical (and value) product curve of *a*. The result is similar to text Figure 8.2. The lower price of one input (here labor type *a*) sets in motion forces that also shift the demand curve to the right (in this case not because more of another input is being used, but because less of it is being used).

3. **a.** If the work day were inflexibly set at 8 hours (= leisure of 16 hours), our friend would receive less total utility (at some point to the right of *C* on budget line *AB*) than at optimum *C*. At such a position, an indifference curve, lying between I_1 and I_0, would *cross* the budget line. The marginal rate of indifferent substitution might then equal $2.50 per leisure hour; certainly any second job offering more than $2.50 per hour net (after extra transportation costs, etc.) would be taken up, moving the worker in the direction of optimum *C*. If the secondary job offered a wage between $5 per hour (implied by budget line slope *AB*) and $2.50 per hour, the total hours worked would be less than optimum *C*. If the secondary job offered a wage in excess of $5 per hour, the total hours worked would exceed optimum *C*. In that case, barring time limits on the secondary job, the secondary one would be substituted for the primary one (note how people often turn their avocation into their vocation). Oftentimes, of course, secondary jobs do have time limitations (e.g., seasonal work, after-hour tutoring that complements the primary job).

b. If our friend worked 16 hours (= leisure of 8 hours), less total utility would be received also (at some point to the *left* of *C* on budget line *AB*). At such a position, an indifference curve, lying between I_1 and I_0, would again cross the budget line. The marginal rate of indifferent substitution might then equal $7.50 per leisure hour. Only steep overtime pay, tilting the budget line upward to the left of *C* until it was tangent, say, to I_2, would bring forth additional voluntary work.

5. **a.** Panel (b) of Figure 8.2, "Rents" might tell the story.

b. The marginal value product might easily exceed the high wage paid. Consider that Joe Namath allegedly drew 10,000 extra fans per game at home and on the road, and he also brought in extra TV broadcasting fees. These two factors were said to have produced extra revenues of well over $590,000 per year. Thus he was a bargain.

ABC television's share of the national news audience fell from 23 rating points in 1973 to 19 in 1976. Each point stands for over 1 million viewers and yields $1.5 million in annual network advertising revenue. When Barbara Walters was lured from NBC with the $1 million annual contract, it was clear that she would be a bargain, if she even raised the ratings by a single point.

c. When there is strong competition for the services of the resource.

d. Once more, Figure 8.12, "Rents" can be used to make the point.

7. In each case, the opportunity cost changes, leading to the behavioral adjustments noted.

Chapter 9

1. The consumer's optimum is still at *H*. The consumer (who has no current income and lots of claims on future goods) can borrow *KH*, promising to pay back larger amount *FK* in the future.

3. **a.** A $1,000 loan without interest for six years is preferable. It is equivalent to a $50 income stream for 6 years. The present value of the stream equals

$$\frac{50}{1.05} + \frac{50}{1.05^2} + \cdots \frac{50}{1.05^6}$$
$$= \$47.62 + \$45.35 + \$43.19 + \$41.14$$
$$+ \$39.18 + \$37.31 = \$253.79$$

b. It depends on the length of time the person can expect to keep the job. If this length is 1 year only, an extra $600 will be earned, hardly as good as $1,000 now. On the other hand, an extra $600 for even 2 years (given the 5 percent interest rate) has a present value of $1,115.65.

c. The $1 million in 50 years is preferable. Its present value equals
$1 million/$1.05^{50}$ = $87,203.79.

d. $20,000 now is preferable. The present value of the $1,000 income stream equals

$$\frac{1,000}{1.05} + \frac{1,000}{1.05^2} + \cdots \frac{1,000}{1.05^{30}}$$
$$= \$15,372.49$$

e. Buying for cash is preferable. The choice is between $4,750 now or (presumably) $5,250 in a year (which, of course, has a present value of $5,000). Even if no interest were charged on the full price, cash buying would be preferable because the present value of $5,000 in a year would be $4,761.90.

5. OPEC had a major impact on the pattern of demand. Thus increased (or decreased) demands for the services of various assets affected not only the prices of these services, but also those of the assets in question. Note the text discussion surrounding Figure 9.6, "How to Capitalize an Income Stream."

7. a. A meaningless statement.

b. True. Consider a copper ore mine. If the net price of, say, $100 per ton rose at 20 percent per year, while the rate of interest was 10 percent per year, an owner would rather hold a ton in the ground now and mine it in a year. At present, $100 would be forgone, but $120 would be gained through sale in a year. This would be better than selling for net $100 now and earning $10 of interest during the year. Yet such action would decrease the supply of copper ore now and, given demand, raise the current price. And it would increase the supply next year, and, given demand, lower next year's price. As a result, the rate of increase in the net price would decline. This postponement of mining now in favor of mining later would continue until the net price, too, was growing at 10 percent per year. Analogously, a net price increase at 5 percent per year, all else being the same, would speed up extraction.

Chapter 10

1. a. You have a 50-50 chance of losing or gaining $1. The expected monetary value is −$1(0.5) + $1(0.5) = 0.

b. You have a 50-50 chance of losing $1 or gaining $10. The expected monetary value is −$1(0.5) + $10(0.5) = $4.50. How much you would pay me would depend on whether you were risk-averse, risk-neutral, or risk-seeking. If you were risk-averse, you would pay less than the expected monetary value, e.g., −$1 for game (a) and $2 for game (b). If you were risk-neutral, you would pay at most the expected monetary value. If you were risk-seeking, you would pay more than the expected monetary value (up to a limit).

3. a. The expected monetary value would be $3,000(0.5) + $27,000(0.5) = $15,000, but the associated expected utility would be less than *D* (on straight line *FG* at *E*).

Figure A-6

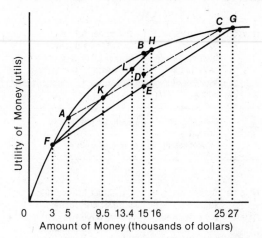

b. The expected monetary value of an equally probable $3,000 or $16,000 would equal $9,500. Its expected utility can be found at *K* on line *FH*. The expected monetary value of $3,000 (p = 0.2) and $16,000 (p = 0.8) would equal $3,000(0.2) + $16,000(0.8) = $13,400. Its expected utility can be found at *L* on line *FH*.

c. As in (a) above, the expected monetary value would be $15,000, but the associated expected utility would be more than *L* (on straight line *MN* at *P*).

Figure A-7

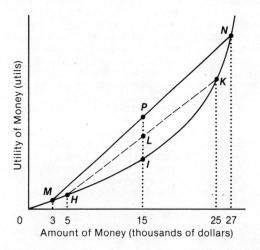

5. Text Table 10.5 modified:

Case III

Nov. 20	Spot price is $2.82 per bushel; farmer sells 10,000 bushels of wheat.	December futures price is $2.85 per bushel; farmer buys two contracts of December wheat
	Gain: 5¢ per bushel	Gain: 2¢ per bushel
	Net result: 7¢ per bushel gain	

Case IV

Nov. 20	Spot price is $2.71 per bushel; farmer sells 10,000 bushels of wheat.	December futures price is $2.94 per bushel; farmer buys two contracts of December wheat
	Loss: 6¢ per bushel	Loss: 7¢ per bushel
	Net result: 13¢ per bushel loss	

7. Marconi, because he put the new ideas into practical use, translating the earlier discoveries into a new product and acting in the face of uncertainty.

Chapter 11

1. Physical force (the murder of key personnel of competitors, the sabotage of their operations) or various forms of collusion (price fixing, tying contracts, etc.) are illegal sources of monopoly power. The student may wish to look ahead to Chapter 17, "Antitrust Policy and Regulation," which discusses various illegal activities designed to gain monopoly power.
3.   **a.** *ATC* must intersect demand at a point vertically below *a* in panel (a) because total cost = total revenue implies average total cost = average revenue (or price).
     b. The total-cost curve's point of inflexion corresponds to minimum marginal cost, because declining *MC* implies total cost rising at a decreasing rate, while rising *MC* implies total cost rising at an increasing rate.
5. If long-run marginal revenue intersected *R*, the firm would produce there.
7. Of course. Consider a monopsony paying, for each unit bought, the lowest possible price at which someone might supply that unit (as along line *ade* in text Figure 11.12, "Bilateral Monopoly"). Note how employers often keep the salary paid to any one employee secret from all other employees or how they pay overtime for extra units of labor.

Chapter 12

1. "Agreed: Each of us will produce 25 units per year and charge a price of $50 per unit." Given zero costs, each firm could expect a profit of $1,250 per year, which would be $138.89 per year better than the $1,111.11 gained under the Cournot equilibrium.
3.   **a.** Major changes in marginal cost and demand might shift the MC-MR intersection to a new quantity and, therefore, a new price. Presumably, the kink is supposed to reestablish itself at the new price-quantity combination.
     b. For a monopoly, any increase in marginal cost lowers quantity and raises price, *ceteris paribus*. The opposites occur for a decrease in marginal cost. Any increase in demand increases quantity and price; any decrease has opposite effects.
     c. For a perfect competitor, any increase (or decrease) in marginal cost lowers (or increases) quantity only, price being market determined. Any increase (or decrease) in demand (presumably meaning market price and horizontal marginal revenue) raises (or lowers) quantity.
5. The hints lead the way. (Goldwater's and McGovern's campaigns, of course, both of which resulted in landslide victories for their opponents, illustrate the dangers of locating at an extreme "right" or "left" position on Hotelling's characteristics space. Taking an extreme position allows an opponent to locate in a position that will attract the vast majority of "customers.")
7.   **a.** Because the firm is making economic profit.
     b. New firms will enter the "industry" (or Chamberlinian product group). This firm's demand will fall until economic profit is eliminated. See panel (b) of text Figure 12.5, "The Monopolistic Competitor," as an example of the end result.
     c. Advertising would raise costs. If successful, it would raise demand sufficiently to recreate economic profit. If unsuccessful, it would fail to raise demand sufficiently and would bring losses.

Chapter 13

1.   **a.**

Number of Workers	Marginal Physical Product	Net Marginal Value Product
1.5	70	$35
2.5	50	25
3.5	40	20
4.5	10	5
5.5	−20	−10

   b. At $20 per day, 3.5 workers.
   At $35 per day, 1.5 workers.
   c. The net marginal value product column would read: $7, 5, 4, 1, and −2. At a wage of $10, nobody would be employed.

3. Panel (a): Unemployment of *ie* would exist. Panel (b): Unemployment would exist equal to the distance, along horizontal line *da*, from *a* to the line's intersection with market supply. Panel (c): Unemployment would exist equal to the distance, along horizontal line *ed*, from *d* to the line's intersection with market supply.

5. Yes. He was monopsonistically exploited, as it is explained in the text section, "Application 1: The Baseball Players' Market."

7. The members of the AFL-CIO are not directly affected by the minimum wage.

Chapter 14

1. Both are correct. A move to a Pareto-superior position involves making one or more people better off in their own estimation (a marginal benefit) without making anyone worse off (a zero marginal cost). Pareto could not support as clearly desirable a positive marginal benefit (making someone better off) at a positive marginal cost (making someone else worse off) because we have no way of measuring either this benefit or that cost and of then comparing them.

3. This allocation almost certainly would *not* be economically efficient because different people's marginal rates of substitution between gasoline and other goods would diverge. Hence the kind of inefficiency depicted in part (A) of text Table 14.4, "The Optimum Allocation of Goods among Consumers of the Same Goods," would exist. Outlawing the trading of rations would perpetuate the inefficiency; allowing it would enable people to overcome inefficiency through exchange, as shown in parts (B) and (C) of Table 14.4.

5. **a.** Text Table 14.4 might be adapted to show the optimum allocation of resources among users of the same resources.

Firm α might initially produce 100 bicycles per day, while using 10 units of labor (*x*) plus 20 units of capital services (*y*). Firm β might initially produce 300 bicycles (or, significantly, 300 lawnmowers), while using 200 units of identical labor (*x*) plus 50 units of identical

capital services (*y*). Given the divergent marginal rates of technical substitution of part (A), the new situation B implies higher outputs for both firms (11*x* plus 15*y* would have produced the same output for α; 199*x* plus 52*y*, the same output for β). . . .

b. *Under perfect competition*, both firms would face identical prices for labor and capital services. To maximize profit, both would use labor and capital services in such amounts as to equate their inputs' marginal value products (MVP_x and MVP_y) with their prices (P_x and P_y). Hence for Firm α:

$$P_x = MVP_x \text{ and } P_y = MVP_y.$$

Therefore,

$$\frac{P_x}{P_y} = \frac{MVP_x}{MVP_y} = \frac{MPP_x \cdot P_0}{MPP_y \cdot P_0} = \frac{MPP_x}{MPP_y},$$

where P_0 is the price of output and MPP the marginal physical product. The same would hold for Firm β. Therefore, the ratio of marginal physical products of the two inputs would be the same for both firms (each being equated with the identical input price ratio). This implies equal marginal rates of technical substitution as well. *Under imperfect competition*, the automatic (and unintended) achievement of economic efficiency would not be assured. Both firms might maximize profit by using input quantities such that the marginal outlay on any input equaled its marginal revenue product. Hence for Firm α:

$$P_x < MRP_x = MO_x < MVP_x$$

and

$$P_y < MRP_y = MO_y < MVP_y$$

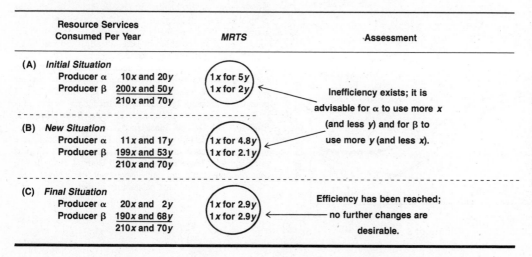

Resource Services Consumed Per Year		MRTS	Assessment
(A) *Initial Situation*			
Producer α	10*x* and 20*y*	1*x* for 5*y*	
Producer β	200*x* and 50*y*	1*x* for 2*y*	Inefficiency exists; it is
	210*x* and 70*y*		advisable for α to use more *x*
			(and less *y*) and for β to
(B) *New Situation*			use more *y* (and less *x*).
Producer α	11*x* and 17*y*	1*x* for 4.8*y*	
Producer β	199*x* and 53*y*	1*x* for 2.1*y*	
	210*x* and 70*y*		
(C) *Final Situation*			Efficiency has been reached;
Producer α	20*x* and 2*y*	1*x* for 2.9*y*	no further changes are
Producer β	190*x* and 68*y*	1*x* for 2.9*y*	desirable.
	210*x* and 70*y*		

Therefore, it would be *possible* that

$$\frac{P_x}{P_y} \neq \frac{MRP_x}{MRP_y} = \frac{MO_x}{MO_y} \neq \frac{MVP_x}{MVP_y} = \frac{MPP_x}{MPP_y}$$

The same would hold for Firm β. Even if both firms paid the same input prices (not a necessity), the ratio of their inputs' marginal physical products and, therefore, their inputs' marginal rates of technical substitution might diverge at the point of profit maximization, eliminating any incentive for change.

7. Pareto wanted to make scientific statements; the speaker here is making moral judgments (see Chapter 15 for further discussion of moral judgments concerning equity).

Chapter 15

1.   a. From *E*, Jones and Smith could move to any point within shaded, lens-shaped area *EDAC*, including points on the indifference curves enclosing this area. From *F* or *G*, they could move to any point within a similar lens-shaped area formed by the two persons' indifference curves (not shown) going through F or G.

b. A cross-cut of the utility mountain above the contract curve is shown by the top line in the graph below, wherein the horizontal axis represents the straightened-out contract curve. Note how various points on the contract curve along the path from 0_J to 0_S (such as *K, D, C,* and *H*) appear in this graph as well. Obviously, Jones's total utility rises along the path from 0_J toward 0_S, while that of Smith rises from 0_S toward 0_J, as ever-higher indifference curves are reached. If utility were not only measurable, but also interpersonally comparable, one could construct the top line of social utility, $U_J + U_S$. Caution: Students should not confuse this graph with text Figure 15.3, "The Equal Income Argument," which measures *marginal* utility (of income).

Figure A–8

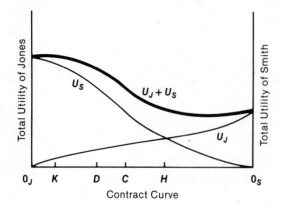

c. Yes, as long as the two consumers' marginal rates of substitution diverged (and they were thus positioned off the contract curve).

d. If they started out on the contract curve, but were determined to move, conflict would be inevitable. Quite possibly, during a long strike or lockout, everyone's tastes would change; that is, two new sets of indifference curves (and thus a newly positioned contract curve) would emerge. As a result, the original position *on* the original contract curve might become a position *off* the new contract curve. Then mutually beneficial trading would again be possible.

e. The two attitudes might be characterized as positions off or on the contract curve, respectively.

f. If this were literally true (and Jack Sprat received infinite disutility from eating fat, while his wife received infinite disutility from eating lean meat), Jack's indifference curves would shrink to the successive dots on the horizontal axis. Those of his wife would shrink to the successive dots on the right-hand vertical axis. Their ideal position would be at *E* (which would represent a shrunk contract curve): Jack would get all of the "lean," his wife all of the fat (see the graph below).

Figure A–9

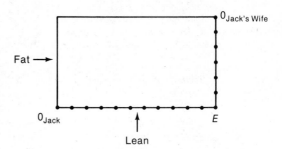

3. Students may wish to review "Application 2: 'False' Wants vs. 'True' Needs" in Chapter 12 of the text. "The government" also consists of people. Why should these people be less fallible than the rest? In addition, it is, of course, far from obvious how *need* is to be defined. Take food. Should one go about it "scientifically," establishing a minimum adequate diet required to keep a person alive? For a moderately active adult male, such diet may involve the annual consumption of the following: 370 pounds of wheat flour; 57 cans of evaporated milk; 111 pounds of cabbage; 23 pounds of spinach; 285 pounds of dried navy beans. This interesting piece of information is taken from George J. Stigler, "The Cost of Subsistence," *Journal of Farm Economics*, May 1945, pp. 303-314. This diet contains the optimum amounts of calories, protein, minerals, and vitamins established by the National Research Council. Thus it is a *physiological* minimum and leaves out of account such "luxuries" as variety and palatability of diet.

5. A variety of arguments can be made to support either position. Besides drawing on this chapter's material about different concepts of equity, students may wish to review "Application 1: Wage Differentials," in text Chapter 8.

7. A variety of arguments can be made to support either position. Note: The $1,250-a-year share of world output equals the per-capita world GNP (a $5 trillion GNP divided by 4 billion people); it does not refer to private consumption goods only. If we excluded investment and government goods from the above figure (to approximate per capita private consumption goods available in a regime of world-wide equality), the per capita figure would be much lower. It would be lower still if we considered the disincentive effects of such a drastic redistribution.

Chapter 16

1. The statement may be overly poetic for some readers, but it does convey the basic truth of economic interdependence. Students should be able to construct any reasonable scenario that shows the statement to be correct.

3. **a.** It rarely would be negative, but it is not impossible, at least for rows (A)-(C). Commodities, for example, could be taken away from households, as has happened in this author's youth in Nazi Germany. (Private cars, cameras, radios, clothing, and stocks of food were confiscated for the war effort.)

 b. The sums of rows would designate total sales revenue (from selling, say, electric power, labor, or machine hours). The sums of rows (D) to (F) would measure the gross national income. The sums of columns would designate total expenditures (on, say, raw materials and primary resources by electric power producers or on consumption goods by households). The sums of columns (4)-(7) would measure the gross national expenditure, as the familiar $C + I + G + (X\text{-}M)$.

5. The statement is incorrect. The production of one more car, for instance, requires extra tires in many places throughout the economy; for instance, on cars to transport extra workers to coal mines to mine extra coal needed for extra steel production to make the extra car. . . . Review the section on "Interpreting the Leontief Inverse Matrix."

7. It would be much more complicated, because the technical coefficients would vary with the volume of production.

Chapter 17

1. These are, indeed, important counter arguments to the Clayton Act provisions.

3. **a.** Consider the graph below, which is a modification of text Figure 11.3(b). By setting a maximum price of $0B$, the regulators would make inaccessible the market demand line to the left of C and make BC into a new marginal revenue and demand line. The firm would produce quantity $0E$, corresponding to point C. The deadweight welfare loss would be gone; there would still be economic profit equal to $ABCD$.

Figure A-10

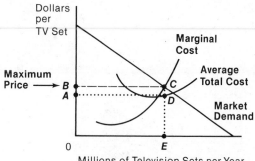

b. Consider the graph below, which again is a modification of text Figure 11.3(b). By setting a maximum price of $0F$, the regulators would annihilate the market demand curve to the left of K and make FK into a new marginal revenue and demand line. The firm would produce quantity $0I$, corresponding to point H. The deadweight welfare loss would then equal GHC; economic profit would be zero. There would also be a shortage of $HK = IL$.

Figure A-11

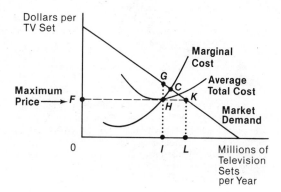

c. Consider the graph below, once more a modification of text Figure 11.3(b). By providing a per-unit subsidy equal to CM (the difference between original marginal cost MC_0 and marginal revenue at the output level which eliminates the deadweight welfare loss), a regulator could get the firm to produce output $0E$, and charge price $0B$. However, this would be equivalent to a parallel downward shift of MC_0 and ATC_0 to MC_1 and ATC_1; hence the firm would make an economic profit of $BCNP$.

Figure A-12

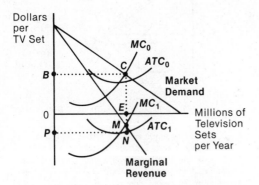

Dollars per TV Set

d. A lump-sum tax of $BCNP$ would eliminate the economic profit, while not affecting marginal revenue and marginal cost and the firm's output/price decision. Such a tax would shift ATC_1 up in a nonparallel fashion, making it go through point C and making it intersect MC_1 at the new ATC minimum (not shown).

5. Sunset laws would probably be a good idea for all three types of regulation discussed in the text.

7. A variety of arguments can be made to support or oppose this position (which paraphrases the position of Milton Friedman—see Biography 2.2).

Chapter 18

1. We can use the same example, slightly modified: Goal: $MRT_{a,b} = MRS_{a,b}$. In the absence of externalities, let $P_a = MPC_a = \$10$, and let $P_b = MPC_b = \$5$. Thus $MRT_{a,b} = 1a$ for $2b$ follows from profit maximization; $MRS_{a,b} = 1a$ for $2b$ follows from utility maximization. Now let the production of a involve a positive externality, such that $MPC_a = \$10$, but $MSC_a = \$5$. Hence true $MRT_{a,b} = 1a$ for $1b$. All else being the same, this implies economic inefficiency. By producing $2b$ less, one could in fact produce $2a$ more, making any consumer better off (because consumers still value $2b$ as much as $1a$ at the margin).

3. It is unlikely that people would be that altruistic. Even if they were, they would not have the knowledge necessary to make the adjustment properly. (This does not mean, of course, that government officials have that knowledge either.)

5. The hint leads the way. The team for which the player would play would be the same regardless of who owned his services. Suppose the reserve clause were not in effect. A player might be playing for Club A for a salary of \$50,000 a year. If Club B offered \$80,000, the player might move to Club B—provided he wasn't worth more than that to Club A, which would make a counter offer. The player would end up playing for the club that most highly valued his services. With the reserve clause, the same would be true. If the above player were worth \$60,000 to Club A, which owned his contract, but \$100,000 to Club B, Club B could offer \$10,000 a year to Club A for the contract and would get it. (Club A would be no worse off than before, gaining *net* revenue of \$10,000 a year in either case.) Club B could then pay the player's \$50,000 annual salary, and the club would be better off, gaining \$100,000 and paying \$10,000 (to Club A) + \$50,000 (to the player) = \$60,000 a year. Once more, the player would be playing for the club that most highly valued his services. (For further reading on this issue, see Harold Demsetz, ''When Does the Rule of Liability Matter?'' *Journal of Legal Studies* 1 (1972):13ff.)

7. Students may wish to study Neher's discussion of mugging, including a number of his fascinating extensions (on computer crime, wolf club bottle collections, and the household encyclopedia market).

Chapter 19

1. There is a lot of truth to this. Public goods can be defined with respect to any society at all, be it all people on earth, all Americans, all residents of Michigan or of Boston, or all the workers in a given firm. Hence a *local* public good is not a self-contradictory term, as students sometimes think. All that matters is that such goods provide nonexcludable and nonrival benefits to all members of the society in question, however defined.

3. Although we do not know it, the city may well have produced the optimal quantity of this public good, such as $0G$ in text Figure 19.2. Although additional benefits might have been procured (totaling $GHFD$ in Figure 19.2), the additional costs might have been larger, as is clearly the case in Figure 19.2 (the area under MSC between G and D exceeds $GHFD$). To prevent the 1,622 murders, for instance, the city might have had to spend $\$x$ billion, which were in fact spent, perhaps, on cardiac arrest units that saved 3,900 lives. (Note: students may wish to review the general discussion of the optimization principle in Chapter 1, and in particular that chapter's Question 6.)

5. Because an economics department receives occasional grants of money from the Treasurer's office, just as government bureaus do from the legislature, there are a lot of parallels. Students might want to reread the text discussion of ''Government Failure: The Problem of Bureaucracy'' and consider where the analogy works and where it breaks down.

7. Almost certainly, this practice was nonsensical. (See the text discussion of benefit-cost analysis.)

Subject Index

Name Index